Handbook
of
African Catholicism

HANDBOOK OF AFRICAN CATHOLICISM

Edited by
STAN CHU ILO

Maryknoll, New York 10545

Founded in 1970, Orbis Books endeavors to publish works that enlighten the mind, nourish the spirit, and challenge the conscience. The publishing arm of the Maryknoll Fathers and Brothers, Orbis seeks to explore the global dimensions of the Christian faith and mission, to invite dialogue with diverse cultures and religious traditions, and to serve the cause of reconciliation and peace. The books published reflect the views of their authors and do not represent the official position of the Maryknoll Society. To learn more about Orbis Books, please visit our website at www.orbisbooks.com.

Copyright © 2022 by Stan Chu Ilo.

Published by Orbis Books, Box 302, Maryknoll, NY 10545-0302.

All rights reserved.

No part of this publication may be reproduced or transmitted in any form or by any means, electronic or mechanical, including photocopying, recording, or any information storage or retrieval system, without prior permission in writing from the publisher.

Queries regarding rights and permissions should be addressed to: Orbis Books, P.O. Box 302, Maryknoll, NY 10545-0302.

Manufactured in the United States of America

Library of Congress Cataloging-in-Publication Data

Names: Ilo, Stan Chu, editor.
Title: Handbook of African Catholicism / edited by Stan Chu Ilo.
Description: Maryknoll, NY : Orbis Books, [2022] | Includes bibliographical references and index. | Summary: "A disciplinary map for understanding African Catholicism today by engaging some of the most pressing and pertinent issues, topics, and conversations in diverse fields of studies in African Catholicism"—Provided by publisher.
Identifiers: LCCN 2021059166 (print) | LCCN 2021059167 (ebook) | ISBN 9781626984745 (trade paperback) | ISBN 9781608339365 (epub)
Subjects: LCSH: Catholic Church—Africa.
Classification: LCC BX1675 .H27 2022 (print) | LCC BX1675 (ebook) | DDC 282/.6—dc23/eng/20220118
LC record available at https://lccn.loc.gov/2021059166
LC ebook record available at https://lccn.loc.gov/2021059167

Dedicated to
Mary Gloria Njoku, DDL (1972–2018), and Jacquineau Azétsop, SJ (1972–2021)

You began this journey with us, but did not live to see its completion; you watch over us from our ancestral home and commune with us in the unbroken bond of love in Christ that cannot be taken away by the physical separation of death.

"Then the wise will shine like the brightness of the heavens, and those who lead many to righteousness will shine like the stars forever and ever." —Daniel 12:3

Contents

Foreword
Anne Béatrice Faye, CIC — xi

Acknowledgments — xv

Acronyms — xvii

General Introduction — xxi
Stan Chu Ilo

HISTORY AND MISSION

A Brief History of the Catholic Church in Africa — 3
Vincent J. O'Malley, CM

Africa — 15
Emmanuel Katongole

Toward a Historical Perspective on African Catholicism in the Era of World Christianity — 28
Paul V. Kollman, CSC

History and Development of African Liturgies in African Catholicism: Liturgical Inculturation for the Future of Catholicism in Africa — 39
Patrick C. Chibuko

Stories of Transformation: African Immigrants to the United States and the Dark Night of St. John of the Cross — 63
Dorris van Gaal

Inculturating the Faith in Africa: History, Context, and Debates — 80
Florence Adetoun Oso, EHJ

Method and Models for Studies in African Catholicism — 95
Nicholaus Segeja

Transformational Servant Leadership in African Catholic Pastoral Ministry — 109
Stan Chu Ilo

The Global Context of African Catholicism — 127
Richard Benson, CM

Contents

African Catholicism and Intellectual History in Africa:
Issues and Disputes 147
Michael Onyebuchi Eze

History and Methods of African Studies of the New Testament:
Protestant and Catholic Dialogue 166
MarySylvia Nwachukwu, DDL, and Zorodzai Dube

FORMATION, EDUCATION, AND COMMUNICATION

Small Christian Communities in Africa: Histories, Themes,
Development, and Challenges 185
Joseph G. Healey, MM

Communicating the Faith in African Catholicism: History
and Development 202
Walter Chikwendu Ihejirika

Catholic Education in Africa and the Agenda of *Africae Munus* 223
Anthony A. Akinwale, OP

Catholic Schools in Africa: Achievements and Challenges 239
Quentin Wodon

Canon Law in African Catholicism: Historical Development,
Challenges, and Prospects 257
Benedict Ndubueze Ejeh

The Changing Face of the Priestly Vocation and Ministry in Africa . . 284
Jordan Nyenyembe

The Impact of the African Laity on Modern African Catholicism:
The Example of Alioune Diop 299
Elizabeth A. Foster

Religious Life in African Catholicism 309
✠ *George Desmond Tambala, OCD*

CHURCH AND SOCIETY

History and Development of Catholic Social Imagination in Africa . . 329
Godswill Agbagwa

Church and Development in African Catholicism 340
Stan Chu Ilo and Gabriel T. Wankar

African Catholicism and Islam: Relationship and Tensions 367
Cosmas Ebo Sarbah

Contents

Alongside One Another: African Catholicism and Ecumenism   381
Ikenna Paschal Okpaleke

Church and Politics in Africa: History, Method of Study, and the Future   397
Aloys Ojore

Catholicism and Fundamental Human Rights to Development in Africa: Looking beyond the Shadows of Legal Norms   415
Wilfred Mamah and Idara Otu, MSP

An African Catholic Approach to Planetary Living   427
Edward Osang Obi, MSP

THE BODY, HEALTH, AND HEALING

Catholic Sexual Morality and Social Ethics in Africa: Contested Questions   449
Hellen Sitawa Wanyonyi and Eunice K. Kamaara

Pentecostal and Charismatic Renewal: A Religious Phenomenon for Transformation in Africa   466
Clement Majawa

Catholicism with a Difference: Popular Catholicism in Kenya   478
Philomena Njeri Mwaura and Beatrice Wairimu Churu

African Catholicism and Health Care in Africa   497
†Mary Gloria C. Njoku, DDL, Sampson K. Nwonyi, and Patrick J. McDevitt, CM

Health and Abundant Life: Catholic Healing amid a Plurality of Healing Paradigms in Africa   511
Bernhard Udelhoven, MAfr

Catholic Health Facilities in Africa: Achievements and Challenges   537
Quentin Wodon

African Catholicism and the Place of Women: Research and Advocacy   551
Ebere Bosco Amakwe, HFSN

The Church as Family of God in Africa   573
Paulinus I. Odozor, CSSp

CATHOLIC THEOLOGICAL AND PHILOSOPHICAL TRADITIONS IN AFRICA

The Changing Faces of Roman Catholic Ecclesiology in Sub-Saharan Africa   589
Josée Ngalula, RSA

Contents

Who Is Jesus Christ for Us? Christology in African Catholicism — 604
Chukwuemeka Anthony Atansi

Dei Verbum in African Catholicism: History and Reception — 621
Paul Béré, SJ

Bible and Society in Africa: African Exegesis for an Effective Catechesis — 634
Daniel Assefa

African Theologies in Dialogue with the West — 647
Emmanuel-Mary Mbam, MSP

African Philosophies in Dialogue with the West — 667
Nathanaël Yaovi Soédé

From Vatican II to the Second African Synod: Themes, Traditions, and Transitions — 685
Anne Arabome, SSS, and Agbonkhianmeghe E. Orobator, SJ,

From *Ecclesia in Africa* to *Africae Munus*: The Synodal Traditions in African Catholicism — 697
Anthony Adawu

Epilogue: Dreaming about the Future of the Church in Africa — 716
Laurenti Magesa

Contributors — 729

Index — 739

Index of Scripture Passages — 788

Foreword

Anne Béatrice Faye, CIC

A proper assessment of the role of African theology in contemporary Africa offers considerable challenges for scholarship. Indeed, African theology is varied and sometimes not easily identifiable with one stream, method, or trend. How can one give an account of the development of theological activities in each country and region of Africa without being forced to take shortcuts, to schematize, and even to simplify? Moreover, we know that for a long time, African theology was engaged in promoting Africa's liberation from colonialism, apartheid, neocolonialism, or, more generally, from external domination.

The fresh perspectives of the fifty contributors to this impressive *Handbook of African Catholicism*, directed and edited by Professor Stan Chu Ilo, take us back to the complexity of the daily life of the African people, the sites of their actual faith, and the anthropological perspectives on faith, as well as the many layers of the sociocultural, political, and economic fractures we experience in the continent of Africa. The most pressing question is to know if Christianity in Africa will become irrelevant to the Africa of the future if the multiple challenges facing this continent persist. How can we understand the mystery of God while remaining attentive to, and being moved profoundly by, the daily realities of our siblings who question if God is present in the daily drama and drudgery of the life of God's people in Africa? How can we Africans speak of God differently, in a way that shows God's concrete presence in our history through the prophetic action and witness of our Christian communities in transforming the difficult situation of life in our continent?

The fields of theological inquiry and scientific study of the Christian mission in Africa are the crossroads where anthropology, hermeneutics, and semiotics meet in the contributions of these authors who are reformulating and redefining the method and object of African theology and Catholic studies, broadly conceived. They reflect on the faith and fate of our people, and they evaluate the different pastoral and theological approaches of the local churches in Africa and jointly develop some best pastoral practices for the renewal and reform of the Catholic Church in Africa. The *Handbook* thus allows us to embrace the intelligibility of faith, starting from the questions and needs of the men and women of our continent. The question, then, is ultimately: How can Christ constitute the foundation on which the reconstruction and liberation of Africa can be done? What conditions should be in place for this urgent task to be realized, and who are the conversation partners with whom Catholic scholars should be undertaking this collaborative exigency of history?

Foreword

We still remember that the African Synod of 1994 encouraged meetings, collective reflections, and very rich regional and continental consultations. As a result, a genuine dialogue was initiated, proposing paths for the future of our churches. The bishops had become aware that they preside in communion over their churches, in solidarity, fraternity, and cooperation,[1] and that they all work for the mission of evangelization and the coming of the kingdom of God and its justice in the world. They embraced at the synod the episcopal collegiality of Vatican II through the renewing experience of the Spirit who is the source and origin for renewing the church.

More than a quarter of a century after the publication of the post-synodal apostolic exhortation, *Ecclesia in Africa* by Pope St. John Paul II, the church and society in Africa have experienced significant shifts and changes. This *Handbook* shows us that the teachings and orientations of that synod have not ceased to be a valid guide for pastoral efforts within the church, the family of God's people in Africa. It is a response to the pope's invitation:

> For all the peoples of Africa, the best preparation for the new Millennium must consist in a firm commitment to implement with excellent fidelity the decisions and orientations which, with the Apostolic authority of the Successor of Peter, I present in this Exhortation. They are decisions and orientations that can be traced back to the genuine heritage of the Church's teaching and discipline and the Second Vatican Council, the primary source of inspiration for the Special Assembly for Africa. (§141)

Progress has been made in the life and mission of the church family of God in Africa. Moreover, the church continues to evolve, to transform, to move forward gradually but realistically. This impressive *Handbook* is of great importance for Africa. It deserves to be read in depth for three reasons.

The first is that the essays in this bold *Handbook* provide a disciplinary map for understanding African Catholicism today. For the church in Africa, it is necessary, through profound catechesis and inculturation, to guide people toward discovering the fullness of the gospel values. Today we have an essential interdisciplinary reference work for Catholic studies in Africa in its broadest sense. This is reflected in the themes addressed in this *Handbook*. The authors explore different pastoral and theological approaches for developing better pastoral practices in Africa. They have surveyed the pastoral concerns of the church in Africa: history and mission; fundamental questions on formation, education, and communication; the relationship between church and society in Africa; morality/spirituality; health and healing; and Catholic intellectual traditions in Africa in theological and philosophical studies.

---

1. Pope John Paul II, *Ecclesia in Africa* [Post-synodal Apostolic Exhortation on the Church in Africa and Its Evangelizing Mission toward the Year 2000; September 14, 1995] (Vatican City: Libreria Editrice Vaticana, 1995; www.vatican.va) §§5, 16, 17, 23, 37, 43, 49, 126, 131–35 (hereinafter *EA*).

Foreword

The second reason is that this *Handbook* will be an effective tool for addressing the expressed need of African bishops, priests, theologians, and lay leaders for a resource of this kind that will foster organic pastoral solidarity throughout the African territory and adjacent islands. This is because the *Handbook* presents important studies that are crucial for an in-depth understanding of current theological questions in Africa as well as of important issues emerging from the challenging African social context and social issues. At the same time, the *Handbook* develops additional important trajectories in areas of church history and African theology—all of which will provide a helpful guide for continuing the task of inculturation. By spreading Catholic intellectual tradition in Africa, this *Handbook* contributes to a scientific study of cultures. This is an urgent and challenging mission today due to the profound and rapid changes that African societies are experiencing and the effects of a civilization that is becoming global (*EA* §73).

The third reason is that this *Handbook* fits with the dynamic role of the universities and Catholic higher institutes in Africa as laboratories of new ideas and centers for producing knowledge that African churches and society need in order to meet the mission of the local faith communities of Africa and the wider public. These institutes

> have a prominent role to play in the proclamation of the saving Word of God. They are a sign of the growth of the Church in so far as their research integrates the truths and experiences of the faith and helps to internalize them. They serve the Church by providing trained personnel; by studying important theological and social questions; by developing African theology; by promoting the work of inculturation, especially in the celebration of the liturgy; by publishing books and spreading Catholic thought; by undertaking assignments given to them by the bishops; and by contributing to a scientific study of cultures. (*EA* §103)

In sum, this *Handbook* proposes and sheds light on the current phase of the reception of the Second Vatican Council in Africa, especially the importance of the Word of God and of Christian prayer, liturgy, mission, and sacraments. In other words, this *Handbook* invites us to transform theology into a very concrete pastoral ministry in which the great visions of sacred scripture and tradition are applied to the daily life and witnessing of the People of God and its pastors, in particular communities and specific contexts.

Many syncretistic movements and sects have emerged in Africa in recent decades. It is sometimes difficult to discern whether they are authentically Christian in inspiration or simply the result of a fascination with a leader claiming to have exceptional gifts. The theology and pastoral care of the church must determine the origins of this phenomenon not only to stem the "hemorrhage" of the faithful from the parishes to join these groups, but also to form the basis of an appropriate pastoral response and a deepening of faith and witness against the attraction of some of these movements and sects. There is also the need for ecumenical relations among churches as presented in some of these essays, but central

Foreword

to ecumenical relations in Africa today will be a proper discernment about church growth and church planting and the commons and canons for validating religious experience and ecclesial leadership across the board. This means once again: to evangelize in depth the African soul and discern "which cultural elements and traditions are contrary to the Gospel," which will make it possible to

> separate the wheat from the chaff (cf. Mt 13:26).... Christianity will thus adopt the face of the countless cultures and peoples among whom it has been welcomed and taken root. The Church will then become a sign of the future that the Spirit of God is preparing for us, a sign to which Africa has a contribution of its own to make. In this process of inculturation, it is important not to forget the equally essential task of evangelizing the world of contemporary African culture.[2]

This *Handbook* offers us the opportunity to remember and recall the words of hope and comfort addressed to the church family of God, which is in Africa (*AM* §15):

> To Africa, which is menaced on all sides by outbreaks of hatred and violence, of conflicts and wars, evangelizers must proclaim *the hope of life rooted in the paschal mystery*. . . . "Christ our hope is alive, we shall live!" Africa is not destined for death, but for life! (*EA* §57)

Burkina Faso
October 2021

---

2. Pope Benedict XVI, *Africae Munus* [Post-synodal Apostolic Exhortation on the Church in Africa in Service of Reconciliation, Justice and Peace; November 19, 2011] (Vatican City: Libreria Editrice Vaticana, 2011; www.vatican.va) §37 (hereinafter *AM*).

Acknowledgments

This book is the fruit of a collaborative effort. It would not have been possible to assemble such a collection of essays from a diverse body of African and international scholars without the cooperation of the authors of the chapters of this *Handbook*. I wish to thank all the contributors for their dedication, sacrifice, and collaboration toward the realization of this book.

This project was shepherded by Prof. Bill Cavanaugh, director of the Center for World Catholicism and Intercultural Theology (CWCIT) at DePaul University, Chicago, and by Prof. Michael Budde, senior research professor at the Center. They contributed ideas to the design of the African Catholicism Project (ACP) and participated in the African palaver process and peer reviews of all the chapters of this *Handbook*. Without their support, encouragement, guidance, and collegial spirit, this work would not have seen the light of day.

I cannot thank Karen Kraft, the managing editor of this project, enough. She was the engine for this project during its five-year duration. Her attention to detail and her editorial, organizational, and project-management skills were invaluable for the successful completion of the *Handbook*. She has worked so hard for this project and made huge sacrifices along the way, which my words are inadequate to capture here. I wish to thank the entire faculty at the Catholic Studies Department, DePaul University, especially our immediate past chair, Emanuele Colombo (who participated in the African palaver in Enugu in 2019), for their spirit of collegiality and friendship.

We thank the Jesuits, students, and faculty at Hekima University College in Nairobi, Kenya, for hosting the contributors to this *Handbook* in 2017 for the African palaver and cohort-based reviews of all the essays in this volume. Special thanks are due to the sisters and management of the Rosa Mystica Spirituality Center in Nairobi for hosting all the contributors during our stay.

I express a special thanks to Dr. Jill O'Brien of Orbis Books for believing in this project and for her professionalism, editorial acumen, and leadership.

I would like to thank Prof. Bradford Hinze, who was a consultant to this project and participated in the African palaver for the *Handbook* in 2017 at Hekima College. I have benefited from the friendship, wisdom, and encouragement of the following scholars and colleagues who served as informal conversation partners for this project: Prof. Paul Murray, Prof. Victor Ezigbo, Prof. Kurt Appel, Prof. Elochukwu Uzukwu, Sr. Mumbi Kigutha, Dr. Felix Nwatu, Bishop Matthew Hassan Kukah, and Dr. John Chan.

Acknowledgments

A special thanks to Greg Black for copy-editing all the chapters of this *Handbook*, and to Bernard Marrocco, my personal editor, who read some of the chapters. I thank Prof. Mary McCain, who took time to read through the General Introduction to the *Handbook* and made some useful suggestions. I wish to thank all of our CWCIT colleagues, particularly our former executive officer, Francis Salinel, who managed the African palaver project for the *Handbook* contributors at Hekima College, and our current budget officer, Marlon Aguilar, for his dedication and commitment. I cannot fail to acknowledge the contribution of a few of CWCIT's student assistants from the last few years who helped with some incredibly tedious, nitty-gritty tasks like document formatting, checking final drafts, and sorting/uploading files to our Google drive. This kind of administrative, editorial support may seem trivial but for a book manuscript with more than fifty authors/chapters, their assistance was truly invaluable for keeping track of the progress of each essay. So, to Elijah Gray, Graciella (Gracie) Saucedo-Rivera, Finnegan Chu, and Morgan Monaghan . . . thank you!

To my mother, Lolo Rose Akunna Ilo, I owe everything—for giving me life and for always being there for me, and for giving me so much encouragement to carry on with this project in those moments when it seemed a near impossibility.

To our African ancestors in the guild who handed over this mission to us and prepared the way for all of us to do this kind of work, we thank you.

Stan Chu Ilo

Acronyms

AACC	All Africa Conference of Churches
AAS	*Acta Apostolicae Sedes*
ACIP	African Christian Initiation Project
ACP	African Catholicsm Project
AEA	Association of Evangelicals in Africa
AECAWA	Association of Episcopal Conferences of Anglophone West Africa
AICs	African Initiated Churches/African Independent Churches/African Indigenous Churches/African Instituted Churches/African Initiatives in Christianity
AMECEA	Association of Member Episcopal Conferences in Eastern Africa
ARCIC	Anglican-Roman Catholic International Commission
ARVs	antiretroviral drugs
ATR	African Traditional Religion
BCC	Basic Christian Community
BEC	Base/Basic Ecclesial Community
BICAM	Biblical Center for Africa and Madagascar
CABAN	Catholic Biblical Association of Nigeria
CALAN	Catholic Liturgical Association of Nigeria
CAMECO	Catholic Media Council
CANAA	Catholic News Agency for Africa
CARA	Center for Applied Research in the Apostolate
CATHAN	Catholic Theological Association of Nigeria
CEAC	Center for Early African Christianity
CEBs	Communautés Ecclésiales de Base
CECOTAPS	Centre for Conflict Transformation and Peace Studies
CEP	Congregation for the Evangelization of Peoples
CEVs	Communautés Ecclésiales Vivantes
CEVBs	Communautés Ecclésiales Vivantes de Base
CHA	Catholic Health Association
CHAG	Catholic Health Association of Ghana
CHIEA	Catholic Higher Institute of East Africa
CIC	Codex Iuris Canonici; Code of Canon Law 1917
CIWA	Catholic Institute of West Africa
CST	Catholic social teaching

Acronyms

CTEWC	Catholic Theological Ethics in the World Church
CUEA	Catholic University of Eastern Africa
CWCIT	Center for World Catholicism and Intercultural Theology
DALY	Disability-Adjusted Life Year
DOV	Decade to Overcome Violence
DRC	Democratic Republic of the Congo
EACUC	East Africa Church Union Consultation
EATWOT	Ecumenical Association of Third World Theologians
EBCs	Ecclesial Basic Communities
ESEAT	Ecumenical Symposium of Eastern Africa Theologians
FECCIWA	Fellowship of Christian Councils and Churches in West Africa
FOCCISA	Fellowship of Christian Councils in Southern Africa
GHS	Ghana Health Services
ICT	Information Communications Technology
IDLC-ISAN	Inter-Diocesan Liturgy Commission of the Igbo Speaking Area of Nigeria
IMBISA	Inter-Regional Meeting of the Bishops of Southern Africa
IMC	International Missionary Council
IRDC	Inter-Religious Dialogue Commission of AECAWA
ITC	International Theological Commission
JCA	Joint Church Aid
JCTR	Jesuit Centre for Theological Reflection
JLIFLC	Joint Learning Initiative on Faith and Local Communities
JNNK	Jumuiya Ndogo za Kikristo (Swahili expression for SCCs)
KDHS	Kenya Domestic Household Survey
MDG	Millennium Development Goals
MPR	Mouvement Populaire de la Révolution
NASCOP	National AIDS and STI Control Programme
NCCK	National Council of Churches of Kenya
NCPD	National Council for Population and Development
NECC	Northeast Catholic community
NECO	Northeast Community Organization
NEPAD	New Partnership for Africa's Development
NGO	Non-Governmental Organization
NHCS	National Catholic Health Services
NIAID	National Institute of Allergy and Infectious Diseases
OECD	Organization for Economic Co-operation and Development
OLA	Our Lady of Apostles (sisters)
PACE/APECA	Pan-African Association of Catholic Exegetes/L'Association Panafricaine des Exégètes Catholiques
PCID	Pontifical Council for Interreligious Dialogue
PNPF	Private-Not-for-Profit
PRB	Population Reference Bureau
RCIA	Rite of Christian Initiation of Adults

Acronyms

RECOWA	Regional Episcopal Conference of West Africa
RTD	Right to Development
SAC	African Society of Culture
SACC	South African Council of Churches
SCCs	Small Christian Communities
SDGs	Sustainable Development Goals
SEC	European Society of Culture
SECAM	Symposium of Episcopal Conferences of Africa and Madagascar
SOCADIDO	Soroti Catholic Diocese Integrated Development Organization
STIWA	Social Transformation Including Women in Africa
SWOT	Strengths, Weaknesses, Opportunities, and Threats
TCCRSA	Theological Colloquium on Church, Religion, and Society in Africa
TOT	Training of Trainers
UCAO	Université Catholique d'Afrique de l'Ouest
UDHR	Universal Declaration of Human Rights
UNAIDS	United Nations Program on HIV/AIDS
UNCTAD	United Nations Conference on Trade and Development
UNDRD	United Nations Declaration on the Right to Development
UNFPA	United Nations Population Fund
USMI	Union of Major Superiors
VMK	Vincentian Ministries, Kenya
VPH	Vincentian Prayer House
VRC	Vincentian Retreat Centre
WAAD	Women in Africa and the African Diaspora
WCC	World Council of Churches
WHO	World Health Organization
WRD	World Religion Database
YSCCs	Youth Small Christian Communities

General Introduction

Stan Chu Ilo, editor

> Anthropologists, sociologists and theologians from foreign churches have been studying us for many years. . . . We have become a fertile field for the kind of research that will enable a person to write an "interesting" thesis and obtain an academic degree. . . . It is therefore not surprising that we do not recognize ourselves in their writings.
> —South African Independent Church Leaders, 1994.[1]

Why the *Handbook of African Catholicism*?

The essays in this *Handbook* provide a disciplinary roadmap for scholars, church leaders, and all those who are interested in understanding African Catholicism today and the momentum of Christian expansion in Africa.[2] Contributors to this volume tell the stories of how the Catholic Church has emerged as a culture-shaping religious tradition in Africa. Readers are invited to follow the footprints of God in Africa as we tell the story of the Christian mission in Africa, which goes back to the first centuries. This mission has opened up multiple theological, doctrinal, social, and pastoral streams in Africa, all of which canalize into the richly diverse spiritual river of both the old and new African Christian traditions today that exude both multiplicities in their expressions and dynamism in growth.

Each chapter introduces readers to the current state of research in specific areas of Christian life and mission in African Catholicism, and to different methodological approaches adopted by practitioners in understanding this Christian tradition as it crosses different cultural, religious, and social frontiers in Africa. The essays are groundbreaking because contributors transgress disciplinary silos and regnant methodological canons in theological studies and in the social sciences. At the same time, contributors weave innovative and refreshing accounts around the central themes, trends, and features of African Catholic communities of faith. They also narrate the stories of the hopes and dreams of these communities of faith as well as their pastoral and social engagement with the challenges and opportunities of the social context in Africa.

Authors identify for readers the intellectual traditions that have developed in the Catholic Church in Africa and some of the persistent issues and paradoxes in this particular Christian tradition vis-à-vis the social condition in Africa. These essays shine a spotlight on African Catholicism as a source of hope and transformative missional praxis in Africa in dialogue and collaboration with other religious, social, and political actors in the continent. The essays also locate African Catholi-

---

1. N. H. Nganda et al., *Speaking for Ourselves: African Independent Churches* (Braamfontein, South Africa: Institute for Contextual Theology, 1985), 5.

2. Paul Avis, in a private email to me inviting me to contribute to the *Oxford Handbook of Ecclesiology*, framed the task of any handbook as that of providing "a disciplinary map" for understanding the continuities and discontinuities in any field of study.

cism within the larger complexity of global history, world Christianity, and the contested notions of modernity. The essays particularly engage some of the bigger issues in the Catholic tradition in the West and the tension between the Roman center and the local Catholic churches in Africa on such issues as the autonomy of local churches, centralization versus contextualization, charism versus authority in the church, new religious movements, Catholic education, inculturation, social concerns, and Catholic intellectual traditions.

These essays are not meant simply to stir people's interests in the peregrination of the gospel message in Africa, and in the multiple paths that divine providence is opening for African Christians in the Catholic Church. Rather, the hope is that these essays will steer conversations about the Christian mission in Africa along the path of greater attention to how Africans themselves faithfully and credibly live their faith, tell the stories of the faith, interpret this faith, and respond to the challenges and opportunities they face in Africa today through the different appeals they make to this faith experience.

The Growth and Prospects of Catholicism in Africa

Flying back to Rome after his five-day "pilgrimage of peace as an apostle of hope" to Africa in 2015, Pope Francis in reply to a question about the most memorable part of his trip said, "For me, Africa was a surprise. God always surprises us, but Africa surprises us too. I remember many moments, but above all, I remember the crowds." Pope Francis spoke of Africa as a continent of hope.[3] Africa always surprises visitors to Africa and Africans themselves because it is a rich continent with immense human and material resources, a rich cultural diversity, multiple religious traditions built on a vibrancy of youth often called "Africa's youth bulge," and creativity in all aspects of human life.[4] The words of Pope Francis evoked happy memories of similar sentiments of hope and joy expressed by previous popes about the beauty of African cultures, civilization, and spiritualities. Pope Paul VI, in his first visit to Africa in 1969,[5] extolled the spirituality and closeness of Africans to God and to a sense of community, which reminds me of the words of the nineteenth-century Scottish missionary to Africa, David Livingstone, "Already Africa is God's. God did not wait for me to bring Him. I found Him in every village."[6]

Writing in his post-synodal apostolic exhortation *Africae Munus*, Pope Benedict XVI proclaimed: "A precious treasure is to be found in the soul of Africa, where I perceive a 'spiritual lung' for a humanity that appears to be in a crisis of faith and hope" (*AM* §13).[7] In a similar vein, Pope John Paul II in his 1994 post-synodal apostolic exhortation, *Ecclesia in Africa*,[8] extolled African Christianity with these words: "Indeed, this continent is today

---

3. Vatican Insider: "Pope opens Holy Door: Today Bangui is the spiritual capital of the world," *La Stampa* (November 29, 2015), https://www.lastampa.it/vatican-insider/en/2015/11/29/news/pope-opens-holy-door-today-bangui-is-the-spiritual-capital-of-the-world-1.35211106.

4. See Alexander Thurston, "Religion, Society, and Conflict," in *The Fabric of Peace in Africa*, ed. Pamela Aall and Chester A. Crocker (Waterloo, ON: Center for International Governance Innovation, 2017), 260: "As of 2014, half of Sub-Saharan Africa's population was under the age of 25, and 'each year between 2015 and 2035, there will be half a million more 15-year-olds than the year before.'"

5. Pope Paul VI, address to the Symposium of Episcopal Conferences of Africa and Madagascar, Kampala (July 31, 1969), 1; *AAS* 61 (1969): 575.

6. See Ogbu Kalu, "Introduction: The Shape and Flow of African Church Historiography," in *African Christianity: An African Story*, ed. Ogbu Kalu (Trenton, NJ: Africa World Press, 2007), 13.

7. Pope Benedict XVI, *Africae Munus* [Post-synodal Apostolic Exhortation on the Church in Africa in Service of Reconciliation, Justice and Peace; November 19, 2011] (Vatican City: Libreria Editrice Vaticana, 2011; www.vatican.va.) §13 (hereinafter *AM*).

8. Pope John Paul II, *Ecclesia in Africa* [Post-synodal Apostolic Exhortation on the Church in Africa and Its Evangelizing Mission toward the Year 2000; September 14, 1995] (Vatican City: Libreria Editrice Vaticana, 1995; www.vatican.va) §6 (hereinafter *EA*).

experiencing what we call a sign of the times, an acceptable time, a day of salvation. It seems that the 'hour of Africa' has come, a favorable time." These expressions—"Spiritual lung," "Spiritual Capital of the world," "new center of gravity of World Christianity," "historical moment of grace," "a sign of the times," "an acceptable time," "creative Africa," "rich Africa," "hour of Africa," and "new home of Christ"—indicate the conviction that the Catholic Church in Africa has not only come of age but is also becoming a strong spiritual force in world Christianity in what has been called "the fourth great age of Christian expansion."[9]

Joel Carpenter and Nellie Kooistra in *Engaging Africa* point out that "Christianity is one of the most dynamic forces on the African continent today.... The Roman Catholic Church is the largest Christian communion on the continent and is growing robustly in many nations, especially in Anglophone Africa, where it had no colonial privileges."[10] The Catholic Church in Africa, indeed, has experienced tremendous growth in recent times. The Center for Applied Research in the Apostolate (CARA), based at Georgetown University, reports that the population of Catholics living in Africa grew from 59 million in 1980 to 199 million in 2012. The share of Catholics living in Africa grew from 7 percent of the world Catholic population in 1980 to 16 percent in 2012. Based on data from the official statistical reports released on June 1, 2015, CARA reports, "If current trends continue, by 2040 there will be about 460.4 million Catholics in Africa and African Catholicism will have more than 20% of the global Catholic population."[11] What these statistics point to is that Africa is the continent witnessing the highest growth of Catholics in the world.[12] This means that, to a large extent, the future of global Catholicism will be shaped by what is happening in Africa and that the Catholicism of the future will look more like Africa than Europe.

It is important to note, however, that scholars should not use these figures to paint an unduly rosy and triumphalist picture of African Catholicism. There is the need for caution and a critical reading of these data. This is because most demographic data on African Catholic population growth do not distinguish what may simply be a numerical growth of the entire population (with Catholic adherents remaining stable, and growing in some countries of Africa and declining in some other countries), from actual gains in the number of people who are converting to Catholicism. Similarly, the increased proportion of African Catholics in world Catholicism may be because of actual growth in African population, or in declining population in North America and Europe and elsewhere in the world, or a combination of other factors.

These statistics also fail to take into account the fact that the exponential growth in Catholic population in the post–Vatican II African church has not been the result of active evangelization or conversion of people from other religions or denominations to Catholicism, as was the case in the Western missionary phase of African Catholicism. The current growth has been more genetic, internal, or genealogical—meaning that African Catholic parents raise their children Catholic and insist on maintaining and handing on the Catholic faith as a family tradition to successive generations. The Catholic churches in African countries like DRC, Nigeria, Kenya, and Ghana, to give a few examples, just as in Brazil and in the Philippines, are losing a significant number of their population, especially the younger generation, to evangelicals and Pentecostals—a fact often lost in these statistics on church growth generated from outside of Africa.

---

9. John D. Y. Peel, "The Christianization of African Society," in *Christianity in Independent Africa*, ed. E. Fasholé-Luke et al. (London: Rex Collings, 1978), 445. See also David Maxwell, "Review Article: New Perspectives on the History of African Christianity," *Journal of Southern African Studies* 23.1 (March 1997): 181.

10. Joel Carpenter, and Nellie Kooistra, *Engaging Africa: Prospects for Project Funding in Selected Fields* (Grand Rapids, MI: Nagel Institute for the Study of World Christianity, 2015), 13.

11. Center for the Applied Research in the Apostolate, *Global Catholicism: Trends and Forecasts*, June 4, 2015 (Washington, DC: CARA, Georgetown University), 25–26.

12. See Pew Research Center's Report, "Global Catholic Population" (2013), https://www.pewforum.org/2013/02/13/the-global-catholic-population/.

General Introduction

Furthermore, this demographic prognosis is predicated on a continuation of current sociological trends. It is, however, worth noting that the Christian mission has historically shown many unpredictable trends that defy mere sociological facts in terms of its survival in particular contexts and its geographical expansion. This fact is evident to most African Christian historians, who know that the African church fathers of the first five hundred years (CE) would not recognize the Islamic religious landscape of North Africa and Egypt today, judging from the expansive growth of the Christian faith in these territories in the first five centuries. The African church father Tertullian sang the praises of Christian expansion in North Africa in the third century CE in these words, "We are but of yesterday, and we have filled every place among you—cities, islands, fortresses, towns, market-places, the very camp, tribes, companies, palace, senate, forum" (*Apologeticus* 37). A more recent example is the prediction made at the beginning of the twentieth century that it was going to be "the Christian century." According to Brian Stanley, "as the twentieth century dawned, many Christians anticipated that the coming decades would witness the birth of a new era. Their expectation was that the accelerating global diffusion of Christianity from its Western heartlands to the rest of the globe will usher in the final phase of human history—the climactic millennial age of international peace and harmony."[13] The project of bringing about the Christian century was to be marked by intense Western missionary activities to the non-Western world, to convert the rest of the world to Western Christianity. The World Missionary Congress of 1910 was convoked to plan the strategies to achieve the "evangelization of the world in this generation" by European churches.[14]

But alas, Christianity, which began the twentieth century as a Western religion, by the end of that century had become a post-Western religion. Given the unpredictable patterns in Christian expansion, scholars must go beyond the binaries of Western contraction and non-Western expansion in world Christianity today to a more expansive cross-cultural and theological interpretation. Merely sociological explanations of these shifts will not suffice. We need theological attention to the work of the Holy Spirit and the gospel's own inherent thrust to grow. Nonetheless, it is notable that the momentum of Christian expansion in some parts of the world and its contraction in others have continued to drive some of the contending narratives of modernity beyond the twentieth century in the following areas: mission and conversion; religion and politics (the relationship between church and state); church and development; interreligious conflicts, religious persecution and violence; Christianity and genocide, racism, and war; reproductive rights, capital punishment, social justice, marriage, and family life; gender issues, ecumenism; women in ministry; same-sex marriages; and immigration.

The truth is that we humans cannot say with certainty how the Christian mission will actually unfold or how it will look in the coming decades and centuries. However, faith leads us to believe that there is a movement of the Spirit in world history. Each of us must play our own part by cooperating with God's grace in making the ambiguities, complexities, and contradictions of present history conform to God's will. This is one way we can bear prophetic witness in the world and thus help bring about the conditions for a new heaven and a new earth of cosmic flourishing in collaboration with people of other faiths and traditions.

In this light, while African Christians are embracing the gospel message with so much enthusiasm, it is also important for us as Africans to listen to what the Spirit is saying to Africa and the world through the reinvention of Christianity in Africa. Particularly of interest for scholars and leaders in today's African Christian communities is the challenge of translating the exuberant faith in Africa into authentic and prophetic witness. This is an urgent mission for today's Africa. The realities and experiences of faith and life mediated through

---

13. Brian Stanley, *Christianity in the Twentieth Century: A World History* (Princeton, NJ: Princeton University Press, 2018), 1.

14. Brian Stanley, "Africa through European Christian Eyes: The World Missionary Conference, Edinburgh 1910," in *African Identities and World Christianity in the Twentieth Century*, ed. Klaus Koschorke (Wiesbaden: Harrassowitz, 2005), 116–80.

the churches in Africa must become a concrete manifestation and realization of integral salvation for God's people in Africa. This is one way through which African Christianity can become Good News proclaimed to the rest of the world on the positive impact of the Christian message, rather than the constant cries of distress for aid and help by millions of our brothers and sisters who are hanging on the cross. African Catholic churches are invited to work critically and consciously to build on the assets and enthusiastic faith of African peoples. This critical and creative function should be directed to translating and transforming the Christian tradition in Africa to serve the needs of Africa, while offering something new and fresh from Africa to the World Church.

There is a need for scholars to confront the contradictions facing Africa today of a continent with an exponential growth in Christian population, on one hand, and a continent with rising poverty, on the other hand. African Catholic scholars must face up to the paradox of a continent that Pope Francis calls the "spiritual capital" of the world, which sadly can also be referred to today as the capital of religious violence, terrorism, religious pathologies, superstition, manipulation through prosperity preachers, religious charlatans, and *pastorpreneurs*, and fragmentation of religious communities and African societies. The growing gap between (1) religious expressions and prophetic religious performance and (2) the sad reality of vibrant religious communities in crumbling, weak, and failing nation-states and fractured local communities is a painful complexity that must be addressed by African Christian scholarship. Many Africans long for "the dawn on high" to shine upon them from the long dark night of suffering, diseases, death, and exploitation. They wish to see in their daily reality and society the signs of the eschatological reign of God in their history. The enormous potentials of Africa in her growing Christian population, youth, human and natural resources, resilient local communities, and women's leadership can be valorized by the church, political actors, and other stakeholders in the continent to bring about a society that reflects the finest values and virtues and dreams of our people.[15]

In order for the Catholic Church in Africa to play a transformative role in meeting the present challenges and opportunities in Africa in a post-COVID-19 world, African local churches, scholars, church leaders, and everyday African Catholics need the space for creative freedom and local agency. This creative freedom will potentiate African local and cultural resources in birthing unique narratives of faith and life and specific forms of prophetic and transformative social engagement to meet the persistent social, spiritual, and political challenges that are features of the so-called African predicament. Creative freedom and local agency will, similarly, strengthen collaborative and mutually respectful partnership among African churches, academies, and social and religious actors in Africa and other traditions outside Africa in reinventing the future on some solid institutional structures, daily practices, and life-giving ecclesial culture.

How the Idea of the *Handbook* Was Born

This *Handbook* fulfills a key aspect of the African Catholicism Project launched by the Center for World Catholicism and Intercultural Theology at DePaul University in Chicago, Illinois, USA, in 2015. The ACP is a collaborative partnership between African Catholic scholars and church leaders, and scholars and professors at CWCIT working with other Catholic scholars in North America and Europe, and frontline social actors, theologians, and churches in the Global South. The partnership was designed to create a capacious space for North–South dialogue in the African Catholic academy. Reports from CWCIT partners in African universities and African scholars in Europe and North America indicate that the church's universities and Catholic scholars in Africa continue to struggle, as scholarly and pastoral resources remain concentrated mainly in the North. The ACP is an international collaborative effort with the overarching goal of expanding the production and distribution

---

15. Cf. World Bank, *Can Africa Claim the 21st Century?* (Washington, DC: International Bank for Reconstruction, 2000), 12.

of scholarly and pastoral resources. Among others, the ACP also identifies the following objectives: (1) to foster collaboration among Catholic scholars working in Africa and between scholars working in Africa and those working in the United States and Europe; (2) to support the work of African scholars teaching in under-resourced institutions in Africa; (3) to encourage interdisciplinary work among scholars studying African Catholicism; (4) to produce written resources, both in print and online, serving both the scholarly community and the pastoral needs of the Catholic Church in Africa; and (5) to ensure the continuity of African scholarship through the mentoring of the next generation of African Catholic scholars.

The ACP offers a forum for African Catholic scholars to collaborate in producing and disseminating significant works for the church and society. ACP has contributed to the formation of scholars in the African church by bringing together different generations of scholars, teachers, and pastoral workers to create academic resources, and by making these resources broadly available for use in both the academy and ministry. Through the ACP and in the process of producing this *Handbook*, CWCIT facilitated three international collaborations between Catholic scholars who are based in Africa and those who reside within Western institutions of higher education and scholarship: in Enugu, Nigeria (December 2015); Nairobi, Kenya (July 2017); and again in Enugu, Nigeria (December 2019).

There is the realization based on this partnership that greater access to library holdings, experts, research funding, and other resources among African scholars will result in measurable increases in the volume and quality of research and pastoral literature that is published. Such partnerships will also increase the overall capacity of African Catholic scholars to carry out an ambitious research and education agenda on behalf of the church in Africa. Altogether, the project supports the growth of African Catholicism with relevant scholarship that accounts for, documents, sustains, and creatively engages the themes and issues that are emerging in African Catholicism. The *Handbook* is the culmination of this effort and is positioned to be one of the most significant and important research resources in the African Catholic Church ever to appear in English or any other language. The hope is that the *Handbook* will fill serious gaps in scholarship in African Catholicism and thus provide for the academy in Africa and in the World Church an important interdisciplinary reference work for studying African Catholicism in its broadest sense.

Telling Our Own Story of What God Has Done for Us

This *Handbook* is an attempt to tell the story of African Catholicism through the lens of Africans themselves in conversation with many scholars from outside Africa, and in collaboration with many universities and other institutions throughout the world. Contributors retrace the redemptive pathway through which the mission of God in Africa began with our ancestors from the beginning of creation and which continues in diverse and dynamic ways today.[16] This effort is thus an attempt to reread this history, while retrieving our African spiritual and theological heritage from the limiting narratives that have often portrayed African Christianity as an appendage to the mission of the Roman Catholic Church or a reproductive prototype of Western Christendom. Many African theologians underscore the importance of a historical turn in African Christian scholarship. For instance, Mercy Amba Oduyoye argues,

> We cannot expect those who cannot tell their story, who do not know where they come from, to hear God's call to his future. We cannot expect a people "without a history" to respond as responsible human beings living in Africa. If their story is the same as the story of those who live in Europe and America, then they can only echo Euro-American responses.[17]

---

16. See Albert Nolan, *Hope in an Age of Despair: And Other Talks and Writings*, ed. Stan Muyebe (Maryknoll, NY: Orbis Books, 2010), 19.

17. Mercy Amba Oduyoye, *Hearing and Knowing: Theological Reflections on Christianity in Africa* (Maryknoll, NY: Orbis Books, 1993), 54.

General Introduction

The *Handbook* is thus an attempt at a liberative historiography—a conscious attempt to tell the story of African Catholicism through a different lens and beyond institutional narratives by giving voice and valence to African agency. This, it is hoped, will be a helpful corrective to some of the partial accounts that have been written in the past.

The need for a liberative historiography in telling the story of Catholicism in Africa cannot be overemphasized. Whenever one hears of mainstream ideas, standard practice, educational models, theological method, research methodology, a distinctive Catholic identity, and unchanging truth, it is important to realize that these are not disinterested claims. Africa still develops her educational systems, contents, and curricula in the Christian academy through a mainstreaming of knowledge and an epistemological framework embedded in the dominant cultural narratives of the West. Indeed, there is a confluence of cultural and historical factors as well as power dynamics that play important roles in the claims people make even in the social and experimental sciences. This is also true in religious studies and in theological accounts of history and theological and ecclesial traditions.

One needs to draw attention to the fact that knowledge, in this case religious knowledge and theological productions, inhabits the domain of power and interests. As a result, those who are able to control knowledge production and dissemination often control the minds of people as well as the kind of history that is told. This has become even more challenging today because of the limitations in documenting the funds of knowledge and knowledge production in Africa, given the digital divide and social media. In addition, research methods and scholarly paradigms on documentation of knowledge, for example, and religious codes and laws often make it difficult for historically dominated peoples to produce their own knowledge, and to tell their own stories, without defaulting to these dominant structures and systems that are the academic legal tender in scholarly circulation in the world. Thus, telling the African stories and documenting the African Catholic heritage in this *Handbook* is an effort to produce a different kind of narrative and resources for Africa and the world that, we hope, will inspire scholars and the general reader to a better appreciation and understanding of the diversity, beauty, resilience, dynamism, challenges, and possibilities of the African Catholic heritage in shaping the future of the Christian mission in Africa and the world.

The *Handbook* chapters show that African Catholic scholarship is transgressing Northern epistemological hegemony. Contributors apply some new methodologies being developed by African Catholic scholars in transmitting Catholic intellectual traditions and the Christian traditions more broadly in Africa. Particularly significant is a conscious attempt to show that the church is a historical subject. Thus, the normativity of institutional history, and particularly the false insistence on an uncritical acceptance of the unity of human knowledge and a distinctive Eurocentric Catholic identity and culture, are being contested by some of the contributors to this volume. This attempt to see all reality and all knowledge as one and the perennial default to the universals pose significant obstacles to finding and appreciating new forms of knowing. We need to hear the suppressed voices within our churches and be open and enthusiastic about the new approaches to the craft of theology, just to give one example. There is a need to embrace in the World Church different experiences of Catholicism and different ways of knowing and of conducting theological or scientific inquiries.

Catholicism as a global religion is best served when the culture of encounter moves us all toward a joyful embrace of different worldviews, new epistemologies, local knowledge, contextual theology, and context-sensitive pedagogy in the one church of God. What this means is that there are important developments in world Christianity and in Africa and in the Global South that invite all discerning Christians to embrace the endless quest of stretching human knowing and thinking to roads less traveled outside the West. Indeed, the future of Christianity and the world will depend on finding a Catholic center in all things. In the face of the ideologies of power and interests that have polarized the church and our world, the new centers of Catholicism in Africa are offering a depolarizing space to encounter the God of surprises at the Catholic center, understood not as the spatial center of Rome but rather the movement to the heart of the Trinity, where all things are held together in love.

However, the battle for the truth and the right faith and the right conduct has continued in the moral and spiritual polarization today in the World Church and the schismatic binaries in local and global politics. In many instances, these battles have made it impossible for deeper encounter with God—beyond the idols of religion, empires, cultures, money, politics, race, and other narrow constructions of identity, social hierarchies, and the social construction of belonging and exclusion in the world.

People often pursue their cultural appropriation of the truth, faith, and identity in an absolute way. Sadly, some of these ideological, cultural, and sociological constructs are often imposed on others as a universal and absolute image of God or truth along the course of Christian history. For us Africans, we are appropriating and celebrating the truths of the Christian faith as our own, and we are unapologetically bringing our own truths and reality into dialogue with the Christian truth claims and assuming ownership of the Christian faith and the Gospel message as a rich tradition that has deep roots in Africa. However, this claim is inclusive because it highlights the rich experience and narrative of the impact of the gospel among African peoples and the shared faith with our brothers and sisters in other parts of the world within the common traits of our Christian and global family.

When we first designed this *Handbook* project in 2016, we were also aware of some disagreements about how to write African Christian history. The question of periodization in African Christian history is taken up in some of the chapters in the *Handbook*, particularly by Paul Kollman in the third article of the volume. However, within the overall thematic structure of this *Handbook*, we have contemporized our research endeavors here from the end of the Second World War to Pope Francis, by concentrating on current themes around the Christianity that emerged in Africa after the missionary work of Western Christians in the continent. The first section of this *Handbook* deals exclusively with African church history, while the rest of the *Handbook* focuses on the developments in the Catholic Church in Africa since the end of the Second World War, the decolonization process in Africa, Vatican II, and post-Vatican II developments. The chapters thus deal with interpretative history rather than providing a chronological account of the selected themes.

Readers will see that the *Handbook* is a unique work of history because of the conscious attempt by contributors to give a historical background to the themes discussed in most of the chapters. But in doing this, we are also conscious of the divergence of meaning in terms of "African Christian history," or the application of the descriptive terms "Africa," "African Christianity," "African church," "church in Africa," and "African Catholicism."[18] As Thomas Oden rightly noted in *How Africa Shaped the Christian Mind: Rediscovering the African Seedbed of Western Christianity*, one must be conscious of a very narrow reading of modern Christian history when it comes to Africa, where often people think that Christianity in Africa was strictly imported from the North. Oden proposes that, whereas many modern African theologians and scholars of religion have fought to give voice to the narratives of faith in God in Africa "in African traditional religious patterns, motifs, rituals, and memories," he thinks that the best weapon for African theologians is the ancient texts of African Christianity.[19]

Another African Christian historian, Elizabeth Isichei, argues differently on how to read early African Christian history. She contends that the Christianity in North Africa, Nubia, and Ethiopia in the first five hundred years and the Christianity in the Kongo and Warri kingdoms, in the West African coastal regions, and in the Zambezi valley, had waned, died, or remained in fragments, especially in Coptic and Ethiopian Christianities. In the

---

18. For more on the theological explication of the complexities involved in these distinctions, see Stan Chu Ilo, "African Ecclesiologies," in *Oxford Handbook of Ecclesiology*, ed. Paul Avis (Oxford: Oxford University Press, 2018), 615–38.

19. Thomas C. Oden, *How Africa Shaped the Christian Mind: Rediscovering the African Seedbed of Western Christianity* (Downers Grove, IL: IVP Books, 2007), 25–26.

light of this reasoning, there is the need for some intellectual humility in universalizing the marginal residues of the Christian influence of these epochs on today's Africa.[20] Thus, a romanticized African past must give way to the realization that today's African Christians need to demonstrate the claim of an unmediated successive connection to ancient African Christianity. The early African church of the first five hundred years should be a source of inspiration to African Christians today because it offers African scholars and leaders in a special way an exemplary model of what is possible in Africa. This is the kind of sentiment expressed by Pope Benedict XVI in a speech in Yaoundé, Cameroun:

> Perhaps this century will permit, by God's grace, the rebirth on your continent, albeit surely in a new and different form, of the prestigious School of Alexandria. Why should we not hope that it could furnish today's Africans and the universal Church with great theologians and spiritual masters who could contribute to the sanctification of the inhabitants of this continent and of the whole Church?[21]

Whereas African Christians should take pride in the glories of the past history of the growth and contribution of African Christianity in the development of Christian doctrines and church structures, I argue that an uninterrupted, diffusionist account of African Christianity is simplistic. Without taking account of cultural mediation, variations, displacements, migrations, the emergence of Islam in Africa, and Western cultural erasures of African histories and religious traditions over a period of fourteen hundred years on the continent of Africa, one might end up producing an emotive history that papers over important disruptions and tragic interruptions from outside Africa that continue to this day. This point, however, only helps readers to appreciate the antiquity of African Christianity.

Indeed, African theological engagement with African stories and histories hark back to the first century, when the Lord Jesus walked the African soil, and even further back to the ancestral past when God spoke to our fathers and mothers in many signs and languages and in shadows and images before the coming of Christianity in Africa. As Augustine of Hippo put it, "That which is called Christian religion existed among the ancients . . . from the beginning of the human race until Christ came in the flesh, at which time the true religion which already existed began to be called Christian" (*Retractationes* 1.13.3). Pope Benedict XVI also spoke in the same vein when he said, "In Jesus, some two thousand years ago, God himself brought salt and light to Africa. From that time on, the seed of his presence was buried deep within the hearts of the people of this dear continent, and it has blossomed gradually, beyond and within the vicissitudes of its human history."[22] Many commentators have observed that, in African Christian religion, the Bible is the dynamic source for connecting both individuals and cultures to the very heart of the Triune God.[23] The goal of this *Handbook* is to leverage the variations in African Catholicism and to give a greater accent to a hermeneutic of multiplicity in this account beyond the often romanticized, univocal, and undifferentiated chronological, diffusionist, theological, and historical accounts.

The birth of modernity in Africa or rather the disruptions caused by modernity in Africa began with the introduction of Western Christianity, slavery, colonialism, and the emergence of nation-states in Africa. All these factors have created the so-called African predicament, which has held Africa down through multiple internal and exter-

---

20. Elizabeth Isichei, *A History of Christianity in Africa: From Antiquity to the Present* (Trenton, NJ: African World Press, 1995), 2.

21. Pope Benedict XVI, address to Members of the Special Council for Africa of the Synod of Bishops (Yaoundé, March 19, 2009); *AAS* 101 (2009): 312.

22. Pope Benedict XVI, address to Members of the Special Council for Africa of the Synod of Bishops (Yaoundé, March 19, 2009); *AAS* 101 (2009): 310.

23. See, for instance, Philip Jenkins, *The New Faces of Christianity: Believing the Bible in the Global South* (Oxford: Oxford University Press, 2006).

nal forces of history. The convergence theory of global history is proving to be a will-o'-the wisp for Africa and is creating greater stress than ever on all fronts. This view is shared by a majority of African scholars, especially those who embrace postcolonial critical social theories of history in writing African Christian history. This is well represented in the words of Ogbu Kalu: "Of all these bearers of the African burden, the missionary was also paradoxically, the best symbol of the colonial enterprise. He devoted himself sincerely to the ideals of colonialisms: the expansion of civilization, the dissemination of Christianity, and the advance of progress."[24] However, Elizabeth A. Foster in *African Catholic: Decolonization and the Transformation of the Church* makes a more nuanced argument regarding Africa and modernity before and after Vatican II. She demonstrates with newly discovered materials that, by the middle of the twentieth century, there was an internal tension between the Vatican and some French missionaries who were inspired by the spirit of Archbishop Lefebvre, who was the pope's vicar for Franco-Africa on the direction of the Catholic mission with regard to modernity in Africa. Whereas most of the French missionaries wanted a greater convergence of the emerging "Franco-African Catholic world" forged by conquest, colonization, missions, and conversions, and knit together by Catholic faith, Catholic education, Catholic press, and Catholic charities to the Metropole, the Vatican was open to reconciling Catholicism with African culture and modernity. This threatened to unhinge the direction of history favored in France, whose mainstream missionaries saw Africa as the extension of the French version of Catholicism. The Vatican, on the other hand, had its own version of modernity in Africa, which was opposed to continuing the "civilizing mission" in Africa, that is, opposed to maintaining the firm relationship of Franco-African Catholicism to the Western heritage.[25] The contestations about different versions of modernity that were implemented by different European nations in Africa are open questions beyond this survey. This *Handbook*, however, is an effort to account for how African Catholic traditions and communities are grappling with the contested notions, projects, and designs of modernity as appropriated through the openness of the Second Vatican Council to cultural diversity and the impetus to contextual histories and ecclesiologies in the Roman Catholic tradition.

The *Handbook*: A Continuing Account of Africa's Reception of Vatican II

One of the ways in which the mothers and fathers of the First African Synod desired to promote the reception of Vatican II was in highlighting the need to make the faith in Africa intelligible. Their proposal was the pathway of inculturation, which aims at transmitting the faith and life of African peoples through an African cultural grammar and African religio-cultural traditions in regard to beliefs and practices, liturgy, morality, and spirituality. In doing this, they also recognized the changes in the movement of the Spirit in the momentum of Christian expansion in Africa (*EA* §8). Particularly significant here is the desire of the synod fathers and mothers to seek ways of integrating faith and life in Africa, through what Pope John Paul II calls an "organic pastoral solidarity" (*EA* §§5, 21).

The Second African Synod, on the other hand, was concerned with realizing the prophetic function of the church, as advanced in Vatican II's call for the church to read and respond to the signs of the times. Thus, whereas the First African Synod dealt with issues of fundamental theology and pastoral life, using the ecclesiological image of the Church as the family of God, the Second African Synod dealt with the same concerns using the ecclesiological image of the Church as salt and light. It embraced this image programmatically, from the perspective of prophetic social ministry. Both the First and Second African Synods called for the

---

24. Olufemi Taiwo, *How Colonialism Preempted Modernity in Africa* (Bloomington: Indiana University Press, 2010), 52.

25. Elizabeth A. Foster, *African Catholic: Decolonization and the Transformation of the Church* (Cambridge, MA: Harvard University Press, 2019), 7.

development of an African theology (*EA* §103; *AM* §136) that will make possible the scientific study of African culture, so that the Christian faith can shed light on African society through Africa's own unique pastoral plan, social praxis, and intellectual heritage. Both synods dealt with issues of culture, communication, dialogue, justice and peace, mission, and ecclesiology and evangelization. Both also encouraged the use of all the gifts of all the members of the church—especially the genius of women, whom the Second Synod called the "backbone" (*AM* §58) of the church—to serve the cause of the gospel in Africa. Both were synods of hope, affirming as they did that the church in Africa must assume agency for her own life. She is called to play an active role in the unfolding of God's plan of salvation in Africa, as both a missionary church and a mission church (*EA* §29).

Building on the themes of the African synods and on the sixteen documents of the Second Vatican Council, the chapters in this *Handbook* offer an account of Africa's reception of Vatican II through the two African synods, the writings of theologians and other church scholars, the evolving methodologies being developed, and the development of themes within a particular field. The essays were produced through a cohort-based African palaver method that lasted for two years, in which each essay went through a rigorous review process through a communal process of correction, revision, and updating. This unique collaborative approach involving cohort-based research support, peer review, and peer learning makes this work a product of a community of learners; in a sense one can say that "we did it together."

Each chapter tells a story—how the theme or issue discussed has developed historically. Then, the contributor examines the methodologies developing in the field and proceeds to "excavate" the data and the range of issues within the church and society around the themes or history under study. The contributor then maps the development of research in that particular field and possible new pathways, while attempting to explore some of the cross-disciplinary connections that are opening in different areas of research, pastoral practice, and other fields outside ecclesiastical studies. All the contributors are leading African Catholic scholars, church leaders, and practitioners. They have worked hard collaboratively over a period of three years to produce works of significant quality, depth, and range.

Themes Covered in the *Handbook*

The themes and topics presented in this *Handbook* are deliberately chosen to reflect the themes, topics, issues, and research interests that have emerged in African Catholicism since the Second Vatican Council. These issues have been articulated in different ways by African theologians, Catholic scholars, social theorists, local church leaders, and everyday Catholics. Some of these issues are not being sufficiently addressed in the Catholic Church in Africa today. In some instances, the African scholars talking about them are not in conversation with one another because of language barriers or the lack of documentary and transferable data. In this *Handbook*, these issues have been thoroughly studied, debated, and developed through the African palaver among a broad range of African and Western conversation partners.

The *Handbook* is divided into five sections according to five broad areas. These five broad areas were chosen to reflect the themes and subjects of the two African synods and the programmatic plan for evangelization in this third millennium from Pope Paul VI to Pope Francis's *Evangelii Gaudium*, namely: (1) the history and mission of African Catholicism; (2) formation, education, and communication in African Catholicism; (3) church and society in Africa; (4) morality/spirituality, health, and healing; and (5) Catholic intellectual traditions in Africa in the areas of theological and philosophical studies. This *Handbook* was designed to transgress disciplinary silos. This is why the contributors employ an interdisciplinary approach in their research and in the development of their chapters. The *Handbook* is thus structured to address different audiences, because in researching and writing on these five themes contributors have integrated multiple perspectives, methodologies, and approaches to harvesting and accounting for the development of African Catholic intellectual traditions.

General Introduction

How to Use the *Handbook*

It is hoped that this *Handbook* can be an aid to scholars, students, practitioners, and the general interest reader studying African Catholicism and the significant momentum of Christian expansion and influence in the continent. We suggest four approaches to reading this work among others that readers might choose.

First, it should be read as *a narrative of hope and a pedagogy of agency*. The chapters tell the story of hope by connecting the African past to the present and providing some blueprints of how the future might unfold. This is a particularly important approach to African studies in general, especially given the negative framing of Africa that could make one lose hope. Indeed, Afro-pessimism is a present temptation for many, given the persistent challenges facing Africa and the suffering of God's people in Africa. Afro-pessimism has its roots in White supremacy and racism, the deficit characterization of African culture, and the general sentiments that Africa's political and religious institutions are retrogressive, leading to the lack of faith in a better future for Africa. However, these sad realities are signs that the continent is still searching for new pathways and new roads to a future, hence the need for moderation of our anger and our pessimism and the need to translate this anger and these negative sentiments into a veritable tool and praxis for reversal. In reading the chapters of the *Handbook*, we hope that readers can appreciate the many significant developments in the past that can serve as an inspiration for us to set out again and put into the deep every new day in the hope that each of us can contribute something to build up the city of God in our continent and in the world.

The second approach is *critical Afrocentric realism away from the popular claim in the World Church that Africa is the new center of gravity for world Christianity*. Readers are invited to read this *Handbook* as a field manual for action on translating faith into action, hope, and enthusiastic faith claims into spiritual agency for changing Africa from this cycle of suffering and pain to a cycle of abundant life and human flourishing. This approach is against one of unrealistic romantic optimism of a better future for Africa through devotions, prosperity gospel, and church growth without taking the time to do the heavy lifting of looking at Africa's past and present history and social conditions and how they have weakened critical, creative, and transformative thinking, knowledge production, and education in Africa. This approach invites readers to critically engage the religious, social, and political institutions, systems, structures, and cultural traditions in Africa and ask the simple question: Is this particular institution generating the kind of knowledge, transformative ethics, and praxis that can bring human flourishing in these rich lands?

Third, the *Handbook* offers *a total-picture approach model in studying African history from the lens of Catholicism*. This approach is analogous to the *nexus mysteriorum*, a principle in Catholic theology that says that, in explicating a particular Christian doctrine, one will inevitably shed light on other doctrines because all the mysteries of faith are intimately connected. The same thing applies here in writing about African Catholic history—there is an organic synthesis to each chapter and an inner connection to all the chapters. The total-picture approach method proposes that we cannot study any reality today in Africa without establishing its linkage to the bigger historical picture of the continent. Every reality in African studies that we study reveals significant insights about other aspects of African history. Therefore, one cannot simply dismiss any African solution without seeing it in its historical and interconnected contexts or interpret Africa through a single narrative. The challenge today for many Africans is that we are often represented in the contemporary world by one thing or another—usually a single narrative, or we sometimes represent present African conditions as originating from a single causative factor. Readers of the *Handbook* are thus invited to this organic and total picture that can be gained by reading each chapter. This is why the chapters are interdisciplinary and cross-disciplinary in nature.

Fourth and finally, the *Handbook* is *the product of a community of scholars and a community of practice*. The hope is that the *Handbook* will attract also a *community of readers and conversation partners in colleges, dioceses, formation houses, and third-sector researchers in Africa and outside of Africa*. What the production of this *Handbook* shows ultimately is a model of how Africans can work together among themselves and with others to do the work of God. Africa's rich harvest of faith and exciting social realities cannot be understood through a single theological method or through the account of one scholar, teacher, or church leader; it has to be accounted for by a network, a coming together of scholars and practitioners. But Africa is also best served when her scholars and leaders are working not only among themselves but with other scholars and leaders in every part of the world. This is the wisdom of the spider's web, an ancient wisdom on solidarity, patience, and teamwork left for us by our African ancestors—"When spider webs unite, they can tie a lion."

HISTORY AND MISSION

A Brief History of the Catholic Church in Africa

Vincent J. O'Malley, CM

The First Seven Hundred Years: The Origin, Expansion, and Decline of the Church in North Africa

The Apostolic Age (First Century)

The New Testament and church tradition identify numerous saintly persons who either originated from Africa or visited there.

The Holy Family fled to Egypt to escape the wrath of Herod, the paranoid Roman-appointed king of Judea. The Gospel reports, "Now when they [the wise men] had departed, behold, an angel of the Lord appeared to Joseph in a dream and said, 'Rise, take the child and his mother, and flee to Egypt, and remain there until I tell you; for Herod is about to search for the child, to destroy him'" (Matt 2:13). Father, mother, and child fled to what traditionally is believed to be Heliopolis. The flight "was to fulfill what the Lord had spoken by the prophet, 'Out of Egypt have I called my son'" (Matt 2:15; see Hos 11:1).

Egypt, Cyrene, and Ethiopia are mentioned in the scriptural stories of the last days of Jesus and the first days of the spread of the church. The "devout Jews from every nation" who were staying in Jerusalem and heard the apostles speaking in the visitors' tongues included Jews from "Egypt, and the parts of Libya belonging to Cyrene" (Acts 2:5, 10). Simon of Cyrene was taken from the crowd to assist Jesus in carrying his cross (Matt 27:32; Mark 15:21; Luke 23:26). At Antioch, Lucius of Cyrene was among the handful of teachers and prophets from whom the Spirit called Barnabas and Paul to serve as missionaries among the diaspora Jews and gentiles (Acts 13:1). The apostle Philip, while traveling on the desert route from Jerusalem down to Gaza, was directed by the Spirit to approach a fellow traveler, an Ethiopian eunuch who was a court official and overseer of the treasury of his country's queen, Candace. Philip instructed the eunuch and the man asked to be baptized (Acts 8:27–39).

Both St. Luke and St. Paul write favorably about Apollos of Alexandria. Luke presents Apollos as "an eloquent man, well versed in the scriptures, . . . [who] spoke with burning enthusiasm and taught accurately the things concerning Jesus" (Acts 18:25, 28). Apollos, it seems, had been baptized by John the Baptist but never received the baptism of the Holy Spirit, until at Ephesus. Priscilla and Aquila "took him aside and explained the Way of God to him more accurately" (Acts 18:26). The Alexandrian later traveled to Corinth, where he was evangelizing at the same time that Paul was rejoicing over the many converts won by Apollos at Ephesus. Returning to Corinth, Paul discovered that cliques had formed around the various preachers of the gospel: Peter, Paul, and Apollos. Paul urged the Corinthians not to focus on the messengers but on the message: "Let no one boast about human leaders. . . . All things are yours, whether Paul or Apollos, or Cephas, . . . you belong to Christ, and Christ belongs to God" (1 Cor 3:22–23). Paul described Apollos and himself as "God's servants" and requested Titus to send Apollos from Crete to continue the ministry of the gospel at Corinth (1 Cor 3:9; cf. Titus 3:13).

Excerpt from *Saints of Africa*, copyright © Vincent O›Malley, published by OSV Publishing, 1-800-348-2440, www.osv.com. Used by permission. No other use of this material is authorized.

According to tradition, St. Mark the evangelist came to Egypt, where he served as the country's first Christian missionary and first bishop of Alexandria. This tradition is recorded as early as the fourth century by both Eusebius, in his *Ecclesiastical History*, and St. Jerome, in the preface of the Latin Vulgate edition of the Gospels. Mark is remembered as the fleet-footed youth who ran away practically naked after he had overheard Jewish leaders at Jerusalem plotting to kill Jesus, as the resident of the home to which St. Peter fled upon his angel-effected escape from prison, and as the missionary who evangelized with Barnabas and Paul in Syria, Crete, and Pamphylia (see Mark 14:51–52; Acts 12:12; 12:25–13:13). Mark became reconciled with Paul and honored his request to visit Rome to assist the apostle of the Gentiles (see Col. 4:10; Phlm 24; 2 Tim 4:11). Mark assisted St. Peter, who affectionately calls the young disciple "my son Mark" (1 Pet 5:13). Churchmen from the second to the fourth centuries, namely, St. Clement of Alexandria, St. Irenaeus, Origen, and Papias, all refer to Mark as "the disciple and interpreter of St. Peter."[1] This is the background and reputation of St. Mark, who tradition teaches evangelized in Egypt.

The Growth of Christianity (Second and Third Centuries)

Martyrdom and monasticism led to the rapid growth of the native church and the intellectual development of the faith.

For almost a century and a half, from 180 to 311, Christians in Africa suffered intermittent waves of imperial persecution. Personal and church properties were confiscated. People of every age and sex were tortured, exiled, or killed on account of their faith. One of the earliest instances of Christian martyrdom ever recorded occurred in 180 at Carthage, where Speratus and eleven companions from the town of Scillium refused the proconsul's order to offer sacrifice to the emperor. For this defiance against paganism and defense of Christianity the dozen persons were beheaded. Two decades later in the same city, the young mothers Perpetua and Felicity, along with three Christian men, were thrown into the amphitheater, where wild animals mauled the men to death and where gladiators, in response to the audience's directions, killed the women. Half a century later and thirty miles to the west, in Utica, the governor ordered numerous Christians to choose between offering incense to the gods and being thrown into a white-hot lime-kiln. The Christians did not wait to be thrown into the fire; instead, they jumped in. A few hundred miles to the east in Alexandria, which was suffering the effects of Roman civil war and citywide violence, it was the Christians who gladly gave up their lives in caring for plague victims. Far removed from Africa, at a battle site on the Rhône River in the Swiss Alps, a legion of Egyptian Christian soldiers from Thebes refused to invoke the protection of the Roman gods before a battle. The emperor's envoy listened to the Christians' explanation and then repeated the order: worship Roman gods or be killed. This happened in 287, when Maurice and countless members of the legion were slaughtered.

The greatest persecution began around 297, became general in 303, and lasted until 311, when the elderly and infirm emperor Diocletian retired from political office to his country villa. In Numidia, a young man named Maximilian refused to be a soldier for the emperor because he had dedicated his life to be a soldier for Christ. Maximilian lost his life on account of this profession of faith. These persecutions were directed toward people of all religions, including Christianity, to foster political unity through religious unity; the order to offer sacrifice "was conceived as an oath of allegiance to the emperor and the Roman state."[2] These persecutions were mandated for particular places prior to 250 and for the entire empire from 250 until 311, although the order was implemented to varying degrees in various places. Only a few of the more than forty emperors who ruled from 180 to 311 mandated persecutions: notably, prior to 250, Marcus Aurelius, Commodus, and Septimius Severus; from 250 onward, Decius, Valerian, Gallienus, and Diocletian. Diocletian applied persecution in an especially thorough way.

Most emperors of the third century had promoted the worship of the sun as a unifying

---

1. McKenzie, "Mark, Gospel of," 543.
2. Scarre, *Chronicle of the Roman Emperors*, 170.

theme, a cult which few of their subjects would have difficulty in accepting. Diocletian instead went back to the traditional Roman gods such as Jove and Hercules. This was to have dire consequences for the Christians, who by now formed a large minority group within the army and the imperial administration. The first blow fell in 297 or 298, when Diocletian issued an order requiring all soldiers and administrators to sacrifice to the gods; those who refused were forced to quit the service. So matters stood for six years. Then on 24 February 303, an edict was issued ordering the destruction of churches and scriptures throughout the empire, and the punishment of leading Christians. Further edicts later that same year ordered the arrest and imprisonment of the entire Christian clergy; they were to be released only after they had sacrificed to the traditional gods. In April 304, a final edict commanded all Christians, clergy and laity alike, to offer sacrifice, on pain of death.[3]

Tertullian, the great African Christian apologist, provides the immortal phrase: "The blood of martyrs is the seed of Christians." Despite the bloodshed, the universal church grew enormously. In Africa, by 225, at least seventy bishops oversaw dioceses in Numidia and proconsular Africa, and shortly thereafter, another seventy bishops served in Egypt. By the time Augustine was appointed bishop of Hippo in 396, over three hundred bishops were serving in Africa, not including the bishops serving in Egypt. Approximately one third of the more than one million population of Egypt's capital city were said to have been Christians.

Martyrdom led to monasticism. During the Decian persecution from 250 to 251, some Christians from the city of Thebes in Upper Egypt fled to the surrounding deserts. Paul the First Hermit (ca. 229–ca. 342) and others like him lived the solitary life there. When Antony (251–356) moved from the city of Memphis to the neighboring desert, so many hermits kept joining him that he kept moving farther and farther out into the desert, eventually to Colzim in 272.

Intense theological discussions took place at this time. Two highly educated converts from paganism to Christianity highlighted the church's intellectual activity: Tertullian (ca. 160–220) and St. Cyprian (ca. 200–258). Tertullian defended the faith against pagans and the heretics of Montanism and Manichaeism. This great apologist was a genius at one-liners; he "is the most quotable of all ancient Christian writers, . . . he had a gift for the phrase rather than the paragraph."[4] Cyprian, the bishop of Carthage, corresponded with three popes. The first, Cornelius, praised the bishop for upholding the need that the *lapsi* do penance as a condition for being reinstated in the Church. The second, Stephen, threatened Cyprian with excommunication for insisting on the rebaptism of heretics. The third pope, Sixtus II, supported the theological position of his predecessor but tolerated the diversity of theological viewpoints and reconciled himself with Cyprian. Both Sixtus and Cyprian were beheaded by Roman authorities within a five-week span in 258.

Institutionalization of the Church in Africa (Fourth and Early Fifth Centuries)

The Edict of Milan decreed in 312 that Christianity, along with other religions, was no longer to be persecuted but was to be tolerated. Not until 395 did Christianity become the official state religion of the Roman Empire. This newfound freedom of religious expression had the effect of shifting popular spirituality from martyrdom to monasticism. And the continuing development of the church's theology led to an ever-increasing precision in the church's statements of its beliefs.

When everybody was nominally Christian, only a portion were practicing Christians. Many of those who wished to live their faith passionately in the more tolerant age thought that they had to leave the lukewarm waters of the churches in the cities. Thousands, therefore, abandoned the urban centers in favor of the remote deserts.

Finally, in 305, Antony organized monks into worshiping communities who gathered on Saturdays and Sundays, while returning to their individual hermitages the rest of the week. This

---

3. Scarre, *Chronicle of the Roman Emperors*, 202.
4. Le Saint, "Tertullian," 1021.

organization is regarded as the earliest expression of Christian monasticism. Pachomius (ca. 292–348) gave full expression to the idea by having monks live, work, and pray together in permanent communities. This movement spread from Upper Egypt to Lower Egypt. Ammon (d. ca. 356) created monasteries in about 330 in the Nitrian mountains about seventy miles southeast of his native Alexandria; Macarius (d. ca. 390) began monasteries about 330 in the desert at Skete, located along the northwestern border of the Nitrian desert. Thousands of men and women joined these monasteries. At any one time at least three thousand followed Antony and seven thousand followed Pachomius.

After Sts. Clement of Alexandria and Cyprian of Carthage had strengthened the foundation of the church in the third century, other fathers of the church—including Sts. Athanasius, Cyril, Isidore, and Macarius in Egypt, and Augustine and Optatus in Carthage—in the fourth and fifth centuries provided further inspiration and insight for the church. In addition, unsainted scholars like Origen in Alexandria and Tertullian in Carthage are included, according to some sources, among the official list of fathers of the church. Ten Africans *in toto* are counted among the church's eighty-seven fathers, while three Africans, namely, Athanasius, Augustine, and Cyril, are included among the church's thirty-three doctors.

The church in Africa, like the church universal, became occupied with explaining and defending the church's teachings against the continuous threats of new heresies, such as Arianism, Donatism, Montanism, and Monophysitism. These heresies focused especially on understanding not only the relation between the divine and human elements in Jesus and the implications for understanding Mary's role as Mother of Jesus but also the Eucharist and the relative authority of the pope in Rome in relation to other bishops.

While the church's first four ecumenical councils, from the Council of Nicaea in 325 to the Council of Chalcedon in 451, took place in Asia Minor (now Turkey), it is noteworthy that Africans played a central role in these councils, especially Cyril of Alexandria at Ephesus and Dioscorus of Alexandria at Chalcedon. During the same period, numerous local and regional councils were held in northern Africa.

Almost halfway through the fourth century, the church conducted its first evangelization efforts into Ethiopia. St. Frumentius, a Christian originally from Tyre, had arrived in Ethiopia decades before and held positions of secretary and treasurer in the court of King Ella Amida before becoming the regent for King Azana.[5] When Azana came of age, Frumentius was released from his responsibilities and, on his trip home, visited Alexandria. Frumentius suggested to Patriarch Athanasius of Alexandria that missionaries be sent to Ethiopia. Athanasius responded that he believed Frumentius would be the ideal missionary. The patriarch ordained the former court official and missioned him to Ethiopia as its first bishop. Significantly, foreign clergy and a foreign mother church continued to dominate the Ethiopian church from its origin until the twentieth century.

Barbarian Invasion and Occupation (429–534)

During the century in which the six Germanic-speaking Vandal kings ruled in North Africa, the church flourished in its desert monasteries but suffered significant persecution in its urban centers.

All of the Vandal kings held to the Arian heresy. They generally aimed to eliminate from North Africa the Christian bishops and to replace them with Arian bishops. The first two kings almost succeeded. In Carthage alone, under Genseric (428–477) the number of Catholic bishops was reduced from 164 to three.[6] Genseric's son Huneric (477–484) took up where his father had left off. The new king ordered all the Catholic bishops remaining in northern Africa to come to Carthage in 484 under the pretext of holding theological discussions with the Arians. Once they were there, however, the king exiled the religious leaders either to Corsica or the surrounding desert. The brutal Huneric scourged and exiled five hundred clerics, five thousand laity,

---

5. Isichei, *History of Christianity in Africa*, 32–33.
6. Gavigan, "North Africa, Early Church In," 504.

and, in an attempt to extirpate the monastic life, ordered all monks and monasteries to be handed over to the dreaded Mauri. When Huneric died, a respite followed with the reign of Gunthamund (484–496), who allowed all the exiled bishops to return home. The worst was yet to come, however. It arrived in the person of Thrasimund (496–523). He prohibited the election of any new bishop. When the province of Byzacena resisted, the king exiled 120 bishops to Sardinia.

> But who could describe in fitting language or confine himself to just a brief account of the different punishments which the Vandals, on the order of the king, inflicted on their own people? If a writer tried to recount the things which were done in Carthage itself one by one, without any ornament of speech, he would not even be able to indicate the names of the torments. The evidence can easily be viewed today. You can look upon people without hands, others without eyes, others who have no feet, others whose noses and ears have been cut off; and you can see others, left hanging for too long a period, whose heads, which used to be held normally, have been plunged between their shoulders, and who have protruding shoulder blades. This occurred because they [the king's soldiers] tortured some by hanging them from high buildings and swinging them to and fro through the empty air by jerking ropes with their hands. In some cases the ropes broke, and those who had been hung so high fell down with great force. Many of these people lost skulls, together with their eyes; others died immediately, their bones broken; while others expired shortly afterwards.[7]

Thrasimund's successor, Hilderic (523–530), recalled the exiles. The last king, Gelmer (530–534), soon was defeated militarily by General Belisarius acting on behalf of Emperor Justinian I, the head of the Roman Empire at Constantinople.

Political antipathies between Africa and the imperial powers at Constantinople evolved into a political vacuum. "The sixth-century Byzantine failure to reunite the Roman world was final. From then on, the Christian world was to be divided, and Islam was to emerge from Arabia in the middle of the seventh century as a third heir to the Hellenic synthesis."[8]

The Second Seven Hundred Years: The Islamic Expansion and Near Elimination of the Catholic Church in North Africa

What began in the middle of the seventh century as a military victory ended half a century later as a religious and cultural victory. "In 642, only ten years after the death of Muhammad, Alexandria was surrendered to the Islamic Arab army, and the province of Egypt, which for centuries had been one of the most important parts of the Roman-Byzantine Empire and of the Christian church, became from then on a central pillar of Islam."[9]

> The most striking of all effects produced by the Arab conquest of North Africa was the gradual but almost complete disappearance of Christianity. The Berbers not only accepted Mohammedanism, they became its most fanatical defenders. Doubtless economic considerations entered: non-Muslims paid a head tax, and converts were for a time freed from it. When in 744, the Arab governor of Egypt offered this exemption, 24,000 Christians went over to Islam. Occasional but severe persecutions of Christians may have influenced many to conform to the ruling faith. In Egypt a Coptic minority held out bravely, built their churches like fortresses, maintained their worship in secret, and survive to this day. But the once crowded churches of Alexandria, Cyrene, Carthage, and Hippo were emptied and decayed; the memory of Athanasius, Cyril, and Augustine faded out; and the disputes of Arians, Donatists, and Monophysites

---

7. Victor of Vita, *History of the Vandal Persecution*, 77.
8. Curtin et al., *African History*, 66.
9. Hastings, *Church in Africa 1450–1950*, 55.

gave way to the quarrels of Sunni and Ismaili Mohammedanism.[10]

With a foothold in Egypt, the politico-military caliphs of Islam extended their hegemony over all of North Africa. During the next fifty years, eight campaigns were launched in order to subdue resistance by the Christian Berbers. The end came when Carthage fell in 694. Christianity was revived briefly by a Byzantine recovery in 695, but the North breathed its last corporate gasp in 698. Catholic Christian North Africa was left to become a shadow of its former self. During the half-century of wars, many Christians had fled across the Mediterranean to Italy, Sicily, and Spain; those who remained succumbed to the active discrimination by a war-calloused people. "New churches could never be built, the public expression of religion was almost always prohibited. Everywhere such a condition has tended over the generations to the annihilation of minorities."[11]

It is one of the more curious facts of African history that Christianity has survived vigorously for many hundreds of years in Egypt. What differences existed between this land and North Africa? One scholar observes, "The strength of the Coptic Church lay in the combination of monasteries, many of them in rather remote places, and a numerous married clergy."[12] The church had extended itself geographically beyond the population centers of the Nile's delta and riverbanks to the surrounding deserts and had rooted itself among common people socially through the priests of the Coptic rite, who were not bound to celibacy like priests of the Roman rite. The numerous desert monasteries provided continuing public legitimacy by their reputations for sanctity, scholarship, and wisdom.

Politically, the Egyptians were accustomed to foreign rule. They had been occupied by the Persians in 525 BC under Cambyses and again, after local reassertion, by Artaxerxes III in 343; by the Greeks ever since the time of Alexander in 332 BC; and by the Romans under Octavian in 30 BC. When the Arabians arrived in 640, the Egyptians received these invaders as one more foreign power.

As a religious phenomenon, Islam was regarded by many, including St. John Cassian (ca. 360–ca. 433), as another Christian heresy, similar to the troubling but temporary challenges of Arianism and Donatism. Even successive dynasties of caliphs tolerated Christians, although in ever-lessening degrees: the Fatimids (967–1171) were quite tolerant, with the notable exception of al-Hakim; the Ayyudid dynasty (1171–1250) was less tolerant; and the Mameluke rule (1250–1517) was least so. In this last dynasty, the church dropped Coptic as its traditional language and, except for liturgies, adopted Arabic. It also changed its episcopal see from Alexandria to Cairo. The church yielded to the new realities of the de-Christianized context in which it struggled to survive. Oppression continued to be waged by the majority against the minority, as demonstrated in 1320, when fifty-four churches were destroyed. When finally the Mameluke Empire lost power, the vacuum was filled by the Ottomans in Constantinople. At that time, the church in Rome had an opportunity to reestablish its influence, when the Copts and the Roman church entered into a short-lived union. Rome, however, had little interest in maintaining the union; and the Copts risked their very survival by allying themselves with a foreign religion and political power. "From the fifteenth to the eighteenth century the Coptic church went through a long dark tunnel about which we know rather little. Yet it survived."[13]

South of Upper Egypt, at the confluence of the Blue Nile and White Nile Rivers in the Sudan, lay the ancient kingdom of Nubia, which had once boasted of a thriving Christianity. Over the course of many centuries, however, the Christian religion lost its vitality and evaporated totally, although imperceptibly. As early as the late fourth cen-

---

10. Durant, *Age of Faith*, 289.
11. Hastings, *Church in Africa 1450–1950*, 65.
12. Hastings, *Church in Africa 1450–1950*, 65.
13. Hastings, *Church in Africa 1450–1950*, 67.

tury and probably sooner, Christianity had taken root. The religion prospered here in the seventh century at the same time that Christianity lost its prominence in Egypt. The Nubians had resisted the Islamic advance and, in 652, signed a treaty whereby the Nubians agreed to pay an annual tribute of slaves to the Muslim leaders at Egypt. The Muslims agreed that no Muslim would ever enter the country. From the eighth to the twelfth centuries, Christian Nubia enjoyed a golden era. In the midst of these centuries, "Christianity in Nubia could be ranked among the healthiest on earth."[14] Cathedrals and monasteries were built and decorated magnificently. Numerous native bishops, who had been ordained by the patriarch of Alexandria, filled the local sees. The Nubian vernacular became the ecclesiastical language used in communicating legal documents and recording the lives of the saints.

In the next few centuries, however, a political change affected the Christian country's religious roots. This development began in the thirteenth century, when a Muslim took over as ruler in Nubia's northern kingdom. The kingdom's central authority had lost its vitality. Disparate local fiefdoms sprang up. The southern kingdom too succumbed to this political disorganization. The hierarchical church had depended on a strong monarchical political government. "Without a strong and supportive monarchy the Church too declined."[15]

Christianity in Nubia maintained itself for many more centuries, but only as a shadow of its former strength. A breakaway kingdom in the north preserved the faith and religion up to the end of the fifteenth century. An isolated island community kept the faith into the middle of the eighteenth century. The die, however, had been cast. In the 1520s, a traveler tells of "150 churches still containing crucifixes and paintings of Our Lady. The people of this country . . . were now neither Christians, Muslims, nor Jews, yet still 'lived in the desire of being Christians.'"[16] This same visitor reported that, while he was visiting Ethiopia, six Nubians requested of the Ethiopian emperor that he send priests and monks to Nubia, which was becoming devoid of priests. The emperor reluctantly refused because, as he explained, even Ethiopia's bishop himself had to be sent from Egypt, and he had no priests in Ethiopia to minister to his own people, let alone send priests to Nubia. Christianity in Nubia lacked priests and lacked influence when the monarchical political system evaporated.

Farther south of ancient Nubia lay Ethiopia, which once had claimed about one quarter of the territory of Africa. This kingdom evidenced international contacts with the Jewish religion as far back as the Old Testament. Jewish ritualistic circumcision and avoidance of women in menstruation still occur in Ethiopia. The Ethiopian eunuch of Queen Candace was converted by the apostle Philip (see Acts 8:27–38). He may have brought the new religion to his native land. Another possibility is the popular story that the two youths Frumentius and Aedesius, when they were sailing from Tyre in Syria to India, stopped in Ethiopia for fresh supplies, but pirates captured them. Most of the crew were slaughtered, but the two youths were sent to serve at the court of the king. Decades later, Frumentius was emancipated from the service at the royal court and, while visiting in Alexandria en route to his home, he asked the patriarch to send native clergy to this people, who were very receptive to the Christian religion. The patriarch responded by ordaining and missioning Frumentius himself. So began the long tradition of Alexandria supplying the head of the church in Ethiopia. The church survived in Ethiopia because of its geographical isolation by its celibate monks, and sociocultural penetration by its married clergy.

One critic comments, "Thus at times violently but more often quietly enough, did Islam advance while Christianity, like an ill-adapted dinosaur, declined and expired in place after place, crushed essentially by its own limitations, its fossilized traditions, and the lack of a truly viable, self-renewing structure."[17]

---

14. King, *Christian and Muslim in Africa*, 9.
15. King, *Christian and Muslim in Africa*, 68.
16. King, *Christian and Muslim in Africa*, 69.
17. King, *Christian and Muslim in Africa*, 70.

The Last Six Hundred Years: The Christianization of Sub-Saharan Africa

Colonization and Frustration at Evangelization (Fifteenth to Nineteenth Centuries)

The Age of Exploration prepared the way for the Christianization of Africa. The Portuguese led the procession of foreign powers, followed by the Dutch, the French, and the English. Accompanying the sailors and governmental administrators were merchants and clergy. Colonization and Christianization went hand in hand. The flag of a European country and the cross of Christianity were planted side by side on the African coast from Morocco westward to the Azores and Cape Verde Islands, southward to the Cape of Good Hope, and northward up to Madagascar and Ethiopia. Catholic dioceses were established at Tangier (1468), Safi (1487), Ethiopia (1555), Cape Verde (1533), and San Salvador (1597). Missionaries began evangelization programs at Ceuta (1415), Benin (1485), Congo (1490), Angola (1550), Monomotapa (ca. 1560), Mozambique (1577), and Sofala (1581). The first native sub-Saharan bishop, Dom Henrique of the Congo, was ordained in 1518. Pope Gregory XV created in 1622 the Congregation of the Faith to organize and expand the church's missionary movement in Africa.

Men's religious orders and secular clergy from colonial countries generously gave of their personnel and finances to increase gradually the church's presence by establishing parishes, then dioceses, schools, and finally seminaries. In the 1400s and 1500s, Augustinians, Carmelites and Discalced Carmelites, Dominicans, Franciscans, and Jesuits spread the word of God in Africa. In the 1600s and 1700s, Brothers of St. John of God, Capuchins, Franciscans, Regular Tertiaries, Holy Ghost Fathers, and Vincentians entered the church's mission in sub-Saharan Africa. The missionary movements of these four hundred years always began with great inspiration and enthusiasm but ended virtually always in failure after a few years or decades of apparent success. Internally, the movement suffered the ill effects of disease, diet, persecution, expulsion, murder, tribal wars, and religious resistance from pagans and Muslims. Many missionaries ended up ministering in coastal cities almost entirely to resident and transient Europeans. Externally, the lifeline of personnel grew quite costly and almost collapsed because of the suppression of the Jesuits in Portugal, the loss of church personnel and church status after the French Revolution, and the cultural impact of the Age of Enlightenment, which promoted the valuation of reason over faith. When the colonial political powers attacked each other in territorial wars, the victors refused to send the clergy needed to support the defeated country's ecclesiastical mission. After the Reformation, Protestants and Catholics strove to impede each other's church work, even within the same country's colony. In a larger context, colonization cast a pall over Christianization because of countries' dominant interest in political and economic benefit rather than religious purpose.

What remained of the church's efforts from 180 to 1800 for the Christianization of Africa? "After the exuberant flowering of the early Christian centuries in Egypt and Roman Africa, and the later attempts during the seventeenth and eighteenth centuries following the Portuguese discoveries, Christianity almost completely disappeared from the African continent by the beginning of the nineteenth century. Everything had to begin anew."[18]

Missionary Revival (Nineteenth to Mid-Twentieth Centuries)

In 1830, when France won military control over Algeria, "many in Europe hailed the event as the harbinger of a new era of Catholicity in Africa."[19] For almost forty years, however, French authorities prohibited Bishops Dupuch and Pavy of Algiers not only from evangelizing the Muslim population but even from hanging crucifixes in Catholic hospitals. The dream of restoring Christianity took on a new excitement in 1849, however, when the Protestant missionary David Livingstone penetrated the interior of sub-Saharan Africa and successfully evangelized the local tribes. Hope for a Christian Africa was reborn.

---

18. Bouchard, "Africa," 176.
19. Johnston, *Church in North Africa*, 22.

Another breakthrough occurred in 1867, when Charles Martial Allemand Lavigerie, the Catholic bishop of Nancy in France, was appointed archbishop of Algiers. Ignoring the limitations imposed by the French and their seductive offer of a principal diocese for him in France if he were to abandon his ministry in Africa, he committed himself wholeheartedly to the evangelization of the continent in the southern hemisphere. He founded the Society of Missionaries of Africa, who became known popularly as the White Fathers because of the color of their cassocks. Archbishop Lavigerie and others like him discovered, however, that they could not crack the Muslim stronghold on North Africa. In half a century from 1873 to 1927, fewer than one thousand conversions were made.[20]

Lavigerie, following the dream envisioned by Livingstone, missioned his priests to equatorial Uganda. In 1879, the archbishop began, against great odds of climate, culture, health, and safety, the great Catholic evangelization of sub-Saharan Africa. Swift and extensive progress was made. Other religious communities joined Lavigerie. By the end of the century, the missionary communities leading the evangelization of Africa included the Capuchins, Holy Ghost Fathers, Jesuits, Marianhill Fathers, Oblates of Mary Immaculate, Scheut Fathers, Society of African Missions, Trappist monks, Verona Fathers, Vincentian Fathers and Brothers, and White Fathers.[21]

Colonization and Christianization fit together like hand and glove. The mother country supplied clergy for her colonies. The Belgian Congo was manned by Belgian missionaries, while Italians served in Ethiopia and Somaliland. French West Africa, North Africa, Equatorial Africa, Senegal, and Madagascar were reserved for the French clergy. South Africa, Rhodesia, Gambia, Nigeria, Gold Coast, Uganda, Sudan, Egypt, British East Africa, and British Congo became the domain of Great Britain. The Portuguese ministered in Portuguese West Africa and Mozambique. Germany missioned their compatriots to German Southwest Africa, German East Africa, and Cameroon. Prior to European colonization, the political map of sub-Saharan Africa consisted of countless tribal lands, but between 1870 and the end of the World War I, the colonial powers carved up and parceled out the continent. While evangelization was not a primary intention of the European colonization, conversion to the religion of the mother country nonetheless occurred and supported the overall vision of the parent country.

Thus it is clear that the Catholic Church has become present everywhere in Africa, and that this presence is the result of only one century of apostolate. The 50,000 Catholics in 1800 increased to 26 million by 1961. In 1800 ecclesiastical divisions were rare; in 1964 there were 312 dioceses, vicariates, or prefectures. . . . The 50 missionaries of 1800 increased to 13,500 priests (2,500 Africans), 5,000 teaching brothers (1,200 Africans), 23,000 religious women (7,000 Africans), and more than 100,000 African catechists or teachers. . . . In a total population of 230 million in 1964, Christians numbered 50 million (26 million Catholics, 19 million Protestants, 5 million Orthodox); Muslims, 95 million; pagans, 85 million. Catholics represented about 12 per cent of the population.[22]

The method of missionizing had shifted with the changes in colonization. Transportation made possible the travel from the capital city into the surrounding countryside. Social development required expansion from the parish church into schools, hospitals, and orphanages.

Independent and Christian Africa (1960 to the Present)

The year 1960 is referred to as "the year of African independence." In that year, eighteen nations declared freedom from European colonial powers.[23] Between 1961 and 1964, another nine nations

---

20. Johnston, *Church in North Africa*, 27.
21. Hastings, *Church in Africa*, 619.
22. Bouchard, "Africa," 185.
23. Belasco and Hammond, *New Africa*, 150–51.

claimed independence.²⁴ In 1990, the last colonial territory in Africa achieved statehood and called itself Namibia. Today, fifty-five African nations enjoy political independence.

Between 1963 and 1965, the Roman Catholic Church conducted its twenty-first ecumenical council, namely, Vatican Council II. The council's originating spirit, *aggiornamento*, meant, as Pope Paul said during the final session, "From now on *aggiornamento* will signify for us a wisely undertaken quest for a deeper understanding of the spirit of the Council and the faithful application of the norms it has happily and prayerfully provided."²⁵ The council's Decree on the Church's Missionary Activity (*Ad Gentes*), Declaration on the Relationship of the Church to Non-Christian Religions (*Nostra Aetate*), and the Declaration on Religious Freedom (*Dignitatis Humanae*) dealt with the church's missionary efforts worldwide and respect for each person's religious conscience.

The council's consequences are having a great impact in Africa. Catholicism and Christianity continue to grow rapidly; approximately fifteen thousand new Christians are added daily to the roles of the Christian churches. Young men and women join the ranks of the Catholic clergy and nuns at very high rates; nonetheless, many regions remain without clergy because the local population burgeons at rates higher than religious vocations. The church in Africa is developing its own identity; it resists Western customs that fail to respect African traditions. None other than Joseph-Albert Cardinal Malula of Zaire challenges non-Africans who attempt to impose Western ways on African culture: "We deny anyone the right to say, in our place, what are the problems we encounter in our faith."²⁶ Because Vatican II has instructed Catholics to value other religions, a temporary missionary moratorium resulted, whereby foreign clergy rethought why and how they would evangelize in a land that abounds with native religions and why Western men and women would leave their secularized post-Christian civilization to evangelize abroad rather than at home.

Regarding respect for popular religion and indigenous expressions of religion, tensions have arisen between theory and practice. "The 'demystification' of folk Catholicism left many troubled and alienated. It was precisely such elements as healing shrines, protective scapulars, statues, candles, and holy water that were closest to traditionalist religion."²⁷ Critics "have warned of a 'tyranny of good taste,' whereby Catholic intellectuals have removed loved statues because they are bad art, and popular devotions because they are of relatively recent origin."²⁸ Despite Vatican II's attempted decentralization of the role of the Blessed Virgin Mary, or perhaps because of this reorientation, alleged appearances of Mary have proliferated worldwide and in Africa as well, specifically in Egypt, Rwanda, Cameroon, and Kenya. In 1994, Pope John Paul II convened the month-long Synod of Africa. A Pan-African assembly had been desired ever since the conclusion of Vatican II, which had focused mostly on developments within the Eurocentric church. Africans wanted to discuss issues especially relevant to Africans. The pope suggested a structure that assured the success of the synod. He appointed as ex-officio members of the synod the two dozen leaders of the Vatican offices, thereby requiring these officials to attend all the synod sessions and to hear what the African bishops were saying. The pope too attended the sessions until an injury prevented him from attending further. Contrary to the original expectation of the African bishops, the pope insisted that the synod be held in Rome; "this 'disaster' turned out to be a blessing in disguise."²⁹ Bishops came and stayed for all the sessions: of the continent's 440 dioceses, 220 were represented by their ordinaries. The synod discussions and teachings provided great fruit.

---

24. Belasco and Hammond, *New Africa*, 151.
25. Shehan, "Introduction," xviii.
26. Isichei, *History of Christianity in Africa*, 328.
27. Isichei, *History of Christianity in Africa*, 327.
28. Isichei, *History of Christianity in Africa*, 328.
29. Baur, *2000 Years of Christianity in Africa*, 509.

The bishops came home from the Synod with the Good News: they had found a new image of the Church, which is corresponding well to African culture and on which one could hinge the whole of African Church life, namely *the Church as family*, the Family of God in Africa. Indeed, this Church model is full of implications: starting with the bishop (no more "his lordship" but an understanding and compassionate father); the laity (no more inferior helpers of the clergy, but sharing an equal responsibility as adult family members with their elder brothers, the priests)—the whole Church a "home," giving a sense of belonging, since it is a community "from which absolutely nobody is excluded," and with a welcome access to the family meal, the holy Eucharist. Moreover, this African Church is an extended family with a diversity of tasks and ministries, ruled by the principles of solidarity and subsidiarity and kept working by dialogue: dialogue with its own members and with other churches and religions.[30]

The issues that the bishops discussed in their sixty-four propositions concerned evangelization, inculturation, dialogue with traditional religions, Christian brethren and Muslims, pastoral care in social areas (including the various crises stemming from the AIDS epidemic), and the challenges presented by modern means of social communication. The central theme of church-as-family was agreed to be a most appropriate symbol for Africans and the church. The critical issue of marriage, however, was not discussed directly. "The most vital subject of marriage was eliminated under the pretext that the question had already been treated in the general Synod of 1980."[31] It was envisioned that at the completion of the synod, study groups would be commissioned on the vital topics of marriage, ancestors, and the spirit world.

Pope John Paul II delivered his post-synodal apostolic exhortation *Ecclesia in Africa* in Cameroon in September 1995. In that document, he reviewed the synod's origins, development, and discussions. He outlined the challenges facing the church in Africa as it approached the Jubilee Year and the millennium. He reminded readers that he had traveled to Africa on ten trips and had visited thirty-six of the fifty-five countries. In reviewing the two-thousand-year history of the church in Africa, the pope recognized and paid homage to the missionaries of the nineteenth century whose efforts at evangelization were particularly fruitful. He lamented the political turmoil and socioeconomic sufferings of the people of the continent. He highlighted evangelization by inculturation.

> Inculturation includes two dimensions: on the one hand, "the intimate transformation of authentic cultural values through their integration in Christianity" and, on the other, "the insertion of Christianity in the various human cultures." The Synod considers inculturation an urgent priority in the life of the particular Churches, for a firm rooting of the Gospel in Africa. It is "a requirement for evangelization," "a path towards full evangelization, and one of the greatest challenges for the Church on the Continent on the eve of the Third Millennium." (*EA* §59)

The pope wrote that family life is being threatened in Africa. He blamed the United Nations Conference on Families, which was held on African soil in Cairo in 1994, for mocking the traditional values of African and universal family life. He echoed the synod fathers' plea to save the family: "Do not allow the International Year of the Family to become the year of the destruction of the family" (*EA* §84). He called on the clergy, religious, and laity, especially the youth, to witness to the faith in Africa. The kingdom of justice and peace, he pointed out, requires the efforts of all people, whom he begs to work in solidarity with each other. The pope concluded by entrusting Africa and its evangelizing mission to Mary, the Star of Evangelization.

As Africa experiences the turn of the millennium, the continent has become a predominantly

---

30. Baur, *2000 Years of Christianity in Africa*, 510–11.
31. Baur, *2000 Years of Christianity in Africa*, 509.

Christian land. Of the continent's 778 million people, 356 million are identified as Christian and 315 million are Muslims.[32] While almost half of the continent's Muslims live in North Africa, which is 90 percent Muslim, almost all the continent's Christians live in sub-Saharan Africa, except for a small percentage who live in Egypt and Sudan. Catholics represent nearly a third of the Christian population.[33]

Bibliography

Baur, John. *2000 Years of Christianity in Africa: An African Church History*. 2nd rev. ed. Nairobi, Kenya: Paulines Publications Africa, 1998.

Belasco, Milton Jay, and Harold E. Hammond. *The New Africa: History, Culture, People*, edited by Edward Graff. Bronxville, NY: Cambridge Book Co., 1970.

Bouchard, Joseph. "Africa." *New Catholic Encyclopedia*, vol. 1. Washington, DC: Catholic University of America Press, 2002.

Curtin, Philip, Steven Feierman, Leonard Thompson, and Jan Vansina. *African History*. Boston: Little, Brown, 1978.

Durant, Will. *The Age of Faith: A History of Medieval Civilization—Christian, Islamic, and Judaic—From Constantine to Dante: A.D. 325–1300*. New York: Simon & Schuster, 1950.

Gavigan, John Joseph. "North Africa, Early Church in." *New Catholic Encyclopedia*, vol. 10. Washington, DC: Catholic University of America Press, 2002.

Hastings, Adrian. *The Church in Africa, 1450–1950*. Oxford History of the Christian Church Oxford: Clarendon Press, 1994.

Isichei, Elizabeth. *A History of Christianity in Africa: From Antiquity to the Present*. Grand Rapids, MI: Eerdmans, 1995.

John Paul II, Pope. *Ecclesia in Africa* [Post-synodal Apostolic Exhortation on the Church in Africa and Its Evangelizing Mission toward the Year 2000; September 14, 1995]. Vatican City: Libreria Editrice Vaticana, 1995. www.vatican.va.

Johnston, T. *The Church in North Africa*. Dublin: Office of the "Irish Messenger," 1930.

King, Noel Q. *Christian and Muslim in Africa*. New York: Harper & Row, 1971.

Le Saint, William. "Tertullian." *New Catholic Encyclopedia*, vol. 13. Washington, DC: Catholic University of America Press, 2007.

McKenzie, John L. "Mark, Gospel of." *Dictionary of the Bible*, 542–46. Milwaukee: Bruce, 1965.

Scarre, Chris. *Chronicle of the Roman Emperors*. London: Thames & Hudson, 1995.

Sheehan, Lawrence Cardinal. "Introduction." In *The Documents of Vatican II*, edited by Walter Abbot, translated by Joseph Gallagher, xv–xix. New York: Guild Press, 1966.

Victor of Vita. *History of the Vandal Persecution*. Translated by John Moorhead. Translated Texts for Historians 10. Liverpool: Liverpool University Press, 1992.

Key Words
African Catholicism
inculturation
martyrdom
missionaries
North Africa

---

32. "Population of the World, 1998," https://www.infoplease.com/culture-entertainment/religion.

33. "Population of the World, 1998." Among the Christians are 114 million Roman Catholics, 74 million Protestants, 34 million Orthodox, 28 million Anglicans, 75 million "other Christians," and 32 million unaffiliated Christians.

Africa

Emmanuel Katongole

Within the Roman Catholic Church, northern dioceses are increasingly likely to use priests from lands in Africa or Latin America, which are still fertile grounds for vocations. . . . African priests are appearing in—of all places—Ireland, that ancient nursery of Catholic devotion. Remarking on this phenomenon, an Irish friend of mine recalled, wryly, how as a child she had been told by the Church to collect pennies to "save Black babies in Africa." She wondered whether some of those babies might have grown up to save Irish souls in recompense.[1]

A brilliant African student goes off to a European seminary. Here he learned German, French, Greek, Latin, Hebrew, in addition to English, Church history, systematics, homiletics, exegesis, and pastoralia. He reads all the great European Bible critics, such as Rudolf Bultmann. Returning home to his native village, the student is welcomed joyfully by his extended family but, suddenly, his sister falls dangerously ill. With his Western training, he knows that her illness requires scientific medicine, but everyone present knows with equal certainty that the girl is troubled by the spirit of her dead great-aunt. Since this fine student has so much theological training, the family knows that it is obviously up to him to cure her. The debate between the student and family rages until the people shout, "Help your sister, she is possessed!" He shouts back, "But Bultmann has demythologized demon possession!" The family is not impressed.[2]

These two quotations nicely capture everything I would like to say about African Catholicism. First, the two stories—of African Catholics reevangelizing the West, and Westernized Africans trying to reevangelize their homes—help to highlight the fact that the story of African Catholicism is indeed the tale of multiple stories. On the one hand, it is a story of great success, of surprise, and a story that holds great potential in terms of its gifts, dynamism, and contribution to the universal church; it is also a story whose performance within Africa continues to be less than impressive, the cause of great frustration and, in some cases, even outright disappointment.

Originally published in *The Blackwell Companion to Catholicism*, edited by James J. Buckley, Frederick Christian Bauerschmidt, and Trent Pomplun, Blackwell Companions to Religion (Malden, MA: John Wiley & Sons, 2007), 127–42. Copyright © 2007. Used with permission.

In memory of Leo Kasumba, the dedicated catechist who first instructed me in the mysteries of the Catholic faith, even though at that young age, I did not understand much of the formulas and prayers he forced us to memorize.

1. Jenkins, *Next Christendom*, 204.
2. Jenkins, *Next Christendom*, 124, citing Mbiti, "Theological Impotence and the Universality of the Church," 6–8.

Understanding the dynamism of African Catholicism and its unique character requires exploring the intersection between these two stories of success and powerlessness, of gifts and challenges. Moreover, the more one does so, the more one appreciates the "catholicity" of African Catholicism. In Africa, the "universal" and the "particular," the "global" and the "local," the "Western" and the "non-Western," the ancient and new mesh, meld, collide, and synthesize in ways at once impressive and not so impressive, at times life-affirming and at other times life-draining. That is why, in order to get a sense of the African Catholic identity, as well as the gifts and challenges of African Catholicism, one must first highlight some of the intersections and apparent contradictions that shape Catholic life and practice in Africa. Only then can one appreciate the unique expression and complex performance of the African Church within Roman Catholicism.

Catholicism in Africa:
A Tale of Many Stories

Catholic Confidence—In a Distressed Continent

The story of African Catholicism is the story of unprecedented growth that has taken place in the past one hundred years or so. While the growth has not been limited to Catholicism, but has been part of the general trend of the southern shift in world Christianity, African Catholicism is in many places at the center of this ferment. In 1900, there were slightly fewer than 2 million Catholics in Africa; by 2000 the number of Catholics had grown to over 130 million, representing a growth of 708 percent (the population of Africa grew during the same period by 313 percent).[3] The rise in African Catholicism is reflected in the number of vocations to the priesthood and religious life, with seminaries and convents in countries like Uganda, Nigeria, and Cameroon registering record numbers. It is also reflected in the number of African churchmen in prominent positions. In 1913, the first African Catholic priest (in modern times) was ordained; in 2000 Africa had 16,962 priests.[4] In 1939, Joseph Kiwanuka was consecrated as the first African Catholic bishop in modern times. In 2000 Africa had 588 bishops and archbishops, and 16 cardinals—a fact that led to speculations about the possibility of an African pope in the April 2005 conclave.

While these developments have rightly led to optimistic projections and widespread confidence about Africa as the future of the church, other developments have not led to the same confidence about Africa. The continent has continued to experience great social, economic, and political distress. Instability, civil unrest, war, violent clashes, poverty, and HIV/AIDS are the realities that African Catholics live with on a daily basis. Accordingly, if the growth of African Catholicism signals the confidence in "the coming of the Third Church,"[5] that church is by and large a church of the poor and marginalized. It is a church characterized by the same unfulfilled dreams and frustrations, the same creative restlessness and destructive madness of a postcolonial Africa. No event depicts these contradictions more acutely than the 1994 genocide in Rwanda, a country that was and still is predominantly Catholic.

The Old and the New in African Catholicism

What is most striking about the growth of the Catholic Church in Africa is that most of this has happened in the past hundred years or so. It would be misleading, however, to think that Catholicism is "new" in Africa. As Pope John Paul II notes in the post-synodal apostolic exhortation *Ecclesia in Africa* (*EA*):

> The spread of the Gospel has taken place in different phases. The first century of Christianity saw the evangelization of Egypt and North Africa. A second phase, involving the parts of the Continent south of the Sahara, took place in the fifteenth and sixteenth century. A third phase, marked by extra-ordinary missionary effort, began in the nineteenth century. (§30)

---

3. Froehle and Gautier, *Global Catholicism*, 4–5.
4. Froehle and Gautier, *Global Catholicism*, 32.
5. Bühlmann, *Coming of the Third Church*.

While the story of present-day African Catholicism might appear to be "recent," the story of Catholicism in Africa is "ancient." That is why in reading various historical accounts of African Catholicism[6] one must keep in mind that the three phases of Africa's evangelization are neither isolated nor self-contained—but rather are moments within the same narrative. The historical continuity and connection between these phases must be constantly explored and highlighted. In this way, it becomes clear that, though much of present-day African Catholicism has grown out of the missionary enterprise of the nineteenth century, what we have here is not "new," either in terms of its presence on the continent or in terms of its key elements. What we see in the twenty-first century is just a recent expression of an ancient story—of Catholicism in Africa, which itself is part of a much bigger story of the universal communion of the Roman Catholic Church. Catholic identity in Africa is shaped and constantly negotiated at this intersection of new and old.

African Catholicism(s): A Tale of Many Stories

One often talks of African Catholicism as though it were a monolith. This, however, is not the case. In fact, anyone looking for a comprehensive historical guide to *African* Catholicism is often frustrated, for there is no single account that can capture the complexity of African Catholicism and its many (hi)stories. From this point of view, African Catholicism is more a patchwork quilt of diverse histories, traditions, and expressions, so it might in fact be more accurate to speak not of African Catholicism but of African Catholicisms. Africa is a huge and complex continent; Catholics in Africa are spread over fifty-four countries, representing diverse colonial and missionary histories. Accordingly, Catholicism in Lusaphone Africa tends to look different from Catholicism in Francophone Africa, which itself looks different from Anglophone Catholicism. To be sure, even within a country or region that shares the same colonial history, the fact that African Catholics are spread over two thousand languages and distinct cultures makes room for significant local differences within African Catholicism. Another factor that contributes to the complexity of Catholicism in Africa is the fact that the evangelization of Africa was undertaken by different missionary congregations that worked either side by side or in competition with one another. Whereas this may not seem to be a significant factor, the differences that the styles, devotions, and spiritualities of the evangelizing societies have had at the level of popular devotions, lay movements, and pious associations can be quite striking. Take the case of Uganda. The spiritual life of Catholics from the south (evangelized by the White Fathers) is organized around Marian devotion (with a grotto and a Marian chapel a regular feature in every parish); the spirituality of northern Catholics (evangelized by the Comboni missionaries) is centered on devotion to the Sacred Heart; and Catholics from eastern Uganda (evangelized mostly by the Mill Hill missionaries) practice a more cerebral type of Catholicism, without much devotional concentration. Similar differences exist in the Democratic Republic of the Congo, where different Belgian orders, the Jesuits, Premonstratensians, Redemptorists, and Benedictines, were each responsible for evangelizing different regions of this huge country. This is what makes any talk of "African Catholicism" either unhelpful or a misleading generalization. On the other hand, the variety of traditions, histories, and expressions within Catholicism in Africa confirm the unparalleled "catholicity" of the African church. Within the African church one comes across every imaginable tradition within Catholicism represented in ways that at once affirm the rich diversity of Catholicism and yet make African Catholicism such a hopelessly fragmented reality.

Western Missionary Dynamic and Local Transmission

The nineteenth century was a great era for both Catholic and Protestant mission as reflected in the growth of missionary fervor and the founding of new missionary congregations in Europe. Africa was the great beneficiary of this missionary move-

---

6. E.g., Baur, *2000 Years of Christianity in Africa*; Hastings, *Church in Africa, 1450–1950*; Sundkler and Steed, *History of the Church in Africa*.

ment. As Adrian Hastings notes, in 1910 there were nearly four thousand Catholic missionaries, over half of them nuns, working in various places in Africa.[7] Apart from the strength of the missionary movement, there were other factors—including increased mobility and even Catholic–Protestant rivalry—that contributed to the growth of the church in Africa. In fact, in cases like Uganda, the rivalry would even take violent forms, fomenting the religious wars of 1887–1895. And, as Hastings claims,[8] without this rivalry, neither side would have worked so hard. Whatever other factors might have been at work, one has to admit that "the splendid growth and achievement of the Church in Africa are due largely to the heroic and selfless dedication of generations of missionaries" (*EA* §35).

Nevertheless, it is equally important to recognize that the evangelization of Africa was as much the work of Western missionaries as of local evangelists, who worked either as translators or catechists. These self-sacrificing and hardworking lay evangelists served as a crucial link between missionaries and local populations, between the parish center and the outlying rural missions. Often illiterate or semiliterate, the catechist depended greatly on memorization and oral skills, often serving as a storyteller. This overlooked factor marks the major difference between Catholic and Protestant mission. Whereas the translation of the Bible into the vernacular was essential to Protestant mission, memory (the question-and-answer drills around the catechism and set prayers) and storytelling were the most important factors in Catholic mission. Here, the case of Uganda is telling, though not unique. Matthias Mulumba and Noa Mawaggali (both of whom were to die as martyrs) were the leaders of a small group of Christians in Singo. Every Monday they would send one of their number to the capital to listen to the priest's sermon, attend the missionary's explanation of the catechism, so that he could repeat what he had learned to his fellow Christians back home.[9]

It is important to acknowledge how the rapid growth of Catholicism in Africa was and continues to be effected at the intersection of missionary transmission and local agency. African Catholicism today is still largely a coming together of missionary gifts and local talents. On the one hand, the Catholic Church in Africa remains very Western in its style and outlook, in its theology, and in its funding. On the other hand, its growth and dynamism, its leadership and expressions are the distinctive working of local gifts and charisms.

A Spiritual Message and Holistic Evangelization
A key feature of the nineteenth-century mission that helped the growth of Catholicism in Africa was the fact that the preaching of the missionaries addressed not just the spiritual life of the person but the whole life of the person. The example of Comboni in the Sudan is very telling, though not unique. Daniel Comboni (1831–1881) believed that "God wills the conversion of Africa." In his vision, however, the conversion went hand in hand with a clear determination to overthrow slavery and to end the slave trade in the Sudan. Like his predecessor Ignatius Knoblecher in the Sudan mission, Comboni believed that education would help defeat slavery in the country. Thus, at mission centers, Comboni encouraged his missionaries to establish schools in which freed slaves would be taught how to read and write, as well as other simple skills like brick making, mechanics, and farming. In some places (e.g., Malbes), the missionaries even set up model agricultural communities. Comboni's missions also included a number of sisters, who opened schools for girls.[10] A similar story was repeated by missionaries everywhere in Africa. Whether it was the Oblates in South Africa, the Holy Ghost Fathers in Tanzania, or the Society of the African Mission in Ghana, the construction of mission schools, the setting up of health centers, and the development of technical institutes were key features and a hallmark of the holistic mission.

The growth, dynamism, and vitality of Catholic life in Africa today is closely connected with Catholic institutions and the provision of such services as education, health care, and development

---

7. Hastings, *Church in Africa, 1450–1950*, 419.
8. Hastings, *Church in Africa, 1450–1950*, 421.
9. Faupel, *African Holocaust*, 180.
10. Baur, *2000 Years of Christianity in Africa*, 155–86.

projects. In the diocese of Soroti in Uganda, the Catholic social services department (Soroti Catholic Diocese Integrated Development Organization [SOCADIDO]) is far more powerful and better known than the diocese itself. This is perhaps not surprising, for given the overall inefficiency, corruption, and mismanagement that characterize many public institutions in Africa, the impact of Catholic social institutions, which by comparison are fairly well run, is often very striking.

Double Identity within a Colonial Setting

By and large, the nineteenth-century evangelization of Africa coincided with the colonial occupation of the continent following the Berlin Conference of 1884–1885. African Catholicism therefore arose from a colonial heritage. This of course is not unique to African Catholicism, for as Thomas Bamat and Jean Paul Wiest note, "Most of those who identify as Catholics today inhabit lands that were once colonized by European powers. Foreign domination, enslavement, and processes of cultural uprooting are part of their historical inheritance."[11]

It would thus be misleading to assume that the reason why Christianity has continued to grow in Africa is that the evangelization of the continent reflected a spiritual movement that had little or nothing to do with the colonialism and imperialism that were going on at the same time. To make such a claim would be to overlook the obvious fact that missionaries were people of their time, shaped by Western history, conditions, and values; and by Western social networks and social, political, and intellectual discourse. As a result, they often found themselves collaborating with, and in some cases even explicitly advancing, colonial interests.

But it would be equally misleading, on account of the observations above, to dismiss the entire Christian mission as nothing but an extension of colonial exploitation. This overlooks the fact that quite often missionaries defended local/native interests against colonial annexation (especially in those places where the coming of missionaries predated the colonial advance). The claim would also gloss over missionary preaching, the study of local languages and customs, and the translation of the Bible/catechism into local languages as factors shaping and mobilizing local resistance to colonialism and the drive toward independence.

It is therefore more helpful to think of missionaries and mission work as bearing a "double identity"[12] within colonialism. John Baur captures this sense of ambivalence quite well when he notes, "Every mission station was an essay in colonization; every mission school was a step to independence."[13] This is quite important, for it somehow helps to explain the "double identity" of many African Catholics, who find the church at once empowering and frustrating, enabling and inhibiting, affirming and denigrating African ideals and aspirations—in much the same way as the colonial regime within whose imagination it took shape. It is this intersection that explains the ambivalent attitudes and relationships of many African Catholics to the church they both love and hate—a church that they will protect at all costs, but also a church whose buildings they would have no qualms about burning down or looting during an insurgency.

Acknowledging the colonial heritage of African Catholicism is also helpful for understanding another aspect of the imagination that Catholicism shapes in Africa. Hastings is right when he notes:

> All the conquerors claimed to be Christian, and at the end of the nineteenth century it seems overwhelmingly obvious that power, riches belonged to Christian nations. It would have been strange if Africans did not, in the situation of conquest, seek to share in the beliefs of their conquerors. If the process of Christianization was now to be greatly accelerated, it was not just that there were vastly more missionaries about, with plenty of privileged opportunities of proselytism, it was because African themselves had been placed in a situation of objective intellectual unsettlement and were thoughtful enough to seek appropriate positive answers of a reli-

---

11. Bamat and Wiest, *Popular Catholicism in a World Church*, 1.
12. Walls, *Missionary Movement in Christian History*, xviii.
13. Baur, *2000 Years of Christianity in Africa*, 284.

gious as well as a technical kind to their current dilemmas.[14]

Having taken root in this context, African Catholicism shares and shapes the same imaginations of power, money, civilizations, and modernity that colonialism embodied.

Official and Popular Catholicism

Catholic identity in Africa is shaped at the intersection of two strong forces: the pull of "official" Catholicism, on the one hand, and the equally strong appeal of "popular" movements and associations, on the other. The missionary evangelization of Africa coincided with the massive institutional revival of the Catholic Church worldwide in the post-Vatican II era.[15] Accordingly, African Catholicism is a very highly hierarchical and, in many ways, stable institution. An account of African Catholicism is thus a story of the different hierarchies, dioceses, parishes, mission centers, education institutions, charitable organizations, religious orders, secular institutes, and lay apostolate movements that make up institutionalized Catholicism. Such an account would be incomplete, however, without taking note of the many fringe movements that arise, more or less spontaneously, away from, and sometimes outside the bounds of officially acceptable Catholic practice.

Within such popular movements as the *Wanamawombi* in Tanzania[16] or the *Movement for the Restoration of the Ten Commandments of God* in Uganda,[17] the perennial themes of visions, prophecy, prayer, and exorcism are compressed into a Catholic spirituality defined by Marian piety and healing. That healing is at the heart of many of the popular movements is not only in response to a felt need (the unavailability of reliable and accessible medical care). It is also a reflection of the deep connection that many African Catholics feel between the spiritual and material worlds. For many Africans, problems of ill health, sickness, and even unemployment do not occur in a vacuum but are ultimately connected to the workings of spiritual forces; therefore, they can be solved only through spiritual intervention.

That is why the tension between the official and the popular forms of Catholicism also reveals a tension between the "modern" and the premodern outlooks operating within African Catholicism. While the theology and practice of the hierarchy are driven by the need to reshape Catholic life in Africa in relation to the reforms of Vatican II, what one witnesses in the popular movements is the resurgence of a traditional Catholic cosmology associated with such practices as exorcism, fasting, the use of holy water, the wearing of religious articles (rosaries, medallions, and scapulas), and a deep, almost magical view of the Eucharist. Thus, in terms of outlook, popular Catholicism in Africa is more at home in a pre-Vatican II world. As Christopher Comoro and John Sivalon note:

> The worldview and cosmology of pre-Vatican II Roman Catholicism were in fact an inculturated understanding based on a culture and consciousness very similar to traditional African culture. Vatican II, while marking an opening up to the world in fact was opening up to a world, worldview, and culture of modernity that are quite different from African culture. As the culture accommodated itself to scientific and secularized culture it moved dramatically away from the cultures of indigenous people around the world.[18]

It is this largely pre-Vatican II outlook centered on the world of spirits, demons, and spiritual forces that pits popular Catholicism against the official hierarchy and creates an element of constant tension within African Catholicism, as the controversy surrounding Archbishop Emmanuel Milingo's

---

14. Hastings, *Church in Africa, 1450–1950*, 405.
15. Hastings, *Church in Africa, 1450–1950*, 419.
16. Bamat and Wiest, *Popular Catholicism in a World Church*, 157–82.
17. Katongole, "Kannungu and the Movement," 108–43.
18. Bamat and Wiest, *Popular Catholicism in a World Church*, 170.

healing ministry reveals.[19] While the members of a popular movement may see themselves as a reform or revival movement, the hierarchy may perceive them as unorthodox, disruptive, and a challenge to their religious authority. On the other hand, many priests are, in their attempts to modernize the church, accused of weakening Christian substitutes for the deep-rooted traditional rites. They may even be perceived as agents being used by Satan to destroy the church.[20]

There are many other intersections to which one may point: sacramental versus non-sacramental versions of Catholicism, rural versus urban varieties, "traditional" versus charismatic expressions. Our treatment here is simply meant to provide an example of the kind of intersections that need to be explored if one is to get a sense of Catholic identity in Africa. Moreover, it is by exploring the complex intersections of Catholic life in Africa that one is able more fully to appreciate the gifts, and grasp the challenges, of African Catholicism.

The Gifts of African Catholicism

A Lived Experience of Hope

In a sermon at the canonization of the Uganda Martyrs in 1964, Pope Paul VI used the words of Tertullian to remind the church that "the blood of martyrs is the seed of Christianity." This is especially true of Catholicism in Africa. The story of the church in Africa is the story of a long witness of martyrs and saints, which is one of Africa's greatest gifts to the world. The list of African saints extends back to the great doctors, martyrs, virgins, and confessors (Athanasius, Tertullian, Cyprian, Augustine, Perpetua, and others) of Roman North Africa; it includes St. Charles Lwanga and companions of the late nineteenth century, and the more recently canonized martyrs and saints: Cyprian Michael Iwene Tansi of Nigeria (beatified 1998); Josephine Bakhita of the Sudan (canonized 2000); Irwa and Daudi Okello from Gulu in northern Uganda (beatified 2002). The list also includes the eloquent witness of many unrecognized martyrs like Archbishop Christophe Munzihirwa of eastern Congo, who was murdered in 1996 for his condemnation of violence in the region, and numerous Christians, many of them young people, who died resisting the genocide in Rwanda. The case of the secondary school girls at Kibuye in Rwanda is particularly striking. Hutu rebels attacked their dormitory, rousing the girls and ordering them to separate themselves, Hutu from Tutsis. When they refused, they were beaten and shot indiscriminately.[21] The witness of such men and women constantly beckons the African church, indeed the universal church, to a sense of heroic witness in the face of trials and persecution. However, the fact that violence, poverty, sickness, and HIV/AIDS are realities that African Catholics deal with on a daily basis means that "hope" is the very identity of African Catholics. Thus, even more than heroic witness, what the African church offers is a lived experience of hope. Where the topic of hope has so much become an academic one in Western theology, Africa offers the church a lived theology of hope.

The Catechist

With his slender qualifications and very modest pay, the African catechist is the unsung hero of African Catholicism. Even with the growth of priestly vocations in Africa, the numbers are not sufficient to cover the wide geographical expanses of many parishes. And so, apart from the small amount of attention that a priest can give on his monthly visits, most local congregations depend on the pastoral leadership of the catechist. He teaches catechumens, instructs Confirmation candidates and First Communion classes, prepares the people for confession, collects tithes, visits the sick, sends out a call for the priest for those in need of anointing, attends parish meetings, and leads the Sunday worship, where he preaches and leads the prayers for the community. The village catechist therefore not only provides the necessary link between the community and the priest; he or she is the recognized pastoral leader and, in many ways, the "agent of conversion" for many African Catholics.

---

19. Hastings, *African Catholicism*, 1989.
20. Kassimir, "Politics of Popular Catholicism in Uganda," 270.
21. Gourevitch, *We Wish to Inform You*, 353.

These selfless and hardworking men and women are a unique gift to the Catholic Church and provide a confirmation, if one was ever needed, that the building up of the body of Christ is sustained through the gifts and ministry of lay leaders, whose leadership and dedication need to be recognized, affirmed, and encouraged. Unfortunately, in Africa as elsewhere, the catechists are often the least appreciated and the most neglected in terms of training and remuneration. Unless this shortcoming is urgently addressed, there is a danger that educated young men and women will turn to more lucrative jobs, thus leaving the ranks of catechists to be filled by school dropouts, who will lack the confidence and moral authority that the vocation of being a catechist demands.

Mission in Reverse: The Development of a New Catholicity

The gift of vocations (priestly and religious) is another gift of the African church. The Bigard Memorial Seminary in Nigeria has over seven hundred young men training for the priesthood. In 2005, the Archdiocese of Kampala in Uganda ordained sixteen priests, numbers that are reflective of a general trend. It is not difficult to imagine that one or two of these priests may in a year or two find themselves spending some time at a parish in either Europe or the United States. For a number of years now, the Comboni congregation has been sending African priests to Latin America and Asia. The quotation at the start of this essay—African priests appearing in (of all places) Ireland—is quite literally true, and very encouraging. Of course there are other ways that one might view this, for example, that Africa itself might need those priests even more than Europe or the United States does. But that would be to fail to recognize the essentially missionary nature of the church, which means that a local church does not give only out of "excess." Mission is about the sharing of gifts and needs, which enriches both the one who gives and the recipient while advancing the communion of the whole.

That is why the issue must move beyond priests and definitely beyond the practice of merely recruiting vocations from Africa to staff needy parishes in the West. It is about forging greater interaction and the sharing of gifts in a way that builds up the Catholicity of the church. It is only through this generous and genuine sharing in the gifts, vocations and otherwise, that the parochialism and isolation ("us" and "them") of nation-state loyalties will, one hopes, begin to break down and a new sense of catholicity will begin to take shape. But just as the presence of missionaries in Africa helps to push the imagination of Africans beyond tribal limitations, the presence of African, Asian, and Latino priests in the West is now critical to push the Western church beyond its tribal (national) loyalties, toward the formation of communities and practices that might genuinely be called catholic.

A Twenty-First-Century Liturgical Movement out of Africa

Worship in Africa is always the occasion for deep celebration involving praise, singing, and dancing. For African Catholics, therefore, worship is not only an event to look forward to; it is the occasion and opportunity for the celebration of the deep spiritual, social, and bodily connection with God. It is therefore hoped that, just as the pre-conciliar liturgical movement helped to both revive and unify the Western churches, the liturgical revitalization evident in the African church may serve a similar role in the coming century. The gifts that come out of this rich dynamism of African liturgical life go beyond its fresh and lively expressiveness. They include a dynamic and ongoing engagement with Christian tradition. The old and new come together in ways that are both fresh and edifying. Latin songs are sung with a new beat, and to the accompaniment of drums. Old liturgical feast days, for example, Corpus Christi, the Assumption, Christ the King, are marked with colorful processions; pilgrimages to holy shrines and other observances of Catholic traditions are celebrated with new contemporary African lyrics. Connected to this creativity is the gift of joy—spontaneous joy and celebration that the African Church displays so well through worship.

African Catholicism as an Embodied Experience

The refusal to separate the realities of body and soul is another distinctive gift that African Catholicism offers, which might draw the church to a renewed appreciation of the deep connection between belief and practice, spiritual matters and material realities. In the context of their African background, where there is no "secular" sphere, African Catholics live, work, and play in a religious environment. They are accordingly very much at home in a world of rituals, mysticism, sacraments, healing, exorcism, devotion, sacrifice, and prayer as a way of securing and sustaining the everyday interaction between the spiritual and material worlds. The full range of liturgical expression through music and dancing also bears witness to this reality of embodiment.

On another level, African Catholicism is not only a Sunday experience since it is as much about schools, health care, hospitals, and development projects as it is about prayer and sacraments. This interaction between material and spiritual realities on a daily basis makes African Catholicism both dynamic and vibrant, and the Catholic parish a hub, a meeting point of bodily and spiritual concerns and realities.

The African Woman

African societies and nations have gone through a number of turbulent transitions and violent upheavals. Given this history, the resilience, resourcefulness, and sheer determination not to give up are simply remarkable. The real, if often invisible, pillars behind this determination and resourcefulness are the women. The most important category here are the mothers—those devout women who look after their homes and families, often in the absence of the husband (due to war or migrant labor), and manage to raise and educate their children. They are the pillars, not only of society but also of the African church, in their care for the local church, in their involvement in its worship, in its leadership on the parish council, in their involvement in lay movements and associations, and even by their regularity in attendance. Increasingly, the leadership and impact of women in the church are felt through the growing number of vocations to the religious life. In the face of Africa's social and political troubles, religious women have often provided a much-needed credible witness and alternative. What Paul Gifford says of religious women in Uganda is in many ways true of Africa as a whole:

> The real strength of Uganda's Catholic Church may turn out to be the congregations of sisters, which are attracting candidates in considerable numbers, and which have always been important for Ugandan Catholicism. The sisters are increasingly well trained, and their training is so un-clerical that they are less concerned with status than with service. They have certain independence and are beginning to organize themselves into an articulate group within the Church. The moral leadership that is not coming from the official Catholic Church may eventually come from this quarter.[22]

One can highlight a number of other gifts of the African church—its youthful dynamism, hospitality, and warmth, its restless creativity, and many other gifts. The list here is not meant to be comprehensive but to offer a sample of what to expect from the African church. Such a sample would also include the challenges, frustrations, and limitations within African Catholicism.

Challenges and Frustrations: In Search of a Way Forward

The single most critical challenge facing the African church is theological, namely, the absence of vibrant and well-developed local theologies that can reflect the growing strength and liturgical dynamism of the African church. The effects of this lacuna are felt in many areas, particularly in the social and political arena, where the African church, its massive presence notwithstanding, is often powerless and thus unable to make any positive difference in the face of the many challenges facing Africa. In this way, African Catholicism often finds itself in the same predicament as the fictional character that Jenkins depicts at the beginning of this essay.[23] First told by John Mbiti,[24]

---

22. Gifford, *African Christianity*, 150.
23. Jenkins, *Next Christendom*, 124.
24. Mbiti, "Theological Impotence and the Universality of the Church," 6–8.

the story recounts the homecoming of an African seminarian who, after many years of studying in Europe and receiving all the necessary training and degrees, is nevertheless disappointingly impotent in the face of the needs of his sister.

Just like Mbiti's fictional character, who has extensive background and training in Western theology but has no ability to think creatively about the local situation (and therefore can only restate what Bultmann has said), the church in Africa, in the face of Africa's social and political challenges, keeps harking back to outdated theological visions and practices. Part of the problem is that theological education in Africa has remained very Western. Both the orientation and content of courses in the seminary closely follow Western models, with just some token overture for "local relevance." As a result, few seminaries have courses on such issues as AIDS, the Rwanda genocide, apartheid in South Africa, violence and nation-state implosions, tribalism, or popular Catholicism—challenges that African Christians face on a daily basis—and yet these seminaries have compulsory courses on critical theory, on Heidegger, and on phenomenology.

This means that, its massive presence notwithstanding, the African church has yet to become a genuine local church. In talking about the conditions of a local church, the Vatican II Decree on the Church's Missionary Activity (*Ad Gentes*) notes: The task of developing a local church reaches to a definite point when

> the assembly of the faithful, already rooted in the social life of the people and to some extent conformed to its culture, enjoys a certain stability and permanence; when it has its own priests although insufficient, its own religious and laity and possesses those ministries and institutions which are required for leading and spreading the life of the people of God under their own bishop. (§19)

While the African Church seems to have attained most of these conditions, it has yet to develop "those ministries and institutions which are required for leading and spreading the life," particularly the ministry of thinking critically and creatively in relation to the challenges facing Africa.

Since Vatican II, inculturation has been the dominant theological trend in Africa, attracting the interest and contribution of many African scholars and theologians. Theologies of inculturation, however, have, on the whole, remained captive not only to issues of culture but to the predictable Western theological methodologies and categories (translation, adaptation, indigenization). As a result, the transforming message of the gospel has not been allowed to explode into the various areas of social life in Africa in a way that provides for new visions and alternatives. A quick overview of the major challenges that African Christians face confirms the need and urgency for the development of such local theologies. The more explicitly political challenges include political instability, civil war, and the general absence, in many African countries, of political structures that ensure a smooth transfer of power. Connected to this are the lack of transparency, blatant abuse of public office, corruption, and a general lack of accountability. Moreover, the abuse of basic human rights, as well as the lack of respect for the rule of law, makes life very cheap in many African countries.

The widespread reality of violence in Africa requires special attention. With many countries in Africa going through one kind of violent upheaval or another, there is an urgent need to focus on the political conditions and histories that create and perpetuate violence in Africa. There is also an urgent need to understand the social effects of constant violence, particularly its tendency to percolate into a cultural pattern and thus become a "way of life." There are many indications that the church in Africa has not only been unable to challenge this culture of violence, but has in some cases itself reproduced and intensified these patterns of life.

Economic challenges include extensive poverty characterized not only by the absence of basic necessities of life but also by the widening gap between the First World and Africa. Within Africa itself, the reality of poverty is heightened by the existence of massive concentrations of the poor surrounded by pockets of wealth. The problem has to do basically with structures—political and economic structures which threaten a "programmed recolonization of the continent"²⁵ by a combination of local economic warlords and international economic structures. The sense of powerlessness and increasing impoverishment combine to destroy any hope for a meaningful future and to make survival, mere survival, the only goal for the majority of Africans.

Among the key social challenges is the problem of AIDS. To date, AIDS has killed over 20 million Africans, and an estimated 26 million people are living with the condition. In sub-Saharan Africa, every individual is either infected or personally affected. This has resulted not only in the rising number of AIDS orphans but also in the drastic reduction of life expectancy in Africa—to an all-time low of below forty years of age in many countries. The reality of AIDS, making death an everyday occurrence, has raised many unanswered questions about sex and marriage, as well as questions about the meaning of friendship and fidelity, the meaning of life, the reality of the church, and the existence of God.

Among the religious challenges is the one posed by the Pentecostal/evangelical wave sweeping through much of Africa. Led by both foreign and local evangelists and charismatic preachers, the evangelical revival in Africa has attracted a large number of young people through lively services, a born-again spirituality, and the promise of miracles. One response to this Pentecostal/evangelical wave has been the revival of the Catholic Charismatic Renewal. The effect of the renewal has, on the whole, been positive: a deepening of faith among members through greater knowledge of the Bible, more enthusiastic and expressive forms of religious practice, sharing of religious experience through small groups, a leveling of authority lines between clergy and laity, an emphasis on the Holy Spirit and the charisms, including the gift of healing. In this way, the Catholic Charismatic Renewal has reattracted a number of Catholics who had been alienated from the church. The church, however, has yet to find ways to face the key challenges raised by Pentecostal revival in Africa, most significantly, the entrepreneurial imagination in which the message of the gospel is uncritically hooked to the expectations and promises of modernity, progress, and prosperity.

No single institution in Africa has undergone so much change and has experienced so much uncertainty as the family. The endless regimes of civil unrest and violence; the genocide in Rwanda; the abductions of young children into rebel armies in northern Uganda and Sierra Leone; the AIDS epidemic; the grinding poverty in the rural areas; growing urbanization; the rabid unemployment in the cities; the growth of cheap media entertainment; all have undermined the traditional values on which the African family is founded. The synod fathers proposed the African family as a model for the church in Africa, reflecting the sense of communion, solidarity, and affirmation of human life that is characteristic of the African family (*EA* §64). With many of these values now threatened, serious attention must be paid to the area of marriage and family life in Africa, if the church is to continue to be God's family in Africa.

Responding to these and many other challenges calls for nothing short of a new reality and a new way of being a church in Africa, a church that can both faithfully discern the signs of the time and embody faithful and hopeful alternatives for the future. Doing so requires moving away from old pre-packaged theologies and calls for the "courage to reinvent Christianity so as to live it with [an] African soul."²⁶ This is possible through the development of local theologies that reflect the yearnings and aspirations of African Catholics.

In order to respond to this challenge, theological education and seminary training in Africa must move away from the overly academic and ivory-tower approach of Western theology and move toward the development of what Jean Marc Éla has called "shade tree theologies"—theologies that develop "among brothers and sisters searching shoulder to shoulder with unlettered peasants for the sense of the word of God in situations in which this word touches them."²⁷

---

25. Éla, "Church—Sacrament of Liberation," 133.
26. Éla, *African Cry*, 120.
27. Éla, *African Cry*, vi.

To be sure, there is already a great deal of this shade tree theologizing going on in informal, quiet, and unwritten ways as African Catholics unconsciously select and reject, mold and transform certain beliefs and practices as they deal with issues of life and death, with AIDS and violence, marginalization and powerlessness, sickness and poverty. The challenge that the church in Africa faces is how to let these shade tree theologies become the basis of a renewed program of Christian education in schools, in the training of catechists and the programs of the local parish, in the social teaching of bishops, and in liturgical renewal at the parish and diocesan level. The challenge is to allow these shade tree theologies to become an integral part of theological education and seminary training in Africa. In this way, as the future leaders of the church in Africa study the rich resources of the Catholic tradition, they are able to press these ancient traditions and dogmas with new questions—questions reflecting the aspirations and frustrations of everyday life in Africa. In the same way that they are able to articulate and engage the yearning and restless ferment within popular Catholicism, they are able to press it into further clarity and consistency and to help it reshape everyday life in Africa in ways that are life-affirming and liberating according to the spirit of the gospel. Only through this mutual and ongoing interaction between the universal and the local, between the ancient and the new, between the Western heritage and the African needs, will the African church truly become a local church—a genuine witness of God's presence in Africa. As this occurs, the results not only will benefit Africa, but will renew the practice and theology of the church universal, while providing it with a fresh vision of the gifts and promises of Catholicism.

Bibliography

Bamat, Thomas, and Jean Paul Wiest. *Popular Catholicism in a World Church: Seven Case Studies in Inculturation*. Maryknoll, NY: Orbis Books, 1999.

Baur, John. *2000 Years of Christianity in Africa: An African History, 62–1992*. Nairobi: Pauline Publications, 1994.

Bühlmann, Walter. *The Coming of the Third Church: An Analysis of the Present and Future of the Church*. Maryknoll, NY: Orbis Books, 1977.

Éla, Jean Marc. *African Cry*. Maryknoll, NY: Orbis Books, 1980.

———. "The Church—Sacrament of Liberation." In *The African Synod: Documents, Reflections, Perspectives*, compiled and edited by the Africa Faith and Justice Network. Maryknoll, NY: Orbis Books, 1996.

Faupel, J. F. *African Holocaust: The Story of the Uganda Martyrs*. Kampala: St Paul Publications, 1962.

Froehle, Bryan, and Mary L. Gautier. *Global Catholicism: Portrait of a World Church*. Maryknoll, NY: Orbis Books, 2003.

Gifford, Paul. *African Christianity: Its Public Role*. Bloomington: Indiana University Press, 1998.

Gourevitch, Philip. *We Wish to Inform You That Tomorrow We Will Be Killed together with Our Children*. London: Picador Press, 1998.

Hastings, Adrian. *African Catholicism: Essays in Discovery*. London: SCM Press, 1989.

———. *The Church in Africa, 1450–1950*. Oxford History of the Christian Church. Oxford: Clarendon Press, 1994.

Jenkins, Philip. *The Next Christendom: The Coming of Global Christianity*. Oxford: Oxford University Press, 2002.

John Paul II, Pope. *Ecclesia in Africa* [Post-synodal Apostolic Exhortation on the Church in Africa and Its Evangelizing Mission toward the Year 2000; September 14, 1995]. Vatican City: Libreria Editrice Vaticana, 1995. www.vatican.va.

Kassimir, Ronald. "The Politics of Popular Catholicism in Uganda." In *East African Expressions of Christianity*, edited by Thomas Spear and Isaria N. Kimambo, 248–74. Nairobi: East African Studies, 1999.

Katongole, Emmanuel. "Kannungu and the Movement for the Restoration of the Ten Commandments of God in Uganda: A Challenge to Christian Social Imagination." *Logos* 6.3 (2003): 108–43.

Mbiti, John. "Theological Impotence and the Universality of the Church." In *Mission Trends No. 3: Third World Theologies*, edited by Gerald Anderson and Thomas Stransky, 6–18. Grand Rapids, MI: Eerdmans, 1976.

Sundkler, Bengt, and Christopher Steed. *A History of the Church in Africa.* Cambridge: Cambridge University Press, 2000.

Vatican Council II. Decree on the Missionary Activity of the Church (*Ad Gentes*), in *Vatican Council II: Constitutions, Decrees, Declarations*, edited by Austin Flannery. New York: Costello, 1996.

Walls, Andrew F. *The Missionary Movement in Christian History: Studies in the Transmission of Faith.* Maryknoll, NY: Orbis Books, 2004.

I am grateful for my former student Jay Carney, PhD, who through many conversations as I supervised his research helped to give shape to the direction, contents, and final shape of this essay.

Toward a Historical Perspective on African Catholicism in the Era of World Christianity

Paul V. Kollman, CSC

The changes in the demography of Christians in the world have been remarkable since the early twentieth century. This global shift in the location of those who constitute the world Christian movement—from a predominantly European and North American population located in the so-called Global North or Minority World, to one mostly found in the Majority World or Global South of Latin America, Africa, and increasingly Asia—is among the largest shifts in religious belonging in human history. Around 80 percent of the world's Christians lived in Europe and North America in 1900 and now well over 60 percent dwell in the Global South, and that percentage is poised to grow.[1] If one measures, moreover, the energy in Christian churches, the discrepancy between 1900 and the present would only be sharper. After all, immense religious vitality exists in Christian bodies in the Majority World, while, despite the ongoing formal Christian affiliation of many people, numerous churches in the Global North are shrinking or disappearing entirely.

Africa's Christian dynamics epitomize this trend. In 1900 there were, by one estimate, perhaps nine million Christians in Africa, nearly all of them in Egypt or Ethiopia. As the fruits of Catholic and Protestant missionary activity that began in the nineteenth century manifested themselves, those numbers have soared, primarily in sub-Saharan Africa: 30 million in 1945, 115 million in 1970, and perhaps 500 million in 2018, with more growth anticipated.[2] Of course, those believers belong not only to churches traceable to missionary activity that are part of global Christian identities linked to those original denominations. In addition, Africans have developed their own churches, some that have global reach; an increasing number of these churches are shaped by Pentecostal-style practices of worship and congregational life.

In the midst of the growth within African Christianity in general, and especially in light of the Pentecostal-linked vitality of many African-initiated churches, or AICs, it can be easy to overlook formal church belonging among African Christians linked to the historical churches founded by missionaries. The older ecclesial bodies can seem staid and uninteresting by comparison to the colorful and enthusiastic AICs and Pentecostal churches. Yet most

---

1. Johnson and Ross, *Atlas of Global Christianity*, 8.
2. Estimates vary for these numbers, of course, and are notoriously hard to verify, especially because denominations present their own numbers. Some of the best data can be found on the Pew Forum's website at www.pewforum.org, or in the two-volume work, the *World Christian Encyclopedia*, ed. David B. Barrett, George T. Kurian, and Todd M. Johnson, 2nd ed. (Oxford: Oxford University Press, 2001). The third edition of this work is currently being produced. Another helpful source of information is the World Christian Database at www.worldchristiandatabase.org.

African Christians continue to belong to Christian bodies traceable to missionary activity, and these churches remain central to the Christian life of the continent. In addition, these churches create and maintain institutional bodies like schools and hospitals with a Christian identity that play important roles in African society, economic life, and politics.

Many people, even many Catholics, are unaware that the largest single religious affiliation among African Christians is, with varying degrees of self-understanding, with the global communion of the Roman Catholic Church. This handbook seeks to advance an understanding of the African Catholic reality and to establish a basis for future research by assessing the past and present. This chapter will seek to place the current situation of the Catholic Church in Africa within a historical perspective that is mindful of Africa's Christian past and present as well as its particularly Catholic past and present. It will do so in light of previous historical approaches to African Christianity as well as more recent revisions to those approaches linked to the emerging field of world Christianity,[3] which seek to allow the new demographic realities to affect how Christianity's story is told.

This chapter will unfold in three parts. First, it will describe one common framework delineating the growth of Christianity in Africa that prioritizes three stages during which external historical forces brought Christianity to the continent. Second, it will present challenges to this three-stage framework from the growing perspective of world Christianity and from a particularly Catholic perspective. Since it is the largest Christian body in the world and in Africa, there is value in thinking of the Catholic Church in Africa by itself, as it were, as well as within larger Christian dynamics, and in considering African Catholicism from a historical perspective that is linked to the emerging field of world Christianity. Thus, the chapter will not separate the Catholic story from the larger story of all Christians, but will highlight what can be seen as distinctive Catholic aspects of the world Christian story in Africa. This, I will argue, reveals certain continuities from the earliest African Christianity to contemporary African Catholic vitality—continuities that are easily overlooked in the absence of a specifically Catholic lens. The chapter thus represents an attempt to provide African Catholics a usable past as they think about their current lives of faith.[4] And finally, third, I will conclude by briefly looking ahead, urging the development of a more serious historical perspective on African Catholic vitality, for the well-being of the global Catholic Church as well as for African and world Christianity moving forward.

A Framework and Its Limitations

One standard historical picture of how Christianity has been present in Africa prioritizes three distinct stages, or "plantings," of the faith on the continent. The first of these plantings coincided with the beginnings of Christianity itself in the vital early church of northern Africa that arose from the first century of the Christian era. The second occurred at various places around the seacoasts of the continent when the Portuguese established themselves there starting in the late fifteenth century. The third refers to the planting that occurred as a result of the rise of the modern missionary movement starting in the nineteenth century, which has generated most of the Christian presence in sub-Saharan Africa today. According to most versions of this story, the first two plantings ended in failure, the first due to the rise of Islam and the second because the Portuguese pursued evangelization only sporadically and then had diminished as an overseas power by the early eighteenth century. As a consequence, in these versions of the story, the contemporary vitality of sub-Saharan African Christianity has little to do with these first two plantings, instead being the result of missionary energy and African initiatives beginning in the third planting—that is, from the nineteenth century and continuing to the present.

---

3. For discussions, see Kollman, "After Church History?" and "Understanding the World-Christian Turn."
4. The term "usable past" was invoked with respect to U.S. history by Van Wyck Brooks in 1915 and more recently by Michel Foucault, among others. See the discussion by searching for "usable past" at www.xroads.virginia.edu.

This three-part framework, which appears in *Ecclesia in Africa* (1995), the post-synodal apostolic exhortation of Pope John Paul II that emerged after the First African Synod in 1994,[5] captures certain indisputable realities. First, stages 1 and 2 witnessed considerable Christian vitality in Africa. Northern Africa was one of the heartlands of the early church, boasting a large number of important thinkers and leaders in the first six centuries after Christ. St. Mark the Evangelist has traditionally been seen as the first bishop of Alexandria, while theological giants such as Origen, Clement of Alexandria, Cyprian, Tertullian, Athanasius, and Augustine all called northern Africa their home. Along with Asia Minor (today Turkey), northern Africa was among the foremost sites of Christian vitality in the church's first few centuries.

In addition, it is equally true that the Portuguese encounter with Africa in the early modern period generated important ecclesial activity, with several dioceses founded in sub-Saharan Africa connected to Portuguese trading posts where Catholic missionaries were active. A remarkable Catholic kingdom emerged in the Kongo, where the son of Afonso I, the first prominent Catholic king, was consecrated a bishop. The Kingdom of the Kongo, which spanned what are today Angola and the Democratic Republic of the Congo, was not alone. Other sites of significant Christian activity during this period included present-day Madagascar, Mozambique, Kenya, Tanzania, and Benin.

Second, as the three-plantings model suggests, historical processes challenged these first two phases, generating setbacks to Christianity. The coming of Islam certainly sapped much of the vitality of Christianity in northern Africa, and the Portuguese-linked Catholic enclaves on the coasts of Africa had shrunk significantly by the nineteenth century. The decline of the latter was the result of several factors, including the limitations of the Portuguese colonial model, European infighting, the rise of the slave trade, and conflicts with emerging political powers in Africa, some of them Muslim.

Finally, it is true that the most vital realities present within—and most of the numerical growth occurring in—sub-Saharan Christianity today, Catholic or not, are traceable to missionary activity that began with the modern missionary movement in the nineteenth century. This movement was led by Protestant voluntary missionary societies in Great Britain and continental Europe as well as a revived Catholic missionary energy after the end of the Napoleonic wars.

Yet this framework also conceals a great deal. An influential essay by Andrew Walls has identified several shortcomings of the framework.[6] First, he emphasizes the persistence of Egyptian and Ethiopian Christianity from the ancient days of the church to the present. Both Egypt's Copts and the venerable Christian churches of Ethiopia have remained vital since their earliest days despite formidable challenges that continue into the present, especially in the case of the Copts. Second, Walls questions the implicit assumption that divides northern Africa from the rest of the continent, recalling that the Sahara Desert was never an insuperable barrier to travel, commerce, and other forms of interaction, including cultural and religious exchanges. Recent research on the dynamic Christian church in Nubia offers support for Walls's contention—this church maintained a vital Christian life until at least the fourteenth, and more likely the sixteenth, century.[7] Third, Walls notes the frequent use of the appellation "Ethiopian" by the founders of AICs in the names of these churches from the nineteenth century to the present. He adduces, in the use of the term by African Christian innovators to apply to their own churches, a felt sense of continuity with the earliest Christians on the continent, something that the three-planting framework might overlook.

One might add to Walls's points that African Christianity has been undergoing a fourth planting

---

5. Pope John Paul II, *Ecclesia in Africa* §§30–37 (hereinafter *EA*). See also Northrup, *Seven Myths of Africa*, 105–9; and Pierli and Ratti, "Pioneers of the Kingdom."
6. Walls, "Africa in Christian History."
7. Bowers, "Nubian Christianity."

of sorts, this time originating in Africa and moving into the rest of the world. This happened previously in some sense, since African Christians were among those trafficked as slaves, bringing their faith with them to Brazil, the Caribbean, and probably even North America.[8] In addition, new forms of Christianity emerged among diaspora Africans who left the continent as non-Christian slaves but became Christian while in bondage. Many of their Christian innovations should be counted as among the most important in Christian history.[9] Recent decades, however, have witnessed a new phenomenon: churches founded in Africa, especially in western and southern Africa, opening branches throughout the world, notably in the metropolitan centers of the Global North.[10]

Other historical work suggests the limitations of the three-planting framework. Noteworthy in this regard have been the efforts of the late Thomas Oden to celebrate and inform others about the abiding achievements of ancient African Christianity. Oden argued passionately that the world Christian movement urgently needs to do more to integrate African Christian achievements into mainstream Christianity, simply in order to get the history right. Among his other efforts, he highlighted seven abiding achievements of ancient African Christianity that shaped all subsequent Christianity: the Christian university, principles of scriptural exegesis, the notion of dogma, the practices of ecumenical councils, monasticism, Christian Neoplatonism, and the principles of Christian rhetoric and dialectic.[11] Oden founded the Center for Early African Christianity (CEAC), which exists, as its website puts it, to educate African leadership in "the depth of African intellectual literary achievements, especially those from the Christian tradition of the first millennium."[12]

These historical challenges to the three-planting framework, however, might not be the most important. Besides the historical realities it overlooks, the framework—and especially the second and third plantings—focuses on external agency in the creation of institutions, stressing the ways in which outside forces brought Christianity to Africa. It too easily overlooks African agency in the growth of African Christianity. Linked to this, it also somewhat unwittingly allows historical understanding to overlook theological realities linked to God's activity in Africa that is not reducible to the three plantings. After all, what God has been about in Africa cannot be limited only to focusing on the efforts of those from outside the continent to bring the Christian message.[13]

A Catholic Perspective on Africa's Christian Past

Some of the important insights coming from the world-Christian turn in historiography arise from the comparative perspectives it offers.[14] These are not limited, however, to Christianity in general. They also devolve to particular forms of Christianity, and the Catholic Church is no exception. African Catholics mindful of the history of Christianity in Africa can gain particular appreciation for the distinctiveness of their experiences as believers by seeing the Christian past through a world-Christian hermeneutic focusing on Catholic aspects of that past in light of the Catholic present in Africa. Three suggestions are offered here for adopting historical perspectives on certain aspects of that past to assist in drawing the Catholic past and Catholic present closer together, helping to overcome the view that the nineteenth century ended what one missionary periodical in 1883 described as Africa's

---

8. Thornton, *Kongolese Saint Anthony*, 212–14.
9. Raboteau, *Slave Religion*.
10. Among many titles discussing the international reach of churches founded in Africa, see Adogame, *African Christian Diaspora*; and Adogame and Spickard, *Religion Crossing Boundaries*.
11. Oden, *How Africa Shaped the Christian Mind*.
12. Center for Early African Christianity (CEAC), "What We Do," www.earlyafricanchristianity.com.
13. Among Catholics, this issue was raised forcefully decades ago by Jean Daniélou, especially in his *Salvation of the Nations* (1950).
14. Kollman, "After Church History?" and "Understanding the World-Christian Turn."

"fourteen-century Christian slumber."[15] These perspectives also draw upon current or recent topics of academic research. The hope is that these might inspire others, scholars as well as ordinary believers, to discern illuminating connections across the centuries of Christianity and Catholicism in Africa.

Discerning the Zeal for Holiness in Christian Roman North Africa

The first necessary historical reconsideration derives from focusing on the part of Christian northern Africa that in the first centuries CE most resembled contemporary Catholicism. This means disaggregating northern Africa into various areas, recognizing that parts of the region took on distinct theological and ecclesiological characteristics that, in retrospect, can be linked to distinct contemporary forms of Christianity. Admittedly, this oversimplifies complex historical processes, yet in the interests of highlighting a Catholic perspective, one can see three distinguishable regions of northern Africa that were centers of Christianity in its first seven centuries, each corresponding with various modes of Christianity still existing today.

First, Ethiopian Christianity and that of the Copts in Egypt can be seen as sharing certain theological features, especially a rejection of the authority of the Council of Chalcedon. They are thus recognized as "non-Chalcedonian" Christians, and contemporary world-Christian historians increasingly appreciate the early vitality and importance of non-Chalcedonian Christianity, not only in Africa but also in Persia, parts of Syria, and into India and China.[16] Today, too, the non-Chalcedonian Christians of Ethiopia, Egypt, Syria, and India are enjoying a renewed prominence. There are important differences between the Coptic Christianity of Egypt and Ethiopian Christianity. Ethiopian Christianity took on forms closer to the deeply Jewish Christianity of the first century (for example, complex rules of fasting, as well as a royal cult that eventually developed national-mythic links to King Solomon through the Old Testament story of the Queen of Sheba), perhaps because it was less exposed to Greek philosophy than the Egyptians farther north—yet it still resembles Coptic Christianity.

Second, a Christian style featuring speculative theological and philosophical reflection in the Greek language also arose in northern Africa. It was centered in Alexandria, also part of Egypt yet with more Greek speakers than the rest of Egypt and thus less Coptic in its Christian features. A firmly Hellenistic city, Alexandria was one of the centers of ancient academic life, and many of early Christianity's great theologians, including Clement of Alexandria, Origen, and Athanasius, called it home. Most of the Christological discussions that formed the creedal formulations claiming the adherence of the majority of today's Christians took place in Greek, and Alexandria was a focal point for those discussions. Alexandria can be seen as prefiguring the Orthodox churches of today, with their historical and theological framework shaped by Greek thought.

Third and finally, there was also Roman or Latin northern Africa—that is, Africa to the west of Egypt. This meant—mindful that names and boundaries changed over time in line with Roman political transformations—the Roman provinces of Libya (with the regions of Marmarica, Cyrenaica, and Tripolitana), Numidia, Byzacena, Proconsularis, and Mauretania (Sitifensis, Caesariensus, and Tingitana); that is, much of the contemporary countries of Libya, Tunisia, Algeria, and Morocco. If the Ethiopian and Coptic Christians of Egypt can be linked to today's non-Chalcedonian Christians, and Alexandrian Egypt to the Orthodox, then Roman northern Africa prefigures most of Western Christianity, and, for present purposes, contemporary Catholic Christianity in Africa.

As J. Patout Burns Jr. and Robin Jensen argue in their remarkable recent study of Roman northern Africa, this part of the ancient Christian world developed a distinctive form of Christian life and reflection. While Greek theologians centered in Alexandria (and also other places like Constantinople and Antioch) formed a distinct school of

---

15. *Annales de la Propagation de la Foi* 44 (1883): 7–9.
16. Jenkins, *Lost History of Christianity*.

thought, an African school of theology in the western part of northern Africa also arose, writing primarily in Latin. Yet the two schools differed not only in the language in which they wrote. As Burns and Jensen put it, the Greek speakers inclined to speculation, the Latin speakers to practical questions.

Whereas the Greeks focused their concern with salvation on the nature of the Godhead and its manifestation in Christ, these Latins worried about the adequacy of human organizations and ministers to mediate the divine life. The Greeks studied the interaction of divine and human in the Savior; the Latins attempted to discern the standards which would guarantee divine operation in the rituals of the church.[17]

Burns and Jensen identify two characteristic themes for these Latinate Africans: "a concern with the holiness of the church and its performing the sanctifying work of Christ."[18] As a consequence, theologians linked to Latin Africa, including Tertullian, Cyprian, and eventually Augustine, concerned themselves with "the role of the church as the medium of Christ's salvific work" and thus "on the church's holiness and effectiveness of its rituals."[19]

The importance of the achievements of these Roman African Christians can be compared to many others in later Christian history. For instance, Roman North Africa was the place of the first Christian writing in Latin—specifically, the narratives composed in honor of the Scillitan Martyrs and the martyrdoms of Perpetua and Felicity in the late second and early third centuries CE, as well as the writings of Tertullian. Besides innovating in Latin Christian writing, they also created a theological tradition by engaging a series of issues that resonate with African Catholics today.

Many aspects of this Roman African theological legacy deserve highlighting in light of contemporary African Catholicism. Here I will mention two. First, the practical attention they paid to the holiness of the church typifies many African Catholics today. For the Christians of Roman Africa, the practical questions they faced arose, at least partially, out of the history of persecution that the Roman African church faced prior to the legalization of Christianity. The reality of apostasy forced church leaders, ordinary Christians, and theologians to consider sacramental validity and the worthiness of ordained ministers. Over time, as the theological tradition grew, the holiness of the church was deemed more important than cultural respectability or the precise modes whereby sacraments became efficacious. Such practical concerns continued after the end of persecution due to controversies linked to Donatism and other movements, many later deemed heretical. Such movements, heretical or not, also concerned themselves with the efficacy of sacramental practice linked to the holiness of the church and its ministers.

Many centuries later, a focus on the church's holiness remains an African Catholic priority. This can be seen in at least two ways. First, African Catholics are drawn to Pentecostalism and its style of prayer, of which personal holiness is a prominent public manifestation. Second, like many Africans, African Catholics show a preoccupation with witchcraft when faced with misfortune and often engage in processes of determining reasons for misfortune, processes that often lead to accusations that a person or persons are engaged in witchcraft. At times, both of these features of contemporary African Catholicism are deemed regressive and unfortunate, signs of the incomplete formation of modern Catholics that have led to the persistence of a pre-Christian worldview. Today's theologians and church leaders show concern about the absence of logic that is part and parcel of certain practices linked to Pentecostal or charismatic religiosity, and the antiscientific assumptions—and at times inhuman cruelty—embodied in accusations of witchcraft. Such pastoral and theological concerns are well taken. At the same time, a historical perspective mindful of early Roman African Christianity would highlight these problematic features of African Christianity as reflective of abiding concerns

---

17. Burns and Jensen, *Christianity in Roman Africa*, xlvi–xlvii.
18. Burns and Jensen, *Christianity in Roman Africa*, xlvi.
19. Burns and Jensen, *Christianity in Roman Africa*, xlviii.

among African Christians from the earliest centuries, and thus allow a better understanding of their existential motivations. As was true for Roman African Christians, for African Catholics today the appeal of holiness and concerns about protecting it motivate their convictions and practices.

A second, related feature of the church of Roman northern Africa also resonates with today's African Catholics, namely, the unusual intensity with which they celebrated their martyrs, their concern for holiness leading to a deep reverence for personal sanctity. This manifested itself early, with the second- and early third-century accounts of the Scillitan Martyrs and of Perpetua and Felicity, and continued, for example, in the theological reflections of Tertullian and Augustine. Today's African Catholics also accord martyrs deep respect, as can be seen in the remarkable devotion to the Ugandan Martyrs and in the popularity of their annual feast on June 3, which gathers over a million people at Namugongo's Uganda Martyrs Shrine every year.

The piety of ordinary believers as shown in their reverence for martyrs is also echoed in contemporary African theological reflections. Theologians like Ugandan Catholic priest Emmanuel Katongole emphasize the role of personal sanctity and heroism in the face of Africa's sometimes difficult circumstances. Katongole recounts the stories of courageous and faith-filled witnesses like Bishop Paride Taban of South Sudan and Angela Atyam of northern Uganda, as well as the Congolese bishop Christophe Munzihirwa, who was killed while supporting local people against violence.[20] Such stories allow for new possibilities in telling the story of African Christian belief and practice.

Inculturation in Kongolese Catholicism

The achievements of the Portuguese period, especially the Catholic kingdom of the Kongo, are a second aspect of the African Christian past that Catholics in Africa can especially appreciate in light of their current circumstances. In particular, the highly inculturated and African nature of the Catholic identity that was lived among the Kongolese has become increasingly appreciated.

The vitality and faithfulness of Kongolese Catholics have long been recognized in the heroism of the first important Kongolese Catholic king, Afonso I, in the development of a Catholic elite and self-sustaining practices of catechesis, and in the role of lay devotional movements in reinforcing piety. Yet Kongolese Catholicism, so promising in the sixteenth century, began to unravel in the seventeenth. Many have seen the devastations of the slave trade, the inability to form Kongolese Catholic clergy (some have seen the cause of this in the insistence on clerical celibacy), and the eventual end of missionaries being sent into the region as combining to undermine the Catholic Church in the Kongo.[21]

The end of a robust Kongolese Catholicism, however, did not undo its abiding achievements. Recently, close historical analysis in dialogue with historical-anthropological fieldwork has shown how Catholicism became a Kongolese religion, not just that many of the Kongolese became Catholic. Key aspects of Kongolese culture shaped the Catholicism that emerged there; for example, distinctive features like the social authority linked to kings, chiefs, and the nobility, as well as the ubiquitous *nkisi*, often rendered "fetish" but referring to any object bearing power, operated before, during, and after the Catholic period of Kongolese history.[22] In 1874, Catholic missionaries returning to the region reported that the Kongolese could still recall the old Kongo mission.[23]

A recent book on Kongolese Christian art has further advanced our understanding of the

---

20. Katongole, *Sacrifice of Africa*.

21. On the rise and fall of Kongolese Catholicism, see Thornton, *Kongolese Saint Anthony*, and Hastings, *Church in Africa, 1450–1950*, 73–77, 79–129. For a recent discussion of the challenges in understanding the Kongolese religious experience over time due to the complexity of the source material, see MacGaffey, "Constructing a Kongo Identity."

22. MacGaffey, *Religion and Society*, 191–216.

23. *Annales de la Propagation de la Foi* 35 (1874): 342. See the discussion in Sundkler and Steed, *History of the Church in Africa*, 287–90.

scope of Kongolese Catholic achievements. Cécile Fromont's *The Art of Conversion: Christian Visual Culture in the Kingdom of the Kongo* shows how the artistic productions of Kongolese Catholics built upon and advanced local aesthetic forms, infusing them with a Christian sensibility and iconography while maintaining cultural continuity with the past. Fromont identifies a number of loci where this cultural work happens: martial dances called *sangamento*s, crosses (which had a pre-Christian history in the Kongo), architectural constructions, and fabric (especially hats). She calls these "spaces of correlation," defined as "cultural creations such as narratives, artworks, or performances that offer a yet unspecified domain in which their creators can bring together ideas and forms belonging to radically different realms, confront them, and eventually turn them into interrelated parts of a new system of thought and expression."[24]

Fromont emphasizes that such creativity was neither amorphous mixing nor motivated by political expediency. Instead, Catholic crucifixes, for example, "naturalized Christianity into a local discourse about the nature of the supernatural and the cycle of life and death and, in turn, transposed Kongo religious signs into visual expressions of Catholic thought." Far from being tools of resistance or compromise, such symbols were the "result of an independent process of cross-cultural inclusion and reinvention."[25]

Understanding Kongolese Catholic achievements certainly serves to increase an awareness of the tragic impact of the Atlantic slave trade, not only on African peoples in general but also on African Christianity. Of less moral importance, but of arguably equal theological importance, early modern Kongo represents a remarkable example of something like inculturation, a phenomenon that has long been underappreciated. Inculturation as a theological program has been endorsed by the Vatican as well as by African bishops' conferences and theologians. Inculturation in practice, however, is a difficult process to prescribe, much less harness and control.[26] Appreciation for how that happened—in many ways—four centuries ago, including through an artistic ingenuity that was firmly Catholic and firmly Kongolese, can only serve to inspire today's Catholics, both church leaders and ordinary believers.

Catholic Missionary Achievements in Africa

A third possible source of inspiration for African Catholics from the past, in addition to Roman northern African Christianity and the richly inculturated Catholicism of the Kingdom of the Kongo in the early modern period, derives from the Catholic achievements of the modern missionary period that began in the nineteenth century. Past studies of mission history in Africa have oscillated between uncritical hagiography and nationalist and anticolonial suspicion, yet recent critical studies of missionary practices and their effects testify to the abiding achievements of numerous Catholic groups that worked in Africa. Such achievements include of course the introduction of the institutional richness of the Catholic Church itself, which continues to provide Africa with a remarkable amount of education and health care.

Less obviously, missionaries—Catholics and others—have often partnered in the creation of social and cultural identity for many people in Africa. This has often been despite the overt racism of missionaries themselves, which led many of them to denigrate Africans and their cultures, with some deplorable consequences. Despite these indefensible tendencies, the processes of translation that missionary Christianity initiated have been instrumental in the adoption into contemporary African languages of written and standardized forms, which has very often been central to the formation of collective identity. As Lamin Sanneh has so persuasively shown, these processes of translation unleashed forces that very quickly grew beyond missionary paternalism.[27] These processes were often empowering—unsurprisingly, the vast majority of the leaders of indepen-

---

24. Fromont, *Art of Conversion*, 15.
25. Fromont, *Art of Conversion*, 108.
26. Magesa, *Anatomy of Inculturation*.
27. Sanneh, *Translating the Message*.

dence movements in sub-Saharan Africa attended schools founded by missionaries. Despite the typical missionary educational goals of shaping docile believers and subjects loyal to colonial regimes, the students often had their own take on the messages that were imparted.

In addition, Catholic missionary strategies in Africa have had impacts on the broader Catholic Church. One important example lies in the procedures used to instruct potential converts that were pioneered by the Missionaries of Africa, or White Fathers, as part of their evangelization efforts beginning in the 1870s. Charles Cardinal Lavigerie, their founder, drew inspiration from the early church in northern Africa, where his society began its work, and sought to reintroduce the catechumenate as it operated in the first centuries of the Common Era. In Uganda and elsewhere, therefore, multiyear processes of Christian initiation developed, a phenomenon that in the late twentieth century has spread all over the Catholic world in the form of the Rite of Christian Initiation of Adults (RCIA).

Implications for the Future of African Catholicism

It seems quite certain that Africa will increasingly become a global center of Christianity in general, and of Roman Catholicism in particular. Most likely this will also mean that one important locus of the church's demographic growth will be far from global economic and political power centers. Pope Francis seems to welcome this, saying shortly after his election that he "would like a church that is poor and for the poor."[28]

Given the vitality of Christianity in Africa today, it can be tempting to overlook Africa's Christian past. Both Christian leaders and ordinary believers can easily focus on growth and novelty while ignoring African Christian precursors. A shortage of resources—fiscal, academic, and institutional—might only increase that risk.

From an admittedly limited perspective, my own experience as a seminarian in Africa and a lecturer in two Catholic seminaries there testifies to reasons for concern, as do aspects of my experience as a researcher into the African Christian past. When I was a seminarian, the church history courses on the syllabus—even courses in African church history—rarely drew much attention from the other students. Later as a professor, teaching other courses myself, I noted once again the scant interest accorded to historical subjects. The state of many archival resources related to the history of Christian communities in Africa is parlous—if they exist at all. One of the goals here, therefore, lies in developing an interest in the Christian—and especially Catholic—past of the church in Africa, both to generate interest and to encourage further research.

That said, there are also signs of hope. Many African Catholic seminaries invite their students to investigate the historical backgrounds of their own families' experiences of faith as part of their academic training. These practices, which often entail interviews with elders in their families or homes, can shed light on the past in ways that allow a personal confirmation of their importance, especially for young Africans predisposed to respect their elders. Such practices ought to be mandatory, in my opinion, for the well-being of the church moving forward.

For both theological and pastoral reasons, the African Catholic past merits deeper consideration, both anecdotal and formally academic. Theologically speaking, all too often Africa's past is treated in two opposing ways, both of which distort the historical record. For some Christians, including some Pentecostal and charismatic Christians—and some, though increasingly fewer,[29] of the scholars who study them—new Christian identities efface believers' pasts, so that testimonies to rebirth substitute for reasoned analysis of the actual behaviors and beliefs of African Christians. On the other

---

28. Joshua McElwee, "The Francis Chronicles," *National Catholic Reporter*, March 16, 2003, www.ncronline.org.

29. For a groundbreaking work, see Meyer, *Translating the Devil*, and further reflection by Robbins, "Continuity Thinking."

hand, there are scholars who argue that Christianity remains a thin veneer over an abiding indigenous substratum that timelessly survives untouched by any historical processes.[30]

The actual social processes whereby Africans have become Catholic yet remain African—as individuals and as communities of faith—have invariably been much more interesting than either of these caricatures. In addition, those involved in these processes are in their own ways transforming the Catholic global presence by their creativity, energy, and faithfulness. Gathering more insight into such African Catholic efforts and thus locating them within longer-term historical processes will only increase our understanding and appreciation of the richness and vitality of African Catholicism. This is an important task for the African Catholic future.

Bibliography

Adogame, Afeosemime U. *The African Christian Diaspora: New Currents and Emerging Trends in World Christianity*. London: Bloomsbury, 2013.

Adogame, Afeosemime U., and James V. Spickard, eds. *Religion Crossing Boundaries: Transnational Religious and Social Dynamics and the New African Diaspora*. Leiden: Brill, 2010.

Bovensiepen, Judith, and Frederico Delgado Rosa. "Transformations of the Sacred in East Timor." *Comparative Studies in Society and History* 58.3 (2016): 664–93.

Bowers, Paul. "Nubian Christianity: The Neglected Heritage." *African Journal of Evangelical Theology* 4.1 (1985): 3–23.

Burns, J. Patout, Jr., and Robin M. Jensen. *Christianity in Roman Africa: The Development of Its Practices and Beliefs*. Grand Rapids, MI: Eerdmans, 2014.

Daniélou, Jean. *Salvation of the Nations*. Translated by Angeline Bouchard. New York: Sheed & Ward, 1950.

Fromont, Cécile. *The Art of Conversion: Christian Visual Culture in the Kingdom of the Kongo*. Chapel Hill: University of North Carolina Press, 2014.

Hastings, Adrian. *The Church in Africa, 1450–1950*. Oxford History of the Christian Church. Oxford: Clarendon Press, 1996.

Jenkins, Philip. *The Lost History of Christianity: The Thousand-Year Golden Age of the Church in the Middle East, Africa, and Asia—And How It Died*. New York: HarperOne, 2009.

John Paul II, Pope. *Ecclesia in Africa* [Post-synodal Apostolic Exhortation on the Church in Africa and Its Evangelizing Mission toward the Year 2000; September 14, 1995]. Vatican City: Libreria Editrice Vaticana, 1995. www.vatican.va.

Johnson, Todd, and Kenneth Ross, eds. *Atlas of Global Christianity*. Edinburgh: Edinburgh University Press, 2009.

Katongole, Emmanuel. *The Sacrifice of Africa: A Political Theology for Africa*. Grand Rapids, MI: Eerdmans, 2010.

Kollman, Paul V. "After Church History? Writing the History of Christianity from a Global Perspective." *Horizons* 31.2 (2004): 322–42.

———. "Understanding the World-Christian Turn in the History of Christianity and Theology." *Theology Today* 71.2 (2014): 164–77.

MacGaffey, Wyatt. "Constructing a Kongo Identity: Scholarship and Mythopoesis." *Comparative Studies in Society and History* 58.1 (2016): 159–80.

———. *Religion and Society in Central Africa: The Bakongo of Lower Zaire*. Chicago: University of Chicago Press, 1986.

Magesa, Laurenti. *Anatomy of Inculturation: Transforming the Church in Africa*. Maryknoll, NY: Orbis Books, 2004.

Meyer, Birgit. *Translating the Devil: Religion and Modernity among the Ewe in Ghana*. Edinburgh: Edinburgh University Press, 1999.

Northrup, David. *Seven Myths of Africa in World History*. Indianapolis: Hackett, 2017.

Oden, Thomas C. *How Africa Shaped the Christian Mind: Rediscovering the African Seedbed of Western Christianity*. Downers Grove, IL: InterVarsity Press, 2007.

---

30. At times, appeals to the need for inculturation seem to make this argument. For criticism, see Bovensiepen and Rosa, "Transformations of the Sacred." For a more nuanced, recent perspective, see Orobator, *Religion and Faith in Africa*.

Orobator, Agbonkhianmeghe E. *Religion and Faith in Africa: Confessions of an Animist*. Maryknoll, NY: Orbis Books, 2018.

Pierli, Francesco, and Maria Teresa Ratti. "Pioneers of the Kingdom in the Sudan." In *Gateway to the Heart of Africa: Missionary Pioneers in the Sudan*, edited by F. Pierli, M. T. Ratti, and A. C. Wheeler, 5–10. Nairobi: Paulines Publications, 1999.

Raboteau, Albert J. *Slave Religion: The "Invisible Institution" in the Antebellum South*. 2nd ed. Oxford: Oxford University Press, 2004.

Robbins, Joel. "Continuity Thinking and the Problem of Christian Culture: Belief, Time, and the Anthropology of Christianity." *Current Anthropology* 48.1 (2007): 5–38.

Sanneh, Lamin. *Translating the Message: The Missionary Impact on Culture*. Maryknoll, NY: Orbis Books, 1989.

Sundkler, Bengt, and Christopher Steed. *A History of the Church in Africa*. Cambridge: Cambridge University Press, 2000.

Thornton, John K. *The Kongolese Saint Anthony: Dona Beatriz Kimpa Vita and the Antonian Movement, 1684–1706*. Cambridge: Cambridge University Press, 1998.

Walls, Andrew F. "Africa in Christian History: Retrospect and Prospect." In *The Cross-Cultural Process in Christian History*, 85–115. Maryknoll, NY: Orbis Books, 2002.

Suggested Reading

Burns, J. Patout, Jr., and Robin M. Jensen. *Christianity in Roman Africa: The Development of Its Practices and Beliefs*. Grand Rapids, MI: Eerdmans, 2014.

Fromont, Cécile. *The Art of Conversion: Christian Visual Culture in the Kingdom of the Kongo*. Chapel Hill: University of North Carolina Press, 2014.

Katongole, Emmanuel. *The Sacrifice of Africa: A Political Theology for Africa*. Grand Rapids, MI: Eerdmans, 2010.

Kollman, Paul V. "Understanding the World-Christian Turn in the History of Christianity and Theology." *Theology Today* 71.2 (2014): 164–77.

Oden, Thomas C. *How Africa Shaped the Christian Mind: Rediscovering the African Seedbed of Western Christianity*. Downers Grove, IL: InterVarsity Press, 2007.

Key Words

African Catholicism
inculturation
Kongolese Catholicism
martyrdom
Roman Africa

History and Development of African Liturgies in African Catholicism: Liturgical Inculturation for the Future of Catholicism in Africa

Patrick C. Chibuko

The year 2015 marked the fiftieth anniversary of the closing of the Second Vatican Council. Another fifty years would bring us to 2065. What will Catholicism in Africa, or indeed in the broader Catholic world, look like in that year? What liturgy will appropriately serve the universal church, of which the church in Africa forms an integral part? It is to be expected that the African liturgy will be linked to the universal liturgy of the church, but downloaded and packaged for the local African churches, guided by the liturgical principles of unity in essence and plurality in expression; unity in diversity; substantial unity and genuine progress; and tradition and progression situated against the backdrop of the historical, theological, liturgical, pastoral, and cultural principles of liturgical inculturation and ecological realities.

In light of the regrettable mishaps that bedeviled the once-flourishing African liturgy in the early history of the church, this chapter argues in favor of a possible redevelopment of an African liturgy that can effectively serve the future of Catholicism on the continent. My argument is based on the premise that theological discussions fulfill their ultimate aim when they lead to inculturated liturgical celebrations in context. This chapter is thus developed along the following lines. It begins by offering operational definitions of some key terms. This is followed by a historical survey of the development of African liturgy, which intends to rediscover what happened to the ancient African liturgy in view of the need to chart a new course for the future, examining the good, the bad, and the ugly phases of the African liturgy. The main thrust of the chapter is a discussion of the missing link between liturgy and other theological and related sciences. Against this backdrop, I examine some of the essential elements that constitute a healthy, inculturated liturgy. I discuss practical attempts by various African ecclesiastical bodies, tertiary institutions and groups, and individual scholars toward a reconstruction of African liturgy/liturgies. The challenges that lie ahead for African liturgists are underscored with recommendations for further scholarly research. The chapter concludes on a note of optimism by affirming the possibility of an inculturated and effective liturgy for the future of Catholicism in Africa because the continent has everything it takes to accomplish this goal if properly enabled in coordination with the entire church.

Definition of Key Terms

The following terms are defined below: *Catholicism*, *context*, *inculturation*, *liturgy*, and *ritualization*. Brief comments are offered for each of these terms to facilitate understanding.

Catholicism

"Catholicism" means the Catholic Church and the totality of its dynamics, especially its form of worship and administrative governance. The term refers also to the intellectual traditions that have developed as part of this visible church since its earliest times, and it includes some forms of spirituality and ethics common to the entire family calling itself Catholic, a commonality that is defined by a distinctive culture existing in diverse sociological forms. Rigorous study of Catholicism so defined is necessary in order to create an authentic African liturgy. The issue to be studied is the process of organic liturgical growth, which is akin to the dynamics of a living organism, whereby a mother gives birth to children who enjoy a certain degree of independence but are still linked with the mother. An African adage has it that "If an egg is broken by an outside force, life ends. If it is broken by an inside force, life begins." The presence of this "inside force" is how great things usually happen, and the argument here is that the resulting processes can give birth to the new African liturgy.

Context

"Context" refers to the circumstances and situations that people face. Here, it refers to the field for testing theological discoveries and conclusions. It is the enabling place of operation (*locus operandi*) where theory and practice can be effectively blended. Theological research without context remains cerebral and sterile. In this article, the liturgical assembly features as the most auspicious context for the specific, as well as the widest, applications of the boundless frontiers of African theology, and for expanding those frontiers. It is in this context that the mutual enrichment of African theology and African liturgy is not only reinforced but also becomes actual. One of the main dynamics relating to "context" in this chapter underscores the fact that every Christian may be understood to be a kind of theologian within his or her environment, a fact that can be celebrated by each individual Christian within that environment.

Inculturation

"Inculturation" means the contextualization of theology by means of mutual enrichment between the gospel of Jesus Christ and the local culture. While the gospel illumines and enlightens the culture, the culture enriches the understanding of the gospel through the genius of the people. This is a process of providing a homely local reception and firm roots to the gospel, which in turn ennobles the local culture. Today, theological research demands contextualization and inculturation as a matter of necessity. Successful inculturation calls for deep knowledge of theology and the culture of the people, beginning with the language, understood as the vehicle of culture.[1]

Liturgy

The term "liturgy" flows logically from the nature of the church, which consists of Christ plus its members. Liturgy means the worship of Christ and the heavenly Father through the unction of the Holy Spirit.[2] In the liturgy, Christ is the liturgy and the liturgist. The liturgy is an efficacious sign of a supernatural reality; however, it is not efficacious because of the great work of the human worshippers, but rather because of the presence of Christ and the actions of the Holy Spirit. Christians participate in this work under the direction of the ministerial priesthood instituted by Christ.

---

1. Authentic inculturation begins with a positive attitude toward change followed by a mastery of the language. The acid test of a person's knowledge of a particular language is the answer to the following question: In what language does one dream, think, pray, greet, and count?

2. The concept of liturgy is based on its classic definition offered by Pius XII in the encyclical *Mediator Dei* (November 20, 1947). The pope stated that "the sacred liturgy is . . . the public worship which our Redeemer as Head of the Church renders to the Father, as well as the worship which the community of the faithful renders to its Founder, and through Him to the heavenly Father. In short, it is the worship rendered by the Mystical Body of Christ in the entirety of its head and members" (*MD* §20). This papal statement generated the conception of the reformed liturgy of the Second Vatican Council—that liturgy is an exercise of the priestly ministry of Christ. See Vatican II, Constitution on the Sacred Liturgy (*Sacrosanctum Concilium*) §7 (hereinafter *SC*).

Liturgical creativity does not mean creation out of nothing or creating an entirely extraneous liturgy. It means the human attempt to participate in and respond with all available human skills and capacities to the unique liturgy of Christ given to the church in the paschal mystery as an inheritance, and to enrich it with the cultural values and genius of the people.

In this chapter, the term "African liturgy" will be used in the singular but with plural connotations and will serve as an umbrella term for African "liturgies" in the same way that Western liturgy is described—that is, including the Roman, North African, Milanese/Ambrosian, Gallican, Spanish/Visigothic/Mozarabic, and Irish liturgies contained in the Bobbio Missal. The same analysis applies to the ancient Eastern liturgies. Even among the ancient "Roman" liturgies, there were sub-liturgies that were Western but not actually Roman, such as the Ravenna liturgy, among others.

Importantly, liturgy goes beyond the frontiers of sacramental celebration. Rather, it touches all expressions of the faith particular to a local church.[3] In this broad sense of the term, liturgy becomes an integral part of the life pattern of a people.[4] Central to the liturgy is the continual celebration of the paschal mystery of Christ in time and space until he comes in glory.[5] The term "liturgy" as theological science and liturgical celebration will be used interchangeably in this chapter.

Ritualization

"Ritualization" allows a historical event to be perpetuated and recalled by means of a lasting concrete form. Ritualization results in a process of reenactment in the context of a celebration by the people in their milieu. The process of ritualization involves the elements of a remarkable event, a celebration, the people in context, and inculturation. It further involves the past, the present, and the future. It ensures the future value and relevance of the remarkable event. Human participation in the liturgy of Christ in context by all the people in their individual roles is an example of ritualization.

Most importantly, the needs of ritualization underscore the synergy that is demanded between sacred liturgy as science and praxis and the theological sciences, as well as other transdisciplinary sciences, for example, communications and psychology. The presence of this synergy will be extremely important in the quest for the future of Catholicism in Africa, as discussed below. Theological discussions must necessarily include a liturgical dimension so that they can practically manifest themselves in celebration, meaning that liturgical theology can be understood as practical theology. The liturgy being discussed here is an inculturated liturgy celebrated in context. It is the argument of this chapter that this is the embodiment of ritualization. First, however, we provide a historical survey of the early African liturgy.

---

3. Uzukwu, *Worship as Body Language*, 267.
4. Searle, *Liturgy Made Simple*, 11–12:
> We shall use this opportunity to clear some misconceptions regarding the liturgy. Most people do not yet seem to understand clearly both the nature of liturgy and its dynamics. Ignorance compels most people to think of liturgy as playing guitars and having joyful pieces of noise, of exuberance, movements, banners and enthusiastic congregations. Some others think of liturgy in terms of strict adherence to rubrics. For them ceremonials and rubricism closely punctuated with strict details define liturgy. Some think of liturgy in terms of gathering of friends and neighbours in someone's home for a careful reading of the Scriptures, for spontaneous prayer, and for intimate sharing of the one bread and the one cup. Some still think of it in terms of solemn ritual and beautiful music, a liturgy of pomp and pleasantries, speaking of concern to put the best of human gifts and talents at the service of worshipping the transcendent God. This is far from the reality of what liturgy means.

5. See Chibuko, *Paschal Mystery of Christ*, 4–24. The paschal mystery consists essentially of the passion, death, and resurrection of Christ. This is the bedrock, the heart, the center, and the firm foundation of the entire life of the church as it is celebrated in the liturgy. The church is built, sustained, nourished, and lives on the foundation of the unique paschal mystery of Christ. Through the liturgical celebrations, the church constantly relives this mystery, making an *anamnesis* of this mystery, particularly in the sacraments and her other liturgical celebrations.

Historical Survey of the Early African Liturgy

What follows is a narrative historical survey featuring a critical interpretation of the historical facts. The importance of history in this article cannot be overemphasized; we need a strong knowledge of the past in the present, in view of the future. Liturgical history offers models of liturgical inculturation and pitfalls to be avoided. History teaches how to take risks with caution in view of the needs of creativity and prudence when something new is introduced.

Historical Traces of the Early African Liturgy: First to Fourth Centuries

Historical narratives furnish us with both the positive and the negative aspects of the early African liturgy. The positive begins with the North African liturgies of the ancient world, which were dominant in their time and determined the character of the major Latin liturgies of the West. Most interestingly, in accordance with Africa's position as the cradle of civilization, the North African liturgies were acclaimed as the premier liturgies of the time, eminently influencing the Latin liturgies, including the Roman, Gallican, and Mozarabic liturgies. It is a matter of liturgical record that early liturgical texts did not originate in Rome. Rather it was in Roman North Africa, the cradle of Latin Christianity, that the first stirrings of liturgical creativity and renewal were felt.[6]

Furthermore, because large numbers of new texts loaded with barbaric expressions, solecisms, and doctrinal errors were appearing, composed by "nonexperts and loquacious people" (*homines imperiti et loquaces*),[7] various African synods tried to control and direct this creative activity, without, however, suppressing it.[8] Liturgical history further shows that at the end of the fourth century and the beginning of the fifth, African collections of *libelli missarum* already existed.[9] It is equally on record that the early African church even had a sacramentary composed by Voconius (d. 460), the bishop of Castellum in Mauretania.[10]

The works of two writers, Tertullian and St. Cyprian, furnish useful information on the African liturgy. Tertullian's writings are especially rich in descriptions of, and allusions to, ecclesiastical customs. The acts of the early martyrs, for example, Sts. Perpetua and Felicity, are also illustrative. Finally, the inscriptions on Christian graveyard monuments provide evidence of the beliefs and practices of the time.

The negative side of the historical development of African liturgies came during the post-Nicene period.[11] Sadly, no African sacramentary or other collection of prayers from this period has survived, not even a single fragment of a eucharistic prayer,[12] and no liturgical codices are extant. These were all

---

6. Vogel, *Medieval Liturgy*, 31–59.

7. Vogel, *Medieval Liturgy*, 34 n. 6.

8. The Synod of Hippo (393), canon 25, stipulated that all prayers at the altar should be addressed to the Father and that one must avoid using prayers compiled in other localities until they could be examined by some of the brother instructors (*fratres instructiores*). The Synod of Carthage (397) took the same line when faced with prayers suspected of containing false doctrine (Mansi, "Council of Carthage [397]," 891). The synod stated that henceforth liturgical prayers would require official approval of some sort. In 407, another Synod of Carthage insisted that a collection of prayers, prefaces, commendations, and formulas for the imposition of hands (*preces, praefationes, commendationes,* and *impositiones manuum*), composed under the supervision of the hierarchy, should become obligatory (Mansi, "Council of Carthage [397]," 1163).

9. *Libelli missarum* is a technical term for a collection of various prayer forms for particular occasions composed for particular churches. The existence of *libelli missarum*, perhaps even of sacramentaries, in this period is certain. See Germain Morin, "Formules liturgiques orientales en occident aux IV–V siècles," *Revue Benedictine* 41 (1929): 70–73.

10. Gennadius of Marseilles, *Liber de scriptoribus ecclesiasticis*, ch. 79, PL 58:1103–4.

11. This period from the Council of Nicaea in 325 CE to the Council of Chalcedon in 451 marked the era of ecumenical councils and spanned the lives of the most important church fathers.

12. Vogel, *Medieval Liturgy*, 35.

lost in the massive destruction occasioned by the Islamic invasion and because of the relatively rural character of the African regions. The loss of these sources has made reconstruction of the ancient African liturgy difficult. According to Paul F. Bradshaw, "Unfortunately, however, because of the Arab conquest of the region at the end of the seventh century and in contrast to other parts of the ancient Christian world, no later Sacramentary or other collection of prayer has survived from which earlier practice might have been inferred."[13]

Comments

Early Catholicism in Africa grew up on a continent endowed with a rich heritage that scholars have ranked as first among equals. African Catholicism's overwhelming influence on the Roman liturgies added gravitas to the African liturgy. The evidence presented above indicates that the early African liturgy was distinguished by a profound spirituality and a powerful capacity to develop every aspect of the human community. This is evidenced by the numerous witnesses to the paschal mystery of Christ offered by the saints and martyrs who lived in the early centuries of the church.[14] In addition, the early African liturgy recognized the preeminence of eucharistic celebration while at the same time appreciating the great importance of other liturgical celebrations.[15]

It must be noted that the similarity of the North African liturgy to the Roman was part of its undoing. The influence of nomenclature[16] was very strong: the North African liturgy was referred to as the "Roman North African Liturgy" from its inception,[17] and Augustine of Hippo was referred to as *Romanus Augustinus* of Hippo. Some conceptual independence and a reasonable degree of freedom of operation would have given the liturgy of North Africa a firmer foundation, authenticity, creativity, and originality than it actually enjoyed. The North African liturgy was unable to be fully itself in both its thinking and execution, and for this reason its capacity for durability and stability was grossly weakened. It became impossible for the North African liturgy to withstand the menace and sweeping influence of rival religions. Like the biblical seeds that fell on rock, having no root, it died without producing fruit (Matt 13:7; Luke 8:14). The factors mentioned made inculturation impossible, and the continent has paid dearly.

Again, as seen above, only remnants of the early African liturgy were preserved; tradition would have led to progression if more of it had survived. However, the challenge given to modern scholars is to learn from history and shift from bemoaning the past to charting a new course, adopting a positive position and working to foster a new, durable, functional, and stable liturgy for the future of Catholicism in Africa. The expectation should thus be an emergent, living liturgy firmly established in theology, context, and culture, well documented and preserved for posterity.

Present-day Catholicism in Africa faces aggressions similar to those it was subjected to in the past. However, it also faces an internal enemy in the form of endless sectarianism, which results in the formation of breakaway ecclesial bodies. The end of these problems is not in sight, largely because the continent has been the worst hit by the global economic recession. Americanization and Europeanization have weakened African values, and Islam is also experienced as a threat to the church on the continent; in addition, there are a number of other sociopolitical and new media challenges.[18] Ansgar

---

13. Bradshaw, *Search for the Origins of Christian Worship*, 98–107.

14. Heffernan, *Passion of Perpetua and Felicity*, 557.

15. The Second Vatican Council refers to the Eucharist as the apex and source (*culmen et fons*) of all the activities of the church (*SC* §10) but acknowledges that the eucharistic celebration does not exhaust all the significant activities of the church (*SC* §9).

16. With regard to the creative renewal of liturgy, the Roman church, a latecomer to using the Latin tongue for liturgy (ca. 380) (the original liturgical language was Greek), was more cosmopolitan than Western, more Eastern than Roman. Rather, it was in Roman North Africa that the creative liturgy took place. See Vogel, *Medieval Liturgy*, 34.

17. Vogel, *Medieval Liturgy*, 34.

18. Chibuko, *Liturgical Inculturation: An Authentic African Response*, chapter 8, Conclusion.

J. Chupungco referred to these factors as inimical forces that must be kept in view lest the authentic cultural values of the African people disappear and fade from memory.[19]

The Rationale for Ritualization in Theological Discussions and Studies

One of the major reasons that the theological achievements of both African theologians and individual African Christians are not widely felt can be traced to the lack of a close nexus between theological discourse and liturgical celebration on the continent. The practical meaning of liturgy is theology in celebration;[20] it must be remembered that what the church believes she teaches, and what she teaches she celebrates, and what she celebrates she lives. African theological achievements, as excellent as they have been, remain, without a liturgical dimension, cerebral, esoteric, and reserved for the "dais people"[21] in the minority; they do not reach the "base people"[22] in the majority. Modern theologians must keep in view this close nexus between liturgy and other theological and related sciences so that theological efforts can achieve their aims. Another problem is that these efforts are few in number and often expensive, and that many of them remain on bookshelves and in archives located outside the continent.

Although theology and liturgy are distinct disciplines, they are interdependent and exist in a relationship of mutuality. Each needs the other. Theology needs liturgy for practical expression in celebration in order to be completed and fulfilled, and liturgy needs theology to provide the content of liturgical celebration. Theology without liturgy is theoretical, and liturgy without theology is empty of substance. The synergy that ought to exist between them has been the subject of serious scholarly debate; some of the arguments in this debate are discussed in the next section.

Debates among Scholars about the Relationship between Liturgy and Theology

Most scholars conceive of liturgy as a *locus theologicus*, a unique source for theology. Others conceive of the reverse, seeing theology as a *locus liturgicus*, a unique source for liturgy. Concerning the former, what really makes liturgy a unique source for theology is that it is a ritual event and therefore can be clearly distinguished from other theological sources, such as statements of the magisterium. For this to be true, however, it is essential to employ a hermeneutic that respects the character of the liturgical event, especially liturgical language and liturgical action.[23] The uniqueness of liturgy lies in the fact that it is the action of the church that mediates the community's experience of God. The liturgy cannot be used as a theological source for the purpose of assembling an arsenal of arguments serving the purposes of apologetics. Instead, it serves as the privileged teaching (*didascalia*) of the church, making use of the fullness of the Christian mystery, the means through which the church continually experiences the paschal mystery.[24]

I. H. Dalmais, in his monograph *Initiation à la liturgie*, gives priority to the liturgy as an ecclesial event over any didactic or informational purpose it may have. He insists that, while sacramental theology deals with what God does for the church in acts of salvation, liturgy deals with the actions of the church in performing acts of worship.[25] While link-

---

19. Chupungco, *Liturgies of the Future*, 28.

20. The relationship between this *Handbook of African Catholicism* and ritualization is akin to that between the Bible and liturgy. The Bible as the written word of God remains ineffective until it is opened, and the most auspicious context for this is in the worshiping assembly. In other words, the Bible as a closed book remains a dead word until it becomes a living word in celebration.

21. A term describing professional theologians.

22. A term describing theologians among the common people, based on the conviction that every believer is fundamentally and to some extent a theologian.

23. Irwin, *Liturgical Theology*, 18.

24. Irwin, *Liturgical Theology*, 19.

25. Dalmais, *Introduction to the Liturgy*, 27–95.

ing liturgy with the deposit of faith, he maintains that the liturgy is the church's permanent work of catechesis because its proper function is to bring alive the mystery of salvation. The liturgy is indeed the privileged place for catechizing the people of God: catechesis is intrinsically linked with the whole of liturgical and sacramental activity, for it is in the sacraments, especially in the Eucharist, that Christ Jesus works most fully for the transformation of God's people.[26] One must therefore be attentive to the complete liturgical action. Each element, text, and rite needs to be interpreted in relation to the other parts of the liturgy.[27]

For Dalmais, liturgy focuses on key moments in salvation history and the believer's contemporary experience of these moments. On the other hand, for him theology is the church's reflection on the work of God in creation. He believes that the liturgy is fundamentally eschatological and doxological, important aspects of the liturgy that are glossed over by both liturgists and theologians. An awareness of the doxological aspect of the liturgy would help theologians appreciate the place of doxological language in theology itself. The liturgy orients the church to its transformation in Christ and to continual formation in Christian living.[28]

Cipriano Vagaggini underscores other important dimensions of the liturgy. He maintains that a proper interpretation of the liturgy requires an understanding that the main purpose of liturgy is to enact the mystery of faith; it also important that one respect the varied literary genres contained in the liturgy.[29] The teaching function in the liturgy is concerned with arousing acts of faith in the believers, not instructing them *about* acts of faith. The chief aim of the liturgy as an act of the body of Christ is to engage the community in an act of prayer. He insists that theological exploration begins and ends by engaging in the liturgy.[30]

For Salvatore Marsili, liturgy is theology par excellence in two ways. First, it is biblical theology in the sense that the Word is revealed in every act of liturgy; and, second, it is fundamentally a liturgical theology because the revealed Word is enacted and operative among the faith community at worship. Marsili's work is Christologically rich and ecclesiologically grounded, insofar as he profoundly articulates the uniqueness of Christ's saving paschal mystery while stressing that Christ's followers experience this divine work again and again in worship.[31] Marsili believes that a theology of liturgy must necessarily include Christology, ecclesiology, and pneumatology, as well as respect each person's present collective experience of the paschal mystery.[32] He links scripture with the liturgy by stating that, just as scripture in all its parts is always the announcement of salvation, so the liturgy in all its moments is always the fulfillment of salvation in ritual.[33] He insists that the sacramentality of revelation and Christ as sacrament containing the totality of revelation, plus the economy of salvation, the paschal mystery of Christ, and an attentiveness to the Word of God, are all actualized through the act of liturgy.[34]

Gerard Lukken holds that the liturgy is both the first theology and the first orthodoxy, *theologia* and *orthodoxia prima*. He notes that, in the early church and especially in the East, the liturgy was known as *theologia prima* and dogmatic speculation as *theologia secunda*. The first meaning of orthodoxy

---

26. *Catechism of the Catholic Church* 1074.
27. Dalmais, "La liturgie comme lieu theologique," 97–106.
28. Dalmais, "La liturgie comme lieu theologique," 102–4.
29. Vagaggini, *Theological Dimensions of the Liturgy*, 512–14. For a thorough review of the different kinds of liturgical witnesses and how to approach their interpretation, see Auge, *Principi di interpretatione dei testi liturgici*, 159–79.
30. Vagaggini, *Theological Dimensions of the Liturgy*, 513–17.
31. Marsili's understanding of liturgical theology can be found in two posthumous works: Marsili, *Mistero di Cristo e liturgia nello Spirito*, 66; and Marsili, *Teologia liturgica dei sacramenti*, 88.
32. Marsili, "Verso una Teologia della Liturgia," 47–48.
33. Marsili, "Verso una Teologia della Liturgia," 102.
34. Marsili, *Teologia liturgica dei Sacramenti*, 1515–19.

was right praise (*ortho-doxia*) in the liturgy, and it is only in a secondary sense that it came to mean right teaching. It is therefore legitimate to speak of an *orthodoxia prima* and an *orthodoxia secunda*.[35] Lukken further maintains that the liturgy is quite properly the first source and norm of faith from which teaching is derived. Since the liturgy is the church's own self-expression through a complex of words and symbols, the liturgical expression of faith is much richer than any intellectual expression or justification of faith in theological argument or dogmatic pronouncement. He establishes a very practical balance in the mutual relationship between liturgy and dogma: he acknowledges that *theologica secunda* can and should stand as an important corrective factor to the liturgy, without which the Holy Spirit is, during the course of the liturgy, always in danger of being extinguished. He posits a relationship of constant dialogue between *theologia* and *orthodoxia prima* and *secunda*, which is essential to ensure that the liturgy does not become isolated from the faith of the church and that the faith of the church does not become sterile and moribund.

For Alexander Schmemann, one's understanding of the church's faith and doctrine is bound to be incomplete without liturgical theology. The purpose of liturgy is to constitute the church, whose foremost expression is the church at Eucharist. It is not the church that exists for the cult, but the cult for the church, for her welfare and her growth into the full measure of the stature of Christ. Schmemann is very much convinced that the liturgy not only has an abstract theological meaning, but is also the living norm of theology; it is in the liturgy that the sources of faith—scripture and tradition—become living realities.[36]

It was Aidan Kavanagh who asserted the primacy of worship over belief—*orandi* over *credendi*. He systematically argues that the statement "*legem credendi lex stataut supplicandi*" ("the law of belief leads to the law of prayer") does not allow for faith and worship to be understood as equal. In addition, he does not believe that the abbreviation *lex orandi, lex credendi* captures the original meaning of the idiom. While admitting that belief shapes worship, he emphasizes that worship founds and even constitutes belief. The liturgy is primarily an *act* as opposed to a theory or a creed; it is a ritual, primarily to be done, not studied.[37] Kavanagh further maintains that hearing the scriptures in the worshiping assembly and acknowledging their anamnetical nature and purpose precede any theological reflection of a specifically doctrinal sort. True pastoral theology involves worship and living sustained by the Word of God.[38]

In the light of this ongoing debate, the Second Vatican Council's Constitution on the Sacred Liturgy, *Sacrosanctum Concilium*, emphasized the special status of liturgy and its interrelationship with other theological sciences. This document clearly states that the study of sacred liturgy should be placed among the compulsory and major courses in seminaries and religious houses of study and should rank among the principal courses in theological faculties. It is to be taught under its theological, historical, spiritual, pastoral, and juridical aspects. In addition, those who teach other subjects, especially dogmatic theology, sacred scripture, and spiritual and pastoral

---

35. Lukken, *Unique Expression of Faith in the Liturgy*, 82.
36. Schmemann, *Introduction to Liturgical Theology*, 40–44.
37. Kavanagh, *On Liturgical Theology*, 7–102.
38. Kavanagh, *On Liturgical Theology*, 7–102. Hence the author's coinage in this article: what the church believes she teaches, what she teaches she celebrates (for celebration includes prayer), and what she celebrates she lives. *Lex credendi, lex docendi, lex celebrandi, lex vivendi*. The parenthetical words are meant to elaborate on the relationship between worship and prayer. Worship and prayer are not dialectically opposed but related, with worship being wider in scope than prayer. In relationship one can worship prayerfully especially when the worship is based on the three theological virtues of faith, hope, and charity. Against this background, prayer and worship are interchangeable. Cf. also *SC* §7 for the essence of liturgical worship, which includes sanctification of the church in her members expressed in integral transformation, the edification of the church in her members, the glorification of God by the church, and witnessing to God through sharing and selfless Christlike service (*koinonia* and *diakonia*).

theology, should—each of them in accordance with the needs of the discipline being taught—expound the mystery of Christ and the history of salvation in a manner that will clearly set forth the connection between their subjects and the liturgy (SC §§15–17).

The future of African Catholicism will depend largely on the quality of the interdisciplinary and transdisciplinary synergy of these disciplines with the sacred liturgy. For this synergy to have the desired effect, all tertiary theological institutions, major seminaries, and universities in Africa will be required to reevaluate the status of sacred liturgy in their curricula of studies.

The Nature of a Future Catholic Liturgy in Africa

Authentic African liturgies demand new forms distinguished by originality, innovation, and novelty. Africa needs to evolve liturgical forms that are indigenous, authoritative, suitable, and appropriate for the African people.[39]

Until now, African forms of worship have worn borrowed garments originating from a cultural background quite different from the African context. Can one speak of an African liturgy in any real sense of the term without introducing an admixture of a superficial and makeshift African liturgy with foreign cultural elements? To be liturgically authentic and self-reliant, Africans need to construct their own original, inculturated liturgy, a liturgy that will be both truly Christian and fully African.[40]

The importance of establishing such a liturgy on the continent of Africa cannot be overemphasized. Liturgy lies at the very heart of self-reliance in the third-millennium church of Africa. "The heart of self-reliance" quickly recalls an image of the heart, which signifies the innermost core or center of an organism, the starting point and endpoint of the circulating blood, the vitalizing center without which life is impossible. The heart supplies all parts of the body, even the most minute, with the blood that is indispensable for life.[41] In the context of this chapter, an authentic and self-reliant African Catholicism of the future needs to derive its growth from a heart, a center—namely, the liturgy. A vibrant church without liturgy is unrealistic because liturgy is the lifeline of the church. The church is built and nourished by the liturgy because of the paschal mystery it celebrates. The church continually relives this mystery through its liturgical celebrations. Her liturgical celebrations make a memorial (*anamnesis*) of this mystery, particularly in the sacraments.

The future of the liturgy in African Catholicism must be essentially and truly Christocentric with all that that implies, and fully inculturated. It must exhibit in its content all that it takes to evolve a "homely" liturgy: a liturgy that speaks meaningfully to both the head and the heart of the people, including linguistic expressions couched in language they understand (head) and love (heart). According to an African saying, "When one speaks the language people understand it goes to the head, when one speaks the language of the people it goes to the heart." For the sake of emphasis, we reiterate with further clarifications some characteristic elements that must distinguish the new African liturgy.

---

39. By speaking of African "liturgies" here, I am expressly not proposing a single mono-liturgy for the entire continent, which is impossible. I formulate the term in the plural against the backdrop of every Christian believer being to some extent a theologian, meaning that everyone should be accommodated at his or her own level. Furthermore, the heterogeneity of the African continent, exemplified by the multiplicity of African cultures, the diversity of peoples, and the numerous languages spoken, makes it impossible to establish a single African liturgy. Most importantly, I do not want to give the impression that there is a superior liturgical expression that would dominate others, especially the liturgies of minority groups.

40. As suggested by Uzukwu in his work *Liturgy, Truly Christian, Truly African;* and Laurenti Magesa in his work "In Search of a New African Spirituality," in *Theological Reimagination: Conversations on Church, Religion and Society in Africa*, ed. Agbonkhianmeghe E. Orobator (Nairobi: Pauline Publications Africa, 2014), 36.

41. Adam, *Liturgical Year*, 19.

Homely Liturgy

The African liturgy must be a liturgy that is within the reach of both people's heads and hearts. In other words, it has to be a liturgy that people can adequately understand and that they can cherish as essentially and fully theirs, a liturgy with the ability to facilitate the comprehension and self-appropriation of the essential aim[42] of liturgical worship. It must be a liturgy exhibiting tremendous dynamism that reflects the social status of everyone who participates. It must be a liturgy whose impact is overwhelming, characterized by a strong spirituality that results in integral transformation issuing in the sanctification and edification of the church and its members and the glorification of God by the church and its members.[43] The effect of such a transformation manifests itself eloquently in authentic witnessing (*martys* in Greek) in both the vertical and horizontal interactions of the faithful. Such a transformation is exemplified in people's enthusiastic communal sharing and Christlike service (*koinonia* and *diakonia*), accomplished through a process of active, conscious, full, and socio-communitarian participation (*SC* §14). Above all, such a transformation will be apparent in the people's positive conception of and response to issues that affect them, and in their actions, reactions, and interactions in inter- and intra-ecological contexts.

Furthermore, a homely liturgy, well celebrated and understood, has the great ability to make people place any given situation in its proper perspective. A homely liturgical celebration instills courage into fainting hearts. It offers confidence in the midst of doubts. It is able to create practical options in the midst of limited alternatives. It opens up new realities, opportunities, and potentialities and suggests Christian courage even in the face of death. It has the power to uplift the mind to a new threshold, from which it can view reality with new eyes, new hopes, and new resistance. It has the capacity to transform radically and above all to make one whole, or holy.

Dynamic Liturgy

African Catholicism deserves a functional and dynamic liturgy. A stereotypical liturgy is moribund and therefore has no place among the lively African people. Guided by the liturgical principle of unity in essence and diversity in expression mentioned above, a new liturgy would entail new texts, new styles, and a new spirit in the liturgical rubrics. This would affect language; songs and other musical forms; ritual gestures, postures, and actions; and material objects of every kind.

Furthermore, a dynamic African liturgy demands new liturgical norms of aesthetics (beauty), dignity, and intelligibility pertinent to the reality of the cult or sacrament, and would affect the relationship of persons participating in the celebration, including the ordained ministers who hold a pastoral office, special lay ministers, and the whole assembly. As a matter of great importance, the new liturgy must be open to a collaborative ministry in which the three essential arms of liturgical celebration are acting optimally—namely, Christ, clergy, and the worshiping community.

Anamnestic Liturgy

Because liturgy is essentially anamnestic,[44] the new African liturgy must facilitate an effective reenactment of the paschal mystery that the people can experience and appropriate personally and collectively as a church in order to promote authentic witnessing on the continent.

In the final analysis, liturgy thus celebrates the glorious power of Jesus's resurrection with all its overwhelming, far-reaching implications and effects. The liturgical celebration of the resurrec-

---

42. According to *SC* §7, this aim is integral transformation of the church and her members. See n. 38 above.
43. See *SC* §7 and n. 38 above.
44. The Greek (and English) word *anamnesis* means, in the context of liturgy, remembrance, memorial, recall, recollection, and reenactment of the paschal mystery of Christ. Christianity in my view is essentially a religion of remembrance, pushing back against the basic human trait of forgetfulness and insisting on a constant reminding and recalling. God reminded the chosen people over and over again to remain faithful, and the most important prayer of the church in the New Testament climaxes in a reminder, a commemoration: "Do this in memory of me" (Luke 22:19).

tion of Jesus proclaims that out of every death, God wills a resurrection. The liturgy proclaims in ritual form that death is swallowed up in victory (1 Cor 15:54–55), that life is changed, not ended,[45] that mortality is sucked up in immortality, that corruptibility is subsumed in incorruptibility, and that perishability is supplanted by imperishability (1 Cor 15:54–55).

Liturgy reassures the church of this truth and reality. It commemorates this tremendous mystery in the life of the church. It renews this mystery in the members of the church. It revives their faith and hope in this promise and reshapes their destinies and thoughts accordingly. It reorients their worldview in accordance with this saving mystery of Christ. It redirects the church's mentality through active participation in her mission in the world and remodels the life of the church following the paschal mystery of Christ.

The new liturgy must be able to challenge the church through her members not just to appreciate and admire the glories of the power of Jesus's resurrection but also to imitate him in their lives. Liturgy invites the church's members to reenactment, participation, and authentic imitation through the witness of their lives (*anamnēsis/metaxy/mimēsis/martys*) to the paschal mystery of Christ.

Liturgy commemorates ritually Jesus's victory in not just a battle but in the whole war, as the church carefully reminds herself in the annual celebration of Holy Week that culminates in the sacred triduum[46] and finally reaches its climax on Easter Sunday. Liturgy truly declares in worship the supreme victory of Christ over sin, death, principalities, forces and powers, thrones, dominions, sickness, pains, poverty, illiteracy, suffering, satanic influences like witchcraft, and other malign realities. Liturgy uplifts and heals Africans exactly where they hurt.

Pedagogical Liturgy

The new African liturgy must fully reflect the pedagogical dimensions of worship.[47] It must teach within the context of celebration that pain and suffering have not only been redeemed but have acquired a salvific meaning through the paschal mystery of Christ. In other words, pain and suffering, although not to be sought, have now acquired a Christocentric meaning and so have become reasonable and acceptable. The new liturgy must teach the contents of the faith of the church for the continuous enlightenment of its members. Liturgy kills the faith-ignorance of the people. It ensures that the people engage in a continual learning process in the faith; to stop learning the faith means the death of the faith.

Transformative Liturgy

In the eucharistic celebration (*SC* §10), which is the apex of the church's liturgical celebrations, bread and wine are transformed at the consecration into the sacred Body and Blood of Christ. The same eucharistic celebration also transforms and renews the worshiping assembly and all other human conditions and realities. There is no aspect of the human condition that is beyond the scope of the transformative power of the liturgy, whose chief act is to represent the paschal mystery. The onus on the new African liturgy lies in making the transformative element of worship evident through authentic enrichment by the proper values and the genius of the people, which are celebrated in the spirit of worship.[48]

Mission-Oriented Liturgy

The new African liturgy needs to underscore the missionary mandate that usually concludes every liturgical or paraliturgical celebration of the

---

45. Preface 1, "Mass for the Dead, The Hope of the Believers," in Roman Missal.

46. The last three days of Holy Week—Holy Thursday evening (the evening of the Last Supper), Good Friday, and Holy Saturday, including the Easter Vigil on Saturday night and Easter Sunday.

47. Pope Benedict XVI very often pointed to the liturgy as an education to the gospel. For him, the true reformer is obedient to faith. The pope thus urged a greater appreciation of the liturgy as a source of education about the "good life of the Gospel" (Assisi, Italy, November 9, 2010 [Zenit.org]).

48. The spirit of worship consists of the right intention to reenact, imitate, and participate in (Greek: *anamnēsis*, *mimēsis*, and *metaxy*) what Christ accomplished, as taught by the church and as contained in the official liturgical books.

church.[49] In the eucharistic celebration, the mandate instructs, "Go forth the Mass is ended" (*Ite Missa est*), which urges the faithful to begin to live the fruits of the mystery just concluded and to bring Christ and his values into the world. It means making a substantial difference in the socioeconomic and political arena; by so doing, witnessing to Christ flourishes and the face of the ecosystem[50] is constantly renewed.

Liturgy Compatible with Information Communications Technology (ICT)

The "in" thing today is the "e-world": e-banking, e-business, e-research, and so on. In his address entitled "Bringing Christ to the Digital Continent," Pope Francis noted that the world of social communications has increasingly become a "living environment" for many, expanding the boundaries of their knowledge and relationships: "The goal in communications is ultimately to dialogue with today's men and women, who sometimes feel let down by a Christianity that to them appears sterile." The pope stressed that in today's globalized age, there is a "growing sense" of isolation and an inability to connect with others that impedes people from building meaningful relationships. It is crucial to know how to dialogue with others in the environments created by technology and social networks "in such a way as to reveal a presence that listens, converses, and encourages."[51]

Liturgical celebration means a reenactment of the person of Christ as the basis for living, a modus vivendi for the Christians of today. ICT has demonstrated a tremendous capacity to record, recall, and preserve the memories of these celebrations for the African Christians of today and the future.[52] In its dynamics, ICT is person-oriented and at the heart of Christian worship is the person of Christ. In the liturgy, the church celebrates a person and a personality, not a theory, philosophy, or ideology.

Thus, there is a point of contact between what liturgy celebrates and ICT. The new African liturgy would necessarily be ICT compatible, which would help us avoid the errors of the early Christian centuries, which were characterized by poor documentation and preservation of information.

Concrete Liturgical Inculturation: Attempts and Experiences in Africa

Liturgical inculturation is a project of the present and future church, particularly on the African continent. Africans have welcomed the Christian message, and Christianity has come to stay. The message of love and peace now needs to become incarnated in the hearts, huts, and hovels of Africans.[53] Together with the traces of the early African liturgy, the reformed liturgy of the Second Vatican Council stirred up a new hope that local churches would wake up and evolve new liturgical forms proper to the culture. Since then, Africans have reached some landmark achievements in this regard. Even before the term "inculturation" came into use, some African churches had made remarkable progress toward inculturation in the realm of liturgy. The achievements of inculturation to date include the introduction of gestures, drums, dances, swaying, and African songs, which are external expressions of the festive African spirit.

According to Jozef Cardinal Tomko, even if much remains to be done, certain African attitudes, including a deep religious sense and reverence for the sacred, and the African way of celebrating and rejoicing in the Lord with others in a joyous, jubilant community, have already been incorporated into the church's liturgical life. These cultural characteristics have already edified, moved, and enriched the faithful of other cultures. In Africa, the Mass is truly a celebration; as Cardinal Tomko

---

49. Chibuko, *"Go the Mass Is Ended,"* 53–63.
50. Patrick C. Chibuko, "Forestation, Deforestation and Reforestation," *African Ecclesial Review* 52.3-3 (2010): 189–212.
51. Junno Arocho Esteves, "Pope Francis Addresses Plenary Assembly of the Pontifical Council for Social Communications," Vatican City, September 23, 2013 (Zenit.org).
52. Chibuko, "Information Communications Technology (ICT) and Liturgical Life of Christians."
53. Ike et al., *Towards an Indigenous African Church*, 102–12.

noted, "You Africans celebrate the Mass while we Europeans attend or participate in it."[54]

The imagery and narratives in sacred scripture are important in inculturating the faith in some places. The mysteries of the Catholic faith, including Jesus's expiatory and propitiatory sacrifice as reenacted in the Eucharist, are easily accepted into the African culture, as is the reality of sin in both its personal and communal forms.[55]

Major seminaries, higher ecclesiastical institutes, and faculties of theology have been founded in various regions and countries of Africa to promote the work of inculturation. These include (together with their dates of canonical erection) the Institut Catholique d'Afrique de l'Ouest (ICAO) in Abidjan, Ivory Coast (1975); the Catholic Higher Institute of East Africa (CHIEA) in Nairobi, Kenya (1984); Facultés Catholiques de Kinshasa, Democratic Republic of the Congo (1987); Institut Catholique de Yaoundé, Cameroon (1991); and the Catholic Institute of West Africa (CIWA) in Port Harcourt, Nigeria (1994). Here we describe the contributions of CIWA as an example of the work being done by these institutions.

The Catholic Institute of West Africa, Port Harcourt, Nigeria

Among these tertiary African institutions and universities,[56] CIWA has become a beacon of hope, especially with respect to the building of liturgical inculturation. CIWA began its work on December 8, 1981. In February 1982, its foundation stone was blessed by Pope John Paul II (now St. John Paul) during his visit to the Bigard Memorial Seminary in Enugu, Nigeria. It will be recalled that CIWA belonged to the former anglophone West African subregion of the episcopal conferences of Gambia, Ghana, Liberia, Nigeria, and Sierra Leone.[57]

The then-bishops of the Association of Episcopal Conferences of Anglophone West Africa (AECAWA) held an important assembly in August 1989, in which they studied the theme for the African synod, which had the subthemes of "Evangelization with Inculturation," "Social Communications," and "Priestly Formation." Thus, inculturation was identified as an important concern in this region. The bishops tasked CIWA with helping the local churches of the region to fully adapt the gospel to the culture; for this reason, contextualization and inculturation became the main thrust of the institute. CIWA as an ecclesiastical institute was given an indult[58] by the appropriate authority to engage in the kind of liturgical inculturation that could serve as a model in the subregion.

The staff, students, and vibrant worshiping community of the institute are fully engaged in the work of inculturation. Practical examples already in place are lectures, the annual Theology Week conference that takes place during the week preceding Palm Sunday, regular colloquia, publications including the *Journal of Inculturation Theology* and the *Proceedings* from Theology Week, the

---

54. Jozef Cardinal Tomko, the then-Prefect of the Congregation for the Evangelization of Peoples, *Auditio* at the Special Assembly of the Synod of Bishops for Africa on the theme "The Church in Africa and Her Evangelizing Mission Towards the Year 2000: 'You Will Be My Witnesses'" (Acts 1:18). The Opening Mass of the Synod was celebrated in St. Peter's Basilica on Sunday, April 10, 1994. For a month, the synod fathers dealt with the general theme of evangelization from five perspectives: proclamation of the message, inculturation, dialogue, justice and peace, and social media.

55. *Bulletin of the Special Assembly for Africa of the Synod of Bishops*, 11–14.

56. The tertiary sister institutions of CIWA on the continent providing the needed personnel and expertise to promote the development of African theology and African liturgies include the Catholic University of Eastern Africa (CUEA) in Kenya; the Catholic University of Ghana; the Catholic University of Ivory Coast; Veritas University in Abuja, Nigeria; Madonna University in Okija, Nigeria; Godfrey Okoye University in Enugu, Nigeria, and others. It is important that these institutions achieve the maximum positive impact on the future of Catholicism in Africa in general and on African liturgies in particular.

57. It now belongs to RECOWA, the Regional Episcopal Conference of West Africa, composed of both the Regional Episcopal Conferences of anglophone and francophone West Africa.

58. In Catholic canon law, a permission given by a church authority.

CIWA *Hymn Book* in its second edition, and the second edition of ten Eucharistic Prayers appropriate for concelebration. Each department prepares a weekly eucharistic celebration. Not only the academic staff and students but also the nonacademic staff of the institute are involved in preparing this celebration in accordance with and enriched by their cultural values.

Attempts at Liturgical Inculturation by Various African Episcopal Conferences

Some remarkable efforts at liturgical inculturation have been made in most African countries. E. Elochukwu Uzukwu has critically examined the various directions taken toward liturgical creativity according to African ecclesiastical region, including anglophone and francophone West Africa, Central Africa, and East Africa.[59] A few of the highlights of Uzukwu's findings are described in the following sections.

CENTRAL AFRICA: CAMEROONIAN AND ZAIREAN MASS

In the Central African region, one can encounter the colorful liturgy developed in the Diocese of Yaounde (Cameroon)[60] called the *Ndzon-melen* Mass. The background of this Mass shows that it is a restructuring of the Roman Order of the Mass as an experiment limited to one parish in Yaounde. It was an individual initiative of Father Pie-Claude Ngumu that received episcopal approval.[61] This Mass contains the familiar divisions of the Liturgy of the Word and the Liturgy of the Eucharist, but there has been some restructuring in the Liturgy of the Word involving the entrance procession; the enthronement of the Book of the Gospels; the readings and homily; and the creed, penitential rite, and collect.

It is, however, in Zaire that one can find a local church that has had the greatest impact on Christian life in Africa. This church has tried to demonstrate that unity not only embraces diversity but is verified in diversity. The Roman Missal for the Dioceses of Zaire (*Missel Romain pour les dioceses du Zaire*) can clearly boast of having achieved remarkable results through the use of an alternative African form of the Order of the Mass popularly called the Zairean Mass. This project began in 1970 with the approval of the Congregation for Divine Worship. Its aim was to give to the Roman Order of the Mass an African and Zairean cultural form, which might explain the reason for its initial name: the Roman Missal for the Zairean Church. Three years later, the conference of bishops presented the project to the Holy See seeking authorization to begin preliminary experimentation with the new Mass. What happened between 1973 and April 30, 1988, when the project was officially approved by the Holy See,[62] is an interesting episode in the history of liturgical inculturation.[63] The present author participated in the rite on one occasion, and it was full of African creativity in its gestures and postures. It enhanced active participation by the assembly and was quite lively. It was very uplifting to the spirit and greatly cherished by the assembly as being truly theirs.

It needs to be noted that the Zairean church calls it "Mass according to the Zairean Rite." Certainly such a designation would create concern in certain quarters. But since the rite embraces more than the eucharistic liturgy, as we said above, and includes the administration of sacraments and sacramen-

---

59. See Uzukwu, *Worship as Body Language*, 265–316.

60. Since the episcopal mandate to experiment with creative liturgies that arose out of the Second Vatican Council was received in Cameroon before Zaire, it is proper to present the Cameroonian experience first. It was here that the first eucharistic liturgy expressing the feelings of Africans was produced—the Cameroonian Mass preceded the Zairean liturgy. See Uzukwu, *Worship as Body Language*, 294.

61. For a more detailed background of this Mass, see Uzukwu, *Worship as Body Language*, 295–305.

62. Congregation for Divine Worship, Decree *Zairensium Diocesium*.

63. The text of this new Order of the Mass with explanatory notes may be found in the dossier presented to the Congregation for Divine Worship. See Conference Episcopale du Zaire: *Rite zairois de la celebration eucharistique*, Kinshasa, August 1985, pp. 1–21. See also Evenou, "Rencontre au Zaire"; Conférence Épiscopale du Zaire, "Le Missel Romain"; Raymond Maloney, "The Zairean Mass and Inculturation," *Worship* 62.5 (1988), 433–42. For a brief analysis of the Zairean Mass, see Uzukwu, *Liturgy, Truly Christian, Truly African*, 59–65.

tals, church discipline, theology, and other things, a Zairean rite as such does not yet exist. Or should we not rather borrow a jargonistic phrase common in Christian eschatology and say that, for Zaire in particular and for Africa in general, the question of an inculturated rite is already and not yet?[64]

Central and East African Charismatic Prayers to Combat Witches

In Central and East Africa, affliction by witches, evil men and women, and spirits may be resolved by participation in the kind of charismatic prayer that is widely diffused in these regions, but the emergent liturgies of these areas have thus far concentrated on the eucharistic celebration and the consecration of virgins.[65]

West Africa

Burkina Faso: The Moore Ritual. In West Africa, the Moore ritual in the Diocese of Diebougou, Burkina Faso, needs to be mentioned. It is a very well-developed combination of traditional and Christian initiation rites and is based on the traditions of the Mossi of Burkina Faso. It is an effort to rediscover the spirit of the reformed Roman Rite of Christian Initiation, which provides for an adult catechumenate in stages and the baptism of adults, adapting it to the traditions of the Mossi people.[66]

Ghana: Corpus Christi Celebration. Among the Ashanti of Ghana the Corpus Christi celebration is adapted to the Odwira festival (the yearly outing of the Asantehene, the Ashanti king). This ceremony is suffused with color and meaning, and this appearance of the king has been integrated into rituals surrounding the consecration during the eucharistic prayer.

Another example of liturgical creativity in Ghana is the Ashanti Mass composed by Bishop Peter Sarpong[67] of Kumasi, which inculturates Ashanti traditions into the Eucharist. According to the commentary accompanying the video titled *The Dancing Church*, the highlight of this Mass is the arrival of the king during the Eucharistic Prayer and the women who, in traditional Ashanti fashion, dance at his arrival. This wonderful act of inculturation means that, in the eucharistic celebration, Jesus our king has come again to us. The blending of the coming of Jesus the king with the symbols used for the Ashanti king is a moment of joy, expectation, and great happiness. Unfortunately, the rite has not been practiced because it has failed to attract the support of the clergy.

Nigerian Eucharistic Prayer. In Nigeria, the creative efforts of Uzukwu in the area of liturgy must be highly appreciated and commended. His contribution to "The All-Africa Eucharistic Prayer"[68] represents a typical Christian Igbo prayer. A typical Igbo prayer is litanic in structure: one prays in the form of incantations and another answers with a specific response. The prayer can be recited or sung. It is similar to the actions of the Christian assembly during the litany of the Blessed Virgin Mary and the litany of the saints. Uzukwu's prayer is at the moment awaiting approval for use in prayer and study.

Igboland: Corpus Christi Celebration. In some parts of Igboland, the Corpus Christi is celebrated as *Ofala Jesu*, meaning Jesus's annual outing as king, especially in the Onitsha area, with fanfare, cannon shots, songs, and dances. According to the universal liturgical calendar, the solemnity of the Body and Blood of Christ with the eucharistic procession usually takes place in the month of June. In Nigeria, however, June is in the rainy season. So, while the celebration of Corpus Christi occurs in union with the whole church in June, the procession is trans-

---

64. Uzukwu, *Liturgy, Truly Christian, Truly African*, 66.
65. Uzukwu, *Worship as Body Language*, 271–72; in pp. 265–316, Uzukwu extensively discusses the emergent forms of liturgical creativity in Africa.
66. For the details of this ritual, see Uzukwu, *Worship as Body Language*, 289–93.
67. Bishop Peter Sarpong is a theologian and anthropologist famous for his blending of theology and liturgy in the service of living. The performances of his cultural groups both at Mass and social evenings during the 2005 African Liturgical Symposium in his Christian village still remain fresh in the minds of the participants.
68. Uzukwu, "All-Africa Eucharistic Prayer," 338–47.

ferred to the last Sunday of the liturgical year, the Solemnity of Christ the King, which is often in the last week of November, in the dry season.

On this day, the church in Nigeria rolls out its drums to joyfully acknowledge Christ, first as the king of the universe and second as being present in the Holy Eucharist. The long, beautiful procession along the major streets of the town features the Blessed Sacrament in a monstrance and various groups of the faithful engaging in dance steps while praying and singing. On seeing the procession passing by, especially with a huge number of young people, even non-Catholics, many people join in.

The twenty-one gunshots that punctuate the procession in places speak eloquently of its power. Credible testimonies also have been given by a number of people regarding the healing benefits they received from a eucharistic procession, especially one taking place on the Solemnity of Christ the King. These healings are spiritual, medical, emotional, psychological, and physical in nature. Some who suffered from various kinds of ailments have testified that, after this long procession undertaken in faith, their ailments ceased. Women who typically experienced hard labor pains in childbirth have testified that their next labor was not only short-lived but went very smoothly after they danced in faith in one of these processions.

What is most striking about this festival is that it is not a single prolonged and monotonous procession—the celebration is enriched by four "stations," or stopping places. These stations are designated and prepared well in advance. At each station a biblical text is proclaimed, a newly composed liturgical prayer is recited, and hymns are sung before the procession continues.[69]

After a benediction at the last station, all enter under their properly marked canopies for a festival of eating and drinking accompanied by music until all disperse. The presence of the clergy and religious is always important and exemplary.

Igboland: The Igbo Christian Rite of Marriage. Recently, the Diocese of Enugu has taken the lead among the Igbo-speaking dioceses in publishing an Igbo Christian Rite of Marriage.[70] This rite was approved by the local ordinary for use in the marriage of Christians in his area of jurisdiction, and he was the first to celebrate it in the diocese.[71] This rite is striking for its blend of African literary forms of prayer, which, as was mentioned above, are essentially litanic. The rite includes the rite of the breaking of kola nuts, which is an essential act in welcoming guests in any traditional Igbo gathering. All the liturgical texts are completely new compositions: the opening prayer, the exchange of consents, the prayer over the gifts, the preface, the Eucharistic Prayer, and the nuptial blessing.

The role of families, especially the parents and in-laws, is highlighted in the rite. It is noteworthy also that the ceremony takes place in the girl's home in the presence of the church, *in facie ecclesiae,* meaning in the presence of the official church witness—the priest who receives the couple's consent on behalf of the church—and in the presence of the sponsors and the people of God. It is a comprehensive rite that combines Igbo cultural heritage with the sacredness of the sacrament of marriage. It provides a suitable alternative to the Roman Rite of Marriage, as recommended by the Second Vatican Council's reform of the liturgy (*SC* §§77–78). The logistics involved in

---

69. For the full details of this celebration, see Chibuko, *Eucharistic Procession on the Solemnity of Christ the King,* 10–22.

70. This marriage rite was created by the present author. The full text of the rite together with scholarship commenting on it are published in Patrick C. Chibuko, *Igbo Christian Rite of Marriage* (Frankfurt am Main: Peter Lang, 1999), while the rite for altar use is published separately as Patrick C. Chibuko, *Church Wedding and Traditional Marriage in One Ceremony* (Enugu: Black Belt Konzult, 2003). Participation in a traditional marriage rite marks the apex of the various stages of marriage in Igbo culture, and at its center is the payment of the bride-price.

71. Uzukwu, "The Word Became Flesh: Areas and Methods of Inculturation in the Twenty-First Century," in *The Church in Nigeria: Family of God on Mission.* Acta of the First National Pastoral Congress. A Publication of the Catholic Secretariat of Nigeria (2003), 89–134, especially 90–91. Also present in Nigeria is the Ebira Christian Marriage Rite, which serves as an instance of liturgical inculturation in the Diocese of Lokoja. A liturgical research group formed in the Awka diocese in Nigeria was permitted to experiment with a proposed Igbo Mass after three years of research. To date, no findings about this experimentation have been published.

celebrating the new rite are straightforward, and it is open to concelebration.

Igboland: An Inculturated Easter Triduum. The Easter Triduum[72] includes Holy Thursday evening, Good Friday, Holy Saturday, and the Easter Sunday celebrations. There are two striking features of African celebrations of Holy Thursday. The first is the provision of the Last Supper meal to the sick and housebound in the spirit of African solidarity and community. The second is an entirely original guide to the one-hour adoration demanded by Christ on this day.

On Good Friday, the faithful venerate the cross all over the world, for example, by kissing it. But, since kissing is culturally alien to Africans, the Rite for the Veneration of the Cross introduced acceptable alternative gestures for veneration,[73] an element that helps make the rite truly and fully African. Depending on the size of the worshiping community, the first alternative is to raise the cross for veneration by all the people with an agreed gesture like kneeling or genuflecting. The second is veneration by the people in the typical form used by the chief celebrant, with triple genuflections and touching the cross with the hands. A third is veneration in the form of adoration. Most Igbo Christians are conversant with the term "adoration": it involves the cross being erected in front of the altar on a well-elevated stand for a good length of time, during which the people are encouraged to assume the common posture of kneeling.

The adoration may last for about half an hour,[74] accompanied by rich theological choruses—songs of praise, adoration, and thanksgiving appropriate for the season (that is, without the alleluia). Then the distribution of Holy Communion follows as prescribed in the rite. At the end of the Good Friday liturgy, the cross is left in front of the altar so that people can genuflect before it while leaving the church, as an opportunity for personal adoration as prescribed.[75] Above all, the rite discourages the appearance of many crosses and insists on a single cross for the Good Friday liturgy.

On Holy Saturday, the readings at the Easter Vigil are punctuated with suitable theological choruses alternating with psalms to keep active participation alive (SC §12). During the renewal of the baptismal promises, the names of the local gods and deities are mentioned so that they may be renounced.[76] Finally, on Easter Sunday, the rite introduces the action of decorating the church and pathways with palm fronds and a procession from the villages to the church carrying palm fronds—palms symbolize victory among the Ndigbo. Finally, there is a feast of eating and drinking and the people go out to provide meals to the sick and housebound.[77]

Igboland: The Covenant among the Ndigbo. Another important example of liturgical inculturation is the *Igba ndu*, or ritual covenanting among the Igbo Christians of Nigeria.[78] This cultural practice of resolving conflicts and reaffirming the faithfulness between two parties is very much in practice and has been Christianized. It is celebrated by the priests and refers to God or the spirits. Its visible signs are symbolic objects like the kola nut, the ogirisi leaf (from *Newbouldia laevis*, or the "tree of life"), and the *ofo* (a consecrated stick cut from the *Detarium senegalense* tree). The celebration presumes that each individual is in relationship to other human beings, the world, and the spirits.

Yoruba and Igboland: Naming Ceremony. The naming ceremony among the Yoruba and other African groups, including Ndigbo, contains a remarkable feature—the giving of a name or names displaying

---

72. Chibuko, *Liturgical Spirituality and Inculturation*, chapter 9, 98–132.
73. For the full details of this rite, see Chibuko, *Veneration of the Cross*, 35–46.
74. When *Ndigbo* (a collective noun for the Igbo people) assemble to worship God, they rarely look at the time, for time spent at prayer is an important moment, especially during the Good Friday liturgy. It took Jesus time to die in order to save humanity; in response and appreciation, humanity must spend time to celebrate his death.
75. Chibuko, *Veneration of the Cross*, 38.
76. Chibuko, *Liturgical Spirituality and Inculturation*, 114.
77. Chibuko, *Liturgical Spirituality and Inculturation*, 115–28.
78. The contents of these ceremonies are beautifully detailed by Uzukwu in *Worship as Body Language*, 274–88.

the web of relationships by which the individual is defined. In this ceremony, neonates are linked to their ancestors, to the day of the week, to prayers made to God or the spirits, and to particular wishes or experiences of the parents. No child is given a name without this close attention to the child's connection with the past. According to Uzukwu, this ceremony is seen as sketching the broad outlines of the newborn's future.[79] It has received the official approval of the Oyo and Ibadan dioceses and is generally practiced all over Yorubaland.

Igboland: The New Order of Eucharistic Celebration. In 2007, the *African Ecclesial Review* published an article[80] in which the author of the present chapter responds to the clarion call of the fathers of the Second Vatican Council regarding liturgical creativity and liturgical alternatives (SC §50). The experience of local churches in the area of cultural adaptation since the council, especially in the missions, has instilled into our consciousness that church unity does not need to be anchored exclusively in the uniform observance of liturgical rites.[81] The various forms of diversity in the church should be seen as positive, for as long as the substantial unity of the faith is maintained, the formal liturgical expression of the faith need not be uniform (SC §38).

The striking feature of the alternative eucharistic rite for Igboland includes a restructuring of the usual Order of the Mass in line with the African Christian format for official gatherings. In this new arrangement, the celebration begins with the invocation of the Holy Spirit and a traditional procession with local musical instruments until the celebration's venue is reached, at which point the choir takes over. The welcoming rite is in a litanic format in which the chief celebrant asks for the best things in life for the assembly, especially the gift of a long and healthy life. The kiss of peace takes place to dissolve any anonymity among the members of the assembly, followed by the rite of the kola nut.

The celebration continues with the liturgy of the Word, including the enthronement of the Book of the Gospels and the homily. The penitential rite takes place after the homily since one does not need to repent to listen to the Word; rather, the Word prompts one to repentance. Having been reconciled with God, the prayers of the faithful and the liturgy of the Eucharist follow, beginning with the Offertory, which includes a display of dancing with joy and happiness while the gifts are brought to the altar. If it is a Sunday Mass, the creed follows the assembly's reception of communion, before the post-communion prayer, in order to remind the worshiping assembly of the summarized contents of the Christian faith. The final blessing and a festive recessional bring the celebration to a joyful close. This Mass is characterized by a high level of active, conscious, and plenary participation, which serves as a prelude to the faithful's full participation in socioeconomic and political witness aimed at the transformation of the world. The liturgical texts for this Mass are entirely new compositions that reflect African values and the genius of the African people.

Igboland: The Igbo Eucharistic Celebration for Peace in the Enugu Diocese. The Adoration Ministry stampede on March 7, 2002, at the Government Technical College in Enugu, Nigeria, which claimed fifteen lives including that of an unborn child, resulted in serious tensions in Enugu State. The Diocese of Enugu promptly intervened with a special eucharistic celebration called the "Mass for Peace," which succeeded in restoring peace. Entirely new liturgical texts were composed for this Mass. The texts, written to suit the occasion, include an opening prayer, a special homily entitled "We Pray for Peace in Enugu State," new prayers of the faithful, a prayer over the gifts, a Preface, and a post-communion prayer. This Mass became an excellent alternative to the general Mass for Peace contained in the Roman Missal.[82]

---

79. Uzukwu, *Worship as Body Language,* 274–88, especially 275.
80. Chibuko, "New Order of Eucharistic Liturgy: A Critical Overview."
81. Chupungco, *Liturgies of the Future,* 65.
82. The present author composed the texts for this Mass for Peace. Approval for use was given by Bishop

Igboland: Emume Uka Nwa—The Igbo Rite of Thanksgiving for a Child. A celebration of thanksgiving after the successful delivery of a child is peculiar to some local churches in Nigeria. The rite is necessitated by the conspicuous absence of such a rite in the official liturgical books of the reformed liturgy of the Second Vatican Council. It cannot be found in the *Book of Blessings* or the *Ceremonial of Bishops*, or in any other Roman ritual. The absence of this rite underscores one of the limitations of the official Roman liturgical books with respect to the needs of the Nigerian church. The fathers of the council acknowledged these limitations and called on local churches to enrich the Roman rite with their cultural values and the resourcefulness of their people (*SC* §§37–40).

A child is normally dedicated at baptism. The celebration of thanksgiving for a child marks the apex of what began at the baptism—it is the formal admission of the child into the church in the presence of other members of the Mystical Body gathered for the eucharistic celebration. The parents bring their child to thank God for the gift of the child and to ask God for his abundant blessings on the child and the family.

The rite is based on combined elements drawn from the Presentation of the Lord (Luke 2:21–40) and Jesus's blessing of the children (Mark 10:13–16). In the Presentation of the Lord, the gestural element was Simeon taking Jesus in his hands and blessing him. In Jesus's blessing of the children, the gestural elements were that Jesus *took* them, *laid hands* on them, and *blessed* them.[83] These actions performed by Jesus are similar to the seven actions that accompany the eucharistic liturgy: with respect to the bread, Jesus "took," "blessed," "broke," and "gave"; for the chalice, he "took," "blessed," and "gave." These actions must be accompanied by appropriate words, and new compositions appropriate to the gestures were devised.

What we have described above is only a sampling of the practical efforts being made by some groups and individuals to show that a future African liturgy is possible, and that in fact, the task has already begun.

Recommendations for the Future of Catholicism in Africa

Many recommendations for further study and research are called for. New ground has to be broken, especially in creating new liturgical rites that address the daily concerns of Africans. These rites could be either alternatives to Roman rites or entirely new African rites; for instance, new rites for exorcism, planting, harvesting, and the empowerment of women in the church.[84] Others include new rites for various sociocultural roles that are open to African Christians, such as chieftain and *ozo*. There is a serious need for Afro-Christian funeral rites for various categories of people, including adults, children, those who died suddenly, and those who died after a protracted illness.[85]

Of special importance is the need for an African Rite of Christian Initiation of Adults. RCIA in Africa should be restructured and patterned after traditional African initiation rites. Christian initiation is an initiation into the paschal mystery of Christ—his life, passion, death, and resurrection—which is celebrated in three stages, through baptism, confirmation, and the Eucharist. Christianity would fare much better if it adopted the methods of initiation already in existence, especially among Ndigbo; these are suitable means for effectively conveying

---

Anthony O. Gbuji, the bishop of the Enugu diocese. He and the priests of the diocese concelebrated the Mass for the first time on April 11, 2002. See Enugu Diocesan Special Bulletin, April 11, 2002.

83. Chibuko, *Rite of Child Thanksgiving*, 19.

84. Women are being honored by the church in Igboland for the special roles they play in their homes, churches, and society. They are being honored as *Nne Okwukwe* (Mother of Faith), *Ezi Nne* (Exemplary Mother), and *Nne Ife* (Mother of Light), the latter a lifetime title. The absence of a proper rite for these honoring ceremonies has led to liturgical abuses that have resulted in the ceremonies being suspended by the Igbo church in some areas. These abuses point to a dire need for proper rites for these important events in the life of women in the church.

85. For more details regarding the need for additional rites, see Chibuko, *Paschal Mystery of Christ*, 101.

the Christian message. The catechumenate period of preparing adults for Christian initiation needs to be restructured in light of the prevailing adolescent, adult, and masquerade methods of initiation. For men, these methods inculcate virility, stability, faithfulness, responsibility, accountability, and the importance of witnessing.[86] The catechumenate period should be focused not only on catechetical and liturgical activities but also on understanding that it is a formative phase for a faithful Christian life (*Ad Gentes* §14). It should inculcate in the candidates the cultural values of the society that are not opposed to Christianity.

The period of the catechumenate should emphasize the virtues of belonging, brotherliness, good neighborliness, human respect and dignity, sensitivity to human feelings, discipline, strong incorporation into the Christian fold, tolerance, identity, obligation, and defense of values. The rigors of cultural initiation should be present in the catechumenate period to produce Christlike Christians—not just nominal and merely pacifist Christians but militant and revolutionary Christians who would fight on the side of Christ, protected by the armor of Christ, which is authentic sacrificial love.[87]

The use of local names should be encouraged in the celebration of Christian rites of initiation. The same applies to the use of local elements like palm oil and palm kernel oil (*ude aku*). These are products of a familiar tree in Igboland and should be considered suitable alternatives for the oil of catechumens and chrism, respectively. These oils, which are readily available and curative, could be imbued with the same theological meanings given to the oil of catechumens and chrism.[88]

RCIA matters a great deal as the decisive point of entry into Christian living. To the extent that RCIA is taught, understood, valued, and celebrated by local churches in Africa, it will be the measure and determine the quality of faith and worship on the continent. Marginalizing RCIA means marginalizing faith and worship, with obvious and devastating consequences.

Concretely, the continent needs a new African Missal similar to *Masses for Various Needs and Occasions* to cater to the needs of Africans, which are not addressed by the current Roman Missal.[89] There is also a need for a new African Book of Blessings with alternative new Euchological texts. An elaborated rite is urgently needed to serve as the Mass for the Development of Peoples (*Populorum Progressio*), which would be a practical adaptation of what is already in the current Roman Missal, but to be celebrated in an African context.

Among Ndigbo, the gesture of striking the chest and saying "through my fault" at the Confiteor has been the subject of serious debate among Igbo theologians arising from the gesture's ambivalence in Igbo culture. This gesture might stand for either admission of fault or defiance; thus, if it is not an admission of fault, it could mean, "Yes I did it and what of it?" The meaning of the gesture is different among Ghanaians—for them, it is a plea for mercy and forgiveness. They adopt a gesture of pleading which corresponds with most Igbo cultural expressions for admission of fault.

Other recommendations include an African pattern for a communal celebration of the Sacrament of Reconciliation; an African pattern for the celebration of Anointing; an enrichment of the rites of Holy Orders and Religious Professions, especially addressing the role of parents at those celebrations; and an enrichment of the liturgical year and calendar with rituals particularly relevant to the African experience. The liturgy must address in ritual form persistent issues of corruption through more effective rites to beef up the existing "Prayer for Nigeria in Distress" and "Prayer against Bribery and

---

86. Chibuko, *Paschal Mystery of Christ*, 101ff.
87. Chibuko, *Paschal Mystery of Christ*, 101ff.
88. Chibuko, *Paschal Mystery of Christ*, 101ff.
89. In addition to women's issues, other concerns that are of particular interest to Africans include leadership, witchcraft, inheritance, accountability, polygamy, polytheism, religiosity, poverty, sicknesses and their cause, and death and its causes, among others. These should not only be discussed theologically but should be addressed in ritualized forms of worship. For instance, a rite for the African church as field hospital would be greatly appreciated.

Corruption in Nigeria." It should include Masses for serious cases like childless couples, couples who have had only girl children, the inheritance rights of girl children, various kinds of sicknesses, unmarried men and women seeking life partners, and those discerning vocations, among others. These are some of the particular issues demanding liturgical attention on the African continent.

Conclusion

African scholars and institutions need to continue their efforts at liturgical inculturation until "we hear them in our own language," as the witnesses declared openly in Acts 2:8. For until Africans begin to act, react, interact, and interpret realities, especially liturgical ones, in their own language, all efforts at inculturation will remain superficial and fake. Every meaningful change begins in the mind and ends in practical results. Universities and other institutions need to establish programs in their curricula to address inculturation effectively. In so doing, they must retain a cautious openness to other cultures, for no one is an island: the dynamism inherent in all cultures demands that the in-depth study of African cultures be mindful of multiple disciplines and other world cultures.

For there to be healthy interdisciplinary and transdisciplinary interaction between liturgy as science and praxis and other disciplines, all tertiary theological institutions, major seminaries, and universities in Africa must begin to emphasize the status of sacred liturgy in their curricula of studies. Intensive liturgical scholarship within this interdisciplinary and transdisciplinary context must not remain in the realm of abstract theory; rather, it must be accompanied by practical results gained from prudent experimentation.

A vibrant future for Catholicism in Africa implies an independent Catholic Church with specifically African rites. This must be properly understood—it does not suggest Africa's isolation or political or ecclesiastical secession from the rest of the worldwide Catholic Church. Rather, the growth of the African church should promote the unity, holiness, catholicity, and apostolicity of the one church of Jesus Christ under the visible headship of the pope as the supreme pontiff. The Eastern Catholic churches that exist today under the leadership of the pope may suggest a model for independent African Catholicism.[90]

An African theology logically leads to an African liturgy in the singular,[91] which could serve as an umbrella for various African sub-liturgies. Africans have before them a golden opportunity to tell their own story and chart their own course for the future. For the best time to chart the course of African Catholicism and its forms of worship was four centuries ago and the opportune time to do this is now.

If Africans fail to plan for the future of the continent's Catholicism and Catholic worship, they are planning to fail. Africa cannot face its future without first dealing with its past. In the midst of various continental challenges we need to stoop to conquer. Brooding over the past woes of the continent and apportioning blame has become all too common, even in the midst of shining new opportunities for the continent.

Against this backdrop, African exegetes, theologians, and liturgists have a sacred duty to lead the continent aright in matters of interpreting and concretely applying new discoveries in their areas of specialization. The continent needs this service so that both dais people and base people can collaborate effectively. African liturgists need to break new ground in research and praxis and to coordinate their individual achievements. This will be possible only through dynamic academic associations characterized by scholarly and practical creativity and innovation. They must work in concert in order to package universal liturgical themes for easy application to and assimilation within the local churches. The unflinching support of the hierarchy is crucial because each local ordinary acts as the chief liturgist in his area of jurisdiction. A healthy

---

90. The twenty-three Eastern Catholic churches or Oriental Catholic churches, also called the Eastern Rite Catholic churches, Greek Catholic churches, or in some cases Uniate churches, are *sui iuris* but in full communion with the Roman pope and part of the worldwide Catholic Church.

91. Without, of course, annihilating any cultural group, especially religious or ethnic minorities.

synergy between the local ordinary and his liturgists is thus required.

In the final assessment, ritualization is all about ensuring that the new theological discoveries imparted by this *Handbook of African Catholicism* will achieve widespread acceptance and lasting relevance through being celebrated. Anything short of this will be business as usual; it will not enter the relevant context and will not achieve the aim of the book.

Tertiary Catholic institutions operating in Africa and African universities are encouraged to participate more actively in the enterprise of making Christianity native to the continent. While these institutions study, research, and critique local efforts at inculturation, the real task of creation is done by those gifted individuals and collaborators who are in touch with the life of each local church,[92] as seen above. These efforts confirm that the work of individuals and groups, if well coordinated, does not introduce confusion but rather reveals the glorious vest of many colors that represents the unity of the body of Christ.[93] The future of Catholicism in Africa and the development of an African liturgy rely on the promise of God that "I will be with you always, yes, even to the end of time" (Matt 28:20).

Bibliography

AA. VV. [Various authors]. *Liturgie de l'Eglise particuliere et Liturgie de l'Eglise universelle, Conference Saint Serge, XXIIe Semaine d'Etudes liturgiques, Paris, 3–30 July 1975*. Paris: Edizione Liturgiche, 1976.

Adam, Adolf. *Liturgical Year*. New York: Pueblo, 1981.

Auge, Matias. *Principi di interpretatione dei testi liturgici*, Anamnesis 1., *La liturgia. Momento nella storia della salvezza*, edited by B. Neunheuser et al. Marietti: Casale Monferato, 1974.

Bradshaw, Paul F. *Search for the Origins of Christian Worship: Sources and Methods for the Study of Early Liturgy*. 2nd ed. Oxford: Oxford University Press, 2002.

Bulletin of the Special Assembly for Africa of the Synod of Bishops, 1994.

Calendarium Romanum. Vatican City: Libreria Editrice Vaticana, 1969.

Chibuko, Patrick C. *Eucharistic Procession on the Solemnity of Christ the King: Its Ceremony, Spirituality and Inculturation (A Celebration in Four Stations to Commemorate the Grand Finale of the Year of Faith: Oct. 11, 2012–Nov. 24, 2013)*. Enugu: Black Belt Konzult, 2013.

———. *"Go the Mass Is Ended, Ite Missa Est": Liturgy for Life: Introduction to Practical Dimensions of the Liturgy*. Frankfurt am Main: IKO, 2005.

———. *Igbo Christian Rite of Marriage: A Proposed Rite for Study*. Frankfurt am Main: Peter Lang, 1999.

———. "Information Communications Technology (ICT) and Liturgical Life of Christians: The Anglophone West African Perspective." *Bigard Theological Studies (BTS)*. June 2014.

———. *Keeping the Liturgy Alive: An Anglo-Phone West African Experience*. Frankfurt am Main: IKO, 2003.

———. *Liturgical Inculturation: An Authentic African Response*. Frankfurt am Main: IKO, 2002.

———. *Liturgical Spirituality and Inculturation: Celebrating Easter Triduum in Africa*. Nos. 210–11. Copublished: Nairobi: AMECEA Gaba Publications; Catholic University of Eastern Africa (CUEA) Press, 2015.

———. "New Order of Eucharistic Liturgy: A Critical Overview." *African Ecclesial Review (AFER)* 49.3-4 (2007): 235–53.

———. *Order of Eucharistic Vigil at the Altar of Repose: Nigerian Response*. Enugu: Black Belt Konzult, 2014.

---

92. Uzukwu, *Worship as Body Language*, 272–73. Associations doing this work are very active. In Nigeria alone, there is the Catholic Theological Association of Nigeria (CATHAN), the Catholic Biblical Association of Nigeria (CABAN), the Catholic Liturgical Association of Nigeria (CALAN), the Canon Law Society of Nigeria, and the liturgical commissions of some Nigerian dioceses, especially the Inter-Diocesan Liturgy Commission of the Igbo Speaking Area of Nigeria (IDLC-ISAN), plus others.

93. AA. VV., *Liturgie de l'Eglise particuliere et Liturgie del'Eglise universelle*, quoted by Uzukwu, *Worship as Body Language*, 265.

———. *Paschal Mystery of Christ: Foundation for Liturgical Inculturation in Africa*. Frankfurt am Main: Peter Lang, 1999.

———. *Rite of Child Thanksgiving—Usoro Emume Uka Nwa*. Enugu: Black Belt Konzult, 2016.

———. *Rite of Church and Traditional Marriage in One Ceremony*. 3rd ed. Enugu: Black Belt Konzult, 2003.

———. *Veneration of the Cross En-route in Africa: A Nigerian Response*. Enugu: Black Belt Konzult, 2011.

Chupungco, Ansgar J. *Liturgies of the Future: Process and Methods of Inculturation*. New York: Paulist Press, 1989.

Conférence Épiscopale du Zaïre. "Le Missel Romain pour les diocèses du Zaïre." *Notitiae* 264 (1988): 454–56.

———. *Rite Zaïrois de la Célébration Eucharistique*, Kinshasa (August 1985): 1–21.

Congregation for Divine Worship. "Decree *Zairensium Diocesium*." *Notitiae* 264 (1988).

Dalmais, I. H. *Introduction to the Liturgy*. Translated by Roger Capel. Baltimore: Helicon Press, 1961.

———. "La liturgie comme lieu theologique." *La Maison Dieu* 78 (1964).

Denzinger, Henricus, and Adolphus Schönmetzer, eds. *Enchiridion Symbolorum Definitionum et Declarationum, De Rebus Fidei et Morum*. 36th ed. Freiburg: Herder, 1976.

Evenou, J. "Rencontre au Zaire avec la Conférence Épiscopale." *Notitiae* 247 (1987): 139–42.

Francis, Pope. *Zenit.org*. Vatican City, September 23, 2013.

Gennadius of Marseilles. *Liber de scriptoribus ecclesiasticis*. In J.-P. Migne, ed., *Patrologia Cursus Completus: Series Latina*, 58:1059–1120. 217 vols. Paris, 1844–1864.

Heffernan, Thomas J. *Passion of Perpetua and Felicity*. Oxford: Oxford University Press, 2012.

Ike, Obiora, et al. *Towards an Indigenous African Church: A Post-Synodal Theological Review of the African Synod in the Context of Nigeria*. Enugu: CIDJAP, 1996.

Irwin, Kevin. *Liturgical Theology: A Primer*. American Essays in Liturgy. Collegeville, MN: Liturgical Press, 1990.

Kavanagh, Aidan. *On Liturgical Theology*. New York: Pueblo, 1984.

Lukken, Gerard. "The Unique Expression of Faith in the Liturgy." *Concilium* 82, edited by H. Schmidt and D. Power, translated by David Smith. New York: Herder & Herder, 1973.

Magesa, Laurenti. "In Search of a New African Spirituality." In *Theological Reimagination: Conversations on Church, Religion, and Society in Africa*, edited by Agbonkhianmeghe E. Orobator, 36. Nairobi: Pauline Publications Africa, 2014.

Maloney, Raymond. "The Zairean Mass and Inculturation." *Worship* 62.5 (1988): 433-42.

Mansi, J. D. "Council of Carthage (397)." In *Sacrorum Conciliorum nova et amplissima collectio* 3. Florence, 1759.

Marsili, Salvatore, *Mistero di Cristo e Liturgia nello Spirito*. Vatican City: Libreria Editrice Vaticana, 1986.

———. *Teologia liturgica dei sacramenti*. Rome: Edizione Liturgiche, 1987.

———. "Verso una teologia della liturgia." *Anamnesis* 1 (Turin 1974): 47–84, 102.

Missale Romanum. Vatican City: Libreria Editrice Vaticana, 2000.

Pius XII, Pope. *Mediator Dei* (Encyclical on the Sacred Liturgy; November 20, 1947). *AAS* 39 (1947).

Schmemann, Alexander. *Introduction to Liturgical Theology*. New York: St. Vladimir Seminary Press, 1966.

Searle, Mark. *Liturgy Made Simple*. Collegeville, MN: Liturgical Press, 1981.

Tertullian. *Apologia*. In J.-P. Migne, ed. *Patrologia Cursus Completus: Series Latina*. Vol. 1. 217 vols. Paris, 1844–1864.

Tomko, Joseph. *Auditio*. Special Assembly for Africa of the Synod of Bishops, Vatican (April 10–May 8, 1994).

Uzukwu, E. Elochukwu. "The All-Africa Eucharistic Prayer: A Critique." *African Ecclesial Review* 21 (1979): 338–47.

———. *Liturgy, Truly Christian, Truly African*. Eldoret: GABA Publications, 1982.

———. "'The Word Became Flesh': Areas and Methods of Inculturation in the Twenty-First Century." In *The Church in Nigeria: Family of God on Mission*, 89–134. Acta of the First National Pastoral Congress. A Publication of the Catholic Secretariat of Nigeria, 2003.

———. *Worship as Body Language: Introduction to Christian Worship; An African Orientation*. A Pueblo Book. Collegeville, MN: Liturgical Press, 1997.

Vagaggini, Cipriano. *Theological Dimensions of the Liturgy: A General Treatise on the Theology of the Liturgy*. Translated by Leonard J. Doyle and W. A. Jurgens from the 4th Italian edition. Collegeville, MN: Liturgical Press, 1976.

Vatican II. *Ad Gentes* [Decree on the Church's Missionary Activity; December 8, 1975]. *AAS* 69 (1976).

———. *Sacrosanctum Concilium* [Constitution on the Sacred Liturgy; December 4, 1963]. *AAS* 1964.

Vogel, Cyrille. *Medieval Liturgy: An Introduction to the Sources*. Translated and revised by William G. Storey and Niels Krogh Rasmussen. Washington, DC: Pastoral, 1986.

Suggested Reading

Bradshaw, Paul F. *The Search for the Origins of Christian Worship: Sources and Methods for the Study of Early Liturgy*. 2nd ed. Oxford: Oxford University Press, 2002.

Chibuko, Patrick Chukwudezie. *Paschal Mystery of Christ: Foundation for Liturgical Inculturation in Africa*. Frankfurt am Main: Peter Lang, 1999.

Uzukwu, E. Elochukwu. *Worship as Body Language: Introduction to Christian Worship; An African Orientation*. A Pueblo Book. Collegeville, MN: Liturgical Press, 1997.

Vahakangas, Mika. *In Search of Foundations for African Catholicism: Charles Nyamiti's Theological Methodology*. Studies in Christian Mission 23. Leiden: Brill, 1999.

Vogel, Cyrille. *Medieval Liturgy: An Introduction to the Sources*. Translated and revised by William G. Storey and Niels Krogh Rasmussen. Washington, DC: Pastoral, 1986.

Key Words

anamnestic liturgy
Catholicism
celebration
Christocentric liturgy
concelebration
context
dynamic liturgy
Easter Triduum
eucharistic celebration

Eucharistic prayer
inculturation
liturgy
missionary-oriented liturgy
paschal mystery
pedagogical liturgy
ritualization
transformative liturgy

Stories of Transformation:
African Immigrants to the United States and the Dark Night of St. John of the Cross

Dorris van Gaal

This chapter presents a closer look at the experience of African Catholic migrants to the United States of America (U.S.), based on a research project that seeks to provide insight into the transformation of identity and faith in the experience of migration. This research project responds to two blind spots, namely, the invisibility of African migrants in U.S. census data and, flowing from that, the lack of the African migrant voice, and, more specifically, the African Catholic voice, in the development of migration theology. These two blind spots will be presented below, followed by an argument as to why storytelling is essential, and then an exploration of how the experience of African migrants can be made more visible by engaging their stories and experiences and appreciating the insights they provide in their own words and on their own terms. In the last part of the chapter some central themes that arise from their stories will be presented as suggestions for further research.

African Migrants and the U.S. Census

This chapter responds to a blind spot in the manner in which American society relates to racial categories. In the U.S., migrants from Africa are practically invisible statistically because they are grouped under the category "Black" as defined by the 2010 census. Even though the "1997 Revisions to the Standards for the Classification of Federal Data on Race and Ethnicity"[1] call for a minimum of five racial categories and allow for an "open" sixth category ("some other race," to be specified on the form), these distinctions do not seem to be taken into account in the analysis of the data related to the Black population. In the 2010 census

---

Parts of this article were incorporated in *Migrant Spirituality: Correlating the Narratives of African Migrants to the USA and the Dark Night of John of the Cross* (Zurich: LIT, 2021). This article draws from the following two published articles of mine: (1) an article that appeared in proceedings of the Pan-African Catholic Congress on Theology, Society, and Pastoral life held in 2019 in Enugu, Nigeria, under the title "A Forgotten Mission in African Catholicism? Migration Experiences from the African Catholic Diaspora in the United States," in *Faith in Action: Reform, Mission and Pastoral Renewal in African Catholicism since Vatican II*, ed. Stan Chu Ilo, Nora K. Nonterah, and Idara Out (Eugene, OR: Pickwick, 2020); (2) "Stories of Transformation: African Immigrants to the U.S. and the Dark Night of St. John of the Cross," in *The Church, Migration, and Global (In)difference*, ed. Darren J. Dias, Jaroslav Z. Skira, Michael S. Attridge, and Gerard Mannion (Cham, Switzerland: Palgrave Macmillan, 2021)—though they share the same title, that article and the present one are substantially different in content.

1. Office of Management and Budget, "1997 Revisions to the Standards for the Classification of Federal Data on Race and Ethnicity," *Federal Register*, vol. 62, no. 210 (October 30, 1997).

the following definition is used to describe "Black" or "African American":

> "Black or African American" refers to a person having origins in any of the Black racial groups of Africa. The Black racial category includes people who marked the "Black, African Am., or Negro" checkbox. It also includes respondents who reported entries such as African American; Sub-Saharan African entries, such as Kenyan and Nigerian; and Afro-Caribbean entries, such as Haitian and Jamaican. Sub-Saharan African entries are classified as Black or African American with the exception of Sudanese and Cape Verdean because of their complex historical heritage. North African entries are classified as White, as OMB defines White as a person having origins in any of the original peoples of Europe, the Middle East, or North Africa.[2]

There is, therefore, no perceived distinction between African Americans and Black African migrants who came after 1965 with the relaxation of U.S. immigration laws. This is also reflected in surveys conducted by the Archdiocese of Baltimore, in which the data, defaulting to the five racial categories used in the national census, ignored the diversity of migrant ethnicities, even though parishes have begun to request that specific attention be paid to this diversity.[3] It was also interesting to see that some of the African participants in the research were already adhering to these racial categories and wrote "Black" on their demographic notecard; I had to ask them to specify their ethnic heritage. This statistical invisibility hinders pastoral outreach to African migrants, as one of the participants affirms in her story: "African immigrants . . . at a national level, . . . are not recognized. It's usually Latinos or Asian Americans . . . how many Africans do we have in this country? Every year they are coming . . . they are everywhere! But again, that stereotyping. And until somebody like you or St. Matthew does something [they] will remain dormant."[4]

This statistical invisibility also hinders theological reflection on the immigration and settlement experience of African migrants. For instance, Peter Phan, in an article in 2013, describes only Hispanic and Asian immigration and mentions only "Latino/a, Asian, and black theologies," but not African migrant cultures, faith, and theology, as resources useful for constructing "a U.S. inter-multi-cultural theology."[5]

African Migrants and Migration Theology

A similar blind spot can be observed in recent theological reflections on how the migrant experience affects a migrant's faith in and understanding of God. Scholars writing about the phenomenon of migration have argued for the need for an interdisciplinary approach to understanding the dynamics of the migration systems and networks that influence a migrant's journey and settlement, and have pointed to the religious as a domain that should not be overlooked in understanding these dynamics.[6] They point out that it is very clear that "religion supports and is itself transformed by all aspects of the migration experience—the journey, the process of settlement, and the emergence of ethnic and transnational ties."[7] Other studies affirm this and show how being part of a religion offers a connection with a network of religious communities, both in the country of origin and the destination country, which are supportive of and oftentimes

---

2. Rastogi et al., *Black Population: 2010*, 2.

3. For example, see "Parish Planning Data—Executive Summary," St. Matthew, Baltimore, MD (May 19, 2016), https://bemissionarydisciples.org.

4. Myizero, interview. The research participants quoted in this article are referred to by pseudonyms to preserve anonymity. The pseudonyms describe their main coping characteristic in their native language.

5. Phan, "Experience of Migration as Source of Intercultural Theology," 180–81, 195.

6. Castles, de Haas, and Miller, *Age of Migration*; Adogame, *African Christian Diaspora*, 1–13; Levitt and Jaworsky, "Transnational Migration Studies."

7. Levitt and Jaworsky, "Transnational Migration Studies," 140.

instrumental in the decision to immigrate, on the journey itself, and during the process of settlement.[8] Afe Adogame's *African Christian Diaspora*, the product of research on three continents, is a thorough presentation of the relevance and significance of African Christian communities for the dynamics of migration. It discusses not only the importance of the global and local networks they have developed that offer support to many immigrants on their migration journey, but it also reveals how this global African Christianity will impact the religious, cultural, social, economic, and political dynamics of the countries where African diasporas emerge. These studies, however, mainly focus on the role of faith and church communities in the dynamics of migration and do so from the perspective of social or religious studies. More research still needs to be done to flesh out the African Catholic migration experience in terms of theology and spirituality.

Daniel Groody and Gemma Tulud Cruz are two Catholic theologians who have undertaken pioneering work on this theological discourse in their description of the characteristics of migrant spirituality and its impact on Christian spirituality.[9] Groody and Cruz have conducted ethnographic work among Mexican immigrants crossing the U.S. border[10] and among Filipino domestic helpers in Hong Kong,[11] but they build their theological reflections solely on the experiences of those migrating from Central and South America to the U.S. and of Asians who immigrate within the Asian continent or to other continents. Although Cruz mentions African migrants in her statistical overviews and refers to the growing number of them in Asia and the U.S., she does not incorporate the experiences of these African migrants into her analysis.[12] The stories and experiences of African migrants to the U.S. still need to be heard and added to the "wealth of migration experiences that has been ignored or left untouched."[13]

This chapter therefore argues for the need to engage the stories of African immigrants to the U.S. as gathered in firsthand interviews, with the goal of contributing to the theological discourse on the characteristics of migrant spirituality. I will explain the importance of these stories as a source of theology and explore how the experience of the "Dark Night" in the spirituality of St. John of the Cross provides a framework to consider the experience of migration. This contemporary experience of the Dark Night involves a process of transition in which identity and faith can be transformed.

Migration Experiences: "A Sign of the Times"

Both the Catholic Church and Catholic theologians have recognized the phenomenon of migration as a "sign of the times," in which one can "decipher authentic signs of God's presence and purpose."[14] This means that the phenomenon of migration offers "a challenge to be discovered and utilized in our work to renew humanity and proclaim the Gospel of Peace."[15] The phenomenon of migration constitutes a *locus theologicus* in which the experiences of migrants become a place of theological reflection generating new theological knowledge.[16]

---

8. Phillip Connor, *Immigrant Faith*; Cruz, *Toward a Theology of Migration*; Adogame, *African Christian Diaspora*; Biney, *From Africa to America*; Olupona and Gemignani, *African Immigrant Religions in America*; ter Haar, "Ghanaians in the Netherlands," 313–30.
9. Groody, "Spirituality of Migrants," 139–56; Cruz, *Toward a Theology of Migration*.
10. Groody, *Border of Death, Valley of Life*.
11. Cruz, *Into the Deep*.
12. Cruz, *Toward a Theology of Migration*, 53, 91, 102, 106.
13. Campese, "Theologies of Migration," 182.
14. Vatican II, Pastoral Constitution on the Church in the Modern World (*Gaudium et Spes*) §11.
15. Pontifical Council for the Pastoral Care for Migrants and Itinerant People, *Erga Migrantes Caritas Christi* §14.
16. Polak, "Migration as a Sign of the Times," 47–78.

The Need for Storytelling

METHODOLOGICAL REFLECTIONS

Recognizing migration experiences as a *locus theologicus* has an impact on the theological approach taken in addressing the phenomenon of migration. In discussing the consequences of the methodology employed in doing migration theology, Gioacchino Campese and Jorge Castillo Guerra suggest a shift from "a more theoretical discourse" about the various dimensions of migration to "a theology grounded in the reality of migration, on the experience of real migrants, a theology for which dialogue with other disciplines that study migration . . . is an imperative," and for which "direct engagement with migrants is crucial."[17] Campese brings to mind Jon Sobrino's insight that "doing theology . . . [is] also to let ourselves be carried by reality in its complexity, because in it, in mysterious and unexpected ways, is present God's Grace."[18] Castillo Guerra suggests following Ignacio Ellacuría, Juan Carlos Scannone, and Sobrino, each of whom considers theological reflection to be a secondary event. Methodologically this means that, for the migrant experience to be able to speak for itself, "the implementation of theological instruments"[19] will, initially, be postponed. This creates a theoretical space in which the experiences of migrants are regarded as "a primary reality" and "the faith and wisdom present in these experiences" as carrying their own theological meaning.[20] Castillo Guerra remarks that seeking to create such a "theoretical space is not limited to the reflection on migrants."[21] Nor, I would add, is seeking to engage with the narratives of the subjects of theological reflection as a "primary reality." I would like to point to a similar method of theology that has been developed by the Circle of Concerned African Women Theologians.[22] This study will, therefore, first listen to the narratives of African migrants to the U.S. and describe their experiences on their own terms and in their own words. In order to break open their stories and analyze their experiences in a systematic manner, I will apply the research strategy of the *grounded theory*.[23]

RESEARCH STRATEGY AND METHOD OF ANALYSIS

Barney Glaser and Anselm Strauss developed the *grounded theory* in 1967 as a strategy for generating knowledge about complex social phenomena.[24] They developed this research strategy in response to what they perceived as a lack of "connection to everyday reality" in the field of empirical research and an emphasis on working with and testing hypotheses rather than explaining social phenomena from the perspective of those who experience them.[25] Grounded theory is a research strategy in the field of qualitative research and works on the assumptions that "knowledge arises through . . . acting and interacting self-reflective beings"[26] (based on the philosophies of interactionism and pragmatism) and that human beings will attempt to give meaning to and explain their social reality and experiences (based on constructivism). Hennie Boeije describes qualitative research from the perspective of grounded theory as follows:

---

17. Campese, "Theologies of Migration," 175–76; Castillo Guerra, "Theologie der Migration," 115–45; and Castillo Guerra, "From the Faith and Life of a Migrant," 107–29.
18. Campese, "Theologies of Migration," 183.
19. Castillo Guerra, "From the Faith and Life of a Migrant," 115.
20. Castillo Guerra, "From the Faith and Life of a Migrant," 115, 123–25.
21. Castillo Guerra, "From the Faith and Life of a Migrant," 125.
22. Phiri and Nadar, *African Women, Religion, and Health*.
23. Boeije, *Analysis in Qualitative Research*; Corbin and Strauss, *Basics of Qualitative Research*; Charmaz, *Constructing Grounded Theory*.
24. Barney Glaser and Anselm Strauss, *The Discovery of Grounded Theory: Strategies for Qualitative Research* (London: Routledge, 1967).
25. Boeije, *Analysis in Qualitative Research*, 8.
26. Corbin and Strauss, *Basics of Qualitative Research*, 2.

The purpose of qualitative research is to describe and understand social phenomena in terms of the meaning people bring to them. The research questions are studied through flexible methods enabling contact with the people involved to an extent that is necessary to grasp what is going on in the field. The methods produce rich, descriptive data that need to be interpreted through the identification and coding of themes and categories to findings that can contribute to theoretical knowledge and practical use.[27]

The chief source of data for the research described in this chapter is the personal narratives of African migrants to the U.S. These narratives were gathered through unstructured interviews. Once the first interview had been conducted and was transcribed, the analysis began. The first procedure undertaken as part of grounded theory is to segment the data by searching for meaningful and relevant fragments that seem to recur. The purpose is to "discover how meanings are formed and to discover rather than test variables."[28] These fragments or segments are assigned descriptive codes and then placed into categories according to the manner in which they describe properties and dimensions of these categories. This is called open coding (segmenting) and axial coding (descriptive categories).

The next step in implementing grounded theory is that of data reassembly. This phase is characterized by constant comparison, asking generative questions, and theoretical sampling. The emerging categories and their evolving relationships are subjected to continuous scrutiny in order to determine "the credibility of those relationships between the categories."[29] This is called "selective coding" (reassembling). It is hoped that the constant comparison of the emerging categories and their evolving relationships will result in "a coherent model or integrated explanation"[30] of, in the case of this study, the transformation of identity and faith in the experience of migration as described by participating African immigrants to the U.S.

Theological Framework: The Migration Experience and the Experience of the Dark Night

MIGRATION: AN EXPERIENCE OF LIMINALITY
A migrant's journey can be described as "a phased process marked by changes,"[31] and scholars agree that one can distinguish three phases that characterize this journey: emigration, immigration, and migration.[32] In each of these three phases a migrant experiences a change in identity.[33] Emigration refers to the movement out of one's place of origin, the place where one's roots are. Depending on an emigrant's means and reasons for leaving (free or forced), this moment can be shorter or longer but sometimes lasts several years. Immigration refers to the movement into a new place. The emigrant becomes an "immigrant," someone who is defined in exclusivist terms such as "foreign," "strange," "alien," or even "illegal"—terms that highlight their difference from their new society's native inhabitants and their strangeness in that society. In the third part of the journey the immigrant becomes a "migrant." A migrant has to negotiate this new reality, settle, and find a new identity that is a healthy synthesis of the migrant's "double identity as emigrant/immigrant."[34]

---

27. Boeije, *Analysis in Qualitative Research*, 11.
28. Corbin and Strauss, *Basics of Qualitative Research*, 12.
29. Boeije, *Analysis in Qualitative Research*, 79.
30. Boeije, *Analysis in Qualitative Research*, 79.
31. Waaijman, *Spirituality*, 34.
32. Castles, de Haas, and Miller, *Age of Migration*, 25–26; Castillo Guerra, "Naar een theologie van de migratie," 241–58; Adogame, *African Christian Diaspora*, 18–27. The way in which the terms "immigration"/"immigrant" and "migration"/"migrant" are used in this chapter differs from their dictionary definitions and instead follows their use by Castillo Guerra, as described in this paragraph.
33. Castillo Guerra, "Theologie der Migration," 118–22.
34. Castillo Guerra, "From the Faith and Life of a Migrant," 113.

These changes in identity carry with them experiences of loss, sadness, grief, or homesickness, which translate into a general feeling of estrangement or of being homeless, displaced, adrift, and uprooted. This feeling is particular to the migration experience: the migrant lives with the physical absence but mental presence of people and places that have been left behind, while also negotiating the shift from living between two worlds to becoming more at home—"refamiliarized"—in the new society.[35] Robert Schreiter describes this latter experience as an experience of liminality: being imprisoned in the in-between, oscillating between participation in the new culture and the feeling of being nowhere. Schreiter points to homesickness as an expression of this experience, an experience of grieving a loss without yet having the perspective of something new.[36] Adogame also refers to the experience of liminality when he speaks of migrants being "betwixt and between" after they have left their home countries and are on the "transitory journey to" but have not yet arrived in the destination country, a situation he calls "the liminal phase of the migratory process."[37] Castillo Guerra and Schreiter, however, argue that the experience of liminality continues upon arrival and may last across generations of migrants.

In the field of spirituality studies, the experience of liminality is seen as a core experience and includes Kees Waaijman's notion of "uprootedness."[38] The experience of liminality constitutes one of three phases comprising a process of spiritual transformation—namely, separation, liminality, and reintegration. For the migrant, these three phases involve moving out of the context of a known social structure (separation), then experiencing a context of antistructure in which the migrant finds him- or herself outside any social structures and living between two worlds (liminality), and then his or her incorporation into new social structures (reintegration). The liminal phase is considered the main phase of this process and is described as oscillating between an experience of a kind of death, in which nothingness prevails, and an experience that brings life and a new sense of wholeness. It is in this "transitional phase of liminality" that a new understanding of a person's faith and relationship with God can develop.[39]

Migration, Liminality, and the Dark Night

St. John of the Cross was a spiritual, mystical thinker whose writings center on illuminating the changes in and transformation of the human–divine relationship. Moreover, in his writings and most especially in his poem and commentary *The Dark Night*, he recognizes and comments on the experience of liminality and the transformation that can happen from within this experience.[40]

Constance FitzGerald, a Carmelite sister and scholar of John of the Cross, speaks of the experience of "impasse" and how in the Dark Night this experience is at the core of a transformation of faith and a new understanding of God. Impasse, according to FitzGerald, is an experience of disintegration and deprivation of worth that can be felt on many levels, both personal and societal. FitzGerald's description of impasse aligns with the experience of liminality as a form of antistructure in which all the conventions or categories of known structures no longer function or apply.[41] Although John of the Cross was a sixteenth-century Carmelite poet and Spanish mystic, FitzGerald claims that his writings and insights continue to speak to contemporary experiences of liminality and can provide people and communities with a framework within which they can "understand, name, and claim [liminality] as an experience of God."[42]

---

35. Castillo Guerra, "Theologie der Migration," 118–22.
36. Schreiter, "Partizipation und Liminalität," 82–94.
37. Adogame, *African Christian Diaspora*, 23.
38. Waaijman, *Spirituality*, 261.
39. Waaijman, *Spirituality*, 213–14.
40. John of the Cross, *Collected Works*; Blommestijn, Huls, and Waaijman, *Footprints of Love*.
41. FitzGerald, "Impasse and Dark Night," 94–95.
42. FitzGerald, "Impasse and Dark Night," 93–94.

Stories of Transformation

In the study of spirituality, transformation is defined as the process in which, through moments of transition characterized by discontinuity and liminality, the relationship between humans and the divine takes shape and humans develop a new understanding or consciousness of God.[43] The migration journey is characterized by a series of transitions, and migrants experience discontinuity and liminality. The question that arises from these experiences is whether and how in their personal narratives the African migrants who participated in this research describe them as experiences of transformation of their identity and faith.

In the remainder of the chapter I will present the context of and the participants in this research. First, I will present the main themes that arise from the analysis of their personal narratives. This will be followed by a summary of how John of the Cross describes the experience of the Dark Night, and finally the migration experiences of the participants and their experience of the Dark Night will be brought together to explore some key concepts that represent the migration experience as a transformation of identity and faith.

Meet the Storytellers

This section will first describe the demographic history of northeast Baltimore, where many African migrants have found a spiritual home in Roman Catholic parishes. Then the participants themselves will be introduced.

The Catholic Community of Northeast Baltimore

Baltimore City was founded as an independent city in 1729. It became a port of entry in 1780 and, in the course of the nineteenth century, grew into the second largest port of entry into the U.S. next to Ellis Island. Baltimore's immigrants initially came mostly from Ireland and Germany, but later immigrants from Italy and a variety of Eastern European countries settled there as well. From 1790 to 1860, the population of Baltimore grew from 13,503 to 212,418.[44] The immigrants established their own neighborhoods or townships there and developed their own social, economic, cultural, and religious life. The landscape in Baltimore is "marked by religious edifices built by immigrant communities from Northern, Southern, and Eastern Europe to honor their God and welcome their faithful."[45] Between 1884 and 1927 these immigrant groups founded five of the seven parishes that are now part of the Northeast Catholic Community (NECC). The remaining two parishes of the NECC were founded in 1949 and 1960 as the inner city started to expand, with new neighborhoods developing to the northeast from the Second World War onward. Before that, "you could walk from 25th Street to Towson along Loch Raven Boulevard and not see a house."[46] What is currently northeast Baltimore was in the early 1940s still quite rural.

In the early 1960s, these new neighborhoods started welcoming another demographic group: African Americans. Baltimore City has its own ambivalent history with African Americans. On the one hand, it played an important role in the abolition movement,[47] but, on the other, "large numbers of Baltimoreans were pro-slavery and rioted when Union troops marched through the city on April 19, 1861, causing the Civil War's first bloodshed."[48] Later Baltimore stood at the forefront of the fight for equality and civil rights, but the city is still known for its neighborhoods that were formed as the result of segregation and continue to show the signs of this segregation.[49] Baltimore City's population demographic is currently 63% Black, 27.7%

---

43. Waaijman, *Spirituality*, 424–26.
44. Connery, "Point of Entry: Baltimore, the Other Ellis Island."
45. *Community of St. Matthew*, 18.
46. *Community of St. Matthew*, 2.
47. Baltimore City, Maryland: Historical Chronology, https://msa.maryland.gov.
48. "A Lasting Legacy: Baltimore's African American History," Baltimore National Heritage area, https://www.explorebaltimore.org.
49. Pietila, *Not in My Neighborhood*.

white, 4.2% Hispanic, 2.5% Asian, 2% mixed, and 0.6% other.[50]

So, when in the early sixties African Americans started moving to the new neighborhoods in northeast Baltimore, this development was met with ambivalence at best and, much worse, with the infamous practice of blockbusting.[51] The communities in the young neighborhoods of northeast Baltimore, however, organized themselves into "groups such as the Greater Northwood Community Council, the St. Matthew Social Action committee, and the Northeast Community Organization (NECO) [working together] to fight blockbusting and achieve peaceful integration."[52] This foreshadowed their later welcoming of the most recent streams of immigrants that settled in their midst, making the northeast neighborhoods one of a few pockets of Baltimore City known for ethnic diversity.[53] During the last three decades, the influx of immigrants, and especially immigrants from various African countries, has grown exponentially.

Parish responses to these newcomers have been varied, ranging from a welcome with the expectation that the newcomers will assimilate, to a warm, intentional embrace. In some parishes one sees immigrants coming for Mass, but they come and go quietly and seem somewhat invisible. One parish opened its doors to an Orthodox Ethiopian community and a Buddhist community from Bhutan, and currently welcomes a small but growing group of African parishioners. Another parish opened its doors to a Nigerian, predominantly Igbo, community who celebrate a monthly Igbo Mass on Sunday afternoon. Although these immigrant communities and newcomers have found a spiritual home in these two parishes, they do not seem to have had a significant impact on the identity of the receiving communities. One of the seven parishes in northeast Baltimore, however, has strongly embraced all newcomers since its founding in 1949. It considers immigrants to be an essential part of its identity, beginning with the founders of the parish—who were descendants of European immigrants and who moved from downtown to northeast Baltimore—and then extending to the descendants of Africans who arrived during the time of slavery and to the new "immigrant groups—from Asia, the Caribbean, and Africa—blessing [their] community with new members, new faith expression, new traditions."[54] The significance of these immigrant contributions can be seen in the importance to this community of storytelling. "Storytelling" is the very first word in the book prepared for the parish's fiftieth anniversary.[55] Storytelling happens everywhere in this parish, even during Mass!

The history of the Catholic communities of northeast Baltimore City and their diverse responses to immigrants are the interesting contexts in which the stories of the participants in this research evolved.

INTRODUCING THE STORYTELLERS

For the case study presented here, my aim was to focus on the most diverse group of African immigrants possible from the Catholic communities of northeast Baltimore City and to aim for an equal representation of women and men. I did not restrict participation on the basis of age, nationality or ethnicity, modes of arrival, immigrant status, or time lived in the U.S.

The search for participants was initiated through announcements in various churches in northeast Baltimore and in two churches in particular. All but two of the participants are affiliated with one of those two church communities. Following the announcement in the two churches, I sought contact and engagement with the African communities present there. It took time for me to develop a trusting relationship with them; although it was clear that the African immigrants had a certain

---

50. United States Census Bureau Quick Facts: Baltimore City, Maryland (county), https://www.census.gov/quickfacts.
51. Pietila, *Not in My Neighborhood*.
52. *Community of St. Matthew*, 8.
53. Yeip, "Baltimore's Demographic Divide."
54. *Community of St. Matthew*, 18.
55. *Community of St. Matthew*, 1.

desire to share their stories, they were also very cautious. I came to understand that, even though they had obtained legal status, there was still a fear of losing that status, especially among the migrants who had received asylum but who might not have disclosed their real reason for coming to the U.S. A year and a half later, a person from the Kenyan Women's Prayer Group, in which I had been participating, volunteered for the first interview. She said that her experience of an interview might spur her to encourage others to share their stories as well. Her willingness helps to explain the fairly large number of participants from Kenya (six). Nine participants came forward from families in the faith formation program of the churches in northeast Baltimore, of which I had become the director. Once we became familiar with each other and they became interested in my research project, the faith formation participants started volunteering for interviews. This group shows the largest national variety (Eritrea, the Democratic Republic of the Congo, Nigeria, Liberia, Sierra Leone, and Rwanda). One man from Nigeria came forward through another network of relationships; he is a resident of northeast Baltimore and was formerly a member of one of the churches.

Stories of Loss and Transformation

Although each story of migration shared by the participants is different and personal,[56] patterns and themes do emerge from their stories as they describe (although not always in chronological order) each of the three phases of the migration experience.[57] First, the participants generously shared the many obstacles and challenges they experienced on this journey, from their experience of departure to their experience of negotiating life in their new country, with an emphasis on the challenges they faced upon arrival and during their adjustment to life in the U.S. They attempted to develop a lifestyle that responded to the demands of their new country but also honored the values of their home country. Second, it became clear from their stories that they had had experiences of loss of many kinds. Central to these experiences of loss is the loss of "the good life"[58] and the sense of vulnerability this engenders. Third, in their efforts to cope with their new situation, the participants sought God's presence, and they shared how their understanding of God transforms and affects their present way of life now that nurturing faith and "the good life" are no longer generated by the comforting support of the community life left behind, but rather depend on the efforts of the individual.

These three main themes arising from the personal narratives shed new light on the spiritual aspects of the participants' migration journeys. For these Catholic migrants from Africa the journey seems to have been a solitary one, and, regardless of whether they were able to find a welcoming and vibrant faith community, they have discovered that faith has become an individual choice that happens in the realm of their private lives. This seems to have intensified their sense of vulnerability and led to a transformation of their relationship with God.

This experience seems contrary to the experience of African immigrants in African-led Christian communities, such as those described by Moses Biney and Adogame.[59] The question arises as to whether the lack of a true spiritual home, in which all the dimensions of an African spirituality can be fully expressed, affects the African immigrant experience and the transformation of identity and faith that is part of this experience. We turn now to what the storytellers shared.

---

56. The reflections below are based on an analysis of the sixteen stories gathered by the author. All the quotations are taken from the interviews of the participants. Transcripts of the interviews are in my research files. The participants quoted here are referred to by pseudonyms to preserve anonymity.

57. Castillo Guerra, "From the Faith and Life of a Migrant," 113; Castillo Guerra, "Theologie der Migration," 119–22.

58. Ter Haar, "Ghanaians in the Netherlands," 325. Ter Haar's references to the concept of "the good life" or "life in abundance" have been helpful in developing my thoughts on the loss of *joie de vivre* and the role of faith in dealing with this loss.

59. Biney, *From Africa to America*; and Adogame, *African Christian Diaspora*.

Emigration, Immigration, Migration: Facing Challenges, Loss, and Vulnerability

The participants described extensively the many obstacles and challenges they faced on their journey, obstacles and challenges that have impacted them economically, culturally, socially, personally, and religiously. The major obstacles, especially at the beginning, were the language barrier (even though African immigrants are multilingual, their unfamiliar accent marks them as outsiders), an unfamiliarity with the workings of American society, an inability to build a network to gain support and knowledge, and a lack of acknowledgment of their educational background and professional experience. Kasala illustrated how these four obstacles affected him by stating that he had become a silent bystander and was not accepted as an active contributor to society: "I am forced to be the quiet guy."[60] Obstacles that prevent immigrants from engaging life in their new country and society include lingering sorrow on the loss of the home country, holding onto an initial plan or goal to return to the home country (like Fda, who initially did not opt to bring his wife and child to the U.S.), and having no goal or purpose at all.

These challenges carry with them many and varied experiences of loss, which I have grouped into two categories: experiences of external loss and, as a result of external loss, experiences of internal loss. Experiences of external loss can be summed up in four subcategories: loss of a social network, loss of one's previous way of life, loss of previous protective tactics, and loss of socioeconomic status.[61]

The loss of a social network is first and foremost experienced in the loss of family and friends left behind in the home country. Those participants who, upon arrival, were not able to connect to an ethnic community experienced a lack of support and some isolation. It seemed to them that nobody was willing to introduce them to the intricacies of life in the U.S. Some participants were left stranded upon arrival, experienced a period of being undocumented and even homeless, or were abused and isolated from society by their host(s); for these participants, the experience of the loss of a social network was even more intensely negative.

All the participants experienced the loss of their previous way of life. They expressed this loss by talking about what they miss from their home cultures, such as food, the way of raising children, or the moral values of those cultures. Participants experience cultural challenges in the already-mentioned language barrier and in their perception that the demands of life in the U.S. are an obstacle to properly attending to family, faith, and the other joys of living. They speak about the good life they left behind, which includes both the established life they had as individuals and the communal life they experienced, which is different from the more individual-oriented society in the U.S. Some also mention the loss of independence, especially during the time they heavily depended on others for their survival or initial settlement (obtaining housing, access to education, and even help with finances).

Arriving in a new society that differs greatly from the society left behind results in a loss of previous tactics for negotiating life. This experience is more intense when immigrants arrive unexpectedly and are therefore unprepared. Everything is different and the known ways of addressing issues like housing, searching for a job, health care, and education do not work in the new setting. Raising children in America is different because the social structure and cultural values in which the parents were raised do not exist or fully apply. And in the midst of all this, the marriage dynamic is challenged. First of all, it is easier to employ women because housekeeping and caregiving are always needed. Second, both spouses have to work to survive economically and so the dynamics of authority and dependency change. Both of these new realities are harder for the husbands to accept than for the wives, especially if the children cope better and have more social and cultural knowledge than their fathers. Participants struggle economically as well. Wirigiro explains, "By the end of the month, bills are looking at you like this. . . . You don't know where to start, where to begin."[62] This quotation illustrates

---

60. Kasala, interview.
61. Keul, "Venture of Vulnerability," 182–83.
62. Wirigiro, interview.

nicely how the socioeconomic system in the U.S. is more complex than what the immigrants are accustomed to and includes multiple unexpected costs of living such as rent, gas and electric; and insurance for liability, house, health, and car. Finding housing is complicated by the checklist of things that need to be lined up correctly before renting or buying a house. Some participants lament the loss of their ability to be self-sustaining, as these much higher costs of living cannot be alleviated by, for example, growing their own small parcels of crops. Participants express feeling ignorant, uncertain, and out of place and say that the "world seems upside down."[63]

A majority of the participants experience a loss of socioeconomic status. This is mostly expressed in their experience of not being able to find a job that recognizes their educational background and professional experience. Most participants start out being underemployed, working manual jobs or low-level caregiving jobs. The majority need to invest time to gain proficiency in American English, redo their secondary education, or achieve new certifications for their professions. Even then a job at their level of education or experience is not guaranteed because their professional experience in their home country might not be accepted. This long journey to achieve a similar level of professional accomplishment is sometimes abandoned, causing the immigrant's socioeconomic status to remain low. As Kasala says, "When I compare myself, I say, 'Oh, I think we are underneath, we are not where we should be.'"[64] On the other hand, participants who arrived as teenagers, or as young adults with educational goals, or who came to receive a particular education, seem to suffer less socioeconomically because they were educated in and integrated into the American system early on. Myizero, who immigrated as the spouse of an American citizen, seems to do well economically but expresses her concern about socioeconomic status as she tries to achieve financial independence.

These experiences of external loss cause experiences of internal loss, which can also be summed up in four subcategories: loss of dignity, loss of hope, loss of faith or faith lived in community, and loss of quality of life. First, participants suffer a loss of dignity, especially when they are perceived as strangers, or even as aliens, and when their life story, their education, and their professional experience are not recognized or appreciated. These experiences hinder their ability to become contributing members of society and move up the socioeconomic ladder, and effect a devaluation of being. Participants face being rejected by friends or compatriots (as Kūohera shares, when her friends, based on a rumor, no longer wished her to be their roommate) or being abused and isolated from the world by a host, as described by Kuriōka. Socially it is a challenge to navigate the optimistic expectations of life in the U.S. when the reality is more complex. Family in the home country expect gifts or remittances from their emigrated family members, and the participants cannot always live up to those expectations. This effects a sense of failure that contributes to a loss of dignity.

Second, participants experience a loss of hope when they try to overcome the challenges they encounter. They soon discover that when one problem is solved there is a new one waiting. This reality is experienced as "a long and painful process." This ongoing effort causes exhaustion and fatigue, feelings of being burdened and unhappy, and sometimes even despair. Kasala expresses this when he says that "the outside is so, so hard."[65]

Third, most participants shared that it is a challenge to nurture one's faith in this new country and that they experience a loss of faith or faith lived in community. Upon arrival, participants are forced to navigate a plurality of denominations and church communities before finding their own denomination and then also a community in which they feel at home and welcomed. Kasala describes the congregants in the first Catholic church he attended as *"gens de marbre,"*[66] meaning marble- or stone-faced

---

63. Kūohera, interview.
64. Kasala, interview.
65. Kasala, interview.
66. Kasala, interview.

people, and Bahlohoi shares how the pastor of the first church his family attended did not even know his name after three years, despite the fact that his family stood out as the only African or Black family in the community.[67] The demands of daily life in the U.S. also make it hard to find time for a life of faith. In American society, the participants experienced that the wider community does not support their faith life. Kuriōka and Ūtana, who work in health care, are shocked that they are not allowed to engage in prayer with their patients. Being a person of faith is an individual choice. When she speaks of this, Kuriōka says that it is "you alone with your journey of faith."[68] And in the midst of trying to cope with all of the challenges posed by being in a new society, there are moments of despair and doubt during which one questions or even risks losing one's faith. As Kuriōka describes it, life in the U.S. challenges one's faith:

> It is a challenging country because many people are not believers. People have no time . . . even to pray because of the nature of the work systems. So you must really, really plan to get time when you are driving and you have to do prayers, or in your quiet time. But the challenges here are many. I never would have thought in my life that Sunday can go without going to church.[69]

Participants share the importance of a welcoming faith community and time to pray on their journey to finding faith and hope.

Finally, the loss of quality of life is seen in the many different feelings participants have. Loss of family and friends and the lack of a support or social network make the participants feel homesick and lonely. The socioeconomic demands of American society are high and navigating its complex social systems, including those relating to education, job, finances and economics, health care, and housing, is very difficult. The race to survive causes exhaustion, fatigue, and stress, and makes participants (especially those who were forced to leave) feel the loss of the good life at home even more strongly. Participants mention feeling unhappy and describe some episodes in their experience as "dark."[70]

The loss of quality of life seems to be a core experience in the stories of the participants. It amounts to the feeling that there is "no time to live," and no time to attend to one's spiritual or family needs. Ustahimili and Kasala voiced this experience most strongly with a French expression: they had lost their *joie de vivre*. Even if the immigrants become socioeconomically successful, all of them express a loss of quality of life. This loss connects both the experiences of external and internal loss and emphasizes the connection between faith and the ability to negotiate a new life. Because participants can no longer depend on the comforting support of the community left behind, they feel that it is their responsibility to nurture their faith and achieve "a good life."[71] All of these experiences of loss effect a sense of vulnerability. Kuriōka describes this when she says that "life [here is] so, so delicate."[72] In their efforts to cope with their new situations, the participants look for God.

Transformation: A New Understanding of God and the Ability to Cope

Asked to reflect on how they had been able to cope in the midst of all these obstacles, challenges, and losses, the participants shared many stories. The coping strategies they mentioned included prayer, contemplation, finding support in the Bible, focusing on the positives, seeking stress relief, and sometimes withdrawing from difficult situations. Doing these things requires a lot of patience, perseverance, and strength and is certainly not easy. But one phrase kept recurring: "It takes God."[73] When one

---

67. Bahlohoi, interview.
68. Kuriōka, interview.
69. Kuriōka, interview.
70. Kasala, interview.
71. Kuriōka, interview.
72. Kuriōka, interview.
73. Hatiri-na-thina, interview.

reflects on the coping strategies participants developed and how they describe them, it becomes clear that their faith and trust in God play a central role in their daily lives and experiences. In all the interviews taken together, the word "God" features 484 times, not counting implicit references to God when participants are talking about prayer, referencing the Bible, or speaking about Christ. Regardless of the depth of their struggles, all participants express that their ability to cope ultimately rests on their ability to trust in God as the source of all their actions.

In the midst of their struggles, participants experience moments in which the fact and manner of God's presence become clear. Unyenyekevu explains that it was in the deep loneliness she experienced that God could reach out to her and rescue her.[74] Hatiri-na-thina describes how leaving behind the comfort of her parents, siblings, and friends, and the experience of being an alien without support affected her faith and relationship with God and how she has learned "to put God first."[75] The participants' changed experiences of God not only change their perspective on the challenges they encounter, but they also share how these experiences have transformed them in their relationships with others and in their overall way of being.

Such experiences of transformation cause real change to take place, both externally and internally.[76] Concrete circumstances are transformed, as in the story of Kūohera: "out of nowhere" she finds a new roommate because of that person's unforeseen need for new housing. Ustahimili has no money to pay for schoolbooks, but God provides when she receives a refund from the IRS. Instances of internal transformation effect a change of perspective or insight, for example when Kuriōka all of a sudden realizes that God does have a purpose for her, and this allows her to take charge of her experience.

Participants also describe a change of attitude, such as in the story of Unyenyekevu, who explains that God showed her that the key to everything is humility and declares that she now works for God, not for the world. This allows her to put her whole heart into her housekeeping job at the hospital, even though she could accomplish so much more given her experience as a national politician. A change in attitude is also recognized in the development of coping abilities like endurance, perseverance, and patience. Another form of internal transformation is finding the strength and courage to cope with difficult and complex circumstances that are or seem impossible to change. Fda expresses this in his ability to accept the current circumstances of his life, which he cannot change; he finds strength from God to sacrifice his own dreams and to "work his heart out" to create better circumstances for his children.[77] Participants also describe a change in themselves. This relates to finding humility, as mentioned above by Unyenyekevu, and in the story of Kūhora, whose humility in her relationship with God allows her to become forgiving, accepting, and generous, even to those who wrong her. This change in oneself allows the participants to put God and others first.

Dark Night: An Experience of Transformation

In his poem and commentary *The Dark Night*, St. John of the Cross describes how God invites humans to go on a journey to grow toward unity with the divine. This is a journey on which all our human understanding, desires, and memories are transformed so that they grow in harmony with divine wisdom, love, and hope. This is not an easy journey, as it asks us to leave behind the life we know to find a new life that prospers in union with the love of God.

---

74. Unyenyekevu, interview.
75. Hatiri-na-thina, interview.
76. Versteegen, *Geleefde Genade*, 184–98. In this dissertation, Versteegen describes moments of transformation that indicate the presence of God's grace, as related in the personal narratives of Dutch women. This is similar to my category of "God's presence" (one of the categories I created during the analysis of the interviews I conducted, in order to gather similar experiences together; as described earlier in this article, creating such categories is part of the process of analysis in qualitative research). The categories and characteristics she describes helped me to distinguish between moments of transformation in the stories of my participants.
77. Fda, interview.

The Experience of Loss in the Dark Night

In the experience of the Dark Night, John explains that, as a favor granted by God, the soul undergoes a process of purification in which "God divests the faculties, affections, and senses, both spiritual and sensory, interior and exterior" (2.3.3).[78] John stresses that this is all the work of God, performed out of love.[79] John describes how the soul suffers aridities and vulnerabilities in this process of purification and transformation. He explains that during this process the soul feels stripped "of the habitual affection of the old self to which the soul is strongly united, attached, and conformed" (2.6.1). With Job, the soul exclaims that it was once "rich and wealthy" (Job 16:12–16) but now feels quite "undone and broken" (*Dark Night* 2.7.2). Convinced that God has rejected it, the soul "feels forsaken and despised" (2.6.3). John also refers to Lamentations 3:1–20, in which a deep sense of desolation is described: "[God] has made my skin and flesh old . . . as those who are dead forever"; "I have forgotten good things"; and "my end, my aim, and my hope from the Lord is frustrated and finished" (*Dark Night* 2.7.3). In this Dark Night the soul remembers and is extremely aware of its own imperfections, miseries, and past prosperity.

Vulnerable in the Face of God: The Blessings of the Dark Night

John explains that, in this experience of the Dark Night, the soul "is humbled, softened, and purified, until it becomes so delicate, simple, and refined that it can be one with the Spirit of God" (2.7.3). Becoming delicate or vulnerable prepares the soul for the union of love that God desires to grant to it (2.7.3). He refers to the Dark Night as "that glad night" and speaks of the "sheer grace" it brings, because "this happy night darkens the spirit . . . to impart light concerning all things [and] it does so only that [these souls] may reach out divinely to the enjoyment of all earthly and heavenly things, with a general spirit of freedom in them all" (2.9.1).

Toward the end of book 1 of *The Dark Night*, John describes the benefits of the night of the senses. Among the many benefits are the ability to live a virtuous life and the awareness that God is the sole source of and satisfaction in doing so:

> These aridities, then, make people walk with purity in the love of God. No longer are they moved to act by the delight and satisfaction they find in a work . . . but by the desire of pleasing God. They are neither presumptuous, nor self-satisfied, as was their custom in the time of their prosperity. . . . Another very great benefit for the soul in this night is that it exercises all the virtues together. In the patience and forbearance practiced in these voids and aridities, and through perseverance . . . the soul practices the love of God. (1.13.12)

John also describes the growth of the love of God in the night of the spirit by setting forth the "successive steps on this ladder of love by which the soul ascends to God" (2.19.1). Here he describes as well the eagerness with which the soul wishes to serve and please God, with humility, patience, and forbearance (2.19–20).

Empowerment through Transformation

Abandonment, Vulnerability, and Transformation

When one reads the migration stories of the participants and John's description of the Dark Night side by side, it becomes clear that in both there is a moment of a departure, whether it is forced (by circumstances)[80] or chosen (as in the religious life or in the seeking of an opportunity). This departure from one's previous life results in experiences

---

78. John of the Cross, *The Dark Night*.

79. FitzGerald, "Impasse and Dark Night," 97. FitzGerald explains that John of the Cross's poems and prose writings "begin and end with love and desire." John of the Cross "is intent on showing what kind of affective education is carried on by the Holy Spirit over a life time."

80. Immigrants escape from various negative circumstances; John escaped from jail (John of the Cross, *Collected Works*, 18–19).

of loss and abandonment. John resonates with the participants' experiences when he employs the metaphor of reaching "a new and unknown land" to describe the soul "getting lost to what it knew and what it tasted" (abandoned), and the need to abandon familiar ways (becoming vulnerable) so that the soul can travel along "these new and unknown roads" (2.16.8). For both migrants and John, the person who sets out on this journey and who engages with loss and surrenders to vulnerability in abandonment experiences a transformation of circumstances, of perspective, and of self in the presence of God.

"Freedom of Spirit," or Empowerment through Transformation

These transformations in the presence of God effect empowerment. This does not necessarily mean that perfect happiness is achieved or that all problems are solved, but that circumstances may be perceived differently and successfully addressing them may become "doable," as some of the participants said. John of the Cross refers to this experience as being able to live with a "freedom of Spirit" in which one "practices the love of God" and finds new joy in both earthly and heavenly things (1.13.12; 2.9.1). A new sense of wholeness may be achieved, and obstacles and challenges encountered are now faced with strength and hope, with patience and perseverance. This experience can be recognized in the stories of the participants—when they speak about their successes and settlement in the new country they express feelings of gratitude and confidence. Even though gratitude is expressed to the people who helped them, the recipient of their gratitude is God. The same goes for their sense of confidence: God is the one who accomplishes things, and who is the source of their strength.

Concluding Remarks

Abandonment,[81] vulnerability, and transformation should be seen as interpretive keys for explaining God's transformative presence when migrants negotiate the loss of what was known while also negotiating life in a new society, as well as for explaining how this transformation empowers the participants to cope and adapt themselves as their new identities emerge.

In the case of African Catholic immigrants to the U.S., the observation that their experience seems to differ from other African immigrant experiences deserves more attention. Regardless of whether they were able to find a more welcoming and vibrant faith community, their journey of transformation seems to be more solitary than that of other immigrants, especially African immigrants in the African-led Christian communities described by Biney and Adogame.[82]

I surmise that taking a closer look at both the experience of the loss of the joyful and abundant life[83] that is such an important part of African spirituality, and the impossibility of Catholic communities offering African immigrants a true spiritual home in which all dimensions of an African spirituality can be fully expressed, could offer deeper insights into the matters considered in this chapter. It would also be interesting to consider the implications of the fact that, rather than seeking recourse in rituals rooted in traditional African "belief in the reality of the supramundane" (composed of spirits, ancestors, lesser gods, and God as the ultimate divine), Catholic African immigrants develop an intensified individual relationship with God as their coping strategy.[84]

---

81. This article was written when the research was still in progress. In the continued correlation between the narratives of the African migrants and the John of the Cross narrative of *The Dark Night* it became clear that both dimensions of "abandonment" function in attaining "poverty of spirit" and "freedom of spirit." The conclusion of the research is that "vulnerability," "spiritual humility," and "God's transformative agency" are the key concepts that explain the dynamics of the process of transformation in the experience of migration. See van Gaal, *Migrant Spirituality*.

82. Biney, *From Africa to America*; and Adogame, *African Christian Diaspora*.

83. Ter Haar, "Ghanaians in the Netherlands," 321–27.

84. Adogame, *African Christian Diaspora*, 86.

Bibliography

Adogame, Afe. *The African Christian Diaspora: New Currents and Emerging Trends in World Christianity*. London: Bloomsbury, 2013.

Biney, Moses. *From Africa to America: Religion and Adaptation among Ghanaian Immigrants in New York*. New York: New York University Press, 2011.

Blommestijn, Hein, Jos Huls, and Kees Waaijman. *The Footprints of Love: John of the Cross as Guide in the Wilderness*. Leuven: Peeters, 2000.

Boeije, Hennie. *Analysis in Qualitative Research*. Los Angeles: Sage, 2010.

Campese, Gioacchino. "Theologies of Migration: Present and Future Perspectives." In *Migration als Ort der Theologie*, edited by Tobias Keßler, 167–88. Regensburg: Pustet, 2014.

Castillo Guerra, Jorge E. "From the Faith and Life of a Migrant to a Theology of Migration and Intercultural *Convivencia*." In *Migration as a Sign of the Times: Towards a Theology of Migration*, edited by Judith Gruber and Sigrid Rettenbacher, 107–29. Leiden: Brill, 2015.

———. "Naar een theologie van de migratie: Context, perspectieven en thematiek." *Tijdschrift voor Theologie* 44.3 (2004): 241–58.

———. "Theologie der Migration: Menschliche Mobilität und theologische Transformation." In *Migration als Ort der Theologie*, edited by Tobias Keßler, 115–45. Regensburg: Pustet, 2014.

Castles, Stephen, Hein de Haas, and Mark J. Miller. *The Age of Migration: International Population Movements in the Modern World*. 5th ed. New York: Palgrave/Macmillan, 2014.

Charmaz, Kathy. *Constructing Grounded Theory: A Practical Guide through Qualitative Analysis*. Los Angeles: Sage, 2006.

The Community of St. Matthew: Rich in Tradition, United in Mission, Blessed with Diversity—Jubilee Year 1999: 1949–1999. Baltimore, MD: Uptown Press, 1999.

Connery, William. "Point of Entry: Baltimore, the Other Ellis Island." http://www.baltimoremd.com.

Connor, Phillip. *Immigrant Faith: Patterns of Immigrant Religion in the United States, Canada, and Western Europe*. New York: New York University Press, 2014.

Corbin, Juliet, and Anselm Strauss. *Basics of Qualitative Research*. 3rd ed. Los Angeles: Sage, 2008.

Cruz, Gemma Tulud. *Into the Deep: A Theological Exploration of the Struggle of Filipina Domestic Workers in Hong Kong*. Manila, Philippines: UST Publishing House, 2006.

———. *Toward a Theology of Migration: Social Justice and Religious Experience*. New York: Palgrave Macmillan, 2014.

FitzGerald, Constance, OCD. "Impasse and Dark Night." In *Living with Apocalypse*, edited by Tilden H. Edwards, 93–116. San Francisco: Harper & Row, 1984.

Groody, Daniel G. *Border of Death, Valley of Life: An Immigrant Journey of Heart and Spirit*. Lanham, MD: Rowman & Littlefield, 2002.

———. "The Spirituality of Migrants: Mapping an Inner Geography." In *Contemporary Issues of Migration and Theology*, edited by Elaine Padilla and Peter C. Phan, 139–56. New York: Palgrave Macmillan, 2013.

Haar, Gerrie ter. "The Religious Dimension in Migration and Its Relation to Development: The Case of Ghanaians in the Netherlands." In *At Home in the World? International Migration and Development in Contemporary Ghana and West Africa*, edited by Takyiwaa Manuh, 313–30. Legon/Accra: Sub-Saharan Publishers, 2005.

John of the Cross. *The Collected Works of St. John of the Cross*. Translated by Kieran Kavanaugh, OCD, and Otilio Rodriguez, OCD. Washington, DC: ICS Publications, 1991.

Keul, Hildegund. "The Venture of Vulnerability: Christological Engravings on Disturbing Questions about Migration." In *Migration as a Sign of the Times: Towards a Theology of Migration*, edited by Judith Gruber and Sigrid Rettenbacher, 167–90. Leiden: Brill, 2015.

Levitt, Peggy, and B. Nadya Jaworksy. "Transnational Migration Studies: Past Developments and Future Trends." *Annual Review of Sociology* 33 (2007): 129–56.

Office of Management and Budget. "1997 Revisions to the Standards for the Classification of Federal Data on Race and Ethnicity." *Federal Register* 62, no. 210 (October 1997).

Olupona, Jacob K., and Regina Gemignani. *African Immigrant Religions in America*. New York: New York University Press, 2007.

Phan, Peter C. "The Experience of Migration as Source of Intercultural Theology." In *Contemporary Issues* of Migration and Theology, edited by Elaine Padilla and Peter C. Phan, 179–209. New York: Palgrave Macmillan, 2013.

Phiri, Isabel Apawo, and Sarojini Nadar. African Women, Religion, and Health: Essays in Honor of Mercy Amba Ewudziw Oduyoye. Maryknoll, NY: Orbis Books, 2006.

Pietila, Antero. Not in My Neighborhood: How Bigotry Shaped a Great American City. Chicago: Ivan R. Dee, 2010.

Polak, Regina. "Migration as a Sign of the Times." In Migration as a Sign of the Times: Towards a Theology of Migration, edited by Judith Gruber and Sigrid Rettenbacher, 47–78. Leiden: Brill, 2015.

Pontifical Council for the Pastoral Care for Migrants and Itinerant People. The Love of Christ towards Migrants—Erga Migrantes Caritas Christi. Vatican City: Libreria Editrice Vaticana, 2004.

Rastogi, Sonya, Tallese D. Johnson, Elizabeth M. Hoeffel, and Malcolm P. Drewery Jr. The Black Population, 2010: Census Briefs 2010. Washington, DC: U.S. Department of Commerce, 2011.

Saint John Neumann Vicariate. Parish Planning Data Executive Summary—St. Matthew-1305—Metro East Region. Based on the Annual Consolidated Report FY 2015 & Parish Planning Survey for the "Be Missionary Disciples" planning process. Report generated on 04/06/2016. https://bemissionarydisciples.org/planning/pastoral-planning-tools/.

Schreiter, Robert. "Partizipation und Liminalität: Liturgie mit Migranten." Theologie der Gegenwart 57.2 (2014): 82–94.

Vatican Council II. Gaudium et Spes [Pastoral Constitution on the Church in the Modern World]. Vatican City: Libreria Editrice Vaticana, 1965. www.vatican.va.

Versteegen, Trees. Geleefde Genade: Een bijdrage aan de theologie van genade vanuit ervaringen van katholieke vrouwen. Gorinchem: Theologische Uitgeverij Narratio, 2013.

United States Census Bureau Quick Facts: Baltimore City, Maryland (county), https://www.census.gov/quickfacts/fact/table/baltimorecitymarylandcounty/AGE29521. Accessed November 27, 2018.

Waaijman, Kees. Spirituality: Forms, Foundations, Methods. Leuven: Peeters, 2002.

Yeip, Randy. "Baltimore's Demographic Divide." Wall Street Journal Graphics, May 1, 2015. http://graphics.wsj.com/baltimore-demographics.

Suggested Reading

Adogame, Afe. The African Christian Diaspora: New Currents and Emerging Trends in World Christianity. London: Bloomsbury, 2013.

Clark, Mary Ann. Then We'll Sing a New Song: African Influence on America's Religious Landscape. Lanham, MD: Rowman & Littlefield, 2012.

Connor, Phillip. Immigrant Faith: Patterns of Immigrant Religion in the United States, Canada, and Western Europe. New York: New York University Press, 2014.

Gruber, Judith, and Sigrid Rettenbacher, eds. Migration as a Sign of the Times: Towards a Theology of Migration. Leiden: Brill, 2015.

Olupona, Jacob K., and Regina Gemignani. African Immigrant Religions in America. New York: New York University Press, 2007.

Phan, Peter C., and Elaine Padilla. Contemporary Issues of Migration and Theology. New York: Palgrave Macmillan, 2013.

van Gaal, Dorris. Migrant Spirituality: Correlating the Narratives of African Migrants to the USA and the Dark Night of John of the Cross. Zurich: LIT Verlag, 2021.

Key Words
faith
identity
liminality
migration (emigration, immigration, migration)
migration theology
spirituality
spirituality studies
transformation

Inculturating the Faith in Africa: History, Context, and Debates

Florence Adetoun Oso, EHJ

This chapter focuses on the process of inculturation in African Catholicism. I will look at the history of the development of inculturation in the African church and the context in which it is being carried out. In the discussion I describe various historical attempts that have been made to contextualize the faith and evaluate how much has been achieved by the process of inculturation in Africa. I also present a number of important realities facing the continent, including the dichotomy between Christian principles and cultural realities, the shallowness of the faith of many Africans, and certain syncretistic practices that are relevant to inculturating the faith. I defend the proposition that true inculturation is not possible without an indigenous African theology. I conclude that although much has been achieved toward inculturating the Christian faith in Africa, there is still much to do to create a truly African Catholic Church.

The cultural realities of Africa pose a challenge to the faith of many African people and to the African church. Though much adaptation has been accomplished in the area of liturgy, including in hymns, vestments, musical instruments, and generally in modes of worship, to reflect the rich elements of African culture, little is being done in the areas of catechetics, sacraments, symbols, concepts, and terms in order to render the faith at home in Africa. The Christian faith is still perceived by many Africans as foreign, and consequently they oscillate like a pendulum between Christian and indigenous cultural practices. The crises of faith and lack of commitment of many African people to Christianity seem to be a direct consequence of the failure on the part of the missionaries to present the faith in ways that answer people's questions. This explains why many African people instinctively return to their traditional practices for answers in times of crises. The faith contexts of Africa reveal an urgent necessity for dialogue between the faith and African culture in such a way that the faith becomes the culture, fully accepted and faithfully lived by African people.

In 1659, in the early days of the missionary enterprise, the Congregation for the Evangelization of Peoples, formerly called the *Sacra Congregatio de Propaganda Fide*, instructed a group of missionaries headed for China as follows: "Do not waste your zeal or your powers of persuasion in getting these people to change their rites unless these be very obviously opposed to faith and morals, for what could be more ridiculous than to import France, Spain, Italy or any other part of Europe into China."[1] What this means should be clear to all: if the customs that are found among the African people are not obviously opposed to morals and faith, the church must protect and promote them. The missionaries were not to destroy indigenous customs and replace them with customs from their own countries; in other words, they were not to engage in cultural domination.

Even though the overall cultural context of

---

1. Flanagan, *New Missionary Era*, 38.

Africa is fairly homogeneous, the continent features many different indigenous beliefs and practices, thereby revealing a certain complexity of cultural expression.[2] Africa is the second largest continent in area, covering about one-fifth of the total land surface of the earth, but a sufficiently encompassing definition of Africa would transcend geographical location and nationality. As a consequence of the forces of history and migration, Africa is present in Europe, in America, and in Asia. It is unquestionable that the forces of slavery extended the boundaries of Africa to these other continents, and all Africans, irrespective of their geographical location, share a common ancestry.[3] The idea of Africa also transcends localized historical-cultural realities. There is the Africa that was part of the Roman Empire, and the Africa of Nubia and Ethiopia with its own distinctive political and cultural history, which is different from that of sub-Saharan Africa.

When we talk of the church in Africa, we are talking about two different things: first, the ancient church of Africa, whose origins go back to apostolic times and which is traditionally associated with the teaching and name of St. Mark the Evangelist and with great doctors and theologians like Origen, St. Athanasius, St. Cyprian, St. Augustine, and many more. The second is the modern African church that came about as a result of evangelization efforts begun in the nineteenth century.

This chapter will refer both to African Christianity and to African Catholicism. By African Christianity, I do not mean a separate form of Christianity, but a Christianity in light of the African faith, which suggests the idea of inculturation. African Catholicism implies the manner and ways in which the Catholic faith is being lived in Africa. It involves an assimilation of the traditions and concepts of African tribal religions into Catholic ceremonies and worship; it is the Catholic faith with an African accent.

Toward a Definition of Inculturation

Many definitions of inculturation have been offered, but I will consider only a few that speak directly to the faith contexts of African people. For Aylward Shorter, inculturation means "the on-going dialogue between faith and culture or cultures. . . . It is the creative and dynamic relationship between the Christian message and a culture or cultures."[4] Another definition holds that inculturation is "the incarnation of Christian life and of the Christian message in a particular cultural context, in such a way that this experience not only finds expression through elements proper to the culture in question . . . but become[s] a principle that animates, directs and unifies the culture, transforming it and remaking it so as to bring about a new creation."[5] Inculturation has its source in the incarnation of Christ the Lord: "And the word became flesh and dwelt among us" (John 1:14). "Incarnation" here also refers to the insertion, planting, or bringing into being of the Christian faith.

Pope St. John Paul II used the word "inculturation" to express "the incarnation of the Gospel in native cultures and also the introduction of these cultures into the life of the Church."[6] Echoing the Extraordinary Synod for the Twentieth Anniversary of the Closing of the Second Vatican Council, he defines inculturation as the "intimate transformation of . . . authentic cultural values by their integration into Christianity and the implantation of Christianity into different human cultures."[7]

The elements included in inculturation theologies vary, but here we identify four reflected in the above definitions of inculturation: universality, diversity, mutual disclosure and dialogue, and the creative reinterpretation of both gospel and culture. Shorter's definition above describes a creative ongoing conversation between the Christian message and the culture it is addressing, suggesting cultural pluralism and legitimizing diversity as

---

2. Tetteh, *What Is Africa?*
3. Tetteh, *What Is Africa?*
4. Shorter, *Towards a Theology of Inculturation*, 1.
5. Arrupe, "Letter to the Whole Society on Inculturation," 172–81.
6. Pope John Paul II, encyclical *Slavorum Apostoli* (June 2, 1985) §21.
7. Pope John Paul II, *Extra-Ordinary Synod* (December 7, 1985), 52.

opposed to uniformity. The second definition above from Fr. Pedro Arrupe also expresses a deep sense of creativity in the harmonization of two cultures, leading to an effective result, while Pope John Paul II's definition describes a mutual exchange between the Christian faith and culture that results in each influencing the other. Taken together, the three definitions presuppose universality, which is not a bland uniformity that disregards the uniqueness of a people and their context. They therefore promote a rendering of the faith that is true and intelligible not only in one part but in every part of the universal church. The second and third definitions apply the word "incarnation," a profound theological term, to the process of inculturation. These three definitions comprehensively capture the task that is expected of the African church if it hopes to incarnate the Christian faith on the continent.

The term "inculturation" was first employed by ecclesiastical thinkers only about sixty years ago. The French theologian Joseph Masson coined the term in 1962 when he called attention to the "need for a Catholicism that is inculturated in a pluriform manner."[8] G. L. Barney used the term in 1973 when he asserted that the supracultural components of the gospel "should neither be lost nor distorted but rather secured and interpreted clearly through the guidance of the Holy Spirit, in 'inculturating' them into the new culture."[9] The term surfaced in the documents of the Second Vatican Council in statements that the incarnation of Our Lord and Savior Jesus Christ needed both a human culture and a divine culture to make it effective. The process of incarnation involves the sower, the seed, and the soil—the sower is God the Father, the creator of heaven and earth. The seed is Christ the Incarnate Word, and the soil is the Jewish people. The action of the Word becoming flesh and dwelling among us is called incarnation; hence, Christ is said to be the true source of every inculturation. In addition, Pope John Paul II declared in 1979 that inculturation "expresses very well one factor of the great mystery of the Incarnation."[10]

Though the term has only recently appeared in official documents of the church, the reality it refers to is as old as the church itself, and in some parts of Africa the penetration of the gospel into the culture is as old as the history of evangelization on the continent. Inculturation is oriented in two different historical directions: the history of missions and the African response they elicited; and the appropriation of both by contemporary African theologians.

It is important to note that, when we talk of inculturation in Africa, it is centered on Christ and the Christian religion—Christ, not God, is what the missionaries brought to Africa: the African peoples already knew and worshiped God before Christianity came. For this reason, the challenge of inculturation in Africa is to discover an authentic and meaningful African face of Jesus Christ that will respond to the questions posed by Africans.

Developments in Faith and Culture in Africa Leading to Developments in the Concept of Inculturation

The concept of inculturation has undergone a number of developments over the years. We have already made reference to the fact that inculturation began with the incarnation. Jesus himself is the originator, the source, the cause, and the inspiration of inculturation, which means that it is nothing more or less than accepting Christ in your own way and passing him on to others. A little window into how the concept of inculturation has developed over the years will better introduce us to some of the challenges facing the inculturation of the faith in Africa.

In the early church, inculturation of the faith was based on a pedagogical methodology, not on actual Christian practice. The early fathers of the church taught the Christian religion in accordance with the religious and philosophical thinking of their age, and even though they have left a wonderful legacy of their teaching in their writings, their

---

8. Chupungco, *Liturgical Inculturation*, 337.
9. Barney, *Supracultural and the Cultural*, quoted in Chupungco, *Liturgical Inculturation*, 25.
10. Pope John Paul II, post-synodal apostolic exhortation *Catechesis Tradendae* §53. The "factor" identified by the pope is the church's work of catechesis.

method was insufficient to truly inculturate the faith.

Beginning in the fifteenth century, when missionaries began to go all over the world, the pedagogical method gave way to a method of imposition of the faith. The missionary methodology was to tell people receiving their message how to do things: how to pray, how to say "I am sorry," and many other things. People were simply given instructions and had to obey. Africans resented many of the changes made by missionaries as foreign impositions.[11]

As a result of Vatican II, imposition gave way to the translation of sacred and ecclesiastical documents into African languages as the primary means of inculturation.[12] The council had allowed the translation of important Latin texts into the vernacular, which led to African people having access to prayers, hymns, catechetical instruction, and the Bible in various African languages, not just English or French; this was accomplished, however, with little contribution from Africans themselves.[13]

The council also opened the door to "adaptation," making it possible for all cultures to truly embrace Christ; in the case of Africa, it became thinkable that the African church might be able to have its own distinct liturgical rites and canon law like the Eastern Catholic churches.[14] The liturgical reforms called for by the council included the creation and use of liturgies adapted to every culture.[15] In the wake of the council, beliefs, rites, symbols, gestures, and institutional forms present in African culture and traditional religion that were similar to those of the Christian faith were employed in order to create stepping-stones toward a better understanding of the Christian faith. This adaptation was mostly carried out by converts to Christianity in the process of accepting the new religion and reconciling it with inherited beliefs and practices. Soon, however, it became clear that adaptation is sometimes worse than imposition. Adaptation implies conforming to somebody's idea and making it your own; it was therefore displaced by the method of inculturation. Adaptation remains, however, a component of the broader process of inculturation.

The concept of "indigenization" attempts to solve the problems posed by other means of inserting the faith into a culture. When we say something is indigenous, it means that it comes from the people. There are indigenous ways of praying, preaching, and explaining the sacrament of the Eucharist; these ways originate with the people engaged in these things and are not taken from another people. However, the concept of indigenization should be used with caution because it implies that culture does not change, that it remains static, when in fact it is a dynamic phenomenon that is always changing. There is no culture that is not continuously borrowing from other cultures, and there is no culture whose traits are solely generated from within in the absence of any external influences. Some of the traits of every culture will eventually disappear.

Nor does substituting "Africanization" for indigenization provide a solution, because the term "Africanization" carries with it racial overtones: it involves a project that seeks to restore Africa to itself. For Africanization to be achieved, the history of African dislocation must be evoked and the entire historical, Western missionary system

---

11. Baur, *2000 Years of Christianity in Africa*, 449.

12. Sanneh, *Translating the Message*, 3. Sanneh underlines the meaning and importance of translation for the relationship between gospel and culture. He describes translation as the intimate and articulate expression of culture, taking it beyond the specialized technical bounds of literal textual work.

13. Baur, *2000 Years of Christianity in Africa*, 74.

14. Vatican Council II, Decree on Eastern Catholic Churches (*Orientalium Ecclesiarum*) (1964) §6. "All members of the Eastern Church should be firmly convinced that they can and ought to preserve their own legitimate liturgical rites and ways of life, and that changes are to be introduced only to forward their own organic development. . . . they are to aim always at a more perfect knowledge and practice of their faith." Beal and Coriden, *New Commentary on the Code of Canon Law*, 27. The Code of Canons of the Eastern churches was promulgated in 1990 and took effect in 1991.

15. Vatican Council II, Constitution on the Sacred Liturgy (*Sacrosanctum Concilium*) (1963) §§37–40.

must be challenged, including the process of transmitting the Christian faith to Africans that was embedded in a culture of conquest, and that, among other things, dismissed the African worldview and system of knowledge as irrelevant and unnecessary to achieving the true salvation of the African subject.

The insufficiency of all of the above concepts led African theologians to adopt the new concept of "contextualization." There are many definitions of contextualization: David Bosch defines it as the church being "incarnated in the life of the recipients"[16] of the Christian faith. L. Luzbetak defines it as the process by which a local community integrates the gospel message with real-life contexts, blending text and context into a single reality, intended for us by God, called "Christian living."[17] Stephen B. Bevans states that contextualization includes everything that is implied in indigenization but that it also includes contemporary secularism, technology, and the struggle for human justice.[18] These three definitions make clear that contextualization means bringing the message of Christ to bear on people's actual situations, but Bosch's is the best definition because it is broad and relates to inculturation (through incarnation).[19]

Contextualization comes with two particular problems. First, the context always has a history: we cannot forget about the past because it is very important for understanding the present. In addition, contextualization widens the scope of the life of the people into which the gospel message is integrated to anything that has to do with the context in which the Christian faith is set, including the political, the economic, and the cultural, while inculturation limits the scope of peoples' lives to the culture alone. The problem with the breadth of the concept of inculturation is that it makes it difficult to address in a research study.[20]

At this time in history, there is no doubt that, as stated by John Paul II, the best opportunity to make the faith our own in Africa is to proceed on the basis of inculturation.[21]

The Historical Development of Inculturation in Africa

The disciples of Christ were first called Christians in Antioch (see Acts 11:26), and the believers who gathered there were largely not Jewish. Cultural adaptation of the faith was necessary in order to accommodate these non-Jewish Christians (see Acts 15). As it spread from Jerusalem to Antioch and from Antioch to Rome, the Christian religion was enriched by the various cultures it encountered. Christianity's spread into Europe involved a passage from the Jewish to the Greek to the Latin cultures. In some of the ancient churches of Africa, including Egypt, which were located in colonies of the Roman Empire, the faith was inculturated in the process of evangelization. Thus, from the beginnings of the church, the cultural element became a medium for the transmission of the gospel message.[22] Many liturgical and other Christian texts were translated into local languages; for example, the Bible was translated into the Sahidic dialect of upper Egypt. In 330 CE, Athanasius preached in the Coptic language, even in Alexandria. In Ethiopia, the monasteries were centers of the faith and exhibited liturgical creativity of a local character; this led to the adoption of a local ecclesiastical language that contributed to the deep foundations of the Christian faith in that country. The acceptance of the gospel message into the local cultural real-

---

16. Bosch, *Transforming Mission*, 421.
17. Luzbetak, *Church and Cultures*, 134.
18. Bevans, *Models of Contextual Theology*, 21.
19. Bosch, *Transforming Mission*, 421.
20. Bosch, *Transforming Mission*, 420–21.
21. Pope John Paul II preferred "inculturation" because of how it incorporates one aspect of the incarnation: "The term 'acculturation' or 'inculturation' may be a neologism, but it expresses very well one factor of the great mystery of the Incarnation" (*Catechesis Tradendae* §53).
22. Lewis, *Middle East*, chap. 13. With the conversion of the Egyptians to Christianity, the Coptic language became the language of Christian Egypt under Roman and later under Byzantine rule.

ity resulted in the birth of the Ethiopic and Coptic churches.²³ The fact that the gospel was transmitted through the cultures of Egypt and Ethiopia enabled their churches to resist the Muslim assault from the seventh to the fifteenth centuries.²⁴ While the church in Egypt and Ethiopia grafted the faith onto local cultural elements, the other churches of North Africa did not; instead, in transmitting the faith they held fast to the Latin culture and language. This failure to indigenize the faith in much of North Africa meant that the Berbers were untouched by the Christian faith, and when the Muslims first launched attacks in the seventh century, Christianity in this part of Africa was almost completely wiped out.²⁵

During the age of patristic creativity in Africa, led especially by fathers of the church like Tertullian, Hippolytus, and Ambrose, inculturation came about through integrating into the faith the rites and linguistic expressions, religious or otherwise, of the contemporary societies. Local rites were the basis of certain liturgical and sacramental practices, including the baptismal anointing, the giving of the cup of milk and honey, and the foot washing of neophytes. These local rites were reinterpreted through a system of biblical topology and were added on to the core of certain liturgical rites, developing the shape of the liturgy. In this way, the rite of baptism developed from the apostolic "washing in water with the word" to an elaborate liturgical celebration that included prebaptismal anointing, an act of renunciation (recited facing west), a profession of faith (recited facing east), the blessing of baptismal water, and postbaptismal rites like foot washing, anointing with chrism, the donning of certain clothing, and the presentation of a lighted candle to the baptized; these are all the result of cultural accretions.²⁶

Hundreds of years later, it became necessary to inculturate the faith in mission territories. Afonso reigned between 1506 and 1543 as the second Christian king of the Congo, and before his conversion to Christianity he was the guardian of the ancestors' holy water. He attempted to continue the cult of ancestors in a Christian way by building a church over the tombs of his forefathers.²⁷ He also had a great desire to establish an indigenous clergy and hierarchy. To effect this, he sent various groups of young people from his kingdom to study in religious houses in Lisbon; among these was his own son, who eventually became the first person to be ordained a priest and then bishop in sub-Saharan Africa.²⁸ The Congolese developed an understanding of the Christian cult by locating it within the context of Nkadi Mpemba, the supreme being and the sky spirit in their traditional belief.²⁹ In addition, the Antonian movement that existed in the kingdom of the Congo in the late seventeenth century attempted to combine Christianity and indigenous religion. The aim of this syncretistic movement was to create a truly Congolese religion, a church of Congolese saints. The leader of this movement, Dona Beatriz Kimpa Vita, was accused of heresy and of being possessed by the devil and was burned to death in accordance with the church's practices in Europe at that time.³⁰ Nev-

---

23. Karotemprel, *Following Christ in Mission,* 278; and Lewis, *Middle East.*
24. Karotemprel, *Following Christ in Mission.*
25. According to Zabbon Nthamburi, "The rise of Islam in the seventh century challenged the existence of Christianity in North Africa.... Within a period of one hundred years after the prophet's death, Islam had overtaken North African Christianity.... The rapid disappearance of the Church in North Africa was due to its not having thoroughly taken root in the Berber population" ("Towards Indigenization of Christianity in Africa," 112).
26. Chupungco, *Liturgical Inculturation,* 335.
27. Baur, *2000 Years of Christianity in Africa,* 58.
28. Baur, *2000 Years of Christianity in Africa,* 59.
29. Cf. Baur, *2000 Years of Christianity in Africa,* 71.
30. The successful inculturation that occurred over a long period in the Democratic Republic of the Congo and that resulted in the Zairean Rite is in some ways similar to the Antonian movement in its desire to create a truly Congolese religion (Ibeka, *Zairian Liturgy as a Paradigm for African Liturgical Inculturation,* 6). This inculturation was promoted by the bishops of the Congo even before the Second Vatican Council. The Bishops' Conference of Zaire encouraged the development of Christian philosophy and theology in Africa, which resulted

ertheless, Dona Beatriz is still venerated in the Congo as a second Joan of Arc.[31] Charles Nyamiti cited the Antonian movement and other evidence to support his argument that inculturation was effected to some degree from the very beginnings of Christianity in much of Black Africa, but often unconsciously and unsystematically.[32]

The process of inculturation in its modern form in sub-Saharan Africa began in the 1960s. Most African nations gained their independence beginning in this decade, and prior to this time, Africa had very few indigenous bishops—most of the first generation of African bishops were ordained in the 1960s.[33] Political independence generated the need for a certain religious independence, which was termed "Ethiopianism"[34] and expressed the relationship between Christian activity and the rise of a nationalistic awareness and cultural identity that accompanied the struggle for independence. According to Ogbu Kalu, Ethiopianism, which had many strands but was rooted in the Bible—specifically Psalm 68:31, a passage that has inspired many generations of Africans, who have freely refashioned it—fueled black nationalism.[35] Politically, Ethiopianism was a movement that sought freedom for Africans, while religiously it tended to support church governance by Africans. For this reason, some have claimed that inculturation is the product of an inferiority complex vis-à-vis the West.[36] The Ethiopianism movement, with its emphasis on nationalistic awareness and cultural identity, led to the emergence of the African Independent Churches (AICs) from their roots in the established churches. The AICs have become one of the most important sources for contextualizing Christianity—they are thriving and growing and are good examples of the dynamism, creativity, and spirituality of the African people.

The modern process of inculturation began with indigenization of church leaders, including the consecration of some African bishops, which was coupled with an explosion in African vocations. The process involved some liturgical adaptations, including hymns being sung in local languages with African tunes. Liturgy has often played a key role in the process of inculturation because, according to John Baur, the foreignness of the Christian faith was most obvious in the European rites and music of the Mass.[37] Some missionaries, together with some pious Africans for whom the foreign liturgy had become a sacred tradition, fought against liturgical innovations; for example, they opposed the use of African musical instruments, especially the drum, because they were used in traditional African religion. In addition, they considered the African melodies and dances improper. These adaptations were sincerely undertaken but were sometimes superficial—some of the traditional African elements that were included, for example, traditional melodies, had previously begun to fade from African culture. With time, however, these adaptations contributed to Christianity's spread throughout Africa.

In 1955, a process was officially initiated at a meeting of theologians in Accra, Ghana, to develop an African theology. In 1960, the necessity and possibility of an African theology was the subject of debate in the faculty of theology at the Louvanium University at Kinshasa.[38] The development of such a theology led some African intellectuals to call on African churches to use only native languages in proclaiming the gospel in Africa.[39] The Second

---

in the success of the Congolese church in making the Christian faith at home in the country. See Baur, *2000 Years of Christianity in Africa*, 72.

31. Baur, *2000 Years of Christianity in Africa*, 72.
32. Vahakangas, *In Search of Foundations for African Catholicism*, 19.
33. Baur, *2000 Years of Christianity in Africa*, 451.
34. Duncan, "Ethiopianism in Pan-African Perspective," 199. "Ethiopianism" became a generic term to describe the whole range of the efforts of Black Africans to improve their religious, educational, and political status.
35. Kalu, *Ethiopianism in African Christianity*, 264.
36. Stinton, *African Theology on the Way*, 4.
37. Baur, *2000 Years of Christianity in Africa*, 448.
38. Baur, *2000 Years of Christianity in Africa*, 431.
39. Baur, *2000 Years of Christianity in Africa*, 431.

Vatican Council insisted on a plurality of theologies; this approach was approved by Pope Paul VI at the inauguration of the Symposium of Episcopal Conference of Africa and Madagascar (SECAM) in Kampala in 1969.[40]

The process of inculturation was initiated in the 1960s, but because the majority of mission personnel were still foreigners, the structures of the Western churches remained unchanged, and foreign missionaries continued to set the church's pastoral policies. This situation led to a growing unease within the African church, which resulted in the "Moratorium Declaration" of the All-Africa Conference of Churches and the statement of the African episcopate at the Fourth Roman Synod of Bishops, both of which came out in 1974. These documents challenged and urged all the local churches in Africa to engage in a process of self-definition and the articulation of a clear identity. This project focused on African theology, liturgical rites, and church structures. Finally, the 1994 Synod of Bishops officially approved the movement and process of inculturation.[41]

The advent of missionary Christianity in Africa resulted in a gradual decline of the indigenous African culture. Colonialism denied Africans their own proper civilization and branded their cultural traditions as barbaric. Missionaries saw Africa as a *tabula rasa*, which created a cultural vacuum for the African Christian. For this reason, the birth of an authentic African Christianity must be closely connected to a renaissance of African cultures.[42]

Criticism of the missionary enterprise's disregard for African culture is reflected in the first chapter of Josiah Young's book *Black and African Theologies: Siblings or Distant Cousins?* Young asserts that (and cites other authors to the effect that) colonialism gave missionaries sanction to systematically undermine African culture and traditions, and that their actions were motivated by white supremacist views that held sway in Europe during the colonial era.[43] Young mentions Edward Fashole-Luke's reference to Edward Blyden and James Johnson, who were both in the vanguard of the development of African nationalism, and how they resisted attempts to impose Western cultural values on African Christians. Fashole-Luke reported Desmond Tutu's assertion about the missionaries' attitude toward African culture that "most . . . missionaries believed the African way of life is thoroughly uncivilized and . . . irredeemably heathen, therefore the missionaries attempted to demolish the African past."[44]

This missionary attitude may at first be perceived as a negative element, but I think we should begin to see it as something positive, because it is a sign that Africa has come of age. The missionaries sent to Africa cannot be blamed for their mistakes because they were captives of a European theological ideology that had forgotten its own history and cultural evolution, but that saw itself as universally valid. What has been the African Christian response to the depredations of, and cultural alienation wrought by, the missions and colonization? One response has been inculturation, which has occurred in a postcolonial context.[45]

The African Context

Africa has had her share of troubles throughout history and continues to face serious challenges today. The present situation in Africa—religious, cultural, social, economic, and political—indeed calls for reconciliation, justice, and peace. The

---

40. Baur, *2000 Years of Christianity in Africa*, 432.
41. Pope John Paul II, post-synodal apostolic exhortation *Ecclesia in Africa* §59.
42. Baur, *2000 Years of Christianity in Africa*, 430.
43. See Young, "The Historical Background: Preludes to Black and African Theologies," chap. 1 in *Black and African Theologies*, 7–30; see 14–16 for Young's discussion of the views of a number of theologians. See also Onwubiko, *Theory and Practice of Inculturation*, 189. In his chapter titled "Christian Mission and the 'Hedgehog Trick' Theologians: Critique of Critics," Onwubiko describes how the earliest missionaries rejected African religion and disrespected African cultural institutions.
44. Fashole-Luke et al., eds., *Christianity in Independent Africa*, 365.
45. Antonio, *Inculturation and Postcolonial Discourse in African Theology*, 1.

negative influences of globalization are robbing Africa of her rich cultural and religious heritage, seeking to banish God from the lives of Africans. According to Jeremy Seabrook, globalization carries with it certain cultural baggage that exercises a profound influence on the lives of peoples everywhere. Globalization eclipses, or at least subordinates, all previous ways of responding to human need and of dealing with the vicissitudes of human life.[46] Kwame Yeboah buttresses this notion by noting that some cultures are being diluted and/or destroyed at the expense of others and that negative values are being spread all over the world with relative ease as cultures interact.[47] All of this has led to a continuing loss of cultural identity in Africa because the younger generation is fast assimilating Western culture and its secularizing tendencies. In short, Africa's experience of modernity has been one of imposition of alien modes of rationality—religious, political, and economic—first in the name of colonization, and now in the name of globalization.

We cannot overlook that certain aspects of the African reality make these problems worse. An inadequate formation in the Christian faith and in their own African culture has prepared rich soil for such negative influences. Africa is the poorest continent in the world.[48] A significant percentage of the world's poor people are Africans, living both on the continent and outside it, yet African leaders are among the richest as well as the most corrupt in the world. Out of the purported 795 million hungry people in the world as of 2015, 232.5 million of them are Africans living south of the Sahara.[49] Though Africa is rich in natural resources, too many Africans live in abject poverty, ravaged by wars, political unrest, tribal strife, religious crises, and corruption, often the victims of social injustice and plagued by pandemics of disease and ignorance.[50] A quick survey of the African continent shows an absence of stability in almost every sector of its societies—economic, political, judicial, social, and demographic. In Africa there are many scars in need of healing and many realities that call for reconciliation; there are many situations calling for justice and many troubled people longing for peace. The old scars left by fratricidal conflicts between ethnic groups (as in the case of the Rwandan genocide), the slave trade, and colonization remain, and unfortunately Africa continues to struggle with new forms of hatred, slavery, and colonization.

In the midst of all these ugly realities, there is, according to at least one scholar, great hope for the future of the continent. Dayo Olopade describes the reasons for an attitude of optimism about Africa's future. Her argument is that the continent has hidden strengths that have caused her to rethink her perception of it.[51]

One of these hidden strengths is Africa's vibrant religiosity; however, taking into account the number of Christians in Africa and the vitality of the African church, one begins to wonder why Christians have generally not been successful in effecting changes in the political, social, economic, and ethical life of African societies. This failure might be because of the absence on the continent of deeply rooted faith, or of a proper integration of the faith with the culture, or of an inadequate understanding of the potentially prophetic effect of Christianity. The problem may also have to do with the church: it offers many aspirational statements, and its theologians offer many reflections and arguments, but these are often unaccompanied by any serious effort to take practical action. Despite being aware of the fact that every deci-

---

46. Seabrook, "Localizing Cultures."
47. See Yeboah, *Impact of Globalization on the African Culture*, 8; Nsibambi, "Effects of Globalization on the State in Africa," 3.
48. Robinson, *Why Is Africa Poor?*, 2.
49. World Hunger Education Service, "Hunger Notes," www.worldhunger.org.
50. Pope Benedict XVI, post-synodal apostolic exhortation *Africae Munus* §9.
51. Olopade, *Bright Continent*, 5. Olopade argues that the continent needs to be seen and heard, not imagined and then dismissed. She maintains that the hidden strengths of the continent come to light in talking to real Africans and listening to their stories.

sion about economic and social life is taken in the political arena, Christians have not been able to effectively position themselves in the political life of the continent so that they can make a difference. Answering to Christian names does not make for Christian participation in national policy formulation.[52] Many Christians in Africa have not allowed their faith to permeate their social and political lives. They wear their Christian faith like a ceremonial coat on Sundays and hang it in the closet during the work week.

The question of people's dual affiliation with both Christianity and traditional African religion is another concern of the African church. It has often been suggested that the church and her sacraments remain foreign to the African experience. This is largely a result of the fact that the gospel in most parts of Africa is presented and interpreted in a theology clothed in words, concepts, and worldviews that are foreign and sometimes incomprehensible to the people. The sacraments too often seem like some kind of magic that does not deeply touch them; the liturgy is still structured around symbols that communicate very little to them. Most churches in Africa, with the exception of the Congolese church and a few other local churches, have not succeeded in inculturating the liturgy except with respect to the use of local hymns and musical instruments. The churches are filled on Sundays, the sacraments are celebrated daily, devotions are on the rise, local church leaders are solidly formed, and vocations to the clerical and religious life are plentiful; yet, despite all of this, the Christian faith is still far from being incarnated in Africa.

Syncretism presents a challenge to and danger for the process of inculturation and is generally seen as something negative. But could there be something positive in syncretism? Cawley Bolt answers this question in the affirmative; for him, a significant number of Africans interpret their religious way of being through the lens of African religion and culture, which offers many elements that Christianity can effectively incorporate. This was seen as syncretism by many missionaries, but for many Africans it is a legitimate way of deepening their understanding of Christianity and meeting their existential needs.[53] Nyamiti makes the reasonable argument that syncretism is an inevitable side effect of inculturation, but it is needed to achieve an inculturated Christianity[54] and is not a reason for African Christians to shy away from inculturation.

The image presented here of the African church is the result of Africa's encounter with the West, which has been both positive and negative, but overall probably more negative. Three damaging aspects of Africa's encounter with Europe are worth highlighting. The first has already been raised—it relates to the missionaries' and colonizers' negation of African identity, considering Africans to be *tabula rasa*, a people without an identity. The second was the European denial of the possibility of an African history; Europeans pretended that Africans had no history outside of the one that began with the discovery of their continent by the West. And the third relates to the European disregard for any culture that does not conform to its own.[55]

The bulk of the work being done in African theology lies in African contextual discourse because "the person who is dressed in other people's clothes is naked, and the person who is fed on other people's food is hungry."[56] This saying by K. A. Opoku pithily expresses the necessity that Christianity be inculturated in Africa. It is an obvious fact that Africa is geographically, historically, culturally, and mentally different from Europe, a fact that both the missionaries and colonizers ignored. Inculturation is certainly a postcolonial phenomenon originating out of Africa's confrontation with Europe over its negation of African difference. Inculturation in this sense is a reassertion of African memory.

The AICs are models of and signs of hope for the incarnation of a real African church that is desired

---

52. Kukah, *Church and the Politics of Social Responsibility*, 29–30.
53. Bolt, "Reluctant or Radical Revolution?," 248.
54. Nyamiti, "My Approach to African Theology," 21.
55. Mundimbe, *Tales of Faith*, 147–48.
56. Opoku, "Skinny but Imperishable Truth," 150.

by Africans. They cater to the spiritual needs of a vast number of Africans, and many Africans hope that one day they will be the national church of Africa.[57] Could the AICs be the ideal inculturation of the faith? Unfortunately, they also face problems, ranging from ethnic strife to a lack of theological clarity to an absence of organizational structure. The major problem, however, seems to be that the positive aspects of their theological tenets come with some negative ones, for example, their focus on the Old Testament, their acceptance of polygamy, and their acceptance of some patriarchal taboos.[58]

The inculturation process must be rooted in the present-day struggles of the African people. It is impossible for Africans to truly understand the Bible and church tradition unless theology takes full account of these struggles. The current situation in Africa is, in fact, an indispensable source of hermeneutical keys.[59]

Current Debates

The relationship between Christ and culture and the inculturation of Christianity in Africa have been the subjects of much debate. In this section, I identify some of the key issues in these debates related to inculturation theology and, more generally, African theology.

First, there is an ongoing debate among theologians as to how Christian theology can reflect the traditional ethos of a people and still remain orthodox. This debate is rooted in the distinction made by African theologians between theologies of adaptation and incarnation. Some theologians fear deviating from church orthodoxy, which causes them to favor theologies of adaptation. But these theologies do not allow the African church to deeply embed African culture into African theology. The bishops of Africa and Madagascar as well as some African theologians have rejected adaptation, but it continues to be the operative theology in Africa,[60] with some African theologians restricting inculturation to liturgical adaptation. Instead, the theologians who have rejected the superficiality of adaptation believe in the need for a theology that is truly indigenous at heart and focused on the experience of the African people. These theologians believe that liturgy is only one aspect of Christian life and that authentic inculturation should involve every aspect of African culture, life, and faith, uniting the socioanthropological and the spiritual. This debate leaves us with the question, How African is African theology? Some of the key voices in this debate are Kwesi Dickson, Ngindu Mushete, Aylward Shorter, F. Eboussi Boulaga, and John Mbiti.[61]

The second debate has to do with the nature of culture. It is clear that culture is a dynamic reality, not static but always changing. The process of inculturation must take account of this fact. What does the word "culture" mean to the present-day African? Which culture should Africa inculturate—incarnate—into Christianity? Nyamiti argues that a single pan-African culture can serve as the basis for inculturation of the faith,[62] but there is a question about whether this is possible on such a diverse continent. The key voices in this debate who believe it is possible to refer to one African culture are Charles Nyamiti, John Mbiti, Geoffrey Parrinder, and Dominique Zahan; key voices emphasizing the need to refer to plural African cultures are John Egbulefu, Mercy Oduyoye, Ralph Tanner, Benjamin Ray, and Aylward Shorter.

Closely related to the debate about culture is the question of whether African religion is plural or singular. Some African theologians opine that traditional African religions are a plural phenomenon because of differences among their cosmolo-

---

57. Baur, *2000 Years of Christianity in Africa*, 489.
58. Beyer, *New Christian Movements in West Africa*, 24–27.
59. Nyamiti, "My Approach to African Theology," 39.
60. See Pope Paul VI, post-synodal apostolic exhortation *Evangelii Nuntiandi* §20; Shorter, *African Christian Theology*, 150.
61. See Young, *Black and African Theologies*, 70.
62. Nyamiti, "My Approach to African Theology," 41.

gies and local differences. Others are of the opinion that, in spite of these variations, there is a certain unanimity of beliefs in traditional African religion and that it should be considered a unified system. Bolaji Idowu, John Mbiti, and Vincent Mulago are the chief contributors to this debate.[63]

Another debate concerns the development of African feminism, and specifically whether Black theology is not credible because it ignores the oppression of Black women. To the extent that African feminism is taken seriously by African theology, certain issues related to inculturation, like male chauvinism, women's roles and bodies, and women's new image of themselves need to be reexamined. Many African women theologians, including Mercy Oduyoye, Jacquelyn Grant, Barbara Smith, Theresa Hoover, and Pauli Murray have already offered reflections on these points, as has James Cone, a male theologian who supports their critique. Following Oduyoye's assertion that theology must accommodate women's new image of themselves, future research in African theology needs to grapple with a pan-African feminist theology.[64]

Another debate involves the relationship between Black theology and African theology. The debate centers on whether Black theology and African theology are in essence the same thing and on the relevance of North American Black theology for Africa. There is certainly a relationship between Black theology and African theology, and two groups of theologians are discussing the extent of their similarities and differences. These thinkers have noted that the two theologies are similar because both are of African origin and focus on traditional African religion, but they differ insofar as Black theology focuses on liberation while African theology focuses on indigenization. Historically, Black theology must be understood in the context of Black oppression in North America, while African theology is born out of the need for Africanization of the Christian faith. To this extent, their histories and discourses are radically different from each other. The key voices in this debate are John Mbiti, Harry Sawyerr, Edward Fashole-Luke, Desmond Tutu, James Cone, and Gayraud Wilmore.[65] A creative direction for the future development of African theology should focus on possible reciprocal contributions between the two theologies.

Inculturation is a response to the intercultural problematics created by the expansion of Christianity into Africa.[66] The pervasive presence of Christianity in Africa testifies to the success of the missionary enterprise, while the existence of the AICs is a sign that African traditions are being recovered by Africans themselves. But is there at present an "African church"? Many Africans have questioned the ends and aims of inculturation, while some African bishops and clerics are indifferent or outright opposed to the movement and process of inculturation.[67] For other Africans, the aim of inculturation is clear—to create a home among the African people[68] for the Christian faith, and to have a truly African church. According to Nyamiti, a truly African church would imply an African liturgical rite and an African Code of Canon Law.

---

63. Bolaji Idowu, *African Traditional Religion: A Definition* (Maryknoll, NY: Orbis Books, 1975); John Mbiti, *African Religions and Philosophy* (New York: Doubleday, 1970); John Mbiti, *Introduction to African Religion* (New York: Praeger, 1975); Vincent Mulago, *Un Visage Africaine du Christianisme* (Paris: Presence Africaine, 1962).

64. Kofi Appiah-Kubi and Sergio Torres, *African Theology en Route: Papers from the Pan African Conference of Third World Theologians, December 17–23, 1977, Accra, Ghana* (Maryknoll, NY: Orbis Books, 1979); quoted in Young, *Black and African Theologies*, 115.

65. Young, *Black and African Theologies*, chap. 4.

66. Mundimbe, *Tales of Faith*, ix.

67. Some are opposed to inculturation because of fears that it will create another, perhaps simpler or inferior, form of Christianity, while others oppose it out of fears of syncretism and possible schism with the Catholic Church. See Walligo et al., eds., *Inculturation*, 13.

68. A question can be raised about what it means to be an African. Although the issues raised by this question are beyond the scope of this chapter, its answer might provide a useful frame for the possibility of a discourse about African identity, culture, and history in general.

It would also mean a church that is no longer Latin but rather simply an African Catholic Church.[69] But even in the context of a truly African church, we must ask ourselves, Has the gospel questioned the heart of African cultures? Are African Christians truly converted? Have African Christians been able to express in preaching, worship, prayer, and writing their experience of salvation as Africans?

I agree that an African church deserves an African liturgy. Different rites are permitted for older churches, and this should be considered for Africa. The mother church may regard the African church as too young for this, but even if it is seen as "too young," it will with time mature. With respect to a separate Code of Canon Law, the church has made provision for the implementation of the universal law for particular churches as in the case of complementary norms (canon 455). Considering the African context, the African church should be allowed a separate canon law, which, of course, does not imply autonomy from Rome. These changes would bring to completion the process of inculturating the faith in Africa.

In his approach to inculturation, Nyamiti proposes that, in order to construct a genuine African theology, there is a need to rid it of all European influences, necessitating a return to the precolonial cultural situation in Africa. But, as Nyamiti asks, "Is it possible to return to an African past, which is undistorted by European contact?"[70] And, is it possible to have a culturally naked Christianity in dialogue with African culture? The absence of a true African theology is one of the great obstacles to a true process of inculturation because as long as "our philosophy is Western, our theology is Western, our prayers and prayer gestures are Western, our liturgy is Western, and the native priests and bishops are Western-educated and think and feel more or less in the Western way, then we are still miles away from the incarnation that the process of inculturation presupposes."[71]

Conclusion

What Africans are trying to do is to plant the Christian message and the Christian life into a given culture, a particular cultural context, and among particular peoples, by using elements proper to those cultures in such a way that an African Catholic Church can emerge. This authentic church would animate, unify, transform, guard, and purify African cultures. The authentic preaching of the gospel message can transform and remake African culture into a new creation that goes beyond the colonial church. The Christian message preached in this way would make a new church.

This chapter has shown that this great African dream and project of having a truly African Christianity is not without its challenges. The future of Christianity in Africa can be guaranteed only by inculturating the Christian faith into the heart of the continent. Let us not presume that what happened in North Africa in Roman times, the disappearance of an entire church, cannot happen again.

The disciples of Christ were to be his witnesses not only in Jerusalem but throughout Judea and Samaria, and indeed to the ends of the earth (see Acts 1:8). In obedience to Christ's command, the church, ever since its birth, has striven to carry out the task of communicating the gospel message to people belonging to clearly defined social groupings, each of which is profoundly linked to a cultural tradition.[72] This means that Christ already had in mind when he was giving his farewell speech to his disciples that the gospel message would be received by various peoples coming from different cultures. The witnesses to this message must render it intelligible, relevant, and credible to everyone to whom it is communicated.

"For God so loved the world that He gave His only son for the salvation of the world" (John 3:16).[73] The fact is that Christ was born a Jew, lived and preached within the Jewish community, and

---

69. Nyamiti, "My Approach to African Theology," 42–43.
70. Nyamiti, "My Approach to African Theology," 34.
71. Muller, "Main Principles of Centralized Government for the Mission," 26.
72. Shorter, *Towards a Theory of Inculturation*, 54.
73. Cf. John 4:42; 1 John 2:2; 4:14.

founded his church among his own people. The church began to spread—first to Antioch, where its members were first called Christians, and from there to the Greek world where it assumed a Greek face, and finally to Rome where it began to wear a Roman garment. These cultural transformations of the faith testify to those scriptural passages that imply the universality of Christ's mission. The same faith has been brought down to Africa, and it is now necessary to give it African attire. Our theologians will therefore need to discover for the African people an African face of Christ. Christ must identify with Africans and be incarnated into the African culture so that the African people can be fully absorbed into a Christian culture.

Bibliography

Antonio, Edward P. *Inculturation and Postcolonial Discourse in African Theology*. New York: Peter Lang, 2006.

Arrupe, Pedro. "Letter to the Whole Society on Inculturation." In *Studies in the International Apostolate of Jesuits*. Washington, DC: Jesuit Missions, 1978.

Baur, John. *2000 Years of Christianity in Africa*. Nairobi: Paulines Publications for Africa, 1994.

Beal, John P., and James A. Coriden. *New Commentary on the Code of Canon Law*: Study Edition. Mahwah, NJ: Paulist Press, 2002.

Benedict XVI, Pope. *Africae Munus* [Post-synodal Apostolic Exhortation on the Church in Africa in Service of Reconciliation, Justice and Peace; November 19, 2011]. Vatican City: Libreria Editrice Vaticana, 2011. www.vatican.va.

Bevans, Stephen B. *Models of Contextual Theology*. Maryknoll, NY: Orbis Books, 1992.

Beyer, Engelbert. *New Christian Movements in West Africa: A Course in Church History*. Ibadan: Sefer, 1998.

Bolt, Cawley. "Reluctant or Radical Revolution?" In *Evangelical Missionaries and Afro-Jamaican Character*. Oxford: Regnum, 2013.

Bosch, David. *Transforming Mission: Paradigm Shifts in Theology of Mission*. Maryknoll, NY: Orbis Books, 1991.

Britannica. "Africa." https;/www.Britannica.com/place/Africa. Accessed on January 11, 2019.

Chupungco, Anscar. *Handbook for Liturgical Studies* Vol. 2. Collegeville, MN: Liturgical Press, 1988.

———. *Liturgical Inculturation: Sacramentals, Religiosity and Catechesis*. Collegeville, MN: Liturgical Press, 1992.

Duncan, Graham A. "Ethiopianism in Pan-African Perspective, 1880–1920." *Studia Historiae Ecclesiasticae* 41.2 (2015): 198–218.

Fashole-Luke, Edward, et al., eds. *Christianity in Independent Africa*. London: Rex Collings, 1978.

Flanagan, Padraig. *A New Missionary Era*. Eugene, OR: Wipf & Stock, 2010.

Ibeka, Valentine. *The Zairian Liturgy as a Paradigm for African Liturgical Inculturation*, https//www.academia.edu.

John Paul II, Pope. *Catechesis Tradendae* [Apostolic Exhortation on Catechesis in Our Time; October 16, 1979]. Vatican City: Libreria Editrice Vaticana, 1979. www.vatican.va.

———. *Ecclesia in Africa* [Post-synodal Apostolic Exhortation on the Church in Africa and Its Evangelizing Mission toward the Year 2000; September 14, 1995]. Vatican City: Libreria Editrice Vaticana, 1995. www.vatican.va.

———. *Extra-Ordinary Synod for the Twentieth Anniversary of the Closing of the Second Vatican Council*. Rome. December 7, 1985.

Kalu, Ogbu. *Ethiopianism in African Christianity*. Pretoria: Pretoria Press, 2005.

Karotemprel, Sebastian. *Following Christ in Mission: A Foundational Course on Missiology*. Boston: Paulines Media Books, 1996.

Kukah, M. H. *The Church and the Politics of Social Responsibility*. Lagos: Sovereign Prints, 2007.

Lewis, Bernard. *The Middle East: A Brief History of the Last Two Thousand Years*. New York: Simon & Schuster, 2009.

Luzbetak, L. *The Church and Cultures*. Maryknoll, NY: Orbis Books, 1988.

Muller, K. "The Main Principles of Centralized Government for the Mission." *Concilium* 13 (1966).

Mundimbe, V. Y. *Tales of Faith: Religion as Political Performance in Central Africa*. London: Athlone, 1997.

Nkomazana, F. "The Development and Role of Pentecostal Theology in Botswana." In *Handbook of Theological Education in Africa*, edited by I. Phiri and D. Werner. Oxford: Regnum, 2013.

Nsibambi, A. "The Effects of Globalization on the State in Africa: Harnessing the Benefits and Minimizing the Cost." Paper Presented at the UN General Assembly Second Committee: Panel Discussion on Globalization and the State (November 2, 2001).

Nthamburi, Zabbon. "Towards Indigenization of Christianity in Africa: A Missiological Task." *International Bulletin of Missionary Research* 3 (1989).

Nyamiti, Charles. "My Approach to African Theology." *African Studies* 7.4 (1991).

Olopade, Dayo. *The Bright Continent: Breaking Rules and Making Change in Modern Africa*. New York: Houghton Mifflin Harcourt, 2014.

Onwubiko, O. A. *Theory and Practice of Inculturation: An African Perspective*. Enugu: SNAAP, 1992.

Opoku, K. A. "Skinny but Imperishable Truth: African Religious Heritage and the Regeneration of Africa." *Studia Historae Ecclesiasticae* 38 (Suppl.) (2012).

Paul VI, Pope. *Evangelii Nuntiandi* [Apostolic Exhortation on the theme of Catholic Evangelization; December 8, 1975]. Vatican City: Libreria Editrice Vaticana, 1975. www.vatican.va.

Robinson, James. *Why Is Africa Poor?* Maddison Lecture, April 8, 2013. University of Groningen.

Sanneh, Lamin O. *Translating the Message*: The Missionary Impact on Culture. Maryknoll, NY: Orbis Books, 2009.

Seabrook, Jeremy. "Localizing Cultures." *Korea Herald*, January 13, 2004.

Shorter, Aylward. *African Christian Theology*. London: G. Chapman, 1975.

———. *Towards a Theology of Inculturation*. Maryknoll, NY: Orbis Books, 1988.

Stinton, Diane B., ed. *African Theology on the Way: Current Conversations*. London: SPCK, 2010.

Tetteh, Daniel. *What Is Africa?* Carleton University, Canada. www.carleton.ca.

Vahakangas, Mika. *In Search of Foundations for African Catholicisim: Charles Nyamiti's Theological Methodology*. Leiden: Brill, 1999.

Vatican Council II. *Orientalium Ecclesiarium* [Decree on Eastern Catholic Churches; November 21, 1964].

———. *Sacrosanctum Concilium* [Constitution on the Sacred Liturgy; December 7, 1963].

Waliggo, J. M., et al., eds. *Inculturation: Its Meaning and Urgency*. Kampala: St. Paul's Publication, 1986.

Yeboah, Kwame. *The Impact of Globalization on the African Culture*. Odense: University of Southern Denmark, 2006.

Young, Josiah U. *Black and African Theologies: Siblings or Distant Cousins?* Maryknoll, NY: Orbis Books, 1986.

Suggested Reading

Barney, G. L. "The Supracultural and the Cultural: Implications for Frontier Missions." In *The Gospel and Frontier Peoples*, edited by R. P. Beaver. Pasadena: William Carey Library, 1973.

Hillman, E. *Inculturation Applied toward an African Christianity*. New York: Paulist Press, 1993.

McGarry, Cecil, and Patrick Ryan, eds. *Inculturating the Church in Africa: Theological and Practical Perspectives*. Nairobi: Paulines Publications Africa, 2001.

Mugambi, J. N. K. *African Heritage and Contemporary Christianity*. Nairobi: Longman, 1989.

Osei-Bonsu, J. *Inculturation of Christianity in Africa: Antecedents and Guidelines from the New Testament and Early Church*. New York: P. Lang, 2005.

Key Words

African theology
appropriation
colonization
culture
evangelization
incarnation
inculturation
indigenization
liturgical adaptation
missionaries
syncretism

Method and Models for Studies in African Catholicism

Nicholaus Segeja

A discussion of the methodology and models for engaging in Catholic studies in the context of African Catholicism ultimately involves a concern about people and their beliefs and practices and is intimately linked to religious systems. In the African context, as John Mbiti asserts, "A study of these religious systems is therefore ultimately a study of the peoples themselves in all the complexities of both traditional and modern life."[1] Thus, this discussion cannot become the monopoly of scholars. In fact, the spirit of communion of the Second Vatican Council (Vatican II), which was a pastoral and ecumenical event, exercises substantial influence over Catholic studies. In addition to making use of the scholastic approach to engaging in theology, Catholic studies also pays heed to the current reality of living the faith and becomes practical, especially in terms of effectiveness, efficiency, and relevance. This essay, therefore, without pretending to be an exhaustive consideration of these issues, envisages a reflection on the challenges, opportunities, possibilities, and trends related to a contextualized method of doing Catholic studies in Africa. I argue that, since looking for solutions together as a family and community is apparently a feature common to most African cultures, a methodology of doing Catholic studies in Africa, especially with an understanding that the church is God's family, should spring from familial-based reverential dialogue.[2]

African Catholicism: Experiences, Challenges, and Opportunities

The Roman Catholic Church is a historical, global community that has often applied certain practices everywhere in the world without regard to context. An example of this is that for centuries, from the Middle Ages up to Vatican II, the scholastic method of doing Catholic studies developed in the Western church forged its way into every corner of the globe, sometimes unchallenged. The practice of Catholic studies in Africa has not been completely free from this influence, which has not always been positive. Of course, after the new insights of Vatican II, we have seen efforts by some scholars, especially theologians, to propose other methods of doing theology. For example, we have seen the introduction of contextual theology (or theologies), including African theology, inculturation, interculturation, liberation theology, and others.[3] Some scholars like Bernard Lonergan, Karl

---

1. Mbiti, *African Religions and Philosophy*, 1.
2. See Pope John Paul II, post-synodal apostolic exhortation *Ecclesia in Africa* §§63, 89 (hereinafter *EA*). The church as *God's family* and also the church as *a family* are guiding ideas for proper evangelization in Africa. These ideas emphasize care for others, solidarity, warmth in human relationships, acceptance, dialogue, and trust. In my research, I always refer to dialogue that reflects a family spirit and is done with respect and reverence as *reverential dialogue*. See Segeja, *Ecclesiology of Reverential Dialogue*. In this document, I discuss the ecclesiology of reverential dialogue in the context of understanding the church as God's family in Africa.
3. See Bevans, *Models of Contextual Theology*, 3.

Rahner, and J. B. Metz have offered certain novel methodological considerations. Still, despite all these innovations, the scholastic method continues to exert strong influence over the practice of Catholic studies in Africa, as if it is part and parcel of divine revelation. Consequently, there are at least two challenges, with some corresponding opportunities, that accompany any search for an appropriate methodology for Catholic studies in Africa. The first challenge is to distinguish, without necessarily separating, the content or theme of a theology from the practice of the scholastic method. The other, perhaps more daunting challenge for Catholic studies in Africa is to clearly describe the features of the method(s) and models or paradigms that should be employed.

The Challenges of Developing an African Catholicism

For the purposes of this chapter, it would have been wonderful to dig into the history and tradition of the church while remaining conscious of the needs of the universal church today. Such a project would, however, have been beyond the scope of the chapter, so the insights that came out of Vatican II will have to suffice as the basis for the discussion. In the light of Vatican II, Pope Paul VI in his encyclical letter *Ecclesiam Suam*, concisely affirms that a rigid adherence to the methods adopted by the church in the past, refusing to countenance practical innovations commonly thought to be in accord with the character of our time, is not required or desirable.[4] This statement by the pope formed the basis for some of the insights of Vatican II concerning the concept and reality of *aggiornamento*, or the renewal of the Catholic Church. Vatican II's Pastoral Constitution on the Church in the Modern World (*Gaudium et Spes*), for example, stresses the church's historical concern that the Christian message be expressed using the concepts and language of various peoples so that it can be adapted to the understanding of everyone, especially in the face of the rapid changes occurring in the contemporary world, at a time when patterns of thought differ widely from place to place.[5]

Adapting the gospel to the understanding of the people has at least three implications. In the first place, it encourages contextualization, meaning placing it into the actual lives of particular people and into their particular social and cultural undertakings. In order to accomplish this, employing the social sciences, especially anthropology, sociology, and even psychology becomes inevitable. Second is the need to preserve the message that is being communicated even while contextualizing it. The gospel message, the Good News of salvation, must remain the same and be communicated as clearly as possible. Thus, an aspect of hermeneutics cannot be avoided—doing Catholic studies in Africa should constitute a hermeneutical activity of the church. Finally, there is a need for concern about the way—the mode and method—of communicating the message. This involves the application of an appropriate methodology guided by the needs of pastoral ministry, because engaging in Catholic studies is essentially related to the ministerial function of the church.

Key to these implications is the church's role in reading the signs of the times as an expression of her pastoral vigilance. Vatican II broadened the church's understanding of this role, conceiving of it as both a personal and a communal effort. As later elaborated by Pope St. John Paul II, it is a human–divine undertaking essentially linked to evangelical discernment of various sociocultural and ecclesial situations, so as to indicate the proper orientation for particular actions of the church.[6] If doing Catholic studies in Africa is to be of any relevance, it needs to employ methods that integrate a reading of the signs of the times, both as a source of divine revelation and a *locus theologicus* in relation to faith-seeking-understanding. Perhaps it is worth recalling here that Vatican II reiterates the need to read the signs of the times precisely because of the church's new understanding of itself as a communion amid the world calling for holiness.[7] Vatican

---

4. See Pope Paul VI, encyclical *Ecclesiam Suam* §50.
5. Vatican II, *Gaudium et Spes* §44.
6. Pope John Paul II, apostolic exhortation *Pastores Dabo Vobis* §57.
7. We encourage a review of the Vatican II Dogmatic Constitution on the Church (*Lumen Gentium*), espe-

II sees the world and its various contexts as a *locus theologicus*—concretely, this implies the relevance and use of inductive methods and approaches in doing Catholic studies. The council's acceptance of inductive methods in doing theology responds to the realities of modernity and perhaps, potentially, postmodernity. The nature of this response is manifested, for example, in the council's acceptance of secularization as a means of illustrating the relationship between the church and the world, as is discussed in the next section.

Modernity and Postmodernity: Challenges and Opportunities

In the wake of Vatican II, and especially beginning in the 1970s, Christian theology began to identify the contemporary social world as "modernity." There is no one theory or view of the precise nature of modernity; however, generally speaking, the term is used to capture the crucial features of an era that began in the seventeenth and eighteenth centuries in Europe and reached its apex only in the mid-twentieth century.[8] We are not able to fully describe these features here, but mentioning some of them may assist in giving us at least some idea of the considerations that must be taken into account in thinking about a proper methodology for doing African studies.

One of the central features of modernity is reliance on science and technology as the main instruments of reason and the achievement of progress. Another important feature, fueled by globalization, is the industrial production of commodities, usually within a capitalist economic system. This feature is also related to the emergence of bureaucratic organizations, both to manage industries and to run the increasingly complex governments of nation-states, and to the advent of total, mechanized war, in turn dependent on constantly upgraded technologies of transport and communication. There seems to be no clear pastoral and practical—that is, effective, efficient, and relevant—method to promote evangelization in the presence of all of these features, a problem that has been addressed in the scholarly literature.[9]

In establishing a methodology for engaging in Catholic studies so as to promote faith-seeking-understanding, it is crucial for the church in Africa and elsewhere to address the nature of modernity. What should underpin this discussion are questions of faith and reason, the relationship between the local church and society, and the proper basis of morals, politics, and pastoral praxis, comprehensively understood. Among discussions of all these matters, a methodology for doing Catholic studies in Africa should aim at creating genuine hope despite the problems, or rather the challenges, humanity faces in Africa and elsewhere.

Of course, modernity may not last forever. In fact, the debate about postmodernity is a clear indicator of the increasing fragility of modernity. Nevertheless, on the level of culture and social outlook, the reality may be completely different. In fact, in the African context the debate between the local church and states is real and, if not well handled and managed, may negatively influence the destiny of the people on the continent. What is vital for the church in Africa is always to propagate a coming into existence of an ever-better society. While this might result largely from the work of experts and intellectuals in their particular areas of specialization, the views of ordinary people cannot be neglected with regard to identification of important priorities and putting into practice whatever may be planned. In fact, the engagement of ordinary people, and therefore the need for a proper method of doing so, maximizes the chances that the signs of the times will be accurately discerned.[10] What is evident today is the influence of modernity and even postmodernity on the contemporary world. Thus, for the church in Africa and Catholic studies in Africa to remain relevant, we need

---

cially articles 1–18 and 39–42, in which the hierarchy is described in terms of its service to the people of God. See also *Gaudium et Spes*, especially articles 1–8, 53–69.

8. Cf. Schluter and Barton, "Modernity and Postmodernity," 597.

9. See Paul Gifford, *Christianity, Development and Modernity in Africa* (Oxford: Oxford University Press, 2016). Gifford discusses the profound impact of religion on African development but laments the fact, as he argues, that Catholic scholars in Africa have not adequately engaged with modernity, especially in their research.

10. See Schluter and Barton, "Modernity and Postmodernity," 598.

a method or methods that can grapple with this reality. Success in this project will not only enable Africans to make a peculiarly African contribution to the universal church, but will influence the destinies of all people for the better.

Modernity and postmodernity have led and are leading to tremendous social transformation. Of course, this transformation is apparently being caused by other factors as well. All of the relevant factors form a systemic and complex *locus* for the practice of theology and African studies. We may not be able to list them all, but the presence and rapid development of new information technologies are evidently a prominent factor. It should come as no surprise, therefore, that Pope Benedict XVI, in contextualizing the church's mission in Africa, identified information technology and communication as a new "world" to be evangelized and a major area for the apostolate.[11] Essentially linked to this reality are phenomena that are leading to changes not only in modes of production but also in modes of consumption. Often, the consumer can hardly be differentiated from the product in the sense that he or she purchases whatever is available in the market without exercising critical and creative thinking, frustrating the practice of genuine reason and positive democracy. This reality is starkly present in Africa, where the global economy, influenced by capitalist enterprise, globalization, and secularization, tends toward a reconstruction of both production and politics. In fact, these phenomena not only eventually reduce political and religious choices to what suits the needs of consumption, but render shaky the very basis of political and moral life. The phenomena described here can impede the search for truth, a fact that should cause concern in those attempting to discern new and appropriate methods and models of doing Catholic studies that favor evangelization. An appropriate method of doing Catholic studies should not only embrace a culture of critical and creative thinking but also foster visionary, prophetic attitudes and leadership.

Discerning the Pastoral Crescendos of Method in Catholic Studies in Africa

In most cases, because of the conditions created by both modernity and globalization, and the tendency to cling to a timeworn scholastic methodology, the practice of Catholic studies is consciously or unconsciously subject to bias. Catholic studies in the African context are usually oriented toward content and themes that are apparently relevant to African life, something that is surely important and necessary. As noted by Rodrigo Mejia, however, "There seems to be, so far, very little concern about the method of producing and teaching theology. It is as if everybody took for granted that, once the theological topic is relevant to Africa and its expression is enriched by African symbols, these ingredients are enough to produce African Theology."[12] There is no doubt that Mejia's analysis is relevant to the whole of Catholic studies in Africa. We need therefore to always identify, as clearly as possible, the areas in which communal concentration and effort should be expended to create pastoral crescendos related to methods and paradigms relevant for Catholic studies in Africa.

Discovering Methodological Motivations and Drivers

Mejia asserts reasonably that "there is no purely objective, neutral and value-free method. Every method implies an interest, a purpose, and an intention."[13] Of course, this is only a part of what is relevant about methods: one's interest in a method includes the content that is being investigated. Although the method and the content can be distinguished, they cannot be separated. These considerations become very significant for Catholic studies when the field makes use of methods or methodologies that have their origin in other natural or social sciences. Perhaps the key challenge is to discover the motivations and drivers behind particular methods and retune them to fit the gospel message in its totality.

---

11. Pope Benedict XVI, post-synodal apostolic exhortation *Africae Munus* §§142–46.
12. Mejia, "Towards an Alternative Way in Teaching Pastoral Theology," 102.
13. Mejia, "Towards an Alternative Way in Teaching Pastoral Theology," 103.

Understanding the motivations and drivers behind a method may involve the pain of acknowledging limits. We always need to be aware that a method cannot be applied without affecting, at least to some extent, the content under investigation. Catholic studies in Africa (and elsewhere) should always strive to employ methods that safeguard the catholicity of revealed truth and that can help faith to discover and understand that truth. In fact, one of the great challenges in choosing a method for engaging in Catholic studies in Africa is always to remain faithful to the gospel message. Another is to retain an openness to and a thirst for always learning more about God's plan of love for humanity, an openness and thirst that derive from a sense of the sacred and the divine nature of the gospel message. In sum, we must be keenly aware that no method, however unimpeachable its motivation, can claim to have a universal, objective, and definitive facility to do justice to every kind of content.

Integrating Lived Faith and Inclusiveness

The self-understanding and spirit of the church as communion in the light of Vatican II have substantially influenced the practice of Catholic studies in various ways. After Vatican II, theology was to be pastorally oriented and practical, and thus effective, efficient, and relevant. All of the biblical images expressing the reality of communion as being like the body of Christ, the temple of the Holy Spirit, and the people of God, leave no room for the exclusion of others in putting the faith into practice. Since the search for an alternative methodology in doing Catholic studies in Africa is basically about faith, it must be open to all people of goodwill. Perhaps rediscovering the original meaning of "method" could prove useful here. The term's etymology points to a "way" or "path." In this context, Bernard Lonergan would simply say, "A method is a normative pattern of recurrent and related operations yielding cumulative and progressive results."[14] In the African context, a way or normative pattern is not the creation of a single individual, and it embraces at least two realities. In the first place, it points to a direction, a destiny open to all. It is a reality that is *spoken*.[15] On the other hand, a way is essentially linked to life, symbolized by a kind of conversation interested in the promotion of life in accordance with the will of God; hence, it embraces a sense of the sacred. Interest in life is another pastoral cornerstone, and Catholic studies should highly esteem any method based on this interest.

Consequently, a shift in the understanding of Catholic studies in Africa should be adopted that embraces the reality of lived faith and life in general. To speak about method in doing Catholic studies, especially in Africa, is at its root speaking about life. Thus, choosing a method cannot in any way be a monopoly of academicians. Besides the need to be inclusive, this has many other implications: one can deduce from this affirmation, for example, the fact that the method should be concerned with the real needs of the people in the search for their destiny, helped by faith. In other words, the method must be concerned with human experience, especially the experience of faith. A way must be sought that can illustrate how human experience enriches Catholic studies in Africa.

Surely, this challenges scholars to rethink the practice of Catholic studies to include people in their life and work environments, as demanded by the call to the new evangelization.[16] Universities and centers of higher learning and schools of thought should be known both for the way they influence and for the way they are influenced by society. Being sensitive to this will overcome the old image of the theologians or scholars living in ivory towers, conceiving a theology *intra muros* with their eyes on the city of God, but far from the city of the people.[17] This approach is not a com-

---

14. Lonergan, *Method in Theology*, 4.
15. Among the Sukuma people, the largest tribe in East Africa, there is a saying that *"Nzilla ili mu nomo,"* literally, "the way is in the mouth." It points to a reality that a way is made or found only when people are ready to engage in interlocution. This is actually what makes life meaningful. In the African context, the significance of words cannot be separated from life itself.
16. Pope Francis, apostolic exhortation *Evangelii Gaudium* §14.
17. See Mejia, "Towards an Alternative Way in Teaching Pastoral Theology," 104.

pletely new one in the church—even in the patristic era, theology, like Catholic studies in general, was a concerted effort of the whole society, unlike that promoted by the world of scholasticism.

Consequently, as Mejia further notes, theology and Catholic studies started not in the university but in the pastoral field and the silence of the monasteries;[18] it was not until the Middle Ages that theology entered the university.[19] And even though it is true that all the early theologians and church fathers and mothers were educated and learned, or at least literate, as were also part of a small elite in their day similar to the later university elites, the example of St. Thérèse of Lisieux, a doctor of the church, is a modern example of someone who is honored for her teaching but had no theological or university training. Thus, it is becoming clearer today, especially after Vatican II, that theology and in fact Catholic studies in general are no longer meant to be only in universities, churches, and monasteries but should also engage people in other strata of society.

The Relevance of the Method in Doing Catholic Studies

The documents of Vatican II, especially *Gaudium et Spes*, declared the church's *practical* solidarity with the human family and the world (§§1–10). The church wanted her actions to be ecumenical and pastorally oriented and therefore practical. As noted above, the concept of "pastoral" here implies practical, which embraces at least three further ideas, namely, effectiveness, efficiency, and relevance. Effectiveness implies doing the right things, while efficiency points to doing those things in the right way. Relevance pertains to the value added by engaging in a practice. The church opened a new era by giving another name to the biblical and traditional practice of doing the right things (*orthodoxy*) in the right way (*orthopraxis*), but also introduced the concept of "relevance," or added value.[20] Theology and Catholic studies since Vatican II have had to rethink the relevance of their methods. With the insights of Vatican II, the scholastic style could no longer serve the purposes of theology and Catholic studies everywhere, since relevance demands addressing real problems and challenges so as to respond to basic human needs comprehensively.

One may recall here some of the characteristics of the scholastic style and method of doing Catholic studies. Without too much simplification, at least three procedural steps were involved, beginning with the reading of a text from the scriptures (*lectio*), from which was developed a question (*quaestio*) or disputation (*disputatio*) to be studied, in order finally to arrive at a result or conclusion to the disputed question. The goal was usually to reconcile the apparently opposing views of two different authorities—namely, the scriptures and the tradition of the fathers and later the position of the magisterium, on the one hand, and, on the other, the worldly knowledge of pagan philosophers like Aristotle, for example. Of course, and especially in the pre–Vatican II context, this procedure usually yielded results that favored the life and mission of the church while deepening its understanding of revealed truth. Consequently, we should perhaps not rely too heavily on the contrast between pre- and post–Vatican II metanarratives in judging scholasticism. There are many other metanarratives in the history of theology that overlap or predate Vatican II, like that of the post-Reformation or Catholic Reformation church arising from the Council of Trent. There are many pre-Trent theologies that impact our present ones—for example, as contained in confessional manuals dating from sixth-century Ireland, well before the start of scholasticism—which are still operative in the underlying attitudes and theologies of the sacrament of confession. Nevertheless, generally speaking the scholastic methodology was the dominant way of doing and teaching Catholic studies and was supported and sustained over a long period of time,

---

18. Mejia, "Towards an Alternative Way in Teaching Pastoral Theology," 104.

19. Of course, without too much generalization one should also remember that there were no universities as such until the Middle Ages.

20. See Foro, "Priority of Orthodoxy in Theology," 42.

seemingly for its own sake.[21] Its major drawback was its flight from real problems and challenges emanating from a lived faith, which minimized its chances of being relevant to the people.

The insights from Vatican II demand more than the motivations underlying the scholastic style and method in order to deepen the understanding of the truth. They demand motivations based on real problems and challenges in living the faith, the *quaestio* or *disputatio* related to the deeper needs and thirsts of the people in given contexts. This is not without certain implications and necessary shifts in attitude. One clear implication is that the research methodologies of the social sciences, especially sociology, anthropology, and even psychology, are needed for Catholic studies. But the use of these methodologies should not embrace the interests of these sciences that are incongruent with the gospel message; instead, there is a need to permeate these methodologies and sciences with gospel values. Another implication is that a relevant methodology for the African context should also consider the transcendent. Concretely this would imply taking into account the features of the kingdom of God, like reconciliation, justice and peace, charity, and even mercy, which are not the result of human effort alone but also require divine intervention. In actual fact, when such features are ignored, society acts to frustrate human destiny.

Properly accounting for these features should reflect the deep and real needs of Africans, which are not limited to geographical location or people of any particular ethnicity. Thus, the method should not result in any kind of neo-tribalism or nationalism (or continentalism). Africa has its own story that may be genuine and true, but Africans have never been able to agree among themselves about the "common good" of the continent, so the story has ended in futility and absurdity. Any method employed should help stop the tendency of Africans to retreat into cocoons of nationalism. African citizens should not give room to xenophobia and intolerance of foreign cultures; in fact, where these things have been present, the smoldering fire of tribalism has often raged. The cases of Rwanda, Darfur, the Central African Republic, and South Sudan should suffice as examples and points of reflection about the need for a relevant method for putting faith into practice.

Of course, the implications of starting from a real *quaestio* or *disputatio* are many. Another is that a methodology for the practice of Catholic studies in Africa should not entangle Christianity with the negative aspects of modernity and postmodernity, leading to a kind of Western cultural domination through, for example, church-based education or missionary expansion. Historically, this seems to have been the case, especially in some places. A method is needed that, as Schluter has observed, can help free the gospel from false alliances with certain kinds of economic arrangements or rationalist arguments or Western thinking, which, however laudable their original intentions, now constitute a millstone around the neck of any meaningful attempt to be "salt and light" today.[22] The church in Africa in doing Catholic studies should employ methods and models containing checks and balances so that these efforts, and

---

21. See Mejia, "Towards an Alternative Way in Teaching Pastoral Theology," 104. Nevertheless, one should not take away from this discussion the impression that the scholastic method is in no way relevant to the African situation. In fact, it has some advantages and is proposed even in some Vatican II documents as a guide for doing Catholic studies, including the Decree on the Ministry and Life of Priests (*Presbyterorum Ordinis*), the Decree on Priestly Formation (*Optatam Totius*), and the Code of Canon Law. See also, "Human Development and Christian Salvation," in *International Theological Commission: Texts and Documents 1969–1985* (San Francisco: Ignatius Press, 1989), 145–62. The voices of African theologians like Charles Nyamiti and many others who argue for the relevance of the scholastic method are also worthy of study. For further reading about Nyamiti, see Frederick Wanjala, "A Compendium of Resources into Nyamiti's Theology," in *Challenges to Religion in Africa in Light of Vatican Council II*, ed. Peter I. Gichure, Frederick Wanjala, and Nicholaus Segeja (Nairobi: CUEA Press, 2016), 303–10. What is emphasized here is that this method *alone* does not suffice to comprehensively address all of the issues facing Africa.

22. See Schluter and Barton, "Modernity and Postmodernity," 599.

Christianity in general, do not enter into collusion with postmodernity but instead can constitute a bold act that will become a real hope for the people.

Toward Methods and Models Based on Reverential Dialogue

Looking comprehensively at the pastoral considerations relevant for an appropriate methodology as discussed above, especially in the context of Africa, where the church understands herself as a family,[23] it is self-evident that sharing the *quaestio* should be the point of departure. Surely, it would be naïve to think that an appropriate method can now be chosen, but some criteria and even an overall orientation can at least be identified. The sharing of the *quaestio* in the African context demands, as its basis and condition, a unique dialogue. In fact, the significance of dialogue in the African context was previously described in the apostolic exhortation *Ecclesia in Africa*. Pope John Paul II observed that "despite the modern civilization of the 'global village,' in Africa as elsewhere in the world the spirit of dialogue, peace and reconciliation is far from dwelling in the hearts of everyone" (*EA* §79). Pope Benedict XVI, in his apostolic exhortation *Africae Munus*, brings the concern for dialogue home to Africa. According to Benedict, reconciliation, justice, and peace, and hence the practice of dialogue is an expression of evangelization. Dialogue is essentially linked to the mission of the church, particularly in Africa, where it operates in a context of the cultural shock of modernity. Benedict strongly confirms that "in this anthropological crisis which the African continent is facing, paths of hope [methods and models] will be discovered by fostering dialogue among the members of its constituent religious, social, political, economic, cultural and scientific communities."[24]

Catholic Studies as an Instance of Reverential Dialogue

Dialogue in the African context is unique because it is intimately connected to family life and building and promoting a good life and healthy relationships. In order to highlight this uniqueness, I will identify this reality as "reverential dialogue." It is called *shikome*[25] by the Basukuma of Tanzania[26] and is commonly referred to by many African scholars as "palaver." Let us briefly explore the characteristics of this reverential dialogue, especially its relationship to family life.

As we have discussed elsewhere, in the context of our research among the Basukuma, reverential dialogue comes with certain implications.[27] In the first place, it implies a maturation or growth. Key to this notion is experience and both personal and communal history. Reverential dialogue also

---

23. Pope John Paul II, post-synodal apostolic exhortation *Ecclesia in Africa* §63 (hereinafter *EA*). See also *Africae Munus* §8. One could say that the African church understands herself as being composed of "families" because of the many cultures present on the continent. It could even be said that the church in Africa sees herself as a confederation of families that share a common faith, rather than a single family that shares a common faith and culture. These semantic issues, however, remain open to debate.

24. *Africae Munus* §11. Insertion mine.

25. The word *shikome* comes from the verb *kukomela*, meaning "getting ready or preparing." Additional study is needed on the reality and practice of *shikome* among the Basukuma of Tanzania and how it can be applied to Catholic studies in Africa. In my doctoral research, a portion of which was published (1998) as *An Ecclesiology of Reverential Dialogue in the Family*, I discussed, among other things, the Basukuma experience of *shikome* as a point of departure for a theological framework, the meaning of *shikome* in light of scriptures, and the achievement of divine *shikome*.

26. Since independence, the Basukuma (or simply Sukuma) people have remained the largest tribe or group among about 120 ethnic groups in Tanzania. Most Basukuma live in northwest Tanzania, and they represent about 20 percent of the total population of the country. See also Frans J. S. Wijsen, ed., *There Is Only One God: A Social-Scientific and Theological Study of Popular Religion and Evangelization in Sukumaland, Northwest Tanzania* (Kampen: Kok, 1993), 49.

27. See Segeja, "Role and Place of Reverential Dialogue (*Shikome*) in the Family Life of the Basukuma," 12–18. See also Segeja, *Ecclesiology of Reverential Dialogue*, 3–11.

implies making strong, fastening, and joining one thing to another so that they remain together, and the idea is especially applicable to relationships. Further, it also includes the notion of drying for future use, including collecting dry cow dung in a heap so that it can be burned to generate heat. Joe Healey refers to this last notion, for example, when he says, "Sukuma *Ha-kikome* is a tradition of gathering family or elders around the fire place to talk. This can be instructional (elders to children) or reflective (on social and economic problems, myths, etc.).''[28] In all of its implications, the family spirit and the interests of the family form the basis of reverential dialogue. A. E. Orobator sees this as a reality practiced not just by the Basukuma: "In Africa, family is the place par excellence for dialogue."[29] Along the same lines, Cecil McGarry states that, in Africa, "[c]ommunication and dialogue are the basis of good relations and understanding within the family."[30]

In doing Catholic studies in the African context as a reverential dialogical reality, therefore, the interest of the family according to God's plan of love is vital. In fact, in Africa, where people are "familied," and where community and reverential dialogue are key, Catholic studies must be done not only *for* the people, but also *with* the people, irrespective of their situation or condition. Catholic studies should be an interdisciplinary reverential dialogical reality first and foremost, and should be entered into with openness and a readiness to engage with the social sciences, including psychology, sociology, economics, political science, and even biology, among others. Providentially, in Africa, the formation of Small Christian Communities (SCCs) as a pastoral priority has proven to be an excellent way of being church. The SCCs have opened avenues for identifying the *quaestio* for doing Catholic studies, and it is through them that families and the local church can effectively, efficiently, and relevantly engage in reverential dialogue.

A Dialectical Relationship between Inductive and Deductive Approaches

Catholic studies in Africa as a reverential dialogical reality should also aim at looking at the future by learning from a lived faith in the past. The fact remains that the scholastic style and method, responding to the *quaestio* by deducing from abstract principles, exercised, at one time in history, a strong influence over the practice of theology and Catholic studies. Frederick Wanjala calls this the noetic approach to theologizing,[31] and it remains an important part of the tradition of the church and its catholicity. In the African context, however, as discussed above, this methodology alone is inadequate, especially today when theology and Catholic studies cannot neglect the importance of context.[32] In actual fact, the inductive approach rather than a noetic or deductive approach would be more appealing to the African mindset and way of doing things. This is because the inductive approach or method is directed at acquiring knowledge from personal and communal experience. Of course, suggesting the employment of the inductive approach here does not mean that the noetic or scholastic style should be abandoned in every case.

In fact, a balance needs to be struck between the two approaches. Both should form a part of reverential dialogue, working simultaneously and harmoniously to respond to human needs in light of the gospel message. A methodology for doing Catholic studies in Africa, while emphasizing a gospel-driven interest in responding to the concrete needs of humanity, should at the same time engage in *dicta probantia* (examining the sayings/words)

---

28. Healey and Sybertz, *Towards an African Narrative Theology*, 104 (brackets by the author [Segeja]).
29. Orobator, "Church in Dialogue as the Family of God," 45.
30. McGarry, "Synod's Vision of an African Church," 171.
31. See Wanjala, "Vitality of Traditional Wisdom in Africa and Beyond," 58.
32. See Jordan Nyenyembe, "Contextual Theology: Unpacking Rebellion Theory," in Wabanhu and Moerschbacher, *Shifting Ground of Doing Theology*, 87–101.

of the scriptures, the tradition and teachings of the church, and the wisdom of the ancestors.[33] This communal exercise, open to examination, would protect Catholic studies in Africa from the consequences of specialized professionalism, fundamentalist readings of the Bible, and the possibility of an overweening exercise of magisterial authority. In fact, *dicta probantia* would result in the opening up of Catholic studies to interdisciplinary reverential dialogue involving collaborative research with the social sciences, research that should be inspired both by the signs of the times and other sources of revelation.

Illuminated Analysis and Research

Scholars working in Catholic studies in Africa should not be content with a kind of automatic application of principles or the mere quotation of texts, even revealed or theologically sound texts. It is not enough to do so without considering the concrete indicators of relevance to contemporary human situations. Any analysis and discernment operating as a methodological focal point and hub for doing theology and Catholic studies needs to connect the work of scholars with the daily lives and reality of the people.[34] Of course, on the one hand, this approach is not completely new—St. Thomas Aquinas, as was noted by Mejia, established the principle of *quidquid recipitur, ad modum recipientis recipitur* ("what is received is received according to the manner of the receiver")—a principle that points to the need for embracing the analysis and interpretation of human situations.[35] On the other hand, however, this approach involves some novelty in that human needs, emanating from a lived faith and comprehensively understood, become the basis for research, a *locus theologicus*; it operates as a communal effort of reverential dialogue.

Accordingly, in addition to embodying reverential dialogue and harmonizing inductive and deductive approaches, a sound methodology for Catholic studies should allow the carrying out of *illuminated* research and analysis. This has quite a number of implications, which, taken all together, require a shift in attitude. In the first place, one should not engage in research guided by the assumption that there are theological positions universally valid for all times and places. In fact, as Stephen Bevans puts it, "The time is past when we can speak of one and right unchanging theology, a *theologia perennis*."[36] It should not need emphasizing that the complexity of the present situation makes necessary a variety of methods for doing Catholic studies. References to context(s) and plural "theologies" are evidence of this development.[37] Since the ultimate purpose of the reverential dialogical method, simultaneously inductive and deductive in nature, is discernment, research, and especially the analysis and interpretation of data in doing Catholic studies in Africa, it must always be open to illumination. We have here in mind divine intervention that provides insights and wisdom in the course of searching for the truth. In the African context, besides the Word of God and the living tradition of the church, identifying relevant concerns, remaining in reverential dialogue with the people and with other sciences, and using narrative and parabolic language, are some possible sources of insights and wisdom. As in the Bible, stories, parables, proverbs, and songs should constitute most of the raw material for doing Catholic studies in Africa.[38]

---

33. See Rahner, "Reflection on Methodology in Theology," 70–71. See also Bevans, *Models of Contextual Theology*, 4.

34. See Ilo, "Wisdom of the Two Cities in Augustine: A Model for Doing Transformational Theology in Africa," in Wabanhu and Moerschbacher, *Shifting Ground of Doing Theology*, 153.

35. See Mejia, *Towards an Alternative Way in Teaching Pastoral Theology*, 108. It is very clear from Thomas Aquinas that theology, and in fact all of Catholic studies, is not just the mechanical repetition or automatic application of formulae, but rather an ongoing interpretation of human situations in light of the Word of God and the living tradition of the church.

36. Bevans, *Models of Contextual Theology*, 4.

37. Bevans, *Models of Contextual Theology*, 3.

38. See Francis Martin, "Biblical Teaching on Human Gender," in Melina and Belardinelli, *Amare nella diffe-*

Because reverential dialogue is by nature inclusive, Catholic studies in Africa should not operate in isolation. In fact, the problems, challenges, and needs of humanity transcend context and geographical location. Thus, as another implication of the need for illuminated analysis and research, remaining in reverential dialogue with discoveries globally is vital because of the communitarian nature of doing Catholic studies in Africa. A key consideration should be unanimity of heart and mind, just as among the first community of believers (Acts 4:43). Thus, in addition to being part of community life, theology, philosophy, and other Catholic studies in Africa should always be open to dialoguing reverentially with the same disciplines elsewhere, both locally and globally, so that everyone can eventually be connected to life and see the wisdom of God. These goals echo St. Augustine, who said that unanimity of heart and mind ends in futility if not focused on the way to God.[39] This leaves us with the quest of illustrating in a systematic way how this reverential dialogical method should be carried out so as to ensure that it always points the way to God, no matter which approaches are employed in the conduct of Catholic studies in Africa.

Conclusion

The reverential dialogical method, which suggests a way of collaboratively doing Catholic studies in Africa, imbues the notion of communion with movement and dynamism. This entails in the first place taking contexts seriously.[40] Since SCCs are a way of being communion, parish, and local church in Africa, every action of the church taken to form such communities presents a graced opportunity for the growth of the local church and raw material for doing Catholic studies. Scholars in Catholic studies in Africa are vigilant in looking for opportunities to feel with and listen to the faithful in their efforts to put faith into practice. Mutual listening open to learning together constitutes the formal start of doing Catholic studies in Africa. Of course, we need to develop skills related to and proper attitudes toward the exercise of free reverential dialogue in the SCCs and other communities, movements, and associations, so that this dialogue can be guided to achieve a consensus. But what underlies all of this, in addition to pastoral considerations, should be reverence for the triune God, witnessed in community life as an expression of "being" as love. In the words of David Schindler, "The point is that love itself, understood in light of the Christian doctrine of creation and the *ontological difference*, demands receptivity and obedience for its integrity."[41] Hence, the insertion into and contact with the people as an aspect of reverential dialogue maximizes not only the putting of love into practice but also the chances of being illuminated by the signs of the times and other sources of revelation in this moment of determining the proper *locus* for Catholic studies.

The reverential dialogical method, understood in a broad sense, is a way of mutual listening and learning at the different levels of being church concerning matters and situations that bear on the internal life of and the mission of the church to put the faith into practice. This method is first grounded in a lived faith. After that, it is based on the theological conviction that all the baptized, and indeed all people of goodwill are graced by the presence of the Holy Spirit and possess the light

---

renza: *Le forme della sessualità e il pensiero cattolico*, 222. The author shows that failure to reverence God is related to the fall of the human person and the effects of sin. See also Mejia, "Towards an Alternative Way in Teaching Pastoral Theology," 109.

39. See St. Augustine, *Rule* 1.3.

40. As an area for further study, it is important to explain the specifics of the reverential dialogical method. What does it look like? Who speaks and how often, who leads, who facilitates, is it moderated, does everyone participate equally, are clerics and lay equally present, are women and men together, are educated and uneducated invited and encouraged to speak? Spelling out the method of reverential dialogue will help the reader not only see and understand its relevance and its possibilities as an authentic African method, but also understand it as a method appropriate to the context of salvation. See Paul VI, encyclical *Ecclesiam Suam* §§70, 78, 81, 93–94.

41. Schindler, "Person, Body and Biology," 347 (emphasis in original).

of faith. As Paul says, such faith comes through personal and communal hearing—*fides ex auditu* (faith from what is heard) (Rom 10:17). Hence, a genuine method of doing Catholic studies that contributes to the search for the truth should integrate mutual listening and learning among those who possess and articulate the faith in a communal discernment toward improved actions by the church. Reverential dialogue as a method provides not only scholars but all the faithful with the possibility of collaboratively obtaining greater knowledge, which is essential both for properly discerned decision-making and for advancement in the search for knowledge and truth.

Since the reverential dialogical method requires thorough research and reflection on concrete issues related not only to the Catholic faith but also to other sets of beliefs and practices, for the purpose of acquiring unique paradigms and models to assist with various facets and expressions of evangelization, scholars in Catholic studies are basically facilitators of the method's movement and dynamism. They are aware and have become convinced that reverential dialogue seeks the truth that exceeds the grasp of each individual participant in the dialogue. Thus, scholars always find relevance in gatherings of the people, from families and SCCs to local and global conferences and symposia, in order to discern with them answers to questions they have identified and identify with. In fact, as Peter Gichure argues, the researcher should consider working among the people while conducting his or her research.[42] As much as they are exercising intellectual charity by sharing the findings of their research in their areas of specialization from their particular perspectives, scholars are also expected to listen to and learn from each other and from the people until a consensus is attained that will lead to reflections in the light of faith and to improved actions by the church.

Bibliography

Atkinson, David J., and David H. Field, eds. *New Dictionary of Christian Ethics and Pastoral Theology*. Nottingham: Inter-Varsity Press, 1995.

Benedict XVI, Pope. *Africae Munus* [Post-synodal Apostolic Exhortation on the Church in Africa in Service of Reconciliation, Justice and Peace; November 19, 2011]. Vatican City: Libreria Editrice Vaticana, 2011. www.vatican.va.

———. *Caritas in Veritate* [Encyclical on Integral Human Development in Charity and Truth; June 29, 2009]. Vatican City: Libreria Editrice Vaticana, 2009. www.vatican.va.

———. *Motu Proprio Data—Porta Fidei* [Apostolic Letter; 2011].

Bevans, Stephen B. *Models of Contextual Theology*. Rev. and expanded edition. Faith and Cultures Series. Maryknoll, NY: Orbis Books, 2016.

Cartledge, Mark J., and David Cheethman, eds. *Intercultural Theology: Approaches and Themes*. London: SCM Press, 2011.

Foro, Emmanuel. "The Priority of Orthodoxy in Theology." In *The Shifting Ground of Doing Theology*, edited by Emmanuel Wabanhu and Marco Moerschbacher. Nairobi: Paulines Publications Africa, 2017.

Francis, Pope. *Evangelii Gaudium* (The Joy of the Gospel) [Post-synodal Apostolic Exhortation on the Proclamation of the Gospel in Today's World; November 23, 2013]. Vatican City: Libreria Editrice Vaticana, 2013. www.vatican.va.

Gichure, Peter Ignatius. "Doing Quality Pastoral Research in the African Context." *Good Shepherd: A Journal of Pastoral Theology* 1.1 (June 2016): 42–51.

Hastings, Adrian, ed. *Modern Catholicism*. London: SPCK, 1991.

Healey, Joseph, and Donald Sybertz. *Towards an African Narrative Theology*. Nairobi: Paulines Publications Africa, 1966.

John Paul II, Pope. *Centesimus Annus* [Encyclical on the Hundredth Anniversary of *Rerum Novarum*; September 1, 1991]. Vatican City: Libreria Editrice Vaticana, 1991]. www.vatican.va.

———. *Ecclesia in Africa* [Post-synodal Apostolic Exhortation on the Church in Africa and Its Evangelizing Mission toward the Year 2000; September 14, 1995]. Vatican City: Libreria Editrice Vaticana, 1995. www.vatican.va.

---

42. See Gichure, "Doing Quality Pastoral Research in the African Context," 42.

———. *Laborem Exercens* [Encyclical on Human Work on the Ninetieth Anniversary of *Rerum Novarum*; September 14, 1981]. Vatican City: Libreria Editrice Vaticana, 1981. www.vatican.va.

———. *Pastores Dabo Vobis* [Apostolic Exhortation in the Formation of Priests in the Circumstances of the Present Day; March 25, 1992]. Vatican City: Libreria Editrice Vaticana, 1992. www.vatican.va.

———. *Sollicitudo Rei Socialis* [Encyclical for the Twentieth Anniversary of *Populorum Progressio*; December 30, 1987]. Vatican City: Libreria Editrice Vaticana, 1987. www.vatican.va.

Lartey, Emmanuel Y. *Pastoral Theology in an Intercultural World*. Peterborough: Epworth, 2006.

Lonergan, Bernard. *Method in Theology*. New York: Herder & Herder, 1972.

Mbiti, John S. *African Religions and Philosophy*. Nairobi: East African Educational Publishers, 1994.

McGarry, Cecil. "The Synod's Vision of an African Church." In *What Happened at the African Synod?*, edited by Cecil McGarry. Nairobi: Paulines Publications Africa, 1995.

Mejia, Rodrigo. "Towards an Alternative Way in Teaching Pastoral Theology." *Good Shepherd: A Journal of Pastoral Theology* 1.2 (December 2016).

Melina, Livio, and Sergio Belardinelli, eds. *Amare nella differenza: Le forme della sessualità e il pensiero cattolico; Studio interdisciplinare*. Vatican City: Liberia Editrice Vaticana, 2012.

Midali, Mario. *Practical Theology: Historical Development of Its Foundational and Scientific Character*. Rome: Libreria Ateneo Salesiano, 2000.

Orobator, Agbonkhianmeghe E. "A Church in Dialogue as the Family of God." In *What Happened at the African Synod?*, edited by Cecil McGarry. Nairobi: Paulines Publications Africa, 1995.

Paul VI, Pope. *Ecclesiam Suam* [Encyclical on the Church; August 6, 1964]. Vatican City: Libreria Editrice Vaticana, 1964. www.vatican.va.

———. *Evangelii Nuntiandi* [Apostolic Exhortation on the Theme of Catholic Evangelization; December 8, 1975]. Vatican City: Libreria Editrice Vaticana, 1975. www.vatican.va

———. *Octagesima Adveniens* [Apostolic Letter; 1971]. Vatican City: Libreria Editrice Vaticana, 1971. www.vatican.va.

———. *Populorum Progressio* [Encyclical on the Development of Peoples; March 26, 1967]. Vatican City: Libreria Editrice Vaticana, 1967. www.vatican.va.

Rahner, Karl. *Foundations of Christian Faith*. London: Darton, Longman & Todd, 1978.

———. "Reflection on Methodology in Theology." In *Theological Investigations,* vol. 11:70–71. Baltimore: Helicon, 1974.

Schindler, David L. "Person, Body and Biology: The Anthropological Challenge of Homosexuality." In *Amare nella differenza: Le forme della sessualità e il pensiero cattolico; Studio interdisciplinare*, edited by Livio Melina and Sergio Belardinelli. Vatican City: Liberia Editrice Vaticana, 2012.

Schluter, M. G. G., and M. J. Barton. "Modernity and Postmodernity." In *New Dictionary of Christian Ethics and Pastoral Theology*, edited by David J. Atkinson and David H. Field. Nottingham: InterVarsity Press, 1995.

Segeja, Nicholaus. "Contextualized Theological Reflection: A Pastoral Perspective." *African Christian Studies* 27.1 (March 2011): 21–42.

———. *An Ecclesiology of Reverential Dialogue in the Family (Shikome)*. Nairobi: CUEA Publications, 1998.

———. "Pastoral Reflection on New Evangelization: A Call for *Communitas Christifidelium*." In *Search for New Paradigms for Evangelization in the 21st Century: 15th Interdisciplinary Theological Session of the Faculty of Theology*, edited by John Lukwata et al., 104–28. Nairobi: CUEA Press, 2013.

———. *Perspectives for the Future in Light of the Synods of the Church in Africa: A Socio-Pastoral Reflection*. Nairobi: CUEA Press, 2012.

———. "Reverential Dialogical Ministry: A Pastoral Paradigm for New Evangelization in the Parish Part I & II." *African Christian Studies* 28.2 (June 2012): 45–88.

———. "Reverential Dialogue-Based Evangelization in Africa." *African Christian Studies* 26.4 (December 2010): 25–41.

———. "The Role and Place of Reverential Dialogue (*Shikome*) in the Family Life of the Basukuma." *African Christian Studies* 13.1 (March 1997): 12–18.

———. "Strategic Pastoral Planning for Deeper Evangelization: A Sign of Vigilance of the Church in Africa." *African Christian Studies* 26.2 (June 2010): 70–88.

Stoddart, Eric. "Current Thinking in Pastoral Theology." *The Expository Times: International Journal of Biblical Studies, Theology and Ministry* 123.7 (April 2012): 323–33.

Sweeney, James, et al., eds. *Keeping Faith in Practice: Aspects of Catholic Pastoral Theology*. London: SCM Press, 2010.

Swinton, John. *Spirituality and Mental Health Care: Rediscovering a "Forgotten" Dimension*. London: Kingsley, 2001.

Synod of Bishops XIII Ordinary General Assembly. "The New Evangelization for the Transmission of the Christian Faith." LINEAMENTA (2011).

Vatican II. *Gaudium et Spes* [Pastoral Constitution on the Church in the Modern World; 1965].

———. *Inter Mirifica* [Decree on the Means of Social Communication; 1963].

———. *Lumen Gentium* [Dogmatic Constitution on the Church; 1964].

Verstraeten, Johann, ed. *Scrutinizing the Signs of the Times in the Light of the Gospel*. Leuven: Peeters, 2007.

Wabanhu, Emmanuel, and Marco Moerschbacher, eds. *The Shifting Ground of Doing Theology: Perspectives from Africa*. Nairobi: Paulines Publications Africa, 2017.

Wanjala, Frederick. "Vitality of Traditional Wisdom in Africa and Beyond: An Exploration in Inculturation Theology." In *The Shifting Ground of Doing Theology: Perspectives from Africa*, edited by Emmanuel Wabanhu and Marco Moerschbacher. Nairobi: Paulines Publications Africa, 2017.

Ward, Pete. *Participation and Mediation: A Practical Theology for a Liquid Church*. London: SCM Press, 2008.

Wijsen, Frans, et al., eds. *The Pastoral Circle Revisited: A Critical Quest for Truth and Transformation*. Nairobi: Paulines Publications Africa, 2006.

Suggested Reading

Lonergan, Bernard. *Method in Theology*. New York: Herder & Herder, 1972.

Orobator, Agbonkhianmeghe E., ed. *Theological Reimagination: Conversations on Church, Religion, and Society*. Nairobi: Paulines Publications Africa, 2014.

Rahner, Karl. "Reflection on Methodology in Theology." In *Theological Investigations*, vol. 11. Baltimore: Helicon, 1974.

Wabanhu, Emmanuel, and Marco Moerschbacher, eds. *The Shifting Ground of Doing Theology: Perspectives from Africa*. Nairobi: Paulines Publications Africa, 2017.

Wijsen, Frans, et al., eds. *The Pastoral Circle Revisited: A Critical Quest for Truth and Transformation*. Nairobi: Paulines Publications Africa, 2006.

Key Words

dicta probantia
disputatio
hermeneutics
illuminated analysis
palaver
pastoral angle components
pastoral angles
pastoral crescendos
pastoral dimension(s)
quaestio
reverential dialogical method
reverential dialogue
shikome
signs of the times

Transformational Servant Leadership in African Catholic Pastoral Ministry

Stan Chu Ilo

> The Christian leader thinks, speaks, and acts in the name of Jesus.
> —Henri Nouwen

This chapter develops the ethical foundation and practices for transformational servant leadership in pastoral ministry for the churches in Africa. It begins by examining the key themes and issues in pastoral leadership in Africa and develops a model of leadership that draws on biblical, pastoral, and sociocultural studies as well as business management and politics. While discussing leadership in general, the chapter will concentrate more on leadership from the perspective of pastoral ministry, with a focus on leadership by clerics and religious who still hold the majority of the leadership positions in the pastoral field in the churches in Africa.

The Challenge of Leadership in Africa

In his apostolic exhortation following on the Second African Synod in 2010, *Africae Munus (AM)*, Pope Benedict XVI called on church and political leaders to embrace a new form of leadership that promotes good governance in Africa (§§81–83, 100–120). During his visit to Africa in November 2016, Pope Francis drew attention to the persistent and unacceptable social conditions in Africa, which remain unchanged despite significant progress made on the continent toward constitutional democracy and the exponential growth in the continent's Christian population.[1] The challenges remain the same: poverty, migration, failed and failing governance at the judicial, executive, and legislative levels, corruption, violence, rising youth unemployment, random epidemics, schizoid faith among Christians who gravitate between multiple religious affinities and identities, war, the semipermanence of humanitarian and refugee problems, seasonal natural disasters, and ecological crises and unpredictable weather patterns, among many others. The truth, however, is that Africa has within her the resources to address these problems and to meet the challenges of the present day. The face of Africa is changing for the good, but Africa cannot realize her potential and God's dream for these blessed lands—in both church and society—without a new crop of ethically driven transformational servant leaders. Africa faces leadership challenges in every societal domain.

Here, however, we are concerned particularly with the challenge of leadership in pastoral ministry, specifically in African Catholic churches. Pope Francis has recognized the insightful proposal of the African bishops that the sacraments of Christian initiation be given to all of God's people as a vocation for the purpose of empowering them to participate fully in the work of the new evangelization and so that they can take up their roles as salt of the earth and light of the world wherever they find themselves.[2] Being salt and light to the world

---

1. "The Pope's First Speech in Kenya," *Rome Reports* (2015).
2. Pope Francis, apostolic exhortation *Gaudete et Exsultate* §33.

is what it means to be a Christian disciple, and the Christian leader is first and foremost a good disciple of Jesus.

Leadership is a form of Christian witness in the church and society by individual Christians through the application of Christian virtues and values to various forms of service to God performed in many settings. The church from its beginnings has always been like a mustard seed in which the gifts and charisms of everyone are fruits of the Spirit and points of light illuminating the city of God. This is why it is important to recognize that leadership is not simply about those at the top; rather, it must be acknowledged that everyone can be a leader because everyone can serve and can influence the behavior of others. Everyone can be a leader because everyone can be a change agent and a source of newness within the church and society. Everyone can be leader because everyone can be the light of Christ and a source of divine love for the world. This is the crux of the matter when it comes to leadership: each and every Christian is called, as William Carey reminded Christians in 1792, to always expect great things *from* God while he or she is attempting to do great things *for* God through service and mission.[3]

Pope Francis has encouraged Christians to go out into the world with courage and firm determination to encounter people and the world of nature with their specifically Christian values and gifts. This emphasis on encountering people, bringing light into their lives, and finding light in the most obscure places is at the heart of the aesthetics of a theology of church I have termed an "illuminative ecclesiology."[4] This is an ecclesiology that answers the question of what form of witnessing and proclamation should be present in our churches among Christians and church ministers that shows the merciful, tender, and loving face of God to the world and brings the diverse faces and conditions of all God's people before God.

I argue that in Pope Francis's priorities and practices, which show a portrait of the church as poor and merciful, we have indications of how the faces of all God's people can be reflected as in a mirror to God and how God can encounter and use the gifts of everyone in the church. This theological aesthetics points to how the light of Christ is mediated in concrete human and cosmic experience and shows how our human condition is shot through with a hidden illumination that the church can discover only through her encounter with the "other." In this kind of ecclesiology, leadership can no longer be restricted to what the clergy and religious do, but rather should be concerned about how all the people of God are sharing in the teaching, healing, liberating, and saving mission of the Lord Jesus through word, service, and witnessing.

A blind spot remains, however, because whenever leadership in African Catholicism is discussed, the focus is mainly on the work of priests and religious.[5] Most of the pastoral and social ministries in African churches are dominated by clerics, even in such areas as the temporal administration of the church's goods and Catholic social ministries like education, health care, justice and peace offices, and marriage and family life. In these ministries, priests and bishops and a few religious are often placed as heads over lay members who may possess better skills and greater competence. Thus, this chapter issues an urgent call for a new and inclusive understanding of leadership and service in the church that overcomes the two-tier ecclesiology that posits a binary in the life of the church, with all that pertains to her spiritual and temporal life (*ad intra* and *ad extra*) being too often placed completely in the hands of clergy and religious, while secular life and concerns are left to the

---

3. "William Carey: Father of Modern Protestant Missions," *Christianity Today*, www.christianitytoday.com.

4. See Stan Chu Ilo, *A Poor and Merciful Church: The Illuminative Ecclesiology of Pope Francis* (Maryknoll, NY: Orbis Books, 2019).

5. See, for instance, the work by multiple authors collected in *Catholic Church Leadership in Peace Building in Africa*, edited by Elias Omondi Opongo and David Kaulemu (Nairobi: Paulines Publications Africa, 2014), which contains the contribution of only one woman, Wangari Maathai, with the rest being priests, bishops, and religious. The initiatives discussed in the study were mainly proposed by bishops, for example, the Amani Mashinani begun by the late bishop of Eldoret, Cornelius Korir.

laity. A more diffused and inclusive understanding of the church's role in Africa today requires a more expanded discussion of leadership in the church that goes beyond the focus of this chapter on the pastoral leadership of the clergy and religious.

Another important point related to the question of leadership in Africa is the challenge of history. It is important to locate the leadership challenges in Africa within the past history of the continent, which in both church and state has not offered role models nor developed mentoring practices aimed at producing leaders. In many African countries, leaders do not create succession plans. This is true not only for heads of state, but also in government, business, and other private and public enterprises. There is a reluctance to create new leaders. As a result, systems and structures are built to ensure that current leaders or people from the leaders' reference or ethnic groups retain power without regard to inclusiveness or merit. A similar dynamic often occurs in the African churches, where in many cases no serious attempt is made to develop young leaders. Existing structures of patronage often lead to the gratification of and subservience to the current leader and stunt the development of mature leadership and responsible following. Within the churches, there is also a strong emphasis on obedience and submissiveness, which often weakens the capacity for the giving and receiving of honest feedback or honest dialogue between those in authority and those they serve or who work for them. As we shall show later in this chapter, this kind of relationship is unhealthy for the church and for the wider society and weakens the capacity of both leaders and led to grow in appreciation of the larger goals of a particular church or society.

This pattern of social relationships goes back many centuries in Africa. Beginning from the fifteenth until the end of the nineteenth century, slavery fundamentally altered something in the social life of Africa. The pattern continued with colonialism and the work of Western missionaries, shaping the character of indigenous African leaders of both church and state. What was altered in the social life of Africa during this long period was the communal and participatory structure of leadership that defined traditional African society, the checks and balances imposed on those in positions of authority, and the merit-based accession to and diffused nature of African leadership. Africa's social life since the slave trade was suffused with the characteristics of a master–servant relationship. Thus, the so-called slave masters, colonial masters/lords, missionary masters, and development experts who came to Africa were not interested in listening to Africans, nor did they respect African agency or leadership or the African social structure, which had previously functioned as an internal control mechanism used to check the excesses of those in authority. This master–servant pattern of leadership was based on a relationship (if one could call it a relationship) of domination, damnation, and command and control. Obedience was an absolute imperative, and there were severe consequences for disobedience, including in many cases death or imprisonment or other harsh punishment. There was no dialogue, consultation, or respect for the people, no mechanism for giving and receiving feedback, and in many cases no honesty, transparency, or accountability. A leader in this kind of structure was the holder of power and privilege and the giver of life and death. The leader was from above and the Africans were from below. Africans could expect to gain anything good from their leaders or from their colonial "motherland" only by praising, glorifying, fearing, or flattering the leaders.

This was the leadership structure in which the modern African state was born and that the indigenous African clergy and religious inherited from the missionaries. This is why what emerged in postindependence Africa generally and in postmissionary African churches resembled the master–servant relationship established in the colonial and missionary periods. This reality was characterized by leaders' obsession with power and control in both church and state, their demands of total obedience and submission, and their tendency to punish rather than correct and to instruct rather than engage in dialogue. This was made worse in many African countries with the emergence of military regimes and other strong rulers whose only means of governing was the giving of orders and the use of violence and threats. These leaders often operated one-party states that did not accept pluralism or diversity. These military strongmen often transformed themselves into civilian presidents even though they still acted in a dictatorial and repressive manner. There was a similar pattern in churches with the emergence of a strong cultic clericalism that made idols out of bishops, priests, and any other religious authority. This history is extremely important for understanding the broader context of the leadership challenges facing the churches of Africa—as the Igbos of eastern Nigeria say, "If you do not know where the rain began to fall on you, you will not know where it stopped."

What Is Leadership?

When we speak about leadership, we immediately think of those in positions of authority or who hold or wield power in society. In hierarchical settings like the church and the majority of traditional African societies, this is how leadership has operated and has been conceived of in modern times. While I will be addressing the question of leadership from the perspective of those who hold positions of authority, I want to preface this by highlighting the importance of leadership starting from the grassroots, that is, shared or communal leadership. Transformation can and does take place from the top down, but the most enduring transformations are not the result of one person's visionary or pragmatic character or leadership skills. Societal change may be driven by a leader but it is ultimately the result of a communal effort from the grassroots in which most members of society commit themselves to a new pathway of service for the greater good and strong ethical practices so that the dream of a particular community can be realized.

As Lao Tzu put it: "A leader is best when people barely know he exists; when his work is done, his aim fulfilled, they will say: we did it ourselves." Harvard scholar Michael Shinagel writes in this regard that the art of leadership consists in its not being about the person of the leader: "This is the art of leadership at its best: the art that conceals art." Good leadership is not about command and control but about being part of a chain in which everyone participates in realizing the common good. According to Shinagel, this was exemplified in the life of Nelson Mandela, who once wrote about leadership that "it is better to lead from behind and to put others in front, especially when you celebrate victory when nice things occur. You take the front line when there is danger. Then people will appreciate your leadership."[6] Pope Francis speaks in a similar vein when he teaches that sometimes the leader should lead from the front, sometimes from the back, and sometimes from the side.[7]

Properly speaking, leadership is about how people can influence the behavior of others in any social interaction. The more power one has, the more opportunity one has to influence others, but the level of influence a leader can exert is not directly proportional to his or her power. If this were so, then we would expect the most powerful people on earth to be the most influential. But this is not always the case! Churches face the perennial challenge presented by gaps existing between a leader's title and his or her power to influence important individual and organizational dynamics. There are many who hold positions of authority in the church but who are not change agents and who do not have any influence on the values embraced by the people of God. For example, being a parish priest confers enormous power and privilege in the eyes of the people, but it does not necessarily follow that the priest is "the source of institutionalized values which, in turn, condition the actions" of his parishioners.[8]

We can note from observation that sometimes church leadership structures face what I term a "triple C" (competence, character, and credibility) problem. This problem emerges from the incorrect notion that simply occupying what Max Weber calls a role of "traditional authority"—whether that role is patriarchal, hierarchical, patrimonial, ecclesial, feudal, or institutional—means that the holder possesses or manifests competence, character, and credibility. People are often chosen for service or a

---

6. Both quotations from Shinagel are from "Paradox of Leadership."
7. Pope Francis, address to the clergy in the Cathedral of San Rufino in Assisi, Italy, October 4, 2013, in Pope Francis, *Church of Mercy*, 75.
8. Podolny, Khurana, and Besharov, "Revisiting the Meaning of Leadership," 65.

position in the church in an informal way; in many cases, the determination of *competence* is made in secret based on the whims of an individual cleric or a group of clerics. Further, how does one determine that a person has the *character* required for an ecclesial position in the absence of an open, transparent, competitive screening process with clearly established benchmarks? The traditional answer is that the Holy Spirit guides the church in making her choices and that God qualifies those who are called, but is that sufficient? And finally, how does a church leader establish his or her *credibility* beyond the validation of authority granted by an institutionalized position?

The challenge emerges in the fact that a parish priest or bishop may not have the competence, the necessary skill set, or the appropriate character for the job. Sometimes the person chosen may not want the position, feeling that he or she may be inadequately prepared or may possess limited skills to carry out the job, but also feeling an obligation to accept it so as not to be disobedient to God or the church. For example, a bishop may be chosen by Rome who does not have the support and respect of the local priests and laity, who may feel that this bishop is being imposed on them or is a puppet of some high-ranking authority in the church. This kind of situation has been a challenge for many churches in Africa. A related example is a parish priest's choice of his friends or cronies for the parish council or parish finance council to ensure that these bodies will carry out his orders without scrutiny or questions. African churches are quite familiar with such situations, which can create serious fissures in the ecclesial community.

However, because church leaders rely on the power derived from their positions, the faithful usually obey and do not question their decisions, even when they may be doing damage to the institution and mission of the church. Most Catholics will obey their pastors because they respect the position that the parish priest occupies within the authority structure of the church. However, the fact that people obey a priest or other authority figure does not necessarily mean that that figure is positively influencing their behavior or having a positive impact on their spiritual and personal development. The point being made here is that possessing power, position, or authority may enhance one's ability to exert influence, but not necessarily influence for the good.

Thus, it is important to explore more deeply the accession to and exercise of power in the church so that its structures can be improved in the service of God and God's people. In the context of leadership, power has been defined as "the capacity or potential to influence. People have power when they have the ability to affect others' beliefs, attitudes and courses of action."[9] However, church leadership represents a spiritual and moral authority that appeals to the deepest values and sense of ultimate meaning held by the faithful. Louis Fry sees spiritual leadership as emerging in a setting in which everyone feels a sense of vocation and mission because they are taught that their lives have meaning and that what they do in obedience to and in cooperation with the leader helps build the community and promote stewardship. Fry argues that spiritual leadership is based on "altruistic love whereby leaders and followers have genuine care, concern and appreciation of both self and others, thereby producing a sense of membership, and feel understood and appreciated."[10]

In spiritual leadership, the person at the top is actually the lowest in rank; this is what the good Lord meant when he said that those regarded as rulers of the gentiles "exercise lordship over them, and their superiors exercise authority over them. But it shall not be this way among you. Instead, whoever wants to become great among you must be your servant" (Mark 10:42). An ethical, spiritual leadership does not rely on power derived from coercion or rewards. Coercive power "is based on the perceived ability of a leader or manager to bring about undesirable or unpleasant outcomes for those who do not comply with expectations, instructions or directives, for example withholding of pay raises or bonuses, promotion or privileges, allocation of undesirable or unpleasant tasks or infliction of physical punishment including pain and death. Coercive power does not bring about

---

9. Northouse, *Leadership*, 7.
10. Quoted in Gill, *Theory and Practice of Leadership*, 82.

voluntary action, only necessary action. Nor does it foster followership."[11]

In the church, coercive power can take many forms; for example, a leader driven by a dictatorial streak may stubbornly insist on carrying out policies, pastoral programs, or construction projects that are not working or have not been clearly thought through and have not been embraced by the people of God. It could also take the form of church leaders taking vindictive and punitive actions (refusing to talk to subordinates or a bishop's suspension of a priest, placing of a priest in residence as a deterrent to other priests, or taking away the priest's faculties without due process, etc.). Reward power, which involves a leader granting privileges and benefits to subordinates or preferential treatment to loyalists and sycophants, is the other side of the coin from coercive power, using positive instead of negative incentives.

Both of these approaches to the exercise of power are unacceptable in the church. They were both condemned in Pope Francis's Christmas speech in 2014 on the fifteen ailments of the Roman Curia. Without exhaustively discussing all of these ailments here, we can capture the heart of those relating to leadership arising out of coercive and reward power and how these forms of power polarize the church and hamper the coming of God's kingdom (in the church, the Curia, the diocesan presbyterate, and the religious community or parish). They create a gulf between those who are beloved by the church leader and those who are outside the cycle of love and must feed on the crumbs from the master's table. As described by the pope, such problems include the following:

- "the disease of those who court their superiors in the hope of gaining their favor. They are victims of careerism and opportunism; they honor persons and not God";
- "the disease of closed circles, where belonging to a clique becomes more powerful than belonging to the Body and, in some circumstances, to Christ himself. This disease too always begins with good intentions, but with the passing of time it enslaves its members and becomes a cancer which threatens the harmony of the Body and causes immense evil—scandals—especially to our weaker brothers and sisters"; and
- "the disease of worldly profit, of self-exhibition. This is the disease of persons who insatiably try to accumulate power and to this end are ready to slander, defame and discredit others, even in newspapers and magazines. Naturally, so as to put themselves on display and to show that they are more capable than others."[12]

John Maxwell points to sociological discoveries concerning the diffuse possibilities of influencing others outside positions of leadership. He argues that even the most introverted individual can influence more than ten thousand people in his or her lifetime because influence is not achieved only by people in the limelight. Influence is often achieved using one's gifts, talents, and spiritual/personal qualities to serve the greater good; it is the function of who we are rather than simply what we do. In this light, he concludes, "Each of us is both influencing and being influenced by others. That means that all of us are leading in some areas, while in others we are being led. No one is excluded from being a leader or a follower."[13]

People are influenced to change by qualities they see in others beyond the positions they occupy. Howard Gardner agrees with this by defining leaders as those who, "by word and/or personal example, markedly influence the behaviors, thoughts, and/or feelings of a significant number of their fellow human beings."[14] In considering leadership, many things come into focus: the leader's personality and personal traits; his or her actions, behavior, and character; his or her engagement with the dynamics of power; and his or her skills and ethical principles and practices. The personal qualities that enable a leader to exercise influence also include an ability to develop people's potential, an ability to connect with people, an ability to communicate honestly

---

11. Gill, *Theory and Practice of Leadership*, 246.

12. Pope Francis, "Presentation of the Christmas Greeting to the Roman Curia" (December 22, 2014), www.vatican.va.

13. Maxwell, *Developing the Leader within You*, 3.

14. Howard Gardner, *Leading Minds: An Anatomy of Leadership* (with Emma Laskin) (New York: Basic Books, 1995), 8. Quoted in Gill, *Theory and Practice of Leadership*, 9. (Original emphasis omitted.).

and openly with everyone, a caring attitude, consistency, fidelity and reliability, integrity, competence, an ability to consult with others, an ability to adopt an experiential approach to problem solving, strong conflict resolution skills, credibility, a proven record of achievement, an ability to create a positive work environment, and trustworthiness.[15]

It has frequently been argued that trust is the most important quality people are looking for in a leader and in every relationship, especially in a world that is ravaged by falsehoods and pretense.[16] Ronald Heifetz, Alexander Grashow, and Marty Linksy argue that the exercise of leadership must be characterized by four important attributes so that it can have a positive influence, adapt to changes in society, and preserve what is essential for any organization's survival and identity: *relevance* (allying vision to mission and mission to purpose); *interpretation* (properly understanding the signs of the times and meeting the needs of the group and the wider society); *relationship* (involving the difference between transaction and transformation—people need to feel wanted and that they are loved and cherished; simply put, to feel that they are friends with the leader and that the leader cares about them);[17] and *implementation* (credibility and creating positive change and bringing successful outcomes for the organization, that is, producing results). Leadership at all levels must achieve these four goals in order to bring about change.[18]

Ethical Transformational Servant Leadership

James MacGregor Burns, the figure regarded as most responsible for developing the transformational leadership model, wrote, "One of the universal cravings of our times is a hunger for compelling and creative leadership."[19] Donald Krause followed up on this idea by stating that "understanding the nature of leadership and developing strong leadership skills is probably the single most important task for society today."[20] Humans have always faced the question of leadership, and it was addressed by both Plato and Aristotle. Plato argued that the reform and transformation of the state can happen only if philosophers become kings or kings become philosophers. Put simply, for Plato leadership requires wisdom, a person who is capable of grasping the essences of things, what truly matters, through an apprehension of the key principles of reality.[21] Aristotle proposed leadership as the most important stabilizing factor in a commonwealth. Many leadership theorists speak of "organizational aesthetics," that is, how leaders, by their decisions, their interpretation of the signs of the times, and their motivations, create a symmetrical integration of values, vision, and judgment for the benefit of all members of a society.[22] These thinkers associate organizational aesthetics, with its exercise of practical judgment, best practices, and effective problem solving in diverse scenarios that goes back to the development of Aristotle's *phronesis* (practical wisdom) and *eudaimonia* (happiness) in the *Nicomachean Ethics*. Aristotle did not clearly articulate how leaders emerge and the form and shape of praxis that flows from *phronesis* to bring about the good of order.[23] But the truth is that all great leaders who are change agents make judgments that bring transformation and happiness to the lives of those they serve. Such leaders embrace the grace of authority and the power conferred on them by a

---

15. See Bass and Bass, *Bass Handbook of Leadership*, 219.
16. Robinson, "New Study Shows a Lack of Trust between Employees and Employers." Concerning the importance of trust, see Gill, *Theory and Practice of Leadership*, 140.
17. This distinction is discussed below in connection with James MacGregor Burns.
18. See Heifetz, Grashow, and Linksy, *Practice of Adaptive Leadership*.
19. Burns, *Leadership*, 1.
20. Donald G. Krause, *The Way of the Leader* (London, 1997), ix. Quoted in Gill, *Theory and Practice of Leadership*, 34.
21. Burns, *Leadership*, 23.
22. See Arja Ropo and Perttu Salovaara, "Spacing Leadership as an Embodied and Performative Process," *Leadership* 15.4 (August 2019): 461–79.
23. Ideas for Leaders #202, "Aristotle, Ethics and the Art of Leadership": https://www.ideasforleaders.com/ideas/aristotle-ethics-and-the-%E2%80%98art%E2%80%99-of-leadership. Accessed September 17, 2021.

position as an opportunity for service and a vocation to influence people toward a higher purpose that aims at a society's attainment of its stated goals.

Burns argues that "the potential for real, intended change that addresses the deepest human needs turns crucially on the extent to which humans are able to separate themselves from their confining social roots and growth experiences and thus manage to control their destinies, to act creatively in pursuit of real change. How far can we free ourselves from becoming pawns of situation and 'slaves of history.'"[24] Burns makes a distinction between transaction and transformation with regard to leadership. This is similar to the distinction between manager and leader, which is well captured in this quotation from Richard Kerr, the former secretary of the U.S. Department of Health, Education, and Welfare:

> People don't want to be managed. They want to be led. Whoever heard of a world manager? World leader, yes. Education leader, yes. Political leader. Religious leader. Scout leader. Labor leader. Business leader. Yes. They lead. They don't manage. The carrot always wins over the stick. Ask your horse. You can lead your horse to the water, but you can't manage him to drink. If you want to manage somebody, manage yourself. Do that well and you'll be ready to stop managing and start leading.[25]

Leadership for Burns is not an exercise in naked power wielding; rather, it is oriented toward the goals and needs of the followers and the common good. Every leadership setting involves interactions, motivations, exercises of authority, and division of labor, among other things, all in pursuit of a common purpose.[26] For Burns's "transactional" leadership does not create binding relationships of enduring value; what is important is the task-related business at hand. This functionalist approach to interactions is often driven by a certain pragmatism governed by strong ethical principles; it has a command structure and brings results. However, it is more about maintaining a process, a protocol, policies, guidelines, and institutional prerogatives than about building people up, bringing to birth new and renewed communities of faith creatively embracing the tension between innovation and the traditions of institutions and systems. This transactional leadership is commonplace in some churches and public institutions. What is important is protecting the institution, making sure that rules are obeyed and formulas strictly followed. There is no transparency and mutual accountability between leaders and followers; often, everything is stage-managed and secretive. There is usually no creative freedom in a church setting that operates according to this model, and often respect for and recognition of individual differences is absent.

Transformational leadership, on the other hand, occurs, according to Burns, "when one or more persons engage with others in such a way that leaders and followers raise one another to higher levels of motivation and morality. Their purposes, which might have started out as separate but related, as in the case of transactional leadership, become fused."[27] Peter Northouse provides a good summary of Burns's development of transformational leadership. According to Northouse, transformational leaders set out to empower followers and nurture them in change. Transformational leaders are concerned with improving the performance of followers and developing them to their fullest potential. They attempt to raise the consciousness of individuals and to help them transcend their own self-interest for the sake of others. "Transformational leaders create vision from the collective interests of individuals; that is, they become social architects. They build trust and foster collaboration with others. Transformational leaders encourage others and celebrate their accomplishments. In the end, transformational leaders make people feel better about themselves and their contributions

---

24. Burns, *Transforming Leadership*, 12.
25. Quoted in Maxwell, *Developing the Leader within You*, x–xi.
26. See Burns, *Leadership*, 19–20.
27. Burns, *Leadership*, 20.

to the common good."[28] Burns's transformational leadership has a connection to servant leadership as developed and popularized by Robert Greenleaf. What are the qualities of a transformational or servant leader?

A transformational leader employs less institutional power and less control while shifting authority to those being served.[29] This is why transformational leaders are also servant leaders. Greenleaf's servant leadership concept proposes that the test of servant leadership is how the person who holds power inspires everyone to service. This is the distinctively Christian approach modeled after Jesus Christ, who came to serve and not be served. The Lord Jesus, by serving humanity through self-sacrifice, mercy, compassion, and care for people, modeled a pattern of service for the church (Matt 20:28). The servant leader is first a servant, making sure that other people's needs and priorities come first. As Greenleaf puts it, "The best test, and difficult to administer, is this: Do those served grow as persons? Do they, while being served, become healthier, wiser, freer, more autonomous, more likely themselves to become servants? And, what is the effect on the least privileged in society? Will they benefit or at least not be further deprived?"[30]

According to Greenleaf's framework, some of the qualities of a servant leader include the following: (1) Servant leaders cherish everyone's contribution to the community or church. The community's interests are placed above those of individuals, especially those of the leader. The community exists to promote abundant life and integral salvation for everyone and is greater than the ego or vision of a leader. In such a community, everyone has a sense of being accepted, respected, and trusted, and everyone's gifts and charisms are affirmed with confidence and joy. (2) Servant leaders place more emphasis on listening, empathy, and the unconditional acceptance of others, especially those who are marginal, voiceless, and poor; the have-nots are considered not as a social liability but as equal stakeholders in the life of the organization.

(3) Servant leaders constantly engage their followers; they see themselves as part of the community and not above it; they are informed, formed, and transformed by being rooted in the community. The joy and pain, the hope and despair, of the community rather than their personal egos, whims, and caprices are the driving forces for their daily choices, decisions, and commitments. And (4) servant leaders are judged by the extent to which they have sacrificed their own egos for the collective good and succeeded in making their followers servants of the greater good of the community, school, church, and other social realities.

The final point to note here is that leadership can be learned. Many have advanced leadership theories based on innate traits, arguing that some people are gifted with certain innate leadership qualities and personality types; hence the popular saying that a certain person is "a natural leader" or is "born to lead." My contention here is that natural traits are not enough to make a leader, nor does personality type or deficiencies of any kind disqualify one from acquiring the qualities, attributes, character, and attitudes that make a good leader. Everyone can be a change agent; everyone can learn to be a leader because in Christian language being a leader means nothing more than being a disciple of the Lord, a servant after the heart of Jesus, and a witness in our different vocations to God's great deeds in the world.

The Ethical Cycle of Transformational Servant Leadership

Five practices of transformational servant leadership developed by James Kouzes and Barry Posner in *The Leadership Challenge: The Most Trusted Source on Becoming a Leader* have become widely accepted by many leadership experts. According to Kouzes and Posner, transformational servant leaders do five things, which they summarize as follows:

---

28. I have relied here on the key aspect of transformational leadership offered in Northouse, *Leadership*, 185–88.
29. See Gill, *Theory and Practice of Leadership*, 50.
30. Greenleaf et al., *Servant Leadership*, 27.

1. *Model the Way.* Transformational leaders establish principles concerning the way people (constituents, peers, colleagues, and customers) should be treated and the way goals should be pursued. They create standards of excellence and then set an example for others to follow. Because the prospect of complex change can overwhelm people and stifle action, they set interim goals so that people can achieve small wins as they work toward larger objectives. They unravel bureaucracy when it impedes action; they put up signposts when people are unsure of where to go or how to get there; and they create opportunities for success.
2. *Inspire a Shared Vision.* Transformational leaders passionately believe they can make a difference. They envision the future, creating an ideal and unique image of what the organization can become. Through their magnetism and quiet persuasion, transformational leaders enlist others in the pursuit of their dreams. They breathe life into their visions and get people to see exciting possibilities for the future.
3. *Challenge the Process.* Transformational leaders search for opportunities to change the status quo. They look for innovative ways to improve organizations. In doing so, they experiment and take risks. And because leaders know that risk-taking involves mistakes and failures, they accept inevitable disappointments as learning opportunities.
4. *Enable Others to Act.* Transformational leaders foster collaboration and build spirited teams. They actively involve others. These leaders understand that mutual respect is what sustains extraordinary effort, and they strive to create an atmosphere of trust and human dignity. They strengthen others, making each person feel capable and powerful.
5. *Encourage the Heart.* Accomplishing extraordinary things in organizations is hard work. To keep hope and determination alive, transformational leaders recognize the contributions of individuals. The members of every winning team need to share in the rewards of their efforts, so leaders celebrate accomplishments. They make people feel like heroes.[31]

FIGURE 1. The Ethical Cycle of Transformational Servant Leadership[32]

---

31. Kouzes and Posner, *Leadership Challenge*, 14–23. See also Kouzes and Posner, "Five Practices of Exemplary Leadership," 8–38.
32. Adapted from Northouse, *Leadership*, 387.

Proposals for Ethical Transformational Servant Leadership in the Church in Africa

Even though African societies are changing in a profound way, exercising leadership in the contemporary church, especially in Africa, presents challenges that are only recently being faced. In the recent past, the Catholic priest was the most educated person in a typical African village; he enjoyed contact with the "white man" and fulfilled many roles—doctor, architect, lawyer, teacher, spiritual leader, writer, banker, social worker, and others. His word was final; his knowledge and judgment were indisputable, and people obeyed him without questioning because he literally had the ability to give life and death.

But things are changing today in Africa in the face of modernization, urbanization, the momentum of Christian expansion, an increase in literacy levels, cultural diversity and differentiation, and other social changes. The challenges facing Africa today are complex, partially because they have become framed and interpreted within the wider picture of the dynamics and problematic of African insertion into global processes, in which Africa has not yet been able to find her voice. This is true especially with respect to Christianity; the African church is witnessing growth and ferment not seen elsewhere and is emerging with diverse and distinctive patterns and models of leadership, organization, and creative tension. In addition to this reality are certain historical exigencies of modernization that have given rise to the gradual abandonment of the assumptions of unquestioned church authority and the traditional norms for legitimizing it. An authority figure is no longer presumed to be right but must persuade people in order to be accepted as *authoritative*, rather than just being followed out of fear of the powers of coercion and reward.

The African Church Leader Should Accompany God's People with Love, Not Threats

The church in Africa through its ministers and lay leaders must learn to influence the behavior of her followers by humble, ethical, and servant leadership. In many dioceses in Africa, we hear of priests being posted to difficult parishes or being stripped of honors because they disobeyed their bishops or because they were critical of a superior general. On the political scene, the patron–client relationship, nepotism, and favoritism often predominate in many African countries, making it impossible for political leaders to receive honest and constructive feedback from their followers or collaborators. Thus, in many settings, what is common is rampant sycophancy, rivalry, gossip, calumny, and all kinds of unhelpful behaviors, which weaken the system and poison relationships, hampering the productive and optimal performance of church and society. The question raised here is whether we can find a better way of eliciting cooperation, collaboration, and participatory and communal living through a transformational leadership that influences people through friendship and healthy and mature relationships of respect, reciprocity, and mutuality.

While the central core of belief in Africa has remained the same in terms of God and the interaction of spiritual forces in the procurement of good, there is a strong competition for whose message, prophecy, or claims of access to the abundant life will prevail. The intersection between conflicting yet plausible solutions offered by various religious groups and the contending narratives of meaning and order that have resulted from the social changes being experienced in Africa today thanks to contending narratives of modernity offer a rich texture of possibilities and complex challenges for leaders. They require adaptive skills and new strategies for engaging people and gaining their trust and confidence. In Africa, every belief system—Catholic, Protestant, Pentecostal, traditional African religion, African Independent Churches, Islam, and so on—must vie for legitimacy and learn to accommodate other approaches. This is why I propose that institutional authority must embrace ethical and transformative servant models; it must also be tempered by motivational techniques and inspirational models that spring from a noncoercive- and nonreward-based leadership approach.

African Church Leaders Should Embrace Ongoing Formation in Leadership

Training in leadership is extremely important in today's church. The church and the Holy Spirit should not be left to fill gaping holes in the formation of church leaders; a conscious effort must be made to find ways and means of training church leaders on an ongoing basis. This is similar to what C. S. Lewis wrote with regard to education and why teachers must first become learners and embody in their lives what they wish to see realized in their students:

> No generation can bequeath to its successor what it has not got. You may frame the syllabus as you please. But when you have planned and reported *ad nauseam,* if we are sceptical we shall only teach scepticism to our pupils, if fools only folly, if vulgar only vulgarity, if saints sanctity, if heroes heroism. Education is only the most fully conscious of the channels whereby each generation influences the next. It is not a closed system. Nothing which was not in the teachers can flow from them into the pupils.[33]

Poor leaders produce poor followers and reproduce themselves in the community. The church in Africa must make formation of the leadership of the Christian community a top priority because failing and failed leadership is at the root of the African predicament.

Church leadership in Africa requires more technical and pastoral expertise than in former days. Church leaders need to be trained in issues of governance and administration. They also must imbibe professional ethics and standards relating to boundary issues when dealing with vulnerable people—widows, orphans, the poor, and all those who come seeking help and assistance from the church. The vulnerable who come to our churches must feel safe and must be protected from all kinds of sexual harassment and exploitation. Dioceses and religious communities in Africa must set clear and enforceable guidelines, monitoring, and protocols applicable to all church establishments, structures, and organizations in order to protect the vulnerable as well as the integrity of pastoral workers.

Leaders must be trained with a deep knowledge of the social, cultural, and economic problems of the times. Furthermore, today's leaders need diverse levels of skills in management and leadership, in crisis management, and in relational and social skills. In addition, church leaders must understand the life span of projects from inception to conclusion. They must hone skills in social entrepreneurship, communications, and appropriate language to be employed in discourse and preaching—all needed for any given church activity.

In addition, leaders in the African church today need basic skills in information technology, the use of social media, and related tools. The most important thing is to connect with people at the deepest level, and to meet them where they are and be immersed in and touched by their social context, or as Pope Francis puts it, to have the smell of the sheep in order to accompany the people in their daily joys and sorrows.[34] The nature of the social context and the religious scene demands greater competence and professionalism among church leaders. Although a leader is not required to become an expert in every area touching on people's lives, sufficient competence should be developed so that the leader is able to identify issues, to be critically aware of risks and benefits related to various courses of action, and to know when it is appropriate to ask for expert help.

African Church Leaders Should Involve Everyone in Leading and Serving

An essential part of the leadership that is needed to transform today's church is the ability to carry everyone along the path. In other words, the church leader must draw from a broad pool of talent present in the church, possessed especially by laypeople and particularly by young men and women. The church in Africa must also begin in a very conscious and deliberate way to address the marginalization of women in leadership positions. How can our churches in Africa draw from the assets and spiritual gifts of African women? How can the voices of our women and their spiritual agency be fully accepted and harnessed for the good of the church and society in Africa? These aspirations cannot be realized in the presence of a patriarchal

---

33. Quoted in Gangel, "Spiritual Formation through Public Worship," 214.
34. Pope Francis, *Church of Mercy*, 87.

and male-dominated leadership structure, one that unfortunately replicates in our churches the sad reality of African politics, in which African women are not very visible.

Nepotism, clannishness, tribalism, patriarchy, favoritism, and the use of ecclesiastical positions to reward loyalty are some of the negative tendencies that make it impossible for all the talents and assets in our churches to be put at the service of God, church, and society. Servant leaders do not run the church as a kind of men's club or exclusive club for a select few, those chosen by the leader; rather, they are at the head of a community of all the beloved of the Lord in which everyone feels needed and appreciated. Leaders who try to carry on with the mindset of the pre–Vatican II church, or worse, notions of authority drawn from a Counter-Reformation mindset, will find that, rather than leading people to God, they will constantly be in crisis management, panic, and fighting mode and may actually be hampering the work of God.

Another serious challenge arises from the fact that authority in the church may be shown greater deference by older people who were socialized to respect authority, but not by younger people who need to know why a given teaching or claim should be binding on them. Pluralism, tolerance of divergent views, and suspicion of hierarchical structures create an environment in which church teachings and authority are considered by many to be suggestions and need to be "marketed" to be accepted as binding. The ability to persuade and communicate Christian ideas and church teaching outside the parameters of catechetical instruction and conventional religious language, imagery, and stories is now of critical importance. This includes the ability to lead and inspire by example. Many in contemporary society will form opinions about leaders based on what they do, not just on what they say. The ability to mobilize people and enlist them to join together on a project that in some way fosters the common good is viewed more highly now than in the past. Although a top-down directive approach may work with some, it will not work with a significant number of people. At a minimum, consultative or participatory methods of decision-making, as well as superior communication skills, will be needed. Given that the church is now competing for time, talent, and resources with many other organizations in society, in the churches, and in other religions, leadership must now, in order to inspire confidence and be attractive to the human resources it needs, be far more sensitive to the quality of its relationships and dialogue with parishioners, priests, volunteers, and church workers, as well as to the quality of its interfaith relationships and dialogue with non-Christians and Muslims.

African Church Leaders Should Adopt Integrated Self-Care in Order to Offer a Healthy Pastoral Ministry to God's People
African church leaders must avoid another "triple C" problem, one that relates to self-care. These problems can destroy pastoral ministry.

Complaining. Pastoral agents must quit complaining and whining. Our rectories, chanceries, and convents have sometimes become dark places where low morale and a negative spirit feed a culture of complaint, gossip, and condemnation of all that is wrong with our churches, superiors, and colleagues, and even God's people entrusted into our care. If a person meets every challenge with a complaint, that person's soul will not be nourished and he or she will only spew out words that do not heal and attitudes that harm individuals and tarnish the ecclesial spirit. You cannot serve people or work with them if you secretly loathe them or think them less than worthy.

Criticism. Too much of this flows from the first attitude. If we do not see our lives and our service as graced opportunities to do something beautiful for God, then every pastoral situation becomes an occasion for criticism and condemnation rather than an opportunity for blessing. God's people in Africa are hungry for joyful and positive church leaders who are slow to judge, criticize, calumniate, and talk about people with a harsh tone. African church leaders must respect the people they serve and listen to them and accept their feedback with joy and deference and treat the laity as adults and discerning believers. Church leaders must be open to sometimes being led by their followers to places they have not been before. A leader must make judgments for sure; indeed, an essential quality of a good leader, as we pointed out in reference to Aristotle's *phronesis,* is the ability to judge situations rightly and choose the right course of action. But wise leaders are humble enough to appreciate the fact that being in a leadership position does not grant them exclusive access to the wisdom of God or the fruits of the Holy Spirit.

Both church and society in Africa are undergoing a period of transition and transformation; these are the birth pangs of a new heaven and a new earth in Africa. This requires that church leaders be slow to put forth definitive judgments and guidelines for the people. Church leaders should not be quick to read people the riot act but should lovingly and mercifully accompany God's people on their journey to the future, the destination of which God alone knows. Furthermore, they must listen to the people, respect them, and treat them as adults. They should not dismiss the people's opinions and perspectives, as well as their time-honored cultural practices, as being uninformed or irrelevant or coming from an anti-Christian worldview because they erroneously conclude that these opinions do not fit into some preconceived notion of what is Christian.

Comparison. This is the killer of joy. Every pastoral agent is unique and has a special calling and special gifts. Everyone must discover his or her vocation within the common vocation of priesthood, religious life, marriage, and so on. The same applies to every Christian and every faith community. People differ and churches differ. An attitude of respecting and embracing diversity is something that church leaders in Africa must learn to adopt so that everyone's unique gifts are embraced. How many bishops are internally suffering because they are comparing their diocese with others or because they think they should be in a bigger diocese? With this negative mindset, bishops and leaders of orders become frustrated with themselves and their perceived opposition, and they gradually become very hard and harsh on their followers, coming down heavily on their priests while neglecting or looking down on the community they have been given the privilege of serving! How many bishops are wasting diocesan money on white elephant projects because they want to be like another diocese or because they are in vain pursuit of a personal legacy, when the resources available to them are incapable of realizing their fanciful folly! How often has the relationship between bishop and priest collapsed because both have failed to enter into a subject-centered relationship; on the priest's side, he might be comparing the way his classmate was treated in another diocese by another bishop to what he perceives as harsh treatment from his bishop. Comparison in pastoral ministry brings unnecessary competition and rivalry; it leads to vain pursuits and can also lead pastoral agents to waste the spiritual or material resources of the people on useless undertakings.

Pastoral self-care for priests and religious and other pastoral agents is vital in the areas of health, lifestyle, eating, and exercise; choice of friends; personal, spiritual, and intellectual development; ongoing formation of character; emotional life; sexual and affectionate maturity; personal and church financial management; management of time and psychological well-being; and social awareness. It will involve abandoning a savior mentality and messiah complex, and developing the capacity to be open to correction and to receiving criticism and positive and negative feedback with gratitude.[35]

A Christian leader should not be wounded by criticism or inflated by praise; everything should be received with joy, humility, and gratitude. Sometimes what trips up a pastoral agent in the face of opposition might simply be that his or her emotional tank has been empty for a long time or that a hole in the heart is crying out for attention and love. Most of the challenges and conflicts in our parishes and chanceries as well as in our social ministry in Africa are not the result of ill will on the part of the laity or the pastoral leader; in most cases, they are the result of failed leadership, the emotional instability of the leader, or knee-jerk reactionary responses to inconsequential matters by pastoral agents—priests, bishops, religious, and others. Pastoral agents who do not know how to deal with people or how to respect the diversity of opinions in the church can do great harm to themselves and to the church. My experience visiting many African

---

35. See, for instance, Paul Midden's essay "I've Spent 30 Years Counseling Priests Who Fall in Love. Here's What I Learned," *Vox* (October 5, 2016), www.vox.com.

churches has taught me that most of the issues that come up could be transformed into opportunities for growth if our pastoral agents would adopt a self-care regimen that helps them to become more critical of their own blind spots, sinfulness, and biases, and more aware of the larger context of their service. A pastoral agent with a good self-care regimen can become a transformational servant leader able to provide a healthy and life-changing pastoral ministry for God's people after the heart of Jesus.[36]

Transformational Pastoral Ministry

Pastoral ministry involves developing various skill sets that will enable ministers to walk with the people they serve in love in such a way that the Christian leader can become all things to all people. Pastoral ministry for an ethical, transformational servant leader begins with seeing each person as embodying the image of Christ. It is all about walking with people so that they can realize their vocations in life. Pastoral ministry proceeds through a deep encounter with others at different stages of their lives and growth so that they can discover the beauty in their lives and in the world, and so that the pastoral minister can discover the beauty in his or her own life through service. The goal of pastoral ministry is to lead the people into the mysteries of God and to allow every encounter with people in the act of pastoral service to become a medium for encountering God. Every meeting becomes a graced opportunity to meet God. Pastoral ministry aims at leading God's people into the mysteries of God's love so that they can live and work in hope, seeing something beautiful for their lives and the light of Christ in every situation, even difficult ones. It is service to the people so that they will want to imitate Christ and find personal fulfillment and purpose through embracing life and other people as gifts. Pastoral ministry aims at making each and every one of us guardians of one another and guardians of the treasures of the gospel, which has been entrusted to us as Christians through the church, our mother.

Simply put, pastoral ministry aims at celebrating and making every member of the Christian community a friend of every other member and a friend of God. This is the offer God has already extended to humanity in Christ when he said to his followers that he calls them friends. Jesus, who is the incarnation of love, calls them friends because of the quality of the love he has for them. In addition, he did not hide anything from them—he reposed his trust in them by giving them the secrets of the kingdom and the mission of bringing about that kingdom to the ends of the earth (John 6:37; 15:15; Matt 13:11; Mark 4:11). The friendship model proposes that loving people deeply, enabling them to act, and encouraging their hearts can happen only when we are learning to love and teaching others to love through selfless acts of service in humble self-surrender. Deepening pastoral ministry involves an ethical transformational servant leader who is able to weave a new level of connection and intimacy animated by love, respect, care, compassion, trust, and hope for the future and to promote the intrinsic beauty of everyone and the world around us. It requires discovering again the divine harmony within the brokenness of our lives and world.

African Church Leaders Should Have People Skills

Finally, it is important to note that the Christian leader must have adequate people skills to be able to persuade and inspire, not just demand and enforce obedience. Given the complex social environment of the present day, the effective leader must have a minimum level of competence in each of the seven "intelligences": cognitive, emotional, social, cultural, moral, spiritual, and behavioral.[37] Because leaders can no longer expect to be followed by most people based on institutional position alone, the integrity of the leader's whole person will be judged in light of his or her deeds, not just words. How the leader treats people figures significantly in this judgment. As a result, effective leadership now requires technical, psychological, spiritual, and relational abilities that will be assessed in the light of personal authenticity. Reliance on one's title is no longer good enough. Successful leadership today requires a wider range of skill sets and a greater

---

36. Some recommended self-care practices were developed in Berry, *When Helping You Is Hurting Me*.
37. Gill, *Theory and Practice of Leadership*, 287–320.

degree of personal integration than in the past when greater deference was shown to authority figures. Effective leadership must start from within and then be validated through both institutional appointment and recognition by the community. It must be sufficiently motivational to inspire service in an environment in which many claims are made on people's time. In short, it requires a fully developed, mature spiritual leader who, as Henri Nouwen put it, can touch both the hand of God and the hand of others to create and transform communities. But this demands a radical change of mentality and also a change in the way we have structured both our churches and positions of authority within them. According to Nouwen:

> The Christian leader of the future is called to be completely irrelevant and to stand in this world with nothing to offer but his or her own vulnerable self. This is the way Jesus came to reveal God's love. The great message that we have to carry, as ministers of God's Word and followers of Jesus, is that God loves us not because of what we do or accomplish, but because God has created and redeemed us in love and has chosen us to proclaim that love as the true source of all human life.[38]

Conclusion

In the early church, the Christian leader was considered a wise person who discerned in the complexities of life and changing times the finger of God in all things. The people listen to the Christian leader and trust him or her not because the leader has coercive, punitive, or vindictive power, but rather because he or she has spiritual power and is the mouthpiece of the Lord of Hosts (Mal 2:7). The Christian leader is a holy person who lives life in imitation of Christ. He or she may not be perfect, but the Christian leader lives in such a way that people can see a light in the leader's way of life that is capable of illuminating the darkness in their own daily lives. Both ways of living—holiness and wisdom—are usually the fruits of prayer, meditation on the Word of God, an insatiable thirst to seek wisdom and personal growth from multiple sources, self-discipline, self-care, ascetic practices, spiritual exercises, humble attention to God, an openness to listening to others, and an ongoing conversion of life by turning to God always. This comes about because the committed Christian leader is constantly in the presence of God and can move readily from this presence into the presence of people and from the presence of people back to the presence of God. It is in this double action of going forth and returning that the Christian leader finds his or her anchor in God, and in fact, to meet a Christian leader is indeed to meet God. This is why we give symbolic titles to our clergy; for instance, priests are called "reverend fathers"—that is, those who are touched by holiness, who make things holy, and who mediate between God and the people. Indeed, one of the earliest characterizations of the clergy in the early church was "those who make Christ present or those who show the divinity of Christ." The Christian leader is thus normed as it were by the words and deeds of Christ.

The two attributes of wisdom and holiness are reflected in the Christian leader's commitment to serving God and people without counting the cost—it could be said that the leader is engaged in washing the feet of the poor in humble service. These attributes bear majestic fruit in the Christian leader's willingness to die for the truth of the gospel, to die to himself or herself so that Christ will rise in him or her. This is the motto St. Paul left us: more of Christ and less of me (Eph 3:8; Phil 3:8). More for the people of God, less for me. One is not called to be a priest or bishop in the church in order, for example, to pursue a personal project, to represent a particular interest, to fill a cultural, ethnic, or clannish quota, or to serve the interests of a select few. The Catholic Church mirrors in her membership, in her ministerial order, and in her sacramental life the eschatological fruits of God's kingdom. The church teaches us all to live in such a way that even here and now we promote through our lifestyle and choices a life beyond tribe, language, and nation. In teaching us to live as one family, Catholicism inspires the hope and anticipates here and now the vision that we will all one

---

38. Nouwen, *In the Name of Jesus*, 17.

day live forever in God's kingdom, where everyone is a firstborn child of God beyond cultural, clannish, or racial identities (Rev 5:9; 7:9). This is what Paul meant when he wrote, "For all of you who were baptized into Christ have clothed yourselves with Christ. There is neither Jew nor Greek, there is neither slave nor free man, there is neither male nor female; for you are all one in Christ Jesus. And if you belong to Christ, then you are Abraham's descendants, heirs according to the promise" (Gal 3:27–29). Our baptism in Christ assures us of God's grace at work in us, helping us to lead and be led into the future, which mirrors the coming reign of God in our families, churches, and wider society, in both Africa and the rest of the world.

There is a need for a greater understanding of the challenges of leadership in the churches in Africa and how these challenges affect the quality of pastoral ministry and the church's own standing and effectiveness as a witness in the African society of today. Greater emphasis should now be placed on the mentoring of future leaders and on equipping and strengthening the agency of the lay members of Christ's faithful for service in the church and society. Catholic scholars should devote greater attention to researching and documenting the best practices exhibited by the life and service of church leaders—both ordained and nonordained—who have demonstrated sound and transformative leadership in various aspects of the church's life.

Bibliography

Allen, John. *Against the Tide: The Radical Leadership of Pope Francis*. 1st ed. Liguori, MO: Liguori, 2014.

Balthasar, Hans Urs von, and Brian McNeil. *My Work in Retrospect*. 1st ed. San Francisco: Ignatius Press, 1993.

Bass, Bernard M., and Ruth Bass. *The Bass Handbook of Leadership: Theory, Research and Managerial Applications*. 1st ed. New York: Free Press, 2008.

Benedict XVI, Pope. *Africae Munus* [Post-synodal Apostolic Exhortation on the Church in Africa in Service of Reconciliation, Justice and Peace; November 19, 2011]. Vatican City: Libreria Editrice Vaticana, 2011. www.vatican.va.

Berry, Carmen Renee. *When Helping You Is Hurting Me: Escaping the Messiah Trap*. New York: Crossroad, 2003.

Burns, James MacGregor. *Leadership*. 1st ed. (paperback). New York: Harper Perennial Political Classics, 2010.

———. *Transforming Leadership*. 1st ed. New York: Grove Press, 2003.

Francis, Pope. *The Church of Mercy: A Vision for the Church*. 1st ed. Chicago: Loyola Press, 2014.

———. Full Text of the Pope's First Speech in Kenya. *Rome Reports*. November 25, 2015, www.romereports.com.

———. *Gaudete et Exsultate* [Apostolic Exhortation on the Call to Holiness in Today's World; April 9, 2018]. Vatican City: Libreria Editrice Vaticana, 2018. www.vatican.va.

———. "Presentation of the Christmas Greeting to the Roman Curia" (December 22, 2014).

Francis, Pope, and Andrea Tornielli. *The Name of God Is Mercy*. 1st ed. New York: Random House, 2016.

Gangel, Kenneth O. "Spiritual Formation through Public Worship." In *The Christian Educator's Handbook on Spiritual Formation*, edited by Kenneth O. Gangel and James C. Wilhoit. Grand Rapids, MI: Baker Books, 1997.

Gill, Roger. *Theory and Practice of Leadership*. 1st ed. Thousand Oaks, CA: Sage, 2013.

Greenleaf, Robert K., Larry C. Spears, Stephen R. Covey, and Peter M. Senge. *Servant Leadership: A Journey into the Nature of Legitimate Power and Greatness*. 1st ed. New York: Paulist Press, 2002.

Heifetz, Ronald, Alexander Grashow, and Marty Linksy. *The Practice of Adaptive Leadership: Tools and Tactics for Changing Your Organization and the World*. 1st ed. Boston: Harvard Business Press, 2009.

Kasper, Walter, and William Madges. *Pope Francis' Revolution of Tenderness and Love*. 1st ed. New York: Paulist Press, 2015.

Kouzes, James M., and Barry Z. Posner. "The Five Practices of Exemplary Leadership." In *Christian Reflections on the Leadership Challenge*, edited by James M. Kouzes and Barry Z. Posner, 8–38. 1st ed. San Francisco: Jossey Bass, 2006.

———. *The Leadership Challenge: The Most Trusted Source on Becoming a Leader*. 4th ed. New York: Wiley, 2007.

Maxwell, John C. *Developing the Leader within You*. 3rd ed. Nashville, TN: Thomas Nelson, 1993.

Northouse, Peter Guy. *Leadership: Theory and Practice*. 5th ed. Thousand Oaks, CA: Sage, 2010.

Nouwen, Henri. *In the Name of Jesus.* New York: Crossroad, 2012.

Poddolny, Joel M., Rakesh Khurana, and Marya L. Besharov. "Revisiting the Meaning of Leadership." In *Handbook of Leadership Theory and Practice*, edited by Nitin Nohria and Rakesh Khurana. 1st ed. Boston: Harvard Business Review Press, 2017.

"Reform of the Roman Curia." *Concilium* 2013.5.

Robinson, Bryan. "New Study Shows a Lack of Trust between Empoyees and Employers." *Forbes,* September 5, 2021, www.forbes.com.

Shinagel, Michael. "The Paradox of Leadership." Harvard Division of Continuing Education. July 3, 2013. dce.harvard.edu.

Key Words
authority
ethical leadership
leadership
pastoral ministry
power
servant leadership
service
transformational leadership

The Global Context of African Catholicism

Richard Benson, CM

The gift you have received, give as a gift.
—Matthew 10:8

The title of this chapter suggests at least four subtopics that need to be addressed, of which perhaps the most intriguing and foundational is the meaning of "Africa," which actually provides a frame and raison d'être for this reflection in the first place. One could say that without an "Africa" there could not be such a thing as "African Catholicism." Second, we will need to explore some elements that define both the secular and Catholic "global" contexts in which Africa and African Catholicism find themselves. Third, we will examine some elements of the global Catholic Church. And, finally, our research into these larger contexts will allow us to contextualize African Catholicism locally and examine the impact of twenty-first-century globalization on the postcolonial church.

In approaching this subject there are several overarching terms, formal in nature, that will be integral to our discussion and so will demand some further attention at various points in the chapter; these are *context, contextualization,* and *inculturation.*

Recognizing Africa: Modernity and Postcolonialism

The context in which African Catholicism finds itself is considerably smaller and noticeably more global than it has been at any point in history. It is imperative that African Catholicism continue to recognize the factors that are part of the global matrix in which it lives and continue to participate as a full dialogue partner with the universal church, while living out the particularity of the African context in which it lives and thrives. Thus, no one should be surprised to see that globalization will allow Africa to raise its own voice in many ways and take ownership of how it chooses "to be church," and that perhaps Africa and African Catholicism may affect the face of the universal Catholic Church in surprising ways.

Out of Africa

The continent of Africa, from which many anthropologists assume the human family first emerged[1] and began its global migration, finds itself in some ways having come full circle. It is surrounded by globalized particularities that have become the particularly global. Are we witnessing the beginning of a new migration from Africa, a migration that is sending ideas, attitudes, and notions, as well as members of local African churches to all corners of the Catholic globe? Clearly, African Catholicism is in dialogue with the local, the particular, and the global church in a number of significant ways. This reality deserves theological investigation. We will first attempt to situate Africa as a locality, a host

---

1. According to James Owen, "Scientists who compared the skulls and DNA of human remains from around the world say their results point to modern humans (Homo sapiens) having a single origin in Af-

of particularities, and then proceed to examine African Catholicism and its global context through the lenses of *solidarity* and *subsidiarity*, which will allow a point of departure for understanding Africa's global context as dialogical in nature.

Modern Africa

We begin by suggesting that too often there are more "myths" about Africa than actual knowledge in the imaginations of non-Africans. Curtis Keim suggests, "Such an imaginary Africa is kept alive by ignorance and by the benefits we get from myths about African difference."[2] Admittedly, he notes, "Africa has more visible problems than any other region of the world, and Africa is the most rural of the continents except for Antarctica. However, Africa's problems are not inherent to Africa. That is, they are not natural. They were created in a history that included Western civilization as well as the civilizations of Africa."[3] Nevertheless, Africa looks more like the rest of the world than different from it. "Africa is 40 percent urban; cities are growing faster in Africa than anywhere else.... An average of 57 percent of adults have cellphones.... Nigeria, Kenya, and South Africa are exploring space programs."[4]

Modern Africa is living in a globalizing and in many ways already globalized world but is challenged in finding a universal welcome in this new reality, to some extent because of the historical impact it has felt from non-African forces, both secular and Christian. In her text *The Challenge for Africa*, Nobel Peace Prize winner Wangari Maathai remarks on this very fact.

The modern African state is a superficial creation: a loose collection of ethnic communities or micro-nations, brought together in a single entity, or macro-nation, by the colonial powers. Some countries include hundreds of micro-nations within their borders; others, only a few. Kenya has forty-two; Nigeria, two hundred and fifty; Cameroon, at least two hundred; Mozambique, more than ten; Gabon, more than forty; Zimbabwe, fewer than ten; and Burundi and Rwanda, three.... With a few exceptions, it is these numbers that determine political power.

Most Africans did not understand or relate to the nation-states created for them by the colonial powers; they understood, related to, and remained attached to the physical and psychological boundaries of their micro-nations. Consequently, even today, for many African peoples, a threat to their micro-nation or those they consider their leaders within their micro-nation carries more weight than a threat to the nation-state. At the same time, each community hopes to have access to the resources of the nation-state should someone from their micronation assume political power [particularly the post of president or prime minister]. In this way, the community will have, as is said in Kenya, its "time to eat."[5]

While some countries in Africa may be substantially constituted of people of a similar language and culture, many others, as mentioned above, made up of multiple micro-nations, were drawn up and given artificial borders, artificial political identities, and even artificial names by colonial powers. There are over two hundred different micro-nations in the Democratic Republic of the Congo (formerly Zaire) and these groups speak at least 210 different languages.[6] While tensions have

---

rica.... The new data support the single origin, or 'out of Africa' theory for anatomically modern humans, which says that these early humans colonized the planet after spreading out of the continent some 50,000 years ago" ("Modern Humans Came Out of Africa, 'Definitive' Study Says," *National Geographic*, July 18, 2007, www.nationalgeographic.com).

2. Keim, *Mistaking Africa*, 80.
3. Keim, *Mistaking Africa*, 81.
4. Keim, *Mistaking Africa*, 81.
5. Maathai, *Challenge for Africa*, 184.
6. *Ethnologue* (https://www.ethnologue.com/country/CG) lists 211 languages spoken in the country. Of these, 210 are living and 1 is extinct. Of the living languages, 205 are indigenous and 5 are nonindigenous. Furthermore, 9 are institutional, 31 are developing, 155 are vigorous, 8 are in trouble, and 7 are dying.

risen among indigenous African peoples because of the artificial constraints imposed by colonial powers, it must be recognized also that some of the political turmoil and violence evident in a number of the African countries is the result of intertribal issues, local pushback between tribes.

Yet even tribalism has a colonial connection. Michela Wrong, in writing about Kenya, suggests that much of the tribalism affecting parts of Africa was not present before colonization and so can be attributed to some extent to colonizers who designed policies that would result in previously nonexistent conflicts between tribes and ethnic groups. Such policies were part of a strategy that was specifically designed to maintain power in the hands of the colonizers and their local collaborators.

> "There's no ideological debate here [in Kenya]," complain incoming diplomats, baffled by a political system in which notions of "left" or "right," "capitalist" or "socialist," "radical" or "conservative" seem irrelevant: "It's all about tribe." . . . A [political] party's only purpose is furthering its tribe's interests. . . . "So," commented a Kikuyu taxi driver when he overheard me expressing skepticism about the likelihood of an Obama win in the 2008 US election, "I see you Westerners have problems with the Luo too." Yet, perversely, the strength of these stereotypes is in inverse proportion to their longevity. Rooted in the country's experience as a British colony, Kenya's acute ethnic self-awareness, far from being an expression of "atavistic tribal tensions" is actually a fairly recent development. While no one would claim that colonialism created the country's tribal distinctions, it certainly ensured that ethnic affiliation became the key criterion determining a citizen's life chances.[7]

Thus, conflicts continue partly as the result of colonial policies that have had a long-term negative effect on the peoples of Africa. Many of the local tribes of Africa, and thus many African Catholics, are unhappy with having been made citizens of nation-states that were not of their own invention. For many African Catholics their most significant contexts likely are religious and tribal, not national. The most important contextual identity is often very local, probably family, village, and tribe. In order to understand Africa and its place in the "global matrix" that envelops it, one must appreciate that, for Africans, the local context is often the deepest part of their identity. While this conclusion may hold a piece of the truth for every person on the planet to one degree or another, the extent and depth to which it is true for Africa is a point that cannot be overlooked. This insight is of course significant for our discussion, as many attempts to contextualize the Catholic Church in Africa have been mostly about deconstructing the colonial linkages between the church and the European cultural addenda that the missionaries saw as almost essential elements of the faith. It is important to note, however, that a postcolonial church is in reality only a stop on the journey to authentic inculturation.

It is also very important to recognize the inherent and essential ethical differences between the terms *tribe* and *tribalism*. An African person's identification with his or her tribe implies a deep experience of community, family, and solidarity. One's very self-consciousness is an interwoven blend of autonomy and tribal identity. The importance of tribal identity is a reality that is very difficult for Westerners to grasp because their self-identity and self-awareness are almost exclusively identified with the principle of autonomy and self-actualization. The full implications of *tribe* or *micro-nation* offer to the world a challenge to identify the ethical foundation of society as something much more than that arising out of a group of autonomous individuals. Whereas Western society is often characterized by autonomy or "enlightened self-interest," traditional tribal identity involves a deep relationship with others as kin, a relationship that includes something like "part-of-me as other." This type of social village is a very different concept from the community that is generally found in the Western world.

---

7. Wrong, *It's Our Turn to Eat*, 44.

Tribalism is not the same reality as *tribe*; it implies the unethical notion that human society is founded on exclusivity rather than on inclusivity. While the notion and reality of *tribe* are established on a deep sense of inclusivity of the other as kin, *tribalism* is powered by a notion of the other as being excluded as kin, as one's equal sister or brother. Thus, while the ethical notion of *tribe* should be welcomed by the West as a corrective to a society based almost exclusively on a right to absolute autonomy, the unethical notion of *tribalism* needs to be rooted out of any society in which it furthers exclusivity and prevents the other from participating in authentic communion in society. Unfortunately, tribalism can be found in some form in every human community and can be fostered in some ways by globalization. Indeed, the chant "America First" is nothing more than tribalism masked as nationalism.

Recognizing Contexts

As far as religious *context* is concerned, African Catholicism, like secular Africa itself, finds itself in the midst of both a global context and a variety of local, continental contexts. A brief review of the history of Catholicism in Africa demonstrates that it came to the continent in four major waves: two precolonial, one colonial, and one postcolonial. Each of these waves represents a different but integral part of the Catholic context of Africa.

The first wave of Christianity came to Africa with the earliest of the missionary disciples, not long after the death of Jesus.

Of all the early centers of Christendom in the first century CE, Alexandria, the commercial capital of Egypt, was perhaps the most important. Alexandria was home to many of the early scholars who first defined the theology of the new religion. It was here that one of the earliest Christian bishoprics was said to have been founded by the apostle and Gospel-writer Mark.[8]

From this beginning, Christianity spread in the second and third centuries throughout North Africa. Eventually, between 500 and 600 CE, Christian missionaries from Egypt pushed south as far as Nubia. "Later Arab writers described the upper Nile valley of Christian Nubia. . . . It is clear that along the upper Nile there flourished a distinct Nubian Christian civilization that long outlived the seventh-century Arab invasion of Egypt."[9] While this first wave of Christianity was confined almost exclusively to North Africa and came to be divided into both Roman and Coptic churches, that early Christian church, which remains alive today, is clearly precolonial and not the result of either colonial or postcolonial missionary efforts.

Later, there was to be a second precolonial Catholic presence to arrive in Africa, this time to sub-Saharan Africa. In the fifteenth and sixteenth centuries, Catholic missionaries were quick to follow the Portuguese traders who were making some headway on the coastlines of southern Africa. However, as Kevin Shillington points out,

> once African rulers realized the strong political motivation behind their presence, the missionaries' initiative was doomed to failure. . . . It was clear that European Christianity, as a vehicle for religious and cultural change, had made virtually no impact at all on the peoples of sub-Saharan Africa. By contrast, the Christian revival of the early nineteenth century was a very different matter. Though initially slow to take effect, eventually its impact proved to be both far-reaching and permanent.[10]

A third significant wave of Christianity came with the founding of the European colonies in Africa. Colonialism was an active imposition of European culture on African people, a culture that too often the Christian evangelizers were not able to separate from the universal nature of their faith. Evangelization assumed the passive acceptance by converts of elements of a European culture embedded in the Catholicism in which they were baptized and catechized. As Shillington notes, "Few Christian missionaries were directly active agents of

---

8. Shillington, *History of Africa*, 73.
9. Shillington, *History of Africa*, 75–76.
10. Shillington, *History of Africa*, 296–97.

European imperialism. But they were an essential ingredient of the increasingly assertive European presence which was a forerunner of imperial control. In a number of cases, Christian missionaries played a significant role in promoting and shaping the advent of European colonialism."[11]

The fourth wave of Christianity is a postcolonial singularity. There has been a literal explosion of Christianity in sub-Saharan Africa since its people were emancipated from their former colonial rulers. This growth in Christianity has involved the entire Christian family, Roman Catholic, Orthodox, and Reformed. "If demography is destiny, then Christianity's future lies in Africa. By 2060, a plurality of Christians—more than four-in-ten—will call sub-Saharan Africa home, up from 26% in 2015, according to a new analysis of demographic data by Pew Research Center. At the same time, the share of Christians living in many other regions—notably Europe—is projected to decline."[12] It is precisely these two facts, the large numbers of baptized Catholics and the phenomenal growth of the church in Africa, that contribute to the identity of the postcolonial Catholic Church in Africa being significantly different from both its precolonial and colonial versions.

These various continental religious contexts in recently evangelized Africa are a complex matrix of particularities of cultures and religious practices and rites that mimic the global family of Eastern and Western Catholic churches, which are themselves joined together in the larger singularity of the universal Catholic Church. Thus, there is room in the rich ecclesiology of the Catholic Church for African Catholicism to make itself both genuinely local and genuinely global. This is part of the project of the growing Catholic Church in Africa as it seeks self-identity and at the same time dialogue with and participation in the globalized world.

On the secular level, this experience of living simultaneously in a global and local context, of being situated in a matrix of horizons is now true for every person on earth. The global and local contexts that make up each person's and culture's horizons are both inherited and of human manufacture

and design. Our contexts, whether local or global, determine our choices, at least to some extent, while at the same time our choices contribute to the makeup of our contexts.

Globalization: A New Paradigm?

The term "globalization" and similar constructs with comparable meanings have certainly become a part of a significant number of business and, especially, academic conversations relating to economics, sociology, law, and of course theology, among other fields. Thomas Friedman, in his book *The World Is Flat: A Brief History of the Twenty-First Century*, is often credited with bringing the issue of globalization into both the boardroom and the classroom. In the book, he makes the argument that the world that is experienced everywhere on the globe has in most respects transcended the local. While it is true that Friedman is almost exclusively discussing the global business experience, almost no personal experience can divorce itself from the global reality in which it finds itself. Friedman's basic thesis is that globalization is the result of ten "flatteners," most of which are new technologies, including hardware, software, and mobile communication platforms. These "flatteners" allow the business world to thrive and of course profit in a global context in a way that was not previously possible. Friedman then suggests a "triple convergence" as the point of departure for the new global world. When these ten "flatteners," like the internet, personal computers, mobile applications, and mobile devices are combined with new ways of doing business and the input of new entrepreneurs, the overall result is a new, global, "flat" earth as far as the world of business and commerce is concerned. Friedman writes,

> It is the triple convergence—of new players, on a new playing field, developing new processes and habits for horizontal collaboration—that I believe is the most important force shaping global economics and politics in the early twenty-first century. Giving so

---

11. Shillington, *History of Africa*, 301.
12. McClendon, "Sub-Saharan Africa Will Be Home to Growing Shares of the World's Christians and Muslims."

many people access to all these tools of collaboration, along with the ability through search engines and the Web to access billions of pages of raw information, ensures that the next generation of innovations will come from all over Planet Flat. The scale of the global community that is soon going to be able to participate in all sorts of discovery and innovation is something the world has simply never seen before.[13]

Friedman's insight is much more than merely the fact that technology is available and being used globally—it is that the technology is a new foundation for a way of "being world." The new way transcends the local, or at least subsumes the local into the global. Thus, for Friedman, we all live in a global context that is, or should be, more and more similar in most ways. Admittedly, he is applying his global context almost exclusively to the world of business and commerce within a clearly capitalistic framework. However, it is not a stretch for us to look beyond the business horizon to see that many of the forces he points to and much of what he says regarding "flatteners" and the "triple convergence" have some currency in almost every aspect of our lives, including our ecclesial contexts. We can reasonably expect that globalization will affect how African Catholics will "be church" (in every dimension of how the baptized are called to be the people of God) in the twenty-first century.

African Catholicism and Global Catholicism

Lamin Sanneh, who has examined the growing globalization of Christianity, especially in Africa, argues that at least some aspects of Friedman's paradigm are accurate and reasonably predictive. Speaking specifically of the changing face of the church of Africa, he writes,

> The current transformation of Christianity in a postcolonial world allows us to track on a global scale the coming structural changes of faith and the public order. In this highly unstable milieu, the real challenge for the churches is no longer what it once so clearly was—namely, the largely conceded case for the populist overthrow of colonial hegemony in favor of uncontested national state power—but rather the still underdeveloped case for a moral bill of rights that would serve as a foundation for new forms of society.[14]

Sanneh is suggesting that globalization is more than a fact; like Friedman, he sees it as an opportunity. The global context is precisely an opportunity to "be church" in a new way, to "be church" in such a way that the gifts that are inherent in the diversity of the peoples of Africa are shared globally through a faith and theology that are not borrowed but are the fruits of the Spirit in an authentically indigenous Christianity.

Over the past century, the number of Catholics around the globe has more than tripled, from an estimated 291 million in 1910 to nearly 1.1 billion as of 2010, according to a comprehensive demographic study by the Pew Research Center.[15] In 1910, Catholics comprised about half (48 percent) of all Christians and 17 percent of the world's total population, according to historical estimates from the World Christian Database. A century later, the Pew Research study found that Catholics still comprise about half (50 percent) of Christians worldwide and 16 percent of the total global population. What has changed substantially over the past century is the geographic distribution of the world's Catholics. In 1910, Europe was home to about two-thirds of all Catholics, and nearly nine in ten lived in either Europe (65 percent) or Latin America (24 percent). By 2010, by contrast, only about a quarter of all Catholics (24 percent) were in Europe. The largest share (39 percent) were in Latin America and the Caribbean, and through 2017 rapid growth has continued to occur in sub-Saharan Africa, which today is home to about 222 million Catholics[16] (16 percent), up from an estimated 1 million

---

13. Friedman, *World Is Flat*, 182–83.
14. Sanneh, "Conclusion: The Current Transformation of Christianity," 221–22.
15. Pew Research Center, "Global Christianity."
16. Vatican bulletin: *The Pontifical Yearbook 2017* and the "*Annuarium Statisticum Ecclesiae*" 2015.

The Global Context of African Catholicism

(less than 1 percent) in 1910. The Catholic population in Africa has grown by 238 percent since 1980 and is now over 220 million. This explosion is outstripping the growth in the number of priests, up 131 percent, and of parishes, up 112 percent. "If current trends in affiliation and differential fertility among religious groups continue, in 2040, 24 percent of Africans will be Catholic. This would result in a Catholic population of 460,350,000 in Africa."[17]

In light of our comments above, perhaps it is possible to use Friedman's ideas as a starting point for focusing on globalization and the Catholic Church, specifically by allowing us to situate African Catholicism in its proper place in the world of global Catholicism. All the available data about the worldwide Catholic population points to the Global South as its new center, and Africa has figured prominently in this shift. Demographic data establish, as we have seen, that Africa has been marked by a phenomenal Catholic growth, well beyond that experienced anywhere else except maybe, to a lesser degree, some areas of Asia. While the number of Catholic parishes has been declining in Europe, the number in Africa has been growing at a rate of more than 100 percent over the past thirty years. During that same time, the Catholic population of Africa has quadrupled. What does this mean for African Catholicism both in its local context and on the global stage? How is African Catholicism, largely a postcolonial church, responding to both phenomenal growth and the impact of globalization? Is African Catholicism redefining itself, gaining a new strength and taking on a new role in global Catholicism? A review of worldwide Catholic demographics from the end of the twentieth century through the first decade of the twenty-first century provides a clear indication of Catholicism's rise in Africa, as seen in the following table:[18]

Continental Catholic Population Changes, 1980–2012

	1980	1990	2000	2010	2012
Africa	58,676,000	88,899,000	130,018,000	185,620,000	198,587,000
Americas	384,816,000	461,264,000	519,391,000	585,998,000	598,819,000
Asia	62,713,000	86,012,000	107,302,000	129,661,000	134,641,000
Europe	271,649,000	285,294,000	280,144,000	284,924,000	286,868,000
Oceania	5,806,000	7,031,000	8,202,000	9,468,000	9,706,000
World	783,660,000	928,500,000	1,045,057,000	1,195,671,000	1,228,621,000

The Global Context: Its Meaning for Africa

Above we examined the demographics of Catholicism in Africa, but in fact, numbers alone are only part of the story of African Catholicism. The *contextualization* of Catholicism is in fact the real story that waits to be told. Authentic contextualization of the faith is much more than evangelization in context or the removal of colonial accoutrements; it involves a church that has found its own voice. African Catholicism is becoming authentically African and authentically Catholic. Sanneh makes the point that "preindustrial primal societies in the Southern Hemisphere that once stood outside the main orbit of the religion have become major Christian centers. They are inducing cultural movements and realignments that only now are coming into their own, especially those in the new urban centers of the global South and East."[19] Continuing his comments on the globalization of Christianity, Sanneh remarks,

---

17. Center for Applied Research in the Apostolate (CARA), "Global Catholicism."
18. Center for Applied Research in the Apostolate (CARA), "Global Catholicism." Used with permission.
19. Sanneh, "Introduction: The Changing Face of Christianity," 3.

Christianity has not ceased to be a Western religion, but its future as a world religion is now being decided and shaped by the hands and in the minds of its non-Western adherents, who share little of the West's cultural assumptions. It is no longer fanciful today to speak of the possibility of say, an African pope, with all that that means for the cultural repositioning of the church.[20]

It would be a mistake to underestimate the impact of the "cultural repositioning" that will take place in global Catholicism because of African Catholicism. The West will need to be ready to engage and take seriously African contributions and challenges to Western anthropology, sexual ethics, ideas about family life, and even liturgical norms, all of which will arise out of the dialogue between African Catholics and Western Catholics in this "flatter" world.

The collaboration at the heart of global commerce that Friedman describes is available and effective within the interpersonal relationships and local interactions of the African church and as part of the global dialogue between African Catholics—engaged in both as Africans and as Catholics—and other Catholics, even though Friedman does not include Africa in his list of globalized countries or continents. We must view African Catholicism as global because neither Africa itself nor African Catholicism is any longer only a local or globally peripheral reality. Africa and African Catholicism exist not in a vacuum but within the ever-smaller global network that defines our world, a world that includes both ecclesial and secular realities. That "the world is flat" was a peculiar statement when it was first suggested by Friedman, but his analysis seems sound, and even though Friedman looks at globalization exclusively through the lens of business, economics, and Western capitalism, we suggest the possibility of using theological concepts to widen his view of the world and the meaning of globalization.

Globalization as a Virtue

In fact, globalization is much more than a business model. Ultimately, it is about community. Globalization, the global context that embraces all the continents and all people, including Africa and African Catholics, is a context that offers significant hope along with significant challenges. The "flatness" of the new globe is not a hermeneutic of homogeneity but instead involves embracing and celebrating the gifts of diversity. It is a lens, a context, that calls for people to recognize the other as both "other" and as kin, as sisters and brothers in true solidarity. Globalization, like solidarity, involves an embrace and is not passive but active. It involves care for the other as "other" and as family. It involves concern for justice, peace, economic opportunity, health care, education, clean water, and adequate nutrition for everyone in the tribe and in the global human community. It involves care for the integrity of creation, our common home. Globalization is about the family of humanity and its environment. It is and must be the globalization of personalism, and that means that globalization must include the notions of subsidiarity and solidarity. Friedman's understanding of globalization is an almost soulless paradigm unless it is expanded to include the priority of persons in the global context. This expanded understanding of globalization may allow us to examine the impact of African Catholicism on the global church and vice versa.

Globalization in Light of Subsidiarity and Solidarity

Since the Second Vatican Council, the concepts of *subsidiarity* and *solidarity* have converged to help create a new context for how the church is church. What these terms imply contributes significantly to a richer understanding of globalization. They suggest an understanding of globalization that is based on the dignity of every individual, of local cultures, and of the local church as it acts in concert with the universal church. Solidarity is the Christian challenge to tribalism, offering a way for the African church to be both one and diverse.

Pope St. John Paul II raised the consciousness of the church regarding the interpersonal and international dimensions of interdependence (i.e., solidarity) when he taught that solidarity was best

---

20. Sanneh, "Introduction: The Changing Face of Christianity," 4.

understood as a virtue, not a political strategy. As a virtue, it is a habitus, an acquired practice that disposes one to live in interdependence, avoiding the extremes of either infantile dependence or suicidal independence.

> Solidarity is undoubtedly a Christian virtue. . . . In the light of faith, solidarity seeks to go beyond itself, to take on the specifically Christian dimension of total gratuity, forgiveness and reconciliation. One's neighbor is then not only a human being with his or her own rights and a fundamental equality with everyone else, but becomes the living image of God the Father, redeemed by the blood of Jesus Christ and placed under the permanent action of the holy spirit. . . . Beyond human and natural bonds, already so close and strong, there is discerned in the light of faith a new model of the unity of the human race, which must ultimately inspire our solidarity. This supreme model of unity, which is a reflection of the intimate life of God, one God in three Persons, is what we Christians mean by the word communion.[21]

This call to communion, the result of a lived solidarity of the people of God, is an integral aspect of the global context in which the Catholic Church and specifically the Catholic Church in Africa must exist.

The church believes that solidarity, living in communion, is intertwined with honoring the dignity of individuals and their cultures. The virtue of subsidiarity is closely aligned with and in fact complements the virtue of solidarity:

> The teaching of the Church has elaborated the principle of subsidiarity, according to which "a community of higher order should not interfere in the internal life of a community of a lower order, depriving the latter of its functions, but rather should support it in case of need and help to co-ordinate its activity with the activities of the rest of society, always with the view to the common good."[22]

The church in her wisdom has come to understand that subsidiarity is recommended for both the external society and the internal life of the church as the people of God. Pope Pius XII speaks clearly about subsidiarity in his social encyclical *Quadragesimo Anno*:

> It is a fundamental principle . . . fixed and unchangeable, that one should not withdraw from individuals and commit to the community what they can accomplish by their own enterprise and industry. So too, it is an injustice and at the same time a grave evil and a disturbance of right order to transfer to the larger and higher collectivity functions which can be performed and provided for by lesser and subordinate bodies.[23]

The bishops of the U.S. picked up this theme and expanded on it in the pastoral letter *Economic Justice for All*:

> This principle [subsidiarity] guarantees institutional pluralism. It provides space for freedom, initiative, and creativity on the part of many social agents. At the same time, it insists that all these agents should work in ways that help build up the social body. Therefore, in all their activities these groups should be working in ways that express their distinctive capacities for action, that help meet human needs, and that make true contributions to the common good of the human community.[24]

The virtues of subsidiarity and solidarity are a call to praxis in the world and in the church. They are complementary factors in the global context that support, enrich, and challenge global Catholi-

---

21. John Paul II, encyclical *Sollicitudo Rei Socialis* §40.
22. *Catechism of the Catholic Church*, §1883 (citing *Centesimus Annus* 48, §4). Hereinafter *CCC*.
23. Pope Pius XII, *Quadragesimo Anno* §79.
24. U.S. Catholic Bishops, *Economic Justice for All* §§99–100.

cism. Specifically, subsidiarity allows us to see more of the global Catholic context that surrounds and enlivens African Catholicism. Inculturation, one mark of subsidiarity, does not separate the local churches from the universal church, nor does it create boundaries based on the local particularities of churches; rather, it allows the individuality of cultures to be a gift to all their sisters and brothers in the church and allows them to play their proper role in the body of Christ. This body of Christ thus lives in subsidiarity and solidarity with all its parts supporting one another. "There is a certain resemblance between the unity of the divine persons and the society that people ought to establish among themselves."[25] This society as a global reality is manifested in solidarity, a lived charity that is the very definition of a people "being church." One error, Pope Pius XII wrote in 1939, "widespread today, is the forgetfulness of that law of human solidarity and charity which is dictated and imposed by our common origin and by the equality of rational nature in all men, to whatever people they belong, and by the redeeming Sacrifice offered by Jesus Christ on the Altar of the Cross to His Heavenly Father on behalf of sinful mankind."[26]

In contemporary political, anthropological, economic, and even theological and religious circles, the term "solidarity" has cachet. In its best sense, it alerts us to the fact that modern communication and travel have made the world smaller. Airplanes, phones, the internet, and social media have enabled people to communicate and interact in ways not imagined even a few decades ago. Conversations can happen and are happening between individuals that are enabling an actual global village. Opportunities for strangers to begin to understand one another, to experience the "other," and to learn to challenge the normativity of their own horizon and culture abound in the present-day world. These are aspects of the dialogue that globalization has allowed the Catholic Church in Africa to enter into.

At the same time, solidarity and globalization can be misunderstood. They should not be seen as realities that dissolve all differences rather than celebrating them. Globalization is not about making the world gray or all one color. This was the mistake of the evangelizers that accompanied the colonizers. Globalization is not a leveling of the mountains and a filling in of all the valleys. Rather, the global context allows a radical stance that accepts the absolute and inherent uniqueness and dignity of each person within his or her cultural horizon. It does not seek to normalize individuals and cultures by means of a single international standard. True globalization is a solidarity woven from different cloths and a celebration of the vibrant tapestry that results. True globalization demands integral dialogue and a deep and abiding, truly catholic, vision.

Pope Francis challenges the limited discussion of globalization found in Friedman's work by pointing out the dangers that come from such a narrow view. While economics and trade are an important and necessary aspect of the growing global world, they are not its only, and certainly not its most vital, aspects. In fact, globalization, if it is truly to be a good for humanity, must not mistake efficiency and profit for the ultimate common good. The church in her social teachings has long proclaimed that people are more important than profit, and that the economy should serve the people, not the other way around. Africa is at great risk when globalization is understood in a restricted, almost exclusively economic, fashion. Nor should globalization be reduced to the phenomenon of instant communication, as achieved, for example, by the ubiquitous mobile phone. Globalization is certainly enhanced by easy and convenient, local and international communication but it cannot be reduced to it. Globalization is as much about the sharing of ideas, hopes, dreams, and gospel faith as it is about the means of that sharing. Africa has much to lose in a world that sees only business and trade as the foundation and sole goal of the global village. Africa is primarily a homeland of peoples, whose individual and communal identities are at risk if globalization is restricted only, or at least primarily, to the horizon of commerce.

Pope Francis gives a clear warning in the encyclical *Laudato Si'* about what happens when globalization is seen only in the horizon of economics and

---

25. *CCC*, §1890.
26. Pope Pius XII, encyclical *Summi Pontificatus* §35. Cf. *CCC*, §1939.

trade with the profit margin teleology that drives it. His warning is of particular interest to Africa.

> The new power structures based on the techno-economic paradigm may overwhelm not only our politics but also freedom and justice.... There are too many special interests, and economic interests easily end up trumping the common good and manipulating information so that their own plans will not be affected. The *Aparecida Document* urges that "the interests of economic groups which irrationally demolish sources of life should not prevail in dealing with natural resources." The alliance between the economy and technology ends up sidelining anything unrelated to its immediate interest.[27]

Authentic globalization embraces the solidarity of difference; it is a globalization that allows the Holy Spirit to speak the same truth in many tongues. Solidarity invites everyone to a place at the table and subsidiarity asks everyone to bring a dish to share. Globalization in the Catholic context is an expression of the Pentecost event. No doubt, Africa also reveals itself as a Pentecost event: with its many tongues, cultures, and religious expressions, it is called to speak the one language of solidarity.

The Postcolonial Call: To Inculturate, Creating a Radically Contextual Catholicism

Our exploration of globalization thus far makes clear that it is a postcolonial reality. This reality, sustained by the dignity of the particular and the challenge of the universal, demands that we recognize *context*.

Stephen Bevans, in his seminal work *Models of Contextual Theology*, suggests that all theology, in order to be done well, must be done in the context of a culture. In fact, he states that there is a "cultural imperative in Christianity itself."[28] This insight has encouraged local Catholic churches throughout the world to find their own voices in order to make their efforts at evangelization more effective.

While it would be correct to understand Bevans's work as being focused on the "local" cultural context, that fact should not distract us from appreciating some of its other important implications. As the title of this chapter suggests, the new global context in which African Catholicism finds itself is my primary focus. I believe that this global context is primarily cultural in nature. How does this global cultural context influence African Catholicism, and how does African Catholicism dialogue with and respond to the realities that the global cultural context has created? While it is both important and necessary to acknowledge the local context in which every Catholic church is embedded, it is the intention of this article to move the reader into the larger, global context and ask questions about how African Catholicism is called to interact with and enrich the universal church in that context. This chapter thus attempts to investigate and identify the major markers of the global context, to investigate how the global culture is interacting with African Catholicism, and to suggest ways in which African Catholicism is in dialogue with the global culture.

Bevans is correct to suggest that any authentic theology must be done within a context that is both acknowledged and taken seriously as a point of departure. However, an indigenous theology is greater than its starting point and must ultimately become a contextualized theology that brings the truth of the particular culture to a place where it can challenge the dark corners of the global culture, while at the same time acknowledging the truths and light the global culture offers, which can challenge the darkness of the particular culture. Wilbert Shenk suggests, in his article on contextual theology, that it is precisely the church's global mission that provides the vital link between the local and global cultures. "To prepare the church to fully enter into the *missio Dei*," he writes, "it must learn to carry out that critical assessment of what makes the context really significant in the light of the *Missio Dei*. To think in context was to engage

---

27. Pope Francis, encyclical *Laudato Si'* §§53, 54. The Holy Father quotes from the *Aparecida Document* of the Fifth General Conference of the Latin American and Caribbean Bishops, 471.
28. Bevans, *Models of Contextual Theology*, 9.

in missiological discernment of the signs of the times. The locus of discernment and action must now be lodged with the local church."[29] In this postcolonial time, churches urgently need to be set free from the burdensome, imported cultural baggage that has proven to be a barrier to effective witness. This entails a radical rethinking of the nature and purpose of the local church in its particular context and of its dialogue with the global culture.

Inculturation is admittedly a complex and important area of theological and ecclesial investigation. Undoubtedly, recognizing and integrating the authentic presence of God that is already evident in the culture of an evangelized people challenges both the local and global church. Authentic inculturation recognizes and raises up proper and authentic elements of the proto-faith that exist in the indigenous culture; however, it does not canonize any human culture in its entirety as the embodiment of a fully developed example of the reign of God. Authentic inculturation is a dialogue in which the gospel of Christ shines its light on a culture so as to recognize and illuminate the goodness and truth already present in it, while simultaneously purifying it of elements that are contrary to the Good News. Inculturation cannot be reduced to integrating mere characterizations and accidentals as an essential part of Catholic worship and catechesis.

Pope Paul VI stated in his apostolic exhortation *Evangelii Nuntiandi* that

> what matters is to evangelize man's culture and cultures (not in a purely decorative way as it were by applying a thin veneer, but in a vital way, in depth and right to their very root), in the wide and rich sense which these terms have in *Gaudium et Spes*, always taking the person as one's starting point and always coming back to the relationships of people among themselves and with God. . . .
> Though independent of cultures, the Gospel and evangelization are not necessarily incompatible with them; rather they are capable of permeating them all without becoming subject to any one of them. The split between the Gospel and culture is without a doubt the drama of our time, just as it was of other times. Therefore, every effort must be made to ensure a full evangelization of culture, or more correctly of cultures. They have to be regenerated by an encounter with the Gospel. But this encounter will not take place if the Gospel is not proclaimed.[30]

The decolonialization of the African Catholic churches following the demise of the European empires in the nineteenth and twentieth centuries has occurred only rather recently, and Catholic churches in former European colonies have struggled with some success to distinguish between the accidental trappings of European culture and the essential and non-negotiable elements of the Good News. There is significant research to demonstrate that Catholic evangelizers, like Protestant missionaries, had a political as much as a religious impact. The missionaries too often presented Christianity and European culture as if they were essentially the same reality. Little authentic inculturation was attempted in most of the colonial models of evangelization, with a few notable exceptions like St. Justin de Jacobis, an Italian Vincentian sent to Ethiopia in the mid-nineteenth century. "De Jacobis is still model and master of a missionary church. Three elements stand out from his line of action: the re-inculturation of the Christian message, ecumenical attention and witness of life."[31]

John Paul II suggested that "inculturation is the incarnation of the Gospel in the indigenous cultures, and at the same time the introduction of these cultures in the life of the Church."[32] The right of peoples to bring to their Catholic worship an authentic integration of both their popular piety and their culture eventually emerged from postcolonial perspectives. In addition, the twentieth-century movement known as *nouvelle théologie*, marked by a new reverence for historical sources, helped Roman Catholics understand that the Catholic Church had always been "diverse in its unity."

---

29. Shenk, "Contextual Theology: The Last Frontier," 207.
30. Pope Paul VI, apostolic exhortation *Evangelii Nuntiandi* §20.
31. See Mazzarello and Micael, *Key to the African Heart*.
32. Pope John Paul II, encyclical *Slavorum Apostoli* §21.

The Global Context of African Catholicism

The one Catholic faith shared by all the baptized has from its beginnings been legitimately celebrated, taught, and grown differently in the different cultural contexts in which it has been planted. While there may be other models of inculturation of the Catholic Church in Africa, one clear example is that of Rome's 1988 approval of the Zairean[33] rite of the Eucharist.[34] In the *Roman Missal for the Dioceses of Zaire*,[35] we see the Roman church recognizing the need to divest the growing, young vibrant church of Zaire of unnecessary vestiges of the Latin rite and to include local symbols that could add rich meaning to the celebration of the Mass. This rite might correctly be seen as an a posteriori attempt by the Latin church to allow the faith to be locally inculturated as it did in a more organic and a priori way in apostolic and patristic times in the various Eastern Catholic churches. Among the changes allowed in the Zairean rite were that the priest is dressed in the robes of a tribal priest, the servers carry spears, the penitential rite is moved to after the creed, people sit at the reading of the Gospel, and there are places for the people to respond during the Eucharistic Prayer. It is perhaps important to note here that possibly the most significant impact of the approval of this new rite by the Latin church in 1988 was not in the changes themselves, but rather in the demonstration that the postcolonial Catholic Church was beginning to see and understand that the Catholic Church in Africa had its own identity, while still being joined to the universal church. In retrospect, it is clear that any liturgical accretions that are nothing more than Roman inculturations have been and continue to be largely useless in communicating the Good News outside the cultural context of the Roman church. This is a point that De Jacobis made clear in his dialogue with Rome when he was a missionary in Ethiopia in the nineteenth century.[36]

In fact, European cultural accretions, which were introduced in many places by Western Catholic missionaries, became a distraction to evangelization efforts in many new cultural contexts. The Latin church was slow to allow the church in Africa to inculturate despite the fact that the universal Catholic Church has always been a federation of local churches. The Catholic Church from its inception has expressed itself locally under the guidance of the Holy Spirit and has consistently encouraged legitimate cultural and vernacular expressions in its prayer and liturgies. This has been a gift of the Spirit from the time of the Pentecost.

At the same time, theologians must ask about the shadow side of this development by asking questions like, To what extent does the Zairean missal authentically inculturate the many different micro-nations of the Democratic Republic of the Congo? If the adage *lex orandi, lex credendi* (how one prays dictates what one believes) has any validity, then it would be expected that the Zairean missal would have become a point of departure for the local church to engage itself in developing and producing an indigenous theology as the fruit of that indigenous liturgy. Has this actually happened?

One might suggest that the *Roman Missal for the Dioceses of Zaire* is actually a double-edged sword. Even though it is an example of the legitimate right that the Good News be embedded into every culture, it may also carry a hint of paternalism. While deconstructing the Latin liturgy with its "accidental" accretions, which, even though reasonable and meaningful in a particular place and time, needed to be replaced by new symbols that more effectively speak to the Catholics in a particular local context, documents like the *Roman Missal for the Dioceses of Zaire* may limit the very meaning of inculturation. Some of the changes that are allowed to the church of the Democratic Republic of the Congo might not be as meaningful and helpful in worship as one might think at first glance. In Kenya, during an ordination ceremony, one tribal elder communicated to another that the tribal symbols

---

33. Since 1997, Zaire has been known as The Democratic Republic of the Congo.

34. Promulgated by the decree *Zairensium Dioecesium*, April 30, 1988, by the Congregation for Divine Worship and the Discipline of the Sacraments, *Notitiae* 24 (1988): 457.

35. Conférence Épiscopale du Zaïre, "Le Missel Romain pour les diocèses du Zaïre."

36. See Mazzarello and Micael, *Key to the African Heart*. De Jacobis was largely responsible for founding the Catholic Church in Ethiopia.

being worn by one of the newly ordained as a sign of inculturation were actually quite inappropriate for the occasion. It was obvious to the elder that the new priest had little understanding of some of the traditional aspects of his own tribe. When a "symbol" becomes merely a caricature of a culture, it has lost its value to communicate.

Finally, in light of our previous analysis of the nation-state and its meaning for Africans, the question must be posed concerning whether the *Roman Missal for the Dioceses of Zaire* makes a perhaps unwarranted assumption that there is or was a "Zaire." Is it only an assumption by the Roman Catholic Church that Zaire represents a reality, a community of people who recognize themselves as "Zaireans"? This Western model of nation-states, and the particular states themselves, as we remarked above, are often inadequate to describe an African's understanding of his or her own social reality.

However important inculturation has been and continues to be to the local Catholic churches spread throughout the world, it would be a mistake to think that an acceptance of the imperative of contextualization was enough. Cultural contextualization might best be perceived as a part of the journey, but certainly not its end point. Culture by its very nature is a living reality, and some aspects of every culture have a limited life span. Icons of culture that may be very fitting and meaningful when they are admitted to a ritual may at some point become antiquated, no longer animating a contemporary meaning but present simply as historical anecdotes that distract from the living liturgy. This kind of fossilization of culture or at least of aspects of culture can actually detract from the message of the Good News at the center of the living church and her liturgies. It is precisely this kind of fossilization that led the fathers of the Second Vatican Council to divest the Latin Rite Eucharist of so much that had become meaningless; for example, the maniple, a meaningless vestment that the priest wore draped over one wrist. Thus, the movement to claim contextual identities, both local and global, was and is important for the continued growth of the church in Africa, but more should be expected.

Local inculturation is important, but is not easy to do properly and it should never be limited to the display of tribal artifacts. African cultures deserve more respect than that.

The Emerging Identity and Global Impact of African Catholicism

A review of the two most recent post-synodal apostolic exhortations, *Ecclesia in Africa* (September 14, 1995), promulgated by Pope John Paul II, and *Africae Munus* (November 19, 2011), promulgated by Pope Benedict XVI, offer a view of the magisterium's balancing act with respect to the challenge of inculturating the faith in Africa. From a formal standpoint, we see that John Paul II offers encouragement for inculturation by focusing on the positive values of the African culture. Here the context is seen as one that can receive the faith authentically because it has many traditional cultural values already in line with the faith and the teachings of the church. The pope writes,

> It [Africa] is endowed with a wealth of cultural values and priceless human qualities which it can offer to the Churches and to humanity as a whole. The synod Fathers highlighted some of these cultural values, which are truly a providential preparation for the transmission of the Gospel. They are values which can contribute to an effective reversal of the Continent's dramatic situation and facilitate that worldwide revival on which the desired development of individual nations depends. (*EA* §42)[37]

Remarkably, here we see the Holy Father not only recognizing the inherent goodness of much of what is culturally African and therefore suitable for evangelization, but even more, suitable for the purpose of "facilitat[ing] a worldwide revival." The church is recognizing that Africa's gift to the global church goes beyond what is obvious, its many religious and priestly vocations and the vibrancy of its youth; rather, its greatest gift is found in the elemental goodness of its peoples and their cultures.

---

37. Pope John Paul II, post-synodal apostolic exhortation *Ecclesia in Africa* (hereinafter *EA*).

These gifts should be effectively shared with the global church. "Africans have a profound religious sense, a sense of the sacred, of the existence of God the Creator and of a spiritual world" (*EA* §43). The same text moves on to point out a variety of positive values in African culture, including the role of the family, love and respect for life, openness to children, veneration of ancestors, belief in the afterlife, respect for the unborn, an acute sense of solidarity and community life, and a deep concern for the elderly (*EA* §43). John Paul II sums up his positive comments by stating that "it is my ardent hope and prayer that Africa will always preserve this priceless cultural heritage and never succumb to the temptation to individualism, which is so alien to its best traditions" (*EA* §43). Here the pope is clearly making a contrast between the positive values of the African peoples versus those found in the North and West.

Nevertheless, this positive and hopeful tone is not found so clearly in *Africae Munus*, authored by Pope Benedict XVI in 2011. Here the text is more tentative about the inculturation of the gospel in Africa. There is a sense of careful warning lest cultural elements contrary to the gospel be accepted too easily into worship and catechesis. "The Synod members," the pope writes, "noted a dichotomy between certain traditional practices of African cultures and the specific demands of Christ's message. In her concern for relevance and credibility, the Church needs to carry out a thorough discernment in order to identify those aspects of the culture which represent an obstacle to the incarnation of Gospel values, as well as those aspects which promote them" (*AM* §36).[38] When this text is compared with John Paul II's *Ecclesia in Africa*, we see a careful attempt to pull back from what may have been perceived as the naïve hopefulness of his approach to the African culture. "Bishops," Benedict says, "should be vigilant over this need for inculturation, respecting the norms established by the Church. By discerning which cultural elements and traditions are contrary to the Gospel, they will be able to separate the good seed from the weeds" (*AM* §37). Benedict does, however, offer some of his predecessor's openness when he states,

"It is imperative therefore to make a commitment to transmit the values that the Creator has instilled in the hearts of Africans since the dawn of time. . . . These positive elements therefore need to be emphasized, lit up from within so that Christians may truly receive the message of Christ" (*AM* §38). Ultimately, we can see that, when taken together, the predominant openness of John Paul II and the predominant caution and concern of Benedict XVI represent a call to a balanced approach to inculturation of the gospel in the local context of African Catholicism.

Contextual African Catholicism: Finding Its Global Voice

While it is evident that Western Catholicism has long enjoyed a prominent place on the global stage, it kept this place primarily through its hierarchical structure. This same structure often muted voices that came up "from the ground" of indigenous churches, even those churches founded by its own missionaries. This was the African experience in the precolonial and colonial periods. However, the power of globalization, driven by various forces, including the new technologies of media and communication, have provided the Catholic hierarchy with the opportunity to evangelize in new and exciting ways. Local Catholics everywhere in the world have begun to network locally and globally in ways that were all but impossible until the twenty-first century.

For example, just as the church began its third millennium, a group of Catholic theologians conceived of an idea for a global dialogue on moral theology and brought it to reality. The title of the conference they produced is telling: "Catholic Theological Ethics in the World Church: The First Cross-Cultural Conference on Catholic Theological Ethics." The mission of the conference was clearly to help a global Catholic voice, made up of a chorus of particular voices from particular churches, articulate itself. One African participant suggested that

> it follows that one of the major tasks of moral theology in Africa consists in stimulating the

---

38. Benedict XVI, post-synodal apostolic exhortation *Africae Munus* (hereinafter *AM*).

intellectual elite to make the most of these energies, this dynamism, this faith and hope which dwell in the hearts of our people, in order to transform its shame—and the challenge which this shame contains—into an opportunity to eradicate once and for all the virus and pandemic of underdevelopment, and the lack of democracy, peace, justice, etc.[39]

Another participant added,

My hypothesis is that the unique and specific situation of Africa compels the ethics inspired by Christianity to engage in a dialogue with the wisdom of the African tradition. This could lead to an ethics that is better adapted, because more incarnate, linking concern for reconstruction to requirements for life in society while refusing to submit to a paradigm that considers only the material means for the reconstruction of Africa.[40]

Truly this was a call to a "concert" that hoped for the possibility of a new song in the church, a beautiful harmony for the faithful created out of their different gifts. The postcolonial church as a post-European context needed to be heard.

The convener of this global conference, James Keenan, SJ, quoted the organization's mission statement in his introduction to its inaugural volume:

Since moral theology is so diffuse today, since many Catholic theological ethicists are caught up in their own specific cultures, and since their interlocutors tend to be in other disciplines, there is a need for an international exchange of ideas among Catholic theological ethicists. Catholic theological ethicists recognize the need: to appreciate the challenge of pluralism; to dialogue from and beyond local culture; and to interconnect within a world church not dominated solely by a northern paradigm. In response to these recognized needs, Catholic theological ethicists will meet to refresh their memories, reclaim their heritage, and reinterpret their sources. Therefore, Catholic theological ethicists will pursue in this conference a way of proceeding that reflects their local cultures and engages in cross-cultural conversations motivated by mercy and care.[41]

This is but one example of the dynamism of the forces of Catholic globalization that respect local cultures. It is an example of solidarity and subsidiarity.

Africa and the Global Catholic Context

At the beginning of this chapter, we reviewed briefly the statistics that demonstrated the growing presence of African Catholicism on the global stage, an impressive presence not just in terms of its numbers but also in its youth and eagerness to join in the work of evangelization. We also saw the challenge to African Catholicism to "own its own skin," and to be both a pre- and postcolonial church that understands its identity, one that is authentic, not inherited.

With its substantial growth, African Catholicism is beginning to have an impact on Catholicism well beyond the shores of Africa. Statistics indicate that this trend will only increase in the near future. With that reality comes the responsibility, the baptismal vocation, to participate fully in the most essential mission of the World Church—defined so clearly by Pope Paul VI in *Evangelii Nuntiandi* as "missionary," that is, the call to bring the Good News to the poor. African Catholicism is being called to move beyond maintenance to mission. African Catholicism is about much more than internal growth, numbers, and local impact. Rather, it is about participating fully in the global context, because the universal Catholic Church is "flattening," as described by Friedman. The African church is transitioning from a voice that shouts against the past, and even at times against its own sisters and brothers, toward being a church that not only contributes to the global Catholic chorus

---

39. Mulombe, "Authenticity and Credibility," 62.
40. Afan, "Main 'Building Sites' of Ethics in West Africa," 48.
41. Keenan, "Introduction: The Conference at Padua," 3.

that sings and dances to the proclamation of the gospel, but that takes a role in global leadership. African Catholicism is called to move from being a mission church to being a church of missionaries. The gift that Africa has received through the proclamation of the Good News, the gift that Africa has embraced, must now be shared. It is called to proclaim the Good News in the global context by sending missionaries, ordained and lay, as pastors and teachers out to the new Areopagi.[42] It is called to share its wisdom by enabling itself not just to take a place at the table but also to enrich the church with the fruits of the African harvest. This is ultimately the journey that African Catholicism has begun, a journey that has been facilitated by globalization. African Catholicism's enriching and being enriched by the universal church are not merely states of being, they are a vocation.

We remember that Friedman suggested that ten "flatteners" and three "convergents" were largely responsible for the phenomenon of globalization and the flattening of the earth at the beginning of the twenty-first century. Friedman's insights fairly clearly demonstrated that the "distance" between local economies and global economies was getting shorter. Perhaps we can conclude our review by suggesting that there may be similar factors in play related to Africa and African Catholicism that are enabling the church of Africa to take its proper place on the world stage of Catholicism. The forces that are flattening the Catholic world are (1) movement of the majority of Catholics from the Global North to the Global South; (2) growth of the Catholic population outside of Europe; (3) growth in the number of Catholics in Africa; (4) growth in the number of African Catholic clergy; (5) growth in the number of African cardinals; (6) youth and vitality of the African church; and (7) growth and development of African theology. The vectors that are converging and leveraging these factors can be traced back to the Second Vatican Council. It has been remarked that one major difference between the First and Second Vatican Councils is that the first had bishops *from* all the continents (some of them missionary bishops), while the second had bishops *of* (that is, indigenous to) all the continents.

The significant growth in the ethnic and cultural diversity of our Catholic bishops is a remarkable sign that the local churches outside of Europe, including those in Africa, are finding their voices. Despite the very real internal issues that continue to challenge African countries and the Catholic Church in Africa, the African church continues to grow at a phenomenal rate. This growth is not only about numbers, but more importantly about impact. For example, we see in the founding of the Catholic University of East Africa (CUEA) by the Catholic bishops of East Africa a wonderful sign of hope in collaboration. The Catholic Church in Africa is itself beginning a Catholic university where teaching and research can serve its needs. The Catholic Church in Africa continues its internal growth as an institution while at the same time taking on the challenge of sending missionaries to all corners of the globe. Globalization and the global context will not wait for Africa to reconstruct itself as a postcolonial reality. The forces, vectors, and convergences that are already present in the global context are clearly at work in Africa. In fact, it is clear that Africa and African Catholicism have already been affected by, are affecting, and are perhaps even creating some of the features of these global forces.

Globalization is, as we have suggested, a dialogue, a two-way street. In this global dialogue, Africa is receiving input and challenges and at the same time is offering its own wisdom and challenges to the world. African Catholicism is clearly being challenged by evangelical, and especially Pentecostal, Christianity; by Western anthropology (especially its acceptance of homosexuality as a normal way of being a person and expressing one's sexuality); by the hegemony of autonomy and individualism in both personal and social interactions; and by the dominance of capitalism in every phase of society. These global forces are certainly challenging the Catholic Church in Africa to define for itself how these forces will affect their dogmatic and moral beliefs. On the other hand, the Catholic Church beyond Africa is challenged by the understandings brought by missionaries from and members of the African Catholic diaspora. African

---

42. See Pope John Paul II, encyclical *Redemptoris Missio* §37b.

Catholics offer the reinvigoration of an eschatological faith; worship as participation, not merely attendance; the central importance of family; the rediscovery of tribal identity in Western cultures; the fact that all life is a gift from God; and the importance of seeing the Catholic faith through a non-European lens.

While the forces mentioned above may complicate the easy entrance of African Catholicism onto the global stage, they cannot ultimately keep it from doing so. At the First Cross-Cultural Conference on Catholic Theological Ethics, several African theologians presented papers and offered interventions. Mawuto Afan, OP, made the insightful remark that "contemporary ethical reflection in Africa deals with complex problems, each of which involves cross-disciplinary work. . . . The anthropological twist that these questions have taken in the context of globalization obliges us to situate our fundamental ethical reflections in a multidisciplinary framework."[43] This framework is part of the matrix making up the global context in which African Catholicism finds itself. However, as African Catholicism continues to look at and understand itself, its particularity and its unique charisms, it will be able to give back to the global church the gifts that it has received from the global church.

African Catholicism very much inhabits a global context. Universal Catholicism itself is being "flattened" by many factors that allow it to act and communicate globally in a way that is not directed by its hierarchical structure. Globalization creates a different reality than that created by a top-down hierarchy or adherence to the Nicene Creed and the Catholic Catechism. While a sustained orthodoxy is at the center of Catholicism, globalization is just as much about how our church acts and evangelizes as what we believe.

Postscript: A Word about Methodology

This chapter is an attempt at a cross-disciplinary work, an approach that is becoming more and more standard in the theological disciplines. One cannot do bioethics without providing both the scientific and moral foundations of any discussion. Similarly, work in the area of catechetics demands attention to psychology, especially developmental models. Here I attempted to borrow the model of globalization from the business world. This allowed me to utilize what could legitimately be transferred to the theological discussion I was developing while at the same time abandoning aspects of the model that did not transfer easily or at all.

The power of cross-disciplinary work is that it uses the "signs of the times" to engage theology. It helps to ground theology and make it more real in the world and for the world. A cross-disciplinary theology demands that theology be taken down from the ivory tower to meet the real world.

If theology is truly "faith seeking understanding," as Anselm suggested in the eleventh century, then I would hope to take his challenge to heart when I write. I write for my future readers, and my hope is that what I write will help them make sense of the theology they encounter in the church we love. I pray that any encounter between my words and the reader will result in a greater understanding of the God we encounter daily in one another. My method begins with a simple approach suggested first by philosophers but then adopted by empirical scientists, social scientists, and even theologians: see, judge, and act. I would hope that the reader can see this method present in this work.

My first step in writing a theological article is to do solid research to "see" accurately the context of my area of research. The historical-critical method suggests that knowing the history and reviewing the full range of writings on the topic at hand provides a solid, academically sound foundation for an article or book. Sometimes this entails research in scripture studies, or the empirical sciences, or history, or the social sciences, among other areas, and of course any theological writings on the subject. The solid research that forms the beginning of my work thus needs to be both broad and deep. Then, I can begin making the creative connections that inform my "judgment" about the research so that I can suggest a new understanding that enlightens the faith. Finally comes the "act." At this point, I have to begin what is to many the most difficult

---

43. Afan, "Main 'Building Sites' of Ethics in West Africa," 39.

task of all—to leap over any psychological barriers that prevent me from writing. Assuming I achieve this, I sit down at my computer and begin to actually put the words on the screen, including synopsizing the results of my research and integrating new contributions suggested by the research into the topic at hand.

As I have said to many, many of my students over the years, papers are not written by the mind but by a pencil (this may tell you how old I am, but "pencil" is just a metaphor). The biggest stumbling blocks I have seen that get in the way of young writers are, first, the inability to know when it is time to stop their reading/research and begin to write; second, finding lots of other interesting things to do rather than writing; and, third, attempting to write without a plan, outline, or method. I strongly suggest that, before someone begins to write, he or she articulate a brief outline of the plan for their work from introduction to conclusion. Once a writer has even a rudimentary roadmap, it is much more likely that he or she will end up at their destination.

Bibliography

Afan, Mawuto R. "The Main 'Building Sites' of Ethics in West Africa." In *Catholic Theological Ethics in the World Church*, edited by James F. Keenan. New York: Continuum, 2007.

Benedict XVI, Pope. *Africae Munus* [Post-synodal Apostolic Exhortation on the Church in Africa in Service of Reconciliation, Justice and Peace; November 19, 2011]. Vatican City: Libreria Editrice Vaticana, 2011. www.vatican.va.

Bevans, Stephen B. *Models of Contextual Theology*. Maryknoll, NY: Orbis Books, 2002.

Catechism of the Catholic Church. 2nd ed. Washington, DC: United States Catholic Conference, 2000.

Center for Applied Research on the Apostolate (CARA). "Global Catholicism: Trends and Forecasts." June 4, 2014. http://cara.georgetown.edu.

Conférence Épiscopale du Zaïre. "Le Missel Romain pour les diocèses du Zaïre." *Notitiae* 264 (1988).

Ethnologue: Languages of the World. https://www.ethnologue.com/country/CG.

Fifth General Conference of the Bishops of Latin America and the Caribbean. *The Aparecida Document*. 2007. English translation and publication, Lexington, KY, 2014.

Francis, Pope. *Laudato Si'* [Encyclical on Care for Our Common Home; June 18, 2015]. Vatican City: Libreria Editrice Vaticana, 2015. www.vatican.va.

Friedman, Thomas. *The World Is Flat: A Brief History of the Globalized World in the 21st Century*. New York: Farrar, Straus & Giroux, 2005.

John Paul II, Pope. *Ecclesia in Africa* [Post-synodal Apostolic Exhortation on the Church in Africa and Its Evangelizing Mission toward the Year 2000; September 14, 1995]. Vatican City: Libreria Editrice Vaticana, 1995. www.vatican.va.

———. *Redemptoris Missio* [Encyclical on the Permanent Validity of the Church's Missionary Mandate; December 7, 1990]. Vatican City: Libreria Editrice Vaticana, 1990. www.vatican.va.

———. *Slavorum Apostoli* [Encyclical "Apostles of the Slavs"; June 2, 1985]. Vatican City: Libreria Editrice Vaticana, 1985]. www.vatican.va.

———. *Sollicitudo Rei Socialis* [Encyclical for the Twentieth Anniversary of *Populorum Progressio*; December 30, 1987]. Vatican City: Libreria Editrice Vaticana, 1987. www.vatican.va.

Keenan, James F. "Introduction: The Conference at Padua." In *Catholic Theological Ethics in the World Church*, edited by James F. Keenan, 1–9. New York: Continuum, 2007.

Keenan, James F., ed. *Catholic Theological Ethics in the World Church*. New York: Continuum, 2007.

Keim, Curtis. *Mistaking Africa: Curiosities and Inventions of the American Mind*. Philadelphia, PA: Westview, 2014.

Maathai, Wangari. *The Challenge for Africa*. New York: Anchor Books, 2009.

Mazzarello, Maria Luisa, and Neghesti Micael. *The Key to the African Heart: Justin de Jacobis*. Nairobi: Paulines Publications Africa, 2006.

McClendon, David. "Sub-Saharan Africa Will Be Home to Growing Shares of the World's Christians and Muslims." Pew Research Center, April 19, 2017, http://www.pewresearch.org.

Mulombe, Sebastien Muyngo. "Authenticity and Credibility: Moral Challenges after the African Synod." In *Catholic Theological Ethics in the World Church*, edited by James F. Keenan. New York: Continuum, 2007.

Paul VI. *Evangelii Nuntiandi* [Apostolic Exhortation on the Theme of Catholic Evangelization; December 8, 1975]. Vatican City: Libreria Editrice Vaticana, 1975. www.vatican.va

Pew Research Center. "Global Christianity: A Report on the Size and Distribution of the World's Christian Population." December 19, 2011. www.pewforum.org.

———. "The Global Catholic Population." February 13, 2013. www.pewforum.org.

Pius XI, Pope. *Quadragesimo Anno* [Encyclical "The Fortieth Year"; May 15, 1931]. Vatican City: Libreria Editrice Vaticana, 1931. www.vatican.va.

Pius XII, Pope. *Summi Pontificatus* [Encyclical "On the Limitations of the Authority of the State"; October 20, 1939]. Vatican City: Libreria Editrice Vaticana, 1939. www.vatican.va.

Sanneh, Lamin. "Introduction: The Changing Face of Christianity" and "Conclusion: The Current Transformation of Christianity." In *The Changing Face of Christianity: Africa, the West, and the World*, edited by Lamin Sanneh and Joel A. Carpenter. Oxford: Oxford University Press, 2005.

Shenk, Wilbert R. "Contextual Theology: The Last Frontier." In *The Changing Face of Christianity: Africa, the West, and the World*, edited by Lamin Sanneh and Joel A. Carpenter. Oxford: Oxford University Press, 2005.

Shillington, Kevin. *History of Africa*, 3rd ed. New York: Palgrave Macmillan, 2012.

United States Conference of Catholic Bishops. *Economic Justice for All: Pastoral Letter on Catholic Social Teaching and the U.S. Economy*. Washington, DC: United States Catholic Conference, Inc., 1986.

Vatican II. Pastoral Constitution on the Church in the Modern World (*Gaudium et Spes*) (1965).

Vatican Bulletin (June 4, 2017). *The Pontifical Yearbook 2017* and the "*Annuarium Statisticum Ecclesiae*" 2015. www.vatican.va.

Wrong, Michela. *It's Our Turn to Eat: The Story of a Kenyan Whistle-Blower*. New York: Harper Perennial, 2010.

Suggested Reading

Bevans, Stephen B. *Models of Contextual Theology*. Maryknoll, NY: Orbis Books, 2009.

Friedman, Thomas. *The World Is Flat: A Brief History of the Globalized World in the 21st Century*. New York: Farrar, Straus & Giroux, 2005.

Hochschild, Adam. *King Leopold's Ghost: A Story of Greed, Terror and Heroism in Colonial Africa*. Boston: Houghton Mifflin, 1998.

Keenan, James F., ed. *Catholic Theological Ethics in the World Church*. New York: Continuum, 2007.

Kirwen, Michael C., ed. *African Cultural Knowledge: Themes and Embedded Beliefs*. Nairobi: Mias Books, 2005.

Maathai, Wangari. *The Challenge for Africa*. New York: Anchor Books, 2009.

Mazzarello, Maria Luisa, and Neghesti Micael. *The Key to the African Heart: Justin de Jacobis*. Nairobi: Paulines Publications Africa, 2006.

Orobator, Agbonkhianmeghe E. *Theology Brewed in an African Pot*. Maryknoll, NY: Orbis Books, 2008.

Sanneh, Lamin, and Joel A. Carpenter, eds. *The Changing Face of Christianity: Africa, the West, and the World*. Oxford: Oxford University Press, 2005.

Key Words

Africae Munus
colonialism
context
Ecclesia in Africa
Economic Justice for All
Evangelii Nuntiandi
globalism
globalization
inculturation
John Paul II
Justin de Jacobis
Laudato Si'
micro-nation
Models of Contextual Theology
neo-colonialism
Paul VI
Pius XII
postcolonialism
Quadragesimo Anno
solidarity
Stephen Bevans
subsidiarity
Thomas Friedman
tribalism
Wangari Maathai
The World Is Flat
Zairean rite

African Catholicism and Intellectual History in Africa: Issues and Disputes

Michael Onyebuchi Eze

In trying to understand or explain unfamiliar historical worlds, scholars and teachers often engage in bold conjectures. These are justifiable or even necessary insofar as the inferences drawn are grounded in an unbiased method of inquiry. When the narratives arising from these conjectures are not historicized, we not only obscure the lives of the people we are seeking to understand but we inflict historical violence upon them. History thus becomes a space for disputes about memories and human recovery. An imposed misrecognition of memories relates to a denial of history, which gives rise to a denial of culture and agency. For example, in antiquity we encounter Pliny speaking about the Ethiopians as "half-animal Goat-Pans." Relying on Homer for archival knowledge, Pliny imposes Greek mythology because he sees it as providing self-evident truths on which he can make characterizations about African anthropology. "The most reliable opinion of Homer," he notes, "tells us that the Ethiopians . . . do not address one another by any names." Because they lack common sense, he continues, "When they behold the rising and setting sun, they utter awful curses against it as the cause of disaster to themselves and their fields, and when they are asleep, they do not have dreams like the rest of mankind." In addition to their cognitive deficiencies, the Ethiopians "live on the flesh of snakes, and *they have no voice, but only make squeaking noises, being entirely devoid of intercourse of speech.*"[1] Notice the irony: "they have no voice" is suggestive of a serious misconception that feeds into Pliny's Afrophobia and similar misconceptions that were dominant during the Western Enlightenment. Such Afrophobism serves as the basis for a claim of Black people's historical nullity: he or she "makes squeaking noises" and is incapable of speech. A subject who is incapable of speech and has no voice *ipso facto* lacks human agency.

Although Pliny served as a procurator in the *Provincia Africa* of the Roman Empire, he lived in an age of benighted ignorance, and his utterances fall into the category of false myth. Such an excuse can hardly be made for Ranulf Higden, a learned Benedictine of the late medieval period, who was commissioned to map the world in 1350. Higden was adamant that Africans were one-eyed, one-legged creatures with three faces and the heads of a lion who used their feet to cover their heads.[2] Such outrageous views are not limited to antiquity or the Middle Ages. Africa's encounter with Catholicism in early Western modernity was equally tainted by willful ignorance, even among the clergy. In 1459, Friar Mauro informed the Italian public of a new discovery in Africa—a bird so large that it could lift an elephant on its wings.[3] It is important to note that these were not fringe views; they were nurtured by doctrinal and pious teachings of the day. St. Isidore of Seville, famously known as the last of the church fathers, characterized Ethiopians and Libyans as creatures "born as trunks, without heads, and have their mouth and eyes on their chest. Others, born

---

1. All of the quotations in this paragraph come from Pliny the Elder, *Natural History* 43–45 (my emphasis).
2. Hochschild, *King Leopold's Ghost*, 6.
3. Hochschild, *King Leopold's Ghost*, 6.

147

without necks have their eyes on their shoulders" (*Etymologies* 11.3.17). Isidore claimed that in Ethiopia people walk like "beasts . . . each having one leg, and marvelous celerity . . . in the summer, lying on their back, they are shaded by the great size of their feet" (11.3.23). Isidore also claimed that these "little men with hooked noses, horns on their foreheads, and feet like those of goats" were also encountered by St. Anthony of the Desert (11.3.21).

As they relate to the church, addressing such misconceptions about Africa draws us into a complex ambivalence. On the one hand is a narrative that actively promotes misconceptions about the African world, offering opinions about what that world ought to be, and on the other hand is our knowledge of a historical church that has benefited from the teachings and theology of African church fathers like Clement, Origen, Cyril, Augustine, Tertullian, Minucius Felix, Cyprian, Lactantius, and Optatus. Among them were even popes: Miltiades, Victor, and Gelasius. As Anna Djintcharadzé explains, these fathers lived in the age of heroic Christianity.

> It was a soil mostly plowed by sufferings from persecutions and fertilized by heresies and threatening schisms. In fact, it was in the middle of all the turmoil of this particular region, where the heroism of numerous martyrs shone most gloriously, that the Latin patristic tradition, although a hundred years younger than the Greek one, took its root. . . . The Fathers originating from North Africa should be seen as the founders of the Latin Church and its proper spirituality.[4]

Any celebration of Africa's era of glorious Christianity needs to be harmonized with Catholicism's encounters with Africa after the early period of the church. The views of Higden and Mauro are typical of Western misconceptions about Africa after this period. A key challenge here is that faith experience becomes synonymous with a sociocultural ideology. Accordingly, this chapter is not concerned with either resolving ideologies or promoting a grand ideological thesis. The purpose of the chapter is instead merely to present a brief historical description of Africa's encounter with Catholic Christianity. A history of Catholicism's encounter with Africa is not just about the past but is also about the future of African Catholicism. But why is this study important? The church we inherited is, after all, a faith experience. Does not subjecting this experience to a historical review constitute a challenge to the fundamentals of our faith? How, then, should we write about our faith in a way that achieves all of the following: (1) escaping the trap of writing about Africa as a residual memory of European historical experience; (2) not undermining the reception of the faith or the experience of conversion; and (3) maintaining the apostolic spirit of the faith we have received without the ideological baggage of racist Christianity.

The hackneyed Hegelian critique that "we learn from history that we have learned nothing from history" is very instructive for my current purposes. One might conclude that the future of Catholicism in Africa lies in our ability to explain ourselves through a historical paradigm. We are not merely products of historical processes but share the same struggles and problems of past historical epochs, not just as objects of history but as subjects, actors, and agents within history. And even as we get lost in the narrative repertoire of the moment, we need to remain conscious of the struggles and conditions of the past in order not to remain captive to them. Part of my aim in this chapter is to treat African intellectual history as a project of *subjective reclamation*. This is not an attempt at the subjective revival of historical structures—that is the role of historical anthropology! I aim instead to trace the interpretative absurdities imposed upon African historiography, which have masked the role of Africans as active agents in historical change.

As was indicated above, Africa's first encounter with the church—the Latin church[5]—occurred during a heroic age. Yet after that age, the faith as

---

4. Djintcharadzé, "African Church Fathers," 2.

5. This is not to say that this encounter with the Latin church was Africa's only early contact with Christendom. The Coptic apostolic throne of Alexandria also extended to northern and western Africa, including Ethiopia.

received has become problematized, idealized, and even transformed. After the encounters with the Latin church of antiquity, not much has been written about Roman Catholicism's encounters with Africa, in particular with sub-Saharan Africa. Accordingly, this chapter is divided into three major sections. In the first section, I will refer to the example of Ethiopia but will largely focus on the Kingdom of the Kongo[6] for a historical illustration and contextual evidence. Moving beyond the Kongo, the second section addresses the church's relationship with sub-Saharan Africa within the secular structures created by the Enlightenment. Historicizing the Enlightenment opens spaces toward an understanding of whether the church was in fact complicit with or merely indifferent to the institutional structures of slavery and colonialism. Historicization also allows us to draw lessons from the past, revealing in the third section what the contemporary African church can learn from its experiences.

The Roman Church in the Medieval Kongo

The dominant strain of scholarship concerning Africa's engagement with Catholic Christianity often accentuates a history of passive reception of the faith without disclosing any creative impulses by Africans. There is support, however, for a view that emphasizes the role of Africans as active historical agents who took initiative and were proactively engaged with their own faith experience. Although my focus here is medieval Kongo, the Ethiopian church also offers a substantive historical parallel that can allow us to understand the extent to which Africans were active agents in evangelization. As Richard Gray explains, the evangelizing came not from Catholic Europe or its missionaries but from African Christians: "from Ethiopia, its Christian tradition which stretched further than many parts of northern Europe; from Kongo, the first African kingdom to respond with a spontaneous enthusiasm to the Portuguese proclamation of the Gospel; from appeals to Rome by African Catholics attempting to reconcile their needs and their culture with the Christian laws brought to them by missionaries."[7]

Ethiopia, already a Christian nation in 333 CE, was important to the early Latin church in part because of its geopolitical partnership with the African church. The Ethiopian church was one of the Oriental Orthodox churches that rejected the doctrine of the Council of Chalcedon (451). For over a millennium, Christianity remained at the center of the country's national imagination and political culture. In 1402, the Ethiopian king sent representatives to the papal court requesting missionaries, a move warmly received in Rome for strategic reasons related to Ethiopia's location and the potential for an alliance. The pressure of the Ottoman wars and the subsequent fall of Constantinople in 1443 increased the urgency felt by the European powers to enter into this alliance because Ethiopia could function as a natural geopolitical buffer.[8]

For their part, Ethiopian rulers were equally desirous of stronger religious and political ties with Europe. The strategic importance of this alliance became clear during the Councils of Constance (1414–1418) and Florence (1431–1449), which Ethiopian ambassadors attended and actively participated in the debates.[9] In an address to the council fathers during the Council of Florence on September 2, 1441, an Ethiopian delegate conveyed his emperor's desire for union with the Roman church and his desire to make an act of royal submission at the feet of the pope.[10] Beyond the expressed desire

---

For my purposes, I focus on the Latin church because of its influence on and relationship with the Roman Catholic Church in Africa.

    6. Located in west-central Africa, the Kingdom of the Kongo included territory that is part of present-day Angola (including Cabinda), Congo-Brazzaville, the Democratic Republic of the Congo, and Gabon.

    7. Richard Gray, cited in Sanneh, "Introduction," 4.

    8. See, e.g., Lowe, "'Representing' Africa," 106.

    9. Gray, "African Origins of the *Missio Antiqua*," 28f.

   10. Hastings, *Church in Africa*, 43.

for spiritual communion, the Ethiopian ambassadors also lobbied for "papal and European financial, technological and psychological help against the Muslim threat in their region, just as all papal contacts with Ethiopia had the underlying motive of trying to enlist Ethiopian manpower against the Muslim threat on another flank."[11]

The Kingdom of the Kongo generated interest in the European imagination chiefly because it was part of a continental route to Ethiopia, needed for trade and commerce. It was also the situs of the legend of Prester John—a wealthy and powerful European Christian king who supposedly relocated his kingdom to a remote region of Africa thought to be in Ethiopia.[12] Like every myth, this legend functioned sociopolitically and historically to move the mind of the people to action, inspiring a wave of missionary activity in Ethiopia among those seeking a chance encounter with "the great Emperor of Aetiopia who is called the Prester John."[13] Thus, Kongo was relevant not just for reasons of trade and commerce but also because it would "open a route to Prester John."[14]

In 1482, the Portuguese under Diogo Cão reached the Congo basin and were warmly welcomed by the visionary Kongo king, Nzinga a Nkuwu (João I). The Portuguese made a deep impression on the king, which influenced him to send his son Nzinga Mbemba (future King Afonso I) to Portugal to become literate.

By 1491, King Nzinga and five nobles had accepted the Roman Catholic faith and become baptized. The burgeoning influence of Catholicism on the political culture of the kingdom inspired the king's wife, Leonor Nzinga a Nlaza, to also demand baptism; she had "learned Christian precepts quickly and very well and was able to answer questions accurately."[15] The king would become an important benefactor of the church, strongly supporting its activities through the royal treasury.[16] A church was built, and when the Portuguese returned to Europe at the end of the century they left a number of priests and craftsmen as a token of goodwill. For King Nzinga, his relationship with the sovereign of Portugal was that of two Catholic kings, religious brothers, so to speak.

Afonso I became king upon the death of his father in 1506. He introduced a Catholic theocracy that would exist for centuries. According to one tradition, he buried his mother alive for refusing to part with an idol, an act he considered sacrilegious in his Christian empire.[17] Centuries later, he is revered as a patron and defender of missionaries in the Kongo and invoked as a saint, as evidenced by an Italian, Father Lorenzo: "Where are you, Afonso the First, King of Kongo, who for love of the Faith buried your own mother alive! Come, O Afonso, come to avenge the injury that these perverse people have done to the Holy Christian Faith in this City."[18]

Afonso's faith was legendary and he was viewed as a mystic. In 1513, he took a special vow of obedience to the pope. A Franciscan described him in glowing terms:

> It seems to me from the way he speaks as though he is not a man but rather an angel, sent by the Lord into this kingdom to convert it; for I assure you that it is *he* who instructs *us,* and that he knows better than we do the Prophets and the Gospel of our Lord Jesus Christ and the lives of the saints and all the things concerning our Holy Mother the Church. For he devotes himself entirely to study, so that it often happens that he falls asleep over his books, and often he forgets to eat and drink in talking of the things of our Lord.[19]

---

11. Lowe, "'Representing' Africa," 111.
12. Lowe, "'Representing' Africa," 115–16; Hastings, *Church in Africa*, 71.
13. Gray, "African Origins of the *Missio Antiqua*," 37.
14. Gray, "Kongo Princess, the Kong Ambassadors, and the Papacy," 149.
15. Thornton, "Elite Women in the Kingdom of Kongo," 442.
16. Thornton, "Elite Women in the Kingdom of Kongo," 442.
17. Thornton, "Origin Traditions and History in Central Africa," 32.
18. Thornton, *Kongolese Saint Anthony*, 192.
19. Oliver and Atmore, *Medieval Africa 1250–1800*, 171 (emphasis in original).

Afonso was a modernizer, a Renaissance statesman. He wanted enlightenment for his people in both religious and temporal affairs and sent many people to study in Lisbon. He appealed for missionaries and craftsmen to come to the Kongo, and, in response, more missionaries and craftsmen arrived in 1512. One of his sons, Dom Henrique, became a priest and was appointed by Pope Leo X as the bishop of Utica[20] in 1518 and vicar apostolic of the Kongo in 1520.[21] Afonso took great interest in Portuguese law, informing himself "in detail about the etiquette of the Portuguese court and the ranking of European society."[22] By the time Afonso died in 1540, Catholicism would constitute a source of imperial authority and dynastic legitimacy in the kingdom.

Although Diogo Cão originally came to the Kongo with only priests, masons, and soldiers, the pressures of the flourishing slave trade changed the rules of diplomatic engagement with Portugal. As Adam Hochschild put it, Afonso was no abolitionist: "He owned slaves and at least once he sent some as a present to a 'brother' King in Lisbon."[23] Yet these were slaves conquered in war, not free subjects. The slaves were often exchanged as gifts but were not part of an institutionalized commercial policy with its associated unimaginable cruelty. He had expressed his hope that the slaves he sent to Lisbon would become educated and be sent back to Africa. For the Portuguese, there was no discrimination involved in the way they thought about the citizens of the Kongo—they were all potential slaves. Horrified by this, Afonso wrote to the Portuguese King João III in 1526 that

> each day the traders are kidnapping our people—children of this country, sons of our nobles and vassals, even people of our own family. This corruption and depravity are so widespread that our land is entirely depopulated. We need in this Kingdom only priests and schoolteachers, and no merchandise, unless it is wine and flour for Mass. It is our wish that this kingdom not be a place for the trade or transport of slaves.[24]

Afonso was concerned about the impact of the materialism that was wrapped up with the slave trade on the temporal and spiritual lives of his Christian subjects. He denounced the European slave merchants, deploring transatlantic slavery as incompatible with Christianity, in a letter to King João of Portugal:

> Many of our subjects eagerly lust after Portuguese merchandise that your subjects have brought into our domains. To satisfy this inordinate appetite, they seize many of our black free subjects . . . they sell them . . . after having taken these prisoners [to the coast] secretly or at night. . . . As soon as the captives are in the hands of white men they are branded with a red-hot iron. . . . These goods exert such a great attraction over simple and ignorant people that they believe in them and forget their belief in God. . . . My lord, a monstrous greed pushed our subjects, even Christians, to seize members of their own families, and of ours, to do business by selling them as captives.[25]

The Portuguese Catholic monarchy, already empowered by the papal injunction of 1491,[26] was not concerned about the demands of Christian social justice. King João responded, "You . . . tell me that you want no slave-trading in your domains,

---

20. A North African Catholic diocese located in present-day Tunisia that was destroyed during the Arab conquest of the region. The diocese was briefly restored during the Spanish reconquest of North Africa and is now a titular see.
21. Oliver and Atmore, *Medieval Africa 1250–1800*, 170; also Clarke, "Brief History of the Kongo."
22. Oliver and Atmore, *Medieval Africa 1250–1800*, 170.
23. Hochschild, *King Leopold's Ghost*, 13.
24. Hochschild, *King Leopold's Ghost*, 13.
25. Hochschild, *King Leopold's Ghost*, 13.
26. The papal bull *Inter Caetera* (1493) granted wide-ranging temporal powers to Spanish and Portuguese monarchs to conquer foreign lands and spread the Roman Catholic faith. See the detailed discussion below.

because this trade is depopulating your country.... [T]he Portuguese there, on the contrary, tell me how vast the Congo is, and how it is so thickly populated that it seems as if no slave has ever left."[27] Disillusioned by what he considered to be a second crucifixion of Christ conducted by Christians and even priests who had become corrupted by the ill-gotten gains of slavery, Afonso was unwavering and "pleaded with his fellow sovereigns as one Christian with another," drawing on the moral content of his Catholic faith: "In this Kingdom, faith is as fragile as a glass because of the bad examples of the men who come to teach here, because the lusts of the world and lure of wealth have turned them away from the truth. Just as the Jews Crucified the Son of God because of covetousness, my brother, so today, He is again crucified."[28]

Neither the Portuguese missionaries nor the laymen with them were interested in Afonso's plea. He wrote to Rome to ask its direct intervention to stop the transatlantic slave trade, but his emissaries were often detained by Portugal before they could reach the Vatican.[29] His activism on this issue caused him to be shunned by the clergy and political elites of Portugal and eventually turned him into a despised enemy of the Portuguese. Ten of his relatives sent to Portugal for religious education were captured and sold into slavery, and while he was attending Mass on Easter Sunday in 1540, an attempt was made on his life.[30]

Despite these challenges the Kongolese church continued to thrive and drive sociopolitical and cultural change. Under the leadership of Alvaro I, Afonso's grandson, new initiatives were undertaken to consolidate and expand the role of the African church. Alvaro I was keen not only to solidify the relationship between the Kongo and the Holy See, but he also made a "firm commitment" by recognizing papal primacy.[31] His diplomatic letter to Rome dated January 15, 1583, underscored his devotion to the papacy. He stated that he wrote "in the first instance to inform His Holiness in detail concerning what happens and takes place in these my kingdoms, to tell him the need that exists for ministers for so many Christian souls, and to ask for relics, indulgences and blessed objects so that with greater courage and devotion we may make progress in the service of God."[32] The bearer of this missive was Duarte Lopes, a Portuguese convert to Catholicism who later became Kongo's ambassador to the papal court from 1584 to 1588. Much of what we know of the inner workings of the royal court and its relationship to the church is derived from the writing of Lopes.[33]

In addition to his alliance with Rome, Alvaro was eager to establish a diocesan rite for eligible Kongolese priests and nuns, and he founded the knighthood of the Order of Christ.[34] This fusion of religion and politics was a critical source of political legitimation enabling the expansion of Kongolese authority. During the leadership struggle following the death of Alvaro I in 1587, his son, Alvaro II, in order to consolidate his claim over the throne, courted political allegiances by giving gifts of Catholic knighthood. As John K. Thornton noted, this "granting [of] Knighthoods in the Order of Christ to [their] supporters and selected rivals"[35] became a common practice of Kongolese kings to bolster their power and influence.

Undeterred by Pope Sixtus V's tepid response to his father's earlier request for a consolidated diplomatic relation with the Holy See, Alvaro II continued with diplomatic overtures to Rome. In 1594, he dispatched a diplomatic delegation led by Antonio Vieira, who successfully negotiated with the papal legate in Lisbon over the creation of a new diocese

---

27. Hochschild, *King Leopold's Ghost*, 14.
28. Hochschild, *King Leopold's Ghost*, 14.
29. Hochschild, *King Leopold's Ghost*, 14.
30. Hochschild, *King Leopold's Ghost*, 14.
31. Gray, "Kongo Princess, the Kong Ambassadors, and the Papacy," 152.
32. Gray, "Kongo Princess, the Kong Ambassadors, and the Papacy," 144.
33. See Pigafetta, *Report of the Kingdom of Congo*.
34. Gray, "Kongo Princess, the Kong Ambassadors, and the Papacy," 145; Thornton, "Origin Traditions and History in Central Africa," 32.
35. Thornton, "Origin Traditions and History in Central Africa," 34.

specifically for the Kongo. The Cathedral of the Holy Savior (Sé Catedral de São Salvador) was dedicated on May 20, 1596. The Kongolese emissaries' understanding of "Christian doctrine and ecclesiastical history" made a huge impact on the papal envoy Fabio Biondi, who offered a benediction for "Christians of this quality."[36] In a letter to the pope's secretary of state, Biondi was full of praises: "They were people of great commonsense . . . those who come from that kingdom give a very good account of their faith, which for me is exceeding wonderful, having so great a lack of priests who can instruct them. One could well say that the harvest is plentiful, but the laborers are few indeed."[37]

In a show of goodwill, Alvaro II was ultimately invited to send a royal ambassador to the papal court "as do all Christian Kings."[38] In June 1604, Antonio Emanuele Nsaku ne Vunda, a cousin of Alvaro II, was chosen as the first Kongolese ambassador to the papal court. Ne Vunda is described as a man "of noble manners and above all pious and devout, also endowed with strength and prudence in diplomacy."[39] Ne Vunda traveled from Brazil to Europe with twenty-five assistants; upon their arrival in Lisbon and Madrid, both the Portuguese and Spanish authorities blocked their passage to Rome and subjected them to extreme privation. After several months of detention by the Spanish authorities, ne Vunda boarded a ship in October 1607 and arrived in Rome on January 2, 1608. Only four of his assistants survived the tragic voyage. Ne Vunda and these assistants were received with pomp and given a reception worthy of princes despite the protestations of the Spanish crown. They were billeted in a palace that had previously been occupied by the famous Jesuit Robert Bellarmine (a saint and doctor of the church), but the hardship of the journey had already taken its toll on ne Vunda's health—he received last rites from Pope Paul V on the eve of the Epiphany, January 5, and died later that day.[40]

The shabby treatment of ne Vunda by Portuguese and Spanish imperial powers set in motion a chain of events in Rome. The papacy was forced to review the *padroado*, the ecclesiastical rights and responsibilities granted to Portuguese kings in 1514 by Pope Leo X for the administration of local churches in the Portuguese sphere of influence. Portugal was at the time of ne Vunda's trip under Spanish authority and the jurisdiction of the *padroado* had been extended to Spain in order to frustrate ne Vunda and his companions, and alternative arrangements were impossible. Further, Kongo was already claimed as a tributary by Portugal, which used all means to dissuade the diplomatic independence of ne Vunda. Since the only means of traveling to Europe was by ship and all the ships were owned by Portugal, the ambassadors were effectively detained upon their arrival in Lisbon.[41]

Pope Paul V not only overruled the Spanish crown's position on the reception of ne Vunda but also ordered Spanish missionaries to be sent to the Kongo. In a resentful reaction to this development, Philip III—whose support for the mission was requested by Pope Paul V—actively obstructed the initiative, causing "great displeasure" to the pope, for whom the obstruction constituted "irreparable harm" not only to the Kongo but to papal authority and the reputation of the church.[42] In the absence of this key support, the papacy's mission to the Kongo could not be successful, and the pope was forced to seek alternative sources of funding this and other missionary initiatives independent of the Portuguese and Spanish crowns. There was also the need to reclaim the church's reputation and reinforce the power of the spiritual sovereign over the temporal sovereign as concerned missions and evangelization. On July 10, 1622, Pope Gregory XV promulgated the bull *Inscrutabili Divinae Providentiae Arcano*, which established an institution that would

---

36. Gray, "Kongo Princess, the Kong Ambassadors, and the Papacy," 45.
37. Gray, "Kongo Princess, the Kong Ambassadors, and the Papacy," 146–47.
38. Gray, "Kongo Princess, the Kong Ambassadors, and the Papacy," 147.
39. Gray, "Kongo Princess, the Kong Ambassadors, and the Papacy," 149.
40. Gray, "Kongo Princess, the Kong Ambassadors, and the Papacy" Cf. Lowe, "'Representing' Africa," 120.
41. Lowe, "'Representing' Africa," 108.
42. Gray, "Kongo Princess, the Kong Ambassadors, and the Papacy," 150, 45.

take responsibility for organizing and spreading the Catholic faith in non-Catholic regions and for the reconversion of Protestants. This body became known as the *Sacra Congregatio de Propaganda Fide* (The Sacred Ministry for the Propagation of Faith). By establishing this body, the church freed itself from the terms of the *padroado* and of individual commissions.

The Kongo offers a *historical address* for understanding the conscious imagination of the church in the relationship it would have with sub-Saharan Africa in the coming centuries. King Garcia II (ruled 1641–1661) berated the teaching Capuchins for insisting that "Christianity was not incompatible with indigenous customs and practices."[43] In 1642, the king also rejected a Dutch invitation to send Calvinist missionaries to the Kongo, insisting that his was a Catholic kingdom.[44] In the centuries that followed, the African church continued to flourish despite the high-handedness of Catholic and Portuguese imperialism. The missionaries mobilized and took advantage of spiritual authority in order to further their domination of the socio-economic, political, and physical space of the people. Spiritual goods were constantly subordinated to immediate material gain and princely privileges. Temporal needs defined the church's evangelization mission. The Catholic faith was invoked only when doing so served temporal power, as John H. Clarke observes:

> The peaceful relations between the Africans and the Portuguese were eventually disrupted by the rising European lust for slaves and gold. . . . [T]he Christian Kingdom of the Kongo began to weaken and was practically destroyed by fortune hunters, pseudo-missionaries and other kinds of free-booters. By 1688, the entire Kongo region was in chaos. By the end of the seventeenth century European priests had declared open war on the non-Christian population of the Kongo. They were attempting to dominate Kongo-

lese courts and had ordered the execution of Kongolese ancestral priests and indigenous doctors. Now the Kongolese Christians were pathetic pawns in the hands of unscrupulous European priests, soldiers, merchants and other renegade pretenders, mere parish priests from Europe were ordering Kongolese kings from their thrones.[45]

The church's indifference to and even complicit involvement in the transatlantic slave trade should be understood in this context. Yet, while the Catholic faith maps the outline of our discussion, the ideological impulse of racist Christianity was typical of all Christendom and all Christian denominations, with the lone exception of the heroic evangelism of the Quakers.

The Transatlantic Slave Trade, the Church, and Colonial Modernity

In 1433 and 1435, Pope Eugenius IV, by means of various papal bulls, threatened to excommunicate any person found guilty of enslaving the converted Catholics of the Canary Islands. A similar ordinance prohibiting the enslavement of Catholics was promulgated by Pope Calixtus in 1456. A few years later, in 1462, Pope Pius II was even more resolute in excommunicating those "wicked Christians who were taking recently baptized adult converts away into slavery."[46] Pius was enraged about the disruption of the church's work of providing a home and refuge for baptized Catholics. For non-Catholics, however, there would be no salvation temporally or spiritually.

The church's antislavery policies are best understood within their peculiar historical context. They were pronounced at a time when Christendom was at war with Muslim kingdoms. The papal edict meant to protect Christians was in part a political maneuver of rebuke against Christian slave-raiders for their "unjust" enslavement of Christians, but did not apply to the enslavement of Muslim

---

43. Sanneh, "Introduction," 12.
44. Thornton, "1706: Dona Beatriz Kimpa Vita, the Kongolese Saint Anthony."
45. Clarke, "Brief History of the Kongo."
46. Maxwell, *Slavery and the Catholic Church*, 51–52.

"Saracens."[47] These policies supported the sociopolitical vision of earlier papal bulls as they concerned non-Europeans. Pope Nicholas V's bull *Dum Diversas* (1452), ratified by *Romanus Pontifex* (1454), promoted the conquest, banishment, and eternal enslavement of pagans and Muslims by the Christian King Afonso V of Portugal:

> We grant you [Kings of Spain and Portugal] by these present documents, with our Apostolic Authority, full and free permission to invade, search out, capture, and subjugate the Saracens and pagans and any other unbelievers and enemies of Christ wherever they may be, as well as their kingdoms, duchies, counties, principalities, and other property... and to reduce their persons into perpetual servitude.[48]

These bulls legitimated the concept of *terra nullius* ("land belonging to no one") as a moral, sociopolitical, and cultural mandate to dominate and occupy non-European lands and spaces, which was expounded by Pope Alexander VI in *Inter Caetera* (May 4, 1493):

> Among other works well pleasing to the Divine Majesty ... this assuredly ranks highest, that in our times especially the Catholic faith and the Christian religion be exalted and be everywhere increased and spread, that the health of souls be cared for and that barbarous nations be overthrown and brought to the faith itself ... we ... recognizing that as true Catholic kings and princes, such as we have known you always to be ... we therefore are rightly led, and hold it as our duty, to grant you even of our own accord and in your favor those things whereby with effort each day more hearty you may be enabled for the honor of God himself and the spread of the Christian rule to carry forward your holy and praiseworthy purpose so pleasing to immortal God.[49]

The *terra nullius* was the prevailing ideological mandate for the Portuguese when they first came to Africa. Already latecomers to the exploration of tropical Africa, the Portuguese desperately needed the logistical and moral support of the church in order to compete with the Muslim explorers "whose trans-Saharan caravans had given them a monopoly on West African gold and ivory trade."[50] The quest to impose perpetual servitude was, according to William Phipps, a clear reference to the peoples of West Africa, who because of their "proximity both to Europe and to the plantations" became "the preferred source of black captives."[51] Thus mandated by the church to "humanize" and Christianize the Africans, the Portuguese explored the hinterlands of West Africa and in 1441 brought their first black slaves back to Portugal. By 1445 they would reach Senegal and Gambia, and when the temporal and spiritual authorities realized how lucrative the Portuguese enterprise was, many of them offered them official sanction and legitimacy.

Although the Catholic Church became actively involved in the limited restoration of the rights and dignity of enslaved peoples in other parts of the world, in Africa, there was no such initiative. While papal bulls outlawed the enslavement of Catholics by fellow Catholics, the European kings ignored these statements as they concerned Africa without fear of any sanction or punishment. In 1514, for example, Oba Ozolua of the Benin Empire sent emissaries to the king of Portugal to show a deep interest in Christianity and trade in firearms. Portugal was willing to send missionaries but only on the condition of a free trade in slavery:

> With a very good will we send you the clergy that you have asked for ... when we see that you have embraced the teachings of Chris-

---

47. Maxwell, *Slavery and the Catholic Church*, 52.
48. Hayes, "Reflections on Slavery," 67.
49. Pope Alexander VI, papal bull *Inter Caetera* (1493).
50. Phipps, *Amazing Grace in John Newton*, 25.
51. Phipps, *Amazing Grace in John Newton*, 25–26.

tianity like a good and faithful Christian, there will be nothing in our realms which we shall not be glad to favour you, whether it be arms or canon and all other weapons of war . . . these things we are not sending you now because the law of God forbids it . . . we earnestly recommend that you order your markets to be opened and trade to be carried on freely.[52]

Within the confines of Catholicism, the initiative for a broad-based abolitionist movement did not emanate from Rome but from the efforts of the African church. In 1684, Lourenço da Silva de Mendonça, an Afro-Brazilian, petitioned Pope Innocent XI about "the horrors being perpetuated by European Christians on and across the Atlantic."[53] A petition by the Capuchin missionaries two years later moved Rome to issue formal condemnation of the transatlantic slave trade. This official condemnation should nevertheless be understood within the historical circumstances of the time. It came out during the Great Turkish War (July 14, 1683–January 26, 1699), and the geopolitical anxiety of the time pressured the church into an unwilling alliance with the African church. On March 20, 1686, a century before William Wilberforce, Pope Innocent XI issued a decree against the transatlantic slave trade. The injunction not only forbade the "violent and fraudulent enslavement of 'Negroes and other natives'" but entreated merchants and dealers to "emancipate and compensate innocent slaves."[54]

If it had been even minimally followed, this proclamation, as Gray notes, would have ended slavery centuries before it actually was.[55] The decree failed to have this effect for three reasons. First, vested interests within the church undermined this exercise of papal goodwill.[56] Second, there was an absence of political will among the European powers and the rest of the Christian world, for whom slavery was a major source of income and political legitimation. And, third, there was no institutional mechanism or temporal clout to enforce the spiritual mandate. The last reason would become even more decisive as an inspiring mandate for the Holy See to change and seek new terms for sociopolitical, temporal, and spiritual relations between itself and the European powers. Derivative lessons thus far provide new insights into the active role of the African church in its relationship with the Roman church throughout history. In this instance, the African church did not accept the official "doctrine" that Africans were subservient slaves of nature. In fact, the African church applied strong pressure on Rome to condemn the reprehensible evil of slave trade, as can be seen in the letters referenced above.

In the nineteenth century, the church's involvement with the abolitionist movements gaining steam in Europe was a consequence of an invitation from British Foreign Secretary Lord Castlereagh. Castlereagh, a Presbyterian, made a plea to Pope Pius VII through cardinals Ercole Consalvi and Bartolomeo Pacca in London to support the Vienna abolitionist congress of 1815. Despite the push of these movements, however, there was a prevalent view in Christian theological circles at this time that Black people were a cursed race, the damned descendants of Ham. This belief was also held in Catholic circles, and in 1873 Pope Pius IX offered a plenary indulgence to redeem the African race of this "natural curse." For the ostensible benefit of "wretched Ethiopians in Central Africa," Pius IX prayed "that almighty God may at length remove the curse of Ham from their hearts."[57]

On December 3, 1839, Pope Gregory XVI in the bull *In Supremo Apostolatus* condemned the enslavement of Africans. While this decree condemned the *future* enslavement of Blacks, it was not proactive in suggesting ways of freeing those already under bondage. In fact, the bull was an exhortation about how to be a good Christian

---

52. Hastings, *Church in Africa*, 77.
53. Gray, "Kongo Princess, the Kong Ambassadors, and the Papacy," 44.
54. Gray, "Kongo Princess, the Kong Ambassadors, and the Papacy," 44–45.
55. Gray, "Kongo Princess, the Kong Ambassadors, and the Papacy," 45.
56. Gray, "Kongo Princess, the Kong Ambassadors, and the Papacy," 45.
57. Maxwell, *Slavery and the Catholic Church*, 20.

slave or master.⁵⁸ This vision of what it meant to be a good slave or master was not peculiar to the church; in fact, it was a residue of the Enlightenment as the intellectual harbinger of colonialism.

Africa's encounter with the European world negotiated a space that privileges the Western understanding of humanity over and above others so that what constitutes a human being was primarily defined within the ambit of Western civilization and cultures. To be human was to be human as seen through a Eurocentric lens. While the Enlightenment championed the rehabilitation of human beings by means of universal rationality, this token of humanity was denied to non-Western peoples. Some Enlightenment spokespersons argued that these peoples possessed neither history nor rationality—key components of Enlightenment humanism.⁵⁹ Rationality and history are characteristics of the highest kind of humanity, but both were the exclusive reserve of the Western world.

For Enlightenment thinkers, Africa symbolizes the primitive condition of nonrational cultures having neither history nor culture nor morality. It is a continent fixated on "childhood," without historical memory, and hence by nature barbaric and savage.⁶⁰ Because the continent and its people have no history, the African is naturally inferior to whites, as we learn from David Hume: "*I am apt to suspect the Negroes to be naturally inferior to the Whites. There scarcely ever was a civilized nation of that complexion, nor even any individual, eminent either in action or speculation.*"⁶¹ Immanuel Kant continued in this vein by stating that because "Negroes" do not exhibit rational traits, they naturally belong to a different human species: "*The Negroes of Africa have by nature no feeling that rises above the trifling. . . . So fundamental is the difference between these two races of man, and it appears to be as great in regard to mental capacities as in color.*"⁶²

According to these authors, an absence of history signifies the nonrational, amoral nature of the Negro. Without rationality the Negro has no culture and possesses neither soul nor humanity. Since the Negro possesses none of these (humanity, culture, or a soul), he or she does not qualify to be treated with the dignity with which we treat other human beings, as stated by Baron de Montesquieu:

> You may obtain anything of the Negroes by offering them strong drink, and may easily prevail with them to sell, not only their children, but their wives and mistresses, for a cask of brandy. . . . It is hardly to be believed that God, who is a wise Being, should place a soul, especially a good soul in such a black ugly body . . . allowing them to be men, a suspicion would follow that we ourselves are not Christians. Weak minds exaggerate too much the wrong done to the Africans.⁶³

---

58. Pope Gregory XVI, papal bull *In Supremo Apostolatus*; also Maxwell, *Slavery and the Catholic Church*, 74.

59. I do not want to fall into the trap of overgeneralization, and so some qualification of this statement is necessary. Not every Enlightenment spokesperson was guilty of racism, and not all Enlightenment traditions emphasized rationality as part of their humanism. One example is the thought of Johann Gottfried Herder in Germany, who argued that it is not rationality but language as an embodiment of culture and tradition that is the key component of humanism. The opinions of Voltaire and Gottfried Wilhelm Leibniz concerning what it means to be a human person vary with respect to China, while August Wilhelm Schlegel offers a different view of what it means to be a person with respect to India. Schlegel argues that language is not just an instinct of nature but a reproduction of the human mind signified through human relations and encounters with other beings. Thus, as with Herder, language becomes a composite signifier of our shared humanity. In France, the unconventional views of Jean-Jacques Rousseau differed from those of René Descartes, Voltaire, and Montesquieu. Rousseau posited the notion of the "noble savage" as a symbol of universal reason; this noble savage was uncorrupted by religious superstition and independent of court civilization, and so could be the basis of a *reasonable* social order [M.O.E.: Although what is considered "rational" here is also contested, for it is judged from the standpoint of the Western epistemic tradition.]

60. Cited in Chukwudi E. Eze, *Race and the Enlightenment*, 35.

61. Chukwudi E. Eze, *Race and the Enlightenment*, 35 (italics mine).

62. Kant, *Observations on the Feeling of the Beautiful and the Sublime*, 110–11 (italics mine).

63. Montesquieu, *Spirit of Laws*, 238.

This is how the Enlightenment became implicated in (1) an epistemic blueprint for the domination of non-Western cultures, and (2) a contemptuous narrative that thrives through denigration of the other. "To *be* [human] is to be *rational* as captured in the Cartesian *Cogito*, 'I think therefore I am (a man).'"[64] But this formula—as I have argued elsewhere—is not extended to Africans, who were conceived of as nonhumans because they were both irrational and nonhistorical beings.[65] Subjective reclamation demands a deep understanding of the sociocultural world of the colonizer. In this world, to become human is to become colonized or assimilated—both processes featuring a special education leading to redemption.[66] "Education" here means education in colonialism and assimilation to European culture. In this view, colonialism becomes an act of charity through which the Black subject is humanized. A colonized subject becomes an educated and civilized subject.

Christianity was not immune to the residual impact of Enlightenment racism. Race was substituted for faith, and institutional Christianity became a cultural expression of Enlightenment racism. Montesquieu gives evidence of this conflation of race and faith in the quotation above: a good Christian knows by faith that *a good and wise God would not put a soul, much less a "good" soul, in a black, ugly body*. This thought summarizes the sociopolitical and cultural mindset of the time. The Black person is not only culturally inferior—he or she is an epitome of the unwanted, an undesired being, a nauseating subject, ultimately a disgrace to humanity, as seen in this passage attributed to Joseph de Maistre:

> There was only too much truth in this first impulse of the Europeans who, in the century of Columbus, refused to recognize as their fellow men the degraded inhabitants of the new world. . . . One cannot gaze upon the savage for an instant without reading the anathema written, I do not say upon his soul alone, but even on the external form of his body.[67]

The African is Black and ugly. *Ugly beings do not belong to a good God*. This Black being is a mistake, an error. To be Black is to be wrong, a wrong kind of human, as was articulated by Bloke Modisane: "White is right, and to be black is to be despised, dehumanized, classed among the beasts, hounded and persecuted, discriminated against, segregated and oppressed by government and by man's greed. White is the positive standard, black the negative. Symbols of wealth . . . are allotted to the whites; . . . inferiority, humiliation and servitude are the lot of the black people."[68]

Where religion is tied to race and race defines the parameters of sociopolitical and cultural praxis, access to Christianity is ultimately defined by color, and blackness is to be excluded. Under such circumstances, Christianity is antithetical to blackness and any attempt to recognize the Black person as human constitutes a crisis of faith, as we learn from Montesquieu above. This is the context in which Christianity became heavily implicated in Enlightenment racism. Africans were not only denied humanity because of their incapacity to be rational, but also because they lacked souls. Even the Jesuits, who attempted to extend Christian brotherhood to Blacks, did so with some uncertainty on this point: "I baptize you, if you have a soul may God have pity on you."[69]

This racialization of Christianity was not restricted to Africa. The Jesuits in Asia between 1574 and 1606 under the Italian Alexandre Valignano opposed the admission of Indians and

---

64. M. O. Eze, "Pan-Africanism and the Politics of History," 679. For a detailed argument, see M. O. Eze, "Humanism as History in Contemporary Africa," 69–70; see also Reckwitz, "Otherness? Towards an Intercultural Literary Anthropology."
65. Ibid.
66. Ibid.
67. Quoted in Césaire, *Discourse on Colonialism*, 49.
68. Modisane, "Why I Ran Away," 26.
69. See M. O. Eze, *Intellectual History in Contemporary South Africa*, 55.

Eurindians as candidates for the priesthood: "All these dusky races are stupid and vicious, and of the basest spirits . . . as for the *mestiços* and *mastiços*, we should receive either very few or none at all; especially with regard to the *mestiços* since the more native blood they have, the more they resemble the Indians and the less they are esteemed by the Portuguese."[70] Nevertheless, as was pointed out by Benedict Anderson, the Jesuits "actively encouraged the admission of the Japanese, Koreans, Chinese and Indochinese to the priestly function."[71] The Jesuits were not alone—the Portuguese Franciscans in Goa, Anderson continues, vehemently refused to admit Creoles into the Franciscan order because "even if born of pure blood white parents [they] have been suckled by Indian *ayahs* in their infancy and thus had their blood contaminated for life."[72]

Even in more recent centuries, Christianity not only has provided a moral mandate in favor of exclusion but also was an embodiment of structural violence. There were many voices like that of Rev. Richard Furman of South Carolina: "The right of holding slaves is clearly established in the Holy Scriptures, both by precept and example. . . . Neither the spirit nor the letter of Scripture demands the abolition of slavery."[73] In some cases, the church banned catechetical instruction to slaves; for example, the Society for the Propagation of the Gospel (Church of England) forbade a certain Dr. Porteus to minister to slaves as "planters argued that 'to teach heathen slaves Christianity would be to barbarize the Gospel.'"[74] When religion and politics are intertwined, slavery is not only an economic necessity, but a religious duty, as we learn from Jefferson Davis:

> Slavery was established by the decree of Almighty God. . . . It is sanctioned in the Bible, in both Testaments, from Genesis to Revelation . . . it has existed in all ages, has been found among the people of the highest civilization, and in nations of the highest proficiency in the arts. . . . Slavery existed then in the earliest ages, and among the chosen people of God . . . you find it recognized, sanctioned everywhere.[75]

These views are of course contrary to the views of the early church with its apostolic commitment to a Christian utopia: "There can neither be Jew nor Greek, there can neither be slave nor freeman, there can be neither male nor female for you are all one in Christ" (Gal 3:28). They also make impossible the profound notion of the Christian faith as a gift, unconditionally given and undetermined by race, culture, gender, or language.

> It is by believing with the heart that you are justified, and by making the declaration with your lips that you are saved. When scripture says: No one who relies on this will be brought to disgrace, it makes no distinction between Jew and Greek: the same Lord is the Lord of all, and his generosity is offered to all who appeal to him, for all who call on the name of the Lord will be saved. (Rom 10:12)

The subjection of Christianity to the cultural ethos of the Enlightenment was problematic for two reasons. First, it reduced Christianity from a religion of utopian universalism to a cultural phenomenon, and, second, the Enlightenment's conflation of culture with race meant that a nonwhite who wished to be a Christian must embrace whiteness and reject his or her own identity. In this way, the racialization of Christianity as a cultural right of white Europeans was justified. This would become a poignant source of moral and epistemic legitimation both of colonization and of the enslavement of Africans. Christianity became a moral handmaid to both colonialism and slavery, making it a

---

70. Anderson, *Imagined Communities*, 59.
71. Anderson, *Imagined Communities*, 59.
72. Anderson, *Imagined Communities*, 60.
73. Jones, *Black Awareness*, 35.
74. Burke and Inalcik, *History of Humanity*, 410.
75. Davis, "Compromise Resolutions," 287–88.

religious duty for Christians to submit to domination. Slavers used St. Paul's epistle to Philemon as a moral justification for their actions, seeing it as a persuasive narrative that runaway slaves should be instructed that being a good Christian involves servile obedience to one's master, as reflected in the following slave catechism:

Q: Who gave you a master and a mistress?
A: God gave them to me.
Q: Who says that you must obey them?
A: God says that I must.[76]

Slaves were also pointed toward this passage of scripture: "Slaves, you should obey your masters respectfully, not only those who are kind and reasonable but also those who are difficult to please" (1 Pet 2:18). The Christianity we inherited through this kind of teaching thrived through the criminalization of Black subjectivity, as Vincent Harding lamented:

> For we first met the [White] Christ on slave ships. We heard his name sung in praise while we died in our thousands, chained in stinking holds beneath the decks, locked in with terror and disease and sad memories of our families and homes. When we leaped from the decks to be seized by sharks we saw his name carved in the ship's solid sides. When our women were raped in the cabins, they must have noted the great and holy books on the shelves. Our introduction to this Christ was not propitious and the horrors continued.[77]

But it is not just the image of the white Christ we encountered—this was our introduction to the church. This Christ was no center of our lives; he was a racist and a bigot. He was no bearer of good news; he was bad news. He was no champion of the poor; he was the exploiter. He was no advocate for the oppressed; he was the oppressor. He was no advocate of justice, but of prejudice. He was no God of compassion, but of cruelty. He was no God of redemption, but of damnation. He was no savior of ours. In fact, this Christ shamed us, he humiliated us. Harding notes in defiance:

> This [white] Christ shamed us by his pigmentation, so obviously not our own. He condemned us for our blackness, for our flat nose, for our kinky hair . . . we are tired of that . . . if this is what your Christ taught you . . . he's no savior of ours. We affirm our homeland and its great black past, a past that was filled with wonder before your white scourge came; you can keep your Christ. We'll take our home.[78]

This was the context in which colonialism came to Africa as a civilizing mission to humanize the "barbarians" through education and Christianization. Hence, to colonize was to civilize, to civilize was to humanize, to impart a full humanity, to give the African a morality for when he or she becomes like the Western "other." The colonizers saw their mission as helping to give Africans a past, a history, a redemptive pilgrimage. Educating the African according to the Western paradigm of knowledge would grant him or her a humanity that would be valued and recognized as such by Europeans. If to civilize is to humanize, to Christianize is to endorse and morally legitimate this humanization. Yet this story must not be told by the African—it must be written and told on his or her behalf. Ernest Renan is revealing here:

> The regeneration of the inferior or degenerate races by the superior races is part of the providential order of things for humanity. . . . Nature has made a race of workers, the Chinese race; . . . a race of tillers of the soil, the Negro; . . . a race of Masters and soldiers, the European race; . . . Let each one do what he is made for and all will be well.[79]

---

76. Fishel and Quarles, *Black American*, 114.
77. Harding, "Black Power and the American Christ," 95–96.
78. Harding, "Black Power and the American Christ," 95–96.
79. Ernest Renan, *La reforme intellectuelle et morale de la France* (1850), quoted in Césaire, *Discourse on Colonialism*, 4.

Beyond Vatican II:
Sentire cum Ecclesia Africae

As shown thus far, the Catholic faith that was received prior to Vatican II in Africa involved a residual narrative of various cultural and social experiences espousing the shared ideals of bringing light and salvation to the darkest corners of Africa. For the most part, the intellectual locus of this missionary zeal was grounded in an Enlightenment-based project of "humanization" to be achieved through the embedded capillaries of what it saw as the truth. Hence, long after Vatican II, we continued to learn in the catechism about *Nnukwu njo* and *obele Njo* (big sins and small sins or, put in the language of the church, mortal and venial sins). Even more important for me was learning as a child that going to a non-Catholic school was one of those big sins: *Iga akwukwo ma o bu uka na abughi nke Catholic* (to attend a church or school that is not of Roman Catholicism). This was the first notion that I understood to be a theological remnant of pre–Vatican II theology, with its emphasis on *Salus extra ecclesiam non est* (there is no salvation outside the church).[80]

As a child, I always wondered if I was perpetually damned to hell since the elementary school I attended, Premier Primary School, Eha–Alumona, Nsukka, was (and still is) a government-owned school. I hated school, and did I need to go to hell doing what I hated? Why couldn't I just skip school and avoid my strict disciplinarian mother who taught in the same school, and then go to heaven?

The old *Catholic Encyclopedia* contains the following entry about attendance at non-Catholic schools:

> The attendance of non-Catholic schools by Catholic Children is something which, for weighty motives and with due safeguards, can be tolerated, not approved. In any case parents must carefully provide for the child's religious instruction. As to higher education, parents have a clear duty to see that the faith of their children is not imperiled by their going to non-Catholic universities and colleges. In the lack of positive legislation before parents can assent to their children attending non-Catholic universities or colleges there must be a commensurately grave cause, and such dangers as may threaten faith or morals are to be rendered remote by suitable remedies. The last-named requirement is obviously the more important. Failure to fall in with the first, provided that means had been taken faithfully to comply with the second, would not oblige the confessor to refuse absolution to such parents. There is an undoubted and under ordinary circumstances inalienable authority to be exercised by parents.[81]

Although the entry here specifies colleges and universities, there is no distinction in the Igbo catechism between attending non-Catholic colleges and schools for younger children. This prohibition was not limited to the catechism. In his encyclical on Christian education, *Divini Illius Magistri,* Pope Pius XI explained why Catholics are forbidden from attending non-Catholic or "neutral" schools or even being educated alongside non-Catholics:

> The so-called "neutral" or "lay" school, from which religion is excluded, is contrary to the fundamental principles of education. Such a school moreover cannot exist in practice; it is bound to become irreligious. There is no need to repeat what Our Predecessors have declared on this point, especially Pius IX and Leo XIII, at times when laicism was beginning in a special manner to infest the public school. We renew and confirm their declarations as well as the Sacred Canons in which the frequenting of non-Catholic schools, whether neutral or mixed, those namely which are open to Catholics and non-Catholics alike, is forbidden for Catholic children, and can be at most tolerated, on the approval of the Ordinary alone, under determined cir-

---

80. This formulation was glossed by the Vatican II Declaration on the Relationship of the Church to Non-Christian Religions (*Nostra Aetate*), which recognized the truth and promise embedded in other religions.

81. Delany, "Parents."

cumstances of place and time, and with special precautions. Neither can Catholics admit that other type of mixed school . . . in which the students are provided with separate religious instruction, but receive other lessons in common with non-Catholic pupils from non-Catholic teachers.[82]

Notice the link between attending only Catholic schools and the internal logic of colonialism as a residue of the Enlightenment. It is also important to note that the catechism we learned had been prepared many years after Vatican II. Besides, these restrictions seem to have applied only to Africa—many missionaries were not restricted to teaching in Catholic schools in their homelands. This is not to discount the value of a Catholic education to which, as a beneficiary, I can testify. But this idea of educating Africans within an enclosed intellectual tradition as a received tradition was merely a means of fulfilling the Enlightenment project.

Thinking differently about the past offers us an intellectual space to deconstruct knowledge that evolved out of northern intellectual edifices. The fundamental premise here is the need to repudiate the episteme of European Christianity. We can draw lessons from the past in order to differentiate faith experience from European cultural experiences often packaged to look like the truths of faith. The work proposed here seeks to strip Catholicism of any aspects of the European Enlightenment that are masquerading as truth. It seeks to reveal—that is unveil—a Catholic faith that is unshackled from all of the rituals and tokens of a colonialist mentality. It seeks to tell a story, not with the intention of undercutting the faith tradition we received, but rather for the purpose of unveiling its apostolic truth within the African experience.

As much as we try, we cannot completely escape the cultural gaze that Europe has imposed on us through its colonization of Africa. I write in English. I speak German and French. I studied in European-style universities. I am recognized as a scholar because I passed through an intellectual furnace grounded in the European intellectual tradition. Yet I also recognize that I am a special kind of historian, an African historian who desires to tell a story from within a particular context. It is not a story told for me or imposed on me. It is not a top-down narrative irrelevant to the African faith experience. My position here is that restricting African Catholicism to received history and tradition enforces homogenized claims not only that are overly simplistic but that actively distort history. Contemporary African Catholicism ought to be explained from the point of view of contemporary cultural and historical transitions. The dangers of telling a story that is purely the residual narrative of Europe's encounter with Africa is that the rich cultural and historical particularities that might be able to enrich our faith experience as African Catholics are distorted.

Religion in the guise of white Christianity was used to smuggle European cultural hegemony into Africa. This fact is reminiscent of Saladin's cautionary warning to Chamcha in Salman Rushdie's *The Satanic Verses*: "They describe us. That's all. They have the power of description, and we succumb to the pictures they construct."[83] Religion is used to convey the idea of a racialized savior—a being we must worship not only for his divinity but for his racialized essence. This image of Christ as a white person is presented as a factual description and not as a mere interpretation. When the image received by a religious person is that of a white Christ (or a white God), a psychosocial condition is created in which the person not only submits to the idea of God because of God's divinity, but to the whiteness[84] associated with God. God is sacred, and whiteness must also be sacred because God chose to come as a white man. My proposal therefore is the urgent recovery and reclamation of the image of a God

---

82. Pope Pius XI, encyclical *Divini Illius Magistri* §79.
83. Rushdie, *Satanic Verses*, 172.
84. Nowhere is this racialized divinity more prevalent than in the holy pictures and religious icons in which Christ, Mary, Joseph, and even the apostles are represented as white Caucasians. These images are blessed as sacramentals and are seen by many Catholics as sources of blessing and symbols of piety. My point here is not about the religious significance of these items but about the associated baggage of a white redemptive teleology that demands decolonization.

that is nearer to each particular context in order to avoid an imposed self-alienation in the name of religion. We can be religious but only insofar as we first reclaim the image of God from racialist essentialism—God is *not* white, God is graced in the sociopolitical, historical, and cultural experiences of *all* peoples. Let cultures find the meaning of Christ (or God) within their own context or, alternatively, let God find God's purpose in our various sociopolitical and economic experiences, and in our graced history.

Writing about African Catholicism should then begin with legitimate inferences from the intellectual and sociocultural context of Africa. It should in addition historicize the overall context within which it operates as a living faith tradition in an ongoing process of recovering African agency and cultural knowledge going back to the first five centuries of Christian history. The epistemic validity of our method is dependent on this relationship between the context of history and the context of culture. Past history is always neutral, constant, and unchanging,[85] but culture is not. Culture is always evolving and nonstatic. We cannot make history subject to culture, but history helps us understand culture. The context of history enlarges and broadens the scope of our investigations, enabling us to draw valid conclusions from the sociocultural and political milieu within which we might speak of any future for African Catholicism. This is a model in which the context of our faith experience becomes our voice.

That is All!

Bibliography

Alexander VI, Pope. *Inter Caetera* [Papal Bull "Among Other [Works]"; 1493]. www.vatican.va.

Anderson, Benedict. *Imagined Communities*. London: Verso, 2001.

Burke, Peter, and Halil Inalcik, eds. *History of Humanity—Scientific and Cultural Development: From the Sixteenth to the Eighteenth Century*. UNESCO, 1999.

Césaire, Aimé. *Discourse on Colonialism*. New York: Monthly Press Review, [1962] 1972.

Clarke, John H. "The Brief History of the Kongo." Africa Federation. http://africafederation.net/Kongo_History.htm.

Davis, Jefferson. "Compromise Resolutions." In Appendix to the Congressional Globe for the First Session, Thirty-First Congress: Speeches and Important State Papers. Vol. 23, part 1, edited by John C. Rives (March 8, 1850).

Delany, Joseph. "Parents." *The Catholic Encyclopedia*. Vol. 11. New York: Robert Appleton Company, 1911. http://www.newadvent.org/cathen/11478c.htm.

Djintcharadzé, Anna. "African Church Fathers." In *The Encyclopedia of Christian Civilization*, edited by George Thomas Kurian. Hoboken, NJ: Wiley-Blackwell, 2011.

Eze, Chukwudi E. *African Philosophy: An Anthology*. Oxford: Wiley-Blackwell, 1997.

———. *Race and the Enlightenment: A Reader*. Oxford: Wiley-Blackwell, 2008.

Eze, Michael Onyebuchi. "Humanism as History in Contemporary Africa." *Taiwan Journal of East Asian Studies* 8.2, issue 16 (December 2011), 59–77.

———. *Intellectual History in Contemporary South Africa*. New York: Palgrave Macmillan, 2010.

———. "Pan-Africanism and the Politics of History." *History Compass* 11.9 (2013): 675–86.

Fishel, Leslie, and Benjamin Quarles. *The Black American: A Documentary History*. New York: Scott Foresman, 1970.

Gray, Richard. "The African Origins of the *Missio Antiqua*." In *Christianity, the Papacy, and Mission in Africa*, edited by Lamin Sanneh. Maryknoll, NY: Orbis Books, 2012.

———. "A Kongo Princess, the Kong Ambassadors, and the Papacy." *Journal of Religion in Africa* 29 (1999): 140–54.

Gregory XVI, Pope. *In Supremo Apostolatus* [Papal Bull; 1839]. www.vatican.va.

Harding, Vincent. "Black Power and the American Christ." In *The Black Power Revolt*, edited by Floyd Barbour. Toronto: Collier Books, 1969.

---

85. Our understanding of the past may change in the light of a new revelation or study, but the event being studied remains a fact that does not depend on new revelations or methodology. Thus, history possesses the aura of mathematical truth.

Hastings, Adrian. *The Church in Africa, 1450–1950.* Oxford History of the Christian Church. Oxford: Clarendon Press, 1994.

Hayes, Diana. "Reflections on Slavery." In *Change in Official Catholic Moral Teaching,* edited by Charles E. Curran. Mahwah, NJ: Paulist Press, 1998.

Hochschild, Adam. *King Leopold's Ghost: A Story of Greed, Terror, and Heroism in Colonial Africa.* New York: Houghton Mifflin, 1999.

Hume, David. "Of National Character" (1748). In *The Philosophical Works of David Hume,* vol. 3. Bristol: Thoemmes Press, 1996.

Isidore of Seville. *The Etymologies of Isidore of Seville.* Translated by Stephen A. Barney, W. J. Lewis, J. A. Beach, and Oliver Berghof. Cambridge: Cambridge University Press, 2010.

Jones, Major J. *Black Awareness: A Theology of Hope.* Nashville: Abingdon, 1971.

Kant, Immanuel. *Observations on the Feeling of the Beautiful and the Sublime.* Translated by John T. Goldthwait. Berkeley: University of California Press, 1960.

Kohn, Hans. *The Idea of Nationalism: A Study in Its Origins and Background.* Piscataway, NJ: Transaction Publishers, 2005.

Lévy-Bruhl, Lucien. *The Notebooks on Primitive Mentality.* Translated by Peter Rivière. Oxford: Blackwell, 1975.

Lowe, Kate. "'Representing' Africa: Ambassadors and Princes from Christian Africa to Renaissance Italy and Portugal, 1402–1608." *Transactions of the Royal Historical Society,* 6th Series, 17 (2007): 101–28.

Maxwell, J. Francis. *Slavery and the Catholic Church: The History of Catholic Teaching Concerning the Moral Legitimacy and the Institution of Slavery.* London: Barry Rose, 1975.

Modisane, Bloke. "Why I Ran Away." In *An African Treasury,* edited by Langston J. Hughes. New York: Crown, 1960.

Montesquieu, Baron de [Charles de Secondat]. *The Spirit of Laws.* 1748. New York: Cosimo Classics, 2007.

Oliver, Roland, and Anthony Atmore. *Medieval Africa 1250–1800.* Cambridge: Cambridge University Press, 2004.

Phipps, William E. *Amazing Grace in John Newton.* Macon, GA: Mercer University Press, 2004.

Pigafetta, Filippo. *A Report of the Kingdom of Congo and of the Surrounding Countries: Drawn out of the Writings and Discourses of the Portuguese, Duarte Lopez, by Filippo Pigafetta, in Rome, 1591.* Cambridge: Cambridge University Press, 1881.

Pius XI, Pope. *Divini Illius Magistri* [Encyclical "The Divine Teacher"; 1929]. www.vatican.va.

Pliny the Elder. *Natural History: Complete Collection in Ten Volumes.* Edited by D. E. Eichholz. Translated by W. H. S. Jones and H. Rackham. Loeb Classical Library. Cambridge, MA: Harvard University Press, 1938.

Reckwitz, Erhard. "Otherness? Towards an Intercultural Literary Anthropology." In *Exploring Humanity: Intercultural Perspectives on Humanism,* edited by Mihai I. Spariosu and Jorn Rusen. Göttingen: V&R Unipress; Taipei: National Taiwan University Press, 2012.

Rushdie, Salman. *The Satanic Verses.* New York: Random House, 2008.

Sanneh, Lamin. "Introduction." In Richard Gray, *Christianity, the Papacy, and Mission in Africa.* Edited by Lamin Sanneh. Maryknoll, NY: Orbis Books, 2012.

Thornton, John K. "1706: Dona Beatriz Kimpa Vita, the Kongolese Saint Anthony." *Executed Today* (July 2, 2008). http://www.executedtoday.com.

———. "Elite Women in the Kingdom of Kongo: Historical Perspectives on Women's Political Power." *Journal of African History* 47.3 (2006): 437–60.

———. *The Kongolese Saint Anthony.* Cambridge: Cambridge University Press, 1998.

———. "Origin Traditions and History in Central Africa." *African Art* 37.1 (2004).

Thornton, John K., and Linda Heywood. "The Treason of Dom Pedro Nkanga a Mvemba against Dom Diogo, King of Kongo, 1550." In *Afro-Latino Voices: Narratives from the Early-Modern Ibero-Atlantic World, 1550–1812,* edited by Kathryn J. McKnight and Leo J. Garofalo. Indianapolis, IN: Hackett, 2015.

Wright, Richard. *Native Son.* New York: Harper & Row, 1940.

African Catholicism and Intellectual History in Africa

Suggested Reading

Eze, Michael Onyebuchi. *The Politics of History in Contemporary Africa*. New York: Palgrave Macmillan, 2010.

Hastings, Adrian. *The Church in Africa, 1450–1950*. Oxford History of the Christian Church. Oxford: Clarendon Press, 1994.

Maxwell, J. Francis. *Slavery and the Catholic Church: The History of Catholic Teaching Concerning the Moral Legitimacy and the Institution of Slavery*. London: Barry Rose, 1975.

Thornton, John K. *The Kongolese Saint Anthony*. Cambridge: Cambridge University Press, 1998.

Thornton, John K., and Linda Heywood. "The Treason of Dom Pedro Nkanga a Mvemba against Dom Diogo, King of Kongo, 1550." In *Afro-Latino Voices: Narratives from the Early-Modern Ibero-Atlantic World, 1550–1812*, edited by Kathryn J. McKnight and Leo J. Garofalo. Indianapolis, IN: Hackett, 2015.

Key Words

African intellectual history
Alvaro II
Black theology
Catholic-Portuguese imperialism
Christian education
Christian messianism
Christian slavery
church fathers
church history
colonial Christianity
colonialism
Enlightenment racism
Ethiopian church history and rationalism
Kongo church
medieval African Catholicism
Nsaku ne Vunda
Nzinga a Nkuwu
political theology
Propaganda Fidei
racialist Christianity
transatlantic slave trade
Western imperialism
imperialism

History and Methods of African Studies of the New Testament: Protestant and Catholic Dialogue

MarySylvia Nwachukwu, DDL, and Zorodzai Dube

This chapter investigates the history and methods of research in studies of the New Testament done by African Catholic and Protestant theologians in order to articulate their contribution to world Christianity. African studies of the New Testament are praxis-oriented, focusing more on contextual issues than on comparative Roman Catholic and Protestant epistemological perspectives. In this overview, we do not pretend to be exhaustive, but rather to describe the prevalent currents of research in African studies of the New Testament, as well as suggestions for the direction of its methodology.

After a brief presentation of the history of Christian Africa, which serves here as a prologue to the history of the contribution of Africa to the Christian theological enterprise, the chapter describes the character, scope, and significance of New Testament studies in Africa.

The History of Christian Africa

The Christian Africa[1] under discussion here is postcolonial Africa, but Christianity was introduced into the African continent as far back as 42 CE.[2] The Gospels and Acts of the Apostles show that the earliest image of the church had a very African color. Egypt was a place of refuge for the infant Jesus (Matt 2:13–15) and the birthplace of the Septuagint, the Bible of the early Christians. Moreover, the list of peoples present at the Pentecost event, among whom were Egyptians and Libyan Cyrenians (Acts 2:10), shows that many Jews from northern Africa had had contact with preachers of the gospel in the first century.[3] The eighth chapter of the book of Acts refers to people from Egypt, Libya, and Ethiopia (Acts 8:27–38). In the first seven centuries of the Christian era, a dynamic Christianity had developed in Africa. This Christian church produced the most theologically important early church fathers[4] and prepared African Christians for heroic martyrdom when Christians on the continent were persecuted.[5] Unfortunately, it was not possible for a specifically African interpretation of the Christian faith to develop in this early period because of Christianity's decline on the continent.

A detailed description of the factors responsible

---

1. In the early period of the church, the term "Africa" initially referred to the peninsula known today as Tunisia, but it came to be applied to all of Mediterranean Africa west of Egypt. During the first Christian millennium, Africa was the term designating lands from Libya to Morocco, from Tripoli to Tangier. For centuries, maps of Africa did not include Egypt, but in due course "Africa" began to refer to the entire continent, including Egypt. See Oden, *How Africa Shaped the Christian Mind*, 81.
2. Tradition has it that the evangelist Mark brought the Christian faith to Egypt in 42 CE.
3. See Mbiti, *Bible and Theology in African Christianity*, 1.
4. These included Clement, Justin Martyr, Tertullian, Cyprian, Augustine, Origen, and Athanasius, to name but a few. See Mbiti, *Bible and Theology in African Christianity*, 1.
5. Christians in Africa were the subject of persecutions by the Romans in the third century, the Arabs in the

for this decline cannot be treated in this chapter.[6] It suffices to point out that the spread of Islam from the seventh century onward led to the conquest and Islamization of previously Christian states in Africa. For centuries, the African church resisted being completely suffocated by the effects of Islamization; in particular, the Ethiopian Orthodox Church with its intense ascetical practices held on tenaciously throughout the medieval period, and continues to serve as a bridge between early and present-day Christian Africa. In the fifteenth and sixteenth centuries, European missionaries mounted an attempt at evangelization, which unfortunately was corrupted by the church's involvement with the slave trade. Beginning in the nineteenth century, however, with renewed European efforts at evangelization, Christianity in Africa began to take geographical shape. By the second half of the twentieth century, two-thirds of Africa had become predominantly Christian.[7]

Although present-day Christian Africa is very different from its earlier version,[8] the church in sub-Saharan Africa today identifies with the honorable and distinguished theological contributions of North Africa, by which it influenced the foundations of Christendom, Europe, and Western civilization. Christianity in Africa has grown to be a dynamic force shaping the lives of more African people than any other faith. John Mbiti rightly says that modern Christian Africa, the product of both political colonization and religious evangelization, is like a granary filled with borrowed grain, and that African Christians, in the gradual process of articulating their own identity, have begun cultivating their own "home-grown grain."[9] By this he means that African theologians have begun to recognize the need to move beyond the Western theological system and Western philosophies and to invest in efforts to develop an indigenous theology. In this regard, the three-volume work *African Theology in the 21st Century: The Contribution of the Pioneers*[10] gathers the contributions of a number of authors who offer appraisals of the theological journey of pioneering African theologians. *African Theology* continues to encourage other theologians to continue the work of inculturation begun by their predecessors for the purpose of discovering the precise identity of a truly African theology.

Characteristics and Scope of New Testament Studies in Africa

The specific characteristics of African New Testament studies can be seen by comparing them with Western approaches to the subject. In general, research on the New Testament involves interpreting the subjects raised by New Testament texts in their Greco-Roman historical and philosophical contexts. One can generalize and say that Western approaches to the study of the New Testament employ one or more modern critical methods in order to draw out the message of the text as understood by its original audience. For African scholars, systematic and scientific research into the New Testament involves the theologian relating the text to African religio-cultural ideas in order to bring that message home to African Christians.[11]

---

seventh century, and the colonial powers in the nineteenth century. See Oden, *How Africa Shaped the Christian Mind*, 117.

6. For a detailed description of these factors, see Groves, *Planting of Christianity*.

7. For statistics about the growth of the new Christian Africa, see Mbiti, *Bible and Theology in African Christianity*, 2–6.

8. The first Christian Africa was evangelized from the eastern Mediterranean and eventually became the seedbed of the universal church's theological tradition, while the new one is the child of later missionary evangelization emanating from Europe beginning at the end of the eighteenth century, and later from America. See Mbiti, *Bible and Theology in African Christianity*, 7.

9. Mbiti, *Bible and Theology in African Christianity*, 7, 12–15.

10. Bujo and Muya, *African Theology in the 21st Century*.

11. See Nyamiti, "Contribution of African Cultures," 29; Idowu, *Towards an Indigenous Church*; Sawyer, *Creative Evangelism*; Mbiti, *New Testament Eschatology in an African Background*.

A question has been raised as to whether the fields of New Testament exegesis[12] and biblical theology[13] are relevant to an African theology. The answer is yes. Although distinct, these two fields are interrelated: while exegesis "draws out" of the text the meaning intended by the human author, biblical theology highlights its divine component, namely, that which makes it part of the Word of God.[14] In general, however, African biblical scholars follow a praxis-oriented interpretation of the Bible.[15]

One can identify various orientations in studies done by African New Testament scholars. Some are fundamentally biblical but also conversational;[16] others follow an approach that presupposes a synthesis of biblical and cultural practices, with the aim of bringing about a contextualized theology. Still others adopt the praxis model, emphasizing action, which seeks especially to touch important concerns in people's lives,[17] while some other scholars believe that African studies must pay close attention to the subjects of liberation, inequality, and reconciliation.[18]

Giving African Studies an Identity

In 1976, John Mbiti remarked that, while there has been considerable theological traffic between the West and two of the new centers of Christianity, Latin America and Asia, there has been an absence of a theological relationship between the West and Africa.[19] This observation has been repeated by more recent authors like John Parratt and J. N. K. Mugambi.[20] A brief comment on this matter is appropriate.

In Latin America and Asia, Christian theologies made their appearance with very clear indigenous identities, languages, structures, and goals and were occasioned by the sociopolitical realities present on these continents.[21] But Africa was unable to become a true partner in evangelization because she still communicates in the foreign languages of the colonial masters, and many Western-trained African theologians offer only the theological traditions and methodologies of their teachers. In addition, Africa is arguably even more pluralistic than Latin America and Asia,[22] a reality that has

---

12. Exegesis, which means "to draw out," investigates the various linguistic, cultural, historical, and literary contexts of a biblical text in order to uncover the original meaning intended by its author. See, e.g., Akonga, "La paix dans la Bible."

13. A theological study facilitates the discovery of the divine reality revealed in the historical event described in the text. It brings the spiritual quality of the message to light, without which the text would have only a literal meaning, merely historical or mythological. See the theological study by MarySylvia Nwachukwu, *Creation-Covenant Scheme and Justification by Faith*, published by Gregorian Press in 2002. For a study that combines the exegetical and the theological, see Béré, "Pourquoi Pierre est-il peiné?," 66–80.

14. See Béré, "Scripture Studies and African Theology," 129.

15. See the proceedings of the Pan-African Association of Catholic Exegetes and similar associations, which offer in-depth interpretations of biblical texts to aid with understanding in academic and pastoral contexts.

16. Although it uses the Bible as a foundational text, this form of research dialogues deeply with the experience of the contemporary African community. Its goal is to highlight the revelatory autonomy of cultures as original bearers of divine truth.

17. See a description of these latter two models in Obeng, "Synthetic and Praxis Models in African Theology," 49. The works of African feminist theologians are praxis-oriented, even though Laurenti Magesa says that "woman defined theology is liberation theology" ("Challenge of African Woman Defined Theology," 89). For Teresa Okure, theological interpretation must be guided by a common search for new inclusive meanings ("Feminist Interpretation in Africa," 77).

18. See Parratt, *Reader in African Christian Theology*; Magesa, "The Political Axis," 144.

19. See Mbiti, "Theological Impotence and the Universality of the Church," 6–18.

20. Parratt, *Reinventing Christianity*, 1; Mugambi, "Theological Method in African Christianity," 26–27.

21. Liberation theology in Latin America, for instance, has emphasized the preferential option for the poor.

22. Despite some common ground, the African continent is characterized by pluralism in the areas of culture, language, political history, and even the theological emphasis of its missionaries. For a useful overview of the multicolored fabric of the African continent, see Mbiti, *African Religions and Philosophy* (1969); Damman, *Die Religionen Afrikas* (1963).

affected the orientation, methodology, and linguistic identity of African theology.

The key that opened the door of theological conversation with the global church was the controversial 1957 book *Des prêtres noirs s'interrogent*.[23] In it, a congress of francophone Catholic theologians sought to determine the scope of the intellectual agenda for the emancipation of the African spirit from Western colonial domination.[24] A second congress, held in Rome in 1959, featured many more Catholic priests and incorporated a subsection for African theologians.[25] A similar initiative was seen in the 1969 proceedings of the All Africa Conference of Churches (AACC) held in Ibadan, Nigeria, published under the title *Biblical Revelation and African Beliefs*.[26] All three of these efforts aimed at a deeper scriptural understanding and vernacular translations of the Bible in order to better implement the desired contextual theology.

Three decades ago, some scholars were calling African theology an "emerging" theology.[27] Although some progress has been made since then, more definite steps must still be taken in order for African theology to assume an authentic identity. An important question that is being asked is whether the road map charting this theological identity is sufficiently clear.[28] Certainly, the path to this identity must pass through a difficult process of deconstructing fixed mental structures and reconstructing them in a way that situates the Christian religion in an African context. This deconstruction will involve clearing a forest of foreign ideological constructs, rites, and structures inherited from missionary times that have been the basis of Christian life in Africa ever since. Early African theologians understood that, as long as the African church remains attached to Western conceptual frameworks, Christianity will remain a stranger to Africa.[29] Deconstruction requires the groundbreaking work of thinkers with a deep experience of faith and deep knowledge of African traditions and cultures who can critically reassess aspects of the African tradition that the missionaries condemned as superstitious.[30] More radically, Laurenti Magesa writes:

> Deconstruction and construction constitute the current vocation of the Church in Africa: it is a process that leads to a new way of being truly African and fully Christian. The process requires an act of the almost sacrilegious deconstruction of certain time honored conceptions of both Africanness on the one hand and Christianity on the other to regain them anew in a more appropriate manner.[31]

We now proceed to a full discussion of African studies on the New Testament—their beginnings, growth, sources, nature, methodologies, and prospects for future research.

The Beginnings of African Studies on the New Testament

Political, cultural, intellectual, and religious factors all inspired the initial steps toward nurturing "home-grown grain" for the emerging store of African New Testament studies and African theology in general.

The first factor was the indigenous political movements that came to the fore between 1950 and 1970, just before and around the time many African nations gained their independence from their former colonial masters.[32] The "Black the-

---

23. A. Abblé et al., eds., *Des prêtres noirs s'interrogent* (Paris: Editions du Cerf, 1957).
24. See Paulin Poucouta's appraisal of M. P. Hebga's contribution to this initial stage of African theology in Poucouta, "Meinrad Pierre Hebga: Theologian and Healer," 84.
25. See Bowers, "African Theology," 111.
26. Dickson, *Biblical Revelation and African Beliefs*.
27. See Parratt, *Reinventing Christianity*, 3.
28. See Magesa, "Truly African, Fully Christian?," 81.
29. See, e.g., Éla and Luneau, *Voici les temp des héritiers*, 165.
30. Lufuluabo, *L'Antisorcier face à la Science*, 7; Lufuluabo, "Orientation préchrétienne," 11.
31. Magesa, "Truly African, Fully Christian?," 81; see also 81–86.
32. See Parratt, *Reinventing Christianity*, 13–14.

ology" of South Africa was produced by these movements in response to situations of inequality and the oppression of Black people. In most colonial African states, the Bible was enlisted as an accomplice in colonialism, racism, and oppression.[33] Faced with this predicament, Black theology undertook to reconstitute an anthropology based on the image of the Christian God, whose will is to liberate people from all forms of oppression.[34] The second factor was the pervasive cultural revolution that occurred mostly in western Africa, which expressed a conscious inward struggle against Western colonization and advocated for an end to European theological imperialism.[35] The third factor comprised certain publications in the field of ethnophilosophy, beginning with Placide Tempels and others,[36] which affirmed that Christianity in Africa could be developed on a substratum of African philosophy. The earliest studies following this line of thought date back to the late 1940s, and John Parratt and Bénézet Bujo agree that Tempels's *Bantu Philosophy* (1945) was the starting point of African theology.[37] Finally, the fourth factor was the universalist message of the Second Vatican Council. Having admitted to the existence in other religions of "rays of that Truth which enlightens all men" (*Nostra Aetate* §2), the council encouraged every area of the world to cultivate indigenous theologies from the seed of the Word of God planted in the customs, traditions, wisdom, art, and disciplines of every people (*Ad Gentes* §22).

Having been encouraged by the presence of these factors to cultivate local expressions of the Christian faith, Catholics and Protestants undertook new initiatives through the formation of denominational, national, and international associations to foster a new theological dialogue. As their names indicate, most of these early associations were ecumenical in orientation. They included the All Africa Conference of Churches (AACC),[38] the Association of Evangelicals in Africa (AEA),[39] the Ecumenical Association of Third World Theologians (EATWOT),[40] the Ecumenical Association of African Theologians,[41] the Catholic Theological Association of Nigeria,[42] the Pan-African Association of Catholic Exegetes (PACE/APECA),[43] and the Ecumenical Symposium of Eastern Africa Theologians (ESEAT).[44]

These associations represent only a small fraction of the movements that have continued to promote the African theological enterprise. The initial efforts to do so were ecumenical and all-encompassing, sometimes involving the participation of Asian theologians, for instance, in EATWOT. Denominational associations began a decade later; the evangelical associations were and are Bible-centered, and in the Catholic associations, biblical scholarship has been significantly influenced by Western research methodologies. The research objectives of PACE, for instance, are (1) to engage in scientific exegesis by means of a rigorous application of universally recognized methods of doing

---

33. See Z. Dube, "Discursive Investigation into John's Internalised Spirit Identity."
34. Mofokeng, "Black Christians, the Bible and Liberation"; Morgenthau, *Politics among Nations*, 4–15.
35. See Hebga, *Emancipation d'Eglises*, 39–40; Idowu, *African Traditional Religions*, xi.
36. See Bujo, *African Theology in Its Social Context*, 56–58; Parratt, *Reinventing Christianity*, 10.
37. For this idea, see Parratt, *Introduction to Third World Theologies*; Bujo, *Ethical Dimension of Community*.
38. Inaugurated in Kampala in 1963 and now comprising more than 120 member churches.
39. Founded in 1966 with its headquarters in Kenya, now comprising forty national evangelical fellowships. The AEA has founded many schools of theology in both francophone and anglophone Africa.
40. Inaugurated in 1976 in Dar es Salaam, Tanzania.
41. Created within the framework of EATWOT and inaugurated in 1977 in Accra, Ghana.
42. Inaugurated in 1985 in Onitsha, Nigeria.
43. In French, L'Association Panafricaine des Exégètes Catholiques. Its origin is traced back to the workshop Journées Bibliques Africaines held in Kinshasa in 1978, but it was formally founded in Yaoundé, Cameroon, in 1987.
44. Inaugurated in 1987 in Sagana, Kenya, its vision was to produce "theological texts which would manifest African theological thinking, as a contribution towards theological consensus in the Church universal" (Mugambi, "Ecumenical Contextual Theological Reflection," 18).

biblical studies; and (2) to perform contextualized exegesis in order to answer the questions that African Christians are posing to the Word of God in their particular contexts. While treating core theological themes in its first three symposia,[45] ESEAT established the goal of enriching the self-understanding of the African church.[46]

Sources of African Studies on the New Testament

It is important to consider here the variety of sources that African scholars draw from in anchoring their study of the New Testament. The primary source, naturally, is the New Testament itself, which is God's Word that demands a human response. A theology worthy of the name must be nourished by scripture, which goes beyond reflections supported by scriptural references to interpretations of experience using the Word of God as a primary source.[47]

The second source used by African scholars of the New Testament is the deposit of faith, which includes the doctrinal and theological traditions of the church. The importance of this source is anchored in the necessity for theological reflections to remain within the mainstream of the church's faith tradition. In giving guidelines as to how indigenous theologies might be cultivated, the Vatican II Decree on the Church's Missionary Activity (*Ad Gentes*) states that "it is necessary that in each major socio-cultural area such theological speculation should be encouraged, in the light of the universal Church tradition, as may submit to a new scrutiny the words and deeds which God has revealed, and which have been set down in sacred scripture and explained by the Fathers and by the magisterium" (§22). Even though some scholars believe that excessive faithfulness to the church's theological traditions accounts for the unwitting captivity of African theology to Western theology,[48] a neglect of this source would necessarily lead to the development of a theology without a historical anchor.

The third source is African Traditional Religion (ATR), from which scholars often derive the proper language to articulate an African understanding of the Christian God and an African cosmology and anthropology. In fact, many African scholars who are experts in the traditional African worldview see the points of similarity between the Bible and ATR and think of the latter as a *preparatio evangelica*, a preparation for the gospel.[49] For instance, Bénézet Bujo and John Pobee interpret Christological themes set forth in the Fourth Gospel from within the framework of an African conception of life.[50] At the same time, the African concept of mediation provides a conceptual framework for interpreting New Testament Christology, pneumatology, and themes of reconciliation, liberation, and healing.[51]

The fourth source used by African theologians is oral theology in the living experience of the church.[52] This refers to the interpretation of scripture going on in Christian churches in various parts of Africa relating the Bible to peoples' experiences of sicknesses and their cures, poverty and wealth, family curses and their cures, witchcraft,

---

45. (1) "Jesus in African Christianity" (1987); (2) "The Church in African Christianity" (1988); and (3) "Moral and Ethical Issues in African Christianity" (1989).

46. Magesa, "Introduction," 8.

47. There is an increasingly popular hermeneutic that appreciates the presence of African characters and places in biblical stories, develops correspondences between the biblical text and the African culture and worldview, and values a narrative approach. See, e.g., Kort, *"Take, Read."*

48. See Muzorewa, *Origins and Development of African Theology*, 94–98; Musopole, "Evangelicalism and African Christian Theology."

49. See Muzorewa, *Origins and Development of African Theology*, 79.

50. Bujo, *Christmas: God Becomes Man in Black Africa*; Pobee, "Jesus Christ—the Life of the World," 5–8; Pobee, "Life and Peace."

51. See the studies by Mbiti, *African Religions and Philosophy*; Bujo, *African Theology in Its Social Context*; Bujo, "Pour une éthique africano-christocentrique"; and Magesa, *African Religion* (1997).

52. This has been called "grassroots theology "and "spontaneous or implicit theology." See Bediako, *Jesus and the Gospel in Africa*, 7.

and other related issues. Special mention should be made in this regard of prayer centers led by Catholic priests and the healing ministries of Protestant pastors from African Independent Churches and religious movements. These groups are united in their concern to find in the scriptures answers to people's needs and anxieties. In doing so, they try to integrate the Christian message into African cultural and ideological values. Present-day African Christianity has been strongly influenced by the Christian spirituality of these groups. The oral theology produced by this spirituality includes melodious songs composed in African languages, songs that narrate people's quest for healing, wealth, and protection from evil spirits and witches—concerns that are not found in traditional written theology. About this source, Kwame Bediako argues that it is an illustration of a spirituality coming from where faith lives and provides clear evidence that Christianity in Africa is a truly African experience:

> In this setting of ubiquitous forces and mysterious powers, the Christian who has understood that Jesus Christ is a living reality, can be at home, assured in the faith that Jesus alone is Lord, Protector, Provider and Enabler. In the struggles and battles of life, the Christian discovers that Jesus goes ahead, and that . . . he alone is capable of fighting and conquering, leading his people in triumph.[53]

This source demands attention from African theologians, who must first and foremost consider it a fertile *locus theologicus*. The neglect of this area of African experience by theologians in mainline churches has often been thought of as one of the main reasons theology is perceived to be unrelated to current African narratives. On this issue, Magesa makes the point that "theological language in Africa that is incapable of following to its internal conclusion the logic and spirituality of witchcraft, polygamy, divination, traditional healing practices, and so on, except to condemn these beliefs and practices, fails miserably to engage with the African person holistically. It addresses culture as a theoretical object outside the person."[54]

Theologians might hesitate to investigate the delicate field of oral theology out of a fear of engaging in syncretism. What is required, however, is a careful synthesis and integration of African cultural meanings and values with those of the gospel, without superimposing one on the other. This source should be valued because it contains concrete expressions of the challenges encountered by African Christians in their living contexts. It is also a fertile ground for narrative theology.

The Nature of African Studies on the New Testament

New Testament studies in Africa can be placed into four distinct categories. The first includes studies deriving from the South African "Black theology" movement. South African Black theology accords with the theological trends of liberation theology in Latin America and the Black theology of North America and is concerned with three things: faith in God in the South African context, the experience of oppression and dehumanization in the face of apartheid, and political liberation and the achievement of social justice.[55] Among the authors who wrote extensively on Black theology are Desmond Tutu, Manas Buthelezi, and Allan Boesak.[56] Now that South Africa is living in a post-apartheid period, this form of theologizing should actually be thought of as reconstruction theology.[57]

The second category of New Testament studies consists of theological speculation about the indigenous cultures of African peoples in order to highlight in their religious traditions rays of God's

---

53. Bediako, *Jesus and the Gospel in Africa*, 9.
54. Magesa, "Truly African, Fully Christian?," 87.
55. See Muzorewa, *Origins and Development of African Theology*, 101. The South African version of Black theology has four focuses: Black theology in general, African theology, African religion, and the independent churches. See Mushete, "Overview of African Theology," 9–26.
56. Tutu, "Black Theology"; Tutu, "Theology of Liberation in Africa"; Buthelezi, "African Theology or Black Theology?"; Boesak, *Farewell to Innocence*; Boesak, "Liberation Theology in South Africa."
57. Mugambi, *From Liberation to Reconstruction: African Christian Theology after the Cold War*, 33.

revelatory truth fulfilled in Jesus Christ. These studies synthesize biblical and African cultural ideas and practices for two very obvious reasons: to make the Christian faith intelligible to Africans and to articulate typical ways in which Africans respond to divine revelation from within their cultures, contexts, and experiences.[58] Primary among this second group are the pioneering works of African scholars in the formative era of African Christianity, who, though trained in Western schools of thought, were able to construct African Christian theologies from the perspective of the traditional African worldview. These include the works of Vincent Mulago of the Congo, Bolaji Idowu of Nigeria, John Mbiti of Kenya, Alexis Kagame of Rwanda, and Meinrad Hebga of Cameroon, among many others.[59] There is also the collection of essays by francophone Catholic theologians published as *Des prêtres noirs s'interrogent*[60] and the collection of essays titled *Biblical Revelation and African Beliefs*.[61] Also in this category are later studies on Christology, pneumatology, and ecclesiology;[62] particular mention should be made of studies by Jean-Marc Éla, Laurenti Magesa, Samuel Kibicho, Gabriel Setiloane, Christian Gaba, and many others.[63] Though crucial to the development of Christian thought in Africa, these studies suffer from some obvious limitations: they have been accused of finding a false correspondence between data relating to ATR and the Christian message, and sometimes of reducing theology to religious anthropology or sociopolitical discourse,[64] or disregarding some syncretistic practices among some African believers.[65]

The third category is studies done by the Circle of Concerned African Women Theologians. These studies have made a huge contribution to ecumenical formation and gender hermeneutics in Africa. The hermeneutical program and vision of the Circle are changing previously male-dominated and patriarchal structures and proposing a socially transformative agenda in contemporary ecumenical theology in Africa. Prominent among these theologians is Mercy Amba Oduyoye, the founder of the Circle. She initiated the idea that women should critique the discursive use of the Bible for the purpose of sustaining patriarchy and oppression of women and at the same create their own theology from their daily life experiences of gender-based injustice and sexual violence.[66] Other significant contributors from the Circle are Musimbi Kanyoro, Teresa Okure, and Mary Getui.[67]

Finally, a fourth category of studies is scientific exegetical studies on the New Testament following Western models of thought and rigorous methodologies. One might include in this category studies done by lecturers and students in biblical and

---

58. This category of studies has been identified by some scholars as involving a theology of reconstruction. See Mugambi, "Theological Method in African Christianity," 24. Others have preferred to identify it as a contextualized theology in a general sense. See Obeng, "Synthetic and Praxis Models in African Theology," 49.

59. Mulago, *Une visage africain du christianisme*; Idowu, *Towards an Indigenous Church*; Mbiti, *African Religions and Philosophy*; Mbiti, *Concepts of God in Africa*; Mbiti, *New Testament Eschatology in an African Background*; Kagame, *La Philosophie Bantu Rwandaise de l'Être*; Kagame, *La Philosophie Bantu comparée*; Kagame, "Une forme de Christianisation"; Hebga, *Emancipation d'Eglises*. For the contributions of other African theologians of this era, see Bujo and Muya, *African Theology in the 21st Century*.

60. A. Abblé et al., eds., *Des prêtres noirs s'interrogent* (Paris: Editions du Cerf, 1957).

61. Dickson, *Biblical Revelation and African Beliefs*.

62. For instance, Bujo, "Pour une éthique africano-christocentrique."

63. Éla and Luneau, *Voici les temps des héritiers*; Éla, *Le cri de l'homme africain*; Éla, *Ma foi d'Africain*; Magesa, "Ethics of Liberation"; Magesa, *African Religion*; Kibicho, "Continuity of the African Conception of God"; Setiloane, *Image of God*; Gaba, "Sacrifice in Anlo-Religion, Part I and Part II."

64. See Akinwale, "African Theology and Dogmatic Responsibility for the Christian God," 213.

65. See Bowers, "African Theology," 117–18.

66. Oduyoye, *Daughters of Anowa*; Oduyoye, *Introducing African Women's Theology*; Z. Dube, "African Women Theologians."

67. Kanyoro, *Introducing Feminist Cultural Hermeneutics*; Okure, "Becoming the Church of the New Testament"; Getui et al., *Interpreting the New Testament in Africa*.

theological faculties of universities. These studies tend to be both thematic and praxis-oriented,[68] but in general they have remained in the academic domain, and so have had no significant impact on the majority of Christians, who do not read them. This is unfortunate because theological themes examined by African scholars often emerge from critical issues present in the sociopolitical context and for that reason warrant serious consideration because of their effect on the lives of the people. In any case, exegetical and theological interpretation of scriptural texts in language that is deeply rooted in the African universe is urgently needed.

Methodological Considerations Relating to African Studies on the New Testament

New Testament scholarship in the twenty-first century has witnessed a great proliferation in emphases, approaches, and methods. Of the many ways in which these studies are conducted, the most common approach is thematic: African scholars have shown an interest in developing biblical themes from African perspectives. The themes that have been most frequently discussed are Christology, salvation, the church as family, the Holy Spirit, reconciliation, gender, morality, liberation, miracles, and healing. In order to determine the best methodology for theologizing in the African context, it is necessary to set forth certain initial considerations.

Initial Considerations

It is necessary to state, first of all, that authentic theology begins with the theologian having faith in what God has revealed. Interpretations of the New Testament that do not spring from the faith of the interpreter and from a deep knowledge of the African context and ways of thinking have created a discernible obstacle to the realization of contextualized theology in Africa. The theologian's faith in what scripture says about divinely revealed mysteries should undergird every exegetical and theological enterprise.[69] This means that the theologian works neither as a disembodied evangelizer nor as a half-breed African. The church fathers offer proof of the fact that a fusion of faith and culture is possible through the Holy Spirit working through those who possess the spirit of Christ. The theologian's ability to comprehend and translate the transcendent truths of the gospel into a particular cultural context depends on his or her deep-rooted insertion into both the gospel and the culture.

Second, it is important to state that theological investigation in every African context should begin with the question of who Jesus Christ is for the people being studied. Is he the Jesus who walks in the midst of his people, revealing his divinity by doing good to everyone, healing the sick, liberating those in bondage, and casting out evil spirits? Is he the Jesus who proclaims the new law from the mountain? Is he the Jesus who encounters the poor and the needy? Is he the Jesus who confronts and confounds the false ideologies and philosophies of rulers and the learned? Who is Jesus for the millions of African Christians whose lands are blessed with beauty and many natural and human resources but who live in a debased and dysfunctional condition? The theologian bears these questions in mind as he or she elaborates the content of people's experience amid the complexities of these life-diminishing realities. The four evangelists are examples of this approach in that each of them presents a Jesus who encounters people in their concrete historical, cultural, and social contexts. If the theologian fails to seriously consider the historical-cultural context of both the Bible and the contemporary culture, Africans will find it difficult to experience the gospel as Good News.

Third, recourse ought to be had to the comprehensive hermeneutics of great church fathers like Augustine, whose first principle of interpretation is the very goal of scripture, that is, to lead its readers to love God and their neighbor. According to Augustine, proper biblical interpretation must first of all focus on a text's literal or historical meaning,

---

68. Ahiwa, "Lavement des pieds (Jn 13:1–17)"; Okure, "Joseph, Husband of Mary"; Ahoua, "Jn 1:14."
69. *Fides quaerens intellectum* ("faith seeking understanding") has been the basis of the research and interpretative activity of the church's great theologians, including Thomas Aquinas, Augustine of Hippo, and Anselm of Canterbury. See Akinwale, "African Theology and Dogmatic Responsibility for the Christian God," 213–18.

which is the real meaning or what the text intends to say.[70] In fact, the literal sense was the basis for the treasury of meanings drawn from scripture by patristic and medieval biblical interpretations, including the allegorical (or doctrinal), moral (or tropological), and anagogical (or eschatological).[71]

Finally, fourth, the theologian should recall the implication of the theophoric names of many Africans. For instance, names like "Chiagoziem," meaning "God has blessed me through this child," and "Chisimdi," meaning "God ordained that I survive," are indicators of a unity of faith and life and demonstrate the presence of God in the lives of Africans. Related to this is the place of oral tradition in African cultures. Africans are storytellers and singers of God's deeds in their midst. This is why church liturgies and worship that nurture faith and spirituality in the African are those that provide for moments of testimony to God's goodness, dance, and communal thanksgiving, but also moments of communal lamentation in which experiences of misfortune are shared. These are theological moments that provide opportunities for interpretation and discernment of the meaning of what God is doing in the midst of the people. A methodological principle suggested by Oduyoye is relevant here: instead of telling people what questions to ask and then furnishing them with answers, the theologian should listen to the questions people ask and then seek the answers.[72]

These four considerations highlight two important foundations for any methodology. First is the necessity of a contextualized study of the New Testament that takes seriously the historical, cultural, and literary contexts and symbolic worlds of both the Bible and the African audience. The second is the need to avoid using a methodology that imports Western paradigms into an African context.[73]

It is clear that the methodology that is most appropriate for African Christian theology is a method of inculturation. This method is not new; it has always been relevant wherever the gospel meets culture. This chapter makes a renewed appeal that the methodology be applied properly.[74] It must be remembered that the primary goal of scripture is that its audience know God and love God and neighbor. Therefore, every interpretation of scripture should aim at leading people to a right knowledge of the God revealed by Jesus Christ and to the cultivation of an ethical and devout Christian life.[75] Any deviation from these goals might lead to corruption of the Christian religion.

The Methodology of Inculturation

African theologians believe that African Christianity must be built through inculturation.[76] This methodology follows two basic orientations: (1) it establishes the priority of biblical revelation as the Word of God that must be announced; and (2) it draws from both the riches and limitations of the culture to contextualize the gospel and evangelize the culture, while remaining deeply faithful to the gospel.

A research methodology that holds to the priority of scripture moves from the meaning of a scriptural text to the application of this meaning to any given situation in the African context. It involves the study of the historical-cultural background of

---

70. See Van Fleteren, "Principles of Augustine's Hermeneutics," 10.
71. Klein, Blomberg, and Hubbard, *Introduction to Biblical Interpretation*, 43, 48.
72. See Oduyoye, *Hearing and Knowing*, 3.
73. Several methodologies are being used in the study of the New Testament across Africa, but most of these have not avoided the problem of importing Western paradigms. In the south of the continent, mostly in South Africa, trajectories of liberation theology in the study of the New Testament have been used. See Speckman, "A Kairos for the Lowly?," which uses Luke's themes related to materialism as a starting point to think about inequality in South Africa. A feminist perspective represented by the voices of the Circle of Concerned African Theologians also raises important questions related to issues affecting African women. See Oduyoye, *Hearing and Knowing*, 3. Related to this are the postcolonial interpretations of Musa Dube in *Postcolonial Feminist Interpretation of the Bible*; and Punt, "Teaching Mark through a Postcolonial Optic."
74. For a detailed review of the history and challenges of inculturation, see Mukuna, "La genèse et l'évolution de la théologie africaine," 51–55.
75. See Klein, Blomberg, and Hubbard, *Introduction to Biblical Interpretation*, 41.
76. See, e.g., Éla, "L'Eglise, le monde noir et le concile"; Waliggo, "Bible and Catechism in Uganda."

the biblical world in order to discover what God intended to communicate through the text. Beginning with this meaning, which was intended for the original recipients, the theologian proceeds to relate it to questions arising out of the African context in order to determine how best to express it in this context.[77] Scholars use the methodology of inculturation to study questions arising from the African context in light of the normative word of God. Justin Ukpong recommends beginning every research project with the question of how it could be founded on Christ,[78] and this is no longer a difficult task, given the growing number of biblical exegetes and theologians in Africa who are well trained in the science of biblical interpretation.[79] It must be noted that some theologians have been accused of abusing the methodology of inculturation through over-spiritualization, that is, by disregarding the historical context of the biblical text and at the same time failing to attribute any positive revelatory value to the African religious tradition.[80]

Contextualization involves the fragile relationship between scriptures, theology, and human experience. How this relationship is managed depends on the theological enterprise, which has the task of defending and safeguarding the ongoing authority, vitality, and relevance of the revealed Word of God for people within their historical context.[81] Done well, theology can avoid the danger that it will merely be an abstract metaphysical explication of divine revelation, bereft of universal and adaptable properties and revelation's character as a living and liberating word. From Vatican II onward, inculturation has been defined from the perspective of the Incarnation; that is, that the Word of God should take flesh in every culture just as Jesus, the incarnate Word of God, took flesh and became human in order to redeem human beings and all of creation.[82]

The Christological character of inculturation compels it to conform to certain related aspects of the hermeneutic of the Incarnation, including an understanding of the Word of God within the context of scripture and tradition, an openness to the Holy Spirit, and the intercultural character of the Word of God, which makes it comprehensible in the symbolic and cultural expressions of every people.[83] Thus, the goal of inculturation becomes more evident—it involves facilitating the fusion of the Word of God and the word of culture, so that by encountering, transforming, and fulfilling each other, African Christians can live an integrated spirituality and find God in their Africanness.[84]

The point of departure for the inculturation methodology can be either the Bible or African reality.[85] Bénézet Bujo and John Pobee, for instance, began their studies of the Gospel of John with an examination of the traditional African concept of

---

77. This methodology was first proposed by E. D. Hirsch; see his *Validity in Interpretation*; and *Aims of Interpretation*.

78. Ukpong, "Christology and Inculturation," 40.

79. This fortunate development contrasts with the anxiety expressed by Edward Fashole-Luke in 1975 about the paucity of African scholars qualified to perform the task of biblical interpretation. See Fasholé-Luke, "Quest for African Christian Theologies."

80. See Musopole, "Evangelicalism and African Christian Theology." Byang Kato, in his book *Theological Pitfalls in Africa*, describes the approach of churches and scholars linked with the Association of Evangelicals of Africa, who often adopt a radical biblicism that fails to appreciate the Bible's historical context (169).

81. Nwachukwu, "Theology and Human Experience," 39.

82. See Vatican II, Dogmatic Constitution on the Church (*Lumen Gentium*) §13; Efoé-Julien Pénoukou uses the terminology of Justin Martyr and Clement of Alexandria, "the seed of the Word" (*Logos Spermatikos*), to explain that inculturation necessarily involves planting the seed of the Word of God in every culture. See Pénoukou, *Églises d'Afrique*.

83. For a detailed presentation of the three aspects of this hermeneutic, see Nwachukwu, "Inculturating Scripture Texts," 382–87.

84. Magesa, *Anatomy of Inculturation*, 159–60.

85. Charles Nyamiti discusses both of these points of departure in the creation of emergent African Christologies; see his "African Christologies Today," 18.

life.[86] It is more appropriate, however, to start from the Bible because useful exegesis should, first of all, understand the original meaning of the Word of God so that it can be best expressed in the language of the contemporary context. Contextualizing the original meaning of the biblical text requires that the interpreter have a strong knowledge of the language, values, and significant symbols of African societies.

Inculturation is not a superficial drawing of parallels between aspects of ATR and the gospel but rather a critical assessment by which theologians situate African thought patterns within the mainstream of Christian theology. Other scholars have defined this methodology as a "theology of adaptation" or "adaptationist theology"[87] because it adapts church teaching and practices to the sociocultural lives of Africans.[88]

Many benefits are derived from using the inculturation methodology. Most importantly, it necessitates a deepened articulation of traditional African concepts such as hospitality, kinship, love for others, and many other practices,[89] the implications of which would have been unknown to modern generations of Africans in the absence of inculturation methodology. It allows the Christian message to be understood in African idioms and symbols. In this regard, Jean-Marc Éla makes the point that African theology must adopt the language of symbolism that permeates life and communication in Africa.[90] When this occurs, African languages become a medium of communicating the gospel, and, at the same time, African ideas can enrich Christian spirituality. As a form of dialogue, the goal of inculturation must be to allow the gospel truth to shine light on African cultures so they can rid themselves of elements that do not align with the gospel message.

Conclusion

This overview of the state of African studies on the New Testament has considered the history of Christian theology in Africa, the contexts of the theologizing enterprise, and the sources and nature of African studies in this field. It raises questions theologians should consider in determining the appropriate methodology for conducting their research and highlights the need to pay attention to four important areas in the course of performing research: biblical revelation, the theological heritage of the church, the nature of African culture, and specific ways of applying the methodology of inculturation. We conclude by identifying other areas that are neglected and need more emphasis.

African theologians should assume a prophetic responsibility in view of the corrupted state of religion in various parts of Africa. The African theologian is required to shun teachings and religious practices that portray God as an unforgiving tyrant or that imply that God can be controlled or bribed to fulfill the material needs and desires of human beings. Biblical interpretation must be in line with dogmatic statements about the nature of the Christian God.[91] Another area needing the urgent attention of theologians relates to life-diminishing realities like illness and the evil effects of witchcraft and malign spirits. There is a need for theologies of healing and for the supreme power of Jesus over evil forces in order to address these realities. To this effect, African theologians should pay attention to oral theology, that is, people's articulation

---

86. Bujo, *African Theology in Its Social Context*; Pobee, "Life and Peace"; and Pobee, "Jesus Christ—The Life of the World."
87. Outstanding early examples of the adaptationist approach appeared in the works of Mulago gwa Cikala, *Une visage africain du christianisme* (1962), and T. Tshibangu, *Le propos d'une théologie africaine*, 1974.
88. See Parratt, *Reinventing Christianity*, 28; Ntakarutimana, "Msgr Tharcisse Tshibangu," 48; Mushete, "History of Theology in Africa," 23–25.
89. This is a basic prerequisite for employing the methodology of inculturation. See Nwachukwu, "Inculturating Scripture Texts," 381.
90. Éla, "Symbolique Africaine et mystère chrétien"; Bujo, "Jean-Marc Éla: Champion of a Theology under the Trees," 192–93.
91. See Akinwale, "African Theology and Dogmatic Responsibility for the Christian God," 220–25, 213, 223.

of their living experience of the divine. There is an abundant supply of raw materials for the creation of narrative theologies and pneumatologies that respond to the African experience. The narrative approach not only corresponds to the African way of articulating a religious and ethical worldview; it also allows the reader to identify with the historical experiences of biblical characters who are models of faith.[92] It is the responsibility of theology to foster faith and give vision and orientation to the traumatized peoples of Africa. It can be argued that theology in Africa has been fulfilling this role since the inception of inculturation theology, but as long as disorientation and disintegration still occupy center stage in the lives of Africans, this theology has simply not achieved its goal of responding to their questions.[93]

Finally, African theologians should bear in mind that every contextualized theology ought to be a contribution to the faith of the entire church; for this reason, the language and content of African Christian theology should be a matter of interest for non-African Christians as well. This is one reason that it is important to explore African Catholicism, in particular, within the confines of the biblical and magisterial traditions. Doing this can help us understand the contributions that African theology could make to world Christianity.

Bibliography

Ahiwa, J. A. "Lavement des pieds (Jn 13:1–17) et leadership dans l'Eglise en Afrique." In *Bible et Leadership en Afrique: Actes du dix-septième congrès de l'Association Panafricaine des Exégètes Catholiques*, edited by Caroline Mbonu et al., 305–26. Abidjan: Presse de l'ITCJ, 2017.

Ahoua, R. "Jn 1:14: Perspective divine et attente africaine de réconciliation à la lumière du mythe Akan de la Femme au pilon." In *Conflicts and Reconciliation in the Bible: The Contribution of African Exegetes; Proceedings of the Fourteenth Congress of the Pan African Association of Catholic Exegetes*, edited by Paul Béré et al., 249–84. Abidjan: Presse de l'ITCJ, 2015.

Akinwale, A. "African Theology and Dogmatic Responsibility for the Christian God." In *God, Bible and African Traditional Religion: Acts of the SIST International Missiological Symposium*, edited by Bede Uche Ukwuije, 212–46. Enugu: Snaap, 2009.

Akonga, E. J. "La paix dans la Bible." *Annales de l'Ecole Théologique Saint-Cyprien* 16 (2005): 51–66.

Appiah-Kubi, Kofi, and Sergio Torres. *African Theology en Route: Papers from the Pan-African Conference of Third World Theologians, Accra, Ghana, December 17–23, 1979*. Maryknoll, NY: Orbis Books, 1979.

Bediako, K. *Jesus and the Gospel in Africa: History and Experience*. Maryknoll, NY: Orbis Books, 2004.

Béré, Paul. "Pourquoi Pierre est-il peiné? Une lecture exégètique et théologique de Jn 21:15–19." *Hekima Review* 17 (1997): 66–80.

———. "Scripture Studies and African Theology: A Critical Overview from an Old Testament Perspective." In *The Church We Want: African Catholics Look to Vatican II*, edited by A. E. Orobator, 121–31. Maryknoll, NY: Orbis Books, 2016.

Béré, Paul, et al., eds. *Conflicts and Reconciliation in the Bible: The Contribution of African Exegetes; Proceedings of the Fourteenth Congress of the Pan African Association of Catholic Exegetes*. Abidjan: Presse de l'ITCJ, 2015.

Boesak, Allan. *Farewell to Innocence: A Socio-Ethical Study on Black Theology and Power*. Eugene, OR: Wipf & Stock, 1997.

———. "Liberation Theology in South Africa." In *African Theology en Route: Papers from the Pan-African Conference of Third World Theologians, Accra, Ghana, December 17–23, 1979*, edited by Kofi Appiah-Kubi and Sergio Torres, 169–75. Maryknoll, NY: Orbis Books, 1979.

Bowers, P. "African Theology: Its History, Dynamics, Scope and Future." *Africa Journal of Evangelical Theology* 21 (2002): 109–26.

---

92. In both biblical and African thought, the narrative method presents the good and the bad within a comprehensive vision of reality. It presents characters as they are without judging them, and, especially in the context of biblical thought, provides openings to God's grace.

93. Cf. Nwachukwu, "Theology and Human Experience," 47–48.

Bujo, Bénézet. *African Theology in Its Social Context.* Eugene, OR: Wipf & Stock, 2006.

———. *Christmas: God Becomes Man in Black Africa.* Nairobi: Paulines Publications Africa, 1995.

———. *The Ethical Dimension of Community.* Nairobi: Pauline Press, 1998.

———. "Jean-Marc Éla: Champion of a Theology under the Trees." In *African Theology in the 21st Century: The Contribution of the Pioneers,* edited by Bénézet Bujo and Juvénal Ilunga Muya, 2:182–214. 3 vols. Nairobi: Paulines Publications Africa, 2003, 2008, 2013.

———. "Pour une éthique africano-christocentrique." In *Combats pour un christianisme africain: Mélanges en l'honneur du Professeur V. Mulago,* edited by A. Ngindu Mushete et al., 21–31. Bibliothèque du Centre d'Etudes des Religions Africaines 6. Kinshasa: Faculté de théologie catholique, 1981.

Bujo, Bénézet, and Juvénal Ilunga Muya, eds. *African Theology in the 21st Century: The Contribution of the Pioneers.* 3 vols. Nairobi: Paulines Publications Africa, 2003, 2008, 2013.

Buthelezi, M. "An African Theology or Black Theology?" In *The Challenge of Black Theology in South Africa,* edited by Basil Moore, 24–35. Atlanta: John Knox, 1974.

Damman E. *Die Religionen Afrikas.* USTL Stuttgart: W. Kohlhammer, 1963.

Dickson, Kwesi. "African Theology: Origin, Method and Content." *Journal of Religious Thought* 30.2 (1975): 34–45.

———. *Biblical Revelation and African Beliefs.* Proceedings of the Ibadan Conference under the Auspices of All Africa Council of Churches. London: Lutherworth, 1969.

Dube, Musa W. *Postcolonial Feminist Interpretation of the Bible.* St. Louis, MO: Chalice Press, 2000.

Dube, Z. "The African Women Theologians' Contribution towards the Discussion about Alternative Masculinities." *Verbum et Ecclesia* 37.2 (2016): a1577. http://dx.doi.org/10.4102/ve.v37i2.1577.

———. "Discursive Investigation into John's Internalised Spirit Identity and Its Implication." *HTS Teologiese Studies/Theological Studies* 72.1 a3113 (2016). http://dx.doi.org/10.4102/hts.v72i1.3113.

Éla, Jean-Marc. "Christianity and Liberation in Africa." In *Paths of African Theology,* edited by Rosino Gibellini, 136–53. Maryknoll, NY: Orbis Books, 1994.

———. *Le cri de l'homme africain: Questions aux chrétiens et aux eglises d'Afrique.* Paris: L'Harmattan, 1980.

———. "L'Eglise, le monde noir et le concile." In *Personnalité africaine et catholicisme,* by Meinrad A. Hebga et al., 59–81. Paris: Présence africaine, 1963.

———. *Ma foi d'Africain.* 1985. Reprint, Paris: Karthala, 2009.

———. "Symbolique Africaine et mystère chrétien, Les quatre fleuves." *Cahiers de recherché et de réflexion religieuse* 10 (1979): 91–109.

Éla, Jean-Marc, and R. Luneau. *Voici les temps des héritiers: Eglises d'Afrique et voies nouvelles.* Paris: Karthala, 1981.

Fasholé-Luke, Edward W. "The Quest for African Christian Theologies." *Ecumenical Review* 27 (1975): 259–69.

Gaba, Christian. "Sacrifice in Anlo-Religion, Part I." *Ghana Bulletin of Theology* 3.5 (1968): 113–19.

———. "Sacrifice in Anlo-Religion, Part II." *Ghana Bulletin of Theology* 3.7 (1969): 1–7.

Getui, Mary N., ed. *Theological Method and Aspects of Worship in African Christianity.* Nairobi: Acton, 1998.

Getui, Mary N., Knut Holter, and Victor Zinkuratire, eds. *Interpreting the New Testament in Africa.* Nairobi: Acton, 2001.

Gibellini, Rosino, ed. *Paths of African Theology.* Maryknoll, NY: Orbis Books, 1994.

Groves, C. P. *The Planting of Christianity in Africa.* London: Lutterworth, 1948.

Hebga, Meinrad P. *Emancipation d'Eglises sous tutelle: Essai sur l'ère post-missionnaire.* Louvain: Présence Africaine, 1976.

Hirsch, E. D. *The Aims of Interpretation.* Chicago: University of Chicago Press, 1976.

———. *Validity in Interpretation.* New Haven: Yale University Press, 1967.

Idowu, Bolaji. *African Traditional Religions: A Definition.* London: SCM Press, 1973.

———. *Towards an Indigenous Church.* London: Oxford University Press, 1965.

John Paul II, Pope. *Ecclesia in Africa* [Post-synodal Apostolic Exhortation on the Church in Africa; 1995]. Nairobi: Paulines Publications Africa, 1995. www.vatican.va.

Kagame, A. "Une forme de Christianisation de notre culture régionale." *Au Coeur de l'Afrique* 5 (1969): 83–98.

———. *La Philosophie Bantu comparée*. Paris: Présence Africaine, 1976.

———. *La Philosophie Bantu Rwandaise de l'Être*. Brussels: Académie Royale des Sciences Coloniales, 1956.

Kanyoro, M. *Introducing Feminist Cultural Hermeneutics: An African Perspective*. Sheffield: Sheffield Academic Press, 2002.

Kato, Byang. *Theological Pitfalls in Africa*. Nairobi: Kisumu, 1975.

Kibicho, S. G. "The Continuity of the African Conception of God into and through Christianity: A Kikuyu Case Study." In *Christianity in Independent Africa*, edited by Edward W. Fasholé-Luke, Richard Gray, Adrian Hastings, and Godwin Tasie, 370–88. London: Rex Collings, 1978.

Klein, William W., Craig L. Blomberg, and Robert L. Hubbard Jr. *Introduction to Biblical Interpretation*. Nashville: Thomas Nelson, 1993.

Kort, Wesley A. *"Take, Read": Scripture, Textuality and Cultural Practice*. University Park, PA: Pennsylvania State University Press, 1996.

Lufuluabo, F. M. *L'Antisorcier face à la Science*. Mbujimayi: Éditions Franciscaines, 1977.

———. "Orientation préchrétienne de la conception bantoue." Ph.D. Thesis in Theology. Rome: Lateran University, 1963.

Magesa, Laurenti. *African Religion: The Moral Traditions of Abundant Life*. Maryknoll, NY: Orbis Books, 1997.

———. *Anatomy of Inculturation: Transforming the Church in Africa*. Nairobi: Paulines Publications, 2004.

———. "The Challenge of African Woman Defined Theology for the 21st Century." In *Challenges and Prospects of the Church in Africa*, edited by N. W. N'dungu and P. N. Mwaura, 88–101. Nairobi: Paulines Publications Africa, 2005.

———. "The Ethics of Liberation." *African Ecclesial Review* 22 (1980): 101–11.

———. "Introduction: Two Decades of Theological Development in Eastern Africa." In *African Theology Comes of Age. Revisiting Twenty Years of the Theology of Ecumenical Symposium of Eastern Africa Theologians*, edited by Laurenti Magesa, 7–12. Nairobi: Paulines Publications, 2010.

———. "The Political Axis of African Liberation Theology." In *Liberation Theologies on Shifting Grounds: A Clash of Socio-Economic and Cultural Paradigms*, edited by Georges De Schrijver, 130–52. Leuven: Peeters, 1998.

———. "Truly African, Fully Christian? In Search of a New African Spirituality." In *The Church We Want: African Catholics Look to Vatican II*, edited by A. E. Orobator, 79–92. Maryknoll, NY: Orbis Books, 2016.

Mbiti, John S. *African Religions and Philosophy*. London: Heinemann, 1969.

———. *Bible and Theology in African Christianity*. London: Oxford University Press, 1986.

———. *Concepts of God in Africa*. London: SPCK, 1970.

———. *New Testament Eschatology in an African Background*. Oxford: Heinemann, 1971.

———. "Some African Concepts of Christology." In *Christ and the Younger Churches*, edited by George F. Vicedom, 51–62. London: SPCK, 1972.

———. "Some Currents of African Theology." In *African and Asian Contributions to Contemporary Theology*, edited by John S. Mbiti, 1–7. Geneva: WCC, 1976.

———. "Theological Impotence and the Universality of the Church." In *Mission Trends 3: Third World Theologies*, edited by Gerald H. Anderson and Thomas F. Stransky, 6–8. New York: Paulist Press, 1976.

Mofokeng, T. "Black Christians, the Bible and Liberation." *Journal of Black Theology in South Africa* 1.2 (1988): 34–42.

Morgenthau, Hans J. *Politics among Nations: The Struggle for Power and Peace*. New York: Alfred A. Knopf, 1978.

Mugambi, J. N. K. "Ecumenical Contextual Theological Reflection in Eastern Africa 1989–1999." In *Challenges and Prospects of the Church in Africa*, edited by N. W. N'dungu and P. N. Mwara, 17–29. Nairobi: Paulines Publications Africa, 2005.

———. "Theological Method in African Christianity." In *Theological Method and Aspects of Worship in African Christianity*, edited by Mary N. Getui, 24–37. Nairobi: Acton, 1998.

———. *From Liberation to Reconstruction: African Christian Theology after the Cold War*. Nairobi: East African Educational Publishers, 1995.

Mukuna, M. M. "La genèse et l'évolution de la théologie africaine." In *Théologie Africaine Bilan et Perspectives: Actes de la dix-septième semaine théologique de Kinshasa du 2–8 Avril 1989*, 27–56. Kinshasa: Facultés catholiques de Kinshasa, 1989.

Mulago, Gwa Cikala. *Une visage africain du christianisme: L'unité vitale bantu face à l'unité vitale écclesiale*. Paris: Présence Africaine, 1965.

Mushete, A. Ngindu. "History of Theology in Africa." In *African Theology en Route: Papers from the Pan-African Conference of Third World Theologians, Accra, Ghana, December 17–23, 1979*, edited by Kofi Appiah-Kubi and Sergio Torres, 23–25. Maryknoll, NY: Orbis Books, 1979.

———. "An Overview of African Theology." In *Paths of African Theology*, edited by Rosino Gibellini, 9–26. Maryknoll, NY: Orbis Books, 1994.

Musopole, Augustine. "Evangelicalism and African Christian Theology." *Africa Journal of Evangelical Theology* 14 (1995): 14–16.

Muzorewa, Gwinyai H. *The Origins and Development of African Theology*. Maryknoll, NY: Orbis Books, 1985.

N'dungu, N. W., and P. N. Mwaura, eds. *Challenges and Prospects of the Church in Africa*. Nairobi: Paulines Publications Africa, 2005.

Ntakarutimana, Emmanuel. "Msgr Tharcisse Tshibangu. Companion of an 'African-Coloured' Theology." In *African Theology in the 21st Century: The Contribution of the Pioneers*, edited by Bénézet Bujo and Juvénal Ilunga Muya, 1:47–63. 3 vols. Nairobi: Paulines Publications Africa, 2003, 2008, 2013.

Nyamiti, Charles. "African Christologies Today." In *Jesus in African Christianity: Experimentation and Diversity in African Christology*, edited by J. N. K. Mugambi and L. Magesa, 17–29. Nairobi: Initiatives, 1989.

———. "Contemporary African Christologies: Assessment and Practical Suggestions." In *Paths of African Theology*, edited by Rosino Gibellini, 62–77. Maryknoll, NY: Orbis Books, 1994.

———. "The Contribution of African Cultures and African Theology to Theology Worldwide." In *The Shifting Ground of Doing Theology: Perspectives from Africa*, edited by E. Wabanhu and M. Moerschbacher, 29–38. Nairobi: Paulines Publications Africa, 2017.

Nwachukwu, MarySylvia. *Creation-Covenant Scheme and Justification by Faith*. Rome: Gregorian Press, 2002.

———. "Inculturating Scripture Texts for Mission Work in Enugu Diocese." In *Renewing Mission and Identity of the Church in Service to Integral Education, Reconciliation and Human Development*, edited by Obiora F. Ike and Benjamin N. Achi, 373–400. Enugu: CIDJAP Press, 2015.

———. "Theology and Human Experience." *African Journal of Contextual Theology* 1 (2009): 33–48.

Obeng, E. A. "Synthetic and Praxis Models in African Theology." In *Theological Method and Aspects of Worship in African Christianity*, edited by Mary N. Getui, 46–49. Nairobi, Acton, 1998.

Oden, T. C. *How Africa Shaped the Christian Mind*. Downers Grove, IL: InterVarsity Press, 2007.

Oduyoye, Mercy Amba. *Daughters of Anowa: African Women and Patriarchy*. Maryknoll, NY: Orbis Books, 1995.

———. *Hearing and Knowing: Theological Reflections on Christianity in Africa*. Maryknoll, NY: Orbis Books, 1986.

———. *Introducing African Women's Theology*. Sheffield: Sheffield Academic Press, 2001.

Okure, Teresa. "Becoming the Church of the New Testament." In *The Church We Want: African Catholics Look to Vatican II*, edited by A. E. Orobator, 83–105. Maryknoll, NY: Orbis Books, 2016.

———. "Feminist Interpretation in Africa." In *Searching the Scriptures: A Feminist Introduction*, edited by Elisabeth Schüssler Fiorenza, 77–89. New York: Crossroad Publishing Company, 1993.

———"Joseph, Husband of Mary (Matt 1:18–25): A Gospel Recipe for Conflict Resolution and Reconciliation for the Church in Africa." In *Conflicts and Reconciliation in the Bible: The Contribution of African Exegetes: Proceedings of the Fourteenth Congress of the Pan African Association of Catholic Exegetes*, edited by Paul Béré et al., 199–232. Abidjan: Presse de l'ITCJ, 2015.

Orobator, A. E., ed. *The Church We Want: African Catholics Look to Vatican II*. Maryknoll, NY: Orbis Books, 2016.

Parratt, John. *Introduction to Third World Theologies*. Cambridge: Cambridge University Press, 2004.

———. *A Reader in African Christian Theology*. London: SPCK, 1987.

———. *Reinventing Christianity: African Theology Today*. Grand Rapids: Eerdmans, 1995.

Pénoukou, Efoé-Julien. *Églises d'Afrique: Propositions pour l'Avenir*. Paris: Karthala, 1994.

Pobee, J. "Jesus Christ—The Life of the World: An African Perspective." *Ministerial Formation* 21 (1983): 5–18.

———. "Life and Peace: An African Perspective." In *Variations in Christian Theology in Africa*, by John S. Pobee and Carl F. Hallencreutz. Nairobi: Initiatives, 1986.

Poucouta, P. "Meinrad Pierre Hebga: Theologian and Healer." In *African Theology in the 21st Century: The Contribution of the Pioneers*, edited by Bénézet Bujo and Juvénal Ilunga Muya, 2:70–92. 3 vols. Nairobi: Paulines Publications Africa, 2003, 2008, 2013.

Punt, Jeremy. "Teaching Mark through a Postcolonial Optic." *HTS Teologiese Studies/Theological Studies* 71.1 (2015): Art. #2970.

Sawyer, H. *Creative Evangelism: Towards a New Christian Encounter with Africa*. London: Lutterworth, 1968.

Setiloane, G. M. *The Image of God among the Sotho-Tswana*. Rotterdam: Balkema, 1976.

Speckman, McGlory. "A Kairos for the Lowly? Reflections on Luke's Story of a Rejected Fortune or Tyche and Lessons for South Africa." *Verbum et Ecclesia* 37.1 (March 2016).

Tshibangu, T. *Le propos d'une théologie africaine*. Kinshasa: Presses universitaires du Zaïre, 1974.

Tutu, D. "Black Theology." *Frontier* 17 (1974): 73–76.

———. "The Theology of Liberation in Africa." In *African Theology en Route: Papers from the Pan-African Converence of Third World Theologians, Accra, Ghana, December 17–23, 1979*, edited by Kofi Appiah-Kubi and Sergio Torres, 162–68. Maryknoll, NY: Orbis Books, 1979.

Ukpong, Justin S. "Christology and Inculturation: A New Testament Perspective." In *Paths of African Theology*, edited by Rosino Gibellini, 40–61. Maryknoll, NY: Orbis Books, 1994.

Van Fleteren, Frederick. "Principles of Augustine's Hermeneutics: An Overview." In *Augustine: Biblical Exegete*, edited by Frederick Van Fleteren and Joseph C. Schnaubelt, 1–32. New York: Peter Lang, 2001.

Vatican II. Decree on the Church's Missionary Activity (*Ad Gentes*) (1965). In *The Sixteen Documents of Vatican II*, edited by Marianne L. Trouvé, 507–63. Boston: Daughters of St. Paul, 1999. www.vatican.va.

———. Declaration on the Relationship of the Church to Non-Christian Religions (*Nostra Aetate*) (1965). www.vatican.va.

Waliggo, John M. "Bible and Catechism in Uganda." In *The Bible in African Christianity: Essays in Biblical Theology*, edited by H. W. Kinoti and John M. Waliggo, 179–95. Nairobi: Acton, 1997.

Wasike, Anne Nasimiyu. "Witnessing to Jesus Christ in the African Context." *Propositum* 3.1 (1998): 17–29.

Suggested Reading

Bujo, Bénézet, and Juvénal Ilunga Muya, eds. *African Theology in the 21st Century: The Contribution of the Pioneers*. 3 vols. Nairobi: Paulines Publications Africa, 2003, 2008, 2013.

Magesa, L. "Introduction: Two Decades of Theological Development in Eastern Africa." In *African Theology Comes of Age: Revisiting Twenty Years of the Theology of Ecumenical Symposium of Eastern Africa Theologians (ESEAT)*, edited by Laurenti Magesa, 7–12. Nairobi: Paulines Publications, 2010.

Mukuna, M. M. "La genèse et l'évolution de la théologie africaine." In *Théologie Africaine Bilan et Perspectives: Actes de la dix-septième semaine théologique de Kinshasa du 2-8 Avril 1989*, 27–56. Kinshasa: Faculté de théologie catholique, 1989.

Nyamiti, Charles. "The Contribution of African Cultures and African Theology to Theology Worldwide." In *The Shifting Ground of Doing Theology: Perspectives from Africa*, edited by E. Wabanhu and M. Moerschbacher, 29–38. Nairobi: Paulines Publications Africa, 2017.

Key Words

Africa's cultural heritage
hermeneutics
inculturation
liberation
method
symbolic world

FORMATION, EDUCATION, AND COMMUNICATION

Small Christian Communities in Africa: Histories, Themes, Development, and Challenges

Joseph G. Healey, MM

Historical Development

At its Sixth Plenary Assembly held from November 20 to December 2, 1961, the Congolese Episcopal Conference approved a pastoral plan to promote "Living Ecclesial Communities" (also called "Living Christian Communities"). The bishops of the country that is now known as the Democratic Republic of the Congo (DRC)[1] decided that the creation of these communities would take precedence over missionaries' construction of buildings (churches, schools, and hospitals). These communities were said to be the only way to make the church more African and close to the people. Thus, the very first Small Christian Communities (SCCs)[2] in Africa started in the DRC in 1961.

Then came the historic Second Vatican Council (1962–1965) with its communion ecclesiology, after which Latin America, Africa, and Asia (especially the Philippines) all further developed the SCC/BCC/BEC model of church. After considerable research and debate, many specialists have concluded that these three continents in the Global South, quite independently of one another, *simultaneously* experienced an extraordinary growth of SCCs. Thus, contrary to some misinformed interpretations, the African experience did not come from Latin America but developed on its own. African SCCs have developed mainly along the lines of a pastoral, parish-based model in a local African context. They are often referred to by Catholics in eastern Africa as "the church in the neighborhood."

In a symposium in Germany in 2013, Sister Josée Ngalula, RSA, a theologian from the DRC, stated that the BCCs were a response to African intuitions about Christianity and a desire that it be rooted in an African reality.[3] At this same symposium, the German lay theologian Marco Moerschbacher made this striking observation:

> Neither from the time of the Second Vatican Council nor from Latin America comes the oldest option of a local church for what is called today Christian Base Community (see *Herder Korrespondenz*, December 2012,

---

1. Formerly Zaire.
2. "Small Christian Communities" is an umbrella term for a number of formulations of this idea and is the most common expression for this new way of being/becoming church in Africa. Even some French writers prefer the term SCCs over the applicable French names because it indicates the scale of the communities. Various terms are used in Africa for these communities: "Basic Christian Community" (BCC); "Base Ecclesial Community" or "Basic Ecclesial Community" (BEC); and in French, Communautés Ecclésiales de Base (CEB) and Communautés Ecclésiales Vivantes de Base (CEVB).
3. Ngalula, "History, Development and Status Quo of Basic Christian Community (BCC) in Africa."

609 ff. and March 2012, 128 ff.). The oldest is rather the option of the Congolese Episcopal Conference at its plenary meeting in 1961—historically between the independence (1960) of the former Belgian colony and the opening of the Second Vatican Council (1962). The Brazilian church's official pastoral plan with such an option dates back to 1962.[4]

During the 1973 study conference of the Association of Member Episcopal Conferences in Eastern Africa (AMECEA),[5] the word "small" was specifically chosen to avoid certain undertones associated with the word "basic." Bishop Raphael Ndingi Mwana'a Nzeki (who would become the archbishop of Nairobi, Kenya) would later state that assigning the African grassroots communities a name different from that used elsewhere ("small" instead of "basic") was another indication that the movement in Africa was growing on its own, quite independent of what was happening along the same lines in other places such as Latin America.[6]

Archbishop Jean-Marie Speich, the former apostolic nuncio to Ghana, has offered an original interpretation. He states that SCCs are an African, not a South American, invention. He emphasizes that the practice of gathering Christian believers in communities began when the first missionaries in Africa initiated contacts with local communities through catechists: "Small Christian Communities started in Africa 150 years ago with the arrival of the first missionaries and with the contacts of the local African catechists who were great witnesses who experienced much suffering, some having suffered martyrdom."[7] The Irish priest and theologian James O'Halloran, SDB, confirms this: "During the 1971 [World] Synod of Bishops the Africans present noted that Small Christian Communities already existed in Africa. And this quite independently of what had happened in Latin America. One cannot say for certain where the modern [SCC] groups began. They sprang up spontaneously throughout the world at roughly the same historical period by the power of the Holy Spirit."[8]

The beginning of SCCs in eastern Africa can be traced back to the parishes of the Luo-speaking deanery (especially the Nyarombo, Ingri, and Masonga parishes) of the Diocese of Musoma in northwestern Tanzania (North Mara region) in 1966. They began based on research on the social structures and community values of the African Initiated Churches (also called *African Independent Churches* and *African Indigenous Churches*) of the Luo ethnic group. The first terms used to describe them were *chama* (small group) and "small communities of Christians." Maryknoll missionaries focused on the formation of natural communities of Luo people living in local and local extended families according to Luo cultural traditions. By 1968, Nyarombo Parish had twenty small communities, and five had been formed in a nearby parish. The concept and praxis of SCCs was first articulated to be a priority in both rural and later urban parishes during the Seminar Study Year in Tanzania in 1969, at which time the SCCs were called "local church communities."

The launching of SCCs in the DRC goes back to the period 1971–1972, when President Mobutu Sese Seko and the Catholic Church were locked in confrontation. Mobutu's "authenticity" campaign had suppressed the missionary institutes and associations. To meet the crisis, the church estab-

---

4. Moerschbacher, "For Fifty Years on the Road."

5. AMECEA is a service organization for the national episcopal conferences of the nine English-speaking countries of eastern Africa, named here with their dates of independence: Eritrea (1993), Ethiopia (1979), Kenya (1961), Malawi (1961), South Sudan (2011), Sudan (1973), Tanzania (1961), Uganda (1961), and Zambia (1961). The Republic of South Sudan became independent on July 9, 2011, but the two Sudans remain part of the same episcopal conference. Somalia (1995) and Djibouti (2002) are affiliate members. AMECEA is one of the eight regional episcopal conferences of the Symposium of Episcopal Conferences of Africa and Madagascar (SECAM).

6. Ndingi, "Basic Communities: The African Experience," 100. Jay Carney notes that "AMECEA intentionally adopted the term 'Small Christian Communities' in 1976 to distinguish the African movement from its Latin American cousin" ("People Bonded Together by Love," 303).

7. Speich, "Africa Is an 'Extended Holy Land.'"

8. O'Halloran, *Small Christian Communities*, 23.

lished the creation and organization of SCCs as a priority. The pioneering cardinal Joseph Malula of the Archdiocese of Kinshasa stated that "the Living Ecclesial Communities are slowly becoming the ordinary place of Christian life, with the parish as the communion of the Living Ecclesial Communities."[9]

The bishops of the neighboring Republic of the Congo closely followed DRC's leadership in their 1973 meeting. SCCs there were built upon the extended family. In 1974, the Episcopal Conference of Cameroon followed suit. The expatriate missionaries in northern Cameroon and neighboring Chad had already begun to channel their work of evangelization into SCCs. In war-torn Burundi and Rwanda, a six-year renewal plan was conceived in 1976 that involved inviting people to attend community meetings. In francophone West Africa, Burkina Faso opted in 1975 for the creation of SCCs on the model of the church as family, and a similar decision was made by other episcopal conferences in Africa. In 1977, Burkina Faso took the lead in making sure that every person would feel part of and fully responsible for the church as a family by putting laypeople in charge of their local neighborhood SCCs. The South African Catholic Bishops Conference had made a decisive step in the same direction toward local lay leadership of SCCs in 1975.[10]

In addition, during the World Synod of Bishops in Rome in 1971 on "Justice in the World," the African delegates noted that SCCs already existed in Africa. At the World Synod of Bishops in Rome in 1977 on "Catechesis," the bishops in Africa declared themselves clearly in favor of SCCs.

The AMECEA study conference on "Planning for the Church in Eastern Africa in the 1980s" in Nairobi, Kenya, in December 1973, stated, "[W]e have to insist on building church life and work on Basic Christian Communities in both rural and urban areas. Church life must be based on the communities in which everyday life and work take place: those basic and manageable social groups whose members can experience real interpersonal relationships and feel a sense of communal belonging, both in living and working."[11] This pastoral policy was in the context of its further statement that "we are convinced that in these countries of Eastern Africa it is time for the Church to become truly local, that is, self-ministering [self-governing], self-propagating [self-spreading] and self-supporting [self-reliant and self-sustainable]."[12]

The AMECEA study conference on "Building Small Christian Communities" took place in Nairobi, Kenya, in 1976. The single most important statement about SCCs that came out of the conference was that "systematic formation of Small Christian Communities should be the key pastoral priority in the years to come in Eastern Africa."[13] The conference went on to affirm the essentially ecclesial character of SCCs: "The [Small] Christian Communities we are trying to build are simply the most local incarnations of the One, Holy, Catholic and Apostolic Church."[14] The Catholic bishops in eastern Africa chose to make SCCs a pastoral priority as the best way to build up local churches. The three "selfs" mentioned in the quotation above ("self-ministering," "self-propagating," and "self-supporting") are essential characteristics of SCCs as the base/basic level of the church and, by extension, of the local church. SCCs are a real self-actualization of the church. The year 1978 saw the birth of Bible sharing/gospel sharing at the Lumko Missiological Institute in South Africa. Excellent SCC training manuals began to be published popularizing Lumko's "seven steps" method of Bible sharing/gospel sharing. These training manuals have been used throughout Africa. Altogether

---

9. Quoted in Éla, "Les Communautés de Base dans les Églises Africaines," 161.

10. A historical review of these developments can be found in Ngalula, "History, Development and Status Quo of Basic Christian Community (BCC) in Africa," 1–2.

11. AMECEA Study Conference on "Building Small Christian Communities," "Guidelines for the Catholic Church in Eastern Africa in the 1980s," 10.

12. AMECEA Study Conference on "Building Small Christian Communities," "Guidelines for the Catholic Church in Eastern Africa in the 1980s," 12. Bracketed insertions mine.

13. AMECEA Study Conference on "Building Small Christian Communities," "Conclusions," 250.

14. AMECEA Study Conference on "Building Small Christian Communities," "Conclusions," 250.

there are eight gospel-sharing methods that can be adapted to local contexts and situations.

The AMECEA study conference on "The Implementation of the AMECEA Bishops' Pastoral Priority of Building Small Christian Communities: An Evaluation" took place in Zomba, Malawi, in 1979. One of the pastoral resolutions that came out of the conference stated that "SCCs are an effective way of developing the mission dimension of the church at the most local level, and of making people feel that they are really part of the church's evangelizing work."[15]

The bishops of Africa placed SCCs at the center of their pastoral strategy in two major documents from SECAM: "Justice and Evangelization in Africa"[16] and "Church and Human Development in Africa."[17] Within this overall pastoral strategy, pastoral centers in Africa have been very important in promoting the SCC model of church, including the AMECEA Pastoral Institute in Gaba, Eldoret, Kenya; the Ave Maria Pastoral Center in Tzaneen, South Africa; the Kenema Pastoral Center in Kenema, Sierra Leone; and the Lumko Missiological Institute in Germiston, Delmenville, South Africa.

The AMECEA study conference on "Evangelization with Its Central Issues: Inculturation, Small Christian Communities and Priestly, Religious and Christian Formation" in Lusaka, Zambia, in 1992 focused on an evaluation of the work of AMECEA. The research findings identified four AMECEA priorities, which included the promotion of SCCs and recommended in-service training for animators of SCCs. This conference reiterated the previous pastoral commitment to SCCs: "So we repeat that SCCs are not optional in our churches; they are central to the life of faith and the ministry of evangelization."

A major step was the First Special Assembly for Africa of the Synod of Bishops in Rome in April 1994 on the theme "The Church in Africa and Her Evangelizing Mission to the Year 2000." The synod featured five main topics: Proclamation of the Good News of Salvation, Inculturation, Dialogue, Justice and Peace, and the Means of Social Communications. Of the 211 interventions during the first two weeks of the synod, there were 29 interventions on SCCs (the fourth highest number after the topics of justice, inculturation, and laity). Bishop Francisco Joao Siloto of the Diocese of Chimoio, Mozambique, said that "these communities are an expression of African communitarianism and the only true way of inculturation for the African Church"; Archbishop Cornelius Fontem Esua of Bamenda, Cameroon, explained that "it is necessary and urgent to put sacred scripture into the hands of the faithful so it can be the source and inspiration for the life and activities of Small Christian Communities"; and Archbishop Zacchaeus Okoth of the Archdiocese of Kisumu, Kenya, noted that "Small Christian Communities help implement the ecclesiology of communion. It is of paramount importance that the Synod on Africa recommends the establishment of Small Christian Communities in the parishes, so that the new model of the parish for the year 2000 will be the one of a community of communities."[18]

Pope St. John Paul II's apostolic exhortation *Ecclesia in Africa* (*EA*) was published and promulgated in Yaounde, Cameroon; Johannesburg, South Africa; and Nairobi, Kenya, in September 1995. Two sections specifically mention SCCs. First, in §23, the pope referred to his statement to the members of the council of the General Secretariat in 1989 that "if this synod is prepared well, it will be able to involve all levels of the Christian Community: individuals, small communities, parishes, Dioceses, and local, national and international bodies." And then in §89, the pope states:

> Right from the beginning, the Synod Fathers recognized that the Church as Family cannot reach her full potential as Church unless she is divided into communities small enough to foster close human relationships. The Assembly described the characteristics of such communities as follows: primarily they should be places engaged in evangelizing themselves, so that subsequently they can bring the Good

---

15. AMECEA, "Conclusions of the Study Conference of the AMECEA Plenary 1979."
16. Sixth Plenary Assembly of SECAM, Yaounde, Cameroon, 1981.
17. Seventh Plenary Assembly of SECAM, Kinshasa, DRC, 1984.
18. Healey, *Building the Church as Family of God*, 72.

News to others; they should moreover be communities which pray and listen to God's Word, encourage the members themselves to take on responsibility, learn to live an ecclesial life, and reflect on different human problems in the light of the Gospel. Above all, these communities are to be committed to living Christ's love for everybody, a love which transcends the limits of natural solidarity of clans, tribes or other interest groups.

SCCs were an important part of the document "National Plans for the Implementation of the African Synod" in the AMECEA countries. *The African Synod Comes Home—A Simplified Text*[19] and other postsynodal documents stressed the importance of SCCs in the follow-up and implementation of the First Synod's recommendations. This included developing SCCs as a concrete expression and realization of the model of church as family. This pastoral priority in favor of SCCs was clear in the Diocese of Ndola, Zambia, whose "Diocesan Guidelines" affirmed that "we share in the universal Church's *missio*. This is achieved through the establishment of active and fully involved Small Christian Communities."

A key turning point for the growth of SCCs in Tanzania was the promotion of a model of church from the bottom up. "The implementation of the new *Constitution of the National Lay Council* in 1998 required that the election of lay leaders in parishes throughout Tanzania start at the level of SCCs and move upwards. This ensured that the parish council leaders would be chosen from those who were already leaders in their SCCs—thus true representation from below. Such decisions gave full confidence to the faithful and opened new possibilities for the laity in the local church." This importance of SCCs can also be seen in diocesan synods at the local level. The booklet for the synod of the Archdiocese of Mwanza in Tanzania in 2002 contains 105 references to *Jumuiya Ndogo za Kikristo* (JNNK), the Swahili expression for SCCs.

Next was the 2002 AMECEA study conference on "Deeper Evangelization in the Third Millennium" in Dar es Salaam, Tanzania. Section 7 of the pastoral resolutions concerned "Building the Church as a Family of God by Continuing to Foster and/or Revitalize the Small Christian Communities," and states, "We recommend that a program on the theological and pastoral value of Small Christian Communities be included in the normal curriculum of the Major Seminaries and houses of formation of both men and women" (no. 43).

The Second Special Assembly for Africa of the Synod of Bishops took place in Rome October 4–25, 2009, on the theme "The Church in Africa in Service to Reconciliation, Justice, and Peace." The "Message of the Bishops of Africa to the People of God" states, "Here we would like to reiterate the recommendation of *Ecclesia in Africa* about the importance of Small Christian Communities (cf. *EIA*, 89). Beyond prayer, you must also arm yourself with sufficient knowledge of the Christian faith to be able to 'give a proof of the hope that you bear' (1 Peter 3:15) in the marketplaces of ideas. . . . We strongly recommend the basic sources of Catholic faith: The Holy Bible, *The Catechism of the Catholic Church*, and most relevant to the theme of the Synod, *The Compendium of the Social Doctrine of the Church*." SCCs are mentioned seven times in the "Final List of [57] Propositions."

The Faculty of Theology of the Catholic University of the Congo under the patronage of the National Episcopal Conference of the Democratic Republic of the Congo sponsored the Twenty-Seventh Theological Week of Kinshasa in Kinshasa, DRC, from February 21 to 25, 2011, on the theme "The Experience of Basic Living Ecclesial Communities in the Democratic Republic of the Congo: Theological and Pastoral Perspectives after 50 Years" ("L'expérience des CEVB en RD Congo: Perspectives théologiques et pastorales 50 ans après"). This conference commemorated the fiftieth anniversary of Living Ecclesial Communities in the DRC (1961–2011). As a sign of unity and solidarity with other parts of Africa, in the day devoted to "Other Experiences of CEVB in DRC and Elsewhere," Father Pius Rutechura, then Secretary General of AMECEA, presented a paper under the heading "Echoes of English-Speaking Africa: AMECEA" entitled, "The Experience of the AME-

---

19. *The African Synod Comes Home—A Simplified Text* (Nairobi: Paulines Publications Africa, 1995).

CEA Region with Small Christian Communities, Pastoral Priority since the 1970s." Father Godefroid Manunga, SVD, the director of the Lumko Missiological Institute, presented a paper on "The Experience of South Africa."

Pope Benedict XVI promulgated the postsynodal apostolic exhortation *Africae Munus* (*AM*) in Ouidah, Benin, in West Africa on November 19, 2011. Four sections mentioned SCCs. In the first, the pope stated, "It can be helpful for you to form associations in order to continue shaping your Christian conscience and supporting one another in the struggle for justice and peace. The Small Christian Communities (SCCs) and the 'new communities' are fundamental structures for fanning the flame of your Baptism" (§131). In most official documents of the Catholic Church the traditional parish is the basic juridical unit of the church, and so the pope's statement that SCCs are "fundamental structures" is significant. The pope continued:

> This [the power of love] is clearly seen in the universal Church, in dioceses and parishes, in the SCCs, in movements and associations, and even in the Christian family itself, which is "called to be a 'domestic church,' a place of faith, of prayer and of loving concern for the true and enduring good of each of its members," a community which lives the sign of peace. Together with the parish, the SCCs and the movements and associations can be helpful places for accepting and living the gift of reconciliation offered by Christ our peace. Each member of the community must become a "guardian and host" to the other: this is the meaning of the sign of peace in the celebration of the Eucharist. (§133)

It is clear from this section that SCCs are places to live Christ's gifts of reconciliation and peace. SCC members exchange the sign of Christ's peace with each other and with others in a spirit of solidarity, unity, and commitment/responsibility to each other.

Then there is this, which confirms the central place of sharing and reflection on the Bible in the life of SCCs in Africa:

> Each member of Christ's faithful should grow accustomed to reading the Bible daily! An attentive reading of the recent Apostolic Exhortation *Verbum Domini* can provide some useful pastoral indications. Care should be taken to initiate the faithful into the ancient and fruitful tradition of *lectio divina*. The Word of God can lead to the knowledge of Jesus Christ and bring about conversions which produce reconciliation, since it is able to sift "the thoughts and intentions of the heart" (Hebrews 4:12). The Synod Fathers encouraged Christian parish communities, SCCs, families and associations and ecclesial movements to set aside times for sharing the Word of God. In this way, they will increasingly become places where God's word, which builds up the community of Christ's disciples, is read, meditated on and celebrated. This word constantly enlivens fraternal communion (cf. 1 Peter 1:22–25). (*AM* §151)

Finally, in the context of the new evangelization, the pope states that "all Christians are admonished to be reconciled to God. In this way you will become agents of reconciliation within the ecclesial and social communities in which you live and work" (§169).

A workshop on the subject of "How Small Christian Communities in Africa Receive and Implement Magisterial Documents with a Special Emphasis on *Africae Munus* and Its Themes of Reconciliation, Justice and Peace" took place in Karen, Nairobi, Kenya, on September 24–30, 2012, organized by SECAM in collaboration with AMECEA and sponsored by Missio in Aachen, Germany. It was the first continent-wide meeting ever held on SCCs,[20] featuring forty-five participants (priests, religious, and laity) from English-speaking,

---

20. After living for fifty years in Africa, I feel the greatest and most difficult challenge is to launch an idea, project, activity, etc., that can succeed, meaning that it can operate permanently and without outside assistance on the local, grassroots level, not just as a "pilot" or "experimental" project. Related to this is another challenge in coordinating meetings and workshops on the national and continental levels in which SCC members from the lo-

French-speaking, and Portuguese-speaking Africa. There were twenty delegates from the AMECEA region, fourteen men and six women. Participants formed seven small groups (similar to SCCs) for prayer and for sharing, reflection, and discussion of the Bible: four English-speaking, two French-speaking, and one Portuguese-speaking.

English bishop Colin Davies, MHM, provided an interesting summary of the period from 1961 to 2018. Along with retired Ugandan archbishop James Odongo, formerly of the Archdiocese of Tororo, Uganda, and retired Tanzanian bishop Gervase Nkalanga, formerly of the Diocese of Bukoba, Tanzania, Davies was one of three still-living bishops in the AMECEA region who participated in the Second Vatican Council. In a wide-ranging interview[21] he recalled that SCCs are the fruit of the council's ecclesiology. The establishment of SCCs in the AMECEA countries in the 1970s "was a marvelous novelty that has made the church grow." He singled out the vibrant church at the SCC level as the greatest mark of ecclesial development on the African continent. Davies also participated in the First African Synod in Rome in 1994 and has witnessed how SCCs have developed as an inculturated model of church from the grassroots.

Pope Francis promulgated the apostolic exhortation *Evangelii Gaudium* (The Joy of the Gospel) in Rome on November 26, 2013, to close out the Year of Faith. It arose out of the synod of bishops on the theme "The New Evangelization for the Transmission of the Christian Faith" held in October 2012. *Evangelii Gaudium* emphasized the role of SCCs: "Other Church institutions, basic communities and small communities, movements, and forms of association are a source of enrichment for the Church, raised up by the Spirit for evangelizing different areas and sectors. Frequently they bring a new evangelizing fervor and a new capacity for dialog with the world whereby the Church is renewed" (§29).

December 8, 2015, was the fiftieth anniversary of the close of the Second Vatican Council, an event that has given rise to many books, articles, and conferences, and a great deal of discussion about its impact. This was an opportunity to revisit recent church history and identify what we have learned from the past fifty years. One thing we have learned is the importance of the two founding fathers of SCCs in eastern Africa, Bishop Patrick Kalilombe, MAfr, of the Diocese of Lilongwe, Malawi, and Bishop Christopher Mwoleka of the Diocese of Rulenge, Tanzania. Their vision of the theology and praxis of Vatican II's model of church and communion ecclesiology based on the notion of the "people of God" helped create the path for the establishment and development of SCCs in that region.

Themes of Small Christian Communities in Africa

Relationships and Community

To a question about the core value of SCCs, African members of SCCs would respond "relationships." Community values are basic to African life and to the foundation of SCCs. When the retired Archbishop of Kumasi, Ghana, Peter Sarpong, was asked what is the central value of African society, he immediately answered with one word: "participation,"[22] a value that is at the heart of the life and activities of SCCs. In recent years, another important word, "solidarity," has emerged. The apostolic exhortation generated by the First African Synod, *Ecclesia in Africa*, states that "African cultures have an acute sense of solidarity and community life" (§43).

The SCC way of life has been described by the Irish theologian and priest Brian Hearne, CSSp, as "essentially a spirituality." George Gichuhu, in *The Spirituality of SCCs in Eastern Africa*, looks at the high priority Africans place on the value of community as expressed in the African proverb "I am

---

cal, grassroots level can actively participate. This requires huge amounts of time, energy, and creativity to manage certain practical issues like language differences, customs, travel arrangements, and currency issues, among others. For people who have not traveled outside their home area there is a wonderful African proverb: "A coconut shell filled with water is like an ocean to an ant."

21. Colin Davies, in an interview with the author in Nairobi, Kenya, March 24, 2012.
22. Peter Sarpong in a conversation with the author, Kampala, Uganda, August 1, 1972.

because we are; we are because I am." SCCs can be described as "truly African, truly Christian."[23] The spirituality of SCCs is rooted in Jesus Christ's new commandment of love and service. SCC members live out their African Christian spirituality by reaching out to others, especially the poor and needy, and in this way African SCCs integrate African values with gospel values.

Biblical

The Bible is central to the mission of SCCs in Africa[24] and forms the foundation for the faith and life of SCC members with regard to such values as participation, solidarity, and social justice. The two essential characteristics of SCCs in Africa are Bible sharing/reflection[25] and practical action/outreach.

There are many important Bible passages on community. First, from the book of Ecclesiastes: "Two are better than one, because they have a good reward for their toil. For if they fall, one will lift up the other; but woe to one who is alone and falls and does not have another to help. Again, if two lie together, they keep warm; but how can one keep warm alone? And though one might prevail against another, two will withstand one. A threefold cord is not quickly broken" (Eccl 4:9–12). The Gospel of Matthew also emphasizes, "For where two or three are gathered in my name, there I am among them" (Matt 18:20).

The Acts of the Apostles provides additional scriptural support for the importance of community and serves as a model of community life in African SCCs. The book of Acts describes a community characterized by a strong witness, praying together, breaking bread together (sharing what we have), and receiving the Eucharist (Acts 2:42–47). Members of the SCCs work together, pray together, and share their lives just as the first Christian communities did. Then there is the profound statement in Acts that "the community of believers was of one mind and heart" (Acts 4:32). In these passages we find the biblical foundations of SCCs. We are called to truly live as the first Small Christian Communities described in the Acts of the Apostles did. Because SCCs are rooted in the New Testament, participants in our SCC workshops and courses are reminded of the oft-heard saying, "Small Christian Communities are a new way of being church that is really a very old (two thousand years old!) way of being church."[26] As the Tanzanian priest and theologian Laurenti Magesa has said, "From its inception as a community after the outpouring of the Holy Spirit at Pentecost, this is what the church in the New Testament was—'the community of believers was of one heart and mind' (Acts 4:32), leading them to share everything they had. To say, then, that SCCs constitute a, or the, '*new* way of being church' is a serious mischaracterization. More correctly, in SCCs, with the help of the Holy Spirit, the African church is pioneering in the rediscovery of the *original manner of being church*."[27]

The Bible sharing and reflection that is a cornerstone of AMECEA's pastoral priority of building SCCs[28] is closely connected to faith sharing and

---

23. This has been the theme of many conferences and symposia on the Catholic Church in Africa.

24. Harking back to St. Jerome, who stated that "ignorance of the scriptures is ignorance of Christ."

25. Among the many basic e-resource materials concerning the study of scripture in SCCs that are available free on the SCC website https://smallchristiancommunities.org are (1) "13 Steps in the Weekly *Bible* Sharing/*Bible* Reflection/Bible—Life Connections Service of Small Christian Communities (SCCs) in Africa"; (2) "Seven-Step Gospel Sharing (Lumko, South Africa)"; and (3) "The Process of *Lectio Divina*."

26. I was vividly reminded of this living history when I visited the city of Philippi, an eastern Macedonian town that was an early center of Christianity in Greece, during the Year of St. Paul in 2009. I stood in the middle of the excavation of one of the house churches (also called small domestic churches), the predecessors of SCCs. The book of Acts recounts how Lydia and her household were baptized and then offered hospitality to traveling preachers. Lydia's house became the site for the local church in Philippi, and she was perhaps its leader.

27. Magesa, "Joy of Community in Small Christian Communities," 24.

28. At the Seventeenth AMECEA Plenary Assembly in Nairobi, Kenya, in June 2011, the Missio Aachen and Missio Munich delegates from Germany praised the African church for three special gifts that can help the Catholic Church in Europe: first, optimism, combined with joy and emotion at liturgical services; second, SCCs, which help address the situation of the declining numbers of priests and also strengthen the personal witness and knowledge of the faithful; and third, important for our discussion here, its methods of reflection on scripture.

faith reflection. Thousands of lectionary-based[29] SCCs in the nine AMECEA countries meet in the middle of the week to reflect on the Gospel of the following Sunday following the three-year lectionary cycle.[30] As the Letter to the Hebrews says, "For the Word that God speaks is alive and full of power [making it active, operative, energizing, and effective]; it is sharper than any two-edged sword, penetrating to the dividing line of the breath of life (soul) and [the immortal] spirit, and of joints and marrow [of the deepest parts of our nature]" (Heb 4:12).

Magesa further explains what is needed in the context of eastern Africa:

> The life of SCCs must be rooted in Scripture—in studying it, seriously reflecting on it, internalizing it, and acting upon it. To spend only a few minutes casually reading and commenting on this or that passage of Scripture once a week, as is the custom in many SCCs, is totally inadequate. SCCs are theological communities and as such they must be scriptural communities. If "the study of the sacred page is . . . the soul of sacred theology," as Vatican II tells us in the *Constitution on Divine Revelation* (*Dei Verbum*, DV 23), then it must form the center of the life of SCCs as well.

How do SCCs sustain their growth and flourishing? Looking at the example of Jesus himself, we can see that the essential factors include listening to and reflection on the Word of God, prayer, and action. These factors form a single movement in the symphony of inculturation as evangelization performed by SCCs. All are necessary for the evangelization of the self (i.e., evangelization *ad intra*, within one's heart, so as to change personal perceptions and attitudes), and neighbor (*ad extra*, which involves the building up of communion, the reign of God on earth).[31]

Ecclesiastical

SCCs developed after the conclusion of the Second Vatican Council by putting the communion ecclesiology and other teachings of the council into practice.[32] The founding fathers of AMECEA and other episcopal conferences in Africa had a vision that focused on communion (*koinonia*), service (*diakonia*), and the development of SCCs as a concrete expression and realization of the model of church as family.

This is rooted in an ecclesiology in which SCCs are not optional but, rather, are the basic unit and most local expression of the Catholic Church. That is why ideally one should greet *all* people as members of SCCs. SCCs are different from traditional parish devotional groups, associations, and sodalities, membership in which is voluntary and often based on international constitutions and guidelines. Unlike these groups, even a priest or religious can become a member of his or her local SCC.

SCCs are characterized by a communion ecclesiology—the family, the SCC, the outstation, the subparish, the parish, and the diocese, all together, reflect a communion-of-communities model of church that starts from below, from the grassroots. SCCs are also characterized by a theology based on the Vatican II notion of "the people of God," which term originated with Dogmatic Constitution on the Church, *Lumen Gentium*.[33] *Lumen*

---

29. Some communities of religious sisters in Africa and other communities meet together daily, often in the evening, to read and reflect on the scripture readings for the next day, following the daily lectionary cycle.

30. To many Catholic laypeople, the expressions "lectionary-based" and "lectionary cycle" are churchy "in" words, jargon that is even difficult to understand. Officially the person who proclaims the scripture readings at Mass or at a Sunday service without a priest, the lector, does so from a book called the "lectionary." The church follows a three-year cycle for the Sunday readings and a two-year cycle for the daily readings. It is sometimes challenging to communicate this fundamental liturgical plan in simple, user-friendly language. "Lectionary-based faith sharing" is also referred to as "faith sharing based on scripture."

31. Magesa, "Joy of Community in Small Christian Communities," 26.

32. Laurenti Magesa boldly stated, "Ecclesiologically they (SCCs) are the best thing that has happened since the New Testament." Private letter to the author, July 1983.

33. The term the "people of God" has its origin in the Old Testament's emphasis on the Jewish people as the

Gentium refers to a trinitarian understanding of the church as "the people of God, the body of the Lord and the temple of the Holy Spirit" (§17) and continues, "This Church of Christ is truly present in all legitimate local congregations of the faithful which, united with their pastors, are themselves called churches in the New Testament. For in their locality these are the new People called by God, in the Holy Spirit and in much fullness.... In these communities though frequently small and poor, or living far from one another, Christ is present. By virtue of Him the one, holy, catholic and apostolic church gathers together" (§26).

In the "Final Message of the Bishops of Africa to the People of God," which was delivered at the end of the First African Synod, and specifically in the section on the "Ecclesiology of the Church as Family," the bishops stated, "The Church, the Family of God, implies the creation of small communities at the human level, living or basic ecclesial communities.... These individual Churches as Families have the task of working to transform society."

Pastoral

Although the term "Small Christian Communities"[34] has many variants,[35] as a new model of church it specifically refers to pastoral, parish-based groups in local neighborhoods that are part of the official structure, leadership, ministry, and life of the parish. Most SCCs in Africa follow this model, which distinguishes them from communities based on the social action and social justice models found in Latin America and parts of Asia. SCCs are a model of church that supports the parish structure—the parish is a communion or network of SCCs within a "communion-of-communities" ecclesiology. SCCs are the central "place" of ecclesial identity, ecclesial life, ministry, and mission. In recent years, a shift has occurred in eastern Africa toward much more of ecclesial life—for example, the celebration of the sacraments, religious education, catechesis, and other ministerial and service activities—taking place in the SCC, not in the outstation church or parish church.

Contextual

This section discusses the social, economic, political, and cultural dimensions of SCCs. The use of the "See, Judge, Act" methodology[36] has transformed many SCCs from inward-looking prayer groups to outward-looking groups interested in issues of justice and peace. The active participation of SCCs in the annual Kenyan Lenten Campaign is a good example of this shift toward facing issues of justice and peace

---

chosen people of God (Yahweh). In the New Testament, the First Letter of Peter says of the newly baptized Christians: "You are a chosen people, a royal priesthood, a holy nation, God's special possession, that you may declare the praises of him who called you out of darkness into his wonderful light. Once you were not a people, but now you are the People of God; once you had not received mercy, but now you have received mercy" (1 Pet 2:9–10).

There are two possible interpretations of this scripture passage depending on the context. The first is inclusive: all human beings are part of the people of God (we are all children of God), while the second is exclusive: only members of the Catholic Church are part of the people of God. These two interpretations have been debated by many theologians including St. Cyprian, Karl Rahner, Edward Schillebeeckx, and Wilbert Gobbo.

34. In eastern Africa, we capitalize the terms "Small Christian Community" (SCC) and "Small Christian Communities" (SCCs) because these communities are a key pastoral priority in our parishes and dioceses and in the official pastoral policy of the Catholic bishops.

35. Described at length with many examples in Joseph Healey, "Evolving a World Church from the Bottom Up: An Analysis and Interpretation of 3,500 Different Names, Titles, Terms, Expressions, Descriptions and Meanings for and about Small Christian Communities/Basic Christian Communities in the World with 11 Case Studies from Six Continents," Background Paper for the International Consultation on "Rediscovering Community—International Perspectives," University of Notre Dame, South Bend, IN, December 8–12, 1991. New research has brought the total number of terms referred to in the title to over 5,000.

36. "See, Judge, Act" is an inductive method of analysis that develops critical thinking. Based on a format of experiential learning, members are encouraged to inquire into the situations that affect them on a daily basis and plan and organize specific actions to bring about a positive change. This method of analysis begins with the everyday lived experience of people—the issues, problems, and challenges that face them every day of the week. The method challenges people to become aware of the reality of their particular situations, and of the situations of others, in the workplace, community and parish, school, home, and broader society.

on a local level. The pastoral spiral process[37] involves reaching decisions by communal discernment, and one step in the process is social analysis, whereby SCC members reflect on the social, economic, political, and cultural aspects of their faith.

God actively participates in this process, as was seen in the call contained in the book of Revelation: "Listen to what the Spirit is saying to the churches" (Rev 2:7). The "churches" referred to there are not just those of two thousand years ago: SCCs are among the "churches," especially the local churches, present in our contemporary world.

Synodal

Pope Francis emphasizes the theme of synodality, a theme that is deeply embedded in the nature of SCCs. He has given a new impetus to the synodality introduced at Vatican II, which involves the entire Catholic Church walking, discerning, and evangelizing together. This means an ongoing process of listening, discussion, dialogue, debate, and discernment, together with proposed pastoral responses, all of which is built on the foundations of collegiality and subsidiarity and develops under the guidance of the Holy Spirit. The pope likes to call this process a "journey" or a "path," following the etymology of the word "synod"; he states that "synodality is the path of the Catholic Church."[38] This process of synodality is a journeying together, which suggests numerous metaphors—one is the story of the road to Emmaus told in chapter 24 of Luke's Gospel; another is summed up by the well-known African proverb "If you want to walk fast, walk alone. If you want to walk far, walk together." SCC members participate in this journeying together by using the "See, Judge, Act" methodology or process and by drawing on pastoral theological reflections and life experiences.

Mission

Practical action, service, social outreach, and mission are foundational aspects of SCCs. Included in these categories are actions for justice and peace and various kinds of evangelization, including primary evangelization, new evangelization, and deeper evangelization, including proclaiming the gospel to people who are not Catholic. SCC members are trying to respond to Pope Francis's call to be missionary disciples, including "reaching out to the marginalized and those on the peripheries." The pope states, "An evangelizing community gets involved by word and deed in people's daily lives; it bridges distances, it is willing to abase itself if necessary, and it embraces human life, touching the suffering flesh of Christ in others. Evangelizers thus take on the 'smell of the sheep' and the sheep are willing to hear their voice" (*Evangelii Gaudium* §24).

The missionary activity of SCCs in the African context includes assuming a prophetic role in the face of the continent's challenges of alienation, corruption, discrimination, division, illiteracy, exclusion, favoritism, inequality, injustice, marginalization, and harmful ethnic strife and tribalism.

The Development of Small Christian Communities in Africa

The last ten years have seen the increasing involvement of SCCs in promoting forgiveness, healing, justice, reconciliation, and peace in Africa. Many of the twenty thousand SCCs were involved in the reconciliation and healing ministry after the 1994 Rwandan genocide. Research on SCCs in Kenya, Rwanda, South Sudan, and Sudan indicates that women are better at peacemaking than men because men tend to emphasize power and control, while women emphasize personal relationships. The Jesuit Centre for Theological Reflection (JCTR) in Lusaka, Zambia, produces guided reflection pamphlets on justice and peace topics so that SCCs can generate faith-based action. In addition, the various reflection methods contained in the Lumko program that are especially related to social justice are used throughout Africa.

SCCs are characterized by an ongoing emphasis on formation and training. Lumko workshops are regularly held throughout Africa, and a workshop on "The Role of SCCs in Civic Education in the DRC" took place in Kinshasa in 2008. The annual

---

37. The metaphor of the pastoral spiral describes better than the circle or the cycle the outgoingness and ongoingness of the process.

38. Pope Francis, "Papal Mass on the Solemnity of Saints Peter and Paul," Homily on June 29, 2013.

Kenya Lenten Campaign trains SCC leaders to use the inductive "See, Judge, Act" methodology of the pastoral spiral and to facilitate Training of Trainers (TOT) workshops on justice and peace. The Biblical Center for Africa and Madagascar, commonly known as BICAM and located at the Catholic University of Eastern Africa in Nairobi, Kenya, promotes training workshops and programs related to reflections on the Bible.

Our research shows that a statistical and analytical evaluation of SCCs in Africa is better done on a diocese-by-diocese basis and even on a parish-by-parish basis, rather than by looking at entire countries. Presently there are 180,000 SCCs in the nine AMECEA countries. Tanzania has 60,000 and Kenya has over 45,000. In Nigeria, some dioceses have active SCCs and some do not. SCCs began in the Archdiocese of Lagos in 1977, but by the late 1980s the number of Nigerian SCCs had nosedived; they made a comeback beginning in 1992, following a typical pattern of fluctuation in their numbers. At present, there are SCCs in sixty parishes in the archdiocese.

SCCs are now a pastoral priority of the Catholic Church in Ghana. In the DRC, statistics from 2006 indicate that the Archdiocese of Kinshasa had 1,800 CEVBs in the city, with many more in the surrounding rural areas. There are many SCCs in southern Africa, especially in South Africa and Zimbabwe. IMBISA (the Inter-Regional Meeting of the Bishops of Southern Africa) conferences and workshops are an important catalyst for SCCs in that region. In Mozambique, the small communities of Sant'Egidio provide another model of SCC.

A recent development is the Network of Small Christian Communities in Africa, which sponsored workshops in Accra in 2014, Ouagadougou in 2015, Nairobi in 2016, and Kinshasa in 2017, organized by Missio Aachen with support from SECAM and AMECEA. The network is a resource forum of experts and practitioners who are passionate about the growth and sustainability of SCCs in Africa.[39] SCCs in Africa try to read the signs of the times and respond creatively. One new initiative has been the creation of workshops, spearheaded in part by SCCs in the Lagos archdiocese, on the subject of child protection, including safeguarding against physical and sexual abuse. Another has been the formation of SCCs in the newer camps for refugees and internally displaced people; examples are present in South Sudan and northern Uganda.

The Challenges of Small Christian Communities in Africa

1. Implementing Pope Francis's Inclusive Vision of the Catholic Church.

Members of SCCs are challenged to be missionary disciples who reach out to the marginalized and those on the peripheries of society. SCCs in Africa need to be on the front lines of the ministry to migrants, refugees, and internally displaced people; the dialogue with Islam; the Catholic relationship with evangelicals and Pentecostals; and prophetic responses to issues involving justice and peace.

2. Responding to the Advent of the Digital Age in Africa.

With respect to using the internet to promote SCCs in Africa, the future is now. Today we see the growing importance of the internet, including online networking, the new media/social media, and other new communication tools. The church and SCCs in Africa need to be adept in the use of interactive websites, online journals, online learning sites, video conferencing, webinars, search engines like Google, Skype, podcasts, video clips, DVDs, apps, e-readers, email, text, smartphones and other mobile devices, and social networking sites like Facebook, Twitter, WhatsApp, YouTube, and Zoom. The social media revolution is changing the way the world—and the Catholic Church in Africa—communicates.

The digital age can enable the African church to dramatically expand its knowledge and understanding on three levels. First, the internet and the new media/social media can help in the formation and training of SCC leaders, animators, facilitators, and coordinators in Africa. Second, they can help members of SCCs to share their experiences with the rest of the world—members of African SCCs can now feel that they are part of the global, world

---

39. See their website, www.africansccsnetworking.org.

church. And third, they can help people all around the world learn about SCCs in Africa.

A concrete example is the Small Christian Communities Global Collaborative Website (www.smallchristiancommunities.org), which shares SCC contacts, information, events, materials, and news for each of the six continents. The section on Africa includes continent-wide material and also material on specific countries, including Burkina Faso, Cameroon, the DRC, Eritrea, Ethiopia, Ghana, Kenya, Malawi, Nigeria, Rwanda, South Africa, South Sudan, Tanzania, Uganda, Zambia, and Zimbabwe. The website also features archives, book reviews, a calendar of events, e-books, links to other SCC websites, a photo gallery, resources, SCC polls, an SCC stories database, a search engine, videos, and sections on vision and what's new.

3. Continuing to Form and Develop Youth Small Christian Communities (YSCCs).
In many countries of Africa, over 60 percent of the population is under twenty-five. The church is challenged to prioritize two major types of YSCCs: parish-based and school- or institution-based. Both types include online, social-media-based YSCCs using What'sApp, Facebook, and so on.

4. Reading and Responding to the Signs of the Times in Africa.
A key challenge is how to respond to the question, What are the various human problems in Africa that we should reflect on in our SCC meetings in the light of the gospel? The response to this question should be based on the section of John Paul II's apostolic exhortation *Ecclesia in Africa* concerning SCCs (§89).

Cardinal Polycarp Pengo, the archbishop of Dar es Salaam, Tanzania, and the former president of SECAM, calls SCCs "a special or privileged instrument of evangelization." Magesa also recognizes this: "For the future of Christian mission, specifically in Africa, we can say without hesitation that the development of small faith communities is an indispensable requirement." Cardinal Berhaneyesus Souraphiel, the archbishop of Addis Ababa, Ethiopia, and the present chairman of AMECEA, describes Africa as a continent with "a great future and a great responsibility, not only for Africans but to the whole world. . . . There is still a need of re-evangelization to make the Gospel planted in the various cultures, to educate the youth in their faith, to prepare Christian Leadership on the level of Small Christian Communities, parishes, deaneries, dioceses, and on the national level."[40]

Nigerian priest and theologian Agbonkhianmeghe E. Orobator, SJ, describes the future development of SCCs in Africa as follows:

> The significant factors of the future development of SCCs include the level and nature of interest from ecclesiastical leadership, the commitment to the formation and empowerment of the lay faithful and the relative strength of negative socio-economic and cultural factors.
>
> Along with the need for ongoing critical reflection on the present organization and practices of SCCs, much still needs to be done to develop the theology of Small Christian Communities as the church in the neighborhood. This theology ought to facilitate the expansion of the missionary focus of SCCs to include attention to socio-political, ecological and economic conditions of their context. In this vein, SCCs in Africa would have much to learn from the history and praxis of the Latin American model, while, at the same time, developing a distinctively African model of Small Christian Communities as a new way of becoming church.[41]

5. Identifying the Task Presented to African Theologians, Researchers, and Scholars by SCCs.
In his well-known book *Models of Church* and in a subsequent book, *Community of Disciples*, Ameri-

---

40. Berhaneyesus Souraphiel in "Church's Presence at the African Union among Priorities of Ethiopia's Cardinal-Designate," Catholic News Agency for Africa (CANAA), January 8, 2015, www.canaafrica.org.

41. Orobator, "Small Christian Communities as a New Way of Becoming Church," 125. For the Latin American model, see Fritz Lobinger, "What SCCs and CEBs Can Learn from Each Other," *East Asian Pastoral Review* 3 (2013): 287–97.

can theologian and cardinal Avery Dulles, SJ, posited six models of the church: institution, mystical communion, sacrament, herald, servant, and community of disciples. Over the years various African models of church have evolved. We need an African Avery Dulles, that is, an African theologian of the new generation who will theologically develop the notion of SCCs as a new model of church in Africa.

Ecclesia in Africa states that "it is earnestly to be hoped that theologians in Africa will work out the theology of the Church as Family with all the riches contained in this concept, showing its complementarity with other images of the Church" (§63). Connected to the model of church as family are community-related African metaphors and ecclesiological images such as the church as the extended family of God, the church as the clan of Jesus Christ, and the church as the universal family in Christ.

6. Working out the Methodology of African Christian Contextual Theology.

The content of African Christian contextual theology today is twofold: it is both rooted in personal experience and based on grassroots research and analysis, and today there is an emphasis on a new and distinct African theological methodology. There are several possibilities involving "conversational theology" and "palaver theology": African conversation theology, African palaver theology, African theology as conversation, African dialogue theology, African Christian palaver theology, and African Christian conversation theology. These are both the names of theological methodologies and the names for the content of the theology (like liberation theology). Methodology heavily influences and determines content and vice versa in a two-way process that illuminates and enriches both African values and Christian values.

Fitting into the SCC model of church, this methodology is African theology as conversation, active dialogue, intensive listening, and learning from each other (described as "listening in conversation") and consensus. This is a new way of doing African Christian theology that is conversational, participatory, collaborative, cross-disciplinary, and multigenerational. It includes oral theological conversation and storytelling related to African narrative ecclesiology.

American priest and theologian Robert Schreiter, CPPS, points out that local theologies can be constructed in such a way that the local community is a theologian:

> The experience of those in the Small Christian Communities who have seen the insight and power arising from the reflections of the people upon their experience and the Scriptures has prompted making the community itself the prime author of theology in local contexts. The Holy Spirit, working in and through the believing community, gives shape and expression to Christian experience. Some of these communities have taught us to read the Scriptures in a fresh way and have called the larger church back to a fidelity to the prophetic Word of God.[42]

SCCs are not a movement in the Catholic Church; rather, they are the church on the move. SCCs can play a major role in the new evangelization. As a new way of being/becoming church and a new model of church (closely related to the models of church as family and communion of communities), African SCCs are influencing the World Church. SCCs in Africa will continue to develop in the spirit of the Spanish proverb that is well known around the world: "We create the path by walking."

Bibliography

African SCCs Networking Website. www.africansccs-networking.org

AMECEA Study Conference on "Building Small Christian Communities." "Guidelines for the Catholic Church in Eastern Africa in the 1980s." *African Ecclesial Review (AFER)* 16.1 and 2 (1974).

AMECEA Study Conference on "Building Small Christian Communities." "Conclusions." *African Ecclesial Review (AFER)* 18.5 (October 1976).

AMECEA. "Conclusions of the Study Conference of the AMECEA Plenary 1979." *African Ecclesial Review (AFER)* 21 (1979).

---

42. Schreiter, *Constructing Local Theologies*, 16. This book has ten references to SCCs.

Bodewes, Christine. *Parish Transformation in Urban Slums: Voices of Kibera, Kenya*. Nairobi: Paulines Publications Africa, 2005.

Carney, Jay J. "The People Bonded Together by Love: Eucharistic Ecclesiology and Small Christian Communities in Africa." *Modern Theology* 30.2 (April 2014): 300–318.

Chimombo, Emmanuel, Joseph G. Healey, Rita Ishengoma, Rose Musimba, Febian P. Mulenga, and Alphonce C. L. Omolo, eds. *Strengthening the Growth of Small Christian Communities in Africa: A Training Handbook for Facilitators*. 2nd ed. Nairobi: AMECEA Pastoral Department; Nairobi: Paulines Publications Africa, 2018.

Éla, Jean-Marc. "Les Communautés de Base dans les Églises Africaines." In J. M. Éla and R. Luneau, *Voici les temps des héritiers: Églises d'Afrique et voies nouvelles*. Paris: Karthala, 1982.

Flynn, Kieran. *Communities for the Kingdom: A Handbook for Small Christian Community Leaders*. Eldoret: AMECEA Gaba Publications, *Spearhead* Nos. 181–182, 2007.

Francis, Pope. *Evangelii Gaudium* (The Joy of the Gospel) [Post-synodal Apostolic Exhortation on the Proclamation of the Gospel in Today's World; November 23, 2013]. Vatican City: Libreria Editrice Vaticana, 2013. www.vatican.va.

———. "Papal Mass on the Solemnity of Saints Peter and Paul," Homily on June 29, 2013, www.vatican.va.

Gichuhu, George. *The Spirituality of SCCs in Eastern Africa*. Eldoret: AMECEA Gaba Publications, *Spearhead* No. 185, 1985.

Healey, Joseph. "Beyond Vatican II: Imagining the Catholic Church of Nairobi I." Nairobi: Privately Printed, 2015. Also a chapter in *The Church We Want: African Catholics Look to Vatican III*, edited by Agbonkhianmeghe E. Orobator. Maryknoll, NY: Orbis Books; Nairobi: Acton, 2016.

———. *Building the Church as Family of God: Evaluation of Small Christian Communities in Eastern Africa*. Eldoret: AMECEA Gaba Publications—CUEA Press Double *Spearhead* Nos. 199–200, 2012. Available free online at the Small Christian Communities Global Collaborative Website: https://smallchristiancommunities.org/wp-content/uploads/2018/04/Build_new.pdf.

———. *A Fifth Gospel: The Experience of Back Christian Values*. Maryknoll, NY: Orbis Books; London: SCM Press, 1981. A Special Edition (Thirty-Second Anniversary Edition printed digitally) was published by Orbis Books in 2013. The Swahili version is *Kuishi Injili (Living the Gospel)* and the German version is *Auf der Suche nach dem Ganzen Leben: Kleine Christliche Gemeinschaften in Tansania*.

Healey, Joseph, and Jeanne Hinton, eds. *Small Christian Communities Today: Capturing the New Moment*. Maryknoll, NY: Orbis Books, 2005; Nairobi: Paulines Publications Africa, 2006.

Healey, Joseph, and Donald Sybertz, eds. *Towards an African Narrative Theology*. Nairobi: Paulines Publications Africa, 1996; Maryknoll, NY: Orbis Books, 1997.

Healey, Joseph, Rose Musimba, and Febian Pikiti. "The Experience of Small Christian Communities (SCCs) in Eastern Africa (AMECEA Region) in Light of the African Year of Reconciliation (AYR) from 29 July, 2015 to 29 July, 2016." Nairobi: Privately published, 2016.

Ishengoma, Rita. *Akamwani: The Challenges of Bible Sharing in Small Christian Communities*. Dar es Salaam: Old East Africa, 2009.

Kalilombe, Patrick. "From Outstation to Small Christian Communities: A Comparison of Two Pastoral Methods in Lilongwe Diocese." Doctoral dissertation. Berkeley: University of California, 1983.

Lumko Institute. Resources and Publications on Small Christian Communities, such as *Training for Community Ministries*. Delmenville, South Africa. 1978–.

Magesa, Laurenti. "The Joy of Community in Small Christian Communities." *New People* no. 149 (March–April 2014).

Mejia, Rodrigo. *Church in the Neighborhood: Meetings for the Animation of Small Christian Communities*. Nairobi: St. Paul Publications Africa, 1992. The Swahili (Eastern and Central Africa) version is *Kanisa la Kimazingira*. The Chewa (Malawi) version is *Mpingo M'Dera Lathu* (Zomba: Montfortian Itinerant Team, 1993).

———. *We Are the Church: Sharing in Small Christian Communities*. Nairobi: Paulines Publications Africa, 2009.

Mobiala, John. "Genèse et situation actuelle des Communautés Ecclésiales Vivantes de Base (CEVBs) dans L'archidiocèse de Kinshasa." https://www.academia.edu/36100468/John_MOBI

ALA_Gen%C3%A8se-situation_actuelle_CEVB_%C3%A0_Kinshasa.pdf.

Moerschbacher, Marco. "For Fifty Years on the Road: The Importance of the Base Communities in Africa's Local Churches." Translated from the German version in *Herder Korrespondenz* 4 (2013): 200–204.

Mugambi, Jesse, and Evaristi Magoti, eds. *Endless Quest: The Vocation of an African Christian Theologian: Essays in Honor of Laurenti Magesa*. Nairobi: Acton, 2014.

Mwoleka, Christopher, and Joseph Healey, eds. *Ujamaa and Christian Communities*. Eldoret: AMECEA Gaba Publications, *Spearhead* 45, 1976.

Ndingi, Raphael. "Basic Communities: The African Experience." In *A New Missionary Era*, edited by Padraig Flanagan, 99–106. Maryknoll, NY: Orbis Books, 1982.

Ngalula, Josée. "History, Development, and Status Quo of Basic Christian Community (BCC) in Africa." In *Proceedings of the International Symposium on In the World of Today? The Church on Her Way in Basic Christian Communities*, Tübingen, Germany, January 17–20, 2012, edited by Marco Moerschbacher. https://www.academia.edu/6456909/HISTORY_DEVELOPMENT_AND_STATUS_QUO_OF_BASIC_CHRISTIAN.

Nunes, José. *Pequenas Comunidades Cristãs: O Ondjanco e a Inculturação em África/Angola*. Monografia. Porto, Portugal: Univ. Católica Portuguesa, 1991.

Nyakundi, Alloys, Nancy Njehia, Everline Nyaituga, and Brian Omondi. "We Create the Path by Walking: Youth Small Christian Communities in Eastern Africa." In *God's Quad: Small Faith Communities on Campus and Beyond*, edited by Kevin Ahern and Christopher Derige Malano, 77–88. Maryknoll, NY: Orbis Books, 2018.

O'Halloran, James. *Small Christian Communities: A Pastoral Companion*. Maryknoll, NY: Orbis Books; Dublin: Columba Press, 1996.

Orobator, Agbonkhianmeghe E., ed., *The Church We Want: African Catholics Look to Vatican III*. Maryknoll, NY: Orbis Books; Nairobi: Acton, 2016.

———. "Small Christian Communities as a New Way of Becoming Church: Practice, Progress and Prospects." In *Small Christian Communities: Fresh Stimulus for a Forward-Looking Church*, vol. 2, edited by Klaus Krämer and Klaus Vellguth. In "Theology of One World" series of Missio Aachen. Quezon City, Philippines: Claretian Publications, 2013.

Radoli, Agatha, ed. *How Local Is the Local Church? Small Christian Communities and Church in Eastern Africa*. Eldoret: AMECEA Gaba Publications, *Spearhead* 126–128, 1993.

Rôle des responsible dans les Communautés Chrétiennes de Base. Ouagadougou: Archdiocese de Ouagadougou, Service diocesain de la formation permanete, 2014.

Schreiter, Robert. *Constructing Local Theologies*. Maryknoll, NY: Orbis Books, 1985.

Segeja, Nicholaus. "Small Christian Communities: A Vital Icon for New Evangelization." *African Christian Studies* 27.4 (December 2011): 7–38.

Small Christian Communities Global Collaborative Website, https://smallchristiancommunities.org

Speich, Jean-Marie. "Africa Is an 'Extended Holy Land,'" Nuncio in Ghana Clarifies." *Catholic News Agency for Africa (CANAA)*, November 27, 2014.

Ugeux, Bernard, and Pierre Lefebvre. *Small Communities and Parishes*. Nairobi: Paulines Publications Africa, 1999.

Wambua, Nzilani Mary. *Enhancing the Spirit of Communion in Small Christian Communities: A Case Study in the Archdiocese of Mombasa, Kenya*. Nairobi: Catholic University of Eastern Africa, privately printed, 2015.

Wijsen, Frans, Peter Henriot, and Rodrigo Mejia, eds. *The Pastoral Circle Revisited: A Critical Quest for Truth and Transformation*. Maryknoll, NY: Orbis Books, 2005.

Zemale, Terese Josephine. *Christian Witness through Small Christian Communities*. Eldoret: AMECEA Gaba Publications, *Spearhead* No. 121, 1992.

Suggested Reading

Chimombo, Emmanuel, Joseph G. Healey, Rita Ishengoma, Rose Musimba, Febian P. Mulenga, and Alphonce C. L. Omolo, eds. *Strengthening the Growth of Small Christian Communities in Africa: A Training Handbook for Facilitators*. 2nd ed. Nairobi: AMECEA Pastoral Department and Nairobi: Paulines Publications Africa, Second Edition, 2018.

Healey, Joseph. *Building the Church as Family of God: Evaluation of Small Christian Communities in Eastern Africa*. Eldoret: AMECEA Gaba Publications—CUEA Press Double *Spearhead* Nos. 199–200, 2012. Available free online at the Small Christian Communities Global Collaborative Website: https://smallchristiancommunities.org/wp-content/uploads/2018/04/Build_new.pdf.

Healey, Joseph, and Jeanne Hinton, eds. *Small Christian Communities Today: Capturing the New Moment*. Maryknoll, NY: Orbis Books, 2005; Paulines Publications Africa, 2006.

Orobator, Agbonkhianmeghe E., ed. *The Church We Want: African Catholics Look to Vatican II*. Maryknoll, NY: Orbis Books; Nairobi: Acton, 2016.

Small Christian Communities Global Collaborative Website: https://smallchristiancommunities.org. Includes theological resources in French and Portuguese under the respective African countries.

Key Words

basic ecclesial communities
Christian contextual theology
Christian conversation theology
Christian palaver theology
church in the neighborhood
communion ecclesiology
community
narrative theology
new model of church
new way of being/becoming church
participation
relationships
Small Christian Communities
synodality
Youth Small Christian Communities

Communicating the Faith in African Catholicism: History and Development

Walter Chikwendu Ihejirika

The Catholic Church believes that the origin of human communication is located in the divine Trinity. The intimate life of God is a profound, ongoing, inexhaustible communication between the three divine Persons. The Father "speaks" or "generates" the Son and communicates everything he is and has to the Son. The Son calls to the Father and gives himself in totality and perfect obedience.[1] The Holy Spirit proceeds from the Father and the Son as the fruit of the love and dialogue between them. Trinitarian communication is the profound communion and exchange that lives in the mystery of God. This is the root of our human communication, which entails sharing (*koinonia*), participation (taking part and sharing), and entering into a mutual bond.

As humans, we are communicative beings because of this trinitarian communication, since we are created in God's image and likeness. Every man and woman in this world is called to take part in this mysterious flow of communication. God's incarnation through Jesus Christ is at the center of any Christian communication. Jesus as communicator is the direct radiance of God's self-communication to people. Jesus is the perfect communicator.[2]

The outpouring of the Spirit and the gift of tongues at Pentecost are a communicative event. Symbolically, Pentecost is the canceling out of the Babel event in which humanity was dispersed because of a lack of understanding (Gen 11:1–9).

The church, born at Pentecost, is now the sign and instrument of the communication between God and the human family, and of the unity of the whole human race. Communication is thus at the heart of what it means to be Christian, and every aspect of the Christian life has a communicative dimension.

Good and effective communication is indispensable for the continued existence of the church as a community made up of human beings in the world. If the main tenets of the faith and its rituals, rites, and other spiritual experiences are not appropriately communicated (in the full sense of the word "communication") to both its members and to outsiders, they will remain meaningless and unknown and will ultimately disappear. There is no gainsaying the fact that a religious body that does not privilege communication is heading toward extinction.

Bernard Lonergan aptly captured this point in his book *Method in Theology*. He first described seven functional specialties in theology, namely, research, interpretation, history, dialectic, foundations, doctrines, and systematic. He presented communication as the eighth functional specialty, as well as the final stage in the theological method—the stage in which theological reflection bears fruit. Noting the link between communication and the other stages, he wrote, "Without the first seven stages . . . there is no fruit to be born. But without the last, the first seven are in vain, for they fail to mature."[3]

---

1. Eilers, *Communicating in Ministry and Mission*.
2. Pontifical Council for Social Communications, *Communio et Progressio* §11.
3. Lonergan, *Method in Theology*, 355.

This chapter seeks to provide an overview of the communicative efforts of the Catholic Church in Africa. In doing so, it adopts the "historical-thematic" approach. Those researching communication in Africa, like their peers in other parts of the world, have a wide range of methods at their disposal, and the choice of a particular method is generally dependent on the nature of the research problem and the questions that the research seeks to answer.

Walter C. Ihejirika and Christy U. Omego noted that the methods employed in communication research can either be qualitative or quantitative, experimental or nonexperimental.[4] Qualitative studies are descriptive in nature and merely describe what is present in the social world, while quantitative studies employ data and numbers to provide statistical explanations of events and behavioral patterns in the social world and to make predictions about the future. Qualitative designs used in communication research include historical studies, case studies, observations, and ethnographies, while quantitative designs include surveys, experiments, and content analysis.

This article has adopted the historical-thematic method, which examines extant documents pertinent to the research objectives in order to draw out relevant conclusions.[5] M. Löblich and A. M. Scheu identified three approaches that have been applied to historical research in communication studies: intellectual, biographical, and institutional.[6] The intellectual approach reviews theories, paradigms, and ideas. The biographical approach focuses on the lives of communicators, while the institutional approach looks at the development of relevant communicating institutions. Each of these approaches can be used in isolation but can also be combined with the others in some cases.

The present study adopts the intellectual approach to historical analysis. Because historical analysis relies heavily on documents, it is closely related to content analysis. At the heart of content analysis is the articulation of content categories, which are basically the themes guiding the analysis.[7] Intellectual historical analysis is best done by delineating relevant themes guiding the study, and thus I term my design "historical-thematic." I used this design in my earlier, detailed review of the African perspective on the field of study known as "media, religion and culture."[8]

This historical-thematic analysis of faith communication is mostly descriptive, following the historical development of the proclamation and lived experience of the Good News on the African continent. These communicative activities in Africa will be discussed under two major themes—evangelizing communication and pastoral communication. I hope this chapter will provide a holistic view of the communication of the Catholic faith in Africa and also facilitate dialogue among scholars from different ecclesial disciplines on the importance of communication in the life and work of the church. I also hope to articulate ways of consolidating the past achievements of communicative efforts in the African church and, where needed, to offer suggestions where there is still work to be done.

Evangelizing Communication

Every communicative process has a goal or aim, and the process is considered effective when that goal or aim is achieved. The most elementary goal of any communication process is enabling the receiver to understand and appreciate the message of the sender as communicated through a channel and then for the receiver to articulate feedback for the sender, which then constitutes a new message and the basis of another response. The first pertinent question to be asked here is, What are the communicative goals of the Catholic Church?

---

4. Ihejirika and Omego, *Research Methods in Linguistics and Communication Studies*, 74–75. See also Jesen, *Handbook of Media and Communication Research*.
5. For a good overview of the historical method, see Mayhead, "Historical Analysis."
6. Löblich and Scheu, "Writing the History of Communication Studies," 3.
7. See Krippendorff and Bock, *Content Analysis Reader*.
8. Ihejirika, "Current Trends in the Study of Media, Religion and Culture in Africa."

The term "evangelization" encapsulates an important communicative goal of the church. Pope Paul VI expressed this succinctly: "The task of evangelizing all people constitutes the essential mission of the Church. . . . Evangelization is in fact the grace and vocation proper to the Church, her deepest identity. She exists in order to evangelize."[9]

The communicative aspect of mission implies bringing the Good News of the gospel to those who have not yet received it, and it signifies everything the church has to do in the world in order to make it conform to the original intention of God. The purpose of evangelization is transforming humanity from within and making it new.

The communicative goals of the Catholic Church could be summarized as proclaiming and witnessing to the reality of the Catholic faith. This is the reality of a group of believers bonded together by their common faith in Jesus and implies both temporal and spiritual aspirations. The ultimate aim or goal of Catholic evangelization is the building up of communities of faith, communities of love, or as the fathers of the First Synod of Bishops for Africa put it, it means building the church as the family of God.[10]

The task of evangelization aimed at bringing the Catholic faith to Africa was and is carried out through evangelizing communication. The form of such communication has as its aim the propagation of kingdom values beyond narrow church boundaries. For the missiologist, Hendrik Kraemer rightly noted, communicating the Christian message involves all of the church's activities, including evangelizing, preaching, teaching, and witnessing in the various areas of life. This incessant communication of the Christian message, he concludes, is what we now call the missionary or apostolic duty of the church.[11]

Evangelizing communication, according to Franz-Josef Eilers, is aimed at sharing and spreading God's love and redemption to people located beyond the physical and mental confines of the established Christian community. Its main thrust is to reach and support those who are not yet fully part of the Christian community. It also involves the preparation given to evangelizers to enable them to reach out to others. This preparation includes mission animation, mission promotion, and the communicative activities of missionary congregations.[12] As current theological and missiological studies in Africa have shown, evangelizing communication also involves the inculturation of the gospel message in the African cultural milieu.[13]

Many church documents, especially those dealing with communication, like *Inter Mirifica*, *Communio et Progressio*, and *Aetatis Novae*, have highlighted the nature of evangelizing communication. In *Aetatis Novae*, for instance, evangelizing communication is presented thus:

> Communications in and by the Church is essentially communication of the Good News of Jesus Christ. It is the proclamation of the Gospel as a prophetic, liberating word to the men and women of our times; it is testimony, in the face of radical secularization, to divine truth and to the transcendent destiny of the human person; it is the witness given in solidarity with all believers against conflict and division, to justice and communion among peoples, nations and cultures.[14]

This understanding of evangelizing communication makes clear that evangelization has two dimensions—evangelization and reevangelization; the latter was identified by Pope St. John Paul II as the "new evangelization." In his encyclical *Redemptoris Missio*, the pope noted that the subjects of the

---

9. Paul VI, apostolic exhortation *Evangelii Nuntiandi* §17.
10. See John Paul II, post-synodal apostolic exhortation *Ecclesia in Africa* (EA).
11. Kraemer, *Communication of the Christian Faith*, 22–24, cited by Eilers, *Communicating in Ministry and Mission*, 212.
12. Eilers, *Communicating in Ministry and Mission*, 212.
13. See, e.g., Magesa, *Anatomy of Inculturation*; McGarry and Ryan, *Inculturating the Church in Africa*; Ilo, "Methods and Models of African Theology."
14. Pontifical Council for Social Communication, *Aetatis Novae*, no. 9.

new evangelization are "entire groups of the baptized who have lost a living sense of the faith or even no long consider themselves members of the Church and live a life far from Christ and His Gospel." He concludes, "In this case, what is needed is a 'new evangelization' or 're-evangelization'" (§34). Both evangelization and reevangelization aim at bringing people into the Christian fold so that they can share in the kingdom values proclaimed by Jesus Christ.

The Good News of salvation was brought to Africa through evangelizing communication. The preaching of the Good News on the continent occurred in phases: "The first centuries of Christianity saw the evangelization of Egypt and North Africa. A second phase, involving the parts of the continent south of the Sahara, took place in the fifteenth and sixteenth centuries. A third phase, marked by an extraordinary missionary effort, began in the nineteenth century" (*EA* §30).

Without adequate communication, the missionary enterprise would have come to naught. In the First Special Assembly for Africa of the Synod of Bishops, the participants noted that the evangelization of the continent was achieved through cooperation between the power of the Holy Spirit and the human agents to whom the message was entrusted (*EA* §21). These agents employed various means of communication to reach out to the people.

The means of communication used in the evangelization of Africa ranged from the traditional to the modern, from interpersonal to mediated communication. We shall examine these means briefly.

Oral Communication

The first means of communication is language, and the missionaries as agents of evangelization used oral communication to interact with indigenous communities. As missiologist Eugene Nida noted, the communication model applied by most Western missionaries was essentially linear.[15] In this source–message–receptor model of communication, the source and content of the message were more important than the receivers of the message. A diagrammatic adaptation of the linear process of evangelizing communication is presented below.

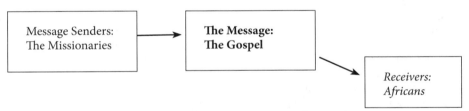

Figure 1: Diagram of the Linear Process of Evangelizing Communication

Nida's criticism of this linear process as being insensitive to the cultural context of the communication exchange is in line with shifts in theoretical discussions generally regarding the relationship between a sender and a receiver in the communication process. Denis McQuail noted the movement from the transmission or linear model to the expressive or ritual models to the publicity and reception models.[16] The ritual and reception models emphasize the convergence of the sender and receiver in a mutual interaction leading to the construction of meaning. These models synchronize with the African model of communication: according to Andrew Moemeka, the philosophical root of African communication is communalism, born out of the traditional communal culture that underlies

---

15. Nida, *Message and Mission*.
16. McQuail, *McQuail's Mass Communication Theory*, 69–75.

the way of life of Africans.[17] Thus, the application of the linear model in communicating the gospel message in Africa in the early period of evangelization was fraught with problems.

Language Barriers to Oral Communication of the Gospel

Language is the central vehicle of oral communication, and participants in oral communication must share the same linguistic code in order to share a common meaning. The early missionaries to Africa were from various parts of the world, and when they arrived in Africa they had to contend with over fifteen hundred native languages found on the continent. Linguists have grouped the different African languages into four distinct families: (1) Niger–Congo; (2) Afroasiatic; (3) Nilo–Saharan; and (4) Khoisan.

The African Language Program at Harvard University presents a brief on these language families:

> Niger–Congo, with approximately 1,350–1,650 languages is the largest of the four; it is also the largest language family in the world. The Niger–Congo languages inhabit Western, Central, Eastern and Southern Africa. The most widely spoken languages of Africa, Swahili (100 million), Hausa (38 million), Yoruba (20 million), Amharic (20 million), Igbo (21 million), and Fula (13 million) all belong to the Niger–Congo family. The next largest family is Afroasiatic with about 200–300 member languages in Africa. The Afroasiatic languages in Africa are found mainly in the Northern regions of Africa, including: northern Nigeria, southern Niger, Somalia, and in the North African countries of Morocco, Algeria, Tunisia, etc. Next in size is the Nilo–Saharan family with about 80 languages. These occupy Eastern Africa and the North Eastern region of Africa, namely: Uganda, Tanzania, Kenya, Chad, the Sudan, etc. Last but not least is the Khoisan family with between 40–70 members. Believed to be the oldest of the four language families, it is the smallest of the four and is found mainly in Southern Africa.[18]

In order to communicate with Africans, the foreign missionaries had to make use of interpreters, mostly liberated ex-slaves. Simultaneous interpretation of oral communication must deal with the issue of fidelity, that is, the closeness of the interpretation to the original speech. Nida notes the linguistic problems confronting language interpretation and translation:

> The major difficulties in communication result largely from the fact that we take communication for granted. Whenever we hear someone speak, we tend to assume that what is meant is precisely what we think they mean, even in our mother tongue, and our seemingly most transparent idioms are rarely translatable into other languages. In a number of languages of Central Africa, the phrase "beat his breast" (used in speaking of the Publican who went into the temple to pray and in great contrition of heart, "beat his breast," Lk. 18:13) can be grossly misunderstood if translated literally and without explanation. To these people, it would mean, "to congratulate oneself" equivalent to our "patting oneself on the back." In that part of the world, a person who is truly repentant will "beat his head," not "beat his breast."[19]

We begin to appreciate the enormity of the task of the missionary interpreters; there were certainly blunders, but, by and large, the outcome of these missionary activities depended as much on the missionaries as their interpreters. The missionary interpreters were merely the linguistic bridges between the senders of the message and its receivers.

Cultural Barriers to Oral Communication of the Gospel

Every communicative activity takes place within a cultural milieu. Communicators and receivers are

---

17. See the following works by Moemeka: "Communalism as a Fundamental Dimension of Culture; "Interpersonal Communication in Communalistic Societies in Africa"; and "Communication in African Culture."
18. The African Language Program at Harvard, "Introduction to African Languages."
19. Nida, *Message and Mission*, 65.

determined in their communicative acts by their cultures and contexts. The more the actors recognize this situation and try to converge toward a common understanding, the more effective they are going to be. If both participate in the same contexts, settings, and frames of reference they will be more effective.

Because the early missionaries were foreigners to Africa, it is clear that they were engaged in some form of intercultural communication, or rather cross-cultural communication. Eilers makes a subtle distinction between intercultural and cross-cultural communication: "Whereas intercultural communication refers to communication partners from different cultures in a partnership way and with partners being at the same level, cross-cultural communication tries to go across cultural borders in a more "selling" approach. The cross-cultural communication wants to convince and change the participant from the other culture, whereas intercultural communication really wants to share."[20]

Charles H. Kraft identified two communicative approaches that arise when actors involved in a communicative activity come from different cultural backgrounds. The first is the "extractionist" approach, in which the communicator demands that his frame of reference provides the communicational categories and the receiver has to convert to the communicator's system. The extractionist approach is founded on the exaggerated self-concept of the communicator, that is, the self-image of being superior, better than others, and so on. The second is the "identificational" approach, in which the communicator accepts the receiver's frame of reference. In identifying with the receiver, the communicator is faced with two possibilities: he can either accept a stereotypical approach, demanding respect and making the receiver dependent on him, or he might reject this stereotype and employ what Kraft calls the "discovery principle." In the discovery mode, the communicator's information and insight come from the receiver's discovery of the substance and value of the message, rather than from the simple transmission of a "prefabricated" message from communicator to receiver. The discovery principle allows the receiver to truly be taken seriously.[21]

Cultural clashes are inevitable when parties to the communicative exchange are blinded by a stereotypical representation of the other party. Teri Kwal Gamble and Michael Gamble present a useful insight into this kind of exchange:

> When we stereotype people, we simply judge them on the basis of what we know about the category to which we feel they belong. The stereotypes we hold affect how we process stimuli around us. For one thing, while we remember more favorable information about in-groups, we retain more unfavorable information about out-groups. Our stereotypes also cause us to disregard any differences individuals may have that set them apart from the stereotyped group. When we stereotype, instead of responding to the communication or cues of individuals, we create expectations, assume they are valid, and behave as if they had occurred. When we stereotype, we judge persons on the basis of what we believe regarding the group in which we have placed them. Stereotyping leads us to oversimplify, overgeneralize, and grossly exaggerate what we observe. Stereotyping leads to prejudices.[22]

There is no doubt that the communicative interactions between the early missionaries and the indigenous Africans were challenged by stereotypical perceptions on both sides. The success of these early missionary activities, as attested to in *Ecclesia in Africa* (§35), shows that both the missionaries and the indigenous people managed to surmount the barriers of language and cultural differences. But this success was dependent to a large extent on the fact that, as Jim Harries highlighted, Western languages and thought patterns were privileged over local languages and cultural values.[23] Noting

---

20. Eilers, *Communicating between Cultures*, 32.
21. Kraft, *Christianity in Culture*, 147.
22. Gamble and Gamble, *Communication Works*, 95.
23. Harries, *Communication in Mission and Development*.

that this is not ideal, Harries argued that missionary and development projects better address current realities when the use of local languages is prioritized.

The following pertinent questions can be formulated about oral communication of the faith:

1. In the proclamation of the Good News, do agents of evangelization endeavor to enter into the host culture and understand its cultural codes and values?
2. Are the perceptions of agents of evangelization about the subjects of their evangelization marred by cultural stereotypes?
3. How faithful are the interpretation and translation of the gospel message?
4. Do the bearers of the message endeavor to acquire the linguistic codes of their host communities in order to enter into a seamless process of oral communication?

An examination of these questions is germane to every epoch of evangelization and will continue to be for as long as human beings interact and communicate orally and across cultures.

Nonverbal Communication

In addition to oral communication, human communication also involves nonverbal or message-conveying activities. There are human actions, artifacts, and environmental objects that carry communicative meaning within a given culture. These activities "speak" meaning in a nonverbal manner to people in the cultural milieu. Nonverbal communication includes sign language, action language, and object language.

These three languages are of interest in the communication of the faith in Africa. The Catholic Church expresses her belief system in symbolic forms. Most of the rites, rituals, and artifacts of the church are encoded with symbolic meaning. Gestures like the sign of the cross, the color of the liturgical vestments worn by the ministers, the architecture of churches, and other things, are rich in symbolism and communicate religious meaning. The sacraments of the church are aptly defined as outward signs of inward grace, and the visible activities performed by the believers in carrying out these sacraments are signs representing a deeper spiritual meaning.

In nonverbal as in verbal communication, the parties to the communication process must be sufficiently grounded in the culture so that the recipients of the communications are able to understand the codes behind the external manifestations. An important part of cultural socialization is the teaching and understanding of these nonverbal codes embedded in appearances, postures, motions, and bodily expressions. One of the difficulties that still persists in the Catholic Church in Africa is that many members may not have a deep understanding of the symbolic actions and gestures of the church.

Cultural artifacts are also channels of nonverbal communication. As Eilers noted, "The whole of material culture, in fact, is a carrier of signs and meanings and thus communicates non-verbally."[24] The erection of physical church buildings, schools, hospitals, and other social amenities by the missionaries communicated to the native Africans the concern of the carriers of the gospel for their well-being, and the social institutions and structures erected during the missionary era were also eloquent in disseminating the Good News as the teaching of the Bible and other catechetical instruction. The point must be strongly made that the oral proclamation of the Good News should be accompanied by concrete gestures through which the recipients of the message see symbols of love, care, and concern, and ultimately see the hand of God working in their lives.

The manifestation of gestures of Christian love and solidarity are powerful ways of letting unconverted people enter into the warm embrace of the Christian family. Pope Benedict XVI, reflecting the views of the Synod of Bishops on the Word of God in the Life of the Church, noted how pastoral care toward the suffering poor, migrants, and the environment are unspoken testimonies of the word of God in the midst of the people:

---

24. Eilers, *Communicating between Cultures*, 66.

Indeed, "the poor are the first ones entitled to hear the proclamation of the Gospel; they need not only bread, but also words of life." The diaconia of charity, which must never be lacking in our churches, should always be bound to the proclamation of the word and the celebration of the sacred mysteries.

Engagement with the world, as demanded by God's word, makes us look with new eyes at the entire created cosmos, which contains traces of that word through whom all things were made (cf. *Jn* 1:2). As men and women who believe in and proclaim the Gospel, we have a responsibility towards creation.... [A]ccepting the word of God, attested to by Scripture and by the Church's living Tradition, gives rise to a new way of seeing things, promotes an authentic ecology which has its deepest roots in the obedience of faith . . . [and] develops a renewed theological sensitivity to the goodness of all things, which are created in Christ.[25]

Nonverbal communication also includes sound and paralanguage: drums can be used for coded information and messages and the qualities of voices and modes of vocalization can be conveyors of nonverbal meaning.

Silence is also an important and powerful aspect of nonverbal communication.[26] The Catholic Church privileges moments of silent reflection in her spiritual life. In silence, one is able to listen to the promptings of the Holy Spirit. Elochukwu Uzukwu champions the cause for the "listening Church in Africa."[27] In fact, the Christian faithful are not only those who proclaim the faith but also those who listen to it. Docility and obedience to the Holy Spirit require the attentiveness of our ears. It is no wonder that the word "obedience" comes from the Latin word *ab-audire* (from listening). In order to communicate well, we must be good listeners.

In *Verbum Domini,* his post-synodal apostolic exhortation on the Word of God, Pope Benedict XVI noted the importance of silence:

A good number of Synod Fathers insisted on the importance of silence in relation to the word of God and its reception in the lives of the faithful. The word, in fact, can only be spoken and heard in silence, outward and inward.... Rediscovering the centrality of God's word in the life of the Church also means rediscovering a sense of recollection and inner repose.... Only in silence can the word of God find a home in us, as it did in Mary, woman of the word and, inseparably, woman of silence. Our liturgies must facilitate this attitude of authentic listening: *Verbo crescente, verba deficiunt.* ("When the Word of God grows, words fall short": §66)

Mediated Communication

Use of the many means of communication available in the present-day world is indispensable in the proclamation of the gospel message. In mediated communication, the instruments of human ingenuity are appropriated as vehicles for spreading the Good News.

Traditional Communication

The first form of mediated communication is the traditional means used in particular cultures. These might include storytelling, songs, drama, drums and other signaling instruments, dance, rituals, cults, or myths. These traditional means of communication were somehow neglected during the early period in which the Catholic faith was communicated in Africa. The Christian message was not adequately crafted using these existing cultural signaling systems. This owed largely to the missionaries' misunderstanding of African culture as idolatrous. Thus, many elements of traditional communication that could have served as viable vehicles for communicating the faith were neglected.

Print, Broadcast, and Social Media

The early missionaries made extensive use of print media, including making the Bible and the litur-

---

25. Pope Benedict XVI, post-synodal apostolic exhortation *Verbum Domini* §§107–108.
26. Eilers, *Communicating between Cultures,* 68.
27. Uzukwu, *Listening Church;* see also Ihejirika, *E-priest.*

gical documents of the church available to the people. The book of the catechism was a simplified form of the major doctrines of the church and was widely used by the missionaries. The use of printed materials was very beneficial for the spread of the Catholic faith, not only in making religious documents available to many people, but because it was appropriate to the nature of the church.

Print media fits well with the institutional or hierarchical model of the church, one of the models of the church articulated by Avery Dulles.[28] This model is concerned with maintaining the integrity of the church's teaching authority and the obligatory nature of adherence to the official doctrines of the church. For the church to maintain her corporate existence in the world, there must be a unified set of doctrines and morals applicable to every believer in every part of the world. The print media is best suited to achieve this unity because it ensures that the same material is distributed from reader to reader. The content of books can be vetted for doctrinal errors or for teachings that could be harmful to faith and morals. Ecclesiastical authorities provide seals of authenticity for print materials through granting *imprimi potest*, when they are assured that the material contains *nihil obstat*, that is, nothing that is against the Catholic faith. All of this explains the early attachment of the church to the print media.

The broadcast media—radio, television, and film—were also used as tools for evangelization in the missionary period, though not as widely as print media. This may be connected with early suspicions the church had toward electronic media, especially film. Pope Pius XI manifested this suspicion in his encyclical letter *Vigilanti Cura*:

> Everyone knows what damage is done to the soul by bad motion pictures. They are occasions of sin; they seduce young people along the ways of evil by glorifying the passions, they show life under a false light, they cloud ideals, they destroy pure love, respect for marriage, affection for the family. They are capable also of creating prejudices among individuals and misunderstandings among nations, among social classes, among entire races. (§24)

Subsequently, Pope Pius XII issued the following cautions about electronic media in his encyclical *Miranda Prorsus*:

> From the time when these arts (motion picture, radio and television) came into use, the Church welcomed them, not only with great joy but also with a motherly care and watchfulness, having in mind to protect her children from every danger as they set out on this new path of progress. This watchful care springs from the mission she received from the Divine Savior Himself; for, as is clear to all, these new forms of art exercise very great influence on the manner of thinking and acting of individuals and of every group of men. (§§4–5).

Despite these earlier suspicions, since Vatican II the church has in various documents recognized the mass media as an excellent tool of evangelization.[29] In line with his predecessors, Pope Benedict XVI stated in the post-synodal apostolic exhortation *Africae Munus*: "The Church needs to be increasingly present in the media so as to make them not only a tool for the spread of the Gospel but also for educating the African peoples to reconciliation in truth, and the promotion of justice and peace" (§145).

Africa is regarded as the "radio continent" because of the pervasive use of the medium there, and the African church has made maximum use of it for evangelization. In his study of community radio used for the purposes of development, Patrick Alumuku discovered that most of the viable community radio stations on the continent are managed by Catholic dioceses or faith-based organizations.[30] The following table presents a good picture of Catholic involvement in radio in Africa.

---

28. Dulles, *Models of the Church*.
29. See *Inter Mirifica*; *Communio et Progressio*; *Evangelii Nuntiandi*; *Redemptoris Missio*; *Ecclesia in Africa*; and *Africae Munus*.
30. Alumuku, *Community Radio for Development in Africa*, 132–37.

East Africa		Central Africa		Southern Africa		West Africa	
Country	No. of Radio Stations	Country	No. of Radio Stations	Country	No. of Radio Stations	Country	No. of Radio Stations
Kenya	22	Burundi	1	Angola	2	Benin	2
Madagascar	2	Cameroon	11	Lesotho	1	Burkina Faso	14
South Sudan	11	Central African Republic	5	Malawi	5	Cape Verde	1
Tanzania	13	Republic of the Congo	3	Mozambique	10	Ivory Coast	9
Uganda	9	Gabon	2	Namibia	1	Ghana	4
		Democratic Republic of the Congo	37	South Africa	1	Guinea Bissau	1
		Rwanda	1	Zambia	10	Liberia	2
		Chad	8			Mali	5
						Reunion	1
						Sao Tome and Principe	1
						Senegal	1
						Sierra Leone	2
						Togo	9
TOTAL	57		68		30		52

Table 1: Number of Radio Stations Operated by the Catholic Church in Africa (by country)[31]

Nigeria is one of the few countries in Africa without a vibrant community radio industry. This is because of government policies barring religious bodies from ownership of broadcast media channels. To overcome this restriction, efforts are being made by the church in Nigeria to enter into partnerships with individuals to make inroads into the industry. Sapentia Radio in Onitsha in southeastern Nigeria is a very good example of such a partnership.

Television is not as widely used by the Catholic Church as radio. In his study of the role of televangelism in the conversion of Catholics to the Pentecostal churches in Nigeria, Ihejirika noted that the Catholic Church, like most of the mainline Christian denominations, has been slow to invest in television ministry for evangelization.[32]

The Catholic Church's attitude toward the electronic media has changed remarkably with the advent of the internet and the new world of social

---

31. Source: The Catholic Media Council (CAMECO). According to the CAMECO database, there are 207 Catholic radio stations in Africa. This figure may be low as the database may have captured only stations that received CAMECO's grants and sponsorships. The stations include Radio Ecclesia in Luanda, Angola; Radio Immaculée Conception in Alada, Republic of Benin; Radio Notre Dame de la Réconciliation in Koudougou, Burkina Faso; Radio Vox Ecclesiae in Bafoussam, Cameroon; Radio Communautaire pour le Développement de la Mvila in Ebolowa, Congo; Radio Progress in Ghana; Icengelo Radio in Zambia; Radio Wa (Our Radio) in Lira, northern Uganda; Veritas Radio in Johannesburg, South Africa; Radio Waumini in Nairobi, Kenya; Radio Espoir in Abidjan, Ivory Coast; Radio for Peace and Local Development in Gbangar, Liberia; and Bakitha Radio in Juba, South Sudan.

32. Ihejirika, *From Catholicism to Pentecostalism*, 277.

media. Unlike the slow and suspicious reception given by the church at the advent of electronic communication technologies, the church has been quick to incorporate the new media into its evangelizing mission everywhere, including in Africa.

This positive appraisal of the new media is evident in church documents, including papal pronouncements. Two examples will illustrate this: first, the Pontifical Council for Social Communication writes that

> it is important, (too), that people at all levels of the Church use the Internet creatively to meet their responsibilities and help fulfil the Church's mission. Hanging back timidly from fear of technology or for some other reason is not acceptable, in view of the very many positive possibilities of the Internet. Methods of facilitating communication and dialogue among her own members can strengthen the bonds of unity between them.[33]

Second, Pope John Paul II stated that "for the Church, the new world of cyberspace is a summons to the great adventure of using its potential to proclaim the Gospel message. This challenge is at the heart of what it means at the beginning of the millennium to follow the Lord's command to 'put out into the deep': *Duc in altum*! (Lk. 5:4)."[34]

The new media have been appropriated by the church in Africa in her evangelizing mission, especially toward the youth, known as the "e-generation" or "digital natives." Many Catholic dioceses and organizations run internet centers, even in rural areas, to facilitate the access of young people to the internet. C. Helland earlier distinguished between "online religion" and "religion online."[35] Online religion is the use of internet facilities to directly promote a particular religion, while religion online is the phenomenon of internet platforms becoming the locus of religious activities. Ihejirika categorized the internet activities of the Catholic Church as "in-line" religion, which he defined as "the application of the new information and communication technologies by a religious group for the benefit of other people, especially the marginal groups in society, which indirectly boosts the image of the group, and sustains the religious consciousness of the users."[36]

Pastoral Communication

Through evangelizing communication, the Catholic faith has been preached to and received by many people in Africa. After Africans accept the teachings of and embrace the faith, they are incorporated into the Catholic family, and, at that point, the communicative approach of the church takes a different direction. The concern is no longer about receiving the Good News, but living it. In sub-Saharan Africa, the era of evangelizing communication (i.e., primary evangelization) could be said to have ended in 1969, the year Pope Paul VI made his historic visit to the continent to canonize the young martyrs of Uganda and also address the Inaugural Assembly of the Symposium of Episcopal Conferences of Africa and Madagascar (SECAM). It was during this visit that the pope told the African church that she had come of age and should now become missionaries to herself. The approach of this new phase becomes one of pastoral communication.

Eilers notes that the concern of pastoral communication is the life and needs of individuals and communities in their present situations and that pastoral communication is like pastoral theology, or the theology of how the Good Shepherd treats his flock.[37] The activities of pastoral communication can be discerned in the church's efforts to consolidate the faith received through evangelizing communication and in actions that tackle the pastoral needs of both the universal church and the local church. The church's activities of pastoral communication to consolidate the faith include

---

33. Pontifical Council for Social Communication, *Church and Internet* §10.
34. John Paul II, "Internet: A New Forum for Proclaiming the Gospel," §2.
35. Helland, "Online-Religion/Religion-Online and Virtual Communitas."
36. Ihejirika, "'In-Line Religion,'" 92.
37. Eilers, *Communicating in Ministry and Mission*, 94.

appropriate celebration of the liturgy, preaching, and the professional management of its corporate image. The African synods have identified two particular pastoral needs of the African church: building the church as the family of God (First Synod for Africa); and engaging the larger African society to foster a culture of justice and peace (Second Synod for Africa). These pastoral concerns come with certain pastoral implications for communication, which we will now examine briefly.

Liturgical Communication

Celebrations of the church's liturgies are great moments of communication. These celebrations align with what James Carey calls the ritual model of communication.[38] Whereas evangelizing communication can be seen in the light of the linear or transportation model of communication, the ritual model is not about passing information, but rather about maintaining the fabric of society. In the ritual model, the actors in the communicative process share, participate, associate, create fellowship, and enjoy their common convictions. The ritual model of communication is all about celebrating the core values of the culture.

The manner and place of liturgical celebrations have much to communicate to the participants. With the liturgical changes introduced by the Second Vatican Council, Africans have been emboldened to inculturate the liturgy into African ways of life. In light of inculturation theology—that is, the theological exercise that seeks to incorporate positive elements of indigenous culture into the life of the church—liturgical celebrations have become participatory and celebrative. The use of local languages and traditional musical instruments and songs have contributed significantly toward making liturgies into not just perfunctory exercises but rather events truly commemorating the faith.

Although the celebrative nature of the liturgy in Africa is a major reason for the active participation of the faithful, care must be taken to ensure that undue exaggeration does not set in and that people do not appreciate the liturgy merely for its celebrative satisfactions while forgetting its spiritual dimension. The liturgy and other sacraments must continue to be outward manifestations of inward grace. Another liturgical area that needs to be under constant surveillance is the healing ministry engaged in by some priests. Although these ministries communicate divine presence and concern for the faithful, there exist possibilities of abuse and infiltration by charlatans. The church's standing tradition of certifying exorcists and spiritual healers must always be enforced.

Another aspect of the liturgy that communicates cultural values is church architecture. The early European missionaries brought with them the architectural designs predominant in their native countries. Christian architecture in Africa was thus the direct heir to European architectural practices. Christianity favored a merging of the longitudinal and centripetal plans, which served the public nature of the Mass and complemented the concept of Christ as king. While the West maintained its preference for the pure basilica design, the East favored the domical basilica design. Most of the early churches in Africa were either longitudinal or cruciform.

Departing from the traditional Gothic cruciform churches and rectangular forms with high rising spires reminiscent of the missionary era, today new churches in many parts of Africa are constructed in an octagonal form, making the interior almost spherical. The following churches are notable examples of this modern African church architecture: the Shrine of Mary Help of Christians in Nairobi, Kenya; the Basilica of the Uganda Martyrs in Namugongo, Uganda; the Igreja Santana in Caxito, Angola; the Don Bosco Catholic Church in Nairobi, Kenya; the Assumpta Cathedral in Owerri, Nigeria; St. Leo's Catholic Church in Ikeja, Nigeria; Mater Ecclesiae Cathedral in Ahiara, Nigeria; and the new St. Gabriel's Chaplaincy Church at the Catholic Secretariat in Abuja, Nigeria. This architectural design reflects the communalistic cultures of Africa, in which the seating for family gatherings and other communal meetings is designed so as to enable every participant to see the faces of others. This new African church architecture communicates the church as a symbol of the family of God.[39]

---

38. Carey, *Communication as Culture*.
39. For an elaboration of the liturgical theology of church architecture, see Chibuko, *Tips on Church Building*.

Preaching

The continuous proclamation of the Good News is necessary for the continued existence of the church. Bishops, priests, deacons, and other pastoral agents are called to preach the gospel in and out of season. Even if these agents testify to the Christian life, the mode in which the message of the gospel is delivered can enhance or mar its reception by the people; thus, the quality of the preaching is in some ways just as important as the content of the testimony. Homiletics that seeks to prepare pastoral agents for accomplishing the task of preaching is a communication-related activity. Preachers of the gospel are expected to be skilled in the act of public speaking.

In *Evangelii Nuntiandi*, Pope Paul VI exhorted the clergy that homilies, especially in the Sunday liturgy, should be "simple, clear, direct, well-adapted, profoundly dependent on Gospel teaching and faithful to the Magisterium, animated by a balanced apostolic ardour . . . full of hope, fostering belief and productive of peace and unity" (§45). The Synod of Bishops on the Word of God in the Life of the Church provided counsel for the preacher that follows appropriate counsel for any public communicator. Drawing insight from the synod, Eilers outlined the following instructions useful for preachers communicating the Word:

1. They should keep the preaching short, focusing on one message, instead of delivering a long lecture on difficult theological problems.
2. Because the preacher is a servant of the Word, he should not behave like a star. This means that he should not exaggerate or overdo his gestures, his style of presentation, or his way of speaking.
3. The preacher should use every available means to make the preaching lively and relevant to the needs and expectations of the people. This might include slides, posters, music, drama, and even films.
4. It is indispensable that the preacher know his audience. This knowledge enables the preacher to select appropriate content, forms, and means of communication.[40]

The need for preachers to be adequately trained is very urgent in Africa—some Catholic preachers have abandoned distinctively Catholic modes of preaching and instead adopted the modes of Pentecostal preaching.

Church communicators must speak with what Pope Francis refers to as the "grammar of simplicity." He explains, "At times we lose people because they don't understand what we are saying, because we have forgotten the language of simplicity and import an intellectualism foreign to our people. Without the grammar of simplicity, the Church loses the very conditions which make it possible 'to fish' for God in the deep waters of his Mystery."[41] Failure to apply the grammar of simplicity may explain why documents from the church's hierarchy, such as pastoral letters from bishops, often do not form part of the lived discussions of the faithful at the grassroots. In his apostolic exhortation *Evangelii Gaudium*, Pope Francis further encourages preachers to ensure that their homilies are rooted in the lives and cultures of the people:

> Christian preaching thus finds in the heart of people and their culture a source of living water, which helps the preacher to know what must be said and how to say it. Just as all of us like to be spoken to in our mother tongue, so too in the faith we like to be spoken to in our "mother culture," our native language (cf. *2 Macc* 7:21, 27), and our heart is better disposed to listen. This language is a kind of music which inspires encouragement, strength and enthusiasm. (§139)

Finally, Pope Francis notes that the close proximity of the preacher to the people, the warmth of his tone of voice, the unpretentiousness of his manner of speaking, and the joy of his gestures are indispensable elements in effective homilies. He calls this disposition "the maternal and ecclesial spirit of homiletics." He notes that "even if the homily at times may be somewhat tedious, if this maternal and ecclesial spirit is present, it will

---

40. Drawn and paraphrased from Eilers, *Communicating in Ministry and Mission*.
41. Pope Francis, "Meeting with the Bishops of Brazil," §3.

always bear fruit, just as the tedious counsels of a mother bear fruit, in due time, in the hearts of her children" (*Evangelii Gaudium* §140).

Professional Management of the Church's Corporate Image

The appropriate management of the church's corporate image is an important pastoral concern at both the local and global level. The promotion of the church's image should be an ongoing task of pastoral communication. The fact is that some people, both within and outside the church, conjure, propagate, and foster erroneous images of the church. Some non-Catholics see the church as a secret organization whose activities are shrouded in a cloak of secrecy.[42] Some of these misguided conceptions are the result of poor communication about the nature and activities of the church. This is the terrain of public relations.

Since the Second Vatican Council, the church has recognized the need for better public relations as an essential component of her pastoral life. Both *Communio et Progressio* (1971) and *Aetatis Novae* (1992), pastoral instructions from the Pontifical Council for Social Communication, highlighted this need. In *Aetatis Novae*, it is clearly stated that "public relations by the Church means active communication with the community through both secular and religious media. Involving readiness to communicate Gospel values and to publicize the ministries and programs of the Church, it requires that the Church do all in its power to ensure that its own true image reflects Christ" (§31; see also *Communio et Progressio* §174).

Eilers itemized the following practical implications of improving the public's perceptions of the church:

1. The need to give proper and timely information, including sufficient background information, explanations, and interpretations concerning the church and the events it sponsors.
2. The need to have proper knowledge of the audiences and contexts of communication and to adjust the communication in such a way as to make it comprehensible to the audience.
3. The need to select the proper means of communicating information about the church to specific audiences in specific environments.[43]

Building the African Church as the Family of God, Fostering Justice and Peace

The two Special Assemblies for Africa of the Synod of Bishops highlighted what should be considered the most urgent pastoral needs of the church on the African continent.

The first need as articulated by the First Synod is building the church as the family of God, a brotherhood and sisterhood that supersedes ethnic and tribal cleavages. The image of the church as God's family emphasizes care for others, solidarity, warmth in human relationships, acceptance, dialogue, and trust. The new evangelization will thus aim at building up the church as family, avoiding all ethnocentrism and excessive particularism, trying instead to encourage reconciliation and true communion between different ethnic groups, favoring solidarity and the sharing of personnel and resources among the different churches (*EA* §63).

To achieve the synod's goals, *Ecclesia in Africa* (1995) exhorted the African church to intensify communication *ad intra* the church, that is, the communication that goes on among the members or other stakeholders of a given church group or organization. This type of communication may be interpersonal, involving only two people at a given time, using face-to-face and nonverbal communication such as conversation, listening, a particular way of dressing, and so on. It may also be a form of group communication, involving two or more people representing different entities. The people in these conversations might pursue shared goals through interaction characterized by dialogue, participation, mutual understanding, and shared meaning and experiences. Internal church communication may thus be summed up as constituting reciprocal love and communion among all the members of the church.

The same communicative actions were invoked as being essential to addressing the second pastoral problem, which was highlighted by the Second Special Assembly. The synod was convened to exam-

---

42. See Shaw, *Nothing to Hide*.
43. Drawn and paraphrased from Eilers, *Communicating in Ministry and Mission*, 50.

ine how the church in Africa as family of God can serve as a positive force opening paths to reconciliation, justice, and peace on the continent. Genuine interpersonal communication among members of the church constitutes what Pope Benedict calls "spirituality of communion." The main elements of this spirituality are

> the ability to perceive the light of the mystery of the Trinity shining on the faces of brothers and sisters around us, to be attentive to our brothers and sisters in faith within the profound unity of the Mystical Body, and therefore as "those who are a part of me," in order to share their joys and sufferings, to sense their desires and attend to their needs, to offer them deep and genuine friendship; the ability as well to recognize all that is positive in the other so as to welcome it and prize it as a gift that God gives me through that person, in a way that transcends by far the individual concerned, who thus becomes a channel of divine graces; and finally, the ability "to 'make room' for our brothers and sisters, bearing 'each other's burdens'" (*Gal* 6:2) and resisting the selfish temptations which constantly beset us and provoke competition, careerism, distrust and jealousy. (*AM* §35)

Through genuine interpersonal communication, the church in Africa will be able to tackle the pastoral problems of ethnocentrism and fratricidal wars and conflicts, and can be a force for the promotion of reconciliation, justice, and peace on the continent.

Training and Formation of Pastoral Agents in Communication

The success of both evangelizing and pastoral communication is largely dependent on the preparedness of those engaged in them. With Vatican II, the church recognized the necessity of having experts at the helm of her communicative activities. This necessity is especially urgent for those training for the priesthood and religious life.

As was stated in *Communio et Progressio*, "If students for the priesthood and religious training wish to be part of modern life and also to be at all effective in their apostolate, they should know how the media work upon the fabric of society, and also the technique of their use" (§111). Later, the Congregation for Catholic Education in its *Guide for the Training of Future Priests Concerning the Instruments of Social Communication* noted the interface between the instruments of social communication and the ministerial priesthood.[44] The *Guide* recommended an integrated course of training in which those studying for the priesthood learn how to effectively use the mass media to help their vocations bear fruit. Alongside this theoretical training, practical experience in using the tools of communication is recommended.

The importance of training is also highlighted by both the African synods and SECAM. In *Ecclesia in Africa*, Pope John Paul II noted that "training in the use of the mass media is a necessity for the preacher of the Gospel" (§71). Before the synod, SECAM in its Plenary Assembly held in Lome, Togo, in July 1990, stated, "The importance of the media makes it necessary for communication studies to be part of seminary formation in all our major seminaries."[45] In this submission, the African bishop re-echoed the position of the Sacred Congregation for Catholic Education, which is that training in communication should be an integral part of the formation of future priests.[46] What comes out clearly in these ecclesiastical documents is that the integration of social communication into the formation curriculum of future priests and religious can no longer be regarded as an option. It is now an essential component of that formation.

The African church has been making remarkable efforts with the assistance of pontifical universities in Rome to train her priests, religious, and lay workers in social communication. Mention must

---

44. Congregation for Catholic Education, *Guide for the Training of Future Priests*.
45. Phillipart, *African Church in the Communications Era*, 147.
46. Congregation for Catholic Education, *Guide for the Training of Future Priests* §§9–13.

be made of the departments and centers of communication in the Pontifical Gregorian University, the Pontifical Salesian University, and the Pontifical University of the Holy Cross. Special mention needs to be made of the American Jesuit priest Rev. Prof. Robert A. White, SJ, the doyen of communications formation in the Catholic Church in Africa. Many priests, religious, and lay Catholics involved in communication both within and outside the continent owe their training to Professor White.

In addition to training provided in foreign universities and training centers, efforts have been made to offer similar training on the African continent. Many Catholic universities and institutes of higher learning have thriving departments of communication. Examples are the Catholic University of East Africa in Kenya; St. Augustine University in Mwanza, Tanzania; the Catholic Institute of West Africa in Port Harcourt, Nigeria; the Catholic University of Central Africa in Cameroon; and Tangaza College in Kenya. Other facilities in Africa that offer church-related communication training include the Catholic Media Service Centre, Kaduna, Nigeria; Bosco Eastern Africa Multimedia Services; and Ukweli Video Productions in Kenya.

Apart from these training centers, efforts have been made to integrate communication training into the curricula of seminaries and houses of formation. In the next section, we describe an example of this from Nigeria.

Pastoral Communication Curriculum for Major Seminaries and Houses of Religious Formation in Nigeria

This program of study, which I helped draft, was proposed for all the major seminaries and houses of formation in Nigeria and could be introduced into the curricula of other African countries. The program was intended only for students in seminaries and religious houses of formation because, unlike in the training available to laypeople, students in seminaries and religious houses do not have access to communication formation in the tertiary institutions of their countries. It is a good example of how communication can become part of the formation program for priests and female consecrated persons.

General Principles
It was agreed that:
1. Communication education should be an integral part of all stages of seminary formation.
2. Efforts should be made to ensure that the training should not merely concern mass media, but also interpersonal, group, and public communications.
3. At each stage, formal instruction should stress the role of communication and media in religious, moral, and spiritual development.
4. Effective communication skills should be acquired within intercultural contexts.
5. Efforts must be made to avoid taxing the already tight academic calendars of some major seminaries with communications courses that may not be necessary or practical.
6. Seminaries and houses of formation must find ways of continuously keeping abreast of new developments in the field if the knowledge they are imparting is to remain relevant.

Proposed Plan
The plan of formation in social communication is divided into two parts: (1) mandatory, not elective, courses within the academic curriculum of the seminary or formation house; and (2) the acquisition of practical experience outside the academic curriculum.

Some of the major seminaries in Nigeria require four years of courses in both philosophy and theology, while others require three years of philosophy and four of theology. Most of the religious formation houses for women provide for one or two years of postulancy and two years of novitiate. For the major seminaries, we propose eight communication courses adapted to the course plan of the institutions. Thus, before priestly ordination, seminarians will complete a total of seven or eight communication courses, and aspirants to the religious life will complete six.

Formation, Education, and Communication

Major Seminaries

A. Philosophy courses
 1. First-year philosophy
    a. Academic course: Introduction to Human Communication
    b. Extracurricular: Practice Exercises (students are to be encouraged to form dramatic and debating groups to practice how to speak well and interact with others).
 2. Second-year philosophy
    a. Academic course: Introduction to Mass Communication
    b. Extracurricular: Practice Exercises (students will have supervised visits at media institutions; they should also be encouraged to engage in such activities as photography and the creation of videos).
 3. Third-year philosophy
    a. Academic course: Mass Media and Society
    b. Extracurricular: Practice Exercises (students will engage in watching both foreign and African films critically and will evaluate their ethical content).
 4. Fourth-year philosophy
    a. Academic course: Media and Youth Cultures
    b. Extracurricular: Practice Exercises (the major practical exercise for this course will involve the youth apostolate in which seminarians are engaged during the period of their apostolic work).

B. Theological Studies
 1. First-year theology
    a. Academic course: Introduction to Pastoral Communication
    b. Extracurricular: Practice Exercises (students will cultivate the capacity to discern communication problems in their local churches; they will also attempt to form small groups in parishes where they do not already exist—this could be done during apostolic work).
 2. Second-year theology
    a. Academic course: Group Communication
    b. Extracurricular: Practice Exercises (students will engage in the formation of Basic Christian Communities during apostolic work).
 3. Third-year theology
    a. Academic course: Homiletics and Public Speaking
    b. Extracurricular: Practice Exercises (students should be required to practice speaking with microphones before their peers, and to practice setting up public address systems and learn the basic components of these systems).
 4. Fourth-year theology
    a. Academic course: Planning Pastoral Communication in a Local Church
    b. Extracurricular: Practice Exercises (students will be required to identify the model of the larger church operating in their local church, and use this as the foundation for designing a pastoral plan).

Houses of Religious Formation

In the stage of postulancy, the number of communications courses will vary according to the number of years of postulancy provided by each house of formation. We propose six and recommend that a minimum of four of these be taught during this period. The six courses proposed are: (1) Use of English and Major Local Languages in Communications; (2) Introduction to Computers; (3) Creative Writing; (4) Introduction to Human Communication; (5) Interpersonal Communication; and (6) Introduction to Mass Communication.

For the period of the novitiate, four courses are proposed, and it is recommended that a minimum of two be taught: (1) Introduction to Pastoral Communication; (2) Group Communication; (3) Media and Youth/Family Apostolate; and (4) Homiletics and Public Speaking.

Conclusion

Generally, when communication is mentioned in relation to the church's mission, people tend to think immediately about the instrumental application of mass media to the work of evangelization.

Throughout this historical-thematic presentation I have shown that communication goes beyond this narrow instrumental conception. Communication embraces every aspect of the church's life and in fact is like the hub of a wheel linking together the various aspects (spokes) of the church's life.

The historical proclamation of the gospel message in Africa was clearly the fruit of the communicative efforts of both missionaries and their indigenous collaborators. During the missionary period, various communicative processes were applied to ensure the successful evangelization of the continent. As we have noted, there is a need to sustain the earlier efforts of the missionaries. This requires the input of various entities within both the local and the universal church.

An ongoing articulation of pastoral plans for communication is indispensable for the church's mission in Africa. These plans should extend from the parish level to the diocesan, national, regional, and continental levels of the church. The articulation and implementation of such pastoral plans will ensure the vibrancy of the Catholic Church in Africa.

We recommend further research to learn how prepared the Catholic Church in Africa is to grapple with the rapid changes occurring in the field of digital media. We noted earlier that Africa is known as the "radio continent," but within the last decade, radio broadcasting has moved from analog to digital, and in some cases has migrated over to the internet.

Another area of further research would be an examination of the impact of digital media on religious authority. During the print era, it was relatively easy for ecclesial authorities to maintain some control over what information was presented to the faithful, but the digital revolution has opened up access to an ocean of information. This has created a need to examine how ecclesial power and authority can be and actually are exercised in the digital world.

Bibliography

African Language Program at Harvard. "Introduction to African Languages." http://alp.fas.harvard.edu/introduction-african-languages.

Alumuku, T. Patrick. *Community Radio for Development in Africa*. Nairobi, Kenya: Pauline Publications, 2005.

Asogwa, Chika, and Amana Damian. "Communication: A Challenge to the Nigerian Church." *Journal of Asian Culture and History* 4.1 (January 2012).

Babin, Pierre, and Angela Ann Zukowski. *The Gospel in Cyberspace: Nurturing Faith in the Internet Age*. Chicago: Loyola University Press, 2002.

Barber, Karin, ed. *Readings in African Popular Culture*. Oxford: James Currey; Bloomington: Indiana University Press, 1997.

Benedict XVI, Pope. *Africae Munus* [Post-synodal Apostolic Exhortation on the Church in Africa in Service of Reconciliation, Justice and Peace; November 19, 2011]. Vatican City: Libreria Editrice Vaticana, 2011. www.vatican.va.

———. "New Technologies, New Relationships: Promoting a Culture of Respect, Dialogue and Friendship" [Message for the 43rd World Communications Day]. Vatican City: Libreria Editrice Vaticana, 2009.

———. "The Priest and Pastoral Ministry in a Digital World: New Media at the Service of the Word" [Message for the 44th World Communications Day]. Vatican City: Libreria Editrice Vaticana, 2010.

———. *Verbum Domini* [Post-synodal Apostolic Exhortation on the Word of God in the Life and Mission of the Church; September 30, 2010]. Vatican City: Libreria Editrice Vaticana, 2010. www.vatican.va.

Carey, W. James. *Communication as Culture*. Boston: Unwin Hyman, 1988.

Catholic Media Council (CAMECO). www.cameco.org.

Chibuko, C. Patrick. *Tips on Church Building for Parish Priests, Architects and Stakeholders*. Enugu: Black Belt Konzult, 2011.

Congregation for Catholic Education. *A Guide for the Training of Future Priests Concerning the Instruments of Social Communication and the Ministerial Priesthood*. Vatican City: Libreria Editrice Vaticana, 1986.

Dulles, Avery. *Models of the Church*. New York: Image Books, 1974.

Eilers, Franz-Josef. *Church and Social Communication: Basic Documents*. Manila: Logos Publications, 1996.

———. *Communicating between Cultures*. Manila: Divine Word Publications, 1992.

———. *Communicating in Ministry and Mission: An Introduction to Pastoral and Evangelizing Communication*. Manila: Logos (Divine Word) Publications, 2009.

Faniran, Joseph. "Towards a Pastoral Plan for Social Communication in the Post-Synod African Church." In *Pastoral Planning for Social Communication*, edited by V. Sunderaj, 133–34. Montreal: Paulines, 1998.

Francis, Pope. "Apostolic Journey to Rio De Janeiro on the Occasion of the XXVIII World Youth Day: Meeting with the Bishops of Brazil." July 28, 2013.

———. *Evangelii Gaudium* [Apostolic Exhortation on the Proclamation of the Gospel in Today's World; November 24, 2013]. Vatican City: Libreria Editrice Vaticana, 2013. www.vatican.va.

Gamble, Teri Kwal, and Michael Gamble. *Communication Works*. 7th ed. Boston: McGraw Hill Custom Publishing, 2002.

Harries, Jim. *Communication in Mission and Development: Relating to the Church in Africa*. Eugene, OR: Wipf & Stock, 2013.

Helland, C. "Online-Religion/Religion-Online and Virtual Communitas." In *Religion on the Internet: Research Prospects and Promises*, edited by J. K. Hadden and D. E. Cowan, 205–23. New York: Elsevier Science Press, 2000.

Ihejirika, Walter C. "Current Trends in the Study of Media, Religion and Culture in Africa." *African Communication Research, A Journal of Information on Current Research in Africa*. 2.1 (2009): 1–60.

———. *The E-Priest: The Identity of the Catholic Priest in the Digital Age*. Owerri: EduEdy Publications, 2011.

———. *From Catholicism to Pentecostalism: Role of Nigerian Televangelists in Religious Conversion*. Port Harcourt: University of Port Harcourt Press, 2006.

———. "'In-Line Religion': Innovative Pastoral Applications of the New Information and Communication Technologies (NICTS) by the Catholic Church in Nigeria." *Politics and Religion Journal* 2 (2008): 79–98.

Ihejirika, Walter C., and Christy U. Omego. *Research Methods in Linguistics and Communication Studies*. 3rd impression. Port Harcourt: University of Port Harcourt Press, 2014.

Ilo, Stan Chu. "Methods and Models of African Theology." In *Theological Reimagination: Conversations on Church, Religion, and Society in Africa*, edited by Agbonkhianmeghe E. Orobator. Nairobi: Paulines Publications Africa, 2014.

Jesen, B. Klaus, ed. *A Handbook of Media and Communication Research: Qualitative and Quantitative Methodologies*. London: Routledge, 2002.

John Paul II, Pope. *Ecclesia in Africa* [Post-synodal Apostolic Exhortation on the Church in Africa and Its Evangelizing Mission towards the Year 2000; September 14, 1995]. Vatican City: Libreria Editrice Vaticana, 1995. www.vatican.va.

———. "Internet: A New Forum for Proclaiming the Gospel" [Message for the 36th World Communication Day, 2002].

Kraemer, Hendrik. *The Communication of the Christian Faith*. Philadelphia: Westminster, 1956.

Kraft, Charles H. *Christianity in Culture: A Study in Dynamic Biblical Theologizing in Cross Cultural Perspective*. Maryknoll, NY: Orbis Books, 1979.

Krippendorff, Klaus, and A. Mary Bock. *The Content Analysis Reader*. London: SAGE, 2009.

Löblich, M., and S. Averbeck-Lietz. "The Transnational Flow of Ideas and *Histoire croisée* with Attention to the Case of France and Germany." In *The International History of Communications Study*, edited by P. Simonson and D. W. Park, 25–46. New York: Routledge, 2016.

Löblich, M., and A. M. Scheu. "Writing the History of Communication Studies: A Sociology of Science Approach." *Communication Theory* 21.1 (2011): 1–22.

Lonergan, Bernard. *Method in Theology*. London: Darton, Longman & Todd, 1971.

Magesa, Laurenti. *Anatomy of Inculturation: Transforming the Church in Africa*. Nairobi: Paulines Publications Africa, 2004.

Massonga, Olga, FSP. "Evangelization and Mass Media: Apostles Communicating without Boundaries in the Footsteps of Paul and Albrione."

Paper presented at the International Missionary Conference, Nairobi, Kenya, May 12, 2015. http://paulinesafrica.org/international-missionary-conference-nairobi-may-2015.

Mayhead, Molly A. "Historical Analysis." In *The SAGE Encyclopedia of Communication Research Methods*, edited by Mike Allen. London: Sage, 2017.

McGarry, Cecil, and Patrick Ryan, eds. *Inculturating the Church in Africa: Theological and Practical Perspectives*. Nairobi: Paulines Publications Africa, 2001.

McQuail, Denis. *McQuail's Mass Communication Theory*. 6th ed. Los Angeles: Sage, 2011.

Moemeka. Andrew. "Communalism as a Fundamental Dimension of Culture." *Journal of Communication* 48.4 (Autumn 1998): 118–41.

———. "Communication in African Culture: A Sociological Analysis." In *Communication and Culture: African Perspectives*, edited by S. T. Kwame Boafo. Nairobi, Kenya: WACC-African Region, 1989.

———. "Interpersonal Communication in Communalistic Societies in Africa." In *Communication in Personal Relationships across Cultures*, edited by W. B. Gudykunst, S. Ting-Toomey, and T. Mishida. Thousand Oaks, CA: Sage, 1996.

Myers, Mary. "Community Radio and Development: Issues and Examples from Francophone West Africa." In *African Broadcast Cultures: Radio in Transition*, edited by Richard Fardon and Graham Furniss. London: James Currey, 2000.

Nida, Eugene. *Message and Mission: The Communication of the Christian Faith*. Pasadena, CA: William Carey Library, 1960.

Paul VI, Pope. *Evangelii Nuntiandi* [Apostolic Exhortation on the Theme of Catholic Evangelization; December 8, 1975]. Vatican City: Libreria Editrice Vaticana, 1975. www.vatican.va.

Phillipart, Michel, ed. *The African Church in the Communications Era*. Nairobi: St. Pauls Publications Africa, 1992.

Pius XI, Pope. *Vigilanti Cura* [Encyclical on Motion Pictures; June 29, 1936]. Vatican City: Libreria Editrice Vaticana, 1936. www.vatican.va.

Pius XII, Pope. *Miranda Prorsus* [Encyclical on Motion Picture, Radio and Television; September 8, 1957]. Vatican City: Libreria Editrice Vaticana, 1957. www.vatican.va.

Pontifical Council for Social Communications. *Aetatis Novae* [Pastoral Instruction on Social Communications]. Vatican City: Libreria Editrice Vaticana, 1992.

———. *The Church and Internet*. Vatican City: Libreria Editrice Vaticana, 2002.

———. *Communio et Progressio* [Pastoral Instruction on Social Communications]. Vatican City: Libreria Editrice Vaticana, 1971.

Rantanen, Terhi. "A 'Crisscrossing' Historical Analysis of Four Theories of the Press." *International Journal of Communication* 11 (2017): 3454–75.

Shaw, Russel. *Nothing to Hide: Secrecy, Communication and Communion in the Catholic Church*. San Francisco: Ignatius Press, 2008.

Uzukwu, E. Elochukwu. *A Listening Church: Autonomy and Communion in African Churches*. Maryknoll, NY: Orbis Books, 1996.

Werner, M., and B. Zimmerman. "Beyond Comparison: Histoire croisée and the Challenge of Reflexivity." *History and Theory* 45.1 (2006): 30–50.

Suggested Reading

AMECEA. *Communication in the Church and Society*. Nairobi, Kenya: Paulines Publications Africa, 1999.

———. Social Communication Department. *Communication for Pastoral Formation*. Nairobi, Kenya: Paulines Publications Africa, 1999.

Anagwo, C. Emmanuel. *Liturgy in the Life of the Faithful*. Onitsha, Nigeria: Laurans Prints, 2012.

Babin, Pierre. *The New Era in Religious Communication*. Minneapolis: Fortress Press, 1991.

Hackett, Rosalind I. J., and Benjamin F. Soares. *New Media and Religious Transformations in Africa*. Bloomington: Indiana University Press, 2015.

Granfield, Patrick, ed. *The Church and Communication*. Kansas City: Sheed & Ward, 1994.

Magesa, Laurenti. *Anatomy of Inculturation: Transforming the Church in Africa*. Nairobi, Kenya: Paulines Publications Africa, 2007.

McGarry, Cecil, and Patrick Ryan. *Inculturating the Church in Africa: Theological and Practical Per-

spectives. Nairobi, Kenya: Paulines Publications Africa, 2001.

Orobator, Agbonkhianmeghe E., ed. *The Church We Want: Foundations, Theology and Mission in the Church in Africa*. Nairobi, Kenya: Paulines Publications Africa, 2015.

———, ed. *Theological Reimagination: Conversations on Church, Religion, and Society in Africa*. Nairobi, Kenya: Paulines Publications Africa, 2014.

Key Words
communication
evangelizing
intercultural communication
mass media
new media
pastoral care
pastoral communication
pastoral plan for communication
public relations
social communications
social media
traditional communication

Catholic Education in Africa and the Agenda of *Africae Munus*

Anthony A. Akinwale, OP

The purpose of this chapter is to reflect on the role of Catholic education in Africa in the implementation of the agenda of *Africae Munus* (*AM*), Pope Benedict XVI's post-synodal apostolic exhortation. The chapter interprets data from the past and present history of Catholic education in some parts of Africa. It is primarily an exercise in what Bernard Lonergan calls "interpretation," the second of his eight functional specialties in academic theology.[1]

The first section of the chapter begins by recalling the history of Catholic education in Africa, from an era of church–state partnership to an era of state monopoly in the education sector. The second section looks to the future of Catholic education in Africa in the light of the agenda of *Africae Munus*. It is my contention that *Africae Munus* offers some relevant proposals for interpreting and realizing the goals of Catholic education in Africa. The third section further specifies the goal of Catholic education in Africa as the cultivation of a Catholic intelligence capable of implementing the agenda of *Africae Munus*. The chapter concludes by proposing steps to be taken toward the attainment of this Catholic intelligence in the academic environment and in the public square in Africa.

We first need to clarify two expressions: "Catholic education" and "Catholic intelligence." Catholic education is not to be understood as a means of making every African adhere to Catholicism. The operative notion of catholicity here has to do with wholeness. Thus, by "Catholic education," I mean the formation of the African in his or her wholeness (*katholos*), involving spiritual, intellectual, moral, and technical formation. The objective of education so conceived is to lead the African to a personal actualization of his or her potential by participation in the intersubjective task of collective actualization. The root of this personal and collective actualization passes through spiritual, intellectual, moral, and technical formation. In more concrete terms, the goal of Catholic education is to be identified in relation to cultivating the African personality so that it can become an agent of fulfilling a threefold duty of reconciliation, justice, and peace. Catholic education in this sense is not merely a matter of providing formation in science and technology. It is rather, fundamentally, about "forming upright consciences receptive to the demands of justice, so as to produce men and women willing and able to build this just social order by their responsible conduct" (*AM* §22).

Catholic intelligence is a fruit of Catholic education. But here again, we must avoid a sectarian connotation. First, intelligence describes human knowing, and, following the medieval distinction, human knowing takes place through the simultaneous operation of discursive thought (*ratio*) and intuition (*intellectus*). In discursive thought, the human being knows by moving from the known to the unknown. Truth offers itself to the human being who is able to see it through intuition, by

---

1. See Bernard Lonergan, *Method in Theology* (1972; repr., Toronto: University of Toronto Press, 1990), chapters 1, 5, and 7.

being attentive to what is given, that is, by being observant.[2] Second, keeping in mind that catholicity has to do with wholeness, intelligence is Catholic when it involves a recognition of and respect for the autonomy and necessity of both faith and reason in their openness to the whole truth. Intelligence is not Catholic if it promotes and reflects an affirmation of faith without reason or of reason without faith—either would be only a partial understanding of both faith and reason. Catholic intelligence involves a movement of the intellect toward knowledge through the cooperation of *ratio* and *intellectus* enlightened and elevated by *fides*, and, conceived of in this way, is able to give birth to authentic African Catholic intellectual traditions as part of a project of inculturation.

Catholic intelligence so understood does not necessarily imply the person's conversion to Catholicism. It may or may not involve Catholic beliefs transmitted by means of Catholic education. While Catholic intelligence arises out of the formation provided by Catholic education, this formation is not necessarily intended to result in the adherence of its recipient to the Catholic faith. Rather, by way of emphasis and intention, it is the purpose of Catholic education to form the whole person so that he or she can make intelligent contributions to the attainment of the common good irrespective of religious affiliation. What makes education Catholic is its formation of the whole person so that he or she searches for what is true and good using multiple means of engaging reality in dialogue with the whole of humanity. It is about forming the whole person to collaborate with the whole of humanity in the intersubjective search for the good. The product of learning the Catholic intellectual tradition of faith and reason through Catholic education is Catholic intelligence.

Here I speak of the Catholic intellectual tradition in the singular. However, this use of the singular is not meant to negate the fact that this tradition is, by virtue of its catholicity, a pluralistic tradition of traditions.[3] It is not a matter of plurality of the *forms* of catholicity, but rather a plurality of its *expressions*. What is handed down in Catholic intellectual tradition may be one, for truth is one, but the ways it is handed down are many, and many are its recipients. They belong to a diversity of cultures, and each receives it according to his or her particular mode. John Henry Newman beautifully illustrates this in his *Essay on the Development of Christian Doctrine*. Catholic intellectual tradition expresses Catholic intelligence in its ability to engage other intellectual traditions in dialogue so that it takes on an expression that is unique to the culture in which one or more other intellectual traditions have evolved. The questions, presuppositions, and language of a culture sew the garb in which the Catholic intellectual tradition is adorned. Thus, within the singular Catholic intellectual tradition, we have a variety of schools—Franciscan, Dominican, Jesuit, and many others. This variety explains why it is possible to speak of a particularly *African* Catholic intellectual tradition, that is, an African expression of catholicity.

Catholicity itself connotes openness to dialogue with other cultures and religions. That is why today, without any intention of sacrificing Catholic beliefs, to be Catholic necessarily imposes an obligation to participate in ecumenical, interreligious, and intercultural dialogue. In the spirit of the Second Vatican Council:

> The Church of the People of God which establishes the kingdom does not take away anything from the temporal welfare of any people. Rather, she fosters and takes to herself, in so far as they are good, the abilities, the resources and customs of peoples. In so taking them to herself she purifies, strengthens and elevates them. . . . The effect of her work is that whatever good is found sown in the minds and hearts of men and women or in the rites and customs of peoples, these

---

2. See Thomas Aquinas, *Quaestiones disputate de veritate* 15.1; Josef Pieper, "Philosophical Education and Intellectual Labor," in his *For the Love of Wisdom: Essays on the Nature of Philosophy* (San Francisco: Ignatius Press, 2006), 13–26.

3. See Yves Congar, *Tradition and Traditions: An Historical and a Theological Essay* (London: Macmillan, 1966).

not only are preserved from destruction, but are purified, raised up, and perfected for the glory of God, the confusion of the devil, and the happiness of men and women.[4]

Only a catholicity that is open to dialogue, as envisioned by the Second Vatican Council, can fulfill the objectives of *Africae Munus*. Catholic intelligence is able to make its contribution in the public square precisely because of its openness to dialogue.

In *Africae Munus*, Pope Benedict articulated an agenda, a threefold duty, of the church in Africa involving reconciliation, justice, and peace. For the church in Africa, being at the service of reconciliation, justice, and peace is a theological and social responsibility (*AM* §15). It is a matter of becoming just and building a just social order. Acknowledging that this duty is not dissimilar to what obtains in the rest of the world, Benedict observes, "Like the rest of the world, Africa is experiencing a culture shock which strikes at the age-old foundations of social life, and sometimes makes it hard to come to terms with modernity" (*AM* §11).[5] He locates the epicenter of this shock in an anthropological crisis, the response to which requires the fostering of dialogue among the members of Africa's constituent religious, social, political, economic, cultural, and scientific communities. He thus invites Africa, and indeed the rest of the world, to embark on a journey of anthropological rediscovery. "Africa," says Benedict, "will have to rediscover and promote a concept of the person and his or her relationship with reality that is the fruit of a profound spiritual renewal" (*AM* §15). This anthropological rediscovery is necessary in the service of reconciliation, justice, and peace and is facilitated by Catholic education.[6] It is in fact the case that, insofar as both aim at the formation of the whole person, the goals of anthropological rediscovery and education coincide. The quest for this rediscovery involves age-old questions: What or who is the human person? Or, what does it mean to be human? What are the rights and duties of the human person? These are questions that must be addressed in Africa's quest for an anthropological rediscovery.

These anthropological questions are especially pertinent in light of Africa's history of dictatorship, which has had a negative impact on education in general and on Catholic education in particular. As I shall show in this chapter, dictatorial regimes and a state monopoly on education in a number of African countries, especially in the years immediately following independence, negatively affected the content and quality of African education and severely impaired the ability and liberty of Africans to address these anthropological questions. Dictatorship made it obligatory but difficult, even dangerous, to raise these questions. *Africae Munus*, for its part, offers a challenge to invest in Catholic education—again, not as a call to have every African adhere to Catholicism, but instead as a call to educate the African in his or her wholeness (*katholos*).

It is necessary to state ab initio that this chapter is necessarily subject to certain methodological limitations. The size, diversity, and complexity of the African continent make it impossible to trace the history of Catholic education on the whole continent in just a few pages. The experience of church–state relations in the education sector differs from one country to another. This chapter will, therefore, limit itself to discussing the experiences of two countries—Congo under Mobutu Sese Seko and Nigeria under military rule.[7] These two countries serve as representative illustrations of how dictatorship militated against the provision of Catholic education and the emergence of

---

4. Vatican II, Dogmatic Constitution on the Church (*Lumen Gentium*) §§13, 17, www.vatican.va.
5. I attempted to show the link between this anthropological discovery and the task of education in my essay "Integral Humanism and the Integrity of Education," *Ibadan Dominican Studies* 1 (January 2015): 37–58.
6. On the role of Catholic education in implementing the agenda of *Africae Munus*, see *AM* §§134–138.
7. These two countries have been chosen for three reasons. First, Congo is francophone, Nigeria anglophone. Second, while Congo has the largest percentage of Catholics of any African country, Nigeria, in spite of having a minority Catholic population, has a history of significant Catholic presence and activity in the education sector. And, third, since I am Nigerian and studied in Congo during the Mobutu era, I have firsthand knowledge of the politics of education in the two countries.

Catholic intelligence in Africa and, by extension, the attainment of reconciliation, justice, and peace.

From Partnership to Monopoly

Education in Africa did not begin with its encounter with Western civilization. Failing to acknowledge and appreciate this obvious fact is to commit an intellectually unsustainable Hegelian faux pas, the denial of African self-consciousness and civilization. The history of flourishing city-states and empires in Africa bears eloquent testimony to the fact that Africans were educated before the arrival of Europeans.[8]

But it is also a well-known fact that Christianity was a major (in some cases the sole) importer and provider of Western education in colonial and postcolonial Africa. During the second and third eras of the encounter between Africa and Christianity, many parts of Africa benefited from schools established by missionaries.[9] In the Bakongo kingdom, during the second era, Mvemba Nzinga, known as King Afonso (ruled 1506–1543), the eldest son and successor of King Nzinga Nkuwu, converted to Christianity. History attests to his Christian piety and concern for justice and education. He ensured that access to education was not limited by gender. According to John Baur, "Even women were to be educated; his own sister, well into her 60s, taught in one of his girls' schools."[10]

In 1906, under Belgian colonial rule, the country known today as the Democratic Republic of the Congo witnessed the Roman Catholic Church's establishment of schools.[11] Hitherto, the Portuguese trained a few Congolese in Europe, teaching them the European way of life. In 1925, as part of an agreement between Belgium and the Holy See, Belgium decided to formally subsidize Catholic education, benefiting the church through grants and land concessions. In 1954, six years before the Congo achieved its independence from Belgium, the Catholic Lovanium University and the Université Officielle du Congo were founded to prepare Africans for civil service in a postcolonial government.

The former Belgian Congo was a place where the church was the state and the state was the church. That the colonizer and the missionary worked hand in hand to provide Western education in the new nation did not obscure the fact that they collaborated in the cultural alienation of the Congolese. The resulting resentment of the people largely explains the antichurch policies of Patrice Lumumba, Congo's first postcolonial prime minister. Upon the Congo's securing its independence in 1960, the Marxist-Leninist Lumumba ended the church–state partnership by secularizing education.

By the time Colonel Joseph-Désiré Mobutu overthrew the government of President Kasavubu in November 1965, the Congo had been fragmented by interethnic strife. Mobutu began as an ally of a church that had been on the receiving end of Lumumba's policies. He reversed Lumumba's decision to secularize education. The country needed reconciliation and a national consciousness, and Mobutu employed his philosophy of *authenticité* to create that consciousness, but also to camouflage the corruption and tyranny he visited on the country. In the name of *authenticité*, the Congolese way of life was promoted, while anything foreign, like wearing Western dress or using foreign names, became unlawful. In 1970, on the occasion of the tenth anniversary of Congolese independence, Joseph Cardinal Malula, then the archbishop of Kinshasa, publicly denounced the political class for its "fascination with the triumphant and the superficial, and a hunger for the lavish."[12] In Mobutu's one-party state, which he renamed Zaire, opposition was viewed with suspicion, and divergent

---

8. Read, e.g., Johnson, *History of the Yorubas*.

9. For a description of the three eras of evangelization in Africa, see Baur, *2000 Years of Christianity in Africa*. See also Pope St. John Paul II, *Ecclesia in Africa* (*EA*) §§30–34. On the role of Christian missionaries in Nigeria, see Ajayi, *Christian Missions in Nigeria 1841–1891*; and Ayandele, *Missionary Impact on Modern Nigeria 1842–1914*.

10. Baur, *2000 Years of Christianity in Africa*, 61–62.

11. On the complex history of the relationship between the church and the state in Congolese education, see the lively narrative in Carney, "'The Bishop Is Governor Here,'" 97–122.

12. Quoted in Carney, "'The Bishop Is Governor Here,'" 101.

opinions were not tolerated. Reprisals against the church followed Malula's speech, and the Roman Catholic Church in the Congo suffered under Mobutu's tyranny, which was sold as *authenticité*. State propaganda presented the church as the promoter of a foreign religion and an opponent of *authenticité*.

In 1971, government agents removed crucifixes from Catholic schools and the celebration of Christmas was banned. Units of the Mouvement Populaire de la Révolution (MPR), the political party founded by Mobutu, were established in Catholic schools, seminaries, and formation houses. Mobutism replaced Christian religious instructions in schools. Congolese bishops, notably Cardinal Malula, resisted these moves and in the ensuing confrontation, Malula's residence was confiscated and turned into an office for Mobutu's party. Malula was forced to live in exile for three months. The Lovanium Catholic University in Kinshasa was confiscated and merged with the Université Libre du Congo and the Université du Congo in Lubumbashi to form the Université Nationale du Zaïre, but Catholic bishops were able to continue their faculty of theology at a different site. Established in 1957 as the Faculté de Théologie Catholique de Kinshasa, it is now the Université Catholique de Kinshasa.

Before examining the history of what transpired in Nigeria, the case of Guinea needs to be cited in passing. The altercation between Mobutu and Malula was replicated in that country, where the dictator Ahmed Sékou Touré arrested Archbishop Raymond-Marie Tchidimbo of Conakry on Christmas Eve 1970.[13] Tchidimbo regained his freedom on August 7, 1979, after the intervention of Pope John Paul II, on conditions stipulated by Sékou Touré: a successor acceptable to Touré had to be appointed, and the archbishop must leave the country upon his release. His successor, Archbishop (now Cardinal) Robert Sarah, assumed office at a time when the church's right to own schools had been violated by Touré's pestilential dictatorship. Touré made it obligatory for all young people to attend schools run by the state. In Sarah's words, "I understood that the State Party revolution was literally destroying all the mainstays of the country. In particular, the educational system was in a chaotic state; the only thing that mattered was the dissemination of official propaganda, inspired by Soviet Marxism-Leninism."[14]

In the case of Nigeria, one of the greatest achievements of Catholic missionaries in all regions of the country was a strong system of schools that lasted from 1890 to 1970.[15] As of 1959, the year northern Nigeria attained self-government, the majority of the primary schools in that part of Nigeria were founded and administered by the Catholic Church. With regard to post-primary education, apart from Government College Barewa, the leading secondary schools for boys in northern Nigeria were St. John's College in Kaduna and Mount St. Michael College in Aliade. The Sisters of Our Lady of Apostles (OLA) established the Queen of Apostles Secondary School in Kaduna for girls, and the Sisters of St. Louis opened secondary schools for girls in Kano and Jos. Dominican sisters from Great Bend, Kansas, in the United States were involved in the education of women in the Muslim-dominated towns of Gusau and Yelwa, and the Holy Rosary Sisters were educating women in Makurdi. There were teachers colleges in Kafanchan, Lafia, and Bazza.

In southern Nigeria, Brother Doyle came from Ireland to open St. Gregory's College on Lagos Island in 1884, while, in 1956, Fr. Denis Slattery of the Society of African Missions opened St. Finbarr's College for Boys in Lagos mainland. Holy Child College for girls on Lagos Island was founded in 1945 by the sisters of the Society of the Holy Child Jesus. In Lagos mainland, the OLA Sisters opened Our Lady of Apostles for girls in 1956. Without presuming to give an exhaustive list, one can mention Loyola College in Ibadan, Christ the

---

13. For an account of the Guinean story, read Robert Cardinal Sarah, *God or Nothing*. Read also Kamil, "Ahmed Sékou Touré," 45–60.

14. Sarah, *God or Nothing*, 62.

15. See Imokhai, "Evolution of the Catholic Church in Nigeria," 11–14. It was not just Catholic missionaries who provided education. On the involvement of other missionary groups, see Braimah, "Church–State Partnership in Education in Nigeria," 111.

King in Onitsha for boys, and a host of schools for girls established and run by the Sisters of St. Louis in the southwestern Nigerian towns of Owo, Akure, Ondo, and Ibadan. It was said of Bishop Shanahan, the father of Catholicism in eastern Nigeria, that he "put all his available funds into the building of schools and the support of teachers for the non-Catholic indigenous people of the territory instead of using the money for the purchase of slaves who would become Catholics."[16] The quality of these schools was a credit to the missionaries, who helped form the first generation of civil servants and technocrats for a Nigeria on her way to independence from Britain.

What was going on in Nigeria with respect to education was replicated in the Congo and elsewhere in Africa. Without the pioneering efforts of the Catholic Church to provide a Western education, it would have been difficult for Nigerians and others in sub-Saharan Africa to interact with the rest of the modern world.[17] African struggles for independence from colonialism were boosted by Christian education in general and Catholic education in particular.

For decades, what obtained in Nigeria and in many African countries was a church–state partnership in the provision of education.[18] This partnership suffered a setback in postcolonial Nigeria, Ghana, Guinea, Congo-Kinshasa, and other places. A number of factors led to a transition to a state monopoly on education.

The primary factor was the installation of dictatorial regimes by both sides in the Cold War, regimes led by greedy and egotistical African tyrants lording it over Africans at the service of foreign neocolonial interests. For example, Ahmed Seko Touré persuaded the people of Guinea to vote in favor of independence from France in 1958, but the independence soon turned out to be a transition to a homemade tyranny. Quite a number of newly independent African nations became one-party states with absolute power held by only one man—the president. In addition to Guinea, such was the case in Kwame Nkrumah's Ghana, Modibo Keita's Mali, and Mobutu Sese Seko's Congo, among many others. The former colonial powers had bequeathed to these newly independent African nations weak constitutions that were unable to secure fundamental human rights and readily allowed political instability. Since many of these countries had been colonized by Western powers, and since most of the Christian missionaries in the second and third eras of evangelization came from these "Christian" countries, the Soviet Union, which presented itself as an ally in the struggle for independence, became a "friend" to Africa. In the midst of the Cold War, it became fashionable for many emerging African heads of state to flirt with Marxism-Leninism or some form of socialism.

This raging inferno of dictatorship in postcolonial Africa was fueled by the political misadventures of African military forces. For about three decades, African soldiers staged coups and countercoups, which sometimes resulted in ethnic cleansing, as was the case with the first two military coups in Nigeria on January 15 and July 29, 1966. Dictatorial regimes failed to appreciate the proper relationship between state and citizen—the purpose of the state should be to protect the land and its people, but totalitarian states in Africa took control of both land and people. Both military and civilian dictatorships had a devastating impact on education in Africa. Since it is the style and practice of dictators to violate fundamental human rights and disregard the principle of subsidiarity—two of the pillars on which the church's ownership of schools was predicated—the confiscation of church-owned schools became the order of the day in a number of African countries.

It is worth repeating that, according to the logic of tyranny, institutions that inculcate learning and shape opinions like schools and the media are the first targets of repression. Dictatorship operates through state-sponsored misinformation and the subjection of education to its ideological agenda.[19] In postcolonial, totalitarian African states, knowl-

---

16. See Imokhai, "Evolution of the Catholic Church in Nigeria," 11.
17. Read Onotu, "Milestones in the Growth of the Catholic Church in Northern Nigeria," 64–66.
18. On this partnership, see Ogunu, *100 Years of Church–State Partnership*; Braimah, "Church–State Partnership in Education in Nigeria," 111–13.
19. See Akinwale, "Knowledge, Power and the State of University Education," 81–90.

edge was subordinated to power, church–state partnerships were replaced by state monopolies, and indoctrination of the people by an ideologized intelligence held sway, while cultivation of Catholic intelligence was effectively outlawed. It is necessary to examine further how this dynamic played out in Nigeria. While the Congo was a one-man dictatorship, in Nigeria, violence against Catholic education was perpetrated by a collective military dictatorship.

The 1967–1970 war against Biafran secession[20] strained the relationship between Nigeria's military junta, led by Yakubu Gowon, and the Holy See, aggravating existing suspicion and envy toward the Catholic Church. The envy can be explained by the fact that an overwhelming majority of Nigerian schools belonged to the Catholic Church. This clearly displeased many Muslims and Christians of other ecclesial communities, and, consequently, these groups were not as vehement as Catholics in resisting the takeover of schools (and medical institutions) that began after the war, together with a strict new visa regime applicable to foreign missionaries.[21]

The real target was the Catholic Church, since there were more Catholic schools than government schools in northern Nigeria. Catholic schools were regarded as the best schools, and many in the Muslim community sent their children to them. Many non-Catholics went to Catholic schools and have remained Muslims or Anglicans or another kind of Protestant up until today. Names like Bola Ige and Lam Adesina, two former governors of Oyo State from 1979 to 1983, and Sanusi Lamido Sanusi, the current emir of Kano, come to mind. Yet there was an alliance against Catholic schools among those who saw them as instruments for winning converts to the faith.[22] There was also a widespread belief that it is the state, not the parents, that is responsible for education.

Leading the takeover of the schools in Nigeria was the civilian administrator of the former East Central State, Ukpabi Asika, who, like Mobutu of Zaire, was Catholic. On May 26, 1970, just five months after the end of the Nigerian civil war, Asika's administration fired the first salvo by formally taking over all primary and post-primary schools established, owned, and administered by voluntary agencies in the East Central State. This came in the form of the Public Education Edict of 1970, promulgated as the East Central State Edict No. 2 of 1971. Its officially stated objective was that government would take over the schools "to secure central control and an integrated system of education which will guarantee uniform standards, fair distribution of educational facilities and a reduced cost of running schools."[23]

Copycats arose as Asika's policy began to be imitated in other parts of Nigeria. The military govern-

---

20. As is the case in almost every war, both sides resorted to propaganda. The war was portrayed in some quarters as a war between Christians and Muslims. Some Spiritan missionaries, rightly or wrongly, sided openly with Biafra. Pope Paul VI invited Catholic bishops from both sides to Rome. The meeting, which took place February 4–7, 1969, had the intention of erasing the impression that it was a religious war and bringing about reconciliation. All three metropolitan archbishops in Nigeria were accompanied by a suffragan bishop. It was the first time in history that bishops from two sides of a war would celebrate the Eucharist together. For an account of the meeting, the address of Pope Paul VI to the bishops, and the position of the bishops, read Makozi, "Contemporary Trends in the Growth of the Catholic Church in Nigeria," 87–94.

21. Many missionaries who went home could not return, and new ones could not come to Nigeria. That largely accounts for the emergence of a wave of very young first-generation indigenous bishops in the early 1970s. They inherited dioceses without personnel that had largely relied on missionaries. That challenge led to a vigorous drive for vocations which largely (but not solely) explains a subsequent "vocation boom" in the Nigerian church. I was in primary school when bishops were making appeals for vocations, and I was one of those who responded to the call. The damage that had been inflicted on the Nigerian church's relationship with the Vatican by the changed visa policy was symbolically mended when President Shehu Shagari invited Pope John Paul II to Nigeria for a visit that occurred on February 12–14, 1982.

22. The Catholic Church did not allow young people to convert without the consent of their parents. My own mother was born into an Anglican family, but she and her siblings converted to Catholicism in primary school with the consent of my maternal grandparents.

23. East Central State Edict No. 2, 1971, quoted in Ogunu, *100 Years of Church–State Partnership*, 11.

ment of the former North Central State (comprising today's Kaduna and Katsina States) followed suit with its Transfer of Post-Primary Schools Edict No. 1 of 1972. By means of this military edict, all post-primary schools established, owned, and administered by voluntary agencies in the state were to be taken over by the state's military government with effect from January 1, 1973.

The epidemic of government takeover of schools by state military governments spread to the whole of Nigeria thanks to the national military government led by Olusegun Obasanjo. By virtue of Decree No. 48 of 1977, the Schools Takeover Validation Decree, the military junta validated and gave nationwide application to this violation of human rights with effect from June 13, 1977. Of course, the military government did not mention its strained relationship with the church; instead, the reason given for the takeover was the "high" cost of education in the mission schools. The government promised to provide tuition-free education.

Thirteen years later, the Ibrahim Babangida-led military junta dressed that decree in the stolen robes of constitutionality when it smuggled it into Nigeria's Statute Books as Chapter 401 of the 1990 Laws of the Federation. Section 2 of this new version of the decree went beyond its 1977 ancestor—not only did it suspend the fundamental rights stipulated in Chapter IV of the 1979 Constitution of the Federal Republic of Nigeria, but it removed the power of the judiciary to adjudicate the matter. Thus, a Nigerian citizen challenging the new law in court would be embarking on an exercise in futility.

Lord Acton's dictum that "power corrupts and absolute power corrupts absolutely" applies perfectly to this governmental takeover of the schools. Nigerian soldiers, by forcibly taking over the reins of government in clear contravention of the democratic principles enshrined in Nigeria's post-independence constitution of 1963, arrogated absolute powers to themselves. With this usurpation and absolutization of powers came catastrophic consequences: ethnic cleansing that led to killings of Igbo people both before and during the 1967–1970 war, the illegal confiscation of school properties—euphemistically referred to as a "takeover" of schools—and the massive destruction of the education sector, which has left Nigeria bleeding to this day.

The inclusion of Decree No. 48 of 1977 among the Laws of the Federation was clearly at variance with the provisions of Chapter IV of the 1999 Constitution of the Federal Republic of Nigeria, which recognizes a citizen's rights to acquire and own property. The recognition of the supremacy of the constitution and the simultaneous retention of this decree among the laws of Nigeria cannot be sustained. As Section 1, subsection 3 of the 1999 constitution states, "If any other Law is inconsistent with the provisions of this Constitution, this Constitution shall prevail, and that other Law shall to the extent of the inconsistency be void." In light of this constitutional provision, it is easy to understand why the decree was removed from the 2004 Laws of the Federation in the legislative activity of a postmilitary government, but any cry of victory was short-lived, for, as Michael Ogunu rightly pointed out,

> Despite the said salutary constitutional developments highlighted above, the selfsame 1979 and 1999 Constitutions have barred and ousted the exercise of the right of access to court to challenge the validity of the takeover of schools. Thus, the military, who in reality enacted and gave Nigerians both the 1979 and the 1999 Constitutions, were scrupulous enough to cover their tracks in such a way that the courts cannot now exercise their judicial powers to question their acts while they were in power starting from the date of the first military coup d'etat in Nigeria on the 15th of January 1966 by the insertion of Section 6(6)(d) in both the 1979 and 1999 Constitutions.[24]

A constitution regulates everyday life in view of the common good and is a nation's foundational document guaranteeing the protection of its citizens' rights. If citizens are satisfied that a constitution fulfills this role, they make it their own by way of referendum. But, as is well known, Nigeria's 1979 and 1999 constitutions were decreed into existence by military fiat. The section being referred to is a singularly infelicitous example of how the military

---

24. Ogunu, *100 Years of Church–State Partnership*, 15.

ensured before leaving the Nigerian political scene that, even though military rule was over, Nigerians would continue to be governed by military rules. According to this notorious Section 6(6)(d), "The judicial powers vested in accordance with the foregoing provisions of this section (d) shall not, as from the date when this section comes into force, extend to any action or proceeding relating to any existing law made on or after January 15, 1966 for determining any issue or question as to the competence of any authority to make any such law."

Thus, acts amounting to simple violations of fundamental human rights by military dictators have been accorded constitutional protection and immunity. Ogunu puts it better by stating that "no court of law in Nigeria has the jurisdiction and competence to adjudicate on the validity of any of the Edicts/Decrees legitimizing the takeover of schools, and the courts would readily decline jurisdiction accordingly."[25]

The takeover of the schools did not happen without a fight. According to Denis Slattery,

> Voluntary agents under the leadership of the principals of their secondary schools banded together to fight for the ownership of their schools. Present at these meetings were Methodists, Muslims, Baptists, Anglicans and Catholics. The private schools proprietors did not attend.
>
> It was my privilege to be chairman of these meetings which on the whole were generally very dull. Certainly, the Muslims were obviously in favor of "take over." The Methodists, Anglicans and Baptists were doubtful; only Catholics were militantly fighting to keep their schools.[26]

Slattery narrates how, in the heat of the crisis, a meeting of the dioceses of the Lagos Ecclesiastical Province was held in Benin City. At the end of the meeting, Slattery was chosen to speak to the press.[27] He unequivocally condemned the soldiers and their civilian accomplices for, in his words, "stealing our property and depriving us of our human rights to educate our children in the religions we chose." He continued:

> Every Nigerian citizen knows that the Catholic Church was famous for buying large tracts of land or receiving gifts of land not just for schools but for greater expansion. We have a plan for each station we opened. A church, a school, a parish hall, a playing ground, a clinic, a library were minimum requirements. Emphatically we did not purchase land just for schools only. It was high class robbery to take all our land where there were other buildings besides primary and secondary schools. The "take over" action prevented us from fulfilling the primary purpose of preaching the message of Christ and consolidating the "faith" of those already converted.[28]

The overall effect of the state monopoly in education has been societal collapse. This is best illustrated by the Yoruba dictum "Aaro meta kii da obe nu,"[29] which involves a tripodal stove securing a pot and the soup being prepared in it. Both will be destroyed if anything untoward should happen to any leg of the tripod. From my personal observation of the way society functions, I propose here the image of a society as standing on a tripod, and that it suffers ruin when any of the three legs is removed. The legs of the societal

---

25. Ogunu, *100 Years of Church–State Partnership*, 15–16.
26. Slattery, *My Life Story*, 191.
27. The details are contained in Slattery's autobiography, *My Life Story*, 61–74. There could not have been a better choice; Slattery was known for his courage in speaking the truth to power. During the struggle for Nigerian independence from Britain, he risked being arrested and deported by the British colonial administration for speaking out alongside nationalists like Nnamdi Azikiwe, the man who would later become Nigeria's governor general and first president, and alongside the first generation of Nigerian journalists and labor leaders.
28. Slattery, *My Life Story*, 192.
29. "The three-faced hearth never overturns the stew" is the loose translation provided by 'Tunji Azeez, "Of Feminism and Yoruba Gender Relations: A Study of Wole Soyinka," in Toyin Falola and Ann Genova, eds., *Yoruba Creativity: Fiction, Languages, Life and Songs* (Trenton, NY: Africa World Press, 2005), 37–55, at 49.

tripod are education, law enforcement, and adjudication of justice; in simpler words, schools, police, and judiciary. Some might think of a quadropod of church, school, family, and state. However, I am of the opinion that church, school, and family *acting as agents of education* properly constitute the first leg of the tripod, while the state is represented by the police and the judiciary, the second two legs. Education, acquired in the family, the school, and the religious community, inculcates civility and forms the citizen to work for the common good by working for his or her own good, and to work for his or her own good by working for the common good. The second leg of the tripod, law enforcement, exists to prevent the citizen from acting in ways that are inimical to the common good, and, if he or she should do so, effects an apprehension so that the citizen must appear before the judiciary, the third leg. Law enforcement agencies attempt to tender credible and admissible evidence to the judiciary to show that the citizen in question has really acted contrary to the common good.

One or more of the three legs on which society stands have been paralyzed, even amputated, broken or cut off by dictatorship in Africa—and specifically in Nigeria and elsewhere—by military dictatorship. There has, however, been one happy development. Since the end of the Cold War and the collapse of dictatorial regimes installed and sustained on the African continent by both sides in that war, there has been a gradual emergence of a network of Catholic universities across Africa.[30] At the same time, however, even though some state governments in Nigeria have returned some of the schools since the country's return to democratic rule in 1999, the education sector is still largely regulated by laws enacted by the military. Education still needs to be rescued from these rules, and, given the fact that the goal of Catholic education and the goal of *Africae Munus* coincide, doing this, and more generally rescuing education from the clutches of dictatorship, would provide an invaluable key that would open the door to addressing Africa's many problems.

The Future of Catholic Education in Africa and the Agenda of *Africae Munus*

The first part of this chapter looked at the past. This second part attempts to look at the future. Given the movement from partnership to monopoly, and given the gradual emergence of a network of universities with a Catholic affiliation in Africa, what can one envisage as the contribution of Catholic education to the agenda of *Africae Munus*?

Rescued from the grips of dictatorship, Catholic education can contribute to articulating the anthropological question and pointing to responses that address it. This becomes clear when the question itself is posed in its African context. The perennial anthropological question referred to earlier in this chapter manifests itself with peculiar intensity in Africa, with its history of interethnic conflicts, political instability, totalitarian regimes, and societal dislocation. Civilization itself represents various attempts to address this question. Diverse cultures and nationalities, races, religions, and philosophies have proffered answers. Catholic education has made and can make its own contribution toward proffering answers, and Aristotle's statement in his *Politics* that the human being is a political animal aggregates these answers. What Aristotle meant is not that the human being is an animal that spends all its life scheming, rigging, or shooting itself into office, but an animal that lives in the polis, a being who does not live alone but lives in communion with others. The human being's

---

30. In addition to the Catholic University of Kinshasa in the Democratic Republic of the Congo, the former Catholic Higher Institute of East Africa has become the Catholic University of Africa in Nairobi, and the former Institut Catholique d'Afrique de l'Ouest in Abidjan has become l'Université Catholique d'Afrique de l'Ouest. The Catholic bishops of Angola have founded a Catholic university in Luanda, while their counterparts in Nigeria have founded Veritas University in Abuja. In addition to Veritas University, Nigeria alone has Madonna University, Caritas University, Godfrey Okoye University, Pan-Atlantic University, Augustine University, Dominican University, and Spiritan University, and the Jesuits are making plans to obtain a license to open their own. It should be noted that none of these Nigerian universities is an ecclesiastical university in the canonical sense of the word; they are, however, Catholic-inspired universities.

relationality necessitates the inquiry: Who is this being and how does he or she to relate to others who also live in networks of relationships? That is the anthropological question.

The two creation narratives in the book of Genesis convey the meaning that the human being is one whose existence originates from and depends on God. Made male and female in the image and likeness of God, and therefore capable of communion with God, his or her existence finds fulfillment in a life lived in communion with others. Faithful to this biblical tradition, the Second Vatican Council answers the anthropological question by affirming in *Lumen Gentium*, the Dogmatic Constitution on the Church, that the human being belongs or is related to the people of God (§13). Echoing the council, the First Special Assembly for Africa of the Synod of Bishops answers that the human person is a member of the family of God (*EA* §63).

Martin Buber's intriguing picture of the dialogical character of the human person points to the twofold attitude of the human person toward the world—the *I–It attitude* and the *I–Thou attitude*.[31] Differentiating between the realm of "It" and the realm of "Thou," Buber speaks of the world of objects—the world of It, and of the world of subjects—the world of Thou. "It" refers to objects I can manipulate. The human being is not an object to be perceived, imagined, willed, felt, thought, used, or abused as a thing, a toy, or a tool, but rather is a subject to be related with, which relationship is facilitated by recognition of the *divine Thou* in others. To love God is to converse with God, and to see God in others is to love and converse with them. Seeing the image and likeness of God in others, I can relate with them without deceit, that is, without insulting their intelligence. Without this recognition, dialogue is replaced by a competition to outfox the other. This recognition is what is missing from dictatorial regimes, even when they do not confiscate schools from their rightful owners. Catholic education must provide an answer to the anthropological question in the consciousness of our common humanity.

In light of Africa's dire need for authentic development, reconciliation, justice, and peace, two urgent and pertinent questions are raised by the anthropological question: What are the rights and duties of the human person? And what is the role of government? These questions involve complex inquiries into human nature, particularly concerning the rights that belong to us as human beings and as citizens, the duties we owe one another as human beings and as citizens, and the duty of government to protect these rights and enforce these duties. The question raised by African conflicts, sometimes accompanied by gratuitous violence, is, What ought to be the relationship between the human person with ethnic, regional, and religious identities, and other human persons who bear different ethnic, regional, and religious identities?

The diverse identities and affiliations that characterize our common humanity compel us to organize our common life with a modicum of intelligence if there is to be any chance of attaining any good. Thus, we constitute a state, we form a government. And the very constitution of a state, meant to regulate the common life of human beings living together while bearing diverse identities, raises other questions: What ought to be the relationship between the state and the human person? And what ought to be the relationship between persons? These questions need to be addressed if we are to coexist harmoniously. But they cannot be adequately addressed without a prior anthropological inquiry into the nature of the human person.

Every human being must participate in the age-old quest to find answers, a task that challenges us to enlarge our vision of the nature and purpose of education. It is in fact the case that the purpose of education is not, primarily, to acquire degrees and academic titles, but primarily to satisfy the pure and unrestricted desire to know what it is to be human in the polis and in the cosmos, that is, in relation to other persons and to the whole of the universe. Education prepares the human person to address the many questions and crises that rear their heads from time to time. It forms the human person so that he or she can articulate the anthropological question and find and reflect on adequate answers. Education forms the human person not just to make a profit by inventing and relating with gadgets, but, fundamentally, to relate with other members of the human community in a quest for

---

31. See Martin Buber, *I and Thou* (New York: Collier/Macmillan, 1955).

a just and equitable social order. Given her history and experience of ethnic and religious conflicts that hamper authentic development, Africa is in dire need of persons formed in this way. It is by forming them that Catholic education in Africa can give birth to agents of reconciliation, justice, and peace and thus contribute to the implementation of the agenda of *Africae Munus*.

Catholic Education and the Cultivation of Catholic Intelligence

Africa's problems will begin to find solutions when education, rightly understood, is given its rightful place on the continent. The cultivation of Catholic intelligence through integral and authentic education anchored in the Catholic intellectual tradition can offer a pathway to addressing some of the most pressing problems facing both church and state in Africa. Contrary to a vision of education that would reduce it solely to formation in science and technology, I argue that, rightly understood, education stands on another tripod, a tripod of intellectual formation, moral formation, and technical formation, with the three legs of the tripod standing on the ground of spiritual, or religious, formation. If any of the legs of the tripod breaks, education will not be able to stand.[32]

The two post-synodal apostolic exhortations, *Ecclesia in Africa* and *Africae Munus*, recognize the vital importance of education (*EA* §§102–103; *AM* §§134–138). The many contributions, past and present, of the Catholic Church to the education sector have been widely recognized; without question, the Catholic Church in Africa has an enviable track record in education. Her schools are present in rural areas and in big cities. In many instances, Catholic schools have demonstrated that there can be harmony in spite of ethnic differences. Admission is not based on ethnic or religious affiliation.

Some of those who fought relentlessly against Catholic education were its beneficiaries. Mobutu of Zaire and Asika of Nigeria were Catholics. Why were some Catholics involved in conceiving and implementing policies inimical to education in general and to Catholic education in particular? How is it that some Catholics have played less-than-noble roles in public life, even in African countries where Catholics are in the majority? These questions remind us that, despite the achievements of Catholic education, and despite the fact that while Africa has Catholic intellectuals and cultural Catholics, the continent needs Catholic intelligence and her own Catholic intellectual traditions. At this juncture, there is a need to further clarify our terms so as to avoid advocating for a sectarian education.

Catholic intelligence is cultivated by a Catholic education. But education is not Catholic simply because it is offered by an institution of learning affiliated with the Catholic Church. Whether the recipient of a Catholic education becomes a member of the Catholic Church is not the test of whether the education is Catholic. Rather, in order to be truly Catholic, Catholic education must be freed from a simplistic conception of catholicity. The notion of catholicity in Catholic education has to do with wholeness (*katholos*). Education is Catholic only if it promotes the dignity of the human person in its integrality; that is, the human person in his or her spiritual, intellectual, moral, and technical dimensions. It is Catholic by its orientation and attention to an integral humanism. Such an education is necessary to the formation of men and women who will undertake the task set forth in *Africae Munus*—the achievement of reconciliation, justice, and peace.

Catholic education in Africa needs to form men and women who not only attend Mass regularly, engage in pious devotions, and make financial contributions to the church, but are also willing and able to integrate their faith into family life, places of work and education, politics, the economy, and international relations, to name only a few. An African Catholic intelligence is what results when the values of the gospel are active ingredients in the way the African knows, thinks, and acts. These values, as the corpus of Catholic social doctrine has

---

32. See Anthony Akinwale, "The Marginalization of the Humanities in Our Educational System," *Ibadan Journal of Humanistic Studies* 17–18 (2007–2008): 36–44.

repeatedly maintained, do not require that those espousing them be members of the Catholic community. They are values anyone can embrace, even on rational grounds. Cultivation of Catholic intelligence fosters knowledge of the content of Catholic social teaching, and especially knowledge of its foundations: human dignity, care for the common good, subsidiarity, and solidarity. One does not have to subscribe to the tenets of the Catholic faith in order to embrace these principles.

Catholic intelligence in Africa is what would come about as a result of what *Africae Munus* describes as "the inculturation of the Gospel and the evangelization of culture." It has the capacity to overcome the "dichotomy between certain traditional practices of African cultures and the specific demands of Christ's message" (*AM* §36). Catholic intelligence takes other points of view seriously in the course of seeking truth.

The goal of education is to facilitate the actualization of each human person's potential. If this occurs, the human person is able to fulfill his or her aspirations and, in the fulfillment of these aspirations, is able to live life to the fullest. Education is thus a process by which the human person is led to full humanization, that is, the actualization of his or her potential and the fulfillment of his or her aspirations in every dimension of human existence: in the spiritual dimension, in which the human person desires God and is capable of having this desire fulfilled; in the intellectual dimension, in which the human person desires truth and is capable of reaching it; in the moral dimension, in which the human being desires the good and is able to attain it; and in the technical dimension, in which the human being desires to work and is capable of working. Thus, the statement above that education stands on three legs—intellectual, moral, and technical—and that these legs stand in turn on a spiritual ground. That is why Catholic education must be inspired not just by anthropological considerations, but ultimately theological ones. It must receive its inspiration from the fact that the truth and the good sought by human beings can be found only in God, and that the human desire to work has its origin in the fact that the human person is made in the image and likeness of God.

There is a relationship between education so conceived and inculturation. Inculturation is the process whereby the word of God, whose authentic interpretation, according to the Second Vatican Council, is the task of the church's teaching office, finds a home in the intellect of the human person. Inculturation is guided by and engenders what Bernard Lonergan describes as a threefold conversion, namely, intellectual conversion, which is a radical reorientation toward the true; moral conversion, which is a radical reorientation toward the good; and religious conversion, which is a radical reorientation toward God. Religious conversion sublates the other two.[33] In other words, the result of the process of inculturation is the formation of Catholic intelligence and Catholic intellectual traditions.

Conclusion

Having looked at the past, at the situation of Catholic education in the context of African dictatorships, and at the future, to the possible contributions of Catholic education to the implementation of the agenda of *Africae Munus*, I conclude by proposing a number of practical steps to be taken toward implementation of this agenda. Let us recall that the vision of education that guides this reflection is inspired by the traditional tripodal African cooking stove. In this vision, education stands on three legs—intellectual formation, moral formation, and technical formation—and these three legs stand on the ground of spiritual formation. The proposals offered here concern how the spiritual foundation of education should be consolidated toward implementation of the agenda of *Africae Munus*.

Implementation of this agenda calls for the cultivation of Catholic intelligence. Catholic education in twenty-first-century Africa must respond by forming men and women who will not only be intelligent cultural Catholics but men and women of Catholic intelligence, products of African Catholic intellectual traditions, who respect the religious

---

33. See Lonergan, *Method in Theology*, 267–69.

liberty of peoples of other faiths studying in our Catholic schools. Such are the men and women who will lead Africa, in her ethnic and religious diversity, from the insecurity of states held together at gunpoint to the harmony of a veritable family of nations. Implementing this agenda through the cultivation of Catholic intelligence imposes a number of obligations on the church. First, as Benedict XVI points out, the Catholic chaplaincy in universities and schools must play an important role (*AM* §138). Here it should be noted that tertiary institutions are incubators of future leaders in various sectors of public life—in politics, the economy, religion, and academia. The Catholic chaplaincy in universities and schools is a special apostolate requiring chaplains with the intellectual tools necessary for fruitful engagement with a community of intellectuals—men and women of the arts and sciences and a future corps of professionals.

A Catholic chaplaincy is more than a place on campus where members of the academic community may go to receive the sacraments. While the sacramental life of the faithful should not be neglected, it would be a great disservice to the Christian faith if pastoral care on campuses were focused only on this life. There is an urgent need to go beyond such a parochial conception of pastoral work to seeing it as leading the people of God to Christ within the Catholic tradition. A Catholic chaplaincy should therefore be a place where people are formed to integrate their faith with learning, a meeting point of the academy and the church, with the chaplain facilitating the encounter between the two. Today's university chaplain should be a person of faith formed by a Catholic intelligence. This poses the challenge of reconceptualizing our Catholic chaplaincies, recreating them away from a schizophrenia whereby professional life and the life of faith walk on opposite sides of the street without exchanging glances. The Catholic chaplaincy must inculcate a familiarity with the principles and contents of Catholic social doctrine.

What has just been said prepares the way for articulating the second obligation of the church in meeting the challenge of *Africae Munus*: the creation of holy, intelligent, and competent pastoral leadership. Benedict XVI observes that the love of God has blessed the church in Africa in many ways. She is a gift with many gifts. In her members—bishops, priests, consecrated persons, lay faithful—she is capable of acting as the salt of the earth and of changing Africa for the better. Indeed, the baptismal grace given to all the faithful is meant for personal renewal in holiness and for the spread of renewal and holiness on the entire continent. Africa's many Catholics, found in various sectors of life on the continent, are capable of transforming it. But to accomplish this, the faithful must be formed in a Catholic intelligence and become inheritors of African Catholic intellectual traditions so that they can carry out the mission of the church.

While there is need to continue emphasizing an updated and adequate formation of the clergy, consecrated persons, and catechists, the formation of the laity, of the man and woman in the pew, young and old, deserves renewed attention. This is the third obligation—that the laity, given the important role they play in the church and in society, needs to be adequately formed. In this regard, these words of Benedict XVI deserve special attention: "To enable [the laity] properly to take up [their] role, it is fitting that centres of biblical, spiritual, liturgical and pastoral formation be organized in the dioceses" (*AM* §128). John Henry Cardinal Newman foresaw this need already in the nineteenth century when he wrote these words, which Benedict XVI would later quote in his homily at Newman's Mass of beatification: "I want a laity, not arrogant, not rash in speech, not disputatious, but men who know their religion, who enter into it, who know just where they stand, who know what they hold and what they do not, who know their creed so well that they can give an account of it, who know so much of history that they can defend it."[34]

A fourth obligation is this: implementing the aims of *Africae Munus* must be the task of the whole church in Africa. But bishops must provide adequate pastoral leadership in this regard. Benedict XVI wisely points out that episcopal leadership is best exercised by those living a life that is out-

---

34. John Newman, *The Present Position of Catholics in England* (Notre Dame, IN: University of Notre Dame Press, 2000), ix, 390.

standing in both holiness and administrative competence. As regards holiness, the bishop must be notable for his exercise of the virtues—of the theological virtues in the first place—and for his exercise of the evangelical counsels and a life of prayer.

It is in recognition of the fact that the task set out in *Africae Munus* rests primarily on the shoulders of bishops that Benedict XVI quotes from Cyprian of Carthage, an African bishop in the early church: "The Church rests on the bishops, and all her conduct follows the direction of those same rulers" (Cyprian, *Epistle* 33.1; quoted in *AM* §101). Cyprian's words warrant the conclusion that the bishop in the local church must be the first educator and chief promoter of Catholic intellectual traditions.[35] It takes adequate formation to create a laity noted for its "active and courageous presence in the areas of political life, culture, the arts, the media and various associations" (*AM* §131). And again, following Cyprian, it takes effective episcopal leadership to ensure that the laity is so formed.

The mission spelled out in *Africae Munus* is inseparable from the Word of God. In fact, there is no mission carried out in the name of God that is not preceded by the proclamation and hearing of God's Word. It is the Word of God that calls to mission. In this regard, the admonition of Benedict must be taken seriously: the first duty of the bishop is to preach the Good News of salvation and to lead the people to a deeper knowledge of Jesus Christ through effective catechesis. One may recall here Paul VI's words that the task of evangelization is to bring about an interior change in the person who hears the word.[36] The first duty of the bishop is to preach the Good News of salvation, enabling the formation of men and women in African Catholic intellectual traditions. The bishop must guide the intellect to a knowledge of Christ, the summit of divine revelation, a revelation to be authentically interpreted by the church.

Benedict enjoins bishops that it is up to them "to support a pastoral outreach to the life of the intellect and reason so as to foster a habit of rational dialogue and critical analysis within society and in the Church" (*AM* §137). He then repeated what he said in Yaoundé about his wish that this century may witness the rebirth, "albeit in a new and different form, of the prestigious School of Alexandria" (*AM* §137). The success of the quest to inculcate Catholic intelligence and establish African Catholic intellectual traditions in the implementation of *Africae Munus* would be nothing short of the fulfillment of this dream of an Alexandrian renaissance. Ongoing efforts to rescue education in the emerging democracies of Africa are the prerequisite for the fulfillment of this dream.

Bibliography

Ajayi, J. F. Ade. *Christian Missions in Nigeria 1841–1891: The Making of a New Elite*. London: Longman, 1965.

Akinwale, Anthony. "Integral Humanism and the Integrity of Education." *Ibadan Dominican Studies* 1 (January 2015): 37–58.

———. "Knowledge, Power and the State of University Education." In *The Idea of a University: A Revisit*, edited by Olatunji Oyeshile and Joseph Kenny. Washington, DC: Council for Research in Values and Philosophy, 2013.

Ayandele, E. A. *The Missionary Impact on Modern Nigeria 1842–1914: A Political and Social Analysis*. London: Longman, 1966.

Baur, John. *2000 Years of Christianity in Africa: An African Church History*. 2nd ed. Nairobi: Paulines Publications Africa, 2009.

Benedict XVI, Pope. *Africae Munus* [Post-synodal Apostolic Exhortation on the Church in Africa in Service of Reconciliation, Justice and Peace; November 19, 2011]. Vatican City: Libreria Editrice Vaticana, 2011. www.vatican.va.

Braimah, Moses. "Church–State Partnership in Education in Nigeria." In *Catholic Education in Nigeria: Proceedings of the First Summit on Catholic Educa-*

---

35. As the first educators and chief promoters of Catholic intellectual traditions, what John Paul II said of formators applies also to bishops: "These contributions presuppose the human, cultural and religious formation of the educators themselves" (*EA* §102).

36. Paul VI, *Evangelii Nuntiandi* [Apostolic Exhortation on the Theme of Catholic Evangelization; December 8, 1975] §14: "Evangelization means the carrying forth of the good news to every sector of the human race so that by its strength it may enter into the hearts of men and women and renew the human race."

tion in Nigeria, 108–22. Abuja: Catholic Bishops' Conference of Nigeria, 2014.

Carney, J. J. "'The Bishop Is Governor Here': Bishop Nicholas Djomo and Catholic Leadership in the Democratic Republic of Congo." In *Leadership in Postcolonial Africa: Trends Transformed by Independence*, edited by Baba Jallo, 97–122. New York: Palgrave Macmillan, 2014.

Imokhai, C. A. "The Evolution of the Catholic Church in Nigeria." In *The History of the Catholic Church in Nigeria*, edited by A. O. Makozi and G. J. Afolabi Ojo, 1–14. Lagos: Macmillan, 1982.

Jallo, Baba, ed. *Leadership in Postcolonial Africa: Trends Transformed by Independence*. New York: Palgrave Macmillan, 2014.

John Paul II, Pope. *Ecclesia in Africa* [Post-synodal Apostolic Exhortation on the Church in Africa and Its Evangelizing Mission toward the Year 2000; September 14, 1995]. Vatican City: Libreria Editrice Vaticana, 1995. www.vatican.va.

Johnson, Samuel. *The History of the Yorubas: From the Earliest Times to the Beginning of the British Protectorate*. Lagos: CSS, 1921.

Kamil, Muhammed. "Ahmed Sékou Touré: The Tyrant Hero." In *Leadership in Postcolonial Africa: Trends Transformed by Independence*, edited by Baba Jallo, 45–60. New York: Palgrave Macmillan, 2014.

Lonergan, Bernard. *Method in Theology*. 1972. Reprinted, Toronto: University of Toronto Press, 1990.

Makozi, A. O. "Contemporary Trends in the Growth of the Catholic Church in Nigeria." In *The History of the Catholic Church in Nigeria*, edited by A. O. Makozi and G. J. Afolabi Ojo, 87–94. Lagos: Macmillan, 1982.

Makozi, A. O., and G. J. Afolabi Ojo, eds. *The History of the Catholic Church in Nigeria*. Lagos: Macmillan, 1982.

Ogunu, Michael. *100 Years of Church–State Partnership in Education in Nigeria (1914–2014): A Critical Analysis*. Benin City: Mabogun Publishers, 2014.

Onotu, J. J. "Milestones in the Growth of the Catholic Church in Northern Nigeria." In *The History of the Catholic Church in Nigeria*, edited by A. O. Makozi and G. J. Afolabi Ojo. Lagos: Macmillan, 1982.

Sarah, Robert Cardinal. *God or Nothing: A Conversation on Faith with Nicolas Diat*. San Francisco: Ignatian Press, 2015.

Slattery, Denis. *My Life Story*. Lagos: West African Book Publishers, 1996.

Key Words

Africae Munus
African Catholic intellectual traditions
Ahmed Sékou Touré
Catholic chaplaincy
Catholic education
Catholic intelligence
church–state partnership
Congo, dictatorship
Ecclesia in Africa
Joseph Malula
Mobutu Sese Seko
Nigeria
Olusegun Obasanjo
Ukpabi Asika

CATHOLIC SCHOOLS IN AFRICA: ACHIEVEMENTS AND CHALLENGES

Quentin Wodon

As is the case for Catholic health facilities, Africa is the continent with the largest and fastest growing number of students in Catholic schools globally. By contrast, in some other areas, especially in developed countries, the number of students in Catholic schools has declined in recent years. If current trends continue, given high rates of population growth and gains in educational attainment, within a decade well above half of all students in Catholic schools globally may live on the continent.[1] This is an opportunity for Catholic schools, but also a challenge. Catholic schools can be proud of their heritage in Africa. Yet, despite the best efforts of teachers and principals and given the constraints they face, the coverage and quality of the education being provided today in the region are insufficient, including in Catholic schools.

This chapter provides a diagnostic of achievements and challenges for Catholic schools in Africa. It is adapted in part from a report on the role of faith-based organizations in education and health in the region,[2] and follows the same structure as a companion chapter in this volume on Catholic health facilities.[3] To facilitate comparisons for readers who may be interested in both topics, these two chapters on schools and health facilities are copycats of each other in terms of basic structure.

In sub-Saharan Africa, where most of the Catholic schools are located, educational outcomes have improved substantially over the last two decades. At the same time, a lot remains to be done. Just above two-thirds of children complete their primary education, according to data from the World Bank's World Development Indicators for 2018. The rates are 70.5 percent for boys and 67.1 percent for girls. Completion rates at the lower secondary level are much lower: 46.6 percent for boys, and 41.6 percent for girls. Apart from low educational attainment, many children are not learning enough in school.[4] Data from international student assessments suggest that fewer than two in ten children in sub-Saharan Africa (13.6 percent for boys and 17.0 percent for girls) are able to read and understand a simple text by age ten.[5] Girls do slightly better than boys on that indicator, but this does not last. At the secondary level, girls are less likely to be in school due in part to a high prevalence of child marriages and early childbearing—indeed,

---

The author is a lead economist at the World Bank. The paper was prepared on the author's own personal time and not as part of his duties at the World Bank. The analysis and views expressed in this paper are those of the author only and may not reflect the views of the World Bank, the countries it represents, or its executive director.

1. Wodon, "Implications of Demographic, Religious, and Enrollment Trends for the Footprint of Faith-Based Schools Globally."
2. Wodon, *Faith-Based Education and Healthcare in Africa*.
3. Wodon, "Catholic Health Facilities in Africa."
4. World Bank, *World Development Report 2018: Learning to Realize Education's Promise*.
5. World Bank, *Ending Learning Poverty: What Will It Take?*

sub-Saharan Africa has today become the region of the world with the largest share of girls marrying as children.[6]

These statistics are dire. Because such a large share of Catholic schools are concentrated in sub-Saharan Africa, the schools have a special role in efforts to reach the fourth Sustainable Development Goal, which is to ensure inclusive and equitable quality education and promote lifelong learning opportunities for all. In many countries, Catholic schools are often perceived as providing a quality education in comparison to other schools. Yet, even if Catholic schools may provide comparatively a good education, this does not mean that they succeed in ensuring good educational outcomes for students. In a context of limited resources and widespread poverty, the challenges are massive.[7] This is true for public schools; it is also true for Catholic schools, private secular schools, and schools associated with other faiths.

A fundamental principle of Catholic social teaching is the preferential option for the poor,[8] which also applies to the mission of Catholic schools.[9] Unfortunately, children from disadvantaged backgrounds are especially at risk of not receiving a quality education.[10] The recent COVID-19 crisis has further exacerbated inequality in educational outcomes between the well-to-do and the much larger group of children who are poor or vulnerable.[11] Projections by the World Bank[12] suggest that Gross Domestic Product in Africa may contract for the first time in twenty-five years. Losses in agricultural production and locust swarms in East Africa may lead to large increases in food insecurity.[13] A detailed analysis of the potential impacts of the COVID-19 crisis on Catholic schools and their students is provided by Wodon in the following two articles: "COVID-19 Crisis, Impacts on Catholic Schools, and Potential Responses, Part I: Developed Countries with Focus on the United States" and "Part II: Developing Countries with Focus on Sub-Saharan Africa." The analysis for developing countries focuses on Africa. It suggests that many children will be affected in severe ways. As schools closed, the crisis is likely to have led children to learn even less during the 2019–2020 school year than they would have normally. Some children probably had to drop out of school altogether because the economic hardship that their family endured led to out-of-pocket and opportunity costs of schooling that were simply too high for parents to be able to afford. Many Catholic schools have a limited capacity to respond to the crisis, whether in terms of distance learning solutions or in terms of their ability to maintain enrollment and thereby financial sustainability in the medium term. As noted in the World Bank's publication *The COVID-19 Pandemic: Shocks to Education and Policy Responses*, achieving the targets set in the fourth Sustainable Development Goal seems even further out of reach. And as the Congregation for Catholic Education affirms, Catholic schools should provide an integral and comprehensive education that contributes to fraternal humanism and a civilization of love.[14] In so doing, quoting *Gravissimum Educationis*, Declaration on Christian Education from Vatican II, the Congregation reminds us that "first and foremost the Church offers its educational service to the poor or those who are deprived of family help and affection or those who are far from the faith." In order to fulfill this promise, Catholic schools in Africa will need

---

6. Le Nestour and Wodon, *Global and Regional Trends in Child Marriage*.

7. Bashir et al., *Facing Forward*.

8. For example, see Pontifical Council for Justice and Peace, *Compendium of the Social Doctrine of the Church*; and Pope Francis, *Laudato Si'* [encyclical On Care for Our Common Home; June 18, 2015].

9. McKinney, "Roots of the Preferential Option for the Poor."

10. Wodon, "How Well Do Catholic and Other Faith-Based Schools Serve the Poor? Part I: Schooling"; and "Part II: Learning."

11. The impacts of the COVID-19 crisis have been severe, but the crisis also revealed opportunities, including the possibility of blending in-person and distance education to improve pedagogy in the classroom.

12. World Bank, "An Analysis of Issues Shaping Africa's Economic Future."

13. Food Security Information Network, *Global Report on Food Crisis 2020*.

14. Congregation for Catholic Education, *The Catholic School*.

to improve the education they provide, again for the children from disadvantaged backgrounds.

The urgency of providing a quality education to Africa's children and youth, and especially the poor, should not be in doubt. Low educational attainment and lack of learning have lifelong consequences for children. In the case of girls, Wodon et al. show how globally and in sub-Saharan Africa not investing in children's education leads to higher rates of child marriage and early childbearing, lower earnings in adulthood, higher risks of intimate partner violence, and lack of decision-making ability within the household, among other issues.[15] When mothers are poorly educated, this also affects their children, including through higher risks of under-five mortality and stunting, lower expected levels of education, and lack of both registration. These are but some of the effects of not educating girls. More generally, the impact of poor education outcomes on human capital is one of the reasons why children do not reach their full potential.[16] This, in turn, has implications for countries' wealth and sustainable development. As demonstrated by Glenn-Marie Lange et al., human capital wealth is the largest component of the wealth of nations, well ahead of natural and physical capital.[17] Not investing in children's education does not enable nations to reach their development potential.

Strong Catholic schools benefit not only students but also communities and societies at large. To discuss the state of Catholic schools in Africa, this chapter reviews some of their achievements and challenges. Relying on data from the annual statistical yearbooks of the church, the first two sections provide simple statistics on trends over time in enrollment in Catholic schools globally and in Africa, as well as country-level data within Africa for 2017. Thereafter, the third section considers some of the achievements of Catholic schools, especially in terms of responding to parental preferences for the education of their children. Finally, the fourth and last section considers where Catholic schools stand in terms of reaching the poor and providing a quality education to students. This is first discussed for the continent as a whole, and next with a brief illustrative case study for Uganda, one of the countries with the largest enrollment in Catholic schools on the continent. A brief conclusion follows.

Aggregate Trends in Enrollment for Africa

Trends in enrollment in K–12 Catholic schools are available in the annual statistical yearbooks published by the church, with the latest yearbook providing data until 2017.[18] At the global level, these trends have been documented in Wodon's 2018 article, "Enrollment in K–12 Catholic Schools: Global and Regional Trends." Here, the focus is on Africa. Data are available on the number of students enrolled and the number of schools for preschools, primary schools, and secondary schools. In addition, data are available on enrollment at the tertiary level for higher institutes and universities, but this is not discussed here.[19]

The data are provided by country and are based on responses by the chancery offices of ecclesiastical jurisdictions to an annual questionnaire. Most jurisdictions reply, and those that do not reply for various reasons tend to have fairly small numbers of students in their schools. Therefore, the data are likely to capture most students. Whether the data are very precise remains open to question, at least in countries with weak data systems. Even governments in low-income countries may not always have very precise data despite implementing annual school censuses. As many ecclesiastical jurisdictions do not have the ability to implement such school censuses every year, especially in sub-Saharan Africa, the data may represent only estimates as opposed to exact figures. Work could be conducted at the country level to check all estimates with other data sources, including national education management systems, but this would be a major undertaking and is beyond the scope of

---

15. See Wodon et al., *Economic Impacts of Child Marriage*; Wodon et al., *Missed Opportunities*.
16. World Bank, *Africa Human Capital Plan*.
17. Lange et al., *Changing Wealth of Nations 2018*.
18. Secretaria Status, *Statistical Yearbook of the Church 2017*.
19. On trends in enrollment, see Wodon, "Enrollment in Catholic Higher Education."

this chapter. Overall, despite some caution, stylized facts emerge from the data and are likely to at least approximately reflect the situation on the ground.

By examining the church's annual statistical yearbooks, we can estimate the yearly total enrollment in K–12 Catholic schools by region, thus including preschools, primary schools, and secondary schools. Estimates are available since 1970, although for preschools, the series starts only in 1979. Data are provided for Africa, the Americas, Asia, Europe, and Oceania. More detailed breakdowns are available in the statistical yearbooks or can be constructed from the country-level estimates, but for the purpose of this chapter, this level of disaggregation is sufficient. Globally, in 2017, 7.3 million children were enrolled in Catholic preschools globally, 34.6 million children attended primary schools, and 20.3 million children attended secondary schools, for a total across the three levels of more than 62.2 million children. This represented a small decline versus estimates for 2016, at 62.4 million. In most years, enrollment increases globally, so the 2017 school year represents somewhat of an outlier given this small decline, which was due to a drop in enrollment in South America, for the most part. Africa accounts for a large and rapidly growing share of total enrollment. In other regions, enrollment has remained flat in recent years, including in Asia, or has even declined.

The church's statistical yearbooks can also help us determine the breakdown of enrollment in Africa by level. In 2017, a total of 27.8 million children were enrolled in K–12 Catholic schools in the region. The largest enrollment by far was in primary schools, with 19.2 million students enrolled, versus 6.4 million in secondary schools, and 2.3 million in preschools. The highest growth rates in enrollment over the last few decades have been observed for preschools and secondary schools. This is good news, as the returns to education in labor markets are higher for secondary than for primary schooling, while the literature also demonstrates that early childhood is a critical period in a child's development.[20]

The yearbooks can also help us determine the share of students enrolled in Catholic schools globally who reside in Africa. Except for a brief period in the early 1970s when the region's share in global enrollment in Catholic schools decreased probably due in part to school nationalizations that were later reversed in some countries like the Democratic Republic of the Congo (DRC), this share has been steadily increasing over time. In 2017, Africa accounted for 44.7 percent of all students in K–12 Catholic schools globally. The share was highest at the primary level (55.5 percent), followed by secondary schools (31.1 percent) and preschools (31.3 percent). In 1970, by contrast, those shares were respectively at 22.8 percent for primary schools, and only 5.9 percent for secondary schools.

This does not mean that the share of students in Catholic schools is increasing. To compute this share, comparisons can be made between enrollment data from the statistical yearbooks of the church and data collected by the UNESCO Institute of Statistics on total enrollment in primary and secondary schools (data for preschools are less reliable). As noted in Wodon's article "Enrollment in K–12 Catholic Schools: Global and Regional Trends," globally, the share of students in Catholic schools increased from 4.1 percent to 4.8 percent at the primary level from 1975 to 2016. At the secondary level, it dropped slightly from 4.3 percent to 3.5 percent due in part to an expansion of private secular schools. In Africa however, the share of students in Catholic schools is much higher. It has remained somewhat stable over time with slight ups and downs, or may have increased slightly, although this depends on the years used for comparisons over time. In 2016, Catholic schools accounted for 10.7 percent of all students in Africa, versus 10.0 percent in 1975. At the secondary level, the share of students in Catholic schools was at 7.4 percent in 2016, versus 7.0 percent in 1980 (the estimated share for 1975 is an outlier and may be affected by data reliability issues). Note that if these shares were computed for sub-Saharan Africa only, they would be higher.

Apart from estimates of the number of students in Catholic schools, the statistical yearbooks of the

---

20. Denboba et al., *Stepping Up Early Childhood Development*; Black et al., "Early Child Development Coming of Age."

church provide data on the number of schools, which can be used to compute the average size of schools. As Wodon notes, growth in the total number of children enrolled in Catholic schools can be decomposed into growth in the number of schools plus growth in the average size of schools.[21] The results of the decomposition for the period from 1995 to 2016 are provided in table 1 for the region. Estimates are also provided for two subperiods, from 1995 to 2005, and from 2005 to 2016. Typically, growth resulted from both an increase in the number of schools, and an increase in the average size of schools. For the full period, enrollment in primary schools increased at a rate of 3.5 percent per year. This resulted from an increase in the number of schools of 1.8 percent per year, and an increase in the size of schools of 1.7 percent per year. At the preschool and secondary levels, as expected, most of the growth came from an increase in the number of schools, but schools also became somewhat larger.

	Annual Enrollment Growth in Catholic Schools			Annual Growth in the Number of Schools			Annual Growth in the Average School Size		
	1995-2005	2005-2016	1995-2016	1995-2005	2005-2016	1995-2016	1995-2005	2005-2016	1995-2016
Pre-primary	5.9	6.1	6.0	4.5	5.0	4.8	1.3	1.0	1.2
Primary	2.9	4.0	3.5	1.7	1.8	1.8	1.2	2.1	1.7
Secondary	7.3	5.1	6.1	4.4	5.1	4.7	2.8	0.0	1.3

Table 1: Enrollment Growth in K–12 Catholic Schools in Africa, 1995 to 2016 (%). Source: Wodon "More Schools, Larger Schools, or Both?"

What can we expect in the next decade in terms of future enrollment? Given high rates of population growth and gains in educational attainment, growth in enrollment in Catholic schools in Africa should continue for some time. In sub-Saharan Africa in particular, women have an average of 4.8 children, about twice the global average. As a large share of Africa's population is young, these high fertility rates lead to high rates of population growth, at 2.7 percent per year for the region versus 1.1 percent globally. Population growth rates are higher among Muslim than Christian populations in the region,[22] but Christian and, in particular, Catholic populations are expanding, too. In addition, because educational attainment is low, education systems will expand to catch up in low-income countries, many of which are in Africa.[23] Enrollment in secondary school may double between 2015 and 2030.[24] For Catholic schools, simple simulations based on recent growth rates in enrollment suggest that, by 2030, Africa could account for 65 percent of all children in Catholic primary schools globally and 44 percent of all children in Catholic secondary schools.[25]

Enrollment Data by Country

There is substantial heterogeneity among countries in the size of their Catholic school networks. Table 2 (pp. 246–47) provides data on enrollment by level in 2017 for fifty countries by groups of five countries. The table also provides data on the number of schools in each country. A few countries or territories are not include because they have no, or virtually no, enrollment (Algeria, Libya, Saint Helena, Seychelles, and Somalia, as well as Western Sahara). Note that Réunion Island is a French territory.

---

21. Wodon, "How Well Do Catholic and Other Faith-Based Schools Serve the Poor?—Part I: Schooling."
22. Pew Research Center, *Changing Global Religious Landscape.*
23. UNESCO Institute for Statistics and Global Education Monitoring Report, *Meeting Commitments: Are Countries on Track to Achieve SDG4?*
24. Bashir et al., *Facing Forward..*
25. Wodon, "Implications of Demographic, Religious, and Enrollment Trends."

The country with the largest enrollment is the DRC, with 6.2 million students, according to the latest statistical yearbook.[26] Some of the first Catholic schools were established when the country was a Belgian colony in the nineteenth century;[27] however, the first Catholic secondary school was established only in 1948, and the first university (Lovanium) in 1954. Catholic schools maintained their autonomy right after independence in 1960, but in 1974, the Mobutu regime nationalized all faith-based schools as part of a policy of "Zaïrianization" in multiple sectors. The policy did not bring its expected results, and in 1977, the management of primary and secondary schools was returned to communities through an agreement signed between the government and the representatives of the Roman Catholic, Protestant, Kimbanguist, and Islamic faiths.

Today, while the schools under this agreement (écoles conventionnées) have substantial autonomy, they are nevertheless considered public schools, and teacher salaries are paid by the government. The size of the network of Catholic and other faith-based schools in the DRC is emblematic of the importance of religion in the country. But it also reflects the fact that decades of conflict led to an inability of the state to provide basic services. The share of students in Catholic schools was especially high at 47.3 percent for primary schools and 33.4 percent for secondary schools during the period of conflict from 1991 to 2004.[28] Today, it is slightly lower but still large at 30.1 percent for primary schools and 27.2 percent for secondary schools (estimates for the year 2015). What may also have played a role in the large number of students enrolled in Catholic schools in the DRC is the fact that despite the principle that the state should pay teacher salaries in both *conventionné* (i.e., religious-run) and *non-conventionné* (i.e., state-run) public schools, in practice a large share of the cost of operating the schools is actually paid by households in both types of schools. This results in smaller differences in out-of-pocket costs for households of faith-based as opposed to public schools.

After the DRC, the country with the second largest enrollment is Uganda, with 5.2 million students. During the colonial period, Catholic schools were owned and managed by the Catholic Church, as was the case for schools operated by the church of Uganda. In 1963, however, the Education Act placed Catholic and most other religious schools under the authority of the government. As a result, most Catholic schools are considered public schools, but some established more recently are private. For public Catholic and other faith-based schools, while religious authorities are consulted on decisions related to the selection of head teachers, or appointments to school management committees or boards of governors, for practical purposes, the schools follow the curriculum taught in public schools and teachers are appointed by the state. This can make it more difficult for the schools to maintain their Catholic identity.[29] At the secondary level, support was provided until recently by the state under an innovative public–private partnership, but this partnership was ended and private Catholic secondary schools participated relatively little in it.[30]

According to data from the Ministry of Education and Sports, data from the ministry indicate that in 2016, 8.7 million students were enrolled in primary school, with 1.5 million in secondary schools. This suggests a share of students in Catholic schools of 56 percent at the primary level, and 29 percent at the secondary level. The latest statistical abstract of the ministry suggests that in 2016, of 4,733 Catholic primary schools that responded to the school census that year, 4,233 schools were government-aided and only 690 were private or not aided by the government. For secondary school, the situation is different, with about two-thirds of Catholic schools being private and only one-

---

26. In 2016, the estimate was at 5.5 million—it is not clear why there was a sizable jump between both years.
27. Wodon, "Catholic Schools in the Democratic Republic of Congo."
28. Wodon, "Catholic Schools in the Democratic Republic of Congo."
29. Heyneman and Stern, "Low Cost Private Schools for the Poor"; D'Agostino, "Precarious Values in Publicly Funded Religious Schools."
30. Wodon, "Benefits from Secondary Education, Public–Private Partnerships, and Implications for Catholic Schools: A Case Study for Uganda."

third public, probably in part because many of the schools were open well after the nationalization, and secondary schools expanded more recently.

The DRC and Uganda make it clear that many Catholic schools in Africa are actually public schools, although in countries with smaller enrollment, including majority Muslim countries, this is less the case. Table 2 on the next page also shows that a few countries account for the bulk of K–12 enrollment in Catholic schools. The DRC and Uganda account for 41.1 percent of total enrollment in the region. When Kenya is added, this increases to 56.0 percent. Malawi and Rwanda round out the top five. Next are Ghana, Nigeria, Burundi, Madagascar, and Zambia. Of the top ten countries in terms of enrollment, seven are considered low income under the World Bank classification (gross national income per capita of $1,025 or less in fiscal year 2020), with the other three (Kenya, Ghana, and Nigeria) classified as lower-middle income (gross national income per capita of $1,026 to $3,995 in fiscal year 2020).

Table 2 finally provides data at the country level on the number of schools, apart from student enrollment. There are large differences in the size of schools between countries. Considering the top five countries, the average size of schools ranges from 308 to 1,051 at the primary level, and 327 to 1,394 at the secondary level. Broadly speaking, Catholic schools tend to have sizable enrollment in many schools at the primary and secondary levels. For preschools, the average size of the schools is much smaller, as expected, at 120 students per school overall in the region, versus 425 students in primary schools, and 418 in secondary schools. As mentioned in the previous section, growth in both the number of schools and the size of schools contributed to rising enrollment over time.

Achievements

Historically, Catholic and other Christian schools played an important role in early formal education systems in African countries, especially during colonial times. In Ghana, for example,[31] missionary "castle" schools in the Gold Coast Colony can be traced back to the sixteenth century, serving European merchants and wealthy Africans with a focus on literacy, arithmetic, and Bible study. By 1529, the settlement of Elmina had been converted to Catholicism, until the (Protestant) Dutch seized the castle in 1637. Later, the country fell under British rule. Over the next few hundred years, many more missionary schools were established, and by independence, the schools were the backbone of the education system. In his 1974 article "African Responses to Christian Mission Education," Edward Berman estimates that, in 1950, missionary schools accounted for 97 percent of school enrollment.[32] In 1957, the British colony of the Gold Coast became the state of Ghana, and in 1962 the government assumed responsibility for the schools, including for teacher salaries.

This story of missionary schools, whether Catholic or Protestant, established in colonial times becoming public schools soon after independence is repeated in many countries. In some countries, the religious identity of the schools was kept, but in others it was not. Historically, the schools often started by serving the elites and thereby were an instrument of colonization. But they also contributed to economic development and later to access to education.[33] In periods of conflict, as mentioned earlier in the case of the DRC, Catholic and other faith-based schools were often the last standing when public education systems collapsed. Still, in education as well as in other areas, the overall (positive and negative) contributions of missionaries remain debated.[34]

Today, many sub-Saharan African countries, especially those with a large network of Catholic schools, have a combination of public and private Catholic schools, with private Catholic schools often established after independence and functioning without state support, but with much more autonomy.

---

31. Olivier and Wodon, "Faith-Inspired Education in Historical Perspective."
32. Berman, "African Responses to Christian Mission Education."
33. Frankema, "Origins of Formal Education in Sub-Saharan Africa."
34. Cagé and Rueda, "Devil Is in the Detail."

Table 2: Number of Students Enrolled and Number of Schools by Country, 2017

	Number of Schools				Number of Students			
	Preschool	Primary	Secondary	Total	Preschool	Primary	Secondary	Total
Total	18,813	45,088	15,238	79,139	2,251,425	19,170,537	6,367,769	27,789,731
Dem. Rep. Congo	712	12,537	5,255	18,504	77,133	4,426,082	1,715,895	6,219,110
Uganda	1,550	5,108	789	7,447	153,208	4,643,008	404,914	5,201,130
Kenya	4,956	5,274	2,177	12,407	396,761	2,685,620	1,073,287	4,155,668
Malawi	404	4,824	160	5,388	451,429	1,486,392	223,084	2,160,905
Rwanda	1,238	1,179	675	3,092	157,793	1,239,035	366,209	1,763,037
Ghana	1,835	2,044	1,207	5,086	212,897	526,193	298,665	1,037,755
Nigeria	1,759	1,851	946	4,556	184,970	419,500	321,118	925,588
Burundi	297	1,407	563	2,267	22,306	613,829	129,000	765,135
Madagascar	1,487	3,880	1,024	6,391	104,195	375,226	202,144	681,565
Zambia	111	96	88	295	11,803	43,521	577,196	632,520
Tanzania	1,012	458	370	1,840	80,726	278,831	138,673	498,230
Cameroon	742	1,077	280	2,099	56,691	230,376	101,144	388,211
Angola	82	286	100	468	15,506	267,726	83,129	366,361
Sierra Leone	101	849	127	1,077	8,378	256,852	72,501	337,731
Gabon	51	234	22	307	18,482	276,416	15,112	310,010
Lesotho	53	529	95	677	15,059	229,203	59,147	303,409
South Africa	224	260	111	595	19,873	129,203	82,538	231,614
Zimbabwe	92	121	114	327	12,947	93,410	56,299	162,656
Ethiopia	315	187	81	583	44,272	88,292	29,128	161,692
Egypt	190	144	79	413	34,710	67,243	44,306	146,259
Togo	195	539	85	819	5,106	107,308	31,698	144,112
Côte d'Ivoire	119	394	54	567	9,302	73,099	30,237	112,638
Mozambique	99	77	64	240	10,522	39,500	57,086	107,108
Burkina Faso	61	176	122	359	8,834	53,333	42,104	104,271
Senegal	128	116	48	292	18,255	55,112	24,277	97,644

South Sudan	70	124	24	218	21,645	59,822	9,107	90,574
Benin	103	228	122	453	6,283	44,307	32,305	82,895
Central Afr. Rep.	78	132	34	244	11,992	43,875	15,130	70,997
Chad	92	133	48	273	4,980	45,409	13,509	63,898
Swaziland	14	47	13	74	900	32,000	11,200	44,100
Eq. Guinea	81	83	62	226	8,865	21,352	13,614	43,831
Mali	20	51	37	108	3,486	25,577	14,626	43,689
Gambia	53	35	42	130	6,858	21,054	10,411	38,323
Sudan	64	160	12	236	5,952	27,613	2,841	36,406
Congo	44	110	65	219	3,671	23,772	7,278	34,721
Mauritius	2	51	21	74	250	18,404	13,989	32,643
Eritrea	69	36	21	126	11,192	10,825	9,927	31,944
Guinea-Bissau	29	64	12	105	5,571	19,651	5,966	31,188
Guinea	40	32	18	90	6,345	15,933	6,183	28,461
Liberia	49	49	34	132	4,393	14,800	6,048	25,241
Niger	14	18	5	37	2,203	7,662	4,634	14,499
Namibia	64	20	8	92	2,501	7,822	2,549	12,872
Morocco	13	13	8	34	2,423	7,797	1,671	11,891
Réunion	24	24	5	53	3,342	5,943	227	9,512
Cape Verde	34	6	3	43	3,580	2,223	2,606	8,409
Botswana	27	11	3	41	1,021	3,248	3,634	7,903
Tunisia	4	7	0	11	500	5,000	0	5,500
Sao Tome & Pr.	3	1	1	5	1,300	650	885	2,835
Djibouti	5	5	2	12	464	1,408	418	2,290
Mauritania	3	-	-	3	420	-	-	420
Comoros	1	1	1	3	130	80	120	330

Source: Statistical Yearbook of the Church, 2019 edition.

What are the achievements of Catholic schools in Africa? One major achievement is their contribution to the transmission and teaching of the faith. While this is not the point of this chapter, transmitting the faith is clearly (and rightfully so) a key area of focus of Catholic school leaders. As noted by Augusta Muthigani in her address as president of the International Office for Catholic Education at the organization's 2019 World Congress, what holds the global network of Catholic schools together is, first and foremost, the faith, values, and educational principles drawn from the Gospels and the social teaching of the church.[35] Contributing to transmitting the faith through Catholic schools is no easy task, not only because this must be done in a way that is respectful of a substantial minority of students that do not necessarily share the faith, but also because the traditional reliance of schools on members of the clergy and religious orders is being tested. Even though the region has seen rapid growth in the number of diocesan priests as well as religious sisters and brothers, given other demands and the ever-growing number of Catholic schools in the region, their availability for the school apostolate has been reduced. This requires training committed laypeople on how to teach Catholicism and the kind of spiritual and moral education that is offered in the evangelizing work of the church through Catholic education.

In terms of their contribution to education systems, Catholic schools often reach children in poverty even if they are not primarily serving the poor, as discussed in the next section. There is also a perception that Catholic schools provide a better education than public schools, although this could be debated again, and the literature on sub-Saharan Africa on this issue is limited. For example, in the landmark 2007 collection of papers by Gerald Grace and Joseph O'Keefe,[36] few contributions deal with the region. In my own work on Catholic and faith-based schools in Africa,[37] in some cases students in the schools seemed to perform better than students in public schools, but this was not always the case. Furthermore, these analyses were based on observational as opposed to experimental studies, so causality is hard to assess. In addition, as will be discussed further below, there is heterogeneity even among Catholic schools.

What is clear, however, is that Catholic and other faith-based schools respond to parental demand for the education provided in the schools since parents often pay higher out-of-pocket costs to send their children to these schools in comparison to public schools. In fieldwork carried out in communities with Catholic or Christian schools as well as public and Islamic schools in Burkina Faso and Ghana, parents were asked why they chose the various types of schools.[38] Parents with children in Islamic schools emphasized the religious education provided by the schools. Parents with children in public schools emphasized their proximity and low cost. Parents with children in Catholic and other Christian schools emphasized first the academic quality of the schools, and next the importance of transmitting strong values to the children. Of note, while Islamic schools had virtually no children from Christian families enrolled, a non-negligible share of enrollment in Christian schools was from Muslim families.

A few statistics help illustrate what drives parents to choose Catholic and other Christian schools.[39] In both Burkina Faso and Ghana, parents could choose, among a wide range of factors, what led them to send their child to the school of their choice. These factors included location, religious knowledge, moral education, learning Arabic (which applied to Islamic schools), learning French or English (depending on the country), teacher quality and discipline, academic performance, ensuring the child's future (good education, jobs), familiarity with the school, and no or low school fees. In Burkina Faso, moral education and reli-

---

35. Muthigani, "How Education Can Save the World."
36. Grace and O'Keefe, *International Handbook of Catholic Education*.
37. For summary results, see Wodon, *Education in Sub-Saharan Africa*; and Wodon, *Economics of Faith-Based Service Delivery*.
38. Gemignani et al., "What Drives the Choice of Faith-Inspired Schools by Households?"
39. Gemignani et al., "What Drives the Choice of Faith-Inspired Schools by Households?"

gious knowledge were ranked third and fourth as factors leading to the choice of the schools by parents after academic performance and teacher quality and discipline. In Ghana, religious knowledge came first, and moral education was third, with teacher quality coming in as the second most cited factor. In Islamic schools, religious knowledge came out even more strongly in both countries as (by far) the most cited factor leading parents to choose those schools. But in public schools, again in both countries, religious knowledge was almost never mentioned, as was the case for moral education. Clearly, from the point of view of parents, the emphasis on religious education and values is a major reason for choosing Catholic schools. Data from nationally representative household surveys for West and Central Africa suggest that Catholic and other faith-based schools manage to respond to these parental priorities. Indeed, satisfaction rates for faith-based schools tend to be higher than for public schools, although they are on a par with the rates observed for private secular schools.[40] Catholic schools are typically not identified separately from other faith-based schools in those surveys, but the results are encouraging. They confirm the implicit revealed preferences of parents who often make financial sacrifices to enroll their children in faith-based schools, as opposed to public school for which there is often no tuition.

Challenges

Despite major achievements, Catholic schools still face challenges in Africa (and elsewhere) in terms of reaching the poor and improving the quality of the education they provide. There should be no doubt that Catholic schools make real efforts to reach the poor and provide a quality education, but this does not guarantee success. To discuss these issues, a few basic facts are first provided across countries before considering an illustrative analysis of challenges faced by Catholic schools in Uganda, one of the countries with the largest enrollment in Catholic schools.

General Considerations

Data for sub-Saharan African countries related to the two challenges of reaching the poor and providing a quality education are visualized in figure 1. The visualization is in terms of protection against the risks of poverty and lack of learning at the national level. The horizontal axis on the figure represents the share of the population not in poverty according to the $1.90 per day threshold in purchasing power parity terms used by the World Bank for international poverty comparisons. Countries further to the right tend to have a smaller share of their population in poverty. The vertical axis represents the expected number of learning-adjusted years of schooling that children can expect to achieve on average. The measure of learning-adjusted years of schooling accounts not only for the average expected number of years of schooling that children are expected to complete but also for how much they actually learn in school as measured through international student assessments.[41] Countries in the upper part of the figure do better in providing educational opportunities to their children. The size of the bubbles in the figure is proportional to the number of students in Catholic schools in each country. Note that for a few countries, data on learning-adjusted years of schooling are not available.

A few stylized facts visible on the figure are worth emphasizing. First, many countries have high rates of poverty. This is the case for the DRC (large bubble on the bottom left of the figure), but also for other countries such as Uganda and Kenya (the other two large bubbles in the center of the figure), as well as several other countries with large enrollment including Malawi and Burundi, as well as, to a lower extent, Rwanda. In many of those countries, as Catholic schools serve a substantial share of the student population, they also tend to reach the poor. In the DRC, for example, Catholic schools enroll students in poverty in roughly the same proportion as public schools[42] (and as mentioned earlier, Catholic schools are themselves considered public schools). In other countries such

---

40. Wodon, *Education in Sub-Saharan Africa*; and Wodon, *Economics of Faith-Based Service Delivery*.
41. World Bank, *World Development Report 2018*.
42. Backiny-Yetna and Wodon, "Comparing the Private Cost of Education at Public, Private, and Faith-Based Schools in Cameroon."

as Sierra Leone,[43] this is also the case. But in some countries where the share of students in Catholic schools is smaller, such as Cameroon, Catholic schools tend to serve more children from more privileged households.[44] Still, overall, given the high rates of poverty in many countries where Catholic schools have a large presence, Catholic schools do manage to reach a large number of children in poverty, and the presence of Catholic schools tends to be stronger in poorer countries.

Second, in most countries, including those with lower levels of poverty, education systems are not providing adequate educational opportunities, in that the expected levels of learning-adjusted years of schooling are very low. Globally, across all countries, children are expected on average to complete 11.2 years of schooling, but this is valued at only 7.9 years of learning-adjusted schooling because many children learn less than what they should for their grade. In sub-Saharan Africa, children in most countries have much lower expected learning-adjusted years of schooling in the three- to six-years range. This means that children are not learning what they should normally learn by the time they complete primary education. The main exception among countries with substantial enrollment in Catholic schools in the figure is Kenya, where children are expected to complete 7.8 years of learning-adjusted schooling. In the DRC and Uganda, the corresponding estimates are 4.7 and 4.4 years, respectively. Note that across countries, there is a positive relationship between lower levels of poverty and better educational outcomes, but this relationship is weak. Education systems across the board tend to perform poorly, with comparatively richer countries not doing much better than poorer countries. When considering all countries in the world, the relationship between economic development and educational outcomes is stronger. In sub-Saharan Africa, this is less the case.

One implicit implication of these data is that, even if it were the case that thanks to a so-called Catholic school advantage the schools were to provide a better education experience than public schools, this could still often result in a somewhat low-quality education.[45] This is not mentioned as a critique against Catholic schools. In some countries, Catholic schools do not benefit from government funding, or when they do, the level of funding received is often lower than for public schools, especially when capital expenditures are taken into account. The fact that, despite limited support, Catholic schools continue to operate and serve many among the poor is a major achievement. In several countries, during periods of conflict, Catholic and other faith-based schools were the backbone of their countries' education systems as public provision collapsed. Finally, while the schools must often recover a large share of their operating costs through tuition paid by parents, household survey data suggest that they are substantially cheaper on average than private secular schools.[46] This being said, the performance of education systems in Africa, including Catholic schools, remains a work in progress.

What can be done to improve the quality of the

---

43. Wodon and Ying, "Literacy and Numeracy in Faith-Based and Government Schools in Sierra Leone."

44. Backiny-Yetna and Wodon, "Comparing the Private Cost of Education at Public, Private, and Faith-Based Schools in Cameroon."

45. As noted in Wodon, "How Well Do Catholic and Other Faith-Based Schools Serve the Poor?—Part II: Learning," there are examples of studies in developing countries suggesting that students in Catholic schools do well, but this is not always the case. For African countries, the extent of the Catholic school advantage seems limited, according to studies by Backiny-Yetna and Wodon ("Comparing the Private Cost of Education at Public, Private, and Faith-based Schools in Cameroon" and "Comparing the Performance of Faith-based and Government Schools in the Democratic Republic of Congo") as well as Wodon and Ying ("Literacy and Numeracy in Faith-based and Government Schools in Sierra Leone"). For Latin America, the performance of Fe y Alegría schools seems very strong, however; see, e.g., Allcott and Ortega, "Performance of Decentralized School Systems: Evidence from Fe y Alegría in Venezuela"; Parra-Osorio and Wodon, "Performance of Fe y Alegría High School Students in Colombia: Is it a Matter of Fe (Faith) or Alegría (Joy)?"; and Lavado et al., "Effect of Fe y Alegria on School Achievement: Exploiting a School Lottery Selection as a Natural Experiment."

46. Wodon, *Education in Sub-Saharan Africa*; and Wodon, *Economics of Faith-Based Service Delivery*.

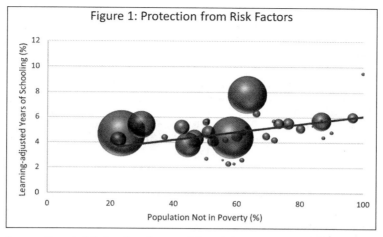

Source: Quentin Wodon, based on World Bank data and the Annual Statistical Yearbook of the Church.

education provided in Catholic schools? It could be that strengthening aspects related to the Catholic identity of the schools would help, but few studies have managed to test this hypothesis in sub-Saharan Africa. It is, however, probably safe to assume that many of the conclusions of the empirical literature on how to improve learning in low-income countries also apply to Catholic schools.[47] For example, in six literature reviews,[48] David Evans and Anna Popova suggest that three types of interventions are recommended across reviews: (1) interventions to ensure that teaching is done at the level at which students are, so that the students can actually follow; (2) in-depth, individualized, and repeated professional development for teachers focusing on the tasks they need to perform in the classroom; and (3) interventions to boost the accountability of schools to parents, so that both teachers and principals can be held accountable for the results they deliver.[49] These are broad recommendations, but they represent a good starting point.

Illustrative Analysis

The context in which Catholic schools operate and how well they perform varies from country to country. To dig a bit deeper, it is useful to consider a brief case study. The focus is on Uganda, a good candidate for additional analysis not only because the country has the second largest number of children on the continent enrolled in Catholic schools but also because data are available to assess how well Catholic schools are doing in comparison to other schools.

Consider first the issue of reaching the poor, in particular for secondary education, where in many countries the demand is not being met. Estimates from Wodon suggest that, while faith-based schools reach the poor in Africa, they do not do

---

47. A discussion of this literature is provided in Wodon, "How Well Do Catholic and Other Faith-Based Schools Serve the Poor?—Part II: Learning."

48. Evans and Popova, "What Really Works to Improve Learning in Developing Countries?" The six studies reviewed by Evans and Popova are the following: Conn, "Identifying Effective Education Interventions in Sub-Saharan Africa"; Glewwe et al., "School Resources and Educational Outcomes in Developing Countries"; Kremer et al., "Challenge of Education and Learning in the Developing World"; Krishnaratne et al., "Quality Education for All Children?"; McEwan, "Improving Learning in Primary Schools of Developing Countries"; and Murnane and Ganimian, "Improving Educational Outcomes in Developing Countries."

49. Evans and Popova, "What Really Works to Improve Learning in Developing Countries?"

so proportionally more than other schools.[50] This is not surprising given that out-of-pocket costs reduce demand for schooling among the poor more than among other groups for all types of schools. However, the geographic location of schools could help. In principle, schools could reach the poor in better-off areas as well as in poor areas because even areas that tend to be better off often have poor households in their midst. In practice, however, it is easier to serve populations in poverty if schools are located proportionally more in poor areas. Is this the case in Uganda, given the challenge of expanding access to secondary education, which is the first objective of the Ministry of Education's strategy? Improving access requires investments in school construction as well as the expansion of existing schools. In that context, Wodon considers two questions. First, where should new secondary schools be built or school expansions considered if the aim is to reduce geographic disparities in access, and how many schools should each geographic area be allocated given limited budgets for school construction? Second, have schools built in recent years by various networks been located in the areas that need new schools the most according to the needs assessment?[51] The analysis is conducted with a data set that distinguishes public schools, private Catholic schools, and other private schools (very few public Catholic schools were created in recent years, hence that category is not considered).

Results suggest that, by and large, new secondary schools have not been located in the areas that need such schools the most based on measures of unmet demand for the schools. There are differences, however, between types of schools, with new public schools somewhat better targeted to areas with the most needs than is the case for Catholic and private schools. This does not mean that new Catholic schools are not serving some among the poor, or that they are not meeting an existing demand for the schools that needs to be met and for which the public schools' response appears to be insufficient. But it does suggest that new Catholic schools are not being created in the areas with the lowest enrollment rates. This could be because the ability of parents to sustain tuition costs in those areas is weaker, although this is only a conjecture. But it does highlight challenges in reaching the poor.

Consider next the issue of learning, with a focus on primary schools since this is where foundational skills need to be acquired by students. National student assessments from Uganda suggest low levels of proficiency for most students. This is confirmed by data for primary schools from the World Bank's 2013 Service Delivery Indicators survey. The data can be used to conduct an assessment of factors affecting student performance. A unique feature of the data is that comparisons can be made not only between public and private schools but also between Catholic and non-Catholic schools, with most of the Catholic schools actually being public schools. In their 2020 World Bank publication, Wodon and Tsimpo look at the performance of primary school students on tests for English, numeracy, nonverbal reasoning, and the student's overall score for the three dimensions combined.[52] The explanatory factors include a wide range of school-level, teacher-level, child-level, and community-level variables.

After controlling for these variables, the analysis suggests that students in private schools, whether Catholic or not, perform better than those in public schools (whether Catholic or not). Students in Catholic private schools are on a par with students in other private schools, and students in Catholic public schools are on a par with students in other public schools. The implications of these findings suggest that, when the schools have autonomy, Catholic schools may be able to perform better, as is the case for other private schools. Still, the results do not necessarily suggest a Catholic school advantage, as they are again of an associative nature and not based on experimental or quasi-experimental evidence.

Conclusion

Africa is by far the continent with the largest number of students enrolled in Catholic schools glob-

---

50. Wodon, *Economics of Faith-Based Service Delivery*.
51. Wodon, "Are New Secondary Schools Built Where They Are Needed Most in Uganda?"
52. Wodon and Tsimpo, "Do Catholic Schools Perform Better in Terms of Student Achievement?"

ally. In 2017, estimates suggest that 19.2 million students were enrolled in primary schools, 6.4 million in secondary schools, and 2.3 million in preschools in the region. That year, Africa accounted for 44 percent of total enrollment in Catholic schools globally. Given high rates of population growth and gains in educational attainment in the region, as well as the possibility of a further decline in the number of students enrolled in Catholic schools in some of the other regions of the world, this share is expected to increase further in coming decades. In many ways, the future of Catholic schools will depend in a substantial way on what happens in the region. It will also depend on how the church navigates the relationship between the church and the state in who controls the quality and content of her faith-based education. The transition from missionary and colonial education to post-independence education where the state played a greater role in the education of the children was fraught with tension in many countries in Africa. This tension is still evident in many countries where there is rivalry among the church denominations for the control of education, as well as tension between Catholic/Christian leaders and Muslim leaders in terms of the degree of autonomy of faith-based schools and the role of the government in exercising an oversight function and providing subvention for the schools.

Relying on data from the annual statistical yearbooks of the church, in this chapter I aimed first to document trends in enrollment in Catholic schools in the region. Next, the objective was to discuss some of the achievements and challenges faced by the schools. A focus was placed in particular on whether the schools manage to reach the poor, and whether they succeed in providing a quality education to students. While there is no doubt that Catholic schools in Africa have achieved a lot, both historically and contemporaneously, the challenges they face remain daunting. Many disadvantaged children remain out of school, and most children who are in school do not learn nearly enough.

There is no magic solution to improve schooling and learning in Africa, including in Catholic schools, but the literature suggests that gains can be achieved with specific interventions, for example, to improve pedagogy in the classroom. The issue of the identity of Catholic schools, and how to maintain or strengthen it, has not been the focus of this chapter, even though it is clear that it is a major motivation for parents to enroll their children in Catholic schools. But it is important to note that, when students acquire strong foundational skills in school, they are probably also more likely to grow in other areas, including in the acquisition of values and socioemotional skills. Cognitive and noncognitive skills often go hand in hand when schools, Catholic or otherwise, aim to educate the whole person.

Perhaps to conclude, it is fitting to mention that the World Development Report on the learning crisis called for three main areas of focus to improve education systems: measuring learning through student assessments, relying on evidence of what works to improve learning, and aligning the actions of stakeholders toward improving learning, which in turn should improve enrollment rates.[53] These recommendations may seem a bit generic, since they essentially call on education systems to measure their performance, adopt proven interventions, and ensure that incentives are provided for stakeholders—parents, teachers, and communities—to act together. But these broad recommendations probably apply as much to Catholic schools as to other schools.

Bibliography

Alcázar, Lorena, and Néstor Valdivia. "Fe y Alegría Schools in Peru: Analysis of the Institutional Management and Pedagogy Model and Lessons for Public Education." In *Faith-Based Schools in Latin America: Case Studies on Fe y Alegría*, edited by J. C. Parra Osorio and Quentin Wodon. Washington, DC: World Bank, 2014.

Allcott, Hunt, and Daniel E. Ortega. "The Performance of Decentralized School Systems: Evidence from Fe y Alegría in Venezuela." In *Emerging Evidence on Private Participation in Education: Vouchers and Faith-Based Providers*, ed. Felipe Barrera-Osorio et al. Washington, DC: World Bank, 2009.

---

53. World Bank, *World Development Report 2018*.

Backiny-Yetna, Prospere, and Quentin Wodon. "Comparing the Performance of Faith-Based and Government Schools in the Democratic Republic of Congo." In *Emerging Evidence on Vouchers and Faith-Based Providers in Education: Case Studies from Africa, Latin America, and Asia*, ed. Felipe Barrera-Osorio et al. Washington, DC: World Bank, 2009.

———. "Comparing the Private Cost of Education at Public, Private, and Faith-Based Schools in Cameroon." In *Emerging Evidence on Vouchers and Faith-Based Providers in Education: Case Studies from Africa, Latin America, and Asia*, ed. Felipe Barrera-Osorio et al. Washington, DC: World Bank, 2009.

Barrera-Osorio, Felipe, et al. *Emerging Evidence on Vouchers and Faith-Based Providers in Education: Case Studies from Africa, Latin America, and Asia*, Washington, DC: World Bank, 2009.

Bashir, Sajitha, et al. *Facing Forward: Schooling for Learning in Africa*. Washington, DC: World Bank, 2018.

Berman, Edward H. "African Responses to Christian Mission Education." *African Studies Review* 17.3 (1974): 527–40.

Black, Maureen M., et al. "Early Child Development Coming of Age: Science through the Life-Course." *The Lancet* 389:10064 (2017): 77–90.

Cagé, Julia, and Valeria Rueda. "The Devil Is in the Detail: Christian Missions' Heterogeneous Effects on Development in Sub-Saharan Africa." In *The Long Economic and Political Shadow of History*, volume 2, ed. S. Michalopoulos and E. Papaioannou. London: Centre for Economic Policy Research, 2017.

Congregation for Catholic Education. *The Catholic School*. Vatican City: Libreria Editrice Vaticana, 1977.

———. *Educating to Fraternal Humanism: Building a "Civilization of Love" 50 Years after* Populorum Progressio. Vatican City: Libreria Editrice Vaticana, 2017.

Conn, Katherine M. "Identifying Effective Education Interventions in Sub-Saharan Africa: A Meta-Analysis of Rigorous Impact Evaluations." Mimeo. New York: Columbia University, 2017.

D'Agostino, T. J. "Precarious Values in Publicly Funded Religious Schools: The Effects of Government Aid on the Institutional Character of Ugandan Catholic Schools." *International Journal of Educational Development* 57 (2017): 30–43.

D'Agostino, T. J., et al. "Faith-Based Education in Changing Social, Economic and Political Contexts: Perspectives from Catholic Educators in Kenya." *Review of Faith & International Affairs* 17.4 (2019): 76–88.

D'Agostino, T. J., and Paolo G. Carozza. "Extending the Research Orientation and Agenda for International and Comparative Studies in Catholic Education." *International Studies in Catholic Education* 11.2 (2017): 140–58.

Denboba, Amina, et al. *Stepping Up Early Childhood Development: Investing in Young Children for High Returns*. Washington, DC: World Bank, 2014.

Evans, David, and Anna Popova. "What Really Works to Improve Learning in Developing Countries? An Analysis of Divergent Findings in Systematic Reviews." *World Bank Research Observer* 31 (2016): 242–70.

Food Security Information Network. *Global Report on Food Crisis 2020*. Rome: Food Security Information Network, 2020.

Francis, Pope. *Laudato Si'* [Encyclical On Care for Our Common Home; June 18, 2015]. Vatican City: Libreria Editrice Vaticana, 2015. www.vatican.va.

Frankema, Ewout H. P. "The Origins of Formal Education in Sub-Saharan Africa: Was British Rule More Benign?," *European Review of Economic History* 16.4 (2012): 335–55.

Gemignani, Regina, et al. "What Drives the Choice of Faith-Inspired Schools by Households? Qualitative Evidence from Two African Countries." *Review of Faith & International Affairs* 12.2 (2014): 66–76.

Glewwe, Paul W., et al. "School Resources and Educational Outcomes in Developing Countries: A Review of the Literature from 1990 to 2010." In *Education Policy in Developing Countries,* edited by Paul W. Glewwe. Chicago: University of Chicago Press, 2014.

Grace, Gerlad, and Joseph O'Keefe. *International Handbook of Catholic Education: Challenges for School Systems in the 21st Century*. Dordrecht, Netherlands: Springer, 2007.

Heyneman, Stephen P., and Jonathan M. B. Stern. "Low-Cost Private Schools for the Poor: What Public Policy Is Appropriate?," *International Journal of Educational Development* 35 (2014): 3–15.

Kremer, Michael, et al. "The Challenge of Education and Learning in the Developing World." *Science* 340:6130 (2013): 297–300.

Krishnaratne, Shari, et al. "Quality Education for All Children? What Works in Education in Developing Countries." Working Paper No. 20. New Delhi: International Initiative for Impact Evaluation, 2013.

Lange, Glenn-Marie, et al. *The Changing Wealth of Nations 2018: Sustainability into the 21st Century*. Washington, DC: World Bank, 2018.

Lavado, Pablo, et al. "The Effect of Fe y Alegría on School Achievement: Exploiting a School Lottery Selection as a Natural Experiment." IZA DP No. 10431. Bonn: Institute for the Study of Labour, 2016.

Le Nestour, A., O. Fiala, and Q. Wodon. *Global and Regional Trends in Child Marriage*. London and Washington, DC: Save the Children and the World Bank, 2019.

McEwan, Patrick J. "Improving Learning in Primary Schools of Developing Countries: A Meta-Analysis of Randomized Experiments." *Review of Educational Research* 85.3 (2014): 353–94.

McKinney, Stephen J. "The Roots of the Preferential Option for the Poor in Catholic Schools in Luke's Gospel." *International Studies on Catholic Education* 10.2 (2018): 220–32.

Murnane, Richard J., and Alejandro J. Ganimian. "Improving Educational Outcomes in Developing Countries: Lessons from Rigorous Evaluations." NBER Working Paper No. 20284. Cambridge, MA: National Bureau of Economic Research, 2014.

Muthigani, Augusta. "How Education Can Save the World." *Journal of Catholic Education* 24.1 (2021): 262–69.

Olivier, Jill, and Quentin Wodon. "Faith-Inspired Education in Historical Perspective: A Case Study." *Review of Faith & International Affairs* 12.2 (2014): 27–37.

Parra Osorio, J. C., and Quentin Wodon. *Faith-Based Schools in Latin America: Case Studies on Fe y Alegría*. Washington, DC: World Bank, 2014.

———. "Performance of Fe y Alegría High School Students in Colombia: Is it a Matter of Fe (Faith) or Alegría (Joy)?" In *Faith-Based Schools in Latin America: Case Studies on Fe y Alegría*, edited by J. C. Parra Osorio and Quentin Wodon. Washington, DC: World Bank, 2014.

Pew Research Center. *The Changing Global Religious Landscape*. Washington, DC: Pew Research Center, 2017.

Pontifical Council for Justice and Peace. *Compendium of the Social Doctrine of the Church*. Vatican City: Libreria Editrice Vaticana, 2004.

Secretaria Status. *Statistical Yearbook of the Church 2017*. Rome: Libreria Editrice Vaticana, 2019.

UNESCO. "Reducing Global Poverty through Universal Primary and Secondary Education." Policy Paper 32 / Fact Sheet 44. Paris: UNESCO, 2017.

UNESCO Institute for Statistics and Global Education Monitoring Report. *Meeting Commitments: Are Countries on Track to Achieve SDG4?* Montreal and Paris: UNESCO, 2019.

UNICEF. *A Future Stolen: Young and Out of School*. New York: UNICEF, 2018.

Wodon, Quentin. "Are New Secondary Schools Built Where They Are Needed Most in Uganda? Comparing Catholic with Public and Other Private Schools." *The Review of Faith & International Affairs* 18.2 (2020): 44–60.

———. "Benefits from Secondary Education, Public-Private Partnerships, and Implications for Catholic Schools: A Case Study for Uganda." *International Journal of Education Law and Policy* 13 (2017): 67–78.

———. "Catholic Health Facilities in Africa: Achievements and Challenges." In *The Handbook of African Catholicism*, edited by Stan Chu Ilo. Maryknoll, NY: Orbis Books, 2022.

———. "Catholic Schools in the Democratic Republic of Congo: Trends, Achievements, and Challenges." *International Journal of Education Law and Policy* 13 (2017): 55–66.

———. "COVID-19 Crisis, Impacts on Catholic Schools, and Potential Responses, Part I: Developed Countries with Focus on the United States." *Journal of Catholic Education* 23.2 (2020): 13–50.

———. "COVID-19 Crisis, Impacts on Catholic Schools, and Potential Responses, Part II: Developing Countries with Focus on Sub-Saharan Africa." *Journal of Catholic Education* 23.2 (2020): 51–86.

———. *The Economics of Faith-Based Service Delivery: Education and Health in Sub-Saharan Africa*. New York: Palgrave Macmillan.

———. *Education in Sub-Saharan Africa: Comparing Faith-Based, Private Secular, and Public Schools*. Washington, DC: World Bank, 2014.

———. "Enrollment in Catholic Higher Education: Global and Regional Trends." *Journal of Catholic Higher Education* 39.1 (2020).

———. "Enrollment in K–12 Catholic Schools: Global and Regional Trends." *Educatio Catholica* 4.3 (2018): 189–210.

———. *Faith-Based Education and Healthcare in Africa*. Washington, DC: World Bank, 2020.

———. "How Well Do Catholic and Other Faith-Based Schools Serve the Poor? A Study with Special Reference to Africa, Part I: Schooling." *International Studies on Catholic Education* 11.1 (2019): 4–23.

———. "How Well Do Catholic and Other Faith-Based Schools Serve the Poor? A Study with Special Reference to Africa, Part II: Learning." *International Studies on Catholic Education* 12.1 (2020): 3–20.

———. "Implications of Demographic, Religious, and Enrollment Trends for the Footprint of Faith-Based Schools Globally." *Review of Faith & International Affairs* 17.4 (2019): 52–62.

———. "Measuring the Contribution of Faith-Based Schools to Human Capital Wealth: Estimates for the Catholic Church." *Review of Faith & International Affairs* 17.4 (2019): 94–102.

———. "More Schools, Larger Schools, or Both? Patterns of Enrollment Growth in K–12 Catholic Schools Globally." *Journal of Catholic Education* 22.1 (2019): 135–53.

Wodon, Quentin, et al. *Economic Impacts of Child Marriage: Global Synthesis Report*. Washington, DC: ICRW and World Bank, 2017.

Wodon, Quentin, et al. *Missed Opportunities: The High Cost of Not Educating Girls*. Washington, DC: World Bank, 2018.

Wodon, Quentin, and Clarence Tsimpo. "Do Catholic Schools Perform Better in Terms of Student Achievement? Evidence on Both Public and Private Primary Catholic Schools in Uganda." *Mimeo*. Washington, DC: World Bank, 2018.

Wodon, Quentin, and Yvonne Ying. "Literacy and Numeracy in Faith-Based and Government Schools in Sierra Leone." In *Emerging Evidence on Vouchers and Faith-Based Providers in Education: Case Studies from Africa, Latin America, and Asia*, edited by Felipe Barrera-Osorio. Washington, DC: World Bank, 2009.

World Bank. *Africa Human Capital Plan: Powering Africa's Potential through Its People*. Washington, DC: World Bank, 2019.

———. "An Analysis of Issues Shaping Africa's Economic Future." *Africa's Pulse* 21 (Spring 2020).

———. *Ending Learning Poverty: What Will It Take?* Washington, DC: World Bank, 2019.

———. "Providing Low-Cost Private Schooling for the Poor." *Inclusive Innovations Notes Series*. Washington, DC: World Bank, 2017.

———. "What Matters Most for Engaging the Private Sector in Education: A Framework Paper." SABER Working Paper Series No. 8. Washington, DC: World Bank, 2014.

———. *World Development Report 2018: Learning to Realize Education's Promise*. Washington, DC: World Bank, 2018.

Suggested Reading

Bashir, S., M. Lockheed, E. Ninan, and J. P. Tan. *Facing Forward: Schooling for Learning in Africa*. Washington, DC: World Bank, 2018.

Wodon, Quentin. "How Well Do Catholic and Other Faith-Based Schools Serve the Poor? A Study with Special Reference to Africa, Part I: Schooling." *International Studies on Catholic Education* 11.1 (2019): 4–23.

———. "How Well Do Catholic and Other Faith-Based Schools Serve the Poor? A Study with Special Reference to Africa, Part II: Learning." *International Studies on Catholic Education* 12.1 (2020): 3–20.

World Bank. *Ending Learning Poverty: What Will It Take?* Washington, DC: World Bank, 2019.

———. *World Development Report 2018: Learning to Realize Education's Promise*. Washington, DC: World Bank, 2018.

Key Words
Catholic schools
learning
primary schools
secondary schools
sub-Saharan Africa

Canon Law in African Catholicism: Historical Development, Challenges, and Prospects

Benedict Ndubueze Ejeh

Canon law as a legislative system[1] is the framework of organizational, disciplinary, doctrinal, and pastoral norms regulating the life of the Catholic Church as a structured community of Christian believers. The church's existence and its sharing of common beliefs, ideals, goals, and activities invariably entail a foundation of common regulatory principles concerning membership, discipline, organization, and faith that is binding on adherents. Thus, though canon law is often associated with the medieval collections of pontifical decrees and jurisprudence, edicts of councils and synods, and the more recent promulgation of a standard codification,[2] a normative or canonical tradition has always been an integral part of the church's life wherever the gospel has taken root. As José Tomás Martín de Agar observes:

> The first Christian communities took the rules of their social life from the Sacred Scripture (principally from the New Testament) and from the teachings of the apostles, passed on by tradition. The bishops also issued norms and decisions for their communities, in which customs and particular traditions originated as well. Evidence of these beginnings of canon law can be found in the documents of that time, in the writings of the apostolic fathers (the first generation of Christian authors after the apostles), and in those of the fathers of the Church (from the second to the eighth centuries). They reflect different ways of understanding Christian life, especially between the East and the West.[3]

In addressing its subject matter, this chapter favors a synchronic historical approach that enables an analytic and critical evaluation of evolving issues and trends in the history of the use of canon law in Africa, as against a diachronic perspective, which would instead concentrate on events and their dates. The scope of the study is to some extent Africa-wide, spanning both northern and sub-Saharan Africa, but the former is seen from the exemplary viewpoint of its glorious Christian past, during which canon law flourished, playing a conspicuous role in the making of its vibrant local Christian communities, until the onslaught of Islam swept away much of its presence and influence.

More detailed attention is dedicated to the present status of canon law as it is lived on the African continent, particularly south of the Sahara. This choice is informed by the fact that African Latin

---

1. As a scientific ecclesiastical discipline also known as "canonistics," canon law deals with studies and scholarship about the juridical essence of the church as elaborated by scholars of different traditions, competing visions, and diverse ideologies.
2. Canon law was first codified in 1917 and significantly revised in 1983.
3. Martín de Agar, *Handbook on Canon Law*, 5–6.

Catholicism, which is the focus of this study, is predominantly present in sub-Saharan Africa.

The chapter offers insights into ways and means of optimizing the use of canon law in African Catholicism as a necessary tool for promoting and enhancing the mission of the church on African soil. Given the limits on a chapter in a handbook of this kind, the very wide scope of the subject matter of this study does not permit a detailed discussion of its various ramifications. It is inevitable, therefore, that the reader may find the content of this work somewhat or maybe even too general. The inevitable limits of this study should be a catalyst for more targeted research into specific areas of interest that have been ignored or merely introduced.

Historical Phases of African Catholicism and Their Canonical Imprint

An agreed, though dated, periodization of the history of the church on the African continent roughly sums up its development into three phases:[4] the early centuries' flourishing of Christianity in the Roman Empire in Africa, extending through Egypt, North Africa, Nubia, and Ethiopia; the superficial attempts at evangelizing the coastal regions of East and West Africa from the era of the great explorations to the eighteenth century; and the "rediscovery" and consolidation of the African missions in the nineteenth and twentieth centuries. A necessary update to this division requires the inclusion of a fourth phase spanning from the Second Vatican Council to the present day. The historical development of canon law in the African church reflects these distinct moments as well. The first phase of this history could be described as the era of legislative canonical autonomy, albeit in universal communion with the church. The second phase can best be described as an era of proxy missionary law, conditioned by partisan colonial policies and interests. The third phase is that of the regime of missionary law, properly so-called, under the jurisdiction of the Congregation for the Propagation of the Faith. A fourth phase is currently ongoing and has been since the inauguration of the ordinary or "common law" regime in the fully fledged particular churches of Africa. This period has been characterized by the impact of Vatican II ecclesiology on the organization of and particular laws governing the churches of Africa.

Canon Law in Roman Africa

In Africa, the canonical tradition of ecclesiastical norms dates back to the earliest Christian centuries, during the era of the Roman Empire's sway in the north of the continent. It is believed that the Christian faith may have taken root in the North African metropolitan city of Carthage by the end of the first century.[5] This would explain the impressive testimony to a flourishing and well-organized body of Christians that, by 180 C.E., already boasted of a documented chronicle of Christian martyrdom[6] and a Latin translation of St. Paul's epistles. By the first quarter of the third century, the church in this region is said to have witnessed the first known gathering of about seventy of its bishops at a council in Carthage, under Bishop Agrippinus, to discuss the controversy regarding the baptism of heretics.[7] The synodal or conciliar gathering of the bishops of the province of Carthage became more frequent, occurring with a certain regularity during the episcopacy of St. Cyprian (ca. 249–58) and even more regularly afterwards. Cyprian presided over not fewer than five councils during his nine-year episcopacy. Later, between the invasion of the Vandals (429) and the conquest of Carthage (439), records indicate that North African bishops celebrated some thirty-eight plenary councils in which issues regarding doctrine, liturgy, discipline, penance, jurisprudence, and even politics were decided.[8] The decisions of these African councils were of

---

4. Chiocchetta, "Verso la conferenza di Berlino," 123.
5. Daniélou and Marrou, "Dalle origini a S. Gregorio Magno," 196; Baus, *Le origini*, 273.
6. The *Acts of the Scillitian Martyrs* records the story of the martyrdom of six North African Christians in July 180.
7. Bardy ("Afrique," 293 and 301) indicates that this occurred in the year 220, while Danielou and Marrou ("Dalle origini a S. Gregorio Magno," 196) place it in 215.
8. Fantappiè, *Storia del diritto canonico*, 47.

particular help to bishops of the suburban dioceses, sustaining and reinforcing their authority, as well as providing them with much-needed assistance in the teaching and governance of their faithful in rural parts of the region, where pastoral tools were often lacking and pastors needed simple authoritative rules in order to exercise effective leadership.[9]

As a part of its thriving ecclesiastical life, the North African church developed a consistent and widely diffused juridical tradition made up of disciplinary and doctrinal norms that were ratified during numerous synods and councils and incorporated into various collections of canonical norms of the regions of the Latin church and beyond. It is on record that in Western Christianity the earliest known chronological collection of canonical norms comes from North Africa,[10] a veritable *liber canonum* of ordinances promulgated by councils of the early African church.[11] The North African church followed a tradition of approving previous synodal decisions at the beginning of each new assembly, which led to the formation of a compendium of normative and judicial dispositions of the synodal sessions. These collections found their way outside the territorial borders of the region and into subsequent collections from other territories in both Eastern and Western Catholicism and became qualified as "'universal' law that greatly influenced the development and composition of the *ius commune*,"[12] or common law. The extensive influence of these norms is attributed to their high juridical quality and the articulate resolution of the existential and legal ecclesiastical issues they addressed.[13] Worthy of particular note among these collections (some of whose various editions have been assembled in C. Munier's volume *Concilia Africae*[14]) are (1) the *Breviarum Hipponense*, containing legislation promulgated during the Council of Hippo in 393, as approved by the Council of Carthage in 397; (2) the *Codex Apiarii Causae* (ca. 419), recording the case of the condemnation, deposition, and excommunication of the priest Apiarius of Sicca by the African bishops for unspecified offenses—probably multiple, as can be deduced from the variety of themes reflected in the norms applied in the trial—and his appeal to Rome;[15] and (3) the *Registri Ecclesiae Carthaginensis Excerpta*, an excerpt from the registry of Carthage containing the norms of previous councils upheld during the Seventh Council of Carthage (419) that related to the above-named controversy surrounding the excommunication of Apiarius. Another early collection, the *Breviatio canonum*, composed around the second quarter of the sixth century by the deacon Fulgentius Ferrandus of Carthage, which assembled the canons of the early Greek and African councils, arranged its decrees under various headings, including Bishops, Priests, Deacons and the Clergy in General, Councils, Heretics, Trials and Punishments, Baptism, Fasting, and Miscellaneous Questions.[16] Regarded widely as the canon law of the earliest church on the African continent, these collections bear witness to the importance that particular councils had in the legislative tradition of local churches.

The collections of the primitive normative traditions of the North African church dealt with issues of various kinds pertaining to the life of the people of God located in that territory. They include doctrinal definitions, canons of sacred scripture, rules pertaining to the reception of sacraments, heresies, ecclesial communion, clerical morals and discipline, clerical celibacy, pastoral jurisdictions, ecclesiastical goods and their administration, ecclesiastical circumscriptions, sanctions, and so on. As noted by Bardy, no important issues escaped the attention of

---

9. Bardy, "Afrique," 305.
10. Van de Wiel, *History of Canon Law*, 45.
11. Bardy, "Afrique," 288.
12. Bardy, "Afrique," 288.
13. Erdö, *Storia delle Fonti*, 35.
14. Munier, *Concilia Africae A. 345–A. 525*.
15. The bishops refused to acknowledge the appellate jurisdiction of the Roman pontiff as exercised in the absolution of the deposed presbyter by Pope Zosimus and later by Pope Celestine I, over a question about which the African prelates considered their decision more faithful to the canons of Nicaea.
16. Bardy, "Afrique," 290.

the synods and councils of the early African bishops: whether heresies, or trials of controversial personal matters, or questions of church discipline, or any other difficult problem, the bishops had a say about them. Citing Auguste Audollent, he affirms that, if the African church was able to resolve its many crises, douse the tensions created by the controversy over the *lapsi* (returning lapsed Christians), resist the assault of heretics, survive the persecution of the Vandals, resist the heretical doctrinal fireworks of Justinian, and flourish tremendously up to the time the Muslim invasion swept away both ecclesiastical institutions and Roman civilization, it is thanks to its numerous councils.[17]

The canons in these collections depict a highly, though by some standards overly, structured local church divided into many dioceses and provinces with numerous bishops, whose large numbers became an issue at some point.[18] The bishops had a strong sense of episcopal solidarity, communion, and collegiality, which translated into regular synodal assemblies, in which common questions were tackled and collective decisions taken that were binding on all, thus ensuring stability, authority, and order. The bishops in council regarded each other as equally responsible before God for their decisions and free to air their views, with none having to lord it over the others.[19] They are known to have jealously guarded the traditions and customs of the early African church.[20] But theirs was also a church in communion with the universal church. The decisions of the general councils were shared with Rome and the other sister churches, who also sent delegates to the assemblies. The early African church also received the canons of the councils of the other churches. It has been observed, however, that the sense of unity and strength provided by frequent assemblies of the African bishops and their overarching authority seemed to have engendered a certain sense of security that led at some point to a defiant stance against the authority of Rome.[21] It has to be taken into consideration, though, that the relationship between Rome and the local churches, in particular with regard to the question of the primacy of the Roman pontiff, was not yet as well articulated as it subsequently came to be, and that this permitted to some degree a loose sense of allegiance to Rome, which was also responsible for bringing about attempts to resist what was considered to be Rome's undue interference.

Canon Law in Africa during the Era of Royal Patronage

Pristine Catholicism in the northern part of the African continent flourished under the foregoing circumstances with a good dose of normative autonomy that to some extent veered toward a posture of independence from and opposition to Rome. In contrast, the beginnings of the church in the sub-Saharan portion of the continent happened in the twin contexts of Rome's established primacy and the Roman pontiff's medieval claim to *plenitudo potestatis*, a privilege of universal jurisdiction acknowledged by Catholic regimes of the period, which granted the pope authority not only in strictly ecclesiastical matters but also in questions relating to the temporal order. Portugal and Spain, which were the first European powers to venture into exploratory conquests of Africa in the fifteenth century, largely subscribed to these principles.

The missionary activity of the church at this time followed multiple approaches. There was as yet no

---

17. Bardy, "Afrique," 305.

18. A letter of Leo the Great (400–461) to the bishop of Mauritania condemned the proliferation of dioceses and bishops, insisting that in areas where the faithful were few in number, the pastoral care of presbyters should be enough, while bishops were to preside in populous cities (*Epist.* 12.10; *PL* 54:654; see Bardy, "Afrique," 296).

19. It is on record that St. Cyprian, during the Council of Carthage of 256, invited his colleagues to freely air their opinions without fear or favor but instead with a sense of responsibility before the Lord Jesus Christ, to whom alone the church and all judgment belong (*Sent.* 87 episc.; *PL* 3:1085; see Bardy, "Afrique," 303).

20. Following a protest against attempted reforms of the customs of the church in the Province of Numidia, Pope Gregory the Great (540–604) addressed a letter to the bishops allowing them to keep to their traditions that were not contrary to the faith, but prohibiting them from elevating Donatists to the dignity of primates, even when such office was due to them by order of seniority (*Epist.* 1.7; *PL* 77:531–32; Bardy, "Afrique," 299).

21. Bardy, "Afrique," 305.

central organ directing programs of evangelization. Indeed, the first missionary enterprise beyond European shores is known to have been championed by religious orders that, with a mandate from or permission of the pope, set out on mission, often under the patronage of Portugal or Spain.[22] Consequently, with the mission territories effectively under the tutelage of these imperial regimes, even in matters of ecclesiastical governance and pastoral life, canon law at the time could, at best, be said to have existed only by proxy. Using the medieval system of patronage, which gave founders extensive privileges over the churches they established, the popes entrusted the Catholic rulers with the responsibility of ensuring the spread of Christianity and of governing ecclesial life in their territories.[23] With the bull (a special papal decree) *Romanus Pontifex* of January 8, 1454, by which Africa was "donated" to the Portuguese king Alphonsus V in recognition of his role in the crusade against the Turks, Pope Nicholas V became the first pontiff to extend the privilege of patronage to African territories. In addition to giving the Portuguese king and his successors possession over the newly discovered and acquired territories, the apostolic edict allowed them to found and build churches, monasteries, and other places of worship and to supply them with ecclesiastics, secular or regular clergy of their choice, to whom the pope granted powers to freely and lawfully administer confessions and other sacraments among the locals. The missionaries were prohibited, under pain of excommunication or interdict, from engaging in all illicit trades and from dealing in arms and in all unauthorized though legitimate merchandise.

Following the successful exploration of the "New World" by Christopher Columbus, the privilege of patronage granted to Portugal over Africa was reviewed at the behest of King Ferdinand and Queen Isabella of Spain, who had sponsored Columbus's expedition. Pope Alexander VI, in response to the request of the Spanish royal crown and eager to prevent a dispute between the two Catholic colonial kingdoms of Portugal and Spain, issued the bull *Inter coetera* (1493), by which he geographically demarcated the regions that were to be subject to each kingdom. Thus, the Spanish kingdom was assigned portions of the globe stretching from Africa to India, discovered and yet to be discovered, in order to lead their peoples to the Catholic faith, so long as such territories did not already belong to other Christian kings.

A study of the system of patronage as applied in the Spanish and Portuguese colonies concludes that it was built around specific rights and duties, which entailed that the task of evangelization was entrusted to civil powers, who were also granted full authority over the church in mission territories.[24] These rights included the establishment of benefices, the admission, designation, and refusal of missionaries by the relevant colonial authorities, and exclusive jurisdiction over ecclesiastical affairs in the regions under their control. Among the duties expected of the royal patrons were to send missionaries to their settlements, to financially support the missionaries, and to build and maintain places of worship.

The patronage arrangement represented an expedient solution to the Holy See's inability to itself reasonably pursue the task of evangelizing the nations, and did achieve some remarkable gains. However, the system also became a grave obstacle to the freedom of the church, to a significant extent hindering the work of evangelization. Not only did imperialistic interests often work at cross-purposes with missionary activity, but even the Apostolic See's own directives were subject to the *placet* of the colonial authorities. The Holy See's bid at some point to send envoys that would directly report to the pope in the capacity of a nuncio was rejected,[25] and royal patrons even appointed subservient clergy to serve as "bishops" without the required pontifical mandate.[26] In this way, missionaries were not allowed unhindered allegiance to the pope's

---

22. Garcia Martin, *L'azione missionaria nel Codex Iuris Cononici*, 245.
23. Marcocchi, "L'evangelizzazione del nuovo mondo," 278–80.
24. Martina, *Storia della Chiesa*, 330–31.
25. Del Re, *La curia romana*, 146; Pastor, *Storia dei Papi*, 8:509.
26. Martina, *Storia della Chiesa*, 331.

governing authority but instead were compelled to vow their fidelity to the terms of the royal colonial patronage.

During this era, the little-known and misunderstood ways of life of African peoples were routinely described as savage, and the peoples themselves were deemed to be urgently in need of conversion. Strong prejudices initially led to postponements of their baptism and, long after, delayed their access to the church's hierarchy through acceptance into the sacred ministries.[27] In fact, papal edicts at the time depicted locals as savage pagans or even as enemies of Christ who needed to be forcefully subdued and Christianized, to the glory of God. The missionaries, propelled by their zeal to convert the indigenes from their "evil" ways and lacking knowledge of the indigenous languages and ways of life and the guidance of suitable, common regulatory norms of evangelization and methods of mission, often showed disdain and intolerance toward the religious and cultural customs of the locals. Backed by the colonial authorities, some missionaries systematically destroyed local religious symbols and rites, resulting in the resentment of the indigenes and leading to frequent scuffles.[28] Some missionaries, like their colonial counterparts, also engaged in the slave trade, which at the time was considered legitimate, even by the church—thus earning her the unfortunate reputation of having aided and abetted this human scourge, rightly regarded as the saddest event in African history.[29]

On a more juridical note, ecclesiastical organization and life at the time existed at only a rudimentary level in Africa, with communities of believers organized into loose parochial units and virtually itinerant pastors trotting between remote villages, administering the sacraments of initiation and celebrating confessions and Masses, assisted by local catechists and interpreters. Canon law was undeveloped, consisting mostly of special pontifical faculties, directives, concessions, and dispensations from common universal norms, all of which were meant to enhance missionary activity and the success of the church among peoples with worldviews, religions, and ways of life that were at best alien to the Christian tradition.

One of the thorny canonical issues missionaries had to deal with at the time was the baptism of married converts. The Pauline privilege came in handy for those in a monogamous marriage. Regarded as naturally valid, such marriages acquired a sacramental character with the baptism of both spouses. If, however, one of them rejected baptism and refused to live peacefully with the converted partner, the latter was permitted, by virtue of the Pauline privilege, to marry anew in order to safeguard the faith. This norm, which has been traced to St. Paul's pastoral directives, featured prominently in Gratian's twelfth-century *Concordance of Discordant Canons*.[30]

But the Pauline privilege could not address the case of polygamous converts. Because of the Catholic doctrine that Christian marriages must involve monogamous unions, which renders other forms of conjugal union illegitimate and adulterous, one could not convert to the faith and receive baptism while remaining polygamous. Some sixteenth-century pontifical edicts proffered solutions to this problem that became the norm in mission territories. Initially, Pope Paul III in his papal bull *Altitudo Divini Consilii* of June 1, 1537,[31] gave preference to the choice of the first wife among the others. Later, Pope Pius V's bull *Romani Pontificis* of August 2, 1571,[32] permitted the husband to choose one of the wives receiving baptism with him while ceasing all conjugal relations with the others. The missionary solution to polygamous marriages was quite problematic because polygamy was at the time socially and culturally legitimate for Africans. Even today, the church's stance on the issue remains one of the most debated by scholars of African culture.

---

27. Magesa, *Anatomy of Inculturation*, 144.
28. Marcocchi, "Le missioni in Africa e in Asia," 317.
29. Magesa, *Anatomy of Inculturation*, 144; Mugambi, *Christianity and African Culture*, 15–16.
30. Friedberg, *Corpus Iuris Canonici*, C. 28, q. 2, d.p.c. 2.
31. Gasparri, *Codicis Iuris Canonici Fontes*, 1:140–42.
32. Gasparri, *Codicis Iuris Canonici Fontes*, I:246.

Another problem the Pauline privilege could not address was that of slaves who had been forcibly separated from their spouses. Pope Gregory XIII's constitution *Populis* of January 3, 1585,[33] allowed these slaves to remarry as Christians, and their spouses also enjoyed the same privilege upon receiving baptism.

In all, however, the initial missionary activity in sub-Saharan Africa was rather sporadic and superficial, unable to survive its many inadequacies and systemic limitations. In most cases it was called off after a short time or resisted by the natives, leaving behind only vestiges of an experience that could not take adequate root. The royal patrons were for all practical purposes unable to administer the enormous territories they were laying claim to, much less sustain the missionary activity in them, and the missions were too ill-equipped to be viable on their own.

These challenges would be addressed during the missionary period of the Sacred Congregation for the Propagation of the Faith, a pontifical missionary outfit with a sweeping mandate to restore the faith and promote primary evangelization. It has to be noted, however, that transition to the full canonical missionary law regime was rather slow and arduous, often having to contend with opposition from royal patrons, new colonial politics and interests, and even resistance from the missionaries themselves. Important gains were made only toward the end of the colonial era.

Colonialism and the Missionary Law Regime of the Congregation for Evangelization in Africa

On the sixth of January 1622, after several inconclusive attempts to establish an arm of the Roman Curia having the responsibility for directly governing the church's missionary activity, Pope Gregory XV finally instituted the Congregation for the Propagation of the Faith.[34] Its purpose was to take charge of the apostolate of restoring and spreading Catholic Christianity universally. The Propaganda Fide, as the congregation came to be simply called, was endowed with all necessary authority and faculties to accomplish, govern, coordinate, and execute all matters related to the task of evangelizing the so-called pagans and defending the faith against heresy.[35] With respect to its responsibility for primary evangelization, the congregation had powers to grant to missionaries sent to all parts of the world the necessary faculties and privileges for the successful accomplishment of their task. It had the responsibility of resolving all disciplinary controversies capable of undermining missionary activity; of promoting and strengthening the missionary apostolate, seminaries, and colleges; of combating doctrinal errors; and especially of bringing some order to the juridical confusion caused by the unlimited faculties hitherto granted to missionaries.[36] This was meant to provide, as much as possible, common juridical principles and structures, and jurisdictional arrangements and modalities of action, for all persons involved in the delicate undertaking of missionary work.[37] In fact, the conflicts of interests, policies, and activities of various missionary groups, coupled with interference occasioned by the privileges of the royal patrons, led Propaganda Fide, in 1655, to issue a terse prohibition against the establishment of new missionary outposts or works by any religious order, under whatever pretext, in places where the congregation had already sent missionaries. The congregation imposed stringent sanctions, including automatic excommunication reserved to the Holy See, against those who established such outposts without express, written permission.[38]

The burgeoning activity of the congregation was strongly hampered[39] by the hostility unleashed

---

33. *Collectanea*, 1:256, n. 1.
34. *Collectanea*, 1:1–2, nn. 1 and 2.
35. Gregory XV, bull *Inscrutabili Divinae Providentiae*.
36. Del Re, *La curia romana*, 150–51.
37. Fantappiè, *Storia del diritto canonico*, 200.
38. *Collectanea*, 1:36, n. 124.
39. On February 10, 1798, the French general Louis-Alexandre Berthier declared the abolition of the congregation, which, however, continued operating even if it was with much difficulty, especially in regard to its economic responsibilities to the missions, which it could no longer fulfill. During this period, many missionary

against the church and her interests by the French Revolution, virtually starving the missions of necessary funds until Pope Pius VII reconstituted the congregation in 1817. This was in the context of a new climate of religious and missionary renaissance driven by the fervor and charity of many faithful, who donated generously, both as individuals and through foundations, to the cause of evangelization in mission lands. With the pontifical edict *Catholicae Fidei Propagatione*,[40] the supreme pontiff assigned additional sources of income to the congregation and exempted it from paying taxes and duties on its real estate in order to bolster its financial strength for missionary purposes. The missionary momentum got a further boost from subsequent popes, leading to the creation of many new missionary circumscriptions and the emergence of more local clergy and missionary colleges for priestly formation. Missionary religious orders and congregations grew exponentially and flourished[41] as increasing numbers of papal policies were being directed toward better formation of missionaries, harmonization of missionary rules, and "indigenization" of the missions.

This was also the era of extensive exploration and colonization of Africa by competing European powers, which led to the dispute over, redistribution of, or outright dispossession of the territories that the royal patrons historically laid claim to but could not effectively occupy. The scramble for African territories by the European powers led to the Berlin Conference (1884–1885), which formally initiated the colonial era in Africa. This ushering in of a new age had both positive and negative impacts on missionary activity in Africa. On a positive note, irrespective of their nationality or confession, the conference guaranteed the protection of all religious missionaries, not only as agents promoting the humanitarian goals that the colonial regimes formally committed themselves to, but also on the basis of the principle of religious freedom upheld by the conference. This was favorable to the modus operandi of Propaganda Fide, for it ensured its role as the only regulator of Catholic missionary activity, shielding it from the undue interference of colonial administrators. In addition, with the abolition of slavery in America, some converted ex-slaves, returning to Africa, became actively involved in the African missions, even as sacred ministers and leaders of new ecclesiastical missionary circumscriptions.[42] Their missionary engagement helped bring the Christian faith to their African brethren, with whom they shared common ancestral, cultural, and ethnological roots. On the flip side, however, each colonial power was understandably more favorably disposed toward its national religious affiliation, and tended to promote it over others.

The missionary activities of competing confessions, therefore, brought about rivalries that to some extent showed missionaries and Christianity as divisive rather than uniting forces. This division played out even in the organization of social life in indigenous communities, as Catholics were often pitched against Protestants and were sometimes physically separated from one other, not just because they attended different churches but also because they lived in different parts of villages, frequenting different markets, schools, and dispensaries. This was a source of constant tension among the people. Likewise, some of the earlier missionary flaws lingered, like misconceptions, prejudices, and ignorance about indigenous culture and improper missionary formation, leading to some abusive practices by missionaries. Greater attention could also have been paid to local value systems, social structures, ethoses, norms, and customs as integral ingredients of the new Christian way of life. These and similar shortcomings would eventually fuel the perception that Christianity was an alien and alienating religion, especially among many of the new African political and academic elite—

---

associations of the faithful in France and elsewhere in Europe rose to the aid of the congregation with prayers and substantial financial support for its initiatives. For more on this see Metzler, "La Santa Sede e le missioni," 27–36.

40. *Collectanea*, 1:425, n. 725.
41. Metzler, "La Santa Sede e le missioni," 44.
42. Chiocchetta recalls that Catholic ex-slaves repatriated from America began the church in Liberia, that others from Brazil founded the church in Lagos (Nigeria) around 1862, and that one of the returnee ex-slaves, Monsignor Bowers, became bishop of Accra (Ghana) ("Verso la Conferenza di Berlino," 133–34).

most of whom were, paradoxically, educated by the missionaries—who often tried to revive the ethnic African cultural, religious, and value systems to the detriment of Christianity.

Overall, however, missionary activity in the African colonies under the pontifical regime of Propaganda Fide was better organized than it had ever been and highly productive.[43] This is attested to by the impressive spread of Christianity in general and Catholicism in particular on the continent, so much so that today Africa is looked up to as *"nova patria Christi."*[44]

The progressive articulation of the canonical profile of the missions in Africa attests to the successful missionary activity of Propaganda Fide during the colonial era. First, the geographically vast apostolic prefectures dating back to the era of royal patronage were upgraded to the status of apostolic vicariates and assigned bishops acting as apostolic vicars, assisted by a handful of missionaries, including indigenous clergy. These vicariates founded other mission outposts far away from their headquarters and formed catechists, other clergy, and religious for the missions. More vicariates and prefectures were created by the Holy See, ordinarily at the request of bishops, to bridge the huge distances and ameliorate the communication difficulties between pastors and their faithful.[45] The prefectures and vicariates were eventually elevated to dioceses, marking the establishment of fully constituted local churches whose pastors were no longer prefects or vicars sharing in the jurisdiction of the Roman pontiff, but bona fide, autonomous diocesan pastors. While deferring to the Holy See in questions reserved to it or subject to the special faculties of the Propaganda Fide, the new bishops received full powers and authority over and responsibility for their episcopal office and for the governance of their dioceses.

The parish and its organization was a vital component of the canonical organization of the missions. The Council of Trent had earlier insisted that territories without clearly defined parish boundaries and duly designated pastors be formally demarcated to reflect this basic structure of ecclesiastical governance, which it regarded as essential for proper pastoral care leading to greater certainty about the salvation of souls.[46] Thus, what were initially somewhat amorphous mission outposts were progressively divided into parochial units and assigned parish priests and also associates or collaborators, the latter of which were ordinarily catechists placed in charge of remote outstations visited infrequently by the pastors, mainly for the purpose of administering the sacraments. The parishioners helped sustain their pastors and parishes economically, not only through freewill offerings and collections taken during liturgical activities, but also by means of levies, sometimes called the "seventh precept," to be paid in cash or kind, and which were often paid willingly by the locals.[47] Parishes also ran schools, dispensaries, and various centers of skill acquisition and formation.

The "Commission" and "Mandate" Systems: Cornerstones of the Canonical Missionary Law Regime of the Propaganda Fide

Faced with the immediate challenge of circumventing the obstacles posed by the existing privileges of imperial patronage granted to the Iberian crowns and the sometimes self-referential structures established by the missionary orders, the congregation

---

43. Garcia Martin, *L'azione missionaria nel Codex Iuris Cononici*, 254.

44. Paul VI, "Homily on the Occasion of the Canonization of the Martyrs of Uganda"; Sarah, "What Sort of Pastoral Mercy," 31.

45. This was the case, for example, of Bishop Carrie of Loango (Congo), who, in his quinquennial report dated September 18, 1890, requested that the Propaganda Fide split his vicariate in two because of large distances and difficulties with communication (A. Koussebila, "Quale stabilità per il parroco nelle chiese di missione," 66).

46. *Conciliorum Oecumenicorum Decreta*, "Concilium Tridentinum (1545–1563)," Sessio XXIV, De Reformatione, can. XIV, 769; "Concilium Tridentinum (1545–1563)," Sessio XXI, De Reformatione, can. IV, 729–30.

47. Pannier, *L'Eglise de Loango 1919–1947*, 224. Reference is made here to what the pioneering bishop of the former French Congo called, in 1890, "the seventh precept," namely, the obligation to faithfully contribute to the maintenance of the church and the sustenance of her ministers. This bishop sought the approval of the Holy See to require the faithful to comply with the precept.

saw among its first tasks in the mission territories the need to replace the existing hierarchical structures with missionary prelates appointed by the Holy See and directly subject to its authority. It most commonly accomplished this by putting in place a special regime of governance in the mission territories based on the so-called system of commissions. This consisted in assigning a specific mission territory without local clergy to the care of a religious institute or local church, which would organize and carry out missionary activity in the territory.[48] Based on this system, new missionary circumscriptions were placed under the pastoral administration of an apostolic prefect or vicar, that is, an ecclesiastical superior appointed by the Holy See to govern a mission territory in the name of the Roman pontiff. The ecclesiastical missionary circumscription was accordingly designated an apostolic prefecture, apostolic vicariate, or in some cases, a *sui iuris* (special or independent) mission. The institute presented a missionary project or plan to the congregation or received one from it. Terms of agreement were incorporated into the project, including such matters as the exclusive or sometimes participatory character of the commission, by which the congregation stipulated the right of one or more religious institutes to govern the mission; the right of the institute to present the ecclesiastical superior of the mission, who would then be appointed by the congregation; and the responsibility of the institute to provide the necessary number of missionaries and economically sustain the missionary activity.[49] The missionaries were subject to the governing authority or jurisdiction of the ecclesiastical superior and assisted him with the pastoral care of the mission.[50] An administrative and/or pastoral council of the mission ordinarily assisted the ecclesiastical superior in the exercise of his duties. By virtue of his power of governance and special faculties received from the congregation, the ecclesiastical superior, a different person than the superior of the missionary religious institute, was in charge of both missionaries and the mission in matters concerning pastoral assignments; administration of temporal goods; and management of missionary foundations, schools, dispensaries, and other missionary initiatives. The religious superior was not allowed, therefore, to transfer, remove, or change a religious missionary without the approval of the ecclesiastical superior except in case of public scandal, about which the latter had to be duly informed.[51]

The ultimate goal of the missionary law was to establish well-adapted, fully equipped, autonomous, stable, flourishing, and viable local churches, governed by an autochthonous hierarchy. Thus, a key aspect of the congregation's policy was the formation of local clergy who would eventually emerge as leaders of the local church, following the examples of the apostles and fathers, as was advocated by papal teaching.[52] Seminaries and colleges were built pursuant to this all-important objective, as stipulated by the Council of Trent. The congregation also recommended the training of catechists to make up for the lack of priests, the foundation of confraternities to aid pastoral activity, and the institution of schools to impart Christian doctrine. Missionaries were also to aid the social development of the indigenes while avoiding interference in local political matters. They were to administer ecclesiastical property in keeping with civil legislation, train local communities to contribute to the sustenance of the missions, and promote charities and Christian publications. All of these undertakings had to be given account of in the reports that superiors of the missions were required to send to the congregation every five years.

The congregation also made considerable use of local synods and councils to drive the effort of building up the missions. As Metzler observes, for Rome the convocation and celebration of synods and councils was strictly related to the estab-

---

48. Garcia Martin, *La formazione del diritto missionario*, 85.

49. Garcia Martin, *La formazione del diritto missionario*, 90–107.

50. *Collectanea*, 2:156, n. 1558.

51. Garcia Martin, *La formazione del diritto missionario*, 109–10; Sacred Congregation for the Propagation of the Faith, "Quum huic Sacrae Congregationi."

52. Sacred Congregation for the Propagation of the Faith, "Neminem profecto," no. 1002.

lishment of the ordinary ecclesiastical hierarchy, with the aim of promoting the spread of the faith and catalyzing the maturation process of locally adapted particular churches.[53] The congregation, therefore, in asserting its right to summon synodal assemblies in mission territories, ordered that said assemblies be convoked regularly to facilitate the proper organization of local churches, including parishes, diocesan curia, schools, and the administration of the church's temporal goods. It instituted a special Commission for the Review of Provincial Councils to examine the acts and decrees of the synods.[54] Following this directive, many provincial synods were celebrated in the mission territories, among which fifty-five are said to have taken place in the African missions between 1559 and 1965.[55]

Over time, the congregation gradually restructured the system of commissions, reducing its prerogatives, rendering the missions transitory, and enforcing the jurisdiction of local prelates over both missions and missionaries. This process was intensified in the mid-nineteenth century, when the missionary law regime was progressively integrated into the common ecclesiastical law, though not without resistance from the missionary institutes and their agents.[56] A significant moment in the process came about in 1969[57] with the abrogation of the system of commissions in the missionary ecclesiastical circumscriptions that had been raised to the status of dioceses and the introduction of a new "mandate" system. This new system was an alternative open to bishops of the mission territories who sought the intervention of the pope to stipulate a missionary agreement with an institute for the pastoral care of some part of the diocesan territory or some missionary endeavor of major importance. This new method of missionary cooperation clearly underscores the responsibility of the bishop, under whose authority missionary activity is accomplished. While it does not prejudice the bishop's right to stipulate simple agreements with institutes of his choice without involving the Holy See, the mandate system concretely manifests the bishop's communion with the Roman pontiff, whose jurisdiction over missionary activity and mission territories is exercised through the Propaganda Fide. It is also meant to safeguard the rights and duties of both the bishops and the institutes in case of dispute.

In all, therefore, the aim of the canonical missionary law regime in Africa and elsewhere is primarily to regulate missionary activity and its agents using special norms, directives, and policies enacted by the congregation or sometimes by the supreme pontiff, ecumenical councils, or local synods and councils.

The Impact of the Ecumenical Councils of the Vatican on Missionary Law

Since the era of the African missions falls within the time period of the two Vatican councils, it seems appropriate to examine, albeit briefly, the impact of these ecumenical assemblies of bishops—as universal organs of ecclesiastical legislation—on missionary activity in Africa.

The First Vatican Council (1869–1870) was prematurely interrupted, but had been poised to provide a suitable platform for the universal college of bishops to regulate the extensive, though beleaguered, missionary activity of the church. Through its preparatory commission charged with examining questions pertaining to the missions, the First Vatican Council was indeed set to address controversial elements of the existing missionary law as well as promote its favorable aspects.[58] One of the proposals of this commission addressed the urgent need for the missions among the blacks of central Africa. This was in response to a passionate appeal for young missionaries to the region made by Daniel Comboni, who was himself a former missionary to the area, even though he depicted a rather bleak and unsavory image of the ways of life of the

---

53. Metzler, "La Santa Sede e le missioni," 62.
54. Metzler, "La Santa Sede e le missioni," 63.
55. Metzler, "La Santa Sede e le missioni," 64. The present study was not able to lay hands on the documents emanating from these synods.
56. See Fantappiè, *Storia del diritto canonico*, 245.
57. Sacred Congregation for the Evangelization of Peoples, "Relationes in territoriis missionum."
58. Metzler, "La Santa Sede e le missioni," 66.

peoples he described as the accursed "descendants of Cam (Ham)"[59] in urgent need of rescue from eternal damnation. The commission also waded into the problematic question of the relationship between missionaries and the ecclesiastical hierarchy, formulating a bill of rights and duties of bishops and apostolic vicars in charge of the missions. It reaffirmed the need to establish seminaries for the training of indigenous clergy, emphasized the duty of the faithful to sustain the missions materially and spiritually, and proposed a code of conduct for missionaries, including their need to adapt to local customs and observe the laws of the state.

Though these issues were never debated on the floor of the council as a result of its sudden interruption, the discussions of the commission consolidated the consciousness of the need for greater indigenization of the local churches, while also opening the eyes of the church as to the delicate issues surrounding the relationship between missionaries, local bishops, and missionary prelates.[60]

The first *Code of Canon Law*, promulgated in 1917, was a child of the First Vatican Council. It articulated the structure and governance of missionary circumscriptions under the heading of "Vicars and Prefects Apostolic,"[61] thereby incorporating missionary law, understood mainly in organizational terms, into the first universal or common legislative instrument of the Catholic Church. At the time the Pio-Benedictine code came into existence, Africa was essentially one huge missionary outpost whose nascent Christian communities were governed by the special provisions laid down in the code's relevant canons and other special rules and regulations found outside the code.

Structured around the fundamental rule that the universal care of missions in non-Catholic territories is reserved solely to the Apostolic See,[62] the canons designated the missions as apostolic vicariates and prefectures; that is, ecclesial communities partitioned into territories whose pastoral governance was directly subject to the Apostolic See through vicars of the Roman pontiff appointed by the Sacred Congregation for the Propagation of the Faith. There were also the so-called independent or *sui iuris* missions entrusted to the governance of prefects or superiors of missions. Though the 1917 code omitted any mention of these units of missionary jurisdiction in its promulgated version, it is a matter of record that the codification process considered canons that were originally intended to regulate them as well as the apostolic vicariates and prefectures.[63] It is believed that the lack of clarity regarding their specific juridical status led to this omission.[64] A special edict of the missionary congregation later declared them to be equivalent to the *servatis servandis* (apostolic prefectures),[65] thus resolving the uncertainty surrounding their definition.

All missionaries, including members of missionary religious orders, were subject to the jurisdiction of the vicars and prefects apostolic in all pastoral matters.[66] Among other responsibilities, the vicars and prefects in turn were bound to make themselves available in their territory of jurisdiction and carry out canonical visits to its various districts;[67] they were also required to give a regular accounting of their stewardship to the Apostolic See.[68] To expedite their duties of governance, vicars and prefects were required to enlist the assistance

---

59. According to Gen 9:20–26, Ham was the son of Noah and father of Canaan, who saw the nakedness of his father and was cursed to be a slave to his brothers.
60. See Metzler, "La Santa Sede e le missioni," 70–74.
61. Cans. 293–311, CIC 1917.
62. Can. 1350 §2, CIC 1917.
63. See Garcia Martin, *La formazione del diritto missionario*, 199–204.
64. Garcia Martin, *La formazione del diritto missionario*, 206.
65. Sacred Congregation for the Propagation of the Faith, "Ad Episcopos, Vicarios, Praefectosque Apostolicos ac Missionum Superiores."
66. Cans. 295–296, CIC 1917.
67. Can. 301, CIC 1917.
68. Can. 300, CIC 1917.

of duly constituted mission councils[69] and could convene local councils and synods whose decisions were subject to the approval of the Propaganda Fide.[70] They were particularly bound in conscience, in view of a sustainable and durable evangelization, to promote vocations to the priesthood among the indigenes and other inhabitants of their territories.[71]

The Second Vatican Council would eventually proffer an articulated position on the missionary activity of the church. In its decree *Ad Gentes*, the council endorsed the phased evolution of the church's missionary work through stages of initial foundation, growth, and consolidation. The goal of the process is to establish a full-blown local church that is properly "rooted in social life and somewhat conformed to the local culture" and that therefore "enjoys a certain firmness and stability": a church that is "already equipped with its own supplies . . . of local priests, religious, and laymen, and is endowed with those institutions and ministries which are necessary for leading and expanding the life of the people of God under the guidance of their own Bishop." A well-established local church is a mature community of the faithful whose congregations are increasingly "more aware of their status as communities of faith, liturgy, and love," a church in which the lay faithful "strive by their civic and apostolic activity to set up a public order based on justice and love," and in which "families become seedbeds of the lay apostolate and of vocations to the priesthood and the religious life." It is a church wherein "the faith is taught by adequate catechesis, . . . celebrated in a liturgy in harmony with the genius of the people, and by suitable canonical legislation, . . . introduced into upright institutions and local customs."[72]

Juridically, missionary activity is simply the effort of the people of God to set up new churches until these take root among a people, becoming fully constituted, that is, adequately endowed with autochthonous members, pastoral agents (*propriis viribus*), structures, and other sufficient means to enable them to be self-sustaining in their evangelization efforts.[73] Canonically, particular churches in sub-Saharan Africa are classified as "mission territory" as a way of identifying the nature of their ecclesial communion with the universal church.

The Present State of Canon Law in African Catholicism: Achievements and Challenges

The Catholic Church is simultaneously universal and particular in all facets of its existence and operation. Both of these aspects of its self-manifestation are entwined in a profound and indivisible communion, in which both the universal and the particular subsist in and through each other in a relationship of reciprocal immanence. This ecclesiology of communion has a special resonance in ecclesiastical law, giving rise to both universal and particular canon law. A review of the status of canon law in African Catholicism, therefore, must embrace two fundamental aspects: the implementation of universal law and the creation of particular law.

The Implementation of Universal Law in the African Church

The elevation of most ecclesiastical circumscriptions in Africa to the status of dioceses brings them under the common law regime, which, in accordance with universal canonical norms, presupposes proper autonomous governance, as is the right of all bona fide particular churches in which and from which (*in quibus et ex quibus*) the one, holy, catholic, and apostolic church of Christ exists and functions.[74] This is without prejudice to some special faculties, which, as a concrete expression of the Roman pontiff's universal pastoral authority and his special care of and jurisdiction over both missionary activities and mission territories, have

---

69. Can. 302, CIC 1917.
70. Can. 304 §2, CIC 1917.
71. Can. 305, CIC 1917.
72. All the quotations in this paragraph are from *Ad Gentes* §19.
73. Cf. can. 786, CIC 1917.
74. Cans. 368, 369, CIC 1983.

been reserved to the Congregation for the Evangelization of Peoples (CEP), which acts on behalf of the pope in matters regarding the missions.

Canon law in its various facets provides the necessary principles and instruments for good governance: it defines roles, ecclesial relationships, offices, duties, and rights of all the faithful (laity, clergy, and consecrated); it regulates the various avenues for fulfilling the church's evangelization mission (official teachings, catechesis, primary mission, and Catholic education); it governs liturgical worship and the proper administration of the sacraments and sacramentals; and it stipulates rules concerning ecclesial temporal goods, penal sanctions for misconduct, and judicial processes for resolving disputes, protecting rights, and enforcing penalties, among others.

The phenomenal growth of the church in Africa since the postcolonial era undoubtedly attests to the significant role of canon law in the creation, organization, and pastoral care of the various communities of the particular churches, even when this is not immediately perceptible.

Based on the records of the 2016 Pontifical Yearbook,[75] Africa presently boasts approximately 518 ecclesiastical circumscriptions (dioceses, missions, vicariates, prefectures) distributed between some ninety-six ecclesiastical provinces. These are further organized into innumerable smaller units of parishes, parish stations, and basic communities. These ecclesial realities, usually brimming with pastoral activity, are sustained by large and growing presbyteries of priests who, with the assistance of other dedicated pastoral workers and volunteers, collaborate with their bishops in the task of building up local churches and fulfilling their mission. The faithful are actively involved in various forms of organized apostolate and ecclesial associations; thriving congregations of religious and consecrated persons are striving to make the evangelical counsels come alive with an African flair; and governing organs and bodies are seeking daily to promote a healthy pastoral life.

Problems, however, abound arising from ignorance or inadequate knowledge of the provisions of canon law, leading to an inability to make effective use of its rich instruments for enhancing pastoral activity and ecclesiastical discipline. There are also issues arising from ignorance of the duties and rights of the faithful that hinder informed and purposeful commitment to the church, and arising from an inadequate or distorted understanding, deliberate disregard, misapplication, or selective application of canonical norms by pastors. There are questions of the abuse of pastoral authority and of the rights of persons with impunity, as well as problems of the maladministration and misuse of the church's temporal goods. There is also a lack of expertise and juridical instruments for establishing and properly utilizing necessary canonical structures for good pastoral governance and administration of justice, as well as an inability or unwillingness to harness the juridical expertise that is present, among other problems.

By way of concrete examples, it can be observed that very often the diocesan curia, which is the center of governance and coordination of the pastoral life of a local church, made up of institutions and persons whose duty it is to assist the bishop in governing the diocese,[76] is poorly staffed and equipped, often hardly functional, and sometimes nonexistent. In many cases, the offices of the curia are not housed in or coordinated from a central administrative structure to enable its effective and harmonized operation. Ecclesiastical administrative acts like the establishment of parishes, institutions, and associations, the designation to and removal from ecclesiastical offices, and the imposition of sanctions, among others, often lack the requisite juridical solemnity and guarantees of due process, giving room for arbitrary action and sometimes illicit or even invalid acts of governance. Established formalities regulating governance are not mere legal niceties to be applied or ignored at will, but rather are long-lived, tested, and proven instruments that ensure propriety of action and due respect for the rights of the faithful, just relationships, and the prevention of abuses of power. The church's judicial ministry in resolving internal ecclesiastical, matrimonial, penal, and other contentious and

---

75. *Annuario Pontificio*, 2016: 1095–1101.
76. Can. 469, CIC 1983.

administrative disputes, problems, and scandals is often applied inadequately. This inevitably leads to a lack of attention to issues capable of undermining the church's credibility in witnessing to the gospel, and may distance people from the church's life of communion, ultimately hindering the salvation of souls. Pastors placed in charge of parish and diocesan communities of the faithful often act without regard for the boundaries of their office because of ignorance, inadequate checks, improperly arrogated powers, or a despotic attitude that engenders a sense of impunity. Prescribed forums for representative assemblies of the faithful to seek a collaborative, shared approach to pastoral policies and programs, including synods and councils, are inadequately and sometimes barely utilized. Instead, quick, ad hoc, and sometimes superficial and arbitrary solutions are applied to problems that require carefully considered solutions capable of withstanding rational scrutiny and the test of time. Even organs of collective pastoral action and planning like pastoral administrative and financial councils are often improperly engaged or altogether ignored. The capacity of the local church to govern itself autonomously is not employed to harness and optimize local resources for the purpose of progressively fostering self-reliance and less dependence on external financial assistance.

Preference is rather often given to the convenience of seeking "missionary" subsidies and grants, which are sometimes misappropriated and improperly accounted for, over local solutions requiring diligent effort regarding, for example, the remuneration of church workers or the execution of particular projects. Practices respecting ecclesiastical edifices and places of worship do not always follow canonical prescriptions and established standards; sometimes they are subject only to the whims and caprices of the reigning pastors. Accountability is largely absent. Diocesan, parochial, and other institutional books, records, inventories, and archives are often poorly kept. In addition to satisfying the exigencies of ecclesiastical bureaucracy, these records are authentic, first-hand sources of local ecclesiastical traditions and history that could permit African Christianity to objectively tell its own story from within, rather than having to rely on the sometimes speculative and biased accounts of third parties or onlookers.

In general, a widespread apathy toward the rule of law and a lethargy toward having recourse to objectively binding normative standards and procedures seem to hold sway within much of today's African ecclesiastical space. This situation is not helped by a certain predisposition toward a rather obsequious, subservient, and supine attitude to authority and superiors, which tends to fear that any form of criticism, dissent, dispute, or even petition to uphold legitimate rights and the rule of law, will be seen as a mark of disrespect or a violation of the sanctity of constituted leadership. This attitude tends to bolster the authoritarian tendencies toward the exercise of governance in both African secular and ecclesiastical institutions. The African disposition, for the most part, seems to expect leadership to be benevolent and self-censuring; but, without checks and balances, those in power are known everywhere to engage in self-dealing. Instead, the duty of Christian fraternal love, communion, and co-responsibility requires that all the faithful help each other enhance the church's mission as the sacrament of salvation to the world, including through legitimate recourse to established juridical instruments.

Though the incidence of these and related juridical, structural, and attitudinal deficiencies capable of mitigating against holistic ecclesial growth and maturity may not exist everywhere in Africa or be restricted to only African churches, they need to be properly addressed if canon law is to achieve its role of fruitfully regulating the organization, governance, life, and activity of the church in Africa, as she seeks to realize her full ecclesial potential.

The Enactment of Complementary Canon Law among African Particular Churches

A certain narrow conception of canon law that hinges on some of the legal principles and traditions underlying the codified norms of the church is often limited to its "Western cultural presuppositions."[77] For this reason, some have dismissed canon law as a tool for the Westernization of

---

77. See Shorter, *Toward a Theology of Inculturation*, 252.

the particular churches.[78] Yet the view that sees the Western ecclesiastical model as "standard" Christianity[79] may not explain or justify the acute lack of African content in local ecclesiastical norms, reasons for which are discussed below. By virtue of its universality, the church presupposes, embraces, and promotes a rich multiplicity of ecclesial traditions and cultures within the unity of its catholicity. As has been aptly noted,[80] though catholicity calls for the uniformity of ecclesiastical law in its fundamental structures and basic principles, it necessarily entails unity in diversity. The structure of ecclesiastical law is endowed with an exceptional capacity to adapt general laws to diverse circumstances and needs, thus ensuring the inclusion of every ecclesial community's peculiar norms that complement, integrate, and sometimes may derogate from universal norms.

Canonically, most areas in Africa still fall under the aegis of the so-called mission territories, as has already been noted. These areas are under the pontifical jurisdiction of the CEP, whose function is to spread the gospel and coordinate and promote missionary cooperation in the church.[81] Generally, the dependence of an ecclesiastical circumscription on one or more dicasteries of the Roman Curia is a valid expression of the vital communion that exists between the Roman pontiff and the bishops, and of the mutual, complementary interdependence that binds the universal and local realities of the one Catholic Church. Being subject to the congregation responsible for primary evangelization particularly implies the special status of a "developing church" still laboring under critical pastoral challenges of varying kinds (cultural, structural, ministerial, financial) and to varying degrees, and is not ordinarily associated with other regional or particular churches belonging to a more established ecclesiastical tradition.[82] In fact, the peculiar status of this canonical regime means that mission territories can, for various reasons, be exempted from some elements of the common or universal canon law and that extraordinary measures can be adopted by the CEP to address urgent or particular pastoral needs. This was the case, for example, for the Chinese church until May 27, 2007, when Pope Benedict XVI ended its regime of special faculties[83] introduced in 1978[84] by the CEP to meet the dire pastoral needs of the persecuted Chinese faithful driven underground. The CEP is, by law, assigned special pontifical faculties that permit it to decide on identified issues of major importance, sometimes with and sometimes without the approval of the Roman pontiff.

Be that as it may, this system of reserved faculties does not supplant the governing autonomy of particular churches. In fact, Vatican II's emphasis on the full pastoral and governing authority of diocesan bishops (*Lumen Gentium* §27; *Christus Dominus* §§8, 11) and on local expressions of collegiality through episcopal conferences, councils, and synods (*Christus Dominus* §§36–38) provide ample opportunity for the emergence of a local African component of canon law. The constitutive sources of particular law that African Catholicism would need to harness in order to evolve its own original normative system that is harmonized with the universal law include (1) pontifical legislation in favor of particular churches in response to specific local needs, sometimes proposed at the behest of the local hierarchy; (2) concordats and other forms of agreement or convention stipulated between the Holy See as the sovereign authority of the Catholic Church with respect to international law and civil authorities, in matters dealing mostly with freedom of religion but possibly also related issues; (3) legislation of particular councils, both plenary and provincial; (4) decrees of episcopal conferences as stipulated by universal law or by a special disposition of the Holy See; (5) diocesan

---

78. Dias, "Accettazione e operatività del diritto canonico," 78–79.
79. Fantappiè, *Storia del diritto canonico*, 316.
80. Feliciani, *Le basi del diritto canonico*, 9–10.
81. John Paul II, Apostolic Constitution *Pastor Bonus* §85.
82. Arrieta, *Diritto dell'organizzazione ecclesiastica*, 349–50.
83. Pope Benedict XVI, letter *Venerati fratres episcopi*, especially §18.
84. Sacred Congregation for the Propagation of the Faith, "Facultates et privilegia," 95–143.

legislation; (6) other local administrative and pastoral provisions; and (7) local customary norms.

While acknowledging the importance of sources of particular law like pontifical norms of local relevance and church–state agreements, instruments of particular episcopal and regional legislation merit special attention.

First and foremost, it is noteworthy that, beyond restating the consolidated norm concerning the governing authority of the diocesan bishop over the entire missionary activity of his particular church, including the power to regulate such activity by means of specific diocesan laws,[85] the *Code of Canon Law* [CIC 1983] also subjects a large number of disciplinary questions to the laws of the diocesan bishop. There are about eighty instances of direct and indirect devolution of normative competence to the diocesan ordinary,[86] which permit the creation of specific local norms that would reflect the concrete ecclesial circumstances and life of a particular church and its faithful. These include (1) the faculty of dispensing with certain universal and particular disciplinary laws;[87] (2) the right to constitute ecclesiastical offices, stipulating their functions and suitability in particular situations;[88] (3) the power to establish a diocesan seminary with its regulatory norms,[89] the power to make rules governing the ongoing formation of priests[90] and concretely determine the special juridical status of permanent deacons;[91] (4) the right to establish the conditions for legitimate absences of and holidays to be taken by clerics of the diocese;[92] (5) the authority to constitute and regulate diocesan associations of the faithful;[93] (6) the responsibility for laying down rules governing pastoral councils and finance committees of the particular church;[94] (7) the power to designate deacons and laypersons for the pastoral care of a parish in the absence of parish priests;[95] (8) the prerogative of defining the roles of assistant pastors,[96] archpriests, and vicars forane;[97] (9) the duty to regulate catechesis and the preaching faculty of clerics,[98] including the propagation of teachings on matters of faith and morals;[99] (10) the responsibility to govern the liturgical and sacramental life of the diocese,[100] including granting the faculty to hear confessions,[101] to determine cases of legitimate general absolution,[102] to erect diocesan holy shrines,[103] to declare individual holy days and days of penance,[104] and to regulate the liturgy of the Word;[105] (11) the power to regulate the faithful's financial support of the local church,[106] including imposing levies on public ecclesiastical

---

85. *Code of Canon Law,* Can. 790, CIC 1983.
86. Dias, "Accettazione e operatività del diritto canonico," 80, n. 33; Beyer, *Dal Concilio al Codice*, 135, n. 5.
87. See cans. 87–88 CIC 1983.
88. Can. 145, CIC 1983.
89. Cans. 243, 259, 263, 277 §3, CIC 1983.
90. Can. 279 §2, CIC 1983.
91. Can. 288, CIC 1983.
92. Can. 283, CIC 1983.
93. Cans. 312 §§1, 3; 312, 320, 322, 326, CIC 1983.
94. Cans. 513, 536, 537, CIC 1983.
95. Can. 517 §2, CIC 1983.
96. Can. 584 §1, CIC 1983.
97. Can. 555, CIC 1983.
98. Cans. 764, 772 §1, 775 §1, 777, CIC 1983.
99. Can. 823, CIC 1983.
100. Can. 838 §§1 and 4, CIC 1983.
101. Can. 967 §2, CIC 1983.
102. Can. 961 §2, CIC 1983.
103. Can. 1230, CIC 1983.
104. Can. 1244 §2, CIC 1983.
105. Can. 1248 §2, CIC 1983.
106. Can. 1261 §2, CIC 1983.

corporate persons in accordance with established norms,[107] regulating the administration of ecclesiastical goods,[108] and supporting pious foundations and their obligations;[109] (12) the faculty to establish canonical penalties within the limits of the ordinary's powers,[110] and to establish exculpatory, attenuating, and aggravating circumstances;[111] and (13) the authority to institute diocesan tribunals[112] and regulate tribunal fees.[113]

The church in Africa also needs to better exploit the ancient tradition of local councils and synods, which were consistently convoked in the patristic church of Roman Africa, to assist as a tool for the creation of local canonical legislation and for ecclesial consolidation, without prejudice to communion with the universal church. The diocesan synod, regulated in canons 460–68 of the *Code of Canon Law* and the *Instruction on Diocesan Synods* jointly issued by the Congregation for Bishops and CEP, is the privileged forum and vehicle for the creation of diocesan legislation under the governing authority of the diocesan bishop as diocesan legislator, in collaboration with the representative and consultative participation of the diocesan clergy and faithful. Through duly promulgated decrees of the diocesan synod (which may not validly contradict superior ecclesiastical laws[114]) the bishop "promotes and fosters the observance of those canonical norms which the circumstances of diocesan life most require; regulates those matters which the law entrusts to his competence and applies the discipline which is common to all of the particular Churches."[115]

The *Code of Canon Law* subjects the convocation of the diocesan synod to the discretionary judgment of the diocesan bishop in consultation with the presbyteral council.[116] Given the importance of this event in the pastoral life and tradition of a local church, in mission territories, where the identity of the particular church is still evolving, it may be proper to establish a regular frequency, say every five to ten years, for celebrating the diocesan synod. Indeed, considerations bordering on mere convenience or subjective perception may ultimately prevail in the bishop's discretionary evaluation of the need for a diocesan synod; however, among the Eastern Catholic churches, whose need to rediscover, consolidate, conserve, and develop their special, *sui iuris* ecclesial identity is comparable to the necessity of missionary churches to foster a mature and properly integrated local Christian community, the convocation of synodal assemblies is not left completely to the discretionary judgment of local pastors. By dint of particular law, it could be made subject to a predetermined, regular, or even yearly, frequency.[117]

A superior instance of particular canonical legislation is offered by the equally ancient and venerable tradition of plenary and provincial councils, currently regulated by canons 439–46 of the *Code of Canon Law*. The former unites all of the particular churches of the same episcopal conference while the latter serves the particular churches of the same ecclesiastical province. These councils, in which representatives of the local clergy and the lay faithful participate with a consultative voice to aid the deliberations of their bishops, are endowed with legislative power without prejudice to universal ecclesiastical law "to decide what seems opportune for the increase of the faith, the orga-

---

107. Can. 1263, CIC 1983.
108. Can. 1276, CIC 1983.
109. Cans. 1304 §2, 1308 §3, 1309, CIC 1983.
110. Cans. 1315–1316, CIC 1983.
111. Can. 1327, CIC 1983.
112. Can. 1327, CIC 1983.
113. Can. 1649, CIC 1983.
114. That is, "The universal law of the Church; the general decrees of particular Councils and of the conference of bishops; the general decrees of the meeting of bishops of Province in matters of its competence" (*Instruction on Diocesan Synods*, V. 4).
115. *Instruction on Diocesan Synods*, V. 4.
116. Can. 460 §1, CIC 1983.
117. *Codex Canonum Ecclesiarum Orientalium*, 1990, can. 104 §2.

nization of common pastoral action, and the regulation of moral and of the common ecclesiastical discipline which is to be observed, promoted, and protected."[118] Decrees emanating from these councils require the approval of the Apostolic See in order to be validly promulgated and must comply with (and express) universal ecclesial communion, in addition to manifesting the local communion of neighboring sister churches that share common pastoral circumstances, needs, and goals. At present, unlike in previous epochs of the church's history, local councils are rarely convoked anywhere in the universal church.[119] For the particular churches of Africa, these councils represent a very important but untapped avenue for maturing a proper ecclesial identity, promoting authentic contextualization of ecclesiastical law, and closing the gap between canon law and local pastoral reality. They, like diocesan synods, could represent a great moment of pastoral reawakening and renewed missionary impetus. Just as the regular convocation of these ecclesial assemblies played a very important role in ensuring the growth of the early church, they should also accompany the progress and consolidation of the more recently established churches in the missionary territories of Africa and elsewhere. For this reason, they should be celebrated on a fixed, regular basis, which could be established and facilitated by CEP to assist with the growth and eventual maturity of young churches through collective, concerted deliberation and legislation on pastoral issues and policies of common regional interest. The present arrangement, whereby the convocation of provincial councils is left to the judgment of the majority of the diocesan bishops of a province,[120] may be partly responsible for the utter disappearance of this highly significant instrument of pastoral organization from the African ecclesiastical landscape since Vatican II. As has already been observed, an unfavorable disposition toward assemblies of this kind may sometimes be inspired by reasons of convenience or personal considerations, which may not necessarily reflect the wishes of the faithful, whom bishops are not bound to consult before making this decision.

The conference of bishops is yet another assembly of ecclesial episcopal collegiality endowed with the faculty of creating ecclesiastical norms on certain issues that have been previously established in the *Code of Canon Law* and other universal legislation, or by a special mandate of the Apostolic See. Legislation emanating from these conferences, whose aim is to adapt general laws to concrete local situations, is subject to the approval of the Holy See. This novel instance of particular episcopal legislation, which is governed by canons 447–59 of the *Code of Canon Law*, is meant to promote "forms and programs of the apostolate fittingly adapted to the circumstances of time and place, according to the norm of law."[121] It also establishes a vital link between the central governing authority of the church and the particular churches of a determined national territory.[122] The *Code of Canon Law* assigns to the conference a series[123] of twenty-one items of compulsory legislation and another twenty-two of optional legislation, which are to be complementary to the universal law, within the territory of the conference. The *Particular Complementary Laws*, as the legislation of the bishops' conferences is called, provides for the regulation of such questions as qualifications for lay ecclesial ministries, formation of candidates for the priesthood and permanent diaconate where they exist, clerical garb, the presbyteral council, the care of retired clergy, doctrinal teachings conveyed by means of the audio and visual mass media, the catechumenate, the confessional, marriage engagements, premarriage investigation requirements and the promises required for mixed marriages, the duty of the faithful to support the church, acts of extraordinary economic administration, and others. It may also address such matters as the tenure of office for parish priests, ecumenical dialogue and sacramental sharing, lay preaching, Catholic religious education in schools, licit conferment of the

---

118. Can. 445, CIC 1983.
119. See Re, "La legge universal," 92.
120. Can. 440 §1, CIC 1983.
121. Can. 447, CIC 1983.
122. Dias, "Accettazione e operatività del diritto canonico," 75.
123. Vatican Secretary of State, *Lettre Certaines*, 458–67.

sacraments of initiation, age requirements for licit ordination and marriage, terms for dispensation from the canonical form of marriage, holy days of obligation, normative fast and abstinence rules, the use of lay judges in ecclesiastical tribunals, and rules for settlement, arbitration, and compromise of disputes.

On account of unverified fears of the possible unpalatable consequences of creating an intermediary national structure between the universal and particular churches and of compromising the autonomy of the diocesan bishops, these provisions fall far short of the more extensive role originally intended for them[124] and have been made subject to rather restrictive conditions.[125] However, they present a significant opportunity for contextualizing the universal canon law that has yet to be properly harnessed by episcopal conferences in Africa.

Records show that the particular churches in the mission territories of Africa are mostly behind in the implementation of the canonical prerogatives discussed here. Very few of them have created any legislation for the *Particular Complementary Norms*. This deficiency is largely attributable to a number of factors[126] that need urgent and proactive attention by the African episcopacy: a dearth of experts whose competence is needed to assist the bishops in their normative responsibilities; difficulties in evolving and articulating a genuine local ecclesiastical identity, often caused by the complexity of regional ethnic differences between the local churches of the same episcopal conference; and lack of purpose, will, and resources to invest in initiatives aimed at rendering ecclesial life and structures more relevant to today's African Christianity.

It will be recalled that during the First Special Assembly for Africa of the Synod of Bishops (1994), African bishops undertook to "be involved in the process of inculturation in an ongoing manner, respecting the following criteria: compatibility with the Christian message and communion with the universal Church"[127] and enjoined the various episcopal conferences, in cooperation with universities and Catholic institutes, to set up commissions to study the three important questions of "marriage, the veneration of the ancestors, and the spirit world, in order to examine in depth all the cultural aspects of the problems from the theological, sacramental, liturgical, and canonical points of view" (*EA* §64). It has been noted that the continued inability to accomplish these projects adversely affects the day-to-day lives of African Catholics,[128] especially in the areas of harmonizing customary matrimonial values and rites with the canonical matrimonial system, and of adequately integrating within the structures of African Christianity the venerable tradition of honoring ancestors.

Worthy of special mention in regard to the contextualization of canon law in Africa is the special role of custom.[129] The *Code of Canon Law* regards custom as the best interpreter of laws and so, even where customs contradict the general law, they are not suppressed unless they breach divine law or are expressly rejected by existing laws. With the approval of a competent legislator, a custom that contradicts or supersedes the provisions of canon law becomes valid for the community living it, but when the custom has been lawfully and continuously observed for at least thirty years, it does not even need this approval to become law; when it has been lawfully and continuously observed for more than one hundred years, or from time immemorial, it acquires a quasi-perennial normative force, even against its prohibition by other customs, unless the said custom is specifically revoked by a specific law or it contradicts divine law. Thus, the provisions of

---

124. About eighty-six instances of normative provisions relevant to the episcopal conferences were proposed in the course of revising the *Code of Canon Law*. For more details, see Dias, "Accettazione e operatività del diritto canonico," 81, n. 35.

125. For example, a qualified quorum of majority, a strict definition of its areas of competence, and the obligatory approval of its decrees by the Holy See, as stipulated in canon 455 of the code.

126. Fantappiè, *Storia del diritto canonico*, 316; Dias, "Accettazione e operatività del diritto canonico," 81.

127. Pope John Paul II, post-synodal apostolic exhortation *Ecclesia in Africa* (*EA*) §62.

128. Fantappiè, *Storia del diritto canonico*, 316.

129. Cans. 5 and 23–28, CIC 1983; D'Auria, "Il diritto consuetudinario nella vita della Chiesa," 65–89.

the universal law do not revoke the binding force of a legitimate local custom.

"Custom is an instrument of extraordinary value for the adaptation of canon law to the real needs of different communities, each of which has its own circumstances: geographical, social, cultural, etc."[130] Indeed, normative dispositions are guaranteed effective and authentic observance if they are integrated into the ways of life of the community. Therefore, to the extent that the provisions of canon law are integrated into customary African life, its norms would no longer be received as an alien legislative culture. To this end, a number of the institutional organs of ecclesiastical organization could, for example, be harmonized with suitable customary structures and practices of community organization, including villages, peer groups, gender-based associations, interest groups, governance and vigilance structures, support groups, arbitration organs, the palaver, and so on, taking care that these cultural realities are seamlessly woven into the ecclesial value system and are channeled toward achieving the intended ecclesial goals. Effective adaptation of suitable customary models of local community governance to the standard ecclesiastical administrative system would no doubt enhance a harmonious blending of local and ecclesiastical institutions into one integrated canonical order. This could help promote such goals of ecclesiastical governance as ecclesial communion and solidarity, ministerial leadership, pastoral collaboration and co-responsibility, the common apostolate, and conflict prevention and resolution. It must be recalled that the existing organizational structures and institutions of the universal canon law are also products of particular cultures and traditions that came to be adopted to achieve the goals of the church.

One particular area in which African customary norms could contribute meaningfully to the making of relevant localized ecclesiastical laws is in the realm of marriage and family life. It is a well-known fact that many of the institutions and practices of present-day canon law are derived from ancient European culture. By the same token, customary African marriage and family traditions and practices should be able to serve the goals of Christian marriage and family life in the African milieu to the extent they conform with these goals and are in accordance with the canonically prescribed institution of marriage. Notwithstanding the existence of some not insurmountable cultural, social, and axiological deficits of the African marriage institution as it concerns some of the essential properties and goals of the conjugal bond, like its monogamic[131] unity and inherent indissolubility, which in any case must be safeguarded as part of any effort at inculturating canonical marriage, there are some core matrimonial and family values and internal defense mechanisms embedded in the customary African marriage institution and practice. These constitute a veritable bulwark for the conjugal life given the pervasive, corrosive influences of a permissive ideology that is threatening the natural and Christian foundations of marriage. These positive attributes, which include the stable, family-friendly, community-allegiant, and value-oriented structure of the traditional African marriage institution, resonate profoundly with the canonical marriage system and would further bolster its authentic integration into the lives of African Christians.

Conclusion

This study underscores the relevance of canon law to the formation of the African ecclesiastical and ecclesiological identity. As is true for the universal church as a whole, the integral structural development and consolidation in Africa of a uniquely African and genuinely Catholic Christianity, in which local value systems, ethoses, and customs dynamically engage and appropriate and integrate

---

130. Lombardia, "Custom," 48.
131. Antoine Ganye argues that polygamy in Africa arises from circumstances and is not structural, while monogamy "constitutes the first anthropological benchmark at the heart of the marital experience in Africa" ("Monogamy and Polygamy," 112). Thus, monogamy remains the ordinary norm while polygamy is a response to certain circumstances, like the infertility of a first wife, the need to demonstrate affluence and virility, the need for more hands for manual labor, incompatibility, and high infant mortality.

gospel values, requires the practical role of canon law as a vehicle by which the dialogue between faith and life may be translated into a lived juridical reality. To this end, the prejudice of antijuridicalism (opposition in principle to the relevance of law in Christian life) needs to be discarded. History has consistently shown that the church may discard canon law only at its own peril. The persistent blight of scandals, misconduct, and abuses of church order, discipline, morals, and authority has long since laid to rest the antijuridical euphoria that greeted the outcome of the Second Vatican Council. Our study has also demonstrated that the church in Africa thrives alongside a healthy juridical tradition. There is a need, therefore, for the church in Africa to explore the extensive areas provided by Vatican II ecclesiology, the *Code of Canon Law*, and other universal ecclesiastical legislation for the creation of pertinent complementary laws that would reflect the rich social and cultural diversity of today's African Catholicism.

This would, however, require a broad-based, consultative, and participatory approach to lawmaking, entailing that only needed, useful, essential, and effective norms that articulate real necessities in the local circumstances are enacted, and that local ordinances are properly disseminated, assimilated, and judiciously integrated into the ways of life of communities, as are those pertaining to the universal church. A knee-jerk approach to regulatory norms and disciplinary measures would only steer governing power in the direction of arbitrariness and abuse. In the same vein, armchair lawmaking is at best a futile effort that will never resonate with lived experience—laws ordinarily draw from life, never the other way around. This may explain why, in the few instances where localized complementary norms have been enacted in Africa, they exist only on paper and are largely unknown in pastoral life. This may not be unrelated to the possible origin of these norms, which seem more to have been composed on the drawing board by episcopal committees simply for the purpose of complying with the demands of universal law.

At the time it is being created, particular law needs to engage the entire gamut of the people of God in a particular place—its hierarchy, institutions, charisms, and culture—in order to discern and articulate genuine measures for living the faith in that place. Local synods and councils are meant to serve this purpose and cannot be ignored as legislative instruments for local churches. The universal church offers an example in this regard: ordinarily its laws and norms are products of councils and synods, or, in exceptional cases, they are the result of a broad-based and patient consultative effort involving pastors, experts, universities, and interest groups. After promulgation, these laws are integrated into the formation program of pastoral agents, whose task it is to disseminate and apply them pastorally. This is also the way to create an authentic African ecclesial and juridical self-expression.

Canon law is not only about lawmaking; it is also science and jurisprudence. All three aspects—legislation, science, and jurisprudence—must be in play in a holistic consideration of canon law in African Catholicism.

In African ecclesiastical studies, the science of canon law, when compared to some of its theological counterparts, lags somewhat behind. It has yet to be meaningfully engaged in the articulation of an integral African ecclesial worldview, thanks to inadequate canonical scholarship and the often simplistic depiction of the discipline among scholars of other African ecclesiastical sciences. As the juridical-ecclesiological self-expression of a living church, canon law is not merely an imposed set of rules and regulations, but necessarily feeds on scientific juridical principles and studies that endow its norms with ecclesial authenticity and historical relevance. The field of African canonical studies exists in some African Catholic universities and tertiary institutions that have canon law departments, but it needs exposure beyond these confines. The field of canonical studies in Africa needs to engage with global academia in order to tap into and contribute to high-quality ecclesiastical scholarship. This would require that canon law scholars in these institutions engage professionally with their colleagues around the continent and beyond it, and publish their studies and research in reputable international journals of ecclesiastical studies. It would also require that the canon law departments of these institutions be upgraded and regularly supplied with relevant academic resources. At present, only a few African Catholic institutions are authorized by the Holy See[132] to confer valid canon law degrees,[133] and from available records only one of them can grant a doctorate.[134] This may not be unrelated to the perceived low level of their canonical scholarship or the relative inadequacy at these institutions of the specialized academic resources required for globally competitive canonical research and studies. Any meaningful effort to promote the science of canon law in Africa must address these limitations, ensuring that students and scholars of the field in Africa have access to quality research and learning tools at the highest possible levels of the discipline, for it is only within a conducive academic and truly African ecclesiastical milieu that the science of canon law can develop in Africa and create a sound canonical legislative tradition and juridical culture in the local churches.

The objective of canon law studies in Africa remains to evolve a juridical culture in tandem with and at the service of African Christian faith identity and self-expression. To achieve this goal there is need for an interdisciplinary approach to canonical research that would enable the cultivation of a peculiarly African canonical science that is in dialogue with mainstream African theological, philosophical, anthropological, legal, and sociological thought, while still engaging universal canonical and related scholarship. In this way, African canonical studies will be in a position to assert its distinctive worldview (even as it engages in mutually enriching dialogue with competing worldviews), especially with regard to those juridical institutions and issues of particular relevance to the church in Africa, including the structures of communion and community life that resonate with and enhance the special African ecclesiology of the family of God; the juridical aspects of the marriage institution; the dynamics of conflict resolution; systems and principles of human formation, initiation, and growth; and the place of customary traditions. As Pope Francis observes, "In various parts of Africa, secularism has not weakened certain traditional values, and marriages forge strong bonds between two wider families, with clearly defined structures for dealing with problems and conflicts."[135] Canonical science that originates in Africa should be able to investigate and articulate African values and social structures as its unique contribution to enriching the juridical patrimony of the universal church.

Regarding canonical jurisprudence, the African sociocultural milieu and lived reality constitute a veritable treasure trove for gaining a unique perspective on the understanding, interpretation, and application of common canonical legal principles and norms. In administering justice, the African canonist entrusted with the ministry of dispensing justice in concrete terms should be able to appropriate and bring to the fore these unique elements to the extent they influence behaviors, ensuring a just application of general canonical norms. Given the particular importance of jurisprudence in resolving real cases and in shaping both legal thought and positive legislation, the bishops of Africa need to invest adequately in promoting it by establishing functional ecclesiastical tribunals that are properly staffed with qualified and competent personnel and endowed with necessary forensic resources. As much as possible, each diocese should operate a functional tribunal to resolve inevitable dis-

---

132. While only the institutions listed in the following footnote are known to have received authority from the Holy See to grant valid canon law degrees, some others, like the Canon Law Department of the Catholic Institute of West Africa, Port Harcourt (Nigeria), offer degrees in theology with a specialization in canon law.

133. These are Département Autonome de Droit Canonique, Université Catholique d'Afrique Centrale, Institut Catholique de Yaounde, Cameroon; Faculté de Droit Canonique, Université Catholique du Congo, Kinshasa; Institut Supérieur de Droit Canonique, Université Catholique de l'Afrique de l'Ouest, Unité Universitaire d'Abidjan, Côte d'Ivoire; and the Institute of Canon Law of the Catholic University of Eastern Africa, Nairobi, Kenya. See https://www.iuscangreg.it/facolta.php?lang=EN.

134. According to https://www.iuscangreg.it/facolta.php?lang=EN, in the whole of Africa only the Faculté de Droit Canonique, Université Catholique du Congo, Kinshasa, is authorized to grant a doctoral degree in canon law.

135. Pope Francis, *Amoris Laetitia* §28 [Post-synodal Apostolic Exhortation on Love in the Family; March 19, 2016] (Vatican City: Libreria Editrice Vaticana, 2016), www.vatican.va.

putes, particularly those arising in marriage cases. The recent reform of the canonical matrimonial process[136] treats this as a very high priority while emphasizing the need for diocesan bishops to exercise their office as judges of first instance for their faithful,[137] particularly in the new abbreviated matrimonial process introduced by Pope Francis.[138] Structures of mediation, conciliation, or arbitration of disputes may also be set up to ensure that effective African conflict resolution mechanisms are integrated with gospel and canonical principles in the search for reliable homegrown solutions to disputes.

All of this will help promote a distinctive canonical jurisprudence that can address pastoral issues peculiar to Africa's particular churches. It will also constitute a special African contribution to the rich variety of universal canonical jurisprudence, ensuring greater recognition for African values and the African worldview within the church's legislative system and praxis.

It is from this threefold perspective (legislative, scientific, and jurisprudential) that any debate about African canon law can be meaningfully and productively engaged. While it may be justifiable to argue for an African canon law understood in terms of homegrown African canonical jurisprudence and canonical studies, the tendency to present this question in terms of advocacy for a *Code of Canon Law* for Africa is, in my view, fundamentally flawed for the reasons stated below. This latter idea is based on the assumption that the present *Code of Canon Law* is a Western legislative document more or less insensitive to the needs of the church in Africa.

It goes without saying that some of the underlying juridical principles of the code originated in the context of Roman law. However, and more importantly, it is equally true that gospel principles and ecclesial values remain the overriding and driving force of the code. Moreover, in recognition of the pluralism of ecclesial contexts and human circumstances, the code makes ample provision for localized and complementary legislation at the level of episcopal conferences and dioceses. I argue that the local churches of Africa need to adequately harness these tools and to make and apply canon law in a manner that adequately addresses the needs of their faithful in the spirit of the gospel and according to universal ecclesial norms ultimately inspired by the gospel. This chapter has made the case for greater recourse to local councils and synods to achieve this objective.

It should be noted that a body of canonical norms that could qualify as African canon law already exists in the form of formally promulgated localized and complementary norms, or simply as de facto rules of pastoral governance of local churches. No doubt, these need to be improved upon. However, a monolithic Code of African Canon Law is not feasible, first because the African continent is not a monolith and, second, because the exigency of ecclesial communion can accommodate only a complementary ecclesial juridical order as between the universal and the particular church, not a structure of concurrent legislative systems established along continental or ethnic lines. Furthermore, because it is already by tradition a part of either the Latin or the Eastern Catholic church tradition, African Catholicism does not lay claim to a different ecclesial tradition that would justify a special juridical order akin to that of Eastern and Western Catholicism. The particular churches of Africa can express their characteristic normative identities only within the framework of the ecclesial tradition to which they belong, and there is enough room to achieve this within the existing canonical order.

Bibliography

Alexander VI, Pope. *Inter coetera* [Papal Bull; 1493]. Taurinensis Editio, 1857–1872: 361–64.

Annuario Pontificio, Vatican City: Libreria Editrice Vaticana, 2016.

Arrieta, J. Ignatio. *Diritto dell'organizazzione ecclesiastica*. Milan: Giuffré, 1997.

Attila, J. Yawovi. *L'azione missionaria della Chiesa ieri e oggi*. Venice: Marcianum, 2015.

---

136. Pope Francis, *Mitis Iudex Dominus Iesus* [Apostolic Letter *Motu proprio*; August 15, 2015].
137. Can. 1673, §§1–2, CIC 1983.
138. Can. 1683, CIC 1983.

Bardy, G. "Afrique." In *Dictionnaire de Droit Canonique*, edited by R. Naz, 1:288–307. 7 vols. Paris: Librairie Letouzey et Ané, 1935–1965.

Baus, Karl. *Le origini: La Chiesa apostolica e sub apostolica—vita e letteratura ecclesiastica dalle persecuzioni all'avvento di Costantino I–IV secolo*. Matrix: Storia della Chiesa 1. Milan: Jaca Book, 1992.

Benedict XVI, Pope. *Venerati fratres episcopi* [Letter; May 27, 2007]. *AAS* 99 (2007): 553–81.

Beyer, J. *Dal Concilio al Codice*. Bologna: Dehoniana, 1984.

Chiocchetta, Pietro. "Verso la Conferenza di Berlino." In *Storia della Chiesa*, 24: 123–45. Milan: Edizione Paoline, 1990.

Code of Canon Law, 1983.

Collectanea S. Congregationis de Propaganda Fide, I (1622–1866). Rome, 1907.

Conciliorum Oecumenicorum Decreta. Bologna: EDB, 2013.

Congregation for Bishops and Congregation for Evangelization of Peoples. *Instruction on Diocesan Synods*. *AAS* 89 (1997): 706–27.

Daniélou, Jean, and Henri Marrou. "Dalle origini a S. Gregorio Magno." *Nuova storia della Chiesa* 1. Turin: Marietti, 1976.

D'Auria, Andrea. "Il diritto consuetudinario nella vita della Chiesa." In *Inculturazione, diritto canonico e missione*, ed. Luigi Sabbarese, 65–89. Euntes Docentes 56.3. Rome: Urban University Press, 2003.

———. "Le facoltà speciali della Congregazione per l'Evangelizzazione dei Popoli." *Ius Missionale* 1 (2001): 257–61.

Del Re, Niccolò. *La curia romana: Lineamenti storico-giuridici*. 4th ed. Vatican: Libreria Editrice Vaticana, 1998.

Dias, Ivan. "Accettazione e operatività del diritto canonico nei territori di missione." In *La legge canonica nella vita della Chiesa*, 64–82. Vatican: Libreria Editrice Vaticana, 2008.

Erdö, Peter. *Storia delle Fonti del Diritto Canonico*. Venice: Marcianum, 2008.

Fantappiè, Carlo. *Storia del diritto canonico e delle istituzioni della Chiesa*. Bologna: Il Mulino, 2011.

Feliciani, Giorgio. *Le basi del diritto canonico*. Bologna: Il Mulino, 2002.

Filoni, Fernando. "Le Competenze della Congregazione per l'Evangelizzazione dei Popoli." Address to St. Damassus University, Madrid. November 10, 2015.

Francis, Pope. *Amoris Laetitia* [Post-synodal Apostolic Exhortation on Love in the Family; March 19, 2016]. Vatican City: Libreria Editrice Vaticana, 2016. www.vatican.va.

———. *Mitis Iudex Dominus Iesus* [Apostolic Letter *Motu proprio*; August 15, 2015].

Friedberg, Aemilius, ed. *Corpus Iuris Canonici*. Vol. 1: *Decretum Magistri Gratiani*. 1879. Reprint, Graz: Akademische Druck- und Verlagsanstalt, 1959.

Ganye, Antoine. "Monogamy and Polygamy: Challenge and Concern for the Truth of Love in African Cultures." In *Christ's New Homeland—Africa: Contribution to the Synod on the Family by African Pastors*, 112–26. San Francisco: Ignatius Press; Nairobi: Paulines Publications Africa, 2015.

Garcia Martin. J. *L'azione missionaria nel Codex Iuris Canonici*. 2nd ed. Rome: Ediurcla, 2005.

———. *La formazione del diritto missionario durante il sistema tridentino (1563–1917)*. Venice: Marcianum, 2013.

Gasparri, P., ed. *Codicis Iuris Canonici Fontes*, I. Rome, 1926.

Gregory the Great. *Epistula* 1. *Patrologia Latina* 77:441–43.

Gregory XV. Pope. *Inscrutabili Divinae Providentiae* [Papal Bull; Bullarium Romanum 12]. Taurinensis Editio, 1857–1872: 690–93.

———. *Romanum decet* [Papal Bull; July 10, 1622; Bullarium Romanum 12]. Taurinensis Editio, 1857–1872: 693–97.

John Paul II, Pope. *Ecclesia in Africa* [Post-synodal Apostolic Exhortation on the Church in Africa and Its Evangelizing Mission toward the Year 2000; September 14, 1995]. In *The African Synod: Documents, Reflection, Perspectives*, 233–86. Maryknoll, NY: Orbis Books, 1996. *AAS* 88 (1996): 5–82. Abbreviated *EA*.

———. *Pastor Bonus* [Apostolic Constitution; June 28, 1988]. *AAS* 80 (1988): 841–912.

Koussebila, André. "Quale stabilità per il parroco nelle chiese di missione." PhD diss., Facoltà di diritto Canonico Pio X Venezia, 2017.

Leo the Great, Pope. *Epistula* 12. Matrix. *Patrologia Latina* 54:656–63.

Lombardia, Pedro. "Custom." In *Code of Canon Law Annotated*, 47–52. 2nd ed. Montréal: Wilson & Lafleur, 2004.

Magesa, Laurenti. *Anatomy of Inculturation: Transforming the Church in Africa*. Nairobi: Paulines Publications, 2004.

Marcocchi, Massimo. "Le missioni in Africa e in Asia." In *Storia della Chiesa (SCh.) XVIII.2*, edited by Luigi Mezzadri, 275–313. Milan: Paoline, 1988.

———. "Le missioni in Africa." In *Storia della Chiesa (SCh.) XVIII.2*, edited by Luigi Mezzadri, 315–53. Milan: Paoline, 1988.

———. "Propaganda Fide." In *Storia della Chiesa (SCh.) XVIII.2*, edited by Luigi Mezzadri, 363–78. Milan: Paoline, 1988.

Martín de Agar, José T. *A Handbook on Canon Law*. Montreal: Wilson & Lafleur, 1999.

Martina, Giacomo. "L'età dell'assolutismo." *Storia della Chiesa da Lutero ai nostri giorni*, vol. 2. Brescia: Morcelliana, 2002.

Metzler, Josef. "La Santa Sede e le missioni." *Storia della Chiesa*, vol. 24, 21–119. Milan: Edizioni Paoline, 1990.

Mezzadri, Luigi. *Storia della Chiesa (SCh.) XVIII.2: La Chiesa nell'età dell'assolutismoconfessionale: dal Concilio di Trento alla pace di Westfalia (1563–1648)*. Milan: Edizione Paoline, 1988.

Mugambi, J. N. K. *Christianity and African Culture*. Nairobi: Acton, 2002.

Munier, C. *Concilia Africae A. 345–A. 525*. Matrix: Corpus Christianorum. Series Latina 159. Brepol: Turnholt, 1974.

Nicholas V, Pope. *Romanus Pontifex* [Papal Bull; January 8, 1454; Bullarium Romanum 5]. Taurinensis Editio, 1857–1872: 114–15.

Pannier, G. *L'Eglise de Loango 1919–1947: Une étape difficile de l'évangélisation au Congo-Brazzaville*. Paris: Karthala, 2008.

Pastor, Ludovico. *Storia dei Papi*, 8. Rome: Desclée, 1924.

Paul VI, Pope. "Homily on the Occasion of the Canonization of the Martyrs of Uganda," October 18, 1964. *AAS* 56 (1964): 907–8.

———. *Regimini Ecclesiae Universae*. *AAS* 59 (1957): 885–928.

Pius IX, Pope. *Romani Pontifices*. *Pius IX P. M. Acta*, 1:402–16. Rome, 1864.

Re, G. Battista. "La legge universale e produzione normativa a livello di Chiesa particolare di Conferenze episcopali e di Concili particolari." In *La legge canonica nella vita della Chiesa*, 84–101. Vatican City: Libreria Editrice Vaticana, 2008.

Sacred Congregation for the Evangelization of Peoples. "Relationes in territoriis missionum." *AAS* 61 (1969): 281–87.

Sacred Congregation for the Propagation of the Faith. "Ad Episcopos, Vicarios, Praefectosque Apostolicos ac Missionum Superiores," April 16, 1922. *AAS* 14 (1922): 288.

———. "Facultates et privilegia sacerdotibus fidelibusque in territorio sinarum degentibus concessa his perdurantibus circumstantiis" (prot. 3242/78). In *Un momento di inculturazione del cattolicesimo in Cina: Le facoltà speciali del 1978*, ed. L. Sabbarese, 95–143. Vatican City: Urbaniana University Press, 2015.

———. "Neminem profecto." *Collectanea*, 1:541–45.

———. "Quum huic Sacrae Congretationi." *AAS* 22 (1930): 111–15.

Sabbarese, L., ed. *Un momento di inculturazione del cattolicesimo in Cina: Le facoltà speciali del 1978*. Vatican City: Urbaniana University Press, 2015.

Sarah, R. Cardinal. "What Sort of Pastoral Mercy in Response to the New Challenges to the Family: A Reading of the Lineamenta." In *Christ's New Homeland—Africa: Contribution to the Synod on the Family by African Pastors*. San Francisco: Ignatius Press; Nairobi: Paulines Publications Africa, 2015.

Shorter, Aylward. *Toward a Theology of Inculturation*. Eugene, OR: Wipf & Stock, 1999.

Van de Wiel, Constant. *History of Canon Law*. Louvain: Peeters, 1991.

Vatican Secretary of State. "Lettre Certaines conférences aux présidents des conférences épiscopales sur la pubblication des norms complémentaires." In *Enchiridion Vaticanum* 9:67–458. Bologna: Dehoniane, 1987.

Suggested Reading

Bardy, G. "Afrique." In *Dictionnaire de Droit Canonique*, edited by R. Naz, 1:288–307. 7 vols. Paris: Librairie Letouzey et Ané, 1935–1965.

Christ's New Homeland: Africa. Contribution to the Synod on the Family by African Pastors. San Francisco: Ignatius Press; Nairobi: Paulines Publications, 2015.

Dias, Ivan. "Accettazione e operatività del diritto canonico nei territori di missione." In *La legge canonica nella vita della Chiesa*, 64–82. Vatican: Libreria Editrice Vaticana, 2008.

Magesa, Laurenti. *Anatomy of Inculturation: Transforming the Church in Africa*. Nairobi: Paulines Publications, 2004.

Marcocchi, Massimo. "Le mission in Africa." In *Storia della Chiesa (SCh.) XVIII.2*, edited by Luigi Mezzadri, 315–53. Milan: Paoline, 1988.

Mugambi, J. N. K. *Christianity and African Culture*. Nairobi: Acton, 2002.

Re, G. Battista. "La legge universale e produzione normativa a livello di Chiesa particolare di Conferenze episcopali e di Concili particolari." In *La legge canonica nella vita della Chiesa*, 84–101. Vatican City: Libreria Editrice Vaticana, 2008.

Shorter, Aylward. *Toward a Theology of Inculturation*. Eugene, OR: Wipf & Stock, 1999.

Key Words

Berlin Conference
briefer matrimonial process
canon law
colonial Africa
commission system
conference of bishops
Congregation for Evangelization of Peoples
customary law
ecclesiastical organization
Gratian's Decree
inculturation
mandate system
marriage
mission, particular/local church
missionary law
particular complementary norms
Propaganda fide
Roman Africa
royal patronage regime

The Changing Face of the Priestly Vocation and Ministry in Africa

Jordan Nyenyembe

At major liturgical celebrations in Kenya and in other places on the African continent, it is now commonplace to see a priest in his Mass vestments leave his concelebrating brothers at the altar to joyously mix it up with the choir members, adding vibrancy and joy to the liturgical celebration by dancing and playing the *kayamba* (a traditional musical instrument that resembles the tambourine). This sight is surely something new! Witnessing such happenings, one gets the idea that the image of the Catholic priest is changing.[1] The Catholic faithful on the continent are being ministered to by a new generation of priests who are full of life and joy, which is one of the fruits of the Holy Spirit. The research of scholars at the Catholic University of Eastern Africa (CUEA) conducted in the three major countries of East Africa (Kenya, Uganda, and Tanzania) in 2009–2010 found that "the majority of the priests were happy and felt fulfilled in their vocation."[2] The same study also noted that priests are more effective in their ministry today because they are closer to the flock than they were in the past.[3]

This chapter highlights the fact that the image of the priest is changing and that the priestly ministry is advancing the reconciliation between God and human beings. New dynamics in pastoral work are promoting collaboration between ordained ministers and laypeople. The people of God are experiencing more joy in ministry today than they did in the past. Pope Francis applauds this renewed joy of the priests, stating that "priestly joy is a priceless treasure, not only for the priest himself but for the entire faithful people of God."[4] This chapter also highlights the image of the priest as a "steward of God's mercy."[5] The Catholic faithful appreciate the ministerial service of the ordained in a special way because they reveal the grace of God's mercy. According to Pope Francis, priests "have the rewarding and consoling task of incarnating mercy."[6] In their service to the people of God, the pope continues, "priests are witnesses to . . . the ever-increasing abundance of the Father's mercy."[7]

The methodology used in this chapter does not follow the rigid pattern of "the pastoral cycle"[8] from insertion to social analysis to theological

---

1. See Nyenyembe, "Conflict and Displacement," 191–211.
2. Lukwata et al., *Assessment of the Effectiveness of the Ministry of Priests in Eastern Africa*, 89.
3. See Lukwata et al., *Assessment of the Effectiveness of the Ministry of Priests in Eastern Africa*, xvi.
4. Pope Francis, "Homily at Holy Chrism Mass" (April 17, 2014), www.vatican.va.
5. Nyenyembe, "Stewards of God's Mercy."
6. Elise Harris, "Your Task Is to Incarnate Mercy, Pope Francis Tells Priests," *Catholic News Agency* (March 24, 2016), catholicnewsagency.com.
7. Pope Francis, "Ambassadors of Mercy" [Homily at Chrism Mass; March 24, 2016], https://zenit.org/articles/pope-francis-homily-at-chrism-mass-2.
8. The pastoral cycle is a process for thinking theologically about a particular issue with the aim of finding new and more effective ways of acting in the future. It starts with the process called "insertion," which is an initial

reflection to pastoral planning. In order to engage squarely with the theme of priestly ministry, it is more appropriate, in this study, to employ a mixed-methods approach borrowed from the social sciences, an approach that makes it possible to include field survey data. The use of mixed methods is not meant to detract from the importance of the pastoral circle process; rather, it is informed by the fact that "the pastoral circle has declared strongly the primacy of reality or experience when, as a matter of fact, it treats these only as having secondary importance, since they are dependent upon some preceding ideal, yet limited, values."[9] In fact, contemporary pastoral theologians are beginning to question the one-size-fits-all methodology of the pastoral cycle—and rightly so, because "not only is the alleged language of 'circle' or 'spiral' inaccurate, the procedural rigidity that it employs can easily lead us into 'methodological imperialism.'"[10]

This chapter starts from the premise that the priestly vocation is a merciful gift from God. The mission of the priest is to extend God's mercy to humanity and to the whole of creation. An understanding that God is the source of a priestly vocation leads us to the notion that "God is our real treasure—that pearl of great price which must be acquired at any cost, even that of great sacrifices."[11] The divine origin of the priestly vocation informs and directs the priestly ministry—priests are agents of mercy performing the work of God on earth, on God's behalf. The second section of the chapter addresses the theme of priests being "stewards of God's mercy" in detail. This characterization highlights the importance of *mercy* in conceptualizing the priestly vocation—the use of the term "mercy" in "steward of God's mercy" makes this phrase much more accommodative and inclusive than "priest as compassionate minister" or "priest as forgiving minister." Mercy incorporates within its meaning other words like "forgiveness," "compassion," "kindness," "generosity," "tolerance," and "patience."[12] The centrality of mercy to the priestly ministry is shown below in two stories of priests who, through the practice of mercy, have exhibited the joy of priestly ministry in their dealings with confreres. Finally, the chapter's conclusion maintains that the new image of priests as agents of God's mercy is likely to reawaken the faith of the global Catholic Church because of the vitality and contagious joy to which it gives birth.

The Priestly Vocation: An Act of God

Priesthood is a call from God for it is God who stirs interest in this vocation in a young man (Isa 6:1–13; Jer 1:5). Because of this, the ministerial priesthood is held to be a privileged gift to humanity. This is summarized well by Stephen Rossetti: "Priesthood is a gift to the people of God, and it is a wonderful gift for the priest himself. Both are blessed."[13] This testimony of Rossetti, who has a rich experience of journeying fruitfully with his brother priests in crisis, is supported by Tim Cullinane, who also asserts that a vocation to the priesthood is a special gift, which is evident from his testimony about what he observed at the ordination of a new priest: "I remember being at an ordination where after the ceremony the parish gave the newly-ordained priest a car and when he was presenting it the chairman of the church council said, 'Today the parish is giving you the gift of a car but God has given you the greatest gift of all, ordination as a Catholic priest.'"[14] Another priest recalled the day of his own ordination while attending the ordination of another priest: "The day of my ordination . . . was a tremendous celebration for my family and my parish and for myself. I was emotional when I blessed

---

stage enabling a researcher to gain experience of what is happening and exploring why is it happening. See Helen Cameron, *Resourcing Mission: Practical Theology for Changing Churches* (London: SCM Press, 2010), 8–13.

9. Adiprasetya, "Towards an Asian Multitextual Theology," 124.
10. Adiprasetya, "Towards an Asian Multitextual Theology," 127.
11. Pope Benedict XVI, post-synodal apostolic exhortation *Africae Munus* §112. Hereinafter *AM*.
12. See Egan, "Understanding Forgiveness," 391–92.
13. Rossetti, *Joy of Priesthood*, 206.
14. Cullinane, *Preparing for Priesthood*, 13.

my mother for the first time. It was heartening to see the joy in so many faces."[15]

It would appear that people are fascinated by the ministerial priesthood for three reasons. First, because "every vocation to the priesthood is a great mystery."[16] It is considered a mystery of divine calling, as in the scriptural reminders that "you did not choose me, but I chose you and appointed you that you should go and bear fruit and your fruit should abide" (John 15:16), and "one does not take the honor upon himself, but he is called by God, just as Aaron was" (Heb 5:4). Since the priestly vocation originates from God, priests rightly feel that they have been shown special favor from above. They are friends of God and are rightly understood as men of God. The divine origin of the call should always remind priests of the fact that they are "not God's friend because we are better than others or because we are spiritually advanced. Rather, we are friends because God has chosen us to be so."[17] On the vigil of their ordination, deacons who are about to be ordained often grapple with feelings that they are not worthy of a priestly vocation. This feeling of unworthiness, though genuine, should not be a cause for discouragement but rather an invitation to the ministry of humility. It is important to acknowledge, as Stephen Rossetti puts it, that "human weakness is the conduit for the power of God."[18]

God intends that each person called to the vocation of ministerial priesthood will perform a particular service for the church. To accomplish this, God bestows on the priest through his ordination a new character that makes him different from laypeople. However, it is good to know that "the priest is different, not because of a humanity that has been elevated beyond human frailty and sinfulness, but because of imbedded grace that shines most brightly through his weakness."[19] Hence, it is important to underscore here the fact that the special favor of mercy granted to the priest through his calling gives him a mission: the ordained are to be the carriers of God's mercy to the people entrusted to their care. Their anointment with chrism oil during ordination marks priests "by *misericordia* to the core of their beings and their lives [bear] the watermark of compassion and deliverance."[20] It is important that the ordained person understand that his vocation is a gratuitous act of God. This reminds priests that "we are called to show mercy because mercy has first been shown to us."[21]

The second reason people admire the priestly vocation follows from the fact that ordained ministers are mediators of divine mercy. Many people are locked into structures of sin and are burdened by a guilty conscience. The priestly ministry of compassion and forgiveness is indispensable to restoring joy and hope in the discipleship of these people. Ministerial priesthood makes the Eucharist the sacrament of love and the greatest of Christian celebrations. Indeed, "so much of ecclesial life depends on priestly vocations."[22] One important aspect of this life happens in seminaries, the institutions established to assist candidates in discerning a possible vocation, and the work of priests in mentoring seminarians is highly valued. In fact, bishops, priests, and the Christian faithful often see the church most clearly through the seminary, which has traditionally (and aptly) been regarded as the heart of the diocese. The word "mercy" in Latin is *misericordia*, which means literally "miserable heart." Thus, a seminary should be a place where future priests are trained to have "miserable hearts," ready to suffer and take on the suffering of others. The seminary must nurture the practice of mercy.

The third reason people esteem the priestly vocation is that, despite the great demand for the

---

15. Moriarty, "Leaving the Priesthood," 35.
16. Pope John Paul II, *Gift and Mystery*, 13.
17. Rossetti, *Joy of Priesthood*, 63.
18. Rossetti, *Joy of Priesthood*, 63.
19. Rossetti, *Joy of Priesthood*, 63.
20. O'Donoghue, "Mercy," 219.
21. Pope Francis, *Misericordiae Vultus* [papal bull of indiction for the Jubilee of Mercy; April 11, 2015] §9, www.vatican.va.
22. Pope John Paul II, *Gift and Mystery*, 114.

agents of God's mercy, there is always a shortage of priests. This is true even though the number of baptized Catholics on the continent continues to rise. It is for this reason that the priestly vocation is regarded by many laypeople as a rare and priceless commodity.

We can understand from the above that the priestly vocation has both a vertical dimension and a horizontal dimension; that is, God initiates it and the Christian faithful respond to it and appreciate it. It is possible to see this in biblical figures like Abraham, Moses, the judges and prophets, Mary, and Paul, to mention just a few who were called by God not for themselves but for others. Thus, a vocation to priestly ministry should not become an excuse for the ordained to seek privileges.[23] The priest should overcome any temptation to use the grace of ordination for personal fulfillment, a goal that might appear to warrant a domineering attitude toward laypeople and that might cause him to forget that his vocation is a gift. Keeping in mind these two dimensions of priestly ministry should spur priests to fulfill their responsibility to serve. This responsibility implies giving an account to God of how faithful they have been to their calling and to the people of God.

Stewards of God's Mercy

We noted above that the image of the priest is changing; now we often find priests with a more human and compassionate face. This is as true in the global church as it is in the regional church in Africa. What one can gather from the experience of many priests working in sub-Saharan Africa is that their ministry requires a great deal of personal sacrifice. Given the harsh situations people face, including poor roads, food shortages, and even famine, pastoral work is never easy in the developing regions of the world. Priests and catechists share in the hardships of the people. Concretely, in dioceses primarily inhabited by farmers such as Lodwar, Garissa, and Kitale in Kenya, to mention only three, priests must grapple with the realities of water scarcity and cattle rustling and its related violence. Pastors of souls working in these areas confront the collateral impacts of marginalization. They do not receive media coverage for the great work they are doing, nor do they receive commensurate financial remuneration. They work prompted by the knowledge that theirs is an office of love (*amoris officium*).

Priests working in dioceses challenged by suffering, misery, and abject poverty can happily carry out their ministry because they have the people of God at the center of their big hearts. The flexibility of their hearts is not symptomatic of high blood pressure or heart attacks but is an expression of affectionate love graced by joy of service for the weakest members of society. Pastoral work in these areas become acts of mercy. The fullest meaning of mercy, *misericordia*, is actually "having a pain in your heart for the pains of others, and taking pains to do something about their pain."[24] For the Catholic faithful in both rural and urban areas of Africa, the church is present not only in the form of the spiritual services pastors provide, but especially in works of charity. In the words of Walter Cardinal Kasper, "The church is alive where corporal works of mercy are performed: feeding the hungry, giving drink to the thirsty, clothing the naked, giving shelter to strangers, freeing the captives, visiting the sick, and burying the dead."[25] However, Kasper further states that in order to offer pastoral services geared toward fully liberating the human person in both body and soul, the corporal works of mercy should be complemented by spiritual ones: "The church is likewise alive where the spiritual works of mercy are performed: correcting sinners, teaching the ignorant, giving good counsel to those in doubt, bearing patiently with those who are burdensome, gladly forgiving those who insult us, and praying for the living and the dead."[26] Mercy and *caritas* cannot be separated. Pope St. John Paul II holds that "mercy is another word for love."[27]

---

23. See Azevedo, *Consecrated Life*, 7.
24. Stackpole, "What Does 'Divine Mercy' Actually Mean?"
25. Kasper, *Leadership in the Church*, 27.
26. Kasper, *Leadership in the Church*, 27.
27. Pope John Paul II, encyclical *Dives in Misericordia* [Rich in Mercy; November 30, 1980] §7.

Recent research findings from the Faculty of Theology of the Catholic University of Eastern Africa (2009) highlight the notion of the priest as a steward of mercy. These findings on what the ordinary Catholic faithful perceive to be the characteristics of a good priest reveal four major categories: his availability to the people (the *ministry of presence*), his compassion (the *ministry of mercy and reconciliation*), his concern for the welfare of the poor (the *ministry of advocacy and prophecy*), and his generosity to the people (the *ministry of charity*).[28] The researchers described their findings with respect to these categories as follows:

> Priests' availability for pastoral service to the people: 72.6 percent (53 respondents) indicated that it is most important, with 27.7 percent (18 respondents) indicating that it is only important. Cumulatively, 97.3 percent (71 respondents) indicated that availability of priests for pastoral ministry for the people is an important quality of a good priest to some extent. Priests being compassionate: 32.9 percent (24 respondents) indicated that it is the most important quality of a priest, with 61.6 percent (45 percent) noting that it is only important. Cumulatively, 97 percent (71 respondents) indicated that being compassionate is important. Charity to the poor: 41.1 percent (30 respondents) indicated that it is the most important, with additional 53.4 percent (39 respondents) noting that it is only important. Cumulatively, 94.5 percent (69 respondents) noted that this aspect is an important quality of a priest. Generosity: 35.6 percent (26 respondents) indicated that it is the most important quality of a priest, with 54.8 percent (40 respondents) indicating that it is only important. Cumulatively, 90.4 percent (66 respondents) indicated that it is important to some degree.[29]

Portraits of Mercy: Tales of Two Clerics

Many Africans who face injustice can ultimately find joy and hope in their lives thanks to the ministry of priests. In situations of brutality, cruelty, exploitation, and the wanton destruction of life, it is crucial for pastors, as they dispense God's mercy, to balance mercy with justice. The two pastors described below have succeeded in this balancing act, thus avoiding turning the granting of mercy into cheap grace. According to St. Thomas Aquinas, "justice without mercy is cruelty, mercy without justice is weakness."[30] Engaging in acts of mercy without considering the injuries suffered by the victims of injustice waters them down. Dietrich Bonhoeffer, a renowned Protestant theologian, argued that "cheap grace means the justification of the sin and not the sinner ... cheap grace is preaching forgiveness without requiring repentance, baptism without church discipline, communion without confession, and absolution without personal confession."[31] In balancing justice and mercy, the two pastors discussed here, one a priest and the other a bishop, have succeeded in demonstrating that Jesus Christ gives sinners a second chance. As Kasper put it, "All application of law in the Church must look at Jesus Christ, the merciful Judge. Its criterion must be the *epikeia tou Christou*, the humanness, kindness, and mildness of Jesus Christ."[32]

The Graceful Seminary Formator

We start with the story of a priest, Fr. John Nchimbi (d. 2012). He served as formator and teacher at the Likonde Minor Seminary in the Mbinga diocese from 1976 to 1985, and will remain in the memory of his students (some of them now priests) for many years. Fr. Nchimbi, nicknamed Socrates for his brilliance in debating and philosophical argumentation, was a charming preacher in church and had a great sense of humor in the classroom. On

---

28. All these findings are taken from Lukwata et al., *Assessment of the Effectiveness of the Ministry of Priests in Eastern Africa*, 80–83.
29. Lukwata et al., *Assessment of the Effectiveness of the Ministry of Priests in Eastern Africa*, 80.
30. St. Thomas Aquinas, paraphrased in Kasper, *Leadership in the Church*, 157.
31. Bonhoeffer, *Cost of Discipleship*, 36.
32. Kasper, *Leadership in the Church*, 157.

account of his jovial character, he developed close relationships with students and fellow teachers.

Fr. Nchimbi was a spiritual physician who regularly accompanied students in manual work and employed humor to relieve their fatigue. He was an able manager of the duties assigned to him at the seminary, which included teacher, bursar, and vice-rector. Although highly intelligent, he was especially admired for his generosity and simplicity of life. The man embodied both spiritual and material poverty. Among all of his good qualities, however, Fr. Nchimbi had a passion for and the guts to practice mercy. Many of his students now acknowledge that without his pastoral sensitivity in dispensing God's forgiveness to them, many of them would not have finished the seminary. Fr. Nchimbi often surprised students with his unexpected visits to the seminarians, which often occurred when other teachers were taking the usual siesta after lunch. He caught several of them committing minor offenses. In serious cases like stealing and engaging in an improper relationship with a woman, the seminary rules were clear: if the seminarian was caught and reported to the rector, he faced summary dismissal.

Fr. Nchimbi grappled with the reality of sin among seminarians using a unique personal approach. He knew about the needs and concerns of young people very well, and so he was never hasty to report their mistakes to the rector or staff; instead, he conducted a "mobile reconciliation service." He would often walk around the seminary compound wearing his priestly stole. If he caught a seminarian committing sin, he asked him to acknowledge the sin—Fr. Nchimbi wanted the seminarian to realize that his actions had caused an offense to God, to the seminary, and to his fellow seminarians. Only after the sinner's acknowledgment that he had sinned would Fr. Nchimbi give the seminarian two choices: either to confess his sins before him and conclude the matter or to reject this "forced reconciliation," which would mean that he would report the matter to the rector and staff for further action. In most cases, seminarians opted to confess and resolve the matter. With his particular pastoral style, Fr. Nchimbi led many seminarians to the mercy of God and allowed them to continue discerning their vocation. Through his ministry of reconciliation, he transformed many young people for the better. His students now look back as priests and cannot help but feel grateful to have been protected by the power of mercy shown by this humble servant of God.

The Fatherly Bishop

The next story is quite similar to that of Fr. Nchimbi. It describes the compassionate heart of a bishop that clearly identifies him as an ambassador of God's mercy. I shall refer to him in this story with the symbolic name of Bishop Huruma.[33] The bishop is appreciated and loved by most of his priests for his fatherly love and friendliness. Bishop Huruma treats the priests in his diocese as true collaborators and friends. He guides them patiently and listens to their concerns with sympathy. He has an open-door policy, and priests and religious men and women can call at his office anytime. He welcomes priests from other dioceses to work in his diocese. He shows special concern for priests experiencing difficulties in their vocation.

Among the priests he once received was Fr. Angelo Kakuma (not his real name). This priest had had difficulties with his priestly ministry in his home diocese. His continuing dissolute life in the ministry had worsened his relationship with the local ordinary, and he was suspended several times. Even after being reinstated, he continued in his immoral ways. Ultimately, his bishop had given him an indefinite suspension. When news of this decision reached the graceful Bishop Huruma, he requested his brother to send the priest to him so he could have another chance in his diocese. Bishop Huruma knew the priest from the major seminary where he had served as spiritual director.

Upon his arrival in the host diocese, Fr. Kakuma was, to his surprise, warmly welcomed by Bishop Huruma. He arrived there totally humbled and was haunted by memories of his sins. Bishop Huruma treated him with love and respect despite his history, and the bishop put him up at his own house for a while. The priest felt deeply honored, and after some time, the bishop sent him to a parish as an assistant parish priest.

---

33. *Huruma* is Swahili word that means mercy, compassion, and forgiveness.

At one point, Bishop Huruma was celebrating the silver jubilee of his ministry as bishop. He invited his brother bishops, priests, religious, and laity and nearly everyone attended. All the guests were served with food and drinks. In the course of the celebration, the bishop spoke to thank all those who had worked to make the event a success. As the bishop spoke, Fr. Kakuma stood up and interrupted him, blurting out: "Bishop, stop your nonsense and leave us to enjoy the drinks!" Everyone in the hall was astonished. The chairman of the priests' association of the diocese confronted Fr. Kakuma and ordered the rude priest to exit the room, but to no avail. The bishops who were seated at the high table were openly upset and the atmosphere was tense. The hosting bishop could only try to calm the invited guests: "Let us continue our feast; I request each one of us to bear with him. He is our son, and we must let him feel accepted like others in his father's house."

With these words, the feasting returned to normal. The priest was allowed to continue working in the diocese. Bishop Huruma did not change his fatherly treatment of the unruly priest nor did he punish him for his behavior at the party; on the contrary, the bishop continued to support Fr. Kakuma to the end of Kakuma's life—the priest was in fact still active in the priestly ministry when he died, and it was Bishop Huruma's fraternal care and concern that graced the priest and allowed him to remain in the ministerial service. Interestingly, when the bishop who had sent him to Bishop Huruma heard of Fr. Kakuma's demise, he traveled to take his body back to his home diocese for burial.

The first story may raise some questions that require answers. How can we justify the forced confessions that Fr. Nchimbi imposed on seminarians he caught in acts of sin? Do we need formators in the seminary who pressure seminarians with forced confessions? It is important to understand that these confessions were not actually "forced." Fr. Nchimbi treated the seminarians he caught in sinful acts gently. He engaged in dialogue with them and often discussed the importance of faithfulness, communal meals, and love for the seminary life. He never began hearing the seminarian's confession until he was certain that the seminarian understood his mistake. He strove to make the seminarians realize that in stealing the property of the seminary or of a fellow seminarian, they were injuring their relationship with God, with the seminary staff, and with their classmates. By administering the sacrament to them, he helped them reconcile with God (he sometimes helped the process of reconciliation along by subjecting the culprits to additional punishments, such as weeding grass on the seminary farm). Confessions were also not heard in public for all to see but rather with pastoral discretion in staff rooms, inside the church, or in a field if the culprit was alone when caught.

In the story of Bishop Huruma, we see a merciful bishop who was never overhasty to take drastic actions against the misdemeanors of his priests. The bishop's decision to allow the priest to serve his canonical penalty in his home diocese follows the thinking of Pope Francis: "Anyone who makes a mistake must pay the price."[34] The story of Fr. Nchimbi is not related to bolster a cause for his canonization, and the story of Bishop Huruma is not meant to give an account of a generous bishop or to humiliate the unruly priest. Bible stories about the sins of great personalities like David and the woman caught in adultery, for example, are not told in order to demonize these people. They are instead meant to teach us important lessons.

The stories of the formator priest and the bishop illustrate the changing image of the African priest. Through their acts of mercy, they move us to trust that the grace of God continues to work through and not simply around our brokenness. They help us understand the mind of Pope Francis when he teaches that "mercy is not opposed to justice but rather expresses God's way of reaching out to the sinner, offering him a new chance to look at himself, convert, and believe."[35] In privileging mercy over judgment, these models invite us to seize the message of the Letter of James: "For judgment is merciless to one who has not shown mercy; mercy triumphs over judgment" (Jas 2:13). The two stories present an encounter between mercy and the

---

34. Pope Francis, *Misericordia Vultus* §21.

35. Pope Francis, *Misericordia Vultus* §21.

sinner. Through the simplicity and humility of pastors approaching sinners with dignity, the church presents itself to the world without pretense of perfection or a know-it-all attitude, but as a "loving mother to all, patient, kind, moved by compassion and goodness."[36] The two pastors model God as the Father who embraces his lost son and welcomes him home from his self-imposed exile, while at the same time helping the self-righteous older son to discover his own kind of self-imposed exile from home in order to regain his true home beyond his narrow point of view (see Luke 15:11–32). Fr. Nchimbi and Bishop Huruma both prescribed what Pope St. John XXIII described as "the medicine of mercy and not severity."[37]

Way Forward and Practical Proposals

The future of the church in Africa depends on how it makes present the reassuring face of God's mercy. Therefore, it is important for the church to put considerable effort into the following three areas.

Pray for Vocations to Priestly Ministry
Priestly vocations originate from God (see John 15:16); they are not the result of our own struggles. The influence of the secular world today makes it hard for gifted young people to join the priesthood. Secular jobs and professions are more materially rewarding and seem to present more of a future. As African economies continue to grow, newly employed graduates are increasingly finding jobs with good salaries, health insurance, house allowances, retirement benefits, and other perks. The church, on the other hand, does not have much to offer materially; rather, it asks those joining the priesthood to devote themselves to the love of God and neighbor. Priests must trust in God and pray without ceasing for vocations. Jesus himself admonished his disciples to pray for vocations: "The harvest is indeed plentiful, but the laborers are few. Pray therefore to the Lord of the harvest to send out laborers into his harvest" (Matt 9:38).

Even though there is much joy and merriment in the beautiful Christian worship and liturgy, it is clear that adequate structures promoting mental and devotional prayer in favor of vocations to priestly ministry do not exist. There is a need to spread the practice of these prayers among the faithful. For such prayer to flourish, an attitude of silence and inner peace is required. Mental prayer presupposes that the Christian faithful are properly catechized and know the Bible. The proper spiritual and physical disposition for mental prayer can be effected by contemplating Christian art; for example, paintings of saints and molded figures of angels. Devotional prayer is stimulated by the experience and needs of both individuals and the society at large, but in Africa, the noisy beats of *tam tam* and top music tones in shops and minibuses make it difficult for people to access the meditative silence needed for mental and devotional prayer.

Traditionally, in parish settings devotional associations like the Sacred Heart of Jesus Group, the Legion of Mary, the Catholic Charismatic Movement, and others have dedicated times for praying for priestly vocations. In some parishes and dioceses founded by the Benedictine missionaries of St. Ottilien (Germany), the Sacred Heart Group has distinguished itself for its promotion of priestly vocations; its members attend holy Mass on every first Friday of the month to pray for this intention. After celebrating the Mass, they recite the litany of the Sacred Heart while offering more prayers for priestly vocations. Inspired by the love and mercy of the Sacred Heart of Jesus, members of this group have distinguished themselves through the practice of corporal and spiritual works of mercy. They visit hospitals, prisons, and the sick, pray with those they encounter, and then share material help with them. The particular mark of their apostolate is the emphasis they place on mercy. Devotions directed to the Sacred Heart constitute a unique appeal for practical acts of mercy.

Unfortunately, the vitality exhibited by the Sacred Heart groups in the past has gradually faded away. In many parishes, the members consist of a few elderly people, and there do not appear to be signs of new membership among the youth; there is a need to study the reason why devotional asso-

---

36. Pope Francis, *Misericordia Vultus* §4.
37. Pope John XXIII, "Opening Address to the Second Vatican Council."

ciations do not attract new members. Given the importance of the lay apostolate groups in praying for vocations, there is a need to awaken enthusiasm for them in parishes. Their disappearance from some parishes robs communities of opportunities for concentrated prayer. Pastoral and liturgical coordinators in dioceses are being challenged to invent new strategies aimed at attracting young people to join these groups. This is crucial if we are determined to revive devotions in favor of priestly vocations.

Train Men after God's Own Heart
Looking at the future of the church in Africa, we trust in the Lord, who promises us, "I will give you shepherds after my own heart" (Jer 3:15). The image of the African priest as a steward of God's mercy is about shepherding the people guided by the merciful heart of God. This image summarizes the whole issue of formation in seminaries. Much has been written about the formation of future priests; still, we need to ask ourselves whether seminaries with their current curricula are veritable nurseries of misericordia for local churches? Are the seminary curricula and lifestyle assisting seminarians to emerge as men after God's own heart as King David was (see 1 Sam 13:14)? As a shepherd and ruler of Israel, King David's heart was informed by the heart of God himself, and the almighty God is full of mercy. "Mercy is God's supreme attribute because, as the absolute superior, the self-existent Creator, he is never self-seeking but acts only with infinite liberality."[38] As was mentioned earlier, the seminary is the heart of the diocese; it must be the place where seminarians are shaped to become shepherds with strong hearts for the people. St. John Chrysostom reckoned that the church during his time had lost touch with the values of the early church. As related by Daniel G. Groody, Chrysostom noted that "in the early days of the church the priests used chalices of wood and had hearts of gold," but in his own day and age, he lamented "that they used chalices of gold and have hearts of wood."[39] The apostles were rich, he said, "not because of their money or possessions but because of their spiritual wealth and charitable deeds."[40] Chrysostom's concern remains critical today, even to the extent that we marvel at the suggestion of the image of a priest as a steward of God's mercy.

Seminary training in Africa as handed down from the missionary church does much good in forming pastors for the people of the continent, and seminaries are doing their best to achieve this end. From the seminaries, parishes are graced with priests, the majority of whom work in the vineyard of the Lord without reserve. Nevertheless, a critical look at the methods of seminary formation inherited from the missionary church shows that seminaries tend to focus much more on intellectual formation than on the formation of the heart. What is at stake is the inner space of the human terrain; in short, human hearts are what need to be set right.[41] The emphasis on intellectual formation has given the minor seminaries in Africa a special status; their academic excellence, as reflected in national examination results, has elevated them in some places to the level of African Cambridge(s) and Oxford(s).[42] But prioritizing intellectual performance over development of the heart has precipitated some negative results.

In the first place, a seminary formation that places too much emphasis on intellectual perfor-

---

38. John Saward, "'Love's Second Name': St. Thomas on Mercy," www.christendom-awake.org/pages/jsaward/mercy. A sacramental presence of the church in the world unleashes God's mercy for humanity, thereby restoring dignity to repentant sinners.
39. Groody, *Globalization, Spirituality, and Justice*, 59.
40. Groody, *Globalization, Spirituality, and Justice*, 59.
41. See Groody, *Globalization, Spirituality, and Justice*, 10–11.
42. This is the case of the Likonde Minor Seminary of Mbinga diocese. This "seminary school, where a huge number of the elite of Tanzania were taught, is often called the 'Cambridge of East Africa'" (Susanne Hardörfer, "The Seminary School in Likonde," in http//diocese-mbinga.bistum-wuerzburg.de/bwo/dem/sites/bistum/extern/mbinga/in. See also Jordan Nyenyembe, "Migrants at the Mining Sector: A Pastoral and Theological Challenges for Africa. A Case Study of Mbinga Diocese (Tanzania)," unpublished doctoral dissertation at the Faculty of the Catholic University, Vienna (Austria), 2012, 112, at https://core.ac.uk/download/pdf/11599201.pdf.

mance has been criticized for favoring the "institutionalization and an emphasis on the Christian life which is over academic."[43] At major seminaries, this trend tends to measure philosophical and theological formation by the same yardstick that secular disciplines use in universities and colleges. Many children from rich families aspire to join minor seminaries, but in the past candidates to minor seminaries largely came from families with modest incomes, for example, children of catechists, farmers, carpenters, and fishermen. At present, applicants include children of government ministers, businessmen, generals, and commissioners. Of course, many of these candidates do not genuinely intend to become priests, and there is a compelling challenge today to discern genuine vocations in new candidates to the seminaries. Some of these applicants want only to benefit from the academic status enjoyed by seminaries and some simply desire to perform well on national examinations. In Nigeria, for example, the challenge facing formators stems from the increasing number of seminarians wishing to be ordained.[44] The workload is too heavy for them to train the seminarians effectively. In his post-synodal apostolic exhortation *Africae Munus* ("Africa's Commitment"), Benedict XVI admonishes bishops and seminary formators thus: "In selecting candidates, careful discernment and quality guidance must be ensured, so that those admitted to the priesthood will be true Disciples of Christ and authentic servants of the Church" (§122).

Some candidates to the priesthood are recruited from among youth who grew up in difficult situations: in the streets, in the slums, some from polygamous families. The challenge for formators is thus enormous. Seminary staff members have to work together to assist such candidates. It is crucial to work closely with and encourage seminarians in order to instill in them human, spiritual, moral, and psychological integrity. All in all, "we must not be afraid to welcome people with lively, rich, or even problematic personalities into our seminaries and houses of formation, provided that they demonstrate clarity of intention or, in the words of *Optatam Totius*, 'proper intention and freedom of choice.'"[45]

The second problem that results from the academic prestige attached to seminaries is the corrosion of priestly vocations. Seminary formators strive to discern genuine vocations, but it would appear that some young men pursue priestly vocations in order to achieve their worldly ambitions. A priestly vocation is a special calling, a special grace, and involves a privileged service. Young men must not join the seminary out of misguided motives that can drive them toward the corrupting influences of worldly temptations. It is in this context that Pope Francis, during his audience with the clergy, men and women religious, and seminarians in Nairobi (2015) warned, "If we want to follow Jesus Christ—in the priesthood or the consecrated life—we have to enter by the door! And the door is Christ! He is the one who calls, who begins, who does the work. Some people want to enter by the window. . . . It doesn't work that way."[46]

The third negative impact of a formation that prioritizes intellectual excellence is that it alienates candidates from day-to-day realities. Seminarians are trained to become bookish and are prepared only for the discipline of sitting, leaving them less time for the discipline of encounter with the people. Availability for itinerancy, which is indispensable to the pastoral and prophetic ministry of the priest, can be frustrated by a bookish pastor.[47] An excessively intellectual priest can become absorbed in a routine of privacy and stability that discourages his leaving the presbytery. He ends up becoming a "parachutist" priest, a term coined by the renowned African liturgist John Lukwata: "A parachutist priest is one who comes to the people for liturgical functions or for a specific duty and moves

---

43. Downey, "Creeping Curriculum," 330.
44. See Uzukwu, *Listening Church*, 94–95.
45. Camisasca, *Together on the Road*, 118, quoting Vatican Council II, *Optatam Totius* (Decree on Priestly Formation) §6.
46. Pope Francis, *Messages of Pope Francis*, 14.
47. See Nyenyembe, "Conflict and Displacement," 194.

away as soon as it is over, avoiding any meaningful contact with the flock."[48]

Moreover, priests who rarely leave the presbytery and spend most of their time away from the realities of the people tend to embrace a spiritualism that can "hinder the development and carrying out of the Church mission."[49] The lifestyle of many office-bound priests favors the bureaucratization of ecclesial life. It "reduces the Christian life to meetings, conventions, and documents. . . . What is missing is the beauty of a life lived in communion here and now."[50] Seminary formators need to be aware of these dangers and respond by fostering a life of communion. They should assist seminarians in developing a spirituality of communion. This is necessary because "the diocesan priest's charism is to live among the people."[51] In fact, "unlike the secular professional, the diocesan priest finds his vocational calling in living with the people. . . . Our vocation calls us to be present to the people in the daily fabric of their lives."[52] It is imperative that future priests be trained to love community life and to love the people they serve. Intellectual life should not be opposed to social life, but rather be a means of living a mature and balanced life, and even to serve the people better. Therefore, Bénézet Bujo rightly advises that "today in Africa, seminaries need to be located where 'seminarians become familiar with the life of the people they will serve as priests.'"[53]

A closely related point is that a rigid intellectual life also distances the priest from places that are hurting. In the face of injustice and suffering, priests cannot remain indifferent. They must take sides to help liberate the suffering from oppression. The sick need healing, and hence, "seminary formation should sufficiently prepare future priests to practice psycho-somatic healing, exorcism, deliverance and pastoral counselling in the face of challenges which include war, ethnic conflict, epidemic diseases, poverty, witchcraft and injustices."[54] This cannot be done by remote control—priests must be in the company of those who cry for justice. Prophets like Jeremiah wept over injustices inflicted on the people. For this reason, Pope Francis directs priests in Africa to "never stop weeping. When priests and religious no longer weep, something is wrong. We need to weep for our infidelity, to weep for all the pain in our world, to weep for all those people who are cast aside, to weep for the elderly who are abandoned, for children who are killed, for the things we don't understand."[55] Therefore, the training of future priests in seminaries must equip them with both a rational mind and a compassionate heart.

It is important at this juncture to say something about the role of women in priestly formation. Beginning with the formalization of seminary training at the Council of Trent (1546–1560), the training of seminarians has lain predominantly on the shoulders of male clerics. However, after the Second Vatican Council (1962–1965), this has changed. Some dioceses in Africa have religious sisters teaching courses in major and minor seminaries. In some local churches, Catholic women participate in the formation of future priests by paying the educational fees of seminarians and otherwise financially supporting the operation of seminaries. This is very encouraging. There is a need, however, to expand the roles that can be played by women throughout the whole process of seminary training. Traditional African cultures regarded women as being secondary to men, and expanding their contribution to seminary training in academic and support staff roles would help to improve their social status. It would also assist priests in relating with women in a more mature and integral manner.

---

48. Lukwata et al., *Assessment of the Effectiveness of the Ministry of Priests in Eastern Africa*, 32.
49. Camisasca, *Together on the Road*, 123.
50. Camisasca, *Together on the Road*, 124.
51. Rossetti, *Joy of Priesthood*, 141.
52. Rossetti, *Joy of Priesthood*, 139.
53. Bujo, *African Theology in Its Social Context*, 104.
54. Lukwata et al., *Assessment of the Effectiveness of the Ministry of Priests in Eastern Africa*, 94.
55. Pope Francis, *Messages of Pope Francis*, 16.

Do Not Condemn Laicized Priests

Jesus Christ, the High Priest and Good Shepherd, defined his ministry as one that does not condemn but instead saves the lost (see Luke 5:31; John 3:17). Based on this model, the priestly domain should be marked by a culture of mercy. The image of priest as a steward of God's mercy calls on every member of the church to engage in soul-searching. Church members need to find ways to show compassion to priests who have left ministerial service. We need to listen more carefully to their stories and accompany them. Some laicized priests and deacons in Africa lead miserable lives, but they are members of the church who yearn for compassion. Spurred by the image of Jesus Christ as the Good Shepherd, the global church has begun to adopt a compassionate approach to its treatment of divorced and remarried couples. The same compassion should also be extended to laicized priests.

Laicized priests are concerned about a number of things, including the very term "laicization." The word "lay" that is at the root of "laicization" is controversial even when it is referring to nonordained members of the church—there has been a scholarly debate about whether the word is appropriate for the nonordained. It is not within the scope of this chapter to present the details of this debate, but suffice it to say that "laicized" priests, in view of their ordination, also dispute the use of the term to refer to their state. They argue that the term "laicization" is improperly applied to them because priestly ordination, like baptism, imbues one with an indelible character, a character that does not change when one is suspended from active ministerial service. Two alternative concepts have been proposed, namely, "dispensed priests"[56] and "transitioned priests,"[57] in recognition of the fact that even if "laicized" priests are not engaged in active ministry, the priesthood continues to define their lives in some way.

They are also concerned that the document setting forth their laicization sounds more juridical than pastoral. It fails to appreciate the service that the priest rendered to the people of God during his years in active ministry. One laicized priest put it this way: "There is no graciousness. In the document there is no mention of the years spent in ministry, no recognition that I applied to be laicized because I wished to live in good conscience. It informs me that I may not minister in any way within the Church and among other things that I may not distribute Holy Communion."[58]

Another concern is the widespread complaint of laicized priests and those serving penalties of suspension that they have been completely abandoned by the church. They feel alienated by the apparent silence of the church at all levels: the hierarchy, religious men and women, and laypeople. It must be stated that laicized priests are not a condemned caste in the church. As Declan Moriarty writes, "The prevailing sense and sound after one leaves is that of silence: the silence of the Church, the silence of priests, the silence of people. . . . The fact that many men have left priesthood and continue to do so ought to merit some sort of research and concern by those in leadership with the Church."[59] Both laicized and suspended priests lament the difficulties they face in getting material assistance for their livelihood. Many laicized priests who come from poor backgrounds languish in poverty. Because they are denied or deprived of assistance by other Christians, some feel that they are regarded as traitors to their vocation, that they have been left to endure earthly penance for abandoning their ministry. The pitiful cry of laicized priests was summarized by one former priest in these words: "A great challenge for us who left was our dependency upon the institution in which we lived. The basic impression given in formation and ordained ministry is 'The Church will take care of you.' This dependency upon the institution is structured into the system with the monastic communal lifestyle of formation, the 'fraternity' of ordained priests, and provided housing."[60]

The image of the priest as steward of God's mercy lasts for a lifetime. Ministerial priesthood is not a

---

56. See Büttner, "Kleine Schritte, große Hoffnungen," 35–37.
57. See "Leaving the Priesthood," www.leavingthepriesthood.com.
58. Moriarty, "Leaving the Priesthood," 37.
59. Moriarty, "Leaving the Priesthood," 37.
60. "Leaving the Priesthood," www.leavingthepriesthood.com.

part-time calling, and laicized priests are aware of the perpetual nature of their calling. On account of the indelible character they received at ordination, they are justified in expecting compassionate attention from the church. As baptized Christians, they too must bear witness to and practice the corporal and spiritual works of mercy even if they are no longer involved in active ministry. The church in Africa must find ways to assist laicized priests and ensure that they lead dignified lives. The church should continue to harness their talents to promote social ministry and other forms of apostolate. Priests in active ministry should be challenged to initiate support mechanisms for those among them who have left active ministry.

Priests leave the ministerial priesthood for a variety of reasons. It goes without saying that many leave because of a lack of dialogue with and respect from their superiors. When priests feel that their human needs are not being cared for, some may be driven to stress-related problems like alcoholism. In addition, priests need and deserve continuous formation. Organizations like AMECEA (Association of Member Episcopal Conferences in Eastern Africa), Pastoral Institutes (Eldoret, Kenya), and the Lumko Institute (South Africa), begun after Vatican II, need to be supported so that priests and religious sisters can experience ongoing pastoral and spiritual renewal. Unfortunately, at present these institutes work with very few people; by and large, ongoing formation and additional study are considered to be a privilege of the few rather than a canonical right and a necessity for the growth of the church. In some dioceses, priests report that they work for years without being granted any sabbatical leave. Clearly, in many dioceses and parishes in Africa, it seems that providing pastoral care to parishioners, as important as that is, is a much higher priority than the welfare of priests. Their health, remuneration, old age insurance, and ongoing formation are treated as secondary. After decades of dedicated service to the church, many priests suffer from "commitment fatigue," and it is important that they be supported. As Benedict XVI exhorts the bishops, "Love and respect your priests! . . . Your priests need your affection, your encouragement and your concern" (*AM* §101). All of this is just as true for laicized priests.

There is also the problem of priests who have defected from the Roman Catholic Church. The church should be sufficiently moved with compassion for these "lost sons" to continue a dialogue with them. There are fifty-four defected priests in Kenya operating under the auspices of the so-called Ecumenical Catholic Church headed by their archbishop Godfrey Shiundu Wasike, and claiming about three hundred thousand followers.[61] In Uganda, twenty priests formed a breakaway sect in 2016 called the Catholic Apostolic National Church, in which priests are free to marry. Worldwide archbishop Emmanuel Milingo (the former ordinary of the Archdiocese of Lusaka in Zambia) is the leader of all the married priests in Africa. Such realities call for the church hierarchy to engage in continuing dialogue. It is important to listen to the stories, questions, anxieties, worries, and insights of these men. Their voices may offer pastoral insights that priests in active ministry *ad intra ecclesia* may not have or may not be able to share.

Conclusion

The image of the Catholic priest in Africa is changing. The growing understanding of the priest as a steward of God's mercy calls for a more eucharistic church that can foster communion because the Eucharist is the sacrament of communion. Because the Eucharist is also the sacrament of love, it can also promote unity and love among the people. And because the Eucharist is the sacrificial anamnesis of the cross, the church can also spearhead a life of forgiveness and reconciliation. A eucharistic church is decentralized, fostering reciprocal relationship. "The Eucharist is an encounter with the merciful Christ in his act of self-sacrifice. More than that, the Eucharist is incorporation into that

---

61. See "South Africa: Married Catholic Priests Grow as Four Join," Kurunzi Afrika: Connecting the Dots (November 10, 2013), https://kurunziafrika.wordpress.com/2013/11/10/south-africa-married-catholic-priests-church-grows-as-4-join.

act of self-sacrifice, for the ecclesial body, as part of the *totus Christus*, is itself the body of Christ."[62]

Understanding the role of the priest as a steward of God's mercy has some implications for the Christian faithful, both ordained and nonordained. First, it should move the Christian faithful to be grateful to God, the creator. The Catholic faithful should be thankful for the gift of priesthood in the church and pray for more vocations. Bishops and laypeople should support priests and deacons materially and spiritually and ensure that they can live out their calling with joy and commitment. In a spirit of thankfulness to God, priests should be accorded the continuing training and formation they need. Their welfare also demands that they be provided with periodic sabbatical leave.

The image of priests as stewards of God's mercy imprints upon them the notion that they are servants of God. What is required of the steward who is aware of his role as a servant (see Luke 17:10) is to remain trustworthy (see 1 Cor 4:1–2). The steward's responsibility, therefore, "has three dimensions; he must please the master, work for the benefit of other servants, and do both by showing a responsible use of the resources entrusted to his care."[63] Within their stewardship of mercy, priests are developing a new consciousness that they are agents of hope and joy to the people. Thanks to its ordained ministers, the African church has become a champion of the message of hope and joy, a "rich laboratory of hope."[64] The presence of hope and joy in people locked in circles of violence and suffering is peculiar to African Christianity. The boldness of faith that grounds the hope and joy of the faithful amid pain and misery is a spiritual gift to the whole church. As Emmanuel Katongole envisions: "When the final story of world Christianity is told as the story of hope, . . . the stories of hope from Africa will be spoken of as those that provided the ink, the much-needed energy, and fresh vitality to bolster the waning prospects of global Christianity."[65]

Bibliography

Adiprasetya, Joas. "Towards an Asian Multi-Textual Theology." *Exchange* 43.2 (2014): 119–31.

Arinze, Francis Cardinal. *Reflecting on Our Priesthood*. Nairobi: Paulines Publications Africa, 2008.

Azevedo, Marcello, SJ. *The Consecrated Life: Crossroads and Directions*. Maryknoll, NY: Orbis Books, 1995.

Benedict XVI, Pope. *Africae Munus* [Post-synodal Apostolic Exhortation on the Church in Africa in Service of Reconciliation, Justice and Peace; November 19, 2011]. Vatican City: Libreria Editrice Vaticana, 2011. www.vatican.va.

Bonhoeffer, Dietrich. *The Cost of Discipleship*. 1948. Reprint, New York: Touchstone, 2018.

Bujo, Bénézet. *African Theology in Its Social Context*. Nairobi: Paulines Publications Africa, 1992.

Büttner, Edgar. "Kleine Schritte, große Hoffnungen: Über ausgeschiedene Priester und ihr Verhältnis zur Kirche." *Würzburger Katholisches Sonntagsblatt*, July 9, 2017, 35–37.

Camisasca, Massimo. *Together on the Road: A Vision of Lived Communion for the Church and the Priesthood*. Pauline Books and Media, 2005.

Cozzens, Donald B. *The Changing Face of the Priesthood*. Collegeville, MN: Liturgical Press, 2000.

Cullinane, Tim. *Preparing for Priesthood: Spirituality for Seminarians*. Nairobi: Paulines Publications Africa, 2015.

Dietrich, Donald, ed. *Priests for the 21st Century*. New York: Crossroad, 2006.

Downey, James. "The Creeping Curriculum." *African Ecclesial Review–AFER* 24 (December 1982).

Egan, Kevin. "Understanding Forgiveness." *The Furrow: A Journal for the Contemporary Church* (July–August 2016).

Francis, Pope. *Messages of Pope Francis: During His Apostolic Journey to Africa* (November 25–30, 2015). Nairobi: Paulines Publications Africa, 2015.

———. *Misericordia Vultus* [Papal Bull for the Indiction of the Jubilee of Mercy; April 11, 2015]. Dublin: Veritas, 2015.

---

62. Schlesinger, "Church's Eucharistic Poverty in the Theologies of Jon Sobrino and Hans Urs von Balthasar," 646.
63. Johnson, *Sharing Possessions*, 151.
64. Katongole, *Born from Lament*, 264.
65. Katongole, *Born from Lament*, 265.

Groody, Daniel G. *Globalization, Spirituality, and Justice: Navigating the Path to Peace*. Maryknoll, NY: Orbis Books, 2007.

Johnson, Luke Timothy. *Sharing Possessions: What Faith Demands*. Grand Rapids, MI: Eerdmans, 2011.

John Paul II, Pope. *Dives in Misericordia* (Rich in Mercy) [Encyclical; November 30, 1992]. www.vatican.va.

———. *Ecclesia in Africa*. [Post-synodal Apostolic Exhortation on the Church in Africa and Its Evangelizing Mission toward the Year 2000; September 14, 1995]. Nairobi: Paulines Publications Africa, 1995. www.vatican.va.

———. *Gift and Mystery: On the 50th Anniversary of My Personal Ordination*. Nairobi: Paulines Publications Africa, 1996.

———. *Pastores dabo Vobis* [Post-synodal Apostolic Exhoration on the Formation of Priests in the Circumstances of the Present Day; March 25, 1992]. Nairobi: Paulines Publications Africa, 1990. www.vatican.va.

Kasper, Walter Cardinal. *Leadership in the Church: How Traditional Roles Can Serve the Christian Community Today*. New York: Crossroad, 2003.

Katongole, Emmanuel. *Born from Lament: The Theology and Politics of Hope in Africa*. Grand Rapids, MI: Eerdmans, 2017.

Lukwata, John, ed. *Year of the Priests: Faithfulness of Christ, Faithfulness of Priest*. Nairobi: CUEA Press, 2014.

Lukwata, John, et al., eds. *Assessment of the Effectiveness of the Ministry of Priests in Eastern Africa: Research Report*. Nairobi: CUEA Press, 2017.

Maliti, Patrick. *Forming Priests in the Modern World*. Eldoret, Kenya: AMECEA Gaba Publications, 1993.

Moriarty, Declan. "Leaving the Priesthood." *The Furrow: Journal for the Contemporary Church* 67.1 (January 2016): 34–38.

Nyenyembe, Jordan. *African Catholic Priests: Confronting an Identity Problem*. Bamenda, Cameroon: Langaa, 2010.

———. "Conflict and Displacement: Plea for Changed Image of an African Priest." *African Ecclesia Review* (September–December 2017): 191–211.

———. "Stewards of God's Mercy: Vocation and Priestly Ministry in Africa." *Journal of Global Catholicism* 1.2 (July 2017): 74–95.

O'Donoghue, Helena. "Mercy." *The Furrow: A Journal for Contemporary Church* 67.4 (April 2016): 218–21.

Rossetti, Stephen J. *The Joy of Priesthood*. Notre Dame, IN: Ave Maria Press, 2005.

Schlesinger, Eugene R. "The Church's Eucharistic Poverty in the Theologies of Jon Sobrino and Hans Urs von Balthasar." *Theological Studies* 77.3 (2016): 627–51.

Stackpole, Robert. "What Does 'Divine Mercy' Actually Mean?," *Divine Mercy News* (October 27, 2010), www.thedivinemercy.org.

Tambudzai, Ignatius, and Chikere C. Ugwanyi, eds. *The Priestly Ministry in Africa: Reflections by Seminarians and Priests*. Nairobi: Paulines Publications Africa, 2011.

Uzukwu, Elochukwu. *Listening Church: Autonomy and Communion in African Churches*. Maryknoll, NY: Orbis Books, 1996.

Vatican Council II. Decree on Priestly Formation (*Optatam Totius*) (1965).

Suggested Reading

Cozzens, Donald B. *The Changing Face of the Priesthood*. Collegeville, MN: Liturgical Press, 2000.

Dietrich, Donald, ed. *Priests for the 21st Century*. New York: Crossroad, 2006.

Kasper, Walter Cardinal. *Leadership in the Church: How Traditional Roles Can Serve the Christian Community Today*. New York: Crossroad, 2003.

Lukwata, John, et al., eds. *Assessment of the Effectiveness of the Ministry of Priests in Eastern Africa: Research Report*. Nairobi: CUEA Press, 2017.

Nyenyembe, Jordan. *African Catholic Priests: Confronting an Identity Problem*. Bamenda: Langaa, 2010.

Key Words

compassionate ministry
mercy
ministry
priesthood
seminary formators
seminary training
servant of God
steward
vocation

The Impact of the African Laity on Modern African Catholicism: The Example of Alioune Diop

Elizabeth A. Foster

In 1957, a blistering editorial entitled "Peut-on dresser le Vatican contre les peuples de couleur" [Can they set the Vatican against peoples of color?] headlined the October–November issue of *Présence africaine*, the leading journal of the negritude movement and the foremost organ of mid-century Black internationalism.[1] The same piece then appeared a few weeks later in *Témoignage chrétien*, a widely circulating, left-leaning French Catholic newspaper.[2] Its author was Alioune Diop, *Présence africaine*'s founder and editor-in-chief, who also established and directed the *Présence africaine* publishing house and the Présence africaine bookstore in Paris's Latin Quarter. Diop wrote the piece as a direct riposte to a strident book by François Méjan, a French Protestant lawyer and civil servant with socialist leanings and secularist sympathies, entitled *Le Vatican contre la France d'Outre-Mer?* [The Vatican against Overseas France].[3] Méjan's work was an angry denunciation of the Vatican for undermining France's rule in its Overseas Territories (most of which were in sub-Saharan Africa) by emphasizing what Méjan termed "de-occidentalization," by calling on French missionaries to renounce their loyalty to France, and by its "rapid" promotion of indigenous bishops to positions of authority over French clergy.[4] For Méjan, this all added up to the church's "abandonment of Western civilization."[5]

Diop objected to Méjan's arguments, his hysterical tone, and his implicit racism, observing that "the Vatican's first treachery apparently consists in admitting that indigenous men can be priests. We are stupefied and wondering how anyone can complain about the church conferring priestly dignity on a yellow or a black man."[6] Diop, in contrast to Méjan, felt that "de-occidentalization" of the Catholic Church was a step toward its realization of its true, catholic universality and was therefore something to be encouraged. Moreover, in Diop's mind, in 1957 the church still had much more to do to disentangle itself from European culture and European colonial rule in Africa.

Diop's response to Méjan was just one of many written and oral public and private interventions he made regarding the mission of the Catholic Church and the nature of Catholicism itself between the 1940s and 1970s. Indeed, Diop was the most prominent of a determined and vocal group of African Catholic lay intellectuals who played a crucial role in the reorientation of the Catholic Church dur-

---

1. Présence africaine, "Peut-on dresser le Vatican contre les peuples de couleur?"
2. Diop, "Peut-on dresser le Vatican contre les peuples de couleur?," 13. *Témoignage chrétien* had been founded as an organ of French Catholic Resistance to German occupation during the Second World War.
3. Méjan, *Le Vatican contre la France d'Outre-Mer?*
4. Méjan, *Le Vatican contre la France d'Outre-Mer?*, 57–63.
5. Méjan, *Le Vatican contre la France d'Outre-Mer?*, 73, 75.
6. Diop, "Peut-on dresser la Vatican contre les peuples de couleur?," 13.

ing the era of decolonization. Diop and his fellow activists were devoutly Catholic, yet nonetheless militantly insistent that the church needed to stop identifying itself solely with Europe and needed to sever its ties with the prevailing colonial order in Africa and elsewhere. They included figures such as Burkinabé historian Joseph Ki Zerbo, Beninese author and activist Albert Tévoéjdrè, Senegalese poet and politician (later President) Léopold Sédar Senghor, and Cameroonian economist and future minister Georges Ngango. Their lives and careers reflect the fact that a disproportionately high percentage of the emerging francophone African elite at mid-century were Catholics.[7] This meant that, as they thought and wrote about the possibility of African political and intellectual independence from Europe, they engaged in debates about the nature of Catholicism itself and its potential to be African in Africa. And thanks to Diop's persistence and organizational skills, they were able to influence the papacy at a crucial juncture. Indeed, without the activism and advocacy of Diop and fellow African lay intellectuals, it is hard to imagine the church pivoting so dramatically toward the wider world at Vatican II and beyond. Their interventions at mid-century thus helped lay the groundwork for the burgeoning African church of the late twentieth and early twenty-first centuries.

Dialogue

A future as a leading Catholic intellectual would have seemed very improbable for a Muslim Wolof boy born in 1910 in colonial Saint-Louis, Senegal, especially one whose first several years of formal schooling consisted of memorizing the Koran in Arabic. Alioune Diop's parents were not highly educated nor particularly prominent, though he had forebears who were aristocrats in the precolonial Wolof kingdom of Kajoor.[8] Saint-Louis was a port town, however, where Muslim Wolof had lived alongside French traders and a devoutly Catholic métis population since the seventeenth century, so Diop knew of other faith communities. Moreover, there was a history of conversion in his family, and Diop had distant Catholic cousins. A great-grandfather had been taken to France as a child and raised in the church before returning to Saint-Louis and marrying there, although his daughter, Alioune's grandmother, converted from Catholicism to Islam to marry her husband. In addition, by virtue of his birth in Saint-Louis, which was one of Senegal's privileged Four Communes, Diop enjoyed French citizenship, which facilitated his movement within the French Empire.[9] Diop entered Senegal's French education system at age ten and excelled at every level, before moving to Algiers to study for a *licence* in classical letters in 1933 and then on to France to pursue a higher degree and a teaching post in the later 1930s.[10]

Diop's conversion to Catholicism took place in the context of the German occupation of France in the Second World War, when he was teaching at the Prytanée militaire de la Flèche, a prestigious military academy in the Loire Valley. While there, Diop undertook a course of religious study and catechism with the Dominican intellectual Jean-Augustin Maydieu, which culminated in Diop's baptism on Christmas Day 1944. Converting while living in war-torn Europe shaped Diop's understanding

---

7. Due to the structurally weak French colonial educational system, mission schools were a major feeder to institutions of higher learning in Africa and France, which explains the high percentage of Catholics among Africans with European diplomas at mid-century. Léopold Senghor started his scholastic career in mission schools and briefly considered becoming a Catholic priest.

8. Coats, "From Whence We Come," 207.

9. After 1879, African men born in the Four Communes of Dakar, Gorée, Rufisque, and Saint-Louis had the right, alongside métis and French male residents of the towns, to vote in municipal elections, in elections to choose a general council for the colony, and in elections to choose a deputy to represent Senegal in the French National Assembly. For more details see Johnson, *Emergence of Black Politics in Senegal*. In contrast to Diop, the vast majority of Africans in French colonies were subjects and had no freedom to migrate to the metropole—indeed many were coerced to go there as soldiers in the World Wars but were then promptly repatriated, even if they wanted to stay.

10. Verdin, *Alioune Diop*, 42–47.

of Catholicism and its relationship with the West and the wider world in significant ways. From the outset, his engagement with Catholicism involved confronting and questioning Europe's place in the world, its dominance within the church, and the church's ambiguous role in colonialism. Before his conversion, he articulated this in a 1943 letter to Marguerite Marteau, his future French godmother. He wrote, "Europe has the rest of the world at its disposition. More riches than it needs to live. However, it is tearing itself apart." Diop felt that the colonized peoples of the world had a special message of peace that Europeans needed to hear, though they were unlikely to heed it. He therefore believed the church should take it up, "purify the faith," and "calm the fever" of Europeans.[11]

Alioune Diop thus believed that dialogue between peoples was the path to a better future, and he devoted his career to facilitating such a dialogue. Throughout his life, Diop distinguished himself by his intellectual curiosity, his openness to new people and ideas, and his desire for exchange with those of other faiths, beliefs, backgrounds, and nationalities. In the course of his peregrinations, he developed a remarkable talent for attracting and bringing together some of the most remarkable thinkers in the francophone world. While in Algiers, he met Albert Camus, who became a good friend. When he then moved to Paris, Diop fell in with the founding trio of negritude: Léopold Sédar Senghor, as well as Aimé Césaire and Léon-Gontran Damas, both from the French Caribbean. After 1939, when Césaire returned to Martinique and Senghor was mobilized to fight in the Second World War (he would spend two years in a POW camp), Diop emerged as a mentor to colonial students in France, organizing them and inviting prominent French thinkers to speak to them. Senghor, Césaire, and Damas had connected Diop to the prominent French Catholic philosopher of personalism Emmanuel Mounier and to the writer and philosopher Jean-Paul Sartre, both of whom addressed Diop's student gatherings.[12] Diop even convinced Mounier to undertake a weeks-long speaking trip through French Africa in 1947, which started with an Easter celebration in Dakar.[13] Diop also came to know Louis Massignon, a Catholic intellectual who advocated Catholic rapprochement with Islam; surrealist writer and ethnographer Michel Leiris; naturalist Théodore Monod; painter Pablo Picasso; and the sociologist and ethnographer of Africa Georges Balandier. In 1946, when Balandier was a young scholar setting out on his fieldwork, he stayed with Diop's family in Dakar. Balandier later described how Diop warmly welcomed an endless stream of visitors for conversation and exchange, including local imams, Islamic scholars, Senegalese political notables, and African and French intellectuals.[14] Subsequently, when Diop opened his bookstore in Paris in 1949, it became a hub for Black intellectuals and the ever-burgeoning numbers of African students who came to the metropole in the late 1940s and the 1950s.[15]

Diop's interest in and talent for organizing and facilitating exchange between intellectuals enabled him to become, in the words of one biographer, "the builder of the Black world,"[16] though today his crucial role in the negritude movement and Black internationalism is largely obscured by scholars' focus on Senghor, Césaire, and Damas. Yet it is highly unlikely that, without Diop's organizational efforts, negritude would have reached a vast global audience. In his journal *Présence africaine*, in the books he published and sold in his bookstore, and in the landmark international conferences of Black artists and writers that he organized in Paris in 1956, in Rome in 1959, and in Dakar in 1966, he gave Black writers, thinkers, and artists venues to share their ideas and connect with one another and a broad international public. In the 1950s, Diop joined the prestigious European Society of Culture (SEC) in order to bring it

---

11. Alioune Diop to Marguerite Marteau, October 31, 1943, quoted in Verdin, *Alioune Diop*, 100.
12. Vaillant, *Black, French, and African*, 213.
13. For more, see Foster, *African Catholic*, 68–77. For Mounier's collected writings on the trip, see Mounier, *L'éveil de l'Afrique noire*.
14. Balandier, *Conjugaisons*, 235–36.
15. Frioux-Salgas, "Entretien avec le poète, romancier et essayiste Daniel Maximin," 158.
16. Mel, *Alioune Diop: le bâtisseur inconnu du monde noir*.

an African point of view, yet he also founded the African Society of Culture (SAC), and served as its secretary-general.

As he argued for the importance of Black perspectives and the inherent value of African culture on the international stage, Diop consistently foregrounded his Catholic faith. Though scholars have long ignored it, there is a great deal of religious discussion in the pages of *Présence africaine* and in the transcripts of the famous conferences of 1956 and 1959. Indeed, Diop's editorials in *Présence africaine*, the many book prefaces he authored, and the books he published, reveal how central the question of Africans' place in the church was for him and for his fellow African Catholic intellectuals. His wide circle of interlocutors on religious questions included the francophone and anglophone Black intellectuals who wrote for and read *Présence africaine*; the many Catholics in the newly emerging francophone African elite; African clergymen and prelates; prominent African Muslims; French and Italian Catholic intellectuals; and European cardinals and popes.

Diop also knew very well that his adopted faith made him vulnerable to the accusation that he had unthinkingly embraced the religion of European colonizers, a charge leveled by critics on the Marxist left.[17] He always maintained, however, that the true essence of Catholicism was its universality—its ability to welcome and nourish all peoples regardless of their race or culture. His goal was to change the Catholic Church from the inside by calling on it to live up to its own universal claims, and he was remarkably successful. Together with lay and clerical allies, he helped to lay the groundwork for the rapid growth of Catholicism in Africa after the Second Vatican Council.

Activism

Through his writings, his publishing, and his organization of conferences and cultural groups, Diop had a profound effect on the reorientation of the Catholic Church during the era of decolonization. He persuaded influential members of the Catholic hierarchy, notably Popes John XXIII and Paul VI, to open the church to the world beyond Europe in new ways. Diop discerned that Europeans, arrogantly and "unconsciously racist," too readily assumed that what was European was "universal."[18] This had implications for their understanding of Catholicism, whose true nature, he argued, they failed to comprehend. In 1955, he wrote in *Présence africaine*, "The serenity of intellectual Europe is betrayed, at the heart of its glorious certainty, by a desire for assimilation, or racism. And thus the fate of culture is tied to the colonial problem. And so is the fate of Christendom (of its habits of thought and its spirituality)." Diop insisted that Christianity was not a civilization and was not wedded to any particular people or culture.[19] The faith itself was indeed universal, but its European adherents too often appropriated it as uniquely their own. For Christianity to survive and flourish, it needed to be rescued from those who defined it too narrowly. Diop wanted to make sure that those at the pinnacle of the Catholic hierarchy comprehended this point.

As the French Empire began to come apart (Indochina won independence by force of arms in 1954, Morocco and Tunisia became independent in 1956, and the Algerian War began in 1954), Diop kept up a steady drumbeat of criticism of the Eurocentrism of his adopted church, and the overweening pride of Europeans in general. For Diop, political self-determination for colonized peoples was akin to the decolonization of Christianity, which he imagined as the decoupling of the faith from European culture and political power. In 1956, he published an article in *Présence africaine* entitled "L'Occident chrétien et nous" [The Christian West and Us] in which he called openly for Christian Europeans to support the independence of African and Asian peoples. He accused European missionaries of long confusing the temporal and spiritual realms as they evangelized colonized peoples. Africans, Diop claimed, were "conscious

---

17. See the critique of *Présence africaine* by Guinean playwright Nénékhaly-Camara, "Conscience nationale et poésie négro-africaine d'expression française," 12.
18. Diop, "Colonialisme et nationalisme culturels," 11.
19. Diop, "Colonialisme et nationalisme culturels," 8, 11–12.

of the immense resources that missionaries could have brought to the liberation of our national cultures, and also conscious of missionaries' desire to 'civilize', that is to say to replace local civilizations, values, cultures, and laws with their European values, cultures, and laws, which are, however, so independent from Christianity."[20] He accused Europeans of confounding might and right—of allowing their dominance in world affairs to persuade themselves that they were the keepers of true, universal knowledge. However, he wrote, "Europe did not invent knowledge, but only accrued the power that knowledge confers. The other peoples of the world only ask to collaborate in the scientific project of humanity. Only colonialism is preventing them at the moment. Not a congenital inaptitude."[21] To his mind, "the fraternal cooperation of the West" in the political liberation of colonized peoples was actually the only "authentically Christian" choice. The church hierarchy and its legions of believers should therefore throw their weight behind political decolonization, and at the same time recognize that the church itself needed to reorient itself to be more hospitable to non-European peoples.

In 1958, major shifts in the francophone African world and in the Vatican gave Diop's arguments more urgency, as well as better opportunities to be heard. With the return of Charles de Gaulle to political power that year, after the French Fourth Republic proved unable to govern amid the rising tensions of the Algerian War, France's remaining Overseas Territories participated in a referendum on whether they would remain part of a "French Community" or accede to immediate independence. All of the sub-Saharan African territories voted to remain in the community except for Guinea, which, under the guidance of its charismatic and violent leader Sékou Touré, thumbed its nose at France and de Gaulle. Guinea paid a steep price for this defiance: the French withdrew all aid immediately, going so far as to cancel existing development projects, take medicines off hospital shelves, and break state dishes.[22] Yet Guinea's independence set a powerful precedent: by 1960 all of the fourteen territories of French sub-Saharan Africa, including Madagascar and the UN mandates of Cameroon and Togo, were self-governing.

The other key shift in 1958 was the election of a new pope: Angelo Cardinal Roncalli, who took the name John XXIII. Roncalli's predecessor Pius XII, who reigned from 1939 until 1958, had begun insisting that European missionaries train increasing numbers of African clergy in the wake of the Second World War, but he kept his distance from African Catholic intellectuals and tried to steer an awkward middle course between their anticolonial stance and European missionaries who saw themselves as implementing a "civilizing mission" in Africa. Roncalli, who had been nuncio to France and the Vatican's representative to UNESCO, understood the intellectual milieu that Diop and his colleagues inhabited and revealed himself to be sympathetic to their aims. On the occasion of the Second Congress of Black Artists and Writers, which took place on Easter weekend in Rome in 1959, John personally received a delegation of the Society of African Culture and affirmed his support for their work. He also insisted on the universality of the church, noting that it was willing to "recognize, to welcome, and even to nourish everything that honors human intelligence and the human heart on beaches of the world other than this Mediterranean basin which was the providential cradle of Christianity."[23] The following year, he welcomed Diop and nine other Black intellectuals, only three of whom were Catholic, to a private audience in which they discussed the Koran, history, travel, and art.[24] John's tenure also coincided with the political independence of all of the French African territories, and he issued words of congratulation and hope on each occasion. Moreover, he elevated many of the first Africans who were promoted

---

20. Diop, "L'Occident chrétien et nous," 143.
21. Diop, "L'Occident chrétien et nous," 147.
22. For details, see Schmidt, *Cold War and Decolonization in Guinea*, 171–72, 178, 182.
23. "S. S. Jean XXIII reçoit les écrivains et artistes noirs," *Présence africaine* N.S. 24/25 (February–May 1959): 427.
24. Diop, "Postface," 114.

to senior posts in the church, including Laurean Rugambwa of Tanzania, the first Black cardinal.[25]

Of course, John's most well-known initiative was his calling of the Second Vatican Council, which surprised many observers who had not expected him, as an older pontiff, to launch into anything overly ambitious. When John announced the council, Alioune Diop discerned immediately that it was an unprecedented chance to advocate for true universalism in the church. Diop devoted a great deal of energy to organizing a coordinated, sustained African response to the council, made up of both lay and clerical voices. In late May of 1962, about six months before the council opened, Diop and the Society of African Culture hosted a two-day symposium of African clergy and laity in Rome to discuss "what Africa could expect from the Council and what it could bring to the Church in spiritual, theological, liturgical, ecumenical, and social matters."[26] In a follow-up interview on Vatican radio, Diop insisted on themes he had developed in the context of war and decolonization in the 1940s and 1950s. On the subject of what Africa expected of the church, he observed that "what people of color, and of Black Africa in particular, complain of, is that their human dignity has never been recognized." In Diop's view, people across the Third World, even those who were not Catholic, expected the church to lead the way in recognizing, celebrating, and protecting that dignity. As for what Africans could bring to the church, he cited, "a certain sense of community life, a spirit of tolerance vis-à-vis all human groups, a profound intuition, poorly expressed but deeply felt, of the spiritual unity of the world." Moreover, he reiterated the idea that exchange between Europe and Africa would benefit the former:

[through exchanges] people will see that some of the virtues that Europe has turned away from can still be found in Africa, and that in the domains of thought, of morality, as well as in the domain of artistic life, in relations between differing communities, Africa will send messages that will be contributions to the creation of a world of peace in which every individual will be respected, recognized, and loved.[27]

John XXIII would reiterate many of these ideas in his own speeches about Africa, including his remarks on the occasion of his reception of Senegal's president Léopold Senghor, just a week before the council opened.[28]

Diop went even further, however, to ensure that Africa was heard at Vatican II. After the preparatory symposium, he launched an epistolary effort to contact hundreds of African clergy and laity, as well as prominent non-Catholic African thinkers, to get their thoughts on Africa's relationship with the church. He did not get as many responses as he may have liked, but he did get enough for *Présence africaine* to put out a 1963 volume entitled *Personnalité africaine et catholicisme* [African personhood and Catholicism], which Diop sent to every African bishop attending the council.[29] In addition, he put in place a permanent committee called the "Catholic Group" of the SAC, which remained in Rome to lobby the council, issuing a bulletin called "Africa at the Council."[30] He therefore made sure that African lay intellectuals, not just the newly promoted ranks of African prelates, would influence the proceedings.

When Pope John XXIII died in the midst of the council in 1963, Diop acted quickly to make sure his successor, Paul VI, would be favorable to African contributions to dialogue within the church. Shortly after Paul's election, Diop traveled to Rome on behalf of the SAC with Georges Ngango and met with the new pope, delivering a

---

25. The Society of African Culture collated all of John XXIII's statements and letters about African independence in *Un hommage africain à Jean XXIII* (Paris: Présence africaine, 1965).
26. See "Résumé des questions discutées au course des deux journées d'études à Rome," 249–54.
27. "A l'occasion du colloque réuni à Rome," 4–5.
28. John XXIII, "Discours du Pape Jean XXIII au Président de la République du Sénégal, Léopold Sédar Senghor, 5 Oct. 1962."
29. Hebga et al., *Personnalité africaine et catholicisme*.
30. Verdin, *Alioune Diop*, 222–23.

summation of African hopes for the council.[31] In Paul VI, Diop found a willing listener who was willing to prioritize and celebrate the African presence in the church. Even well before his elevation to the throne of Saint Peter, Paul, the former archbishop of Milan Giovanni Cardinal Montini, had taken an interest in Africa. In the summer of 1962, he took a month-long trip across francophone and anglophone Africa, becoming the first future pope to meet Africans on their own soil.[32] He then became the first sitting pontiff to visit Africa when he made a personal pilgrimage to Namugongo in 1969. Namugongo was the site of execution of the "Ugandan Martyrs," a group of Catholic and Protestant converts who had been burned alive by Mwanga II of Buganda for their refusal to renounce their faith. Beatified by Benedict XV in 1920, they had not advanced on the path to canonization by the start of the council in the early 1960s. In the 1950s, Diop had taken up their cause, denouncing the lack of Black saints in the church as evidence of its Eurocentric bias: "the Ugandan martyrs are not saints. . . . Even God, a prisoner of European civilization, seems not to know of us."[33] Paul addressed the situation in 1964, canonizing them during the council in a highly symbolic gesture that indicated the church was opening its doors to the world, and to Africans in particular.

Well after Vatican II, Alioune Diop continued to push for his vision of an inclusive church that would not only embrace believers outside Europe but would advocate for all people in Africa and the "Third World" more generally, regardless of their faiths. Over time, he developed the argument that the church was the most natural protector of African cultures and peoples, and the best hope for a path to economic development that would not crush the unique "personalities" of the world's peoples. Though it had been coopted by Europeans for centuries, he felt the church's universal vocation meant it could see and help to safeguard the human wisdom in all cultures and could therefore assume a role of moral leadership that no other international organization could aspire to fill. While he felt that the United Nations undertook some worthy initiatives, he felt it was too often ignored by the great powers, including those that had founded it. Alternatively, he felt that Western communism was limited by its ongoing Eurocentrism, which only contemplated the redistribution of resources within the boundaries of the Occident and not between the Occident and the rest of the world.

Indeed, Diop believed that development in the Third World "was linked to the changing of economic structures in the Western World," and in his mind, the only institution with a broad enough vision to grasp this reality was the Catholic Church.[34] As he put it in a 1965 article in *Le Monde*, "In this explosive century, where man cannot find a guarantor of justice anywhere, the church, more than any other institution, has a powerful capital of moral discipline, acquired through trials and often unknown sacrifices."[35] Diop's interest in simultaneous cultural preservation and economic development became part of his ongoing dialogue with Pope Paul VI, who issued his landmark encyclical on development, *Populorum Progressio*, in March 1967. Diop's reaction to the encyclical was typical: he felt that the church could have gone even further to embody its universal vocation, but he nonetheless saw it as an important step toward his vision of a Catholicism that was true to itself.[36]

Diop held fast to that vision for the rest of his life. Amid his myriad other projects, he carried forward the work of trying to make the Catholic Church more welcoming to Africans. For example, in Abidjan in 1977, he presided over a colloquium hosted by the African Society of Culture on "Black Civilization and the Catholic Church," whose stated goal was "to define the conditions in which African identity could flourish at the heart of the Catholic Church."[37] By then, though nearly

---

31. Messina, *Evêques africains au concile Vatican II*, 43.
32. Hebblethwaite, *Paul VI*, 301–2.
33. Diop, "On ne fabrique pas un people," 13 n. 5.
34. Diop, "Note sur le poids de l'occidentalité dans l'expérience chrétienne," 577.
35. Diop, "'Tiers-monde' et Eglise," 13.
36. Diop, "Note sur le poids de l'occidentalité dans l'expérience chrétienne," 577.
37. Lock, *Alioune Diop et le dépassement du conflit identité africaine-catholicisme*, 234–35.

all of Africa had shed its colonial bonds and numbers of African clergy had increased, Diop felt that many African Catholics still wrestled with a disconcerting tension between their African and Catholic selves, because the church as a whole did not yet fully embrace them and their cultures.[38] At the Abidjan conference, the Cameroonian Jesuit Fabien Eboussi Boulaga called for the convocation of a church "Council of Africa" which would have "no model or precedent." Eboussi Boulaga did not picture a mere gathering of bishops, but rather a much broader group of participants.[39] Diop embraced this idea enthusiastically and directed his organizational talents toward promoting it. He founded a new magazine under Eboussi Boulaga's direction entitled "For an African Council" and announced that "clerics and laity, indeed all those who have ideas on the conduct of an African Council in Africa, are freely invited to collaborate."[40] This initiative would not come to fruition—Eboussi Boulaga would leave the clergy and the publication fizzled almost immediately.[41] Diop himself would die in 1980 and not live to see the African Synod of 1994. Nonetheless, his activism continued to inspire both African clergy and laity who imagined and worked toward a Catholic Church that was truly African in Africa.[42]

Legacy

Alioune Diop and his allies embodied an elite strand of African Catholic lay activism that was able to convince Europeans, including Popes John XXIII and Paul VI, of the importance of an African Catholicism for Africa, and of the wisdom and experience Africans could bring to the church. Diop circulated easily among the European intellectual elite, whose leading lights he both befriended and critiqued. Yet he simultaneously nurtured his project to bring African culture, knowledge, and wisdom to the world's attention, creating the vehicles to publish and showcase African writing and art. He facilitated exchange and collaboration among Black artists and writers, as well as between them and their European counterparts. As he did so, Diop explored Africa's troubled relationship with Christianity, and Catholicism in particular, in his own writing and in that of the African Catholic clergymen, students, and intellectuals he published, encouraged, and mobilized.

In the late 1940s, when Diop was founding his journal, publishing house, and bookstore, Catholicism in Africa was still a missionary faith, carried by European clergy into colonized territories. Europeans justified their rule in Africa through their belief in their own racial superiority, coupled with a civilizing mission to bring their wisdom and expertise to the continent's "benighted" peoples. These impulses were not absent from the missionary church—many European missionaries condescended to their African converts and saw little of value in African cultures. The Vatican, wary of the possibility that political decolonization would result in the expulsion of European missionaries, pushed against missionary reluctance for the Africanization of the clergy after the Second World War. Yet, even by 1955, when Rome erected the church hierarchy across the vast territories of French Africa, the overwhelming majority of prelates and clergy in them were Europeans, and European viewpoints continued to hold sway in the church in Africa.[43]

A mere two generations later the picture looked strikingly different, however. By the early twenty-first century, the flow of Catholic movement from Europe to Africa had completely reversed. By then, African clergymen traveled to Europe in droves to fill empty pulpits and reinvigorate missionary societies that were withering from a lack of local vocations. The explanation of this sea change is multivalent, but there is little doubt that the era of

---

38. Lock, *Alioune Diop et le dépassement du conflit identité africaine-catholicisme*, 235.
39. Eboussi Boulaga quoted in Lock, *Alioune Diop et le dépassement du conflit identité africaine-catholicisme*, 237.
40. Lock, *Alioune Diop et le dépassement du conflit identité africaine-catholicisme*, 239.
41. Lock, *Alioune Diop et le dépassement du conflit identité africaine-catholicisme*, 239 n. 368.
42. For evidence of this ongoing influence, see many of the contributions in Becker, Lopis-Sylla, and Ndiaye, *Actes du Colloque international 50 ans après Vatican II*.
43. See Foster, *African Catholic*, 28–34, 155–71.

"decolonization" between the end of World War II and the end of Vatican II was a crucial period of reorientation from a Eurocentric colonial church to one that could be African in Africa. This realignment came about because African Catholics demanded it and successfully made their case at the highest levels of the church.

As the leader and publisher of militant African Catholic lay activists who called upon the church to disentangle itself from European colonialism and European culture at mid-century, Alioune Diop played a starring role in this lobbying and the transformations it wrought. He challenged the church and its leaders to decolonize Catholicism itself by living up to its universal premise to embrace all peoples and cultures of the world, and not just the "West." He demanded African clergy, African prelates, and African saints in the church, and asked the church to support the self-determination of African peoples. Even after French and British territories in Africa became independent, he continued to argue that the church had a particular moral responsibility to protect the vulnerable peoples of the Third World, regardless of whether they were Catholic. He continually denounced the ongoing Eurocentrism of the church, yet nonetheless felt that the church was capable of realizing its true universality and of playing a moral role that no other international body could. Looking backwards from the twenty-first century, one can see how important Diop's voice was at a moment that proved to be the beginning of the great shift in Catholicism from Europe to Africa.

Bibliography

"A l'occasion du colloque réuni à Rome, M. Alioune Diop précise ce que l'Afrique attend de l'Eglise," *Informations catholiques internationales* 171 (July 1, 1962): 4–5.

Balandier, Georges. *Conjugaisons*. Paris: Fayard, 1997.

Becker, Charles, Jeanne Lopis-Sylla, and Aloyse-Raymond Ndiaye, eds. *Actes du Colloque international 50 ans après Vatican II, l'Afrique et l'héritage d'Alioune Diop: Le dialogue des religions et les défis du temps present, Dakar, 26–29 janvier 2016*. Numéro doublé de la Revue *Présence africaine*, 195–96. Paris: Présence africaine, 2019.

Coats, Geoffrey. "From Whence We Come: Alioune Diop and Saint-Louis, Senegal." *Research in African Literatures* 28.4 (1997): 206–19.

Diop, Alioune. "Colonialisme et nationalisme culturels." *Présence africaine* N.S. 4 (Oct.–Nov. 1955): 5–15.

———. "Note sur le poids de l'occidentalité dans l'expérience chrétienne." *Parole et Mission* no. 39 (1967): 569–78.

———. "L'Occident chrétien et nous." *Présence africaine* N.S. 6 (Feb.–Mar. 1956): 143–47.

———. "On ne fabrique pas un people" *Présence africaine* 14 (1953): 7–14.

———. "Peut-on dresser le Vatican contre les peuples de couleur?," *Témoignage chrétien* (December 20, 1957): 13.

———. "Postface." In Société africaine de culture, *Un hommage africain à Jean XXIII*. Paris: Présence africaine, 1965.

———. "'Tiers-monde' et Eglise." *Le Monde,* October 3–4, 1965, 13.

Foster, Elizabeth A. *African Catholic: Decolonization and the Transformation of the Church*. Cambridge, MA: Harvard University Press, 2019.

Frioux-Salgas, Sarah. "Entretien avec le poète, romancier et essayiste Daniel Maximin." *Gradhiva* 10.2 (2009): 156–63.

Grah Mel, Frédéric. *Alioune Diop: Le bâtisseur inconnu du monde noir*. Abidjan: Presses Universitaires de Côte d'Ivoire, 1995.

Hebblethwaite, Peter. *Paul VI: The First Modern Pope*. New York: Paulist Press, 1993.

Hebga, Meinrad P., et al. *Personnalité africaine et catholicisme*. Paris: Présence africaine, 1963.

John XXIII, Pope. "Discours du Pape Jean XXIII au Président de la République du Sénégal, Léopold Sédar Senghor, 5 Oct. 1962." www.vatican.va.

Johnson, G. Wesley. *The Emergence of Black Politics in Senegal: The Struggle for Power in the Four Communes, 1900–1920*. Stanford, CA: Stanford University Press, 1971.

Lock, Etienne. *Alioune Diop et le dépassement du conflit identité africaine-Catholicisme*. Paris: L'Harmattan, 2018.

Méjan, François. *Le Vatican contre la France d'outre-mer*. Paris: Librairie Fischbacher, 1957.

Messina, Jean-Paul. *Evêques africains au concile Vatican II, 1959–1965: Le cas du Cameroun*. Paris: Karthala, 2000.

Mounier, Emmanuel. *L'éveil de l'Afrique noire*. Paris: Éditions du Seuil, 1948.

Nénékhaly-Camara, Condotto. "Conscience nationale et poésie négro-africaine d'expression française." In *Les étudiants africains et la littérature négro-africaine d'expression française*, ed. Amady Aly Dieng, 8–17. Oxford: African Books Collective, 2009.

Paul VI, Pope. *Populorum Progressio* [Encyclical on the Development of Peoples; March 26, 1967]. Vatican City: Libreria Editrice Vaticana, 1967. www.vatican.va.

Présence africaine. "Peut-on dresser le Vatican contre les peuples de couleur?," *Présence africaine* N.S. 16 (Oct.–Nov. 1957): 3–8.

"Résumé des questions discutées au course des deux journées d'études à Rome (26 et 27 mai 1962) sur la présence et l'expression de la personnalité africaine dans la vie catholique." *Présence africaine* N.S. 44 (4th trimester 1962): 249–54.

Schmidt, Elizabeth. *Cold War and Decolonization in Guinea, 1946–1958*. Athens, OH: Ohio University Press, 2007.

Société africaine de culture. *Un hommage africain à Jean XXIII*. Paris: Présence africaine, 1965.

Tévoédjrè, Albert. *L'Afrique révoltée*. Paris: Présence africaine, 1958.

Vaillant, Janet G. *Black, French, and African: A Life of Léopold Sédar Senghor*. Cambridge, MA: Harvard University Press, 1990.

Verdin, Philippe. *Alioune Diop: Le socrate noir*. Paris: Lethielleux, 2010.

Suggested Reading

Becker, Charles, Jeanne Lopis-Sylla, and Aloyse-Raymond Ndiaye, eds. *Actes du Colloque international 50 ans après Vatican II, l'Afrique et l'héritage d'Alioune Diop: Le dialogue des religions et les défis du temps present, Dakar, 26–29 janvier 2016*. Numéro doublé de la Revue *Présence africaine*, 195–96. Paris: Présence africaine, 2019.

Foster, Elizabeth. *African Catholic: Decolonization and the Transformation of the Church*. Cambridge, MA: Harvard University Press, 2019.

Grah Mel, Frédéric. *Alioune Diop, le bâtisseur inconnu du monde noir*. Abidjan: Presses Universitaires de Côte d'Ivoire, 1995.

Lock, Etienne. *Alioune Diop et le dépassement du conflit identité africaine-Catholicisme*. Paris: L'Harmattan, 2018.

Verdin, Philippe. *Alioune Diop, le socrate noir*. Paris: Lethielleux, 2010.

Key Words
Alioune Diop
Catholic intellectuals
decolonization
laity
Présence africaine/Presence africaine
Vatican II

Religious Life in African Catholicism

✠ George Desmond Tambala, OCD

Saint Anthony of Egypt is considered by some to be the founder of religious life in the Latin church. He was born in Cooma in Lower Egypt around 252 CE.[1] and died around 356 CE. The life of this "African man" was recounted by another African saint, Athanasius, born in Alexandria, Egypt. Unfortunately, the life of this early African Christianity has often been shrouded in mystery, because most of it was wiped away by Muslim Arabs spreading their religion through conquests of that region. There has also been a recurring theory that this church did not survive in history apart from the North African church because it was not "inculturated" enough into the life of the people. For example, the Bible was never translated into the local North African languages in which the majority of the people communicated. For the Latin church, Latin was at that time an exclusive language of the very educated people in the cities. The presence of the heresies of *monophysitism* and *donatism* and the confusion and wrangling they caused among Christians, together with the Vandal persecution inflicted upon the Christian community, contributed to the fact that, when the Muslim Arabs arrived in 643, they were able to prevail over Latin Christianity by the thirteenth century.[2] What is interesting is that religious life on its own has never been examined as a life until after Vatican II. What I mean to say is that from the reintroduction of the church's missionary expansion in the sixteenth century, religious life was mostly surpassed and engulfed by the missionary task of converting more people and bringing them into the church. During this age of missionary expansion, many religious congregations were founded beginning in the sixteenth century purely for this evangelizing task, while the contemplative religious congregations remained in Europe.

Model of Religious Life as a Missionary Enterprise

Many history books dedicate numerous chapters to the "missionary enterprise of the Catholic Church" and to the "growth of Catholicism in Africa." They are historically correct, although these men and women missionaries were primarily religious who offered themselves, feeling compelled by God to embark on the mission of baptizing and expanding the Catholic Church. The initial motivation was not to spread their charisms. Recruitment of vocations came later on during the twentieth century. For almost four hundred years, the missionary call and work were the most important issues at hand. These religious were motivated by a very deep Christian experience and understanding of universal salvation offered by the Father to all in the incarnated Son; therefore, the obligation to proclaim salvation in Jesus Christ offered to all was paramount in the church.[3]

A reformer of the Carmelite order and founder of the Order of the Discalced Carmelites, St. Teresa of Ávila was to lament her incapacity to participate in the great mission to the Americas that was ongoing during her time. Many Spanish religious priests joined the colonialists from Spain and engaged in the expansion of the church in South America,

---

1. De Lignerolles and Meynard, *Historia de la Espiritualidad Cristiana*, 43.
2. *Lineamenta* for the preparation of the African Synod, no. 4.
3. Karoptemprel, *Following Christ in Mission*, 204.

which today is one of the strongest churches within Catholicism. She could not join in this enterprise because, at that time, there were no active-life women religious; all women who wanted to be religious had to be cloistered. About this missionary work, St. Teresa says:

> Four years later, or I think, a little more than that, a Franciscan friar happened to come to see me, whose name was Fray Alonso Maldonado, a great servant of God, who had the same desires for the good of the souls as I, but he was able to transfer them into deeds for which I envied him greatly. He had recently come back from the Indies. He began to tell me about the many millions of souls that were being lost there for want of Christian instruction, and before leaving he gave us a sermon, or conference, encouraging us to do penance. I was so grief-stricken over the loss of so many souls that I couldn't contain myself. I went to a hermitage with many tears. I cried to the Lord, begging Him that He give me the means to be able to do something to win some souls to His service, since the devil was carrying away so many, and that my prayer would do some good since I wasn't able to do anything else. I was very envious of those who for love of our Lord were able to be engaged in winning souls, though they might suffer a thousand deaths. This is the inclination the Lord has given me, for it seems to me that He prizes a soul that through our diligence and prayers we gain for Him, through His mercy, more than all the services we can render Him.[4]

This same passion for "saving souls" is what lies behind the great missionary expansion in Africa during the nineteenth and twentieth centuries, through the founding of special forms of consecrated missionaries such as the famous Missionaries of Africa (until recently known as White Fathers) founded by Charles Cardinal Lavigerie in 1868; Comboni Missionaries founded by St. Daniel Comboni in 1857; the Society of African Missions founded in 1856 by Blessed Melchior Marion de Bresillac (1813–1859); Missionaries of the Consolata founded by Blessed Giuseppe Alamano in 1901; and the Congregation of the Holy Spirit (Holy Ghost or Spiritan Fathers and Brothers) in 1703.[5] Another missionary society that made a huge impact on evangelization in eastern Africa is the Mill Hill Missionaries, founded by Henry Vaughan in 1866. All of these groups were founded with a specifically African mission in mind, and the African evangelization is part of their founding charism. Of course, over the years they have also taken on a global face and mission while remaining very strongly attached to and identified with Africa. The White Fathers, Comboni Missionaries, Spiritans, Consolata Missionaries, and Mill Hill Missionaries also had their female religious counterparts in the form of Missionary Sisters of Our Lady of Africa, Comboni Sisters, and Consolata Sisters, just to name a few. The nineteenth and early twentieth centuries found Africa greatly in need of primary evangelization understood as the preaching of the gospel, conversion and baptizing of people, building of new church structures, and direct involvement in the teaching, health ministries, and development of the diocesan local clergy.[6]

Querying the Mission Enterprise as a Model of Religious Life

The question that perhaps we can ask today as we focus on the elements of religious life itself, apart

---

4. St. Teresa of Ávila, *Foundations*, in Kavanaugh and Rodriguez, *Collected Works of St. Teresa of Avila*, 3:101–2.

5. The Spiritans or Holy Ghost Fathers were initially founded by a French priest by the name of Claude-François Poullart des Places in 1703, but later they were joined by Francis Libermann, a convert from Judaism who founded another society of priests for the emancipation of black slaves. This society was dedicated to the Virgin Mary. After some time, there was a fusion of Libermann's society with the congregation founded by Poullart des Places, giving birth to the Congregation of the Holy Ghost. The Spiritans are among pioneer missionaries to many parts of Africa.

6. Other notable religious congregations that have made a huge impact on Africa are the Jesuits, Salesians of Don Bosco, Montfort Missionaries, Medical Missionary of Mary, Medical Missionary Sisters, Marist Brothers,

from the pastoral engagement, is this: How did the continent of Africa view the elements of religious life as they emerged through the witness of the missionaries? Was it primarily a matter of seeing and appreciating just a group of pastorally engaged priests and sisters? Today, some African Catholics and non-Catholics do not see anything specifically "religious" about consecrated men and women; they see them rather as pastoral agents of the church whose reason for existence is to do work for the church. African Catholics would say that all the religious men and women are the same but simply wear different habits and have different founders. For them, vocation to religious life is about choosing one congregation among many similar ones: "They are all the same, but pick one that best suits you." This mentality stems from a certain history of religious life in Africa, whereby religious life was introduced into Africa through the faces of providers of pastoral care and social work. Today, in many parts of post-independence Africa, governments are appropriating most of the social services like education and health, and many religious are having a sort of identity crisis, examining how to refocus their charisms in the church of today. The growing indigenous diocesan church, with its own proper autonomy and authority over church structures and apostolate, is another challenge to the religious who used to run the church from the bishopric down to the village church. The diocesan church in Africa is gradually affirming its proper role by taking over most of the ministries previously run by missionary religious. The task now is for the religious to rethink their identity and role in the church of today. Is there anything specifically "religious" apart from pastoral work and the administration of institutions? If so, what is it, and how can it be lived on a daily basis in a religious community of Africans?

The "Institutionalization" Model

To understand how religious life has come to have such a huge and positive impact on ecclesiastical life in Africa, we need to see the model of missionary life that the religious missionaries of Europe became part of as they were sent to Africa. The Berlin Conference of 1884–1885 divided the African continent among European nations wishing to expand their colonizing efforts in order to gain economic and nationalistic advantage. Thus, Africa was divided up into countries that, prior to this, had never existed except as kingdoms and tribal areas. Right up to the Second World War, European activity in Africa increased or accelerated to such an extent that the face of the continent completely changed. In this surge of Europeans going to Africa, we also find many religious congregations who join in the venture as Catholic missionaries, many of them following their colonial brothers and sisters. By 1920, we find the following statistics of religious on the continent working as missionaries:[7]

- 31 religious congregations of men, among whom 14 congregations were founded just prior to that time with the express purpose of evangelizing Africa
- 24 religious congregations of women
- 9,500 African catechists.

This contingent basically dedicated itself to the following visions and plans:[8]

- Imposition of methods of evangelization that were more or less uniform, through which the preaching of the gospel went hand in hand with human promotion and development.
- Study of local languages, so that the Bible, catechism, and other liturgical books could be translated and made understandable to local people. We find that, in many countries, missionaries compiled the first local dictionaries and grammars.
- Education of the people, from basic knowledge of reading and writing to more advanced systems of education like primary, secondary, and college education.

Christian Brothers of the Schools, Benedictines, Oblates of Mary Immaculate, Society of Divine Word, Maryknoll Missionaries, Passionists, and Sisters of Mercy.
 7. *Compendio di Storia della Sacra Congregazione per l'Evangelizzazione dei Popoli*, 163.
 8. Menin, "Modelli di Presenza missionaria nella storia della Chiesa."

- Establishment and running of hospitals that eventually became very important centers of health care in Africa.
- Establishment of centers of Christian formation for catechists and seminaries for training local African priests.
- Construction of social infrastructure that included roads and bridges.

The following are statistics of the church in Africa, reflecting its development over a span of one hundred years:[9]

- 130 million Catholics in Africa (representing a 6,708 percent growth rate and 13 percent of the world's Catholic population)
- 16,178 health centers
- 1,074 hospitals
- 5,373 outpatient clinics
- 186 leper colonies
- 753 homes for the elderly and physically/mentally less able
- 979 orphanages
- 1,997 kindergartens
- 1,590 marriage counseling centers
- 2,947 social reeducation centers
- 1,279 other centers
- 12,496 nursery schools
- 1,266,444 registered children learning in nursery schools
- 33,263 primary schools with 14,061,000 students
- 9,838 high schools with 3,738,238 students
- 53 national chapters of Caritas
- 34 National Commissions of Justice and Peace.

The missionary and religious individuals who emerged from this time up to the 1990s can be described as constructors and providers of social and religious services. It is important to understand this model of religious life because, more recently for African religious, it has been a struggle to understand the vow of poverty as they have received it from their congregation's European brothers and sisters. This type of religious life accessed and administered massive funds that, in many ways, gave it the image of a rich institution. This model was important for its time because Africa had nothing in terms of social infrastructure and services, and there was no local government to take charge of these issues.

The other thing we see with this type of religious missionary enterprise is that the identity of a developing local church was often linked to the history of a particular religious congregation in such a way that the missionary congregation's spirituality and devotions also became those of the local church. This diversity of local spiritualities helped to bring about a richness in the local church of Africa, but it was also a serious limiting factor in that sometimes the Africans did not see Catholicism any more broadly than as the spirituality of the religious congregation in that area. This was due to the *ius commissionis* right given to some congregations over a particular area, whereby the Congregation for the Propagation of Faith in Rome would give a particular religious congregation of men jurisdiction over a particular mission territory.

Religious Life as a "European Spiritual Enterprise"

The other factor is the interplay and strong connection between European nationalism and the presence of missionaries in a particular area. As stated earlier, many colonists took with them their own missionaries. This made it almost automatic that the missionary in a particular location would be of the same nationality as the colonist. This friendship and collaboration had both positive and negative effects. In places where the colonists were Protestants, Catholicism never prospered, because Catholic missionaries were never given much freedom to operate. The opposite happened also in countries with Catholic colonial masters. In some cases, even though the colonists would be of the same religion as their missionaries, they would not allow missionaries of their church from countries considered to be "enemy" countries. In this context, it is difficult to find a process of understanding religious life in and of itself, without colonial national biases.

The result of this immense missionary enterprise is that, as of 2010, the Catholic Church in

---

9. *Compendio di Storia della Sacra Congregazione per l'Evangelizzazione dei Popoli*, 6.

Africa "represents a major moral, spiritual, economic and political force in today's Africa. It also has a potential to profoundly impact the lives of Africans in many ways."[10]

Understanding the Radicalism of Religious Life in Africa

The Unexamined Concept of "Radicalism"
One day during a seminar on religious life, we were reflecting on the expression "radical following of Christ," and during discussion time we were asked to give our own views on how this can be lived today in the twenty-first century. I remember several reactions and positions that came out of this discussion. A good number of us repeated what we had learned from the novitiate, and we were really impressed at seeing how well we knew the "theory" of following Christ by "selling everything, giving the money to the poor, and going to follow him." After reminding each other of these principles, one of the participants posed a very tough and honest question: "Yes, we all know that, but have we at any time believed in all this stuff? Is this something we can die for?" A silence followed, and someone in a weak voice said, "Of course, we do, but we are also human and we realize our own limitations in front of this ideal."

I still remember this question, and whenever we find African religious discussing religious life or presenting it to people who do not understand, what comes across, in my view, is that I am hearing a well-rehearsed formula that is not reflected in the face of the person. It does not seem to be a deeply held conviction. All the classes of formation, from novitiate to final profession, seem to be geared toward inculcating theories of the radicalism of religious life but do not provoke any spark in the one learning them. In the face of the scandals today that involve religious, the picture is even more discouraging. Coupled with this mechanical understanding of religious life, we now find religious with a considerable amount to apologize for whenever they have to present religious life to others, whether it be youth or laypeople. In other contexts, there is even a perceived collective guilt that appears to say to people, "We have failed you. We were supposed to be saints." This understanding is very damaging to vocations and to a credible witness in Africa. The call to go back to the radicalism of following Jesus according to the Gospels is the first step in building a new understanding of religious life in the modern world, especially in Africa.

The other phenomenon we witness regarding evangelical radicalism as lived by religious in Africa is that the heroic examples we have among us may not attract the young people of the twenty-first century because the young people do not feel that it is possible or livable. For example, when some young people in one particular place were asked about their view of religious individuals, many of them considered the religious to be self-sacrificing heroes in many areas like education, hospital work, or help offered to street children and prostitutes, but they did not feel that they themselves could make it in the religious life. They admired what we may call "pedestal heroic religious," but these were not necessarily people they could personally identify with. Was this a problem of presenting religious life as a kind of obstacle race for only the "special forces" among us? Everybody admires the Navy SEALs of the United States, the *Spetznaz* of Russia, and the Foreign Legion of France in their military exploits, but of course not everyone can be among these special forces. These individuals are special elites coming from a very small minority among us, and their human capacity for endurance is far above the rest of us. Is this the way religious life in some parts of Africa may be presenting itself? In this case then, religious life can be admired but not emulated; it is not livable.

This is a real issue that African religious life of the twenty-first century needs to address. While religious life may be viewed as a life of "hypocrites" or "failed saints" hanging their heads in shame, it may also be presented as a life lived by superhuman ascetics who are totally removed from society: a perfect life for perfect people. In the church's history, religious life has always tended to fluctuate between these two extremes. In cases where it has

---

10. See Stan Chu Ilo, "Clerical Sex Abuse and the Presumed Innocence of African Catholicism," https://pan-africantheologyandpastoralnetwork.org/essays/Clerical%20Sex%20Abuse.pdf.

become lukewarm and compromised, saints have always appeared on the scene to recall religious life to its radicalism. We have many of examples of this: St. Benedict, St. Francis, St. Catherine of Siena, St. Dominic, St. Teresa of Ávila, St. John of the Cross, the Cistercian monastic reformers, and St. Ignatius of Loyola. The church has also known extreme figures like Simeon the Stylite, who is said to have lived on top of a narrow pillar for thirty-six years.[11] Whether such stories are really true is beside the point, but surely this type of radicalism is not representative of what we want to see evolve among men and women religious in Africa.

What Is Evangelical Radicalism?

The word "radical" comes from the Latin term *radix*, which means "root." In the Gospels, Jesus invites his disciples to a life of radicalism. He is asking them to go all the way to the root in following him, by which he means going the whole way without any compromise or cutting corners.[12] In fact, cutting corners is condemned by the Lord in the book of Revelation: "I know your works; you are neither cold nor hot. I wish that you were either cold or hot. So, because you are lukewarm, and neither cold nor hot, I am about to spit you out of my mouth" (Rev 3:15–16 NRSV). In the study of the Gospels, we find that, at the beginning of everything, there is the call of Jesus, often uncompromising, for the disciples to "leave everything" and follow him:

- "If anyone would come after me, let him deny himself and take up his cross daily and follow me" (Luke 9:23).
- "It will not be so among you; but whoever wishes to be great among you must be your servant, and whoever wishes to be first among you must be your slave; just as the Son of Man came not to be served but to serve, and to give his life a ransom for many" (Matt 20:26–28 NRSV).
- "For those who want to save their life will lose it, and those who lose their life for my sake . . . will save it" (Mark 8:35 NRSV).

- "'Teacher, I will follow you wherever you go.' And Jesus said to him, 'Foxes have holes, and birds of the air nests, but the Son of Man has nowhere to lay his head.' Another of his disciples said to him 'Lord, first let me go and bury my father.' But Jesus said to him, 'Follow me, and let the dead bury their own dead'" (Matt 8:19–22).
- "Jesus, looking at him, loved him and said, 'You lack one thing; go, sell what you own, and give the money to the poor, and you will have treasure in heaven; then come, follow me.' When [the man] heard this, he was shocked and went away grieving, for he had many possessions" (Mark 10:21–22).

This radicalism centered on "leaving behind" and "selling" attachments to *one's blood family, money, wealth,* and *possessions* and finally the attachment to *one's own ego, pride,* and *self-direction.* Some people have paraphrased these to mean centers of human happiness and attachment, sources from which we draw our existential meaning—for example, money, power, and sex—but I feel that the best paraphrasing should be blood family, wealth/possessions, and oneself. According to Donna Orsuto, such radical following of Christ does not mean putting into effect some type of reform program, strategic plan, or system of doctrinal and ethical control.[13] The call to follow Jesus in this form of radicalism was originally addressed not to consecrated religious but to ordinary men and women who were listening to him. They were meant to live this radicalism in their own world, environment, and work conditions. These radical maxims are for all Christians and not specifically for the religious.

The specific nature of religious consecration consists in living these maxims in the context of vows, community, and an apostolate lived in the church. For religious, their radicality means that they live it by leaving their blood families and joining the community of like-minded followers of Jesus, with the understanding that, by joining this community, they are actually living the call of Jesus in John: "'Rabbi . . . where are you staying?' He said

---

11. See "St. Simeon Stylites the Elder," *Catholic Encyclopedia,* www.newadvent.org.
12. See, e.g., Matt 13:3–8.
13. Orsuto, *In obsequio Jesu Christi,* 73.

to them, 'Come and see'" (John 1:38–39 NRSV). "Come and see" is interpreted as "come and live with me where I stay." This community of followers of Jesus is then modeled after the twelve apostles that he called to himself.

The church has always recognized that there are different vocations to follow Jesus. Each vocation is grounded in the radical sayings of Jesus but lived within a unique context. This is what we term the "call to holiness," and, in front of God, all vocations then are equal in dignity. Prior to Vatican II, religious life was explained in terms of the "state of perfection," and there was a much-diffused belief that virginity or chastity was superior to marriage. Today, we have moved beyond this and accorded all vocations equal dignity. The vocations are diverse and unique, and through them one realizes one's following of Christ. Nevertheless, a religious especially in Africa now needs to feel her vocation as the best for her, without looking down on the vocations of others who are not religious.

The Concept of Religious Life as "My Radical Response" and the "Best for Me"

The old concept of looking at religious life as a "state of perfection" has deep roots in Africa, and perhaps we might rightly say that it still pervades many Catholic minds in Africa today. Gradually, however, the mentality is changing, perhaps because the so-called state of perfection has suffered greatly from scandals of all types, and the religious of today no longer enjoy such an image of perfection.[14]

Over the past one hundred years, ever since Christianity was introduced to the African continent in a massive way, the radicalism of the gospel has been evident in many saintly laypeople, mostly catechists who bore the brunt of living and witnessing to the radicalism of the gospel through a very concrete way of preaching it. As a result, the religious life now in Africa cannot claim a history of the "perfect way" or the "superior and more perfect way." Over the years, some African religious have attempted to explain the concept of consecration and vows in order to explain as well the radicality behind the consecration experienced by Africans. These writers include Matungulu Otene, a Jesuit from the Democratic Republic of the Congo, and F. Kabasele Lumbala.

The African Concept of Consecration

From the very early days of the insertion of consecrated life into the cultures of Africa, it has been lived with much richness and taken many forms that were not foreseen by those who brought it to the continent from Europe. Africans have always understood the concept of radicality in the same way the Europeans have; the only difference is that, in the African context, the concept of consecration explains better the religious concept of radicalism. African culture has always had consecrated persons who were "set apart" to be at the service of the community in a mediation role with God. But they were not set apart in the eremitical sense of St. Anthony, who permanently withdrew into the desert. The consecrated persons of African traditional culture were asked to be set apart so that they could go back into community in a mediatory role with God. All the rites of initiation are also rites of consecration and transition back into community, fully integrating the person back into the community.

If we are to understand the concept of "leaving everything and following Jesus," we need to ask an honest question as to whether our African family members truly understand the concept we present to them, that we are consecrated. Being set apart for God does not present a problem for them, but perhaps, instead, they may have questions like "Consecrated for what? For whom? What social value and benefit is one's consecration?" We live now in a utilitarian, postmodern world where the value of a career is assessed in terms of how much it contributes to social and personal development. In my

---

14. The "State of Perfection" argument is extensively treated by St. Thomas of Aquinas in his *Summa Theologica*, question 184, where he addresses questions including "Whether the perfection of Christian charity life consists mainly in charity"; "Can one be perfect in this life?"; "Does the perfection of this life consist chiefly in observing the counsels and commandments?"; "Is whoever is perfect in the state of perfection?"; "Are prelates and religious especially in the state of perfection?"; "Are all prelates in the state of perfection?"; "Which is the more perfect, the Episcopal or the religious state?"; and "the comparison between religious and parish priests and deacons."

view, the only way religious life can be understood in Africa is through the concept of consecration understood as being called, set apart, and brought back into the community with a mission that benefits the community, especially the poor and broken. All unnecessary misunderstandings of the vows stem from this view, which is neither good nor bad in itself; it is the reality, and if we want religious life to make sense, we need to listen to it seriously. We may refuse and wish to continue our antisocial radicalism, but sooner or later we will face the same reality as in Europe: society will reject us. It might be nice to talk about consecration as being set apart and forsaking the world, but when people know us only for having a good life, protected behind fences with little hard work and nothing for the people, then we are surely preaching a concept of formation that might be good in novitiate manuals but would not be understood by the people. It is one thing to be prophetic against our own cultures and another thing entirely not to try to make ourselves understood.

The African context is holy and must be taken seriously by taking off our shoes before we talk of the vows. We remember Moses when he was told to remove his shoes, because the ground on which he stood was holy ground. Consecrated life in Africa from the twentieth century onward is both complex and "sacred ground," and therefore we need to treat its history with respect.

This, however, does not mean that we naïvely overlook the many limitations that have come about in the course of its introduction. We need to be very critical, then, as we face our history. When we talk about the introduction of consecrated life in Africa, we are considering two very big camps: on the one hand, we have the *consecrated life with its long history, experiences, and traditions,* and, on the other, we have the camp of *African cultures with their long history* (customs, rites, religion, etc.). It is not easy to do a study comparing these two realities without losing ourselves in the "branches," that is, in examples and other particular experiences. The history has been very rich and diverse, taking different forms. We are trying to do something that can be talked about only by those who have experienced this history themselves. To explain what it has meant to be an African consecrated person is something that only Africans can do.

Throughout the course of European history, consecrated life has had to explain to the European cultures what it means to be "consecrated." Among some of the biblical and ecclesial models it has used are the following:

- Mary, who said "Yes" to the message of the angel: the Annunciation;
- John the Baptist and his retreat into the desert: the contemplative, eremitical life;
- the rich young man of the Gospels, who was asked to sell everything, give the money to the poor, and follow Jesus; and
- the itinerant and poor life of Jesus, who had nowhere to lay his head and preached the gospel: the mendicant model of the Franciscans.

The Prophetic Role of Religious in African Cultures

Africa is a continent full of songs and dances. In this way, the celebration marks our communities as unique among many cultures of the world. A community that celebrates is a place where life is lived in its fullness. In Psalm 137:1–4, the exiled people of God ask a question that remains to this day: "How can we sing in a foreign land?" The question asked by our people is the same one as that of the exiles in Babylon who felt it inappropriate and a mockery to sing a joyful song in the midst of deportation, exile, slavery, and oppression. Without a song to God, there is no life. A song is an expression of love, appreciation, gratitude, and prayer. In Africa, consecrated life is lived in the midst of untold misery and suffering, in the form of AIDS, poor education, and orphans. How can the evangelical counsel of poverty be understood as "kenosis" (self-emptying) and proclaim itself in such a context?

According to Fr. Engelbert Mveng, most of our people are poor. Our people can be characterized by the condition of "not knowing what will happen tomorrow, or what the future keeps in store. Everything escapes them. They are sure neither of their independence, nor of their earthly riches. Their bread for the next day is not assured. They have no control over their treasure or crops."[15] Poverty, as we know, among our people carries another meaning from the spiritual one. Material poverty in itself is a relative term. It has to be measured according to local standards and according to the local social context.[16] The truly poor person is the one who lacks the basic or minimum necessary conditions or means for a life of dignity.

We are speaking about people living "below the poverty line." These people form the highest percentage in our populations. In this, we are reminded that consecrated persons are not the only ones who follow the "poor Christ." Some live the condition of indigence by the mere fact of belonging to the bottom rung of the social ladder. Poverty in this sense is something degrading, a thing to be fought against and discarded at any cost; it is an evil.[17] Our people in Africa have not chosen to live this kind of indigence. In the scriptures, material poverty is a scandalous situation and condition that runs contrary to human nature, and, as a fruit of injustice, it cries to God for justice. Here we have the known groups of the widow, the orphan, and the foreigner among the protected ones of God.

Rediscovering the Biblical Roots of Prophetic Consecrated Vowed Poverty in Africa

In the Old Testament, the term used for the poor person is *'ebyon,* which means the "one who desires," "the one who begs, and the one who lacks something and expects of it from another."[18] The term "poverty" is also represented by the word *dal,* which signifies "the weak, the thin." The poor is the person who is "bent double under weight on his/her back," following the meaning of the Hebrew word, *'ani.*[19]

Another term, *'anaw,* stands for the person "bent double" but it has also the added meaning of "humble one in front of God." In the New Testament, most of which was written in Greek, the poor person is represented by the term *ptōchos,* which means "the one who does not have the necessary things for survival, the miserable one obliged to live by begging."[20] Even today, the words "needy," "beggar," and "bent double under a weight" all reflect a person who is in a very difficult life situation.

These are terminologies that automatically evoke in us the sense of protest. Another sense of poverty is what has been traditionally called the "spiritual childhood." In the Bible, the poor is also one we can call the "client" of God. Poverty here is understood as the attitude by which the one disposes oneself, opening oneself to God in humility. Even though the same terminologies are used for material poverty, more and more the words take on a meaning that is understood now more in a spiritual sense. For instance, in some passages, the typical word *'anawim,* the plural form of *'anaw,* takes on a spiritual sense. The *'anawim* are those poor and simple-minded, humble people who are open to the salvific power of God. The ones opposed to the poor in spirit are the proud ones who are clearly identified as the enemies of Yahweh, a God in solidarity with the crippled and the lame (Ps 10:2; 18:28; 37:10; 86:14). Spiritual poverty has its highest expression in the beatitudes of the New Testament.

In the beatitudes in Matthew, the sense of poverty is that of spiritual poverty as it is understood in the book of Zephaniah: "Seek the LORD, all you humble of the earth, who have observed his law; seek justice, seek humility" (Zeph 2:3); and "But I will leave as a remnant in your midst a people humble and lowly, who shall take refuge in the name of the LORD" (Zeph 3:12). This kind of poverty is, above all, the reception with an open heart of the will of God. To receive the grace of God, our hearts are supposed to have this attitude grounded within. In the words of Aylward Shorter, consecrated poverty has come to mean different things

---

15. Mveng, *Identidad Africana y Cristianismo,* 141.
16. Shorter, *Religious Poverty in Africa,* 9.
17. Gutiérrez, *Teología de la liberación,* 323.
18. *'Ebyon* is used sixty-one times in the Old Testament, above all, in the Psalms and prophets. See Gutiérrez, *Teología de la liberación,* 326.
19. Gutiérrez, *Teología de la liberación,* 326.
20. Gutiérrez, *Teología de la liberación,* 326.

in practice. What do we mean when we say that this vow of poverty must be lived in the African culture, or, in other words, that it must be "inculturated"? In Africa, people are poor; and for him to say that African consecrated persons are born in a "culture of poverty" is to be gravely wrong.[21] Culture can be said to be an inherited system of concepts, images, and norms that orient a group of people cognitively, emotionally, and behaviorally to the world in which they live. To deprive one of one's culture is to deny one the basic right to live meaningfully in this world.[22]

Prophetic Solidarity with the Poor

People of a given culture, as are the cases with many Africans, may be factually poor, but this is incidental to their culture. It is only a material deprivation. We cannot then say that poverty is part of the culture of Africa. When we look at the gospel values connected with spiritual and material values from an African point of view, we can say that, in the middle of a new culture of grabbing and getting rich over others' misery, consecrated poverty points to a value of solidarity with those who are downtrodden by the system and riches of others. Wealth seeking can be a counter-witness, and bad news for the poor.

In the same measure that God is on the side of the downtrodden, religious poverty is built on Christ as the poor as well as on the African sense of family, solidarity, and sharing: "I am because we are, and because we are, I am." The following words said in the early 1970s are now a reality all around here in Africa:

> The traditional solidarity in which the individual says, "I am because we are, and since we are, therefore I am," is constantly being smashed, undermined and in some respects destroyed. Emphasis is shifting from the "we" of traditional religion corporate to the "I" of modern individualism. Schools, churches, economic competition and the future dimension of time with its real and imaginary promises, are the main factors which,

jointly or singly are working to produce an orientation towards individualism and away from communalism. So then, for example, amidst the many people who live in the cities, the individual discovers that he/she is alone. When he/she falls sick, perhaps only one or two other people know about it and come to see him, when he is hungry he finds that begging for food from his neighbour is either shameful or unrewarding or both; when he/she gets bad news from his relatives in the countryside, he/she cries alone even if hundreds of other people rub shoulders with him in the factory or bus. This individualism makes a person aware of him/herself, but his/her self-consciousness is not founded upon either traditional solidarity which by its nature and structure allowed little or no room for individualism, or another solidarity since nothing concrete has yet replaced what history is submerging. The individual simply discovers the existence of his individualism but does not know of what it consists. He has not language with which to perceive its nature and destiny.[23]

Religious Life in Africa and Its Prophecy in Front of Materialism

In the apostolic exhortation *Vita Consecrata*, Pope John Paul II identified materialism as the reality destroying the fabric of African community life. Materialism is a craving for possessions at any cost: "another challenge today is that of a materialism which craves possessions, heedless of the needs and sufferings of the weakest, and lacking any concern for the balance of natural resources" (§89). The values proposed by consecrated life all over the world in the face of materialism are the same as those of Africa, namely solidarity and charity (§89); solidarity is what is meant by the expression, "I am because we are, and because we are, I am." In Africa, the vow of poverty launches the consecrated person into the midst of the continent's underprivileged and downtrodden. This evangelical life is a defense of life in its fullness.

---

21. Shorter, *Religious Poverty in Africa*, 9.
22. Shorter, *Religious Poverty in Africa*, 9.
23. Mbiti, *African Religions and Philosophy*, 224–25.

Life here is a fundamental reality. It is life in its pure state and one that is found only in God, who is the author and source of this life. In the worldview of the Africans, poverty represents a diminishment of life, and there is a need for liberation from the wounds and scars that poverty leaves in our people through sickness and hunger: "Consecrated persons fight to overcome hunger and its causes; they inspire the activities of voluntary associations and humanitarian organizations; and they work with public and private bodies to promote a fair distribution of international aid" (§89).

In Africa, there is a need for what has been called the "preferential option for the poor" on the part of consecrated persons. This phrase, borrowed from South America and made popular there in the 1970s, has been well explained by Donal Dorr;[24] such an option, seen in a biblical perspective, would mean some special care or preference for people or groups who are marginalized in human society. It is quite true that there is a sense in which everybody is "poor before God." But this idea can be invoked as a way of evading the central thrust of the biblical teaching about poverty. The meaning of the word "poor" can be extended and redefined to a point where the challenge of the scriptural position gets lost.[25] Talking about evangelical poverty most of the time results in a mere accumulation of words. Analyzing what poverty is, its context, and so on, makes us lose track of the practical side of this option for the poor. The exhortation *Vita Consecrata* has indicated what this practical side can mean:

> The option for the poor is inherent in the very structure of love lived in Christ. All of Christ's disciples are therefore held to this option; but those who wish to follow the Lord more closely, imitating his attitudes, cannot but feel involved in a very special way. The sincerity of their response to Christ's love will lead them to live a life of poverty and to embrace the cause of the poor. For each institute, according to its charism, this involves adopting *a simple and austere way of life*, both as individuals and as a community. (§82; italics original)

Prophetic Common Ownership

The simple and austere way of life in Africa has been understood as part of what we call "African common ownership of goods and property." Some have called it not "common ownership" but "common non-ownership."[26] We have a history of our people, which can be called a "migratory history." Here, we are not talking about a nomadic existence. In Malawi, as in other African countries of southern Africa, strictly nomadic peoples like the Maasais of East Africa are not found. However, the history of *kusamuka* is as ancient as the peoples themselves. This is what we may call a mobile life caused by famine, nonproductive land, witchcraft fears, family disputes, and many other factors. One of the results of this kind of life among our people is that they developed a philosophy of "traveling light."

Property was seen as bondage in some ways, for it prevented people from moving on when necessary. In our consecration, we can talk of consecrated poverty from the point of view of Africa as "traveling light" on our way to the Father. The kingdom of the Father is the destination of all consecrated people, and everything in front of this goal loses its absolute value. This is our treasure to which we look forward, without losing sight of our incarnation in this world; "where your treasure is, there will your heart be also" (Matt 6:21 NRSV). The unique treasure of the kingdom gives rise to desire, anticipation, commitment, and witness (*Vita Consecrata* §26). If we are aiming at the house of our Father, consecrated poverty is a sign to the materialistic culture of today that life is not only about accumulating wealth and power—there is greater value for which we live in this world. This is a very difficult message to communicate to the modern world. In the sense of the urgency of the kingdom, everything else is relative. To travel to

---

24. Dorr, *Option for the Poor*.
25. Dorr, *Option for the Poor*, 6.
26. Shorter, *Teología de la Liberación*, 13.]

our destination, consecrated poverty reminds us that we need to "travel light and faster":[27]

- The first important thing in our option for the poor is to be aware that the poor need to have the sympathy and support of the consecrated person vowed to Christ through the evangelical counsel of poverty.
- Second, the poor need the professional expertise of consecrated persons, their spiritual and moral strength as well as their training in medicine, education, and social work to help them in their struggle for life, in their fight to come out of degrading and inhuman poverty.
- The poor need the fraternal love, understanding, and solidarity of the consecrated. This involves sharing our "precious time" with them. The selfless giving of our time is very important in Africa. That is why we say that "availability" is a sign of a genuine, consecrated, poor person.
- One of the truths about consecrated poverty involves a process of "learning from the poor." The poor evangelize us through their patient and faith-filled attitude of their own participation in Christ's passion.

Traveling light in the following of Christ through evangelical poverty involves the following fundamental presuppositions about the "excess luggage" that impedes an easy climb and walk through life toward Christ. This kind of poverty is what we can call "spiritual poverty."

Prophetic Mysticism and Religious Life in Africa

The famous theologian of the Vatican II era, Karl Rahner, made the following statement about the future Christian: "The Christian of tomorrow will be a mystic, or he will not exist at all."[28] Many people tried to interpret this statement and how it can be applied to the changing world of today, which we are experiencing even here in Africa. The word "mystic" as we know it has had a very negative connotation; it has come to mean a person who experiences extraordinary favors in prayer and life, like visions, stigmata, and so on. All these elements do not make a mystic. The consecrated person of the twenty-first century will have to be a mystic in a true sense of the word: "a person with a radical openness towards the life of Christ, Son of the Father in the Spirit."[29]

Many have associated consecrated life with habits, apostolates, and constitutions. These are good in the sense that they promote the experience of God. On this point, we can say that the consecrated person of today is caught up with an excess luggage of emphasis on external signs. Rahner was speaking to a church that was and still is in some ways caught up with emphasis on external signs. The sacraments are in many ways not presented in many circles as vehicles of God's experience. The realization that we are all mystics at heart and have to recover this idea at any cost is supported by this definition of grace. As Leonardo Boff asserted,

> The word "grace" refers to the most basic and original Christian experience. It is an experience of God, whose sympathy and love for human beings runs so deep that he has given himself. It is an experience of human beings, who are capable of letting themselves be loved by God, of opening up to love and filial dialogue. The result of this encounter is the beauty, gracefulness, and goodness that is reflected in all of creation—but especially in human beings and their history.... If grace is all that we have described above, then it is ever threatened by what we can call disgrace: i.e., lack of encounter, refusal to dialogue, and closing in upon oneself. Grace and disgrace are two possibilities of freedom. This is the mystery of creation, an absolute mystery to which reason does not have access.[30]

In Africa, God is calling on consecrated people to be first "God-filled" persons.

---

27. The following points are drawn from Aylward Shorter's book on consecrated poverty, *Religious Poverty in Africa*.
28. Karl Rahner, *Theological Investigations* (Baltimore: Helicon, 1961–), 20:149.
29. Tambala, "Will Africa Survive Secularism?," 53.
30. Boff, *Liberating Grace*, 3–4.

Luggage I: The Temptation to Avoid Sharing in the Life Situations of Our People

The exhortation *Vita Consecrata* mentions the need for what has been called "insertion" in recent years. One example of the excess luggage carried by current forms of consecrated life in Africa is the consecrated individuals' sparse participation in the life situations of the people. The accusation that they live in "ivory towers" amid misery and deprivation holds, in many ways, some truth. However, it is not all who are living like this; some have made a great effort to live with the poor themselves. "This witness will, of course, be accompanied by a preferential option for the poor and will be shown especially by sharing the conditions of life of the most neglected. There are many communities which live and work among the poor and the marginalised; they embrace their conditions of life and share in their sufferings, problems and perils" (*Vita Consecrata* §90). For the future of consecrated life in Africa to be prosperous, the ones embracing it will have to be bound and inserted in real-life situations, in which their lives will be conformed to the Gospels. This is what we call a real incarnation and reading of Christ from within the culture itself. Patrick Ryan has elaborated a few things that can be considered fundamentals of any insertion by consecrated people:[31]

1. Exposure to various pastoral-mission situations of the local church and society, and being able to interpret them in the light of our charisms and spiritualities.
2. Deepening of our sensitivity to the marginalized and dispossessed; more realistic awareness of the individuals and structures responsible for poverty and oppression.
3. Introduction of strategies of empowerment of the oppressed at the parish, school, and institutional levels.
4. Becoming a balanced and self-reflective person, content in sharing one's personal story, including one's personal history, family and cultural background, faith journey, and personal gifts in service of the building-up of the church.
5. Developing the basic values of listening, challenging, self-disclosure, confidence keeping, conflict resolution, and sensitivity and warmth toward people under stress.
6. Growth in appreciation of one's own culture and traditions, as well as a gradual opening to the riches of the different levels of society.
7. Identifying one's expectation and presuppositions toward one's congregation and charism and the way they are integrated into the mission of the founders and one's life.

Luggage II: The Temptation to Ignore Self-Knowledge of Our Human Nature as a Vehicle for Grace and Self-Transcendence

In the years after Vatican II, many people have accused religious life of creating "dehumanized" consecrated people. These are people who have been labeled as "cold," "unfeeling," and "distant." For consecrated life to be well-grounded in the vow of poverty as well as in the vows of chastity and obedience, knowledge of the human within us is extremely important, and this knowledge can help us to live poverty positively. An awareness of our nature as redeemed by Christ moves us to appreciate our nature and to strive for the conversion of its many dark sides, the parts which we have called "dis-grace." The qualities of communication and friendship will cement a genuine solidarity and commitment to the poor Christ. It is impossible to be truly poor if consecrated poverty is not lived in solidarity with members of the community who are friends. We cannot truly love the poor if we have not experienced love at home and in the community in which we live. We may be hardworking and living in the midst of the poor, but this will eventually wither if we do not have a shared experience of the same poverty with others who are friends.

Consecrated Poverty and Detachment in Africa

In our consecration, we come across the part of poverty that we can classify as "detachment" from possessiveness and materialism:

---

31. Ryan, "Pastoral Insertion as a Component of the Theological Studies Curriculum," 72–73.

Its primary meaning, in fact, is to attest that God is the true wealth of the human heart. Precisely for this reason evangelical poverty forcefully challenges the idolatry of money, making a prophetic appeal as it were to society, which in so many parts of the developed world risks losing the sense of proportion and the very meaning of things.... Consecrated persons are therefore asked to bear a renewed and vigorous evangelical witness to self-denial and restraint, in a form of fraternal life inspired by principles of simplicity and hospitality, also as an example to those who are indifferent to the needs of their neighbor. (*Vita Consecrata* §90)

The Future of Religious Life in Africa

From the reflections I have made in this essay, I feel that religious life has a future and that the church in Africa needs it. Having said so, I believe that, if religious life is to retain its relevance, it must change to align itself with its evangelical inspirations as well as its fidelity to the praxis or context in which it finds itself not only in Europe but across the globe. The following, in my opinion, are key to the meaningful survival of the religious life.

Rediscovery of the Evangelical Inspiration
While it is not historical to claim that religious life already started with Jesus in the Gospels, the Gospels contain enough inspiration for a life that was later to be called religious life. In the Gospels we not only find a "formula of life" but also a view of the human person who is driven by values that can be called "values of the kingdom of God." Conforming to these values, there is a type of man and woman who decides to live a certain unique way of life not followed by the rest of the population. In the Gospels, there is room for a personalized interpretation and for the way that many have called "the road less traveled." To deny this possibility for the people of God is a form of reductionism that cripples the fullness of gospel living. I have met many Protestant friends who lament the absence of religious life as we have it in the Catholic Church. The death of religious life will result in a church that, in my opinion, will not be Catholic as we have known it from its beginnings. The Gospels spell out some key values like servanthood, taking up the cross, community, and attention to the marginalized and poor. The ministries of Jesus as recounted by the Gospel writers all attest to the need for a specific group that takes up these ministries with a lifelong and twenty-four-hour dedication. If religious life is to continue, there is a need to root it constantly in the Gospels. The Gospels have always inspired a *sequela christi* or "following of Christ." All reforms of religious life have come about in the church because in many ways religious life has deviated from this Gospel path into various forms of enslavement. The Gospels represent a very good antidote to the negative secularization of religious life.

Rediscovery of Community Life
The death of religious life in many parts of the world is partially due to the collapse of community life. Individualism has led to many religious no longer inspired by their charism, spirituality, and community but by individual tastes and external human ideologies. Community life in Africa needs to build on healthy aspects of African community and family life without sliding into a negative uniformity. It must be a religious life that allows the individual to flourish while at the same time to be committed to the congregational spirit. There is a need for African religious to strike a balance that, in many ways, has not been achieved by Western forms of religious life. This is the balance between the individual and the community—a healthy dialogue between the interior life and the community. If African religious life can achieve this, it will become a very powerful and attractive life in the world.

Rediscovery of a Truly Christian and Truly African Spirituality and Mysticism
We can say that mysticism, understood correctly, is at the heart of the call to religious life as well as the imaging of the evangelical counsels. We just have to look at the "nuptial or spiritual marriage" symbolism that is now part of religious vows. Starting from the image of being consecrated to Christ, as symbolized by the ring, the habit, and the candles, to the whole rhythm of prayers at a personal as well as a community level, religious life is heavily mysti-

cal. As I have stated earlier on, mysticism has little to do with supernatural experiences or visions. It is the daily life lived in prayer experiences. This is where, in Africa, either religious life becomes a school of prayer or it will cease to be. African religious need to discover their proper African mysticism, which they can integrate into their formation as well as the whole of religious life. This is crucial if religious life is to have a future in Africa. The people of God will look to religious life not because of its specialized social services but because of its experience of God lived in a healthy mysticism. There is a need to image the whole trajectory or journey of prayer, devotions, spiritual direction, sacred music, and the Divine Office in a truly African way. This is not to be done in the ways we have done *inculturation* up to now, but in a new way to be discovered by the young religious of today.

Rediscovery of a New Global Solidarity
Religious life in Africa will need to avoid being a ghetto type of religious life that can be lived only on the African continent. This is extremely important if it has to be open to the global mission of the church. There is much talk of Africans becoming missionaries to the churches of the West. From my little experience, there is not much of a "missionary school" on the continent. Most of these Africans find themselves thrown into other cultures without much prior preparation. It is very hard to expect that a religious who has been formed on a purely local view will suddenly find himself/herself open to other cultures. I think that all houses of formation need to include missiology as a compulsory topic in their programs. Superiors and formators need to discourage candidates for mission outside the continent if they are driven solely by the financial benefits that can be obtained "overseas." African religious life should not allow itself to be turned into a kind of "sacred emigration bureau." We must learn to live the words of Our Lord: "freely you have received, freely give" (Matt 10:8).

Rediscovery of the Marginalized and the Poor
In religious life, there has always been a bitter tug of war in choosing between being on the side of the poor or on that of power, riches, and pleasure, and this has led to countless reforms in the history of religious life in the church. If African religious life is to survive in the future, it will need to have a clear option and solidarity with the marginalized and the poor. Otherwise, we can be very sure that religious life will become irrelevant. The African continent is home to the most extreme forms of social and economic inequalities. The gap between the poor and the rich is going to continue as various forms of exclusive forms of capitalism will drive our economies. Industrialized and "Big-Tech" Africa will have its own form of the poor.

A Truly Prophetic Religious Life
While Africa is blessed with many positive things, it is also plagued by superstition, corruption, tribalism, the oppression of women and children, and many other social ills. For religious life in Africa to survive, it must make a difference in these areas. The continent is undergoing a revolution of justice that will not forgive a form of religious life that is cowardly or part of these negative realities. If religious life does not raise a prophetic voice against these negatives, the people will not accept it as relevant. This prophetic stand must also be reflected in the interior of religious life (attitudes, structures, and decisions).

Suggestions for Scholars

For scholars of religious life in Africa as well as theologians, I think the following areas may be interesting and important to explore for a deep and serious reflection on religious life in Africa.

Research on Truly Indigenous Forms of Christian Religious Life in Africa
The last century has seen the birth of many forms of consecrated life in dioceses as well as episcopal conferences across the continent. These forms of female as well as male religious life need to be examined in a well-researched way to determine which have been successful and the reasons behind their success. The opposite also needs to be studied. The findings can greatly assist bishops, as well as religious themselves, to perform a proper self-analysis. Without this academic exercise, we will continue to see religious congregations that merely mimic their Western counterparts.

A Study of the Concept of Charism in Africa

Charism forms the heart of all pastoral motivation. There is a need for scholars to examine how this motivational motor in religious life can be grounded in a properly African terminology and worldview. If this is not done, religious life will be reduced to "social works and habits," and the very religious themselves will continue to have identity crises as to who they are.

A Proper Canonical Setting for Religious Life in Africa

Religious life has a juridical nature in the church with a proper language found in the Code of Canon Law. While this remains universal, it often lacks an African praxis. Issues like membership, vows, formation stages, rights and obligations, government, exclaustration/dismissal, and expulsion need to have a proper context in Africa where they can be applied. I feel that positive African community values need to prevail over a purely rigid and inflexible application of aspects of canon law. African scholars must research a proper praxis and language for applying canon law in religious life.

Research into Theology of Religious Life in Africa

Scholars must explore ways to develop a theology of religious life that will inspire many of our religious in Africa to live their consecration happily. Most of the language describing religious life is still couched in Western terminologies.

Bibliography

Berzosa Martínez, Raul. *Hacia el año 2000: que nos espera en el siglo XXI?* Bilbao: Desclee de Brouwer, 1998.

Boff, Leonardo. *Liberating Grace.* Maryknoll, NY: Orbis Books, 1979.

Castillo, José María. *Los pobres y la teología.* 2nd ed. Bilbao: Desclee de Brouwer, 1998.

Compendio di Storia della Sacra Congregazione per l'Evangelizzazione dei Popoli. Rome: PUU, 1974.

Dorr, Donald. *Option for the Poor: A Hundred Years of Vatican Social Teaching.* Dublin: Gill & Macmillan, 1985.

Downey, Michael, ed. *The New Dictionary of Catholic Spirituality.* Collegeville, MN: Liturgical Press, 1993.

Dupuis, Jacques, and Josef Neuner, eds. *The Christian Faith: Doctrinal Documents of the Catholic Church.* Bangalore: Theological Publications in India, 1987.

Galilea, Segundo. *Following Jesus.* Maryknoll, NY: Orbis Books, 1981.

González Faus, José Ignacio. *La humanidad nueva: Ensayo de gristología,* Vol. 2. Madrid: Sal Terrae, 1974.

Groody, Daniel G. *Globalization, Spirituality and Justice.* Maryknoll, NY: Orbis Books, 2009.

Gutiérrez, Gustavo. *Teología de la liberación.* Salamanca: Sigueme, 1994.

John of the Cross. *The Collected Works of St. John of the Cross.* Translated by Kieran Kavanaugh and Otilio Rodriguez. Washington, DC: ICS Publications, 1991.

John Paul II, Pope. *Vita Consecrata* [Post-synodal Apostolic Exhortation on the Consecrated Life and Its Mission in the Church and in the World; March 25, 1996]. Vatican City: Libreria Editrice Vaticana, 1996. www.vatican.va.

Kabasele Lumbala, François. *Celebrating Jesus Christ in Africa: Liturgy and Inculturation.* Maryknoll, NY: Orbis Books, 1998.

Karoptemprel, Sebastian, ed. *Following Christ in Mission.* Nairobi: Paulines Publications, 1995.

Lignerolles, Philippe de, and Jean Pierre Meynard. *Historia de la espiritualidad cristiana.* Burgos: Monte Carmelo, 2007.

Mbiti, John. *African Religions and Philosophy.* London: Heinemann, 1969.

Menin, Mario. "Modelli di Presenza missionaria nella storia della Chiesa." *Ad Gentes* 12.2 (2008): 209–32.

Mveng, Engelbert. *Identidad Africana y Cristianismo: Palabras de un creyente.* Estella, Spain: Verbo Divino, 1999.

Orsuto, Donna. *In obsequio Jesu Christi: Comunidad orante y profetica en un mundo que cambia.* Rome: Carmelitane, 2007.

Ryan, Patrick. "Pastoral Insertion as a Component of the Theological Studies Curriculum." In *Tangaza Occasional Papers, No. 6: Religious Formation in International Communities,* 72–73. Nairobi: Paulines Publications Africa, 1998.

Shorter, Aylward. *Religious Poverty in Africa.* Nairobi: Pauline Publications, 1999.

Tambala, George, OCD. "Will Africa Survive Secularism?," *Africa Tomorrow* 16.1 (2014): 33–64.

Teresa of Ávila. *The Collected Works of St. Teresa of Ávila.* Vol. 3. Translated by Kieran Kavanaugh and Otilio Rodriguez. Washington, DC: ICS Publications, 1985.

Suggested Reading

Burke, Joan F. *These Catholic Sisters Are All Mamas! Towards the Inculturation of Sisterhood in Africa: An Ethnographic Study.* Leiden: Brill, 2001.

Kalonga, Joachin, ed. *Inculturation de la vie consacrée en Afrique a l'aube du troisieme Millénaire: Acte du cinquième colloque international.* Kinshasa: Editions Carmel Afrique, 1998.

Kianziku, Vincente Carlos. *Consecrated Life in Bantu, Africa.* Nairobi: Paulines Publications Africa, 2007.

Otene, Matungulu. *To Be with Christ: Chaste, Poor, and Obedient; An Essay in a Bantu Spirituality of the Vows.* Nairobi: St. Paul Publications Africa, 1986.

Schneiders, Sandra M., IHM. *Buying the Field: Catholic Religious Life in Mission to the World.* Religious Life in the New Millennium 3. New York: Paulist Press, 2013.

Key Words

celibacy
charism
community life
consecrated
culture
evangelical counsels
evangelical poverty
formation
founder(s)
inculturation
indigenous
marginalized
mission
mysticism
praxis
radicalism
religious life
solidarity
tribe
Vita Consecrata

CHURCH AND SOCIETY

History and Development of Catholic Social Imagination in Africa

Godswill Agbagwa

Catholic social imagination refers to the distinctive way Catholics express the social demands of their faith. It is the Catholic way of engaging social questions and imagining social possibilities. Catholic social imagination is basic to the salvific mission of the church because it responds to the challenges of human sociality, which is a fundamental dimension of the human person. As noted in the *Compendium of Catholic Social Doctrine*, the salvation offered to humanity in Jesus Christ by God the Father's initiative and brought about and transmitted by the Holy Spirit is an integral and universal salvation—that is, salvation for all people and of the whole person. It concerns the human person in all human dimensions: personal and social, spiritual and corporeal, historical and transcendent.[1]

Indeed, nothing that concerns the human person is foreign to the salvific mission of the church. Whether it is situations and problems regarding justice, freedom, development, relations between peoples, family, politics, economics, law, or peace, the salvific mission of the church cannot be accomplished if it does not take into account the simultaneous demands of the gospel and of the concrete, personal, and social life of human beings.[2] Catholic social imagination is an ensemble of Catholic approaches to these demands that dates back to the early church. From apostolic times, the church has always imagined social possibilities; however, these may have varied in nature, scope, and effectiveness from age to age, place to place.

This chapter examines the history and development of Catholic social imagination in Africa. The aim is to understand how African Catholics have engaged with social concerns since the church's first appearance in Africa. As I will argue, although Africa is a very large and diverse continent with millions of Catholics, African Catholics have tended to share a similar social imagination in any given historical period. There are two reasons for this. First, African cultures are quite similar, and so the chances of their engendering a similar social imagination are high; and, second, the missionaries who evangelized Africa shared a similar Catholic culture and social imagination. They all came from Europe and were influenced by the existing Catholic social imagination.

For clarity, I will begin with a brief explanation of my research method. Since this is a historical study that also seeks to reconstruct history, the method of historical reconstruction seems appropriate. The idea is to look back at the history of Catholicism in Africa with an eye toward practices that fall within the categories of Catholic social imagination. Joseph Palacios has conducted systematic work on approaches to Catholic social imagination in the United States and Mexico. In this chapter, I will examine these approaches in the light of the entire history of the Catholic Church in Africa, which stretches back to the patristic period in North Africa.

---

1. Pontifical Council for Justice and Peace, *Compendium of the Social Doctrine of the Church*, no. 38.
2. Pope Paul VI, apostolic exhortation *Evangelii Nuntiandi* §29.

At the conclusion of the historical study, I will offer a brief examination of the current Catholic social imagination in Africa, focusing on Catholic political engagement in Nigeria. The goal is to identify current challenges facing Catholic social imagination in an area that is key to authentic development and Christian flourishing. The prospects and challenges facing Catholic social imagination in the area of politics in Nigeria are not too different from those of other African countries. Thus, the discourse will provide modest insight into similar situations elsewhere in Africa.

Method

While it is beyond the scope of this work to provide an exhaustive study of the history and development of Catholic social imagination in Africa, I will attempt to identify and briefly discuss its various forms since Catholicism arrived in Africa. Methodologically, because of the absence of a thematic study of the history and development of Catholic social imagination in Africa, I will follow the path of historical reconstruction.

Based on the work of Joseph Palacios on the history of Catholic social imagination in the United States and Mexico, I will examine very closely the historical dynamics of Catholic social imagination in Africa, including the African social imagination in antiquity and in the medieval, modern, and contemporary eras. Palacios has identified four approaches to Catholic social imagination that fairly represent the various ways the church has imagined and imagines social possibilities.[3] As Palacios explains, these four approaches are based on the Catholic social doctrine that has developed since the first social encyclical, *Rerum Novarum*, by Pope Leo XIII, in 1891.

Though these four approaches are based on Catholic social doctrine, they also reflect Catholic social imagination as it existed prior to the announcement of that doctrine, in light of the fact that much of the doctrine reechoes earlier Catholic social imagination. Indeed, and as the *Catechism of the Catholic Church* affirms, the church's concern for social matters certainly did not begin with *Rerum Novarum*, for the church has never failed to show interest in these matters. Nonetheless, the encyclical marks the beginning of a new path. Grafting itself onto much older traditions, it signaled a new beginning and a singular development in the church's teaching with respect to social matters.[4] The four approaches are (1) the integral church or ecclesial approach; (2) the integral world or Christian-inspired approach; (3) the structural church or social ministry approach; and (4) the structural world or faith-based citizen approach. Although Palacios used these four approaches in analyzing Catholic social imagination in North America (U.S. and Mexico), they capture the various approaches to Catholic social imagination employed at various stages of the life of the Catholic Church in Africa.

The integral church or ecclesial approach is about implementing Catholic social imagination within the church with the hope of building an internal solidarity that will reflect outward to the world. Catholics in this category tend not to imagine social possibilities beyond the Catholic Church. In fact, for them, involvement in social issues beyond the confines of the church is considered sinful and even an obstacle to salvation. As we shall see, this approach to Catholic social imagination was common in the early Catholic Church in Africa, which stretches back to the arrival of the faith in North Africa in the first and second centuries CE (culminating in its temporary disappearance around the eleventh century).

The integral world or Christian-inspired approach seeks to infuse Christian values into the social reality. Catholics in this category imagine social possibilities in what they see as an integral part of the Catholic mission. They not only engage social issues but seek to Christianize social reality because they believe that, just as the soul gives life to the body, so does that reality have its roots in the spiritual world. This approach was common in the medieval Catholic Church in Africa, which began with the arrival of Portuguese missionaries in Kongo around 1482.

---

3. Palacios, *Catholic Social Imagination*, 212.
4. *Catechism of the Catholic Church* §2421.

History and Development of Catholic Social Imagination

The structural church or social ministry approach imagines social possibilities for civil society acting only on its own. Unlike the integral church or ecclesial approach, which considers involvement in social issues sinful, the structural church approach considers social issues to be important to human flourishing, but, according to this approach, it is not the duty of the church to become involved in these issues. This approach does not in any way seek to Christianize the social reality as the integral world approach does. Rather, Catholics in this category seek to make helpful contributions to addressing social and political issues. This approach was common in the modern era, which began toward the end of the eighteenth century, coinciding with the colonial era in Africa.

The structural world or faith-based citizen approach, like the integral world approach, imagines social possibilities as an integral part of Catholic mission. However, unlike the integral world or Christian-inspired approach, the structural world approach does not seek to Christianize the social reality. Rather, it engages social issues based on Catholic social teaching, which practitioners of this approach are not shy to appeal to in the public square. This approach is becoming more prevalent in the contemporary Catholic Church in Africa. The contemporary era, which began in the mid-twentieth century, has been the era of indigenous leadership in the African church. Let us now examine in detail Catholic social imagination in Africa beginning from antiquity.

African Catholic Social Imagination in Antiquity

A complete history of Catholic social imagination in Africa must start from the beginnings of the church in Africa. The Catholic Church came to Africa in the first century. Besides the fact that some Egyptians were present at Pentecost, there is growing scholarly consensus that the evangelist Mark brought the Catholic faith from Jerusalem to Alexandria around 60 CE.[5] Several scholars speak of the rich Catholic faith that flourished in Cyrenaica (Libya), Alexandria (Egypt), Carthage (Tunisia), and Hippo (Algeria) from the first to the seventh centuries CE.

For example, Elizabeth Isichei speaks of the vibrant theological discourse against Gnosticism at the catechetical school of Alexandria, as well as other theological debates on the Trinity and the nature of Christ. According to Isichei, the vibrancy of the Catholic faith in Africa at this time led to the emergence of remarkable African Catholic theologians like Origen and Augustine, among others.[6]

Thomas Oden has observed that, not only did the Catholic faith flourish in Africa at this time, but it also helped shape Western Christianity. In his book *How Africa Shaped the Christian Mind,* Oden shows that the birth of the European university was anticipated in African Christianity; the historical and spiritual exegesis of scripture first matured in Africa; African thinkers shaped the very core of the most basic early Christian dogmas; the early ecumenical councils followed African conciliar patterns; Africa shaped Western forms of spiritual formation through monastic discipline; the Neoplatonic philosophy of late antiquity moved from Africa to Europe; and influential literary and dialectical skills were refined in Africa.[7] These and similar narratives of vibrant theological and spiritual imagination dot the pages of many books about this history of early Catholicism in Africa.

One wonders, then, whether social imagination had any place in the Catholic Church in Africa at this time. The answer is yes—the Catholic social imagination of Africa at this time was highly suspicious of social realities and material things. This way of imagining social possibilities was shaped by their common perception of material things as sinful and inimical to salvation. Catholic theologians and clerics encouraged Catholics to fly away from worldly realities and social issues and focus on their spiritual lives. This led to an attitude of austerity and separateness from "the world" in the Catholic Church of North Africa,[8] which accounts for the surge in monastic, hermitic, and ascetic life

---

5. Baur, *2000 Years of Christianity in Africa,* 21.
6. Isichei, *History of Christianity in Africa,* 22–23.
7. Oden, *How Africa Shaped the Christian Mind,* 45.
8. Isichei, *History of Christianity in Africa,* 22–23.

at this time. "The inward focus of the North African Catholic Church," says Isichei, "is reflected in the striking density of ecclesiastical administration in 411. No fewer than 286 Catholic bishops and 284 Donatist ones held a debate."[9]

The attitude of Catholics was to shy away from social issues rather than engaging them; and, when they did engage them, it was only to the extent that such issues were considered necessary for salvation. Whether Catholics were fighting battles against the pagans, speaking up against political injustices, or even buying and selling, their actions had to be theologically and doctrinally necessary for salvation.[10] Thus, the famous saying about this place and time: "If you ask for your change, the shopkeeper theologizes to you about the Begotten and the Unbegotten."[11] Even with his great vision of justice and politics, Augustine hesitated to preach Christianity beyond Roman boundaries because the Christian empire was seen as the mirror image of the heavenly kingdom. Thus the teaching, "Outside the church, there is no salvation."

African Catholic social imagination in antiquity may be considered to have been integral church or ecclesial in approach. This is because African Catholics at this time imagined social possibilities strictly within the church. This point of view was championed by Catholics who believed that salvation could be attained only through belief in church doctrine and reception of the sacraments. For them, social imagination was about implementing Catholic social concerns within the church with the hope of building an internal solidarity that would reflect outward to the world.[12] African Catholics identified with this kind of social imagination, and the majority shied away from any form of public involvement in civil associations. Instead, they sought to build ecclesial communities as alternatives to civil society. This way of imagining social possibilities was common not only in the Catholic Church of Africa at this time, but also in other churches beyond Africa.

This kind of social imagination still has a hold on some Catholics today and has been reinforced by the misconception that the notion of the separation of church and state means that the church should steer clear of social and political issues. Catholics following the ecclesial approach to Catholic social imagination believe that they are in the world but not of the world. They make little effort to engage the social dimension of the human person beyond the confines of the church.

African Catholic Social Imagination in the Medieval Era

Although pockets of Christians may have survived in North Africa until the eleventh century, by the ninth century the Cyrene Cathedral had been converted to residential homes and Catholic North Africa had effectively become extinct in the wake of the Arab invasion. Catholicism returned to Africa through the Portuguese, who arrived in Kongo in west-central Africa in 1483. The Portuguese came to do business and to make Christians.

Adrian Hastings remarks that for the Catholic Church in Portugal there was an intimate relationship between religion, politics, and commerce. The king dominated the church, while trade was seen as a religious, even missionary activity.[13] That is to say, there was no separation between the church and the state. This was not peculiar to Portugal—in Spain and elsewhere in Europe, and in fact across the globe, there was at that time an intimate relationship between religion and the state. In Kongo, as in Portugal, the king dominated religion.

This attitude toward religion and politics in the medieval era made it easier for the Catholic missionaries to succeed in Africa. Given the powerful role played by kings in religion, the first step the missionaries usually took was to try to convert the native kings to Catholicism. In the mind of the people, Europeans and Africans alike, religious conversion was dependent on a royal decision. "In

---

9. Isichei, *History of Christianity in Africa*, 41–42.
10. Lanctatius, *Divine Institutes*, VI, 9 and 6.
11. Gregory of Nyssa, *Oratio de deitate Filii et Spiritus Sancti* (*Oration on the Deity of the Son and of the Holy Spirit*), PG 46, 557b.
12. Palacios, *Catholic Social Imagination*, 213.
13. Hastings, *Church in Africa 1450–1950*, 75.

Benin, Kongo, and Mutapa," says Hastings, "we have a common pattern. Missionaries are sent from king to king. Baptism is a matter of high policy. Accepted by the king, it is then offered to his subjects, more or less *en masse*."[14]

This intimate relationship between religion, politics, and commerce shaped Catholic social imagination in Africa at this time. For African Catholics, the social, political, and material worlds were intimately bound up with religion and spirituality. All aspects of life fell under the authority of the kings, who were also the spiritual leader of their kingdoms. Unlike the Catholics of North Africa in antiquity, who shied away from social concerns, medieval African Catholics engaged these concerns as an integral part of their spirituality. Nothing social, political, or material happened by chance. Everything had a spiritual connection.

This animistic mentality, which medieval African Catholics carried over to Catholicism, put the African church right at the center of social issues and defined her approach to social imagination in Catholic kingdoms. Catholic priests, monks, and nuns guided kings, passed laws, and conducted adjudications of various political, business, and cultural disputes; all of this was seen as integral to the Christian faith. Catholic kings carried out their kingly duties from the perspective of the faith. As John Baur explains, this can be seen in the report of a Portuguese parish priest, Rui de Aquiar, about King Afonso of Kongo in 1516. He praises not only Afonso's piety but also his ardent desire to bring progress to his people and his concern for justice and education.[15]

Here, one sees an integral world approach to Catholic social imagination in Africa. As Palacios explains it, this approach seeks to bring Christian values into the civil sphere. Catholics who follow this point of view desire to infuse their communities with Christian values regardless of whether these values are in conflict with other religions and cultures. The emphasis of the medieval African church led by the missionaries was on Christian faith and values as the norm for all social, political, moral, and other questions. Catholics who shared this view of Catholic social imagination identified Christianity with the Catholic faith and insisted that Catholic doctrine serve as a standard for civil activities. They wanted to infuse society with their Christian values even when they conflicted with other religions.

African Catholic Social Imagination in the Modern Era

In the early seventeenth century, there was a shift in the Catholic missionary approach. The new missionary norms developed by Propaganda Fide[16] under the guidance of Francesco Ingoli stressed that missionaries should avoid politics and instead focus on the formation of clergy, learning local languages, and printing books in the vernacular, all as tools for the propagation of the faith.

The Portuguese Jesuits, Carmelites, and Capuchins had begun implementing the new norms by focusing on the teaching of doctrine and Christianization prior to the Dutch conquest of Angola and Elmina in 1637. This conquest freed Kongo from the Portuguese, making it possible for Dutch Protestants and other non-Portuguese missionaries to enter Kongo, an eventuality that Lisbon had tirelessly worked against. In 1640, Rome established an apostolic prefecture for the Kongo and confided it to the Italian Capuchins.

Unlike the Portuguese missionaries, who came to colonize, trade, and evangelize at the same time, the primary task of the Capuchins, following the new Propaganda Fide directives, was simply to evangelize. Their ministry was one of administering the sacraments and teaching. Their focus was on destroying indigenous African religion and enthroning Christianity. They were most interested in destroying shrines and other articles of worship used in traditional African religion and replacing them with rosaries, statutes of saints, and other Catholic images. From Kongo to Warri, from Mutapa to Sierra Leone, the approach was the same. As Adam Hochschild puts it, "the missionaries had come to the Congo eager to evangelize, to

---

14. Hastings, *Church in Africa 1450–1950*, 79.
15. Baur, *2000 Years of Christianity in Africa*, 61.
16. Also formerly called the Sacred Congregation for the Propagation of the Faith, now called the Congregation for the Evangelization of Peoples, or CEP.

fight polygamy, and to impart to Africans a Victorian sense of sin."[17]

It is not clear what led to this shift in missionary approach, but some commentators point to the proceedings of the Council of Trent and the increasing determination of Rome to recover some measure of control over missions from the governments of Portugal and Spain. Some others suggest that the agitation for the separation of church and state in Europe and America may have contributed to the shift.

Recall that the end of the eighteenth century saw the beginning of the era of colonialism and the emergence of nation-states. The French Revolution ending the country's monarchic rule took place at this time, inspiring agitation for an end to monarchies across Europe, which led to the emergence of the nation-states. In Africa, colonialism was spreading, and the scramble for Africa becoming more intense. With the rise of nation-states, however, missionaries were no longer the political emissaries of the colonizing states. France, Britain, Portugal, and other nations that were scrambling for Africa sent colonial masters to oversee the colonies in Africa. These historical circumstances may have contributed to the shift in missionary approach. One of its most visible impacts was on Catholic social imagination in Africa at this time.

From the seventeenth century up to the early twentieth century, the Catholic Church in Africa imagined social possibilities as the exclusive responsibility of the civil society, an approach that began with the missionaries. Unlike their medieval counterparts, modern missionaries in Africa did not get involved in social issues because they thought that the mission of the church was purely spiritual; they focused on the spiritual life of the people, leaving the sociopolitical issues to the state. They understood the separation of church and state to mean that the church should focus on the soul, while the state focuses on the body. Although the missionaries often worked closely with the colonial masters, and many enjoyed their support, the sphere of politics and other social realities was left to the colonial masters. When the missionaries did get involved, the actions were usually indirect, either in the form of charitable services or prayers. There was hardly any direct engagement with politics and other aspects of the society because the church in Africa, led by the missionaries, did not see these things as an integral part of the church's mission. As Hastings has noted, "A large number of missionaries and African Christians doubtless believed that there was little or no connecting link between their religious concerns and the present political state or future constitutional prospects of the lands where they lived and worked."[18]

In his book *The Sacrifice of Africa: A Political Theology for Africa*, Emmanuel Katongole paints a picture of Catholic social imagination in Africa during the missionary and colonial era that clearly reveals a structural or social ministry–based church. The Catholic Church in Africa, led by Western missionaries, imagined social possibilities based on the assumption that "the social and material conditions of life properly belong to the jurisdiction of politics. Christianity, which belongs to the realm of religion, can only make a helpful contribution to the field of politics."[19] Speaking of the church's "helpful contribution" approach to social issues, Hochschild's report in *King Leopold's Ghost* of the attitude of the Catholic missionaries in Congo during Leopold's reign is instructive:

> Thousands more children perished during the long journeys to get there. Of one column of 108 boys on a forced march to the state colony at Boma in 1892–1893, only sixty-two made it to their destination; eight of them died within the following weeks. The mother superior of one Catholic colony for girls wrote to a high Congo state official in 1895, "Several of the little girls were so sickly on their arrival that our good sisters couldn't save them, but all had happiness of receiving Holy Baptism; they are now little angels in heaven who are praying for our great king."[20]

---

17. Hochschild, *King Leopold's Ghost*, 172.
18. Hastings, *History of African Christianity: 1950–1975*, 21.
19. Katongole, *Sacrifice of Africa*, 1–2.
20. Hochschild, *King Leopold's Ghost*, 172.

As Katongole explains, this way of imagining social possibilities was inspired by an existing vision of the church as an institution whose competence lies in spiritual and pastoral fields of life and surrenders the determination of social and material processes to the realm of politics.[21] Here, one can sense the structural approach to Catholic social imagination. As Palacios explains, Catholics following this trend engage the society indirectly as they do not see the sociopolitical as a fundamental part of the church's mission.

Pope Benedict XVI echoes this approach in his encyclical *Deus Caritas Est*. In his analysis of the relationship between church and state, the pontiff insists that the pursuit of social issues is basically a political task, and so is a basic norm and direct responsibility of the state.[22] The church does not supplant the state when it comes to social issues, since her mission is fundamentally not political, cultural, or economic, but rather religious and spiritual. Though it is not the direct duty of the church to manage social issues, the church shows great concern for these problems. The church can neither remain indifferent to social problems nor be at the periphery of efforts geared toward the good of society and human flourishing.

Pope Benedict XVI explains that, with its indirect involvement in social issues, the church helps to illuminate the human reasoning behind false ethical systems so that the state's pursuit of social well-being may be protected from parochial interests, power, and greed. The church assists in the formation of right political consciences in order to inform public opinion and revive in the hearts of people those moral values necessary for establishing and preserving just structures. He challenges public officeholders to think first of the common good rather than personal gain in managing community resources.[23]

Some of the indirect ways that the Catholic Church in Africa under the leadership of the missionaries engaged sociopolitical concerns were through the building of schools, hospitals, orphanages, and soup kitchens, among other things. Although some have argued that these social service centers were built by the church as a means of evangelization, they have served a useful sociopolitical purpose in the civil society. They were means of forming the kind of social consciousness that Pope Benedict points to in his analysis.

This approach to Catholic social imagination outlived the missionaries and can still be found today in many African churches. Those following this approach want to remain in the institutional church while engaging the civil society in some way. In many parts of Africa this approach is growing, and many parishes have strong social ministries that provide church members with the opportunity to imagine social possibilities beyond the confines of the church yet from the perspective of Catholic social doctrine. These social ministries often work well with other social actors because the other actors see the church contributing to the resolution of social issues, not attempting to take over society.

African Catholic Social Imagination in the Contemporary Era

Although the social ministry approach is still flourishing in Africa, since the exit of the missionaries in the mid-twentieth century, Catholic social imagination in Africa is gradually taking the form of the structural world or faith-based citizen approach. Some indigenous African clergy have engaged the civil society on a variety of sociopolitical issues facing the continent. Episcopal conferences and many Catholic lay organizations have taken a hands-on approach to social issues. Here is how Paul Gifford captures it:

> The explicit involvement of Africa's churches in the public sphere was drawn to the world's attention in the late 1980s, when francophone countries began national conferences and Catholic bishops were appointed to chair them. In Benin, Mgr. Isidore de Sousa, Archbishop of Cotonou, presided over the

---

21. Katongole, *The Sacrifice of Africa*, 21.
22. Pope Benedict XVI, encyclical *Deus Caritas Est* §§ 26, 28.
23. Pope Benedict XVI, encyclical *Deus Caritas Est* §§ 26, 28.

national conference, and then as president of the Haut Conseil de la Republique overseeing the transition process, was the highest authority in the land for the thirteen months leading up to elections. In Gabon it was Mgr. Basile Mve Engone, Bishop of Oyem. In Togo, Mgr. Sanouko Kpodzro, Bishop of Owando, presided over the three-month-long national conference and then the entire transitional process. In Zaire, Mgr. Laurent Monsengwo Pasinya, Archbishop of Kisangani, was elected in 1991 to preside over the national conference attempting to halt that country's decline into anarchy.... In Malawi, the process of terminating President Banda's rule was begun by the 1992 Lenten Pastoral of the Catholic Bishops, etc.[24]

In the post-synodal apostolic exhortation *Ecclesia in Africa*, Pope St. John Paul II recognized and praised the strides that have been taken: "In spite of its poverty and the meagre means at its disposal, the Church in Africa plays a leading role in what touches upon integral human development. Its remarkable achievements in this regard are often recognized by governments and international experts" (§45).

The Catholic Church in Africa is imagining social possibilities beyond the restricted point of view that care for social reality is only a concern of politics. Rather, the church is imagining social possibilities from the perspective that social engagement is an integral part of the church's mission. There are several reasons for this, but many think that the social encyclicals, beginning with *Rerum Novarum*, which brought social concerns to the forefront of the church's mission, are the main reason for this change in the African mentality.[25] Pope John Paul II describes this change in the African church in *Ecclesia in Africa*:

In Africa, the need to apply the Gospel to concrete life is felt strongly. How could one proclaim Christ on that immense Continent while forgetting that it is one of the world's poorest regions? How could one fail to take into account the anguished history of a land where many nations are still in the grip of famine, war, racial and tribal tensions, political instability and the violation of human rights? This is all a challenge to evangelization. All the preparatory documents of the Synod, as well as the discussions in the Assembly, clearly showed that issues in Africa such as increasing poverty, urbanization, the international debt, the arms trade, the problem of refugees and displaced persons, demographic concerns and threats to the family, the liberation of women, the spread of AIDS, the survival of the practice of slavery in some places, ethnocentricity and tribal opposition figure among the fundamental challenges addressed by the Synod. (§51)

As Palacios explains it, the structural world approach allows Catholics to imagine social possibilities fully. Whether they are lay or clergy, Catholics having this mindset are able to bring Catholic theological, doctrinal, and sacramental languages to bear on social issues. They imagine social issues as authentically Catholic issues and engage them squarely through the lens of Catholic social doctrine.

This approach takes as normative Pope Benedict's prescription that lay Catholics must be directly involved in civic activities, bringing with them their Catholic social imagination. He insists that lay members understand that, as citizens of the state and of the human family, they have a direct and personal responsibility to engage in social issues. He tells the laity that they are to carry out this responsibility by participating actively and ethically in all aspects of temporal affairs, and that they should nurture a genuine passion for and shared commitment to the common good.[26]

Contemporary African Catholics are imagining social possibilities as an integral part of Catholic mission, but questions remain: How well are they

---

24. Gifford, *African Christianity*, 2.
25. Ugorji, *The Memoirs of a Shepherd*, 35.
26. Pope Benedict XVI, *Deus Caritas Est* §§28–29.

doing this, and can it be sustained? What is the impact of this approach on the everyday African Catholic person? These and many more questions squarely raise the challenges facing Catholic social imagination in Africa.

Contemporary Catholic Political Engagement in Nigeria in Light of African Catholic Social Imagination

Before concluding this chapter, I would like to briefly discuss the issues that are emerging as African Catholics imagine political engagement to be an integral part of Catholic mission. Across the continent, Catholics are becoming increasingly involved in politics. Bishops, priests, nuns, and lay Catholics are no longer looking at politics as something inimical to the Christian faith.

In Nigeria, there is an increasing awareness that one of the ways Catholics are called to work toward the kingdom is through civic engagement, especially political involvement. In the past five years, the number of Catholics playing active roles during elections has increased dramatically. Some dioceses have created diocesan platforms for priests and laypeople to participate in politics. For instance, the Justice, Development and Peace Office of the Archdiocese of Owerri has in the past ten years hosted campaign debates for gubernatorial candidates and other elective offices in the state. That a Catholic archdiocese is organizing a political debate is a clear indication that politics is no longer something on the periphery of the life of the Catholic Church in Nigeria, but rather an integral part of its life and liturgy.

In this same archdiocese, Catholic votes have for the past two decades played a major role in who emerges as governor. In fact, eight years ago, Catholics *decided* who became governor. Despite his power of incumbency, the then governor of Imo state, Mr. Ikedi Ohakim, was voted out by Catholics because his entourage manhandled a Catholic priest. Today, there is the perception in this archdiocese that whoever the archbishop anoints during elections will secure Catholic votes. Catholic priests across Nigeria are also engaging the political system, speaking up on social media and from the pulpit.

In the 2015 presidential elections, a popular Catholic priest, Fr. Mbaka, preached several homilies in which he supported the current Nigerian president. Although these homilies were presented as merely making a statement about the outcome of the elections, the express endorsement of one political candidate over another by a Catholic priest has put the church in the spotlight. Although it has not yet taken any explicitly stated political positions, the Catholic Bishops Conference of Nigeria has on many occasions issued communiques urging Catholics to get involved in government as part of their calling as Catholics.

In a communique issued on September 15, 2017, the bishops stated, "While not permitted to participate in partisan politics, clerics are urged to foster among people peace and harmony based on justice (cf. Canon 287). The lay faithful, on the other hand, are expected and encouraged to bear witness to the Gospel in their private, public and political lives."[27] The bishops quoted Pope Benedict from his encyclical *Deus Caritas Est*: "The Mission of the lay faithful is . . . to configure social life correctly, respecting its legitimate autonomy and cooperating with other citizens according to their respective competence and fulfilling their own responsibility" (§22), and concluded with the following:

> We therefore earnestly call on the Lay Faithful to intensify their efforts in bringing the light of the Good News to those places only they can reach. They are by their life of witness to bring Christ into the temporal order such as politics, business, and in their places of daily engagements (*Christifideles Laici* 42). By their vocation they are to challenge government policies that negate fundamental human rights and their individual and collective rights as Christians.[28]

While the Nigerian church is seeing Catholics become increasingly interested in politics, ques-

---

27. Catholic Bishops Conference of Nigeria, "Our Hope in Despair."
28. Catholic Bishops Conference of Nigeria, "Our Hope in Despair."

tions have arisen as to whether this involvement is helping the church accomplish its salvific mission. Catholic social imagination envisions an ordered society in which the one goal of political officeholders should be working toward the common good. As Pope John Paul II described it, the common good is "the good of all and of each individual."[29] This involves, but should not be limited to, protecting the dignity of the human person, a commitment to human equality, the preservation and protection of the family, a balancing of rights and responsibilities, a call to community and participation as citizens, the dignity of work and workers' rights, solidarity with the human community, and an option for the poor.[30]

Contemporary Catholic political engagement in Nigeria has yet to meet these demands of the Catholic social imagination, largely because of the country's culture of corruption and ethnoreligious rivalries. Like their fellow citizens, Catholic politicians and public servants still see Nigerian politics as an opportunity to get a piece of the national cake. This attitude may not be unconnected to the fact that Nigerian Catholics do not yet have an adequate understanding of the proper Catholic attitude to political and social issues. A Catholic political imagination has not yet found its way into the psyche of Nigerian Catholics. The challenge facing the Nigerian church as Catholics become increasingly involved in politics is the development of a clear political vision, a vision that reflects Catholic social imagination in the arena of politics. Nigerian Catholic theologians must take the lead in providing systematic Catholic political education that accurately reflects African Catholic social imagination.

Conclusion

Catholic social imagination in Africa has a long history that dates back to the church of the first century in North Africa. Though the Catholic Church had not yet articulated any systematic thought about social matters, the North African Catholics saw engagement with society as sinful and an obstacle to salvation. They dismissed social and material realities as being inimical to salvation, choosing instead to lead lives of asceticism and martyrdom. In contrast, medieval African Catholics led by the early missionaries imagined social possibilities as being integral to their Catholic mission and sought to Christianize the social, material, and political.

In the modern era, the missionary-led church in Africa recognized the importance of social issues to salvation but did not believe it was the duty of the church to address them. They thought that doing so was the duty of the state but that the church could make helpful contributions. Today, the African Catholic social imagination recognizes that social issues are an integral part of Catholic mission. While not seeking to Christianize all of social reality, they are not afraid to engage social issues in the public square from the point of view of Catholic social teaching.

It is hoped that this essay will provoke conversation about how the church can best engage social issues in line with the present-day Catholic social imagination.

Bibliography

Baur, John. *2000 Years of Christianity in Africa: An African Church History*. Nairobi: Pauline Publications, 1994.

Benedict XVI, Pope. *Deus Caritas Est* [Encyclical "God Is Love"; December 25, 2005]. Vatican City: Libreria Editrice Vaticana, 2006. www.vatican.va.

Catechism of the Catholic Church. 2nd ed. Washington, DC: USCCB Publishing, 2000.

Catholic Bishops Conference of Nigeria. "Our Hope in Despair: Towards National Restoration." September 15, 2017.

Gifford, Paul. *African Christianity: Its Public Role*. Indianapolis: Indiana University Press, 1998.

Hastings, Adrian. *The Church in Africa 1450–1950*. Oxford History of the Christian Church. Oxford: Clarendon Press, 1994.

———. *History of African Christianity, 1950–1975*. Cambridge: Cambridge University Press, 1979.

---

29. Pope John Paul II, *Sollicitudo Rei Socialis*, §38.
30. Pontifical Council for Justice and Peace, *Compendium of the Social Doctrine of the Church*, 6.

Hochschild, Adam. *King Leopold's Ghost: A Story of Greed, Terror, and Heroism in Colonial Africa*. Boston: Houghton Mifflin, 1998.

Isichei, Elizabeth. *A History of Christianity in Africa: From Antiquity to the Present*. Grand Rapids, MI: Eerdmans, 1995.

John Paul II, Pope. *Ecclesia in Africa* [Post-synodal Apostolic Exhortation on the Church in Africa and Its Evangelizing Mission toward the Year 2000; September 14, 1995]. Vatican City: Libreria Editrice Vaticana, 1995. www.vatican.va.

———. *Sollicitudo Rei Socialis* [Encyclical on Social Concern; December 30, 1987]. Vatican City: Libreria Editrice Vaticana, 1987. www.vatican.va.

Katongole, Emmanuel. *The Sacrifice of Africa: A Political Theology for Africa*. Grand Rapids, MI: Eerdmans, 2011.

Lanctatius. *Divine Institutes*, volume VI. Translated by Anthony Bowen and Peter Garnsey. Liverpool: Liverpool University Press, 2004.

Oden, Thomas. *How Africa Shaped the Christian Mind: Rediscovering the African Seedbed of Western Christianity*. Downers Grove, IL: InterVarsity Press, 2010.

Palacios, Joseph. *Catholic Social Imagination: Activism and the Just Society in Mexico and the United States*. Morality and Society. Chicago: University of Chicago Press, 2007.

Paul VI, Pope. *Evangelii Nuntiandi* [Apostolic Exhortation on the theme of Catholic Evangelization; December 8, 1975]. Vatican City: Libreria Editrice Vaticana, 1975. www.vatican.va. *AAS* 68 (1976).

Pontifical Council for Justice and Peace. *The Compendium of the Social Doctrine of the Church*. English translation. Washington, DC: United States Conference of Catholic Bishops, 2004.

Ugorji, Lucius. *The Memoirs of a Shepherd: On Social Problems and Theological Themes of the Day*. Enugu: SNAAP Press, 2000.

Church and Development in African Catholicism

Stan Chu Ilo and Gabriel T. Wankar

This chapter is divided into two parts. In the first part, we will explore issues related to church and development in Africa. We will also present some of the fundamental themes of the development of Catholic Social Teaching (CST) since the Second Vatican Council as they relate to the social mission of the church in Africa. The second part looks at how this social mission is actually being carried out and the limitations and strengths of the approaches that will be identified. The concluding sections of the second part will critically analyze various theologies of development current in Africa through the writings of selected African theologians. We will propose some pathways for performing social analysis in Africa, highlighting the need for a greater attention to and respect for the agency of the poor, especially women, and for a more contextual reading and appropriation of the social paideia of the church in grassroots evangelization and in the Catholic academy. The chapter will finally indicate some pertinent methodological issues related to research on church and development in Africa and what Africa would look like with a renewed commitment to CST and integral salvation by the churches in Africa.

Crises of State and Church in Africa

We suggest that two crises have accompanied Africa's turbulent march toward modernity. They have not only defined Africa's social context but also shaped and determined the proposals that theologians in Africa have made and continue to make with respect to church and development. These two crises are the postcolonial state and post-Western missionary Christianity in Africa.

With respect to the crisis of the postcolonial state, we are referring to the failure of African nations to build strong national institutions and structures that promote, protect, and preserve the common good and equally and fairly guarantee social mobility for all citizens. Elias Bongmba demonstrates that the human crisis in Africa is directly related to the crisis of the postcolonial state. He characterizes this crisis using four *p*'s that are typical of the abuse and misuse of power in contemporary Africa: privatization of power, pauperization of the state, prodigalization of the state, and proliferation of violence.[1] After the emergence of independent nations in Africa in the 1960s, unworkable paradigms of development were imposed on these nations by their former colonial oppressors in collaboration with emerging indigenous economic and political elites. What emerged in postindependence Africa is what George Ayittey described as a "religion of development."[2] This involved a kind of development that "propelled African nationalist leaders and elites to opt for obtusely expensive and inappropriate capital-intensive techniques of production when simple, less costly techniques were available. It also contributed to the neglect and consequent decline of African agriculture. Peasant agriculture was too 'backward' and was simply excluded from the grandiose plans drawn

---

1. Bongmba, *Dialectics of Transformation in Africa*, 9–37.
2. Ayittey, *Africa Unchained*, 87.

by the elites to industrialize Africa. Nor was any role envisaged for Africa's peasant majority—the *Atingas*. Derided as 'uneducated,' 'slow to change,' and 'bound by traditions,' 'primitive implements' were shunned."[3] This was only one problem facing postindependence Africa. There was also the innocent romantic ideal that the "poisoned chalice" of nationhood given to the now defunct Western colonies of Africa would function well because it had been modeled on the characteristics of Western governmental systems—constitutional democracy, rule of law, separation of powers, and free and fair elections, among others. Instead, in the first decade following independence, the governments of most African countries either became one-party states, were taken over by military coups, or both.

The soldiers who assumed control of governments in Africa as well as the dictators who emerged either from military takeovers or the suppression of opposition in a one-party state often triggered the unraveling of the inchoate social compact and false identity and foundation of postcolonial African states. These figures also unconsciously triggered the inevitable emergence of the multiple fault lines that were already present in many African nations, fault lines that have spawned wars, genocides, ethnic conflicts, government corruption, failed and failing states, refugee crises, and generalized suffering and poverty—all of which continue to convulse the continent today. The problem has not been the emergence of the state per se in Africa—traditional African communal societies and ancient kingdoms always implied some form of social compact and the accompanying values and virtues required of every person. The problem has been the lack of cohesion and unity among the diverse ethnic and religious groups of the postcolonial states of Africa. As Adebayo Olukoshi rightly argues, the autonomy of African states has eroded, with Western governments, corporations, financial institutions (like the International Monetary Fund and the World Bank), and aid agencies delegitimizing local development and social policies and practices. This has led to a lack of harmonization between economic policies and locally driven instruments and agencies for social renewal.[4]

We see similar processes at work in the post-Western missionary phase of the history of Christianity in Africa. Just like the Western gift of nation-states, which was a prepackaged product made abroad and delivered to Africa without respect for Africa's own narratives and forms of social arrangement, the missionary churches in Africa—particularly the Roman Catholic, Anglican, Methodist, Baptist, Presbyterian, and churches of the Reformed tradition—were also established without paying serious attention to local processes and cultural and religious traditions. What the soldiers did with their armored tanks, bullets, and cannons in bringing down the state, and what the dictators did in expropriating the wealth of the state for themselves and their cronies, also happened in mainline Christianity in a related but parallel context through preachers, prophets, priests, the big men/daddies and thick madams/mamas of these burgeoning churches.

The Pentecostals had no guns or bullets, but they had the Bible and their ability to harvest the riches of God and the powers of the Holy Spirit. With these tools, what were once considered fringe movements led by "uninformed and false" pastors, preachers, and prophets have now become the new African Reformation, offering, as religious subalterns, an alternative to the missionary churches that has attracted many, competing with these groups for social space and membership.[5] The Pentecostal revival in Africa has revealed that the fragmentation of the churches of Africa is a religious version of what has happened in African states, with ethnic groups, rebel leaders, and factions of political parties, among others, breaking away, and communities forming to provide social capital for themselves outside the formal apparatus of the failed social agencies and institutions of the state.

The crisis of the postcolonial state and the crisis of the post-Western missionary churches in Africa have resulted in the same consequences—namely, the continued predominance of Western ideas

---

3. Ayittey, *Africa Unchained*, 87–88.
4. Olukoshi, "Africa and the Process of 'Underdevelopment,'" 2–4.
5. On the Pentecostalization of African Christianity as the "African Reformation," see Anderson, *An Introduction to Pentecostalism*, 104.

and ideals with respect to development, failed and even disastrous aid and development industries, death-dealing economic policies imposed by the West, and mission projects initiated by Western faith-based groups that end up harming Africa by creating an unbroken chain of dependency and reinforcing negative and racist representations of Africa and Africans as poor, benighted, crisis-ridden, and always in despair.

This double crisis of state and church points to the absence of strong institutions in Africa. With regard to the state, it is clear that its structures and bad actors are contributing to the worsening of Africa's social and economic predicament.[6] With regard to the churches, it is equally clear that a truly inculturated African church promoting structures of development and grassroots evangelization grounded in local processes and contexts, in the local church's social mission, and in context-specific pastoral plans, has not fully emerged in Africa. There is a need to work toward the emergence of African churches that will bring about a faith and Christian praxis that go beyond enchantment, devotionalism, and false claims. Such churches would offer spiritual and religious services to God's people while at the same time acting as strongly prophetic entities in the fight against bad state actors (and the unholy alliance that exists in some places between these actors and African churches), checking the excesses of religious fundamentalism and reversing the failures of churches to achieve the goals of their social mission.

For most regular Africans, access to the common good involves a highly competitive, volatile, and destructive run to the top, often without any institutional framework or best practices developed over time. Thus, as the state increasingly abdicates its responsibility for the common good because of so-called state capture by families, political parties, and ethnic groups, the result is greater fragmentation and competition. The multiple and ever-increasing appeals to nonstate actors to provide social integration and hope largely explain the metastases of rebel movements, secessionist uprisings, militia groups, terrorist cells, and migrant crises in Africa. The presence of such actors has, on the other hand, also led to positive developments, including the emergence of strong microcredit groups, small groups in villages focusing on social activism, and camps for refugees/internally displaced persons. Many nonstate actors in Africa are constructing new narratives through their resilience and daily personal and communal solidarity in fighting poverty and fragmentation.

The struggle between the existing faiths and emerging faiths in the churches of Africa, taking place in the various religiocultural contexts of the continent, is ongoing. Both the mainline and new churches in Africa continue to witness increasing internal tensions, scope creep in their social mission, signs of abuses and a lack of transparency, and the presence of splinter groups and competing teachings and doctrines. All of these affect how the churches approach issues of poverty and its causes and wealth creation, and how they may be contributing to the widening of the dry desert of poverty in Africa. There are questions about the preaching and ministries of the churches with respect to how people can access the riches of God, including good health and cures for sickness. These problems also affect the churches in their construction of a praxis of hope and their ability to strengthen the agency of regular people attempting to deal with the adverse social conditions and limiting situations in Africa. These various churches offer many different narratives in responding to fundamental questions about being and belonging, life and death, and poverty and wealth, among other things. The competition for membership among the churches, their various problem-solving approaches in resolving difficult situations, and the forms of control they adopt to exploit the poor and the vulnerable continue to limit the ability of people to find a social space for survival, as each group constructs their own sites for enacting narratives of being and belonging. Some of these narratives may not be able to find a home within the mainline churches because of their relationships to their founding Western churches and their formal, top-down structures of authority.

The challenge in creating any discourse on theology and development in Africa must be seen in this context. It is helpful to examine African developmental methodologies through the lens of CST,

---

6. Assefa et al., *Globalization, Democracy, and Development in Africa*, vii.

and we will focus below on this teaching. We will consider the writings of theologians and development theorists. We will also explore the obstacles blocking the Catholic Church's social mission in Africa, which are the result of the church's social legacy in Africa. And, significantly, our analysis stresses the importance of listening to the voices of the poor and those on the margins. Our goal here is to provide a survey of various approaches to development and to make intelligible some of the principles operative in the narratives of the African Christian social mission and in African theologies of development.

Development Discourse in Africa and the Social Agency of the Church

There are two related questions that must be answered in any discussion about the church and development, not only with respect to Africa but also with respect to world Christianity. The first is about the meaning and scope of the term "development"; it is a word that has proven to be contentious in the way it has been understood and applied both locally and globally. The second is about the role of religion in development and specifically why and how churches play a role in bringing about integral development in Africa.

Regarding the first, there is a need for a more critical reading of developmental theories and their modernizing, secularizing, and social evolutionist claims, stratagems, and failed predictions as put forth by experts about Africa. As Frederick Cooper noted regarding development programs in Africa, between 1960 and 1973 notions of progress, the eradication of poverty, intellectual and educational advancement, building up of capital to compete in world markets, and entering a new history in the world order were central to the persistent and so-called African predicament.[7] These Western notions have remained central to many analyses of Africa to this day. This narrow set of ideas based on a Western reading of history was most cogently described by Francis Fukuyama in an essay titled "The End of History,"[8] which later became a book of the same title. The main thesis of this essay reflects to a great extent this Western reading of history, which goes back to Hegel in political philosophy and to Eusebius in ecclesiastical history. It involves the notion that the West is the center of global progress—economic, political, religious/Christian, cultural, civilizational, and in other ways—and the rest of the world is mere periphery that must follow the center in order to assume its rightful place in this Eurocentric conception. This idea is characterized by the racist mindset of both pre- and post-Enlightenment Europe and was at the heart of the American and European creation of an imaginary world order after World War II. This conceptual framework has, through the law of unintended consequences, brought about many of the crises crippling the world. This can be seen in how "helping" the non-Western "other" gain access to wealth and institute democracy through a process of economic, cultural, social, and religious identification and convergence with the West has played out in many countries in Africa, Asia, Latin America, and the Middle East. This was also the mindset that informed the Christian missions to Africa and still informs missionary Christian aid and international development interventions and assistance moving from North to South in today's era of world Christianity.

Fukuyama argued that there is a strong case to be made for the evolution of all political institutions everywhere in the direction of liberal democracy based on a correlation between economic development and stable democracy. In the world's most economically advanced countries, liberal political and economic institutions have converged over time, leading Fukuyama to the conclusion that there are no obvious good alternatives to these institutions. Fukuyama argues that the fundamental question that needs to be asked is about the bases of the "unabashed victory of economic and political liberalism."[9] Fukuyama asks why all other twentieth-century political systems that confronted Western liberal democracy—fascism, communism, monarchism, authoritarianism, autocracy, and despotism, among others—had crumbled by the end

---

7. Cooper, *Africa since 1940*, 91–92.
8. Fukuyama, "The End of History," 3–18.
9. Fukuyama, *Political Order and Political Decay*, 48.

of the century. The victory started in the realm of consciousness; it was an ideological triumph that is reflected also at the material level, in the long run leading to more freedom and greater material wealth in lands once held under the stranglehold of dictatorship. The material aspect of the triumph of liberal democracy, according to Fukuyama, is yet to be fully and concretely instantiated, which explains the conflicts and wars in places like Africa, based on the argument that the presence of "conflicts correlates very heavily with poverty."[10]

The question of history is central to the discourse about development, culture, and poverty. Even though Catholicism has rejected this false Hegelian notion of history and the false economic determinism of either socialism or liberal capitalism,[11] African Christianity faces a challenge concerning how history should properly be read and how church leaders and ministers should interpret what is happening in people's lives. Many questions come to mind concerning how African churches are and should be interpreting the movement of history and constructing a praxis for the future; for example, should churches be more involved in healing ministries without also fighting for the provision of basic health care services for everyone in Africa as part of a holistic biosocial approach to human well-being? Should churches in Africa spend more time healing family roots in the wake of persistent tragedies in a family rather than seeking a more holistic healing of families through reconciliation and restoration of broken and fraying relationships? Should church ministers and healers spend more time destroying ancient ecological spaces and forests in search of the roots of ancestral curses rather than developing an ecospirituality in which health and wholeness go hand in hand with restoring human and cosmic harmony? Should churches in Africa preach prosperity for the people without seeing themselves as called to be concretely involved in pulling down the structures of oppression that are present in both church and state and that contribute to poverty and marginalization, and instead embrace a praxis of historical reversal? African theologies are rejecting Western progressivist history and theories of development based on "modernization," but it seems that Africans have not yet sufficiently developed African theologies of abundant life that could serve as both foundation and praxis for reversing the unacceptable trajectory of history in Africa, a history that has nailed most of our people to a cross of suffering and pain.

African theologies of abundant life should move toward a critical and broader account of creation, history, political theories and praxis, and development by examining the root causes of poverty and the African predicament in the light of God's dream for Africa and the many gifts and assets of the continent. They should seek the spiritual, cultural, historical, and economic causes for the African condition and propose solutions through prophetic proclamation. This proclamation should not simply consist of claims and promises of deliverance, but should describe a credible ecclesial life that draws, for instance, on an African Christian humanism that offers a concrete praxis to reverse the challenging social conditions on the continent. This will require offering alternative pathways to the future through the narratives of hope created by the subalterns of counterdevelopment—new stories of belonging, healing, and restoration in local communities away from the limelight. Ogbu Kalu proposes that African Christians are reappropriating in Christianity the African traditions of abundant life because for African Christians "salvation manifests itself in the transformation of material, physical and psychic spaces."[12] In the words of Francis Young, "salvation . . . is God's rescue operation, recreation, the restoration of a wholeness which involves transformation into 'Christs', into bearers of the divine image."[13]

---

10. Fukuyama, *Political Order and Political Decay*, 48–49. Paul Collier notes that social upheavals, state failures, and wars harm development because "war is development in reverse" ("Development and Conflict," 1).

11. See Pope John Paul II's speech to UNESCO in 1980, "Man's Entire Humanity Is Expressed in Culture"; see also Gremillion, *Church and Culture since Vatican II*, 317–28; and Pope John Paul II, encyclical *Centesimus Annus* §§13 and 33.

12. Kalu, *African Pentecostalism*, 261.

13. Young, "Salvation and the New Testament," 35–36.

Development is not about movement from one state of underdevelopment to another. Theologies of development in Africa must give an account of the unfolding of God's gift of integral salvation in Africa as the realization of God's creative purpose in history. They must explore what works against integral salvation in Africa and how Christians and churches working with other faith and nonfaith groups in Africa can help bring God's purposes for Africa to fruition through a holistic mission of transformation. An authentic African theology of development seeks to identify the bases for societal wholeness and for the process of societal and individual conversion, which will remove the structures, systems, and false ethical standpoints that work against human and cosmic flourishing. These negative factors are often found in the kinds of choices people make as individuals as well as the kinds of systems, cultural traditions, and practices these choices bring about, working in tandem to lead the people away from a realization of the fruits of God's reign in history. An African theology of development must also be grounded in a social justice critique, which concentrates on an analysis of power and oppression. Particularly significant is to identify through immersion in the people's social context how power differentials everywhere, ranging from local communities to the world order, take freedom away from the people and how people are reduced to objects and pawns in certain unjust structures of the state and certain sinful structures of the churches. This is not only a question of history, but an anthropological one that must address what it means to be an African in the world and what it means to be a child of God, made in the image and likeness of God, when one's life is unfulfilled because of, among other things, one's place of birth, sex, sexuality, location in the social structure, or religious or ethnic identity.[14]

Viewed in this light, for many people in Africa today, "development" signifies everything that is wrong about North–South relations as well as all that is wrong with African societies—including, with respect to the latter, racism, classism, sexism, crass materialism, conspicuous consumption, exploitation, cultural imperialism, destruction of natural habitats, industrial pollution, dumping of toxic wastes, and the presence of substandard goods. Development has meant the destruction of African people's agency and freedom to become agents in their own history, a fact that is related to the unbroken cycle of dependency that African governments have created through their slavish, wholehearted embrace of Western economic orthodoxies. This destruction of agency is also related to a lack of vision and sacrifice among African leaders in failing to seek a truly African version of development that is free from the "religion of development," with its Western high priests. "Development" thus refers to the wreckage of the free market, modernization, and progressive history, and to the products of neoliberal capitalism and globalization, whose priests inhabit the iniquitous heights of the buildings that house the World Trade Organization, the International Monetary Fund, the World Bank, and the United Nations and the Organization for Economic Co-operation and Development (OECD), among others. It is about COVID-19, Ebola, and HIV/AIDS and how these diseases affect Africa because of its marginal place in the world created by ongoing structural, social, and commercial determinants of health. Development in Africa is also about the destruction of Africa's beautiful forests by international conglomerates, the resource curse in Africa which has given rise to wars, child soldiers, blood diamonds, unsafe mines and oil wells, corruption, and environmental degradation; state collapse in oil-rich countries like Libya and South Sudan; an unbroken cycle of frustration, violence, and terrorism in other countries like Nigeria and Algeria; and the failure of many political and social institutions all across Africa. "Development" for many Africans is about condoms, abortion, population control, the hypersexualization of African youth, radical feminism, new forms of social engineering, and charitable donations tied to embracing some one-sided Western ideologies on family, marriage, gender, sex education, and others.[15]

---

14. Young, "Salvation and the New Testament," 35–36.
15. See Ekeocha, *Target Africa*.

Many young Africans are restless as they watch their dreams dying. Their natural instinct is that Africa should embrace the logic, plan, and promises of Western development and they wonder "why are we not like the West? Why are we suffering in this way?" Indeed, many young Africans are groaning in despair because of their false conviction that their failure to be gainfully employed after graduation and the absence of any ladder of social mobility is caused by their countries not being like European nations or the United States and Canada. For this reason, they would rather risk death on perilous trips across the Sahara and the Mediterranean in order to escape from Africa to Europe, even if it means living in modern forms of slavery. The stories of such young people and the way our churches and societies have failed them are the new gospel, which the churches cannot ignore in proclaiming and living out the Good News today.

It is obvious that the time has come for people to imagine a "church after development."[16] Such a church will have to discover again the heart and praxis of the social gospel and holistic salvation. It must embrace the authoritativeness of local process and engage in grassroots evangelization that will build on the assets and cultural and material resources of Africans. Such a church in Africa must also develop a political theology, praxis, and engagement against the bad politics and bad social ethics that define the modern state in Africa. This will require a lot of hard work and sacrifice that go beyond mission appeals by African church leaders and social workers in Western-based churches. In addition, this vision of development will not be constructed on a constant cry for help by African bishops in Rome, New York, Brussels, or London; or on top-down, Western, faith-based initiatives and programs designed without the input of Africans. As Robert D. Lupton wrote concerning a needs-based, top-down approach to what he calls "toxic charity,"

> the giver–recipient relationship is doomed from the start. Such relationships hardly foster trust. Usually they breed resentment. The recipient must figure out the rules of the system, determine the kind of appeal most likely to secure the maximum benefit, learn the language that best matches the dispenser's values, and, above all, be sincere. Half-truths are acceptable. Fabrication may be necessary. It doesn't really matter since this is about working a system, not joining a community. Givers, then, continually tighten the rules, close off loopholes, guard against favoritism, and be ever vigilant to detect manipulation or outright fraud. The system lends itself to adversarial relationships.[17]

What is notable, then, is that a top-down, rule-based charitable relationship between churches in Africa and their Western counterparts is for the most part hurting Africa. Particularly in the Catholic Church, keeping African Catholic dioceses under the control of the office of the Congregation for the Evangelization of Peoples hampers African churches from developing their own contextual educational programs and curricula, their own social and pastoral programs, and their own administrative and church structures that will build on the assets and agency of the people. The canonical principles of subsidiarity and solidarity must be applied fully in the relationship between the African churches and officials in Rome as well as other church agencies who are actively involved in the burgeoning "helping industries" in Africa.

In light of the foregoing, we would like to offer a basic definition of an African Christian notion of development. In the following discussion, it will become clear how this basic definition is like and unlike some notions that are prevalent in development literature and current scholarship. This definition is built on the fundamental values of African humanism, which

> emphasizes vitality of life and abundant life as the chief goals for daily living. These are the ends of every religious ritual: to preserve, enhance, and protect life. Abundant life among the Akan resonates with the Hebrew

---

16. See Michael L. Budde, "The Church after Development," in *Foolishness to Gentiles: Essays on Empire, Nationalism, and Discipleship* (Eugene, OR: Cascade, 2022), 94.

17. Lupton, *Toxic Charity*, 62.

concept of *shalom*, denoting total wholeness that is physical, psychological, spiritual, and social. For the African, it describes peace with God, the gods, ancestors, fellow human beings (family and community), and the natural world. Natural forces cooperate by yielding their fruits or "increase."[18]

Based on this theological anthropology, it is proposed that *an African notion of development is the presence of those social, cultural, religious, economic, and political conditions that make human and cosmic flourishing possible by the daily unfolding of the reign of God in African history through the agency of Africans themselves.* An African theology of development, in this light, is concerned with demonstrating the relevance and place of the African Christian faith as an agency for constructing communities where the human and material resources of the people are being applied to meeting the needs of the people in that community. This will require the translation of the social gospel into a politics and praxis of social transformation for all people in the community, state, or nation. The mission of the church in development in Africa should become more instrumental in valorizing the agencies of individuals, cultures, systems, and structures for bringing about human and cosmic flourishing. Theologies of development in Africa must develop the rational and practical conditions and road map for the realization of human and cosmic flourishing, which is essential to the fulfillment in history of God's saving will for creation and the people of Africa, as revealed through Christ. It is a theology of accountability that renders praise to God by showing how the assets of Africa in all their richness and diversity need to be employed in order to realize human and cosmic fulfillment. It is a theology that proposes a pathway for a missional praxis and offers a foundation for the kind of daily actions, witnesses, and proclamations by Christians and churches in Africa for the purpose of bringing about a continuing realization of the mission of God in Africa's evolving history.

The second question raised at the beginning of this section concerns the place of the church and religion in development. In his post-synodal apostolic exhortation *Evangelii Gaudium*, Pope Francis makes the connection between theological anthropology and the Christian vocation in social transformation when he teaches that "the very mystery of the Trinity reminds us that we have been created in the image of the divine communion, and so we cannot achieve fulfilment or salvation purely by our own efforts." He adds, "From the heart of the Gospel we see the profound connection between evangelization and human advancement, which must necessarily find expression and develop in every work of evangelization" §178). Just as the church and people of faith have a role to play in social transformation, the pope also teaches that faith does not simply relate to "the private sphere" (§182), but must be applied in bringing conversion to the world, especially with respect to those aspects of social life related to the pursuit of the common good. This is necessary because in creating an option for the poor the church must not only be concerned with charitable works but must also confront the structural elements of societies that sustain violence; these are structures of sin and injustice. Faith, in this teaching, should lead us to God, to seek the things of heaven, but it should also make us uncomfortable about suffering in the world, about the cries of the poor and the destruction of the earth through human agency, the latter of which has given rise to climate change and environmental crises that hurt the poor and vulnerable. Faith in this sense relates to justice and transformation and should propel Christians to work hard with others in leaving the earth better than they found it (*Evangelii Gaudium* §§182–83, 195–98, 202–15).

Bob Mitchell, writing about the marginalization of religion in Western notions of development (inspired by Max Weber's relegation of religion to "private ethics"), posits that "religion in some cultures is not about a set of abstract doctrinal or theological arguments that can be neatly quarantined. Rather, it is experienced as permeating and influencing everyday life."[19] In Africa, religion is

---

18. Kalu, *African Pentecostalism*, 262.
19. Mitchell, *Faith-Based Development*, 11.

the dominant discourse and a holistic approach to life is already woven into the people's worldview, in contrast to Western dualism. Asonzeh Ukah and Tammy Wilks wrote about how Peter Berger's "market model" of religion—that is, the idea that religious groups are like economic units engaging in competition within a free market, together with associated concepts like "privatization," "enchantment," "secularization," and others—was very confusing to their students in South Africa because it did not resonate with their experience. Ukah and Wilks propose that "Western theories of religion, therefore, that aim at the hegemonic interpretation of the fate of religion and religious consciousness in the face of rapid social transformation are only partially or tentatively relevant to the African situation and require local (empirical) content to refine and bolster them."[20]

It is an understatement to say that religion plays an important role in African societies. In a very real sense, religion and religiously inspired concepts, worldviews, and praxis have a better chance of impacting the evolution of history in Africa than in the West. In Africa, religious narratives impact the state, and what happens in the state in turn affects the ideas of religious people—the narratives of the state in Africa are often discussed in the courts of priests, prophets, fortune-tellers, imams, and marabouts. Thus, with respect to the crisis of the post-Western missionary church and the postcolonial state, which are at the root of the African predicament, the factors that hamper the church's effectiveness are also in play in undermining the state's effectiveness. This is why the churches and the state must work together. What this means is that an effective and strong church with credible, dynamic, and creative structures and transformational ethical leadership at all levels that is immersed in the daily lives of the people and stays with and on the side of the poor could be a strong agency for healing Africa through social transformation. It is true that, despite the internal challenges facing the continent, there is still a great measure of trust in, goodwill toward, and deference given to religious and spiritual leaders in African Christianity and African religion in general.

In addition, African Christian churches have played and continue to play an important role in such things as resolving conflicts, the settlement and care of refugees and migrants, eradicating poverty, health care and social services, support for those living on the margins, and civic engagement. In a real sense, African churches are helping to reverse history in Africa by bringing the Good News to the poor and hope to all people, fighting poverty and healing the physical, spiritual, and moral sickness in our societies. What is obvious is that the churches in Africa are well positioned to expand the range of their activities and to formalize and streamline these activities into social capital in meaningful, strategic, and helpful ways.

It is not surprising that there is a huge scholarly production in Africa rebutting the negative characterization of the Pentecostal, charismatic, and evangelical revival in Africa and of the generalized explosion of churches in Africa. Pentecostal groups should not simply be dismissed as fundamentalist groups led by false prophets who water down the Christian message through the prosperity gospel; in fact, in some instances they have offered alternative models of wealth creation.[21] As Nimi Wariboko proposes, these groups are "sites of the social, the contexture in which social life hangs together, in which practices cluster and congeal to produce domination, oppression, and derailment of destiny."[22] Wariboko argues further that these groups are contesting state powers that are seen as corrupt and decrepit, satanic and demonic, and they are seeking new forms of power built on a spiritual praxis that is "sustained in a network of persons and within the internal and immanent social dynamic of the community and its immediate and remote larger contexts."[23] Wariboko's ideas are shared by J. Kwabena Asamoah-Gyadu, who proposes that the Pentecostals in Africa are concerned with confronting "the structures of

---

20. Ukah and Wilks, "Peter Berger, The Sacred Canopy, and Theorizing the African Religious Context," 1150.
21. See, for instance, Heslam, "Christianity and the Prospects for Development in the Global South."
22. Wariboko, "Political Theology from Tillich to Pentecostalism in Africa," 132–33.
23. Wariboko, "Political Theology from Tillich to Pentecostalism in Africa," 132–33.

oppression that consign Africa to backwardness, mediocrity, and non-achievement."[24] The works of these scholars reinforce the argument that Pentecostals are arising as subalterns because of the failures of both church and state in Africa, and that they are now major players in Africa at all levels—in civic life, economics, education, politics, and in efforts directed at social transformation.[25] According to Dawid Venter, these new groups offer bridges that allow modernity to be represented in older forms, while cloaking older forms of tradition in newer guises. They are thus attempting to recover a lost African religious past, reinventing and adapting it to meet the challenges of creating Africa's own version of modernity. In a sense, they are a bridge between the past and the present and between the present and the future in sub-Saharan African Christianity.[26] This positive dynamic could be harnessed in generating a theology of development in Africa that valorizes the agency of these groups as social capital.

Pope Benedict XVI points toward this possibility very clearly in his post-synodal apostolic exhortation *Africae Munus*: "Before the obstacles, both physical and spiritual, that stand before us, let us mobilize the spiritual energies and the material resources of the whole body which is the Church, convinced that Christ will act through the Holy Spirit in each of her members" (§98). This is the language of social capital: mobilizing the spiritual energies of groups within our churches, removing physical and spiritual obstacles as well as economic and social bondage, and nurturing a faith that can help to develop solidarity and creativity for the purpose of relieving the heavy burdens weighing down on African people. The pope also pointed out that the church must speak out in favor of an economy that cares for the poor and is resolutely opposed to an unjust order; the present economic order has, under the pretext of reducing poverty, often aggravated it (§§79–80). Thus, there is a need for the church to build networks with other components of the civil society to fight against an unjust order that prevents African people from shoring up their economies and developing along the lines of their culture.

Pope Benedict strongly invites African Christians and theologians to find new languages and categories for understanding and appropriating the gospel message and the transformative presence of grace in the vast and challenging social context of Africa. There is also a need to reconceive the ways and means of being church in today's Africa. This calls for expanding the horizons of our understanding of what it means to be a Christian in Africa, and how we can use the resources of the faith to work with people of other faiths, including practitioners of traditional African religions, to create a better society. This will require using the tools and categories available in the social sciences together with native African wisdom enriched by the gospel to find concrete answers to the challenges of our times. We think that it could be helpful to conceive of religion in Africa as social capital and to promote the transformation such a conception could bring by identifying how the faith of individuals and churches could become agencies for constructing a new and better history for Africa.

The former president of the World Bank, James D. Wolfensohn, describes the importance of religion for the economic and general well-being of society as follows:

> Religion is an omnipresent and seamless part of daily life, taking an infinite variety of forms that are part of the distinctive quality of each community. Religion could thus not be something apart and personal. It is, rather, a dimension of life that suffuses whatever people do. Religion has an effect on many people's attitudes to everything, including such matters as savings, investment and a host of economic decisions. It influences areas we had come to see as vital for successful development, like schooling, gender equality, and approaches to healthcare. In short, religion could be an important driver of change, even as it could be a brake to progress.[27]

---

24. Asamoah-Gyadu, "'Born of Water and the Spirit,'" 351.
25. Asamoah-Gyadu, "'Born of Water and the Spirit,'" 351–54.
26. Venter, "Introduction," 9.
27. Wolfensohn, "Foreword," xvii.

Along the same lines, the World Social Forum's document "Faith and the Global Agenda: Values for the Post-Crisis Economy" highlights the role of religion in helping humanity rethink the development of the moral framework and the regulatory mechanisms that underpin a just economy and politics and global interconnectedness.[28] It is obvious that religion can offer the spiritual capital as well as reshape the construction of meaning with regard to values, virtues, social justice, ecology, the notion of the good of order, and the nature and direction of history.

In a very real sense, there is no organization in Africa better positioned than the churches to play this very important role. In this regard, it is possible for every parish and small mission outpost in Africa to create at least six important socioeconomic and spiritual outreach groups/programs, each of which is an instance of social capital: an agricultural development committee (Gen 2:5), a women's microcredit cooperative group, a parish mentoring and support group for the youth, poverty eradication outreach programs, a parish village or community bank, and a parish food bank to feed the hungry. An example of a socioeconomic and spiritual outreach program is Songhai Farms in the Republic of Benin, which has been designated as a center of excellence by the United Nations. It demonstrates how a combination of science, religion, innovation in agriculture, and locally driven practices can be mediated through the church to achieve food security and wealth creation in local communities.

The idea of social capital also finds some basis in the practice of the early church. The early Christian community worked and lived together, making sure that through their common efforts the needs of everyone were met. The early Christian community did not depend on any external sources and donors in order to accomplish this. They did not need to appeal to governments or politicians in making the needed sacrifice through solidarity to ensure that none of their members went to bed with empty stomachs. Everyone in the early church brought what he or she had to help others and to the support the wider community in its creation of wealth and establishment of provisions for the poor. Paul reported on these support networks in his Second Letter to the Corinthians (2 Cor 8:1–24), showing how first-century churches employed social capital in these networks of encouragement, hope, praxis, and wealth creation. About the life of the early Christian community, the Acts of the Apostles gives this account, "The whole group of believers was united, heart and soul; no one claimed for his own use anything that he had, as everything they owned was held in common. The apostles continued to testify to the resurrection of the Lord Jesus with great power, and they were all given great respect. None of their members was ever in want, as all those who owned land or houses would sell them and bring the money from them to present it to the apostles, and it was then distributed to any members who might be in need" (Acts 4:32–35).

The example of the early church was the inspiration for the Small Christian Communities (SCCs). The truth is that poor people have agency and subjectivity, and their otherness must be affirmed in our churches. Indeed, one of the sad realities of our times in terms of church and development in the Catholic tradition is the utter neglect of local parish initiatives and grassroots groups, especially SCCs, parish wards, and those comprised of women. Preference is given to diocesan structures, while parishes serve as outposts of the diocese rather than strong local agencies for grassroots evangelization of the poor, culture, and traditions. Churches in Africa do not need to create new bodies; there are time-tested social structures in African communities (age-grade groups, women's groups, etc.) that can be used as the basis for social networking, solidarity, and wealth creation inspired by faith commitments. Furthermore, many parishes have strong zonal, age-grade, and peer groups (e.g., confirmation classes, Holy Communion classes, women's groups, men's groups, and youth groups) that do not fit into the model of the SCCs. These are the groups upon which parish fundraising is built, and they could also act in the role of social capital providing "otherworldly" insights informing a "this worldly" proclamation and living out of the gospel of abundant life.[29] These groups can serve as means

---

28. World Economic Forum, "Faith and the Global Agenda," 9.
29. For an analysis of Paul Gifford's "imaginative rationality," which contrasts notions of globalization and globalizing Christian entrepreneurship, see King, "Godly Work for a Global Christianity," 79.

for creating new ways of building solidarity, creating wealth, supporting and empowering the poor, and confronting the sinful structures present in local communities and national life. These groups can play specific roles in the following areas:

- Mobilizing community resources and valorizing the people's agency by making use of their strengths, entrepreneurial skills, resources, and wisdom
- Creating linkages and networks among various church and church-related social groups that engage in activities inspired by their faith related to eradication of poverty, wealth creation, civic engagement, participatory practices, solidarity with the poor and those on the margins or facing difficulties, and cultural revival and participation
- Empowering and enlisting church and church-related social groups that are often focused solely on spiritual development and devotions, and therefore have little influence on the social agenda, to fight against ecological crises, pollution in our cities, and the destruction of natural vegetation and forests
- Developing institutional structures and frameworks emanating from the church and church-related organizations that will undertake agricultural projects and foster the creation of support networks and beneficial linkages with agencies, communities, governments, and other sources of social capital, all for the purpose of stimulating grassroots development
- Developing and training leaders who will help heal divisions, contribute to bonding and the bridging of differences, and lead smaller groups and the wider community to ask fundamental questions about the direction of society, including strategizing about how to propose and implement workable and concrete solutions to social problems, with the aim of developing leaders whose reflections will bring about concrete praxis and who can influence others by their passion, purpose, and proposals for change
- Transforming faith-based organizations into sources of social capital by linking their acts of faith to social, economic, and political issues, such as providing efficient, cost-effective services, reaching the poorest people in the society, providing an alternative to a secular theory of development, igniting advocacy for the betterment of civil society, and motivating and inspiring ordinary Christians to empowering activities inspired by their faith[30]
- Transforming church groups into social capital, which will require gradual and integrated training and conscious efforts by church leaders to include five kinds of development (spiritual, socioeconomic, intellectual, physical, and ecological) in their preaching, advocacy, and praxis

All of these aspects of development should be emphasized without sacrificing the explicitly religious aspects of faith or undermining the intimate link between faith and life.[31]

A Short History of the Social Mission of the Church in Africa from Vatican II to African Synod II

Pope Paul VI offered the first magisterial teaching on the role of the church in African development in recent times. He also set the trajectory of discourse for the application of CST in Africa in the post–Vatican II church. Unlike Pope Pius XII, who was more concerned that Africa should acknowledge and embrace Europe's contributions to Africa's progress—warning African bishops in the 1950s against "blind nationalism," which might lead Africa into "chaos and slavery"—Paul VI was a strong advocate for Africa's own unique narratives of faith, life, and society.[32] He became the first modern pontiff to visit Africa, where he experienced firsthand, as he did in India, some of the pressing social questions facing the newly independent countries of Africa and Asia. During this 1969 visit, Paul VI uttered the now famous battle cry

---

30. See Aiken, "Assessing the Impact of Faith," 3.
31. We have relied here on the typology from the 2002 report by the University of Glasgow, *Churches and Social Capital*.
32. Calderisi, *Earthly Mission*, 108.

that the time was ripe for a truly African church.³³ He underlined in his speech in Kampala the need for African solutions to African problems—social, political, economic, theological, and cultural. He had previously visited Africa in 1962 as Cardinal Montini and in 1964 as pope had canonized the Ugandan Martyrs at St. Peter's Basilica, where he suggested in his homily that the history and contribution of African Christianity were central to the ongoing conversation at the council about the contributions of non-Western churches to the future direction of world affairs and world Christianity.

Paul VI's homily at the canonization was remarkable in many ways. It highlighted the spiritual treasures of Africa and pointed to Africa's central place in salvation history and in the history of humanity. But, at the same time as he emphasized the fact that human suffering and persecution still afflicted Africa, especially as part of the decolonization process, he made a very painful assertion about Africa that confirmed earlier prejudices about the continent being backward and primitive, needing integration into Western Christian civilization in order to overcome the incubus of the continent's benighted past.³⁴ This idea, that Africa is trapped, backward, and needy, is still prevalent in projects of Western humanitarianism in Africa.

The most developed and comprehensive version of Paul VI's vision for African development, however, in which he develops key themes explored in his encyclical *Populorum Progressio*, with a specific focus on the African condition, is the papal message *Africae Terrarum*.³⁵

Populorum Progressio (1967) had decisive and far-reaching effects in articulating and stimulating the church's social ministry everywhere in the world, but particularly in Africa. The pope unequivocally rejected many of the basic precepts of capitalism, including unrestricted private ownership of the means of production, the uncontrolled pursuit of profit to the detriment of the poor, and the worst consequences of free trade. He also drew attention to the slow pace of improvement in the lives of people in the developing countries, the scourge of poverty, and imperialism, all of which continued to bind many peoples and nations in chains.³⁶

The encyclical gave new impetus to the work of the newly constituted Pontifical Commission for Justice and Peace, created by Paul VI in January 1967 as an ecclesial initiative and structure authorized by Vatican II. This commission fostered a global Catholic movement that led to the church's greater involvement in worldwide causes promoting justice and peace.³⁷ It helped deepen the global Catholic conversation about the role of the church in the world, and helped with the establishment of justice and peace commissions in parishes, dioceses, and episcopal conference offices.

In the wake of *Populorum Progressio*, the church moved faster in Latin America than in Africa to translate its message into local idioms having a strong emphasis on the option for the poor, including the work done at the 1968 Medellín conference and the emergence of liberation theology as a distinctive social analysis and praxis of transformation informed by the Christian gospel.

---

33. Pope Paul VI, "Address to the Symposium of Episcopal Conferences of Africa and Madagascar," Kampala, 575.

34. "These African martyrs open a new epoch. . . . The tragedy which devoured them is so unheard of and expressive as to offer representative elements sufficient for the moral formation of a new people, for the foundation of a new spiritual tradition, to symbolize and to promote the passage from a primitive civilization, not lacking in magnificent human values, but infected and weak and almost a slave of itself, to a civilization open to the superior expressions of the spirit and to superior forms of social life." (My translation; the Latin version of the homily can be found at www.vatican.va.)

35. This message was released in Latin. We have referred to the French translation; the numbering in both the French and Latin versions is the same. See Message à l'Afrique, de 1967: *Africae Terrarum*, Adresse à la hiérarchie de L'Eglise Catholique d'Afrique et tous les people de ce continent, in Tharcisse T. Tshibangu, *Le Concile Vatican II et L'Eglise Africaine* (Paris: Epiphanie-Karthala, 2012), 103–22.

36. See O'Brien and Shannon, *Catholic Social Thought*, 238–39.

37. For a more detailed discussion of the worldwide Catholic movement for justice and peace, see Joseph Gremillion, *The Gospel of Peace and Justice: Catholic Social Teaching since Pope John* (Maryknoll, NY: Orbis Books, 1976), 188–90.

In Africa, *Populorum Progressio* led only to the creation of diocesan and national offices for justice and peace and a more coordinated organization of the church's charities. In 1981, the African bishops admitted that they had not done enough to advance and contextualize the message of *Populorum Progressio* within the broader social mission of the church.[38] Significant progress was made, however, between the first and second African synods (which occurred in 1994 and 2009, respectively) in deepening the theology and praxis of the church's social mission in Africa.

Many factors led to this period of progress. First was the work of theological development of the themes of CST and the social analysis of theologians like Adrian Hastings, Engelbert Mveng, Jean-Marc Éla, Elochukwu Uzukwu, Bénézet Bujo, Laurenti Magesa, and Peter Henriot, among others. Added to this was the introduction of CST into the curricula of many African seminaries, colleges, and universities led by religious orders; for example, the Jesuits in eastern, southern, and central Africa, the Comboni and Maryknoll Fathers in eastern Africa, the White Fathers in western Africa, and the Loretto sisters in southern Africa. In particular, these predominantly foreign congregations and missions began to introduce into their congregations, especially after the 1974 synod on evangelization, reflective practices as part of their charitable work. Also significant in this regard was the pastoral, biblical, and social formation taking place in the flourishing SCCs present in African parishes and local communities. However, not all Africans warmed up to missionaries leading the development of the church's social mission in Africa, and there arose between 1971 and 1974 a strong movement for a self-governing, self-reliant, and self-reproducing African church.

This movement led to the 1974 declaration at the meeting of the All Africa Conference of Churches (AACC) in Lusaka of a moratorium on additional missionaries and money being sent to Africa. This declaration, which was supported by a number of Catholic clerics, stated in part that "to enable the African church to achieve the power of becoming a true instrument of liberating and reconciling the African people, as well as finding solutions to economic and social dependency, our option as a matter of policy has to be a moratorium on external assistance in money and personnel. We recommend this option as the only potent means of becoming truly and authentically ourselves while remaining a respected and responsible part of the Universal Church."[39] The Catholic Church was not (and currently is not) a member of the AACC, but the document submitted by the African Catholic bishops on coresponsibility to the 1974 synod spoke about the need for Africa to assume full responsibility for its mission and social life.

Another important development worthy of note was the publication and dissemination of Catholic literature and magisterial documents through the *African Ecclesiastical Review*, the first English-language Catholic journal in Africa. The first edition of this journal in 1959 contained a special section on recent papal and magisterial teaching. The publication of *AFER* as the main English-language channel for disseminating the teachings of the church was complemented by the work of Pauline Publications Africa, which, since its inception, has been the most important disseminator of Catholic literature in Africa.

But the most important factor driving this period of progress was that some of the most pressing problems being discussed in CST were already ravaging Africa in the 1970s, including wars, grinding poverty, dictatorial governments, drought, locust invasion, tension over mission and money, foreign aid with stringent conditions, neocolonialism, and the impacts of Cold War ideological battles. These factors led international organizations as well as Catholic and papal charities to intervene repeatedly in Africa. There was an urgent need for these institutions to articulate how to proceed with aid initiatives in Africa, as well as a need to articulate a development discourse in African Catholic theology. All of this required specifically African approaches to social analysis informed by CST against the backdrop of the growing number of African voices espousing liberation theology

---

38. Calderisi, *Earthly Mission*, 60.
39. All Africa Conference of Churches (AACC), "Living No Longer for Ourselves but for Christ."

and a Black liberationist discourse, both of which were becoming suspect to leaders in the church hierarchy.

Also during this period, the Catholic Church, inspired by *Populorum Progressio*, was heavily involved in efforts to build civil society and protect human rights. These efforts were (and are) a disputed area in CST because the church is supposed to be neutral and nonpartisan in political matters, but it was difficult for the church to remain silent in the face of misrule, corruption, inexcusable human suffering, and the collapse of law and order. How could the church remain neutral in Africa in the face of genocide, a culture of waste and corruption, and glaring cases of injustice perpetrated against minorities because of their ethnicity, gender, religion, or social class? Many Catholic clerics became champions of human rights, often not through their writings, but instead through the witness of their lives. The Catholic archbishop Christophe Munzihirwa of Bukavu (DRC), who was one of the most vocal critics of the misrule of Mobutu Sese Seko, was assassinated by Rwandan troops in eastern Zaire and his corpse left on the streets for many days in October 1996. In 1977, Archbishop Luwum of Uganda was murdered on the orders of Idi Amin, the so-called "butcher of Uganda," because of his open condemnation of Amin's malfeasance. In the same year, Cardinal Biayenda was murdered in the political strife in the two Congos; he was a defender of human rights and a culture of good governance and justice for ordinary people. In West Africa, the heroism of Cardinals Yago of Abidjan, Paul Zoungrana of Ouagadougou, and Olubunmi Okogie of Lagos are still remembered as prophetic witnesses to the social gospel.[40] Many Catholic clerics headed or served on constitutional conferences and truth and reconciliation commissions that ushered in constitutional democracies in the DRC, Sierra Leone, Liberia, Nigeria, Benin, and the Ivory Coast. These were the first examples of many instances of Catholic involvement in Africa's emerging democratic processes, but unfortunately the voices of women were absent from these efforts, which was and is a major challenge facing the church in realizing the goals of its social mission in Africa.

By the time of the Second African Synod, the Catholic Church in Africa was the most important Non-Governmental Organization (NGO) working on the social mission in Africa. At the time of the second African synod in 1994, the Catholic Church operated more private hospitals and clinics than any other religious organization or private agency. These facilities served pregnant women and people suffering from malaria and other tropical diseases and, in some cases, provided free medical treatment for HIV/AIDS. Today, the church is still predominant in the health care sector in Africa, even in those African countries where the Catholic population is in the minority. In Ghana, for instance, Catholics make up about 30 percent of the population but the church runs more hospitals than any other private agency in the country. In Uganda, the Catholic Church provides 28 percent of the country's hospital beds.[41] The impact of the Catholic Church is also visible in many other social sectors in Africa. In Uganda, for example, the church is the second largest provider of vocational, technical, teacher, and business training (22 percent of students in these areas, compared to the government's 42 percent).

Scholarly Dialogue among African Theologians on Church and Development in Africa

There has been an increase in scholarly output in the area of CST, which has enunciated a clear and consistent vision of integral development in Africa. This work provides the theoretical and practical foundations for the church's involvement in development. There is a noteworthy disconnect, however, between what African theologians are writing about church and development and what the official church is saying about it. There is also a disconnect between what the church is adopting as its official approach to development and local practices of development. In both scholarly and practical work, the voices of the poor are largely being ignored; discussions and choices relating to development

---

40. Jenkins, *The Next Christendom*, 182–84.
41. Calderisi, *Earthly Mission*, 112.

have appeared to objectify the poor, pushing them further down in the social and ecclesial hierarchy. Bridging these power differentials between, on the one hand, African theologians and the official church, and on the other, the official church and the poor is a needed first step, because theologies of development must be a narrative of the people and how they are farther from or closer to the abundant life that approximates the reign of God in history. These theologies must also arise from and strengthen the church in its understanding of its mission and in its pastoral and social efforts, which are all part of the evangelizing mandate given to it to preach the Good News to the poor, to liberate those held in captivity, and to announce that the *kairos* (critical time) of God has come.

The first point to note is that these theologies about church and development in Africa are grounded in Catholic theological anthropology, Christian humanism, and the biblical teaching of the *imago Dei* (Gen 1:26–27). The church's teaching about integral development hinges on the dignity of every human person, endowed with intelligence and freedom to be responsible for his or her self-fulfillment. This vision seeks to promote the solidarity and community of human beings in their diverse social, economic, political, ethnic, class, and gender identities.[42] This vision and the need for collaborative effort in the quest for human and cosmic flourishing have attracted the interest of many African scholars. It was also a constant in the teaching of the two African synods, as can be seen in the recurrent themes discussed in some of the literature, to which we now turn.

The First and Second African Synods[43] were the most significant events in the life of the African church in recent times. Here, we are particularly interested in their impact in shaping the African social imagination and the church's social mission in Africa. The synods expended remarkable amounts of effort and resources in order to articulate the interrelatedness of the personal and social aspects of Christian faith. The First Synod, with its central theme of building the church in Africa as the "Family of God," proclaimed the necessity of bridging the gap between the proclamation of the gospel and the lived life experience of the people, as well as the gap between faith and culture (*EA* §51). The First Synod involved a reexamination of the church's approach to evangelization in the face of the dehumanizing conditions faced by many and the failed leadership endemic to Africa. The Second Synod dealt specifically with reconciliation, justice, and peace, emphasizing the church's theological and social responsibility, and inviting the church to reflect on its public role in the Africa of today (*AM* §17).

According to Pope St. John Paul II, the First African Synod of 1994 "was convoked in order to enable the church in Africa to assume its evangelizing mission as effectively as possible in preparation for the third Christian Millennium" (*EA* §141). In *Ecclesia in Africa*, his apostolic exhortation following the First Synod, the pope declared that "the main question facing the Church in Africa consists in delineating as clearly as possible what it is and what it must fully carry out, in order that its message may be relevant and credible" (*EA* §21).

---

42. Iber, "Church and State in Nigeria as Partners in Development," 73–75.

43. The official names of these gatherings were the First (and Second) Special Assembly for Africa of the Synod of Bishops. Given the limited scope of this chapter, we draw selectively from sections of the papal exhortations that emanated from the synods (Pope John Paul II, post-synodal apostolic exhortation *Ecclesia in Africa* [1995; here *EA*]; Pope Benedict XVI, post-synodal apostolic exhortation *Africae Munus* [2011; here *AM*]), sections that are pertinent to our suggestion that the church's social mission in Africa should be thought of primarily in terms of prioritizing social analysis over charitable and aid initiatives, a prioritization that is able to build on the assets of Africans. The First Synod focused on respect for human life and the family, with a special emphasis on the right of women to be actively involved in church ministries and decision-making processes, the promotion of dialogue with traditional African religions, developing a theology of the African church as family, and denouncing arms sales to Africa. The Second Synod dwelled largely on the need to work toward reconciliation, justice, and peace; to achieve this, it is necessary for the church to engage in dialogue with diverse groups, especially in regions of Africa characterized by significant religious and social pluralism. For a detailed treatment, see Wankar, *The Dual Reality of Salvation and the Church in Nigeria*, 121–84.

Acknowledging the rapid growth of Christianity in Africa south of the Sahara, this document asks pointedly, "In a Continent full of bad news, how is the Christian message 'Good News' for our people? Amid an all-pervading despair, where lie the hope and optimism which the Gospel brings?" (*EA* §40). Notably, the synod did not limit itself to proclaiming the Good News solely to win new converts. It called for a religious imagination that can fashion concrete ideals to respond critically and prophetically to the restless desire for the advent of the reign of God in Africa, noting that "in Africa, the need to apply the Gospel to concrete life is felt strongly. How could one proclaim Christ on that immense Continent while forgetting that it is one of the world's poorest regions? How could one fail to take into account the anguished history of a land where many nations are still in the grip of famine, war, racial and tribal tensions, political instability and the violation of human rights? This is a challenge to evangelization" (*EA* §51).

Underscoring the necessary connection between the quality of life of the faithful and the life-giving essence of the gospel, the synod acknowledges the yearning of Africans to make this connection manifest, noting how "the winds of change are blowing strongly in many parts of Africa, and people are demanding ever more insistently the recognition and promotion of human rights and freedoms" (*EA* §44). To respond to this challenge, the pope noted:

> It is therefore essential that "the new evangelization should be centered on a transforming encounter with the living person of Christ." "The first proclamation ought to bring about this overwhelming and exhilarating experience of Jesus Christ who calls each one to follow him in an adventure of faith." This task is made all the easier because "the African believes in God the creator from his traditional life and religion and thus is also open to the full and definitive revelation of God in Jesus Christ, God with us, Word made flesh. Jesus, the Good News, is God who saves the African . . . from oppression and slavery." (*EA* §57)

This call of the synod implies a sound understanding of the nature and causes of poverty, the neglect of the masses and, in most of the nations of Africa, corruption. Thus, the First Synod categorically teaches, "To proclaim Jesus Christ is therefore to reveal to people their inalienable dignity, received from God through the Incarnation of his Only Son" (*EA* §69). The church cannot ignore a concern for the concrete personal and social situations of Africans, since these earthly conditions bear upon their pilgrimage toward heaven.

The Second Synod, in building on the first, called specifically for a "transformation of theology into pastoral care, namely into very concrete pastoral ministry in which the great perspectives found in sacred scripture and Tradition find application in the activity of bishops and priests in specific times and places" (*AM* §10). Pope Benedict XVI hinges his understanding and interpretation of the entire Second African Synod on a realization that "the three principal elements of the theme chosen for the Synod, namely reconciliation, justice and peace, brought it face to face with its 'theological and social responsibility,' and made it possible also to reflect on the Church's public role and her place in Africa today" (§17).

Clearly, the church in most of Africa today is facing complex and interrelated systems of injustice that are calling it to more active engagement in the structures that plague the living conditions of Africans. These structures have undermined every political and economic endeavor aimed at promoting the common good. The Second Synod acknowledges this fact:

> [In Africa] situations demanding a new presentation of the Gospel, new in ardor, methods and expression, are not rare. In particular, the new evangelization needs to integrate the intellectual dimension of the faith into the living experience of the encounter with Jesus Christ presently at work in the ecclesial community. Being Christian is born not of an ethical decision or a lofty ideal, but an encounter with an event, a person, which gives life a new horizon and a decisive direction. (*AM* §165)

At the heart of the Second African Synod, therefore, is the call for a meaningful and enduring transformation of the African structures of injustice. To accomplish this, "the disciple of Christ, in union with his Master, must help to create a just society where all will be able to participate actively, using their particular talents, in social and economic life" (*AM* §26). In this light, the Second African Synod poignantly stressed the necessity of the churches to forge alliances toward the creation of a liberating spirituality and witness, emphasizing that "for her part, the Church will make her specific contribution on the basis of the teaching of the Beatitudes" (*AM* §27).

In order to dialogue fruitfully about issues affecting the common good, Catholics need to be informed about their faith tradition. Yet, for the most part, the African church is still not fully immersing rank-and-file Catholics in the Catholic intellectual tradition of which the CST is an essential plank. Pope Benedict XVI decries illiteracy on the continent:

> Illiteracy represents one of the principal obstacles to development. It is a scourge on a par with that of the pandemics. True, it does not kill directly, but it contributes actively to the marginalization of the person—which is a form of social death—and it blocks access to knowledge.... I ask Catholic communities and institutions to respond to this great challenge, which is a real testing ground for civilization, and in accordance with their means, I ask them to multiply their efforts, independently or in collaboration with other organizations, to develop effective programmes adapted to people's needs. (*AM* §77–76)

The faithful need to know that it is not an article of faith that they should remain poor. They need to know that it is not an article of faith that they be subservient to self-serving leadership. Instead, they need to be made aware that it is a legitimate demand of the faith that they oppose bad leadership in both the church and the state for the purpose of enhancing the common good. This understanding could form the basis for a dialogue that would foster common action among the various churches. A basic theme following on the two synods concerns the agency of Africans to identify, through their daily experiences, their developmental challenges and the need to fashion ways to overcome them.

In what way have theologians, guided by CST, reflected on African social questions and the proper response of the church and African peoples to the challenges they pose? Jozef D. Zalot, in his outstanding account, *The Roman Catholic Church and Economic Development in Sub-Saharan Africa: Voices Yet Unheard in a Listening World*, argues that the temporal impact of theology is just as important as its spiritual impact. From his critical analysis of leading voices in the discourse of church and development in Africa, including the voices of African bishops and African theologians (among the latter group are Engelbert Mveng, Jean-Marc Éla, and Laurenti Magesa), Zalot draws the conclusion that "if the Catholic Church is to be a relevant force in the lives of Africans, ... it must draw upon both the principles of CST and the insights of the African people themselves in order to articulate a theology of development that will help to create a more just and equitable society for all."[44] In an approach that departs from the age-old mentality of development workers and groups coming from the West to "develop" the "underdeveloped" Africans, Zalot crafts a vision of the church's involvement that is mindful of "development's intimate relationship to both justice and peace and to the broader issues facing the sub-Saharan Catholic Church."[45] While recognizing that neither African bishops nor theologians have the final word in regard to development in Africa, he opines that their contributions to the debate constitute an invaluable resource for any proposed theology of development and should be listened to. In addition to incorporating the principles of CST and distinctively African Catholic contributions, Zalot proposes the inclusion of "theologians who write from other Christian traditions," "the ethical principles of traditional African religion," and "the contributions of Islam," since "there are certain commonalities between the African Catholic Church's teachings on economic issues and those of other religious traditions."[46]

---

44. Zalot, *Roman Catholic Church and Economic Development in Sub-Saharan Africa*, ix–x.
45. Zalot, *Roman Catholic Church and Economic Development in Sub-Saharan Africa*, xii.
46. Zalot, *Roman Catholic Church and Economic Development in Sub-Saharan Africa*, 226–32.

Indeed, Zalot advocates a more fundamental collaborative effort between the Catholic Church in Africa and other religious traditions, not only in providing material relief in times of need and distress, "but also in formulating theological and practical responses to the foundational development questions facing the African people."[47]

Stan Chu Ilo, drawing from theological, ecclesial, social scientific, and historical sources, proposes an approach to the question of development in contemporary Africa that is focused on a transformative theological praxis. Grounding his work, *The Church and Development in Africa: Aid and Development from the Perspective of Catholic Social Ethics,* in the creative vision of Pope Benedict XVI's encyclical *Caritas in Veritate* (Charity in Truth) and in the African synods, Ilo agrees with Zalot in what he calls a creative appropriation of CST and proposes principles for the functional integral development of Africans. This approach involves "building on the assets of ordinary Africans through pro-active evangelically driven initiatives in the areas of education, capacity-building, co-operative groups, and various support networks which empower the poor, especially women and children."[48]

Thus, in place of the many aid and development programs on the African scene, which over the years have ended up creating a circle of dependency and privileging the donors instead of those in need, Ilo insists on a new model of development that includes, among other things, "participatory practices that place at the center the active involvement of the people in articulating the vision, setting out goals, and day-to-day implementation of the vision through solidarity."[49] The specific role of the church in Africa in this effort is to form the faithful in a new vision and mission; in other words, the accumulation of human capital through education, enabling Africans to build on their particular assets and move toward self-sustenance. While the principles advanced by Ilo may theoretically not be entirely new to CST, his specific proposals for intervening around education by way of context education, the quality of teachers, the priority afforded to education, and developing a pedagogy of hope,[50] all for the purpose of creating better social policy and greater attentiveness to African history, is a novel recipe for advancing a balanced theology of development in Africa.

In *The Sacrifice of Africa: A Political Theology for Africa,* Emmanuel Katongole insists on a retelling of the story of Africa, including the African Christian story, casting Christian social ethics in the role of uncovering "the underlying stories of key social institutions in Africa that affect both their performance and the types of characters they produce."[51] Reviewing the colonial past of a few African nations, including Congo, Rwanda, Burundi, and Uganda, as typified in works like Adam Hochschild's *King Leopold's Ghost,* Katongole, like many African scholars, believes that "at the heart of Africa's inception into modernity is a lie. Modernity claims to bring salvation to Africa, yet the founding story of the institution of modern Africa rejects Africa itself."[52] Thus, the urgent task for Christian social ethics in Africa is to pay attention to how the institution of nation-state politics works on the continent and why it works the way it does. A theology of development for Africa will necessarily need to fashion a strategic transformational approach to evangelization by engaging "the layers of memory through which the performance of the colonial imagination continues to live in the present."[53] While it is simplistic to blame all of Africa's woes on colonialism, Katongole has established that overlooking the interwoven narrative of the colonial project and the story of Christianity in most of Africa would indeed amount to a colossal deceit.

---

47. Zalot, *Roman Catholic Church and Economic Development in Sub-Saharan Africa,* 235.
48. Ilo, *Church and Development in Africa,* 224.
49. Ilo, *Church and Development in Africa,* 225.
50. Ilo, *Church and Development in Africa,* 232–36.
51. Katongole, *Sacrifice of Africa,* 3. See also Adam Hochschild, *King Leopold's Ghost: A Story of Greed, Terror, and Heroism in Colonial Africa* (Boston: Houghton Mifflin, 1998).
52. Katongole, *Sacrifice of Africa,* 20–21.
53. Katongole, *Sacrifice of Africa,* 12.

In the documents of the two synods and in the works of the authors reviewed above, there is a common, discernible trajectory: identifying relevant models for African theologies of development based on the needs of Africans and proposing practical steps to be taken, with a strong emphasis on the agency and assets of Africans in the development process and their capacity to effect social change. In other words, these scholars are concerned with what the churches of Africa can do through their social mission as an alternative to the developmental models pursued by governments and aid agencies. Both the synods and the reviewed authors express a fundamental rejection of the classical development paradigms of modernization and dependency. There is unanimity among church leaders and African theologians on the need to seek fitting development orthodoxies grounded in local cultures and local pastoral initiatives. These leaders and thinkers privilege local cultures and local knowledge as well as solidarity and support for grassroots movements. However, these alternative approaches have remained largely theoretical. Indeed, the sad reality of the development debate in Africa is that the many proposals of the synods and of African scholars have not been implemented on the ground. Some of the analysis of theologians concerning development in Africa is subject to the criticism that it is overly sociological and not grounded in the eschatological thrust of the mission of God in history, of which the church is an instrument.

A Critical Analysis of and Methods Pertaining to Development in Africa

Zalot's important analysis proposes a balance between CST and listening to the unheard voices of Africans in determining how the church should empower the faithful to assume responsibility for their own economic well-being. He charges Africans with the role of speaking out to the international community about what works best for Africans. Indeed, Ilo credits Zalot's work as "the most authoritative from the practical aspect of showing how the Catholic Church in Africa has been playing a prophetic role in development."[54] Zalot, however, sees the call by African theologians for the African church's self-determination as a fundamental problem as it relates to communion with Rome, in addition to questioning the theologians' understanding of liberation ecclesiology.[55] Even though he advocates for Africans to tell the international community what works for them, a crucial question for Zalot concerns who determines which African voices are to be listened to. Zalot's approach offers another good example of an approach to African development that is not grounded in local processes in which development is a gift Africa receives or a model for Africa to embrace. In any case, it is our belief that the right to self-determination, to which Africans are entitled, is the basis for any true development, since agency implies in the first place respect for differences of opinion and diversity.

Both Katongole and Ilo have the distinction of writing from their experiences as Africans as well as from informed contact with the West, and they call for participatory people-centered approaches to development. While Katongole's assertions are valid for much of Africa, he tends to assume that the continent is a homogenous whole and fails to acknowledge the varying experiences of different African communities, even with colonialism. There is truth in Katongole's argument that at the heart of Africa's insertion into modernity is a lie, a lie that has perpetuated the dependency of African governments and economies on the West. This is a fitting explanation for why nation-state politics functions the way it does in Africa. However, the fact that the likes of Nelson Mandela and Thomas Sankara, as well as a few others, could manage to function differently from the mass of other African leaders ipso facto means it is possible to be different. It is therefore problematic to assume that all theories of development and development practices in Africa are strains of modernization and dependency, even if this may have often been true.

---

54. Ilo, *Church and Development in Africa*, 224.
55. Zalot, *Roman Catholic Church and Economic Development in Sub-Saharan Africa*, 216–17.

Moreover, as Elias Bongmba argues with respect to Katongole's *Sacrifice of Africa*, "The notion of narrative and lament [in Katongole's book] could be strengthened by adopting a dialectical approach to political theology which must continue to examine institutions and structures as aspects of sovereignty broadly defined."[56] According to Bongmba, the church in Africa must engage state actors and work toward civic engagement in order to build political institutions, without which alternative sites of hope will remain marginal, without national or local impact beyond their founding narrative. The church in Africa must engage in critical and creative dialogue with the institutions of the state. In discovering and affirming narratives of hope in the community, the church must realize that the hope for Africa lies not in these local narratives, which are often made possible by outside donors, but in institutional reforms both in the state and in the churches that can make possible a liberating and transformative movement to transcend Africa's present failures. In addition, while Katongole's follow-up book, *Born from Lament*, offers a strong portrait of what hope looks like in modern Africa through the narratives emerging from these marginal sites, it does not offer a strong social analysis of why such sites exist.[57] Thus, the norming of these sites as portraits of hope may inadvertently serve to excuse the failed institutions and structures that generate them in many parts of Africa. Could there emerge from such a social analysis an African theology of hope that shows what hope looks like in the presence of strong religious and political institutions? Could this theology of hope become a portrait of what God's dream for Africa looks like, involving the collaboration of an inclusive state (as opposed to an extractive and centralized state) with a prophetic and poor church (as opposed to a church hosting a bazaar of spiritual claims and endless devotions to salve the wounds of a bleeding people)?

Like Katongole, Ilo consistently holds that the church's approach to development in Africa must begin from a counternarrative and praxis that privilege the agency of the people. This position is consistent with the long tradition of CST, but in the specific context of Africa, Ilo's proposal for a context-driven education marks a specific point of departure in the current debate. From the First African Synod through the work of numerous contemporary writers on this issue, a common thread has been a call for the education of the faithful in CST, but the context of this education has often been overlooked, leaving the impression that what applies to Europe, or even other "Third World" countries, can be extrapolated and applied to Africa. As Ilo notes, this oversight has been in the background of many failed development initiatives in Africa. In calling for a context-driven education, however, caution must be exercised against romanticizing local knowledge and cultural practices, especially where local forms of exclusion, particularly the oppression of women and children, are implied in some of these contexts.

Ilo's account of theology and development has been criticized by Paul Gifford. While Gifford affirms that Ilo's analysis of church and development in Africa is the best representative work in this area, so much so that it could serve as a kind of handbook on the subject, he argues that Ilo's book faces the same shortcomings as many current works by African theologians: a failure to address the dominant worldview in African Christianity that the world is ruled by spirits and demons, the constant assigning of blame to the West for all of Africa's woes, and "proof-texting" of CST in Africa. In his view, because of these problems, African theologies of development are divorced from the world of ordinary Africans, including their world of meaning. This explains why these theologies have failed to make any significant impact in changing the African social context.[58]

In a review essay, Briana Wong disagrees with Gifford's claims that African Christianity is a captive of an enchanted view of reality and that theologies like Ilo's are detrimental to African development and modernity because they ignore the African fascination with the spirit world. Wong

---

56. Bongmba, "Lament and Narrative," 407.
57. Emmanuel Katongole, *Born from Lament: The Theology and Politics of Hope in Africa* (Grand Rapids, MI: Eerdmans, 2017).
58. Gifford, *Christianity, Development and Modernity in Africa*, 104–6.

agrees with Ilo that mission and development practices in Africa must respect the African worldview. With regard to Gifford's claim that the "enchanted Christian religious imagination" has been ignored by Ilo and other African Catholic theologians, Wong states,

> The irony lies in the fact that Gifford critiques what he sees as Ilo's willful excision of the "enchanted dimension" from his description of African Christianity, while Gifford himself fails to recognize Ilo's endorsement of a fair amount of the so-called enchantment in Christianity, simply without the aspects Ilo finds as abusive—some, by no means all of which overlap with Gifford's own list of unsettling characteristics in African Pentecostalism. It seems therefore that Gifford unintentionally has placed himself among those at whose arguments Ilo takes umbrage, due to their "not taking Africa seriously or . . . not listening to Africans."[59]

Renewal and Reform of Church Structures for Effective Mission to the Poor

The Catholic social mission in Africa is alive and active; however, certain obstacles have hindered the church's efforts to make this mission more effective. As a sacrament of Christ's presence and an instrument of salvation and self-fulfillment in the present-day reality of Africa, what would be an appropriate approach for the church to adopt with respect to development? In what areas of research should African theologians focus their attention in order to realize the potential of this social mission as part of Africa's march toward a better future?

Current structures of governance in the Catholic Church in Africa stand in the way of achieving the proper goals of African development for two major reasons: First, in everything from decision-making to its management of finances, African church governance lacks transparency, with no mechanisms for checks and balances, especially with respect to the actions of bishops and priests. This is particularly worrying as it concerns the church's administration of its temporal goods intended for the poor. Second, church governance is affected by an increasingly prevalent patriarchy that has its origin in traditional African society. This patriarchy has legitimated stratification in the life of the church in Africa, making the problems of accountability and transparency in church leadership worse and obstructing the most effective use of its members' talents.[60] Patriarchal role differentiations in church administration and leadership undermine accountability and probity and have led to the failure of many development projects in Africa. Poor accounting practices and instances of corruption relating to aid and development projects have persisted because, from a sociological perspective, the African church operates as, in the words of Leonardo Boff, an authoritarian system.[61] A system is authoritarian when those in power exclude their subordinates from the free and spontaneous acknowledgment of that authority.[62] True authority, as opposed to power and domination, is typically characterized by the *uncompelled* submission of a group of people to an individual or an institution. Without natural conditions in place allowing for equal, respectful, and mutual relationships to flourish in an atmosphere of dialogue and coresponsibility, authority becomes ever more authoritarian. Because the exercise of power within most of the Catholic Church is effected through a structured catechesis and theological formation, and because of deference to forms of transmitting traditions that are accepted from generation to generation, transparency becomes a huge concern.

Contemporary society finds absurd the authority of a gospel, upon which the church stands, that sharply denounces every abuse of power, calling for the equality of all of God's children, while at the same time upholding stratifications in its own

---

59. Wong, "Review Essay," 46.
60. See Egan, "Facing the Crisis," 247–58.
61. Boff, *Church, Charism and Power*, 40.
62. Boff, *Church, Charism and Power*, 40.

structures. Just as the church previously took on Roman and feudal structures, it has become clear that in our times she needs to incorporate structures found in today's civil societies that are more compatible with the growing sense of our common humanity and that favor a fraternal community with the participation of the greatest number of people.[63] "Civil society has learned over the last two centuries that good government calls for (1) the elimination of nobility; (2) the separation of powers; (3) the principle of subsidiarity (what can be done at a lower level of society should be done there); and (4) a system of checks and balances."[64] A centralized government making every important decision is now recognized as a recipe for failure.

Also in need of reform are the church's structures of patriarchy, which fuel the marginalization of women's agency and voice in shaping the vision and praxis of reversing the trajectory of Africa's tragic history. The role of women and questions of gender equity were strongly raised in *Africae Munus*, as well as during the deliberations at the Second African Synod. "The Church has the duty to contribute to the recognition and liberation of women, following the example of Christ's own esteem for them" (*AM* §7).[65] Pope Paul VI's encyclical *Humanae Vitae* (1968), while rightly highlighting the challenges posed by various theories of and approaches to population control, was not successful in developing workable principles of social ethics promoting and protecting the rights of women. The discussions of the dignity of women in society and in the family in subsequent papal documents also failed to achieve this goal. According to Henriot, a number of feminist scholars have pointed out that this failure

> may be the result of an emphasis on "proper nature" and "proper role" of women—seeming to imply that women have a "nature"

distinct from men's. As a result, insufficient attention is paid both to the massive contributions made by women to economic development (e.g. food production and health care) and social development (e.g., education), and to the massive obstacles they face (e.g. suffering disproportionately from poverty, illiteracy and malnutrition).[66]

We agree with Musimbi R. A. Kanyoro that

> the witness of the Church in Africa will not be credible unless the Church takes into account the traumatic situation of the millions of women and the perilous conditions of the outcast of our societies. What meaning can faith have in churches that seek to be liberated without sharing the people's battles with the forces of oppression assaulting their dignity? . . . These questions frighten churches and communities with long established traditions and practices of injustices to women. They threaten our institutional comfort as churches, our invested privileges, our secure situations and they threaten the security of our judgment of what is right and what is wrong.[67]

The subjugation and marginalization of women, a phenomenon that is deeply rooted in a patriarchal ethos, has contributed to the violation of women's rights in Africa. The various forms of abuse of women include domestic violence, payment of the ritual bride-price, forced marriages, sexual harassment, punitive widowhood rites, female genital mutilation, rape, prostitution, and enforcement of gender-biased laws. In Africa about 51 percent of African women have been victims of violence; 11 percent have suffered violence during pregnancy; 21 percent marry before the age of fifteen; and

---

63. Gal 3:28: "You are one in Christ"; Matt 23:8: "You are all brothers."
64. Reese, "Reforming the Vatican," 216.
65. We are grateful to Pete Henriot for sharing the original draft of his article in which he critically analyzes and creatively appropriates *Africae Munus*. We also owe him a debt of gratitude for inspiring us with his pioneering work of social analysis within the CST tradition and his work as an activist in Zambia and Malawi.
66. Henriot, "Who Cares about Africa?," 229.
67. Kanyoro, *Introducing Feminist Cultural Hermeneutics*, 80.

24 percent have experienced genital mutilation.[68] These oppressive practices degrade the dignity of the African woman and are exacerbated by the socioreligious, economic, and political arrangements that obtain in Africa. The life of an African woman unfolds along the trajectory of vassalage: at home she serves everyone in the family, in society she has limited opportunities, and in the culture she is a victim of unjust traditional practices.[69]

According to a survey of nine African countries by the Food and Agriculture Organization in 1996, about 80 percent of the economically active female labor force is employed in agriculture. Food production is the major activity of rural women, and their responsibilities and labor inputs often exceed those of men. Women also provide much of the labor for the cultivation of export crops, from which they derive few benefits. Women are responsible for 70 percent of food production, 50 percent of domestic food storage, 100 percent of food processing, 50 percent of animal husbandry, and 60 percent of agricultural marketing.[70] About 50 percent of women in Africa are married by the age of eighteen, and one in every three women in Africa lives in a polygamous marriage. The fertility rate for women in Africa is about 5.7 children per woman. What is clear is that the social mission of the church in Africa must largely be anchored on the shoulders of African women and therefore must address those factors that make it impossible for women to use their assets to further the transformation of Africa.[71]

The most promising future thus lies in a concerted effort by the church to become more actively involved in shaping a moral vision for a new African society. It must do this, at least in part, by looking inward to resolve practices that contradict its ideals. When the church liberates itself from the allure of power and its perceived need for self-preservation by providing the faithful with a truly sound education, it will be better enabled to proclaim the truth that God does not desire the evil of poverty and want in African society, but that indeed these and other ills facing that society are human-made and should be resisted and reformed.

Africae Munus made many recommendations for a better formation of church members at every level toward a mature, adult faith relevant to meeting the challenges of faith and life in Africa. It proposes that all members of the church be educated in CST (*AM* §§109, 128, 134, 137) and that catechesis become deeper and more relevant to the historical exigencies of the moment (*AM* §§32, 165). In the words of Pope Benedict:

> Dear brothers and sisters in Catholic universities and academic institutions, it falls to you, on the one hand, to shape the minds and hearts of the younger generation in the light of the Gospel and, on the other, to help African societies better to understand the challenges confronting them today by providing Africa, through your research and analyses, with the light she needs. (*AM* §135)

The social paideia of the church in Africa must be integrated through daily praxis into preaching in the churches, into the work of the SCCs, and into the sacramental life of the church. The church in Africa must embrace practical and concrete social mission at the local level in the areas of agriculture, civic education, empowerment of women, grassroots networking, and leveraging local initiatives for sustainable development in the areas of ecology, health care, and sanitation, among others.

The social paideia of the church does not exist only in papal documents, the *Catechism of the Catholic Church*, the *Compendium of the Social Doctrine of the Church*, the occasional statements of the episcopal conferences, and in works of theology—it extends beyond written documents. While the social paideia of the church is embodied by these documents, Mary Elsbernd observes that it begins as reflections on local situations by local

---

68. See Arabome, "Woman, You Are Set Free!," 119.
69. See Arabome, "Woman, You Are Set Free!," 120.
70. Manuh, "Women in Africa's Development," 4.
71. See Swanee Hunt's account of how the empowerment of women in Rwanda has led to the valorization of their agency and to the gradual transformation of Rwandan society, in *Rwanda Women Rising* (London: Duke University Press, 2017).

faith communities.[72] The community of faith is the locus of dialogue between social conditions, social context, the people's daily existence, and the reality of faith. The community of faith can be a parish, an SCC, a Christian women's self-help group, or a Catholic university. The community of faith continually engages in theological reflections that give birth to a contextual social paideia based on the experience of and the stories of suffering and hope told by the community. This paideia draws insight from scripture, the social doctrine, the community's social ministry, the traditions of the church, and local traditions. CST is hidden when it is abstracted from the community of faith and history, but when it is engaged in a context of faith and action, a hopeful and concrete praxis of social transformation emerges, and grows like the mustard seed.

Conclusion

In this chapter, we have offered a comprehensive outline of the role of the church in African development within the context of the double crises of the postcolonial state and post–Western missionary church in Africa. We have done this through a historical survey of the Catholic social mission in Africa and CST in Africa, and by looking at some of the arguments for and against the various theories and theologies of African development. We proposed some helpful approaches to overcoming the obstacles we identified to the church's accomplishing its social mission, particularly the social capital approach as a possible route for engaging the voices of the poor at the grassroots level. We have described various methodological approaches for studying the church and development in Africa and set forth the challenges facing scholars in the field, especially those related to developing a praxis that can address the issues facing Africa today through the agency of the Christian faith and the African churches.

African scholars must take seriously this task of developing a useful praxis. Their work needs to go beyond critical studies of prevailing theories and practices to the development of theologies of hope grounded in local and ecclesial processes and in the sources of faith. Some areas requiring additional research include: (1) developing the theology and praxis of the social gospel to reveal its intimate connection to integral salvation and holistic mission; (2) conceiving a better relationship between the local and the global in the era of world Christianity, so that aid and mission outreach to Africa from other parts of the world are understood and organized as a mutual exchange rather than a top-down hierarchical relationship of dependency between Western churches and their African counterparts; (3) developing ecumenical and interreligious approaches as part of political theologies and prophetic traditions that can help unify the masses of African people around the common good rather than parochial interests; (4) understanding the phenomenon of multiple groups being involved in sometimes duplicative charitable efforts in Africa, which appears to be the consequence of the fragmentation and competition for social space in Africa; (5) finding ways to best use the assets of women and young people in Africa; (6) addressing the ideological and doctrinal impasses affecting Catholic charities that relate to questions of population, reproductive health and reproductive rights, the use of contraception in the fight against HIV/AIDS, and the rights of children and families; and (7) developing a political theology for democratization of Africa; and a global health ethics that addresses health inequity in Africa in a world that will have to deal with new infectious diseases and the double tragedy of both infectious and non-infectious diseases ravaging Africa in these times of the pandemic.

Bibliography

Aiken, Anna. "Assessing the Impact of Faith: A Methodological Contribution." International NGO Training and Research Center, June 2010.

All Africa Conference of Churches (AACC). "Living No Longer for Ourselves but for Christ." Lusaka, Zambia, 1974.

Anderson, Allan. *An Introduction to Pentecostalism*. Cambridge: Cambridge University Press, 2008.

---

72. Quoted in Gaillardetz, "Ecclesiological Foundations of Modern Catholic Social Teaching," 76.

Arabome, Anne. "Woman, You Are Set Free! Women and Discipleship in the Church." In *Reconciliation, Justice, and Peace: The Second African Synod*, edited by Agbonkhianmeghe E. Orobator. Maryknoll, NY: Orbis Books, 2011.

Asamoah-Gyadu, J. Kwabena. "'Born of Water and the Spirit': Pentecostal/Charismatic Christianity in Africa. In *African Christianity: An African Story*, edited by Ogbu Kalu. Trenton, NJ: Africa World Press, 2007.

Assefa, Taye, Severine M. Rugumamu, and Abdel Ghaffar M. Ahmed. *Globalization, Democracy, and Development in Africa: Challenges and Prospects*. Addis Ababa: Organization for Social Science Research in Eastern and Southern Africa, 2001.

Ayittey, George B. N. *Africa Unchained: The Blueprint for Africa's Future*. New York: Palgrave Macmillan, 2005.

Benedict XVI, Pope. *Africae Munus* [Post-synodal Apostolic Exhortation on the Church in Africa in Service of Reconciliation, Justice and Peace; November 19, 2011]. Vatican City: Libreria Editrice Vaticana, 2011. www.vatican.va.

Boff, Leonardo. *Church, Charism and Power: Liberation Theology and the Institutional Church*. London: SCM Press, 1985.

Bongmba, Elias K. *The Dialectics of Transformation in Africa*. New York: Palgrave Macmillan, 2006.

———. "Lament and Narrative: A Review of Emmanuel Katongole's *The Sacrifice of Africa*." *Modern Theology* 30.2 (April 2014): 403–7.

Calderisi, Robert. *Earthly Mission: The Catholic Church and World Mission*. New Haven: Yale University Press, 2013.

Churches and Social Capital: The Role of Church of Scotland Congregations in Local Community Development. Department of Urban Studies, University of Glasgow, 2002.

Collier, Paul. "Development and Conflict." Paper for The Center for the Development of African Economies, 2004.

Cooper, Frederick. *Africa since 1940: The Past of the Present*. Cambridge: Cambridge University Press, 2006.

Egan, Anthony. "Facing the Crisis: On the Continent, in the Church; An Ecclesiology for an Africa in Distress." In *The Church We Want: Foundations, Theology and Mission of the Church in Africa*, edited by Agbonkhianmeghe E. Orobator, 247–58. Nairobi: Pauline Publications, 2015.

Ekeocha, Obianuju. *Target Africa: Ideological Colonialism in the Twenty-First Century*. San Francisco: Ignatius Press, 2018.

Fukuyama, Francis. "The End of History." *The National Interest* (Summer 1989): 3–18.

———. *Political Order and Political Decay: From the Industrial Revolution to the Globalization of Democracy*. New York: Farrar, Straus & Giroux, 2014.

Francis, Pope. *Evangelii Gaudium* (The Joy of the Gospel) [Post-synodal Apostolic Exhortation on the Proclamation of the Gospel in Today's World; November 23, 2013]. Vatican City: Libreria Editrice Vaticana, 2013. www.vatican.va.

Gaillardetz, Richard R. "The Ecclesiological Foundations of Modern Catholic Social Teaching." In *Modern Catholic Social Teaching: Commentaries and Interpretations*, edited by Kenneth R. Himes. Washington, DC: Georgetown University Press, 2004.

Gifford, Paul. *Christianity, Development, and Modernity in Africa*. London: Hurst, 2015.

Gremillion, Joseph. *The Church and Culture since Vatican II: The Experience of North and Latin America*. Notre Dame, IN: University of Notre Dame Press, 1985.

Henriot, Peter J. "Who Cares about Africa? Development Guidelines from the Church's Social Teaching." In *Catholic Social Thought and the New World Order*, edited by Oliver F. Williams and John W. Houck. Notre Dame, IN: University of Notre Dame Press, 1993.

Heslam, Peter S. "Christianity and the Prospects for Development in the Global South." In *The Oxford Handbook of Christianity and Economics*. Oxford: Oxford University Press, 2014.

Iber, Simeon Tsetim. "The Church and State in Nigeria as Partners in Development." *Aquinas' Journal* 4 (June 2011).

Ilo, Stan Chu. *The Church and Development in Africa: Aid and Development from the Perspective of Catholic Social Ethics*. Eugene, OR: Pickwick, 2011.

Jenkins, Philip. *The Next Christendom: The Coming of Global Christianity*. 3rd ed. Oxford: Oxford University Press, 2011.

John Paul II, Pope. *Centesimus Annus* [Encyclical on the Hundredth Anniversary of *Rerum Novarum*; September 1, 1991]. Vatican City: Libreria Editrice Vaticana, 1991. www.vatican.va.

———. Speech to UNESCO: "Man's Entire Humanity Is Expressed in Culture" (1980).

Kalu, Ogbu. *African Pentecostalism: An Introduction*. Oxford: Oxford University Press, 2008.

Kanyoro, Musimbi R. A. *Introducing Feminist Cultural Hermeneutics: An African Perspective*. Cleveland, OH: Pilgrim Press, 2002.

Katongole, Emmanuel. *The Sacrifice of Africa: A Political Theology for Africa*. Grand Rapids, MI: Eerdmans, 2011.

King, David P. "Godly Work for a Global Christianity: American Christians' Economic Impact through Missions, Markets and International Development." In *The Business Turn in American Religious History*, edited by Amanda Porterfield, Darren E. Grem, and John Corrigan, 72–107. New York: Oxford University Press, 2017.

Lupton, Robert D. *Toxic Charity: How Churches and Charities Hurt Those They Help*. New York: Harper One, 2011.

Manuh, Takyiwaa. "Women in Africa's Development." *Africa Recovery* 11 (April 1998).

Mitchell, Bob. *Faith-Based Development: How Christian Organizations Can Make a Difference*. Maryknoll, NY: Orbis Books, 2017.

O'Brien, David J., and Thomas A. Shannon, eds. *Catholic Social Thought: The Documentary Heritage*. Maryknoll, NY: Orbis Books, 1992.

Olukoshi, Adebayo. "Africa and the Process of 'Underdevelopment': Neo-Liberal Globalization and Its Social Consequences." In *African Voices on Development and Social Justice: Editorials from Pambazuka News*, edited by Firoze Manji and Patrick Burnett. Dar es Salaam: Mkuki na Nyota, 2005.

Paul VI, Pope. "Address to the Symposium of Episcopal Conferences of Africa and Madagascar," Kampala, 1969 (*AAS* 61).

———. *Africae Terrarum* (The Land of Africa), 1967 (*AAS* 61).

———. *Populorum Progressio* [Encyclical on the Development of Peoples; March 26, 1967]. Vatican City: Libreria Editrice Vaticana, 1967. www.vatican.va.

Reese, Thomas J. "Reforming the Vatican: The Tradition of Best Practices." In *Catholics and Politics: The Dynamic Tension between Faith and Power*, edited by Kristin E. Heyer, Mark J. Rozell, and Michael A. Genovese, 213–20. Washington, DC: Georgetown University Press, 2008.

Ukah, Asonzeh, and Tammy Wilks. "Peter Berger, The Sacred Canopy, and Theorizing the African Religious Context." *Journal of the American Academy of Religion* 85.4 (2017): 1147–54.

Venter, Dawid. "Introduction." In *Engaging Modernity: Methods and Cases for Studying African Independent Churches in South Africa*, edited by Dawid Venter. London: Praeger, 2004.

Wankar, Gabriel T. *The Dual Reality of Salvation and the Church in Nigeria*. New York: Peter Lang, 2017.

Wariboko, Nimi. "Political Theology from Tillich to Pentecostalism in Africa." In *Paul Tillich and Pentecostal Theology: Spiritual Presence and Spiritual Power*, edited by Nimi Wariboko and Amos Yong, 126–40. Bloomington: Indiana University Press, 2015.

Wolfensohn, James D. "Foreword." In *Religion and Development: Ways of Transforming the World*, edited by Gerrie ter Haar. London: Hurst, 2011.

Wong, Briana. "Review Essay." *Journal for the Study of the Religions of Africa and Its Diaspora* 2.1 (October 2016): 43–54.

World Economic Forum. "Faith and the Global Agenda: Values for the Post-Crisis Economy." Geneva: World Economic Forum, 2010.

Young, Francis. "Salvation and the New Testament." In *Windows on Salvation*, edited by Donald English, 28–41. London: Darton, Longman & Todd, 1994.

Zalot, Jozef D. *The Roman Catholic Church and Economic Development in Sub-Saharan Africa: Voices Yet Unheard in a Listening World*. New York: University Press of America, 2002.

Key Words

African Church	*Populorum Progressio*
African Synod	poverty
Catholic Social Teaching	social capital
development	social mission
Evangelii Gaudium	Vatican II

African Catholicism and Islam: Relationship and Tensions

Cosmas Ebo Sarbah

Just within a century, the religious demographics of sub-Saharan Africa have undergone a major transformation. In the early twentieth century, Muslims and Christians constituted a small minority in the region. The vast majority of the people on the continent were adherents of African indigenous religions. The Christian and Muslim populations together made up just a quarter of the entire population.[1] Recent reports, however, indicate that the Muslim population of the region has dramatically increased, from just about 11 million in 1900 to an estimated 240 million in 2010. The Christian population has seen even faster growth within the same period, increasing from about 7 million to almost 457 million. Today, about one-fifth of the world's Christians and one-seventh of the world's Muslims live in sub-Saharan Africa. Even though the Christian population appears to be twice that of the Muslim population in sub-Saharan Africa, on the whole the two religious traditions are roughly balanced.

Africa is considered to be not only a major stronghold of the Catholic Church; it is also her great resource.[2] Several reasons account for this fact. First, there has been rapid growth in the Catholic population on the continent. Second, African Catholicism has a powerful influence both on the continent and globally. And, third, the African missionary societies and the dioceses across the continent continue to send many missionaries to other areas of the world. Thus, increasing numbers of priests and religious men and women from Africa offer their services to needy dioceses across the world in what is often described as reverse evangelization.

The relationship between African Catholics and African Muslims has generally been positive. Despite this, the Vatican has recognized that sub-Saharan Africa has been a place of sporadic confrontation between Muslims and Christians.[3] The church has assigned a high priority to ensuring that Catholic–Muslim interactions do not lead to open conflict. It has encouraged African Catholics to actively engage in dialogue with Muslims. This process of engagement is not simple. Islam in Africa, like Christianity, is not a homogenous entity; it is composed of many branches and sects with doctrinal differences, some of which are quite ethnocentric. Many members of these groups are at any one time migrating from one place to another.[4] The essential internal differences characterizing both Islam and Christianity in Africa have produced many Muslim and Christian identities, which offer both opportunities and challenges for dialogue.

---

1. The World Religion Database (WRD) contains detailed statistics on religious affiliations for every country in the world.
2. Pope John Paul II, post-synodal apostolic exhortation *Ecclesia in Africa* §38 (hereinafter *EA*).
3. "Francis in Africa: Conquering Conflict with the Medicine of Mercy," *Catholic Voices Media* (November 24, 2015), https://cvcomment.org.
4. Brenner, *Muslim Identity and Social Change in Sub-Saharan Africa*, 11.

The Two Aspects of Evangelization in the Catholic Church: Proclamation and Dialogue

The church in Africa, as elsewhere, is mandated to engage in evangelization. The evangelizing mission of the church, which is derived from the Great Commission of the apostles (Matt 28:16–20), is a complex reality. The complexity of the church's mission or evangelism was underscored by Pope St. John Paul II in his address to the members of the Plenary Assembly of the Pontifical Council for Interreligious Dialogue in 1984. In this assembly, the pope declared, "Just as interreligious dialogue is one element in the mission of the Church, the proclamation of God's saving work in Our Lord Jesus Christ is another. . . . There can be no question of choosing one and ignoring or rejecting the other."[5] The Pontifical Council for Interreligious Dialogue identified the two main elements of the evangelizing mission of the church as proclamation and dialogue, describing them as two sides of the same coin. These two elements evolve from the two senses in which Pope Paul VI's apostolic exhortation *Evangelii Nuntiandi* understands evangelization.[6] In the transmission of the Christian faith, sincere attention must always be paid to the essential bond between these two elements. As it was put in *Evangelii Nuntiandi*, evangelization as proclamation and interreligious dialogue, far from being opposed, mutually support, complement, and nourish one another (§24). This means that in her evangelizing mission to Muslims, the church in Africa has to adopt a two-way approach: (1) proclamation; and (2) interreligious dialogue.

Proclamation is rooted in the narrow definition of evangelization, which is "the clear and unambiguous proclamation of the Lord Jesus" (*Evangelii Nuntiandi* §22), performed as a response to Jesus's Great Commission to the apostles (Matt 28:18–20; Mark 16:15–20). Proclamation has the sense of kerygma, the communication of the gospel message, and it may take a solemn and public form as on the day of Pentecost (see Acts 2:5–41), or it may occur in a simple private conversation (see Acts 8:30–38). It must be noted that proclamation usually has an institutional objective in the sense that it involves an invitation to make a commitment of faith in Jesus Christ and to enter through baptism into a community of believers, the church, which exists as an institution. Proclamation aims, ultimately, at effecting change in this community/institution and leads naturally to the work of catechesis in order to deepen the faith of the people. In the historical development of the church, proclamation has not only become the foundation and summit of evangelization (*Evangelii Nuntiandi* §27), but is almost synonymous with it.

According to the Pontifical Council for Interreligious Dialogue, interreligious dialogue, in the context of religious plurality, means "all positive and constructive interreligious relations with individuals and communities of other faiths which are directed at mutual understanding and enrichment in obedience to truth and respect for freedom."[7] This definition makes it clear that the quest for interreligious dialogue is essentially the quest for proper relationship between two or more religions.[8] Thus, interreligious dialogue is different from proclamation in the sense that it does not focus on immediate change in religious traditions. It seeks simply to engage people of other religions for mutual benefit. It also seeks to discover new spiritual insights and possibilities in the tradition of the other to enrich one's own community.[9] Interreligious dialogue as an aspect of evangelization seeks, above all, to "impact society" and the individuals within it even as they remain non-Christian. It targets the transformation of all humanity, even non-Christians, into a new human and spiritual reality (*Evangelii Nuntiandi* §27). Interreligious dialogue

---

5. Pope John Paul II, Address to the Plenary Assembly of the Pontifical Council for Interreligious Dialogue (1984).
6. Sarbah and Antwi, "Inter-Religious Dialogue," 39.
7. Cf. Segretariato per i Non-Cristiani, "L'atteggiamento della Chiesa di fronte ai seguaci di altre religioni."
8. Trouve, *Sixteen Documents of Vatican II*.
9. World Council of Churches, "Mission and Evangelism: An Ecumenical Affirmation," 43.

is grounded in the idea that institutional obstacles emanating from religious differences must not be allowed to impede the all-important evangelizing mission of the church.

Engaging in Dialogue with Muslims

Consequently, the church in Africa has become increasingly conscious of the "widening scope of her mission" to all people regardless of religious affiliation.[10] The participating bishops of the 1986 Association of Episcopal Conferences of Anglophone West Africa (AECAWA) acknowledged that the Catholic Church not only recognizes herself as the people of God (the leaven of society and the instrument of salvation for humanity); the church also exercises her mission outside her visible dimensions on a wide scale. The church engages in dialogue with members of other faiths and actively "cooperates with all and sundry in the social, educational, medical, and other fields of activity in order to promote love, justice, and peace."[11]

The two elements of evangelization described above took center stage at two major and relatively recent synods of bishops: the 1994 Special Assembly for Africa of the Synod of Bishops; and the Second Special Assembly for Africa of the Synod of Bishops (2009). The fathers of both synods stressed the need for evangelization in Africa as proclamation and dialogue, in light of the fact that the continent is plagued on all sides by outbreaks of hatred and violence, conflict and war (*EA* §59). In his post-synodal apostolic exhortation *Ecclesia in Africa* (1995), Pope John Paul II tasks African Catholics to commit to engaging in dialogue with all Muslims of goodwill, considering such engagement to be an integral part of the proclamation of the gospel (*EA* §66). A commitment to dialogue with members of other religious traditions, which hinges on the fundamental truth that all human beings belong to one great family because of the one Father of all, should be grounded in three principles: (1) respecting the values and religious traditions of each human based on the principle of freedom; (2) working together toward human progress and reconciliation, justice, and peace; and (3) raising our voices against unfair policies and practices, as well as against a lack of reciprocity in matters of religious freedom.[12]

While acknowledging and commenting on the complexity of the Muslim presence on the African continent, in his post-synodal apostolic exhortation *Africae Munus* (2011), Pope Benedict XVI recommends a multifaceted approach to both proclamation and interreligious dialogue on the continent.[13] This document highlights the unique role played by the social apostolate of the church in the socioeconomic lives of the African people. Stressing the non-institutional objective of interreligious dialogue, the pope highlights the need for the social apostolate, which provides key health and educational facilities. The church comes to the aid of those in need, be they Christian, Muslim, or animist.

It must be noted that Africa is the most religiously diverse continent in the world. In such an environment, religion is a double-edged sword. On the one hand, religion has been a source of tension and conflict both within and between religious traditions; on the other, it is a source of hope in sub-Saharan Africa, where religious leaders and movements are a major force in civil society and a key provider of relief and developmental assistance for the needy, particularly because of the widespread reality of failed states and collapsing government services. In this regard, relations with Muslims should involve the following three considerations: (1) Priority must be given to a dialogue of life and a partnership in social matters, with the aim of reconciliation, and initiatives promoting respect, friendship, collaboration, and reciprocity; (2) Models of dialogue ought to take into consideration the variety of situations and experiences relevant to people on the African

---

10. Association of Episcopal Conferences of Anglophone West Africa, *AECAWA Directory 1986*, 128.
11. Association of Episcopal Conferences of Anglophone West Africa, *AECAWA Directory 1986*, 128.
12. Dadosky, "Methodological Presuppositions for Engaging the Other in the Post-Vatican II Context," 9–24; Pope Francis, encyclical *Fratelli Tutti* §203.
13. Pope Benedict XVI, post-synodal apostolic exhortation *Africae Munus* (2011) §94 (hereinafter *AM*).

continent; and (3) Efforts must be made to honestly confront misunderstandings and difficulties by providing a better knowledge of Islam in the formation of priests, men and women religious, and the lay faithful.

Relationships with Muslims

No doubt, there are difficulties standing in the way of Christian–Muslim dialogue in Africa on both sides, including the Christian fear of political subjugation, on the one hand, and the Muslim suspicion of attempted spiritual domination by Christians, on the other.[14] Yet it must be said that there are Christians and Muslims who overcome these difficulties, who meet together, talk together, live together, work together, and pray together.[15] Though people who are engaging in dialogue in both faiths are in the minority, at least for now, the fact that they exist at all raises a question about the source of their courage to persevere despite criticism and setbacks.[16]

In spite of the small number of people actually participating in Christian–Muslim dialogue, there are notable regions of peaceful coexistence between Catholics and Muslims in sub-Saharan Africa.[17] These regions include Ghana, southwestern Nigeria (mainly populated by the Yoruba ethnic group), and some parts of Kenya. In all these regions, Catholics and Muslims live together for the most part peacefully, sometimes sharing certain aspects of material culture such as dress, eating habits, and language, sometimes celebrating festivities together, and sometimes even sharing clergy. John Cardinal Onaiyekan of the Nigerian Catholic Bishops' Conference notes that "80 million Muslims and 80 million Christians live side by side in Nigeria in relative peace and harmony."[18] Various reasons have been given to explain the generally peaceful relations between Christians and Muslims in Africa. Some believe that it is because both of these missionary religions have been given about the same opportunity to engage constructively with Africans.[19] Others stress the pluralistic nature of African society.[20] Still others note that the faith and practices of both Christians and Muslims in most parts of Ghana, the Ivory Coast, Kenya, Tanzania, Benin, and southwestern Nigeria retain aspects of indigenous religion, which engenders a certain transreligious attitude and even doctrinal apathy.[21] Africans are noted for holding onto indigenous kinship structures that even today sometimes transcend religious ties.[22]

Various programs and activities focus on Catholic–Muslim dialogue and on building a citizenry in both faith traditions that possesses a communal consciousness and can sustain peaceful encounters for mutual benefit. For example, the Inter-Religious Dialogue Commission of AECAWA (IRDC)[23] undertakes activities like joint study sessions and joint research. A three-day study session organized by the IRDC once every year offers an opportunity for study papers to be presented and discussed by Muslims, Christians, and practitioners of African traditional religions.[24] These study sessions, which

---

14. Fitzgerald and Borelli, *Interfaith Dialogue*, 89–90.
15. Ratzinger, *Truth and Tolerance*; Fitzgerald and Borelli, *Interfaith Dialogue*, 29.
16. *AECAWA Directory 1986*, 161.
17. Trimingham, *Islam in West Africa*; Samwini, "The Need for and Importance of Dialogue of Life in Community Building."
18. Onaiyekan, *Seeking Common Grounds*, 88.
19. Bediako, "Christianity, Islam and the Kingdom of God," 4.
20. For Bishop Joseph Osei Bonsu's comments on the topic, see National Catholic Secretariat, *Ecclesia in Ghana*, 157.
21. Onaiyekan, *Seeking Common Grounds*.
22. Sanneh, *West African Christianity*, 221.
23. This commission is responsible for interreligious affairs under the Department of Ecumenical Relations and Inter-Religious Dialogue.
24. Some of the themes of the study sessions have been African Traditional Religious Movements (Lagos, Nigeria, 1996); Islam and Christianity on Human Development in West Africa (Nsawam, Ghana, 1997); Religion and Pursuit of Peace and Social Justice (Lagos, Nigeria, 1998); Christians, Muslims and Believers of African Traditional Religion and the Great Jubilee (Accra, Ghana, 1999); Inter-Religious Dialogue and Nation Building

highlight the need for peaceful coexistence among the religions, are especially relevant because both African Christianity and African Islam are still open to being influenced, positively or negatively, by Christian and Islamic ideas and faith from other continents.

The Catholic and Muslim communities of Africa are not walled off from other Africans. Each lives in the context of a larger community of nation, town, and village. Because of this, the activities, beliefs, practices, and laws of each should address not only the daily challenges of their own community, but the wider community as well. A Muslim or Catholic community that does not concern itself with the needs of non-Muslims or non-Christians falls short of what is needed. The two communities must strive to become more deeply rooted in the broader human community of Africa. This calls for Catholic–Muslim cooperation and collaboration.[25]

Toward the Holistic Development of Christians and Muslims

In order to promote the holistic development of Christian and Muslim students, the Catholic Church in Africa engages Muslims in dialogue.[26] The Catholic side of this dialogue adopts approaches that look beyond the institution of the church or the Catholic fold to bring out the best in people outside its boundaries. The church's interlocutors include imams, sheikhs, and others from strong Muslim families, for whom Islam is not only a cherished, inherited tradition and a source of pride but also a means of livelihood. They also include everyday people whose ethnic groups (the Fulani, the Hausa, and the Kotokoli, among others) are traditionally linked with Islam in sub-Saharan Africa and who have been socialized to reject essential Christian doctrines like the Trinity and the Incarnation as human innovations and to reject the Bible as a fabrication.[27] This approach to dialogue entails making available to Muslims church facilities like schools and health and retreat centers, and providing for other pastoral needs.[28]

Educating the Population

This spirit of dialogue includes human resource development; as part of this, the church in Africa has embarked on a journey to transform societies by establishing educational facilities.[29] As in other places in the world, Catholic education in Africa has seen increased enrollment, not only of Christians but also of Muslims. Muslims patronize Catholic schools in Africa because of the high-quality education they offer at both the pretertiary and tertiary levels. The increased number of Muslims in Catholic schools can also be explained by the fact that these schools have virtually abandoned their objective of open proselytization and conversion.[30] Although Catholic schools were established in the past primarily to support evangelization efforts, this is no longer the case.[31]

Catholic mission primary and high schools in Ghana, Nigeria, Egypt, Kenya, and Tunisia, both private and public, no longer cater mainly to Christian children. They enroll a significant number of Muslims every year. In some Catholic schools in Muslim majority areas in Ghana such as St.

(Ibadan, Nigeria, 2000); Religion, Violence and Peace in West Africa (Accra, Ghana, 2002); Offer Forgiveness and Receive Peace: A Challenge to Multi-Religious Society (Kaduna, Nigeria, 2003); and Peace: Preachers and Politicians (Tamale, Ghana, 2004).

25. See Taylor, "Community Relationship between Christians and Muslims."
26. Samwini, *Muslim Resurgence in Ghana since 1950*, 76.
27. Dharmaraj and Dharmaraj, *Christianity and Islam: A Missiological Encounter*, 78.
28. Vatican II, Dogmatic Constitution on the Church (*Lumen Gentium*) §17.
29. Akyeampong, "Christianity in Ghana," x.; see also Buah, *A History of Ghana*, 100; and Foster, *Education and Social Change in Ghana*, 81; Garnier and Schafer, "Educational Model and Expansion of Enrolments in Sub-Saharan Africa," 153–75.
30. Reichmuth, "Islamic Learning and Its Interaction with 'Western' Education in Ilorin, Nigeria," 179–97; Nuamah, *Case for Educating the Muslim Girl-Child*, 36; Abubakre, "Academic and Non-Academic Study of Islam in Sub-Saharan Africa," 258.
31. Zinsou, "Compendium and the Pastoral Promotion of Human Rights in Africa," 210, 211.

Martha's Catholic (Kasoa) and Abura Roman Catholic primary schools, Muslim pupils sometimes make up more than 50 percent of the students. Prestigious Catholic high schools like Holy Child College, St. Rose's Senior High, and St. Augustine College admit non-Christians, some of whom are Muslims. Catholic teacher-training colleges such as OLA Training College (Cape Coast) and Holy Child Training College (Takoradi) admit Muslim teacher-trainees, some of whom, upon completion, offer their services in Catholic schools.

In these schools, students are exposed to, among other things, Catholic practices and in particular the Mass. They say the Angelus and the Lord's Prayer at the morning assemblies. The ultimate purpose for these Catholic observances is, as has already been stated, not conversion—most of the Muslim students remain Muslim even upon completion of their courses. Students are introduced to these Catholic practices solely because these practices are part of the routine at a Catholic school for the purposes of enhancing knowledge and discipline. Still, religious rights issues are occasionally implicated by introducing non-Christians, and Muslims in particular, to these practices and to compulsory church activities in the schools. Many have argued, on the basis of concerns about religious rights, that Catholic schools should be open only to Catholics and Christians. Suffice it to say that Catholics train non-Christian students in their schools not only for the benefit of these students and their communities but also as part of their Catholic mission. Non-Catholic Christian and Muslim students are trained in Catholic schools to embrace universal principles, not only those grounded in Christian values and professional ethics. Many Muslims trained in this environment may not turn out to be Christians, but they are certainly imbued with core values they will retain in their future lives and careers.

Hospital and Clinic Apostolate

In addition to educational facilities, the church, as part of its apostolate, operates hospital and clinic services, which, in the course of strengthening the health of all citizens, help build the basis for peaceful coexistence between Christians and Muslims. The Catholic Church operates 17 percent of the health care institutions present on the continent.[32] In order to coordinate the services and activities of these facilities, National Catholic Health Services (NCHS) has branches in archdioceses and dioceses in almost every African country. Catholic health facilities have been established as a continuation of the public healing ministry of Jesus Christ. The goal is to provide health care services for the poor, the neglected, and the marginalized segments of society regardless of religious affiliations. These various health centers seek to empower the people they serve to take ownership of their own individual and collective health needs through consulting medical professionals who operate on the basis of solid ethical and moral standards, and who are conscientious, professionally competent, strongly motivated, and united in their common respect for fundamental human values. Among the policy objectives is the application of Catholic ethics and morals in the delivery of health care in as many situations as possible. Those working in Catholic health centers all over Africa, including doctors, nurses, and ancillary staff, promise to abide by the Christian principles of these centers, no matter their religious backgrounds.

Catholic mission hospitals and clinics abound in Ghana, the Ivory Coast, Senegal, Kenya, and Botswana. St. Dominic Catholic Hospital (Akwatia), the Obstetric Fistula Centre (Mankessim), and Eikwe Catholic Hospital (all in Ghana) provide health services to all regardless of religious persuasion. Some facilities like St. Francis Xavier Hospital (Assin Fosu) and St. Luke Catholic Hospital (Apam) in Ghana are the only hospitals in their districts. The Mankessim facility provides specialized help for women. St. Dominic Catholic Hospital, established in 1960 by the Dominican Sisters of Speyer (Germany), operates a special clinic for the 25 percent of outpatient cases that are eye-related. The personnel of eye clinics operated by the Catholic Church across Africa undertake intensive outreach programs to surrounding villages and schools to enhance access to eye care services for all people.

---

32. Nsiah, "Catholicism in Postcolonial Ghana," 5.

Encounters Leading to Spiritual Growth

In Africa, Catholics, other Christians, and Muslims have reached a stage in their relationships in which they need to find a way of making basic, necessary demands of each other. These demands include challenging each other to concentrate their resources on programs and activities that promote the core values (togetherness and friendship, forgiveness, patience, peace, love and mercy, and hospitality) of their religious traditions as enshrined in their sacred texts. Muslims and Catholics ought also to challenge each other to learn the tenets of their respective faiths and to speak about them truthfully.[33] Thus, an appropriate, non-institutional Christian approach should be to acknowledge the presence of the "seeds of the word" in Islam and the "riches which a generous God has distributed among them too" (*Ad Gentes* §11). Christians should assist Muslims to live in accordance with the riches that are readily available to them, and even hold them accountable for doing so. The leaders of the two faith communities need to acknowledge the essential differences inherent in the doctrines, practices, and spiritualities of these faiths in their sermons and teachings, noting that differences between Catholicism and Islam should not always be seen as a liability, but are sometimes an asset.

Tensions between Catholics and Muslims

Despite the numerous programs and activities put in place by both Catholic and Muslim communities to actively engage each other for peaceful coexistence and mutual advancement, there have been instances when tensions and even open confrontations have seriously impaired the relationship between them in Africa. According to a report by the German Institute of Global and Area Studies, the last two decades have seen an upsurge in religious tensions and sometimes violence in West, Central, and East Africa.[34] Some tensions have been contained by the efforts of Christians and Muslims, but it is also true that many other situations have escalated. Christian–Muslim clashes are becoming a major concern on the continent because they have the potential to generate instability and insecurity.

Consequently, Catholics and Muslims are engaged in dialogue to address these tensions. Some of these issues are particularly frequent between communities that identify themselves solely according to their religion, ethnicity, language, sect, or race. Of all these tensions, the ones that are most difficult to confront are the ones generated by historical antecedents.[35] The communal violence between Christians and Muslims in northern Nigeria is largely caused by historical antecedents that date back to the period of slavery and the slave trade in the thirteenth and fourteenth centuries. Muslim traders and herders (mostly from the Hausa-Fulani ethnic group) preyed on other indigenous groups for slaves. The indigenous people found in Christianity an attractive alternative to Islam, their oppressors' religion. The eventual suspicion and mistrust engendered between the two religious communities have existed to this day.[36] In southern Ghana, Muslim communities of Wangara, Kotokoli, and Fulani are usually found in the Zongo settlements that are often located on the outskirts of mainly Christian and indigenous villages and towns, including Akan, Ewe, and Ga. The failure of these Muslims, unlike their Muslim counterparts in the northern parts of the country, to integrate and become involved in local politics and socioreligious affairs has created long-standing and worsening tension between Christians and Muslims.[37] As a result, Ghanaians have seen eruptions of violence between Christians and Muslims and among Muslims in towns like Agona Nyakrom, Takoradi, Kumasi, Oda, and Wenchi.[38] According

---

33. Abashiya and Ulea, *Christianity and Islam*, vii.
34. Pew Research Center, *Tolerance and Tension: Islam and Christianity in Sub-Saharan Africa*; Basedau and Vüllers, "Religion and Armed Conflict in Sub-Saharan Africa, 1990 to 2008."
35. Onaiyekan, *Seeking Common Grounds*, 45.
36. Brenner, *Muslim Identity and Social Change in Sub-Saharan Africa*, 124.
37. Schildkrout, *People of the Zongo*, 69–265.
38. Amoah, "African Indigenous Religions and Interreligious Relationships," 4.

to James Anquandah, between 1987 and 1989 there were twenty reported cases of intra- and interreligious clashes in Ghana that resulted in the loss of life and property.[39]

In Ghana, as in other African countries, migration, especially from other West African countries, particularly Niger, Mali, Sudan, Burkina Faso, Nigeria, and the Ivory Coast, has led to significant increases in the Muslim population of the Zongo communities. Migrants engage in small trading ventures in these communities and eventually settle there. Muslim migrants also work in the mining areas and on farms, sometimes tending herds of cattle or goats. They eventually make demands on lands and other services that some local Christians deem outrageous.[40] The activities of the Muslim Fulani herdsmen on farmlands have been a particular cause for concern among Christian farmers in Ghana, the Ivory Coast, Kenya, and Nigeria. It is noteworthy that misguided suspicion fueled by ethnic migrations is often at the heart of Christian–Muslim communal tensions in Africa.

Tensions Caused by Dysfunctional Governments

Dysfunctional governments have led to a more recent wave of communal religious tensions in sub-Saharan Africa.[41] Governments in the region have repeatedly proven to be incapable of providing much-needed social infrastructure facilities. Thus, underlying the religious rage and conflicts in these countries are genuine, long-standing political grievances as a result of failures of the political elite and their attendant evils of corruption, acute lack of social infrastructure, unemployment, and abject poverty. Minority religious extremist groups such as Boko Haram in Nigeria and Cameroon, Ansar Dine in Mali, and al-Shaba'ab in Kenya and Somalia often exploit these already dire situations to their advantage. Such groups have become a threat to national and communal security. Boko Haram, which began as a peaceful religious movement in the northeastern city of Maiduguri in Bono State, has introduced a new dimension of religious tension and conflict into Nigeria. In 2011, the group orchestrated and claimed responsibility for the bombing of a United Nations office building in Abuja, which killed eighteen city dwellers. In the same year, the group staged a bomb attack on the police headquarters in Abuja and another attack at St. Theresa Catholic Church on Christmas Day, in Madalla, Niger State, which killed more than forty worshipers.[42] Often we hear that the members of Boko Haram are not Muslim, which means that the group has transformed itself, over time, from a religious movement into a political one.

Tensions between Christians and Muslims in 2013 in the Central African Republic led to serious political upheaval, which turned into savage violence. The politico-ethnic failure there resulted in interethnic and interreligious conflict between two main militia groups: the Anti-Balaka (militia groups of predominantly Christian and indigenous religions) and the Seleka (an Islamic rebel group). The Seleka took over the government in late 2013 and attacked and massacred non-Muslim villages, plunging the country into a brutal sectarian war.[43] The United Nations' 2013 report on conflict in the sub-Saharan Africa indicated that the communal religious war that ensued in the Central African Republic took the lives of thousands of inhabitants, displacing over 440,000, a significant number of whom became refugees in neighboring Cameroon, the Democratic Republic of the Congo, Chad, and the Republic of the Congo.

Christian and Muslim leaders actively engage governments in the sub-region in order to counter and prevent the spread of violence triggered by defective regimes. The Catholic Bishops Conferences are at the forefront of over twenty-three national interreligious councils in sub-Saharan Africa who are in ongoing discussions with gov-

---

39. Anquandah, *Agenda Extraordinaire: 80 Years of the Christian Council of Ghana*, 70.
40. Sarbah and Antwi, "Inter-Religious Dialogue."
41. Sturm, "Crossing the Boundaries," 1–19.
42. Onaiyekan, *Seeking Common Grounds*, 91.
43. The United Nations announced in 2013 that it was dispatching another one thousand soldiers to bring the total peacekeeping force in this desperately impoverished country to 13,000.

ernment officials for the purpose of resolving interreligious conflicts.[44] Suffice it to say that some governments in Africa have adopted pragmatic policies to address the concerns of the marginalized in their countries. For instance, in 2018 the government of Ghana set up a fund with $50 million seed money for critical interventions in deprived communities in the Zongos. The fund, according to the sector minister, Dr. Mustapha Abdul Hamid, has succeeded in recruiting over three thousand Arabic instructors for some basic schools in inner-city communities. With critical support from the World Reader (a Non-Governmental Organization), the fund also built or renovated schools across the country and donated a mobile library and books to a school at Sabon-Zongo in Accra. In order to develop interest of the youth in football and other sporting activities, several modern AstroTurf football pitches have been put in place by the fund in the Walewale (Northern Region), Kyebi (Eastern Region), Asewase (Ashanti Region), and the Fadama (Greater Accra Region), in addition to green parks in Oda, Salaga, Bolgatanga, Yeji, and other places. The Catholic Bishops' Conference of Ghana has applauded the government's establishment of a Ministry of Inner City and Zongo Development and is keen on monitoring the efficient implementation of the fund and its policies.

Tensions Resulting from Aggressive Evangelization

To avoid confrontation and ensure cordial relations, Christian and Muslim missionaries in Africa avoided direct conversion of the other faith's members for years. Instead, the Christian missionaries of evangelization and Muslim *da'wah*[45] agents have concentrated all their efforts, resources, and time on "winning" practitioners of African Indigenous Religions. The Catholic Church, one of the first Christian churches to establish missions in the northern part of Ghana, worked primarily among ethnic groups who for various reasons had developed an aversion to Islam. In northern Ghana, the Roman Catholic mission was begun by the missionaries commonly known as the White Fathers in 1906, at Navrongo among the Kassena-Nankana people.[46] Thus, the church in Ghana directed all its activities toward the evangelization of non-Muslims, particularly adherents of indigenous religions. On the Muslim side, until the advent of the Ahmadiyya Movement in 1921, very little was known about active Muslim *da'wah* involving Christians in the country. Their main target groups were also indigenous religious believers. The Muslims were probably influenced by the *dhimma* (People of The Book) status of Christians,[47] which ensured their protection and made them not the prime targets of Islamic *da'wah* or even jihād.[48]

However, this nonconfrontational strategy adopted by both Christian and Muslim missionary agents, which gave rise to a generally cordial Christian–Muslim relationship in sub-Saharan Africa, is fast changing with a rise in attempts by each faith to gain converts from the other side.[49] More extreme forms of Christian evangelization and Islamic *da'wah* are gaining strength in Africa, raising the risk of more confrontation, especially as the two sides compete for converts from each other's camps, in light of the shrinking numbers of followers of indigenous religions.

The aggressive conversion efforts of both Christians and Muslims have often been met with violence. One wonders how Christians and Muslims will be able to undertake their unique "missionary mandates" without necessarily endangering communal peace and security. In this case, it is important that the concept of "mission" be properly understood by missionary agents and carried out in a manner that demonstrates respect and integrity.[50] Christian missions and Islamic *da'wah* operate in their lowest forms when they are orchestrated on the basis of religious propaganda that is often will-

---

44. Onaiyekan, *Seeking Common Grounds*, 68.
45. *Da'wah* is an Islamic term for proselytizing non-Muslims.
46. Sackey, *Beginnings of Mission on the Gold Coast*, 279.
47. The Holy Qur'an, Sūrah 29:46.
48. Ye'or, *Dhimmi*, 45.
49. Onaiyekan, *Seeking Common Grounds*, 44.
50. Arne, "The Concept and Practice of Christian Mission," 16–26.

fully ignorant and engenders malignant prejudice against the other community.

Missionary activities carried out in such negative manners are not only depraved and vile but also defective. They tend eventually to create tension and acrimony, with dire consequences for the larger community. In the light of this, John Paul II, in his encyclical *Redemptoris Missio*, places "life of witness" at the heart of evangelization. The pope touts a "witness of a Christian life" as the most effective missionary tool in contemporary times, a tool that ought to be described as "the very life of the missionary, of the Christian family, and of the ecclesial community" (§42). It is not a stretch to say that a witness of a good Muslim life should be at the heart of the Muslim missionary as well.

Many scholars and commentators, however, have been highly critical of much of what occurs in contemporary missions and *da'wah* activities. Farid Esack, a South African Muslim scholar, contends that much of the current discourse about African theology and Christian–Muslim dialogue in Africa could be interpreted as an effort to continue the nineteenth-century colonial fight for territory in Africa. Esack asserts that this time, the fight is between the Christian-Europe and Muslim-Arab worlds.[51]

Since the oil boom of the 1970s, oil-rich Arab countries like Saudi Arabia and Iran have sponsored a renewed campaign to Islamicize Africa through missionary, philanthropic, and governmental activities, especially in countries with Muslim heads of state.[52] Sudan, for instance, experienced a twenty-one-year civil war that has been attributed to Muslim-Arab government imposition of strict Sharī'a (Islamic) law on that country, where over four million Catholics constitute approximately 13 percent of the entire population. The Sudan war claimed over two million lives. Furthermore, tens of thousands of Muslims and Christians have been killed across religious lines during conflicts in Liberia, Ivory Coast, and Nigeria.[53] In Nigeria, riots erupted in the year 2000 when mainly Muslim northern states with a significant Christian and Catholic population implemented the Shari'a, with entrenched provisions for punishments of amputation and death by stoning.[54]

The implementation of Sharī'a either at the regional or national level in general in Africa and in particular northern Nigeria and Sudan has been described by the Ghanaian scholar Rabiatu Ammah as a "search for a voice, a search for justice and a search for identity," over and against the Christian and colonial legacy of the African continent.[55] However, Ammah wonders whether the mode and manner in which and the extent to which Sharī'a has been applied to African societies thus far does not "undermine or contradict the very principle of justice which the Sharī'a espouses," and whether this has been done to advance Muslim and Arab control.[56] Muslims have often maintained that the Sharī'a in no way limits the religious freedom of Christians, as it is meant to apply only to Muslims,[57] but human rights issues have nevertheless been raised in areas in Africa where the Sharī'a has been implemented. On the other hand, Josiah Idowu-Fearon, the bishop of Sokoto, has voiced the concerns of some Nigerian Muslims who feel that the state and the Christian faith are inseparable, with one being an extension of the other,[58] especially given the organization of the week with Saturday and Sunday as the weekend days off, the long school recesses for Christmas and Easter and short breaks for Id al-Fitr and Id al-Adha, and the design of school uniforms for children. To this, Christians often retort that public funds are used to sponsor the Hajj. Situations where Christian or Islamic structures and ideals are forced on citizens

---

51. Esack, "Islamic Da'wah and Christian Mission," 27.
52. Hiskett, *Course of Islam in Africa*, 74.
53. Konate, "Question of Religion in the Ivorian Crisis," 8–44.
54. Konate, "Question of Religion in the Ivorian Crisis," 8–44; Ammah, "Christian-Muslim Relations in Contemporary Sub-Saharan Africa," 150. See also Ryan, "In My End Is My Beginning."
55. Ammah, "Christian and Muslim Relations in Contemporary Sub-Saharan Africa," 150.
56. Ammah, "Christian and Muslim Relations in Contemporary Sub-Saharan Africa," 150.
57. Mahmoud, "When Shari'a Governs," 275–86.
58. Idowu-Fearon, "The Shari'a Debate in the Northern States of Nigeria," 7–8.

as common norms must be immediately addressed to ensure an even playing field for all, irrespective of religious backgrounds.

In 2002, more than two hundred people died in Christian–Muslim riots triggered by Muslim opposition to the staging of the Miss World competition in Nigeria, which was interpreted by Muslims as an attempt to unduly spread Western dominance and modern values. It is arguable that al-Qaeda's terrorist bombings of the U.S. embassies in Kenya and Tanzania in 1998, which claimed the lives of hundreds of Muslims and Christians, were bolstered by the idea that diplomatic establishments and missions constitute evidence of and extensions of Western and Christian dominance and continuing control over the African continent.[59] This kind of thinking, engaged in by some religious practitioners, is a major obstacle to interreligious dialogue as well as to peace and security. In an era when missionary activities are seen as efforts to perpetuate European and Arab control over the African continent, African Christian–Muslim dialogue has become all the more relevant. African Christians and Muslims must make the effort to join hands and deal with the repercussions of the Europe-Arab onslaught. Interreligious or intercultural dialogue is the best means to preserve what is purest, best, and noblest in Africa's multifaceted indigenous cultures.[60]

Conclusion

Catholic–Muslim dialogue in Africa aims ultimately at promoting peaceful coexistence on the continent. Thus, models of dialogue focus on building up both the Catholic and Muslim citizenry for the betterment and continued survival of the larger society. In addition to pursuing initiatives that will build on and sustain existing good relations, Catholic and Muslim organizations and networks have adopted crisis-driven models focusing on certain regions and situations of religious tension and conflict. Such models explore the possible causes of intra- and interreligious controversies and propose solutions for calming or addressing them. The Catholic Church, for example, is at the forefront of providing relief initiatives and services in Cameroon and is being besieged by refugees fleeing Christian and Muslim militias in that country, who have killed indiscriminately, sparing neither Muslim nor Christian, adult nor child, since the overthrow of a Christian president by an ostensibly Muslim coalition.[61] In an earlier era, South African Muslims joined South African Christians in their fight against apartheid, and both played a vital role in the period of national reconciliation.[62] In the early 1990s Muslim and Christian leaders in Liberia took the initiative to set up the Interreligious Council of Liberia to work toward peace in that country.[63] The Christian Council of Ghana established peace committees at regional and local levels in the northern part of that country in 2002 after war broke out. These committees, which were non-partisan, non-ethnic, and non-religious, were able to carry out their duties with a high level of impartiality.[64] The Centre for Conflict Transformation and Peace Studies (CECOTAPS), supported by Catholic Relief Services, was founded in 1999 by the Catholic Diocese of Damongo in response to the growing number of violent conflicts in the three northern regions of Ghana. CECOTAPS is a faith-based, nonprofit, peace-building institution committed to the just and peaceful resolution of violent conflicts.[65]

Future academic research should be geared toward critical studies of both the positive and neg-

---

59. Onaiyekan, *Seeking Common Grounds,* 44.
60. Dixon, "What Causes Civil Wars?," 4; Møller, *Religion and Conflict in Africa.*
61. Sarbah, "Interrogating the Approaches of Interreligious Dialogue in West Africa," 378.
62. Haron, "Christian–Muslim Relations in South Africa," 265.
63. York, "Christian–Muslim Collaboration in Liberia"; Abimbola, "Religion, World Order and Peace," 307. See also Ayandokun, "Beyond the Religious Crisis," 285.
64. Anquandah, *Agenda Extraordinaire: 80 Years of the Christian Council of Ghana,* 75.
65. Despite the effectiveness of these and other initiatives, the Catholic Church failed the test of peacemaking during the 1994 genocide in Rwanda, where some churches that offered sanctuary were turned into slaughterhouses and some Catholic priests participated in the killings. Longman, "Church Politics and the Genocide in Rwanda."

ative effects of the activities and initiatives of interfaith networks across the continent. Other research should explore critical models for advancing the interests of African societies in general. A strong sense of communitarianism is necessary to resolve any excessive competition and tension between the Christian and Muslim communities and to help them see themselves as partners or associates whose activities ought to complement each other to promote the common interest.

Bibliography

Abashiya, Chris Shuhris, and Ayuba Jalaba Ulea. *Christianity and Islam: A Plea for Understanding and Tolerance*. Nigeria: Justice, Peace and Reconciliation Movement, 1999.

Abimbola, Wande. "Religion, World Order and Peace: An Indigenous African Perspective." *Cross Currents: 2010 Association for Religion and Intellectual Life* (September 2010).

Abubakre, Razaq Deremi. "The Academic and Non-Academic Study of Islam in Sub-Saharan Africa: Nigeria as a Case Study." In *Study of Religions in Africa: Past, Present and Prospects*, edited by Jan Platvoet, James Cox, and Jacob Olupona. Cambridge: Roots & Branches, 1996.

Akyeampong, Emmanuel K. "Christianity in Ghana: An Introduction." In *Christianity in Ghana: A Postcolonial History*, Vol. 1, edited by J. Kwabena Asamoah-Gyadu. Legon-Accra: Sub-Saharan Publishers, 2018.

Al-Faruqi, Ismama. *Islam and Other Faiths*. Leicester: Islamic Foundation, 1998.

Ammah, Rabiatu. "Christian–Muslim Relations in Contemporary Sub-Saharan Africa." *Islam and Christian–Muslim Relations* 18.2 (2007): 139–53.

Amoah, Elizabeth. "African Indigenous Religions and Interreligious Relationships." Paper presented at Westminster College, Oxford, October 22, 1998.

Anquandah, James. *Agenda Extraordinaire: 80 Years of the Christian Council of Ghana*. Accra: Asempa, 2009.

Arne, Ruvin. "The Concept and Practice of Christian Mission." In *Christian Mission and Islamic Da'wah: Proceedings of the Chambesy Dialogue Consultation*, 16–26. Leicester, UK: Islamic Foundation, 1982.

Asamoah-Gyadu, J. Kwabena, ed. *Christianity in Ghana: A Postcolonial History*, Vol. 1. Legon-Accra: Sub-Saharan Publishers, 2018.

Association of Episcopal Conferences of Anglophone West Africa. *AECAWA Directory 1986*. Lagos: AECAWA Secretariat, 1986.

Ayandokun, O. Esther. "Beyond the Religious Crisis: Building a Tension-Free Society in Nigeria." In *Our Burning Issues: A Pan-African Response*. Nairobi: All Africa Conference of Churches, 2013.

Basedau, Matthias, and Johannes Vüllers. "Religion and Armed Conflict in Sub-Saharan Africa, 1990 to 2008—Results from a New Database." Paper prepared for presentation at the Standing Group on International Relations (SGIR), 7th Pan-European Conference on IR, Stockholm, September 9–11, 2010, German Institute of Global and Area Studies, Neuer Jungfernstieg, Hamburg, Germany, https://standinggroups.ecpr.eu/sgir/.

Bediako, Kwame. "Christianity, Islam and the Kingdom of God: Rethinking Their Relationship from an African Perspective." *Journal of African Thought* 7 (2004).

Benedict XVI, Pope. Address to the Roman Curia (December 21, 2012): *AAS* 105 (2006).

———. *Africae Munus* [Post-synodal Apostolic Exhortation on the Church in Africa in Service of Reconciliation, Justice and Peace; November 19, 2011]. Vatican City: Libreria Editrice Vaticana, 2011. www.vatican.va.

Brenner, Louis, ed. *Muslim Identity and Social Change in Sub-Saharan Africa*. London: Hurst, 1994.

Buah, F. K. A. *History of Ghana*. Revised and updated. Malaysia: Macmillan, 1998.

Dadosky, John D. "Methodological Presuppositions for Engaging the Other in the Post-Vatican II Context: Insights from Ignatius and Lonergan." *Journal of Inter-Religious Dialogue* Issue 3 (Spring 2010): 9–24.

Dharmaraj, Glory, and Jacob Dharmaraj. *Christianity and Islam: A Missiological Encounter*. Delhi: ISPCK, 1999.

Dixon, Jeffrey. "What Causes Civil Wars? Integrating Quantitative Research Findings." *International Studies Review* 11 (2009): 707–35.

Esack, Farid. "Islamic Da'wah and Christian Mission: A Muslim Perspective." In *Christian–Muslim Encounter in Africa*, edited by K. T. August and C. Sauer, 21–30. Johannesburg, South Africa: AcadSA Publishing, 2007.

Fitzgerald, Michael L., and John Borelli. *Interfaith Dialogue: A Catholic View*. Maryknoll, NY: Orbis Books, 2006.

Foster, Philip. *Education and Social Change in Ghana*. London: Routledge & Kegan Paul, 1965.

Francis, Pope. *Fratelli Tutti* [Encyclical on Fraternity and Social Friendship; October 4, 2020]. Vatican City: Libreria Editrice Vaticana, 2020. www.vatican.va.

Garnier, Maurice, and Mark Schafer. "Educational Model and Expansion of Enrolments in Sub-Saharan Africa." *Sociology of Education* 79.2 (2006): 153–75.

Haron, Muhammad. "Christian–Muslim Relations in South Africa (circa 1986–2004): Charting Out a Pluralist Path." *Islam and Christian Muslim Relations* 18.2 (2007): 257–73.

Hiskett, Mervyn. *The Course of Islam in Africa*. Edinburgh: University Press, 1994.

Idowu-Fearon, J. "The Shari'a Debate in the Northern States of Nigeria and Its Implication for West African Sub-Region Ghana." In *From the Cross to the Crescent*, edited by J. A. Mbillah and J. Chesworth, 15–24. Nairobi: PROCMURA, 2004.

John Paul II, Pope. Address to the Plenary Assembly of the Pontifical Council for Interreligious Dialogue, 1984.

———. *Ecclesia in Africa* [Post-synodal Apostolic Exhortation on the Church in Africa and Its Evangelizing Mission toward the Year 2000; September 14, 1995]. Vatican City: Libreria Editrice Vaticana, 1995. www.vatican.va.

———. *Redemptoris Missio* [Encyclical on the Permanent Validity of the Church's Missionary Mandate; December 7, 1990]. Vatican City: Libreria Editrice Vaticana, 1990. www.vatican.va.

Konate, Yacouba. "The Question of Religion in the Ivorian Crisis." In *Conflict: What Has Religion Got to Do with It? An African–European Dialogue*, 8–44. Accra: Woeli Publishing Services, 2004.

Longman, Timothy. "Church Politics and the Genocide in Rwanda." *Journal of Religion in Africa* 31.2 (2001): 163–86.

Mahmoud, M. "When Shari'a Governs: The Impasse of Religious Relationships in Sudan." *Islam and Christian–Muslim Relations* 18.2 (2007): 275–86.

McAuliffe, Jane Dammen. *Qur'anic Christians: An Analysis of Classical and Modern Exegesis*. New York: Cambridge University Press, 1991.

Møller, Bjørn. *Religion and Conflict in Africa, with a Special Focus on East Africa*. DIIS Report 2006: 6. Copenhagen: Danish Institute for International Studies, 2006.

National Catholic Secretariat. *Ecclesia in Ghana: On the Church in Ghana and Its Evangelising Mission in the Third Millennium*. First National Catholic Pastoral Congress, 1997.

Nsiah, Alice M. "Catholicism in Postcolonial Ghana." In *Christianity in Ghana: A Postcolonial History*, Vol. 1, edited by J. Kwabena Asamoah-Gyadu. Legon-Accra: Sub-Saharan Publishers, 2018.

Nuamah, Ishaak Ibrahim. *A Case for Educating the Muslim Girl-Child*. Accra-Ghana: Dezine Focus, 2001.

Onaiyekan, O. John. *Seeking Common Grounds: Inter-Religious Dialogue in Africa*. Nairobi: Paulines Publications Africa, 2013.

Paul VI, Pope. *Evangelii Nuntiandi* [Apostolic Exhortation on the theme of Catholic Evangelization; December 8, 1975]. Vatican City: Libreria Editrice Vaticana, 1975. www.vatican.va.

Pew Research Center. "Tolerance and Tension: Islam and Christianity in Sub-Saharan Africa." April 15, 2010. www.pewforum.org.

Ryan, P. J. "In My End Is My Beginning: Muslim and Christian Traditions at Cross-Purposes in Contemporary Nigeria." In *Muslim–Christian Encounters in Africa*, edited by B. F. Soares, 187–220. Leiden: Brill, 2006.

Ratzinger, Joseph Cardinal. *Truth and Tolerance: Christian Belief and World Religions*. Translated by Henry Taylor. San Francisco: Ignatius Press, 2004.

Reichmuth, Stefan. "Islamic Learning and Its Interaction with 'Western' Education in Ilorin, Nigeria." In *Muslim Identity and Social Change in Sub-Saharan Africa*, edited by Louis Brenner, 179–97. London: Hurst, 1994..

Sackey, Anthony Kofi. *The Beginnings of Mission on the Gold Coast*. Zurich: LIT, 2018.

Samwini, Nathan. *The Muslim Resurgence in Ghana since 1950: Its Effects upon Muslims and Muslim–Christian Relations*. Berlin: LIT, 2006.

———. "The Need for and Importance of Dialogue of Life in Community Building: The Case of Selected West African Nations." *Journal of Interreligious Studies* 6.6 (2011).

Sanneh, Lamin. *West African Christianity*. Maryknoll, NY: Orbis Books, 1983.

Sarbah, Cosmas Ebo. "Interrogating the Approaches of Interreligious Dialogue in West Africa." *Journal of Ecumenical Studies* 51.3 (2016): 364–85.

Sarbah, Cosmas Ebo, and Emmanuel Kojo Ennin Antwi. "Inter-Religious Dialogue: A Non-Institutional Approach to the New Evangelisation in Ghana." *International Journal of African Catholicism* 11.1 (2021): 25–46.

Schildkrout, Enid. *The People of the Zongo: The Transformation of Ethnic Identities in Ghana*. Cambridge and New York: Cambridge University Press, 1978.

Segretariato per i Non-Cristiani. "L'atteggiamento della Chiesa di fronte ai seguaci di altre religioni: Riflessioni e orientamenti su dialogo e missione." In *Enchiridion Vaticanum: Documenti Ufficiali della Santa Sede 1983–1985*, 9:928–43. Testo ufficiale e versione Italiana. Bologna: Centro Editoriale Dehoniano, 1987.

Sturm, Douglas. "Crossing the Boundaries: On the Idea of Interreligious Dialogue and the Political Question." *Journal of Ecumenical Studies* 30.1 (Winter 1993): 1–19.

Taylor, John B. "Community Relationship between Christians and Muslims." In *Christian–Muslim Dialogue: Papers Presented at the Brooumana Consultation, July 12–18, 1973*, edited by S. J. Samartha and J. B. Taylor. Geneva: World Council of Churches.

Trimingham, J. Spencer. *Islam in West Africa*. Oxford: Clarendon Press, 1961.

Trouve, Marianne Lorraine, ed. *The Sixteen Documents of Vatican II*. Boston: Pauline Books and Media, 1999.

Vatican Council II. *Ad Gentes* [Decree on the Church's Missionary Activity; 1965]. www.vatican.va.

———. *Lumen Gentium* [Dogmatic Constitution on the Church]. www.vatican.va.

World Council of Churches. "Mission and Evangelism: An Ecumenical Affirmation." 1982.

Ye'or, Bat. *The Dhimmi: Jews and Christians under Islam*. Rutherford, NJ: Fairleigh Dickinson University Press, 1985.

York, St. John. "Christian–Muslim Collaboration in Liberia." In *PROCMURA at 50 (1959–2009): Where We Came from, Where We Are Today, Where We Go from Here*, edited by Sigvard von Sicard, David Bone, and Johnson Mbillah, 236–42. Nairobi: PROCMURA Publications, 2009.

Zinsou, Anna Kone de Messe. "The Compendium and the Pastoral Promotion of Human Rights in Africa." In *Towards a New Evangelisation of African Society*, 210–11. Proceedings of the Continental Conference on the Presentation in Africa of the Compendium of the Social Doctrine of the Church, Dar es Salaam, Tanzania, August 27–30, 2008.

Suggested Readings

Gioia, Francesco, ed. *Interreligious Dialogue: The Official Teaching of the Catholic Church (1961–1995)*. Boston: Pauline, 1994.

Mazrui, Ali A. *The Africans: A Triple Heritage*. Boston: Little, Brown, 1986.

Michel, Thomas F. *A Christian View of Islam: Essays on Dialogue*. Edited by Irfan Omar. Maryknoll, NY: Orbis Books, 2010.

Troll, Christian W., and C. T. R. Hewer, eds. *Christian Lives Given to the Study of Islam*. New York: Fordham University Press, 2012.

Zinsou, Anna Kone de Messe. "The Compendium and the Pastoral Promotion of Human Rights in Africa." In *Towards a New Evangelisation of African Society*, 210–11. Proceedings of the Continental Conference on the Presentation in Africa of the Compendium of the Social Doctrine of the Church, Dar es Salaam, Tanzania, August 27–30, 2008.

Key Words

Africa
Christianity
dialogue
Islam
relationship
religious encounters
tension

Alongside One Another: African Catholicism and Ecumenism

Ikenna Paschal Okpaleke

Vatican II's Decree on Ecumenism, *Unitatis Redintegratio* (*UR*), marked the official endorsement of Catholic participation in ecumenism, but it is quite doubtful if it had any impact in Africa at the time it was issued on November 21, 1964. The council was convoked (1962–1965) at a time when most African countries were struggling with both political and religious emancipation.[1] Ecumenism in African Catholicism, as a result, has been shaped by the teachings of the Second Vatican Council, particularly by certain theological principles of ecumenism. Yet how these principles have been appropriated contextually in response to Africa's historical, cultural, and sociopolitical realities is open to diverse theological interpretations.[2]

In examining the approaches of the Catholic Church in Africa to ecumenism and theological development in African ecumenism, this chapter historically explores the various ecumenical practices, methods, as well as dispositions, that can be discovered in the faith and witnesses of African Catholics and churches. Central to our concern here is to raise the question of the possibility of "receptive ecumenism" as a principle of ecumenical learning that can guide churches of Africa in faith and action for and in developing ecumenical theologies in African Christianity.

The chapter also looks into the future of ecumenism in Africa through historical developments in the application of the teaching of Vatican II on ecumenism, beginning in Vatican II and extending into the papacy of Pope Francis. The chapter will particularly explore, in this regard, a version of intercultural hermeneutics that could offer an approach to doing ecumenical theology with a spirituality of openness. The chapter concludes by articulating some challenges facing the development and practices of ecumenism in African Catholicism. The objective is to provide both an overview and a more focused attention to ecumenism in Africa, in the hope of realizing the ecumenical mission of socially transforming the continent through the collaborative efforts of all the churches in Africa.

Ecumenism in African Christianity Today: Methods and Trajectory

What began as robust ecumenical enthusiasm following the incorporation of Africa into the World Council of Churches (WCC) in the first decade of the WCC's existence appears to have lost its steam. Qualified as being in a state of "despair" and "crisis," and as "disorganized" and "struggling" in several parts of Africa,[3] it is fair to say that ecumenism

---

1. Melady, "Impact of Africa on Recent Developments in the Roman Catholic Church," 147–56.
2. In this regard, some of the significant theological conversations taking place in Africa are presented by the following: the Circle of Concerned African Women Theologians; Theological Colloquium on Church, Religion, and Society in Africa (TCCRSA); Catholic Theological Ethics in the World Church (CTEWC): African region; and the Pan-African Catholic Congress on Theology, Society, and Pastoral Life.
3. Tsele, "African Ecumenism within the Context of NEPAD," 111. [NEPAD = New Partnership for Africa's Development.]

is hardly thriving in Africa. In South Africa, for instance, the South African Council of Churches (SACC), which witnessed the struggle against apartheid, has weakened considerably today.[4] The same situation applies to many parts of Africa and has led to a certain level of ecumenical apathy among churches.

Ecumenical apathy in Africa suggests misplaced foundations.[5] In many cases, churches are rather preoccupied with competition and political rivalry among themselves, denominational differences in doctrine and teaching, mutual suspicions and attacks, leadership struggles that in some cases lead to increasing fragmentations, and social problems in Africa that already create another layer of problems and lack of cohesiveness. These attitudes further weaken the attempts to promote collaboration, dialogue, and unity among churches in Africa.

To map out the practice of ecumenism in Africa, one could consider two broad operative streams with multiple trajectories. The first stream is the African ecumenical scholarship that articulates the emergence, mission, challenges, and future of ecumenical projects and movements on the continent. Scholars approach African ecumenism in constructive or descriptive ways.[6] Of course, this does not suggest that scholars are categorized into either group since both approaches could be identified in the works of a single author. The constructive approach critically interrogates history, practices, and methods with a view to advancing ecumenical engagement through new methods of dialogue, reception, and collaboration. The descriptive approach focuses on presenting and mapping out what is obtainable in the African ecumenical sphere in terms of its historical development and practices. The information provided by this approach is not knowledge-producing in terms of redefining and advancing an ecumenical agenda in Africa. Yet it remains relevant by laying out the landmarks and the complexities of past approaches with a catalogue of the efficient and inefficient, the progress and retrogression, and the necessities and nonessentials. Both the constructive and the descriptive approaches are necessary in the project of African ecumenism.

The second stream is represented by the practical ecumenical initiatives and projects in Africa. This paradigm is largely captured by the history of the ecumenical movement in Africa, beginning with initiatives such as the 1908 Kajabe Conference that predates the 1910 Edinburgh Conference.[7] Ecumenical agendas differ as much as the number of initiatives. While groups such as the Gambia Christian Council (1963) and the Christian Association of Nigeria (1976) respond to the political survival of the Christian community, regional bodies such as the Fellowship of Christian Councils and Churches in West Africa (FECCIWA) and the Fellowship of Christian Councils in Southern Africa

---

4. Pillay, "Faith and Reality." Pillay blames the weakening of SACC, especially in struggles toward social justice, on the fragmentation of the ecumenical movement in South Africa.

5. See Dina, "Life-Giving and Healing Ecumenism in Africa," 382; Pillay, "Ecumenism in Africa," 637–38.

6. Some examples of constructive works would include Byamungu, "Constructing Newer 'Windows' of Ecumenism for Africa"; Kwame A. Labi, "Transforming Ecumenism in Africa in the 21st Century: The URM Experience and Challenge," *Ecumenical Review* 53.3 (2001): 366–73, which proposed the so-called "renaissance paradigm"; and Ilo, "Receptive Ecumenism in Africa." Examples of the descriptive approach would include essays such as Isabel Apawo Phiri, "The Circle of Concerned African Women Theologians: Its Contributions to Ecumenical Formation," *Ecumenical Review* 57.1 (2005): 34–42; Kwabena J. Asamoah-Gyadu, "'Hearing in Our Own Tongues the Wonderful Works of God': Pentecost, Ecumenism and Renewal in African Christianity," *Missionalia* 35.3 (2007): 128–45; Pillay, "Ecumenism in Africa"; Priscille Djoumhoué, "Manifestations of Ecumenism in Africa Today: A Study of the Mainline and Pentecostal Churches in Cameroon," *International Journal for the Study of the Christian Church* 8.4 (2008): 355–68; and Jesse N. K. Mugambi, "Ecumenism in African Christianity," 232–51, in *The Routledge Companion to Christianity in Africa*, ed. Elias Kifon Bongmba (New York: Routledge, 2016).

7. Kobia, "Denominationalism in Africa," 299. Equally significant are the Kikuyu Conference of 1913, the formation of the national Christian Councils of Kenya (1943) and Zambia (1945), and the 1959 conversations between Catholic priests and Lutheran pastors in Arusha (Tanzania). 1959 was the same year that saw the formation of the East Africa Church Union Consultation (EACUC) by the Protestants, with a focus on theological deliberations on mission and unity.

(FOCCISA) tend to focus exclusively on issues of poverty and social justice. There are also a few instances of bilateral dialogues among churches in Africa, particularly between Catholics and Anglicans (in Nigeria and South Africa) that promote the contextualized reception of results of the Anglican-Roman Catholic International Commission (ARCIC). Outside the institutional structure, practical ecumenical projects are also conceptualized in so-called grassroots ecumenism, a relatively new aspect of ecumenical studies[8] that is said to have its roots in Pentecostalism.[9] Some examples include the Full Gospel Businessmen's Fellowship International, and Catholic groups like Chemin Neuf, the Focolare Movement, and Sant'Egidio, all of which operate in Africa. As a caveat, the two-stream categorization of the practice of ecumenism in Africa provided here is far from being quintessential. Finally, the activities of the All Africa Conference of Churches (AACC) show a multivariant and multilevel ecumenical engagement.

Nevertheless, these broad categories capture the basic approaches to ecumenism within Africa, with its inherent tensions between the institutional and grassroots, and between ecclesiology and ethics, both in scholarly articulations and in concrete practices. In fact, the history of ecumenism in Africa reveals the tension between an ecclesiological attention to Christian unity (Sam Kobia, Kwesi Dickson, Emmanuel Katongole)[10] and the "reconstruction paradigm" that focuses on social transformation (Jesse Mugambi, Kä Mana, Charles Villa-Vicencio).[11] Given the peculiarity of Africa, I propose that social ecumenism offers the best entrée into spiritual, practical, and theological ecumenism—as long as it is not reduced to activities and projects but rather provides a foundation for socializing people in the faith and offers practical steps on how unity serves the cause of justice and peace. In learning *why* they ought to work together, believers are led to work together for social justice, and in doing so they are further led to know, understand, and learn about and from one another, and thus to be able to pray and celebrate together.[12]

The WCC and the Commitment to Justice and Peace

Taking social ecumenism as a starting point is to recall that the commitment to social transformation, specifically to justice and peace, has always been central in the ecumenical movement. The 1925 Stockholm gathering, which birthed the Life and Work Movement that was later integrated into the WCC, pointed to an agenda that preceded the formal existence of the WCC in 1948. Indeed, the existence of the WCC in the aftermath of the Second World War speaks volumes about the goal of justice and peace, which is perfectly aligned with the WCC's program of unity. This connection is highlighted in a short essay by a former vice moderator of the Faith and Order Commission, Paul A. Crow, titled "Ecclesiology: The Intersection between the Search for Ecclesial Unity and the Struggle for Justice and Peace, and the Integrity of Creation."[13] This work clearly expressed the link between unity and justice within an understanding of the church as *koinonia*.

---

8. Some of the few scholarly works on this grassroots ecumenism include Ernst Conradie, ed., *South African Perspectives on Notions and Forms of Ecumenicity* (Stellenbosch, South Africa: Sun Press, 2013); a collection of articles in the 2018 special edition of the *Journal of South African Studies* 44.2; and Bennetta Jules-Rosette, "Grass-Roots Ecumenism: Religious and Social Cooperation in Two Urban African Churches," *African Social Research* 23 (1977): 185–216.

9. Werbner, "Grassroots Ecumenism in Conflict," 207.

10. See Sam Kobia, *The Courage to Hope: A Challenge for Churches in Africa* (Nairobi: Acton, 2003); Kwesi Dickson, *Theology in Africa* (Maryknoll, NY: Orbis Books, 1984); and Emmanuel Katongole, *The Sacrifice of Africa: A Political Theology for Africa* (Grand Rapids, MI: Eerdmans, 2011).

11. Cf. Sakupapa, "Ecclesiology and Ethics."

12. While these are laudable ideas, one admits that they are dangerously impaired by the shallow structure and disposition of the many Christian denominations operating in Africa.

13. Crow, "Ecclesiology," 53–58.

The WCC has always operated with the understanding that the commitment to justice and peace is at the same time a commitment to Christian unity. Held in Nairobi in 1975, the WCC's Fifth Assembly addressed, among other issues, structural systems of injustice designed by the powerful against the weak. In extending this concern, which had already begun in the preceding assembly (Uppsala, 1968), the Nairobi assembly deliberated extensively on issues concerning human rights, the plight of women, and racism.[14] As a follow-up, the Sixth Assembly (Vancouver, 1983) invited member churches "to make a clear covenanting commitment to work for justice and peace" and to resist the abhorrent powers of "racism, sexism, class domination, caste oppression, and militarism."[15] The Vancouver assembly roundly condemned all forms of domination as diabolical and hinged its covenantal invitation on the dual foundation of "confessing Christ as the life of the world" and "Christian resistance to the powers of death." These two commitments, as Preman Niles argues, should be seen as "one and the same activity."[16] They both belong to the single goal of bringing about Christian unity.

Once again, the WCC took up the challenge of this double commitment at its Tenth Assembly (Busan, 2013) under the theme "God of life, lead us to justice and peace." In his report, WCC General Secretary Olav Fyske Tveit highlights the double pathway of prayer and action that is required in this renewed commitment.[17] Indeed, we cannot admit a bifurcation of these pathways since a prayer for peace is at once an action against injustice. It is an action, however, that begins with the transformation of the one who prays, while leading to action on behalf of the oppressed, the marginalized, and the vulnerable as its inevitable consequence. The WCC's efforts to promote justice and peace in Africa, as can be seen, are an important contribution to the goal of furthering Christian unity in Africa.

Even before the WCC held its Fifth Assembly in Nairobi, Africa had already played host to the world ecumenical movement with the International Missionary Council (IMC) meeting of 1957 in Achimota (Ghana) that ratified the proposal for the integration of the IMC and the WCC in 1961. Meanwhile in 1960, the WCC's central committee met in Enugu, Nigeria, where a president of the WCC, Sir Francis Akanu Ibiam, was serving as the first African governor of colonial Eastern Nigeria. This was the beginning of the WCC's history of involvement in issues of justice and peace in Africa. Hardly had the Nigerian–Biafran War (1967–1970) begun when the WCC, at the behest of Ibiam, stepped into the fray. The WCC collaborated with the Vatican and the ecumenical Joint Church Aid (JCA) to provide aid to the Biafrans, who faced food blockades by the Nigerian Federal Forces. Ibiam led the Biafran Christian delegation to the WCC's assembly in Uppsala in 1968 (while Bola Ige represented Nigeria) to appeal for an intervention by the WCC.[18] The WCC has since been involved in aid distribution to conflict victims across Africa and in working toward overcoming violence, efforts that led to the decision to inaugurate the Decade to Overcome Violence (DOV) at the 1998 Harare assembly. That assembly, which commemorated the WCC's fiftieth anniversary, provided an opportunity for the council's rededication to the African dream and agenda of justice and peace in the twenty-first century, with recommendations that sought to deepen the WCC's program of dialogue and solidarity in Africa.[19] The assembly further requested the churches to engage with the government and civil society and international institutions to bring about "respect for human rights, the promotion of an alternative economic

---

14. World Council of Churches, *Work Book for the Fifth Assembly of the World Council of Churches, Nairobi 75*, 50–62. Section V of the workbook deals with "structures of injustice and struggles for liberation."
15. Gill, *Gathered for Life*, 89.
16. Niles, *Resisting the Threats to Life*, ix.
17. Tveit, "Report of the General Secretary," 225.
18. Otieno and McCullum, *Journey of Hope*, 10–11. See also the article by Annegreth Schilling on the Uppsala assembly: "The Ecumenical Movement and 1968: The Uppsala Assembly as the Beginning of a New Era?," *Ecumenical Review* 70.2 (2018): 194–215.
19. Kessler, *Together on the Way*, 226.

order, debt relief, reductions in the arms trade, and urgent measures to bring about peace and justice in . . . areas of conflict in Africa."[20]

Today, despite the great efforts directed toward these issues, we have yet to see significant changes. Instead, the crisis in Africa has deepened. What exactly is responsible for this failure? Are churches in Africa unable to work ecumenically to realize these dreams and agendas? It is worth noting that the WCC's assembly in Harare presented its recommendations as the primary responsibility of the churches in Africa. The WCC understood its duty as "a commitment to work *with* and *through*" the churches in "*accompanying* . . . African brothers and sisters in their journey of hope."[21] Of course, the WCC avoids any superintendent role since it conceives of itself as a fellowship of churches; as such, it must always take a position that would ensure *mutual accountability* among the churches. What is obvious is that the churches in Africa have a vital role to play in some of the persistent social issues facing Africa. The perennial conflicts, violence, and wars in many parts of the continent could be addressed by churches in Africa if they mirror unity in their ranks and work together in ecumenical dialogues and in joint action for peace, transformation of conflict, national unity, and good governance. All of these can be achieved through robust ecumenical collaboration. It is important, then, to examine ecumenical commitment in Africa, particularly in the Catholic Church, with fresher insights, such as the one that emerges from the method of receptive ecumenism.

Yet this proposed method must be grounded in intercultural hermeneutics that sufficiently accounts for the African context. What is today known as intercultural theology is constituted by the cultural interplay of identity and the *other*, or difference.[22] Primarily, the objective is to reject any unintended reduction of either the *other* or the self, the consequence of which is a homogenization of some sort. Accordingly, intercultural hermeneutics is best understood as "a comparative search for common meaning between different culturally defined subjects."[23] Characteristically, such hermeneutics is tension-laden since it "immerses itself in the phenomenology of faith and life, using multiple and interdisciplinary historical and theological approaches in order to achieve a valid explanation of the local processes, movements, and tensions in their dialectical and mutual relations."[24] As a comparative way of searching and interpreting reality, intercultural hermeneutics engages with the faith experiences of African Christians within the overwhelming flux of realities on the continent.

The only constants here are faith and life. Faith and life emerge as dynamic realities to be lived out rather than a set of propositions simply to be followed. Thus, with attention to the individual African believer, intercultural hermeneutics refers to *the interpretative disposition of a cultural subject in its search for meaning, within the complexities of lived experience, before the horizontal cultural realities it encounters*. An unapologetic open-mindedness, formed in a *readiness to encounter* and *to learn from the other*, thus becomes a defining attribute of this subject. This is against any version of intercultural hermeneutics that pitches the cultural subject within the limiting spaces of the "in-between" or "double-belonging."[25] In the context of African ecumenism, therefore, intercultural hermeneutics grounds the method of receptive ecumenism with the fundamentals of mutual openness and mutual learning.

---

20. Kessler, *Together on the Way*, 227.
21. Kessler, *Together on the Way*, 226 (emphasis added).
22. Gruber, *Intercultural Theology*, 40. For Gruber, the central task of intercultural theology is the "unsilencing of interculturality" that invariably "denaturalizes and de-essentializes the normative texts of ecclesial tradition and reveals the contingent histories of their formation." Gruber's analysis rests on the understanding that "the definition of Christian identity cannot be negotiated in terms of idealistic abstractions but proceeds via the production of texts that embody the delineations between ecclesial identity and those it defines as its others" (123).
23. Ilo, "Crosscurrents in African Christianity," 189.
24. Ilo, "Crosscurrents in African Christianity," 189.
25. Marotta, "Intercultural Hermeneutics and the Cross-Cultural Subject," 273.

Receptive Ecumenism, Appropriate to the African Context

Paul Murray's principle of "receptive ecumenism" places a great premium on mutual openness and learning. Conceived of as a new way of overcoming the slow progress in ecumenical dialogue, receptive ecumenism has become a popular framework for carrying out structured, institutional dialogue with the values of "responsible hospitality" and "dynamic integrity," to use Murray's expressions.[26] According to Murray, receptive ecumenism sets before the churches the question, "What, in any given situation, can one's own tradition appropriately *learn* with integrity from other traditions?"[27] Each church is expected to pose this self-critical question "without insisting, although certainly hoping, that these other traditions are also asking themselves the same question."[28] By not insisting on a criterion of reciprocal learning, receptive ecumenism places the burden of transformation on one's community while acting *in spe* as regards the response of one's dialogical partner. However, the timeline of the proposed ecumenical learning may need to be clarified. Even at the risk of redundancy, one may ask, Does receptive ecumenism, as a form of ecumenical learning, guarantee some sort of openness both *in-dialogue* (during the process) and *post-dialogue* (after the process)?

Beyond the question posed above is a recognition of what is really at stake here, namely, the intended transformation that constitutes the central objective of bilateral dialogues. If dialogue does not bring about change but instead reconfirms the representative communities in their ideological and doctrinal fortresses, then what value does it have?

For Murray, receptive ecumenism exactly serves to highlight the disposition toward the intended transformation in dialogue. Hence, he argues that "unless this commitment to transformational receptivity be made the explicit driving-motor of ecumenical engagement then no amount of refined conceptual clarification and reconciliation of differing theological languages alone will lead to real practical growth and change in the respective lives of the participating churches."[29] So important is this understanding that the ARCIC (III) eventually adopted receptive ecumenism as its methodological framework, especially in the context of its historical setting and challenges.[30] However, the act of limiting the application of receptive ecumenism to the structural institutional dialogue of experts,[31] despite its merits, may not promote a more robust "transformational receptivity" beyond the circle of experts in some contexts, such as Africa. The result would be a top-down process of reception that does not sufficiently consider the participatory role of the entire Christian community, or what could be considered grassroots Christianity.

Receptive ecumenism in African Christianity ought therefore to be redefined in such a way that ecumenical learning is promoted across the institutional and the grassroots levels. However, it must begin by engaging in intraecclesial conversations that will lead to a conversion that transcends "ecclesial narratives of contamination," according to which particular churches fortify their ecclesial boundaries so as not to be influenced by the religious practices and dispositions of other churches. Rather, these conversations would be focusing on "redemptive narratives of what God is doing" in the Christian *other*.[32] This shift aligns with what could

---

26. Murray, "Receptive Ecumenism and Catholic Learning," 12.
27. Murray, "Receptive Ecumenism and Catholic Learning," 12 (italics mine).
28. Murray, "Receptive Ecumenism and Catholic Learning," 12.
29. Murray, "Receptive Ecumenism and Catholic Learning," 14.
30. See Murray, "Reception of ARCIC I and II in Europe," 199–218; and ARCIC III, *Walking Together on the Way: Learning to Be the Church—Local, Regional, Universal* (London: SPCK, 2017), §18.
31. Murray insists that receptive ecumenism intends to draw out only the "interpersonal and structural institutional dimensions" of dialogue (see Murray, "Receptive Ecumenism and Catholic Learning," 15). This does not imply that both cannot be conceived of as operating alongside each other, since in practice a certain level of personal approach is operable during a dialogue of experts in their "off-the-record" interaction with each other as well as in the various moments of common prayers, relaxation, and reflection.
32. Ilo, "Receptive Ecumenism in Africa," 74. Ilo frames this in the context of the possibilities of receptive ecumenism that are provided by the Charismatic and Pentecostal groups in Africa.

be considered the core of ecumenical spirituality, namely, openness, with its pneumatological and Trinitarian grounding.

Two observations are to be made here. On the one hand, to foster ecumenical learning at the institutional level, African Catholicism must be willing to make this transition. At this point, the *other* is no longer threatening to ecclesial identity since the "gift exchange" of "what God is doing in the *other*" is no longer perceived as impositional. Rather, this gift is appropriated as an offer by the Holy Spirit, which happens through the Christian *other* as the church listens and discerns communally. Interestingly, ecumenical learning comes with a measure of freedom that does not impose on the Christian *other* the condition of reciprocity. Construed as an openness to the Holy Spirit, ecumenical learning primarily serves the internal life of the church. On the other hand, ecumenical learning at the grassroots level appears to be already at work in Africa, as many Catholics freely participate in or appropriate the religious practices of other Christian churches. This is evident in the Charismatic movement, which has firmly established itself within African Catholicism today.[33]

Equally, many Christian groups now identify as nondenominational, interdenominational, or transdenominational, and they seek to provide answers to the spiritual and social concerns of African Christians across denominations.[34] In a place like Nigeria, for example, the annual gospel musical concert, "The Experience," hosted by the House on the Rock Ministries, is perhaps the biggest noninstitutional platform of spiritual ecumenism for Christians. Today, it has motivated other churches, including the Catholic Church, to host similar "open" events. There is significant ecumenical learning here, which emerges from the openness of the grassroots and eventually reshapes the response of the magisterium. Hence, the intention here is not to present the institutional and the grassroots as diametrically opposed to each other but to insist on the possibility of ecumenical learning across both levels, with implications for the inner renewal and transformation of the church.

Looking into the Future

The task of this chapter is not only to provide a historical account of ecumenism in Africa, particularly from the Catholic perspective but also to map out an agenda for the future. Importantly, the program for the future must be theologically rooted in Scripture and Catholic tradition, beginning with the Second Vatican Council but interpreted from an African Christian worldview and a reimagination of a new future of global solidarity and joint collaborations needed to meet the challenges we face to human and cosmic health and peace.

Vatican II provides a theological grounding for approaching ecumenism in Africa. The paradigm shift in the council's understanding of revelation as not just a set of propositional statements about God but as the communication of Godself (*Dei Verbum* [*DV*] §6) radically disposes the Christian to an open dialogue with God, with others, and with the world. In this way, dialogue is deeply rooted in revelation and not merely in the sociological, philosophical, and even theological arguments of the entanglement between the self and the other.[35] In revelation, the mystery of God's will (*DV* §2; Eph 1:9) is communicated as a person, Christ, with the full existential, pragmatic, relational, and embodied implications for salvation. Reimund Bieringer explains that, through revelation, "God enables human persons to accept God's invitation to friend-

---

33. Ilo, "Receptive Ecumenism in Africa," 77.

34. Some of these groups have equally displayed "unusual practices" that emerge from multilayered factors (theological, socioeconomic, and psychological), aided by the manipulability of the religiosity of Africans. See Mookgo S. Kgatle, "The Unusual Practices within Some Neo-Pentecostal Churches in South Africa: Reflections and Recommendations," *HTS Theological Studies* 73.3 (2017): 1–8.

35. For the philosophical and theological study of the idea of entanglement between the "self" and the "other," see Gregor Maria Hoff, *Die prekäre Identität des Christlichen: Die Herausforderung postmodernen Differenzdenkens für eine theologische Hermeneutik* (Paderborn, Germany: Schöningh, 2001); and Bernhard Waldenfels, *Phenomenology of the Alien: Basic Concepts* (Evanston, IL: Northwestern University Press, 2011).

ship and partnership," and, consequently, "monologue is replaced by dialogue and encounter."[36] This understanding of dialogue accounts for both its vertical and its horizontal dimensions, which ought to be held in constant tension. Without absolutizing the claims of Vatican II's excellent approach to this understanding, one could, however, identify an underlying *communio* ecclesiology that follows from this understanding of revelation. *Lumen Gentium* (*LG*), the Dogmatic Constitution on the Church, with its theology of the "people of God" (§§9–17), which topples the hierarchical ecclesiological model, and documents such as *Unitatis Redintegratio* and *Nostra Aetate,* the Declaration on the Relationship of the Church to Non-Christian Religions, further deepen the ecumenical disposition in the church. There is, of course, so much to say about the period between Vatican II and the present, but one significant development is a continuity of teaching and a renewed emphasis on ecumenical dialogue in Africa.

In a post-conciliar tradition of continuity and contextuality, the ecclesiological model of "Family of God,"[37] which is an African interpretation of Vatican II's understanding of the church as communion of the "people of God" (*LG*, chapters 1 and 2) emerges as the African gift to the universal church. The 1994 Synod of Africa highlights the "Family of God" as an ecclesiology that is marked by "care for others, solidarity, warmth in human relationships, acceptance, dialogue and trust" (Pope John Paul II, post-synodal apostolic exhortation *Ecclesia in Africa* [*EA*] §63). Dialogue, which is critical in this ecclesiology, is possible only when it opts for the intercultural hermeneutics in which openness and readiness to accept and learn from the other remain the basic norm (*Lineamenta* for the synod §78). The argument here further chimes into Pope John Paul II's exhortation to African theologians to work out the "Family of God" ecclesiology in continuity with scripture and tradition (*EA* §63). Stephanie Lowery's *Identity and Ecclesiology* demonstrates how African theologians have been developing different ecclesiological models inspired by the spirit of Vatican II and the two African Synods.[38] Central to these ecclesiologies is the emphasis on the identity of the church as a community of solidarity, diversity, interdependence, and equality. Such diverse images of the church in *Ecclesia in Africa* and some of the writings of African theologians open new pathways for developing an ecumenical theology. For instance, *EA* suggests some dialogue initiatives like "ecumenical translations of the Bible, theological study of various dimensions of the Christian faith or by bearing common evangelical witness to justice, peace and respect for human dignity" (§65) as ways of common Christian witnessing in the continent.

Theological engagement in Africa implies a constant imagination and reconstruction of how African ecclesiology serves the social transformation of our society as well as an unyielding interrogation of structures of dialogue in our church. Questions such as the following need to be constantly posed: How can we present the model of "Family of God" in a way that frees it from the dysfunctional attributes of some models of family in Africa? How ecumenical are African communities or families? How can African Catholicism fruitfully engage in a dialogue mission that aims at socially transforming the continent? These questions are not entirely new given that they remain the object of investigation of many African theologians today.[39]

---

36. Bieringer, "Biblical Revelation and Exegetical Interpretation According to *Dei Verbum* 12," 5–6.
37. Cf. Orobator, "Church in Dialogue as the Family of God," 33, 34.
38. Some of the African ecclesiologies examined by Lowery include those of Elochukwu Uzukwu, Kwame Bediako, Mercy Amba Oduyoye, Agbonkhianmeghe E. Orobator, Bernard Ukwuegbu, and Augustin R. Bishwende. See Stephanie A. Lowery, *Identity and Ecclesiology: Their Relationship among Select African Theologians* (Eugene, OR: Pickwick, 2017). Besides Lowery's, publications from the *Theological Colloquium on Church, Religion, and Society in Africa* (TCCRSA) equally address Catholic African ecclesiology in the light of Vatican II.
39. See Orobator, *Church as Family*; Mercy Amba Oduyoye, "The African Family as a Symbol of Ecumenism," *Ecumenical Review* 43.4 (1991): 465–78; Jesse N. K. Mugambi and Laurenti Magesa, eds., *The Church in African Christianity: Innovative Essays in Ecclesiology*, African Challenge (Nairobi: Initiatives, 1990); Stan Chu Ilo, Joseph Ogbonnaya, and Alex Ojacor, eds., *The Church as Salt and Light: Path to an African Ecclesiology of Abundant Life*, African Christian Studies 1 (Eugene, OR: Pickwick, 2011).

These theologies are further enriched by the emphasis of Pope Francis in his teaching and practical examples on the need for ecumenical dialogue and Christian unity. In relating Pope Francis's dialogical approach to the specific African context, the connection between the common good and the quest for justice and peace in his post-synodal apostolic exhortation *Evangelii Gaudium* (*EG*) becomes particularly important.[40] This connection is made against the backdrop of ecumenical dialogue expressed through the metaphor of "companionship of pilgrims"[41] in the Christian quest for unity: "We must never forget that we are *pilgrims journeying alongside one another*. This means that we must have sincere trust in our *fellow pilgrims*, putting aside all suspicion or mistrust, and turn our gaze to what we are all seeking: the radiant peace of God's face" (*EG* §244; emphasis added). But how can churches in Africa overcome the temptation to mistrust one another? An atmosphere of mutual suspicion greatly hampers any attempt to promote unity. Indeed, African churches must find a way to come together before even they can partner with external or international ecumenical bodies (such as the WCC) in the task of promoting social transformation in Africa. Perhaps this requires that the Catholic Church in Africa initiate the dialogue by first cultivating an internal disposition to openness, dialogue, and solidarity (*EA* §65). In that way, dialogue becomes an organically and internally transformed asset that is transferred to the encounter with the ecumenical other.

The principles advanced by Pope Francis offer some insights on how African solidarity and interdependence could be deployed by African Catholicism in its ecumenical engagement. The first principle, "Time is greater than space" (*EG* §222), disavows the obsession with dominating "all the spaces of power and of self-assertion" (§223) and challenges the church to engage in "generating processes of people building" (§224) that endure with time. To build the church as a "Family of God" is to build a people that live in sincere solidarity and trust with one another. The second principle—"Unity prevails over conflict" (§226)—is a rejection of any romanticized form of solidarity. African solidarity is intensified when it is pursued in spite of conflict. Interestingly, the pope joins the Congolese episcopal conference in affirming that "our ethnic diversity is our wealth," since it testifies to the power of the Holy Spirit to "harmonize every diversity" (§230). The third principle—"Realities are more important than ideas" (§231)—radically challenges "conceptual elaborations," namely, theological and even ecumenical ideas that are totally detached from action. This explains the failure of most leadership even within the church. In other words, it is not enough to lay claim to the model of church as "Family of God" as the specific African ecclesiology without translating that into action in ecclesial, ecumenical, and social settings. The fourth principle—"The whole is greater than the parts" (§234)—calls the church in Africa to broaden its horizon and to avoid unbridled particularism. To do otherwise is to fall into the trap of ethnocentrism and parochialism that prevents the church from being open and ready to learn from both its members and others. According to Pope Francis, this principle serves the "intrinsic principle of totality" of the gospel (§237), which seeks the abundant life for all. These principles further deepen the dialogical task of the church, not only within itself but equally with the ecumenical other in the service of justice and peace in the society.

On the basis of the foregoing, Catholic ecumenism in Africa can proceed in three main steps. First is the task of further deepening the African appropriation of the Roman Catholic ecclesiology and commitment to ecumenism in a way that balances the relationship between the universal church and local church. By so doing, ecclesial solidarity is imbued with a unique African contribution.

Second is to approach ecumenism from an understanding that dialogue is the main way of "putting solidarity into practice" (*EA* §138). This requires being aware of the complexities of dialogue, such as the fear of fundamentalism and of loss of identity. Yet a focus on the "bigger picture"

---

40. See *EG* chapter 4:III, "The Common Good and Peace in Society."
41. Mayer, "Ecumenical Vision of Pope Francis," 159. Mayer summarizes Pope Francis's ecumenical vision as one in which "unity is created in the journeying itself," provided everyone is "on the move together" (169).

(*EG* §225) of building human relationships and of how the lack of unity stokes conflict is a way of overcoming ecumenical apathy among African churches.

Third, African Catholicism must work out, in clear terms, the social implications of the "Family of God" ecclesiology. As an ecclesiology that emerges *from* the African worldview of communality (*EA* §43), it must reach beyond a narrow self-understanding of the church. Indeed, the credibility of this ecclesiology must be tested against its power to offer social transformation in Africa.[42] Overall, the ecclesial learning for African Catholicism in this regard is the celebration of diversity both *ad intra* and *ad extra*, which is necessary for ecumenical dialogue that sufficiently promotes human flourishing in Africa.

Path to African Catholic Ecumenism: Solidarity, Friendship, and Participation in the Family of God

At the core of the ecumenical principles of Pope Francis is something that transcends denominational identities (metaphorically expressed as "space," "conflict," "ideas," and "parts") in the search for social transformation in Africa. What is left to determine is whether we can reconcile the African concept of solidarity with the pope's principles—thus constituting an enrichment of the treasure of African solidarity, community, and interdependence. Stan Chu Ilo offers practical reflections in the context of the African church that could be applied here. His intercultural hermeneutics of friendship and participation provide the needed praxis to sustain an ecumenical commitment founded on African solidarity. He roots his vision of participation and friendship in the Trinitarian life of communion that all humans are called to share. Sharing in the life of God takes the mode of this life of God—it is sharing in the life of divine communion. This sharing in the life of God is made possible by Christ who "gives us access" and by the Holy Spirit who leads us "to share in the inner life of the Trinity."[43] Critical in Ilo's analysis is the concept of *life* (vital union, vital bond) that affords a common participation by men and women.

Ilo's principle of participation resonates in the African philosophy of *ubuntu* ("I am because we are") and can be related as the core principle of unity in the ecclesiology of the "Family of God" in Africa where all are welcome.[44] *Ubuntu* recaptures the fundamental relationship that exists among all created realities. All are interconnected. Thus, it is about a sharing, a participation that is at once communal and personal. But most essentially, it is existential. The intrinsic nature of this participation could mean that we ought to understand ourselves as existentially open to one another in the form of solidarity. For Pope Francis, Christian communities ought to be spaces of "living communion and participation" (*EG* §28). According to him, the church's task of fostering "a dynamic, open and missionary communion" (*EG* §31) requires the indispensable elements of participation and dialogue. It is important to note that it is the Holy Spirit that opens the heart to believe in Christ (1 Cor 12:3), thus making solidarity and communion possible. It is the Holy Spirit that forms the church as a community gathered around, and for, God (*LG* §12). This explains why this solidarity has guided the church all through history as it communicates and transmits the faith it has received. It is obvious that some of the barriers to ecumenical solidarity could be considered to be artificially constructed and ought to be dismantled as much as possible, with great care and patient discernment.

---

42. Orobator, *Church as Family*, 31.
43. Ilo, "Crosscurrents in African Christianity," 192.
44. Ilo presents *ubuntu* as follows: "We are through other people; I am related therefore I am; I am loved therefore I exist; I exist in order to participate in community, and I am nothing if I am not in community and friendship with others—nature and humans (living, dead, and those not yet born)" ("Crosscurrents in African Christianity," 194). Although it has a South African (Bantu) origin, *ubuntu* is generally accepted as reflecting the African worldview. See John S. Mbiti, *African Religions and Philosophy*, 2nd ed. (London: Heinemann, 1989); Pieter H. Coetzee and Abraham P. J. Roux, eds., *Philosophy from Africa: A Text with Readings* (Cape Town: Oxford University Press, 2002); and Michael Battle, *Ubuntu: I in You and You in Me* (New York: Seabury, 2009).

Christian solidarity as a call to relearn the existential openness among ecclesial communities expresses its dynamism not only in terms of participation but also in friendship. An ecclesial friendship that is built on love is, after all, a central command in the Christian faith (John 13:34; UR §2). Pope Francis captures this well when he argues that God's love "blossoms into an enriching friendship" that liberates us from our "narrowness and self-absorption" (*EG* §8). From the perspective of *ubuntu*, Ilo asserts that this friendship presupposes "a certain equality, autonomy, shared life, respect, and acceptance; it also presupposes solidarity, collaboration, and cooperation."[45] It is perhaps instructive to note that dialogue usually first leads to conflict, which is a necessary passage on the path to healing and restoring justice to the oppressed and marginalized. Friendship can happen only if conflict is resolved through dialogue. Conflict can be long, however, and often means that there are no easy answers.[46] In friendship, therefore, we participate in the *life* of the *other*. We become open to the other, and the other becomes open to us as well. Dialectically, this process reflects "a losing and discovery of self and the other and a redemptive step towards fulfillment of the promise of life at the heart of the Trinity, the Christian faith, and the entire cosmos."[47] Pope Francis also captures this sense of reflexivity and reciprocity in the idea of friendship. He asks quite poignantly, "[I]f we have received the love which restores meaning to our lives, how can we fail to share that love with others?" (*EG* §8). There is, therefore, an interrelation between life, community, and friendship (*EG* §§49, 228, 248, 265). Friendship with God flows out into friendship within human communities, carrying with it the meaning of life. With regard to the two principles of participation and friendship, then, Pope Francis's understanding of dialogue and the common good resonates with the African concept of solidarity in a way that can promote Catholic ecumenism in Africa.

Pope Francis's principles, which are also emphasized by the WCC's quest for harmony in communities, reflect an antidote against actions and practices that upturn peace and create injustice in society. Faith is the precise resource for this antidote. The church in Africa has the responsibility to promote these ideals, but to do so it must embrace dialogue that is built on the principles of participation and friendship. Pope Francis's understanding of dialogue as reflected in the four principles of *Evangelii Gaudium* reminds African churches to tap into their worldview to address issues of conflict and divisions. For instance, a reappraisal of the prevalence of "unity" and the greatness of "the whole" in Africa, as further captured in some nuggets of traditional wisdom,[48] is a key incentive of Pope Francis's ecumenical perspectives that could serve the agenda of Catholic ecumenism in Africa. Such reappraisal is echoed in the African concept of *ubuntu*, which, with its emphasis on the interrelatedness of all things, constitutes a very powerful resource for ecumenical engagement toward justice and peace in Africa.

Path to African Catholic Ecumenism: Ecumenical Spirituality in the Family of God

Sustaining the ecumenical agenda in Africa requires a corresponding ecumenical spirituality. Ecumenical spirituality is intrinsically linked to ecumenical reception and is captured in the "spirituality of openness"[49] that is rooted in the Trinitarian life of communion in which believers participate. The identity of a believer is that of someone who is called to share the life in the Trinity—in the Father's offer of life at creation, in the Son's "new life" in the

---

45. Ilo, "Crosscurrents in African Christianity," 194.
46. The persistent Christian–Muslim conflict in Africa weakens the enthusiasm for dialogue, but friendship as a dialogical approach could help, as we see in the case of Imam Mohammed Ashafa and Pastor James Wuye, founders of the Interfaith Mediation Center in Kaduna, Nigeria. See the description of the film *The Imam and the Pastor* at https://www.iofc.org/imam-pastor.
47. Ilo, "Crosscurrents in African Christianity," 194–95.
48. In Igbo culture, for example, concepts such as *igwebuike* (community/unity is power) and *ofu obi* (unity of minds) articulate the ideas of unity and solidarity.
49. Okpaleke, "On the Borderline between Consensus and Reception," 348–70.

Incarnation, and in the Holy Spirit's unceasing vivification. What we receive from the Trinity is *life* in its profundity. Reception as "the movement from God to human beings," therefore, "constitutes a basic structure of personal and corporate faith,"[50] with its Christological and pneumatological implications.[51] The spirituality of openness should exist at every area of dialogue if reception is to be maintained. It should exist not only at the horizontal level of the different churches that engage in bilateral/multilateral dialogue, but also within the inner-ecclesial life of the individual churches in Africa. Dialectically, this process reflects "a losing and discovery of self and the other and a redemptive step towards fulfillment of the promise of life at the heart of the Trinity, the Christian faith, and the entire cosmos."[52] This openness should be evident in the disposition of the relevant structures of life within the church to receive this result in the liturgy, teaching, and devotional practices of the faithful, that is, in "the *kerygma*, the *didache*, and the *praxis pietatis*," as Cardinal Willebrands would describe it.[53] At this level, reception is no longer the problem of the theological experts. It involves everybody, and the primary concern is to welcome the result in the life of the church in such a way that aligns with the preexisting mechanism of intra-ecclesial renewal and transformation (*ecclesia semper reformanda*—"the church always reforming").

To guarantee inner-ecclesial reception during ecumenical dialogue, there must be a predisposition to receive positive feedback from the church. Without such a predisposition, which in itself is a fundamental reception, dialogue among the churches will not yield any significant results in theology, unity, or joint social actions. This further implies that the spirituality of openness should be cultivated within churches as a minimal, yet fundamental, process of reception. It is a form of reception *in spe*, which, however, is not eclipsed *ad finem*, since it remains relevant not only for reception *ad extra* but also for the ever-needed inner renewal of ecclesial life. Alluding to this spirit of openness, William Rusch remarks that "official reception should open the possibility of further steps and have its influence in other situations or later generations."[54] Reception as a transgenerational process is guaranteed by the spirit of openness.

The spirituality of openness within the African ecclesial community would serve as a sign of healing. This could be manifested in being approachable with the disposition to dialogue (*EG* §165). It is equally evident in the readiness to enter into friendships with the concomitant exchange of gifts (*EG* §§228, 246); to engage in common social projects (*UR* §12, *EG* §258); and to participate in common spiritual activities (*UR* §8) like the Office of the Hours or the aforementioned worship event, "The Experience." Such significant expressions of openness give frontline ecumenists the courage to continue patiently to work together even when the results of dialogue are not manifesting as quickly as they wish. Sometimes, unity occurs not in the anticipated official manner but more subtly, as the conditions for unity permeate the different Christian communities over time, signaling the informal success of ecumenism. A spirituality of openness also points to an admission of lack of self-sufficiency of a particular church, which saves it from taking a triumphalist attitude toward others. For instance, despite its claims to fidelity in preserving the essential elements of Christ's church (*LG* §8; *UR* §4), the Roman Catholic Church does not claim to be totally self-sufficient.[55] The implication is that ecumenism and reception call for learning by the churches from one another. This is what William Henn refers to as the "receivability" of ecumenical documents (as the object) and the "receptivity" of the people of God (as the subject).[56]

---

50. Gassmann, "From Reception to Unity," 127.
51. See John 11:51–52; 1 Cor 12:1–3, 12–13; Eph 1:11–13; Heb 13:15; 1 Thess 2:13–14; *LG* §§4, 12.
52. Ilo, "Crosscurrents in African Christianity," 194–95.
53. Johannes Cardinal Willebrands, *Origins* 14:44 (April 18, 1985): 722, quoted in Gros et al., *Introduction to Ecumenism*, 126.
54. Rusch, *Reception*, 59.
55. Henn, "Reception of Ecumenical Documents," 391.
56. Henn, "Reception of Ecumenical Documents," 392.

It is clear from the above discussion that ecumenical reception presents challenges to African Catholicism, the churches, and all Christians. In Africa, as elsewhere, these challenges arise from hesitance to openness toward the other. They emerge from factors that may be purely psychological, built on the fear of loss of identity, or from sociopolitical restraints that emerge from particular ecclesiologies,[57] or even from what one could consider as "irreducible differences,"[58] which are indicated by the "non-negotiables" in ecumenical conversation. In the praxis of Catholic ecumenism in Africa, the ecumenical spirituality of openness is best fostered and intensified through the praxes of participation and friendship and an account of solidarity in which there is an open narrative of identities and traditions.

Challenges for the Future of Ecumenism in Africa

The challenges facing Africa today are at once the challenges facing the church in Africa (see *Gaudium et Spes* §4). These challenges imply that ecumenical collaboration is constitutive of the church's mission. As such, the objective of Christian unity articulated in ecumenical encounter is to be taken seriously by African Catholicism with a theological conviction that is not simply notional or conceptual but rather existential, contextual, and lived.[59] In a continent where the Christian identity and mission are distorted by the ravages of communal conflict, ethnocentrism, poverty, corruption, disease, and occasions of religious and denominational conflicts and rivalries, the future of ecumenical dialogue is thus confronted by factors that are not only internal (intra-ecclesial and inter-ecclesial) but also external (interreligious and intercultural). I shall limit the future challenges to four critical concerns that should occupy African theologians of all stripes and Christian leaders:

The first challenge is *the socioeconomic and political realities that negatively impact the Christian faith in Africa*. Poverty, corruption, and unemployment affect the general well-being of the people of the continent in a nondiscriminatory manner and, as such, have disastrous consequences for a divided Christian community. One has to recognize that social ecumenism is as important as theological and spiritual ecumenism, and both must be held together as the churches jointly act as the "salt" and "light" in Africa (see Matt 5:13–15). Ecumenical collaboration on social and political issues that affect society invariably help redirect the continent toward abundant living for all. The church in Africa cannot exclude this responsibility from its salvific mission without risking being aloof toward its missional reality (*sine fundamentum in re*—"without foundation in reality").

The second challenge is *the need to overcome the "ecclesial denominational arrogance" that forestalls ecumenical learning*. There are claims by some Catholics that they are superior to other denominations. Such claims proceed from a certain ahistorical reading of the history of Roman Catholicism as an undifferentiated development from the Council of Jerusalem to its embodiment in its Western missionary implantation in Africa. Some African Catholics, thus, make an appeal to the Roman Catholic Church's unbroken tradition, its well-organized structure and hierarchy, and global influence rooted in its long claims to the legacies of historical Christendom as signs of its superiority to other churches. This can drive a wedge into ecumenical dialogue and relations in Africa between the African Catholic faithful and Africans of other church traditions. Yet the missionary attitude of the church, even in an ecumenical context, requires that we be the first to "boldly take the initiative" to "go out to others" (*EG* §24) with attention to what God is doing in the other.[60] Indeed, this attitude of superiority invites all Christians to internal conversion, since ecumenical learning as a pathway to transformation is fundamentally *ad intra* and is not imposed from the outside. In other words, ecumenism's "spirituality of openness" has

---

57. McGrail, "Fortress Church under Reconstruction?," 320.
58. Okpaleke, "On the Borderline between Consensus and Reception," 364.
59. Ilo, "Receptive Ecumenism in Africa," 69.
60. Ilo, "Receptive Ecumenism in Africa," 74–76.

a fundamental internal theological and pastoral function. Added to this is the need for ecumenical education that guarantees such openness.

The third challenge involves *understanding internal diversity as constitutive of the African ecclesiological models of community or family as the ground of ecumenism*. This demands a culture of internal dialogue and self-criticism by African Catholics (as well as any Christian group) as a prerequisite for ecumenical dialogue. Any assumption or enforcement of homogeneity of opinions, understandings, and processes ill-disposes a church to an ecumenical encounter with the other. A "cultural hermeneutics" that opens up to the inclusive participation of all believers, particularly women, is needed.[61] Further highlighted in this challenge is the task of embracing the validity and legitimacy of ecclesial dissent as a litmus test for determining the congruence between the institutional exercise of authority and the perception of its effectiveness in reality, as well as between the operational ecclesiological model and the theorized ecclesial identity.[62]

The fourth challenge is *determining the appropriate theological or interdisciplinary hermeneutical and methodological instruments of ecumenical engagement*. The ecumenical engagement that is required in Africa must recognize the complexity of the issues and agencies that affect communal flourishing in Africa. In constructing its methods and approaches, insights from Africa's historical, cultural, and religious heritage must be considered. Social analysis of contemporary existential challenges must be accounted for as well. This will require paying attention to what is already happening among Christians who are working together across denominational boundaries in many parts of Africa, as exemplified in the "Action Plan for Peace" by the South Sudan Council of Churches; the ecumenical collaboration behind the anonymous *Kairos Document* (1985) in South Africa; the work of the Christian Association of Nigeria against military dictatorship and religious extremism in Nigeria; and the interchurch collaboration for development by Lifeline in Zambia. It is equally important that such approaches avoid the dualism between the institutional *versus* grassroots, the theological/expert *versus* the social/spiritual, and the elite *versus* non-elite forms of dialogue. To do so is to ensure an effective reception process.

While these challenges do not refer to eucharistic communion, which is at the center of the ecumenical quest for Christian unity (*UR* §§2, 4, 22), they do make possible such a level of communion in the future. The suggestions amount, therefore, to a strategic Catholic approach to the question of Christian unity in Africa in line with the existential and contextual factors that define the contemporary African reality. With a focus on building up a community that guarantees the flourishing of all, the future of ecumenism in Africa is eschatologically eucharistic so long as the Eucharist remains the signifier of both ecclesial and Christian unity (*UR* §2).

Bibliography

Bieringer, Reimund. "Biblical Revelation and Exegetical Interpretation according to *Dei Verbum* 12." *Studien zum Neuen Testament und Seiner Umwelt* (SNTU) A:27 (2002): 5-40.

Byamungu, Gosbert T. M. "Constructing Newer 'Windows' of Ecumenism for Africa: A Catholic Perspective." *Ecumenical Review* 53.3 (2001): 341–52.

Crow, Paul A. "Ecclesiology: The Intersection between the Search for Ecclesial Unity and the Struggle for Justice and Peace, and the Integrity of Creation." In *Costly Unity: Koinonia and Justice, Peace and Creation*, edited by Thomas F. Best and Wesley Granberg-Michaelso, 53–58. Geneva: WCC, 1993.

Dina, Titi. "Life-Giving and Healing Ecumenism in Africa." *Ecumenical Review* 53.3 (2001): 380–84.

Francis, Pope. *Evangelii Gaudium* (The Joy of the Gospel) [Post-synodal Apostolic Exhortation on the Proclamation of the Gospel in Today's World; November 23, 2013]. Vatican City: Libreria Editrice Vaticana, 2013. www.vatican.va.

Gassmann, Günther. "From Reception to Unity: The Historical and Ecumenical Significance of the Concept of Reception." In *Community—Unity—Communion: Essays in Honour of Mary Tanner*,

---

61. Kobia, "Denominationalism in Africa," 305.
62. O'Gara, "Shifts below the Surface of the Debate."

edited by Colin Podmore, 117–29. London: Church House Publishing, 1998.

Gill, David, ed. *Gathered for Life: Official Report, VI Assembly World Council of Churches, Vancouver, Canada 24 July – 10 August 1983*. Geneva: WCC, 1983.

Gros, Jeffrey, et al. *Introduction to Ecumenism*. Mahwah, NJ: Paulist Press, 1998.

Gruber, Judith. *Intercultural Theology: Exploring World Christianity after the Cultural Turn*. Göttingen: Vandenhoeck & Ruprecht, 2018.

Henn, William. "The Reception of Ecumenical Documents." *Jurist* 57.1 (1997): 362–95.

Ilo, Stan Chu. "Crosscurrents in African Christianity: Lessons for Intercultural Hermeneutics of Friendship and Participation." In *Pathways for Interreligious Dialogue in the Twenty-First Century*, edited by Vladimir Latonovic et al., 183–96. London: Palgrave Macmillan, 2016.

———. "Receptive Ecumenism in Africa: Lessons Learned from the Actual Faith of Everyday Christians." In *Leaning into the Spirit: Ecumenical Perspectives on Discernment and Decision-Making in the Church*, edited by Virginia Miller et al., 65–84. Cham, Switzerland: Palgrave Macmillan, 2019.

John Paul II, Pope. *Ecclesia in Africa* [Post-synodal Apostolic Exhortation on the Church in Africa and Its Evangelizing Mission toward the Year 2000; September 14, 1995]. Vatican City: Libreria Editrice Vaticana, 1995. www.vatican.va.

Kessler, Diane, ed. *Together on the Way: Official Report of the Eighth Assembly of the World Council of Churches*. Geneva: WCC, 1999.

Kobia, Sam. "Denominationalism in Africa: The Pitfalls of Institutional Ecumenism." *Ecumenical Review* 53.3 (2001): 295–305.

Marotta, Vince. "Intercultural Hermeneutics and the Cross-Cultural Subject." *Journal of Intercultural Studies* 30.3 (2009): 267–84.

Mayer, Annemarie. "Ecumenical Vision of Pope Francis: Journeying Together as Fellow Pilgrims—'The Mystery of Unity Has Already Begun.'" *International Journal for the Study of the Christian Church* 17.3 (2017): 156–72.

McGrail, Peter. "The Fortress Church under Reconstruction? Sociological Factors Inhibiting Receptive Catholic Learning in the Church in England and Wales." In *Receptive Ecumenism and the Call to Catholic Learning: Exploring a Way for Contemporary Ecumenism*, edited by Paul D. Murray, 319–32. New York: Oxford University Press, 2008.

Melady, Thomas Patrick. "The Impact of Africa on Recent Developments in the Roman Catholic Church." *Race & Class* 7.2 (1965): 147–56.

Murray, Paul D., ed. "The Reception of ARCIC I and II in Europe." *Ecclesiology* 11.2 (2015): 199–218.

———. "Receptive Ecumenism and Catholic Learning—Establishing the Agenda." *International Journal for the Study of the Christian Church* 7.4 (2007): 279–301.

———. *Receptive Ecumenism and the Call to Catholic Learning: Exploring a Way for Contemporary Ecumenism*. New York: Oxford University Press, 2008.

Niles, Preman D. *Resisting the Threats to Life: Covenanting for Justice, Peace and the Integrity of Creation*. Geneva: WCC, 1989.

O'Gara, Margaret. "Shifts below the Surface of the Debate: Ecumenism, Dissent and the Roman Catholic Church." *Jurist* 56 (1996): 361–90.

Okpaleke, Ikenna Paschal. "On the Borderline between Consensus and Reception: The Spirituality of Openness as a Necessary Criterion for Ecumenical Reception." *Journal of Ecumenical Studies* 53 (2018): 348–70.

———. "'With New Eyes': Towards Advancing the Commitment of the World Council of Churches to Justice and Peace in Africa." *Ecumenical Review* 70.3 (2018): 455–69.

Orobator, Agbonkhianmeghe E. *The Church as Family: African Ecclesiology in Its Social Context*. Hekima College Collection 5. Nairobi: Paulines Publications, 2000.

———. "A Church in Dialogue as the Family of God." In *What Happened at the African Synod?*, edited by Cecil McGarry, 33–50. Nairobi: Paulines Publications Africa, 1995.

Otieno, Nicholas, and Hugh McCullum. *Journey of Hope: Towards a New Ecumenical Africa*. Geneva: WCC, 2005.

Pillay, Jerry. "Ecumenism in Africa: Theological, Contextual, and Institutional Challenges." *Ecumenical Review* 67.4 (2015): 635–50.

———. "Faith and Reality: The Role and Contributions of the Ecumenical Church to the Realities and Development of South Africa since the Advent of Democracy in 1994." *HTS Theological Studies* 73.4 (2017): 1–7.

Podmore, Colin, ed. *Community—Unity—Communion: Essays in Honour of Mary Tanner*. London: Church House Publishing, 1998.

Rusch, William G. *Reception: An Ecumenical Opportunity*. Philadelphia: Fortress Press, 1988.

Sakupapa, Teddy Chalwe. "Ecclesiology and Ethics: An Analysis of the History of the All Africa Conference of Churches (1963–2013)." PhD diss., University of Western Cape, 2016.

Siegwalt, Gérard. "Vatican II between Catholicism and Catholicity." *Concilium* 3 (2012): 62–74.

Tanner, Norman P., ed. *Decrees of the Ecumenical Councils*, vol. 2: *Trent to Vatican II*. London: Sheed & Ward, 1990.

Tsele, Molefe. "African Ecumenism within the Context of NEPAD." In *African Christian Theologies in Transformation*, edited by Ernst Conradie, 111–18. Stellenbosch, South Africa: EFSA, 2004.

Tveit, Olav Fykse. "Report of the General Secretary." In *Encountering the God of Life: Official Report of the 10th Assembly*, edited by Erlinda N. Senturias and Theodore A. Gill, 213–32. Geneva: WCC, 2014.

Vatican Council II. *Lumen Gentium* [Dogmatic Constitution on the Church; 1964]. www.vatican.va.

World Council of Churches. *Work Book for the Fifth Assembly of the World Council of Churches, Nairobi 75*. Geneva: WCC, 1975.

Werbner, Richard. "Grassroots Ecumenism in Conflict—Introduction." *Journal of South African Studies* 44.2 (2018): 201–19.

Suggested Reading

Amanze, James. *A History of the Ecumenical Movement in Africa*. Gaborone: Pula Press, 1999.

Byamungu, Gosbert T. M. "Constructing Newer 'Windows' of Ecumenism for Africa: A Catholic Perspective." *Ecumenical Review* 53.3 (2001): 341–52.

Katongole, Emmanuel. *Born from Lament: The Theology and Politics of Hope in Africa*. Grand Rapids, MI: Eerdmans, 2017.

Odeyemi, John Segun. *Pentecostalism and Catholic Ecumenism in Developing Nations: West Africa as a Case Study for a Global Phenomenon*. Eugene, OR: Wipf & Stock, 2019.

Orobator, Agbonkhianmeghe E. *The Church as Family: African Ecclesiology in Its Social Context*. Hekima College Collection 5. Nairobi: Paulines Publications, 2000.

———, ed. *The Church We Want: African Catholics Look to Vatican III*. Maryknoll, NY: Orbis Books, 2016.

Key Words

African Catholicism
ecumenism
Family of God
receptive ecumenism
transformation

Church and Politics in Africa: History, Method of Study, and the Future

Aloys Ojore

African politicians are known to remind church leaders to leave politics to politicians and concern themselves with strictly religious matters. As Laurenti Magesa notes, however, the Christian church "has not only been involved in politics, but has also had to struggle for her identity from the very beginning of her inception."[1] Initially, she had to try to fit within the Jewish religious and political structures, and, later, the Roman imperial religious power tried to force the church to follow the empire's religious dictates. Christians rejected this and "took a relative view of the Emperor and the Empire, which were only to be obeyed when they were in harmony with the will of the one true God, which had been revealed to his Church."[2] Eventually, Christianity triumphed following its recognition by Emperor Constantine in or around 312 CE. The marriage between the Catholic Church and the Roman state led some popes and emperors to act as coleaders of both church and state. Consequently, Magesa writes, "The question of contestation of power between the emperor and the bishop, the prince and the priest, the earthly ruler and the divine representative became constant."[3] Sometimes the political authorities reigned supreme and at other times clerics directed the political realm.

This relationship between church and state has been viewed differently by various commentators through the centuries. St. Augustine of Hippo (354–430), characterized politics as belonging to people "who are impious and proud . . . , who strive after certain privileges of their own, and who seek divine honors from their misguided subjects" (*City of God* 11.449).[4] For Augustine, the church should, therefore, have nothing to do with politics. St. Thomas Aquinas, however, held that "politics was good for the purpose of both human happiness and development. Aquinas recognized that the state and the Church are intertwining institutions of the same social reality. Consequently, there is only a division of labor between the two since they serve the same purpose, that is, human happiness on earth which is important for their connection to God."[5]

In line with this view of Aquinas, it was entirely appropriate for Pope Leo III (795–816) to anoint and declare Charlemagne the first Christian emperor of the Holy Roman Empire in 800 CE. During the Reformation, Martin Luther insisted, on the contrary, that the "Church should deal with matters of faith and morals and leave matters of money, property, life and honor to the temporal

---

1. Magesa, *Post-Conciliar Church in Africa*, 97.
2. Bokenkotter, *Concise History of the Catholic Church*, 36.
3. Magesa, "Taking Strategic Positions," 10.
4. Augustine, *The City of God against the Pagans*, ed. W. R. Dyson. See also Mhandara et al., "The Church and Political Transition in Zimbabwe," 104.
5. Mhandara et al., "The Church and Political Transition in Zimbabwe," 104.

judges."⁶ He raised the notion of "the wall of separation between Church and State."⁷

The struggle to push the Christian church out of public life reached its climax with the French Revolution in 1789. The revolution was anti-Catholic and anti-monarchy. The church and her clergy were identified with the royals who oppressed and exploited the people. The confusion in the aftermath of the revolution gave Napoleon Bonaparte an opportunity to stage a coup d'état, leading to the political reorganization of France. Because of his fear of being controlled by Rome, at his coronation as emperor of France in the Cathedral of Notre-Dame de Paris in 1804, Napoleon grabbed the crown from the hands of Pope Pius VII and "placed on his own head the crown which the people's armies had won for him."⁸ Napoleon subsequently made sure that the Roman pontiff did not meddle in his political business.

Toward the end of the nineteenth century, at a time when Catholicism was being vigorously introduced into Africa, the church adopted an antiliberal and authoritarian mindset. This attitude arose from the fact that "when Rome was taken away from the pope by military force in 1870, the then-Pope Pius IX excommunicated the king and the leaders of the Italian government and forbade good Catholics from recognizing its legitimacy, running for office, or voting in parliamentary elections."⁹ The serious tension between the Roman church and the Italian state explains why the early Catholic missionaries were, all over the world, slow to support democratic ideals, social activism, and movements for independence. They kept away from politics and wanted their converts and would-be converts to do the same.

The chief subject of this chapter is how the Catholic Church has related to the political domain in Africa. The continent is home to fifty-four countries today, and it would be impossible to cover all of them here. Even though references to other African countries are made in the discussion, I have chosen to focus primarily on the church–state relations in Uganda, Kenya, Tanzania, and Zimbabwe. There are several reasons for this choice. First, each of these countries contains a good representation of members from all the Christian churches present in Africa; second, these countries were colonized and evangelized by the same country, Great Britain, which makes them interesting for comparative studies; and third, the unique political circumstances of each of these countries has involved interesting political and religious personalities.

Since the Catholic Church in Africa has always acted in collaboration with other Christian churches in all spheres of African life, the word "church" is not restricted to references to the Catholic Church. Throughout the chapter, when the term "church" refers to the Catholic Church, such usage will be understood from the context. When I apply the term generally, it will refer to the Christian church (or churches). When appropriate, I will mention a specific Christian church by name.

The chapter is divided into the following sections: (1) the Christian church, her mission in the world, and her relationship to politics; (2) why the Christian church participates in politics; (3) the relationship between church and state in colonial Africa; (4) church and politics in postcolonial Uganda, Kenya, Tanzania, and Zimbabwe; (5) African politicians and the church; (6) the prophetic mission of the church; (7) African churches and the future; and (8) a conclusion. In discussing church–state relations in Africa, the first critical issue we need to address is the mission of the Christian church on earth.

The Christian Church, Her Mission in the World, and Her Relationship to Politics

The Second Vatican Council's Dogmatic Constitution on the Church, *Lumen Gentium*, defines the church as "the people of God" (§9; see also 1 Pet 10–2:9) who are "anointed by the Spirit at baptism to become active participants in Jesus Christ's

---

6. Luther, "Open Letter to the Christian Nobility of the German Nation," 60.
7. Magesa, "Taking Strategic Positions," 12.
8. MacCulloch, *Groundwork of Christian History*, 253.
9. David Kertzer, quoted in "'Pope and Mussolini' tells the 'Secret History' of Fascism and the Church," *Fresh Air*, NPR (January 27, 2014), www.npr.org.

prophetic, priestly, and kingly ministry."[10] As stated in the Gospel of Luke (4:16–32), Christ's ministry was, in fact, a ministry of liberating all human beings from oppressive sinful social structures. Christians are all called to serve the least, to live for the sake of both close and distant neighbors, and "to do justice, to love mercy, and walk humbly with God" (1 Pet 2:24). It is clear that God, as preached by Jesus Christ, is radically social. The Christian church, therefore, has the obligation to uncover why basic human needs and rights are not being met in Africa. Since a mission of liberation was in the forefront of Christ's ministry, we can conclude that our mission on earth as church is "first of all God's" mission.[11] The church cannot compromise this divine mandate in the face of political pressure, no matter how strong the pressure may be. Both the council and the *Compendium of the Social Doctrine of the Catholic Church* explain, "The Church, by reason of her role and competence, is not identified with any political community nor bound by ties to any political system. . . . The political community and the Church are autonomous and independent of each other in their own fields. Nevertheless, both are devoted to the personal vocation of man, though under different titles."[12]

In the modern world, therefore, the church understands politics as

> that science which teaches people to seek the common Good at both the national and international levels. Its task is to spell out the fundamental values of every community in the temporal sphere and to enable leaders of a nation to provide the community with ways and means for honest, just and peaceful life, combating elements . . . such as lawlessness, poverty, hunger, ignorance, disease and corruption.[13]

It follows that "politics is generally supposed to be concerned with the distribution of power in society"[14] and moderating the relations among citizens. The church urges her members to be good citizens who live in accordance with the demands of national constitutions and laws and to pay their taxes so as to enable the government to provide necessary services. The church holds and teaches that "in their proper spheres, the political community and the Church are mutually independent and self-governing" (*Gaudium et Spes* §76).[15]

According to the *Compendium*, "The Church cares for and provides spiritual welfare while the state cares for and provides everything that is part of the temporal common good."[16] The state should therefore see the church as a responsible partner and not a reckless critic. The church accepts and supports legitimate political authority but vehemently rejects corrupt political authority. In Romans 13, the apostle Paul tells all citizens, church leaders included, that they have a duty to obey rulers; but when it is time to say no to a tyrant, the church must stand firm. The church gives to Caesar what belongs to him and to God what belongs to God (Mark 12:13–17). Due respect must be shown to leaders because citizens have given them the mandate to govern. "In a democracy, the people transfer their exercise of authority to those whom they freely elect. The people also preserve the prerogative to replace those elected when they do not fulfil their functions satisfactorily."[17] This is because the sovereignty of the state inheres in its own citizens.

Although the church and state have mutual interests, there should be a clear separation between their respective powers. The principle of separation of powers between the state and the church should be understood as follows:

---

10. Hinze, "Listening to the Spirit," 4.
11. Bevans and Schroeder, *Prophetic Dialogue*, 15.
12. Vatican II, Pastoral Constitution on the Church in the Modern World (*Gaudium et Spes*) §76. See also Pontifical Council for Justice and Peace, *Compendium of the Social Doctrine of the Church*, no. 424.
13. Tarcicio, *Every Citizen's Handbook*, 373.
14. Ellis and ter Haar, "Religion and Politics in Sub-Saharan Africa," 178.
15. See also *Catechism of the Catholic Church*, no. 2245.
16. *Compendium of the Social Doctrine of the Church*, no. 424.
17. Harrington, *Religion and Politics for Everyone*, 19.

If it [the principle of the separation of church and state] means that the state has autonomy in regulating matters of governance, without undue interference by the church, the principle is impeccably sound and is at the best service of democratic rule. It prevents religious tyranny. But, then, if it is taken to imply the total removal of religious consciousness (morality or ethics) from the political and economic processes, then it must be rejected because it easily leads to political impunity.[18]

The "mutual autonomy of the Church and the political community does not entail a separation that excludes cooperation. Both of them . . . serve the personal and social vocation of the same human beings."[19] In other words, "since the state and the Church have society as their context, absolute categories of separation of involvement and activities cannot be sustained."[20]

Christians believe that "authority must be guided by the moral law. All of its dignity has to be guided and exercised in the context of the moral order, which in turn has God for its source and final end" (*Gaudium et Spes* §74).[21] Political authority is "an instrument of coordination and direction by means of which the many individuals and intermediate bodies must move towards an order in which relationships, institutions and procedures are put at the service of integral human growth."[22] The church, therefore, has a divine mandate to intervene in the political life of her members.

Why the Christian Church Engages in Politics

As Charity Mhandara et al. note, "The fact that the Church's influence is mainly on spiritual aspects does not stop its leaders from involvement in national politics."[23] The church must participate in the political life of the people for at least eight reasons. First, human nature calls for the proper organization of daily activities that can be achieved only by politics. Aristotle (384–322 BCE) wrote, "It is evident that the state is a creation of nature, and that man is by nature a political animal. He who by nature and not by mere accident is without a state, is either above humanity, or below it" (*Politics*, Book 1, 1253a). Second, long before the arrival of the Christian church, "[i]n all known pre-colonial African political systems and states, religious performance played an important role."[24] The concept and practice of the priest-king were known in Ghana among the Ashanti and in Uganda among the Baganda. That the king in each of these countries was both a "political and a religious leader was an indisputable fact."[25] Combining religion and politics is, therefore, part of African culture. Third, "[b]oth the Church and the State are focused on the same human being."[26] In other words, those who are the subjects of political authority are the same people as the congregations that gather in places of worship. When politics are unjust, it is the responsibility of the people of God (the church) to raise their voices.

The fourth reason the church must participate in politics is that otherwise it is unclear how millions of African citizens can express their views to their political leaders on matters affecting them. They "must have at least some organization which speaks up for the rights of all regardless of what happens tomorrow," Henry Okullu writes, and "[o]ne cannot think of any other organization better placed than a church to play that role."[27] The fifth reason was explained by the Symposium of Episcopal Conferences of Africa and Madagascar (SECAM),

---

18. Magesa, "Taking Strategic Positions," 13.
19. *Compendium of the Social Doctrine of the Church*, no. 425.
20. Magesa, *Post-Conciliar Church in Africa*, 103.
21. See also Pope John XXIII, encyclical *Pacem in Terris* §270.
22. *Compendium of the Social Doctrine of the Church*, no. 394.
23. Mhandara et al., "Church and Political Transition in Zimbabwe," 106.
24. Ellis and ter Haar, "Religion and Politics in Sub-Saharan Africa," 187.
25. Magesa, "Taking Strategic Positions," 9.
26. Harrington, *Religion and Politics for Everyone*, 23.
27. Okullu, *Church and Politics in East Africa*, 10.

which stressed that, with respect to the Catholic faithful, "[t]here can be no dichotomy between their Christian conscience and their political conscience. Even in political matters, they should remember that they are the salt of the earth and the light of the world."[28] Sixth, both church and state are creations of history. It is within history that the Christian church exists and carries out her saving mission, and it is an interest in the common good that explains the church's involvement in the affairs of the society and the state. It has to be stressed, however, that the church "has no desire to replace human and political leadership. The mission of the church is much greater, for she stands over and against society, irreducible to it, challenging it, even judging it in the world but not finally of it."[29]

Seventh, as Emily Choge argues, the church is a powerful and reliable "instrument for bringing the change that God wants in the world and not the state."[30] Part of the prophetic role of church leaders in Africa is to make this clear to political leaders. Jesus told Pilate to his face that he had no power over him except that given by God (John 19:11). Christians believe that Christ is far above all rule and authority and power and dominion, and above every name that is named, not only in this age but also in the age to come (Eph 1:21). In obedience to her master, it is required that the church be everywhere in the world (Matt 28:18–20).

Finally, eighth, the Universal Declaration of Human Rights (1948) states, "All human beings are born free and are equal in dignity. All are entitled to rights and freedoms regardless of . . . religion and political affiliation, and all have rights to take part in the governing of one's country."[31] Christians are not excluded from the enjoyment of such rights. Christians uphold that human beings are created in the image and likeness of God (Ps 8:5–7; Gen 1:27; *Gaudium et Spes* §12). "Aware of their dignity, people are demanding a proper political, social and economic order that affirms this" (*Gaudium et Spes* §9). Wherever the church goes she helps people discover their rights, enhances the dignity of the human person, and preaches the unity of the human family *Gaudium et Spes* §§40, 41, 42). This was the message the missionaries brought to Africa, even if the politics of colonization marred it.

Church and Politics in Colonial Africa

Evangelization of Africa was intimately connected with the process of colonization. "In French and Portuguese colonies . . . the Catholic Church had a much closer relationship with colonial authorities than it did in the British areas,"[32] and this was also true in the Belgian Congo, a largely Catholic colony. Similarly, the Anglican Church missionaries belonging to the established Church of England tended to work closely with the British colonial authorities. This was replicated in Ghana, Nigeria, Kenya, and Uganda. Consequently, "Christian mission churches were perceived by many African elites to be the vanguard of the advance of European hegemony."[33] It is no wonder that President Jomo Kenyatta of Kenya once quipped, "The white man in Africa was very clever: he came with his Bible, he preached and sung hymns, and we Africans were very amused. He then said, 'Close your eyes and let us pray.' When he said 'Amen,' we opened our eyes; he had taken over our land and we were holding the Bible."[34]

It is important to note, however, that "relations between Church and State have always varied from place to place, according to particular history, culture and circumstances."[35] The relationship between church and state in Africa, for example, was always guided by instructions from Rome. In his encyclical *Ad Beatissimi Apostolorum*, Pope Benedict XV seemed to suggest that it was not prudent to

---

28. SECAM, *A Letter to the Christians of the Great Lakes Region*, 40. See also Matt 5:14.
29. McDonagh, *Church and Politics*, 34.
30. Choge, "Pilgrim Motif," 98. See also Kasenene, "Relation between Religion and Politics," 15.
31. United Nations, Universal Declaration of Human Rights, arts. 1, 2, and 21.
32. Haynes, *Religion and Politics in Africa*, 43.
33. Haynes, *Religion and Politics in Africa*, 42.
34. Burton, "Blessings of Africa," 89.
35. Ellis and ter Haar, "Religion and Politics in Sub-Saharan Africa," 188.

divorce religion from the political life and development policies of a country. He wrote:

> Let the Princes and Rulers of peoples remember this truth, and let them consider whether it is a prudent and safe idea for governments or for states to separate themselves from the holy religion of Jesus Christ, from which their authority receives such strength and support. Let them consider again and again, whether it is a measure of political wisdom to seek to divorce the teaching of the Gospel and of the Church from the ruling of a country and from the public education of the young. (§11)

Surprisingly, in his apostolic letter *Maximum Illud* of 1919, Benedict denounced the political activities of the missionaries as "a plague" that would "infect the apostolate," saying that missionaries should not "busy themselves with the interests of their terrestrial homeland instead of with those of their homeland in heaven and faith" (§19). This caution was again repeated by Pope Pius XI in 1938, at the start of the Second World War.[36] Suddenly, the most important task of the Catholic missionaries "was to establish the Church of Christ, which was supranational and above politics."[37]

In the 1930s, African Catholic bishops often sent telegrams to governors in which they pledged their loyalty.[38] The "missionaries realized their precarious position as foreigners. They depended on the colonial government for granting visas, for buying and renting land, and subsidizing schools and hospitals."[39] Collaboration was needed to achieve success in all sectors of society. This explains why in "the 1930s, 1940s and 1950s when the nationalistic movements came into being, the basic principle that the Church was above politics also applied to African nationalism."[40] It is known that "the Catholic Church was initially highly suspicious of African nationalism, as it was often equated with communism"; and "[c]onsequently, Catholics were urged to avoid joining political parties and to remain obedient to the colonial authorities. After World War II, the attitude of the mission church toward African nationalism changed: the missionaries chose to forge close ties with nationalist leaders and, later, independent governments."[41]

Two main reasons can be cited for this change on the part of the mission churches. First, the Universal Declaration of Human Rights of 1948 stressed that all peoples of the world have the right to self-determination. Second, in the 1950s, African bishops and priests were increasing in numbers and were better placed to call for equality and better treatment for the African peoples. Prior to that time, the Catholic missionaries in South Africa, for example, did not confront the apartheid system because "there was a continuing fear that, since the Hierarchy and clergy were until the 1970s predominantly expatriates, any serious Catholic ... resistance to apartheid could lead to the deportation of prominent leaders of the Catholic Church from South Africa, leading to the virtual collapse of Catholicism in the country."[42]

In the late 1960s, the Christian churches in Africa began to support local political movements that would eventually lead to independence. Right after the independence of many African countries, the Catholic Church became very actively involved in the political life of the people. Examples from Uganda, Kenya, Tanzania, and Zimbabwe will help to illustrate the relationship between church and state in Africa.

Church and Politics in Postcolonial Uganda, Kenya, Tanzania, and Zimbabwe

The interplay between church and politics in Uganda was characterized by tension and even violence from the beginning. Religious wars were

---

36. De Jong, "Church and Politics in Tanzania," 26.
37. De Jong, "Church and Politics in Tanzania," 26.
38. De Jong, "Church and Politics in Tanzania," 25.
39. De Jong, "Church and Politics in Tanzania," 25.
40. De Jong, "Church and Politics in Tanzania," 27.
41. Haynes, *Religion and Politics in Africa*, 61–62.
42. See Kean, "Church Growth and Development in South Africa," 3, 4.

fought between Protestants and Catholics in 1865 and from 1888 to 1892. However, when Kabaka (King) Mwanga became despotic and murderous, "Catholics, Protestants and Muslims joined forces and overthrew him in 1888."[43] Mwanga had killed his young pages (the Ugandan Martyrs), who chose to disobey him out of loyalty to Christ and the church.

During the period of British control over Uganda from 1894 to 1962, the colonizers favored the Protestant Baganda people to the displeasure of Catholics and minority Muslims. For this reason, "[t]he rivalry between Protestants and Catholics was the main political issue in the 1950 and 1960s. The conflict focused on the role of the Baganda and their King in the political structure of the country."[44] The Kabaka was a Protestant but many of his chiefs were Catholics. In Uganda, therefore, the "Anglican and Catholic churches are an essential part of the social fabric, and have become fused at a deep level into political, social and cultural life."[45] Uganda became independent from Britain in 1962; Milton Obote became its first prime minister and Edward Mutesa II its first (nonexecutive) president. Soon afterwards, a power struggle arose between the two and reached a critical point in 1965 when Obote deposed Mutesa and forced him into exile in Britain. The then Catholic archbishop Kiwanuka condemned Obote for this action. Obote took power as an executive president from 1966 to 1971, when he was deposed by General Idi Amin Dada.

Amin's despotic regime was accused of involvement in numerous murders and of persecuting the church. In 1976, the bishops of the Anglican Church of Uganda, the Catholic bishops, and prominent Muslim leaders met under the chairmanship of the Anglican archbishop of Kampala Janani Luwum. They categorically condemned the atrocities of Amin, with Luwum reading the statement prepared by the religious leaders. He was later found tortured and murdered. The Anglican Church appeared to have been cowed by this killing because after Luwum's murder, it elected Silvanus Wani, who was from Amin's ethnic community, to succeed him. When Obote returned to power after the overthrow of Amin, the Anglican Church elected Yona Okoth, an Obote supporter, to succeed Wani.

In response to the killing of citizens in Uganda, SECAM said in a statement, "We condemn all the crimes committed in the name of the security of the State, as if the State were absolute and not at the service of the citizen, that is to say, the human person. It is the human person and not the State which has a transcendental character."[46] However, after Amin's exit, during successive regimes the church in Uganda became more and more silent. The Christian churches have been unable to stand up against President Yoweri Museveni, who has ruled Uganda since 1986 and is bent on serving as president for life.

The situation in Kenya unfolded in a somewhat different way. After a volatile colonial period and many conflicts during the struggle for liberation in the 1950s, the relationship between church and state in post-independence Kenya was largely cordial. In an address to the Catholic Association of Member Episcopal Conferences of Eastern Africa in 1976, President Jomo Kenyatta reminded the Catholic bishops that the "church is the conscience of the society, and today a society needs a conscience. Do not be afraid to speak. If we go wrong and you keep quiet, one day you will answer for our mistakes."[47] Bishop Okullu also said, "A nation without a conscience is like a ball bouncing on the waves."[48] Agbonkhianmeghe E. Orobator observes that, from 1963 to 1978, the Catholic bishops and other church leaders in Kenya admirably fulfilled their role as the conscience of Kenyan society.

During the dictatorial regime of President Daniel arap Moi (1978–2002), however, "collaboration shifted to opposition."[49] According to Orobator,

---

43. Gifford, *African Christianity*, 112.
44. Haynes, *Religion and Politics in Africa*, 62.
45. Gifford, *African Christianity*, 116.
46. SECAM, *A Letter to the Christians of the Great Lakes Region*, 40.
47. Kenyatta quoted in Mejia, *Conscience of Society*, 50.
48. Okullu, *Church and Politics in East Africa*, 10.
49. Orobator, "Church, State, and Catholic Ethics," 182.

"the opposition was spearheaded by individual church leaders renowned for the strident denunciation of political figures, usually in the form of political sermons."[50] Gifford notes that "Catholics and Protestant Church leaders from the main-line churches took the lead."[51] President Moi played the ethnic card against all church leaders who opposed his dictatorial regime with much success, but, Gifford notes that "the churches that supported him received parcels of land to build church structures, schools and hospitals." In addition, "[t]he President contributed a lot of money to help build many church structures in Kenya."[52] Moi stoked ethnic tensions to divide opposition political parties prior to the 1992 and 1997 elections, leading to the infamous ethnic violence in the Rift Valley. Eventually, all of the Christian churches united in condemning Moi's regime and openly urged their faithful to vote Moi out of office in 2002.

After the contested elections in Kenya in 2007, "the top leadership of the Catholic Church in Kenya was publicly divided along ethnic lines, thus putting exclusionary tribal identities ahead of inclusive Christian identity and commitment. The Church's credibility and capacity to challenge the political class was deeply dented."[53] Both the Catholic and Protestant churches failed to take a stand against the ethnic cleansing that was taking place in Kenya. In 2008, the Protestant National Council of Churches of Kenya (NCCK) publicly apologized to Kenyans, saying, "We regret that we as church leaders were unable to effectively confront these issues because we were partisan,"[54] but Catholic Church leaders never apologized. The failure of the Christian churches to respond to political crisis in Kenya was repeated in the 2013 and 2017 presidential elections.

The Christian churches in Uganda have traditionally been paralyzed by an excessive fear of the power of the state, and the churches in Kenya have been rendered impotent by their obsession with ethnic loyalties. Unlike Uganda and Kenya, the church and the Tanzanian state have had a very healthy relationship that deserves the emulation of other African countries.

In the Trust Territory of Tanganyika (now Tanzania), "the Catholic Church recognized the legitimacy of the Colonial state."[55] This recognition continued until agitation for independence began. In 1953, the Tanzanian Catholic Episcopal Conference issued a pastoral letter entitled "Africans and the Christian Way of Life." The bishops told Tanzanians that the "people of the territory may rest assured that in their efforts to build their homeland, they will have the full support of the Church."[56] The bishops were categorical that they would not support the current political authority, and they recognized the people's right to self-determination.

On the eve of independence in 1960, the Catholic bishops wrote another pastoral letter, *Unity and Freedom in New Tanganyika*. They called for a separation between church and state but appealed for collaboration in the development of human services. When Julius Nyerere became the first president in 1961, he called for closer links between the Tanzanian church and state, and warm relations and mutual respect existed until Nyerere retired in 1985. Throughout the period of Nyerere's presidency, church and state collaborated to create a peaceful, harmonious, and developing nation that promoted brotherhood, sisterhood, and respect for human dignity. He fostered good relations in part by establishing a Council of Elders made up of three Catholic bishops, one Anglican bishop, one Lutheran bishop, representatives of Pentecostal churches, the secretary general of the Tanzanian Evangelical Federation, and representatives of the Islamic faith.

---

50. Orobator, "Church, State, and Catholic Ethics," 183.
51. Gifford, *African Christianity*, 36.
52. Choge, "Pilgrim Motif," 109.
53. Orobator, "Church, State, and Catholic Ethics," 183.
54. See "Hope for Kenya," NCCK Executive Committee Press Statement. See also Gichure and Stinton, *Religion and Politics in Africa*, 8.
55. Gichure and Stinton, *Religion and Politics in Africa*, 24.
56. Tanzanian Catholic Episcopal Conference, *Africans and the Christian Way of Life*, 1953, cited in Gichure and Stinton, *Religion and Politics in Africa*, 8.

In 1967, Tanzania opted for the "villagization" (*Ujamaa*) system of government following Nyerere's publication of the Arusha Declaration.[57] Rural populations were relocated to huge villages in order to promote more efficient agricultural production and to protect an African social system that was being threatened by the pressures of the modern world. The following year, the Catholic bishops issued a pastoral letter entitled *The Church and the Developing Society of Tanzania*. In it, the bishops declared their support for *Ujamaa* insofar as it upheld the Christian principles of justice, unity, and equality.

However, when it was clear that the system was not working, the Catholic leaders told the president as much. When Nyerere retired in 1985, he publicly admitted that his experiment had failed and asked Tanzanians to forgive him for the mistakes his government had made. But his relationship with the church was always strong. Even after his retirement, "Nyerere was the point of reference in the relations between Church and state, to whom Church leaders had easy access in case of conflicts."[58] The church in Tanzania exercised vigilance over post-Nyerere governments, never failing to condemn corruption where it was present. Tanzania is an exception to the generally poor church–state relations in Africa, which particularly obtained in Zimbabwe.

In 1963, when Ian Smith of what was then called Southern Rhodesia (now Zimbabwe) declared independence from Britain, the Anglican bishop Kenneth Skelton and his Catholic counterpart Donal Lamont were playing an active role in "denouncing racial segregation, human rights abuses and other excesses of the state."[59] When Robert Mugabe declared the War of Liberation against Smith's government in 1964, all the Christian churches in Zimbabwe held meetings with politicians in an attempt to mediate the conflict, but they met with little success. In 1979, the churches called upon all the political parties to end the war and to accept national unity and reconciliation. When independence came on April 18, 1980, the church had become an important part of political life in Zimbabwe; in fact, the first two presidents of Zimbabwe were Protestant clergymen: Rev. Canaan Banana and Bishop Abel Muzorewa.

Zimbabwe's "first decade of independence was guided by a socialist ideology deriving its basic thought and principles from Marxist-Leninist philosophy."[60] President Robert Mugabe, who had become president in 1987, and his vice president Canaan Banana, called upon the Zimbabwean Christian churches to completely support the government's policies, and the churches responded by cooperating with the state in the provision of education and health services. Despite this collaboration, the "Protestant Zimbabwe Council of Churches and the Catholic Commission for Justice and Peace adopted a watchdog position in the endeavor to promote civic consciousness."[61] Criticism of government policies by the churches was perceived to be a Western imperialist attack to be ruthlessly repelled, and the churches began to cave in after experiencing brutal reprisals at the hands of Mugabe's forces.

In 1997, for example, government forces moved into Matabeleland to crush demonstrations against Mugabe. The Catholic Commission for Justice and Peace documented the atrocities and the abuses committed there and submitted their report to the Catholic bishops, but the bishops refused to adopt it. The report was later smuggled out to Britain and published in the newspaper *The Independent*, to the embarrassment of the Catholic Bishop's Conference. Frustrated by the church's inability to address the problems facing the country, the lay-led Catholic Commission for Justice and Peace undertook to advocate for the reform of Mugabe's government amid harassment from his security forces.

In 1998, Zimbabwe launched an interventionist war in the Democratic Republic of the Congo. The Catholic Justice and Peace Commission organized and executed a demonstration against it, but the bishops refused to join. In the same year, the World

---

57. Nyerere, *Ujamaa Essays on Socialism*, 13–37.
58. De Jong, "Church and Politics in Tanzania," 29.
59. Munemo and Nciizah, "Church in Zimbabwe's Peace and Reconciliation Process," 63.
60. Gundani, "Church's Mission in the Building of Zimbabwe," 24.
61. Gundani, "Church's Mission in the Building of Zimbabwe," 29.

Council of Churches held its conference in Zimbabwe and called upon the churches to be courageous in their dealings with the government. In 1999, the government drafted a constitution and called a referendum to ratify it; the Catholic Justice and Peace Commission campaigned against it. Sensing that the draft constitution would be rejected and that the people might rebel, the Zimbabwe Council of Churches, together with the Catholic Church, urged the National Constitutional Assembly and the people to reject it. The draft constitution was defeated in the referendum in 2000, humiliating Mugabe's government. After this defeat, Mugabe had to win in the elections scheduled later that year in order to hold on to power, but the opposition party of the late Morgan Tsvangirai was poised for victory. Mugabe "resorted to . . . accelerated land reform to win back the rural and peri-urban vote constituting the majority of the eligible registered voters."[62] Mugabe was successful, but the elections were massively rigged and marred by violence.

After this election, the Catholic Church, as well as other Christian churches, remained rather ambivalent and afraid to challenge Mugabe's government. The only Catholic bishop who dared to take on Mugabe, Pius Alick Mvunda Ncube, the archbishop of Bulawayo, was forced to resign in September 2007 after Mugabe's secret service implicated him in a serious sex scandal. The other bishops learned their lesson from this event and avoided politics even as the inflation rate in Zimbabwe reached levels not seen anywhere in the world. There seemed to be no hope for the people of Zimbabwe, but political change came from an unexpected quarter.

On November 14, 2017, the Zimbabwean military put Mugabe under house arrest. Shortly before this, Mugabe had ousted his vice president and heir apparent Emmerson Mnangagwa in an attempt to pave the way for his wife, Grace, to take power. The move by the military thwarted this plot. In their address to the nation, the generals who led the coup pleaded: "To all Churches and religious organizations in Zimbabwe, we call upon you and your congregations to pray for our country and preach the Gospel of love, peace, unity and development."[63] Mugabe was forced to resign and the deposed and self-exiled Mnangagwa was invited to return to the country from South Africa, whereupon he was sworn in as the new president of Zimbabwe.

The churches were unable to influence this regime change because Mugabe had managed to divide them, and they maintained a low profile during this period of sudden change in Zimbabwe. Despite the weakness of the church as described here, it "can be argued that the Christian Churches have played an important role towards the . . . birth of a vibrant multi-party politics in Zimbabwe."[64]

Despite the strained relations between church and state in many African countries, politicians often invite church leaders to play crucial roles in government. In addition, in South Africa, Kenya, Uganda, Nigeria, Mozambique, and South Sudan, "the majority of the structures of dialogue for reconciliation have called on prelates and high religious personalities of the Church"[65] to take the lead. This involvement is proper because the "main role of the Church in politically disturbed areas is peacemaking that is based on justice."[66] In South Africa, for example, the late Archbishop Desmond Tutu led the famous Truth, Justice, and Reconciliation Commission, which investigated the atrocities committed during the apartheid regime. In Kenya, the committee that drafted Kenya's new constitution was chaired by Philip Sulumeti, then the Catholic bishop of the Diocese of Kakamega. The late Reverend Prof. John Mary Waliggo served on the Uganda Constitution Commission. On January 23, 2017, the retired archbishop Eliud Wabukala of the Anglican Church of Kenya was appointed chairman of the Ethics and Anti-Corruption Commission. Church leaders are preferred for these positions because "they enjoy a broad consensus among citizens and political actors who appreciate

---

62. Mhandara et al., "Church and Political Transition in Zimbabwe," 103.
63. "Zimbabwe Military's Statement after Seizing Power" (Reuters).
64. Mhandara et al., "Church and Political Transition in Zimbabwe," 108.
65. Ndiaye, "Leadership/Governance and Religion in Africa," 279.
66. Byrne and Rayan, "Church and the Dilemma of Development," 33.

their impartiality."⁶⁷ But, as is discussed in the next section, it is also clear that African politicians often use the church for their political interests.

How African Politicians Use and Abuse the Church

Some African politicians believe that the church should stay out of politics. However, the same politicians are known to align themselves with the church "for purposes of mobilizing voters, creating clienteles or organizing constituencies."⁶⁸ It was with this aim that "South Africa's President P. W. Botha attended and addressed the Easter gathering of the Zion Christian Church in 1985," and that "some years later the same event was attended by Frederick W. de Klerk, Nelson Mandela and Chief Mangosuthu Buthelezi."⁶⁹ They were all seeking political support from this church, which had millions of followers in towns and cities all over South Africa. Anecdotal evidence reveals that all over Africa, politicians usually visit churches and other places of worship in order to solicit votes. President Félix Houphouët-Boigny of Togo built one of the largest basilicas in Christendom in his village town of Yamoussoukro, and one of the reasons he did so was that "politicians are ready to do anything to win elective positions."⁷⁰

Other politicians invite or visit important church personalities to win the support of the faithful, using the church as a platform to gain political notoriety. For example, "[i]n order to ensure huge support of Christians . . . in elections, President Shehu Shagari invited Pope John Paul II and the then Head of Anglican Church, Archbishop Runcie, on state visit to Nigeria in 1981. Millions of Christians in Nigeria were jubilant when the Pope arrived."⁷¹ In 2011, the retired archbishop of Canterbury Lord Rowan Williams visited Zimbabwe and met with Robert Mugabe to discuss land issues that had been raised by the Anglican Church. African politicians have even used African Instituted Churches (AICs, also called "African-Initiated Churches" or "African Independent Churches") to undermine and control mainline Christian churches.

It is no wonder that African governments identify with AICs, which often support politicians rejected by other Christian churches. President Moi of Kenya, for example, appointed the late Archbishop Stephen Ondiek of the Legio Maria Church of Africa to his cabinet. Legio Maria supported Moi throughout his twenty-four years of rule. Members of AICs tend to see African presidents as God-given leaders who fought for the rights of Africans against racial discrimination during white rule.

In the 1970s, Catholic bishop William Patrick Whelan argued that apartheid was not contrary to Catholic teaching⁷² and became a darling of the apartheid regime. In the 1990s, a Catholic bishop of the Diocese of Kabale in Uganda "used his links with the security forces to harass his priest opponents, and even had them arrested. . . . The Bishop could not enter eight or nine parishes without threat of serious violence."⁷³ The bishop eventually stepped down, and a foreign missionary was appointed to replace him. In 2017, the late Catholic bishop of the Diocese of Eldoret in Kenya received a state funeral because of his close links to President Uhuru Kenyatta and his deputy William Ruto. The two politicians had raised funds so that the bishop could salvage his diocese from imminent financial collapse; in return, the two leaders received unswerving loyalty and support from the prelate. It should be noted that some church leaders in Africa have used the powers of the state for personal gain and that African politicians have often tried to influence and control the church by taking advantage of this fact.

---

67. Ndiaye, "Leadership/Governance and Religion in Africa," 279.
68. Ellis and ter Haar, "Religion and Politics in Sub-Saharan Africa," 188. See also Mhandara et al., "Church and Political Transition in Zimbabwe," 111.
69. Ellis and ter Haar, "Religion and Politics in Sub-Saharan Africa," 188.
70. Gichure, "Religion and Politics in Africa: The Rise of Ethno-Religions," 46.
71. Chukwu, "Religion as a Factor in the Nigerian Political Culture," 58.
72. Egan, *The Politics of South African Catholic Student Movement*, iv.
73. Gifford, *African Christianity*, 123.

Magesa notes that "Marxist leaning African leaders like Kwame Nkrumah of Ghana and Ahmed Sékou Touré of Guinea Conakry called for total separation of powers between state and church."[74] According to Samuel Kobia, "Whereas the Church urged members to seek first the Kingdom of God, Nkrumah coined the call: 'Seek ye first the political Kingdom.'"[75] Nkrumah was convinced that the Christian churches had deliberately colluded with colonial powers to defraud African peoples. In 1961, he "ordered the mission churches in Ghana to open branches of his Convention Peoples' Party in each community church building."[76]

Churches began to fear that the new independent governments would demand that they support their political agenda, a demand to which some church leaders appeared willing to accede. In 1965, for example, the respected cardinal Joseph-Albert Malula of Kinshasa wrote to Mobutu, "Mr. President, the church recognizes your authority, because authority comes from God. We will loyally apply the laws you establish. You can count on us in your work of restoring the peace towards which all of us desire."[77] Malula lived in a mansion given him by Mobutu in 1974.

Many church leaders, however, opted to remain loyal to their prophetic role and challenged high-handed political leaders. The consequences were varied, ranging from exile, as in the case of Catholic bishop Patrick Kalilombe of Malawi under Kamuzu Banda, to the murder of Ugandan archbishop Janani Luwum under Amin. In 1990, the Anglican bishop of Eldoret was killed in a car accident. Later, a member of Kenyan intelligence confessed to the Truth, Justice, and Reconciliation Commission that the bishop was actually killed following an order from then-President Moi. In 1997, Kenyan police attacked the Anglican All Saints Cathedral in Nairobi and threw tear gas at worshipers. Later, Kenyan police, supported by political thugs called *Jeshi la Mzee* (the old man's army), grabbed the outspoken Presbyterian church minister Timothy Njoya and beat him senseless in the streets of Nairobi. As was mentioned above, in 2007, the Catholic archbishop of Bulawayo was double-crossed by Mugabe's intelligence and publicly embarrassed by a sexual scandal. He was forced to resign. In December 2017, forces loyal to President Joseph Kabila of the Democratic Republic of the Congo attacked and arrested worshipers in Catholic churches who were opposed to his attempts to stay in power. Each African country has its own story about how politicians have dealt with church leaders who criticize them, and indeed "the tendency in many states of Africa has been to lean heavily towards absolutism."[78] The caution to be exercised is that the church must "not work too closely with any form of government as if it has been blessed or endorsed by God."[79] The church must instead remain faithful to her prophetic role.

The Prophetic Role of the Church in Africa

With respect to its relationship to governments, Okullu notes,

> The church is called upon to point out the wrongs and sins, though many may not like it. If it fails to do this, it is no longer the church. The church has a message from God which must be proclaimed whether people like it or not. The fact that some people will not like it does not matter. The church cannot soften that message to make it palatable to those people.[80]

Catholic bishops in Africa have stated clearly that they "condemn . . . political system[s] based on falsehood as well as intolerance, . . . system[s] of informers, political murders, corruption and the shameless enrichment of a small class at the

---

74. Magesa, "Taking Strategic Positions," 11.
75. Kobia, *Courage to Hope*, 35.
76. Haynes, *Religion and Politics in Africa*, 58.
77. Haynes, *Religion and Politics in Africa*, 110.
78. Okullu, *Church and Politics in East Africa*, 13.
79. Choge, "Pilgrim Motif," 97.
80. Okullu, *Church and Politics in East Africa*, 16.

expense of broad masses."[81] This is the prophetic role of the Christian church that she must never shy away from. At this moment in Africa, "[t]he mission of preaching the Gospel dictates . . . that we should dedicate ourselves to the liberation of people, even in their present existence in this world. For unless the Christian message of love and justice shows its effectiveness through action in the course of justice in the world, it will only with difficulty gain credibility with the people of our time."[82]

How can our churches maintain their credibility in the eyes of God? Bishop Kobia stresses:

> We must note how our own praxis all too often falls short of the ideal, and more troublingly, how it echoes the social dysfunctions of the Continent. . . . First, we have sometimes been complicit in war and genocide. . . . In an earlier era, the Catholic Church also played a highly ambivalent role in anticolonial wars of liberation, particularly in Francophone countries in which the hierarchy was close to the colonial regimes. Second, the Church has courageously proclaimed to all the importance of good governance in African society, organized campaigns ecumenically against corruption, and stood up to dictators. But many features of church governance, including finances, mirror less-than-democratic practices that can be often thrown back at us by those we criticize.[83]

Christian churches cannot ask the world to do that which they are unable or unwilling to do. This is why the Catholic Church insists that "while the Church is bound to give witness to justice, she recognizes that anyone who ventures to speak to the people about justice must first be just in their eyes. Hence we must undertake an examination of the modes of acting and the possessions and life style found within the Church herself."[84] As the people of God, we must first put our own houses in order before we can speak to governments with moral authority.

Urgently Needed Actions for the Future of the African Church

As Elias Opongo notes, "While the Church's commitment to social justice has evidently led to social change in a number of African countries, there is need to invent creative ways to address the ever-changing dynamics of the challenges Africa faces."[85] There are many possibilities for improving the relationship between the Catholic Church and the states in Africa. One is the effective use of electronic, print, and social media to engage the African faithful in seeking, demanding, and nurturing good governance (of both church and state). Pope Benedict XVI stressed that "the media can make an important contribution towards the growth in communion of the human family and the ethos of society when they are used to promote universal participation in the common search for what is just."[86] In this regard, some national bishops' conferences, like that of Kenya, have succeeded in establishing radio stations. These stations, however, spend much more time on strictly religious content than on issues touching on politics. Matters related to corruption and good governance, for example, need to be discussed more frequently.

Corruption in all aspects of life has impeded the development and provision of needed services to the African people. John Mukum Mbaku has written extensively on corruption in Africa, its consequences, and ways of dealing with it.[87] He

---

81. SECAM, *Letter to the Christians of the Great Lakes Region*, 40.
82. Synod of Bishops, *Justice in the World*, art. 35. See also Egan, *Politics of South African Student Movement*, 2; Pope John Paul II, *Ecclesia in Africa* §70; and Gremillion, *Gospel of Peace and Justice*, 521.
83. Kobia, *Courage to Hope*, 160. See also Egan, *Politics of South African Catholic Student Movement*, 251.
84. Synod of Bishops, *Justice in the World*, art. 40.
85. Opongo, "Ecclesiology for Africa in Distress," 271. African scholars who have suggested possible ways of addressing these challenges include Orobator, "Church, State, and Catholic Ethics"; Magesa, "Taking Strategic Positions"; Ilo, *Church and Development in Africa*; and Opongo, "Ecclesiology for Africa in Distress."
86. Pope Benedict XVI post-synodal apostolic exhortation *Africae Munus* §142.
87. Mbaku, *Corruption in Africa*.

rightly maintains that corruption is equivalent to genocide—when government health officials, for example, steal billions of shillings meant for the purchase of drugs, this leads to the avoidable early death of many citizens. What should the churches in Africa that have corrupt politicians among their members do? What actions might they take against them?

Since Christ came for sinners, excommunication is not an option; however, there should be public rebuke and condemnation of such behavior. Church leaders need the courage of Bishop Ambrose of Milan, who publicly denied communion to Emperor Theodosius II after he had ordered the massacre of seven thousand citizens in Thessalonica in 390 CE. The emperor accepted the resulting public humiliation and performed a public penance for his actions. Those who claim to be Christians cannot be allowed to perpetrate crimes against humanity and still hope to be in communion with the other members of the body of Christ. As Magesa states, "The Church should be built on the principle that Christians are people who identify themselves primarily by their concern for justice and truth."[88] Practically speaking, Christian politicians who succumb to corruption could be subjected to automatic loss of their seats. In addition, Opongo notes, "it is equally the responsibility of the Church to create structures that support and encourage public officials to be more ethical in carrying out their duties."[89] The church could take steps to sponsor prominent women and men who want to participate in politics, and Catholic universities could also do more to influence political behavior in Africa.

It has been proven, as George Kuh points out, that "education increases knowledge, which can break down barriers to social participation. It can also expand perspectives, values and aspirations and encourage critical and analytical thinking beyond individual circumstances."[90] It has been deeply disappointing, however, that Africa's educated elite often connive with corrupt political leaders to defraud the people of Africa rather than improve their lot. Catholic universities and institutes in Africa could add clauses to their statutes that would encourage their graduates to remain upright and responsible in the places they serve by spelling out circumstances that would lead to the recall of an advanced degree. This recall would affect any graduate who has become a national disgrace because of child abuse, corruption, or any other unacceptable behavior.

Catholic universities could also promote the concept of "popular university" as conceived by the French Catholic priest Fr. Joseph Wresinski. Fr. Wresinski founded the Fourth World Movement in France, which, by means of well-organized demonstrations and protests, forced the French government to extend social welfare benefits to the poorest. He tells us, "I vowed to myself that if I stayed at La Grange camp, I would see to it that one day these poor families could go to the Vatican, the Élysée Palace, and the UN."[91] One of the secrets of Fr. Wresinski's success was the concept of a "popular university" for the poor who have no formal education. In France, these institutions provide the poor with civic education about the qualities of good leadership and productive collaboration between church and state. They are taught their rights in the church and informed about how to hold leaders accountable. They gain the confidence needed to speak out and form solidarity groups that fight for justice. In the face of numerous conflicts in Africa, popular universities could be venues for the acquisition of peace-building and reconciliation skills. They would be ideal places to tackle the religious extremism that is affecting Nigeria, Egypt, Libya, Mali, Sudan, and Kenya. Attendees would have an opportunity to learn about how African leaders should exercise servant leadership instead of oppressive authoritarian rule.

Another area in which the church can make an impact concerns matters of justice. Activities of Justice and Peace Commissions could be strengthened and better coordinated to address continent-wide issues rather than just local ones. Gifford remarks that, "despite the statements of Catholic

---

88. Magesa, *Post-Conciliar Church in Africa*, 109.
89. Opongo, "Ecclesiology for Africa in Distress," 275.
90. Kuh, "Other Curriculum." See also White, "Philosophy and the Aims of Higher Education."
91. Anouil, *Poor Are the Church*, 49.

bishops in Ghana, the Justice and Peace Commission is a mere shadow of what it could be."[92] African bishops could recruit well-educated, well-paid, and courageous lay Catholics to serve on these commissions. This has been rather difficult to achieve because of the chronic problem of the poor pay the Catholic Church offers those working in her institutions. There is an urgent need for professional clergy working side by side with the professional laity to engender positive change in Africa. The church continues to be absent from the core places where political decisions affecting Africa are made, but when politicians have broken the peace, it is always the churches that are the first to welcome the victims of violence all over Africa.

The church in Africa also needs to put resources into theological training and formation of church ministers and laypeople. In 1978, the Catholic bishops in Africa noted that "to lead Africa to her development and to establish peace, we need men and women who are effectively well predisposed and inspired by a spirit of service and who love and respect their fellow men and women. It is in this sense that the Church in Africa and Madagascar is committed to participate in training such people."[93] Those already in ministry need ongoing formation to prepare them for the urgent demands of the continent. Douglas Munemo and Elinah Nciizah assert that "African Churches should improve on theological formation of pastors to include politics and economics skills, promote civic education, equip the faithful with peace building and reconciliation skills, and prepare women and youth to take part in politics and to groom future leaders who share the vision of the Church for human society."[94]

Conclusion

From what we have seen in this chapter, it is clear that there have been moments when the Catholic Church and, indeed, other Christian churches have buckled under the pressures applied by political authority. Africa must change in order to achieve a better future, and in the course of embracing this change the church is required to stand up for the truth, convinced that "society must be rooted in truth, and that God's truth must be defended against brute power and political expediency—even if it costs the defenders their liberty and their lives."[95] All baptized Christians in Africa are challenged to respond to this demanding call.

It is thus necessary to propose some methodological approaches for African scholars hoping to positively influence the African future. Scholars should not only analyze the problems and challenges of the relationship between the church and politics, but must also come up with proposals relating to how the church can be an active agent of social transformation. African scholars can enhance the potential of the church to unleash the boundless faith and momentum for social justice welling up in the hearts of Christ's African lay faithful. I have shown in this essay that for centuries the church used confrontational methods to respond to political authorities who tried to limit her ministry in the world. History has provided ample evidence that confrontation only leads to a hardening of positions and can even lead to loss of life, as happened in South Africa under apartheid, Uganda under Amin, and Zimbabwe under Mugabe. Because the church stands for justice, peace, and love and is the mediator to which states revert in times of crisis, her methods of relating to the world should be above reproach. For this reason, the church in Africa needs to adopt better methods of enhancing healthy church–state relations. I propose three: mutual acceptance, constructive engagement, and critical collaboration.

The method of mutual acceptance is based on two facts. First, both church and state are here to stay; one cannot wish away the other. Second, both have the same citizens as their objects of interest, service, and ministry. Mutual acceptance leads to the second method, constructive engagement, which we saw employed in the relationship between church and state in Tanzania. President Nyerere's involvement of a Council of Elders from mainline and Pentecostal churches and from Islam gave reli-

---

92. Gifford, *African Christianity*, 66.
93. SECAM, *Letter to the Christians in the Great Lakes Region*, 42.
94. Munemo and Nciizah, "Church in Zimbabwe's Peace and Reconciliation Process," 69.
95. Duffy, "Reimagining the Reformation," 5.

gious groups an opportunity to voice their concerns directly to the president. This model could be expanded to include the youth, academics, professionals, and civil society groups. African presidents would then have an objective outside consultative group that would tell them the facts that their self-seeking cabinets and cronies may not.

The third method I propose, critical collaboration, would call upon the church to remember her prophetic role each time she engages with the state or with politicians. Orobator advocates for this method.[96] We have already seen how the churches in Kenya failed to reconcile a divided nation after the highly contested elections of 2007, 2013, and 2017. Instead, church leaders remained silent, implying recognition of presidents whose elections were contested by many. In order to ensure its credibility in the future, the church must take certain deliberate actions now. This chapter has discussed a number of best practices of and prophetic footprints left by the church on our continent. We can learn from such examples and from our failings as people of faith, both individually and as ecclesial communities, in order to secure a more peaceful and prosperous Africa.

Bibliography

Anouil, Gilles. *The Poor Are the Church: A Conversation with Fr. Joseph Wresinski, Founder of the Fourth World Movement*. Mystic, CT: Twenty-Third, 2002.

Augustine, *The City of God against the Pagans*, edited by W. R. Dyson. Cambridge: Cambridge University, 2002.

Benedict XV, Pope. *Ad Beatissimi Apostolorum* [Encyclical appealing for peace; November 1, 1914]. Rome: Libreria Editrice Vaticana, 1914. www.vatican.va.

———. *Africae Munus* [Post-synodal Apostolic Exhortation on the Church in Africa in Service of Reconciliation, Justice and Peace; November 19, 2011]. Vatican City: Libreria Editrice Vaticana, 2011. www.vatican.va.

———. *Maximum Illud* [Apostolic Letter on the Propagation of Faith throughout the World; November 30, 1919]. Vatican City: Libreria Editrice Vaticana, 1919. www.vatican.va.

Bevans, Stephen B., and Roger P. Schroeder. *Prophetic Dialogue: Reflections on Christian Mission Today*. Maryknoll, NY: Orbis Books, 2011.

Bokenkotter, Thomas A. *Concise History of the Catholic Church*. New York: Image, 1990.

Burton, Keith Augustus. "The Blessings of Africa: The Bible and African Christianity." *Journal of African American History* 94.1 (2009): 87–91.

Byrne, Tony, and Samuel Rayan. "The Church and the Dilemma of Development." In *Spearhead No. 50*. Eldoret: Gaba, 1977.

Catechism of the Catholic Church, 1992.

Choge, Emily J. "The Pilgrim Motif and the Role of the Church in Kenya in Politics." In *Religion and Politics in Africa: Theological Reflections for the 21st Century*, edited by Peter I. Gichure and Diane B. Stinton. Nairobi: Paulines Publications, 2008.

Chukwu, Cletus N. "Religion as a Factor in the Nigerian Political Culture." In *Religion and Politics in Africa: Theological Reflections for the 21st Century*, edited by Peter I. Gichure and Diane B. Stinton. Nairobi: Paulines Publications, 2008.

De Jong, Albert. "Church and Politics in Tanzania from Colonial Times to the Third Phase Government." In *African Christian Studies* 15.1. Nairobi: CUEA, 1999.

Duffy, Eamon. "Reimagining the Reformation." *The Tablet* [London], January 31, 2015.

Egan, Anthony. "Facing the Crisis: On the Continent, in the Church: An Ecclesiology for an Africa in Distress." In *The Church We Want: The Church We Want: Foundations, Theology, and Mission of the Church in Africa*, edited by Agbonkhianmeghe E. Orobator. Nairobi: Paulines Publications, 2015.

———. *The Politics of South African Catholic Student Movement, 1960–1987*. Cape Town: Centre for African Studies, 1991.

Ellis, Stephen, and Gerrie ter Haar. "Religion and Politics in Sub-Saharan Africa." *Journal of Modern African Studies* 36.2 (1998): 175–201.

Francis, Pope. *Evangelii Gaudium* (The Joy of the Gospel) [Post-synodal Apostolic Exhortation on the Proclamation of the Gospel in Today's World; November 23, 2013]. Vatican City: Libreria Editrice Vaticana, 2013. www.vatican.va

Gichure, Peter I. "Religion and Politics in Africa: The Rise of Ethno-Religions." In *Religion and Politics in*

---

96. Orobator, "Church, State, and Catholic Ethics," 182–85.

Africa: Theological Reflections for the 21st Century, edited by Peter I. Gichure and Diane B. Stinton. Nairobi: Paulines Publications, 2008.

Gichure, Peter I., and Diane B. Stinton, eds. *Religion and Politics in Africa: Theological Reflections for the 21st Century*. Nairobi: Paulines Publications, 2008.

Gifford, Paul. *African Christianity: Its Public Role*. London: Hurst, 2001.

Gremillion, Joseph. *The Gospel of Peace and Justice: Catholic Social Teaching since Pope John*. Maryknoll, NY: Orbis Books, 1976.

Gundani, Paul H. "The Church's Mission in the Building of Zimbabwe." In *Reconstruction, the WCC Assembly in Harare 1998 and the Churches in Southern Africa*. Utrecht: Meinema, Zooetermeer, 1998.

Harrington, Patrick, ed. *Religion and Politics for Everyone*. Nairobi: Paulines Publications, 2012.

Haynes, Jeff. *Religion and Politics in Africa*. London: Zed, 1996.

Hinze, Bradford E. "Listening to the Spirit." *The Tablet*. Vol. 271, no. 9203, June 2017: 4–5.

Ilo, Stan Chu. *The Church and Development in Africa*. Eugene, OR: Pickwick, 2014.

John XXIII, Pope. *Pacem in Terris* (Peace on Earth) [Encyclical on Establishing Universal Peace in Truth, Justice, Charity, and Liberty; April 11, 1963]. Vatican City: Libreria Editrice Vaticana, 1963. www.vatican.va.

John Paul II, Pope. *Ecclesia in Africa* [Post-synodal Apostolic Exhortation on the Church in Africa and Its Evangelizing Mission toward the Year 2000; September 14, 1995]. Vatican City: Libreria Editrice Vaticana, 1995. www.vatican.va.

Kasenene, P. "The Relation between Religion and Politics, Church and State in Africa: The Role of African Theologians." In *Religion and Politics in Africa: Theological Reflections for the 21st Century*, edited by Peter I. Gichure and Diane B. Stinton. Nairobi: Paulines Publications, 2008.

Kean, H. M. "Church Growth and Development in South Africa: The Catholic Experience." In *Pangs of Growth: A Dialogue on Church Growth in Southern Africa*, edited by Gabriel M. Setiloane and Ivan H. M. Peden. Johannesburg: Rosenberg, 1988.

Kobia, Samuel. *The Courage to Hope: The Roots of a New Vision and the Calling of the Church in Africa*. Geneva: WCC, 2003.

Kuh, George D. "The Other Curriculum: Out-of-Class Experiences Associated with Student Learning and Personal Development." *Journal of Higher Education* 66.2 (1995): 123–55.

Luther, Martin. "Open Letter to the Christian Nobility of the German Nation, Concerning the Reform of the Christian Estate." 1520.

MacCulloch, Diarmaid. *Groundwork of Christian History*. London: Epworth, 1987.

Magesa, Laurenti. *The Post-Conciliar Church in Africa: No Turning Back the Clock*. Nairobi: CUEA, 2016.

———. "Taking Strategic Positions: Church, Media, Politics, and Society in Contemporary Africa." *Hekima Review* 49 (2013): 8–18.

Mbaku, J. M. *Corruption in Africa: Causes, Consequences, and Cleanups*. Lanham, MD: Lexington, 2007.

McDonagh, Enda. *Church and Politics: From Theology to a Case History of Zimbabwe*. Notre Dame, IN: University of Notre Dame Press, 1980.

Mejia, Rodrigo, ed. *The Conscience of Society*. Nairobi: Paulines Publications, 1995.

Mhandara, Charity M., et al. "The Church and Political Transition in Zimbabwe: The Inclusive Government Context." *Journal of Public Administration and Governance* 3.1 (2013): 102–14.

Munemo, Douglas, and Elinah Nciizah. "The Church in Zimbabwe's Peace and Reconciliation Process under the Government of National Unity." *Journal of Humanities and Social Sciences* 19.5 (2014): 63–70.

National Council of Churches for Kenya. "Hope for Kenya": NCCK Executive Committee Press Statement. February 13, 2008, http://rescuekenya.wordpress.com.

Ndiaye, Aloyse R. "Leadership/Governance and Religion in Africa: Is Religion an Asset or an Obstacle?" In *Theological Re-Imagination: Conversations on Church, Religion, and Society in Africa*, edited by Agbonkhianmeghe E. Orobator. Nairobi: Paulines Publications, 2014.

Nyerere, Julius K. *Ujamaa Essays on Socialism*. London: Oxford University Press, 1968.

Okullu, Henry. *Church and Politics in East Africa*. Nairobi: Uzima, 1974.

Opongo, Elias. "An Ecclesiology for Africa in Distress: Time to Change Our Pastoral Strategy." In *The Church We Want: Foundations, Theology, and Mission of the Church in Africa*, edited by Agbonkhianmeghe E. Orobator. Nairobi: Paulines Publications, 2015.

Orobator, Agbonkhianmeghe E. "Church, State, and Catholic Ethics: The Kenyan Dilemma." *Theological Studies* 70.1 (2009): 182–85.

———, ed. *The Church We Want: Foundations, Theology, and Mission of the Church in Africa*. Nairobi: Paulines Publications, 2015.

———, ed. *Theological Re-Imagination: Conversations on Church, Religion, and Society in Africa*. Nairobi: Paulines Publications, 2014.

Pontifical Council for Justice and Peace. *Compendium of the Social Doctrine of the Church*. Washington, DC: United States Conference of Catholic Bishops, 2004.

Reuters. "Zimbabwe Military's Statement after Seizing Power." Reuters. November 15, 2017, www.reuters.com.

SECAM Bishops. *A Letter to the Christians of the Great Lakes Region*. Accra: SECAM, 1997.

Setiloane, Gabriel M., and Ivan H. M. Peden, eds. *Pangs of Growth: A Dialogue on Church Growth* in Southern Africa. Johannesburg: Rosenberg, *1988*.

Synod of Bishops. *Justice in The World*. Vatican City: Libreria Editrice Vaticana, 1971.

Tarcicio, Agostoni. *Every Citizen's Handbook*. Nairobi: Paulines Publications, 1997.

United Nations. Universal Declaration of Human Rights. Paris, 1948.

Vatican II. *Gaudium et Spes* [Pastoral Constitution on the Church in the Modern World]. Vatican City: Libreria Editrice Vaticana, 1965.

———. *Lumen Gentium* [Dogmatic Constitution on the Church]. Vatican City: Libreria Editrice Vaticana, 1964.

White, John. "Philosophy and the Aims of Higher Education." *Studies in Higher Education* 22.1 (1997): 7–17.

Suggested Reading

De Jong, Albert. "Church and Politics in Tanzania from Colonial Times to the Third Phase Government." *African Christian Studies* 15.1. Nairobi: CUEA, 1999.

Egan, Anthony. *The Politics of a South African Catholic Student Movement, 1960 – 1987*. Cape Town: Centre for African Studies, 1991.

Ellis, Stephen, and Gerrie ter Haar. "Religion and Politics in Sub-Saharan Africa." *Journal of Modern African Studies* 36.2 (1998): 175–201.

Gichure, Peter I., and Diane B. Stinton, eds. *Religion and Politics in Africa: Theological Reflections for the 21st Century*. Nairobi: Paulines Publications, 2008.

Harrington, Patrick, ed. *Religion and Politics for Everyone*. Nairobi: Paulines Publications, 2012.

Magesa, Laurenti. "Taking Strategic Positions: Church, Media, Politics, and Society in Contemporary Africa." *Hekima Review* 49 (2013): 8–18.

Okullu, Henry. *Church and Politics in East Africa*. Nairobi: Uzima, 1974/2002.

Key Words
Africa
African church
Catholic Church
Christian churches
church and politics
colonial Africa
future actions
methodologies
prophetic role

Catholicism and Fundamental Human Rights to Development in Africa: Looking beyond the Shadows of Legal Norms

Wilfred Mamah and Idara Otu, MSP

Human rights consciousness on the African continent predates the formal proclamation of the Universal Declaration of Human Rights (UDHR) in 1948, and subsequent legal norms. Some scholars view "rights" from a strictly "legal" perspective, in which they define "legal norms" as exhaustive of norms, leading to traps and contradictions. Moreover, there are limitations of legal norms concerning the enforcement of human rights. Though legal norms are a significant tool for organizing human society, religion remains a formidable force, since it appeals to the supernatural. The Christian Bible, for example, as a normative framework offers a clear definition of what promotes human flourishing. As the central foundational teaching of the scripture, love is the determining factor for the experience of abundant life. Witnessing love to all peoples is the criterion for those who will be "saved" or "damned" (Matt 25:31–46).

This chapter undertakes a theological-*cum*-jurisprudential task of reflecting on the role of the Christian faith in the promotion and protection of Right to Development (RTD) in Africa. Drawing from the Nigerian social context, this chapter argues for a renewal in the approaches to the vision of human rights for sub-Saharan Africa, in four unique but interrelated parts. The first examines the Catholic teachings on human rights and RTD. The second draws from the Nigerian social context to identify traps to the promotion of RTD. The third briefly presents the historical context of RTD and describes its use as an instrument for promoting integral development in Africa. In the fourth, we contend that Catholic social teaching provides significant insights for helping African Catholicism to become a credible, prophetic, and effectual voice of the African voiceless.

Catholic Theology and Human Rights

Understanding a right as a theological concept oscillates between considerations of moral rightness and the right as a claim. Though a right is conventionally connected with the claim dimension, moral rightness offers a fundamental underpinning.[1] A right is conceived as a moral claim, which enables each person to achieve his or her desired destiny. With this underlying presupposition, Michael Himes and Kenneth Himes envision "human rights as moral claims to some good which

---

This chapter drew inspiration from Wilfred Ukanwoke Mamah, "Traps and Tools: A Contextual Critique of the Right to Development in International Law" (PhD thesis, London: University of Westminster, 2013); and Idara Otu, *Communion Ecclesiology and Social Transformation in African Catholicism: Between Vatican Council II and African Synod II* (Eugene, OR: Pickwick, 2020).

1. Vincent, *Politics of Human Rights*, 10.

can be provided and which should be provided in light of the moral ideal of establishing communities which can mirror the trinitarian life of self-giving."[2] Human rights are rights that are inherent and inalienable, and essentially belong to all individual persons. Without such rights, humans cannot fulfill their life goals.

Human rights do not owe their existence merely to declarations or institutional laws; rather, they are ascribable to the individual person as a being created in the image of God and sharing in a common humanity. Human rights as an integral dimension of the church's mission emerged from the civil and social rights revolutions, and movements for indigenous peoples in the New World.[3] However, a watershed in the Catholic vision of human rights was the pontificate of John XXIII and the convocation of the Second Vatican Council (1962–1965). The intertwining of the inspiring personality of Pope John XXIII and the conciliar assembly propelled a clear theological understanding that situated human rights as a fundamental and integral dimension of the morality and mission of the Catholic Church.

Love for the human person is at the heart of the momentous social encyclical *Pacem in Terris* (1963), presented by Pope John XXIII and addressed to all people of goodwill. This encyclical's Catholic vision of human rights is remarkable in its affirmation of universality, inalienability, inviolability, and the attendant duties (§9). Rights and duties are concurrent dynamics in the Catholic vision of human rights: "Hence, to claim one's rights and ignore one's duties, or only half fulfill them, is like building a house with one hand and tearing it down with the other" (§30). It is the defense of human rights that contributes to the enhancement of basic human needs, integral development, the promotion of universal common good, and peaceful human community. This foundational understanding is accentuated in *Gaudium et Spes*, a document that stresses the church's mission to proclaim human rights "by virtue of the Gospel committed to her."[4] These include the rights to "choose a state of life freely and to found a family, the right to education, to employment, to a good reputation, to respect, to appropriate information, to activity in accord with the upright norm of one's own conscience, to protection of privacy and rightful freedom even in matters religious" (*GS* §26).

The overarching justification for the promotion and protection of human rights is rooted in two interrelated foundational principles. The first is the dignity and sacredness of the human person, created in the image and likeness of God (*Imago Dei*): "Then God said, 'Let us make humankind in our image, according to our likeness.... God created humankind in his image, in his divine image he created him; male and female he created them" (Gen 1:26–27). This dignity of the human person is elevated by Christ, who through his incarnation and paschal mystery united himself with humans and reconciled humanity back to God (*GS* §22).

The second foundation is the social and communitarian nature of the person. The human person, created in the dignity of God, lives out his or her life in a community with other persons, and with the entirety of creation (*GS* §§40, 63). The human person can be viewed as a being in relationship, with the Trinity as the model par excellence for human community. Jesus Christ prayed: "The glory that you have given me I have given them, so that they may be one, as we are one, I in them and you in me, that they may become completely one, so that the world may know that you have sent me and have loved them even as you have loved me" (John 17:22–23). The communitarian and social nature of the person, in contrast to the claims of individualistic liberalism, necessitates that human dignity be realized in a community. The church and state serve as major intermediate institutions protecting and preserving human dignity.

David Hollenbach describes the Catholic Church's linking of human rights and human nature as a core tenet of the Christian faith. Reflecting on the challenge of chronic poverty in many parts of

---

2. Himes and Himes, *Fullness of Faith*, 73.
3. See Hollenbach, "Global Human Rights."
4. Vatican II, Pastoral Constitution on the Church in the Modern World (*Gaudium et Spes*) §41 (hereinafter *GS*).

Africa, Hollenbach draws attention to the implication of structural discrimination imposed by poverty in Africa, and how this situation makes the notion of human rights untenable. Consequently, the poor and most vulnerable "are being told that they simply do not count as human beings."[5] Catholic social teaching aims at reversing this trend of dehumanization by recognizing the inherent dignity and rights of every single human person. This teaching, if adopted in theory and practice by people of goodwill, would go a long way in resolving the contradictions in both national and international law with regard to promotion of human rights nationally and globally.

Human rights theories span academic fields, including jurisprudence, history, philosophy, economics, culture, ethics, and international relations. Amid the diversity of these disciplines there exist types of human rights theories, including Marxist, liberal, libertarian, feminist, and communitarian. Nevertheless, the two major approaches to human rights discourse are the universalist and the relativist. Universalists study human rights through a transcultural perspective, affirming the validity of a right as a moral claim that is applicable to every human person and promotes the common good of society.

The universal approach considers the individual as a social subject—thus the emphasis on a universal human nature.[6] The universalist, according to Simon Ilesanmi, "holds that from the conception of human rights we can generate acceptable principles for both the criticism and defense of the economic, diplomatic, cultural, humanitarian, and military policies of nation-states."[7] This approach draws on international declarations, conventions, and charters to provide foundations for moral judgment about the unrestrictive applicability of human rights norms. Since there is a "universal human nature" common to all human beings, human rights are applicable to all peoples.[8] Universalists, therefore, argue that human rights apply to every person, irrespective of race, gender, and religion.

The relativist approach to human rights focuses conversely on how human rights can be adapted and applied to a specific cultural context.[9] It contends that morality is culture-specific or contextual, and that conceptions of human rights must bear the seal of cultural specificity. The relativist approach disapproves of the conception of a common human-rights principle. It considers the community to be the basic social unit and places less emphasis on the individual, because the interest of the community is paramount. This approach disapproves of the application of human rights as a universal norm to different cultures.[10]

Distinct from secular frameworks, an African perspective on human rights is more communal and communitarian, rather than exhibiting individualistic liberalism. It stresses both the rights of the person and the individual's obligations toward the common good of the community. According to Chris Mojekwu: "African concepts of human rights are very different from those of Western Europe. Communalism and communal right concepts are fundamental to understanding African culture, politics and society."[11] This communal view of human rights is discernible in the wording of the 1998 African charter of rights—the "African Charter on Human and Peoples' Rights"— which is different from the UDHR of 1948. While the charter emphasizes the communal dimension of humanity with the use of the plural "peoples," concern for the rights and duties of the individual is articulated using the umbrella noun "human," thereby demonstrating the dynamic interplay between the person and community in the conceptualization of rights.

African anthropology conceives of the person as inextricably related to the community, and thus human rights are correlated to human responsibilities toward the well-being of society. The complementarity and homogeneity of Afri-

---

5. Hollenbach, "Accompaniment, Service, and Advocacy," 11.
6. See Panikkar, "Is the Notion of Human Rights a Western Concept?"
7. Ilesanmi, "Human Rights Discourse in Modern Africa," 294.
8. Panikkar, "Is the Notion of Human Rights a Western Concept?," 80–81.
9. Ilesanmi, "Human Rights Discourse in Modern Africa," 294.
10. Ilesanmi, "Human Rights Discourse in Modern Africa," 295.
11. Mojekwu, "International Human Rights," 92.

can communities are grounded in the concept of the person, expressed in the Zulu (South African) phrase *umuntu ngumuntu ngabantu*—a person through other persons. The anthropology of *ubuntu* expresses interconnectedness and interpersonal relationships as implied in the envisioning of the human person.[12]

The African understanding of personhood and human community enriches both Catholic social teaching and secular approaches to human rights discourse. The value of the African communitarian view of human rights is the expression of the global responsibility to protect the dignity and rights of the individual, the rights of all peoples, and the societal common good. This is not dissimilar to the Catholic vision of rights that extends to all aspects of human life, such as the civil, cultural, political, religious, and economic realms of society. Human rights equally assign rights and responsibilities to the poor, oppressed, and marginalized.

Right to Development and Catholic Social Teaching

Right to Development articulates a rights-based model for integral and sustainable development, as well as government responsibilities and citizens' obligations toward their realization. The United Nations Declaration on the Right to Development (UNDRD) describes RTD thus: "An inalienable human right by virtue of which every human person and all peoples are entitled to participate in, contribute to, and enjoy economic, social, cultural and political development, in which all human rights and fundamental freedoms can be fully realized."[13] Since the human person is the primary subject of development, each individual and community has a responsibility to participate and contribute toward the actualization of RTD.[14] This communal dimension to RTD captures the essence of human rights from an African perspective. This framework strikes at the heart of the powerlessness, inequality, and dehumanization that weigh on Africa, despite the seeming triumphs of decolonization and democratization. It is not surprising that the progenitor and forerunner of the modern articulation of RTD was the Senegalese jurist Kéba M'Baye. In 1972, Judge M'Baye clearly proposed that development be defined as a right.[15] Five years later, M'Baye inspired the United Nations Commission on Human Rights to authorize a study on "the international dimensions of the right to development as a human right in relation with other human rights based on international cooperation, including the right to peace, taking into account the requirement of the New International Economic Order and the fundamental human needs."[16] Subsequently, in 1979, the UN secretariat articulated the principles for what became the UNDRD, adopted in 1986.

Catholic social teaching advocates a right to integral development that upholds the dignity of the human person, created in the image and likeness of God, with an emphasis on the fair use of the earth's resources.[17] The Catholic understanding of RTD promotes integral human development and empowers people to fulfill their potential and reach their desired destiny.[18] The church critiques any aspect of RTD that dehumanizes persons or degrades the ecosystem.[19] As Pope Francis writes, "Authentic human development has a moral character. It presumes full respect for the human person, but it must also be

---

12. See Otu, *Communion Ecclesiology and Social Transformation in African Catholicism*, 20–28.
13. United Nations, "Declaration on the Right to Development," Article 1:1.
14. United Nations, "Declaration on the Right to Development," Article 2:1.
15. Kéba M'Baye was the Chief Justice of Senegal, and later a judge at the International Court of Justice. He proposed RTD in his 1972 address at the International Institute of Human Rights in Strasbourg, France. See M'Baye, "Le droit au développement comme un droit de l'homme."
16. See E/CN. 4/1334, "UN-Secretary Report to the Thirty-fifth Session of the Commission on Human Rights on February 21, 1977," https://digitallibrary.un.org/record/6762.
17. Pope Paul VI, encyclical *Populorum Progressio* §14; Pontifical Council for Justice and Peace, *Compendium of the Social Doctrine of the Church*, no. 172 (hereinafter *CSDC*).
18. Ogbonnaya, *Lonergan, Social Transformation, and Sustainable Human Development*, 18.
19. Pope John Paul II, encyclical *Sollicitudo Rei Socialis* §46.

concerned for the world around us and 'take into account the nature of each being and of its mutual connection in an ordered system.'"[20] The Catholic vision of RTD places a premium on the integral development of the person, without undermining the socioeconomic, ecological, political, cultural, or spiritual aspects of human society.[21]

Catholic social teaching envisions RTD as based on the following principles: "unity of origin and a shared destiny of the human family; equality between every person and between every community based on human dignity; the universal destination of the goods of the earth; the notion of development in its entirety; and the centrality of the human person and solidarity."[22]

These principles are based on a theological anthropology that promotes human dignity, integral human development, and the common good. The common good "must take account of all those social conditions which favor the full development of human personality."[23] RTD demands that every person and society have a role to fulfill. This means "cooperation among individuals and political communities," and "collaboration in the development of the whole person and of every human world: East and West, North and South."[24]

Right to Development in Nigeria

Undertaking a comprehensive survey of the current state of RTD in Africa is needed in constructing an appropriate theology of rights for African Catholicism. Given the commonalities in the human-rights situations in African nations, a case-study approach of a single nation will help to articulate a model relevant to the African continent.

The choice of Nigeria as a suitable case study for RTD in Africa is multifaceted. Nigeria can be envisioned as a microcosm of Africa. It is the most populous black nation in the world. It has one of the largest populations of youth in the world, is one of the largest producers of crude oil in Africa, and is a key political player in West Africa.[25] Yet the UN's Human Development Index designates Nigeria as a relatively poor nation despite its potential wealth, with attendant social issues that betray poor economic sustainability and a lack of progress in integral human development. Closely related to deficiencies in Nigeria's developmental progress is its record of human rights abuses and violations, which the current democratic climate has not succeeded in overturning. Human rights abuses occur unabated, to which physically and mentally challenged persons, the poor, children, and women are the most vulnerable.

A comparative analysis by a 2021 Human Rights Watch World Report discredits a positive human rights image of Nigeria, by pointing to violence by the Boko Haram terrorist group; killings and conflicts fueled by nomadic herdsmen; restrictions of gender identity; violation of women's and children's rights; lack of freedom of expression and media; intercommunal violence and ethnic conflicts; misconduct of police and armed forces, including arbitrary arrests and detention; inadequate foreign policy; limited protection of citizens' rights; and endemic corruption. These constraints to the implementation of RTD are present in most nations in sub-Saharan Africa. The Nigerian government, as in many other African nations, is an accomplice in allowing the law to align with the forces of oppression against rights at the local and national levels.

Nigeria has been labeled an underdeveloped nation, and key development reports support this categorization. With a population of over 180 million, about 83 million Nigerians live below the poverty line, and another 53 million are vulnerable.[26]

---

20. Pope Francis, encyclical *Laudato Si'* §5.
21. See Benedict XVI, encyclical *Caritas in Veritate* §§43–52; Ogbonnaya, *Lonergan, Social Transformation, and Sustainable Human Development*, 16.
22. Pontifical Council for Justice and Peace, *CSDC*, no. 446.
23. Pope John XXIII, *Pacem in Terris* §58.
24. Pontifical Council for Justice and Peace, *CSDC*, no. 446.
25. World Bank, "Nigeria in a Glance."
26. World Bank, "Nigeria in a Glance."

In the wake of the COVID-19 pandemic, many of these 53 million vulnerable people could fall deeper into poverty and exclusion. Notwithstanding the ratification and domestication of the United Nations' Convention on the Rights of the Child, the child-protection system remains weak.[27] Recent global development indices reveal that six of ten Nigerian children will suffer at least one form of violence (sexual, physical, or psychological) before the age of eighteen.[28] A World Health Organization report shows Nigeria's estimated maternal mortality ratio at 800 deaths per 100,000 live births. With the COVID-19 pandemic, 950 more Nigerian children under five could die every day. (The average life expectancy for Nigerians stands at about fifty-four years.)[29] Corruption remains endemic, fueled by both local and international greed, with poorly rated governance. A review of Corruption Perception Index reports published by Transparency International ranks Nigeria quite low among the nations surveyed.[30] The Mo Ibrahim Governance Report rated Nigeria as one of the ten worst-governed nations in Africa, using the index of "Safety and Rule of Law, Participation and Human Rights, Sustainable Economic Opportunities, and Human Development."[31]

The Nigerian social context calls into question the notion of "common humanity," as expressed in Article 1 of the UDHR: "All human beings are born free and equal in dignity and rights. They are endowed with reason and conscience and should act towards one another in a spirit of brotherhood."[32] In the context of the overall human population and socioeconomic wealth of Africa, Nigeria provides a crucial window to identify obstacles to RTD in Africa. The UNDRD places a significant duty of the realization of RTD at the doorstep of the state.[33]

The obstacle trap to RTD is the absence of political will and legal enforcement by governments toward promoting the rights of citizens to development. Though many African countries have ratified RTD, Africans, and especially the African poor, are not given pride of place in the scheme of development. The second obstacle is the systemic corruption that impoverishes Africans even amid abundant human capital and natural wealth. Sadly, the political class often conspires with foreign investors to siphon national resources, to the detriment of the country's citizens.[34] The third obstacle is the gradual erosion of the African cultural values of preserving human dignity and fostering community, contributing to the loss of social responsibility by the government toward its citizens, and citizens toward the poor and most vulnerable.

Overcoming these selected obstacles to the realization of RTD in Africa demands a paradigm shift from legal norms to concrete actions that appeal to the human conscience and are geared toward addressing underlying structural challenges. The implementation of RTD is not the onerous responsibility of the government alone; the church, as a forerunner in promoting the articulation of right language and declaration, has an important role to play as well. When RTD is conceived of as merely a legal instrument and not as a development vision for integral human and social progress, there will likely be no commitment by government or citizens toward its actualization.

It is important to note that the duties and obligations of RTD described by the UN are not antithetical to Catholic social teaching. In articulating the church's role in promoting RTD, it is relevant to review the historical development of RTD.

---

27. See Nigeria's Child's Rights Act 2003; Otu, "Child Labour and the Nigerian Children's Rights Acts in the Light of Catholic Social Teaching," 167–85.

28. UNICEF, "Child Protection."

29. World Health Organization, "Maternal Health in Nigeria"; UNICEF, "COVID-19: 950 More Nigerian Children under 5"; World Bank, "Life Expectancy at Birth, Total (years)."

30. For corruption index reports of 2020, 2019, 2012, 2005, 2004, 2003, and 2000, see Transparency International, https://www.transparency.org/en/; World Bank Human Capital Index, www.worldbank.org.

31. "Mo Ibrahim Governance Report, 2019–2021," https://mo.ibrahim.foundation/iiag/downloads.

32. United Nations, "Universal Declaration of Human Rights."

33. See United Nations, "Declaration on the Right to Development," Articles 4–8.

34. See Baker, *Capitalism's Achilles Heel*, 57–68.

Historical Synopsis of Right to Development

The advent of RTD came in the wake of the earliest "development decades."[35] Development decades categorize the different epochs of the global community in order to initiate agendas for social progress toward integral human development and sustainable social transformation. The 1945 UN Charter affirms the preservation of human dignity and human rights as fundamental to any developmental vision for society. Frithjof Kuhnen's categorization situates the first development decade (1960–1969) as growing out of the concept of industrialization.[36] Deliberations at the first United Nations Conference on Trade and Development (UNCTAD) in 1964 revealed that industrial nations were unwilling to make trade concessions to poor nations. Many nations turned to agriculture production as a stimulus for the process of economic growth, leading to the birth of the Green Revolution. The Green Revolution was not entirely a blessing, however, because although it made it possible to reduce food shortages, it did so at high social and ecological costs. The rich became richer, regional differences became more significant, and the start of oil crises raised questions about the suitability of an agrarian strategy based on the use of high-yield crops.[37]

This first decade was characterized by the growth of new theories of development, such as the influential "dependency theory," which persisted throughout the second (1970–1979) and third (1980–1989) development decades. Dependency theories affirm that any surplus produced at the periphery (poor nations) is extracted and expropriated by the few (wealthy nations), to the advantage of the latter. The mechanisms used include access to cheap raw materials, subsistence output and low wages, increased demands for imports from the center, increasing budget deficits and foreign investment, and repatriation of profits to the center.[38]

Against this backdrop, the UN General Assembly adopted the third UN Development Decade (at its 83rd Plenary Meeting on December 5, 1980), in which nations pledged individually and collectively to fulfill their commitment to establish a "New International Economic Order" based on justice and equity. The third development-decade strategy set forth goals for the accelerated expansion of developing countries. A key component of this strategy was a rapid and substantial increase in official development assistance provided by all developed countries, to reach or exceed a target of 0.7 percent of the GNP of developed countries. This development target, like many others, was largely unmet. The failure of three development decades to narrow the deepening gulf between poverty and wealth led to the promotion of RTD; a counter-hegemonic initiative championed by states on the periphery, with a view to challenging the notion of development as charity, and instead constructing a new model of development as freedom.

One attempt to implement RTD was through the UN's Millennium Development Goals (MDGs). In 2000, this popular framework was introduced at the UN Millennium Summit, with the overwhelming support of 191 nations. It outlined eight goals, with defined targets. The First Goal, considered the cardinal goal, proposed to halve the proportion of people living in abject poverty by 2015, while the Eighth Goal provided for international cooperation as a prerequisite for development. Needless to say, many African nations failed to realize the MDGs.

Phillip Alston, an advocate of RTD, described the MDGs vis-à-vis human rights as "ships passing in the night, each with little awareness that the other is there and with little if any sustained engagement with one another."[39] This apparent disconnection in practice between "development" and "rights" raises questions regarding the utilitarian value of a rights framework that cannot be employed as a tool of emancipation. The failure of the MDGs contributed to the 2015 drafting of the UN's "2030 Agenda for Sustainable Development,"

---

35. See Koehler, "Seven Decades of 'Development,' and Now What?"
36. Stiglitz and Charlton, *Fair Trade for All*, 41–56.
37. See Collier, *The Bottom Billion*, 79–96; Zalot, *The Roman Catholic Church and Economic Development*, 1–32.
38. See Kambhampati, *Development and the Developing World*, 55.
39. Alston, "Ships Passing in the Night," 825.

which provides a shared blueprint for prosperity for all peoples. Central to its seventeen Sustainable Development Goals (SDGs) is an emphasis on global partnership among nations.[40] It is difficult to speculate as to whether Africa will meet the 2030 deadline for the full realization of these goals.

The history of development shows that RTD was conceived as a universal right. The idea of universal human rights has been critiqued by scholars, with Costas Douzinas, Bonny Ibhawoh, Sandra Fredman, and Reza Banakar being among the most recent voices. Earlier, cultural relativism had posited that the idea of universal human rights was another form of imperialism. In failing to factor in history and particular cultures, relativists distance themselves from the grand narrative of universal human rights. Critical legal scholars such as Douzinas and Radha D'Souza argue that the rights discourse presents a "paradox" and a "conundrum," respectively.[41]

Ibhawoh critiques RTD as a language of power and resistance. He believes that "[a]nalysis of the polemics and politics of power and resistance on the right to development offers important lessons on the uses and misuses of human rights language."[42] Continuing, Ibhawoh contends that "[d]isagreement over meanings and priorities, differences over the nature and extent of entitlements and responsibilities, as well as narrow and distorted interpretations have all had undesirable impacts on the promotion of human rights," and hence the urgency to "seriously consider the morally troubling outcomes that arise when human rights are co-opted by authority structures in ways that serve more to enhance their powers than alleviate human suffering."[43] Ibhawoh also draws attention to the paradoxes underlying the discourse of human rights in Africa. He juxtaposes the metanarratives of universal and transcendental rights with the historical experiences of colonialism, with a view to capturing the nuances that underlie the notion of human rights.[44] Ibhawoh develops a metanarrative approach to RTD, which intersects with the stories of Africans and the works of scholars and rights experts, in a conversation that is truly contextual and universal.

Some scholars have expressed misgivings about the rights regime, observing that the notion of universal human rights has not, in fact, fostered the liberation of the poor and powerless. Douzinas captures this stunning reality:

> There is no greater insult to victims of natural or man-made catastrophes, of famines and war, of earthquakes and ethnic cleansing, of epidemics and torture, there is no greater scorn and disregard than to be told that, according to the relevant international treaty, they have a right to food and peace, to shelter and home or to medical care and an end to maltreatment.[45]

There is a growing consensus among critical legal scholars, legal historians, post-structural thinkers, and an array of social and legal theorists that the top-down nature of the universal regime of human rights renders it largely unhelpful for the poor, the weak, and the powerless, for whom "rights" actually means "survival." For those in dire need, according to these critical perspectives, a human-rights framework, far from promising justice, may in fact perpetuate the notion of "justice lost!"[46] In contrast, the Catholic vision of RTD prioritizes an approach to the promotion of human rights that seeks to give voice to the African voiceless. Giving voice to the poor, marginalized, oppressed, and most vulnerable in Africa is constitutive of the social mission of the Catholic Church. The section that follows explores two methodological approaches that particular churches in Africa can contextualize to support and amplify the woes and griefs, cries and tears emerging from the African continent.

---

40. See United Nations, "Sustainable Development Goals," https://sdgs.un.org/goals.
41. D'Souza, "'Rights' Conundrum," 55.
42. Ibhawoh, "Right to Development," 103.
43. Ibhawoh, "Right to Development," 104.
44. See Ibhawoh, *Imperialism and Human Rights*.
45. Douzinas, *The End of Human Rights*, 153.
46. See Hafner-Burton and Tsutsui, "Justice Lost!"

Giving Voice to the African *Wananchi*

Contextual theological discourse on RTD must not overlook the failure of the realization of human flourishing in developing nations. This is true of a Catholic theology of rights, for "the progressive development of peoples is an object of deep interest and concern to the Church."[47] Overcoming the barriers to the implementation of RTD demands the promotion of human dignity and interpersonal relationships within society, so as to propel an integral human development and the common good of society.[48] African Catholicism has contributed in many ways toward the integral development of Africa, including upholding the dignity and equality of human persons, committing to the provision of basic amenities and social welfare services, protecting human rights, and speaking out against injustices and violence.[49] According to Idara Otu, "In most cases, Catholic dioceses have intervened through their social ministry far beyond the private sector and civil governments in their countries."[50] Such social interventions are provided freely to rural communities and the poorest of the poor.[51] Other ecclesial interventions toward promoting RTD include income-generating investments; agricultural initiatives; socioeconomic development projects; advocacy through pastoral letters, statements, and communiqués; and the establishment of centers for social justice and development, as well as the Justice and Peace Commissions.[52]

Without diminishing the social mission of the church, there is a need to foster renewal and reform of pastoral praxis so as to guard against reinforcing structures of marginalization, abuses, oppression, and injustice in Africa. We are proposing two approaches to complement existing praxes for the church in Africa toward the realization of RTD in the continent.

The first pastoral praxis is *the identification of victims of underdevelopment in Africa*. A communitarian dimension of RTD, rooted in an African anthropology and community and embodied in the church in Africa's self-understanding as a family of God, remains a relevant starting point. The communitarian view of RTD situates the poor as humans with dignity and rights, and as our fellow brothers and sisters, not merely as isolated persons removed from the social construct and commonwealth of any nation. In other words, the poor and marginalized are members of the community, even though they may be caught in a social web that degrades their dignity and human flourishing. Otu describes the poor in Africa as:

> persons who are insignificant in the ecclesial community and secular society, persons who are ethnically and tribally despised, and persons who are socially, economically, politically and culturally marginalized . . . the men and women embarking on a treacherous journey across the Sahara Desert and the Mediterranean Sea to the Global North . . . the men and women held hostage as slaves and in refugee camps across the world . . . families who cannot afford a meal, and who lack access to basic necessities of life . . . children dying daily from curable and preventable diseases, and children forced into labour and prostitution . . . the aged abandoned by their families and government, and who cannot fend for themselves. In the African Swahili language, these groups of persons could be referred to as *wananchi* (the common men and women of society), though in the eyes of God they are not insignificant (Mt 5:3).[53]

The church in Africa has to rediscover the humanity of the poor, and see in them persons with inalienable dignity and rights to human flourishing. Pov-

---

47. Pope Paul VI, *Populorum Progressio* §1.
48. Pope Paul VI, *Populorum Progressio* §11.
49. See Otu, *Communion Ecclesiology and Social Transformation in African Catholicism*, 20–23.
50. See Otu, *Communion Ecclesiology and Social Transformation in African Catholicism*, 21.
51. Zalot, *The Roman Catholic Church and Economic Development*, 1–32.
52. See Orobator, *Church as Family of God in Its Social Context*, 86–89; Otu, *Communion Ecclesiology and Social Transformation in African Catholicism*, 14–49.
53. Otu, *Communion Ecclesiology and Social Transformation in African Catholicism*, 223.

erty, marginalization, and injustice are sometimes interpreted as consequences of sin, ingratitude to God's blessings, or insufficient faith in God. The rise of the "prosperity gospel" in Africa, which in some cases has crept into the church, often overlooks the roots of poverty and the structural factors that support its existence. The church in Africa must recognize the poor as Christ, and as members of the family of God. According to Pope Francis, the poor are "the privileged recipients of the Gospel," and "there is an inseparable bond between our faith and the poor."[54] In this first pastoral praxis, African theologians have a duty to encounter and engage the poor, to see them not as statistics but as persons created in the image and dignity of God, who are loved by God.

The second pastoral praxis is *ecclesial advocacy for victims of underdevelopment in Africa*. According to Otu, "In some African nations, the voices of those living on the margins are not accounted for in the scale of social progress. Pastoral aid initiatives often lack a real human connection with the aspirations of the poor, because they are excluded from conversations about their liberation."[55] The practical effect of excluding the poor from conversation that would lead to their liberation creates a dependency posture in the church–poor relations. Pope Francis, in *Evangelii Gaudium*, calls on the faithful to become God's instrument of help to the poor, which requires docility and attentiveness to the cry of the poor (§187). It demands that the church in Africa contribute toward the actualization of RTD through education, realized by a conscientization process that empowers the poor, oppressed, marginalized, and most vulnerable. As a group, the disadvantaged of society are to become architects of their own humanization and freedom, as well as of their destiny and future.[56] This will bring about citizen participation in the political, economic, and social spheres of their nations, as they demand equity, justice, transparency, and accountability. Catholic non-governmental and faith-based organizations must move away from a handout model and knee-jerk approach to poverty, and instead toward empowering the African *wananchi* to be active participants of sustainable development. These ecclesial institutions have an indispensable role in strengthening civil society in order to confront the structures of injustice and poverty.

Conclusion

The inherent constraints in the implementation of RTD could be transcended through applying Catholic vision and principles toward the realization of human rights. These principles appeal to human consciousness, and they are indispensable for the African continent. In African Traditional Religion, it is difficult to forget the advocacy of African chief priests, who dared not approach the supreme deity with any form of taboo, such as violation of the rights of others. Similarly, the ecclesial hierarchy in Africa is highly regarded and revered. The church in Africa should not wane in its advocacy for the poor, oppressed, marginalized, and vulnerable. Particular churches must embrace true prophetic proclamation and transformative witness to build a social order in which RTD serves the integral development of the person and the common good of the community. Entrusted with the task of transforming the social order, the lay faithful cannot jettison collaborating with legitimate governments, civil societies, faith traditions, cultural institutions, global institutions, and the international community. This is a constitutive role for African theologians and Catholics, especially in the face of increasing conditions of poverty, inequality, injustice, underdevelopment, and human-rights violations.

This chapter has presented a historical excursus and the emerging concerns of "rights" and "development." It demonstrated the appropriation of a multilevel interdisciplinary approach to RTD, revealing the obstacles that can confound efforts to live up to the true notions of rights and development, and these make it difficult to address the systemic inequalities that negate the core ideals of human rights. In an effort to transcend these normative barriers, this chapter drew on sacred scrip-

---

54. Pope Francis, post-synodal apostolic exhortation *Evangelii Gaudium* §84.
55. Otu, *Communion Ecclesiology and Social Transformation in African Catholicism*, 237.
56. See Freire, *Pedagogy of the Oppressed*, 75–76.

ture and magisterial teachings to offer insights toward reconstructing a theology of rights that promotes the integral development of Africans, and the common good of Africa. The enduring challenge that confronts the church in Africa—and the universal church—is to truly become "the salt of the earth" and "the light of the world"' (Matt 5:13–14).

Christian social praxis is indispensable, if efforts toward RTD are to bear abundant fruit in Africa. Particular churches should move beyond exhortatory words and posturing to concrete action, in order to heal Africa of the scourge of destitution and underdevelopment. The church in Africa has a responsibility to offer credible and transformative witness toward the full realization of RTD in the African continent.

Bibliography

Alston, Philip. "Ships Passing in the Night: The Current State of the Human Rights and Development Debate Seen through the Lens of Millennium Development Goals." *Human Rights Quarterly* 27 (2005): 755–829.

Baker, Raymond. *Capitalism's Achilles Heel: Dirty Money and How to Renew the Free-Market System*. Hoboken, NJ: Wiley, 2005.

Benedict XVI, Pope. *Caritas in Veritate* [Encyclical on Integral Human Development in Charity and Truth; June 29, 2009]. Vatican City: Libreria Editrice Vaticana, 2009. www.vatican.va.

Bernstein, Richard. *Praxis and Action: Contemporary Philosophies of Human Activity*. Philadelphia: University of Pennsylvania Press, 1971.

Collier, Paul. *The Bottom Billion: Why the Poorest Countries Are Failing and What Can Be Done about It*. Oxford: Oxford University Press, 2008.

Douzinas, Costas. *The End of Human Rights: Critical Legal Thought at the Turn of the Century*. Oxford: Hart, 2000.

D'Souza, Radha. "The 'Rights' Conundrum: The Poverty of Philosophy amidst Poverty." In *Rights in Context: Law and Justice in Late Modern Society*, edited by Reza Banakar, 55–69. Farnham: Ashgate, 2010.

Escobar, Arturo. *Encountering Development: The Making and Unmaking of the Third World*. Princeton, NJ: Princeton University Press, 1995.

Francis, Pope. *Evangelii Gaudium* (The Joy of the Gospel) [Post-synodal Apostolic Exhortation on the Proclamation of the Gospel in Today's World; November 23, 2013]. Vatican City: Libreria Editrice Vaticana, 2013. www.vatican.va.

———. *Laudato Si'* [Encyclical On Care for Our Common Home; June 18, 2015]. Vatican City: Libreria Editrice Vaticana, 2015. www.vatican.va.

Freire, Paulo. *Pedagogy of the Oppressed*. Harmondsworth, UK: Penguin, 1972.

Government of Nigeria. "Child's Rights Act, 2003."

Hafner-Burton, Emilie M., and Kiyoteru Tsutsui. "Justice Lost! The Failure of International Human Rights Law to Matter Where Needed Most." *Journal of Peace Research* 44.4 (2007): 407–25.

Himes, Michael J., and Kenneth R. Himes. *Fullness of Faith: The Public Significance of Theology*. New York: Paulist Press, 1993.

Hollenbach, David. "Accompaniment, Service, and Advocacy: Responding to Global Poverty and Displacement." *Conversations on Jesuit Higher Education* 44 (2013): 1–12.

———. "Global Human Rights: An Interpretation of the Contemporary Catholic Understanding." In *Human Rights in the Americas*, edited by Alfred Hennelly, SJ, and John Langan, SJ, 9–24. Washington, DC: Georgetown University Press, 1982.

Ibhawoh, Bonny. *Imperialism and Human Rights: Colonial Discourses of Rights and Liberties in African History*. SUNY Series in Human Rights. Albany: State University of New York Press, 2007.

———. "The Right to Development: The Politics and Polemics of Power and Resistance." *Human Rights Quarterly* 33 (2011): 76–104.

Ilesanmi, Simeon O. "Human Rights Discourse in Modern Africa: A Comparative Religious Ethical Perspective." *Journal of Religious Ethics* 23.2 (1995): 293–322.

John XXIII, Pope. *Mater et Magistra* [Encyclical on Christianity and Social Progress; May 15, 1961]. Vatican City: Libreria Editrice Vaticana, 1961. www.vatican.va.

———. *Pacem in Terris* [Encyclical on Establishing Universal Peace in Truth, Justice, Charity, and Liberty; April 11, 1963]. Vatican City: Libreria Editrice Vaticana, 1963. www.vatican.va.

John Paul II, Pope. *Sollicitudo Rei Socialis* [Encyclical for the Twentieth Anniversary of *Populorum Progressio*; December 30, 1987]. Vatican City: Libreria Editrice Vaticana, 1987. www.vatican.va.

Kambhampati, Uma. *Development and the Developing World.* Cambridge: Polity Press, 2006.

Koehler, Gabriele. "Seven Decades of 'Development,' and Now What?," *Journal of International Development* 27 (2015): 733–51.

"The Lottery of Life: Where to Be Born in 2013." *The Economist,* November 21, 2012, www.economist.com.

Mamah, Wilfred Ukanwoke. "Traps and Tools: A Contextual Critique of the Right to Development in International Law." Doctoral thesis. London: University of Westminster, 2013.

M'Baye, Kéba. "Le droit au développement comme un droit de l'homme." *Revue des droits l'homme* 5 (1972): 505–34.

"Mo Ibrahim Governance Report, 2019–2021." https://mo.ibrahim.foundation/iiag/downloads.

Mojekwu, Chris C. "International Human Rights: The African Perspective." In *International Human Rights: Contemporary Issues,* edited by Jack L. Nelson and Vera M. Green, 85–95. Stanfordville, NY: Earl M. Coleman, 1980.

Ogbonnaya, Joseph. *Lonergan, Social Transformation, and Sustainable Human Development.* Eugene, OR: Pickwick, 2013.

Orobator, Agbonkhianmeghe E. *The Church as Family of God in Its Social Context.* Nairobi: Paulines Publications, 2002.

Otu, Idara. "Child Labour and the Nigerian Children's Rights Acts in the Light of Catholic Social Teaching." *Journal of Inculturation Theology* 13.2 (2012): 167–85.

———. *Communion Ecclesiology and Social Transformation in African Catholicism: Between Vatican Council II and African Synod II.* Eugene, OR: Pickwick, 2020.

Panikkar, Raimundo. "Is the Notion of Human Rights a Western Concept?," *Diogenes* 30 (1982): 75–102.

Paul VI, Pope. *Populorum Progressio* [Encyclical on the Development of Peoples; March 26, 1967]. Vatican City: Libreria Editrice Vaticana, 1967. www.vatican.va.

Pogge, Thomas. "The First United Nations Millennium Development Goal: A Cause for Celebration?," *Journal of Human Development* 5 (2004): 377–97.

Pontifical Council for Justice and Peace. *Compendium of the Social Doctrine of the Church.* Rome: Libreria Editrice Vaticana, 2005.

Smith, Linda Tuhiwai. *Decolonizing Methodologies: Research and Indigenous Peoples.* London: Zed Books, 1999.

Stiglitz, Joseph, and Andrew Charlton. *Fair Trade for All: How Trade Can Promote Development.* Oxford: Oxford University Press, 2007.

UNICEF. "Child Protection," https://www.unicef.org/nigeria/child-protection.

———. "COVID-19: 950 More Nigerian Children under 5." May 13, 2020. www.unicef.org/nigeria.

United Nations. "Declaration on the Right to Development." 1986. www.un.org.

———. "The Universal Declaration of Human Rights." 1948. www.un.org.

Vatican II. *Gaudium et Spes* [Pastoral Constitution on the Church in the Modern World; 1965]. www.vatican.va.

Vincent, Andrew. *The Politics of Human Rights.* New York: Oxford University Press, 2010.

World Bank. "Life Expectancy at Birth, Total (years)." www.worldbank.org.

———. "Nigeria in a Glance." www.worldbank.org.

Williams, Lucy. "Towards an Emerging International Poverty Law." In *International Poverty Law: An Emerging Discourse,* edited by Lucy Williams, 1–13. London: Zed Books, 2006.

World Health Organization. "Maternal Health in Nigeria: Generating Information for Action." 2019. https://www.who.int/reproductivehealth/maternal-health-nigeria/en/.

Zalot, Jozef. *The Roman Catholic Church and Economic Development in Sub-Saharan Africa: Voices Yet Unheard in a Listening World.* Lanham, MD: University Press of America, 2002.

An African Catholic Approach to Planetary Living

Edward Osang Obi, MSP

The need for an African Catholic discourse on planetary living is becoming urgent in our time. The clock is ticking ever more rapidly toward an imminent ecological disaster occasioned by human-induced climate change. As lakes recede and give way to advancing deserts, and rivers burst their banks with increasing volumes of water every year, arable land in many parts of sub-Saharan Africa is scarce and the food supply is insecure. This is a recipe for region-wide instability unless something is done soon.

Among the many things that can be done at the level of government policy and social and economic life is to go beyond technological fixes and undertake a determined retrieval of the spiritual values of African religion and culture, which includes the profound respect Africans have for tradition and social continuity. Built into this is intergenerational regard, which means that past generations of the family and tribe are considered to be still-present members of the community. This regard is neither formally taught nor even thought about—Africans drink it in with our mothers' milk. This respect for tradition, Bénézet Bujo notes,

> in the African way of thinking, is not to be regarded in a deterministic, much less in a fatalistic, way. It is to be regarded rather as a potency, which the individual may choose to actuate or not. Success or failure depends on a personal choice: in freely recalling the life-giving actions and words of the ancestors, a person is choosing life; but in neglecting these things, that person is choosing death.[1]

Coming to terms with the notion and practice of planetary living may require a conscious bid to recover this traditional and original harmony in African societies and in their natural ecologies. This harmony has been severely disrupted by modernity's so-called progress toward the new forms of life made available by science and technology.[2] Africans must now consciously relearn and reclaim the ethical values that previously undergirded and sustained their harmonious relationship with nature; these values no longer come to us naturally, thanks to the good intentions of everyone who labored to bring Africans scientific and technological ideas by means of Western education. These ideas, which have affected the social, religious, and cultural realms, have contributed a great deal to making us who we are today. Thanks also to Western education, we can communicate and share life experiences with other people and cultures and also benefit from the developments resulting from a globalized world. Yet, in the same breath as we recount the great benefits provided by these new ideas, we must also state that we have, somehow, lost the common understanding of a spiritual and ecological relationship with creation. The so-called civilizing influences of this exposure to new ideas by those who explored the African continent, first out of curiosity, then for trade, and later for political self-aggrandizement, have come

---

1. Bujo, *African Theology in Its Social Context*, 25.
2. See Pope Paul VI, apostolic letter *Africae Terrarum*.

with a price. Often that price has been the loss of ecological innocence, epitomized by the loss of the original sense of "all living beings and visible nature itself as linked with the world of the invisible and the spirit,"³ a world in which everything supports and sustains everything else in a "creative process of ecological wholeness and solidarity."⁴

Traditional African societies always conceived of nature as a place of both physical and spiritual harmony, an inexhaustible pool of human sustenance, and they lived accordingly. Nature was to be approached with the utmost care and respect, and used only as was necessary for survival and well-being. The bark and roots and every single leaf of a shrub in the forest were enchanted, pregnant with good and a potential source of healing; hence, the African's traditional belief that "the *human person and the cosmos have a vital connection* and . . . both influence and depend on each other."⁵ Even when commutative exchanges (*commutatio*) were done, the purpose was never to amass a lot of anything; instead, it was to barter something that one had plenty of for something else that was needed. In that way, natural equilibrium was maintained and nothing was exhausted, and because nothing was exhausted, it was possible to satisfy one's needs again and again.

With modernity's new ideas, however, came the economic values of mass production, accumulation of resources, competition, economic advantage, and profit. Economic life became adversarial rather than communitarian, as was the case in more socially minded economies. On its face, there was nothing wrong with capitalism as it was envisaged by the so-called Great Transformation⁶ of mid-nineteenth-century England—its purpose was to liberate economic life from social and political control. That was good and necessary at the time, but in order to accomplish this, the free market became necessary. The free market resulted in a new kind of economy in which social considerations were disregarded in favor of a market imperialism in which the prices of all goods, including labor, fluctuated without regard to societal effects.⁷

When free market thinking is taken to its logical end, as in neoclassical economics, it results in the kind of propaganda expressed by Milton Friedman early in his career: "Few trends could so thoroughly undermine the very foundations of our free society as the acceptance by corporate officials of a social responsibility other than to make as much money for their stockholders as possible."⁸ The global world order has enabled many Africans to attend schools of economics in Europe and North America, where they have imbibed these ideas of market supremacy and social irresponsibility. They have propagated these ideas in some form or other in our more prestigious citadels of learning, thereby capturing the imagination of younger generations of the African intelligentsia. Thus, it comes as no surprise that modern Africans cannot readily grasp the planetary perspective of a communal life involving responsibility, mutuality, reciprocity, and interdependence, or have never acquired a sense of gratitude for what the earth gives us.⁹ This chapter addresses this disjuncture as a way of helping the African Catholic reconnect with his or her environment and to undergo the ecological conversion necessary for planetary living.

An *African* Catholic Approach?

In proposing my topic in this way, I have perhaps made the same mistake that many of our European and American friends make when describing a journey to Africa. They say, "I am going to Africa" or "I have been to Africa," but Africa is a huge continent of more than 11.7 million square miles. There are thousands of miles separating Egypt, South Africa, and Nigeria. So when we speak of

---

3. Pope Paul VI, apostolic letter *Africae Terrarum*.
4. Orobator, *Religion and Faith in Africa*, 110.
5. Orobator, *Religion and Faith in Africa*, 110 (emphasis in original).
6. See Polanyi, *Great Transformation*, 140.
7. See Gray, *False Dawn*, 1.
8. Friedman, *Capitalism and Freedom*, 113.
9. See Orobator, *Religion and Faith in Africa*, 111.

an African Catholic approach to planetary living, we need to keep in mind that there is in fact no such approach that we can pick up and study. We have the task of birthing one by deploying the vast resources of our forebears.

We also must bear in mind that many religions are practiced in Africa, not just those having a "book" like Christianity, Judaism, and Islam, and that these religions exercise varying degrees of influence in different parts of Africa. There are those, however, who believe that there is a recognizable religion, a so-called traditional African religion embodying a distinctively African religious culture. Pope St. John Paul II describes it as "the living expression of the soul of vast groups of people" in Africa.[10] The basis for this claim comes from the pope's candid articulation of the value of the African religious disposition: "Africans have a profound religious sense, a sense of the sacred, of the existence of God the Creator and of a spiritual world. The reality of sin in its individual and social forms is very much present in the consciousness of these peoples, as is also the need for rites of purification and expiation" (*EA* §42).[11] Coming from the pope, this is an important sign of the integrity of African tradition and religious culture, and a good reason for us to consider an African Catholic approach to planetary living. Perhaps to underscore Africa's importance and its significance in the historical development of the universal church, John Paul II recalls these words of Paul VI:

> In recalling the ancient glories of Christian Africa, we wish to express our profound respect for the Churches with which we are not in full communion: the Greek Church of the Patriarchate of Alexandria, the Coptic Church of Egypt and the Church of Ethiopia, which share with the Catholic Church a common origin and the doctrinal and spiritual heritage of the great Fathers and Saints, not only of their own land, but of all the early Church. They have labored much and suffered much to keep the Christian name alive in Africa through all the vicissitudes of history. (*EA* §31, quoting *Africae Terrarum* §4)

With such sentiments of high regard for the ancient origins of the church in Africa, it becomes easier to see why the fathers of the African synods saw the need for the universal church to be a place of refuge for the African church against the veritable and present danger of being overwhelmed by post-Enlightenment ideas, especially the profit-oriented mentality of modern capitalism.

The diversity of African tribes and tongues notwithstanding, Africans throughout the continent know that planetary living is a matter of survival. This knowledge springs from an African culture that continues to be influenced to its core by a tradition that binds Africans to their ancestors, to the community, and to the earth or soil. The importance of this triad seems to be a common characteristic of all African cultures, and upon it hang the faith and fate of the traditional African society. Bujo captures this well when he describes the closeness of the relationship between those living on earth and their ancestors. On the one hand, he says, the living owe their existence to these ancestors, from whom they receive everything necessary for life, and, on the other hand, the "living dead" can "enjoy" their role as ancestors only through the living clan community. In this way a kind of interaction is created between the two communities, with the goal of this interaction being the increase of the clan's vitality.[12] What many see as Africans' lively, expansive, almost exaggerated faith and religiosity "proceeds from the affirmation of creation and culminates in the proclamation of the existence of a creator."[13]

---

10. Pope John Paul II, post-synodal apostolic exhortation *Ecclesia in Africa* §47 (hereinafter *EA*).
11. This African sense of the sacred has been referred to in the past by the derogatory term "animism," as if there were no substance to the sacred milieu of Africa.
12. See Bujo, *Ethical Dimension of Community*, 16.
13. Orobator, *Theology Brewed in an African Pot*, 49.

The Wisdom of the Pioneers[14]

One of the earliest pioneers of African ethics and the Christian faith was Vincent Mulago, a Congolese born in Birava, near Bukavu, and Shi by tribe and culture.[15] He developed a distinctively anthropomorphic ethical framework in which "Being" is a synthetic whole; it is composed of separate elements brought together to form a coherent whole in which [wo]Man occupies center stage. According to Bujo, who has read and translated Mulago's original French,

> There is a hierarchy of beings, from God to the inferior levels of nature; but between God and human beings on earth there are all the dead, particularly the ancestors. Within this hierarchy there exist relations and interactions, so that one can speak of a "global, cosmic philosophy." The whole universe is called to contribute towards keeping and increasing human life. Everywhere and in everything in the world there are means that can influence life, but one must capture them in order to make them beneficial.[16]

This conception of a hierarchy grounding the African understanding of the interdependence of the human person and other creatures is quite common in African thought. Mulago described this interdependence thus: "The *ntu*, a substance scholastically speaking, is not given separately from other beings. There is no created substance existing independently of other *ntu*: every *ntu* remains open to other beings so as to receive from them a supplement and reinforcement of vital being."[17] The hierarchy of being concerns created things, with the human person at the top and other creatures below. But the supreme being, whom Mulago describes as "*Uncreated Life, Happiness by Essence, Principium et Finis of all being*,"[18] is *other* in relation to this hierarchy. The supreme being does not have a creator and is the only complete being, needing nothing, not even needing to increase or augment itself, as no competitor exists to deplete it.

This *principium et finis* commands the vertical axis of the relationship. But on the horizontal axis, [wo]Man has competitors in creation with whom s/he must contend, and must share the space and all of the resources of creation. For this reason s/he has a tendency, an innate drive, to expand and make other creatures serve her/his interests and thereby increase her/himself. Though these instincts manifest naturally, [wo]Man knows that s/he cannot attain the fullness s/he desires unless s/he participates in communion with others, either vertically (with the supreme being) or horizontally (with other persons and creatures). [wo]Man often sins and transgresses the boundaries created by the ethics of "participation and communion with another."[19] To forestall this predicament and reduce (or eliminate) the impact of his/her sin on the community, s/he is regulated by taboos and totems and other religious and cultural artifacts, including appeasement rituals; s/he can even be afflicted with bad dreams, sicknesses, and evil spirits to torture her/him and curb his/her excesses. In this regard, Bujo, a pioneer in his own right, sees the purpose of ethics as highlighting the fact that "every conscience has always a communitarian dimension."[20] Thus, as long as [wo]Man's excesses are curbed, there is social and ecological equilibrium, and the peace thus achieved leads to an all-around fecun-

---

14. In formulating this section, I have studied the entries about some of those considered to be pioneers of African theology in the rich three-volume anthology *African Theology*, edited by Bujo and Juvénal Ilunga Muya, vol. 1.

15. The Bantu culture and religion can be considered to be the strongest influence in sub-Saharan Africa, and one can rightly refer to it as "African culture." Vincent Mulago was a Muntu from the Shi extraction, one of numerous Bantu tribes, and I find his thought as narrated by Bujo to be quite representative of African thought.

16. Bujo, "Vincent Mulago," 33.

17. Bujo, "Vincent Mulago," 33.

18. Bujo, "Vincent Mulago," 17 (emphasis in original).

19. Bujo, "Vincent Mulago," 33.

20. Muya, "Bénézet Bujo," 141.

dity in the land and in the procreative power of human beings in community.

A remarkably similar sentiment is expressed by Pope Paul VI in his apostolic message *Africae Terrarum* when he explains that African religion "has never considered man as mere matter limited in earthly life, but recognizes in him the presence and power of another spiritual element, in virtue of which human life is always related to the after-life" (§8). A fitting locus of that recognition that is given to the human person for her/his welfare is the family. The family in Africa is "the natural environment in which man is born and acts, in which he finds the necessary perfection and security, and eventually through union with his ancestors has his continuity beyond earthly life" (§10).

We have already established, following Mulago, that the supreme being is not in contention with the *ntu* or human being. The creator exists far above the human sphere and allows [wo]Man to carry on virtually undisturbed. As a result, everything in creation tends to be centered around [wo]Man, and s/he sources everything s/he needs from the environment. This anthropocentric approach to life is common to all African cultures, but Martin Nkafu Nkemnkia thinks of this unified vision of life (unified around the *anthropos*) as "vitalogy," in which [wo]Man is expected to live in harmony with God, ancestors, the world, and other people.[21]

Obviously each of the many different peoples of Africa has had its own unique historical development, cultural adaptations, and unique experiences of the supreme being, and its own particular interactions with the supreme being and with other creatures. Through folklore, anecdotes, proverbs, fables, and parables, every African people comes to learn of how they came to be where they are. This process of gaining self-knowledge is crucial to the formation of ideas about religion and ethics. "African religious traditions admit of multiple creative agents with some playing the role of intermediaries or secondary agents who actually complete the process of creation. This highlights the relationship between the so-called 'secondary' or 'lesser' or 'economic' gods and goddesses and the 'Supreme Being.'"[22]

In any case, human beings are at the center of creation and own everything that was ever created—it was created *for* them! The African sees the universe from the perspective of how it is related to her/him. Even the smaller gods or deities paid respects to the human person, as can be seen from this Yoruba creation myth, narrated by Geoffrey Parrinder:

> The first man was the giver of morality and family order, and he has been respected as ancestor and lawgiver ever since. He imposed taboos and punished anybody who broke them. His tutelary deity was Great God, since he had formed his body. Some of the other gods came down to earth, and one of them it is said did not pay his respects to the first man but acted with disdain toward him. . . . [A]t last the god came begging to man to heal him. The man was skilled in medicine and he demanded respect and repentance from the god before healing his daughter.[23]

It can be deduced from this Yoruba myth that the power of the human being to make and to destroy was immense, and that is why the supreme being made him the keeper of the law and the source of ethics. This implicit belief in the power of [wo]Man subsists unchanged in any significant way in the lives and interactions of present-day Africans. The words, actions, instruments, vessels, and other tools employed in these interactions may vary from one part of Africa to another, yet in all three thousand ethnic groups and twenty-one hundred languages,[24] the African understanding of life and of human beings does not. Orobator's cautionary words that "to attain a meaningful engagement with Africa, it is important to shed the misconception that Africa is a simple entity, and to keep in mind the fact that

---

21. See Nkemnkia, *African Vitalogy*.
22. Orobator, *Religion and Faith in Africa*, 109.
23. Parrinder, *African Mythology*, 39.
24. Cf. Amadiume, "Igbo and African Perspectives on Religious Conscience and the Global Economy."

Africa is a complex reality,"²⁵ must be heeded, but it is possible to identify a number of fundamental structures that all African religiosity has in common and that can allow us access to the African understanding of God, human beings, and the cosmos.

Bujo provides much more than an inkling of these fundamental structures, beginning with the African notion of life,²⁶ especially life that is not limited to earth but takes place in the whole of the relationship between the living and the dead, a relationship that is inescapable because it is so important. The realities of ancestors, community, and ecology are intrinsic to the African's understanding and expression of life. The African notion of life bestrides all of the other fundamental structures of the African worldview—Africans look to ancestors for life, are embedded in community in order to receive life, and respect created reality because of its life-giving potential. In short, one cannot live life fully and happily unless s/he has an a priori belief in ancestors and the community and an openness to the cosmos.

In Bujo's thought, life is not just a biological exercise; rather, it integrates both the animal and plant worlds into a life current that includes human beings, who share it with other beings.²⁷ The deep quest of [wo]Man for life also has an eschatological dimension, which is what makes her/him desire communication with, and the mediation of, ancestors. Bujo opines that, "every act and every reality has a communal dimension in the Black African world. It is a relation, human-to-human and human to nature, which in the end is founded in God. The whole of the community then extends to the living as well as to the dead."²⁸

The discussion will now proceed to a consideration of the three most important elements of the African worldview and traditional ethics: ancestors, community, and soil.

Key Elements of the African Worldview and Traditional Ethics

The Role of Ancestors

Who is an ancestor? Pioneers of African thought are agreed that belief in the importance of ancestors is a common denominator and starting point of the African worldview. Bujo even goes so far as to make the extraordinary claim that ancestral belief is determinative of every facet of African life, including the religious, political, and socioeconomic.²⁹ Bearing in mind the highly anthropocentric picture of the [wo]Man and her/his relationship on the vertical level with the supreme being that generates all things, there is good reason for the African to consider God the supreme progenitor, almost in the sense of an original ancestor who gives the dead human ancestor a power that transcends the earthly order with a commanding authority and honor and measure of moral definition.³⁰

But this view of the supreme being as original ancestor is not popular among scholars. Mulago has a different approach in which ancestry does not begin with God. For Mulago, the influences of the various *ntu* are never interrupted, not even by death, among those who share the same vital source. The first ancestors are always at the head of their community, and their descendants are but the extensions of the primordial chief. In a participated political-social economy, power passes from the supreme being to ancestors and from them to heads of families, communities, clans, and tribes, usually all male. Mulago divides the notion of participation in two: the principal participated and the secondary participated: "The first foundation of . . . Bantu solidarity, vital union and fraternity is the unity of life, the identity and indivisibility of the founding ancestor's blood. The secondary participated is in function of the first and subordinated to

---

25. Orobator, *Religion and Faith in Africa*, 6.
26. See Muya, "Bénézet Bujo."
27. Muya, "Bénézet Bujo," 121.
28. Muya, "Bénézet Bujo," 121.
29. Cf. Muya, "Bénézet Bujo," 122.
30. Agbakwuo, *African*, 65.

it: it is all that sustains life and the means towards maintaining it."[31]

Binding ties of blood with the living members of the family, clan, or community are, therefore, the sine qua non of the relationship of ancestors to their living human offspring. According to Bujo, the ancestor is the man who, through death understood as a rite of passage, has entered the hereafter and thus is both in contact with God and actively engaged in the affairs of the family and in village events. The ancestor's engagement with village or community events comes from the fact that even in death he is still a member of the community in the eyes of his family and of others in the community.[32] This is why values like family, hospitality, brotherhood, and respect for others extend out in concentric waves, creating the so-called enlarged family, which dissolves itself in the community of the people and in the entire human family.[33] This is reflected in the fact that, in Africa, death never occurs to only one family. The entire community or clan is bereaved ipso facto, and mourns or celebrates (depending on the age of the deceased and circumstances of the death) at the passing of one of their own.

However, not just anybody is venerated as an ancestor; there are criteria, even if they vary from place to place: "The deceased must have lived an exemplary life of virtue, have respected the laws received from the ancestors; he must not have been a quarrelsome man or involved in sorcery, he must have been a principle of unity within the community. He must not have died a violent death and he must have left progeny."[34] Ancestors are not all of the same grade; depending on their contribution to the life of the community and the example of their lives, some are more important than others. A clan or community founder is seen as a first-class ancestor, as are community heroes and others who sacrificed their lives for the survival of the community, for example, by engaging in warfare with other tribes. There are also family ancestors whom one is obliged to mention in libations, invoking some good omen. The one thing common to all these paragons is that they are publicly acknowledged.

Orobator mentions four traits of African ancestorship, including the fact that the experience of death offers the ancestors a privileged place of closeness to God. Other traits include the ancestors' ability to mediate or intercede on behalf of living family or clan members; the ancestor is therefore entitled to mandatory and regular communication and consultation through invocations, libations, ritual offerings, sacrifices, and so on; and, as noted above, not just anybody is raised to the status of a living dead: "A person must have distinguished himself or herself in service and led an exemplary life in the community. This is precisely what allows him or her to become a model for the entire family and community of the living."[35] In other words, the ancestor is seen as an important model and guarantor of the present and future moral life of the community. Thus "the descendants must, beginning from the advice, deeds and experience of the ancestors, search for and point towards ways of solving today's problems."[36]

It can be clearly seen that there is affinity between the African concept of ancestors and the Christian meaning of the triumphant church, that is, those whom the church refers to as "those who have gone before us marked with the sign of faith."[37] Because the ancestors have spiritual power over living humans for all the reasons mentioned above, the fear of contravening the ethical code or the example of the ancestors becomes an additional restraint on [wo]Man yielding to his/her natural instinct to usurp and dominate other creatures. The notion of community, as we shall see presently, also plays a moderating role on the selfish and individualistic tendency of [wo]Man to satisfy her/his human instincts.

---

31. Bujo, "Vincent Mulago," 19.
32. Cf. Muya, "Bénézet Bujo," 122.
33. See Nkemnkia, *African Vitalogy*, 8.
34. Muya, "Bénézet Bujo," 122.
35. Orobator, *Theology Brewed in an African Pot*, 75.
36. Muya, "Bénézet Bujo," 123.
37. Eucharistic Prayer 1, The Roman Canon.

The Centrality of Community

The second element of the worldview and traditional ethics of Africans that we must attend to is that of the centrality of community in African religion and culture. Orobator sees community as

> the space where the human person is situated, where he or she strives through personal action to realize his or her full potential in cooperation with other members of the community. Because life is construed as a shared value or the ultimate common good . . . African spirituality allows for a wide participation of all members in setting the criteria for determining the common good and for judging people's actions.[38]

Both good and bad deeds are appraised in the context of the community because they are done not only to a single individual. That individual is the father, brother, or son of somebody; the mother, sister, or daughter of somebody.

In this same way Bujo aligns the notion of community with that of the family relationship in a "threefold body of relations: the ancestors, the living and the not-yet-born," in which "the happiness of those who leave this life for the next, consists in their remaining alive in the memories of their descendants."[39] There is a *sensus communis*, therefore, by which everything that happens to the individual also happens to the community, and vice versa. Thus, that there are communal effects of good or bad deeds is well accepted by Africans, and this puts a further check on the excesses of individuals, who are well advised not to commit infractions that would negatively impact the whole community.

This community perspective on sin is supported by Harry Sawyerr, who observes that God does not directly enter into any discussion about sin or wrongdoing among African people. These things are seen within the context of community life, in which the clan relationship embracing the living, the dead, and the unborn is essentially one of covenant. Any breach that punctures the communal relationship amounts to sin. Thus, the corporate solidarity of the family, the clan, and the tribe becomes a fundamental factor of life, crucial for ensuring ethical conduct and a common standard of behavior.[40] Orobator breaks this down expertly to three dimensions comprising Africans' focus on community.

> First, it prioritizes the human person as the privileged recipient of the gift of creation, and it underscores the centrality of the human person within the ecological framework. Second, community is the privileged space for manifesting the sacred, for celebrating in ritual and worship, where the living and the world of the spirits intertwine and interact for the common good of the members of the community. To deny the community of this vital interaction is to bring about its potential destruction, because the spirit world and the natural environment are part of a vital ecological pact. Third, . . . life is inclusive of our ecological siblings and other constituents of nature, and, thus, the experience of healing in its fullness occurs within this wider communitarian framework.[41]

There are consequences of being a member of a community. Whenever the community is targeted by evil deeds, each individual is also targeted. There are people in every community who are suspected of working maliciously against their relatives and neighbors through the use of magic, sorcery, and witchcraft. "Mystical power is neither good nor evil in itself; but when used maliciously by some individuals it is experienced as evil. This view makes evil an independent and external object which, however, cannot act on its own but must be employed by human or spiritual agents."[42] Martin

---

38. Orobator, *Religion and Faith in Africa*, 177.
39. Muya, "Bénézet Bujo," 125.
40. See Sawyerr, *Creative Evangelism*, 30–32.
41. Orobator, *Religion and Faith in Africa*, 117–18.
42. Daniel, "Psychological and Religious Understanding of Wrong Doing in African Perspective," 188.

Nkafu Nkemnkia, arguing from the point of view of his notion of "vitalogy" as "a conceptual vision of the whole of reality, where there are no spaces for irreducible dichotomies between matter and spirit, religious commitment and daily life, soul and body, the world of the living and the world of the dead (world of the ancestors),"[43] warns about the possible erosion of the value of "community." The requirements of "vitalogy" are reposed in and possessed by the whole community, and "if each and everyone does not maintain a personal identity in his dialogue with others, there will be a risk of presenting a false image of oneself and by so doing, annihilate the riches and positive cultural differences which offer to each one the possibility of constructing a world community rooted on cooperation, solidarity, sharing and communion."[44]

The idea of community, as I pointed out earlier, is closely linked with the idea of life and the giving of life. This is true not only for those living here and now but also for the dead living in the "village of the ancestors" and the yet-to-be-born. It is also true not only in our relationship with other human beings but also in our relationship with the animal, plant, and mineral worlds that are constitutive elements of life. "Everything that lives, guarantees, and promises life on earth is included in the concept" of community.[45] It is clear, therefore, that blood ties are not the only criterion for community membership. In addition to relationships of marriage, friendship, and neighborhood, even a foreigner can be admitted into the community with the full benefits and responsibilities of communitarian living. The community opens to the universal and guarantees respect for the otherness of others.

> God's radical otherness towards everything that is not God founds and guarantees transcendence in respect of his creatures. The foreigner relates to the absolute otherness of the origin of all created reality and to the unity of humankind with the whole cosmos, thus establishing absolute respect for the whole of creation. One can assert that the clan or tribe is open to the universal. The relation towards others and the cosmos is contemplated from the viewpoint of transcendence, in God's spirit.[46]

Attachment to Earth (Land or Soil)

The third element that lies at the core of African religious belief and the African worldview is the earth, or the land or soil. On account of his subsistence living conditions, the traditional African looked upon the land as the sole source of all that gives life. His/her attachment to the land far outweighed anything else that s/he considered of benefit to her/his life. The land and everything that is in it was always considered a gift of the supreme being and had a sacred character of its own. Unlike the Western idea of land as a commodity to be bought and sold, sometimes in order to aggrandize the owner's social status, in Africa land was the ultimate equalizer—needed by all, available to all, and used by all. Even when parcels of land were owned by families, it was merely for their use, since true ownership of land was always invested in the community. Membership in or affiliation with a community was the only thing that gave anyone access to any land.

The testimony of one Mr. Z. Nkosi from South Africa at a World Council of Churches forum addressing the issue of land in Africa is very instructive:

> Our belief that land is a gift from God and from our ancestors has not left us. We continue to see ourselves as stewards of God's resources, especially of communally owned land.... In many African families the umbilical cord of a new born baby is buried. In other communities when a boy is circumcised, the foreskin and blood is also buried. The sacredness of land in Africa is further linked to the fact that our ancestors are buried in it. Without land, we would not have a home for a

---

43. Nkemnkia, *African Vitalogy*, 9.
44. Nkemnkia, *African Vitalogy*, 9.
45. Muya, "Bénézet Bujo," 125.
46. Muya, "Bénézet Bujo," 126.

dead body. That is why we kneel barefooted next to the grave when we want to communicate anything to our ancestors, showing a lot of respect for the land on which they lie.[47]

From the details of this narrative, most of which are still applicable among traditional Africans all over sub-Saharan Africa, one can sense an African spirit of enchantment with the land. The land here refers not only to the soil but also to the flora and fauna, the watercourses and arable portions, and indeed the insects and microbes invisible to the human eye; it refers also to minerals on the surface of or underneath the land. It refers to everything associated with the earth, including the human beings that walk upon and till it for sustenance. Thus, "the earth, our mother, is the outcome of an intentional act by an agent who is deeply involved and invested in the process of creating the world and human beings."[48] What this implies is that human beings were created as part of a package that includes earth's others. These others were also loved into being in their own right, not just to satisfy the needs of human beings. The next section grapples with how to understand [wo]Man's place as the apex of creation.

The Human Person as the Apex of Creation

It has been stated more than once here how anthropocentric African cosmology is. Be that as it may, the African approaches and utilizes his/her primacy with respect to the earth's resources in a markedly different way than modernity's *Homo consumens*. It is not in doubt that God created only the human person *in God's image and likeness*. There are some, however, who blame the workings and dysfunctions of the present global order, especially the ecological crisis, on the extraordinary place accorded the human person in the Judeo-Christian story of creation.[49]

The anthropocentrism that overshadows most of the ecological discourse to this day is based on a wrong interpretation of the divine intent concerning creation. The power to subdue and dominate was not meant to be an unbridled power of lordship over other creatures. Drawing on James Lovelock's Gaia hypothesis, Celia Deane-Drummond identifies "cooperation and symbiosis" as implicit values in that hypothesis, but warns in the same breath that "it is equally possible to interpret Gaia's theory along more Darwinian lines, which includes the idea that those species that are the most influential in setting the environmental state become the most dominant."[50]

But, as we have come to know, the divine injunctions of "dominion" and "subduing" in the first chapter of the book of Genesis (1:26–28) were more about stewardship of creation than lordship over it. Neither of these injunctions are absolute, nor do they grant a unilateral right; reciprocal stewardship was intended between human beings and other creatures.

> Although this may sound positive, in Judeo-Christian tradition, nonetheless, stewardship seems a one-directional reality that flows from human beings toward other creatures. . . . [I]t assumes that other creatures or constituents of nature do not have any equal or reciprocal responsibility of stewardship toward human beings. Herein lies a critical difference: African religion emphasizes the mutuality and interdependence that underlie the communion and solidarity of human beings and the rest of creation.[51]

Denis Edwards has done a fantastic job of assembling resources from the Christian tradition to support the notion that humans are made in the image of God in a distinctive way, not over and against other creatures, but precisely in an evolutionary interrelationship and ongoing relationship with

---

47. World Council of Churches, "Land and Spirituality in Africa."
48. Orobator, *Religion and Faith in Africa*, 108–9.
49. See White, "Historical Roots of Our Ecological Crisis."
50. Deane-Drummond, *Eco-Theology*, 11.
51. Orobator, *Religion and Faith in Africa*, 109.

them. Edwards, for instance, found in the theological anthropology of St. Athanasius an excellent explanation of being created in the image and likeness of God: "Athanasius reserves the word 'image' to the eternal Word. Christ, for him, is the Image, the Radiance, the Word, and the Son of the Father. Humanity, then is 'in the image' of the Image. Athanasius situates humanity in the midst of God's creation, all of which is completely dependent on the creative Word for its existence."[52] With this explanation it becomes less arduous a task for us to scrutinize and challenge notions and assumptions of human exceptionalism. Thus, so that human beings can truly understand planetary living that accommodates all other creatures, Edwards suggests that "first, humans are 'persons oriented toward communion' with the triune God and with one another; [and] second, [that] human beings occupy the unique place of 'sharing in the divine governance of visible creation.'"[53] In this thinking, the earth must remain the subject of an ongoing renewal in time and space. Orobator affirms that "creation was not a definitive act sequestered in the impenetrable and irretrievable historical past. Creation is an enterprise continually being fulfilled, in mutuality and reciprocity." In this sense, therefore, planetary living is not about the origin of the earth, but about how "it is to be continued and sustained, how it survives. The plan can go awry, and human beings can mistreat the earth. . . . Conversely human beings can chart a different course, one of care and protection of mother earth."[54]

Obviously, anthropocentrism has been the bane of ecological rectitude. And when people are thinking about and shaping the world according to the values of economism,[55] there will always be ecological and human consequences to anthropocentrism, including, as Mary Evelyn Tucker says, "[e]nvironmental destruction, marginalization of large numbers of people, endemic poverty and control of wealth by the few."[56] Tucker challenges the way globalization has led us to put our planet in disrepair:

> Our radical dependence on interrelated ecosystems is being made abundantly clear as we are unraveling the web of those ecosystems in ways that reflect multiple motivations—including blindness and ignorance as well as greed and arrogance. . . . [W]e have had cornucopian expectations of nature's limitless capacity for use and renewal and an abundant faith in the saving power of science and technology as agents of progress. These have led us to the brink of destruction—not only of human life but also of all other forms of life.[57]

Ecological poverty comes from the attitude that what can be exploited must be exploited—now. This attitude overlooks the fact that the earth has a certain carrying capacity, beyond which there can only be diminishing returns. In this view, all other creatures are made for human beings and are available for their use, and possible abuse, as long as human beings are happy. This is an attitude I have described elsewhere as "anthropogenia."[58] Unfortunately, however, by our nature, human beings are never fully satisfied with anything on earth. Of course, human beings were never meant to be satisfied here on earth, since God's intention was to have them reunite with God in heaven, where all need and desire will be fully satisfied.[59] This lesson

---

52. Edwards, "Humans, Chimps and Bonobos," 20. Edwards is quoting from the International Theological Commission, "Communion and Stewardship: Human Persons Created in the Image of God," paras. 25 and 57.
53. Edwards, "Humans, Chimps and Bonobos," 19.
54. Orobator, *Religion and Faith in Africa*, 109.
55. Cobb, "Will Economism End in Time?"
56. Tucker, "Globalization and the Environment," 88.
57. Tucker, "Globalization and the Environment," 92.
58. See Obi, "Fragile Ecosystems and the Pressures of Anthropogenia," 176. Here we denounce "an apparent hegemony of the humanum, in which everything is subject to and determined by human beings and our need, or the value we place on it. . . . [O]ur belligerent *be*-ing and voracious *act*-ing in the natural environment is what constitutes anthropogenia." Emphasis in original.
59. St. Augustine of Hippo famously said, "You have made us for yourself, O Lord, and our heart is restless until it rests in you" (*Confessions* 1.1.1).

is, however, lost on the human person of modern times, and the result is manifest in all the problems of our time, the solutions to some of which are proving insurmountable to human knowledge and technique. But how do we reorganize the world in such a way that the present situation can be met by purposive action geared at recovering our ecological losses?

At this point it is necessary to introduce the notion of ecological economics as a hermeneutical key to understanding the predominant anthropology of economism. As explained by Sallie McFague nearly twenty years ago, ecological economics is economics for the well-being of the whole *oikos* (household) of planet Earth and all its creatures:

> This model claims that human beings, while greedy to be sure, are even more needy. After all, they, we, depend on the health of all the other parts of the planet for our existence.... Ecological Economics claims that market economics denies one huge fact: unless the limited resources of the planet are justly distributed among its myriad life forms so they all can flourish, there will be no sustainable future for even the greediest among us. We cannot live without these other sources of our existence.... Of all creatures alive, we are the neediest.[60]

Planetary Living—What It Involves

Planetary living is a way of looking at how human persons live on the Earth, one of several planets in our solar system, and how they can evaluate the impact of their lifestyles on the support structures of the environment and ecosystem of the planet. Though the development of this construct is somewhat new, vestiges of it can be traced all the way back to the beginnings of environmental awareness in the 1970s. With the Club of Rome's publication of *Limits to Growth* in 1972, and its work to disseminate its dire message of the consequences of exponential economic and population growth as against a finite supply of resources, an awareness of sustainable and thoughtful consumption was born. Between then and now the global economic wheel has spun furiously and the world's ecosystems have sad stories to tell of denuded forests, overmined and scarred mountainsides, polluted waters, intense and rapid desertification, frequent flood events, endangered ecosystems, extinct species, overflowing landfills, and possibly more pieces of plastic in the sea than fish!

These and many more effects of globalization have increasingly led scholars to draw a distinction between the "global" and the "planetary," and to reach a consensus that a "global" point of view is not only limited in time and space but is also unsustainable. The "planetary" recognizes and invokes an inevitable and inalienable alterity (otherness), which our mechanics and techniques cannot evade or control by the sheer fact of our proximity, interrelatedness, and intersubjectivity, and which opens up more to life, in community. In other words, the circumstances of our common existence will compel us to planetary living whether we actively accept these circumstances or not. In the words of Kwok Pui-lan, "Planetarity signifies an alterity that does not derive from us, a system that is beyond us and yet we inhabit." That is to say, thinking in terms of planetarity is to situate oneself as a person who offers prudent stewardship of an alterity that is above and beyond our reach, that implies an inexhaustible taxonomy, and that offers us the chance to imagine the best possible scenarios for the flourishing of all.[61]

Planetary living, thus, forces us to be mindful of the welfare of others and of alterity as such, because "identities are formed through relationships with others (or through that which is different from oneself), not in isolation."[62] Whitney Bauman explains the distinction between a global mentality and planetary mentality by stating that a global mentality tries to solve all the world's problems with a single (preconceived or prejudiced?) solution, whereas a "'planetary mentality' acknowledges that the planet is made up of many different places,

---

60. McFague, "God's Household," 121.
61. See Lai, "Planetary Loves."
62. Bauman, "Developing a Planetary Ethic," 222 n. 1.

peoples, ecosystems, terrains, and problems."[63] Living a planetary existence, therefore, has the feeling of participating in something greater than oneself. The notions of participation and inclusion, which are central to understanding planetarity, point to an affinity between planetary living and the notion of common good as described in Catholic social thought. Even more interestingly, both planetarity and Catholic social thought are, in turn, accommodated by an understanding of being bonded through a community as traditional African religion conceives of it.

Though everyone participates in building the common good, each does so in a different way. On account of the differences that alterity brings, it is only right that different measuring sticks are used for evaluating different issues and problems as they arise. The poverty of the global mentality, therefore, lies in drawing a false equivalence between all present-day contexts under the pretext that we are one world and must all contribute equally to addressing its problems. As Bauman further clarifies, "A planetary perspective pays much deeper attention to the differences that make up populations, places, histories, geographies, and so on, while a global perspective seeks to apply a one-size-fits-all solution to everything from industrialization to technology to solutions for ecological and social ills."[64]

Planetary Living and African (Catholic) Perspectives on Ecology

Whereas in the Global North the notion of planetary living has developed almost as a protest against the unwholesome experience of all-consuming global capitalist greed, with its attendant impacts on the common space we share with other creatures in nature, in the Global South, and particularly in sub-Saharan Africa, this concept already has deep cultural and religious roots. In other words, Africans have long accepted and accommodated themselves to the fact that they must live, survive, and thrive in and with nature, and that other creatures and their habitats and well-being are of as much consequence as those of human beings. This intricate, interlocking, inalienable, and mutually supportive relationship of ecological interaction with numerous natural ecosystems is for the African the very key to survival. Taboos, totems, and cultural anecdotes are woven around these ecosystems in order to protect them from human greed. In this way, a morality of care for nature and its resources—based on certain principles, attitudes, and dispositions—is created and sustained in the imagination of young and old alike. Though not contained in a set of rules written in a book, Africans imbibe these principles, attitudes, and dispositions through careful attention to the examples of the ancestors, giving them due credit for preserving and sustainably handing on these ecological goods to successive generations.

The *Catechism of the Catholic Church* (*CCC*) recognizes and affirms "a *solidarity among all creatures* arising from the fact that all have the same Creator and are all ordered to his glory" (§344). This solidarity is preserved by divine providence, as all creation is in a "'state of journeying' (*in statu viae*) toward an ultimate perfection yet to be attained, to which God has destined it" (§302). According to the *CCC*, the creator God "not only gives [his creatures] being and existence, but also, and at every moment, upholds and sustains them in being, enables them to act and brings them to their final end" (§301). Furthermore, taking into consideration the fact that the International Theological Commission (ITC) speaks of the close relationship between the human person and other creatures when it states that "human beings are beings who share the world with other bodily beings but who are distinguished by their intellect, love and freedom and are thus ordered by their very nature to interpersonal communion,"[65] one can assume that human exceptionalism, in the way in which it has been employed to justify and support some of the basest instincts of the human person, like barefaced greed, selfishness, consumerism, and eco-

---

63. Bauman, "Developing a Planetary Ethic," 223.
64. Bauman, "Developing a Planetary Ethic," 223–24.
65. International Theological Commission, *Communion and Stewardship* §56.

logical displacement, has no place in Christianity. Though there are still unresolved issues of human, and specifically male, dominance in the ITC text, it is clear that the experts acknowledge, and are at pains to make clear, that human beings are part of and within creation, not outside of it.

An African Relational Ethic of Planetary Living

Different from the Western paradigm of economism is the African relational ethic that stresses bonds with and between created reality rather than an adversarial relationship in which the *anthropos* is dominant and domineering. The notion of the "bondedness of life" has been employed by Harvey Sindima to describe an African worldview that opposes the Western dualistic, mechanistic, and deist assumptions that have hitherto predominated and are still very much the basis of present-day Western economic models that place growth over sustainability and efficiency over effectiveness. Inevitably, these models have largely been blamed for any number of ongoing crises, including poverty and climate change.[66] In this notion of bondedness, "the issue is the re-establishment of community, the re-establishment of the circulation of life . . . [so that it] can go on transcending itself, go on bursting the barriers, or the intervals, the nothingness . . . [so that it can] go on being superabundant."[67] This African perspective comes from centuries of attempts by Africans to answer fundamental questions about their place in and relationship with the universe of created reality, searching as it were for an African worldview.

Martin Heidegger noted that "a worldview (*Weltanschauung*) grows out of an all-inclusive reflection on the world and the human Dasein, and this again happens in different ways explicitly and consciously in individuals."[68] Similarly, Emefie Ikenga Metuh conceived of an African worldview as consisting of "the complex of their beliefs and attitudes concerning the origin, nature, and structure of the universe and the interaction of its beings—with particular reference to man."[69] For African peoples, and probably other communitarian societies, this worldview is necessarily connected with a tradition embedded within their religious consciousness. Thus, when they explain the universe and its creation, they do so in an automatically religious way.[70] Sindima further clarifies this: "Since the cosmos is spiritual, all considerations about human life have religious and moral implications as well as political ramifications. This means that the question of human life cannot be fully addressed until the religious and moral and political questions have been answered. Life always has to be seen in its totality."[71] It is this totality that is at stake when we engage in dualisms that divide nature from culture and mind from body. Western ecological semantics has tended to create two distinct realities with little or no relationship between them, which "created a dramatic new narrative about humanity's exalted and exceptional place in a cosmos increasingly perceived as having no other moral significance or divine purpose than its material value to humans. Approaching the rest of creation in this utilitarian way effectively deifies, idolizes and, consequently, absolutizes the *anthropos* . . . one out of the many different species on earth."[72] This is the basis of all idolatry!

Because of Africans' profound consciousness of living in the presence of God, who is the owner of all created things, their activities in and with the land, the soil, the environment, and their relationships with one another in those contexts, are governed by alterity, an ethic of reverence for the unknown "other." It is not because the other (*alter*) is absent or unknown, but because his/her ever-present spiritual aura is itself the abode of God, who is unknowable. These relationships assume covenantal sanctity when viewed in this way. This "participation-sharing," according to Laurenti

---

66. See Sindima, "Community of Life" (1989), 538.
67. Sindima, "Community of Life: Ecological Theology in African Perspective" (1990), 145.
68. Heidegger, *Basic Problems of Phenomenonology*, 4.
69. Metuh, *God and Man in African Religion*, 76.
70. Mbiti, "African Views of the Universe," 175.
71. Sindima, "Community of Life" (1989), 544.
72. Obi, "Fragile Ecosystems and the Pressures of Anthropogenia," 184.

Magesa, is the way in which "balance in life" is preserved.[73]

Most African cultures south of the Sahara have an idiom, a metaphor, or an anecdote that conveys and encourages participation-sharing. Folklore shared around the fireplace is a good source of anecdotes that teach moral lessons about this concept. More recently this has been recaptured as the notion and spirit of *ubuntu*, which was popularized by the Nobel laureate Desmond Tutu in the context of the new "rainbow" nation of South Africa (as opposed to the old, individualistic, exclusivist, white supremacist one). The concept of participation-sharing simply states that "I am because we all are!" In other words, my *be*-ing and flourishing derive from and depend on others, in the same way that I also undertake responsibility for others' be-ing and flourishing. In terms of the environment, Africans woo and protect the productivity of earth and nature by imposing taboos that may be contravened only on the pain of bad luck and misfortune to the contravener.[74]

Ritual appeasement sacrifices have been used to ensure people's purity of intention and action toward one another and the environment because their very survival depends on the continued bounty of nature or, effectively and ultimately, on the bounty of God as evidenced in created good. Orobator makes the point that "African religious traditions allow for multiple creative agents with some playing the role of intermediaries or secondary agents who actually complete the process of creation."[75] He follows up this assertion by underscoring the fundamental "mutuality and interdependence that underline the communion and solidarity of human beings and the rest of creation."[76] This is central to an *ubuntu* worldview.

When Africans extend glorious appellations to God in praise of her/his creative activity, they do so as a conscious reminder to God of his/her responsibility to bring them sustenance from the goods of the earth, which s/he, God, has made abundant and universally accessible. At the same time, they bind themselves to do justice to mother earth in order to protect and prolong her fecundity. This is a mutual support ethic that extends to, and envelops, relationships between and among humans and between and among humans and other creatures. When evil ruptures these relationships, the African expects that the ritual cleansing of the earth will appease the creator. The king, because he represents God and is guardian and custodian of the earth/land, is worthy of the same appellations as those showered on God; these do not belong to him personally, but to his role, his throne.[77]

In the African worldview, the line of distinction between the human and the divine is blurred: "The dichotomy which is so characteristic of the Graeco-Christian world-view is strikingly absent. . . . There is no clear-cut distinction or opposition between the visible and invisible, the material and spiritual, the temporal and non-temporal, the sacred and the profane."[78] Thus, even though the African worldview is anthropocentric, the relational harmony that exists between human beings and the rest of creation leads to the mutual strengthening of both and promotes life. According to Metuh,

> The main object of an African is to live a life in harmony with humanity and with nature. Man strives to be in harmony with God, the deities, and his fellowmen both living and dead. He feels himself in intimate rapport and tries to maintain harmonious relationship with the animal, vegetable, and other elements and phenomena in the universe. For him, the first evil is disintegration, for this would spell disaster both for himself and his immediate world. The ideal thing is integration, communion and harmony.[79]

---

73. Magesa, *African Religion*, 67.
74. See Ayisi, *Introduction to the Study of African Culture*, 92. Such bad luck or misfortune can, of course, be obviated by a priest or medicine man through a prescribed ritual exercise.
75. Orobator, *Religion and Faith in Africa*, 109.
76. Orobator, *Religion and Faith in Africa*, 109.
77. Ntreh, "Survival of Earth," 98.
78. Metuh, *Comparative Studies of African Traditional Religions*, 51.
79. Metuh, *Comparative Studies of African Traditional Religions*, 71.

African Catholicism and the Pauline "Principle of Universal Access"

My purpose in describing this relational aspect of traditional African ethics is to show that as a people we are quite well grounded in a natural theology that allows, at its core, universal and common access to the goods of the earth. There is no pretense here to absolutize this ethic as though it were an ideal of some sort. It is evident that Africans themselves may have lost this traditional ethic in the intense onslaught of the global capital markets. The result of this onslaught is clear: exclusion, or the desire to grow and expand by excluding others. The famines, wars, political upheavals, economic woes, and environmental catastrophes that have become part of our experience in the last century can be traced to these exclusionary tendencies. The relevance of such an ethical framework here is that it creates a basic structure of life in which the environment is treated so as to leave open the possibility of self-fulfillment to as many people as possible, including future generations.

The present scourge of climate change, or indeed any one of numerous other catastrophes facing us, forecloses that possibility to those least able to adapt and survive them. This has to do with the diminishment of life in its various forms at different levels, by reason, among other things, of the excessive indulgence of human beings in the use (or abuse) of created things. In tackling ecological scourges it might help to remind people in sub-Saharan Africa of the religious values that stood their ancestors in good stead in the past, by which it was believed that the creator God created the human person as one among many creatures. Though s/he is the lead or head creature, the human person cannot and should not remove him/herself from the rest of creation. Being a part of, and living in community with, the rest of creation makes her/him not only one of them but also the primary life-giver and life-preserver among them. The ethical quandary in which this situation places the African religious person is profound, to say the least.

There is a Christian version of this religious ethic in what I see as a "principle of universal access" in the writings of St. Paul. Students of St. Paul can recognize a consistent, recurring allusion to the boundlessness of the salvation wrought by Christ. In fact, in reading Paul, one gets the impression that inclusion, not exclusion, is at the core of the Christ-event and its effects. What some have described as the most important passage in the letter to the Romans,[80] for instance, proclaims that *all* have been justified freely by God's grace "through the redemption that comes in Christ Jesus" (Rom 3:22). This is necessary because all people have sinned and fallen short, and are thus equally condemnable (see Rom 2:11; 3:23). God's grace, therefore, is universally destined, and with it, the privilege of being righteous in Christ. That the death and resurrection of Christ make all of humanity righteous is further supported by the fact that Christ's work effectively "broke down the dividing wall of hostility" (Eph 2:14) between Jews and gentiles, slaves and freepersons, men and women (Gal 3:28). On account of these boundary-breaking actions of Christ, we are a "new creation," "no longer strangers or sojourners, but fellow citizens"; and consequently, the Christian community is "one body" in Christ, the "one Lord," sharing "one faith" in "one God the Father of all" (see Eph 2:19–22; 4:1–7). A community of this sort would be bonded not only by the joys, but also by the sufferings or limitations, of its members. Paul's conviction about the universal character of salvation in Christ emboldened him to stand up to and challenge Peter and James for their obvious hypocrisy in curtailing their consumption of the foods of non-Jewish believers (see Gal 2:12–13). It would seem, therefore, that Paul would stop at nothing in emphasizing the universal, all-inclusive character of salvation in Christ. This salvation cannot merely be a spiritual reality experienced only by human beings. It must include the rest of creation as well, which, though it has been subjected to futility, awaits the glorious rising of the children of God (see Rom 8:19). This universal access to salvation in Christ is the key to revamping all of our relationships—ecological, social, economic, and political.

From the above discussion, it can be deduced that both the Catholic Christian understanding of creational solidarity and planetary living and the African relational ethics of responsibility for cre-

---

80. Onwukeme, *Being All Things to All People*, 143. Onwukeme in this instance cited Fitzmyer, *Romans*.

ation function on the same principle—the preservation of life. Where the lack of attention to this principle has led to climatic conditions that ultimately threaten all life forms on the planet, it is possible to consider a broad convergence of these thought systems into a possible African Catholic approach to planetary living. This approach relies on a great deal of evidence showing that human activity is indeed compromising the planetary environment, and, as described here, may hold the key to regaining what has been lost.

A Return to Ecological Virtue

None of the arguments here in favor of recovering traditional African values as they relate to the environment should be construed to mean that I am opposed to science and technology. Nothing could be further from the truth. The great achievements of science and technology are there to see, but science is also instructing us that "the heightened entropy around the earth system bodes a future that may be literally unbearable, a situation in which we would have become victims of our own success."[81] Nobody, I believe, wants this to happen. There is surely common ground for us to find meaning in our lives and for discovering equitable ways of sharing the burdens and benefits of planetary existence. This chapter serves as an effort to recover that which has been good and sustainable along the way, and also, I hope, to denounce what has not been so helpful. The recovery of what is good will lead us to construct an ethical framework in which virtue once again becomes the natural tendency of human beings toward nature and the environment.

The numerous Christian voices raised in favor of virtue as the way of being and acting in a truly human way will, it is hoped, benefit from an African relational ethic aimed at creating and maintaining a balance between humans and the biosphere. If for no other reason, the Christian theological understanding of the divine act in creation, and the solidarity that this act engenders among creatures, is quite similar to the ethical perspectives of traditional African religion. These perspectives give a primary place to the relational notion of giving life. Living life to the full as a creature and giving life in its fullness to creation as a whole seem to be at the center of African religious ethics; thus, according to Magesa, whatever gives or promotes life should be considered good, just, ethical, desirable, and even divine. In the same way, whatever diminishes life is wrong, bad, unethical, unjust, and detestable.[82]

I contend, therefore, that the subject of planetary living is consanguineous with African ecological morality, a morality that is embedded in the African cultural consciousness. The "integral ecology" that Pope Francis talks about[83] is a good fit with and a Christian foundation for this morality, and should be the basis for the solution to a myriad of contemporary problems including those associated with climate change. To the contrary, and by implication, a certain contractarian Western paradigm that pursues economic growth at all costs and propagates a model of development that ultimately exhausts the pool of natural resources our generation inherited from previous ones goes against this ethical disposition. This is as un-African as it is unsustainable. African Catholicism, in my opinion, needs to imbibe this ethic, propagate it, and, I hope, be in a position to hold in check or even overcome prevalent Western assumptions that make impossible a right relationship with created reality.

Bibliography

Agbakwuo, John Obinna. *The African: His Religion and Cosmology*. Umuahia: Lumen, 2013.

Amadiume, Ifi. "Igbo and African Perspectives on Religious Conscience and the Global Economy." In *Subverting Greed: Religious Perspectives on the Global Economy*, edited by Paul F. Knitter and Chandra Muzafar, 15–37. Maryknoll, NY: Orbis Books, 2002.

Ayisi, Eric O. *An Introduction to the Study of African Culture*. London-Ibadan: Heinemann Educational Books, 1979.

---

81. Obi, "Fragile Ecosystems and the Pressures of Anthropogenia," 177.
82. See Magesa, *African Religion*, 77.
83. See Pope Francis, *Laudato Si'*, chapter 4.

Bauman, Whitney A. "Developing a Planetary Ethic: Religion, Ethics and the Environment." In *Religious and Ethical Perspectives for the Twenty-First Century*, edited by Paul O. Myhre, 222–37. Winona, MN: Anselm Academic, 2013.

Bujo, Bénézet. *African Theology in Its Social Context*. Eugene, OR: Wipf & Stock, 1992.

———. *The Ethical Dimension of Community: The African Model and the Dialogue between North and South*. Nairobi: Paulines Publications Africa, 1998.

———. "Vincent Mulago: An Enthusiast of African Theology." In *African Theology in the 21st Century: The Contribution of the Pioneers*, edited by Bénézet Bujo and Juvénal Ilunga Muya, 13–38. Nairobi: Paulines Publications Africa, 2003.

Bujo, Bénézet, and Juvénal Ilunga Muya, eds. *African Theology: The Contribution of the Pioneers*. Vol. 1 of 3. Nairobi: Paulines Publications Africa, 2002.

Cobb, John B., Jr. "Will Economism End in Time?," *Religion Online* (1998). http://www.religion-online.org/article/will-economism-end-in-time/.

Congregation for the Doctrine of the Faith. *Catechism of the Catholic Church*. Vatican City: Liberia Editrice Vaticana; Dublin: Veritas, 1995. www.vatican.va.

Daniel, Kasomo. "Psychological and Religious Understanding of Wrong Doing in African Perspective." *International Journal of Psychology and Behavioural Sciences* 2.6 (2012): 185–95.

Deane-Drummond, Celia. *Eco-Theology*. London: Darton, Longman & Todd, 2008.

Edwards, Denis. "Humans, Chimps and Bonobos: Towards an Inclusive View of the Human as Bearing the Image of God." In *Turning to the Heavens and the Earth: Theological Reflections on a Cosmological Conversion*, edited by Julia Brumbaugh and Natalia Imperatori-Lee, 7–25. Collegeville, MN: Liturgical Press, 2016.

Fitzmyer, Joseph A. *Romans: A New Translation with Introduction and Commentary*. Anchor Bible 33. New York: Doubleday, 1993.

Francis, Pope. *Laudato Si'* [Encyclical On Care for Our Common Home; June 18, 2015]. Vatican City: Libreria Editrice Vaticana, 2015. www.vatican.va.

Friedman, Milton. *Capitalism and Freedom*. Chicago: University of Chicago Press, 1963.

Gray, John. *False Dawn: The Delusions of Global Capitalism*. London: Granata, 1998.

Heidegger, Martin. *The Basic Problems of Phenomenology*. Translated by A. Hofstadter. Bloomington: Indiana University Press, 1982.

International Theological Commission. *Communion and Stewardship: Human Persons Created in the Image of God*. Vatican City: Libreria Editrice Vaticana, 2002.

John Paul II, Pope. *Ecclesia in Africa* [Post-synodal Apostolic Exhortation on the Church in Africa and Its Evangelizing Mission toward the Year 2000; September 14, 1995]. Vatican City: Libreria Editrice Vaticana, 1995. www.vatican.va.

Lai, Alan Ka Lun. "Planetary Loves: Spivak, Post-Coloniality and Theology (Book Review)." *Consensus* 36.1 (2015).

Magesa, Laurenti. *African Religion: The Moral Traditions of Abundant Life*. Nairobi: Daughters of St. Paul, 1998.

Mbiti, John S. "African Views of the Universe." In *This Sacred Earth: Religion, Nature, Environment*, edited by Roger S. Gottlieb, 174–80. New York: Routledge, 1996.

McFague, Sallie. "God's Household: Christianity, Economics and Planetary Living." In *Subverting Greed: Religious Perspectives on the Global Economy*, edited by Paul F. Knitter and Chandra Muzafar, 119–36. Maryknoll, NY: Orbis Books, 2002.

Metuh, Emefie Ikenga. *Comparative Studies of African Traditional Religions*. Onitsha: IMICO Books, 1987.

———. *God and Man in African Religion: A Case Study of the Igbo of Nigeria*. Enugu: Snaap Press, 1999.

Muya, Juvénal Ilunga. "Bénézet Bujo: The Awakening of a Systematic and Authentically African Thought." In *African Theology: The Contribution of the Pioneers*, ed. Bénézet Bujo and Juvénal Ilunga Muya. Nairobi: Paulines Publications Africa, 2002.

Nkemnkia, Martin Nkafu. *African Vitalogy: A Step Forward in African Thinking*. Nairobi: Paulines Publications Africa, 1999.

Ntreh, Abotchie. "The Survival of Earth: An African Reading of Psalm 104." In *The Earth Story in the Psalms and the Prophets*, edited by Norman C. Habel, 98–108. Sheffield: Sheffield Academic Press, 2001.

Obi, Edward Osang, MSP. "Fragile Ecosystems and the Pressures of Anthropogenia: Recovering a Theo-Ethic of Relationality in Our Common Home." In

Fragile World: Ecology and the Church, edited by William T. Cavanaugh, 175–91. Eugene, OR: Wipf & Stock, 2018.

Onwukeme, Victor. *Being All Things to All People: Knowing St. Paul through His Journeys and Writings*. Iperu-Remo: Ambassador, 2008.

Orobator, Agbonkhianmeghe E., SJ. *Religion and Faith in Africa: Confessions of an Animist*. Maryknoll, NY: Orbis Books, 2018.

———. *Theology Brewed in an African Pot*. Nairobi: Paulines Publications Africa, 2008.

Parrinder, Geoffrey. *African Mythology*. London: Hamlyn, 1967.

Paul VI, Pope. *Africae Terrarum* [Apostolic Letter]. Vatican City: Libreria Editrice Vaticana, 1967. www.vatican.va.

Polanyi, Karl. *The Great Transformation: The Political and Economic Origins of Our Time*. Boston: Beacon Press, 1944.

Pui-lan, Kwok. "What Has Love to Do with It?" In *Planetary Loves: Spivak, Postcoloniality, and Theology*, edited by Stephen D. Moore and Mayra Rivera, 31–45. New York: Fordham University Press, 2011.

Sawyerr, Harry A. E. *Creative Evangelism: Towards a New Christian Encounter with Africa*. London: Lutterworth, 1968.

Sindima, Harvey. "Community of Life." *Ecumenical Review* 41.4 (1989): 537–51.

———. "Community of Life: Ecological Theology in African Perspective." In *Liberating Life: Contemporary Approaches to Ecological Theology*, edited by Charles Birch, William Eakin, and Jay B. McDaniel. Maryknoll, NY: Orbis Books, 1990.

Tucker, Mary Evelyn. "Globalization and the Environment." In *Globalization and Catholic Social Thought: Present Crisis, Future Hope*, edited by John A. Coleman and William F. Ryan, 88–112. Maryknoll, NY: Orbis Books, 2005.

White, Lynn. "The Historical Roots of Our Ecological Crisis." *Science* 155 (March 1967): 1203–7.

World Council of Churches. "Land and Spirituality in Africa." *Echoes—The Earth as Mother* (1998). www.wcc-coe.org/wcc/what/jpc/echoes-16-05.html.

Suggested Reading

Bauman, Whitney A. "Developing a Planetary Ethic: Religion, Ethics, and the Environment." In *Religious and Ethical Perspectives for the Twenty-First Century*, edited by Paul O. Myhre. Winona, MN: Anselm Academic, 2013.

Bujo, Bénézet. *The Ethical Dimension of Community: The African Model and the Dialogue between North and South*. Nairobi: Paulines Publications Africa, 1998.

Magesa, Laurenti. *African Religion: The Moral Traditions of Abundant Life*. Nairobi: Daughters of St. Paul, 1998.

Metuh, Emefie Ikenga. *Comparative Studies of African Traditional Religions*. Onitsha: IMICO Books, 1987.

Nkemnkia, Martin Nkafu. *African Vitalogy: A Step Forward in African Thinking*. Nairobi: Paulines Publications Africa, 1999.

Orobator, Agbonkhianmeghe E., SJ. *Religion and Faith in Africa: Confessions of an Animist*. Maryknoll, NY: Orbis Books, 2018.

Key Words

African relational ethic
African spirit of enchantment
alterity
ancestral tradition
anthropogenia
communitarian
community bondedness
commutative
continuity triad
economism
fecundity
human ascendancy
human exceptionalism
intergenerational regard
interpersonal communion
original harmony
Participial Unparticipated Vital Source
planetarity
planetary living
participation sharing
Pauline Universal Access Principle
sensus communis

THE BODY, HEALTH, AND HEALING

Catholic Sexual Morality and Social Ethics in Africa: Contested Questions

Hellen Sitawa Wanyonyi and Eunice K. Kamaara

In 2015, the United Nations declared sexual violence a global moral crisis, one that is made worse by "the culture of impunity" for those who commit these crimes.[1] It singled out eight countries in which sexual violence is most rampant, and six are in Africa. While the UN was discussing atrocities committed in conflict situations, the crisis is widespread in other settings as well. The rape of a young female physical therapy intern in South Delhi on December 16, 2012, comes to mind. Commenting on the incident, Deepak Tripathi observes:

> The violent and sustained rape of a 23-year-old woman by a gang of youths in Delhi before the eyes of someone who, according to reports, she was to marry is a particularly gruesome act. That it happened in an upmarket area of the Indian capital was worse. It has serious implications for the nation's reputation in the eyes of the world. . . . The brutal assault on the couple, and the events leading up to the woman's death at a Singapore hospital, has been one of the most widely covered topics outside India about the country, and rightly so. When a crime prompts the United Nations Secretary General, Ban Ki-moon, to castigate India, and to remind the government that "every girl and woman has the right to be respected, valued and protected," it must be taken as a matter of national shame.[2]

Sexual violence can occur anytime and anywhere, even at home among family members, the very place in which people usually expect to find peace and love.

In sub-Saharan Africa, both premarital and extramarital sexual activity is common, sometimes with multiple partners. In many situations, marriage is a predisposing factor to HIV infection, especially among women, due to what is commonly known in Kenya as "*mpango wa kando*" (extramarital affairs) and other cultural factors.[3] Add to this fact the prevalence of gender-based violence, and one can begin to understand why HIV infection is almost uncontrollable in the region.

Africans claim to be deeply religious, with a majority of them confessing and practicing a specific faith.[4] Religious institutions are some of

---

This chapter was made possible through the support of a grant from Templeton World Charity Foundation, Inc. The opinions expressed herein are those of the author(s) and do not necessarily reflect the views of Templeton World Charity Foundation, Inc.

1. United Nations Security Council, Meetings Coverage, April 2015.
2. Tripathi, "India and Its Moral Crisis."
3. For example, a "sponsor" is a euphemism for "sugar mummies" and "sugar daddies"—older, wealthy women and men (who themselves may be married) with whom young people have sexual relationships in exchange for financial support.
4. Mbiti, *African Religions and Philosophy*, 1.

the most influential actors in Africa given their numerical strength, regular public presence, expansive social networks, and continued standing as agents of respect and authority.[5] Christianity is numerically the strongest religion in Africa and the Roman Catholic Church is the largest denomination.[6] Although morality and religion are not synonymous, there is a relationship: many religions offer an ethical framework guiding the personal and social behavior of their adherents, but even within religious groups there are frequent disagreements about what is right and what is wrong.

Against this background, in this chapter we explore Catholic sexual morality in relation to the socioeconomic realities of contemporary Africa. We begin with a brief history of the development of Catholic sexual morality, followed by a presentation of the essential teachings of that morality. Then the discussion moves to an analysis of some of the controversies surrounding Catholic sexual morality as it relates to the realities of poverty and HIV/AIDS in the African context, with the objective of generating critical reflection among Christians in general as well as among church leadership. We deliberately raise more questions than answers and propose some methodological trajectories African scholars might follow in order to further develop themes and insights pertaining to sexual morality as taught by African Catholicism.

The Historical Development of the Church's Teaching about Sexual Morality

The teachings of Christian and Catholic sexual morality may be traced back to the patristic period. Patristic theology refers to the work of early Christian writers who reasoned systematically about the Christian faith. The most influential and outstanding of these is Augustine of Hippo (354–430 CE). As is well known, St. Augustine lived as a sexually promiscuous hedonist during his early life, believing that human beings should have sex for pleasure and not just for procreation. Later in his youth, he became an adherent of Manichaeism, which taught a doctrine of moral dualism involving simplistic choices between good and evil and advocated for rejection of the material world, including sexual activity. He later converted to Christianity. He describes the Christian turning point in his views of sexual morality:

> For, compared with Your sweetness, and the beauty of Your house, which I loved, those things delighted me no longer. But still very tenaciously was I held by the love of women; nor did the apostle forbid me to marry, although he exhorted me to something better, especially wishing that all men were as he himself was. 1 Corinthians 7:7. So quickly I returned to the place where Alypius was sitting; for there had I put down the volume of the apostles, when I rose thence. I grasped, opened, and in silence read that paragraph on which my eyes first fell: "Not in rioting and drunkenness, not in chambering and wantonness, not in strife and envying; but put ye on the Lord Jesus Christ, and make not provision for the flesh, to fulfil the lusts thereof." Romans 13:13–14. No further would I read, nor did I need. (*Confessions* 8.12.29)

After his conversion to Christianity, Augustine wrote extensively on sexuality. Even though he lived in the patristic era, he has been described as a "master of medieval thought for through him, the Middle Ages were furnished with a framework of ethical reference in the area of sexuality. Right up to the twelfth century, theologians, jurists and moralists systematically referred to him when discussing these ethical issues."[7] Augustine developed a Christian sexual morality which taught that the sole lawful purpose of sex was procreation. For him, any "sexual intercourse even with one's legitimate

---

5. Green, *Faith-Based Organizations*; JLIFLC, "Evaluation of the Impact of Christian Aid's Support of Faith-Based Responses to HIV"; Lazzarini, "Human Rights and HIV/AIDS."
6. Pew Research Center, "Sub-Saharan Africa."
7. Fuchs, *Sexual Desire and Love*, 111.

wife is unlawful and wicked where conception of the offspring is prevented."[8] He held that all sexual desires, pleasures, and relationships that were not related to procreative sex were lustful and sinful. Even though his theology allowed for procreative sex, Augustine personally grew to despise sexual acts after baptism. This animus likely contributed to a negative attitude toward sexuality within the church; in fact, some early church theologians equated sexual love with death.[9] It was from within this negative view of sexual love that the tradition of Christian sexual ethics was developed. Paula Fredriksen discusses how various cultural realities at the time of the early church shaped its understanding and development of the concept of sin. In so doing, she raises complex questions about how cultural forces influenced Augustine and affected his views of Christian sexual morality.[10]

In the medieval period, the church generally followed Augustine's negative attitude toward sex, even within marriage, if it was engaged in for nonprocreative purposes.[11] Medieval thinkers discussed the question of when sexual intercourse was or was not allowed, and eventually it was disallowed on feast days, Sundays, during menstruation, before receiving communion, during pregnancy, and even for a period after childbirth. In fact, sexual intercourse was forbidden on about 40 percent of the days of the year.[12]

Scholastic theologians of the Latin church later took a more moderate position by adopting a policy toward sexual relations that was not based on prohibited times but rather on the intention or motive behind engaging in the act.[13] The Council of Trent (1566) and other synods did not insist on abstinence from sexual intercourse at specific times as an "obligation," but rather as an "admonition."[14]

These gatherings of the church formulated rules governing sexual intercourse, affirming the rule of celibacy for priests and indicating that the sole purpose of married sex is procreation.

St. Thomas Aquinas made significant contributions to the church's teachings about sexual morality in the medieval period. Relying on scripture, he maintained that chastity is an important virtue for moderating sexual appetite,[15] and he considered sexual morality to be an aspect of the virtue of temperance. His views have strongly influenced the present-day views of the Catholic Church that sexual intercourse in marriage is chaste only when engaged in for both unitive and procreative purposes, and that unmarried people are expected to express chastity through sexual abstinence.[16] These views were echoed by Pope St. John Paul II:

> At the center of the spirituality of marriage, therefore, there lies chastity not only as a moral virtue (formed by love), but likewise as a virtue connected with the gifts of the Holy Spirit—above all, the gift of respect for what comes from God (*donum pietatis*). This gift is in the mind of the author of the Ephesians when he exhorts married couples to "defer to one another out of reverence for Christ" (Eph. 5:21). So the interior order of married life, which enables the manifestations of affection to develop according to their right proportion and meaning, is a fruit not only of the virtue which the couple practices, but also of the gifts of the Holy Spirit with which they cooperate.[17]

In line with the church's long-standing positions, the *Catechism of the Catholic Church* (*CCC*) enu-

---

8. Augustine, *The Catholic and Manichean Ways of Life*, 109–11.
9. Ranke-Heinemann, *Eunuchs for the Kingdom of Heaven*.
10. Fredriksen, *Sin*.
11. Salzman and Lawler, *Sexual Person*, 175.
12. Ranke-Heinmann, *Eunuchs for the Kingdom of Heaven*, 140.
13. Ranke-Heinmann, *Eunuchs for the Kingdom of Heaven*, 140.
14. Ranke-Heinmann, *Eunuchs for the Kingdom of Heaven*, 140.
15. See O'Riordan, "Chastity."
16. Thomas Aquinas, *Summa Theologica* I–II q. 60 a.5.
17. Pope John Paul II, "Christian Spirituality of Marriage Possible Only by Living according to the Spirit."

merates several offenses against chastity, including fornication, rape, lust, masturbation, and prostitution (§§2351–56).

The Protestant Reformation led to significant changes in the medieval Christian view of sex. The Reformers critiqued and challenged the church's moral teachings; in fact, the Reformation can be seen as a conflict both over morality and over authority. Erich Fuchs observes that it was during the early period of the Reformation that sexuality was recognized as central to the fundamental human experience of conjugality.[18] The Reformation spurred a shift in the Christian tradition away from exalting celibacy as the royal road to salvation to promoting the primacy of marriage; it lent to sexuality a positive dimension in which husband and wife were charged with a co-responsibility for conjugal and family life and for exercising moral and social responsibility within marriage.

But what exactly is the content and meaning of Catholic sexual morality today? To this we now turn.

Catholic Sexual Morality

Catholic sexual morality is grounded in divine revelation and natural law as expressed in canonical scripture and sacred tradition, as these are interpreted authoritatively by the magisterium (the teaching authority) of the Catholic Church. It is derived from the teaching that "sexual pleasure is morally disordered when sought for itself, isolated from its procreative and unitive purposes" as between spouses (*CCC* §2351). The Catholic apologist Dave Armstrong, in a blog post appearing on the website of the *National Catholic Register* titled "Sex and Catholics: Our Views Briefly Explained," affirms the church's position that God created the sex act first and foremost for procreation, but also for the purpose of pleasure and enjoyment to enhance marital unity.[19] In 2016, Pope Francis, in revisiting and affirming the teaching of Pope Paul VI's encyclical *Humanae Vitae* (1968), held that married couples can enjoy and celebrate sex, but he also offered the following observation: "We also know that, within marriage itself, sex can become a source of suffering and manipulation."[20]

The teachings of Catholic sexual morality are clear that human sexuality is not simply a biological urge but rather concerns the innermost being of the human person. This view is predicated on the Sexual Spiritualism Theory, which advances the notion that sexual activity has a spiritual function that distinguishes it from its practice by animals, and which holds that the complementarity of male and female becomes complete in sexual intercourse.[21] As observed by Karl Peschke, when male and female are joined in the sexual act, they complete one another biologically but also spiritually, because sexuality reaches deep into the human soul.[22] The anthropological foundation of Catholic sexual morality is the biblical creation account in the book of Genesis, which affirms that God created human beings to reflect his own image and likeness and that everything God created was "very good" (Gen 1:31), meaning that the human body and sex must also be good. Having been created in the image of God, human beings are not mere products of nature, with their sole origin and destiny in the dust of the earth; rather, they are able to and expected to transcend their biological and sociological makeup so that they can take part in shaping their being and identity as co-creators with God.

There is no sexual act that is exempted from the moral law. In evaluating whether any particular sexual act is to be considered moral, it is necessary to consider the three basic determinants of ethical behavior: the object of the act, the circumstances of the act, and the end of the act. The morality of any sexual act is hence dictated by its intention, its moral object, and its consequences. The good and positive consequences of any sexual act must always outweigh any bad or negative consequences.

Here we propose a combination of deontological and teleological approaches to reach a concrete

---

18. Fuchs, *Sexual Desire and Love*, 115.
19. Armstrong, "Sex and Catholics: Our Views Briefly Explained."
20. Pope Francis, post-synodal apostolic exhortation *Amoris Laetitia*, §154.
21. The theory was first described in Kamaara, *Gender Relations*.
22. See Peschke, *Christian Ethics*, 391–95.

basis for the relevant moral norm. We argue that it is not possible to arrive at a judgment about the morality of an action without careful study of the nature of beings (deontological approach) and without proper regard for the end of the act being judged (teleological approach). We consider these two approaches to be complementary, not mutually exclusive.

The teachings of the church categorically stress that, for a sexual act to be morally acceptable, it must be engaged in within marriage and be both unitive and procreative in nature. The Catholic Church considers any sexual act that does not satisfy these conditions evil and morally wrong. The *CCC* provides that "conjugal love . . . aims at a deeply personal unity, a unity that, beyond union in one flesh, leads to forming one heart and soul" (§1643), eventually resulting in the marriage bond becoming a true sign of the love between Christ and the church (§1617). The conjoining of husband and wife through sexual intercourse is sacred and life-giving, with their biological differences being divinely designed to complement each other for the purposes of reproduction and mutual sexual pleasure. Hence, sexuality in the Catholic discourse is ordered to the conjugal rights and obligations between man and woman in marriage (1 Cor 7:3–5). Sexual intercourse is performed in a truly human way only if it is an integral part of the love by which a man and woman commit themselves totally to one another until death. This is why the church is categorical in its teaching that if sexual intercourse is performed outside the context of marriage it contradicts its God-given purpose, and why sex is considered chaste only in marriage.

Despite the many variations in marriage throughout the centuries in different cultures and social structures, and in the presence of different spiritual attitudes, marriage has never been seen as a purely human institution. Marriage is not a chance event; rather, it is ordained by God. Hence, the intimate community of life and love that is the married state has been established and endowed with its own proper laws by the creator. God is seen as the author of marriage, and the vocation to marriage is written in the very nature of man and woman, a nature generated by the hand of the creator.

The church considers the expression of love between husband and wife to be an exalted expression of humanity. Husband and wife are joined in complete, mutual self-giving, and they open up their relationship to new life. As Paul VI wrote in *Humanae Vitae*: "The sexual activity, in which husband and wife are intimately and chastely united with one another, through which human life is transmitted, is, as the recent Council recalled, 'noble and worthy'" (§11). This union demands indissolubility and faithfulness in definitive mutual giving that is open to fertility. The marriage union not only purifies and strengthens married couples but also raises them to a place where they can express specifically Christian values. For the church, polygamy is contrary to the demands of an undivided and exclusive conjugal love. This is a love that seeks to be definitive, not an arrangement maintained "until further notice."

Children are believed to be the supreme gift of marriage, and the fruitfulness of conjugal love extends to the moral, spiritual, and supernatural life that parents hand on to their children by educating them. In this sense, the fundamental task of marriage and family is to always be at the service of life. The *CCC* states that "by their very nature, the institution of matrimony itself and conjugal love are ordained for the procreation and education of the offspring, and it is in them that it finds its crowning glory" (1652). Even for spouses to whom God has not granted children, the church is clear that they can still have a conjugal life full of meaning that radiates the fruitfulness of charity, hospitality, and sacrifice.

The church expresses grave moral concern about any sexual expression taking place outside sacramental marriage, including premarital sex, homosexual practices, or sexual violence, or in which the procreative function of sexual expression within marriage is deliberately frustrated, for example, by the use of artificial contraception like pills or condoms. Regardless of (or perhaps because of) this clear teaching about sexual morality, "sexual negativism" (a negative attitude toward sex) still abounds in the contemporary church around the world, and sexual love is not openly discussed. This reality is particularly poignant in Africa, especially because the teachings of Catholic sexual morality seem to contradict African social values as they apply to sexuality. This has generated many controversies that remain unresolved more than a hundred years after the latest wave of missionary activity in Africa. In the next section, we analyze some of these controversies in the context of the most significant modern challenges facing Africans: poverty and HIV/AIDS.

African Controversies Related to Catholic Sexual Morality

This section presents a brief outline of controversies that have emerged related to the teachings of the church on sexual ethics and morality in the context of contemporary Africa, in particular with respect to contraception and, more specifically, condom use.

The Church's Historical and Current Teaching on Contraception

The practice of contraception dates far back into human history. It refers to the intentional use of any one of a number of chemical or physical methods, including devices, agents, drugs, surgical procedures, or even coital practices that manage the sexual act so as to prevent pregnancy. These include oral contraceptives, barrier methods (like intrauterine devices, commonly known as IUDs), spermicides, condoms, tubal ligation, and vasectomy, among others. There is historical evidence of the practice of coitus interruptus (commonly known as withdrawal); it is referred to in the story of Onan in Genesis 38 and was also known in the Greco-Roman world and in medieval Europe.[23]

The Catholic Church has been opposed to contraceptive practices for as far back as one can historically trace:

> The anti-contraception rule by the Catholic Church developed through various historical periods was necessitated by the need for the Church to protect fundamental values of procreation, life, human dignity and marital love; a move that was justified especially at a time when procreation was under attack by heretical groups such as the Gnostics and Marcionists in the first three centuries of Christianity.[24]

Gnostics encouraged sexual practices only if they did not result in procreation, arguing that having children was a senseless perpetuation of creation, and Marcionists saw procreation as supporting the sadistic work of the evil God of the Old Testament.[25] They saw the Old Testament God as taking delight in the discomfort and suffering of women during pregnancy and labor.

The first school of Christian theology, the Catechetical School of Alexandria, was developed as a reaction against these heretical teachings. The theologians of this school argued that procreation was not only good but holy because through it man and woman cooperate with God in the work of creation. The larger church affirmed that only married couples should engage in sexual intercourse, but that in marriage procreation becomes a good. Most early theologians believed that sexual intercourse was for the sole purpose of procreation and was the primary end of marriage. This opinion gave rise to a debate over contraception, in which Augustine participated and which continued through the medieval period.

Augustine condemned sexual intercourse between married couples during the sterile period of the wife's menstrual cycle, as was promoted by the Manicheans, since conception is impossible during this period. For this position, he relied on the aforementioned biblical story of Onan (Gen 38:8–10), who was killed by God for withdrawing during sexual intercourse with his brother's wife.[26] Augustine's reliance on this story to support his position is, however, questionable in light of the fact that God may have condemned Onan for refusing to procreate on behalf of his brother as had been directed by his father, not for withdrawing during sexual intercourse.

The Catholic Church developed its teaching against contraception in line with the Augustin-

---

23. Noonan, "Contraception," 271.
24. Chadwick, *Early Church*, 39.
25. Chadwick, *Early Church*, 39.
26. Augustine, *Catholic and Manichean Ways of Life*, 109–11.

ian philosophy that sex should be for procreation only. Political interests often welcomed the teaching because population levels played a crucial role in the balance of power—the higher its population, the more powerful a country was. It was not until the nineteenth century that the contraception debate appeared as an issue of international concern.[27] Many people began to see contraception as a social good because the high global rate of population growth was threatening the socioeconomic situation of some nations. Social organizations began to advocate for birth control as a solution for high population growth, a move that the Catholic Church saw as a direct attack on its teaching. The church most strongly defended its position in Pope Pius XI's encyclical *Casti Connubii* in 1930. Prior to the release of this encyclical, the pope announced that he intended to deliver a speech that "would deal with the most important subject affecting more than any other the family, the state, and the whole human race."[28] In *Casti Connubii,* the pope acknowledged that children are gifts and blessings from God, adding that "the blessing of the offspring however is not completed by mere begetting of them, but something else must be added, namely the proper education of the children."[29]

There was opposition to *Casti Connubii* even within the church, and a discussion ensued that led, in 1951, to Pope Pius XII's approval of couples facing serious economic, medical, or social constraints using the sterile period to avoid the conception of children. Vatican II also approved the method of natural family planning, asserting that it does not involve the destruction of life. The council document, however, rejected all other family planning methods, stating that "sons of the Church may not undertake methods of birth control which are found blameworthy by the teaching authority of the Church in its unfolding of the divine authority" (*Gaudium et Spes* §51). In approving the method of natural family planning, the council thus appears to have differed from Augustine's view that sex should be for procreation only but held the line against all artificial methods of family planning, including sterilization, condoms, and other barrier methods, spermicides, coitus interruptus, and the birth control pill, with a view toward strongly defending human dignity, marital love, and the transmission of life. At the time these positions were announced, they sat well with the majority of the African faithful because the African culture prescribed that couples should have many children.

Pope Paul VI found it necessary to affirm the church's traditional teaching on sexual morality and the sanctity of life in *Humanae Vitae*. In the face of the allegedly Malthusian consequences of population explosion and the attendant family planning campaigns of the 1960s, the pope restated the twofold purpose of conjugal relations: procreative and unitive. He declared that artificial contraception was intrinsically evil and that natural family planning, in which sexual activity is restricted to times in a woman's menstrual cycle when conception is unlikely to take place, is the only licit method of contraception.

On November 22, 1981, Pope John Paul II released the postsynodal apostolic exhortation *Familiaris Consortio*, in which he affirmed that using artificial contraception is an intrinsically evil act that is against the natural order (§32). He also delivered a series of over 120 lectures in which he reflected favorably on *Humanae Vitae*.

Pope Benedict XVI explicitly reaffirmed the church's position on contraception on one occasion, at the international congress organized by the Pontifical Lateran University on the fortieth anniversary of *Humanae Vitae* in 2008. The pope characterized *Humanae Vitae* as "controversial, yet so crucial for humanity's future.... What was true yesterday is true also today."[30] Pope Francis too has affirmed the Catholic teaching on contraception

---

27. Noonan, "Contraception," 271.
28. Augustine, *De Conjug, Adult.* 2.21, cited in McLaughlin, *Church and the Reconstruction of the Modern World*, 115.
29. Augustine, *De Conjug, Adult.* 2.21, cited in McLaughlin, *Church and the Reconstruction of the Modern World*, 115.
30. Pope Benedict XVI, International Congress organized by the Pontifical Lateran University on the fortieth anniversary of the encyclical *Humanae Vitae*, May 12, 2008.

and praised *Humanae Vitae*, describing Paul VI as "prophetic," and noting "he had the courage to take a stand against the majority, to defend moral discipline, to exercise a cultural restraint, to oppose present and future Neo-Malthusianism."[31]

Despite these statements, some of the recent popes have subtly suggested that the church's teaching might be flexible in certain situations. Pope Paul VI, who stated in *Humanae Vitae* that artificial contraception was in fact intrinsically evil, was the first to hint at this when he observed that it was necessary for nuns raped in the context of civil wars. But the most explicit suggestion of this possible flexibility has come from Pope Francis. On May 1, 2014, in the course of praising *Humanae Vitae*, he observed that "everything depends on how *Humanae Vitae* is interpreted. Paul VI himself, in the end, urged confessors to be very merciful and pay attention to concrete situations.... The question is not of changing doctrine, but of digging deep and making sure that pastoral care takes into account situations and what is possible for persons to do."[32] Francis's emphasis on the need for careful interpretation of *Humanae Vitae* demonstrates sympathy for contexts in which poverty and other challenges are present.

We turn now to the implications of the Catholic position on contraception in the African context.

Contraception in the Context of Poverty and Youth Sexual Activity

The church's position throughout the ages has been that artificial contraception is not "natural" and that it is anti-life. But what is meant, exactly, by "natural"? What is "natural" to human sexuality? Are sexual instincts not natural to both men and women? Is it not natural that women generally feel more sexually aroused during the fertile period than during the infertile period of their menstrual cycle? Is it not unnatural then for women to engage in sexual intercourse when they are not naturally aroused and to avoid the act when they are most aroused? The church's approval of "natural" family planning would thus seem to contradict the natural order of things. These and many other questions have been raised by other African scholars, including Bénézet Bujo and Laurenti Magesa.[33]

The anti-contraceptive position of the church raises certain questions in the African context: In the context of the poverty present in developing countries in Africa, what should be the way forward in the contraception debate? Should couples accept children as they come as gifts from God? What about married Christians who cannot afford to provide education for their children? Should they continue to live as husband and wife without having a sexual relationship? Indeed, the church does not seem to offer practical solutions to materially poor couples even though procreation and education are inseparable. The church should not require couples to procreate who cannot afford the cost of educating their children—sexuality should not be regarded as only a biological fact, but as something that implicates human reality as well. Even though African Catholic couples are taught to surrender to each other in marriage and follow the teachings of church authorities, they need to be realistic and mindful of their moral obligations in their particular socioeconomic situations.

International development organizations like the World Health Organization (WHO) and the United Nations Population Fund (UNFPA) associate poverty with high populations at the national level and many children at the family level. They recognize that high population growth comes with other socioeconomic impacts like crime, prostitution, and overcrowding in educational and health facilities. Poverty in contemporary Africa is associated with inadequate resources, unemployment, and other socioeconomic factors. This poverty manifests itself in an inability to meet basic needs like food, education, health care, and shelter. In order to alleviate this poverty, international organizations and others encourage African couples to engage in family planning, but many of these couples are Catholic. Is it realistic in this context for the Catholic Church to forbid the use of contraceptives? Is the argument that contraception is anti-life valid when many people are dying of hunger and other problems associ-

---

31. Sandro, "Francis, the Pope of *Humanae Vitae*."
32. Sandro, "Francis, the Pope of *Humanae Vitae*."
33. See Bujo, *Foundations of an African Ethic*; Magesa, *African Religion*.

ated with poverty? Should people die rather than practice contraception?

It would appear that the church is not able to offer practical advice to couples who cannot rely on natural family planning, and for this reason some Catholics do not perceive the use of contraceptives as evil. In view of the realities facing African couples, Peschke observes that artificial methods of family planning are not necessarily gravely sinful and should not therefore warrant excommunication from the church.[34] The church should seek out the views of the married couples who are directly affected by the church's teaching on contraception—these couples would be able to explain their reasons for using artificial contraception and perhaps be able to suggest ways of doing so that would limit its negative moral implications. As argued by Joshua Akong'a, there is a need to differentiate between provision of information and communication; information involves a one-way flow of knowledge, while communication is two-way, aiming at the active involvement and cooperation of the target group.[35] Catholic married couples need to be convinced of the relevance to their lives of the church's message about contraception so that they can understand it as being for the good of their lives and not merely as a way of pleasing church authority.[36]

As noted above, the church has told poor families in Africa that they have the option of natural family planning. But how effective is natural family planning in contemporary African contexts? The method requires proper instruction in order to be effective, and many Catholic families who practice it without this instruction end up with unplanned pregnancies. These failures result in hostility toward Catholic teachings.

In January 2015, a German journalist sought Pope Francis's opinion during his visit to the Philippines concerning polls indicating that population growth in that country was the major reason for its poverty and finding that many Filipinos disagree with the Catholic teaching on contraception. The pope stated simply that the key is "responsible parenthood." He directs those who need guidance in natural family planning to consult experts and marriage groups for help.

The pope is correct that we should not bend rules to suit the circumstances. However, the church should do more than just call for couples to become educated about how to engage in natural family planning; it should take steps to improve this education. On the one hand, the education provided in Africa in the proper use of natural family planning has been inadequate. On the other, in order for natural family planning to be effective, both husband and wife are expected to work together in agreement and with mutual respect, and to exercise self-control and discipline. In the context of the patriarchal societies of Africa in which unequal gender relations characterize marriages and sexual violence in and out of marriage is rife, it is unrealistic to expect mutual respect and agreement. Perhaps the church should be placing more emphasis on gender justice as the foundation on which natural family planning is laid.

Since the church and governments serve the same people, it is useful to consider the church teaching on contraception in relation to government policies, like those of the National Council for Population and Development (NCPD) and other family planning programs. In Kenya, for example, various family planning programs aim at ensuring that contraceptives are provided to all people of reproductive age; the Catholic Church criticizes these programs on the grounds that they provide contraceptives to unmarried people, thereby encouraging premarital sex and promiscuity. The government and the church do not, however, seem to be in total disagreement about family planning—they have a common goal but they differ on the means for achieving that goal. Couples should be enlightened as to both the advantages and disadvantages of each of the various methods of family planning, and both the government's and the church's efforts in this regard should be encouraged and improved upon. Unlike the artificial methods, the natural method is said to have no

---

34. Holdren and Gagliarducci, "Full Text In-Flight Interview from Manila to Rome."
35. Akong'a, "Functional Communication Model for Family Planning Extension Services in Kenya."
36. Akong'a, "Functional Communication Model for Family Planning Extension Services in Kenya."

side effects, though it is not very effective and is not easy to practice. The magisterium is aware of these problems, and scientists are continuing to research how the method might be made more effective. But until a breakthrough is achieved, should people just watch as more families plunge into poverty? Every effort should be made, by all religious bodies, nongovernmental and private organizations, and even individuals to provide more education about the natural method, but education should also be provided about artificial methods.

Statistics suggests that young unmarried people in Africa are sexually active, often with multiple partners. A review of national surveys showed that 25 percent of young people aged fifteen to nineteen had had sex by age fifteen, with more than 20 percent of females having been pregnant by the same age.[37] Multiple sexual partners are common, which explains the high incidence of HIV infection among the same age group. Over time, parents have gone from less than 10 percent supporting condom use among young people to 60–65 percent. A recent study in Kenya has examined the hashtag #SexMoneyFun; it suggests that for fourteen- to twenty-four-year-old Kenyans, these three are so complicatedly interrelated "that they deserve to be connected not just into a single concept, but into a single word. And not just any word but a digitally interactive hashtag word."[38] According to this report, 65 percent of Kenyan youth consider it acceptable to have a "sponsor" even when in a relationship and 33 percent of all youth interviewed indicate that they in fact do have a "sponsor."[39] Another study from Kenya found that 50 percent of all the women aged fifteen to twenty-four involved in the study had had sex by the time of the study; the mean age of their first sexual encounter was 17.7 years, and 15 percent had previously been pregnant, with the mean age of first pregnancy being 18.3 years. Of those who had previously been pregnant, 76 percent said that the pregnancies were unwanted at the time.[40]

In spite of the huge amount of money spent by international health organizations on information, education, and services to promote the use of contraceptives across Africa, the overall rate of contraceptive use among young people continues to be low. This is the case even though the risk of dying during childbirth for women aged fifteen to nineteen is double that for women in their twenties and five times that of girls under the age of fifteen.[41]

In light of these facts one can understand the growing acceptability of condom use among the parents of young people. Parents know their children better than the church does, but the Catholic Church insists that condom use is unreliable in preventing pregnancy and HIV infection, and therefore is not the solution. The church argues that the prevalence of a behavior does not make it morally acceptable, and that no conclusions can be drawn from these statistics by themselves. Instead, they indicate a deeper problem of weakened moral values. The answer therefore does not lie in promoting condom use because that addresses only the symptoms of the real problem; the more rational response is to address the root causes of sexual promiscuity among young people by promoting values education. This is a valid point, especially in light of the fact that in contemporary African society, there are emerging issues related to the ignorance of and erosion of the meaningfulness of African values, which are now being evaluated using Western criteria. This has led to a disintegration of the moral fabric of society, a breakdown of the synergies of the African family, and the alienation of individuals and societies from their roots.

Responding to these emerging issues is important. To begin with, we need to salvage the synergies of the African family as a foundation for recovering and perpetuating African values. This needs to happen in an interactive way that supports the integration and incorporation of values from other cultures so that they enrich African value systems rather than destroy them. A healthy

---

37. Doyle et al., "Review: The Sexual Behaviour of Adolescents in Sub-Saharan Africa," 796.
38. Kubania, "What the Youth Really Think about Dating and Sugar Daddies."
39. For the definition of this term, see n. 3 above.
40. Okigbo and Speizer, "Determinants of Sexual Activity and Pregnancy among Unmarried Young Women in Urban Kenya."
41. UNFPA & PRB, 2012, "Status Report, Adolescents and Young People in Sub-Saharan Africa."

interaction between African value systems and the value systems of other cultures is likely to lead to integral development that can adequately meet the needs of African people. For example, Christianity does not teach African moral values but rather clarifies, purifies, and confirms them. This can be seen in the goals of the African Christian Initiation Project (ACIP), which seeks to promote values education for early adolescents in western Kenya through modern initiation rites.[42] ACIP is involved in a doctoral study that seeks to investigate how these rites can function to integrate traditional African values and Christian values.

Condom Use in the Context of HIV/AIDS and Gender Violence

The Catholic Church opposes the use of all barrier methods of contraception, which includes condoms. The position of the church to date is that condom use during sexual intercourse is morally evil because sexual acts must be open the creation of life.[43] In this section, however, we focus on condoms not as a contraceptive but as a disease-prevention device.

It has been over forty years since the first case of AIDS was reported, but HIV/AIDS remains a global health challenge and priority. At the end of 2011, 34.2 million people were living with HIV globally, a slight increase from 33.5 million at the end of 2010.[44] A persistent trend of HIV infection is its geographic variation between and within nations and regions. Sub-Saharan Africa continues to be the epicenter of the disease, with the staggering figure of over 90 percent of all global cases of children under fifteen living with HIV.[45] In Africa, while national HIV infection rates suggest that HIV infection has significantly declined, HIV/AIDS-related deaths continue to be high in some parts of some African nations. In Kenya, for example, even though the rate of HIV infection has declined from its peak of 10.5 percent of the population in 1995/1996 to 6.7 percent in 2003, 5.6 percent in 2012, and 4.9 percent in 2017, the rate in Homa Bay and Siaya counties was over 20 percent in 2017.[46] New infections continue to be registered throughout the continent, and people are continuing to die of new AIDS-related opportunistic diseases.

The HIV/AIDS situation in Africa is made worse by gender-based sexual violence. Sitawa Kimuna and Yanyi Djamba explored factors associated with the physical and sexual abuse of wives among 4,876 married women from fifteen to forty-nine years of age.[47] Their findings suggest that 13 percent of all married women in Kenya have experienced sexual violence. The Kenya Domestic Household Survey (KDHS) 2014 also estimates that 14 percent of women in this age range experience sexual violence in marriage. Sadly, multivariate analysis showed that a woman's status as a Christian significantly increased her risk of physical and sexual abuse.

Despite scientific evidence supporting a positive relationship between condom use and HIV prevention, and in spite of the continuing high rate of HIV/AIDS in Africa, condom use remains low, especially in marriage relationships. The 2012 Kenya AIDS Indicator Survey, for example, suggests that married women are more at risk of HIV infection than unmarried women because of *"mpango wa kando"* ("side plate").[48] The high number of married "sponsors" involved in extramarital sexual relations confirms this. Yet, generally, married women in Africa are unable to insist on their partner's use of a condom even in high-risk HIV infection situations because of unequal gender relations.[49]

Against this background, the church, with its

---

42. Okigbo and Speizer, "Determinants of Sexual Activity and Pregnancy among Unmarried Young Women in Urban Kenya."
43. See Pope Benedict XVI and Seewald, *Light of the World*, 117–19.
44. UNAIDS/WHO Epidemic Updates, 2011.
45. UNAIDS/WHO Epidemic Updates, 2011.
46. NASCOP, *Kenya HIV Estimates Report 2014*; NASCOP, *Kenya AIDS Indicator Survey, 2012*.
47. Kimuna and Djamba, "Gender-Based Violence."
48. NASCOP, "Kenya AIDS Indicator Survey."
49. Tenkorang, "Negotiating Safer Sex among Married Women in Ghana"; Atteraya, Kimm, and Song, "Women's Autonomy in Negotiating Safer Sex to Prevent HIV."

teaching about contraception, appears not to be concerned about HIV/AIDS and, by extension, not to be concerned about women in Africa.[50] Upon returning to Rome from a visit to Kenya, Uganda, and the Democratic Republic of the Congo, Pope Francis was asked by a journalist whether the church should reconsider its position on condom use in the fight against HIV/AIDS. While we appreciate his response that "the problem is bigger" than can be addressed by condom use, his dismissive attitude seems insensitive to the deadly challenge facing millions of Africans. In addition, in his post-synodal apostolic exhortation *Amoris Laetitia* (The Joy of Love) addressing pastoral challenges related to the family, Francis was silent about condom use. It would have been better if he had, at a minimum, affirmed Pope Benedict's position that condom use may present a step in the right direction,[51] or better still explained why the condom is an effective weapon in the fight against HIV/AIDS. He could have cited scientific evidence to rebut the idea that condom use is not positively related to HIV/AIDS prevention and control. He also could have discussed the inconsistent and incorrect use of condoms as well as the challenge of "risk compensation"[52] (the assumption that the use of condoms eliminates all risks associated with sexual behavior, thus promoting sexual promiscuity). We appreciate the pope's cautious way of dealing with such a complex issue, but he would have done well to indicate his awareness of special situations in which condom use may be a necessary evil; for example, among couples with one infected partner where the threat of HIV infection is a daily reality.

Condom use as a way of preventing disease, especially in the context of HIV/AIDS, has been controversial among theologians.[53] In contrast to drugs and surgical procedures intended for therapeutic purposes, many prominent Catholic leaders have openly declared that they do not support the use of condoms to prevent disease because of its contraceptive effect.

Pope Benedict stated in 2010 that, although condom use may be seen as a responsible act in very special cases such as among male prostitutes for the purpose of reducing the risk of infection from HIV, and therefore saving lives,[54] it is not a truly moral solution. He emphasizes that, in such situations, the use of a condom becomes a responsible act only as a first step to raise awareness of the act which is later followed by the benefit of not contracting a deadly condition. For Benedict, a truly moral solution would be to advise these prostitutes to cease their immoral activities; however, it is far from clear that all of them would take this advice. For those who would not, for whatever reason, would it be Christian to insist on the nonuse of condoms? Would it not be loving to allow them to use condoms?

The church has also been consistent in raising problems of leakage and breaking of condoms during sexual intercourse, which may result in the non-infected partner being exposed to infection. While condom manufacturers consistently claim that condom use prevents the spread of HIV, in 2003 the president of the Vatican's Pontifical Council for the Family claimed that condoms are permeable to the HIV virus; he argued that the HIV virus is about 450 times smaller than the spermatozoon and that there is a possibility that it can pass through the "net" formed by the condom,[55] an allegation that has since been disputed. However, according to international health organizations that promote condom use, for example UNFPA, condoms have a 98-percent success rate in preventing pregnancy; real-world studies suggest a lower

---

50. See, for example, "Pope Francis Indicates Little Interest in Condom Use in the Fight against AIDS," *The Guardian*.

51. See "Catholic Church Tries to Clear Confusion over Condom Use," *The Guardian*, November 23, 2010, www.theguardian.com.

52. Farrow, "Pope Francis Was Right about Condoms and HIV."

53. Guevin and Rhonheimer, "Debate on the Use of Condoms to Prevent Acquired Immune Deficiency Syndrome."

54. See "Catholic Church Tries to Clear Confusion over Condom Use."

55. Bradshaw, "Vatican: Condoms Don't Stop AIDS."

85-percent success rate.[56] Whatever the case, the 2 to 15 percent who experience condom failure are 100 percent exposed to the life-threatening HIV virus while thinking that they are protected. Thus, condom use may not absolutely guarantee that the user is protected, a fact that the church has trumpeted in arguing that condoms provide a false sense of security. But does the 2- to 15-percent failure rate justify ignoring the 85 to 98 percent for whom the condom provides effective protection against HIV?

The church is opposed to condom use to prevent the spread of disease; instead, it advocates for the formation and education of people toward proper behavior. It teaches sexual abstinence before marriage and advocates for a faithful, monogamous marriage. Rather than the use of condoms as an "easy" means of preventing the transmission of AIDS, the church advocates education toward sexual responsibility, that is, to have sex only within marriage. So that it can respond to those affected by the scourge of AIDS, the church offers health care personnel, including doctors, plus chaplains and volunteers. This entire approach might make sense if the church had already established regular and effective institutions through which education toward sexual responsibility is promoted, but in fact it has not.

The position of the Catholic Church on condom use has generated considerable criticism from secular entities involved in global health care services like the United Nations Program on HIV/AIDS (UNAIDS) and WHO, raising questions about its ability to collaborate with these organizations. These bodies and others have criticized the church's stance against condom use, arguing that it is the best available means to prevent infection among sexually active people. The church's position has been criticized as being unrealistic, irresponsible, and immoral by some public health officials and AIDS activists. In 2014, the United Nations Committee on the Rights of Children stated that there is a need for the church to "overcome all the barriers and taboos surrounding adolescent sexuality that hinder their access to sexual and reproductive information, including on family planning and contraceptives."[57] Public health officials advocate for comprehensive sex education as opposed to the abstinence-only sex education advocated by the church, but it needs to be asked whether the indiscriminate provision of sexual knowledge and contraceptives in the name of "comprehensive" sex education merely addresses the symptoms rather than the root causes of youth sexual activity and, in so doing, actually promotes irresponsible sexual behavior.

In view of these criticisms, one may ask, What is the position of the church with respect to HIV/AIDS? Should the church be blamed for not responding to the HIV/AIDS crisis? It is simply not true that the Catholic Church has not done much in response to the AIDS crisis. The church is the largest private provider of HIV care, treatment, and support to victims of the epidemic, providing, according to UNAIDS, approximately 25 percent of such services worldwide.[58] The church has cooperated with UNAIDS through Caritas Internationalis,[59] a confederation of 164 Catholic relief, development, and social service organizations operating in most countries of the world. The church has cooperated with a number of international organizations to provide patient care, antiretroviral treatment, home-based care, and visits and counseling to those infected and affected by HIV/AIDS even though it takes a different view of condom use than these organizations.

Turning back to Africa, some countries like Uganda have reported that the spread of the epidemic has declined drastically. It may be interesting to know whether this decline in many places in Africa was primarily the result of the use of condoms, and the Ugandan experience is instructive. In the early 1990s, HIV/AIDS in Uganda was

---

56. See, for example, National Institute of Allergy and Infectious Diseases (NIAID), *Scientific Evidence on Condom Effectiveness for Sexually Transmitted Disease (STD) Prevention*; and Holmes et al., "Effectiveness of Condoms in Preventing Sexually Transmitted Infections."

57. Wooden, "U.N. Committee Presses Vatican on Child Abuse, Some Church Teaching."

58. "UNAIDS Congratulates Newly Elected Pope Francis."

59. See Caritas Internationalis, "Memorandum of Understanding between UNAIDS and Caritas Internationalis."

spreading fast like a bush fire; the horrifying death rate necessitated the taking of serious measures. President Museveni initiated a concerted community mobilization strategy that included the church, businesspeople, and even rock stars. The entire Ugandan nation saw the epidemic as their crisis. The mobilization efforts widely promoted the message that it was possible to prevent AIDS through "ABC" (Abstinence, Be faithful, and Condom use), which was later supplemented by offering people testing and counseling. The campaign's message was clearly articulated to the people of Uganda, and the primary solution offered was sexual responsibility. This was of course in harmony with the church's teaching and has been credited with helping to reduce the spread of the virus in Uganda. The Ugandan experience demonstrates that promoting the use of condoms may be one aspect of an effective solution but by itself may not be enough.

Although the position of the church on condom use may be an effective response to sexual immorality with all of its resulting challenges, it raises concerns especially among married couples with only one infected partner. When a Catholic married person realizes that he/she has contracted HIV, should that person continue a sexual relationship with the non-infected partner without using a condom? The church's opposition to condom use poses great challenges to such marriages. Hence, the direction in which this struggle and debate are ultimately resolved is key to finally controlling AIDS, especially on the African continent. Moreover, the approach will affect the future credibility of the Catholic Church because the core of all the problems around HIV/AIDS is being able to deal squarely and adequately with sexuality.

Conclusion

In this chapter, we have presented the Catholic Church's teachings on sexual morality with specific reference to contraceptive use. From the time of Augustine of Hippo through the Reformation and up to the contemporary period, highlighted by Pope Pius XI's encyclical *Casti Connubi*, the Second Vatican Council, Paul VI's encyclical *Humanae Vitae*, John Paul II's *Familiaris Consortio*, and the comments of Benedict XVI and Francis, the position of the Catholic Church has not changed: artificial contraception is against the moral law because it frustrates the procreative purpose of sex. But there have been some recent indications that the church may be backing off its position that artificial contraception is intrinsically evil.

In this chapter, we also interrogate the church's anti-contraception position in the context of contemporary Africa. In spite of the explosion of family planning campaigns driven essentially by Malthusian considerations in the 1960s, the church's position found acceptance among many Africans perhaps because it affirmed procreation as a natural God-given gift, a position that resonated with African values about the family. Many Africans and others, however, began to question the church's position, necessitating that the church reaffirm its position in *Humanae Vitae*, *Familiaris Consortio*, and other official pronouncements.

It is our view that the Catholic Church is right that morality is not dependent on popular acceptance or majority practices. The church is clearly called to condemn sin, but it is also called to love the sinner. It is the argument of this chapter that it would be an act of love for the church to continue proclaiming its teaching that condom use is in general evil while allowing for it in certain specific situations. Further, we concur with the church that the promotion of condoms as a response to the sexual activity of young people has in fact promoted sexual promiscuity. We stand with the church's magisterium that what should instead be promoted is values education, especially for young unmarried people, so that they can make right and reasonable choices. In this regard, we make reference above to the African Christian Initiation Program, which seeks to reconstruct African initiation rites with the aim of promoting Christian values, including Christian sexual values. Yet we acknowledge that, even with educational programs of this kind, the right and reasonable thing is not always chosen. In such situations, condom use would be a lesser evil than sexually promiscuous behavior without condom use, with its attendant dangers.

A number of scientific findings, including those of condom-use promoters like UNFPA, concur that condoms, even when correctly and consistently used, are not 100 percent effective in preventing either pregnancy or HIV infection. Pregnancy and HIV are matters of life and death whose acceptability should not be dependent on issues of probability: even though condoms provide an 85–98-percent probability of success for preventing pregnancy and HIV, for those who conceive or become infected while using a condom, the chance that these things would happen was effectively 100 percent. Yet we cannot refute that, in light of its rather high success rate, the condom remains the most efficacious means of controlling HIV infection.

We appreciate that the Catholic Church is one of the major providers of HIV/AIDS care and support services in Africa. Nevertheless, we are discouraged that the church's recent message that artificial contraception may not be intrinsically evil has not been strongly affirmed. In the context of contemporary Africa, which is characterized by poverty, HIV/AIDS, gender violence, and various problems faced by married couples, and where over 60 percent of young people engage in sex, the church's lukewarm affirmation of this new position suggests an inability to appreciate the value of practical moral theology based on the "lesser evil."

In this chapter, we raise more questions than answers in order to prompt further research by African scholars working with their colleagues from other parts of the world. We suggest a methodological approach that applies critical thinking and an analysis of the church's position in the context of certain complex realities, and which raises the following questions: (1) Should poor families who cannot afford to educate many children continue to procreate without regard for the consequences? (2) Where only one partner in a marriage is infected by HIV, should the couple refrain from sexual relations even while continuing to live as husband and wife? (3) Should spouses face moral condemnation for using condoms to protect each other from disease? Pope Francis realistically acknowledges the social reality of spousal sexual violence. For couples where only one partner is HIV-positive, sexual abstinence may not be realistic, and the partners may have no option but to use condoms. This is food for thought not only for church leaders, but also for the Christian faithful and those outside the Christian community. The need to appreciate context cannot be overemphasized.

Bibliography

Akong'a, Joshua. "Functional Communication Model for Family Planning Extension Services in Kenya." *Journal of East African Research & Development* 18 (1967).

Armstrong, Dave. "Sex and Catholics: Our Views Briefly Explained." Blog post, *National Catholic Register,* February 2, 2018, www.ncregister.com/blog.

Atteraya, M. S., H. Kimm, and I. H. Song. "Women's Autonomy in Negotiating Safer Sex to Prevent HIV: Findings from the 2011 Nepal Demographic and Health Survey." *AIDS Education and Prevention* 26.1 (February 2014): 1–12.

Augustine, Saint. *The Catholic and Manichean Ways of Life.* Translated by Donald A. Gallagher and Idella J. Gallagher. Washington, DC: Catholic University of America Press, 1966.

Benedict XVI, Pope. International Congress Organized by the Pontifical Lateran University on the 40th Anniversary of the Encyclical *Humanae Vitae.* May 12, 2008.

Benedict XVI, Pope, and Peter Seewald. *Light of the World: The Pope, the Church, and the Signs of the Times.* San Francisco: Ignatius Press, 2010.

Bradshaw, Steve. "Condoms Don't Stop AIDS." *The Guardian,* October 9, 2003, www.guardian.co.uk/world/2003/oct/09/aids.

Bujo, Bénézet. *Foundations of an African Ethic: Beyond the Universal Claims of Western Morality.* New York: Crossroad, 2001.

Caritas Internationalis and Joint United Nations Programme on HIV/AIDS. "Memorandum of Understanding between UNAIDS and Caritas Internationalis." Caritas Internationalis (1998), www.caritas.org.

Chadwick, Henry. *The Early Church.* London: Penguin, 1967.

Congregation for the Doctrine of the Faith. *Catechism of the Catholic Church.* Vatican City: Libreria Editrice Vaticana, 1995.

Doyle, Aoife M., Sue Napierala Mavedzenge, Mary L. Plummer, and David A. Ross. "Review: The Sexual Behaviour of Adolescents in Sub-Saharan Africa: Patterns and Trends from National Surveys." *Tropical Medicine and International Health Volume* 17.7 (May 18, 2012): 796–807.

Farrow, Mary. "Pope Francis Was Right about Condoms and HIV." *Catholic News Agency*, December 13, 2015, www.catholicnewsagency.com.

Francis, Pope. *Amoris Laetitia* [Post-synodal Apostolic Exhortation on Love in the Family; March 19, 2016]. Vatican City: Libreria Editrice Vaticana, 2016. www.vatican.va.

Fredriksen, Paula. *Sin: The Early History of an Idea*. Princeton, NJ: Princeton University Press, 2012.

Fuchs, Eric. *Sexual Desire and Love: Origins and History of the Christian Ethic of Sexuality and Marriage*. New York: Seabury, 1963.

Green, E. *Faith-Based Organizations: Contributions to HIV Prevention*. Washington, DC: The Synergy Project, 2003.

Guevin, Benedict, and Martin Rhonheimer. "Debate on the Use of Condoms to Prevent Acquired Immune Deficiency Syndrome." *The National Catholic Bioethics Quarterly* (Spring 2005): 35–48.

Holdren, Alan, and Andrea Gagliarducci. "Full Text In-Flight Interview from Manila to Rome." *Catholic News Agency*, January 19, 2015, www.catholicnewsagency.com.

Holmes, K. K., et al. "Effectiveness of Condoms in Preventing Sexually Transmitted Infections." *Bulletin of the World Health Organization* 82 (2004): 454–61.

John Paul II, Pope. "Christian Spirituality of Marriage Possible Only by Living According to the Spirit." Address at the weekly General Audience, November 14, 1984, www.ewtn.com.

———. *Familiaris Consortio* [Post-synodal Apostolic Exhortation on the Role of the Christian Family in the Modern World; November 22, 1981]. Vatican City: Libreria Editrice Vaticana, 1981. www.vatican.va.

Joint Learning Initiative on Faith and Local Communities. "Evaluation of the Impact of Christian Aid's Support of Faith-Based Responses to HIV." 2014. www.jliflc.com.

Kamaara, Eunice Karanja. *Gender Relations, Youth Sexuality and HIV: A Kenyan Experience*. Eldoret: AMECEA Gaba Publications, 2005.

Kimuna, Sitawa R., and Yanyi K. Djamba. "Gender-Based Violence: Correlates of Physical and Sexual Wife Abuse in Kenya." *Journal of Family Violence* 23.5 (July 2008): 333–42.

Knox, R. J. *The Documents of Vatican II*. New Delhi: St. Paul's Publications, 1966.

Kubania, Jacqueline. "What the Youth Really Think about Dating and Sugar Daddies." *Daily Nation*, May 19, 2016, www.nation.co.ke/news.

Lazzarini, Z. "Human Rights and HIV/AIDS, Discussion Paper on HIV/AIDS Care and Support." In *The Synergy Project: Health Technical Services (HTS) Project*. USAID, 1998.

Magesa, Laurenti. *African Religion: The Moral Traditions of Abundant Life*. Nairobi: Paulines Publications Africa, 1997.

McLaughlin, Terence P., ed. *The Church and the Reconstruction of the Modern World: The Social Encyclicals of Pope Pius XI*. New York: Image Books, 1957.

Mbiti, John S. *African Religions and Philosophy*. Nairobi/London: Heinemann, 1969.

National AIDS and STI Control Programme (NASCOP). "Kenya AIDS Indicator Survey 2012: Final Report." Nairobi: NASCOP.

———. "Kenya HIV Estimates Report." June 2014. Nairobi: NASCOP.

National Institute of Allergy and Infectious Diseases (NIAID). *Scientific Evidence on Condom Effectiveness for Sexually Transmitted Disease (STD) Prevention*. NIAID, 2008.

Noonan, John T., Jr. "Contraception." In *The New Catholic Encyclopedia*, vol. 4. Washington, DC: Catholic University of America, 1967.

Okigbo, C. C., and I. S. Speizer. "Determinants of Sexual Activity and Pregnancy among Unmarried Young Women in Urban Kenya: A Cross-Sectional Study." *PLOS ONE* 10.6 (2015).

O'Riordan, S. "Chastity." In *The New Catholic Encyclopedia*, vol. 3. Washington, DC: Catholic University of America, 1967.

Paul VI, Pope. *Humanae Vitae* [Encyclical on the Regulation of Birth; July 25, 1968]. Vatican City: Libreria Editrice Vaticana, 1968. www.vatican.va.

Peschke, Karl. H. *Christian Ethics*. Alceister: C. Goodliffe Neale, 1985.

Pew Research Center. "Sub-Saharan Africa" (April 2, 2015), http://www.pewforum.org/2015/04/02/sub-saharan-africa/.

Pius XI, Pope. *Casti Connubii* [Encyclical on Christian Marriage; December 31, 1930]. Vatican City: Libreria Editrice Vaticana, 1930. www.vatican.va.

"Pope Francis Indicates Little Interest in Condom Use in the Fight against AIDS." *The Guardian*, November 30, 2015, www.theguardian.com.

Ramjee, Gita, and Brodie Daniels. "Women and HIV in Sub-Saharan Africa." *AIDS Research and Therapy* 10.30 (December 2013).

Ranke-Heinmann, Uta. *Eunuchs for the Kingdom of Heaven: Women, Sexuality, and the Catholic Church*. New York: Doubleday, 1990.

Salzman, Todd A., and Michael G. Lawler. *The Sexual Person: Toward a Renewed Catholic Anthropology*. Washington, DC: Georgetown University Press, 2008.

Sandro, Magister. "Francis, the Pope of *Humanae Vitae*." *L'espresso* 18 (2014), chiesa.espresso.repubblica.it.

Tenkorang, E. Y. "Negotiating Safer Sex among Married Women in Ghana." *Archives of Sexual Behavior* 41.6 (December 2012): 1353–62.

Tripathi, Deepak. "India and Its Moral Crisis." *Counterpunch* (January 24, 2013), www.counterpunch.org.

UNAIDS. "UNAIDS Congratulates Newly Elected Pope Francis." March 14, 2013, www.unaids.org.

———. "UNAIDS Requests Pope Benedict XVI for Support in Efforts to Stop New HIV Infections in Children." April 11, 2012, http://www.unaids.org/en/resources/presscentre/featurestories/2012/april/20120411afaithbasedresponsetohiv/.

UNAIDS/WHO Epidemic Updates, 2011, www.unaids.org.

UNFPA & PRB. Status Report, 2012. "Adolescents and Young People in Sub-Saharan Africa: Opportunities and Challenges," www.prb.org.

United Nations Security Council. "Fight against Sexual Violence in Conflict Reaches 'New Juncture,' Security Council Told." 7428th Meeting, April 15, 2015, www.un.org.

Wooden, Cindy. "United Nations Committee Presses Vatican on Child Abuse, Some Church Teaching." *Catholic News Service*, February 5, 2014.

Suggested Reading

Bujo, Bénézet. *Foundations of an African Ethic: Beyond the Universal Claims of Western Morality*. New York: Crossroad, 2001.

Fuchs, Eric. *Sexual Desire and Love: Origins and History of the Christian Ethic of Sexuality and Marriage*. New York: Seabury, 1963.

Kamaara, Eunice Karanja. *Gender Relations, Youth Sexuality and HIV: A Kenyan Experience*. Eldoret: AMECEA Gaba Publications, 2005.

Magesa, Laurenti. *African Religion: The Moral Traditions of Abundant Life*. Nairobi: Paulines Publications Africa, 1997.

Paul VI, Pope. *Humanae Vitae* [Encyclical on the Regulation of Birth; July 25, 1968]. Vatican City: Libreria Editrice Vaticana, 1968. www.vatican.va.

Peschke, K. H. *Christian Ethics*. Alceister: C. Goodliffe Neale, 1985.

Salzman, Todd A., and Michael G. Lawler. *The Sexual Person: Toward a Renewed Catholic Anthropology*. Washington, DC: Georgetown University Press, 2008.

Key Words

Catholic Christianity in Africa
condom use
contestations
cultural contexts
gender relations
HIV/AIDS
sexual morality
values
youth

Pentecostal and Charismatic Renewal: A Religious Phenomenon for Transformation in Africa

Clement Majawa

The socioanthropologist Maxwell George Zithatha expresses great concern about the socioreligious direction that sub-Saharan Africa is taking in the era of globalization:

> Africa is at a cross-road because it is experiencing conflict of beliefs between Christianity and Traditional religious heritage; misunderstandings between Western civilization and African worldview. Thus, Africa is presently in search of genuine integration between Christian and African spirituality. She is looking for socioreligious globalized identity. The people want self-sustenance in cultural and religious values so that they can determine their mission and destiny in life.[1]

How can this be achieved in a changing world? Pope Francis warns about the greatest threats facing Christianity today in his 2018 apostolic exhortation *Gaudete et Exsultate*. He discusses the dangers of a contemporary Gnosticism that favors purely subjective truth, atheism, relativism, rationalism, the exaltation of the self, and the absolutizing of theories and ideologies over Christian doctrine. Gnosticism prefers "a God without Christ, a Christ without a Church, a Church without her people" (§37). He also discusses the dangers of a new Pelagianism involving excessive pride in human intelligence and effort, leading to self-justification, self-dependence and self-glorification, eliminating the need for God (§§47, 57–59).

Eugene Kamanga, the former archbishop of Lubumbashi in the Democratic Republic of the Congo, provides an important insight on African values in the light of the presence of the Holy Spirit, which offers a good starting point for the subsequent development of this chapter. For Kamanga, the African conception of life and relationships comes from the power provided by the dynamism of the Spirit as revealed in the scriptures, the tradition of the church, and African history. The African continent is called to renew itself by embracing the spirituality of its ancestral beliefs and the harmonious spirit of the land.[2] Allan Anderson, arguing in the same vein, proposes that the Holy Spirit is revisiting Africa so as to engage and renew the traditionally benevolent spirit of the people.[3] South African charismatic theologian Jameson Zakahlana concludes that Africa's traditional spirit of communality has paved the way for the African spirit world to become a fertile ground for the "'New Pentecost' of Transformation."[4] Indeed, it is true to say that the Holy Spirit is becoming flesh in Africa. This chapter aims at showing how this is happening in

---

1. Zithatha, *Challenges of Christian Faith in Africa in the Times of Globalization*, 67–68.
2. Cited in Howard, *Values on African Heritage and Religious Pluralism in Context*, 56.
3. Anderson, "African Spirituality in African-Initiated Churches," 146.
4. Zakahlana, *African Churches and the Phenomenon of Pentecostal and Charismatic Experiences*, 88–90.

the Catholic churches in Africa and how scholars are developing the theological navigational tools to follow the movement of the Spirit in African Christianity in general.

Pentecostal Charismatic Expressions

In the Mass of Pentecost Monday in 1975, Pope Paul VI thanked the worldwide Pentecostal charismatic groups with these words: "In the name of the Lord, I thank you for having brought Charismatic Renewal into the heart of the Church." Leo Joseph Cardinal Suenens acknowledges that pneumatic gifts are real and are effective in the process of deeper evangelization and societal transformation. Thus, he writes:

> Pentecostal believers are modern Christians who believe they can share in the same personal relationship with Jesus and pneumatic sanctification as did the apostles over hundreds of years ago. The transformative event that indicates pneumatic sanctification, transformation and therefore religious conversion, has come to be known as Baptism in the Holy Spirit. In their highly enthusiastic approach to worship the manifestation of charismatic power is indicated by enacted gifts of the Holy Spirit ("spiritual gifts"), which include wisdom, knowledge, faith, healing, miracles, prophecy, discernment of spirits, speaking in tongues and interpretation of tongues. The aforementioned pneumatic gifts are real in the world and effective in the process of deeper evangelization.[5]

Baison Mahumbulele asserts, along similar lines, that Africa and the global world of today are in need of these gifts to rebuild, renew, and transform the life of all peoples.[6] Archbishop Paul Cordes has argued that, from the inception of the church, charismatic gifts have functioned as powerful tools for missionary activities and for building God's kingdom in people's hearts.[7] According to St. Thomas Aquinas (1225–1274), charismatic religiosity uses the gifts of the Holy Spirit to become an agent of spiritual initiative and human opportunity.[8] Pope St. John Paul II has referred to a Pentecostal awareness that is now present worldwide, an awareness that is playing a vital role in uniting all peoples and cultures.[9] Charismatic Pentecostalism is truly a special grace to the world.[10]

It is obvious in the changing momentum of Christian expansion in Africa that the pneumatic power and influence of the Holy Spirit cannot be stopped, nor can it be attributed to one culture or nation or a single factor. The wind blows where it pleases (John 3:8). "People worldwide are praying to experience the power of the Holy Spirit in their life."[11] The Pentecostal movement today comprises over 30 percent of the world's Christians.[12] Estimates for the number of adherents of Pentecostalism and other charismatic Christian expressions range from five hundred to six hundred million.[13]

---

5. Leo Joseph Cardinal Suenens, "Pneumatic Gifts in the Church." This was echoed by Prof. Raniero Cantalamessa, OFM, in the foreword to Cordes, *Call to Holiness*, 56–58; Cantalamessa, *Come, Creator Spirit*.
6. Mahumbulele, *Transforming the Church in Africa through Charismatic Values*, 55–58.
7. Cordes, *Call to Holiness*, 1–4.
8. See John and Cameron, *Gifts of the Holy Spirit according to St. Thomas Aquinas*, 2, 9. See also John, *Spurred by the Spirit*, 145–46; *Catechism of the Catholic Church* §800 (hereinafter *CCC*); Pope John Paul II, "Champion of the Charisms."
9. Pope John Paul II, "Message to the Great Gathering of the Catholic Charismatic Family."
10. Pearson, *The Church of Christ and Charismatic Experiences*, 24.
11. Pope Paul VI, "Address to the Second International Leaders' Conference." See also Pesare et al., *"Then Peter Stood Up,"* 17.
12. Robeck, "The Holy Spirit and the Unity of the Church," 14–20; see also Robeck, *Azusa Street Mission and Revival*, 64–69.
13. "Report of the 5th Phase of the International Dialogue between Some Classical Pentecostal Churches and the Catholic Church (1998–2006)," 216. Cf. Philip Jenkins, *The Next Christendom: The Coming Global Christianity* (New York: Oxford University Press, 2011). According to the Pew Research Center's 2011 Global Christianity

Following Christ's mandate of making disciples of all nations, the number of Pentecostal Christians continues to grow rapidly.

This chapter seeks to investigate the nature and significance of charismatic Pentecostalism in Africa. It presents the reasons for the fact that many mainstream Christians are dissatisfied with the formalism of the church's liturgy, prayer, spirituality, sacraments, and discipline and are finding an alternative in Pentecostal or "born again" churches. They are searching for dynamic liturgical celebrations, healing ministries, and the gospel of prosperity. The discussion further investigates how such challenges might be addressed through a Pentecostal formation rooted in the African spirituality of *ubuntu*. The conclusion will discuss some approaches to transforming charismatic Pentecostalism in Africa and elsewhere.[14]

The Foundations of Charismatic Pentecostalism

Charismatic Pentecostalism has roots in the scriptural, apostolic, and patristic traditions. Beginning with the experiences of the day of Pentecost, this pneumatic phenomenon has evolved over the course of history to become a worldwide reality influencing every aspect of religious, human, and social life.[15] It is evident that the growth of the Charismatic Renewal movement in the Catholic Church is one of the fruits of the Second Vatican Council.[16]

In calling for the council, Pope St. John XXIII intended to open the windows of the church so that fresh air and new experiences could renew its life.[17] The pope suggested that Christians should read the account of the Pentecost in the Acts of the Apostles (Acts 2:1–13) and relive it with the disciples in the upper room. His call marked the beginnings of a fundamental renewal in the church, a renewal that targeted the whole of the church and society.[18] Vatican II was a new Pentecost for the church and society.[19] It created an ecclesial benchmark for *aggiornamento* and the transformation of Africa.

The subsequent development of charismatic spiritualities and Pentecostal movements in Africa has strong roots in African religious and spiritual traditions. Pope John Paul II's post-synodal apostolic exhortation, *Ecclesia in Africa* (*EA*; 1995), notes that African values were a preparation for the continent's reception of the gospel and that the Holy Spirit is working in all African cultures. The presence of the incarnate Son of God through the Holy Spirit was the foundation for the church's deeper evangelization of the African continent on the eve of the third millennium (*EA* §60). Pneumatic movements and spiritual organizations initiated and guided by the Holy Spirit have become pillars of the new evangelization. In Africa, this new evangelization aims at building the church as Family of God so that she can become a true "Temple of the Holy Spirit" in the context of the continent's cultural heritage (*EA* §63).

Malawian theologian Patrick Kalilombe has observed that African spirituality is increasingly being inculturated in Christianity in Africa. This is particularly reflected in the features and identities of African Pentecostalism. The ongoing attraction to African spirituality in the light of charismatic Pentecostalism throughout Africa is not confined to the historical mainstream churches alone but is also manifested in many religious and independent churches. Furthermore, with strong roots in the Holy Spirit and inculturated pneumatology, African Initiative Churches are focusing on transformational practical and extraordinary gifts of the Holy Spirit such as healing, miracles, prophecy, speaking in tongues, and so on. Thousands of African Christians are attracted annually to spiritual sites of pilgrimage and worship for socio-spiritual

---

Report, online at https://www.pewforum.org/2011/12/19/global-christianity-exec, 305 million Christians worldwide follow the charismatic movement. As of 2019, the growth was still significantly increasing.

14. Martin, "Interpretations of Latin American Pentecostalism," 111–36.
15. International Catholic Charismatic Renewal Service, *Charismatic Renewal*, 44–46.
16. John, *Spurred by the Spirit*, 14.
17. Pope John XXIII, encyclical *Ad Petri Cathedram* on Truth, Unity and Peace in a Spirit of Charity (1959).
18. Walters, *John XXIII*, 56.
19. Jordan, *Theology and Mission of Vatican II*, 111.

renewal and integrated witness of faith.[20] Pope John Paul II understood this spread—like "wildfire"—of charismatic churches in Africa as a sign that "Pentecostal grace was at work and needs communal discernment."[21] African spirituality transformed by Pentecostal spirituality is playing a major role in helping the church become self-reliant, self-propagating, self-governing, and self-renewing.

Challenges and Questions Facing Charismatic Christianity in Africa

A popular street preacher, Brighton Bamubamu, was heard preaching passionately in the streets of Blantyre in Malawi:

> Through baptism, we are born again and are charismatic. No church has a monopoly on charisma. Yet in this city, some churches deny this. How can a congregation be a church it if has no Holy Spirit, no tongues, no miracles. Look here, I have thousands of followers. When I preach: "Halleluja! Shaba! Shabata! Shabalalakata!" even those from mainstream conservative churches come to me for healing, guidance, wives, husbands, jobs, prosperity, counseling, and miracles. I am the lightening tongue of the prophet Moses who is living with you in this new Sinai desert full of snakes and vipers. Do not be afraid. I am here to protect you. Nobody, no religion, no politician, no witch, no prostitute, no devil-worshipper, etc. can snatch you away from *Chauta* (God) our Lord.[22]

This episode is a manifestation of some of the challenges facing the phenomenon of Pentecostalism.

Thomas Rausch observes that despite the significant success of charismatic Pentecostalism, there are still misunderstandings and challenges surrounding it.[23] It is evident that there are many differences among Pentecostal churches and charismatic groups, and it cannot be denied that on occasion the spirituality of the Holy Spirit is abused. The African movement faces many challenges with regard to its identity, mission, and strategies of expansion, in addition to questions about its place in global Pentecostalism.

Abuses in African Pentecostalism

The wave of misunderstanding and abuse of the gifts of the Holy Spirit has become a global phenomenon, and Africa has not been spared. Negative experiences are distorting the image of the Holy Spirit's transformative role on the African continent. A renowned Kenyan media consultant recently warned:

> Beware of materialistic fake evangelists who swindle and become millionaires in God's name and religion. There are many mobile and television preachers who con and impoverish millions of Kenyans in broad daylight as they are cheered on by their followers. They promise glory and fleece unsuspecting individuals. They purport to perform miracles that even Jesus Christ will marvel at. For some money, they promise to turn one's poverty and miserable life into a paradise. To instil awe and fear in people, they organize a legion of false witnesses. These self-anointed men and women of "God" chant: "Hallelujah! Praise the Lord! Amen! Alleluia plant more seed [give more money!]" as their supporters lie in supplication, while others retreat into fake delirium. Indeed, one will be a stranger in Jerusalem if he/she has not seen or met them in Nairobi, Mombasa or Eldoret cities in Kenya. They are really like wolves in sheep's skin: Mt 7:15.[24]

---

20. Kalilombe, "Relevance of Contextual Theologies for Deeper Evangelization and Societal Transformation in Africa."
21. John Paul II, "Address to the Bishops of Malawi."
22. Bamubamu, "Local Preachers Scrambling for the People of God," 2–3.
23. Rausch, *Catholics and Evangelicals: Do They Share a Common Future?*, 37.
24. Ogallo, "Fake Evangelists Swindling in God's Name and Religion," 15.

There is a flood of sham pastors of "Pentecostal" churches who are involved in the crimes of extortion, religious impersonation, murder, drugs, and human trafficking. They abuse the name of the church and the gifts of the Holy Spirit, conjuring fake "miracles," coaching witnesses to their amazing deeds, and selling fake "blessed" oils, among other things. In response, the Kenya Conference of Catholic Bishops, the Evangelical Alliance of Kenya, and the National Council of Churches of Kenya have asked the government to investigate, regulate, and possibly deregister deceitful churches, dubious evangelists, rogue prophets, and errant ministers for the good of Kenya.[25]

In addition, as Aluko Chimbotosya observes, because of high levels of ignorance, poverty, sickness, and underdevelopment in Africa, the gospel of prosperity is becoming a more lucrative business. If the government cannot address the challenge of unemployment among the youth and if the church opts to be silent in the face of socioeconomic injustices perpetrated on the poor and the voiceless, then many of these marginalized people will join such "unrighteous" churches and movements.[26] Divine wisdom is good and so is material wealth, but the latter should be used to serve God. In summary, there is a need for the discernment of spirits when it comes to religious groups in Africa.

All of this raises an important question: Why are many Christians leaving the mainstream churches—Catholic, Lutheran, Methodist, Anglican, Presbyterian, and so on—to join the Pentecostal churches or religious groups that might mislead or mistreat them? There are a number of reasons for this. First, Pentecostalists highly value what they see as a "democratic" pneumatic experience. Pentecostal churches and groups in Africa tend to be more diffused, more fluid in their systems and organizations, and more flexible in their structures, all of which help to explain why they attract many who are seeking more religious diversity, freedom, and creativity in doctrine, morality, and liturgy. Second, many see charismatic Pentecostalism as offering spiritual integrity, the final goal of their search for meaning.[27] And, third, people are always on the move, in search of personal and communal identity, religious satisfaction, and material security. If they are unable to find it in one place, they migrate to another in their ceaseless quest for abundant life.[28]

Pentecostal Religiosity for Evangelization and Public Life

Kenneth Okomatani Dube reports that the journals of the first evangelizers of Malawi, Zambia, and Zimbabwe (formerly the Federation of Rhodesia and Nyasaland) show their great zeal for missionary success. They believed that the Holy Spirit was guiding them in the most challenging circumstances. Historical studies of evangelization reveal that missionary activity has three main dimensions: the proclamation of the Good News, bearing witness, and seeing the gifts of the Holy Spirit bearing fruits in the transformation of societies.[29] This early evangelization was "pneumocentric" in that it reached out to people of various ethnic and religious backgrounds in order to bring them to a communion of faith through the Holy Spirit.

African religiosity promoted an ongoing relationship between the unborn, the living, the living dead (ancestors), and the creator. Religious leaders, societal chiefs, and traditional healers and mediums played a crucial role in interpreting the will of the supernatural being and the mysteries of life. They safeguarded traditional practices, secrets, taboos, and community values. They ensured that unity of purpose, justice, peace, and progress prevailed in the community. People believed that religious values and spiritual gifts are from God and should be used for the common good. Personal spirituality and integrity had a communitarian dimension.

---

25. See Njoroge, "Churches in Kenya Have Asked the Government to Regulate Deceitful Churches," 24.
26. Chimbotoysa, *Seeking God in the Contexts of Material Exploitation and Spiritual Degradation*, 96.
27. "You have made us for yourself, and our hearts are restless until they can find rest in you" (Augustine, *Confessions* 1.1.1, trans. Rex Warner [New York: Mentor, 1963]).
28. Pfeiffer, *Pentecostal Conversations for the Changing Societal Dynamics*, 135; Cordes, *Call to Holiness*, 1–3; Barrett, *Century of the Holy Spirit*, 381–414.
29. Dube, *Evangelization of Central Africa*, 35.

One can say that African spirituality was rooted in social and public life. African religious leadership, chieftains, and spirit mediums were a means of communicating public interests and the common good. Public life and religion were rooted in each other and determined human behavior and relationships between society and the supernatural.

Barry Smart argues that charismatic religiosity and witness in Africa is increasingly becoming a public affair, a public religion that addresses broad-based cultural, socioeconomic, political, and moral issues as a means of evangelization.[30] Charismatic religiosity and pneumatic gifts are being used to unify people so that the world may believe (John 17:21), and thus they are becoming public. Pentecostal charismatic religions with public value should be interrogated by and should learn more from the traditional African heritage.

The public nature of Pentecostalism implies a number of important conclusions. First, there is an urgent need for a religious paradigm that embraces the African worldview and its complexities and is in dialogue with contemporary issues in charismatic religiosity and with the wider African society. Such a paradigm would embrace the need for religious groups to bring their gifts to the table in search of gospel-driven practices and approaches to addressing issues of ignorance, poverty, disease, bad governance, injustice, abuse of human rights, and underdevelopment. Second, in addressing itself to public issues of socioeconomics, politics, the environment, and globalization, public religiosity with a Pentecostal orientation needs to focus on the ethos and character of African societies in the light of their traditional spirituality. In order to bring holistic transformation,[31] public Pentecostalism must develop a relevant language and witness to the truth about African societies.[32] Finally, the public role of Pentecostalism is important because in Africa, "public religion should guide public life."[33] A public religious identity may be able to contribute to Africa's goal of sustainable development. Africa is fast becoming a world of many diverse sociocultural, political, and religious interactions. In this environment, there is a need for openness, dialogue, engagement, and mutuality between culture and religion, all of which can be influenced by charismatic Pentecostalism with an African spiritual twist.

The Spirituality of Discernment in Pentecostalism

The documents of Vatican II affirm the legitimacy of charisms both ordinary and extraordinary.[34] The church teaches that a charism (a spiritual gift) is a grace given freely by God through the Holy Spirit for the service of God and the building up of the church as opposed to the graces given to sanctify an individual.[35] Paul lists true charisms that should not be distorted or abused.[36] These charisms do not themselves make a person holier; rather, they enable him or her to serve others.[37] The apostle John encourages us to "test the spirits" (1 John 4:1), which in this context can refer to charisms. Over the course of history, the church has developed criteria (discussed below) for determining whether the fruits of a person or community are good or bad, whether they are from God or evil spirits (see Matt 7:15–29).

Pope Benedict XVI taught about the importance for Christian identity of discernment of faith and the recognition of charismatic gifts.[38] On March 27, 2007, Tarcisio Cardinal Bertone, the Vatican's Secretary of State, said that the "overall goal" of Benedict XVI's papacy was to defend authen-

---

30. Smart, *Facing Modernity*, 3–9.
31. Tracy, *Analogical Imagination*, 10–15.
32. Norris and Inglehart, *Sacred and Secular Religion and Politics Worldwide*, 15–28.
33. Casanova, *Public Religion in the Modern World*, 20–28.
34. Vatican II, Dogmatic Constitution on the Church (*Lumen Gentium*) §12.
35. Rom 1:11; 5:15; 6:23; 1 Cor 1–11; 2 Cor 1:11.
36. Healing, miracles, tongues, and deliverance. See 1 Corinthians 12.
37. CCC §§688, 798–800, 809, 1508, 2003, 2024, 2684.
38. Allen, *Ten Things Pope Benedict Wants You to Know*, 26.

tic Christian and charismatic identity in a world marked by religious relativism.[39] Every religious belief, charism, and practice needs a discernment of the Spirit and a witness. This is urgent today because of the evident misunderstandings, abuses, and scandals surrounding Pentecostalism and the gifts of the Holy Spirit.

Many televangelist apostles, prophets, and pastors are misinterpreting and misusing the Bible to enrich themselves while, in some cases, engaging in sexual affairs with the members of their churches. A particularly notorious example is the case of the thirty-three-year-old televangelist "prophet" Victor Kanyari from Kajiado County, Kenya, who leads the Salvation Healing Ministry, a Pentecostal church with over two thousand members. In October 2015, he conducted a "healing" that involved fondling a woman's breasts in full view of national television. He simulates blood coming from his fingers by using potassium permanganate mixed with water when performing fake "miracles" in the name of Jesus. He urges his followers to "plant the seed" of 310 shillings each so that he can perform his "miracles" and maintain his church.[40] Obviously, such activities need the discernment of the Spirit, a discernment that was described in the council's Decree on the Apostolate of the Laity (*Apostolicam Actuositatem*).[41] Consistent and proper discernment in Pentecostal churches and charismatic groups would guide the evolution of authentic evangelization in Africa and elsewhere.

There is grave danger today that the scriptures will be misused and abused by some for fame and personal gain, conduct that calls into question the credibility of the gospel and Christian teaching.

There are today many so-called gospels that place more emphasis on outward material prosperity than on spiritual transformation. There is a need for a new paradigm of discernment that can check the growth of these "gospels."[42] The promises of healing, miracles, deliverance, and exorcism need discernment and scientific verification.[43]

This discernment should take place in local contexts and particularly in diocesan pastoral programs. Here are some of the pastoral guidelines that should be followed: (1) inclusive language should be used; for example, ministers should not say things like "only certain people are anointed and saved"; (2) only ordained priests should anoint with the holy oils; (3) only ordained priests should lay hands on people for the purposes of healing; (4) the gospel of prosperity should not be overemphasized; and (5) there should not be an excessive focus on miracles, healings, and deliverance. The activities of charismatic groups are meant to strengthen people's faith; thus, it is important that Pentecostal movements be approved by legitimate church authority.[44]

Lumen Gentium teaches that, since there are many charisms that can be misused, those who have charge over the church should judge their genuineness and proper use for the common good (§12; see also 1 Thess 5:12, 19–21). Thomas Aquinas teaches that the exercise of a charism requires the intervention of divine power, the Holy Spirit, who accomplishes it through the mediation of the holy angels. However, when a charism is within the power of the angelic nature, this power is capable of demonic imitation. Therefore, great caution, humility, prudence, discernment, and prayer are necessary.[45]

---

39. Allen, *Ten Things Pope Benedict Wants You to Know*, 26.

40. Ng'enoh, "Singer Betty Bayo Left Me but We Expect Things to Turn Round—Pastor Victor Kanyari."

41. Paul VI, *Apostolicam Actuositatem* §3: "For the exercise of this pneumatic apostolate, the Holy Spirit who sanctifies the people of God through ministry and the sacraments gives the faithful special gifts also (cf. 1 Cor. 12:7), 'allotting them to everyone according as He wills' (1 Cor 12:11) . . . in the freedom of the Holy Spirit who 'breathes where He wills' (Jn 3:8) . . . the true nature and proper use of these gifts not to extinguish the Spirit but to test all things and hold fast to what is good (cf. 1 Thess. 5:12, 19, 21)." Cf. Moltmann, *Theology Today*. See also Moltmann, *God for a Secular Society*.

42. *Apostolicam Actuositatem*, 7–10. See also Mark 11:23–24; 10:29–30; Phil 4:9.

43. Majawa, *Holy Spirit and Charismatic Renewal in Africa and Beyond*, 385–95. See also Ps 103:1–3; Matt 4:23–24; 8:1–3; Mark 11:23–24; Acts 3:16; 5:12–16; 10:38; 1 John 3:8.

44. Majawa, *Holy Spirit and Charismatic Renewal in Africa and Beyond*, 2–6.

45. St. Thomas Aquinas, *Summa Theologica*, II–II q 172, a 2.

The Contribution of African Spirituality to Global Pentecostalism

Africa contributes important human values, social integrity, and religious community to enhance the well-being of the international community. Pope John Paul II expressed this view on a pastoral visit to Malawi on May 6, 1989: "I urge you in Africa to look critically inside yourselves. Look at the traditional wisdom and values of your own African traditions. Look at the faith which you celebrate profoundly. Share the good spirituality in Africa with the global church and community."[46] *Ecclesia in Africa* mentions the role of the Holy Spirit in defining, inspiring, guiding, and transforming the activities of the African church and society (§6). The Special Assembly for Africa of the Synod of Bishops (1994) was a historic moment of ecclesial grace inspired by the Holy Spirit. The synod provides a framework for how charismatic Pentecostalism ought to be understood, guided, and experienced for the good of all Africans.

Traditional African cultures are characterized by many values that are similar to Christian values. There are traditional cultural values rooted in African spirituality that are righteous and can be inculturated in developing African theologies of Pentecostalism; such values can guide the church and her members in strengthening the foundations of charismatic belief, mission, and outreach to Africa's people in their search for health, wealth, and hope.

Over the course of Christian history, traditional African values and religion have ceased to have a monopoly over the continent; these elements of African tradition no longer exist in isolation from those present in other places. Jesus's message, as delivered by the apostle John, sets the agenda that determines the fate of all world religions: "And I, when I am lifted up from the earth, will draw all people to myself" (John 12:32). The phrase "all people to myself" is instructive. It provides a reason for discussing not only traditional African religion but also all world religions. It concerns the message of a global God who calls people into relationship with God and with one another through the Holy Spirit.[47]

The African socioreligious heritage provides Africans with the fundamental task of establishing a harmonious relationship between the unborn, the living, their ancestors, and the creator. In this spiritual universe, there is a deep connection and bond between the spirits of the living and the witness and communion with the supernatural world as a basis for harvesting those rich springs of life that lead to human and cosmic flourishing. African spirituality strives to achieve meaning, peace, liberation, progress, and communion in society, values that connect men and women to the supernatural world. Throughout its history, Africa has experienced the extremely dehumanizing experiences of slavery, colonialism, and cruel exploitation. Amid these circumstances, Africans have persevered because of their connectedness with the power of the supernatural spirit that gives them hope, even in the face of these challenges and the unjust global world order.

Patrick Mitchell writes that Pentecostal and charismatic values are spiritual-redemptive mechanisms for the liberation of oppressed and suffering people.[48] Africa is in need of a permanent agenda of freedom, liberation, and sustainable development, all of which are manifested in Pentecostal ecclesial structures and charismatic movements. Matthews Cooper argues that Jesus Christ founded the church through the Holy Spirit so as to liberate the poor and marginalized in body, mind, and spirit.[49] Jesus continually liberates and transforms the poor, the oppressed, and the suffering in Africa and similar contexts through charisms of healing, deliverance, exorcism, justice, peace, and the prophetic gospel. African spiritual experiences of both pain and goodness have created positive wisdom that can help people in Africa to make sense of the complexities of the divine–human opportunities that open up in present history. Anderson agrees that the most important contribution of African spirituality to global Pentecostalism is that it is an

---

46. Cited in Majawa, *Holy Spirit and Charismatic Renewal in Africa and Beyond*, 116.
47. Spencer, *Transformation of Religions in Global Contexts*, 10.
48. Mitchell, *Religious Institutions and Pentecostal Communities*, 99–101.
49. Cooper, *Christology of the Oppressed*, 114–15.

"enacted spirituality" enriched by the gifts of the Holy Spirit.[50] Pentecostal spirituality must not only be an African experience; it must also be applied to every aspect of religious and social life and must be seen as one of the values that can help enrich our common human experience in the search for those values that ennoble the human spirit and promote justice and the good of order.

Pentecostalism and African Humanness (*ubuntu*)

The socioreligious phenomenon of African spirituality may be understood through the lens of *ubuntu*. It is a spiritual value that I propose should be developed as a key to understanding African Pentecostalism as an African spiritual worldview which affirms that the Holy Spirit gives life and new dynamism to creation, and inspires believers to see the intimate connection of life in all things. Paul Oliver Zaphwanyika observes that "in Africa, to be is to be ubuntu."[51] *Ubuntu* or *umunthu* ("African humanness") is rooted in the book of Genesis 1:27: "God created man and woman in his image." God placed in men and women the dignity and sacredness of both divinity and humanity. *Umunthu* posits that both of these dimensions account for the origin, mission, vocation, and destiny of the human person. The *umunthu* or *ubuntu* paradigm begins with the human person immersed in the exigencies and dynamics of history. It is not a model that a priori implies the glory of the person, as is the case for the models of the African king, chief, village headman, diviner, healer, medicine man/woman, dream interpreter, counselor, or ancestor.[52] This African value is about the life of the world, the truth of which is revealed to human beings by the Spirit of God. Here we see a link between the wisdom to see clearly the footprints of God in creation—through the Holy Spirit—and the courage that the Holy Spirit gives to all believers in their prophetic witnessing in the world. These are values whose traces can be seen in African Pentecostalism beyond the aberrations and exaggerations that are noticeable in many Pentecostal sites in Africa. Charismatic Pentecostalism in Africa can be a veritable source for socio-moral-pastoral praxis for promoting personal renewal, deeper evangelization, and holistic transformation. The *ubuntu* philosophy-spirituality opens a new way of understanding the African relationship with the supernatural world. Pentecostalism has much to learn from this worldview.

Kgalushi Koka writes:

> ubuntu is not an "African" peculiarity. It is a universal concept that is characterized by an attribute of omnipresence. It is in, and embraces, all persons alike. It is an endowment from the "One" (Supreme Principle of Principles) to the human race. It transcends all human-made barriers. It permeates and transforms ethnicity, tribes, race, groupings, religious affiliations, cultural settings, political ideologies, human frailty, etc. It makes interpersonal communication, international mutuality, global communion and relations possible.[53]

Pentecostalism enriched by *ubuntu* values would present an opportunity for real, transformative progress for the person, the church, and the state.

Conclusion

The Ugandan scholar Gerald Maxwell Mpalanyi has observed that the Pentecostal reality is present in Africa to stay. Whereas the task of this chapter was to look at this phenomenon through an African lens, the proposal is that, at the cultural level, it is hard to make a distinction between Protestant forms of Pentecostalism and African Catholic charismatics. However, given the very structures and hierarchical nature of the Catholic Church, one notices that the Catholic charismatics are more

---

50. Anderson, "African Spirituality in African-Initiated Churches," 147.
51. Paul Oliver Zaphwanyika, *Ubuntu: An Ethic and Worldview for Africa* (Pietermaritzburg: Cluster Publications, 2009), 42.
52. Chigona, *Umunthu Theology,* 74; see also Magudumu, *Umunthu Anthropology and New Vision of Africa,* 41–44.
53. Koka, "African Renaissance in the Context of African Humanism," 6.

structured and, in many instances, controlled by local authorities. The perennial challenge between charism/gifts and authority continues to affect the way the Catholic charismatics have functioned in Africa along with the "healer priest" and "healing ministries" of priests, nuns, and laity in the Catholic Church. This is an area of critical importance to which African theologians should give more attention than it has received up to the present.

It must be pointed out, however, that Pentecostal charisms and charismatic gifts manifest differently in different contexts, and how these gifts are received varies from one church tradition and denomination to another. The Catholic groups in Africa maintain a more normative mediation of the gifts, while Africa's Pentecostal and evangelical groups show a greater flexibility and creativity in the use of the gifts and their application of "dominion theology" in translating the gifts to political and economic praxis.[54] The many instances of both ordinary and extraordinary charisms within Pentecostalism will never be fully submitted to the exhaustive scrutiny of the church. Bishops, priests, religious leaders, and the laity working with the renewal movements need ongoing training and personal renewal because of the complexity of the Pentecostal phenomenon. They are called upon to discern each charismatic manifestation in accordance with the church's demanding criteria for discernment.

Pentecostal and charismatic experiences need special attention in Africa. An ongoing and open conversation regarding the catechesis and spirituality of Pentecostalism in Africa and in global contexts is required. It is through this discernment process that the African church can gradually achieve its own brand of *ubuntu* Pentecostalism and define its own destiny as self-reliant, self-propagating, and self-governing—all for the greater glory of God, the transformation of creation, and the salvation of humanity.

Africa needs a new paradigm of inculturated Pentecostalism and charismatic catechesis and spirituality. Africa should embark on a collaborative new vision for education and evangelization through fostering the reception and proper use of the spiritual gifts[55] within the context of *ubuntu*, not only in the charismatic groups but everywhere in the universal church and international community. This new vision will play a major role in the establishment of an ongoing transformation of humanity toward holiness.[56]

Bibliography

Allen, John. L. *Ten Things Pope Benedict Wants You to Know*. London: Catholic Truth Society, 2007.

Anderson, Allan. "African Spirituality in African-Initiated Churches." In *Inculturation in the South African Context*, edited by Patrick Ryan et al. Nairobi: Paulines Publications Africa, 2000.

———. *An Introduction to Pentecostalism: Global Charismatic Christianity*. London: Cambridge University Press, 2004.

———. *Spreading Fires: The Missionary Nature of Early Pentecostalism*. Maryknoll, NY: Orbis Books, 2007.

Bamubamu, Thokozire B. "The Local Preachers Scrambling for the People of God: A Pastoral Challenge: A Pastoral-Catechetical Study in Blantyre Archdiocese." Limbe, Malawi: Pastoral Department, 1998.

Barrett, David. *Century of the Holy Spirit: 100 Years of Pentecostal and Charismatic Renewal, 1901–2001*. New York: Thomas Nelson, 2012.

Cantalamessa, Raniero. *Come, Creator Spirit*. Pretoria: Protea Book House, 2003.

Casanova, John. *Public Religion in the Modern World*. Chicago: University of Chicago Press, 1994.

Chigona, Gerald. *Umunthu Theology: Path of Integral Human Liberation Rooted in Jesus of Nazareth*. Balaka, Malawi: Montfort Media, 2002.

Chimbotoysa, Aluko G. *Seeking God in the Contexts of Material Exploitation and Spiritual Degradation*. New York: Patrick Publishers, 2005.

Congregation for the Doctrine of the Faith. *Catechism of the Catholic Church*. Vatican City: Libreria Editrice Vaticana, 1995.

Cooper, Matthews. *Christology of the Oppressed*. Kearney, NE: Morris, 2010.

---

54. Mpalanyi, *Scrutiny and Inclusion of the Pentecostal Spirituality in Africa*, 77–79.
55. For these *charismata*, see 1 Cor 12:4–11.
56. Lev 11:44–45; 19:2; 20:7, 26; 1 Pet 1:15–16.

Cordes, Paul. *Call to Holiness: Reflections on the Catholic Charismatic Renewal.* New Delhi: NCO Publications, 1996.

Dube, Kenneth O. *Evangelization of Central Africa.* London: Geoffrey Chapman, 1967.

Francis, Pope. *Gaudete et Exsultate* [Apostolic Exhortation on the Call to Holiness in Today's World; March 19, 2018]. Vatican City: Libreria Editrice Vaticana, 2018. www.vatican.va.

———. *Laudato Si'* [Encyclical On Care for Our Common Home; June 18, 2015]. Vatican City: Libreria Editrice Vaticana, 2015. www.vatican.va.

Howard, George D. *The Values on African Heritage and Religious Pluralism in Context.* London: Dorrace, 1998; 2nd ed., 2018.

International Catholic Charismatic Renewal Service. *Charismatic Renewal: A Grace, a Challenge, and a Mission.* Vatican City: ICCRS, 2000.

John, Cyril. *Spurred by the Spirit: The Catholic Charismatic Renewal in the Millennium.* New Delhi: NCO Publications, 2007.

John, Cyril, and Peter John Cameron. *The Gifts of the Holy Spirit according to St. Thomas Aquinas.* New Haven, CT: Knights of Columbus Press, 2002.

John XXIII, Pope. *Ad Petri Cathedram* [Encyclical on Truth, Unity and Peace, in a Spirit of Charity; June 29, 1959]. Vatican City: Libreria Editrice Vaticana, 1959. www.vatican.va.

John Paul II, Pope. "Address to the Bishops of Malawi." Archbishopric of Blantyre. May 5, 1989. www.vatican.va.

———. "Champion of the Charisms: Seminal Address to the Lay Movements and Ecclesial Communities at Pentecost." May 31,1998. http://www.ccr.org.uk/old/champion.htm.

———. *Ecclesia in Africa* [Post-synodal Apostolic Exhortation on the Church in Africa and Its Evangelizing Mission toward the Year 2000; September 14, 1995]. Vatican City: Libreria Editrice Vaticana, 1995. www.vatican.va.

———. *Fides et Ratio* [Encyclical on the Relationship between Faith and Reason; September 14, 1998]. Vatican City: Libreria Editrice Vaticana, 1998. www.vatican.va.

———. "Message to the Great Gathering of the Catholic Charismatic Family Organized by the Italian Association *Rinnovamento nello Spirito Santo* and Sponsored by the ICRRS." Rimini, April 28–May 1, 2000.

Jordan, Erick. *Theology and Mission of Vatican II.* London: Mill City Press, 1982.

Kalilombe, Patrick. "The Relevance of Contextual Theologies for Deeper Evangelization and Societal Transformation in Africa." Presentation at the Silver Jubilee celebration of the Catholic University of Eastern Africa's Faculty of Theology, Nairobi, 2009.

Koka, Kgalushi. "The African Renaissance in the Context of African Humanism." Paper presented at International Conference "Ubuntu: From Philosophy to Practice," organized by the Democracy Development Programme in association with the Centre for African Humanism. Durban, Republic of South Africa, August 1999.

Magudumu, Lawrence. *Umunthu Anthropology and New Vision of Africa.* Oxford: Intellect Books, 2009.

Mahumbulele, Baison Dick. *Transforming the Church in Africa through Charismatic Values.* Philadelphia: Westview, 2010.

Majawa, Clement. *The Holy Spirit and Charismatic Renewal in Africa and Beyond.* Nairobi: AIC Kijabe Printing Press, 2007.

Martin, Bernice. "Interpretations of Latin American Pentecostalism: 1960s to the Present." In *Pentecostal Power: Expressions, Impact, and Faith of Latin American Pentecostalism,* edited by Calvin L. Smith, 111–36. Leiden: Brill, 2011.

Mitchell, Patrick. *Religious Institutions and Pentecostal Communities.* Bangalore: Theological Publications, 2005.

Moltmann, Jürgen. *God for a Secular Society: The Public Relevance of Theology.* London: SCM Press, 1999.

———. *Theology Today: Two Contributions towards Making Theology Present.* London: SCM Press, 1988.

Mpalanyi, Gerald M. *Scrutiny and Inclusion of the Pentecostal Spirituality in Africa.* Bloomington: Indiana University Press, 2009.

Ng'enoh, P. Kemmoi. "Singer Betty Bayo Left Me but We Expect Things to Turn Round—Pastor Victor Kanyari." *The Nairobian,* October 6, 2015.

Njoroge, Kiarie. "Churches in Kenya Have Asked the Government to Regulate Deceitful Churches." *The Daily Nations Newspaper.* Nairobi: The Nations Media Group, 2012, 24.

Norris, Pippa, and Ronald Inglehart, eds. *Sacred and Secular Religion and Politics Worldwide*. Cambridge: Cambridge University Press, 2004.

Ogallo, Gladys. "Fake Evangelists Swindling in God's Name and Religion." *The Daily Nations Newspaper*. Nairobi: The Nations Media Group, 2012, 15.

O'Malley, John W. *A History of the Popes: From Peter to the Present*. New York: Sheed & Ward, 2011.

Paul VI, Pope. "Address to the Second International Leaders' Conference." Rome, May 19, 1975.

Pearson, Henry. *The Church of Christ and Charismatic Experiences*. Nairobi: Kijabe, 2011.

Pesare, Oreste, et al. *"Then Peter Stood Up . . . .": Collections of the Popes' Addresses to the CCR from Its Origin to the Year 2000*. Vatican City: ICCRS Publications, 2000.

Pfeiffer, Marcel. *Pentecostal Conversations for the Changing Societal Dynamics*. Birmingham: Westview, 2002.

Rausch, Thomas. *Catholics and Evangelicals: Do They Share a Common Future?* Mahwah, NJ: Paulist Press, 2000.

"Report of the 5th Phase of the International Dialogue between Some Classical Pentecostal Churches and the Catholic Church (1998–2006)." PCPCU Information Service 129 (2008/III).

Robeck, Cecil M. *The Azusa Street Mission and Revival: The Birth of the Global Pentecostal Movement*. Nashville, TN: Thomas Nelson, 2018.

———. "The Holy Spirit and the Unity of the Church: The Challenge of Pentecostal, Charismatic and Independent Movements." In *The Holy Spirit, the Church, and Christian Unity: Proceedings of the Consultation Held at the Monastery of Bose, Italy (14–20 October 2002)*, edited by Doris Donnelly et al., 353–81. Leuven: Leuven University Press, 2005.

Smart, Barry. *Facing Modernity: Ambivalence, Reflexivity, and Morality*. London: Sage, 1999.

Spencer, Duncan. *Transformation of Religions in Global Contexts*. The Hague: Mouton, 1998.

Suenens, Cardinal Leon-Joseph. "Pneumatic Gifts in the Church." *CHARISINDIA: A Magazine for Renewal and Spiritual Growth* [New Delhi: Tagore Garden] (September–October 1996).

Tracy, David. *The Analogical Imagination: Christian Theology and the Culture of Pluralism*. London: SCM Press, 1981.

Vatican II. *Lumen Gentium* [Dogmatic Constitution on the Church; 1995].

———. *Apostolicam Actuositatem* [Decree on the Apostolate of Lay People; 1995].

Walters, Kerry. *John XXIII: A Short Biography*. Cincinnati, OH: Franciscan Media, 2013.

Zakahlana, Jameson. *African Churches and the Phenomenon of Pentecostal and Charismatic Experiences*. Nairobi: Heinemann, 2010.

Zaphwanyika, Paul Oliver. *Ubuntu: An Ethic and Worldview for Africa*. Pietermaritzburg: Cluster Publications, 2009, 42.

Zithatha, Maxwell G. *Challenges of Christian Faith in Africa in the Times of Globalization*. New York: Harper & Row, 2008.

Suggested Reading

Anderson, Allan. *An Introduction to Pentecostalism: Global Charismatic Christianity*. Cambridge: Cambridge University Press, 2004.

Asamoah-Gyadu, J. Kwabena. *Contemporary Pentecostal Christianity: Interpretations from an African Context*. Eugene, OR: Wipf & Stock, 2013.

Cox, Harvey. *Fire from Heaven: The Rise of Pentecostal Spirituality and the Reshaping of Religion in the Twenty-First Century*. London: Cassell, 1996.

John, Cyril. *Spurred by the Spirit: The Catholic Charismatic Renewal in the New Millennium*. New Delhi: NCO Publications, 2007.

John Paul II, Pope. *Dominum et Vivificantem* [Encyclical on the Holy Spirit in the Life of the Church and the World; May 18, 1986]: Vatican City: Libreria Editrice Vaticana, 1986. www.vatican.va.

Majawa, Clement. *The Holy Spirit and Charismatic Renewal in Africa and Beyond*. Nairobi: AIC Kijabe Printing Press, 2007.

Vähäkangas, Mika, and Kyomo Andrew, eds. *Charismatic Renewal in Africa: A Challenge for African Christianity*. Nairobi: Acton, 2003.

Yong, Amos. *Discerning the Spirits: A Pentecostal/Charismatic Contribution to Christian Theology of Religions*. Sheffield: Sheffield Academic Press, 2000.

Key Words

charismatics
conversation
divisions
evangelization
Pentecostalism
religious crossroads
renewal
transformation

Catholicism with a Difference: Popular Catholicism in Kenya

Philomena Njeri Mwaura and Beatrice Wairimu Churu

Since the 1960s, Kenya has witnessed the phenomenal growth of the Catholic Church, whose numbers now stand at 33 percent of the total Christian population, with 26 dioceses and 925 parishes. There are currently 38 bishops,[1] 2,744 priests, 6,303 religious (798 male and 5,505 female), 11,343 catechists, and 5,501 seminarians.[2] The Catholic News Agency for Africa has noted that the church has 12,195 Catholic education centers from the preschool to the university level. The church has contributed immensely to the country's health care and social support systems through its 513 hospitals and clinics; 21 "leper colonies"; 117 homes for the elderly, sick, or people with disabilities; 1,713 orphanages and nurseries; and 110 family advisory centers.[3]

Gone are the days when there were very few vocations of Africans to the priesthood and religious life; in those times, the church was overwhelmingly led by white missionaries with little or no inculturation of the faith and very little lay participation. The liturgical reforms of the Second Vatican Council,[4] among other later reforms, resulted in a pastoral revolution in terms of popular participation. It can now be said that Kenya is a major location of growth and vitality in the Catholic Church. Kenyan Catholics have strongly embraced the church. Numerous lay Catholic associations have taken root in Kenya, which, though generally responsive to the calls of the episcopate and the clergy, are largely self-driven and self-governed. The leadership of these associations operates with the approval of the teaching hierarchy, but the tasks they engage in and how they engage in them are largely up to the lay membership. Regardless of whether their founders were lay or clergy, many of these groups, such as the Catholic Women's Association, Catholic Men's Association, Marriage Encounter, and the Christian Life Community (among many others), have become the particular way in which the Catholic laity live their membership in the church. They have acquired a life of their own as support groups for their members and channels for spiritual growth. Nevertheless, despite this dynamism, social problems continue to pose challenges to the church's identity and mission as a sacrament of God's peaceable kingdom. These problems include violence in all its manifestations, which has become a permanent feature of social life; debilitating disease; social, economic, and political injustice; and a lack of food security leading to hunger, environmental degradation, gender injustice, and poor management of national affairs and resources.

It is true that many of these issues are not the charge solely of the church, and in fact the instrument most responsible for progress on these frontiers is the government. Yet the concerns of the

---

1. Two bishops, the Rt. Rev. Bishop Cornelius Korir of the Eldoret diocese and the Rt. Rev. Bishop Emanuel Barbara of Malindi, died in recent years (2017 and 2018, respectively).
2. Onyalla, "Vatican Publishes Church Statistics of Kenya, Uganda, and CAR ahead of Pope's Visit."
3. Onyalla, "Vatican Publishes Church Statistics of Kenya, Uganda, and CAR ahead of Pope's Visit."
4. Hastings, *African Catholicism*, 129.

people in any given context are the same as those of the church, and therefore the church is engaged in ameliorating and eradicating at its roots the suffering that results from these problems. Catholic social teaching recognizes that the laity have a strong role to play in this work. In his apostolic exhortation *Christifideles Laici* (The Vocation and Mission of the Lay Faithful), Pope St. John Paul II noted that the social, economic, political, and cultural circumstances of the contemporary world urgently call for the work of the lay faithful. Their vocation is to be "labourers in the Lord's vineyard," the "salt of the earth," and the "light of the world" (§14). In the conciliar and postconciliar documents of the Second Vatican Council, the council fathers clearly stated that the Christian mission is a divinely ordained and fundamental obligation of the entire church. Every Christian is a member of the "Family of God" regardless of gender, age, or status and is therefore called to be an apostle.

Christifideles Laici states further that, by virtue of their baptism and confirmation, the laity are called to participate in evangelization and to radiate belief (§14). During the Fourteenth Plenary Session of the Association of Member Episcopal Conferences of Eastern Africa (AMECEA), Archbishop Robert Sarah, the secretary of the Congregation for the Evangelization of Peoples, emphasized the need for the laity to be given priority by the local church. He acknowledged that in Africa, where there are few clergy for the number of the faithful, it is the leaders of the lay faithful who are the true force of evangelization. He reiterated the need to equip them for their varied roles in the affairs of the world.[5] In the apostolic exhortation *Gaudete et Exsultate* (On the Call to Holiness in Today's World), Pope Francis underscores the fact that the call to discipleship and holiness is for the entire Christian community. Those more educated in the faith should not consider themselves to be more important than their less-educated brothers and sisters. The call to holiness is received by all and can be lived heroically even by the laity (§10).

From these statements, it is clear that the days when the lay faithful are looked upon as backbenchers and spectators in the life of the church are long gone. A variety of lay associations sanctioned by the church have played crucial roles in training Christian leaders for integral evangelization in the apostolate of the laity. In addition to the groups mentioned above, these include Catholic Action, Young Christian Students, The Grail, Focolare, the Association of St. Monica, the Association of St. Anne, the Lay Carmelites, the Legion of Mary, and the Catholic Charismatic Renewal. Popular devotions to the saints, the Blessed Virgin Mary, the Sacred Heart of Jesus, and the Immaculate Heart of Mary, among others, have also intensified since the year 2000, especially in the Archdiocese of Nairobi. In these groups, some focusing on personal piety, Christians grow and mature at the spiritual, intellectual, and emotional levels of the faith—Christians encounter Christ.

There are, however, other popular religious expressions and mobilizations within Kenyan Catholicism with strong lay and sometimes clerical participation that we call "popular Catholicism." These are not outside the purview of the official church, but neither are they like the more traditional Catholic movements that have been in existence for decades. These new movements were founded in the late 1980s and are often local, sometimes present in only a single diocese. They seek to respond to a need among the laity for a more radical spirituality, especially as expressed in rigorous prayer, healing, and deliverance. Because they are without a long tradition, they develop quickly as they grow. This "popular Catholicism," while remaining inside the wider tent of the Catholic Church, responds to specific spiritual needs.

This chapter explores some of these new popular Catholic groups in the Archdiocese of Nairobi. It examines their origins, characteristics, concerns, and how they have contributed to the reshaping of Catholicism in that diocese and in Kenyan Catholicism in general. It begins by conceptualizing the meaning of the terms "popular Catholicism," "popular piety," and "popular religion" in order to examine how appropriate these terms are in describing and contextualizing the phenomenon under consideration. The article will then provide a brief review of the literature on the Catholic Charismatic Renewal and articulate the theoretical framework for understanding two case studies that fall under

---

5. AMECEA 14th Plenary, 239.

the aegis of that movement. The chapter will then reflect on the case studies and draw conclusions.

Conceptualizing Popular Catholicism

In an article entitled "Varieties of Popular Catholicism: A Parish Study," Anna Peterson describes the complexities involved in defining popular Catholicism but arrives at the following definition: the "religiosity of the laity, distinguished from 'official' or 'institutional' Catholicism."[6] Peterson adds that this distinction implies that popular religiosity emerges from and remains largely determined by the people outside the authority structures of the church.[7] She also cites the definition of Jesus Delgado that popular Catholicism/popular religiosity is "the devotion inculcated by the clergy which later the people take on and cultivate as their own."[8] Another view is that of the *Encyclopedia of Christianity*, which avers that, "in the Catholic Church, the popular religion of ordinary believers concerns the practice of rites and customs in the life cycle and festivals in the church year. Popular Catholicism seems to be synonymous with religious folklore and antiquated traditions with a kind of . . . superstition."[9] A more general (and generous) view may be adopted that popular Catholicism is simply the faith of the average Catholic. In the forefront of his or her mind are not doctrinal or intellectual forms but religious life and practice. The faith of "everyday piety takes a simple form. It is not based on the complex structures of theologies or persons of the clergy."[10] In this reading, popular Catholicism is identical with the piety or spirituality of ordinary people. It is spontaneous, oral, and emotional. The *Encyclopedia of Christianity* further observes that the manifestations of popular piety include, but are not limited to, priestly participation, forms of worship, sacraments, fraternities, observance of various church festivals, pilgrimages to shrines, veneration of the saints, Mariology, prayers, and benedictions. There are also inward dimensions of the faith for ordinary people like ethics, dogma, beliefs about sexuality, beliefs about demons, and fears about end times.[11]

The Catholic Church considers popular piety to be a treasure of the people of God. The council fathers asked that popular Catholic devotions be drawn up in such a way that "they harmonize with the liturgical seasons, accord with sacred liturgy, are in some fashion derived from it and lead the people to it, since in fact, the liturgy by its very nature far surpasses any of them."[12] The *Directory of Popular Piety and the Liturgy: Principles and Guidelines* defines popular piety as "those diverse cultic expressions of a private or of a community nature which, in the context of the Christian faith are inspired predominantly not by a sacred liturgy but by forms deriving from a particular nation or people or from the culture" (§9). The document views popular piety as a "treasure of the people of God, manifesting a thirst for God known only to the poor and to the humble and rendering them capable of generosity and sacrifice to the point of heroism in testifying to the faith while displaying an acute sense of the profound attributes of God" (§9). The document further calls for the need to appreciate the many riches of popular piety and the commitment to Christian life that it inspires (§12). Popular piety has also been a means of preserving the faith in situations in which Christians have been deprived of pastoral care. In his apostolic exhortation *Evangelii Nuntiandi*, Pope Paul VI expounds on the power of popular piety as follows: "Popular piety manifests a thirst for God which only the poor and the simple know. It also makes people capable of generosity and sacrifice" (§48). According to the *Aparecida Document*, examples of popular piety

---

6. Peterson, "Varieties of Popular Catholicism," 399.
7. Peterson, "Varieties of Popular Catholicism," 399.
8. Peterson, "Varieties of Popular Catholicism," 399.
9. *Encyclopedia of Christianity*, vol. 4, 282.
10. *Encyclopedia of Christianity*, vol. 4, 282.
11. *Encyclopedia of Christianity*, vol. 4, 282.
12. It is important to note that in the Middle Ages, the public functions of the church and the popular devotions or piety of the people were intimately connected. This waned over time, pushing popular devotions to the periphery of the liturgy.

in the Latin American context include "patronal saint celebrations, novenas, rosaries, the Way of the Cross, processions, dances and songs of religious folklore, affection for the saints and angels, solemn promises and family prayer."[13]

Speaking about Latin America, Pope Benedict XVI pointed out that popular piety is a precious treasure of the Catholic Church in which we see the soul of the Latin American people. In his post-synodal apostolic exhortation *Evangelii Gaudium*, Pope Francis links popular piety to inculturation of the gospel, saying that it "enables us to see how the faith once received becomes embodied in a culture and is constantly passed on" (§112). The pope further says that "expressions of popular piety have much to teach us; for those who are capable of reading them, they are a 'locus theologicus' which demands our attention especially at a time when we are looking to the New Evangelisation" (§126). Regarding the new evangelization, Pope Francis says that it is the responsibility of everyone, lay and clergy. In addition, in his apostolic exhortation *Evangelii Gaudium*, the pope calls the whole Christian community to a life of holiness and says that the "Church must be a place of mercy freely given where everyone should feel welcome, loved, forgiven, encouraged to live the good life of the Gospel" (§§113, 114).

From the above definitions of popular piety and explanations of what it entails, we can conclude that it is the spirituality of the people of God as they live their faith in their own particular social-cultural context. Their spirituality can be lived and expressed individually in personal prayer and devotions, and it can also be lived and expressed communally in lay associations. This spirituality must be in accord with Catholic doctrine, and therefore the clergy have a role in guiding it.

Historically, "popular religion" has been distinguished from "popular piety." *The Directory of Popular Piety and the Liturgy* views popular religion as a universal experience. It states that there is "always a religious dimension in the hearts of people, nations and their collective expressions. All people tend to give expression to their totalizing view of the transcendent, their concept of nature, society, and history through cultic means" (§10). This is of course not limited to Christianity and is therefore different from popular piety, which in its common usage is particularly connected to Christianity.

There is no single definition of the term "popular religion." Some scholars have regarded it as a rural phenomenon in contrast to urban forms of religion—that is, the religion of the peasants as opposed to that of the dominant ruling classes. Others see it as a religion of the masses as opposed to that of the intellectual or sophisticated classes.[14] Popular religion can also mean the religion of ethnic or minority groups located in a context dominated by one major religion.[15]

According to Ronald Kassimir, as an analytical construct, popular religion has three basic variants: "(a) popular religion as belonging to a particular social group, or a dominated class, (b) popular religion as a deviation from a canonical set of beliefs, symbols, and practices and (c) popular religion as a rejection of the authority of designated religious specialists and the institution they represent."[16]

The first variant reflects the situation in Latin American Catholicism and is useful for suggesting an elective affinity between certain individuals and classes within the structure of religious power and practice. The second two are usually construed by the church as mutually reinforcing. "Evidence of this assertion can be found in the institution's own practice of tolerance of 'misrepresentations' of doctrine which in some cases are either accommodated or dealt with through catechism and pedagogy but others are suppressed when those beliefs take autonomous organizational form, or deny clerical authority."[17] Kassimir's variants, however, do not explain the groups that are the focus of this article.

---

13. *Aparecida Document*, 258. The *Aparecida Document* is the proceedings from the Episcopal Conference of the Catholic Church in Latin America that was held in Aparecida, Brazil, in 2007.
14. *Encyclopaedia of Christianity*, vol. 4, 283.
15. See Swatos, "Popular Religion," in *Encyclopaedia of Religion and Society*.
16. Kassimir, "Politics of Popular Catholicism in Uganda," 255.
17. Kassimir, "Politics of Popular Catholicism in Uganda," 255–56.

We agree with Kassimir that the problem raised by the above three variants can be dealt with by creating a fourth variant of popular religion.[18] This fourth category can be called "official popular Catholicism." This is because many of the aspects that are called "popular," for example, Marian devotion, are openly encouraged by church leadership. The idea of "official popular" religion is akin to what is often called "folk Catholicism" in Latin America.[19] In this chapter, "popular Catholicism" will be used in this sense of "official popular" since the popular Catholic groups discussed here are not antagonistic to but in fact operate within the framework of the Catholic Church in Kenya. The term "popular Catholicism" will also be used with reference to popular piety, for as seen in the first part of this section, the Catholic Church perceives popular piety as a spirituality that is experienced individually and in groups, communities, and associations under the umbrella of the Catholic Church.

Literature Review and Theoretical Framework

This study concerns Catholic charismatic Christianity. In this section, a brief literature review of the Catholic Charismatic Renewal will be presented and a theoretical framework will be discussed.

Literature Review

The Catholic Charismatic Renewal is regarded by scholars as part of the global Pentecostal renewal movement that originated in the late nineteenth and early twentieth centuries in the United States, Europe, the United Kingdom, and Asia. The story began in 1901 when Agnes Ozman, a student in Charles Parham's Bible school in Topeka, Kansas, received the power of the Holy Spirit upon being prayed over, and then spoke in tongues.[20] Many others received the gifts of the Holy Spirit shortly thereafter, including during an event in April 1906 in a Los Angeles church led by the African American Pentecostal preacher William J. Seymour. The phenomenon subsequently spread throughout the world.[21]

Pentecostalism has become a strong force in Christianity all over the world and especially in Africa. According to Kwabena Asamoah-Gyadu, "Africa has become a hot-bed of Pentecostal/charismatic Christianity."[22] In Africa, this form of Christianity began with the emergence of the African Instituted Churches (AICs) at the beginning of the twentieth century. Commenting on the rise of the AICs and their contribution to the church in Africa, John Taylor remarked, "In Africa today it seems the incalculable Spirit has chosen to use the Independent Church Movement for another spectacular advance. This does not prove that their teaching is necessarily true, but it shows they have the raw materials of which a missionary church is made—spontaneity, total commitment, and the primitive responses that arise from the depths of life."[23] Taylor connects the emergence of the AICs to the agency of the Holy Spirit. Asamoah-Gyadu has also observed that the AICs' "religious and theological emphases on practical salvation, charismatic renewal, innovative gender ideology, and oral and interventionist theologies have found new lease on life among contemporary Pentecostals on the continent. Their emergence led to the renewal of Christianity in Africa and inspired the process of 'Pentecostalization' currently underway in contemporary African Christianity."[24]

Philomena Mwaura argues that, when the Pentecostalist Nigerian missionaries evangelized Kenya in the 1990s and early 2000s, they found a context that had already been exposed to Pentecostal Christianity and the experiences it engenders.[25] The African context had in the first quarter of the twentieth century experienced an outpouring of

---

18. Kassimir, "Politics of Popular Catholicism in Uganda," 256.
19. Kassimir, "Politics of Popular Catholicism in Uganda," 256.
20. O'Connor, *Pentecostal Movement in the Catholic Church*, 15.
21. O'Connor, *Pentecostal Movement in the Catholic Church*, 15.
22. Asamoah-Gyadu, *Contemporary Pentecostal Christianity*, 9.
23. Taylor, *Go-Between God*, 54.
24. Asamoa-Gyadu, *Contemporary Pentecostal Christianity*, 9.
25. Mwaura, "Nigerian Pentecostal Missionary Enterprise in Kenya," 273.

the Holy Spirit that resulted in the formation of the AICs.[26] Other groups had reinforced the growing revival in the mid-twentieth century, including evangelical and Pentecostalist preachers from the US who preached in Nairobi, Mombasa, and Kisumu in the 1950s, '60s, and '70s.

The East African Revival Movement that evolved within missionary churches involved another trajectory that created a context open to the Pentecostal and charismatic revival. Mark Winters defines this movement as "a revival in which nominal or 'backslidden' Christians are 'revived' in their commitment to the faith; it is not primarily a movement of charismatization affecting non-Christians."[27] The movement was interdenominational, interracial, and interethnic. It was a response to the perceived lethargy of missionary Christianity and its having been compromised by worldliness. It emphasized the experience of personal salvation through the blood of Jesus, personal holiness, asceticism, confession of sins, hard work, and reliability. It involved weekly—and, for larger groups, monthly and yearly—fellowship meetings. The fellowship meetings included Bible readings, expositions of Bible passages, personal testimonies, confession of sins, and offers of repentance and response by those to be saved. The Balokole Movement, which evolved from within the East Africa Revival Movement, empowered the laity, literate and illiterate, to testify for Jesus. Patterns of ministry evolved that were different from those of mainline churches.

Yvan Droz adds that the songs sung as part of the revival drew on traditional African tunes that appealed to the sensibilities of African converts, unlike the staid foreign music in the mission churches.[28] The revival also involved the laity in the leadership of fellowship groups, thus empowering them. In a seminal article, Ogbu Kalu argues that gospel music (which has now taken over secular music in Africa) strongly contributed to the appeal of the Pentecostal and charismatic revival.[29] This was true also for the Catholic Charismatic Renewal in Kenya—as we shall see later, music and singing are central to the activities and meetings of the Vincentian Prayer Houses and the Patrick and Rosalia Family Prayer Group.

According to scholars of Pentecostalism, the Catholic Charismatic Renewal emerged during the second wave of Pentecostalism in the mid-1960s, which occurred chiefly in the mainline churches. Specifically, it is traced to a weekend retreat in mid-February 1967 involving a group of twenty people on the staff and faculty of Duquesne University in Pittsburgh in the US. They met for a Bible study,[30] and, according to Edward O'Connor, they experienced a profound religious transformation and "were brought into real personal contact with the living Christ."[31] The event was marked by charismatic manifestations similar to those that occurred on the day of Pentecost. Many of them received the gift of tongues and others received other gifts, including prophecy, discernment of spirits, and the power of exorcism. Within a month, the Charismatic Renewal had spread to many Catholic institutions in the US[32] and, by the early 1970s, had spread to countries in Africa, including Kenya, Uganda, Cameroon, Nigeria, Ghana, the Ivory Coast, and South Africa, and to other places in the world.

According to Matteo Calisi, there were antecedents to the Catholic Charismatic Renewal. He traces the movement to Pope St. John XXIII, who, at the opening of the Second Vatican Council, prayed, "Divine Spirit, renew your wonders in our time as in a new Pentecost."[33] Further, Calisi argues that the Second Vatican Council opened the way for the acceptance of a Catholic Pentecostalism by

---

26. Mwaura, "Nigerian Pentecostal Missionary Enterprise in Kenya," 271–72.
27. Winters, "Balokole and the Protestant Ethic," 69.
28. See Droz, "Local Roots of the Kenyan Pentecostal Revival," 23–44.
29. Kalu, "Holy Praiseco," 87–88.
30. Synan, *Twentieth Century Pentecostal Explosion*, 20. See also O'Connor, *Pentecostal Movement in the Catholic Church*.
31. O'Connor, *Pentecostal Movement in the Catholic Church*, 16.
32. O'Connor, *Pentecostal Movement in the Catholic Church*, 16.
33. Quoted in Calisi, "Future of the Catholic Charismatic Renewal," 69.

recognizing the relevance of charismatic gifts to the church.[34] One of the initiatives that led to the Catholic Church's acceptance of the Charismatic Renewal was Pope Paul VI's audience with its leaders in Rome in 1973. Leo Joseph Cardinal Suenens of Belgium was asked to head a theological and pastoral commission to study the evolution of the Charismatic Renewal in the Catholic Church and to explore its theological, pastoral, and social implications for the church.[35] The Charismatic Renewal has been supported by subsequent popes, and, at the invitation of Pope Francis, members celebrated the golden jubilee of the movement in Rome from May 31 to June 4, 2017. Pope Francis described the movement as embodying the preaching of the gospel and the joy of the Holy Spirit.

In his seminal work *Catholic Pentecostalism and the Paradoxes of Africanization*,[36] Ludovic Lado decries the absence of research on the Catholic Charismatic Renewal in Africa in contrast to the many studies of Pentecostalism in Africa. His book was on the ethnography of Ephphatha, a charismatic healing ministry begun by the Jesuit priest Meinrad Hebga in Cameroon in 1987. Hebga had been introduced to the Catholic Charismatic Renewal on a visit to the United States in 1975 and had received baptism in the Holy Spirit.[37] Gerrie ter Haar conducted a study on the healing ministry of Archbishop Emmanuel Milingo, who in 1973 had an experience of being filled by the Holy Spirit and founded a charismatic prayer group, the Divine Providence Community.[38] He later established links with charismatic groups in the West.[39] Katharina Wilkens studied the Marian Faith Healing Ministry in Tanzania and concluded that the movement appeals to Tanzanians because it incorporates traditional healing elements into the Catholic liturgy of exorcism.[40] These three movements are similar in that they include a therapeutic component that addresses elements of the African worldview like witchcraft and haunting by ancestral spirits. These are the only three in-depth studies of the Catholic Charismatic Renewal movement in Africa, meaning that there is ample room for additional work.

As for Kenya, there are no available statistics on the membership of the Charismatic Renewal, but it is generally acknowledged that there are over four hundred thousand members of the movement with over one thousand prayer groups. According to David Karanja, on February 20, 2009, the archbishop of Nairobi, John Cardinal Njue, suspended the movement fearing that some of its activities, including holding all-night vigils, were a threat to the family and that the types of singing and prayer methods they engaged in were not Catholic.[41] Karanja further observes that, in 2004, Pope John Paul II sent Fr. Raniero, a Capuchin priest, to help strengthen the Charismatic Renewal movement in Kenya. Fr. Raniero presided over a crusade attended by the then-archbishop of Nairobi, Raphael Ndingi Mwana N'zeki, who was also the patron of the movement.[42]

In a 2010 work, Daniel Kasomo explored why the Catholic Charismatic Renewal has been growing at such a tremendous rate, and he concluded that the causative factors are sociological, including

---

34. Calisi, "Future of the Catholic Charismatic Renewal," 70.
35. Calisi, "Future of the Catholic Charismatic Renewal," 74.
36. Lado, *Catholic Pentecostalism and the Paradoxes of Africanisation*, 23.
37. Lado, *Catholic Pentecostalism and the Paradoxes of Africanisation*, 21–23.
38. Gerrie ter Haar, *Spirit of Africa: The Healing Ministry of Archbishop Milingo* (Trenton, NJ: Africa World Press, 1992).
39. Lado, *Catholic Pentecostalism and the Paradoxes of Africanisation*, 19.
40. Wilkens, *Holy Water and Evil Spirits*.
41. Karanja, "Kenya Prelate Lifts Suspension of Charismatics." Karanja notes that on July 31, 2009, the cardinal lifted the ban and that the movement is alive in many parishes despite the fact that some bishops are still wary of it and its activities. Karanja reports further that Fr. John Muindi, the chaplain of the Nairobi Catholic Charismatic Renewal, stated that any person interested in joining the movement should participate in a week-long seminar that features a Bible study. Members of the movement are trained in guidance and counseling and how to worship and run prayer groups. During their training, they are reminded of their commitment to their baptism and to the sacraments, and about the purpose and importance of prayer.
42. Karanja, "Kenya Prelate Lifts Suspension of Charismatics."

widespread stress, isolation, poverty, and marginalization experienced by many. He sees the movement's Pentecostal and charismatic ethos as being attractive to people because it involves the "democratization" of charismatic gifts and the absence of hierarchical leadership.[43] But he discusses the dangers posed by the movement without showing its positive impact on the Catholic Church or elaborating on its beliefs and practices, and he also fails to acknowledge the revivals within mission churches at the beginning of the twentieth century in Kenya and especially in the Quaker mission in 1927, or the rise of the AICs and the East African Revival Movement. Nevertheless, despite its faults, overall his study is a fair attempt at exploring the Catholic Charismatic Renewal movement.

Theoretical Framework

While there is very little literature explaining the rise of the Catholic Charismatic Renewal, there is a huge body of literature concerning the rise of Pentecostal and charismatic movements in general. Allan Anderson, a prominent scholar of Pentecostalism in Africa, argues that, in discussing the factors behind the growth of Pentecostalism and charismatic Christianity in Africa, one must distinguish between "causal factors" related to the founding of a church or movement and "reasons for [its] growth."[44] He observes that the rise of Pentecostalist and charismatic movements should be seen within the social, political, cultural, and economic contexts of nineteenth- and twentieth-century Africa. In this period Africa, and Kenya in particular, was subjected to colonialism and Western missionary Christianity, which involved racism, forced labor, land alienation, violations of human rights, paternalism in both church and society, and poor education aimed at strengthening the bonds of servitude, among other evils.

By the mid-1960s when the Catholic Charismatic Renewal emerged, most African countries, with the exceptions of South Africa, Namibia, and the lusophone countries had attained political independence, and the appearance and growth of the movement may not be directly linked to the colonial experience. But, as Kasomo highlights, the socioeconomic and political context was important for the rise of the renewal, a context that was characterized by social anomie, poverty, illness, political intolerance, social inequality, crime and unemployment, experiences of alienation, and the absence of loving communities. Kasomo observed that the Charismatic Renewal "seems to restore control of the individual over important aspects of life through the various gifts of the Spirit."[45]

The Charismatic Renewal's emphasis on the experience of the Holy Spirit and the gifts of healing, discernment of spirits, and prophecy resonate with both a biblical and an African worldview. The growth of the Charismatic Renewal should therefore be seen as the result of the proclamation of a relevant message, the empowerment of Christians, and the fact that it gave them a place to feel at home in their Catholic faith. Anecdotal evidence suggests that the Charismatic Renewal and other similar groups of popular Catholicism have stemmed the tide of Catholics leaving the church in search of a meaningful and fulfilling spirituality.[46]

This chapter will utilize Ogbu Kalu's conceptual framework, which traces the rise and proliferation of Pentecostal and charismatic Christianity in Africa through three explanatory models: the cultural-historical, the providential, and the functionalist/instrumentalist. With respect to the cultural-historical model, Kalu argues that Pentecostal and charismatic Christianity enjoyed rapid growth because of "its cultural fit into indigenous worldviews and its response to the questions that are raised within the interior of the worldviews."[47] He makes the point that Pentecostalism and charismatic Christianity took seriously certain African beliefs concerning evil, haunting by ancestral spirits, evil eye, bad omens, and witchcraft. Missionary Christianity saw these beliefs as mere superstitions that would fade away as Africans became more "civilized."

---

43. Kasomo, "Assessment of the Catholic Charismatic Renewal."
44. Anderson, "Stretching Out Hands to God," 54.
45. Kasomo, "Assessment of the Catholic Charismatic Renewal," 175.
46. Kasomo, "Assessment of the Catholic Charismatic Renewal," 175.
47. Kalu, "Holy Praiseco," 92–93.

Kalu's providential model incorporated the notion that the rise of Pentecostal and charismatic Christianity is the work of God through the Holy Spirit,[48] and he acknowledged the appeal for Africans of the gifts of the Holy Spirit. The functionalist/instrumentalist model emphasizes the rise of dictatorships and the increase in poverty on the continent from the 1960s to the 1990s. During that time, poverty was exacerbated by the Structural Adjustment Programs imposed on Third World economies by the World Bank and the International Monetary Fund. These programs resulted in African governments withdrawing subsidies from the public sector, which resulted in worsening poverty, poor health, food insecurity, and wars and conflicts.[49] Networks of international Pentecostal and charismatic groups like Christ for All Nations, led by Reinhardt Bonnke from South Africa, and charismatic preachers like Sr. Brigit from Ireland and Fr. Bill of the Vincentian Congregation of India appeared during this period. These networks and preachers and the worship and healing crusades of the Charismatic Renewal appealed widely to Kenyan Christians, both Catholic and Protestant. As has been alluded to, the Catholic Church in Kenya was wary of what it viewed as the unorthodox practices and teachings of the renewal, but these fears have largely been allayed. The Charismatic Renewal appeals to Catholics in all walks of life, both lay and religious, unlike the broader Pentecostal movement, which is said to appeal mostly to upwardly mobile youth and women.[50]

The contribution of these movements to the piety of the lay faithful is not only considerable but also laudable, as seen in the consolation and hope they kindle among the faithful. Reginauld Alva has documented many of the good fruits of the Catholic Charismatic Renewal,[51] one of these being the diversification of options for communal prayer; all of these fruits were the result of the Vatican Council's renewal of the church.[52]

The ministries of the Charismatic Renewal have been a blessing to many lay Christians and even to many clergy, and religious and have helped African people connect with their indigenous spirituality. The presence and action of the spirit manifested in them have been experienced as being strong and accessible, providing the power to overcome challenges and endure great difficulties. They should be seen as a means by which a vulnerable and suffering people can celebrate the presence and action of God in their lives. Accordingly, following the church's affirmation of these ministries as described by Stan Chu Ilo,[53] they have become an important part of the church's mission of healing and reconciliation in Africa today. The prayers and ministries of the Charismatic Renewal call forth the spiritual and social resourcefulness of the African continent in order to chart new ways of encountering God and creating communities of faith.

The First Special Assembly for Africa of the Synod of Bishops (1994) described the church as the "Family of God in Africa." Just as parents do for families, the African church must do everything it can to steer the faithful in fruitful directions. Ignoring the needs of some members of a family can lead to grave consequences. To disempower through ignorance the gifts of some family members can lead to their unhappiness and even to their harm. It is for this reason that the church's openness to new expressions of popular Catholicism is to be appreciated and encouraged.

Research Location and Research Methodology

Fieldwork for this article was carried out in the Archdiocese of Nairobi and specifically in parts of Kiambu and Nairobi counties between October 2016 and February 2017. We have also drawn on fieldwork data collected by Prof. Mwaura, one of the authors, in March 2014. The study is focused on

---

48. Kalu, "Holy Praiseco," 92–93.
49. Kalu, "Holy Praiseco," 92–93.
50. Anderson, "Stretching Out Hands to God," 71.
51. Alva, "Catholic Charismatic Renewal Movement and Secularization," 124–39.
52. Orobator, "'After All, Africa Is Largely a Nonliterate Continent.'"
53. Ilo, "*Africae Munus* and the Challenges of a Transformative Missional Theological Praxis in Africa's Social Context," 116–31.

two groups. The first, Vincentian Ministries Kenya (VMK), has been approved by the Catholic hierarchy in Kenya and so may be described as "official popular." The second, the Patrick and Rosalia Family Prayer Group, is a more informal entity that calls on its participating members from Kiambu and Nairobi to grow in their faith and take control of their spiritual growth. The data collection methods included participant observation of worship services in both groups and in-depth interviews with the groups' participants and leaders. The sampling method built on itself when interviewees referred the authors to others with knowledge of the groups. In total, twenty people were interviewed and ten worship/meeting services were attended. A brief description of each group is presented below.

Vincentian Ministries Kenya: Origin and Spread

VMK traces its origin to the ministry of Fr. Dr. Joseph Kuruppamparambil (usually shortened to Fr. Bill), Sa who was a priest of the Sacred Heart Region of the Vincentian Congregation of Kerala, India, which was established by Fr. Varkey Kattarath in 1904.[54] Fr. Bill, an international retreat preacher who conducted popular missions and healings all over the world, went to Uganda in the early 1990s at the invitation of a Ugandan Catholic priest, Fr. Expedito Magombe. The latter hoped that Fr. Bill's preaching "would revive the church."[55] In an entry for the *Dictionary of African Christian Biography*, Diogratias Kabagombe noted that Fr. Bill joined the seminary of the Vincentian congregation soon after graduating from high school. During his seminary training, he studied the lives of the saints and was impressed by their piety, prayerfulness, and endurance. He was intent on emulating the life of St. Vincent de Paul and his concern for charitable works of mercy. He was ordained on October 12, 1958, and during his life of ministry held several important appointments in his congregation and initiated charitable projects like orphanages and schools.[56]

Fr. Bill had a life-transforming experience in 1976 following three heart attacks. During a period of recuperation, a friend told him about a six-day Charismatic Renewal retreat that was to take place in Kerala. He decided to go, and during prayers at the retreat for healing, the presiding bishop Sebastian laid hands on Fr. Bill; he experienced the "touch of Jesus"[57] and was miraculously healed, a fact that was confirmed by his medical doctor. After this experience, Fr. Bill began a public ministry of evangelizing and healing, organizing retreats for clergy, youth, lay faithful, religious, and married people. This ministry spread to other parts of India and Africa, and even to the US. He is said to have reformed the concept of popular mission originally conceived by St. Vincent de Paul, which was the particular charism of the Vincentian Congregation. He added elements of the Catholic Charismatic Renewal movement into his mission retreats. Africans in India who attended his retreats asked him to consider taking his mission to Africa. He accepted this challenge and, in 1992, conducted his first African retreat and healing Mass in Kigoma, Tanzania. Soon invitations followed from other parts of Africa, including Uganda and Kenya. Fr. Bill first went to Uganda in the early 1990s, and his work there led to the revitalization of the Catholic Charismatic Renewal, which, although in existence in Uganda for twenty-six years, had become virtually dormant. He promoted a devotion to Our Lady within the Charismatic Renewal movement in Uganda, and by 2008 when he died, all the Catholic dioceses in Uganda had embraced the movement.[58]

Fr. Bill also visited Kenya in the 1990s,[59] conducting numerous retreats all over the country, which

---

54. Fr. Anthony, oral interview, Vincentian Retreat Center, Thika, February 3, 2014.
55. Kabagombe, "Fr. Joseph Kuruppamparambil."
56. Kabagombe, "Fr. Joseph Kuruppamparambil."
57. Kabagombe, "Fr. Joseph Kuruppamparambil."
58. All of the material in this paragraph was drawn from Kabagombe, "Fr. Joseph Kuruppamparambil."
59. The Catholic Charismatic Renewal movements in Kenya and Uganda are very closely connected. For example, Fr. James Burasa, a priest of the Holy Cross Congregation in Uganda, is a frequent visitor to Kenya and works in Dandora Parish in Nairobi. He holds one-day healing prayer services in Karen Nairobi every quarter at the Apostles of Jesus Shrine of the Sacred Heart. One of the authors of this chapter, Philomena Mwaura, has par-

drew huge crowds. Some of the retreats were held at the former Kenya Science Teachers College and at Kenyatta University in Nairobi. After Fr. Bill's death in 2008, the demand for his style of ministry continued, resulting in the Vincentian Congregation in India establishing the Vincentian Prayer House (VPH) on Amboseli Road, Lavington, in Nairobi. In 2011, the Vincentian Retreat Centre (VRC) was opened in Thika and another VPH followed in Kisumu in 2014. Fr. Anthony Parankimali, then the director of the VRC in Thika, told the authors that other prayer houses were to open in Ngong', Murang'a, Nyeri, and Makueni in due course.[60] Fr. Anthony further reported that the prayer houses were given permission to operate in the Archdiocese of Nairobi by Auxiliary Bishop David Kamau. They were later given five acres of land in Thika town by George Thuo, the now-deceased Catholic member of Parliament from the area. When asked if he considered the Vincentian ministries a form of popular Catholicism, Fr. Anthony said that, even though they are not charismatic, the ministries are popular in the sense that they involve evangelizing the people.[61] In his words, "This is a prayerful congregation that invites Catholics and non-Catholics—Protestants, AIC members, Muslims, and Hindus. We welcome even atheists to know the love of God. We minister through the inspiration of the Holy Spirit whereas the charismatic movement is for a renewal within the Catholic Church." He further said that the Vincentian ministries teach basic Catholic doctrine and speak about a God who saves: "People come, pray, and worship in an African way, singing, praising and dancing."[62] When asked what people find appealing in this ministry, Fr. Anthony said, "Jesus brings them here to find life changes, healing, forgiveness, and reconciliation."[63] He added that he has seen broken marriages restored, lapsed Catholics finding their way back into the church, and the faithful learning the doctrines of the church.[64]

The Activities of Vincentian Ministries Kenya

VMK conducts numerous three- or five-day retreats in their prayer houses and retreat centers among students and youth, unmarried men and women, religious, priests, seminarians, debtors, the jobless, the sick, prisoners (women and men), and refugees. The ministers conduct the retreats for parishes, for family renewal meetings, and for Bible conventions. Services are held regularly every Saturday in Nairobi and Kisumu, and every Friday in Thika. On Sundays, the faithful are encouraged to attend their parishes because VMK is not meant to supplant the work of the parishes but rather to supplement it. The Friday and Saturday activities and those occurring during the retreats are focused on conviction of sin, repentance, forgiveness, healing of memories, reconciliation, ailments (whether social, economic, cultural, or spiritual), and other personal challenges facing people.[65]

---

ticipated in several of these events and has spoken to participants who claim that they have received physical and emotional healings as a result of their participation. In Fr. Burasa's sermons, he focuses on issues like anger and its consequences, generational curses, and the importance of deliverance.

60. Fr. Anthony, oral interview.

61. It would be fair to describe VMK, due to its roots in the Charismatic Renewal, as having charismatic elements. These elements, like the gifts of prophecy, discernment, knowledge, wisdom, teaching, leading retreats, prayer, preaching, healing, and miracles are quite evident to a visitor to these ministries. The pneumatic element, however, has to some extent been muted, especially in the Archdiocese of Nairobi. Many of those who spoke to us told us that the cardinal discourages this type of ministry and even had VMK investigated. It was not possible to verify this information with archdiocesan authorities.

62. Fr. Anthony, oral interview.

63. Fr. Anthony, oral interview.

64. It should be noted that the Vincentian Fathers have developed an excellent ministry in media, both print and electronic. They have published several books, including *We Are More Than Conquerors*; *All Glory to Jesus*; *Why Turn to Jesus Christ?*; *All Glory to Abba Father*; *The Catholic Answer Bible*; *You Are Not Rejected*; and the *Catholic Catechism*. Some of the books have been translated into Kishwahil to achieve wider circulation. The Vincentians have also uploaded teachings and announcements about their activities to YouTube.

65. Participant observation by the authors, November 2017.

Services are structured to include silent perpetual adoration of the Blessed Sacrament, counseling, confession, reciting of the Chaplet of Divine Mercy, preaching of the Word, and recitation of the Holy Rosary, culminating in a healing and penitential Mass. Throughout these activities, the importance of confession and forgiveness is emphasized. Fr. Anthony or another presiding priest urges the congregation to

> forgive and pray every time we forgive; God promises us forgiveness of our sins and that our prayers will be answered. We cannot experience the resurrection in our lives if we are binding many people in our lives without forgiving them; sin is a failure to be what we might have been and could have been; are we good husbands, wives, mothers, fathers, sisters, friends, brothers, priests, nuns?[66]

The priest then takes the congregation through each of the Ten Commandments, asking them to examine their consciences and repent of their failures. He also urges them to pray the Lord's Prayer, but not before they have confessed and are willing to or have forgiven their debtors. The teachings and homilies derived from various biblical texts, especially from the Gospels, seek to spur individual moral reform and living according to the values of the gospel. The challenges people experience in families and relationships, plus joblessness, childlessness, jealousies, fear of witchcraft, and lingering illnesses are all attributed to sins of anger, failure to forgive, bitterness, resentment, improper sexual behavior, abortion, and hate, among other things.[67] The congregation is urged literally to cry out to God for forgiveness and healing. A song is sung prayerfully many times during the day-long services that goes like this: "Forgive me (heal me, cleanse me) Father (Jesus, Spirit), forgive me, heal me, cleanse me again." This song is sung in English and Kiswahili, the most widely spoken Kenyan languages. The penitential service held every Friday or Saturday or during retreats is aimed at spurring congregants to cry for God's mercy and liberation from all that binds them. Scriptural texts that promise forgiveness and renewal for the repentant like Jeremiah 13:13–14, Isaiah 43:25, and Psalm 55 are read and claimed. Peace is said to follow those who heed the call.

The Eucharistic Life of Vincentian Ministries Kenya

The Mass—that is, the celebration of the Holy Eucharist—is the central liturgical ritual in the Catholic Church. The church describes the Mass as the "source and summit of the Christian life."[68] It is also the highlight of all the activities of VMK, especially on Fridays and Saturdays. Just before the Mass begins, the priest walks down the aisles of the church hall and compound exposing the Blessed Sacrament in a monstrance to stimulate the faithful's awareness of the presence of Christ and to invite them to spiritual communion with Christ. This is a very solemn occasion, and the congregation, especially the women, spread their outer clothing (wraps) on the aisles for the priest to step on so that they can appropriate the blessings bestowed by Christ in the Blessed Sacrament. Experiencing Christ in the Blessed Sacrament is a source of nourishment, healing, and sustenance for the congregation.[69]

All participating Catholics are urged to live a eucharistic life by frequent attendance at and participation in the eucharistic celebration and by reception of the Holy Eucharist. Through the Mass they are told something that was reiterated in the interviews: God gives the congregation the grace, strength, and perseverance to carry out each of their unique and personal missions. Time spent before the Blessed Sacrament exposed in the adoration chapel as part of the "holy hour" observance is said to enable each congregant to receive the graces to know, love, and serve God more fully.

---

66. Participant observation by the authors, November 2016.
67. Participant observation on several occasions in 2017. See also Fr. Anthony, *You Are Not Rejected!* (Nairobi: VPH, 2012).
68. *Catechism of the Catholic Church* §1324.
69. Participant observation by the researchers, November 2016.

Congregants are given peace and encouragement to continue walking with Jesus, which leads to an experience of God's mercy and personal love.

The services at the VPHs and the VRC are frequented not only by Catholics but also by members of other faiths and denominations, but only Catholics receive Holy Communion. The spirituality offered in these places, which is centered on the Eucharist, has, according to many people we talked to, transformed the lives of many who have lived in discord, pain, bitterness, anger, and resentment with an inability to forgive, or with physical, social, or psychological illnesses.

Testimonies by Participants in Vincentian Ministries Kenya

Testimonies abound of liberation from every kind of disease, evil, difficulty, and spiritual hunger. Many who have not been to confession for decades are able to seek God's forgiveness and experience healing, and thus liberation and peace. One interviewee who requested anonymity had the following to say about a VPH:

> I am living proof that everything is possible before God. I suffered an asthmatic attack awhile back which not only threatened my career but also my life. My condition deteriorated after admission to the MP Shah Hospital. A friend introduced me to Fr. Anthony when I had lost all hope of living another day. At first I was hesitant, but my desperation pushed me to grab the opportunity. Fr. Anthony gave me some scriptures from the Holy Bible to read for a whole month, which I obediently did. Immediately after I finished the assignment, I attended a five-day retreat at the Prayer House, and Fr. Anthony asked those of us experiencing bodily pain to stand up. I did not because I was very weak, but he prayed for all of us. The following morning, I suddenly gained miraculous strength and stood without support. I jumped up and down happily, and my relatives could not believe what had happened to me. My doctor could also not believe when I excitedly broke the news to him that I had fully recovered. It is a big miracle that God has given me another chance to live.

We put this question to the interviewees: "What do you find distinctive about the VPH and the VRC?" One person said:

> The centrality of the Word of God. They make the members read the Bible a lot until they are steeped in it. There is counseling, which is personalized with guidance to read scriptures in order to solve problems. A person can be told to read a passage every day for a month. There is very profound prayer. They are eucharistic in focus. They encourage marriage in church and reception of the sacraments. There is the time in the service for witnessing when great experiences are reported. People are healed, consoled, strengthened, and reconnected with God. When during prayer moments some people fall, it is usually very striking for newcomers, but eventually we come to expect that it will happen due to the strength of the spiritual experiences that happen here.[70]

Another interviewee said:

> The Vincentians are very devoted priests. I like their way of worshiping—prayers, reading scriptures, singing at length, and praise. The power of God is experienced in this place. There are no Sunday services so people must keep to their parishes for Sunday services. There is no money talk, which there is annoyingly too much of in the parishes. Participating in the VPH has increased my faith. The fathers are servant leaders who selflessly give their all. The ushers and servers are very devoted, kind people and they work without complaining. Theirs is a different Catholicism![71]

---

70. Anonymous interviewee.
71. Anonymous interviewee, VPH, Nairobi, February 2017.

Many respondents related how they had benefited by learning about the importance of the Eucharist in their lives and how they can read the Bible on their own for edification. The poor have access to counselors at any time but do not have to pay for their services. There is no doubt that VMK is filling a gap in the offerings of the official church and that the demand for its services will continue to increase. They appeal not only to the marginalized, but to people from all walks of life.

Patrick and Rosalia Family Prayer Group

This is a charismatic prayer group that was begun in Nairobi in 2008[72] by a group of young multiethnic men and women who felt called to contribute to the renewal of the church by ministering to other young people. The founders were formerly employed full time but have left their jobs to minister to God's people. Like the VPHs, their spirituality is centered on experiencing Christ through adoration of the Blessed Sacrament, participating in the eucharistic celebration, preaching the word, and calling people, especially lapsed Catholics, to repentance.

John Maina,[73] one of the leaders of the group, says that the reason for its focus on the Eucharist is that "many people know about the Eucharist but they have never experienced it. They need to know that the Eucharist is not Jesus being symbolically present in the Tabernacle but receiving an actual person. It is encountering Jesus, receiving someone into your life."[74] He himself has moved from knowing about the Eucharist to actually living it. He now understands what perpetual adoration is, having been taught by Fr. Edward from Uganda. Fr. Edward is the priest who, with the blessing of the official church, was responsible for the establishment of adoration chapels all over Kenya.

Maina has learned and teaches others that "in the Eucharist there is healing, blessings, and peace."[75] To him the blessings that come with adoration of the Blessed Sacrament and participation in the celebration of the Eucharist include living a life of perpetual prayer, experiencing Jesus as a close friend, protection from evil, and living a life guided by the Holy Spirit. He has witnessed many people be healed or receive Jesus as their personal savior after reception of the Eucharist or spending time in the presence of the Blessed Sacrament.

Regina Wambui, another leader, says that she has experienced the transformative power of the gospel through her involvement.[76] She is a high school teacher and has organized prayer rallies in her school featuring itinerant Catholic evangelists. She has seen the lives of the students transformed, resulting in better behavior, more focused concentration on their studies, and diminished fears. In the company of priests, the prayer group's deliverance and exorcism ministries have brought relief through the gospel to families and individuals plagued by demon possession. A Mass for healing is always offered in connection with the work of these ministries. Asked if the clergy approve of this kind of ministry, she responded that some make fun of the Christians who participate in them, calling them "fanatic retreat goers." She says that the parish priests have no time to meet the needs of the faithful for healing because they are too bogged down by administrative duties, raising money for schools, churches, and clinics, and performing works of mercy. Apparently they are not able to offer adequate catechesis or initiate healing ministries.

Another interviewee, Michael Wanjau, said that there is a lot of hunger for the word of God and a great need for attention to problems like witchcraft, demon possession, harassment by ancestral spirits, unexplained misfortunes and illnesses, bad marriages, difficult children, and other kinds of evil.[77]

---

72. The group was named in remembrance of some of the members' grandparents, who were among the early converts to Catholicism in Kiambu and were very pious.
73. Not his real name; he did not want his identity disclosed.
74. John Maina, oral interview, Nairobi, October 20, 2016.
75. John Maina, oral interview, Nairobi, October 20, 2016.
76. Regina Wambui, oral interview, Kiambu town, December 15, 2016.
77. Michael Wanjau, oral interview, Thika, July 21, 2016.

Wanjau says that the official church does not take these problems seriously and some priests explain them away as superstition. The interviewees were unanimous that the official church in Nairobi and in the whole of Kenya must take these issues more seriously if its ministry is to be effective.

The ministries offered by the Patrick and Rosalia Prayer Group are now present in other parts of Kenya, and their meetings draw people from every denomination. The men and women involved in these ministries have devoted their lives to providing services that are needed by the people. To help them reach more people, these ministers have attended training sessions in evangelism in Uganda and other training sessions offered by the official church. Their work is financially supported by the lay faithful.

Members of the group organize various activities like pilgrimages to the Subukia Marian Shrine (Nakuru), the Komorock Marian Shrine, and the Padre Pio Shrine in Nairobi, retreats at the VPH and at Resurrection Gardens in Karen, Nairobi,[78] and Fr. James Burasa's quarterly retreats. Another interviewee, Margaret Njagi, told us that, through participating in events like these, she has come to realize that God is real and that God answers prayers. She has also learned how to relate Christianity to life, how to forgive, and how to pray for herself and others. She has come to recognize her weaknesses and now sees that miracles come from inner healing.

These two cases of the VPHs and the Patrick and Rosalia Prayer Group are representative of the many other forms of spirituality centered on the Eucharist evolving in Kenya that complement what the Small Christian Communities (SCCs) and other associations are doing. The multiethnic composition of the membership and clientele of these groups and their experience of unity through partaking in the Holy Eucharist are indicative of the power of the Eucharist to heal and promote unity among the people of God. What conclusions can be drawn from the experiences described in these two case studies? What do they reveal about popular Catholicism in Kenya? It is to this that we now turn.

Discussion and Reflection

It is evident from these case studies that popular Catholicism exists in Kenya in varied forms. The case studies show that one significant manifestation of this popular Catholicism is its charismatic nature. Catholic Christians are being drawn to it because of its combination of Catholic spirituality and pneumatic experiences. Catholics are experiencing the transformative power of the gospel and the Eucharist, and their spirituality is being deepened by the popular Catholicism offered by these groups, including the regular prayer meetings and reading and understanding of the Word of God. The testimonies of participants in these two groups witness to the evolution of a different kind of Catholicism. As a result of the work of groups like these, the Charismatic Renewal movement and the broader Catholic Church in Kenya have been growing tremendously.

It seems that the laity, the clergy, religious, families, youth, and all members of the church require a deeper and a more meaningful spirituality. They do not want to participate mechanically in the rituals of the church. They want to understand what they believe. It is not enough for them to recite set prayers, go to Sunday Mass, and participate in the meetings of SCCs once a week. Besides the need for deeper understanding, the faithful are experiencing an urgent need to meet God at the points of greatest vulnerability in their practical lives. Issues like illness and childlessness and fears concerning such things as witchcraft and spirit possession are all matters of great need in the community and merit ministerial attention. The official church, despite its noble work, does not seem able to meet these demands. Yet, when these needs are not addressed by regular worship services, a big gap is felt. There is a need, for example, to create homegrown youth groups in order to keep the youth, who are not adequately targeted and involved, in the church. It is to such needs that the VPHs and the Patrick and Rosalia Prayer Group attend. For this reason, they have attracted a dedicated following.

The activities taking place in the groups of popular Catholicism require continuous monitor-

---

78. These sites are important to the spirituality of Kenyan Catholics.

ing by local church authorities to guard against unorthodox teachings and practices. The decision, for example, that VPH activities should not take place on Sundays encourages participants to be active members of their parishes and protects against what might be seen as schismatic tendencies. In addition, the groups' focus on the Eucharist encourages participants to be faithful to the sacraments and to adhere to the life of the local church.

Scholars of religion, and particularly of Christianity in Africa, have viewed the rise of popular Catholicism in light of the proliferation of other Christian expressions, including the twentieth-century wave of neo-Pentecostalism and AICs. These expressions coincided with the stresses of rapid social change occasioned by the colonial and missionary enterprises in the late nineteenth and early twentieth centuries, which resulted in the destruction of African social, religious, political, and cultural systems, creating anomie among the people. The turmoil continued in the late twentieth and early twenty-first centuries, and, as Kalu argues, religion contributed to the creation of spaces for the relief of the resulting tensions.[79] As was introduced above, Kalu identifies three explanatory models for the rise of neo-Pentecostalism, which we believe can be useful for explaining the appeal and vivacity of the VPHs, the Patrick and Rosalia Prayer Group, and other forms of popular Catholicism: the cultural-historical model, the providential model, and the functionalist/instrumentalist model. Kalu's cultural-historical model emphasizes two discourses—the African roots of Pentecostalism and the profound revivalism that characterized the initial African response to the gospel.[80] This model perceives this African response to the gospel as a continuation of traditional African religiosity and as an attempt to solve problems endemic to the indigenous African worldview. It resonates well with the activities of the VPHs and the Patrick and Rosalia Prayer Group. Despite the VPHs' rejection of their links to the Catholic Charismatic Renewal, there is no doubt that Fr. Bill, their founder, had roots in that movement. The problems that have been addressed in the healings conducted by these groups are typically the same ones presented to traditional healers and prophet healers in AICs, for example, witchcraft, haunting by ancestral spirits, unexplainable misfortunes, lingering illnesses that have defied modern medical treatment, barrenness, marital problems, and difficult children.

The providential model is a religious explanation that has been employed by scholars like Allan Anderson[81] to explain the rise and expansion of global Pentecostalism. As noted above, this model posits that renewal movements are the result of an outpouring of the Holy Spirit. Most studies in Africa agree that there have been spontaneous explosions of revivalism on the continent during particular periods, for example, the 1910s, the 1970s, and the mid-1980s to the present. Paul Gifford argues that the explosion of Pentecostal churches in Liberia and elsewhere in Africa was linked to the spiritual lethargy of mainline churches, their collusion with corrupt government forces, the collapse of African economies, and various conflicts and civil wars. All of these things elicited a pneumatic response[82] evident in the proliferation of charismatic and Pentecostal churches. The two groups under study have their origins in this environment as it existed in Kenya.

The functionalist model is related to the providential model insofar as it focuses on the context in which religious movements occur. This model explains the rise of Pentecostalism in Africa by its appeal to what Kalu identifies as "materialist" and "instrumentalist" factors. This means that the context in which conversions or the joining of religious groups takes place is crucial because religion is seen as the solution to certain problems. We can say that the social, economic, and political upheavals of the 1990s and 2000s resulted in a quest for well-being, including healings, an escape from poverty, and an ability to cope amid civil strife,

---

79. Kalu, *Power, Poverty and Prayer*.
80. Kalu, *Power, Poverty and Prayer*, 141. See also Kalu, *African Pentecostalism*, 102ff.; Kalu, "Holy Praiseco," 87–88.
81. Anderson, *African Reformation*.
82. See Gifford, *New Dimensions in African Christianity*, chapter 2.

war, and other negative societal circumstances, all of which led people to begin or join charismatic or Pentecostal groups. Judging by the needs identified by participants in the VPHs and the Patrick and Rosalia Prayer Group, we are persuaded that these two groups have provided space for participants to find solace, healing, and the ability to cope with life's challenges. We are aware of the risks of reductionist explanations for the appeal and growth of popular Catholicism—as noted above, there are purely spiritual reasons people join these groups. Nevertheless, the presence of a religious or social group or movement cannot be viewed outside the relevant social, political, economic, and cultural milieu and historical context.[83]

Whatever explanation is given, popular Catholicism with its focus on combining Catholic doctrine with elements of the Catholic Charismatic Renewal has stemmed the tide of African Catholics streaming to neo-Pentecostal churches. Our study has shown that parishes with innovative and creative clergy who have read the signs of the times have incorporated charismatic elements into the Mass, like "praise and worship"[84] and Bible study. These parish leaders have been able to transform parish life and the lives of the faithful through innovative programs addressing their spiritual, social, physical, and moral needs. Like the groups discussed above, parishes should, in order to remain relevant, offer a holistic ministry that creates a sense among the faithful that they belong and are loved. In this way, the groups we have discussed and others like them are able to introduce elements of renewal into the lives of parishes. Also, for the Catholic Church to remain relevant in Kenya, it must take seriously the ministry of healing, not in the sense of scientific medicine, which it already does, but in the sense of the healing of souls, memories, and societies at large. Only then can it embody the words of Jesus that "I have come that you may have life and have it abundantly" (John 10:10).

Conclusion

As the core members and citizens of the church, the laity are called to animate social, political, and cultural life, that is, to usher in fairness and justice in public life, promote equal rights for all citizens, advocate for a spirit of pluralism, and create inclusive governments and accountable public servants and institutions. Through the apostolate of the laity, the power of Christ and his liberating spirit penetrates the various environments of politics, trade, and culture. For these reasons, Kenya needs a dynamic and committed laity to promote and defend the rights of the marginalized, the poor, internally displaced persons, refugees, children, and victims of gender-based violence, among others. The laity need to be proactive and vigilant in the exercise of their charismatic gifts of prophetic leadership and discernment so that they can intervene against policies and practices, whether emanating from governments or from other institutions, that violate human dignity.

The church, through the lobbying and advocacy of the laity, needs to be part of the decision-making processes of societies, in collaboration with other people of goodwill, especially those in civil society and in other faith-based institutions and churches. The church, of which the laity are the pillar, has a role in providing concrete solutions for the liberation of humanity. The church is an explicit sign, instrument, and sacrament of the communion between God and humankind. Through its evangelical mission, the church as people of God promotes the integral development and liberation of the whole person. The laity as the primary agents of the new evangelization, acting in various capacities, promote inner conversion through their living of the gospel values of goodness, honesty, justice, forgiveness, and reconciliation. Family life is the basis of both church and society and demands untiring devotion, discernment, and self-sacrifice.

---

83. See also Magesa, "Charismatic Movements as 'Communities of Affliction.'"

84. "Praise and worship" is a concept borrowed from African Pentecostalism. It involves the congregation singing songs and choruses of praise for half an hour or an hour before Mass, songs and choruses that are common in most Pentecostal and mainline churches in Kenya. Musical instruments are played and people dance to the music.

It is the laity that forms and sustains these families by their ongoing commitment, prayer, and action.

In order to effectively accomplish all these tasks, the laity need not only human and professional formation but also spiritual fortitude, which requires spiritual nourishment. It is for this reason that the work done by the popular Catholic renewal movements is neither shallow nor ephemeral. These movements provide an opportunity for the church to grow in authenticity and inclusiveness.

Popular Catholicism in its various manifestations and themes has not been adequately researched in Kenya. It should be studied further from various perspectives, including those that are anthropological, theological, religious, and gender-focused.

Bibliography

Alva, R. "Catholic Charismatic Renewal Movement and Secularization." *Pentecostal Studies* 14.1 (2005): 124–39.

AMECEA. 14th Plenary, "Deeper Evangelisation in the 3rd Millennium: A Challenge for AMECEA." Gaba Publications, Eldoret. *African Ecclesial Review* 44.5 and 6 (October–December 2002): 239.

Anderson, A. H. *African Reformation: African Initiated Christianity in the Twentieth Century*. Trenton, NJ: Africa World Press, 2011.

———. "Stretching Out Hands to God: Origins and Growth of Pentecostalism in Africa." In *Pentecostalism in Africa: Presence and Impact of Pneumatic Christianity in Postcolonial Societies*, edited by Martin Lindhardt. Leiden: Brill, 2014.

Anderson, David M., and Douglas H. Johnson, eds. *Revealing Prophets*. London: James Currey, 1995.

Asamoah-Gyadu, Kwabena. *Contemporary Pentecostal Christianity: Interpretation from an African Context*. Oxford: Regnum Books International, 2013.

Bellagamba, A. *Mission and Ministry in the Global Church*. Maryknoll, NY: Orbis Books, 1992.

Calisi, Matteo. "The Future of the Catholic Charismatic Renewal." In *Spirit-Empowered Christianity in the 21st Century*, edited by H. Vinson Synan. Lake Mary, FL: Charisma House, A Strang Company, 2011.

Congregation for Divine Worship and the Discipline of the Sacraments. *Directory on Popular Piety and the Liturgy: Principles and Guidelines* (2001). www.vatican.va.

Congregation for the Doctrine of the Faith. *Catechism of the Catholic Church*. Vatican City: Libreria Editrice Vaticana, 1995.

Droz, Yvan. "The Local Roots of the Kenyan Pentecostal Revival: Conversion, Healing, Social and Political Mobility." *Les Cahiers de l'IFRA* 20 (2001): 23–44.

Encyclopedia of Christianity, volume 4. Grand Rapids, MI: Eerdmans; Leiden: Brill, 2005.

Francis, Pope. *Evangelii Gaudium* (The Joy of the Gospel) [Post-synodal Apostolic Exhortation on the Proclamation of the Gospel in Today's World; November 23, 2013]. Vatican City: Libreria Editrice Vaticana, 2013. www.vatican.va.

———. *Gaudete et Exsultate* [Apostolic Exhortation on the Call to Holiness in Today's World; March 19, 2018]. Vatican City: Libreria Editrice Vaticana, 2018. www.vatican.va.

Gifford, Paul. *New Dimensions in African Christianity*. Nairobi: AACC Press, 1992.

———. *Christianity and Politics in Doe's Liberia*. Cambridge: Cambridge University Press, 1993.

Haar, Gerrie ter. *The Spirit of Africa: The Healing Ministry of Archbishop Emmanuel Milingo of Zambia*. Trenton, NJ: Africa World Press, 1992.

Hastings, Adrian. *African Catholicism: Essays in Discovery*. London: SCM Press, 1989.

Ilo, Stan Chu. "*Africae Munus* and the Challenges of a Transformative Missional Theological Praxis in Africa's Social Context." *Transformation* 31.2 (2014): 116–31.

John Paul II, Pope. *Christifideles Laici* [Post-synodal Apostolic Exhortation on the Vocation and the Mission of the Lay Faithful in the Church and in the World; December 30, 1988]. Vatican City: Libreria Editrice Vaticana, 1988. www.vatican.va. Nairobi: Paulines Publications, 1994.

Kabagombe, D. "Fr. Joseph Kuruppamparambil." In *Dictionary of African Christian Biography*. www.dacb.org.

Kalu, Ogbu U. *African Pentecostalism: An Introduction*. Oxford University Press, 2008.

———. "Holy Praiseco: Negotiating Sacred and Popular Music and Dance in African Pentecostalism." In *Collected Essays of Ogbu U. Kalu*, edited by Wilhelmina Kalu, Nimi Wariboko, and Toyin Falola, volume 3. Trenton, NJ: Africa World Press, 2010.

———. *Power, Poverty, and Prayer: The Challenges of Poverty and Pluralism in African Christianity, 1960–1996.* Trenton, NJ: Africa World Press, 2006.

Kalu, W., Nimi Wariboko, and Toyin Falola, eds. *African Pentecostalism: Global Discourses, Migrations, Exchanges and Connections.* Trenton, NJ: Africa World Press, 2010.

Karanja, David. "Kenya Prelate Lifts Suspension of Charismatics." OVS *NewsWeekly*, May 8, 2009.

Kasomo, Daniel. "An Assessment of the Catholic Charismatic Renewal: Towards Peaceful Co-Existence in the Roman Catholic Church." *International Journal of Sociology and Anthropology* 2.8 (2010).

Kassimir, Ronald. "The Politics of Popular Catholicism in Uganda." In *East African Expressions of Christianity*, edited by Thomas Spear and Isaria N. Kimambo. Oxford: James Currey, 1999.

Lado, L. *Catholic Pentecostalism and the Paradoxes of Africanisation.* Leiden: Brill, 2009.

Magesa, Laurenti. "Charismatic Movements as 'Communities of Affliction.'" In *Charismatic Renewal in Africa: A Challenge for African Christianity*, edited by Mika Vahakangas and Andrew Kyomo. Nairobi: Acton, 2003.

Mwaura, Philomena Njeri. "Nigerian Pentecostal Missionary Enterprise in Kenya." In *Religion, History and Politics in Nigeria: Essays in Honour of Ogbu U. Kalu*, edited by Chima Korieh and Ugo G. Nwokeji, 270–89. Lanham, MD: University Press of America: 2005.

O'Connor, Edward. *The Pentecostal Movement in the Catholic Church.* Rev. ed. Notre Dame, IN: Ave Maria Press, 1974.

Omenyo, C. N. "Charismatization of the Mainline Churches in Ghana." In *Charismatic Renewal in Africa: A Challenge for African Christianity*, edited by Mika Vihakangas and Andrew Kyomo, 171–77. Nairobi: Acton, 2003.

Onyalla, D. B. "Vatican Publishes Church Statistics of Kenya, Uganda, and CAR ahead of Pope's Visit." *Catholic News Agency for Africa*, November 19, 2015.

Orobator, Agbonkhianmeghe E. "'After All, Africa Is Largely a Nonliterate Continent': The Reception of Vatican II in Africa." *Theological Studies* 74 (2013): 284–301.

Paul VI, Pope. *Evangelii Nuntiandi* [Apostolic Exhortation on the theme of Catholic Evangelization; December 8, 1975]. Vatican City: Libreria Editrice Vaticana, 1975. www.vatican.va.

Peterson, Anna. "Varieties of Popular Catholics: A Pilot Study." *Social Compass* 45.3 (1998).

Spear, Thomas, and Isaria N. Kimambo, eds. *East African Expressions of Christianity.* Nairobi: East African Publishers, 1999.

Swatos, William H., Jr., ed. *Encyclopaedia of Religion and Society.* Lanham, MD: AltaMira Press, 1998. http://hirr.hartsem.edu/ency/.

Synan, V. *The Twentieth Century Pentecostal Explosion: The Exciting Growth of Pentecostal Churches and Charismatic Renewal Movements.* Altamonte Springs, FL: Creation House, 1987.

Taylor, John V. *The Go-Between God: The Holy Spirit and the Christian Mission.* London: SCM Press, 1972.

Wilkens, Katharina. *Holy Water and Evil Spirits: Religious Healing in East Africa.* New Brunswick, NJ: Transaction Publishers, 2011.

Winters, M. "The Balokole and the Protestant Ethic: A Critique." *Journal of Religion in Africa* 14.1 (1983).

Suggested Reading

Anderson, David M., and Douglas H. Johnson, eds. *Revealing Prophets.* London: James Currey, 1995.

Hastings, Adrian. *African Catholicism: Essays in Discovery.* London: SCM Press, 1989.

Kalu, Ogbu U. *Power, Poverty, and Prayer: The Challenges of Poverty and Pluralism in African Christianity, 1960–1996.* Trenton, NJ: Africa World Press, 2006.

Spear, Thomas, and Isaria N. Kimambo, eds. *East African Expressions of Christianity.* Nairobi: East African Publishers, 1999.

Key Words
Catholic Charismatic Renewal
Pentecostalism
popular Catholicism
popular piety
popular religion
revivalism

African Catholicism and Health Care in Africa

†Mary Gloria C. Njoku, DDL, Sampson K. Nwonyi, and Patrick J. McDevitt, CM

A contemporary understanding of health and wellness integrates a number of different aspects of the human person, including the biological, cognitive, emotional, social, moral, and spiritual. Achieving health and wellness involves a balanced lifestyle with adequate leisure time that incorporates fun and an ability to laugh at oneself. Additionally, an ability to appreciate and be comfortable with one's own body are signs of wellness. It is also important to learn to listen to our bodies, to exercise, to enjoy the outdoors, and to notice and appreciate beauty. A holistic model of health and wholeness provides for a balance of body, mind, and spirit.[1] In this model, disease is seen as a disruption of that balance and healing involves its restoration.[2] Health care is the set of services provided by a country or organization for the treatment of physical and mental illnesses.[3]

In 1947, the World Health Organization (WHO) defined health in terms of "wellness," or "physical, mental, and social well-being, not merely the absence of disease."[4] WHO later defined "optimal health" as "a state of complete physical, mental, and social well-being and not merely the absence of disease or infirmity."[5] The later definition added the term "complete" to refer to a sense of wholeness. Critics of this definition have argued that such "optimal health" is a utopian goal that can never be practically achieved, even by the richest people on the planet, and that attempting to achieve this goal would turn everyone into a patient. The critics have asserted that everyone is in need of better health and that attempting to achieve "optimal health" would be economically impossible and would result in the medicalization of life.[6]

Africa, with 11 percent of the world's population, has a high illness burden, including the highest incidence of malaria and HIV/AIDS in the world. Ensuring access to clean water and sanitation, battling communicable diseases, and reducing preventable deaths still dominate the health care agenda in many countries of Africa. However, according to a report by the Economist Intelligence Unit,[7] the demands of health care in Africa are changing. The rising incidence of chronic diseases is creating a new matrix of challenges for Africa's health care workers, policy makers, and donors.

The Catholic Church has always been at the fore-

---

1. Gordon, *Holistic Medicine*.
2. Engel, "Clinical Application of the Biopsychosocial Model."
3. *Cambridge Advanced Learner's Dictionary*.
4. Hattie, Myers, and Sweeney, "Factor Structure of Wellness."
5. WHO, "Preamble to the Constitution of the World Health Organization."
6. Illich, *Medical Nemesis*, 15. The "medicalization" of life is the consequence of both insufficient health education and insufficient health care. People will assess ordinary and everyday experiences as pathology or disease. Consequently, the boundaries of normalcy are narrowed and everyone become a patient.
7. Economist Intelligence Unit, "Value-Based Healthcare in Europe."

front of holistic care for the physical, spiritual, and emotional well-being of African people through its health care networks[8] and the efforts of individual dioceses, including the sacramental ministry. The church's efforts in Africa have historically focused on the health needs of the poorest and the marginalized, rather than aiming at "optimal" or "complete" well-being for everyone.

In the new health care environment in Africa, it is necessary that the church improve and expand its health mission in Africa. It must continue with its network-based health care model but must also foster a system that promotes actions targeted at influencing the determinants of health and well-being. An integrated biopsychosospiritual perspective on health and health care delivery is recommended.

This chapter examines the contributions of the Catholic Church to African health care. It begins with a theoretical description of the evolving understanding of the etiology of diseases, illnesses, and conditions. It then shifts to a general overview of the Catholic Church's conception of its mission to provide health care. It discusses the healing ministry of Jesus and the continuation of that ministry by the Catholic Church. Following that is a brief overview of the health profile of Africans and a brief history of the Catholic Church's involvement with health care in Africa. Finally, we review the church's current health care efforts in Africa with a focus on its programs in southern Africa and Nigeria, and conclude by considering the challenges facing Catholic health care in Africa.

The methodology for this research is empirical and quantitative, as well as discussing theoretical criteria for effective health care and holiness health in Africa. The focus of this chapter is to describe and promote a biopsychosospiritual model[9] within the context of Catholic social teaching, the health care mission and values of the church, and the current situation of health, illness, and health care on the African continent.

Evolution of the Understanding of the Etiology of Health Problems

The understanding of the etiology of health problems has progressed from the supernatural to the biological (biomedical) to the biopsychosocial and, finally, to what we now call a biopsychosospiritual perspective. In the first of these paradigms—the supernatural—health problems were understood as resulting from supernatural forces, and treatment required supernatural intervention. Demons, witches, the effects of the moon and stars, and other supernatural forces were thought to be at the root of illnesses.[10] This supernatural perspective has been replaced by other paradigms in most countries of the world. In Africa, however, it is still recognized as having explanatory power as to the causes of diseases, illnesses, and conditions. It is not unusual to hear African patients or their relatives speaking of demons, witches, and other spiritual forces afflicting them with all kinds of illnesses. In some cases, adherents of the supernatural perspective turn to spiritual solutions as their first line of treatment.[11]

A "disease" is defined as a disorder of structure or function in a human, animal, or plant which is associated with specific symptoms or which affects a specific location on the afflicted subject. Disease is thus viewed as a medical condition with specific signs and symptoms. Some critics of this definition, however, have posited that it is difficult to define disease, because sometimes it is dependent on the context, including the temporal context—

---

8. Catholic Health Care Association of Southern Africa, "Annual Report 2015."
9. This term was coined by the co-author, Sr. Gloria Njoku, DDL, who died in 2018 before the publication of this work. It represents her unique discovery that holistic health care requires an integrative interaction of all the channels through which Africans procure and promote wellness—*bio* (promoting all the things that give abundant life and combating all things that diminish the quality of life), *psychological* (paying attention to the mental health and well-being of people in diagnosing and treating any health condition), *social* (the communal dimension of healing and restoration of the condition of the sick), and *spiritual* (integrating spirituality as part of healing and wellness). All these, she argues, must be taken into consideration in holistic healing of the mind, body, soul, emotions, physical and social life of a sick person and in understanding what ails people.
10. Barlow and Durand, *Abnormal Psychology*, 7–25.
11. Barlow and Durand, *Abnormal Psychology*, 7–25.

what constitutes a disease changes with time.[12] For example, osteoporosis was traditionally viewed as an unavoidable part of normal aging, but in 1994 WHO officially recognized it as a disease. "Illness" is considered to be related to the consequences of the presence of disease. "Conditions" like seizures, obesity, and asthma do not imply the presence of illness or disease. Obesity is a condition that has been implicated in the development of heart disease and some forms of diabetes, but seizures are not directly linked to any illness or disease. In essence, the terms "disease," "illness," and "condition" are ways of classifying health problems, but there is considerable ambiguity and dynamism in determining what falls into each category. Research and medical advancements influence how we categorize and treat diseases, illnesses, and conditions. Health care, as discussed in this chapter, is intended to address all three of these phenomena.

The biomedical (or biological) model that came to eclipse the supernatural paradigm in most places understands good health as being devoid of defects, diseases, and all forms of pain. As its name implies, this model is exclusively centered on biological factors. It does not consider the role of environmental, psychological, or social factors in its conceptualization and treatment of health problems.[13] Whereas the supernatural perspective was closely linked to religion, the biomedical model distinguished itself as a discipline distinct from religion,[14] in which the process of healing was largely considered to be mechanical. The position of adherents to this model is aptly captured by Lewis Thomas: "For every disease there is a single, central, causative mechanism that dominates all the rest, and if you are looking for effective treatment or prevention you have to find that mechanism first, and start from there.... I am an optimist, and a true believer in the effectiveness and indispensability of the science of medicine."[15]

The biomedical model was introduced into Africa by missionaries and was partially successful, especially in the treatment of yellow fever, malaria, meningitis, tuberculosis, and other illnesses. It was only partially successful, however, because these illnesses and diseases and others are still prevalent in Africa. For example, a WHO report in 2015 estimated that malaria was responsible for the deaths of 403,000 persons in Africa.[16] One major challenge that arose from the implementation of the biomedical model was the role of traditional African medicine in the prevention and treatment of illnesses. These traditional practices refer to native approaches to health care, including the use of natural leaves, roots, and seeds to treat specific conditions, diseases, and illnesses. They also include divination (*igbaafa*) and offerings to spirits (*ikwaaja*). The discourse on the role of African native medicine was made more problematic by the attitudes of the early missionaries toward it.[17] Because the biological model did not typically look to environmental, psychological, and social factors causing illness, the missionaries did not consider the potential for integrating African native medicine into the predominant model. After years of dominating the health discourse, the biomedical model fell out of favor, because it refused to consider disease-causing factors other than biological ones. Contemporary psychiatry and medicine then shifted to the biopsychosocial model in order to address some of the limitations of the biomedical model.

The biopsychosocial model promoted by George Engel first gained prominence in the Western world,[18] and the term "biopsychosocial" was first used by R. R. Grinker, in 1954.[19] Engel was a specialist in internal medicine—specifically, gastrointestinal medicine—and Grinker was a neurologist and psychiatrist. Engel posited that psychosocial factors must be integrated into the biomedical model

---

12. Bayer and Spitzer, "Edited Correspondence on the Status of Homosexuality in DSM-III," 32–52.
13. Annandale, *Sociology of Health and Medicine*.
14. Koenig, "Religion and Medicine," 385–98.
15. Thomas, "Medicine in America," 25–26.
16. World Health Organization, "Global Health Estimates 2015."
17. Mohr, "Missionary Medicine," 429–61; Gundani, "Views and Attitudes of Missionaries," 298–312.
18. Engel, "Need for a New Medical Model."
19. Grinker, "Struggle for Eclecticism," 451–57.

to produce a holism. Engel and other supporters of biopsychosocial holism posited that a holistic approach is better than a single-factor model; this biopsychosocial holism is heuristically meaningful in that it addresses all three aspects of health: mind, body, and spirit. Engel viewed the biopsychosocial model as the best model for health research, teaching, and practice.[20] Grinker's biopsychosocial model emphasized the place of biological factors and not just psychosocial factors in the practice of psychiatry. Grinker did not subscribe to biopsychosocial holism for psychiatric treatment and research, because psychiatric illnesses must be analyzed on a case-by-case basis. Grinker favored an eclectic model for psychiatric treatment, in which the biological, the psychological, or the social could be the primary approach for a particular case.

The challenge with the actual implementation of the biopsychosocial model in research and practice is determining the ordering or prioritization of the factors to be investigated. The absence of a definite mechanism by which the model operates makes it difficult for both researchers and practitioners to adopt a uniform modality to ensure rigor and comparability of outcomes. N. Ghaemi sees this absence of a specific prioritization mechanism as a problem of eclecticism.[21] In light of the limitations of the biopsychosocial model, there was a need for alternative approaches that might take into consideration a full range of humanistic factors. One alternative is the biopsychosospiritual model proposed by Mary Gloria C. Njoku,[22] which expands on the biopsychosocial model and accepts William Osler's proposal that science and art be applied to health care research and practice.[23]

The biopsychosospiritual model posits that a proper understanding of health must take into account the biological, psychological, social, and spiritual dimensions of the human person. It suggests that all these dimensions are affected by any given illness and ought to be considered in the prevention, treatment, and management of health-related problems. Njoku agrees with Osler that, if an illness or disease can be traced to a specific biological factor, the body should be treated. If the biological problem can be further traced to a spiritual issue, then the spiritual issue ought to be treated. For example, if a patient presents with biological symptoms like headache and insomnia that are secondary to issues of spiritual belief (e.g., believing that spirits are in the house that will attack if the patient goes to sleep), the spiritual issue should be treated. On the other hand, if a person is undergoing a spiritual crisis that is primarily driven by a curable biological problem, the body should be treated. In the same way, if a biological symptom like a headache is due to a psychological or social problem, that problem should be treated. If all the factors—biological, psychological, social, and spiritual—require attention, then the treatment should incorporate all of them. In proposing this model, Njoku understands that there may be difficulties in deciphering which factor or factors are the primary source of the presenting symptoms. This is where the gathering of background information is absolutely necessary. Njoku posits that the background information will facilitate the process of deciding the primary source or sources of health problems. The biopsychosospiritual model is consistent with a holistic approach to medicine. The treatment of many illnesses, including the twenty leading causes of mortality in Africa, can benefit from the application of this model.

There are two other models that share some of the attributes of the biopsychosospiritual model: the sustainability model and the anthropological model. Both of these models attempt to address health from a larger perspective, but they fail to address important human, cultural, and spiritual variables. Global health programs in Africa and other developing countries are often ineffective, because they are hampered by governmental bureaucracies and poor needs assessments and data analyses. A. Yang, P. Farmer, and A. McGahan discuss how the management of global health programs and NGOs that are addressing critical health threats facing Africa (like HIV/AIDS, malaria,

---

20. Engel, "Need for a New Medical Model."
21. Gaemi, "Rise and Fall of the Biopsychosocial Model," 3–4.
22. Njoku, "Behavioural Health."
23. Osler, *Aequanimitas*.

Ebola, and others) are often funded based on the sustainability model.[24] The sustainability model has come to define global health programs by the longevity of the programs themselves instead of by how they address the underlying causes of disease, not just the symptoms. However, if global health programs were managed based more on effective medical outcomes, the sustainability model could serve as a powerful vehicle for addressing the root causes of disease. The virtue of the sustainability model is that it can provide the necessary time to form relationships in the community and collect significant longitudinal data on biological, psychological, spiritual, and cultural factors. The anthropological approach is helpful, because it looks at the real local needs of individuals and communities through the experiences of marginalized and powerless people. Anthropologists recognize the need for both global and local action, community relationships, and broad international networks. In Uganda, the anthropological approach resulted in successful health programs which thrived at multiple levels. The research paid attention to moral experiences, social relationships, and culture, all of which create a capacity for action and results.[25]

Health, Health Care, and the Catholic Church

The Catholic Church as an institution recognizes the vital role of promoting health and health care in its mission. For instance, in a pastoral letter on health and health care, the United States Conference of Catholic Bishops (USCCB) postulates that "health and the healing apostolate take on special significance because of the church's long tradition of involvement in this area and because the church considers health care to be a basic human right which flows from the sanctity of human life."[26] Pope John XXIII, in his encyclical letter *Pacem in Terris*, wrote that the church sees health care as a basic human right, along with life, food, clothing, and shelter.[27] In addition, the *Catechism of the Catholic Church* explains that the political community has a duty to ensure the right to medical care[28] and that the pursuit of the common good must include health care so that people can attain acceptable living conditions.[29]

Unfortunately, bishops' conferences in Africa have provided little direction or leadership on health care, aside from statements regarding contraception, abortion, and the eradication of HIV/AIDS. There is a critical need in the African Church for a comprehensive anthropology, theology, and spirituality of social justice as it relates to health care that is specific to the African experience.

The Catholic perspective on modern health care and its ethical dimension is concerned with promoting and protecting the patient's dignity and autonomy. For this reason, information regarding a patient's values, beliefs, commitments, wishes, preferences, life-defining historical events, and hoped-for life goals is as crucial to health care decisions as information about the patient's physical condition. Yet these aspirations are rarely reached in Catholic health care facilities and, to some extent, this may be the result of inadequate human and other resources. Many countries in Africa suffer from inadequate health care systems due to poor infrastructure, management, and human resources, and a lack of essential medicines. Oftentimes, these systems operate in a purely survival mode and cannot afford to address the humanistic, cultural, and spiritual aspects of health. There are some health care professionals who take these dimensions of care seriously, but doctors and nurses are often so overworked that they forgo an inquiry into their patients' commitments, life goals, and life-defining historical events.

As alluded to above, another significant aspect of health care relates to the foundational principle that adequate health care is a human right, suggesting that it must be available and affordable

---

24. Yang, Farmer, and McGahan, "Sustainability in Global Health."
25. Feierman, Kleinman, Stewart, Farmer, and Das, "Anthropology, Knowledge-Flows and Global Health."
26. USCCB, "Health and Health Care," 3.
27. Pope John XXII, *Pacem in Terris* [Encyclical on Establishing Universal Peace in Truth, Justice, Charity, and Liberty; April 11, 1963] (Vatican City: Libreria Editrice Vaticana, 1963; www.vatican.va) §11.
28. *Catechism of the Catholic Church* §2211.
29. *Catechism of the Catholic Church* §2288.

to all, regardless of the person's health condition, age, legal status, or ability to pay. During the time of the early missionaries, health care services were delivered to sick people in an empathetic manner that was focused first not on money but on saving life. The promotion of health and the saving of lives has continued to guide the work of the Catholic Church in health care.

With the rise of lay leadership, a growing percentage of non-Catholic employees, and an increasingly interdependent and collaborative health care system, a question arises that the early missionaries did not face: What does it mean for a health care organization to have a Catholic identity? This question elicits a variety of responses. Surely, a Catholic identity is more than just the presence of religious pictures and symbols in patient rooms, edifices, common spaces, and signage. Those who emphasize Catholic social teaching distinguish Catholic health care by its commitment to justice and charity—for example, the Catholic Health Association of the United States, Ascension Health, and Catholic Health Care Association of South Africa. Catholic identity should define the ethos and culture of an institution through its moral and policy norms, social teaching, rituals, and religious symbolism. These things on their own, however, understate the full meaning and foundation of Catholic identity in health care. At the heart of a health care organization's Catholic identity is a belief in God's love and in the meaning of Jesus's healing ministry.[30]

Jesus's Healing Ministry

There is no doubt that illness and healing are among humankind's most fundamental challenges. The exemplary life of Jesus and his teaching and preaching were not done in isolation—they were accompanied by frequent manifestations of Jesus's power to heal mind, body, and spirit. His healing power, as reflected in the Gospels, involved personal and concrete encounters with a wide diversity of people from various economic, social, and religious groups. Jesus shows us that it is in relationships that people receive holistic healing. No matter the situation, Jesus brought healing and wholeness to every human encounter by his very presence and his interest in and love for people. His healing ministry exemplifies the biopsychosospiritual model: in the physical, biological realm, for example, Jesus cured every disease (Matt 9:35). He cured the leper (Matt 8:1–4), healed the hemorrhaging woman (Matt 9:20–22), gave sight to the blind (Matt 9:27–31), and enabled the lame to walk (Luke 5:17–26). In the psychological and spiritual realms, he brought peace to troubled hearts (John 14:27) and rest to the weary and the burdened (Matt 11:28–30); he invited all to freedom and spiritual growth (John 4:1–42).

The USCCB elucidated the relevance of Jesus Christ's ministry to the health care practices of the Catholic Church when it asserted that "the mystery of Christ casts light on every facet of Catholic health care: to see Christian love as the animating principle of health care; to see healing and compassion as a continuation of Christ's mission; [and] to see suffering as a participation in the redemptive power of Christ's passion, death, and resurrection."[31] The biblical interpretation of health is that it signifies wholeness—a combination of physical, spiritual, and psychological wholeness—and that health is needed by both individuals and communities. Jesus is a divine healer who restores health to all human beings. When he was present on earth, Jesus not only healed people's physical, spiritual, and psychological illnesses—he restored people to wholeness. Throughout his earthly ministry, Jesus unceasingly proclaimed the kingdom of God as he reached out to heal our wounded humanity.

The Church's Continuation of the Healing Ministry of Christ

The church's healing apostolate has traditionally been a continuation of the healing ministry of Christ. The USCCB has made clear that, from the earliest church to the present day, healing was a major part of the mission of evangelization to which Jesus commissioned his followers.[32] Jesus himself stressed the importance of continuing his healing ministry: "Into whatever city you go, after they welcome you . . . cure the sick there. Say to them,

---

30. Trancik and Barina, "What Makes a Catholic Hospital Catholic?"
31. USCCB, "Health and Health Care."
32. USCCB, "Health and Health Care."

"'The reign of God is at hand'" (Luke 10:8–9). In his remarks about the final judgment day, he held out the promise of God's blessings to all who comfort the sick: "Come. You have my Father's blessing! For I was . . . ill and you comforted me. . . . I assure you, as often as you did it for one of the least of my brothers and sisters, you did it for me" (Matt 25:34–40). The church and her members follow Jesus's example in various acts like healing and visiting the sick. In doing so, the faithful not only provide care for the physically ill but also work to restore health and wholeness to all aspects of the human person and the human community. Christians understand that the sacraments, including the rite of the anointing of the sick, are an important part of today's healing ministry in the church. This rite, as well as pastoral care for the sick, are of particular significance as a sign and prayer for the restoration of health, which was part of the mission preached by Jesus.[33] Church members place much importance on these actions, not only because they bring relief from illness but also because they help Christians communicate that human sickness must be understood in the context of the whole mystery of salvation.

The sacrament of the anointing of the sick is strong proof of the church's continuation of Jesus's healing ministry. This sacrament ensures that those who are seriously ill and in need of special help from God's grace can avoid the temptations and weakening of faith that come from anxiety and a broken spirit. Additional evidence of the church's commitment to healing and health is shown in the availability of the presbytery for sacraments, the laying-on of hands, and prayers of faith. The church understands that celebrating the sacraments provides the sick with the grace of the Holy Spirit and, through this grace, the whole person receives the gift of health.

The mission of the church is to follow Jesus Christ, the healer, the comforter, the liberator, and teacher. Therefore, every action of the church's ministry must include healing of body, soul, and spirit. The church carries out its work of healing in other ways—for example, by providing local places of care and comfort for its members in need of healing[34] and by operating programs for those in need, including the sick, orphans, widows, the elderly, the poor, the homeless, and people with various physical and mental challenges.

Having explored the church's general outlook toward healing and health, it is now appropriate to examine in more detail the role of the Catholic Church in African health care. First, however, it is necessary to briefly outline the health care needs of Africans.

Health Care Needs in Africa

Africa is the second most populous continent in the world with 1.392 billion people, which accounts for 16.72 percent of the world's population.[35] Rich in natural resources, Africa also has a high rate of poverty and a high burden of illness. Nearly 50 percent of people in the sub-Saharan region live on less than $1.25 a day.[36] In terms of illness burden, more than 90 percent of the three hundred thousand to five hundred thousand cases of malaria worldwide occur in Africa, and 60 percent of the global HIV/AIDS cases occur on the continent.[37] Of the one million Africans who die of malaria each year, 85 percent are children aged five and below. Africa has the highest neonatal death rate in the world, as well as high rates of life-threatening communicable diseases and noncommunicable diseases like hypertension, coronary heart disease, and diabetes.[38] Of the twenty countries with the highest mortality rates in the world, nineteen are in Africa.[39] See table 1 below for a summary of the twenty leading causes of mortality in Africa in 2015. The high poverty and mortality rates on the continent call for global attention.

---

33. USCCB, "Health and Health Care."
34. USCCB, "Health and Health Care."
35. World Health Organization, "Global Health Estimates 2015."
36. Bunson, "Church in Africa."
37. World Health Organization, "Global Health Estimates 2015."
38. World Health Organization, "Global Health Estimates 2015."
39. World Health Organization, "Global Health Estimates 2015."

Rank	Cause	Deaths (000s)	% of total deaths	Cumulative % of total deaths	CDR (per 100 000 population)
0	All Causes	9,207	100.0	100.0	930.8
1	Lower respiratory infections	1,007	10.9	10.9	101.8
2	HIV/AIDS	760	8.3	19.2	76.8
3	Diarrheal diseases	643	7.0	26.2	65.0
4	Stroke	451	4.9	31.1	45.6
5	Ischemic heart disease	441	4.8	35.9	44.5
6	Tuberculosis	435	4.7	40.6	44.0
7	Malaria	403	4.4	45.0	40.8
8	Preterm birth complications	344	3.7	48.7	34.7
9	Birth asphyxia and birth trauma	321	3.5	52.2	32.5
10	Road injury	269	2.9	55.1	27.2
11	Congenital anomalies	218	2.4	57.5	22.0
12	Meningitis	210	2.3	59.8	21.3
13	Maternal conditions	195	2.1	61.9	19.7
14	Protein-energy malnutrition	181	2.0	63.8	18.3
15	Cirrhosis of the liver	174	1.9	65.7	17.6
16	Neonatal sepsis and infections	174	1.9	67.6	17.6
17	Diabetes mellitus	169	1.8	69.5	17.1
18	Chronic obstructive pulmonary disease	105	1.1	70.6	10.6
19	Interpersonal violence	102	1.1	71.7	10.3
20	Sickle cell disorders and trait	99	1.1	72.8	10.0

Table 1: Twenty Leading Causes of Death in Africa[40]

The History of Health Care Services Offered by the Catholic Church in Africa with Examples from Nigeria

Western-style colonial health care services were introduced to Africa during early European incursions on the continent. As articulated by Seggane Musisi and Nakanyike Musisi, these incursions had three objectives: to open up the continent for trade, to conquer and occupy it, and to civilize it by means of Christian evangelism.[41] Western medical facilities were established in order to assist with these objectives but were initially intended only for the European explorers, missionaries, and colonial administrators and their families. Later, missionary groups—including those associated with the Catholic Church—established

---

40. World Health Organization, "Global Health Estimates 2015."
41. Musisi and Musisi, "Legacies of Colonialism in African Medicine."

churches, schools, hospitals, and other health care facilities that were open to Africans. Some of these health care facilities were confronted with human-resources challenges, which were in part addressed by the establishment of schools of nursing and midwifery to train native Africans. Most of the Catholic health care facilities were established by religious men and women. For example, the Holy Rosary Sisters established maternity hospitals in Onitsha and Emekuku in Nigeria; Mother Kevin established a hospital for lepers in Nyenga, Uganda, in 1932; and Sr. Eletta Mantiero started a dispensary in Kalongo, Uganda, in 1934.

Western-style health care services were first introduced into Nigeria by Western explorers and traders, specifically to serve their own health needs; they were not accessible to Nigerians. Later on, Catholic, Anglican, and Baptist missionaries began to establish health care facilities available to Nigerians as part of their mission to gain converts. The first hospital in Nigeria, named the Sacred Heart Hospital, was built in 1885 by the Catholic mission at Lantoro Abeokuta in Ogun State.[42] Other health care facilities established during the early days of the Catholic Church's presence in Nigeria include the Holy Rosary Hospital Maternity Clinic, Waterside, which opened in Onitsha in 1889; St. Luke's Hospital in Anua; Mater Misericordiae Hospital in Afikpo; the Holy Rosary Hospital in Emekuku; and St. Gerard's Hospital in Kaduna.[43] Many Catholic religious communities and congregations of women are actively involved in charitable works in the health sector in Nigeria. The efficiency and dedication of these religious sisters are visible in both their state-of-the-art nursing homes and simple rural clinics. Much importance is given to rural and community health programs, with special attention paid to the curative, preventive, and social aspects of medicine.

Current State of the Health Care Services Provided by the Catholic Church in Africa

Responding to the mandate of Jesus Christ to heal the sick, the Catholic Church has been at the forefront of health care services in Africa, playing a significant role in combating the disease burden on the continent.[44] The church's health care services are found in the sub-Saharan region of Africa, which has the largest Catholic population, and in other regions of Africa as well.[45]

A health care system includes agencies (organizational and individual) and actions targeted toward the promotion, restoration, and maintenance of health.[46] It encompasses activities aimed at influencing the determinants of health and those that are targeted toward treating health problems.[47] These activities include direct health care, awareness campaigns, informal and formal education, and other actions that promote health and wellness. The determinants of health include "the social and economic environment, the physical environment, and the person's individual characteristics and behaviours."[48]

The church works assiduously to alleviate the effects of diseases, illnesses, and health conditions in Africa. During the recent Ebola epidemic, Catholic medical care contributed significantly to the treatment of those who were affected in Liberia, Nigeria, Sierra Leone, and Guinea.[49] The church in Africa has continued to be active in supporting the treatment of persons with HIV/AIDS and in developing prevention programs—for example, the Reach Out Mbuya program in Kampala, Uganda.[50] The Catholic Church in Africa provides social spaces, care, support, and other kinds of health care services for various groups of Africans. Table 2 presents a summary of the health care facilities operated by the church in Africa.

---

42. Schram, "History of Nigerian Health Care Services."
43. Ferdinand Nwaigbo, "The Church and Repositioning the Maternal Care in Africa," 118.
44. Bunson, "Church in Africa."
45. Bunson, "Church in Africa."
46. WHO, "Everybody's Business."
47. WHO, "Everybody's Business."
48. Engel, "Clinical Application of the Biopsychosocial Model"; WHO, "Everybody's Business."
49. Bunson, "Church in Africa."
50. Calderisi, *Earthly Mission*; PBS Newshour, "Catholic Church Looks to Lead Conversation on Combating HIV/AIDS"; Stahl, "AIDS and the Catholic Church."

Health Care Facility Type	Number
Hospitals	1,100
Dispensaries and Primary Care Centers	5,250
Leprosy Colonies	200
Homes for the Elderly	750
Orphanages	1,300
Nurseries	2,600
Marriage Counseling Centers	1,590

Table 2: Health Care Facilities Operated by the Catholic Church in Africa[51]

Health Care Type	Number
Hospitals	3
Hospices	18
Clinics	26
Care of the Elderly	7
Care of Orphans and Vulnerable Children	26
Parish Nurse Programs	2
Diocesan Health Ministry	12
Home-Based Care Projects	121
Mental Health	1

Table 3: Health Care Services of the Catholic Health Care Association of Southern Africa (CATHCA)[53]

Examples of Catholic Health Care Programs in Africa

The health care programs of the Catholic Church in Africa are typically organized by individual dioceses or consortia of dioceses. For example, the bishops of southern African countries formed a consortium, the Catholic Health Care Association of Southern Africa (CATHCA), for the purpose of "playing a facilitating role in promoting, supporting, and developing effective Catholic healthcare" in their region.[52] This consortium encompasses the nations of Botswana, Swaziland, and South Africa. CATHCA's 2015 annual report describes significant health care activities ranging from hospitals to home-based care. Table 3 presents statistics related to the health care services provided within the CATHCA network. CATHCA also conducts training in maternal and child health, as well as in gender-based violence, for government and NGO community health workers. See table 4 for details about this training. In addition, in recognition of the importance of providing holistic services encompassing a full range of spiritual, physical, and emotional needs, CATHCA launched an intervention focused on providing spiritual care and training to community health workers. The goal was to integrate spirituality into the Catholic health care system.

Another, larger consortium is the Southern African Regional Network of Catholic Health Care Providers, which covers eight southern African countries: Zimbabwe, Zambia, Malawi, Lesotho, South Africa, Swaziland, Botswana, and Namibia. This network was established in 2014 in order "to share information on the work being done by the Catholic Church in Southern African countries in health, to strengthen partnerships between the various church bodies and to consider ways to tackle common health issues across the region."[54] This network has largely focused its work on training aimed at achieving these goals.

West African countries have also benefited from the church's efforts in health care. In Nigeria, individual dioceses develop and implement health care services. For example, the Diocese of Enugu has taken steps to provide quality health care services to people in the diocese. Under an insurance initiative established in 2015 by the diocese known as Ndubuisi Community Mutual Based Health Insurance (NMBHI), individuals from both urban and rural areas are able to access health services regardless of age, ethnic group, or religious affiliation.

---

51. Data drawn from Bunson, "Church in Africa."
52. CATHCA, "Annual Report 2015," 1.
53. CATHCA, "Annual Report 2015," 1.
54. CATHCA, "Annual Report 2015," 13.

District	Province	Total Number Trained in 2015					
		Church Community Health Workers	Government Community Health Workers	Leadership	Public Participation	Gender-Based Violence	Maternal and Child Health
Tshwane	Gauteng	1	88	49	19	37	75
Bojanala	Northwest	144	77	55	48	48	66
Vhembe	Limpopo	29	37	24	21	21	-
Mopani	Limpopo	30	15	31	17	17	-
Total		204	217	159	105	123	141

Table 4: Health Training Services Provided by CATHCA in 2015

Enrollment in the scheme costs ₦100 (Nigerian naira), and the total cost to receive the full benefit of the program is ₦6,000 per year. There is also the extended scheme for chronic illness costing ₦18,000.[55] The Enugu Diocese is responsible for the expenses of administering the system as well as for identifying health providers and credibility for the participants. Participants are not required to receive care from diocesan hospitals, which are among the options they could choose to cater to their health care needs.[56]

Furthermore, committed in its constitution to implementing Catholic social teachings,[57] the Enugu Diocese's Catholic Institute for Development, Justice, and Peace (CIDJAP) operates a primary health care program with four health centers spread across Enugu State. The program offers services to more than sixty communities. The community health center in Akegbe-Ugwu covers more than twelve communities, and the centers at Akpakwume and Nze cover sixteen and twelve communities, respectively. The people in these communities enjoy regular hospital, primary health care, and maternity services focused on health education, HIV/AIDS awareness and treatment, maternal health and childcare, and family planning. The health centers also provide essential drugs, a supply of food and water, treatment of minor ailments, dental care, mental health care, domestic accident prevention, prevention and treatment of endemic diseases, and environmental and occupational health care. As of 2017, the centers featured resident doctors and were open twenty hours a day. Their services are available to both the rich and the poor in the rural areas.[58] The health care centers are coordinated by CIDJAP, which employs more than three hundred health professionals working to make health care services accessible to more than one million people in both the rural and urban areas of Enugu State.[59]

Other dioceses in Nigeria also make health care services available through their local CIDJAP. In addition, religious congregations of women and men have continued to provide leadership in health care in Nigeria. Their leadership is demonstrated through health education, preventative medicine, local clinics, and health advocacy with government. The Catholic health system strives to work with and collaborate with the wider community.

---

55. Enugu Diocesan Secretariat, 2016.
56. Enugu Diocesan Secretariat, 2016.
57. CIDJAP, "Health Care."
58. CIDJAP, "Health Care."
59. CIDJAP, "Health Care."

Challenges Facing Catholic Health Care in Africa and the Way Forward

The health care programs of the Catholic Church in Africa face several challenges, which should become the subject of research and publications and should be met by a pastoral response from community leaders. One of the challenges identified by Barbara Mann Wall is the problem of inadequate human resources to maintain the church's health care services.[60] Despite the fact that the church has established schools to train health professionals to meet this challenge and despite the gains achieved by these schools, issues of adequate staffing remain. It is possible that a paucity of funds may be limiting the capacity of health care facilities to attract and retain adequate numbers of health professionals.

Another challenge faced by Catholic health care facilities in Africa concerns the availability of modern medical equipment and supplies. This is a challenge that affects some facilities, but not all. In addition, maintaining the equipment poses a further challenge. Just as the church established schools of nursing and midwifery to increase the available pool of human resources, it might be beneficial to consider the establishment of schools to train people in medical physics and engineering, so that there will be a crop of professionals who can both invent and maintain hospital equipment.

A major problem the church's health care programs might need to address is the role of native African medicine in health and healing. In the early missionary period, native medicine was demonized, and Christians were barred from using it.[61] In light of a better understanding of native medicine and in the spirit of inculturation, however, there is a great need for the Catholic Church to explore the uses (and limitations) of native medicine.

Another major challenge facing the Catholic Church in its health care ministry is the fact that many people attribute illnesses or diseases to spiritual forces and make spiritual healing their first line of treatment, even for health issues that have known medical causes. Before Christianity and Islam, many African nations practiced the worship of ancient native gods, and these practices persist to this day in some people's reliance on witch doctors, healers, and herbalists promising miracle cures. These ancient beliefs, embedded in the culture, are more about magic and miracles than any real, significant relationship with a God or gods. This challenge requires that the church mount regular awareness campaigns for its health programs. The church also needs to reinvent its health care facilities by adopting the biopsychosospiritual model discussed earlier in this chapter. There are two possible ways to make this model an integral part of health care practice. One way is to modify the curriculum for training medical professionals to include all dimensions of health, which would enable trainees to develop appropriate skills in managing these dimensions in collaboration with relevant professionals. Another way is to create multidisciplinary consulting rooms, where a patient could be seen by a team made up of a medical doctor, a psychologist, a sociologist, and a pastoral counselor.

Conclusion

The health care needs of Africa are enormous. The Catholic Church in Africa has contributed to the provision of health care through its establishment of health care networks and through the efforts of individual dioceses. The range of health care services delivered by the Catholic Church in Africa supports a holistic approach to health, and it might be additionally helpful to make these services integrative following the biopsychosospiritual model.

The southern African network-based model described above, which includes both the provision of health care services and the training of health professionals, might be helpful in ensuring that health care services are properly coordinated and delivered to those in need. The health care model of the Enugu diocese is another example of how the Catholic Church in Africa is contributing, and can continue to contribute, to health care for the African people. As stated by the World Health Organization, the challenges of African health care call for

---

60. Wall, *Into Africa,* 53–56.
61. Musisi and Musisi, "Legacies of Colonialism in African Medicine."

a systemic approach to health care services. Coordinated models such as the southern African network-based model and the Enugu diocesan health program might be the key to the implementation of a systemic approach.

Bibliography

"Africa Population (Live)." http://www.worldometers.info/world-population/africa-population.

Annandale, Ellen. *The Sociology of Health and Medicine: A Critical Introduction*. Cambridge: Polity Press, 1998.

Arinze, Ani. "Even Witch-Doctors Create Churches." *The Southern Cross: Southern Africa's Catholic Weekly*, October 6, 2018. https://www.scross.co.za/2018/10/even-witch-doctors-create-churches.

Barlow, D. H., and V. M. Durand. *Abnormal Psychology: An Integrative Approach*. 4th ed. Belmont, CA: Thomson Wadsworth, 2005.

Bayer, R., and R. L. Spitzer. "Edited Correspondence on the Status of Homosexuality in DSM-III." *Journal of Historical Behavioural Science* 18 (1982): 32–52.

Bunson, Matthew. "The Church in Africa: A Story of Challenges and Hope." *Our Sunday Visitor*, August 9, 2015. https://www.osvnews.com.

Calderisi, Robert. *Earthly Mission: The Catholic Church and World Development*. New Haven, CT: Yale University Press, 2013.

Cambridge Advanced Learner's Dictionary, 4th ed. Cambridge University Press, 2013.

Catholic Bishops Conference of Nigeria. "Bishop Dunia Tasks Government on Health Care Delivery Service." October 15, 2013. http://www.cbcn-ng.org/newsdetail.php?tab=253.

Catholic Bishops Conference of Nigeria (2012). Communique issued at the end of the Second Plenary Meeting. https://www.cbcn-ng.org/articledetail.php?tab=12.

Catholic Health Care Association of Southern Africa (CATHCA). "Annual Report 2015." https://cathca.org/wp-content/uploads/2018/08/2015-annual-report.pdf.

CIDJAP. "Health Care" (2017). http://www.cidjap.org/healthcare.html.

Congregation for the Doctrine of the Faith. *Catechism of the Catholic Church*. Vatican City: Libreria Editrice Vaticana; Dublin: Veritas, 1995.

de la Porte, A. "Spirituality and Healthcare: Towards Holistic People-Centred Healthcare in South Africa." *HTS Theological Studies* 72.4 (2016): 1–9.

Economist Intelligence Unit. "Value-Based Healthcare in Europe: Laying the Foundation." 2011. https://www.eiuperspectives.economist.com/sites/default/files/ValuebasedhealthcareEurope.pdf.

Engel, George L. "The Clinical Application of the Biopsychosocial Model." *American Journal of Psychiatry* 137.5 (1980): 535–44.

———. "The Need for a New Medical Model: A Challenge for Biomedicine." *Science* 196 (1977): 129–36.

Feierman, S., A. Kleinman, K. Stewart, P. Farmer, and V. Das. "Anthropology, Knowledge-Flows and Global Health." *Global Public Health* 5.2 (2010): 122–28.

Gaemi, N. "The Rise and Fall of the Biopsychosocial Model." *British Journal of Psychiatry* 121 (2009): 3–4.

Gordon, James S. *Holistic Medicine*. New York: Chelsea House, 1988.

Grinker, R. R. "A Struggle for Eclecticism." *American Journal of Psychiatry* 121 (1964): 451–57.

Gundani, P. "Views and Attitudes of Missionaries toward African Religion in Southern Africa during the Portuguese Era." *Religion & Theology* 11 (2004): 298–312.

Hattie, John, Jane E. Myers, and Thomas J. Sweeney. "A Factor Structure of Wellness: Theory, Assessment, Analysis and Practice." *Journal of Counseling & Development* 82.3 (2004): 354–64.

Illich, Ivan. *Medical Nemesis: The Expropriation of Health*. New York: Pantheon Books, 1976.

Koenig, Harold. "Religion and Medicine: Historical Background and Reasons for Separation." *International Journal of Psychiatry in Medicine* 30 (2000): 385–98.

Mohr, Adam. "Missionary Medicine and Akan Therapeutics: Illness, Health, and Healing in Southern Ghana's Basel Mission, 1828–1918." *Journal of Religion in Africa* 39 (2009): 429–61.

Musisi, Seggane, and Nakanyike Musisi. "The Legacies of Colonialism in African Medicine." https://www.who.int/global_health_histories/seminars/nairobi02.pdf.

Njoku, Mary Gloria C. "Behavioural Health: Application of Biopsychosocial Model of Prevention and Treatment." Inaugural lecture delivered at Godfrey Okoye University, Enugu, Nigeria, March 2014.

Nwaigbo, Ferdinand. "The Church and Repositioning the Maternal Care in Africa: A Project of the Millennium Development Goals," IGIRISI 6 (2009): 118.

Osler, William. *Aequanimitas*. 3rd ed. Philadelphia: Blakiston, 1932.

PBS Newshour. "Catholic Church Looks to Lead Conversation on Combating HIV/AIDS." May 27, 2011.

Schram, R. *A History of Nigerian Health Care Services*. Ibadan: Ibadan University Press, 1971.

Scully, J. "What Is a Disease?," *EMBO Reports* 5.7 (2004): 650–53.

Stahl, Brittany. "AIDS and the Catholic Church," *NYC Pavement Pieces*, December 14, 2008. journalism.nyu.edu.

Thomas, Lewis. "Medicine in America," *TV Guide* (December 31, 1977): 25-26.

Trancik, E., and R. Barina. "What Makes a Catholic Hospital Catholic?," *U.S. Catholic*, March 2015. www.uscatholic.org.

Travis, John W., and Regina Sara Ryan. *The Wellness Workbook*. Berkeley, CA: Ten Speed Press, 1988.

United States Conference of Catholic Bishops. "Health and Health Care: A Pastoral Letter of the American Catholic Bishops." Washington, DC: United States Catholic Conference, 1981.

Wall, Barbara Mann. *Into Africa: A Transnational History of Catholic Medical Missions and Social Change*. New Brunswick, NJ: Rutgers University Press, 2015.

Weigel, D. D. "Justice Perspective: From a Catholic Perspective, Health Care Is a Basic Human Right." Catholic Charities of Buffalo, 2017.

"Wholeness." In *American Heritage Roget's Thesaurus*. Boston: Houghton Mifflin Harcourt, 2014. www.thefreedictionary.com/wholeness.

World Health Organization (WHO). "The African Regional Health Report: The Health of the People." 2015.

———. "Everybody's Business—Strengthening Health Systems to Improve Health Outcomes: WHO's Framework for Action." 2007.

———. "Global Health Estimates 2015: 20 Leading Causes of Death by Region, 2000 and 2015." 2015.

———. "Preamble to the Constitution of the World Health Organization." 1946.

Yang, A., P. Farmer, and A. McGahan. "Sustainability in Global Health." *Global Public Health* 5.2 (2010): 129–35.

Suggested Reading

Feierman, Steven. "Struggles for Control: The Social Roots of Health and Healing in Modern Africa." *African Studies Review* 28 (1985): 73–147.

Gordon, James S. *Holistic Medicine*. New York: Chelsea House, 1988.

Ventegodt, S., M. Morad, H. Eytan, and M. Joav. "Clinical Holistic Medicine: Use and Limitations of the Biomedical Paradigm." *Scientific World Journal* 4 (2004): 295–306.

Werner, Dietrich. "WCC Consultation on Mission, Health and Healing, Accra, Ghana, 4–8 December 2002 Reflector's Report." *International Review of Mission* 93 (2004): 379–88.

Key Words

Africa
anointing of the sick
biblical interpretation of health
biomedical
biopsychosocial
biopsychosospiritual
Catholic Health Care Association of Southern Africa
Catholic Hospital Association of Nigeria
Catholic Institute for Development, Justice and Peace
communicable diseases
curative medicine
determinants of health
disease
global health estimates
health care
health insurance
health system
HIV/AIDS
holistic model
home-based care
human rights
illness
illness burden
malaria
mission
missionary
mortality
Nigeria
non-communicable diseases
pastoral care
Southern African Regional Network of Catholic Health Care Providers
sub-Saharan region
supernatural perspective
visitation of the sick
wellness
wholeness
World Health Organization

Health and Abundant Life: Catholic Healing amid a Plurality of Healing Paradigms in Africa

Bernhard Udelhoven, MAfr

> The issue of healing, understood in the wider sense of the word . . . will indeed be the central missiological topic of the 21st century. This requires a paradigm shift in missiology. The central soteriological framework and religious mindset in which the search for God is expressed and God's power is experienced no longer constitutes justification (as it did in the period of the Reformation), or sanctification (as in the holiness movement), or liberation (as in the period of decolonization and the struggle against military dictatorships in the 70s and 80s of the 20th century). At the end of the historical phase of modernity that ever more dissociated body, mind and spirit in the understanding of the human being, a new tendency is making itself known and felt everywhere to correct the dichotomies at work in the 19th and 20th centuries.
>
> —Dietrich Werner, commenting on the World Council of Churches' consultation on healing, Accra, 2002[1]

Today the quest for healing is seeking new forms and expressions that touch people's experiences of suffering and alienation in more existential ways. Examples from the Catholic Church include novenas, pilgrimages to healing sites, new forms of eucharistic adoration, and other healing liturgies. Another manifestation is the rapid growth of the Catholic Charismatic Renewal in Africa with its ministry of healing and deliverance. Care for the sick and the fight against disease have always been fully part of the evangelization efforts of churches across the Christian spectrum. Going a step further, many ministries today see in healing the paradigm for God's salvific actions and the church's purpose, the lens through which to understand the paschal mystery: "By his stripes you are healed" (1 Pet 2:24, quoting Isa 53:5). For these ministries, healing restores access to "abundant life" or the "fullness of life" (John 10:10b) that Jesus promised to the believer. They understand health in the widest sense, not just as absence of disease but as a positive way of life in God's presence. This includes the social, financial, political, and environmental dimensions of life, as well as the forgiveness of sins, reconciliation, inner and outer freedom from oppression, finding one's place in society, and the quest for justice. This may all be expressed in the *shalom* of God, whose absence affects the human body in one way or another.

If Werner is right, however, and if healing today is indeed the prime focal point for seeking and finding God's presence and intervention, it has also become a sign and cause of divisions within Christianity. Different ministries understand the human condition of sickness and its causes in fundamentally different ways.

The historical mission churches in Africa understood sickness mainly from a biomedical perspective. The Christianity of Europe and America, shaped by the Western Enlightenment, gradually

---

1. Werner, "WCC Consultation," 380.

downplayed beliefs in the spiritual bases of illness, preferring to look to the natural world for explanations of conditions that were at one time considered evidence of the workings of the supernatural. After Sigmund Freud's explanation of demonic possession in terms of neurosis, autosuggestion, and repressed wishes and impulses,[2] many psychologists came to regard belief in demons and exorcism as not only superstitious and outmoded but also as dangerous because it discouraged people from pursuing mainstream medical treatment and sanctioned irrational behavior.[3] Theologians began using the social sciences to explain what the demons described in the Bible "really" were. "Jesus healed people who had various kinds of mental or psychosomatic illnesses," wrote Paul Hollenbach. "[T]he question of the miraculous need no longer be a serious issue because the phenomena of possession and exorcism are now examined and understood via the social sciences as common world-wide phenomena throughout most of history."[4]

The missionary churches tended to categorize African conceptions of the spirit world and their spiritual experience of illness as superstition.[5] For this reason, the churches often overlooked or misrepresented the spiritual concerns of sick people. I do not mean to say that there was (or is) no such thing as superstition in Africa. I understand superstition as an inflexible attitude of mind that does not want to let go of cherished beliefs even when confronted with evidence to the contrary. If such beliefs cannot be attuned to a person's view of life and religion, that is all the more reason that they should be unmasked as superstitious and overcome, or at least engaged in a critical way. According to this understanding, most people's views of sickness are loaded with superstitious beliefs, and not only in Africa. Even if that is true, popular African conceptions of sickness often pointed to (and continue to point to) dimensions of illness to which the church was (and is) blind. When the human body, the self, and the soul are understood in relational ways, the experience of being ill cannot be isolated from the social environment in which it is lived. In this way, the experience of illness encompasses a moral dimension that is often interwoven with spiritual notions. If we strip away these popular conceptions of sickness, we may even lack the vocabulary to describe its moral and spiritual aspects.[6] In many traditional African healing rites, healing the sick and healing the sick person's surroundings and social environment are one and the same thing. Such an understanding of sickness and healing should also be relevant beyond Africa and will remain the focus of this chapter.

---

2. Freud, *Eine Teufelsneurose*.

3. For example, Trethowan, "Dangers Present in Exorcism."

4. Hollenbach, "Jesus, Demoniacs, and Public Authorities," 567. For Hollenbach, demonic possession is a neurotic condition caused by coercive social structures. He cites Frantz Fanon's opinion that the phenomenon of demon possession is symptomatic of a divided mind that arises from the alienation of the uprooted masses, a reaction to oppressive circumstances and totalizing structures. Hollenbach reads Jesus's unsanctioned exorcisms, which brought him into conflict with the religious and political authorities, as provocative, prophetic actions meant to disturb the fake peace upheld by repressive and authoritarian structures. I will take up this argument later in an examination of the prophetic understanding of spiritual afflictions.

5. It would be wrong to say that Western missionaries did not believe in the existence of the devil and demons. Many did, but regarded demonic possession as being very rare. The African spirit world did not fit into their demonology, especially because Scholastic theology defined demons and angels in terms of their essentially inert characteristics and ignored that the "goodness" or "badness" of a spirit in Africa often depended on specific social relationships. (See Udelhoven, *Unseen Worlds*, chapter 2.) Because missionaries saw themselves as part of the civilizing mission of a superior culture, or later, in postcolonial times, of a discourse about development, African beliefs were usually seen as backward, immoral, or superstitious. See Mohr, "Missionary Medicine and Akan Therapeutics," for examples of changing attitudes about the African spiritual world among the missionaries of a Protestant missionary society.

6. Emmanuel Milingo called these the "mysteries of life," affirming that the Catholic faith itself works miracles among its faithful because it has access to these mysteries (*Are Zambians Superstitious?*).

Pastoral Dilemmas in Dealing with Spirits[7]

Despite the fact that African Catholic theologians refer so often to African culture and to the project of inculturation, Paul Gifford has accused them of ignoring the religious imagination of the rank-and-file African Catholic, who lives in what he calls, following Max Weber, an "enchanted world."[8] Though I would be able to cite a few examples to the contrary, I want to highlight the divided understanding that has indeed hampered the Catholic Church's grassroots pastoral engagement with people's demons and with witchcraft.

One example is the so-called Milingo Affair of the early 1980s. With his popular healing ministry and mass exorcisms, Emmanuel Milingo, the archbishop of Lusaka, directly addressed the world of spirits that afflict people.[9] While many found relief and healing from Milingo's ministry, the reaction to it polarized laity and clergy, revealing within the church a great difference of opinion about the nature of the spiritual world and its effects on people and their health.[10] Many of Milingo's critics feared that he was opening a Pandora's box of validations for a belief system that needed to be overthrown. Those who connected their illnesses to spiritual afflictions and who looked at Milingo's evident success could not understand the reaction of the church hierarchy. After his removal from Lusaka, any further popular engagement by Catholics with the spirit world became a "hot iron" that many feared to touch, in Zambia and elsewhere.

Many Catholic dioceses and parishes have experienced divided reactions to charismatic deliverance ministries in other places in Africa. The vibrant forms of healing offered by the fast-growing Catholic Charismatic Renewal movement do not always follow Vatican guidelines for the healing ministry[11] and are often practiced away from the watchful eye of the church. They address a popular demand for deliverance and, following the example of Pentecostal healing ministries, have exorcised multitudes of spirits on a daily basis. While the charismatic prophets discerned in the spirit world the root cause of many sufferings, Western-trained skeptics devalued the encounters as hysterical episodes in the lives of troubled people. On both sides of the divide, the actual experiences of people did not always count—the skeptics dismissed them as phantasms and many exorcizing healers molded them according to their own conceptions of the demonic.[12]

Meinrad Hebga (1928–2008), a pioneer in African theology and also a popular exorcist, attempted to bridge the gap between the language of the sick and the language of the church's healing ministry.[13] First, Hebga believed that moral and spiritual afflictions accompanying serious illness, including witchcraft and spirits, are complex realities that the church in Africa needs to acknowledge, even when these phenomena cannot be fully comprehended in terms of Enlightenment rationality. He held that the church's approach to such challenges should not be reduced to the concepts that obtain in Western cultural settings. Second, he believed (and prac-

---

7. Note that I use terms like "spirits" and "witchcraft" in a person-centered way, in which the meaning depends on the affected person using the terms.

8. Gifford, *Christianity, Development, and Modernity,* 144. According to Gifford, one of the reasons for this is the Catholic Church's cozy relationship with and financial dependence on development agencies.

9. I refer here to Milingo's healing ministry in Zambia that was active from 1973 to 1983, when he was removed by the Vatican. He continued his healing ministry in Europe, partly under the umbrella of the Catholic Charismatic Renewal.

10. Ter Haar, *Spirit of Africa.*

11. Congregation for the Doctrine of the Faith, *Instruction on Prayers for Healing.*

12. Many exorcists strongly shape the form of the testimonies that the delivered persons are encouraged to give to the congregation. See especially Johanneke Kamps's work on the testimonies of delivered satanists in Zambia (*Speaking of Satan in Zambia*).

13. I was not able to engage directly with Hebga's work; his major publications have not yet been translated into English and were unavailable to me. I have consulted the information about and views of Hebga contained in Lado, *Catholic Pentecostalism,* and Poucouta, "Meinrad Pierre Hebga: Teacher and Healer," and have reviewed E. E. Uzukwu's comments in *God, Spirit, and Human Wholeness.*

ticed the belief) that prayer, exorcism, and diverse spiritual gifts given to the church provide answers to these forces. In his view, the power of the Holy Spirit in the church is greater than the power of witchcraft and evil. Third, he insisted that a pastoral approach to these afflictions needs to include the insights of the medical and social sciences as well as psychology, but as part of a nonreductionist, multidisciplinary approach. Finally, he saw that the church's theology and pastoral language need to embrace African mystical experiences and connect with key concepts relevant to these experiences, for example, the "mystical shadow," the "breath," and "life forces." Such openness demands a positive engagement with the African cultural understanding of body, soul, the human self, the community, and the world of the spirits and ancestors.

The first three of these convictions resonate rather well with the church's official teaching on demonology, which affirms the existence of the devil and demons against the Western world's growing skepticism and its tendency to reduce the phenomenon of spirits to psychological or social categories.[14] However, the last has been insufficiently embraced as part of the project of inculturation. One reason may be a lack of theological concepts that do justice to African relational and situational notions of the spiritual world. Hebga developed an alternative view of body and spirit(s) rooted in the African experience, but his practice of ritual healing and exorcism in the Ephphatha Movement (founded in Cameroon), which was inspired by the Charismatic Renewal in the U.S. (as was Milingo's ministry in Zambia and Europe), has been strongly criticized for misunderstanding diverse African spiritual realities by gathering them together into a single, undifferentiated evil empire. The critics have compared this misunderstanding with the early missionaries' demonization of the entire African spiritual world.[15] These criticisms would also apply to many practices of Pentecostal and charismatic deliverance throughout Africa, which are embedded in a strongly dualistic framework.[16] If, however, we understand exorcism and deliverance in the context of prayer, therapy, and ritual and view it as a drama of faith, the divided views of the ontological reality of afflicting spirits may to some extent be brought together. In this way, the goodness or badness of a spiritual affliction is found not in its intrinsic characteristics but in its helpfulness or hindrance with respect to living the Christian vocation. The overriding concern of exorcism should not be demonology, but rather bringing the alienating forces (whether spiritual, sociocultural, or psychological) into the presence of the risen Christ.

More pressing from a pastoral angle are the ethical concerns that arise when healing prayers closely follow people's expectations and concepts, trapping them in webs of fear and dependency. Providing relief from witchcraft may reinforce certain beliefs about witchcraft by confirming that it is the root of all human suffering.[17] Too often, sessions of deliverance and healing have resulted in witch-hunts or the scapegoating of individuals or even of entire minority groups; some Catholic deliverance ministries in Africa have been guilty of provoking violent witch-hunts.[18] The drama of deliverance and exorcism often portrays the image of utterly evil powers that have intervened in the lives of totally innocent victims. While deliverance is supposed to culminate in a public demonstration of Christ's powers and the defeat of the devil, one may express doubts about whether a victim mentality leads to spiritual growth when repentance and conversion are meant for others (the witches), not oneself.

Other ethical concerns range from subtle forms of group pressure to have unquestioning faith in

---

14. Congregation for the Doctrine of the Faith, "Christian Faith and Demonology."

15. Lado, *Catholic Pentecostalism*, 71, 90.

16. About the resulting hybrid character of the figure of the devil embracing both Christian and traditional concepts, see Meyer, *Translating the Devil*.

17. Akrong, "Neo-Witchcraft Mentality in Popular Christianity," 1–12.

18. One of many documented examples concerns the witch-hunting activities of the Catholic Uganda Martyrs Guild (Behrend, "Rise of Occult Powers," 41–58). Also noteworthy is the panic over satanism in Zambia, which generated a great deal of fear, plus accusations and mob killings. The panic was exacerbated, if not created, by charismatic and Pentecostal deliverance ministries (Udelhoven, *Unseen Worlds*, 327–44).

the healer to explicit forms of exploitation (financial, sexual, and reputational) of people who come in very vulnerable states with very high hopes in priests, pastors, or prophets.[19] Many people have died as a result of deciding or being persuaded, after experiencing the euphoric effects of trance-like states, not to seek available medical treatment because they wanted to prove their faith in the healing they had received. Others attended healing services, stood before the audiences with their visible disabilities, and were prayed over, yet nothing remarkable happened. After all the testimonies of healing, they felt out of place and without faith in front of the expectant crowd.[20] These ethical concerns can be addressed when the healing ministry agrees to be subjected to an evaluation that, while acknowledging the ministry's gifts and benefits for the sick, also maintains some critical distance.

In the maze of competing healing paradigms and today's shifting denominational boundaries, there is a rather pressing question about the direction and dynamics of a Catholic understanding of the healing ministry. In order to pursue this question, I will first look at the challenges that the history of evangelization in Africa poses to the healing ministry. A Catholic understanding of healing should strive to learn from its own experiences as well as from the insights of other traditions, but it will also challenge popular notions of health and healing from the point of view of Catholic tradition and faith. I will elaborate on the transformative and prophetic character of the Catholic healing ministry and how it impacts on an understanding of the "abundant life" that is its goal.

As a way of embracing people's mystical experiences with illness, I follow the person-centered method of Carl Rogers, which is based on unconditional positive regard, empathy, and congruence.[21] This leads me to an approach that, while never denying the existence of afflicting spiritual agencies, remains indeterminate about the essential or ontological nature of them. We resist the temptation to quickly translate the afflicted person's notions (for example, about particular types of witchcraft or spirits) into our own neat conceptual categories (for example, by declaring them to be related to angels, demons, or superstitious beliefs); instead we focus on the specific contexts and historical contingencies in which these notions make sense. From a pastoral angle, we link people's spiritual beliefs specifically to their broken relationships, with respect to which the Christian faith needs to prove itself. The sick person and the caring community are called jointly to become agents of reconciliation and, in doing so, will also respond justly to the demands of the spiritual entities, without regard to the latter's ultimate ontological status as spiritual, psychological, or social realities. The advantage of this person-centered approach is its inclusivity in a pluralistic world.

Healing Contests

The historical mission churches excelled in the founding of health facilities that, following Western medicine, provided African populations with effective treatment options for many acute diseases. The establishment of dispensaries and mission hospitals during the history of evangelization in Africa attests to the Christian compassion for and dedication to the sick. At the same time, the missionaries also saw these facilities as a precondition for effective evangelization, legitimizing the bearer of the Good News.[22] They became beacons of religious and social power, demonstrating the superiority of the Christian worldview. Many hoped that the new health facilities would undermine superstitious thinking, which was seen as posing barriers both to the acceptance of the Christian faith and

---

19. See, for example, Agazue, "Sexual Exploitation of Female Church Members." In addition, the familiar sight in the healing ministry of male pastors delivering mainly female victims of demons in trancelike states on the floor has raised ethical questions.
20. See especially Clifton, "The Dark Side of Prayer for Healing," 204–25.
21. See Cain, *Person-Centered Psychotherapies*, for a good explanation.
22. This aim was expressed, for example, in 1938 by the then president of the American Catholic Medical Mission Board (Garesché, "Catholic Medical Missions," 111–24).

to development.[23] The drums of traditional healing rites beating next to the mission station were often silenced. Unfortunately, there can be a thin line between healing out of compassion and healing as part of a contest for attaining hegemony over the discourses that produce truth and meaning.

Africans used the churches' health care institutions for ordinary sicknesses that could be cured by Western medicine. However, illnesses that were not easily curable were not always seen as "ordinary." The failure of these institutions to engage positively with popular notions of sickness meant that often attempts were made to cure the body without regard for the needs of the mind and the soul. For this reason, neither the mission hospital nor secular health facilities rendered the traditional African healers obsolete. These healers often understood a sickness through its effects on the soul. They appropriated for their healing rites the powers of nature and tradition and employed ever-more-creative methods to diagnose the spiritual root causes of difficult illnesses, including forces like witchcraft, spells, curses, ancestors, and spirits, all of them closely tied to the person's relationships and environment. At the same time, the sick and their families, including many nurses and local clinical staff, understood Western technical medical vocabulary in terms of their own local healing discourses.[24] When whole families avoided the hospitals because they knew that their sicknesses were caused by witchcraft or spirits, and instead participated in African healing rites, they confirmed an interstitial political space with its own authority figures in which one could deal with illness away from the prying eyes of the church and state. African Initiated Churches (AICs), often arising (like the traditional healers) from very humble origins, offered an implicit or explicit critique of the mainstream churches' failure to recognize and deal with the spiritual components of sickness in a way that "clicked" with popular ideas and experiences.

The quest for a healing ministry that could deal with the spiritual issues underlying sickness and misfortune also became a driving force for the exponential growth of the Pentecostal and charismatic churches. Pentecostals in Africa rarely shared Western uneasiness about spirits and healing miracles; direct contact with the Holy Spirit was (and is) a power that should be enlisted in battles with spiritual realities that can determine a person's health and future.[25] Not only did Pentecostals take up the unfulfilled demand for diagnosing and curing spiritual diseases in which the modern Catholic priest did not believe, but many discovered their own giftedness in the healing ministries.[26] By dealing directly with spirits and witchcraft, these ministries had the power to name these forces; they actively played a part in the discernment processes that the sick and their families went through in order to make sense, spiritually and morally, of what was going on in their social environment. The Catholic Church found herself largely outside of this ritual space of discernment.

Initially, Pentecostal healers engaged in polemics with the Catholic Church as well as with other historical mission churches, whom they accused of having settled too comfortably into the Western secular worldview, failing to understand the spiritual dimensions of the Christian faith and live it in their worship. When the historical churches became open to integrating charismatic elements, the debate became more complex, but healing is

---

23. Kalusa, "Language, Medical Auxiliaries," 60–62. Receiving hospital treatment also often clashed with local norms against ritual and sexual pollution, cultural ideas about human development, and taboos in the context of pregnancy and childbirth, such as perceived dangers connected to bodily fluids and the placenta.

24. Kalusa gives examples of clinical staff translating Western medical terms into local languages and thereby introducing Western concepts into local healing discourses and procedures of diagnosis. Some sought X-rays and examination by stethoscope in order to discern witchcraft and ancestral shades. In general, Western medication found its way into local usages not imaginable to European doctors (Kalusa, "Language, Medical Auxiliaries"). Audrey Richards documented that, already in the early 1930s, Western medical terms and procedures (e.g., census, registration, the use of stoppered chemist's bottles for medicines) had begun to migrate into indigenous healing rites in northern Rhodesia (Richards, "Modern Movement of Witchfinders," 448–61).

25. Gifford provides many examples in *Christianity, Development, and Modernity in Africa*.

26. Cheyeka, Hinfelaar, and Udelhoven, "Changing Face of Zambia's Christianity."

still a contested domain.[27] Miracles of healing in Africa are widely advertised and televised. The noise level during healing prayer goes beyond what is needed for therapeutic purposes and attests to a struggle for public recognition. Similarly, Pentecostal affinity for nighttime healings may be the result of a need for spectacle, but they also convey the notion of testing one's faith in a sphere of darkness, a metaphor for witchcraft and Satan and his demons, to which the sleeping priests are often seen as oblivious.[28]

Among Africa's plural cultures and competing modernities, people have many choices—they can opt for treatment in a modern hospital, or seek Catholic prayers, or visit a traditional healer in order to identify the responsible witch, or go to a Zion church in which one can appease or exorcise afflicting spirits, or seek Pentecostal prayers that break the powers of Satan. Whatever choice they make, they have to adapt their situation and their conceptualizations to the chosen channel of treatment, participate in its discourse, cooperate with its authority figures, and believe that it will work. Africans have successfully learned the languages of plural and conflicting discourses about healing.

Dialogue on Healing

Even though healing is a contested platform, Werner speaks of an agreement among various churches about the necessity of dialogue. He witnessed in the World Council of Churches Conference renewed efforts of the churches to listen to the pain and the experiences of afflicted people, their families, and those supporting them, calling for a language of prayer that touches the depth of present-day suffering. "There is a growing conviction that the different churches and denominations need each other to complement, correct and enrich their understanding of Christian healing. In the wider fellowship of churches there are different gifts of healing alive. None of them should be excluded or marginalized."[29] As examples of complementary gifts in different churches, Werner mentions the healing aspect of the Eucharist in Orthodox, Catholic, and Protestant traditions, the relevance to healing of counseling and confession in Protestant churches, the healing effect of the sung and celebrated liturgy, as well as that of images and icons in Orthodox churches, of prolonged silence as practiced in monasticism or by the Quakers, and the joyful expectation of the direct intervention of the Holy Spirit as practiced in Pentecostalism.

The Catholic Church has committed herself irrevocably to this dialogue, which she needs for the sake of her own catholicity. Walter Kasper as secretary of the Pontifical Council for Promoting Christian Unity stressed the duty to encounter the other using the method reflected in the life of the Master, who came not to dominate but to serve.[30] There is no place for organizational arrogance or a crusading mentality in the healing ministry. If God humbles the mighty and raises up the small, then it is possible to learn from the experiences of every healing ministry, no matter how seemingly insignificant it may be.

There may not be only a single cause of a particular illness. Theological insights allow for multiple causes of sickness operating simultaneously, including biological, moral, and spiritual. For example, the doctrine of original sin allows us to see illness as a result of our fallen nature, thus making it part of a moral discourse without linking it directly to personal sin. At the same time, sickness can be seen as fully embedded in the spiritual realm, in which life, even in the presence of sickness and sin, is always upheld by God and transformed by grace.

Dilemmas of the Medical Paradigm

For the most part, the historical mission churches gave the task of healing to institutions that treated sickness according to the prevailing medical para-

---

27. This is not the case for churches involved in health care institutions; this sector is characterized by remarkable cooperation.
28. About Pentecostal preferences for nocturnal events, see van Dijk, "Testing Nightscapes," 41–57.
29. Werner, "WCC Consultation," 383.
30. Kasper, "Nature and Purpose of Ecumenical Dialogue," 293–99. See especially the unabridged version of this article on the Vatican website, www.vatican.va.

digm. In Europe, medicine had, by the time of the Renaissance, established itself as a system of knowledge that was independent from religion, breaking a long tradition in which the understanding of sickness and health was an intrinsic part of religious discourse.[31] Under the new paradigm, the human body became an object of investigation in isolation from the sick person's social environment and relationships. The biological model sees various kinds of sickness as objective and testable phenomena accompanied by specific symptoms and considers the sick person's own understanding, experiences, or beliefs to be irrelevant. Medicine was no longer a healing art but became a healing science, giving rise to a corresponding "medical gaze" (Michel Foucault) operating from a "sealed off position" (Stanley Cavell), fully detached from the experience of the sick person, who had become an object of treatment.[32]

The Bacteriological Revolution of the 1880s, in the course of which the pathogens that caused disease were identified and the first vaccinations developed, validated the germ theory, rendering other general theories about health and sickness obsolete. With further important discoveries, including that of antibiotics, and other scientific and technological developments such as the industrialized fabrication of medicines, plus the establishment of complex national health systems with interconnected, institutionalized training and facilities, modern Western medicine brought evident successes in the treatment of diseases, first to Western societies but then to people around the world. A general change in outlook within the institutions that determined the medical discourse away from plural and often religious conceptions of sickness toward a much more singular conception had been concluded. The scientific space related to healing had become centered on the biomedical model, which understands disease in terms of intruding pathogens (bacteria, viruses), biochemical and physiological malfunctioning of organs, and genetic predispositions. This change of outlook strongly affected the prevailing view of healing in the historical mission churches.

In Africa, the biomedical model was very successful in treating or controlling killer diseases like intestinal sicknesses, leprosy, tetanus, yellow fever, sleeping sickness, bubonic plague, dysentery, meningitis, typhoid, and malaria—diseases that periodically decimated African populations up to the 1920s, especially in times of famine and mass migrations.[33] However, the unquestionable success of the biomedical model and especially the germ theory also had the effect of pushing African models into the realm of superstition (or the primitive, the pagan, or the demonic), making it difficult to positively engage with local understandings of sickness.[34]

The biomedical model of disease is rooted in the Enlightenment's quest for empirical knowledge. However, several generations of post-Enlightenment philosophers, including Wilhelm Dilthey, Edmund Husserl, Martin Heidegger, Maurice Merleau-Ponty, Hans-Georg Gadamer, Meinrad Hebga, and Emmanuel Chukwudi Eze, have deconstructed Enlightenment methods for reaching the truth about reality, arguing that they unwittingly and implicitly accept a mind–body dualism that makes preconceptual human ways of experiencing, being, and knowing unreachable.[35] This means that medical knowledge of sickness grounded in "facts" has become isolated from knowing as a process that involves concrete bodily experience, leaving little room for the spiritual aspects of illness.

The biomedical model of disease, which has dominated faculties of medicine for more than a century, has subsequently been challenged by psy-

---

31. Koenig, "Religion and Medicine," 385–98.

32. Foucault, *Birth of the Clinic*; Cavell, *Claim of Reason*.

33. Note, however, that in 2015 malaria still claimed an estimated 395,000 lives in Africa, according to the World Health Organization's *World Malaria Report 2015*.

34. Prior to the 1880s, missionaries had varied attitudes toward African medicine. Contrast, for example, Mohr, "Missionary Medicine," 429–61, with Gundani, "Views and Attitudes of Missionaries," 298–312.

35. See, for example, Schoeller-Reisch, "Thinking Changes," 299–315. Emmanuel Eze has suggested further that racial prejudice and Eurocentrism were an integral part of the Enlightenment project ("What Remains of Enlightenment?," 281–88).

chosomatic, preventive, and behavioral medicine and has been found in need of revision—even in the West.[36] It has become clear that the strictly biological components of disease are affected by stress, lifestyles, and coping mechanisms, all of which are related to social factors like behavioral norms, social pressures and expectations, economic class, and ethnicity. States of mind have become increasingly important in the treatment of chronic disease. In the past, placebos were not thought of as real medicines. ("They just work in the mind!") Today they have become important for the management of various conditions like migraines, depression, anxiety disorders, hypertension, congestive heart failure, sleeping disorders, severe pain, Parkinson's disease, and multiple sclerosis. They may come in the form of medication, but they also relate to treatment surroundings, the quality of interactions with doctors and other medical personnel, and other subtle cues triggering responses in the mind that have real physiological effects.[37] Placebos by themselves may not cure cancer or acute diseases, but they have changed the balance in favor of success with respect to many forms of medical treatment in which the mind is needed to set in motion a whole chain of positive biochemical responses. Involving the mind in medical treatment was and is the reason that many traditional African therapies and rituals have been successful.

This challenge to Western medicine has given rise to the biopsychosocial model first formulated by George L. Engel, which looks at the human being as part of a wider social system and environment that is crucial for properly understanding health and disease.[38] The biopsychosocial model builds on the scientific achievements of the biomedical model but refuses to look at disease exclusively in terms of biology. It has given rise to "holistic medicine," a term that has found its way into the health institutions operated by churches.

HIV management in Africa is an example of the biopsychosocial model in action. Antiretroviral drugs (ARVs) remain a central factor in the management of HIV, but it is taken for granted today that they need to be accompanied by appropriate patient self-care, including lifestyle and diet. The patient's behavior is often affected by the various barriers created by poverty, the demands of marriage partners, cultural traditions (which, if evaded, can result in shaming), and the stigma attached to the use of ARVs. Multinational institutions see faith-based organizations as critical to the treatment of HIV, which has led to massive donor funding of home-based care and other church-monitored health programs all over Africa. The church seems finally to have found a medical paradigm that is sound from a biological angle but also recognizes the positive contributions of faith and spirituality in the healing process, and pastoral care strives to foster this component of healing.

Yet, despite the positive contributions of the holistic model, in practice it often lacks integrative principles on which medical care can focus.[39] This also applies to pastoral care. The Catholic healing ministry often lacks a language of prayer that addresses the spiritual needs of the patients *in relation to their bodily experiences*. Prayer and medical treatment have become separated from each other. Many programs based on holistic medicine have been phased out, in part because of the bureaucratic demands placed on both caregivers and donors. The impact of social factors on health are unquestionably crucial, but their precise contribution remains evasive and difficult to quantify.

The Problems of an All-Embracing Health Discourse

The notion of holistic health care comes with philosophical, theological, and ethical dilemmas. According to the World Health Organization, "Health is a state of complete physical, mental and

---

36. Africa has been rather slow to accept this challenge and implement necessary changes in its medical training institutions (Gukas, "Global Paradigm Shift in Medical Education," 887–92).
37. Hedges and Burchfield, "Placebo Effect and Its Implications," 161–79.
38. Engel, "Need for a New Medical Model," 129–36.
39. McLaren, "A Critical Review of the Biopsychosocial Model," 86–92.

social well-being and not merely the absence of disease or infirmity."[40] While such an all-embracing concept of health with quasi-religious overtones is well intentioned, it has also made a number of commentators uncomfortable. As one theologian rightly put it, "It is a mistake to equate health with the totality of human well-being. . . . Attempts to define health and disease in objective, value-free terms also fail. . . . Health and disease must be understood in terms of the goods and goals to which human lives are directed."[41] For a Christian, he adds, these goods and goals can be understood only in terms of God's purposes as reflected in the life of Christ.

Since very few people on the planet inhabit a blissful state of complete well-being in all areas of life, the question of moral hegemony over the health discourse is rather pressing. Ivan Illich saw an enormous proliferation of health discourses in the West and warned long ago about the medicalization of life, by which the general public is increasingly forced to rely on the medical profession in order to cope with life.[42] Michel Foucault worked with the terms "biopower," "biopolitics," and "governmentality" in order to show the mechanisms of a new form of power in the Western world by which health systems, on behalf of the modern state, came to regulate populations en masse.[43] He argued that this form of biopower, by working simultaneously in the realms of the human body (health care), subjective selves (through processes of self-identification and self-monitoring governed by categories established by the health discourse), and the collective body (population management), has become a precondition for the functioning of the modern state and the neoliberal labor market. Biopower, for Foucault, is concerned with the individual subject and human welfare and is not "repressive power" but "productive power" that creates ever-new discourses about various problems of human life. At the same time, it is much more elusive than other forms of power; it is no longer linked to specific social groups or persons who are allowed to exert power over others but constitutes itself through processes of human interaction in which subjectivities are established based on the prescriptions of scientific experts, health experts, and the modern state. When the human body became subject to programs of medicalization from conception to death, the discourse about health became a dominant force for regulating social life, controlling the standards for diet and nutrition, prescribing the proper developmental stages of human life, and determining the suitability of a person for school and employment, the healthfulness (and thereby also the appropriateness) of diverse practices related to sexual and reproductive life, the management of aging, and in many cases the right to be born or to die. Moral issues like sexuality and crime were turned into medical issues. Biopolitics was directed at keeping privileged populations healthy and economically productive, thereby defining the ideal state, and at the same time setting the boundaries of human desire, motivation, and ideals. It also became the engine defining the "other" who is a threat to the integrity of the privileged population and who is therefore excluded from membership in the state (whether inside or outside its borders) by unspoken rules, giving rise to what Foucault called "state racism"—a concept he used to explain the inconceivable genocides of the twentieth century.[44]

Of course, there are limits to the application of Illich's and Foucault's ideas to the realities of the health sector in Africa. As we have seen above, many people make themselves subject only in very partial ways to the public health discourse (and thus to biopolitics and programs of medicalization), or

---

40. Preamble to the constitution of WHO as adopted by the International Health Conference, New York; signed on July 22, 1946, by representatives from sixty-one states (Official Records of WHO, no. 2, p. 100) and entered into force on April 7, 1948. The definition has not been amended since 1948.

41. Messer, "Toward a Theological Understanding of Health and Disease," 162. See also the polemical account of Domaradzki, "Extra Medicinam Nulla Salus," 21–38.

42. Illich, *Medical Nemesis*.

43. Foucault, *History of Sexuality*, vol. 1, 140.

44. Foucault, *History of Sexuality*, vol. 1, 137.

make themselves subject simultaneously to a variety of fundamentally different health discourses.[45] Africans have greatly benefited from the modern health discourse and want to benefit more—in Foucault's terminology, they want to be part of the "privileged population" whom this discourse "makes live." At the same time, access to modern medical care remains grimly uneven. Many of Africa's social upheavals are related to people's attempts to become part of the privileged population that has access to the promises of modern life, including health care. Examples are the "brain drain" from the economically weaker to the economically stronger regions, the breakdown in solidarity of the extended family (the existence of which often clashes with the realities of the market economy), and, ironically, the appearance and permanence of Africa's fast-growing slums: when the real or imagined privileged population lives in town, so does its shadow and antithesis. I have elsewhere provided examples of people who have been uprooted from their traditional way of life but failed to appropriate the promises of modern life, and who felt that the processes of medicalization made them dependent on modern medicine and robbed them of their traditional ways of seeking cures without adequately addressing their medical needs.[46]

Where the health industry and health policies follow the laws of the market, they are shaped by the needs of those who have invested the money. Sicknesses that become a potential threat to the West receive much more attention, while the fight against vector-borne diseases in Africa is still too expensive.[47] As part of a process of "othering," these diseases are easily "naturalized," seen as the inevitable result of African geography and the tropical environment.[48] Despite this global neglect, Africa has greatly benefited from philanthropy and private financial initiatives in the health sector—maybe, however, at the cost of weakening local governments and increasing dependency.[49]

The concepts of medicalization and biopolitics have powerful explanatory power with respect to these contradictions and blind spots and the mechanisms of exclusion. Emma Whyte Laurie, for example, criticizes the categories of measurement used in the global health discourse that justify the reasonableness of certain medical interventions as being strongly biased with respect to gender and toward economic activities that can easily be described in monetary terms.[50] She refers to Giorgio Agamben's concept of "bare life" (human life that develops outside the protected or privileged status assigned by social rights)[51] to describe those

---

45. See especially Vaughan, *Curing Their Ills*, 8–12. According to Vaughn's argument, colonial medicine was geared toward whole populations and was relatively unconcerned with shaping subjectivities through the care of individuals, and we may extend her argument to the postcolonial settings of weak governments, donor-driven health agendas, and plural and conflicting health ideologies. At the same time, we need to acknowledge that alternative health discourses, as long as they can be practiced in the open, need some connection to governmental health institutions or to be policed by and thus become partially subject to biopolitics. See Kelly, "International Biopolitics." Note also that Foucault's concept of biopower underwent many developments and that there are also interesting non-Foucauldian ways of understanding biopower in various situations of social pathology (Renault, "Biopolitics and Social Pathologies").

46. Udelhoven, *Christianity in the Luangwa Valley*, 36: "The clinics made us sick. . . . We had fewer sicknesses before the clinics came."

47. Kelly, "International Biopolitics," 10. See also Farmer et al., *Reimagining Global Health*, chapter 5, which discusses the mechanisms that finally allowed the successful treatment of HIV/AIDS in Africa. About the failures of the malaria eradication programs of the 1950s and '60s, see chapter 3 of the same book.

48. About the ways that "Africa" and "the tropics" have since colonial times been constructed as places of disease, see Vaughan, *Curing Their Ills*; and Farmer et al., *Reimagining Global Health*, chapter 3.

49. See Buntaine, Parks, and Buch, "Aiming at the Wrong Targets."

50. Whyte Laurie, "Who Lives, Who Dies, Who Cares?" Laurie discusses the example of the "disability adjusted life year" (DALY) used to measure time and productivity lost because of sickness.

51. For a critical treatment of Agamben's notion of "bare life," see Bennett, *Technicians of Human Dignity*, 165–98.

who fail to qualify for membership in a health category that attracts support, or fall between two or more categories and are thus rendered voiceless and unable to represent themselves.[52] Paul Farmer describes the situations of those whose medical conditions are not amenable to "reasonable" (meaning cost-efficient) treatment options; he discusses the example of drug-resistant tuberculosis and suggests that many could be helped if the "reasonable" treatment categories were more flexible and patient-centered.[53]

In Africa, many of the most vulnerable fail to make proper use of available public health facilities. They often do not have enough time to visit them (until such a visit is too late), fail to secure the required funds for sustained and regular treatment, are excluded because of their lack of formal education from decision-making processes related to their treatment, lack essential connections to seek better options, fail to supplement their treatment with appropriate diet or rest, or are forced to balance the cost of their treatment against other necessities of life in a way that is not required of more affluent people. Many become sick in the first place because poverty places them in the situations of highest risk to contract illness, and this poverty means that they have limited opportunities to receive suitable treatment once they have done so. For these reasons, Farmer speaks about the structural violence that a health system driven by the neoliberal market system inflicts on the poor.[54]

Africa's health institutions, including those operated by the church, are often guided by well-intentioned mission statements that state their objectives of holistic care and health care for all. But these mission statements do not inoculate these institutions against processes of exclusion that manifest themselves not only in understaffed facilities with long queues of patients but also in the clinical staff—for whom health care is a job that may be divorced from a strong ethical commitment—lacking any sense of urgency and dedication to the welfare of patients. Some patients are subjected to such strong implicit disapproval—the result of their failure to follow up on a prescribed regime of medication, to understand the reasons for a certain treatment, or who appear to have taken traditional medicines in their quest for healing—that they may never visit a particular facility again. Neoliberal ideologies emphasize a person's own responsibility to look after his or her health, a responsibility that cannot be assumed by the health institution. This is not unreasonable, but this attitude can also lead to the exclusion of those who do not adequately buy into the logic of the health regime ("It is their own fault!") or whose choices are overpowered by other demands. They become less worthy of treatment and there is little concern for what they think about their situation. All of this led Farmer to ask the question, "If access to health care is considered a human right, who is considered human enough to have that right?"[55]

Health and healing belong to a discourse that also embraces rights, economics, and politics. Where people are somehow excluded from the privileged population that is the subject of a particular health discourse, they will look for alternatives that also promise to "make them live," whether in the form of ever-flexible traditional healers or faith healers in the multitudes of old and new Christian churches. Earlier in this chapter, we considered healing as a contest. Healing *has to be* a contest because there is no such a thing as a neutral, aphilosophical, and apolitical concept of health, especially if it aims to be holistic.

I want to link the point about indirect ways of excluding people from a health discourse to the main argument of this chapter, namely, that the language and vocabulary a patient employs to describe the spiritual component of his or her experience of illness (including the vocabulary of spirits or demons) are very often a sign of a rupture

---

52. An example would be children in Africa who are in need of support for education or major medical treatment yet fall outside the categories of "orphan," "AIDS victim," or other categories established by donor or health organizations that would attract such support.
53. See, for example, Farmer's discussion in chapter 4 of *Pathologies of Power* of "untreatable tuberculosis" in Russia's prisons.
54. Farmer, *Pathologies of Power*, chapters 1, 5, and 9.
55. Farmer, *Pathologies of Power*, 206.

with the official health discourse, indicating dramatically that this discourse is not working for that person—medically, socially, or spiritually. A careful reading of spiritual afflictions, including their gendered patterns, can help us point to the areas of exclusion that play themselves out in the lives of the sick. With this in the background, I now turn to the political and prophetic dimension of the Catholic Church's teaching on healing.

The Catholic Theology of Healing: Transformation versus Restoration

The *Catechism of the Catholic Church* (*CCC*) outlines the healing ministry in very brief terms.[56] The sick person, in living his or her sickness before God and turning to God for healing, knows that "Christ has given a new meaning to suffering: it can henceforth configure us to him and unite us with his redemptive Passion" (§1505). Not all sicknesses are healed even in response to sincere prayer, and while praying for healing the suffering person is called to share in Christ's mission. "By following him they acquire a new outlook on illness and the sick. Jesus associates them with his own life of poverty and service. He makes them share in his ministry of compassion and healing" (§1506). In Catholic teaching the healing ministry clearly has a transformative nature, changing both the sick and the church. The sick person becomes more Christlike and attains a new sense of mission, while the church, which becomes the caring community, is affected as was Christ by the suffering of the sick. This aspect of healing requires faith and is essentially the work of the Holy Spirit. The healing character of the sacraments (more specifically of the Eucharist, penance, and the anointing of the sick) shows that the church continually reconstitutes herself by care and prayers for the sick—the church makes the sacraments but also the sacraments make the church (§1118). The accompanying community through their care and intercession share in the transformation brought about by God's healing, thus gaining a greater understanding of the mysteries of life.

The transformative character of healing may be illustrated by a scene from the Gospel of John (5:1–14). When Jesus met a cripple who was complaining about unhelpful people, he told him, "Get up, pick up your sleeping mat and walk!" Since it was the Sabbath day, Jesus also asked him to take a position in front of the hypocritical religious system in which he was immersed. The narrative does not describe whether the man was transformed beyond his physical healing; however, Jesus clearly hoped for this ("Go and sin no more"). This inner transformation seemed, for Jesus, more important than the cure ("Lest something worse will happen to you"). Healing in this story, and in many others in the Gospels, is related to a moral response, to living fully one's vocation in life, which is the opposite of assuming the role of a victim. In other words, it is better to enter the kingdom with one eye or one hand than to be thrown out with both (Mark 9:43–48). The hope radiated by the Christian healing ministry must go beyond physical restoration.[57]

This transformative understanding of healing in Catholic teaching contrasts somehow with the restorative bias of the biomedical model. In germ theory, once the invading pathogen is destroyed, the body can go back to its normal way of operating; healing means going back to an original healthy state. The casting out of evil spirits in many Christian ministries in Africa often follows the same bias: once the invading demons are gone, normal

---

56. The instruction in *CCC* should not be seen in isolation from the church's social teaching about the dignity of the poor and the responsibility of the rich toward the poor. See for example Pope Leo XIII's encyclical *Rerum Novarum* on capital and labor (May 15, 1891) §§23 and 29; Pope John XXIII's encyclical *Mater et Magistra* on Christianity and social progress (May 15, 1961) §157; Pope Paul VI's encyclical *Populorum Progressio* on the development of peoples (March 26, 1967) §§24, 53, and 75; and the Second Vatican Council's Pastoral Constitution on the Church in the Modern World (*Gaudium et Spes*) §63.

57. This transformative paradigm of healing is evident also in the Synoptic Gospels. They present Jesus as healing all types of sicknesses (Matt 15:29–31; etc.) while expecting faith and repentance in return, and he cursed whole towns that failed to accept the new reality he was bringing (Matt 11:20–25). Many healing narratives go hand in hand with exorcisms, which also aim at the transformation of faith and life, lest the evil spirit return "with seven other spirits more wicked than itself" (Matt 12:43–45).

life is restored. Both types of healing remain within a theology of restoration, not of transformation. "Restoration" is a key term in the Word of Faith movement, which looks back to a quasi-divine state of human nature that was lost when humanity was expelled from the Garden of Eden.[58] Unfortunately, when the lost paradise fails to return, many sick people blame themselves for their lack of faith or even die a kind of death that proves that Satan has triumphed.[59]

Political Acquiescence versus the Prophetic Voice in the Healing Ministry

A restorative as opposed to a transformative healing ministry can also be characterized by an absence of political protest. "It is a matter of empirical observation that healing Churches [in Africa] lean heavily towards political acquiescence," wrote Matthew Schoffeleers.[60] His observation provoked criticism and, in a way, should be discounted by the complex social agendas that accompanied some of the healing ministries he wrote about. Still, there is an urgent need to engage with his observation, the more so in situations where the political powers are corrupt or oppressive. Schoffeleers looked for a causal link between healing and political acquiescence and found one in the functionalist sociology of Talcott Parsons, who examined illness as a form of deviance from societal expectations. The argument is worth exploring: a sick person can no longer fulfill the work and duties imposed on him or her by family and society; in this way, illness is a challenge to the established order of things. Hence, while the sick will be cared for and dispensed of their duties, they also fall under society's scrutiny and are required to submit themselves to an accepted regime of treatment. The established and recognized doctor (or, alternatively, the prophet or healer) becomes the family's and the society's "gatekeeper," who gives a name to the illness. The *illness*, understood in medical anthropology as a subjective experience of ill feeling, thereby becomes a *sickness*, a socially recognized concept of a condition that determines the status and future social role of the sick person.[61] The doctor or healer in this analysis has an intrinsically restorative function for family and society—they are agents for maintaining the status quo.[62]

The theological concept of healing must go beyond restorative mechanisms and embrace an unsettling, prophetic character.[63] While good health is a condition everyone rightly desires, and while the church has always been committed to fighting disease and maintaining health, her healing mission points beyond these things toward eternal life. Precisely by giving her healing ministry an otherworldly dimension, the church can maintain a prophetic role that is outside the scope of the dominant health discourse and biopolitics and, if necessary, in tension with the dominant politico-religious culture.

Serious illness is also a challenge to an uncritical

---

58. In the simplified version of the story told by this movement, man and woman were created in the image of God; they were gods and given dominion over the earth, but by sinning they came under the authority of Satan, who rules them by means of illness and death. Jesus has overcome Satan, and he restores the believer to this original state where God is in charge and where they can rid themselves through faith of sickness and poverty and gain health and prosperity.

59. For examples, see Udelhoven, *Unseen Worlds*, chapter 4.

60. Schoffeleers, "Ritual Healing and Political Acquiescence," 1–25. He focuses on the apolitical role of the Zionist churches in South Africa during the time of apartheid.

61. This anthropological distinction between illness and sickness (which does not exist in ordinary English) is taken from Boyd, "Disease, Illness, Health, Healing and Wholeness," 9–17.

62. Note that Schoffeleers's argument does not consider that visible political protest is often not possible for many healers, and that political convictions can also be subordinated to a healing ministry's focus on the healing of individuals.

63. Paul Hollenbach's thesis of the politically unsettling character of Jesus's exorcisms—which I mentioned above at n. 4—again becomes relevant here. We follow Hollenbach in stressing the social and political dimensions of exorcisms and of healing in the wider sense, but we depart from him when he reduces demons to unreal social and psychological phenomena.

acceptance of a reduced meaning of life.[64] The healing ministry aims to be transformative not only for the individual but also for society. A restorative approach aims at reintegrating a sick person back into a functioning society, but a transformational approach aims at marking society itself by the experiences of existential sickness. When a Christian healing ministry follows a restorative bias, it will prevent sickness from shaking the foundations of social life. Juanne Clarke highlighted the tendency among many doctors and nurses in the hospital settings she studied to brush aside the disturbing nature of sickness and death, radiating the appearance that "all is under control!" behind a façade of medical instruments, even when their expertise was spent or when their colleagues made fatal mistakes. Patients were subtly subjected to a medical management strategy that suppressed radical questions about life and death.[65] A Christian healing ministry can fall into the same trap when the promise "all will be well in Jesus' name!" lulls the sick into a false sense of confidence that life and faith no longer pose any challenge to the status quo.

This does not need to be the case. I want to focus now on a theology of "abundant life," in which fundamental Christian hope is also the engine that makes a healing ministry transformative and prophetic.

Abundant Life

The theology of "abundant life"—taken up by Pentecostals but also by mainstream churches—can be read as a Christian critique of a secular understanding of health. Similar to the WHO's health discourse, it looks at health from the broadest possible point of view, but not isolated from a faith in God, the author of life. The theology of abundant life has been expressed in a variety of terms—I am not engaging here with the popular theology of the Word of Faith movement widely known as the "prosperity gospel," except to mention that earthly blessings and healings will never eliminate decay and death; even the sick whom Jesus healed eventually died (many probably at a young age). A healthy Christian focus will always subject the search for the fullness of life to the ultimate challenge of gaining eternal life.

Instead, I draw attention to an important aspect of abundant life theology that can be discerned in the lived experience of many charismatic ministries all over Africa: the centrality of joy to the healing ministry. It may not seem appropriate to speak to the sick about joy, but, in practice, joyful Pentecostal and charismatic ministries in Africa have attracted the sick like a magnet. Sick people are not always helped by putting on gloomy faces in recognition of their sufferings! Many critiques have reduced the Pentecostal and charismatic success of making the sick at home in their ministries to mere emotionalism, or to giving false hope and promises to the sick, or to confusing the effects of trance with the Holy Spirit. Such criticisms of charismatic worship are in many cases well founded and need attention and correction, but they can also be throwing out the baby with the bathwater. Engaging with charismatic experience reveals a reality of hope and joy that goes beyond the intellectual layer of well-formulated prayers that have dominated the formal Catholic healing ministry. At a grassroots level, charismatics have brought to the church an experience of worship in which existential joy cannot be omitted from the notion of salvation. This joy has brought healing to many sick people.

Let me give the example of two Reformed theologians who have dedicated their lives to outlining a persuasive theology of joy and expressing it in a very approachable language: John Piper ("God is most glorified in us when we are most satisfied in Him") and Jürgen Moltmann ("Joy is the meaning of human life").[66] Both position themselves against any prevailing system of thought that reduces or diminishes life in any way. Piper's theology does not make gods out of pleasure, happiness, prosperity, or health, and he has been one of the most outspoken evangelical critics of the prosperity gospel. But, since we all make a god out of what we take most pleasure in, the raison d'être of the Christian

---

64. See especially Taussig, *Devil and Commodity Fetishism in South America*.
65. Clarke, "Multiple Paradigm Approach," 89–103.
66. Piper, *Desiring God*, 10; Moltmann, *Living God and the Fullness of Life*, 195. Hugo Rahner offers a Catholic example of a theology of joy and playfulness in *Man at Play*.

ministry should be to help people to make God their God by looking for the greatest joy and pleasures they can find in God, even in times of illness. This is also true of Moltmann; life in fellowship with Christ is always life marked by an existential joy that affirms the human senses and that is constitutive of a human nature created in the image of God. He quotes St. Athanasius: "The Risen Christ makes of life a never-ending festival."[67] For Moltmann, a person who lives in the presence of the living God whose face is Jesus Christ will, even when faced with illness, be hopeful, creative, think across borders and barriers, and make the right use of memory in order to anticipate the future.

When Catholic theology encourages the sick person to unite with Christ in his or her suffering, it does not idealize the silent sufferer (as some polemics hold) but encourages the sick person to join in Christ's wish for his disciples "that my joy may be in you and your joy may be complete" (John 15:11). Christ prayed for his disciples to have this joy the night before his suffering from an anticipation of the fulfillment of his life and mission. We are then not wrong to say that abundant joy is tied to living out and fulfilling one's life mission. The promise of abundant life is also related to the shepherd laying down his life for his sheep (John 10:10-11). A life mission, then, is something for which, when accepted, one is ready to suffer and lay down one's own life—as did the Master. It is a way of being and a way of doing that needs no justification before people. It comes out of an inner depth that connects with the determinative aspects of one's life history and reflects the dignity of who one is before God. Serious illness poses radical questions for a person's life mission, which can (and should) become the focal point to mediate between the biological, moral, and spiritual dimensions of a sickness. Søren Ventegodt proposed with his colleagues a comprehensive alternative medical model in which a person's primary mission, his or her purpose in life, or life mission, becomes an integrative tool for the whole medical enterprise—an understanding that is absent from the biopsychosocial model.[68]

In the lived charismatic experience, this joy also has to do with the connected, connecting, and mediating capacities of the human body. Joy not only comes as a gift for the sick person, but is always a "joy with" that reaches out to others. In this way, the brokenness of the social body can be reflected and symbolized in the illness of the sick person.[69] However, when the Christian healing ministry attempts to bring the sick in touch with this connecting joy, it is important that we be aware of an opposite set of dynamics working within serious illness: blame.

From Blame to the Acceptance of a (New) Life Mission

Beneath illness looms an unsettling concern about its moral dimension. "Who has sinned, he or his parents?," the disciples asked Jesus when they were faced with the reality of a man born blind (John 9:2). In his answer, Jesus took the blind man's condition out of the context of personal sin, but he did not take it out of a moral discourse. Blindness and healing became signs of disbelief and faith and a challenge to the prevailing moral order. Healing asked for a response: to accept or reject the new reality of grace brought by Christ.

In Western health institutions and also in mission hospitals, the moral dimension is usually bracketed out from an understanding of sickness. Sickness follows biological, not moral, laws, but the moral question cannot be so easily shoved aside. The complex stigmatization processes that surround the HIV and AIDS crisis have shown that issues of blame remain deeply interwoven into experiences of sickness, asking to be recognized, often by means of spiritual concepts.

Unlike witchcraft, belief in evil spirits or demons initially shifts the blame away from human

---

67. Moltmann, *Living God and the Fullness of Life*, 195.
68. Ventegodt et al., "Clinical Holistic Medicine," 295–306. He proposed his model from a medical, not theological, perspective.
69. St. Paul's analogy of the human body and the emphasis in charismatic practice on spiritual gifts for the benefit of others and of the church, as expressed, for example, in 1 Cor 12–14, illustrates this awareness of the fundamental interconnectedness of believers.

agency, and for this reason it is often a relief for the community when a spirit or a devil is responsible for an illness and not a family member or neighbor. But spirits and demons are closely tied to social structures, and their presence always becomes part of a broader moral dialogue. New concepts of satanism in Africa as well as other notions of the occult not only constitute causal explanations for misfortune (e.g., illnesses, failures, accidents, and mysterious deaths); they are also complex moral commentaries about Africa's modern society, its colossal inequalities, and the lack of transparency in its modern politics, which often involves nepotism and other forms of favoritism.[70] According to E. E. Uzukwu, "Ecstasy, trance or possession in AIC practice is always a mystical experience with a social agenda."[71] When a root cause is located in the spiritual sphere, it will almost certainly attain to an issue involving moral dimensions in the social sphere. The presence of spiritual agents, at the end of the day, also prompts the moral question, Who is to blame? Christians all over Africa visit famous diviners and also modern Christian prophets not only to be delivered from spiritual afflictions but also to be acquitted from the blame that sticks to them beneath the quiet surface of day-to-day relationships. Refusing to participate in the discourse of the diviner is often understood as an admission of guilt.

When witchcraft and demons bring out the disruptive and unsettling implications of sickness, they point to those dimensions in which the Christian faith needs to prove itself. They demonstrate that life cannot go back to "business as usual," as if all was well. A sound healing ministry will help the person escape the role of victim and end the discussion of blame, helping him or her assume agency and responsibility—not for the illness but for how to deal with it from a depth that reflects what the person's life and faith are about. At the same time, a sound healing ministry will help the person become a reconciling and healing force in his or her surroundings. A sound healing ministry transforms the moral question of blame into the moral question of identifying one's life mission.

Pelagia's Snake

To illustrate the desired shift from a restorative to a transformative healing ministry, one that poses a challenge to a person's life mission, I present a case study that was narrated to me by the priest who appears in the story. He had recently appointed Pelagia M. as the sacristan of their parish in Ndola, one of Zambia's larger towns. She was also a member of a prominent lay group. Being a sacristan was a volunteer service, not a paid job, but somehow Pelagia found herself at the center of a lot of gossip. People in her lay group wondered why she, of all people, had been entrusted with this role. Pelagia was single, which also provoked gossip. She fell seriously ill and could no longer eat or defecate. In the hospital she was told that she had an intestinal obstruction with severely twisted bowels and that she needed an emergency operation. The operation was successful and saved her life. Two days after the operation, the priest visited her in the hospital, and Pelagia told him about an issue they could not treat there in the hospital:

> The night after the operation I had a very bad dream: Mrs. B. [a fellow member of her lay group] came to me wearing her church uniform, and said, "You think, because you are the sacristan, you are above us? You see now what we can do! I have tied your bowels in a knot. This time I will allow you to live, but the next time it will be for real!" Yesterday, our lay group came to visit me. Mrs. B was the last one to greet me. She looked at me in a strange way, and when she greeted me it was as if electricity flowed through my body. I can't hide it from you, father, she is a big witch. We all know it in the church. Yet she is always the first to receive Holy Communion. If you stand in her way, you will see!

---

70. For a discussion of the integration of Christian spiritual notions into West African religious consciousness and the resulting moral issues, see Meyer, *Translating the Devil*; Meyer, "'Delivered from the Powers of Darkness,'" 236–55; and Uzukwu, *God, Spirit, and Human Wholeness*.

71. Uzukwu, *God, Spirit, and Human Wholeness*, chapter 7.

The priest was quite aware that Mrs. B. had a strong character and that some members found it difficult to work with her, but that would surely not make her a witch. He tried to convince Pelagia not to link the dream directly to Mrs. B. but instead concentrate on getting better. Yet when she was discharged from the hospital, she resigned from her position as sacristan. A few weeks later she moved to another part of town and another parish. She had come to regard her old parish and lay group as a place that was fully enmeshed in the world of witchcraft; for her, witches were evidently more powerful than the protective prayers of the church. She explained her move to the priest in very rational terms: "My children need me. I also look after orphans who depend on me. If I die now, where do they go? I can't take the risk of staying. Anyway, I will continue to be active in the church. The Catholic Church is everywhere. I love my lay group, and I will be an active member in the new parish."

For her, the decision to move did not contradict her Christian faith in any way. It even seemed to correspond with her life mission of bringing up her children. The priest continued to stay in touch with her and her family. More frightening dreams came to her, however, even after she moved away. She felt pain in her stomach and went to the doctor. Afterwards, she said that "the doctors didn't find anything!" which confirmed for her that her condition was the result of witchcraft. She continued to ask the priest for his prayers, even though she no longer lived near him.

One day the priest found a Pentecostal pastor who brought a choir to her house, which sang lively songs around her, while he prayed over her and started to cast out demons. He invoked a whole arsenal of demons, casting out spiritual husbands, spirits from the mountain, spirits from the ocean, spirits of confusion, and spirits of witchcraft. While she sat relatively quietly during the prayers, upon hearing the word "witchcraft" her body started to shake slightly. The pastor continued, rebuking various forms of witchcraft, until he rebuked the "snake of witchcraft that they implanted in you," upon which Pelagia fell onto the floor in a violent trance.

The pastor, with the choir, continued to cast out the "snake." After five minutes the woman came back to her senses, tired but somewhat relieved. The pastor said that she needed more prayers and left.[72]

Pelagia had always been somehow passive and even indifferent during prayers with the priest, while the prayers of the charismatic pastor, once he touched on witchcraft, produced an amazing bodily reaction, which proved to everyone present that witchcraft was indeed the root cause of her afflictions.

The priest did not hear from Pelagia for some months. He wondered whether she had become Pentecostal. But then she called again, asking him to bless her new home saying, "You never know who lived here before!" He went reluctantly. Pelagia told him that her afflictions had stopped for a while after the pastor's prayer, but now they were back and were even affecting the children; one had just dreamt of a snake while another had also had a "bad dream." The priest challenged Pelagia in a blunt way:

> You told me that you ran away from our parish for the sake of your children. You asked, "Who will care for them?" But now what have your children learned from you? One day you will indeed be dead. What will they remember about you? That witchcraft is stronger than Jesus Christ. And your lay-group, what have they learned from you? That you can come to church and pray and receive Holy Communion for your entire life, but you cannot overcome a witch. You will be buried in your church uniform while you yourself know that it has no power whatsoever!

In his prayers with the family, the priest read the story of God sending deadly snakes to the people of Israel in chapter 21 of the book of Numbers. But instead of "binding" and "rebuking" the snakes, he asked God to continue to haunt the family with snakes in their dreams until they looked up to the cross and stood up for what they believed in! His

---

72. See especially Kamps, *Speaking of Satan in Zambia*, 91–94, for a detailed example of a Pentecostal discernment of a spiritual affliction in which the healer asks the patient leading questions and follows the patient's bodily reactions.

prayers were rather unconventional—he tortured the family with their own dreams and fears, and then blessed the house in a formal ritual.

Not long afterward, the family told him that the dreams had stopped bothering them. The priest hoped that she had developed an inner conviction of the need to show her faith in a new way. At a medical review, Pelagia was told that the pain arising from the scars of the operation would come back from time to time. She did not stop believing in witchcraft, nor did people stop gossiping about her, but her fear strangely was gone. She had discovered an inner strength that she could bring into a bodily awareness, linked to the very scar that she had previously associated with witchcraft. Pelagia eventually went back to visit her old church group in a free and open manner, and the group in turn organized an official farewell party for her, which brought the episode to a close.

Discussion of the Meaning of Pelagia's Snake

Illness and healing are mysteries that escape neat explanation. Their meaning cannot be provided solely by the patient, nor is it in the hands of the medical doctor or the priest. An important component in the process of discerning sickness is what John Janzen called the "therapy management group" and Steve Feierman, "lay therapy management."[73] These groups include the family members who bear the social and economic costs of treatment. They spend a great deal of time with the sick—hours, days, and weeks—bathing and feeding them, washing their clothes, and performing other tasks. The presence and support of important family members and friends around the sickbed is essential. However variable the membership of such a group may be, it crucially includes acknowledged authority figures who can say yes or no to proposed methods of treatment, although it usually includes others whose opinions are simply ignored. This group is not constituted on the basis of medical or theological expertise. Its members understand the communications of doctors and priests in their own way, and their decision-making is often not based on these communications but rather on all of the complex issues relating to social life. The moral dilemma of sickness plays itself out in this arena. Pelagia and her family understood her dream as a clear sign of witchcraft, no matter what the doctor or the priest said.

Though his advice was not heeded at the beginning, the priest remained relevant to the therapy management group throughout Pelagia's episode of illness. Healing in this case was accompanied by the priest's attentiveness, his readiness to be thrown off of his own routine, and his confidence in the power of prayer—even if it did not seem very effective at first. The priest was careful to frame his prayers in a way that would not assign blame. The prayers of the Pentecostal group allowed Pelagia's experience with witchcraft (whatever its ontological reality) to express itself in a clear bodily manifestation—something the priest could not offer her. However, in the restorative paradigm of healing offered by the charismatic Pentecostal prayer, this bodily awareness could not be transformed into a challenge for growth; the focus was on exorcism, not transformation. It was the challenge posed by the priest that switched the long healing process into a transformative mode that allowed for Pelagia's spiritual growth, making her reflect on the faith and values for which she would be ready not only to live but also to die. By staying with and dwelling on the symbols of the attack, she allowed her awareness of a mystical snake in her belly to shift into an awareness of her own power and a personal vocation, which put the jealousies of others out of her mind. She became clearer about what she wanted to live for instead of what she wanted to avoid. She still had pain in her bowels, but she no longer symbolized it in terms of a snake brought about by witchcraft; instead she saw it as something that belonged to her and that even reminded her of what her life was about.

In Africa, witchcraft and demons are not felt in an abstract way—they are felt through the body. Some people's descriptions of bodily states associated with spiritual attacks may refer to pathological medical conditions. Very often, however, they arise also out of a process of symbolizing a life situation in one's own body.[74] Thus, while Pelagia had

---

73. Janzen, "Therapy Management", 68-84; Feierman, "Struggles for Control," 73–147.
74. For examples, see Udelhoven, *Unseen Worlds*, chapters 8 and 9.

connected her snake to her relationship with Mrs. B., with whom she felt uncomfortable, it was also woven into a crisis within her Catholic lay group. The snake caused by witchcraft seemed to be moving around freely not only in her belly but also in the lay group, whose Christian life and prayer meetings often revolved around gossip and social position. Pelagia had embodied an experience of poisoned relationships that was also felt by others in the church. Sunday worship in Pelagia's parish, with its nice singing, processions, and gift giving had little to do with faith or love. The "snake," when freed from Pelagia's belly, soon began to figure as a prophetic image in the priest's homilies, through which he attempted to address the hidden jealousies and climate of backbiting in the congregation.

A Person-Centered Approach to Dealing with Spiritual Realities

Many charismatic and Pentecostal ministries focus on the world of demons and witchcraft and on exorcising the demons. In our own approach, we remain uncertain or agnostic about their ontological status. When a person knows that he or she has been attacked or possessed, we recognize that the person's own words best describe his or her spiritual and mystical experiences. Whatever our specific beliefs and concepts about the spiritual world, none of us can avoid the influence and even the control exercised by certain powers, whether they are located in the unconscious mind, in social pressures and norms, in the mind-shaping forces wielded by institutions, or in spiritual realms (heaven and hell). As Carl Jung said, "The one thing we refuse to admit is that we are dependent upon 'powers' that are beyond our control."[75] In our own approach, which I am presenting here only in a brief form,[76] we link people's mystical experiences with illness to wounded life situations to which their concepts of spiritual realities often point. Like experiences with serious illness, those with witchcraft and demons pose moral questions about the purpose of life. They pose serious challenges to a person's life vocation. By focusing our approach on addressing broken relationships from the viewpoint of the demands of Christian duty, we can leave the question about the ontological nature of the demons, about which it is impossible to reach consensus in a pluralistic world, in the background. There are unresolvable questions about whether experiences with demons are caused by outside spiritual forces, or whether they are the result of overly anxious communities or inner psychic constellations that impose themselves on the conscious mind and appear to be coming from the outside, like dreams. Regardless of the nature and cause of demonic possession (or witchcraft in that regard), I propose an approach that moves the afflicted person away from victimhood toward a Christian agency that operates from the core of his or her life vocation.

The shift in focus from outer demons to demonic conditions is prophetic in that it seeks to identify the wounded life situations that the Christian faith always seeks to name and address. We call afflictions "demonic" when they have the potential to seriously derail a person and even a community from their source of life in a Christian vocation. Painful illnesses can be demonic if they lead people into despair, denial, or the search for scapegoats. Money and wealth can be demonic when they erode family solidarity and assume the role of idols.

In my own ministry of accompanying people who have experienced demons or attacks from witchcraft, I have witnessed that many of them had an extraordinary ability to absorb tensions that other members of their family, or even the wider community, also experienced yet could not express, and to reenact those tensions in dreams, visions, and trances. When we appreciate that many people under attack, with whom there is "something wrong," have an extraordinary capability to absorb and symbolically or spiritually reveal a society's tensions, we see that they become the suffering artists of a community, expressing realities for which there were previously no words. Yet one needs an intelligent way of listening to them and bringing them into prayer.

The way we listen can enhance a restorative or

---

75. Jung, *Man and His Symbols*, 21.
76. For a more extended discussion, see Udelhoven, *Unseen Worlds*, chapters 5–7.

a transformative course. The transformative way, as described by Carl Rogers, allows, in a pastoral and confidential setting, the patient's narrative to stand on its own—even with its disturbing dimensions—without explaining, judging, or deforming it through the interpretations of others.[77] Empathetic listening, but also appropriate prayer rituals, help the patient to feel the rightness of his or her own words and to be in touch with his or her own experience. As Eugene Gendlin explained in his approach of "focusing": for an experience to transform itself, it first needs to be "felt anew" in a "bodily felt awareness."[78] The listener recognizes in the sick person's own words the best possible way of communicating the experience of the illness at that point in time, even when this includes the language of witchcraft and demons. The listener is present not as a neutral person, but as a person of faith. Events are no longer felt in the same way when another person, a person of faith, listens to them. Also, the ritual dimension of prayer is very important. Instead of always depending on the terminology of spiritual warfare that is very popular today in Africa, communitarian rituals may bring out more clearly the dimension of the power of the believing community's faith, while also providing a peaceful atmosphere of prayer with an emphasis on growth, not on extraordinary spiritual battles.[79]

Where people speak about experiences with spiritual forces, the categories of "true" and "false," "real" and "not real" are problematic. We prefer to speak of "inner" and "outer" worlds as an ad hoc method for distinguishing between statements describing an attack that refer to a person's inner experiences, to which the listener has no personal access (inner world), and statements that refer to empirical realities that can be checked or that others also witnessed. It is not the goal of this terminology to create a dualism involving the "experienced" world over and against the "real and objective" world; we must humbly confess that the latter remains largely beyond our knowledge. The distinction is made in order to identify the parts of a story that need to be worked with and discerned in a confidential setting as opposed to those that, if verified, call for a drastic change in life circumstances that also involves other people, for example, in scenarios where a person's experiences of spiritual attacks stand in an obvious relationship to physical or sexual abuse, public threats concerning witchcraft, or abusive relationships. The church has a long and important tradition in pastoral care of separating internal and external forums. We deal with inner worlds in the internal forum and with outer worlds in the external forum.

The outer world is populated by those statements that are considered objective by those talking to each other (they are observable or testable using common criteria); that is, they are considered to be their (and our) common world. Dialogue across different beliefs will push certain areas of disagreements into the inner world, seeing them as subjective to the believer—and this is our starting point. Communications about realities that transcend the ordinary world, a dream, an intuition, or an awareness that other persons present did not have are also part of the inner world, as are visions of a diviner or of a Christian prophet, regardless of whether people see them as true or false. In the internal, confidential forum, negative spiritual experiences, including those resulting from witchcraft, can be talked about freely with the aim of discerning a response shaped by the gospel. We work toward a changed attitude toward an alleged witch, look at concrete issues that need to be clarified with that person, and work toward reconciliation.

When Pelagia in our case study experienced Mrs. B. as a witch in her inner world, the priest had to protect her from accusations that might be made in the outer world, but the method allowed him to address public patterns of unsettling behavior that Mrs. B. may have exhibited in her lay group without labeling her a witch. This point has often been lost in those approaches that denied the existence of witchcraft and failed to address public behavior that the community associated with witchcraft. The

---

77. Rogers, "Theory of Therapy," 184–256.
78. Gendlin, *Focusing-Oriented Psychotherapy*.
79. It is important to note that there exist pastoral challenges in which the language of warfare and catharsis can be important in order to create a rupture leading to a new life. For examples, see Udelhoven, *Unseen Worlds*, chapter 11.

method of "nonviolent communication" as worked out by Marshall Rosenberg is a very good guide on how behavior in the outer world can often be successfully addressed without using labels taken from a person's inner world.[30]

The inner world always deserves respect. It is shaped by a person's life history and beliefs, and is the world in which, it is hoped, God meets the person. The experience of the patient with witchcraft or spirits touches very personal and intimate layers of the patient's being that have unfolded within his or her own or his or her family's frame of reference—not within those of the helper. While one does well to unmask superstition, one also needs to acknowledge the aspect of mystery in the patient's experience. We acknowledge that every deep experience that shapes the "inner autobiography" of the person affects the soul and is therefore spiritual in nature; as such, it should be brought into the realm of prayer.

The inner world is often concerned with existential truth, but our approach refuses to transform a truth in a person's inner world into a truth in the outer world. In the Catholic Church, the discernment process of the spiritual truth of a person's visions and experiences is not in the hands of that person but in those of the larger church, guided by the bishops. Biblical visions or private revelations to saints became canonical only on account of their being finally accepted by the wider community of the church.

At the same time, a meaningful Christian ministry will also be attentive to the appeal and level of plausibility to others of a sick person's inner experiences of ghosts and witches. When a narrative of spiritual events becomes the subject of public concern, it may carry within itself prophetic dynamics. New types of ghosts and witches that populate the world of many sick people in Africa may be dismissed by the public in some circumstances as illusions but may be very plausible and real in other circumstances. Some scholars have suggested that economic and political conditions that are marked by sharp and rising inequalities, lack of access to economic opportunities, or disintegrating family solidarity provide a fertile ground for witches and vampires and that rituals of dealing with these phenomena are also ways of (re-)negotiating globalizing forces, even if only partially.[81] Others have described African imaginings about satanic worlds and creatures as the prosperity gospel's moral discourse about sinful ways of becoming rich.[82] Ghosts and witches afflicting the sick may point to injustices that people have experienced yet cannot describe. These experiences often have a much greater popular appeal than Catholic discourses on social justice formulated in a dry language, which should be an encouragement to listen more attentively to the spiritual language of the sick.

Conclusion

The Catholic theology of healing confirms that the human body is a medium through which a suffering person can symbolize aspects of the broken world while uniting it with Christ and his body, which is the church. Because the death and resurrection of Jesus, to whom the sick person is united, is known theologically in its cosmic dimensions, his or her mystical experiences during sickness can point toward the lack of God's *shalom*, which may be expressed in the prayers of the believers and may be addressed in the healing ministry together with the medical issues of the afflicted. In Africa, spiritual afflictions affirm the inherent interconnectedness of human life. This interconnectedness has been expressed, for example, in the *ubuntu* philosophy of Desmond Tutu, which teaches that life, health, and healing are relational. Charismatic healing ministries that are marked by joy and in which people are also allowed to cry and fall into a trance have tapped into dimensions of ritual healing that cannot be easily reached by well-formulated intellectual prayers alone. In these ministries, a person's spiritual aware-

---

80. Rosenberg, *Non-Violent Communication*.
81. See, for example, the various contributions in Comaroff and Comaroff, *Modernity and Its Malcontents*. Note that healing rituals and exorcisms seek to deal with witches and ghosts, not with globalizing forces; but when the former "live" in the latter it is futile to exclude one from the other. To link spiritual forces to wider social forces is not the same as reducing one to the other.
82. For example, see Meyer, "Power of Money," 15–37.

ness is allowed to manifest itself in bodily awareness—they are not two totally unrelated things. A transformative paradigm of healing can link spiritual afflictions to the challenge of spiritual growth, especially embracing a new vision of and commitment to one's life mission and, at the same time, addressing larger social rifts, concerning which the Christian faith needs to prove itself and for which the followers of Christ are called to be agents of reconciliation. The ghosts and witches of the sick, always pointing to a moral dimension, affirm the mediating, connected, and connecting capabilities of human beings and can attain to a prophetic role if the helper is able to work with them intelligently without sparking a witch-hunt. When a sick person comes to symbolize forces that are also felt by others in the community, healing rituals can renew the community as much as the individual person who needs its support.

I have stressed in this chapter the advantages of an approach that respects the sick person's own language about spiritual matters. I may add as a concluding remark that doing so opens up the possibility of transforming people's spiritual beliefs. Hidden discourses about witchcraft have led to a great deal of violence in many countries in Africa and have also undermined trust in many Christian communities. Christian attempts to marginalize these discourses into the realm of the superstitious have thus far not succeeded in eradicating them—their power may only have increased underneath the quiet surface of Christian life. It is apparent that beliefs change through active and intelligent engagement with them, especially by acknowledging and protecting the moral dimensions of life to which they point, while working against all dehumanizing tendencies.

Further research may be able to draw conclusions concerning the nature of an engagement with belief in witchcraft that actually leads to its transformation, even if achieved in small steps. This should start with the language and conceptual world of the sick in the various social contexts of Africa. This research may reveal more clearly how the church's teaching about healing, spiritual afflictions, and the mystery of sickness is actually understood on the ground by people who are not trained in theology, and how the language of everyday Africans could in turn be allowed to influence theology. This would help to narrow the gap between the high theological language used in teaching institutions and the language that can be most helpful in the real-life situations of the African faithful.

Bibliography

Agazue, Chima. "'He Told Me That My Waist and Private Parts Have Been Ravaged by Demons': Sexual Exploitation of Female Church Members by 'Prophets' in Nigeria." *Dignity: A Journal on Sexual Exploitation and Violence* 1.1 (2016): article 10.

Akrong, Abraham. "Neo-Witchcraft Mentality in Popular Christianity." *Research Review* 16.1 (2000): 1–12.

Behrend, Heike. "The Rise of Occult Powers, AIDS and the Roman Catholic Church in Western Uganda." *Journal of Religion in Africa* 37.1 (2007): 41–58.

Bennett, Gaymon. *Technicians of Human Dignity: Bodies, Souls, and the Making of Intrinsic Worth.* New York: Fordham University Press, 2016.

Boyd, Kenneth M. "Disease, Illness, Health, Healing and Wholeness: Exploring Some Elusive Concepts." *Med Humanities* 26 (2000): 9–17.

Buntaine, Mark T., Bradley C. Parks, and Benjamin P. Buch. "Aiming at the Wrong Targets: The Domestic Consequences of International Efforts to Build Institutions." *International Studies Quarterly* 61.2 (2017): 471–88.

Cain, David J. *Person-Centered Psychotherapies.* Washington, DC: American Psychological Association, 2010.

Cavell, Stanley. *The Claim of Reason: Wittgenstein, Skepticism, Morality, and Tragedy.* Oxford: Oxford University Press, 1999.

Cheyeka, A., M. Hinfelaar, and B. Udelhoven. "The Changing Face of Zambia's Christianity and Its Implications for the Public Sphere: A Case Study of Bauleni Township, Lusaka." *Journal of Southern African Studies* 40.5 (2014): 1031–45.

Clarke, Juanne N. "A Multiple Paradigm Approach to the Sociology of Medicine, Health and Illness." *Sociology of Health & Illness* 3.1 (1981): 89–103.

Clifton, Shane. "The Dark Side of Prayer for Healing: Towards a Theology of Well-Being." *Pneuma* 36 (2014): 204–25.

Comaroff, Jean, and John Comaroff, eds. *Modernity and Its Malcontents: Ritual Power in Post-Colonial Africa*. Chicago: University of Chicago Press, 1993.

Congregation for the Doctrine of the Faith, "Christian Faith and Demonology." *L'Osservatore Romano*, English Edition, July 10, 1975.

———. *Instruction on Prayers for Healing*. Vatican City: Libreria Editrice Vaticana, 2001. www.vatican.va.

Dijk, Rijk van. "Testing Nightscapes: Ghanaian Pentecostal Politics of the Nocturnal." *Etnofoor* 20.2 (2007): 41–57.

Domaradzki, Jan. "Extra Medicinam Nulla Salus: Medicine as a Secular Religion." *Polish Sociological Review* 181 (2013): 21–38.

Engel, George L. "The Need for a New Medical Model: A Challenge for Biomedicine." *Science* 196.4286 (1977): 129–36.

Eze, Emmanuel C. "Answering the Question, 'What Remains of Enlightenment?'" *Human Studies* 25.3 (2002): 281–88.

Farmer, Paul. *Pathologies of Power: Health, Human Rights, and the New War on the Poor*. Berkeley: University of California Press, 2003.

Farmer, P., J. Y. Kim, A. Kleinman et al. *Reimagining Global Health: An Introduction*. Berkeley: University of California Press, 2013.

Feierman, Steven. "Struggles for Control: The Social Roots of Health and Healing in Modern Africa." *African Studies Review* 28.2/3 (1985): 73–147.

Foucault, Michel. *The Birth of the Clinic: An Archeology of Medical Perception*. Translated by A. M. Sheridan Smith. London: Routledge, 2003.

———. *The History of Sexuality*, volume 1. Translated by Robert Hurley. New York: Vintage Books, 1978.

Freud, Sigmund. *Eine Teufelsneurose im 17. Jahrhundert*. Vienna: Internationaler Psychoanalytischer Verlag, 1928.

Garesché, Edward F. "Catholic Medical Missions." *Irish Quarterly Review* 27.105 (1938): 111–24.

Gendlin, Eugene. *Focusing-Oriented Psychotherapy: A Manual of the Experiential Method*. New York: Guilford Press, 2012.

Gifford, Paul. *Christianity, Development and Modernity in Africa*. London: Hurst, 2015.

Gukas, Isaac D. "Global Paradigm Shift in Medical Education: Issues of Concern for Africa." *Medical Teacher* 29.9 (2007): 887–92.

Gundani, P. H. "Views and Attitudes of Missionaries toward African Religion in Southern Africa during the Portuguese Era." *Religion & Theology* 11.3/4 (2004): 298–312.

Hedges, Dawson, and Colin Burchfield. "The Placebo Effect and Its Implications." *The Journal of Mind and Behavior* 26.3 (2005): 161–79.

Hollenbach, Paul W. "Jesus, Demoniacs, and Public Authorities: A Socio-Historical Study." *Journal of the American Academy of Religion* 49.4 (1981): 567–88.

Illich, Ivan. *Medical Nemesis: The Expropriation of Health*. New York: Pantheon Books, 1976.

Janzen, John M. "Therapy Management: Concept, Reality, Process." *Medical Anthropology Quarterly* 1 (1987): 68–84.

Jung, Carl G. *Man and His Symbols*. N.p.: Turtleback Books, 1968.

Kalusa, Walima T. "Language, Medical Auxiliaries, and the Reinterpretation of Missionary Medicine in Colonial Mwinilunga, Zambia, 1922–51." *Journal of Eastern African Studies* 1.1 (2007): 57–78.

Kamps, Johanneke. *Speaking of Satan in Zambia: The Persuasiveness of Contemporary Narratives about Satanism*. PhD diss., University of Utrecht. Published in *Quaestiones Infinitae* 108 (2017).

Kasper, Walter. "The Nature and Purpose of Ecumenical Dialogue." *Ecumenical Review* 52.3 (2000): 293–99.

Kelly, M. G. E. "International Biopolitics: Foucault, Globalisation and Imperialism." *Theoria* 57.123 (2010): 1–26.

Koenig, Harold G. "Religion and Medicine I: Historical Background and Reasons for Separation." *International Journal of Psychiatry in Medicine* 30.4 (2000): 385–98.

Lado, Ludovic. *Catholic Pentecostalism and the Paradoxes of Africanization: Processes of Localization in a Catholic Charismatic Movement in Cameroon*. Leiden: Brill, 2009.

Laurie, Emma Whyte. "Who Lives, Who Dies, Who Cares? Valuing Life through the Disability-Adjusted Life Year Measurement." *Transactions of the Institute of British Geographers* 40.1 (2015): 75–87.

McLaren, N. "A Critical Review of the Biopsychosocial Model." *Australian & New Zealand Journal of Psychiatry* 32.1 (1998): 86–92.

Messer, Neil. "Toward a Theological Understanding of Health and Disease." *Journal of the Society of Christian Ethics* 31.1 (2011): 161–78.

Meyer, Birgit. "'Delivered from the Powers of Darkness': Confessions of Satanic Riches in Christian Ghana." *Africa: Journal of the International African Institute* 65.2 (1995): 236–55.

———. "The Power of Money: Occult Forces, and Pentecostalism in Ghana." *African Studies Review* 41.3 (1998): 15–37.

———. *Translating the Devil: Religion and Modernity among the Ewe in Ghana*. Edinburgh: Edinburgh University Press, 1999.

Milingo, Emmanuel. *Are Zambians Superstitious?* Lusaka: Teresianum Press, 1975.

Mohr, Adam. "Missionary Medicine and Akan Therapeutics: Illness, Health and Healing in Southern Ghana's Basel Mission, 1828–1918." *Journal of Religion in Africa* 39.4 (2009): 429–61.

Moltmann, Jürgen. *The Living God and the Fullness of Life*. Translated by Margaret Kohl. Louisville, KY: Westminster John Knox, 2015.

Onwuanibe, Richard C. "The Philosophy of African Medical Practice." *Quarterly Journal of Africanist Opinion* 9.3 (1979): 25–28.

Piper, John. *Desiring God: Meditations of a Christian Hedonist*. Rev. ed. Colorado Springs, CO: Multnomah Books, 2011.

Poucouta, Paulin. "Meinrad Pierre Hebga: Teacher and Healer." In *African Theology in the 21st Century: The Contribution of the Pioneers*, edited by Bénézet Bujo, 2:70–92. Nairobi: Paulines Publications Africa, 2006.

Rahner, Hugo. *Man at Play*. Translated by Brian Battershaw and Edward Quinn. New York: Herder & Herder, 1967.

Renault, Emmanuel. "Biopolitics and Social Pathologies." *Critical Horizons* 7.1 (2006): 159–77.

Richards, Audrey I. "A Modern Movement of Witchfinders." *Africa* 8.4 (1935): 448–61.

Rogers, Carl. "A Theory of Therapy, Personality and Interpersonal Relationships as Developed in the Client-Centered Framework." In *Psychology: A Study of a Science*, vol. 3: *Formulations of the Person and the Social Context*, edited by S. Koch, 184–256. New York: McGraw Hill, 1959.

Rosenberg, Marshall B. *Non-Violent Communication: A Language of Life*. 2nd ed. Encinitas, CA: Puddledancer Press, 2003.

Schoeller-Reisch, Donata. "Thinking Changes: Stanley Cavell and Eugene Gendlin." *Existential Analysis* 19.2 (2008): 299–315.

Schoffeleers, Matthew. "Ritual Healing and Political Acquiescence: The Case of the Zionist Churches in Southern Africa." *Africa: Journal of the International African Institute* 61.1 (1991): 1–25.

Taussig, Michael T. *The Devil and Commodity Fetishism in South America*. Chapel Hill: University of North Carolina Press, 1980.

Trethowan, W. H. "Dangers Present in Exorcism." *The Times* [United Kingdom], March 25, 1975, 19.

Udelhoven, Bernhard. *Christianity in the Luangwa Valley: Where Faith and Culture Meet and Don't Meet*. Lusaka: FENZA, 2007.

———. *Unseen Worlds: Dealing with Spirits, Witchcraft, and Satanism*. Lusaka: FENZA, 2015.

Uzukwu, Eugene Elochukwu. *God, Spirit, and Human Wholeness: Appropriating Faith and Culture in West African Style*. Eugene, OR: Pickwick, 2012.

Vaughan, Megan. *Curing Their Ills: Colonial Power and African Illness* (Stanford University Press, 1991).

Ventegodt, S., M. Morad, H. Eytan, and M. Joav. "Clinical Holistic Medicine: Use and Limitations of the Biomedical Paradigm." *Scientific World Journal* 4 (2004): 295–306.

Werner, Dietrich. "WCC Consultation on Mission, Health and Healing, Accra, Ghana 4–8 December 2002: Reflector's Report." *International Review of Mission* 93.370/371 (2004): 379–88.

Suggested Reading

Kamps, Johanneke. "Speaking of Satan in Zambia: The Persuasiveness of Contemporary Narratives about Satanism." PhD diss., University of Utrecht, 2017. Published in *Quaestiones Infinitae* 108 (2017).

Meyer, Birgit. *Translating the Devil. Religion and Modernity among the Ewe in Ghana*, Edinburgh: Edinburgh University Press, 1999.

Udelhoven, Bernhard. *Unseen Worlds: Dealing with Spirits, Witchcraft, and Satanism*. Lusaka: FENZA, 2015.

Uzukwu, Eugene Elochukwu. *God, Spirit, and Human Wholeness: Appropriating Faith and Culture in West African Style*. Eugene, OR: Pickwick, 2012.

Ventegodt, S., M. Morad, H. Eytan, and M. Joav. "Clinical Holistic Medicine: Use and Limitations of the Biomedical Paradigm." *Scientific World Journal* 4 (2004): 295–306.

The Body, Health, and Healing

Key Words

- abundant life
- African Initiated Churches
- Agamben, Giorgio
- Bacteriological Revolution
- biomedical paradigm
- biopolitics
- biopower
- biopsychosocial paradigm
- blame
- body–mind dualism
- Cavell, Stanley
- charismatic healing ministry
- deliverance
- demons
- Enlightenment
- evil spirits
- exorcism
- Farmer, Paul
- Foucault, Michel
- Gendlin, Eugene
- germ theory
- healing ministry
- Hebga, Meinrad Pierre
- HIV/AIDS
- holistic medicine
- home-based care
- inner forum
- inner world
- lay therapy management
- life-mission paradigm
- medical health discourse
- mission hospital
- Moltmann, Jürgen
- national health systems
- nonviolent communication
- original sin
- Orthodox Churches
- outer forum
- outer world
- overdetermined concept of healing
- Pentecostal churches
- Pentecostalism
- Piper, John
- placebos
- political acquiescence
- prophetic healing ministry
- prosperity gospel
- Protestant churches
- restorative paradigm of healing
- Rogers, Carl
- Rosenberg, Marshall
- satanism
- structural violence
- therapy managing group
- traditional healers
- transformative paradigm of healing
- Ventegodt, Søren
- Western medicine
- witchcraft
- Word of Faith movement
- World Health Organization (WHO)

Catholic Health Facilities in Africa: Achievements and Challenges

Quentin Wodon

As is the case for Catholic schools, Africa is the continent with the largest and fastest growing number of Catholic health facilities globally. By contrast, in some other areas, especially in developed countries, the number of Catholic health facilities has declined in recent years. If current trends were to continue, given high rates of population growth and gains toward universal access to health care, close to half of all Catholic health care facilities globally might be located on the continent within a couple of decades. This is an opportunity, but also a challenge. Catholic health facilities can be proud of their heritage in Africa. Yet, despite the best efforts of health personnel and given the constraints they face, the coverage and quality of the care being provided today are insufficient in the region, including in Catholic health facilities.

This chapter provides a basic diagnostic of achievements and challenges for Catholic health facilities in Africa. It is adapted in part from a report on the role of faith-based organizations in education and health in the region,[1] and follows the same structure as a companion chapter in this volume on Catholic schools.[2] To facilitate comparisons for readers who may be interested in both topics, the two chapters on schools and health facilities are copycats of each other in terms of basic structure.

In sub-Saharan Africa, where most of the Catholic health facilities are located, health outcomes have improved substantially over the last two decades. At the same time, a lot remains to be done. According to data from the World Bank's World Development Indicators for 2018, the region has the highest under-five mortality rate in the world, at 78 per 1,000 live births versus 39 globally. For under-five stunting, an indicator of malnutrition associated with long-term negative consequences including risks for brain development in early childhood,[3] the proportion is 33.0 percent versus 21.3 percent globally. Life expectancy at birth in sub-Saharan Africa stood at 60.9 years in 2018 versus 72.4 years globally. The prevalence of child marriage and early childbearing is higher in the region than elsewhere and declining more slowly than elsewhere, leading to negative consequences not only for young mothers but also for their children.[4] Access to care is much lower across the board, leading to wide-ranging consequences. As just one example, the maternal mortality ratio in the region stood at 534 per 100,000 live births in 2017 versus 211 globally.

These statistics are dire. Because such a large share of Catholic health facilities are concentrated in sub-Saharan Africa, the facilities have a special role in efforts to reach the third Sustainable Devel-

---

The author is a lead economist at the World Bank. The paper was prepared on the author's own personal time and not as part of his duties at the World Bank. The analysis and views expressed in this paper are those of the author only and may not reflect the views of the World Bank, the countries it represents, or its executive director.

1. Wodon, *Faith-Based Education and Healthcare in Africa*.
2. Wodon, "Catholic Schools in Africa: Achievements and Challenges."
3. Denboba et al., *Stepping Up Early Childhood Development*; Black et al., "Early Child Development Coming of Age."
4. Wodon et al., *Economic Impacts of Child Marriage*; Wodon et al., *Missed Opportunities*.

opment Goal, which is to ensure healthy lives and promote well-being for all at all ages.[5] In many countries, Catholic health facilities are often perceived as providing quality care in comparison to other health facilities. Yet, even if Catholic health facilities may indeed provide comparatively good care, this does not mean that they succeed in ensuring good health outcomes for patients. In a context of limited resources and widespread poverty, the challenges exist for improving health outcomes, including through universal health care.[6] This is true for public health facilities. It is also true for Catholic facilities as well as private secular facilities and those associated with other faiths.

A fundamental principle of Catholic social teaching is the preferential option for the poor,[7] which also applies to the mission of Catholic health facilities. There is some evidence that Catholic and other Christian facilities in Africa aim to serve the poor. In Uganda, untied grants provided by the government to nonprofit (mostly religious) health facilities in Uganda were used to provide more services at lower costs to vulnerable groups as opposed to increased benefits for health workers.[8] Unfortunately, despite efforts by health facilities, patients from disadvantaged backgrounds remain at high risk of not receiving quality care.

The recent COVID-19 crisis has further exacerbated inequality in health outcomes between the well-to-do and the much larger group of individuals and households who are poor or vulnerable. For the first time in twenty-five years, sub-Saharan Africa will suffer from a recession according to projections by the World Bank.[9] Losses in agricultural production may be especially severe. Together with the devastation caused by locust swarms in East Africa and widespread insecurity in the Sahel, this will lead to food insecurity.[10] Children will suffer, not only in terms of their health and nutrition, but also in terms of losses in learning and higher risks of dropping out of schools. Catholic schools themselves may be affected as they may suffer from losses in tuition due to lower enrollment.[11] Similar losses in revenues may affect Catholic health facilities too, especially when they do not benefit from substantial state support. Pandemics tend to have a wide range of negative effects on children in multiple areas. As evidenced in Sierra Leone during the 2014 Ebola outbreak,[12] the negative effects can be wide-ranging, including with a lower likelihood that parents will seek care when children need it. Overall, Africa is especially ill-equipped to deal with the health consequences of the crisis. As a result, achieving the third Sustainable Development Goal seems even further out of reach.

The urgency of providing better care to Africa's population, and especially the poor, should not be in doubt. Apart from reducing morbidity and mortality—the first priority—better health systems could dramatically improve standards of living. The impact of poor health outcomes on human capital is one of the reasons why children do not reach their full potential.[13] This, in turn, has implications for countries' wealth and sustainable development. Human capital wealth is the largest component of the wealth of nations, well ahead of natural and physical capital.[14] Not investing in people's health does not enable nations to reach their development potential.

Strong Catholic health facilities benefit not only individuals and households but also communities

---

5. See United Nations General Assembly, "2030 Agenda for Sustainable Development," https://sdgs.un.org/goals.

6. World Health Organization, *Primary Health Care on the Road to Universal Health Coverage: 2019 Monitoring Report*.

7. For example, see the Pontifical Council for Justice and Peace, *Compendium of the Social Doctrine of the Church*; Pope Francis, encyclical *Laudato Si'* (On Care for Our Common Home).

8. Reinikka and Svensson, "Working for God? Evidence from a Change in Financing of Not-for-Profit Healthcare Providers in Uganda."

9. World Bank, "An Analysis of Issues Shaping Africa's Economic Future," *Africa's Pulse* 21 (Spring 2020).

10. Food Security Information Network, *Global Report on Food Crisis 2020*.

11. Wodon, "COVID-19 Crisis, Impacts on Catholic Schools, and Potential Responses, Part II."

12. United Nations, *Policy Brief: The Impact of COVID-19 on Children*.

13. World Bank, *Africa Human Capital Plan*.

14. Lange et al., *Changing Wealth of Nations 2018*.

and societies at large. To discuss the state of Catholic health facilities in Africa, this chapter reviews some of their achievements and challenges. Relying on data from the annual statistical yearbooks of the church, the first two sections provide simple statistics on trends over time in the number of health facilities globally and in Africa, as well as country-level data within Africa for 2017. Thereafter, the third section considers some of the achievements of Catholic health facilities, especially in terms of providing care with deep respect for the humanity of patients. Finally, the fourth and last section considers where Catholic health facilities stand in terms of reaching the poor and providing quality care. This is first discussed for the continent as a whole and, next, with a brief illustrative case study for Ghana, one of the countries with a substantial number of Catholic health facilities on the continent. A brief conclusion follows.

Aggregate Trends in the Number of Health Facilities for Africa

Trends in the number of Catholic health facilities are available in the annual statistical yearbooks published by the church, with the latest yearbook providing data until 2017.[15] Data are available on the number of hospitals, dispensaries (I will use the term "health centers" here[16]), leproseries, nursing homes, and facilities for people with disabilities[17] managed by the church. The focus in this chapter is only on the first two categories, but it is worth noting that the role of the church is also massive in the other two categories. Globally, the church manages 5,269 hospitals and 16,068 health centers, as well as 646 leproseries and 15,735 nursing homes and facilities for people with disabilities.

The data are provided by country and based on responses by the chancery offices of ecclesiastical jurisdictions to an annual questionnaire. Most jurisdictions reply, and those that do not reply for various reasons tend to have fairly small numbers of health facilities. Therefore, the data are likely to capture most facilities. Whether the data are very precise remains open to question, at least in countries with weak data systems. Even governments in low-income countries may not always have very precise data when they implement annual censuses of health facilities. As many ecclesiastical jurisdictions do not have the ability to implement such censuses every year, especially in sub-Saharan Africa, the data may represent only estimates as opposed to exact figures, although the issue of under- or over-counting may be less salient than in the case of schools, since there are fewer Catholic health facilities than Catholic schools in most countries. Work could be conducted at the country level to check all estimates with other data sources, including national health management systems, but this would be a major undertaking and is beyond the scope of this chapter. Overall, despite some caution, stylized facts emerge from the data and are likely to reflect, at least approximately, the situation on the ground.

Globally, in 2017, the church managed 23,354 health facilities. As mentioned above, this includes 5,269 hospitals and 16,068 health centers. The total number of facilities has not changed dramatically over time, since in 1980 the church already managed 20,469 facilities. However, there have been major changes across regions. Africa accounts for a large and rapidly growing share of the total number of facilities; in most other regions, the number of facilities has declined in recent years. This does not mean that the number of patients served also declined, since facilities may have expanded their capacity, and some of the facilities that closed may have been merged. Unfortunately, data on the number of patients served are not available in the statistical yearbooks. Trends also differ by type of facilities between regions. In the Americas and Europe, for example, there was a sharp reduction in the number of hospitals managed by the church between 1980 and 2017, but the number of health centers remained steady (it increased slightly in the Americas and decreased slightly in Europe). In Asia, both the number of hospitals and health

---

15. Secretaria Status, *Statistical Yearbook of the Church 2017*.
16. Another option would be to use the term "clinics," but in Africa many health centers may not have the type of equipment that clinics often have.
17. The terminology used in the yearbooks is somewhat outdated, as the following terms are used: "homes for the old, the chronically ill, invalids, and the handicapped."

centers increased, although less so than in Africa.

Next, we can consider the breakdown of health facilities in Africa by type. In 2017, the church managed 1,367 hospitals and 5,907 health centers in the region. This compares to 978 hospitals and 3,115 health centers in 1980. In other words, most of the growth in the number of facilities took place through health centers (increase of 89.6 percent in the number of facilities over the period) as compared to hospitals (increase of 39.8 percent over the period). This is good news in terms of the likelihood that the health facilities reach the poor in remote areas where health centers are more likely to operate than full-blown hospitals.

Finally, let us consider the share of Catholic health facilities globally that are located in Africa. From 1980 to 2010, changes in shares were relatively modest, but by 2017, there was a large increase in the share of all facilities located in the region, not only because of growth in Africa but also because of a decline in some of the other regions, as mentioned earlier. In 2017, Africa accounted for 25.9 percent of all hospitals managed by the church, 36.8 percent of all health centers, and 34.1 percent of all health care facilities. This compares to 14.6 percent, 26.4 percent, and 22.1 percent in 1980 for hospitals, health centers, and the combined total, respectively.

The increase in the number of health facilities managed by the church globally and especially in Africa does not mean that the share of patients using Catholic health facilities has increased. Ideally, estimates of this share should be based on the number of patients going to Catholic facilities as a share of total visits. These types of data are available in household surveys and are discussed in my 2015 book, *The Economics of Faith-Based Service Delivery: Education and Health in Sub-Saharan Africa*. While Catholic health facilities—and, more generally, Christian health associations that also federate facilities managed by other Christian denominations—account for a substantial share of hospital beds in many countries, their share of overall health care provision tends to be lower, because there are many other providers of care.[18] It is not fully clear whether, over time, the share of patients using Catholic health facilities has increased or decreased, yet because of a large expansion of public health facilities in many countries in recent decades, it is unlikely that the share of patients using Catholic facilities would have increased markedly. A decline in this share seems more likely, even if the networks have expanded.

What can we expect in the next decade in terms of future growth and the importance of Africa for the provision of health care by the church? Given high rates of population growth and efforts to increase access to health care, growth in the number of Catholic health facilities in Africa could continue for some time. In sub-Saharan Africa in particular, women have an average of 4.8 children, about twice the global average. As a large share of Africa's population is young, these high fertility rates lead to high rates of population growth for the region, 2.7 percent per year versus 1.1 percent globally. Population growth rates are higher among Muslim than Christian populations in the region,[19] but Christian and, in particular, Catholic populations are expanding, too. This growth in the population puts pressure on health systems to expand, and this is also the case for Catholic facilities. If one were to use recent growth estimates to forecast growth in the next ten to twenty years, close to half of all Catholic health care facilities globally might be located on the continent within a couple of decades.

Health Facilities Data by Country

There is substantial heterogeneity between countries in the number of Catholic health facilities. Table 1 provides data on health facilities in 2017 for forty-nine countries by groups of five countries. A few countries or territories are not included because they have no Catholic health facilities. This is the case for Cape Verde, Mauritania, Saint Helena, Seychelles, Somalia, Tunisia, as well as West-

---

18. Statements have been made by church officials that the church may provide a fourth of all health care worldwide. As noted by Olivier and Wodon in a series of three Health-Nutrition-Population working papers in 2012, these statements are, however, difficult to reconcile with other data, including data from household surveys as documented in Wodon, *Economics of Faith-Based Service Delivery*.

19. Pew Research Center, *Changing Global Religious Landscape*.

ern Sahara. The country with the largest number of Catholic health facilities by far is the Democratic Republic of the Congo (DRC), with 2,185 facilities, followed by Kenya with 1,092 facilities and Nigeria with 524 facilities according to the latest statistical yearbook. These three countries alone account for more than half (52.3 percent) of all Catholic health facilities in the region, and the proportion is even higher when considering only hospitals. Tanzania, Cameroon, Uganda, Angola, Madagascar, Zambia, and Ghana round out the top ten.

In the case of Catholic schools, estimates suggest that, over time, the share of students going to Catholic schools in Africa has remained fairly stable.[20] Such data are not available for Catholic health facilities, but it is likely that the share of all health facilities in countries that are Catholic has declined over time as public health facilities have expanded. A comparison with Catholic schools may be instructive. In Africa between 1995 and 2016, the number of Catholic schools operated by the church grew by 4.8 percent per year for preschools, 1.8 percent for primary schools, and 4.7 percent for secondary schools. The growth in enrollment was even larger as the average size of the schools grew as well.[21] By comparison, the rate of growth for the number of Catholic health facilities between 1980 and 2017 is estimated at only 0.9 percent per year for hospitals, and 1.7 percent per year for health centers. While schools and health facilities are different in terms of catchment areas, and while the periods for computing the growth rates are different, the difference in the growth of facilities is still large.

The fact that the growth in the number of Catholic health facilities may not be sufficient for them to maintain their footprint is noted in Ghana by the Christian Health Association (CHA) for that country.[22] CHAs are national-level umbrella networks of Christian health providers that help improve coordination in service provision, reduce duplication, and provide a platform for dialogue with governments (the membership of the CHAs is typically the individual health facilities in the country).[23] Competition from public facilities is also noted for Uganda in a 2018 journal article by Aloysius Ssennyonjo et al.,[24] which looks at trends in government resource contributions to private-not-for-profit (PNFP) health providers in Uganda, most of which are faith-based and federated by the Uganda Catholic Medical Bureau, the CHA for Uganda. Their analysis focuses on funding for primary health care from 1997 to 2015. They identify three phases in the funding: initiation, rapid increase, and then decline. The share of the government's health budget allocated to PNFPs peaked in 2002–2003, while amounts adjusted for inflation disbursed to PNFPs peaked in 2004–2005. The concern is that as countries expand their public health system, the ability of Catholic facilities to maintain their activities and have an influence on overall provision may decline.

The DRC is a bit of a special case in terms of the rapid growth of Catholic health facilities observed over time. In 1980, the country had 236 hospitals and 795 health centers. As shown in table 1, in 2017 the country had 432 hospitals and 1,753 health centers, suggesting annual growth rates of 1.6 percent for hospitals and 2.2 percent for health centers, both of which are well above the growth rates observed for the continent as a whole. As noted by Brunner et al. (2018), the number of faith-based facilities grew in part because of an inability by the state to provide services during periods of conflict. As a result, only 54 percent of hospitals are state-run, 35 percent belong to the faith-based and non-profit sector, and 11 percent are operated by other private institutions.[25] What may also have played a role in the comparatively faster growth of Catholic health facilities in the DRC as compared to the region is the fact that for health care as for education, a large share of the cost of operating health facilities is paid out-of-pocket by households. This may result in smaller differences in out-of-pocket costs for households in choosing faith-based as opposed to public facilities.

---

20. Wodon, "Enrollment in K–12 Catholic Schools: Global and Regional Trends."
21. Wodon, "More Schools, Larger Schools, or Both."
22. Christian Health Association of Ghana, *Strategic Framework 2017–21*.
23. Dimmock et al., "Network Development for Non-State Health Providers."
24. Ssennyonio et al., "Government Resource Contributions to the Private-Not-for-Profit Sector in Uganda."
25. Ministère de la Santé Publique, *Formations hospitalières de la République Démocratique du Congo*.

Table 1: Number of Health Facilities by Country, 2017

	Hospitals	Dispensaries/Health Centers	Total
Democratic Republic of the Congo	432	1753	2185
Kenya	84	1008	1092
Nigeria	269	255	524
Tanzania	68	406	474
Cameroon	32	286	318
Uganda	32	279	311
Angola	30	224	254
Madagascar	20	217	237
Zambia	39	118	157
Ghana	59	68	127
Egypt	15	107	122
Rwanda	9	99	108
Benin	18	85	103
Ethiopia	23	65	88
Togo	12	76	88
Burundi	10	74	84
Malawi	28	55	83
Senegal	2	78	80
Côte d'Ivoire	8	69	77
Chad	8	63	71
South Africa	3	58	61
Zimbabwe	37	23	60
Lesotho	4	55	59
South Sudan	14	44	58
Burkina Faso	7	45	52
Congo	5	44	49
Mozambique	24	21	45
Central African Republic	13	30	43
Guinea-Bissau	5	34	39
Eritrea	9	28	37
Mali	6	27	33
Liberia	8	16	24
Sierra Leone	8	13	21
Gabon	0	13	13
Namibia	6	7	13
Gambia	10	2	12
Guinea	2	10	12
Equatorial Guinea	0	11	11
Sudan	3	7	10
Morocco	1	7	8
Swaziland	1	7	8
Comoros	2	5	7
Niger	0	7	7
Botswana	0	2	2
Libya	0	2	2
Sao Tome & Principe	0	2	2
Algeria	0	1	1
Djibouti	0	1	1
Mauritius	1	0	1
Total	1,367	5,907	7,274

Source: *Statistical Yearbook of the Church*, 2019 edition.

Achievements

Historically, Catholic and other Christian health facilities played an important role in early health systems in African countries, especially during colonial times. Yet the expansion of the number of facilities operated by the Catholic Church and other denominations took place for the most part after the 1930s or even later and until independence.[26] In the case of Ghana for example, the number of mission hospitals increased from three to twenty-seven between 1951 and 1960.[27] As a result, at the time of independence or shortly thereafter, a large

---

26. Asante, *Sustainability of Church Hospitals in Developing Countries*.
27. Arhinful, "Solidarity of Self-Interest."

share of health facilities were managed by Catholic and other Christian denominations.

James McGilvray, the first director of the Christian Medical Commission, discusses events that affected faith-based health facilities in the region from the 1960s to the 1980s, including the Tübingen meetings that led to the creation of the CHAs.[28] As mentioned earlier, the CHAs help federate the experience of individual facilities or groups of facilities by faith denomination—Catholic and Protestant—into a coherent voice for the sector as a whole, including for negotiations with governments for public-private partnerships and funding. The first CHAs were created in the 1950s and 1960s in countries such as Cameroon, Ghana, Kenya, Malawi, and Uganda. International support for mission hospitals decreased after independence, in part because the resources available to the religious bodies that had founded hospitals were also decreasing. The CHAs were instrumental in seeking government funding.

McGilvray estimated that in Tanzania, Malawi, Cameroon, and Ghana, Christian health facilities accounted at the time for one-fourth to one-half of all health care facilities (estimates were lower in South Asia). These estimates have often been used to claim that up to half of all health care in Africa is still today provided by faith-based organizations, but this claim does not stand up to scrutiny, especially when a broader definition of health care provision is accounted for as in household surveys.[29] Nevertheless, there is no doubt as discussed above that Catholic and, more generally, Christian health facilities remain an essential part of health systems in many African countries.

Today, CHAs operate in two dozen countries in Africa, and internationally many CHAs are members of the African Christian Health Associations Platform, which facilitates exchanges between countries. The CHAs can be categorized according to their level of development and sophistication as emergent, professionalized, or integrated.[30] Emergent CHAs are still being formed or have not been very active yet. Professional CHAs have entered into formal relationships with Ministries of Health and provide capacity-building support to their members (health facilities). Integrated CHAs are fully part of the national health system.

While there is no one-to-one relationship between the level of development of CHAs and that of their country, emergent CHAs tend to be located in countries that have been affected at one point or another by fragility and conflict over the last two decades.[31] This would include CHAs in the DRC, Liberia, the Central African Republic, Sierra Leone, Togo, Rwanda, Sudan, and Zimbabwe. Professionalized CHAs tend to be in low-income countries, although a few are in lower-middle-income countries. This group would include CHAs in Benin, Cameroon, Chad, Kenya, Lesotho, Malawi, Nigeria, Rwanda, Tanzania, Uganda, and Zambia. Finally, integrated CHAs would be mostly in lower-middle-income countries. This would include Botswana, Ghana, Namibia, and Swaziland. The CHA of Ghana (CHAG), one of the first to be established with many of its members being Catholic facilities, is a great example of what has been accomplished. CHAG has a memorandum of understanding with the Ministry of Health and benefits from state support for staff salaries.[32] Over time, in its relationship with government, beyond an initial focus on securing funding, the CHAG has managed to be involved in broader policy making.

At the level of individual facilities, achievements often include an ability to provide quality care at low out-of-pocket costs for patients. Cost of care remains a barrier to seeking care for many households in Burkina Faso.[33] Based on qualitative fieldwork, analysis shows that low cost of care is one of the reasons why patients seek care in faith-based facilities, but so is the perception that the quality of care, including respect for patients, is higher in

---

28. McGilvray, *Quest for Health and Wholeness*.
29. See Wodon et al., "Market Share of Faith-Inspired Health Care Providers in Africa."
30. Dimmock et al., "Network Development for Non-State Health Providers."
31. Dimmock et al., "Network Development for Non-State Health Providers."
32. Buckle and Yeboah, "Evolving Partnership between the Government of Ghana and National Faith-Based Health Providers."
33. Gemignani et al., "Making Quality Care Affordable for the Poor."

those facilities than in public facilities. How are the facilities able to provide quality care at low cost? Part of the story is the support in kind and in cash from religious groups and other donors, but the dedication of nuns working for very low wages is also a factor.

Importantly, and contrary to what is observed for parents choosing Catholic schools for their children, as discussed in the companion chapter on education in this *Handbook*,[34] the reasons leading patients to choose faith-based facilities are not related directly to religion but rather to the quality of care received and its affordability. This finding emerges from qualitative work conducted in areas of the country where patients have access to public, Catholic or other Christian, and Islamic health facilities. In the 2014 article, "Faith-Inspired Health Care Provision in Ghana: Market Share, Reach to the Poor, and Performance," a similar finding is observed for Ghana, using the same research design.[35] As reported by the authors, two-thirds of patients relying on Christian clinics and hospitals state that quality of care is the main reason for choosing the facilities, with the second factor cited most often being the fact that staff at the facilities are knowledgeable as well as dedicated. In particular, respect by staff for the dignity of patients is a strong factor leading patients to choose Christian as well as Islamic facilities. Thus, while religion itself is not a driver of the choice of faith-based facilities, the religious inspiration of the staff, which leads them to provide services in a caring way, does make a major difference.

To try to triangulate these results using different questions, patients in both Burkina Faso and Ghana were asked to mention what they saw as the main reason for relying on faith-based health facilities for care. The quality of the staff, the affordability of services for the poor, and the quality of the care received were cited most often for Catholic and other Christian facilities. Similar responses were provided for patients relying on Islamic facilities, although location came in as more important. Interestingly, patients had no problem using services provided by health facilities affiliated with a different faith than their own. In fact, patients from other faiths respected the faith-related motivation of staff in the clinics for providing them with quality and affordable care. On the other hand, public facilities were often not perceived as positively.

The relative satisfaction of patients with faith-based facilities, including Catholic facilities, also emerges from nationally representative household surveys for West and Central Africa. Satisfaction rates with faith-based health facilities tend to be higher than for public health facilities, although on a par with the rates observed for private secular health facilities.[36] Catholic health facilities are typically not identified separately from other faith-based health facilities in those surveys, but the results are encouraging.

Challenges

Despite major achievements, Catholic and other faith-based health facilities still face challenges in Africa (and elsewhere) in terms of reaching the poor and ensuring good health outcomes. There should be no doubt that Catholic health facilities make real efforts to reach the poor and to improve health outcomes, but this does not guarantee success. To discuss these issues, a few basic facts are first provided across countries before considering illustrative analysis of challenges faced by Catholic and other faith-based health facilities in Ghana, one of the countries with the largest number of Catholic health facilities on the continent.

General Considerations

Figure 1 illustrates data for sub-Saharan African countries related to the two challenges of reaching the poor and ensuring good health outcomes. The visualization is in terms of protection against the risks of poverty and poor health outcomes. The figure's horizontal axis represents the share of the population not in poverty according to the $1.90 per day threshold in purchasing power parity terms used by the World Bank for international poverty

---

34. See Wodon's essay on education in this volume, "Catholic Schools in Africa: Achievements and Challenges."
35. Olivier et al., "Faith-Inspired Health Care Provision in Ghana."
36. Wodon, *Economics of Faith-Based Service Delivery*.

Catholic Health Facilities in Africa

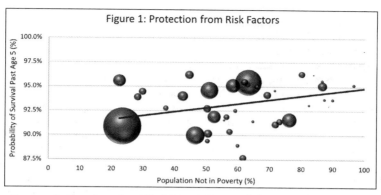

Source: Author, based on World Bank Data and the *Annual Statistical Yearbook of the Church*

comparisons. Countries further to the right tend to have a smaller share of their population in poverty. The vertical axis represents the likelihood of survival past age five, hence one minus the under-five mortality rate as a proxy for broader health outcomes. Countries in the upper part of the figure do better in reducing under-five mortality and thereby ensuring good health outcomes. The size of the bubbles in the figure is proportional to the number of Catholic health facilities in each country. Countries without Catholic health facilities are not displayed.

A few stylized facts visible on the figure are worth emphasizing. First, many countries have high rates of poverty. This is the case for the DRC (large bubble on the bottom left), but also for other countries such as Uganda and Kenya (the other two large bubbles in the center), as well as several other countries with a large number of Catholic health facilities, including Malawi and Burundi, as well as to a lower extent Rwanda. In many of those countries, as Catholic health facilities serve a substantial share of the population, they also tend to reach the poor. Given the high rates of poverty in many countries where Catholic health facilities have a substantial presence, it is fair to say that, overall, Catholic health facilities do manage to reach a large number of children in poverty. Overall, the presence of Catholic health facilities also tends to be stronger in poorer countries, due in part to the large number of facilities in the DRC.

Second, in most countries, including those with lower levels of poverty, health systems are not ensuring adequate health outcomes, in that survival rates past age five remain too low. As mentioned in the introduction, 39 children die globally by age five per 1,000 live births. In sub-Saharan Africa, the rate is twice that at 78 deaths per 1,000 live births. But in the DRC, the country with the largest number of Catholic faith facilities, the rate is 88 per 1,000 live births. Note that, across countries, there is a positive relationship between lower levels of poverty and better health outcomes, but this relationship is not very strong. Most health systems in Africa perform poorly. When considering all countries in the world, the relationship between economic development and health outcomes is stronger. Within sub-Saharan Africa, this is less the case.

Even if it were the case that Catholic health facilities were to provide better care than public health facilities, one implicit implication of these data is that this could still result in poor health outcomes. This is not mentioned as a critique against Catholic health facilities. Despite some support received through advocacy by CHAs—especially for salaries, as mentioned above—in many countries, Catholic health facilities still do not benefit from government funding, or at least the level of funding received is often lower than for public health facilities, especially when capital expenditures are taken into account. The fact that, despite limited support,

Catholic health facilities continue to operate and serve many among the poor is a major achievement.

In several countries, during periods of conflict as public provision collapsed, Catholic and other faith-based health facilities were the backbone of their countries' health systems. Finally, while the health facilities must often recover at least some of their operating costs through fees paid by households, household survey data suggest that these facilities are substantially cheaper on average than private secular health facilities.[37] This being said, the performance of health systems in Africa, including Catholic health facilities, remains a work in progress.

What can Catholic health facilities do to improve health outcomes? This is a complex question, and answering it is beyond the scope of this chapter. But, as noted by the World Bank, a key priority is for governments to renew their commitment toward ensuring universal health coverage so that the whole population can get care without financial hardship.[38] Given the large role of Catholic and other faith-based facilities in the provision of care, it would be natural to include these facilities in national plans to reach universal health coverage, but to do so more sustainable core funding would be needed than is the case.[39]

Illustrative Analysis

The context in which Catholic health facilities operate and how well they perform varies from country to country. To dig a bit deeper, it is useful to consider a case study. The focus is on Ghana, a country with a substantial number of Catholic health facilities, an established CHA, and better-than-average data to assess where Catholic and other Christian health facilities are located and how they may be performing, at least according to some metrics.

Consider first the issue of reaching the poor, which is often a core objective of Catholic health facilities given the church's preferential option for the poor and vulnerable. Estimates suggest that, while faith-based health facilities reach the poor in Africa, they do not do so proportionately more.[40] This is not surprising given that out-of-pocket costs reduce demand for health care among the poor more than among other groups for all types of facilities. However, the geographic location of facilities could help. In principle, health facilities could reach the poor in better-off areas as well as in poor areas because even areas that tend to be better off often have poor households in their midst. In practice, however, it is easier to serve populations in poverty if health facilities are located proportionately more in poor areas. Is this the case in Ghana? Using poverty mapping techniques, Harold Coulombe and Quentin Wodon assess whether CHAG facilities, many of which are Catholic facilities, are located proportionately more in poor areas, as is often suggested by the CHAG.[41] If the CHAG were to look only at the distribution of its own facilities across districts, it could conclude that, among the areas it serves, its facilities are indeed located proportionately more in poorer areas. Yet, from a national point of view, there may still be other areas that are poorer and not served by CHAG's facilities, in which case it might not be correct to state that, nationally, facilities are located in poorer areas. The authors find that this is indeed the case—CHAG facilities are not proportionately located more in poor areas at the national level.[42]

What could be the reasons why CHAG facilities are not located proportionately more in poor areas despite a stated intention to do so? One suggestion is that CHAG facilities may have been located in poor areas in the past, but faster development in those areas may have rendered the areas less poor in comparison to other areas.[43] In particular, there

---

37. Wodon, *Economics of Faith-Based Service Delivery*.
38. World Bank, *Universal Health Coverage (UHC) in Africa*.
39. Dimmock et al., "Network Development for Non-State Health Providers."
40. Wodon, *Economics of Faith-Based Service Delivery*.
41. Coulombe and Wodon, "Mapping Religious Health Assets." For example, in one of its annual reports, CHAG stated that its "member institutions are located predominantly in the rural areas and are aimed at reaching the marginalized and poorest of the poor" (CHAG *Annual Report*, 2006).
42. See also Grieve and Olivier, "Towards Universal Health Coverage."
43. Coulombe and Wodon, "Mapping Religious Health Assets."

have been profound changes in the geography of poverty in the country as poverty rates were substantially reduced, but not everywhere. Poverty is now increasingly concentrated in the northern and rural savannah part of the country, which tends to have a higher share of the population that is Muslim and where CHAG facilities have traditionally had a smaller footprint. The combination of differences in population growth, migration, and development in various areas may have led to CHAG facilities being progressively located less in poor areas, not because of changes in the location of the facilities themselves but because of changes in their environment. This illustrates how difficult it is to maintain a presence in poor areas for facilities—especially hospitals that were often built decades earlier and whose location cannot be changed easily.

Consider next the issue of the quality of the care being provided. In health care, there are fewer commonly agreed-upon and comprehensive quality metrics for the performance of facilities than is the case in education, where student and, by extension, school performance can be measured through standard student assessments.[44] But studies provide insights on particular metrics that may be related to a particular type of illness. A recent study in Ghana, for example, looks at the availability of basic equipment for visual impairment–related care.[45] The study's authors find that CHAG facilities tend to be better equipped than similar public facilities managed by the Ghana Health Service (GHS). For example, for hospitals, more CHAG facilities had a slit lamp and an applanation tonometer[46] than GHS facilities. On the other hand, while basic equipment for refraction could be found in most facilities, specialized eye care equipment was often not available at the subdistrict and community level whether the facilities were operated by CHAG or GHS. This example suggests that, even if CHAG facilities are able to provide better care than other facilities, they still often do not have the resources to provide the care that would be needed.

The issue of lack of resources comes out strongly in CHAG's annual reports and its strategic framework for 2017–2021.[47] The plan for 2017–2021 notes a series of difficulties in the implementation of the previous strategic framework for 2014–2016, the first two of which relate to lack of funding for key activities in the plan and delays in receiving reimbursement for service provision from the National Health Insurance System. The plan for 2017–2021 also includes a nice SWOT (Strengths, Weaknesses, Opportunities, and Threats) analysis. Beyond the issue of funding for some programs, weaknesses include lack of structures for effective monitoring and supervision and for communications and collaborations within the CHAG network. As for concerns, a first issue is the fact that new partnerships by GHS may lead to the creation of three thousand new health facilities. While this will increase the availability of care in the country, it will also dilute the role played by CHAG within the sector, and thereby, possibly, its influence. This is a challenge encountered in other countries as well. While there has been an expansion in the number of Catholic and other Christian health facilities in Africa, the resources for such expansion pale in comparison to the resources available to governments for expanding public health facilities, thus possibly resulting in losses in the shares of patients relying on CHA facilities. While maintaining such shares is not a primary objective of the CHAs, if their role in countries is diluted given a faster expansion of public facilities, this may weaken their overall position and sustainability.

Conclusion

Africa is by far the continent with the largest number of Catholic health facilities globally. In 2017, estimates suggest that the church managed 1,367 hospitals and 5,907 health centers in the region. That year, Africa accounted for 25.9 percent of all hospitals managed by the church globally and 36.8

---

44. On the type of metrics used to assess performance by CHAG, see its annual reports (e.g., CHAG, *Annual Report 2016*).

45. Morny et al., "Assessing the Progress Towards Achieving 'VISION 2020: The Right to Sight' Initiative in Ghana."

46. An instrument used to measure the intraocular pressure of the eye.

47. CHAG, *Strategic Framework 2017–21*.

percent of all health centers. Given high rates of population growth and efforts to increase access to health care in the region, as well as the possibility of a further decline in the number of Catholic health facilities in some of the other regions of the world, this share is expected to increase further in coming decades. In many ways, the future of Catholic health facilities will depend in a substantial way on what happens in the region.

Relying on data from the annual statistical yearbooks of the church, this chapter aimed first to document trends in the number of health facilities in the region. Next, the objective was to discuss some of the achievements and challenges faced by Catholic and other Christian health facilities, considering that many of these facilities are federated at the national level through CHAs. A focus was placed, in particular, on whether the health facilities manage to reach the poor and whether they succeed in ensuring good health outcomes for patients.

Qualitative work and other data sources, including satisfaction rates as measured in nationally representative household surveys, suggest that within the constraints they face, Catholic and other faith-based health facilities manage to provide quality care, especially in terms of the respect and dignity with which patients are treated. There are also indications that Catholic facilities try to serve the poor to the best of their ability by making their services affordable. While there is no doubt that Catholic health facilities in Africa have achieved a lot, both historically and contemporaneously, the challenges they face today remain daunting. Many households still lack access to care, and even when they have access, health outcomes are poor.

There is no magic solution to improve health outcomes and the quality of health care in Africa, including in Catholic health facilities. The literature suggests, however, that gains can be achieved with specific interventions, including especially efforts to provide universal health care, although those efforts are driven mostly by governments, even if Catholic facilities can contribute. At the country level, challenges will depend on local context, but the issues of funding and coordination among facilities are likely to be high on the agenda, as are proper evaluation and monitoring to assess performance. The strategic framework produced in Ghana by the CHAG is a great example of how to conduct an analysis of strengths, weaknesses, opportunities, and threats to enable faith-based health facilities to thrive. Finally, the question of the identity of Catholic health facilities, and how to maintain or strengthen it, has not been the focus of this chapter. But it is important to note that qualitative work suggests that identity clearly plays a central role in both the ability of health personnel to serve patients with dignity and the choice by patients of faith-based facilities when seeking care.

Bibliography

Arhinful, Daniel K. "The Solidarity of Self-Interest: Social and Cultural Feasibility of Rural Health Insurance in Ghana." Doctoral thesis. University of Amsterdam, 2003.

Asante, Rexford Kofi Oduro. *Sustainability of Church Hospitals in Developing Countries: A Search for Criteria for Success.* Geneva: World Council of Churches, 1998.

Black, Maureen M., et al. "Early Child Development Coming of Age: Science through the Life-Course." *The Lancet* 389:10064 (2017): 77–90.

Brunner, Bettina Marie, et al. *The Role of the Private Sector in Improving the Performance of the Health System in the Democratic Republic of Congo.* Bethesda, MD: Abt Associates, 2018.

Buckle, Gilbert, and Peter Yeboah. "The Evolving Partnership between the Government of Ghana and National Faith-Based Health Providers: Leadership Perspective and Experiences from the Christian Health Association of Ghana." *Development in Practice* 27.5 (2017): 766–74.

Christian Health Association of Ghana (CHAG). *Annual Report: June 2005–May 2006.* Accra: Christian Health Association of Ghana, 2006.

———. *Annual Report 2016.* Accra: Christian Health Association of Ghana, 2016.

———. *Strategic Framework 2017–21.* Accra: Christian Health Association of Ghana, 2017.

Coulombe, Harold, and Quentin Wodon. "Mapping Religious Health Assets: Are Faith-Inspired Facilities Located in Poor Areas in Ghana?," *Economics Bulletin* 33.2 (2013): 1615–31.

Denboba, Amina, et al. *Stepping Up Early Childhood Development: Investing in Young Children for High Returns*. Washington, DC: World Bank, 2014.

Dimmock, F., J. Olivier, and Q. Wodon. "Network Development for Non-State Health Providers: African Christian Health Associations." *Development in Practice* 27.5 (2017): 580–98.

Food Security Information Network. *Global Report on Food Crisis 2020*. Rome: Food Security Information Network, 2020.

Francis, Pope. *Laudato Si'* [Encyclical On Care for Our Common Home; June 18, 2015]. Vatican City: Libreria Editrice Vaticana, 2015. www.vatican.va.

Gemignani, Regina, et al. "Making Quality Care Affordable for the Poor: Faith-Inspired Health Facilities in Burkina Faso." *Review of Faith & International Affairs* 12.1 (2014): 30–44.

Grieve, Annabel, and Jill Olivier. "Towards Universal Health Coverage: A Mixed-Method Study Mapping the Development of the Faith-Based Non-Profit Sector in the Ghanaian Health System." *International Journal for Equity in Health* 17.1 (2018): 97.

Lange, Glenn-Marie, et al. *The Changing Wealth of Nations 2018: Sustainability into the 21st Century*. Washington, DC: World Bank, 2018.

McGilvray, James. *The Quest for Health and Wholeness*. Tübingen: German Institute for Medical Mission, 1981.

Ministère de la Santé Publique. *Formations hospitalières de la République Démocratique du Congo*. Kinshasa, Democratic Republic of the Congo: Ministère de la Santé Publique, 2017.

Morny, Enyam Komia Amewuho, et al. "Assessing the Progress Towards Achieving 'VISION 2020: The Right to Sight' Initiative in Ghana." *Journal of Environmental and Public Health* (2019): Article ID 3813298.

Olivier, Jill, and Quentin Wodon. "Network Development for Non-State Health Providers: African Christian Health Associations." *Development in Practice* 27.5 (2017): 580–98.

———. "Playing Broken Telephone: Assessing Faith-Inspired Health Care Provision in Africa." *Development in Practice* 22.5–6 (2012): 819–34.

Olivier, Jill, and Quentin Wodon, eds. *The Comparative Nature of Faith-Inspired Health Care Providers in Sub-Saharan Africa: Strengthening the Evidence for Faith-Inspired Engagement in Africa*. Vol. 2. HNP Discussion Paper. Washington, DC: World Bank, 2012.

———. *Mapping, Cost, and Reach to the Poor of Faith-Inspired Health Care Providers in Sub-Saharan Africa: Strengthening the Evidence for Faith-Inspired Engagement in Africa*. Vol. 3. HNP Discussion Paper. Washington, DC: World Bank, 2012.

———. *The Role of Faith-Inspired Health Care Providers in Sub-Saharan Africa and Public-Private Partnerships: Strengthening the Evidence for Faith-Inspired Engagement in Africa*. Vol. 1. HNP Discussion Paper. Washington, DC: World Bank, 2012.

Olivier, Jill, et al. "Faith-Inspired Health Care Provision in Ghana: Market Share, Reach to the Poor, and Performance." *Review of Faith & International Affairs* 12.1 (2014): 84–96.

———. "Understanding the Roles of Faith-Based Healthcare Providers in Africa: Review of the Limited Evidence with a Focus on Magnitude, Reach, Cost, and Satisfaction." *The Lancet* 386:10005 (2015): 1765–75.

Pew Research Center. *The Changing Global Religious Landscape*. Washington, DC: Pew Research Center, 2017.

Pontifical Council for Justice and Peace. *Compendium of the Social Doctrine of the Church*. Vatican City: Libreria Editrice Vaticana, 2004.

Reinikka, Ritva, and Jakob Svensson. "Working for God? Evidence from a Change in Financing of Not-for-Profit Healthcare Providers in Uganda." *Journal of the European Economic Association* 8 (2010): 1159–78.

Secretaria Status. *Statistical Yearbook of the Church 2017*. Rome: Libreria Editrice Vaticana, 2019.

Ssennyonjo, Aloysius, et al. "Government Resource Contributions to the Private-Not-for-Profit Sector in Uganda: Evolution, Adaptations and Implications for Universal Health Coverage." *International Journal for Equity in Health* 17:130 (2018).

United Nations. *Policy Brief: The Impact of COVID-19 on Children*. New York: United Nations, 2020.

Wodon, Quentin. "Catholic Schools in Africa: Achievements and Challenges." In *The Handbook of African Catholicism*, edited by Stan Chu Ilo. Maryknoll, NY: Orbis Books, 2022.

———. "COVID-19 Crisis, Impacts on Catholic Schools, and Potential Responses, Part I: Developed Countries with Focus on the United States." *Journal of Catholic Education* 23.2 (2020): 13–50.

———. "COVID-19 Crisis, Impacts on Catholic Schools, and Potential Responses, Part II: Developing Countries with Focus on Sub-Saharan Africa." *Journal of Catholic Education* 23.2 (2020): 51–86.

———. *The Economics of Faith-Based Service Delivery: Education and Health in Sub-Saharan Africa*. New York: Palgrave Macmillan, 2015.

———. "Enrollment in K–12 Catholic Schools: Global and Regional Trends." *Educatio Catholica* 4.3 (2018): 189–210.

———. *Faith-Based Education and Healthcare in Africa*. Washington, DC: World Bank, 2020.

———. "More Schools, Larger Schools, or Both? Patterns of Enrollment Growth in K–12 Catholic Schools Globally." *Journal of Catholic Education* 22.1 (2019): 135–53.

Wodon, Quentin, et al. *Economic Impacts of Child Marriage: Global Synthesis Report*. Washington, DC: ICRW and the World Bank, 2017.

———. "Market Share of Faith-Inspired Health Care Providers in Africa." *Review of Faith & International Affairs* 12.1 (2014): 8–20.

———. *Missed Opportunities: The High Cost of Not Educating Girls*. Washington, DC: World Bank, 2018.

World Bank. *Africa Human Capital Plan: Powering Africa's Potential through Its People*. Washington, DC: World Bank, 2019.

———. "An Analysis of Issues Shaping Africa's Economic Future." *Africa's Pulse* 21 (Spring 2020). Washington, DC: World Bank, 2020.

———. *Universal Health Coverage (UHC) in Africa: A Framework for Action*. Washington, DC: World Bank, 2016.

World Health Organization. *Primary Health Care on the Road to Universal Health Coverage: 2019 Monitoring Report*. Geneva: World Health Organization, 2019.

Suggested Reading

Christian Health Association of Ghana (CHAG). *Strategic Framework 2017–21*. Accra: Christian Health Association of Ghana, 2017.

Dimmock, F., J. Olivier, and Q. Wodon. "Network Development for Non-State Health Providers: African Christian Health Associations." *Development in Practice* 27.5 (2017): 580–98.

Reinikka, Ritva, and Jakob Svensson. "Working for God? Evidence from a Change in Financing of Not-for-Profit Healthcare Providers in Uganda." *Journal of the European Economic Association* 8 (2010): 1159–78.

Wodon, Quentin. *The Economics of Faith-Based Service Delivery: Education and Health in Sub-Saharan Africa*. New York: Palgrave Macmillan, 2015.

World Health Organization. *Primary Health Care on the Road to Universal Health Coverage: 2019 Monitoring Report*. Geneva: World Health Organization, 2019.

Key Words
Catholic health care
Christian Health Associations
health outcomes
health centers
hospitals
sub-Saharan Africa

African Catholicism and the Place of Women: Research and Advocacy

Ebere Bosco Amakwe, HFSN

The hour is coming, in fact has come, when the vocation of women is being achieved in its fullness, the hour in which woman acquires in the world an influence, an effect and a power never hitherto achieved. That is why, at this moment when the human race is undergoing so deep a transformation, women impregnated with the spirit of the Gospel can do so much to aid mankind in not falling.[1]

The above statement by Pope Paul VI at the close of the Second Vatican Council about the importance of the role of women indubitably reechoes today. It is no surprise that the subject of women in the twenty-first century holds ever-greater interest.[2] Apart from the fact that women make up half of the world's population,[3] the reason for this interest is related to the crucial place women occupy both in society and in the church. The present research is part of that growing interest, especially as it pertains to women in Africa. This chapter investigates the fact that, despite the many and varied roles played by African women in the African church and society, the contributions of women are understudied, their works are less published and less read, and their representation in positions of leadership is lagging. In order to address these problems, I propose some methodological approaches for African researchers that might facilitate a better understanding of the roles played by women in Africa. I suggest that the relative lack of attention paid to women in Africa is the result of a lack of interest in engaging in an in-depth conversation about "African women's palaver"[4] on the part of both African and non-African scholars, African church authorities, and even African women themselves.

This chapter will look closely at the role of women in the African church and society. I will examine how, following the council, the role of women everywhere in the world, but particularly in Africa, has become more prominent. With a focus on the period that began in 1959 with the planning for the council, this research will analyze (1) the impact of the council on the African church; (2) the impact of the council on the roles of African women; (3) the current situation of women on the continent; and (4) the way forward for research about how to ensure that women can assume their place as full members of God's family in both the African church and society.

Many theories have emerged for discussing the role of women in society, including "Feminism, Black Feminism, African Feminism, [and] Alice

---

1. Pope Paul VI, "To Women" §1.
2. Kemdirim, "Towards Inclusiveness for Women," 71.
3. UN WOMEN, *Progress of the World's Women*, 3.
4. Okonjo Ogunyemi, *Africa Wo/Man Palava*, 106 and 114.

Walker's Womanism,"[5] Chikwenye Okonjo Ogunyemi's African womanism,[6] Catherine Acholonu's "Motherism,"[7] and Molara Ogundipe-Leslie's "Stiwanism."[8] Critics have viewed these concepts as being "female-centered" and focused on the quest for "female empowerment,"[9] and thus oriented to the experience of Western women; according to the critics, use of these terms connotes "European domination/White supremacy."[10] For this reason, a more appropriate theoretical tool is Clenora Hudson-Weems's "Africana Womanism Theory"[11] with its African "epistemic identity."[12] Her use of the term "Africana" stresses a celebration of the African culture and heritage of togetherness, family life, and hard work, all of which are focal points for African women. Hudson-Weems's theory celebrates women as victors and emphasizes the complementarity of women and men, in contrast to the other theories mentioned above, which are concerned only about presenting women as victims of a patriarchal system. Even though this is unquestionably true, women have, as this study will show, made many advances in the direction of emancipation and in successfully asserting their presence in and contributions to church and society. These gains have, however, not been the subject of much research or discussion. In order to address this gap, in this chapter I discuss the present situation of African women in light of the theory of Africana womanism because it allows African women to be celebrated and highlights their potential and uniqueness.[13]

Africana Womanism as a Theoretical Framework for Assessing the Roles of African Women

The most important thing to note about Hudson-Weems's groundbreaking theory is its Africanness—the term "Africana" establishes the African cultural identity of the women being studied.[14] As noted by Nahed Mohammed Ahmed, "There is no substitute for centering oneself in one's own culture and speaking one's own cultural truth." Ahmed called African womanism "an authentic African-centered paradigm."[15] The model is universally applicable to the study of all women of African origin regardless of their precise place of origin on the continent. As noted by Hudson-Weems herself, "Africana Womanism is an ideology created and designed for all women of African descent. It is grounded in culture and, therefore, it necessarily focuses on the unique experiences, struggles, needs, and desires of Africana women.[16]

In this sense, "Africana womanism is not ahistorical";[17] rather, the struggles of African women are not divorced from the larger African problems of poverty, underdevelopment, marginalization, exploitation, the struggle for acceptance, and the need to reform both the African church and the African society.[18] In addition, "African womanism is centered on the need for positive gender self-definition within religious, historical, geographical and cultural contexts,"[19] each of these contexts complementing and giving meaning to the others. This

---

5. Alexander-Floyd and Simien, "Revisiting 'What's in a Name?,'" 67.
6. Okonjo Ogunyemi, *Africa Wo/Man Palava*, 106.
7. Acholonu, *Motherism*.
8. This word is born out of the acronym STIWA, which stands for "Social Transformation Including Women in Africa." Ogundipe-Leslie coined this term and advocates using it in place of the term "feminism." See Ogundipe-Leslie, *Re-Creating Ourselves*.
9. Ahmed, "Africana Womanist Reading," 61.
10. Ahmed, "Africana Womanist Reading," 61.
11. Hudson-Weems, *Africana Womanism*.
12. McDougal, "Africana Studies' Epistemic Identity," 236.
13. The words "African" and "Africana" in reference to woman/women are used interchangeably.
14. Africana Womanism Society, http://africanawomanismsociety.webs.com/aboutaws.htm.
15. Ahmed, "African Womanist Reading," 58–59.
16. Hudson-Weems, *Africana Womanism*, 155.
17. Kolawole, *Womanism and African Consciousness*, 203.
18. Kolawole, *Womanism and African Consciousness*, 203.
19. Kolawole, *Womanism and African Consciousness*, 203.

process involves a positive harnessing of the aptitudes of the African woman.

As part of this discussion of Africana womanism, it is important to mention "continental African" women.[20] This study is about who these women really are, what they do and have done, how their potential can be better harnessed, and how further research into the issues they face can benefit the entire African continent. This is crucial because "placing African ideals at the center of any analysis" involving women and their activities, whether the analysis is "social, political . . . economic," or religious, can shed light on African women's "suppressed contributions"[21] to their societies. Under the umbrella of African womanism, this study analyzes continental African women as "agents," actors who have roles in the creation of history and culture not simply as spectators or "passive recipients of someone else's actions."[22] Hudson-Weems echoed Pope Paul VI in the opening words of this chapter when she stated that "the chief role of the Africana woman is to aid in bringing to fruition the liberation of her entire race."[23] To achieve this, Hudson-Weems identified eighteen "descriptors" that should guide an informed analysis of the presence and actions of Africana women,[24] as follows: "A self-namer; A self-definer; Family-centered; Genuine in sisterhood; Strong; In concert with the Africana man in Struggle; Whole; Authentic; A flexible role player; Respected; Recognized; Spiritual; Male Compatible; Respectful of elders; Adaptable; Ambitious; Mothering; and Nurturing."[25]

For "self-namer and self-definer," Hudson-Weems urged the Africana woman to name and define herself based on her context. This means accessing herself and explaining her reality within her community in terms of her cultural experiences.[26] Citing herself as an example in an interview, Hudson-Weems explained that "in naming, she tries to be reflective of two things, 'Africana' and 'Womanism' which gives a cultural connection with the continent Africa, and the idea of being a woman that is developed in that context."[27] In another passage, quoting Toni Morrison, an Africana Womanist, Reed emphasized that Africana women talk about naming and defining themselves because,

> Definitions belong to the definers, not the defined, historically. So, it is up to us to define ourselves. If we don't, someone else will, and they will do it miserably. . . . We have to name ourselves. In the African cosmology, the word *nommo* is critical to existence. It is through the proper naming of a thing that it gains its existence, its essence. So there it is. We have to name ourselves properly.[28]

It has become evident in recent times that women are heeding this clarion call. Today, around the globe unlike ever before, women are deciding for themselves what they should be called, whether married or not. They are choosing and thereby naming their areas of study and careers. They are choosing and thereby naming the particular cities and countries in which they want to pursue these things. The act of naming is of great importance to African women, especially in the case of newborn babies, because names have meanings attached to them. Names are given to events and circumstances, whether joyful or sad, and women are always involved in the naming. The names women give to their babies or to places can be an expression of faith or a reflection of their immediate or past experiences, all of which reveals a state of mind. Emphasizing the importance of this process for African women, Okonjo Ogunyemi observed, "Naming ourselves meaningfully as we have always

---

20. Kolawole, *Womanism and African Consciousness*, 169.
21. Ahmed, "African Womanist Reading," 58.
22. Ahmed, "African Womanist Reading," 58.
23. Hudson-Weems, *Africana Womanism*, 51.
24. Hudson-Weems, *Africana Womanism*, 168.
25. Hudson-Weems, *Africana Womanism*, 154.
26. Africana Womanism Society, http://africanawomanismsociety.webs.com/aboutaws.htm.
27. Reed, "Africana Womanism and African Feminism," 169.
28. Reed, "Africana Womanism and African Feminism," 169.

done in our cultures historicizes our circumstances and focalizes our politics."[29]

Based on Hudson-Weems's eighteen indicators, Marquita Pellerin affirmed that the essential principles of an Africana womanist methodology must include the following:

1. A pledge to the wholeness of Africana womanhood; 2. An acceptance of the interconnectedness of Africana women and humanity; 3. Consciousness of the Africana woman comes through the African family and community; 4. Recognition of the centrality of motherhood; 5. Acknowledgment that Africana women are inherently tied to the struggle for social justice; 6. The inseparability of the Africana woman and her race; 7. An awareness of . . . spiritual and moral grounding; and 8. A commitment to the beauty and strength of the Africana woman's body, mind, and soul. Thus, what defines an Africana womanist methodology is holistically engaging in an agency-driven investigation of Africana womanhood in order to conceptualize and unshackle her realities.[30]

Its holistic and complementary nature is what makes Africana womanism "different from any other female-based theory."[31] In further explaining the dissimilarities with other theories, Hudson-Weems noted that "Africana Womanism as a theoretical concept and methodology defines a new paradigm, which offers an alternative to all forms of feminism. It is a terminology and a concept that consider both ethnicity (Africana) and gender (Womanism). . . . It critically addresses the dynamics of the conflict between the mainstream feminist, the Black feminist, the African feminist, and the Africana Womanist."[32]

The first difference between these theories involves the terms "woman" and "female." Africans prefer the term "womanism" over "feminism" because the latter carries a negative connotation. According to Edith Miguda, womanism resonates with African women's "politics of location,"[33] that is, their womanhood. As noted by Okonjo Ogunyemi, "Feminism appears more rhetorical, polemical, and individualistic in its thrust"[34] in comparison to womanism, and "since feminism is inevitably rooted in the democratic and economic systems of the West, which affect Africans adversely, the African woman has no viable position in such an affiliation."[35] Further, Hudson-Weems explains that

the term "woman," and by extension "womanism," is far more appropriate than the term "female" (feminism), as only a female of the human race can be a woman. "Female," on the other hand, can refer to a member of the animal or plant kingdom, as well as to a member of the human race. Finally, in electronic and mechanical terminology, there is a female counterbalance to the male correlative. Hence, the terminology derived from the word "woman" is more suitable and more specific when naming a group of the human race.[36]

The second difference is that, as already mentioned, the theory of Africana womanism analyzes women as victors, as opposed to feminist theories that see them only as victims of an oppressive society. Worthy of note here is Okonjo Ogunyemi's African womanism theory, which is critical of Hudson-Weems's methodology, referring to it as "utopian," arguing that it romanticizes "male-female relationships, ignoring its myriad dangers for women."[37] Okonjo Ogunyemi further explained that

---

29. Okonjo Ogunyemi, *Africa Wo/Man Palava*, 116.
30. Pellerin, "Defining Africana Womanhood," 76–77.
31. Pellerin, "Defining Africana Womanhood," 76–77.
32. Hudson-Weems, "Africana Womanism: An Historical, Global Perspective," 1814.
33. Miguda, "View from Womanism," 454.
34. Okonjo Ogunyemi, *Africa Wo/Man Palava*, 119.
35. Okonjo Ogunyemi, *Africa Wo/Man Palava*, 118.
36. Hudson-Weems, "Africana Womanism: An Overview," 205.
37. Okonjo Ogunyemi, *Africa Wo/Man Palava*, 119.

women tried to bear whatever they experienced in their fathers' houses and later in their husbands,' because it was impolitic, sometimes forbidden, to mention unspeakable experiences, though women have always tried to share such experiences, if only with limited audiences. This female heritage of occasional defiance, complicity, grumbling, secrecy, silence, conformity, suffering, and unwitting collusion with the male has perpetuated gross misbehavior by men.[38]

According to Okonjo Ogunyemi, the African woman is hapless because she "is not only a native born in her father's house, but is born again as a slave in her master/husband's house."[39] In contrast, Hudson-Weems argues that one of the indicators of an Africana womanist is that she is strong in light of the fact that she "comes from a long tradition of psychological as well as physical *strength*. She has persevered centuries of struggling for herself and her family,"[40] which gives her the ability to improve her life conditions and those of others.

Related to the second difference is Africana womanism's conceptualization of gender relations as "Wo/Man."[41] Other feminist theories argue that women's subjugation is the result of patriarchy, and therefore a feminist should be anti-men and should promote and prefer the culture of women exclusively.[42] As mentioned above, however, an Africana womanist is pro-men. She sees the man–woman relationship as involving a necessary complementarity. She is "in concert with males in struggle,"[43] both encouraging the other so that they can "emancipate and empower one another together."[44] Miguda has affirmed that it is important for women "to acknowledge difference, not as opposition but as a paradigm,"[45] and Okonjo Ogunyemi has emphasized that women's resistance should shift from the "idea of *palava*, or trouble, to consensus, compromise, complementarity, and cooperation," which in turn "tackles sexism, totalitarianism," and cultural prejudice.[46] Hudson-Weems concurred with Okonjo Ogunyemi's conception of the issue:

> I am a full-blown Africana Womanist, dealing with gender any time I want to—because we're all trapped in a patriarchal system, but it's the way in which we deal with those gender issues that makes us different. I deal with it authentically. I am not anti-male. My daddy was a male. My husband is a male. My brother is [was] a male. I have cousins, friends, ... who are male. ... I'd be the last one to exclude a male from a discussion because he's a male. They should be welcomed instead of excluded from the meetings or discussions on gender issues. I think the feminists have missed it. ... You can't be anti.[47]

The problem is that because of the patriarchal system, the very existence of women has been relegated to the shadows. By propounding Africana womanism, Hudson-Weems urged women to "reclaim themselves."[48] She argued that the "framework for a world free of patriarchal oppression already exists within the traditional African philosophical worldview" of a matrilineal-patrilineal

---

38. Okonjo Ogunyemi, *Africa Wo/Man Palava*, 120.
39. Okonjo Ogunyemi, *Africa Wo/Man Palava*, 8.
40. Hudson-Weems, *Africana Womanism*, 66.
41. Okonjo Ogunyemi, *Africa Wo/Man Palava*, back cover.
42. Reed, "Africana Womanism and African Feminism," 169.
43. Hudson-Weems, *Africana Womanism*, 61.
44. Ukagba et al, *The Kpim of Feminism*, back cover.
45. Miguda, "View from Womanism," 454.
46. Okonjo Ogunyemi, *Africa Wo/Man Palava*, back cover.
47. Reed, "Africana Womanism and African Feminism," 171.
48. Hudson-Weems devised her innovative theory in the mid-1980s. She presented her seminal work in 1992 at the International Conference on Women in Africa and The African Diaspora (WAAD) held at the University of Nigeria, Nsukka. Her ideas were applauded by all the women present. The theory was published in the 1993 book *Africana Womanism: Reclaiming Ourselves*.

culture, a "harmonious dualism accepted by both sexes ... [in order] to build a ... society where each and every one could fully develop by following the activity" best suited to his or her "physiological nature."[49] What African women need to do, then, is to rediscover this framework because it celebrates their spiritual, social, and intellectual strength and their crucial role in the family. The aim of this chapter is to highlight the accomplishments of African women in these areas; I begin with an analysis of the impact of the Second Vatican Council on realizing these accomplishments.

The Impact of the Second Vatican Council on African Catholicism

John Allen describes the African church as "Catholicism's most dynamic growth market," stating that "Africa, in many ways, symbolizes" the vitality of the Catholic Church around the world. Much of this vitality can be attributed to the energy and devotion of her female members.[50] For Africans, and especially African women, religious life and social life are tightly interwoven. "Prior to the advent of the missionary enterprise,"[51] Africans were conscious of and believed in something greater than themselves—a higher being that intervenes positively or negatively in every situation. The expressions of this religiosity continue into the present in many ways; one of them is in the names Africans give to people, places, and things. It is this strong consciousness of the divine that leads people to affiliate with a particular religious group; for example, African traditional religion (traditionalists), Islam (Muslims), or Christianity (Christians).

The situation in the church began to be transformed in 1959 when Pope St. John XXIII (the Good Pope) convened the Second Vatican Council.[52] One important accomplishment of the "Catholic revolution"[53] effected by the council was the renewal of the church, transforming it into "a Church with great elasticity and creative adaptability."[54] A good example of this was the decision of the church to familiarize itself with and then to integrate into the African culture, a process referred to as "inculturation."[55] This approach helped African Catholics understand "the reality of the Church within the gravitational center of African spirituality and religious consciousness."[56] It also helped the Roman church to "respect the pluralities and dynamism of African religiosity, culture, and philosophy."[57] Inculturation came to be defined as the "cultural contextualization"[58] of Catholic teachings in Africa or the "indigenization of Catholicism"[59] on the continent or even the "Africanization of Catholic Christianity."[60] This twentieth-century phenomenon made the "alien Church" into "the African Church,"[61] the Latin Church into a vernacular church; and it also "promoted a theology based on community and personal values."[62] The process of inculturation has made it easier for the universal church to understand the Afrocentric perspective and community-oriented nature of Hudson-Weems's methodology.[63]

---

49. See Reed, "Africana Womanism and African Feminism," 175 (bracketed insertion mine). See also Diop, *The Cultural Unity of Black Africa*, 108.
50. Allen, "Pope Benedict Needs to Show That He 'Gets' Africa," 1 and 6.
51. Edusa-Eyison, "Trio of African Academics," 76.
52. Hebblethwaite, *Pope John XXIII*, 292.
53. Sweeney, "How Should We Remember Vatican II?," 255.
54. Peters et al., *De Ecclesia*, 14.
55. Duncan, "Inculturation," 1.
56. Nkurunziza, "Ethnicity and Evangelization," 19–36.
57. Thomas, "Anthropology, Mission, and the African Woman," 12.
58. Kolawole, *Womanism and African Consciousness*, 11.
59. Peel, "Reviewed Work: African Catholicism," 92.
60. Hastings, *African Catholicism*, 124.
61. Hearne, "Roman Catholicism or African Catholicism?," 101–2.
62. Hearne, "Roman Catholicism or African Catholicism?," 101–2.
63. Hudson-Weems, "Africana Womanism and the Critical Need," 79.

The Role of African Women in the African Church

As was previously mentioned, the Second Vatican Council achieved "a renewed vision of what it means to be the Church." The council's vision that the church is the "People of God" reflected a new appreciation of laypeople,[64] of which women are a significant part. The typical twenty-first-century Christian is no longer European, "but a Latin American or African woman"; if "we want to visualize a . . . contemporary Christian, we should think of a woman living in a village in Nigeria or in a Brazilian *Favela*."[65] Among the Maasai in Tanzania, Dorothy Hodgson found that there is a "preponderance of female adherents to Christianity" over men.[66] In the whole of eastern Africa, J. M. Waliggo observed that women are the "greatest source of energy to the Church . . . the core of any Church community."[67] Since Vatican II, women have become "more religious than men" as measured by church attendance and their devotions.[68] Ana Cristina Villa B noted that, among the participants in the 2012 Synod on the New Evangelization held at the Vatican, there were "nearly the same number of female auditors as male, and a considerable number of female experts. They spoke, participated, worked, compiled, intervened . . . and their coffee bar wasn't separate" as it was during the council.[69] They were from all walks of life, representing the various capacities in which women serve in the church, including women who have consecrated their entire lives to the service of the church.[70]

Any discussion of particularly African women in this new church must consider their spirituality. According to Hudson-Weems, an Africana womanist "demonstrates a definite sense of spirituality, a belief in a higher power that transcends rational ideals, which is an ever-present part of Africana culture."[71] African women, who bring to worship all aspects of African culture, including their respect for ancestors and the way they dress and dance, have made African Catholicism into a "genuinely . . . African religion," a living African "religious reality . . . reinterpreted with Christian paradigms."[72]

Women Religious

One way to understand the new gender realities in world Catholicism is to examine the enthusiasm for the religious life among non-Western women. Even as the number of nuns is dropping in the West, the number of women religious has increased in Africa, where studies show that there are "one-third fewer Catholic priests and brothers than there are religious sisters."[73] For instance, Jane Wakahiu et al. found that in ten African countries (Kenya, Uganda, Tanzania, South Sudan, Ghana, Nigeria, Cameroon, Zambia, Malawi, and Lesotho) there are more than 40,400 women religious[74] engaged in various ministries in both the church and society.

Before the council, church officials treated women religious as nobodies. They were invisible and voiceless and "often relegated to the background";[75] they were seen as "mere appendages of their male counterparts."[76] There were many pioneering missionary women religious who came to Africa and lived, worked, and died on the continent, but they were not treated any better. They were completely at the service of the clergy, a fact that was reflected in the work they were assigned.

---

64. Aymond, "10 Ways Vatican II Shapes the Church," 1.
65. Robert, "World Christianity as Women's Movement," 180.
66. Hodgson, "Engendered Encounters," 758.
67. Waliggo, "The Practice of Democratic Principles," 91.
68. Stuart, "Freedom of Religion and Gender Equality," 439.
69. Villa B, "On the Laywomen Auditors at the Council," 2.
70. Villa B, "On the Laywomen Auditors at the Council," 2.
71. Hudson-Weems, *Africana Womanism*, 69–70.
72. Hastings, *African Catholicism*, xi.
73. Robert, "World Christianity as Women's Movement," 181.
74. Wakahiu et al., *Voices of Courage*, 14.
75. Amakwe, "Globalization and the African Woman," 103.
76. Amakwe, *Factors Influencing the Mobility of Women*, 3.

Carmel McEnroy's description of the American situation captures well what was going on in the rest of the Catholic world.

> Prior to Vatican II, women could clean Church sanctuaries, and after Church hours they could come close enough to strip altars and spend long hours mending, washing, starching, ironing, and replacing linen altar cloths, priests' amices, albs, and purificators (the last only after the priest had given them the initial rinse, lest women's hands should come in contact with any residue of consecrated wine). Women sacristans could remove, clean, and polish the sacred vessels—chalice and ciborium—but only while wearing white gloves. They could arrange flowers, remove candle grease, and replace candles, especially in the long white metallic interior-sprung variety, which were lit mainly for High Mass, Benediction, and Forty Hours Exposition.[77]

All of this changed in the wake of the council. Paul VI called women religious "consecrated virgins" at the close of the council, and commissioned them, as did Christ with his apostles, to go into the world "for the service of all."[78] This resonates with Hudson-Weems's notion that the Africana womanist "embraces the concept of collectivism"[79]—she exists for the good of all in the community.

Today, women religious no longer confine their service to the boundaries of the parish or diocese but instead are "concerned about the needs of the people of God dispersed throughout the world."[80] For example, women religious in Africa, in addition to working as missionaries in great numbers outside the continent, also own and run schools, hospitals, homes for the elderly, shelters for battered women, and orphanages, and direct diocesan catechetical programs. They are involved in non-governmental organizations (NGOs) that are engaged in the alleviation of poverty and misery on the continent. In Nigeria, for instance, the Conference of Women Religious established an NGO for the rehabilitation of Nigerian ex-prostitutes and victims of human trafficking who were deported from Italy, working with an Italian counterpart, the Union of Major Superiors (USMI). Since 2007 they have operated a shelter called the Resource Centre for Women[81] in Benin City, the capital of Edo State (the home of most of the girls). It is the first of its kind to be built in the whole of Africa. In Italy, Nigerian and Italian women religious, by networking with government authorities, were able to enter into the "complexity of the world of the night and of the streets"[82] to free young girls and women who had become slaves of the sex industry. It is no wonder that Pope Benedict XVI said, in praising African sisters, that "they are a necessary and precious aid to the Church's pastoral activity but also a manifestation of the deepest nature of our Christian vocation."[83]

Unlike in earlier times, it is currently a common practice in Africa for women religious to assist in the distribution of Holy Communion. Indeed, Philomena Njeri Mwaura notes, "In the absence of priests on some occasions, they assume responsibility for the para-liturgical assembly, preside over it and direct it on Sundays and weekdays. During these occasions, they preach to parishioners about their duty as Christians."[84]

Another great contribution of women religious to the African church is their founding of local religious orders. Prior to Vatican II and in the years immediately after the council, almost all of the diocesan religious congregations of women on the continent were founded by bishops and priests,

---

77. McEnroy, *Guests in Their Own House*, 16.
78. Paul VI, "To Women."
79. Hudson-Weems, *Africana Womanism*, 44.
80. Vatican II, Decree on the Apostolate of the Laity (*Apostolicam Actuositatem*) §10 (hereinafter *AA*).
81. Bonetti, "Women Helping Women," 271.
82. Bonetti, "Women Helping Women," 262.
83. Pope Benedict XVI, post-synodal apostolic exhortation *Africae Munus* §118 (hereinafter *AM*).
84. Mwaura, "Women and Evangelization," 135.

the majority of whom were expatriates, but that is changing. For example, in recent years, Nigerian women religious have formed many orders (both active and contemplative). Some of these sisters are either still members of the congregations in which they professed their religious vows or left to begin new congregations based on the expression of a new charism focused on charitable works.[85] The story is the same in other parts of Africa.[86]

Jane Wakahiu noted that the foundation of indigenous orders of women religious in Kenya, Uganda, and Tanzania is "vital in defining and understanding" evangelization in Africa.[87] In general, women religious on the continent are leading with courage, strength, and a desire to bring social change and economic empowerment to their people. Their approaches to leadership incorporate the concepts of spiritual and servant leadership. Through the work of these sisters, something good is happening in Africa.[88] This reechoes the "humanist and communal approach" described in Africana womanist theory, an approach that is concerned with the liberation and well-being of everyone in the community, women, men, and children alike.[89]

Catholic Women's Organizations (CWOs)

You, Catholic women, carry on the Gospel tradition of those women who assisted Jesus and the apostles (cf. Lk 8:3). In the local Churches, you are a kind of "backbone," because your numbers, your active presence and your organizations are a great support for the Church's apostolate. When peace is under threat, when justice is flouted, when poverty increases, you stand up to defend human dignity, the family and the values of religion. May the Holy Spirit unceasingly call forth holy and courageous women in the Church, who can make their precious spiritual contribution to the growth of our communities! (*AM* §58)

These words of Pope Benedict XVI to women in Africa sum up the role of Catholic women in today's church, not only in Africa but around the world. Before the council, things were different. Catholic women were more like spectators, not fully involved in the activities of the church. This is why, according to Teresa Berger, "in 1962, many of the then 300 million Catholic women worldwide greeted" the coming of the council with a sense of excitement and hope.[90] More than fifty years after the conclusion of the council, CWOs are pillars of Catholic communities, especially in Africa, and are continuing to grow. Philomena Njeri Mwaura found that in Kenya, "the national Catholic Women Association has a membership of over 600,000 and the number continues to increase."[91] These women are "life transmitters, effective agents of communication and fervent religious adherents"[92] in their local churches.

---

85. Examples of these are the Benedictine Word Incarnate Abbey, founded on January 6, 1974, by Mother Mary Charles Anyanwu, OSB, a contemplative order of pontifical right in the Enugu diocese; the Queen of Peace Benedictine Monastery, founded on November 22, 1997, by Rev. Mother Patricia Alufuo, OSB, also a contemplative order of pontifical right in the Nnewi diocese; the Missionary Sisters of Divine Mercy, founded on June 21, 2003, by Mother Amaka Osegbo in the Nnewi diocese of diocesan right; the Missionary Daughters of Blessed Michael Iwene Tansi, founded on April 2, 2004, by Rev. Mother Dr. Susana Uzoamaka Obineli in the Onitsha archdiocese of diocesan right; and the Dei Verbum Institute, founded by Mother Angela Uwalaka, DDL, on December 8, 2006, in the Ibadan archdiocese of diocesan right.

86. For example, the Daughters of the Sacred Passion Congregation was founded in 2009 by Mother Dorothy Mbonu in the Diocese of Beua, Cameroon, of diocesan right, and the Missionary Servants of Our Lady of Roses Congregation was established of diocesan right in the Diocese of Dakar, Senegal, in 2012 by Mother Maryann Chinazo Umeh.

87. Wakahiu, "Foundation of Religious Institutes," 34.
88. Wakahiu et al., *Voices of Courage*, 15.
89. Ahmed, "Africana Womanist Reading," 63.
90. Berger, "Spying in the Promised Land," 28.
91. Mwaura, "Women and Evangelization," 135.
92. Ishengoma, "The Need to Tap the Potential in African Women," 97.

It is a widely acknowledged fact that all over Africa CWOs are the lifeblood of parishes and dioceses. They raise money for humanitarian projects in their communities such as the construction of orphanages, multipurpose halls, guest houses, schools, and clinics. They assist their fellow women in obtaining credit to begin small businesses. These things are signs of what Hudson-Weems calls "genuine sisterhood," a reciprocal sisterly bond "in which each gives and receives equally . . . all reach out in support of each other, demonstrating a tremendous sense of responsibility for each other."[93] Women in CWOs make home and hospital visitations as well as help clean the churches. Because they are "whole, authentic, and "spiritual,"[94] Catholic women in CWOs often act as special kinds of mothers to priests and nuns and those training to become priests and nuns, providing both spiritual and material help.

Women Theologians

More than any other field, it was unthinkable before the council for women to study theology, much less teach or write about it. McEnroy recalled that women were not permitted to earn degrees in theology in the US. Even when they were accepted into the doctoral program at the Catholic University of America, they were permitted to hear the lectures only while sitting in the hallway outside the classroom.[95] As can easily be imagined, things were worse in Africa. But today, thanks to the empowerment and freedom brought about by the council, women in various places in the world have studied and do study theology; and, what is even more remarkable, many women teach it in seminaries, colleges, and other institutions of learning, and are engaged in writing about it.

The Vatican's International Theological Commission now has women members.[96] Mary Luke Tobin, who was one of the "conciliar women,"[97] recounted that, after the council, there was an "emergence of a number of outstanding women theologians and biblical scholars"[98] around the world. Currently among these are African Catholic women theologians who are using their status to address "the place of women in African Society and the Church."[99] "They also teach Christian doctrine, Catholic attitudes, prepare people to receive the sacraments, and to cultivate piety, especially Eucharistic piety" (*AA* §17) in churches and other Catholic settings, and they engage in humanitarian works, especially in the fight against HIV/AIDS.[100]

The Role of African Women in Society

Women's roles in society (and in the church) are "formative" (meaning shaping or molding), reformative (improving what is wrong), and transformative (psychologically, spiritually, and behaviorally). We see the capacity of being "flexible role-players"[101] reflected in all aspects of women's lives on a daily basis. It is little wonder, then, that the council described women as "leaven in the world," describing them as natural educators who can engage in the "evangelization and sanctification of men and . . . penetrat[e] and perfect[] the temporal order through the spirit of the Gospel" (*AA* §2). Women are instructed by the documents of the council to collaborate with people to help them "govern their activities with a sense of responsibility, and strive for what is true and right, willing always to join with others in cooperative effort."[102]

---

93. Hudson-Weems, *Africana Womanism*, 65.
94. Hudson-Weems, *Africana Womanism*, 65.
95. McEnroy, *Guests in Their Own House*, 18.
96. Berger, "Spying in the Promised Land," 31.
97. McEnroy, *Guests in Their Own House*, 5.
98. Tobin, "Women in the Church: Vatican II and After," 297.
99. McElwee, "African Women's Journeys of Faith," 2a.
100. Haddad, "South African Women's Theological Project."
101. Hudson-Weems, *Africana Womanism*, 63.
102. Vatican II, Declaration on Religious Freedom (*Dignitatis Humanae*) §8.

Hudson-Weems described an Africana womanist as "adaptable" and "respectful of elders."[103] African women are capable of holding in "high esteem professional skill, family and civic spirit, and the virtues relating to social customs, namely, honesty, justice, sincerity, kindness, and courage, without which no true Christian life can exist" (*AA* §2). In line with this, the council documents affirmed that "women now work in almost all spheres. It is fitting that they are able to assume their proper role in accordance with their own nature."[104] And Pope St. John Paul II noted that "in our day women have made great strides in . . . attaining a remarkable degree of self-expression in cultural, social, economic, and political life, as well as, of course, in family life."[105]

Addressing African women in particular, John Paul II observed that "one of the characteristic signs of our times is the growing awareness of women's dignity and of their specific role in the Church and in society at large. . . . Their rights and duties in building up the family and in taking full part in the development of the Church and society were strongly affirmed [at the Synod on Africa]."[106] Similarly, Pope Benedict XVI, speaking to African women during his first apostolic visit to the continent, said, "Women in Africa make a great contribution to the family, to society and to the Church by their many talents and unique gifts" (*AM* §55). Because the family is the epicenter of women's many roles, I will dedicate the next section to discussing it.

Scholars have argued that one of the changes the council brought to the church was its emphasis on the importance of the family, "the domestic church" which "provides a strong foundation for each believer."[107] Women, as ardent believers themselves and as great nurturers, carry out their responsibilities in their families first. As has already been mentioned, one of the most important characteristics of the theory of Africana womanism is that it is family-oriented. Hudson-Weems explains that the Africana womanist is "family-centered as she is more concerned with her entire family rather than with just herself." She is "male compatible, and seeks a relationship in which each individual is mutually supportive, an important part of a positive Africana family," and she is "committed to the art of mothering her own children in particular and humankind in general."[108] The reason for this, as noted by Hudson-Weems, is that "the African woman comes from a legacy of fulfilling the role of the supreme Mother Nature—provider and protector," which makes her "a nurturer and consistent in doing what must be done for the survival of the family."[109] Traditionally, the family is the natural, the first, and the main workplace for every African woman. Every other role begins and revolves around the family because of its importance as the bedrock of African society. Nahed Mohammed Ahmed noted that Africana womanism emphasizes the "centrality of family" because "the success of a nation depends inevitably on family."[110]

Similarly, Josephine Dibie and Robert Dibie noted that men generally "acknowledge that the physical, psychological . . . and mental health of each member of their family depends" on the mother.[111] It is clear that there would be no society or church without the family. The council affirmed that the family is "the first and vital cell of society" (*AA* §11) and "the domestic Church" (*Lumen Gentium* §11). Pope Benedict XVI, addressing families in Africa, called it the "sanctuary of life" and poetically explained that it is in the family that "the features of a people take shape; it is here that its members acquire basic teachings. They learn to

---

103. Hudson-Weems, *Africana Womanism*, 70–71.
104. Vatican Council II, Pastoral Constitution on the Church in the Modern World (*Gaudium et Spes*) §60.
105. Pope John Paul II, *Genius of Women*, 12–13.
106. Pope John Paul II, post-synodal apostolic exhortation *Ecclesia in Africa* §121 (bracketed insertion mine).
107. Aymond, "10 Ways Vatican II Shapes the Church Today," 1. See also *Lumen Gentium* §11.
108. Hudson-Weems, *Africana Womanism Society*, http://africanawomanismsociety.webs.com/aboutaws.htm
109. Hudson-Weems, *Africana Womanism Society*, http://africanawomanismsociety.webs.com/aboutaws.htm.
110. Ahmed, "Africana Womanist Reading," 61.
111. Dibie and Dibie, "Non-Governmental Organization (NGOs)," 107.

love inasmuch as they are unconditionally loved, they learn respect for others inasmuch as they are respected, they learn to know the face of God inasmuch as they receive a first revelation of it from a father and a mother full of attention" (AM §42). On the same note, Pope Paul VI affirmed that "women's role in the family is the most important and the beginning of all that happens in the society."[112] He encouraged and empowered women to do more:

> You women have always had as your lot the protection of the home, the love of beginnings and an understanding of cradles. You are present in the mystery of a life beginning. You offer consolation in the departure by death.... Reconcile men with life and above all, we beseech you, watch carefully over the future of our race.... Wives, mothers of families, the first educators of the human race in the intimacy of the family circle, pass on to your sons and ... daughters the traditions, prepare them for an unsearchable future. Always remember that by her children a mother belongs to that future which perhaps she will not see.[113]

Even though it is often believed that a man is the head of the family and the breadwinner, especially in Africa, in reality the woman is the pivot of the family. Recent research from South Africa shows that many women have overcome traditional notions of gender roles by "becoming primary breadwinners in their homes and providing primary financial support for their families."[114] Of course many women carry out their roles alone, or in troubled homes, or in abusive marriages. Pope Paul VI addressed women who live in difficult situations:

> And you, women living alone, realize what you can accomplish through your dedicated vocation. Society is appealing to you on all sides. Not even families can live without the help of those who have no families. Especially you, consecrated virgins, in a world where egoism and the search for pleasure would become law, be the guardians of purity, unselfishness and piety. Jesus who has given to conjugal love all its plenitudes, has also exalted the renouncement of human love when this is for the sake of divine love and for the service of all. Lastly, women in trial, who stand upright at the foot of the cross like Mary, you who so often in history have given to men the strength to battle unto the very end and to give witness to the point of martyrdom, aid them now still once more to retain courage in their great undertakings, while at the same time maintaining patience and an esteem for humble beginnings.[115]

As the traditional African family system is becoming increasingly weakened because of globalization (which has, ironically, made it "possible for Africans to interact with many social systems"[116]), women as nurturers must be present to shape the African family and protect its values for generations to come. At this juncture, there is no doubt that women are the heart of the church and society, but is their noble role sufficiently appreciated and celebrated? Has it been adequately researched? The next section will discuss some of the progress that has been made with regard to the latter.

The State of Research on the Role of African Women

As this chapter has shown, many scholars, especially women scholars, are doing a lot to fight whatever demeans the African woman culturally, socially, or religiously in order to raise her to her rightful place. Recent years have witnessed an upsurge in the number of scholars and commentators studying women from historical and contemporary perspectives. Africanists and African women scholars in particular have expended considerable efforts to help African women assert their identities and

---

112. Paul VI, "To Women."
113. Paul VI, "To Women."
114. Parry and Segalo, "Eating Burnt Toast," 182.
115. Paul VI, "To Women."
116. Nyaundi, "Contemporary African Family," 78.

to lay bare their contributions to African societies.[117] Mary Modupe Kolawole emphasized that "many African women scholars are unfolding the visibility of the African woman as an important step in speaking out. Self-healing entails correcting the representation of African women as if they exist in some subterranean world, tongue-tied and demobilized."[118]

There is a "growing but still scant literature"[119] on African women's participation in the religious sphere, especially in Christianity. Most important has been a breakthrough toward women refusing to allow themselves to be seen as "headless chickens"[120]—a breakthrough achieved by the research framework of Africana womanism.[121] The theory has been described as an "intellectual paradigm grounded in knowledge and values" derived from African women's cultural experiences.[122] This new paradigm places the African woman at the center of any analysis and therefore makes her both the "self-namer and self-definer."[123] In other words, the time is gone when women spoke through intermediaries. Today, African women act, speak, and write for and about themselves in the way they want using the terminologies that define them best. Today, the African woman is conscious of her unique role: "That of speaking to her gender, for her gender, and on behalf of her gender without the risk of solipsism."[124]

For these reasons, African womanism has replaced feminism as the operative framework for African women to express themselves and has provided a "universal voice of all."[125] The theory is important because feminism is seen as "problematic and incapable of addressing all the needs" of women, especially African women.[126] In fact, African women see feminism as "the destroyer of homes, imported mainly from America to ruin nice African women."[127] Importantly, the "independence/self-advocacy"[128] of African women advanced by Africana womanist ideology is indicative of their intellectual, ecclesial, and societal emancipation. With Hudson-Weems's theory, there exists today in the African scientific world an "African gender theory" which is "dialogic or accommodationist"[129] in nature. Above all, in accord with Sotunsa Mobolanle Ebunoluwa, I see the theory of Africana womanism as involving researchers in women's issues, especially African women scholars themselves, in a "healthy appreciation of African cultures, a recognition of the heterogeneity of African cultures, and realistic and wholesome strategies devoid of unnecessary aggressiveness." According to Ebunoluwa, this method, which focuses on communalism, family, marriage, and motherhood as positive experiences for African women, saved gender discussions on the continent from "becoming irrelevant, static, rigid and dogmatic."[130]

As Pamela Yaa Asantewaa Reed notes, "Leading African women writers and scholars . . . have all staked out ideological and philosophical positions on the matter of the overall condition of the African female and the African family."[131] Their approach "empowers women and men to actualize a humanist vision," which has led to the development of an emancipatory epistemology of African

---

117. Korieh and Nnaemeka, "Introduction," vii.
118. Kolawole, *Womanism and African Consciousness*, 25.
119. Bevans, review of *Putting Names with Faces*, by Christine Lienemann-Perrin, 264.
120. Evans, "In Praise of Theory," 225.
121. Okonjo Ogunyemi, "Womanism," 72.
122. Muwati et al., "Africana Womanism and African Proverbs," 1.
123. Hudson-Weems, *Africana Womanism*, 55.
124. Hudson-Weems, *Africana Womanism*, 55.
125. Tsuruta, "Womanish Roots of Womanism," 3.
126. Ntiri, "Reassessing Africana Womanism," 164.
127. Phillips, *Womanist Reader*, 44.
128. Tsuruta, "Womanish Roots of Womanism," 3.
129. Ebunoluwa, "Feminism," 232.
130. Ebunoluwa, "Feminism," 232.
131. Reed, "Africana Womanism and African Feminism," 168.

women's struggles[132] as they "grapple with family and community survival and growth."[133] This drive for epistemological adventure is the result of African women attempting to avoid idle theorizing; instead, it is their goal to address the "practical consequences of any theoretical speculation"[134] about women on the continent.

The work and contribution of African women theologians, already mentioned, is paramount in this regard. "Through their biblical and anthropological research, several remarkable women scholars are uncovering new data regarding women in history, scripture, and the early Church community."[135] Their scholarship "is winning acclaim in theological" circles,[136] for example, the Circle of Concerned African Women Theologians.[137] The aim of this group is to "promote theological thinking, research and publishing"[138] in a continuous "search for a new cultural identity" for modern African Christians, which "includes a critical and positive view of African traditional practices, and the continuation" of some of these practices they have "identified as not being oppressive"[139] to women. Because of their initiative, there is now "African women's theological scholarship" through which women theologians "interact with African religious culture in two ways: . . . giving literary expression to religious aspirations, and . . . reformulating African women's intimate life with God in the context of African culture."[140] In their works, women theologians "critique old theologies in such a way as to make apparent the marginalization of women in the collective religious consciousness of former African writers."[141] Through their writings, these women contribute to a clear "understanding of widowhood, polygamy, sexuality, prostitution, and marriage that helps to define the faith systems of African Christian culture," and above all, of the lives of women on the continent.[142]

The work of women theologians has made possible a recent development in African women's Christology, one that proposes a "method for doing contextual theology, namely, the 'pastoral circle' or 'pastoral cycle'" with "its four key dimensions of encounter, social analysis, theological reflection, and pastoral planning."[143] This methodology allows for a "flexible framework for probing the causative factors, the contextual nature, the theological methods, and the central motifs of African women's Christologies, as well as their contributions to social transformation through the impact of individuals and institutions."[144] Through this methodology, women theologians are insisting on Christologies rooted in the praxis of Jesus as it relates to their own experiences in context. For instance, they are asking questions like, "What would Jesus do in the midst of people who are suffering so much from poverty, oppression, sexism, and stigmatization, aggravated by the HIV and AIDS pandemic?," and "What does confessing Christ mean for the African woman in their particular sociopolitical, socioeconomic, sociocultural and socioreligious context?"[145] In fact, these women are asserting that "a key criterion for assessing the worth of a theology is the extent to which it challenges and transforms lives within its context."[146] Through

---

132. Temple, "Cosmology of Afrocentric Womanism," 24.
133. Ntiri, "Reassessing Africana Womanism," 163.
134. Vähäkangas, *In Search of Foundations for African Catholicism*, 18.
135. Tobin, "Women in the Church: Vatican II and After," 299.
136. Tobin, "Women in the Church since Vatican II," 24.
137. Vähäkangas, "African Feminist Contribution," 171.
138. Vähäkangas, "African Feminist Contribution," 171.
139. Vähäkangas, "African Feminist Contribution," 170.
140. Cannon, "Foreword," vii.
141. Cannon, "Foreword," viii.
142. Oduyoye and Kanyoro, "Introduction," in *The Will to Arise*, viii.
143. Stinton, "Encountering Jesus at the Well," 267.
144. Stinton, "Encountering Jesus at the Well," 267.
145. Stinton, "Encountering Jesus at the Well," 267.
146. Stinton, "Encountering Jesus at the Well," 280.

this gospel-conscious approach, African women theologians are contributing to many changes in the African church. They and the women to whom they minister are digging deep within to find the moral and spiritual resources to transform their lives and those of their communities. The changes these women are working for are happening slowly but continuously as they give themselves to God in prayer, to their communities in love, and to a constant study of their contexts.[147]

African women theologians have through their scholarly works inspired other women to become theologians. The number of African women reading and studying the scriptures has increased; women have begun to see that "God's call to them is not passive. It is compelling and compulsory. It is a call to action and it is a call to wholeness that challenges the will and the intellect."[148] Not only do African women theologians write; they are also involved in narrative theology expressed through oral communication and stories in order to promote dialogue that will bring togetherness and ease the "challenge of being both African and Christian,"[149] especially for their fellow women. Mercy Amba Oduyoye and Musimbi R. A. Kanyoro explained this better in the introduction to their anthology, *The Will to Arise*:

> Our purpose is to seek, find, examine, and expose the historical and cultural aspects that are the roots of belief systems that continue to dehumanize women. We are also attempting to bring to the attention of the Church in Africa the truth about the love of God, who considers all women and men . . . needful of grace that comes through Jesus Christ. We are only starting our long journey of faith. We will need to think about methodologies and strategies that will help us achieve our purposes. In this anthology we share experiences in our own lives, of our families, and in those of our sisters, aunts, mothers, and grandmothers. We begin to see patterns emerge as African women search for wholeness and transformation of both the African culture and the church. We see patterns in our desire to share experiences, to reflect together on our respective practices, and to analyze historical events.[150]

Hence, African women theologians believe that, when women have a sound and deep knowledge of the scriptures, they will also be empowered to voice their concerns and make their case in matters that affect their lives as Christian women. This is exactly why, apart from the "production of theological literature,"[151] African women theologians hope also to inspire and stimulate more women to take an interest in the study of theology. In addition, since the "majority of worshipers in the Churches of Africa are women, a deeper grounding in theology and better understanding of the Scripture will affect the way they worship."[152]

Further, as women relate their own experiences to biblical events, "the church in Africa will be . . . enriched by talents and gifts that have remained untapped until today."[153] Thus, to Naomi Schor's question "Can females theorize?,"[154] or, better put, "Can Afro-women theorize?" Hudson-Weems has provided an affirmative answer and has at the same time bolstered our belief in women's ability to do so. Today, African women "can proclaim, without shame or false pride" that the theoretical framework of womanism "is ours in the first place"[155] and has come to stay. At present, women can and in fact are singing about their "own heroic deeds."[156] The

---

147. Bowers, "Women Transforming Communities," 14.
148. Oduyoye and Kanyoro, "Introduction," in *The Will to Arise*, 1.
149. Oduyoye and Kanyoro, "Introduction," in *The Will to Arise*, 2.
150. Oduyoye and Kanyoro, "Introduction," in *The Will to Arise*, 4.
151. Pemberton, *Circle Thinking*, 12.
152. Pemberton, *Circle Thinking*, 5.
153. Oduyoye and Kanyoro, "Introduction," in *The Will to Arise*, 5.
154. Schor, "Female Paranoia," 206.
155. Tsuruta, "Womanish Roots of Womanism," 9.
156. Nnaemake, "From Orality to Writing," 137.

"past four decades have witnessed a rapid change in the trends and quality of research on African women"[157] in every relevant area. Today, African "women's palava"[158] is a thing for papal discourses, and the scientific, social, and theological research being performed by women attests to their emancipation and their many contributions to church and society. This momentum "shows no signs of slowing down. Indeed, the very love of the church which women profess and manifest" urges them on in their difficult and demanding work.[159] A great deal more needs to be done for women in Africa to reach their full potential in every area of human endeavor.

The State of Advocacy for African Women: Areas Needing Further Development

At this point, I want to state the obvious: the place of African women in the church and in society is still a "domain that has not been adequately explored despite an increasing interest."[160] We are well into the new millennium, and the African woman is still underrepresented in positions of leadership in both church and society. Her potential has still not been fully met. In my opinion, this is the result of an "it's a woman thing" mentality endemic to the African culture.

Auli Vähäkangas believes that African missiologists "need in-depth anthropological and theological analyses to understand the variety of cultures in their societies and to contextualize the Gospel" in order to understand the plight of women in African cultures.[161] This means that Africans themselves need to be "missionized by the scholarship of Africans, primarily women."[162] Unfortunately, there is a "shortage of female researchers for case studies"[163] in this area.

As has already been observed, scholars studying African Christianity will have more success if they put women at the center of their research.[164] In order to accomplish this, however, it is crucial to continue probing the unexplored absences of African women from positions of responsibility in order to assess the contours of their invisibility and voicelessness, especially in the Catholic Church. The church hierarchy in Africa should champion this kind of work, but, unfortunately, leaders of the church in Africa are still using what Mercy Oduyoye called "the theology of 'the Bible says'" to define accepted norms for African Christian women.[165] The many feminine qualities described in this chapter (strong, authentic, flexible role player, adaptable, ambitious, nurturing, spiritual, etc.) "are desperately needed for evangelization"[166] or, better said, for a "new evangelization" in Africa. Increasing the number of women in various areas of service in the church, but especially in the church's leadership positions, would add value to the effectiveness of its structures because the "Church needs to blend both female and male attributes in its leadership structures."[167] If the man–woman complementarity works in the family, as is emphasized by Africana womanism, it should also work in the family of God, the church.

Going back to the Afrocentricity of Hudson-Weems's theory, the matrilineal family system is the predominant model and functions well in many parts of Africa. Both men and women in this system relate in perfect harmony for the good of their families and communities. This model can also work in the African church; for example, on the parish level, there should be a significant

---

157. Korieh, *African Women*, 1.
158. Amakwe, "Infertility in the African Culture," 33.
159. Tobin, "Women in the Church: Vatican II and After," 304.
160. Oduyoye, *Womanism*, 3.
161. Vähäkangas, "African Feminist Contribution," 170.
162. Thomas, "Anthropology, Mission and the African Woman," 12.
163. Thomas, "Anthropology, Mission and the African Woman," 12.
164. Robert, "World Christianity as Women's Movement," 181.
165. Oduyoye, "Calling the Church to Account," 480.
166. Mbabazi, "Leadership Alternatives for Women," 489.
167. Mbabazi, "Leadership Alternatives for Women," 491.

number of women, both religious and lay, on parish councils and in other leadership bodies. It is equally important that priests, nuns, and CWOs partner in the leadership of diocesan chaplaincies. For instance, having a team of three—one priest, one nun, and one member of a CWO—working as chaplains to various organizations and bodies in the diocese as needed would enrich this pastoral work. On the national level, a joint leadership body should be formed with participation from the episcopal conferences, the CWOs, and the conferences of women religious. Similarly, on the regional and interregional levels, bodies like the Episcopal Conferences of Central Africa, the Association of Member Episcopal Conferences in Eastern Africa, and the Symposium of Episcopal Conferences of Africa and Madagascar, working together with CWOs and bodies of women religious on the continent, should form a joint leadership body.

In addition, African women's studies should focus on how women have engaged, do engage, and will engage in the self-conscious shaping of their reality and of the world at large in the past, present, and future.[168] This means that African women cannot be studied without putting their experience into proper historical context.[169] This is why recent works like *African Women: Early History to the 21st Century*, by Kathleen Sheldon, are so important.[170] More such studies are needed. Finally, in studying African women, it is important to recognize their continuing struggle against oppression of all kinds and their desire for liberation. The oppression of women in Africa, more than in any other part of the world, is the result of what Serie McDougal referred to as "intersectionality"[171]—they are both African (a culture in which the oppression of women is the norm) and women (often considered to be the weaker and inferior sex). Additional topics that should be studied include how African women create "intersectional social systems to shape their own lives,"[172] such as obtaining an education, entering into leadership positions, and becoming mothers.[173] Unless this method of analysis is followed, the Africanity of women will not be understood.[174]

Three things are necessary to remedy this lack of research about and by women: more women should be trained in higher education; more women should be present in academia; and bibliographies of works by African women should be compiled.[175] But the push to do this must come from women themselves. Pope John Paul II challenged women: "If anyone has this task of advancing the dignity of women in the Church and society, it is women themselves, who must recognize their responsibility as leading characters."[176] Pope Benedict XVI advised women as follows:

> Dear daughters of the Church, sit constantly at the school of Christ, like Mary of Bethany, and learn to recognize his word (Lk 10:39). Grow in knowledge of the catechism and the Church's social teaching, so as to acquire for yourselves the principles that will assist you in acting as true disciples. Thus you will be able to engage with discernment in the various projects involving women. . . . Help young girls by your counsel and example, so that they may approach adult life serenely. Support one another! . . . The Church counts on you to create a human ecology through your sympathetic love, your friendly and thoughtful demeanor. (*AM* §59)

---

168. Mbabazi, "Leadership Alternatives for Women."
169. Mbabazi, "Leadership Alternatives for Women," 246.
170. Sheldon, *African Women: Early History to the 21st Century*.
171. Mbabzi, "Leadership Alternatives for Women," 247.
172. McDougal, "Africana Studies' Epistemic Identity," 247.
173. McDougal, "Africana Studies' Epistemic Identity," 247.
174. McDougal, "Africana Studies' Epistemic Identity," 243.
175. Josée Ngalula has created such a bibliography of works by women in theology, titled *Production Théologiqué Chrétienne Africaine: 1956–2010; Bibliographie sélective de 6000 ouvrages et articles des théologiens/nes africains; Informatisés dans le cédéron "LARETHEA"* (Kinshasha: Edition Mont Sinaï, 2011).
176. John Paul II, post-synodal apostolic exhortation *Christifideles Laici* §49.

Women can achieve all of this if they are "trusted, sensitized, animated and empowered."[177] Benedict XVI explained the importance of women's empowerment as a catalyst in carrying out their roles:

> Giving women opportunities to make their voice heard and to express their talents through initiatives which reinforce their worth, their self-esteem and their uniqueness would enable them to occupy a place in society equal to that of men—without confusing or conflating the specific character of each—since both men and women are the image of the Creator (cf. Gen 1:27). Bishops should encourage and promote the formation of women so that they may assume their proper share of responsibility and participation in the life of society and . . . of the Church. Women will thus contribute to the humanization of society. (*AM* §57)

Conclusion

It has been the argument of this chapter that African women play important roles in the African church and society, but that these are not adequately acknowledged or celebrated because of the African cultural mentality that sees women as being inferior. The chapter has documented the many changes in the church that can be traced back to the emphasis of the Second Vatican Council on the empowerment of the laity, in which women are the majority, and on the importance of the family as domestic church, in which the role of women is of course very prominent. A good portion of this chapter employed a content analysis methodology to showcase the works and contributions of women in the church acting in various capacities, including as religious, theologians, and members of CWOs. The chapter also highlighted the transformative impact of African women on the church and the society, beginning from their work in the family. Thus, it has been a celebration of women as victors, as opposed to many previous studies that have presented them as victims. More work needs to be done to combat the dehumanization and subjugation of women in Africa.

This research has shown how women have asserted significant influence through their scholarship. It has raised new awareness of an old yet new African-centered methodology—Clenora Hudson-Weems's Africana womanism. It is argued that this methodology is superior to other frameworks used to study women on the continent because it centers on the person of the African woman (her womanhood) and on her context (Africa). This paradigm offers a clear typology for analyzing women as self-namers and self-definers who are family-centered, reliable partners with men in the struggle for the common good, flexible role players who are capable of creating and enjoying genuine sisterhood, strong, compatible with men, respected and recognized, whole and authentic, spiritual, respectful of elders, adaptable, ambitious, mothering, and nurturing. Unquestionably, in any state and at any stage of life, these are the true qualities of African women.

Research on the subject of African women should continue until their full potential is achieved, their dignity and freedom promoted and protected, and their persons respected, appreciated, and celebrated. It must always be remembered that "whatever diminishes, denies or distorts the full humanity of women does not reflect the divine and therefore is not redemptive; by the same token, whatever promotes the full humanity of women is of the Holy."[178] Long live women and long live the continent of Africa.

Bibliography

Acholonu, Catherine O. *Motherism: An Afro-Centric Alternative to Feminism*. Owerri: Afa Publications, 1995.

Ahmed, Nahed Mohammed. "An African Womanist Reading of the Unity of Thought and Action." *IOSR Journal of Humanities and Social Science (IOSR-JHSS)* 22.3 (2017): 58–64.

Alexander-Floyd, Nikol G., and Evelyn M. Simien. "Revisiting 'What's in a Name?': Exploring the

---

177. Ndunguru, "Role of Women in Peacebuilding and Reconciliation," 286.
178. Tobin, "Women in the Church since Vatican II," 24.

Contours of Africana Womanist Thought." *Frontiers: A Journal of Women Studies* 27.1 (2006): 67–89.

Allen, John L., Jr. "Pope Benedict Needs to Show That He 'Gets' Africa." *National Catholic Reporter* 45.11 (2009): 1–6.

Amakwe, Bosco Ebere. *Factors Influencing the Mobility of Women to Leadership and Management Position in Media Industry in Nigeria*. Rome: Pontifical Gregorian University, 2006.

———. "Globalization and the African Woman: A Socio-Cultural Analysis of the Effect of Information and Communication Technology (ICT) on Women." In *The Church as Salt and Light: Path to an African Ecclesiology of Abundant Life*, edited by Stan Chu Ilo et al., 99–129. Eugene, OR: Pickwick, 2011.

———. "Infertility in the African Culture: Women's Palava?," *Encounter: Journal of African Life and Religion* 9 (2011): 33–61.

Aymond, Gregory, Archbishop. "10 Ways Vatican II Shapes the Church Today." http://www.usccb.org/news/2012/12-155.cfm.

Benedict XVI, Pope. *Africae Munus* [Post-synodal Apostolic Exhortation on the Church in Africa in Service of Reconciliation, Justice and Peace; November 19, 2011]. Vatican City: Libreria Editrice Vaticana, 2011. www.vatican.va.

Berger, Teresa. "Spying in the Promised Land: Sacramental Sights through Women's Eyes." *CTSA Proceedings* 67 (2012): 28–41.

Bevans, Stephen. Review of *Putting Names with Faces*, by Christine Lienemann-Perrin. *International Review of Mission* 102.2 (2013): 264–66.

Bonetti, Eugenia. "Women Helping Women: The Prophetic Role of Women Religious in Counter-Trafficking in Persons." *Revista Interdisciplinar da Mobilidade Humana* 19.37 (2011): 261–73.

Bowers, Esmé. "Women Transforming Communities." *Mutuality* 16.2 (2009): 12–14.

Cannon, Katie G. "Foreword." In *The Will to Arise: Women, Tradition, and the Church in Africa*, edited by Mercy Amba Oduyoye and Musimbi R. A. Kanyoro, vii–viii. Maryknoll, NY: Orbis Books, 1992.

Dibie, Josephine, and Robert Dibie. "Non-Governmental Organizations (NGOs) and the Empowerment of Women in Africa." *African and Asian Studies* 11 (2012): 95–122.

Diop, Cheikh Anta. *The Cultural Unity of Black Africa: The Domains of Matriarchy and of Patriarchy in Classical Antiquity*. London: Karnak House Publishers, 2000.

Duncan, Graham A. "Inculturation: Adaptation, Innovation and Reflexivity: An African Christian Perspective." *HTS Theological Studies* 70.1 (2014): 1–11.

Ebunoluwa, Sotunsa Mobolanle. "Feminism: The Quest for an African Variant." *Journal of Pan African Studies* 3.1 (2009): 227–34.

Edusa-Eyison, Joseph M. Y. "The Trio of African Academics in Theological Education and Missions: The Contributions of Harry Sawyerr (Sierra Leone), Bolaji E. Idowu (Nigeria) and Kwesi A. Dickson (Ghana)." *Ogbomoso Journal of Theology* 15.2 (2010): 73–98.

Evans, Mary. "In Praise of Theory: A Case for Women's Studies." In *Theories of Women Studies*, edited by Gloria Bowles and R. Duelli-Klien, 219–28. London: Routledge, 1983.

Flannery, Austin P. *Documents of Vatican II*. Grand Rapids, MI: Eerdmans, 1975.

Haddad, Beverley. "The South African Women's Theological Project: Practices of Solidarity and Degrees of Separation in the Context of the HIV Epidemic." *Religion & Theology* 20.1/2 (2013): 2–18.

Hastings, Adrian. *African Catholicism: Essays in Discovery*. Philadelphia: Trinity Press International, 1989.

Hearne, Brian. "Roman Catholicism or African Catholicism?," *African Ecclesial Review* 14.2 (1972): 97–107.

Hebblethwaite, Peter. *Pope John XXIII, Shepherd of the Modern World: The Definitive Biography of Angelo Roncalli*. New York: Image Books, 1984.

Hodgson, Dorothy. "Engendered Encounters: Men of the Church and the 'Church of Women' in Maasailand, Tanzania, 1950–1993." *Comparative Studies in Society and History* 41.4 (1999): 758–83.

Hudson-Weems, Clenora. "Africana Womanism: An Overview." In *Out of the Revolution: The Development of African Studies*, edited by Delores P. Aldridge and Clarence Young, 205–17. Lanham, MD: Lexington Books, 2001.

———. "Africana Womanism: An Historical, Global Perspective for Women of African Descent." In *Call & Response: The Riverside Anthology of* the African American Literary Tradition, edited by Patricia Liggins Hill et al., 1812–15, Boston: Houghton Mifflin, 1998.

———. Africana Womanism: Reclaiming Ourselves. Troy, MI: Bedford, 1993.

———. "Africana Womanism and the Critical Need for Africana Theory and Thought." Western Journal of Black Studies 21.2 (1997): 79–84.

———. Africana Womanism Society. http://africanawomanismsociety.webs.com/aboutaws.htm

———. Africana Womanist Literary Theory: A Sequel to Africana Womanism: Reclaiming Ourselves. Trenton, NJ: Africa World Press, 2004.

Ishengoma, Rita. "The Need to Tap the Potential in African Women." African Ecclesial Review 38.2 (1996): 97–101.

John Paul II, Pope. Christifideles Laici [Post-synodal Apostolic Exhortation on the Vocation and the Mission of the Lay Faithful in the Church and in the World; December 30, 1988]. Vatican City: Libreria Editrice Vaticana, 1988. www.vatican.va.

———. Ecclesia in Africa [Post-synodal Apostolic Exhortation on the Church in Africa and Its Evangelizing Mission toward the Year 2000; September 14, 1995]. Vatican City: Libreria Editrice Vaticana, 1995. www.vatican.va.

———. The Genius of Women. Washington, DC: United States Conference of Catholic Bishops, 1997.

Kemdirim, Protus Otitodirichukwu. "Towards Inclusiveness for Women in the African Churches." Mission Studies 12.1 (1995): 71–78.

Kolawole, Mary E. Modupe. Womanism and African Consciousness. Trenton, NJ: Africa World Press, 1997.

Korieh, Chima J. African Women: A Reader. San Diego, CA: University Readers, 2009.

Korieh, Chima J., and Obioma Nnaemeka. "Introduction: Long Journeys of Impediments and Triumphs." In Shaping Our Struggles: Nigerian Women in Historical, Cultural and Social Change, edited by Obioma Nnaemeka and Chima Korieh, vii–xxv. Trenton, NJ: Africa World Press, 2011.

Mbabazi, Veneranda. "Leadership Alternatives for Women in the Catholic Church." African Ecclesial Review 53.3-4 (2011): 468–96.

McDougal, Serie. "Africana Studies' Epistemic Identity: An Analysis of Theory and Epistemology in the Discipline." Journal of African American Studies 18.2 (2014): 236–50.

McElwee, Joshua J. "African Women's Journeys of Faith." National Catholic Reporter (December 21, 2012): 2a–3a.

McEnroy, Carmel. Guests in Their Own House: The Women of Vatican II. New York: Crossroad, 1996.

Miguda, Edith. "A View from Womanism: A Comment on Hester Eisentein's 'Feminism Seduced' Employing Chilla Bulbeck's Re-Orienting Western Feminisms." Australian Feminist Studies 25.66 (2010): 453–58.

Muwati, I., Z. Gambahaya, and T. Gwekwerere. "Africana Womanism and African Proverbs: Theoretical Grounding of Mothering/Motherhood in Shona and Ndebele Cultural Discourse." Western Journal of Black Studies 35.1 (2011): 1–8.

Mwaura, Philomena Njeri. "Women and Evangelization: A Challenge to the Church in the Third Millennium." In Challenges and Prospects of the Church in Africa: Theological Reflections of the 21st Century, edited by Nahashon W. Ndung'u and Philomena N. Mwaura, 119–44. Nairobi: Paulines Publications Africa, 2010.

Ndunguru, Bernadette. "The Role of Women in Peacebuilding and Reconciliation in the AMECEA Countries." African Ecclesial Review 51.3 (2009): 279–87.

Nkurunziza, Deusdedit R. K. "Ethnicity and Evangelization: An African Perspective." African Ecclesial Review 49.1-2 (March 2007): 19–36.

Nnaemeka, Obioma. "From Orality to Writing: African Women Writers and the (Re)Inscription of Womanhood." Research in African Literatures 25.4 (1994): 137–57.

Ntiri, Daphne W. "Reassessing Africana Womanism: Continuity and Change." Western Journal of Black Studies 25.3 (2001): 163–67.

Nyaundi, Nehemiah M. "The Contemporary African Family in the Light of Rapid Social Change Theory." In Challenges and Prospects of the Church in Africa: Theological Reflections of the 21st Century, edited by Nahashon W. Ndung'u and Philomena N. Mwaura, 71–87. Nairobi: Paulines Publications Africa, 2010.

Oduyoye, Mercy Amba. "Calling the Church to Account: African Women and Liberation." Ecumenical Review 47.4 (1995): 479–89.

Oduyoye, Mercy Amba, and Musimbi R. A. Kanyoro, eds. *The Will to Arise: Women, Tradition, and the Church in Africa*. Maryknoll, NY: Orbis Books, 1992.

Ogundipe-Leslie, Molara. *Re-Creating Ourselves: African Women & Critical Transformations*. Trenton, NJ: Africa World Press, 1994.

Okonjo Ogunyemi, Chikwenye. *Africa Wo/Man Palava: The Nigerian Novel by Women*. Chicago: University of Chicago Press, 1996.

———. "Womanism: The Dynamics of the Contemporary Black Female Novel in English." *Signs* 11.1 (1985): 63–80.

Parry, Bianca Rochelle, and Puleng Segalo. "Eating Burnt Toast: The Lived Experiences of Female Breadwinners in South Africa." *Journal of International Women's Studies* 18.4 (2017): 182–96.

Paul VI, Pope. "To Women" [Message to Mark the Close of Second Vatican Ecumenical Council; 1965]. Vatican City: Libreria Editrice Vaticana, 1965. www.vatican.va.

Peel, J. D. Y. "Reviewed Work: *African Catholicism: Essays in Discovery* by Adrian Hastings." *Journal of Religion in Africa* 21.1 (1991): 90–92.

Pellerin, Marquita. "Defining Africana Womanhood: Developing an Africana Womanism Methodology." *Western Journal of Black Studies* 36.1 (2012): 76–85.

Pemberton, Carrie. *Circle Thinking: African Woman Theologians in Dialogue with the West*. Boston: Brill Academic, 2003.

Peters, Edward H., et al. *De Ecclesia: The Constitution on the Church of Vatican Council II*. Glen Rock, NJ: Deus Books, 1965.

Phillips, Layli. *The Womanist Reader: The First Quarter Century of Womanist Thought*. London: Routledge, 2006.

Reed, Pamela Yaa Asantewaa. "Africana Womanism and African Feminism: A Philosophical, Literary, and Cosmological Dialectic on Family." *Western Journal of Black Studies* 25.3 (2001): 168–76.

Robert, Dana L. "World Christianity as Women's Movement." *International Bulletin of Missionary Research* 30.4 (2006): 180–88.

Schor, Naomi. "Female Paranoia: The Case for Psychoanalytic Feminist Criticism." *Yale French Studies* 62 (1981): 204–19.

Sheldon, Kathleen. *African Women: Early History to the 21st Century*. Bloomington: Indiana University Press, 2017.

Stinton, Diane B. "Encountering Jesus at the Well: Further Reflections on African Women's Christologies." *Journal of Reformed Theology* 7.3 (2013): 267–93.

Stuart, Alison. "Freedom of Religion and Gender Equality: Inclusive or Exclusive?," *Human Rights Law Review* 10.3 (2010): 429–59.

Sweeney, James. "How Should We Remember Vatican II?," *New Blackfriars* 90.1026 (2009): 251–60.

Temple, Christel N. "The Cosmology of Afrocentric Womanism." *Western Journal of Black Studies* 36.1 (2012): 23–32.

Thomas, Linda E. "Anthropology, Mission, and the African Woman: A Womanist Approach." *Black Theology* 5.1 (2007): 11–19.

Tobin, Mary Luke. "Women in the Church: Vatican II and After." *Ecumenical Review* 37.3 (1985): 295–305.

———. "Women in the Church since Vatican II." *America* (1999): 22–28.

Tsuruta, Dorothy Randall. "The Womanish Roots of Womanism: A Culturally-Derived and African-Centered Ideal (Concept)." *Western Journal of Black Studies* 36.1 (2012): 3–10.

Ukagba, George Uzoma, Obioma Des-Obi, and Iks J. Nwankwor. *The Kpim of Feminism: Issues and Women in a Changing World: A Reader*. Studies in African Philosophy, Culture and Development. Victoria, BC: Trafford Publishing, 2010.

UN WOMEN. *Progress of the World's Women 2015–2016: Transforming Economies, Realizing Rights*. http://progress.unwomen.org/en/2015/pdf/UNW_progressreport.pdf.

Vähäkangas, Auli. "African Feminist Contributions to Missiological Anthropology." *Mission Studies: Journal of the International Association for Mission Studies* 28.2 (2011): 170–85.

Vähäkangas, Mika. *In Search of Foundations for African Catholicism: Charles Nyamiti's Theological Methodology*. Boston: Brill, 1999.

Vatican Council II. *Apostolicam Actuositatem* [Decree on the Apostolate of the Laity, 1965].

———. *Dignitatis Humanae* [Declaration on Religious Freedom, 1965].

———. *Gaudium et Spes* [Pastoral Constitutuion on the Church in the Modern World, 1965].

Villa B, Ana Cristina. "On the Laywomen Auditors at the Council." http://www.laici.va/content/laici/en/sezioni/donna/tema-del-mese.html, 1–3.

Wakahiu, Jane. "Foundation of Religious Institutes and Impact of Technology Innovation on Sisters in Africa: A Socio-Cultural Approach." In *Voices of Courage: Historical, Socio-Cultural, and Educational Journeys of Women Religious in East and Central Africa*, edited by Jane Wakahiu, Peter Gichure, and Ann Rita Njageh, 34–99. Nairobi: Paulines Publications Africa, 2015.

Wakahiu, Jane, Peter Gichure, and Ann Rita Njageh, eds. *Voices of Courage: Historical, Socio-Cultural, and Educational Journeys of Women Religious in East and Central Africa*. Nairobi: Paulines Publications Africa, 2015.

Waliggo, J. M. "The Practice of Democratic Principles by the Catholic Church in AMECEA Countries." In *New Trends for the Empowerment of the People*, edited by David Kyeyune. Nairobi: Paulines Publications Africa, 1997.

Suggested Reading

Bowles, Gloria, and R. Duelli-Klien, eds. *Theories of Women Studies*. London: Routledge, 1983.

Haddad, Beverley. "The South African Women's Theological Project: Practices of Solidarity and Degrees of Separation in the Context of the HIV Epidemic." *Religion & Theology* 20.1/2 (2013): 2–18.

Hastings, Adrian. *African Catholicism: Essays in Discovery*. Philadelphia: Trinity Press International, 1989.

Hudson-Weems, Clenora. *Africana Womanism: Reclaiming Ourselves*. Troy, MI: Bedford, 1993.

———. *Africana Womanist Literary Theory: A Sequel to Africana Womanism: Reclaiming Ourselves*. Trenton, NJ: Africa World Press, 2004.

Kolawole, Mary E. Modupe. *Womanism and African Consciousness*. Trenton, NJ: Africa World Press, 1997.

Korieh, Chima J. *African Women: A Reader*. San Diego, CA: University Readers, 2009.

Lienemann-Perrin, Christine, Atola Longkumer, and Afrie Songco Joye. *Putting Names with Faces: Women's Impact in Mission History*. Nashville, TN: Abingdon, 2012.

McEnroy, Carmel. *Guests in Their Own House: The Women of Vatican II*. New York: Crossroad, 1996.

Ntiri, Daphne W. *One Is Not a Woman, One Becomes: The African Woman in a Transitional Society*. Boston: Bedford, 1988.

Oduyoye, Mercy Amba, and Musimbi R. A. Kanyoro, eds. *The Will to Arise: Women, Tradition, and the Church in Africa*. Maryknoll, NY: Orbis Books, 1992.

Phillips, Layli. *The Womanist Reader: The First Quarter Century of Womanist Thought*. London: Routledge, 2006.

Sheldon, Kathleen. *African Women: Early History to the 21st Century*. Bloomington: Indiana University Press, 2017.

Uzoma Ukagba, George, Obioma Des-Obi, and Iks J. Nwankwor. *The Kpim of Feminism: Issues and Women in a Changing World; A Reader. Studies in African Philosophy, Culture and Development*. Victoria, BC: Trafford Publishing, 2010.

Vähäkangas, Mika. *In Search of Foundations for African Catholicism: Charles Nyamiti's Theological Methodology*. Boston: Brill, 1999.

The Church as Family of God in Africa

Paulinus I. Odozor, CSSp

A significant challenge facing the African church (and indeed the global Catholic Church) in these early years of the new millennium is the degree to which it will approach its mission with a deep understanding of its nature, its past, and its knowledge of the present realities with which it is confronted. The questions are how accurately the church in Africa can read "the signs of the times," and what tools it has to face these times. These challenges are not unknown to the church in other places; in this article, however, the focus is on Africa in light of the First Special Assembly for Africa of the Synod of Bishops, which took place in Rome in 1994. This event was motivated by an increasing need in the church in Africa to articulate more consciously a rationale and method for conversation with postcolonial and post-independence Africa. The synod was singularly focused on mission, and in the post-synodal apostolic exhortation *Ecclesia in Africa,* Pope St. John Paul II eloquently indicated the important mission challenges facing the church in Africa. In addition to evangelization and inculturation, the church must help Africa overcome its endemic divisions, ensure stable and enduring Christian marriages, engender vocations to the priesthood and the religious life, tackle the massive poverty on the continent, and help the continent tap into the promise of the modern mass media while avoiding its many pitfalls.[1] These issues outlined in the First Synod for Africa continue to be challenges for the African Catholic Church.[2]

In what follows, I will discuss some issues that I consider still very important and of ongoing concern for the church in Africa since the first African synod. My argument is that attending to the full implications of the pivotal metaphor of the church as "family of God"—which is how the first African synod describes the church in Africa—is crucial for the proper growth of the church in Africa in the foreseeable future.

The Church as Family of God in Africa: The Power of a Metaphor

One of the enduring legacies of the First Synod for Africa was the use of the metaphor of church as "family of God" as a reality of African life. This metaphor has become, in the minds of many, the guiding ecclesiological characterization of the church of Africa. Therefore, a primary objective in this commemorative essay will be to revisit the idea of the church as family of God in Africa and to discuss, albeit cursorily, some of the implications of this metaphor and the challenges associated with it as a theological descriptor of the African church today. Although "family" would normally connote some sort of consanguinity or affinity, it can also sometimes metaphorically describe close relationships that are built on other grounds.

The metaphor "church as family of God" has biblical roots and a long history in the Christian tradition, as the Vietnamese theologian Ngo Dinn Tien has shown.[3] In the African theological context, the

---

1. Pope John Paul II, *Ecclesia in Africa*, especially §§46–54 (hereinafter *EA*).
2. See Pope Benedict XVI in his post-synodal apostolic exhortation after the second African synod, *Africae Munus* (hereinafter *AM*).
3. Tien, "The Church as Family of Development and Implications for the Church in Vietnam."

metaphor first appears prominently in §25 of the *Instrumentum Laboris* of the first African synod. This text provides several references to support the biblical origin of the concept of the church as family of God, including 1 Tim 3:15, where the author speaks of the "household of God," and Eph 2:19–22, where the biblical writer again refers to Christians as "no longer strangers and aliens" but "citizens with the saints" and also members. In the message that the synod sent to the Christians of Africa at the end of their deliberations, the synod fathers wrote that they were sending a "word of hope and encouragement" to "the family of God" in Africa, and indeed to "the family of God all over the world." Their message was simple and direct: "Christ our Hope is alive: we shall live!" (*EA* §13).

In *EA* §43, Pope John Paul II speaks glowingly of the African family and its high esteem in African communities, thus providing further anchoring for the use of family as metaphor to describe the church of God in Africa. In African culture and tradition, he says, "the role of the family is everywhere held to be fundamental. Open to this sense of the family, of love and for life, the African loves children, who are joyously welcomed as gifts of God." As evidence that Africans have deep regard for family life this text further emphasizes that Africans show respect for human life until death; they keep elderly parents and relatives within the family; and they have a sense of solidarity and community life. In Africa, the pope asserts, it is impossible to celebrate a feast without the participation of the whole village. Thus, community life in Africa expresses and involves the whole extended family. The pope then tasks the African community to preserve "this priceless cultural heritage and never succumb to the temptation to individualism which is so alien to its tradition" (*EA* §43).

In a later context, Pope Francis speaks generally of the church as the "family of families," constantly enriched by the lives of the various domestic churches. He adds that "in virtue of the sacrament of matrimony, every family becomes in effect a good for the Church. From this standpoint, reflecting on the interplay between the family and the Church will prove a precious gift for the Church in our time. The Church is good for the family and the family is good for the Church." [4] One big question is, How can this be true in the case of Africa? Some African scholars who have taken up the theme of the church as family of God in Africa point out that the family metaphor has its strengths and its limitations, which must be thoroughly examined to make it yield the results desired by the synod.

Purifying the Metaphor

Family is the fundamental unity or organizational nucleus of human society. It is the primary human experience and expression of *communio*. At its best, the African family, like families elsewhere, can be "a place of care for others, solidarity, warmth in human relationships, acceptance, dialogue, and trust" (*EA* §63). But the African family, like families everywhere, is also sometimes beset with many problems and difficulties—abuse, neglect, infidelities, violence, lack of care, poverty, destitution, and so on. Therefore, as Elochukwu Uzukwu insists, the family metaphor should not be taken to imply that African cultural experience could set the terms for the construction of this new family of God. The metaphor must first be stripped of patriarchal dominance and of other negative characteristics that can sometimes be evident in the life of African families (as is the case in many families around the world).

> The novelty of the gospel introduces a mode of being into the African family experience similar to the way Jesus lived family life in order to reassemble the new family of God or new people of God based on a new kind of relationship. This may not exclude division (Lk 12:52f), and it will certainly include an openness that knows no limits (Mk 3:31–35).[5]

To continue to use the expression church as "family of God," therefore, we must first "purify" the metaphor in some ways. First, it must be realized that the church as family of God is not simply a collection

---

4. Pope Francis, post-synodal apostolic exhortation *Amoris Laetitia* §87.
5. Uzukwu, *Listening Church*, 66–67.

of clans and peoples who have consanguinity and thus are bonded to each other on this basis. Rather, it is a brotherhood and a sisterhood "beyond the frontier of blood relationship, clan, ethnic group, or race."[6] The church as family of God is a family with one Lord, one faith, one baptism as its basis. This family has no earthly father because it has one true and real father, God himself, and all others are brothers and sisters. This is to say that an ecclesiology of church as family of God is built on the understanding of the creation of every member in the image and likeness of God, a reality that confers not only the essential equality of all persons before God but also the dignity of sonship and daughtership to all people, and on the idea of incorporation into the body of Christ through one baptism. The universal church is "a people brought into unity from the unity of the Father, the Son, and the Holy Spirit," as the Second Vatican Council states.[7]

There are two other noteworthy sides to the metaphor of the church as family of God. On the one hand, it alludes to a sociological reality, a concrete living institution of people who have found faith in Jesus Christ. "Called together from all the nations . . . all the members of the Church form one body" (*LG* §7).

[This is] the one Church of Christ which in the Creed is professed as one, holy, catholic and apostolic, which our Savior, after His Resurrection, commissioned Peter to shepherd, (Jn 21:17) and him and the other apostles to extend and direct with authority (cf. Matt. 28:18, etc) which He erected for all ages as "the pillar and mainstay of the truth" (1 Tim. 3:15). This Church, constituted and organized in the world as a society, subsists in the Catholic Church, which is governed by the successor of Peter and by the Bishops in communion with him, although many elements of sanctification and of truth are found outside of its visible structure. These elements, as gifts belonging to the Church of Christ, are forces impelling toward catholic unity. (*LG* §8)

This visibly present and established entity is also the family of God in which each member receiving life through baptism is formed into the likeness of Christ and is taken up in the breaking of bread into communion with him and with one another (*LG* §7). Sociologically, this family, like every other organization, has visible structures of governance, which are set up by Christ or have developed over the ages for carrying out the mission of the church. The African church, bearing the marks of the universal church—apostolicity, unity, and catholicity—professing one faith, proclaiming one Lord, and sharing the same sacraments, is truly a family of God in Africa as everywhere else.

On the other hand, the metaphor of church as family of God in Africa must not be taken as an expression or as an assertion of a theological truth already achieved or evident in the life of the church on the African continent. It is still rather for the most part a statement of theological hope, a pivotal guide. Indeed, it is the goal of evangelization in Africa, as *Ecclesia in Africa* states, "to build up the church as the family of God, an anticipation on earth, though imperfect, of the kingdom." The Christian families of Africa will thus become "true domestic churches, contributing to society's progress towards a more fraternal life" (*EA* §85). This is how African societies will be transformed through the gospel. The aspirational nature of this metaphor must not be overlooked because the reality on the ground in Africa is often vastly different from the aspirational dream: African Christians are sometimes as disunited as their societies and sometimes even more so; African churches are sometimes as un-Christlike as the societies in which they are found; and African church men and women can be as sinful as their secular or non-Christian counterparts on the continent. All this is to say that one cannot look unambiguously to the history of the church in Africa or to current practices or modes of being church on the continent to validate the assertion of the church as truly and really a family of God.

---

6. Uzukwu, *Listening Church*, 67.
7. Vatican II, Dogmatic Constitution on the Church (*Lumen Gentium*) §4 (hereinafter *LG*).

What I have said here must be qualified. There is no perfect family anywhere on earth, and there is no family without its heartaches, sorrows, and traumas, some of which are imposed by the realities of life but many of which arise from self-inflicted wounds due to sin, such as the now endemic worldwide scourge of clerical sexual abuse of minors. These negativities do not nullify the relatedness that fashions families. As already indicated above, theologically and ecclesiologically a church family comes into existence wherever there are people who have been baptized into the death and resurrection of Christ, who share one faith in one God, the father of our Lord Jesus Christ, who partake of the Body and Blood of Christ, and who have one hope. Thus, despite the many negative realities of the church in Africa, the metaphor describes an existing sociologically bounded theological reality that can be real and evident, as in a real family going through thrills and thralls of what it means to be a family and discovering through this process both its strengths and its dysfunctionalities, and, it is hoped, struggling with the help of the Holy Spirit to do something about its inadequacies.

Finally, the metaphor of the church as family of God must not be taken in isolation from the other metaphors that the Second Vatican Council used to describe the reality of the church, as even *Ecclesia in Africa* insists (§64). Vatican II, which was very much an ecclesiological council, used several other metaphors to describe the church: the church as a mystery or sacrament; the church as people of God; the church as servant; the church as collegial; the church as ecumenical; and the church as eschatological.[8] As people of God, the church is called to proclaim justice and must be exemplary in its just treatment of peoples and persons. As the synod fathers said in 1971, "While the Church is bound to give witness to justice, she recognizes that everyone who ventures to speak to people about justice must first be just in their eyes. Hence we must undertake an examination of the modes of acting and of the possessions and lifestyles found within the Church herself."[9] The church as people of God is constituted by all the faithful and not just the hierarchy. This fact has implications for the consultative process and for the free flow of ideas in the church. A servant church serves human needs both spiritually and materially. A collegial church is made manifest in the parish assembly, in the diocese and in the universal church. The collegial nature of the church helps "to raise and rephrase the question of the use and limits of authority" and the meaning of subsidiarity. As an eschatological reality, the church is in via, in the world but not of the world, open to mistakes in some of its decisions. Thus, the church as family of God is just one metaphor among many (see *LG* §§6, 29, 32), a reality to which anyone who wants to discuss fully the challenges that the church faces in Africa must advert if one must do justice to the topic. One metaphor alone, however important it is, cannot carry the reality of the church in Africa or elsewhere. It must be supplemented by other metaphors and imageries.

Taken together, these designations of the church provide a very complex but more complete image of the challenges that face the church as family of God in Africa. Even so, it is clear that Pope John Paul II had the clear intention of making the concept of the church as family of God in Africa a pivotal concept, a guiding metaphor, so to speak, when in *Ecclesia in Africa* he declared that "it is earnestly to be hoped that theologians in Africa will work out the theology of the Church as family with all the riches contained in this concept, showing its complementarity with other images of the Church" (§63). In the words of Nigerian theologian Teresa Okure, one would regard the metaphor as a "recipe" for growing a particularly effective and Christlike community of Christians in Africa. And, as Okure notes, a recipe "remains only an idea until persons use it to produce the dish it prescribes."[10] The question, then, is whether and to what extent the church in Africa has used, is using, or is capable of using this recipe to produce or to build up the church "as an anticipation on earth, though imperfect, of the kingdom . . . [and] contributing to society's progress towards a more fraternal life"

---

8. See McBrien, *Church*, especially 163–81. On this issue, see also McCormick, "Moral Theology from 1940–1989," 5–6.

9. 1971 Synod of Bishops, "Justice in the World," 295.

10. Okure, "Gospel-Based Personal Identity and Life," 45.

(*EA* §85). The answer to this question is not clear, in part because twenty-five years is a very short period in which to gauge progress on such matters, and in part because it is hard to determine what constitutes progress.

Although there are many signs of hope wherever one looks within the African church, such as increasing interactions between the various churches at various levels, and the increasing involvement of the church in issues of development and situations of social justice all over the continent, there are also many troubling signs of dysfunctionalities which lead to the question of whether the family metaphor is indeed the best one to use for the African church. One of the dysfunctional situations in the African church relates to appointments to ecclesial offices. In some African churches, appointments to high ecclesial offices, whether in the dioceses or in religious communities, are marked by inter- and intra-ethnic quarrels. Ahiara and Makeni dioceses are good examples of the situations I am describing.[11] These situations are characterized by "ethnic prejudice, sectionalism and discrimination," and, as Okure points out, they exist partly because "church leaders in particular use them rather than the gospel as the operative fundamental of their life, their mindset about themselves, their view of Church and of their ministry as Church leaders. They use ethnicity as a yardstick for relating to the different ethnic groups in their parishes, dioceses, and religious communities and in the country as a whole."[12] Many years after the synod it is still the case, as the late Archbishop Albert Obiefuna of Onitsha quipped at the synod in 1994, that the blood of ethnicity in Africa is still thicker than the waters of baptism, even among Christians. This is to say that the realization of the promise of the synod's guiding metaphor appears in many cases to be still a distant dream. It is my argument in this chapter that the failure of this metaphor to ignite African Christianity is a result of a much deeper failure to attend to the theological issues that would provide proper grounding and effectiveness for the idea of the church as family in Africa. High on this list is the failure to articulate a properly Christian theology of God in Africa. Put positively, the desire to build up the church family of God in Africa "as an anticipation on earth, though imperfect, of the kingdom . . . [and] contributing to society's progress towards a more fraternal life" (*EA* §85) can happen only from and through explicitly theological intentionality.

The Theological Challenge Facing the African Church

Perhaps the most important challenge facing the church as family of God in Africa is one of theological self-awareness and identity. This challenge in turn creates a few others, both internal and external to the African church, which I will discuss below. Many of these issues were identified by the two synods on the African church.

The challenge of self-awareness and identity has been ever-present since the dawn of Christianity and seems to be especially urgent today as Christianity everywhere confronts many divergent voices and many questions: What does it mean to be a Christian today? Who is Jesus Christ and what relevance does he have for me and the way I live? What is the church and how is it different from or related to other associations and groups to which I belong? Which of them has or should take priority when they make competing claims about reality and about life itself? These questions are at the heart of the problem of Christian identity, in Africa and everywhere.

The church in Africa is growing at an annual rate of nearly 3 percent, a rate unparalleled anywhere else in the world, and it is estimated that by the end of the next decade there will be more Catholics in Africa than in all of Latin America. Today, there are 800 million people in Africa; 370 million are Christians and 124 million are Catholics. By 2025, the number of Catholics will increase to more than 228 million.[13] With this growth comes increased

---

11. These are cases from Nigeria and Sierra Leone, where people rejected candidates appointed to these dioceses on ethnic grounds.
12. Okure, "Gospel-Based Personal Identity and Life," 46.
13. Barrett et al., *World Christian Encyclopedia*, 13–15.

anxiety about what it means to be a Catholic Christian, especially in the face of the rise of Pentecostalism, the emergence and growth of militant Islam, the increase of ethnic tensions everywhere on the continent, and the increased destitution present on the continent, among other pressures. The African church has repeatedly been called upon to prove its relevance to African societies by helping find answers to the problems of ethnic tension and poverty. For example, in the late twentieth century, then president Julius Nyerere of Tanzania warned that, unless the church participated actively "in the rebellion against those social structures and economic organizations which condemn man to poverty, humiliation and degradation, the church will become irrelevant to man . . . the Christian religion will be identified with injustice and persecution . . . it will die."[14] Nyerere argued that the church in Africa must help people rebel against the slums they live in; share hardships, knowledge, and progress with the people; and help find solutions to the problems of national unity, which plagued nearly every African country at the time (and now). He said that the church should do this by presenting itself as a "great family . . . which transcends tribe and clan."[15] To a large extent, the African church has vigorously attempted to respond to these challenges through the work of various charitable outreaches and interventions and through its words and deeds addressing the dysfunction of Africa's political structures, even to the extent that some have wondered whether the ancient work of the church—"arousing, strengthening and maintaining faith"—has not been sometimes "supplanted by charitable work, social commitment, involvement in development aid, revolt against economic and racial tyranny." While this has not yet occurred in Africa, it is an issue that the African church must watch with vigilance.

African churches have devoted significant attention to the so-called social question facing African societies. This is as it should be. But I want to suggest that the biggest problem facing the African church is the theological problem I have identified. This problem is evident on two important fronts—the doctrine of God and the question of anthropology. I have written extensively about this in other places and will not go into these issues here at any length. Suffice it say that the African church suffers from a deficiency of God-knowledge. African theologians and churches have often made the mistake of insisting that, when Africans talk about God, they are referring to the God of Jesus Christ. This is only partially true. The God of Jesus Christ is not like the deities that are talked about in African religions or in any other religion present in the world.

The Unique Understanding of God in the Christian Faith

As Pope Benedict XVI points out in the first volume of his three-volume work, *Jesus of Nazareth*, the most important thing Jesus contributed to the world is his unique sense of God. As the pope puts it, Jesus has brought God to the world.[16]

> He has brought the God who formerly unveiled his countenance gradually, first to Abraham, then to Moses and the Prophets, and then in the Wisdom Literature—the God who revealed his face only in Israel, even though he was also honored among the pagans in various shadowy guises. It is this God, the God of Abraham, Isaac, and Jacob, the true God, whom he has brought to the nations of the earth. He has brought God, and now we know his face, now we can call upon him. Now we know the path that we human beings have to take in this world. Jesus has brought God and with God the truth about our origin and destiny: faith, hope, and love.[17]

In an earlier book, *Introduction to Christianity*, then Cardinal Ratzinger argued that an essential characteristic of God, the one whom Jesus calls "Father," is that he is personal. God is personal by

---

14. Nyerere, "Christian Rebellion," 83.
15. Nyerere, "Christian Rebellion," 85.
16. I have used the views of Pope Benedict XVI here and in some other writings on this matter because I find his views on God and God-language very compelling.
17. Pope Benedict XVI, *Jesus of Nazareth*, 1:44.

his name. This implies not only that we can experience God beyond all other experiences but also that he can express and communicate himself.[18] In Jesus Christ, God has become quite concrete but even more mysterious. God is always infinitely greater than all our concepts and all our images and names. "The fact that we now acknowledge him to be triune does not mean that we have meanwhile learned everything about him."[19] Even so, the fact is that "this God now shows us his face in Jesus Christ (Jn 14:9)—a face that Moses was not allowed to see (Ex. 33:20)."[20]

According to Pope Benedict XVI, in bringing the gift of the God of Israel to the nations, Jesus has brought the gift of universality, so that through him all the nations "recognize Israel's Scripture as his word, the word of the living God." This was the one gift God had promised Abraham, Isaac, and Jacob:

> This universalization, this faith in the one God of Abraham, Isaac and Jacob—extended now in Jesus' new family and all nations over the bonds of descent according to the flesh—is the fruit of Jesus' work. It is what proves him to be the Messiah. It signals a new integration of messianic promise that is based on Moses and the prophets, but also opens them up in a completely new way.[21]

The vehicle of Jesus's universalism is the new family of God, that is, the church,

> whose only admission requirement is communion with Jesus, communion in God's will (cf. Mk 3:34ff). . . . This universalization of Israel's faith and hope, and the concomitant liberation from the letter of the law for the new communion with Jesus, is tied to Jesus' authority and his claim to Sonship. It loses its historical weight and its whole foundation if Jesus is interpreted merely as a liberal reform rabbi.[22]

Pope Benedict's position must not be interpreted to mean that those cultures unfamiliar with the God of Israel, including in Africa, have no idea of God or of his presence in human history. Catholic tradition has always acknowledged God's presence and revelation in human societies everywhere. In fact, Pope Benedict himself, in his homily at the opening Mass of the Second Special Assembly for Africa of the Synod of Bishops on October 4, 2009, said as much: "The absolute Lordship of God is one of the salient and unifying features of the African culture. Naturally in Africa there are many different cultures, but they all seem to agree on this point: God is the Creator and the source of life."[23] In this regard the pope referred to Africa as "the repository of an inestimable treasure for the whole world."[24] However, what he is inviting readers of *Jesus of Nazareth* to do is something very necessary for our work here—to pay attention to the unique features of Jesus's particular revelation of God. The God of Jesus is new in every culture, including African culture, and the content of our belief about him has important implications for the way we live our lives and the way we organize society. As one writer has pointed out, "What African Christians need is not the African concept of God. What African Christians need is a clear picture of the Christian view of God."[25] Yet this is what is often lacking in much of African theological discourse. It is not often clear what difference belief in the God who manifested himself in Jesus Christ

---

18. Ratzinger, *Introduction to Christianity*, 23.
19. Ratzinger, *Introduction to Christianity*, 25.
20. Ratzinger, *Introduction to Christianity*, 22.
21. Pope Benedict XVI, *Jesus of Nazareth*, 1:116–17.
22. Pope Benedict XVI, *Jesus of Nazareth*, 1:117, 119. For a more detailed discussion of this topic and of Pope Benedict XVI's position, see also my book, *Morality, Truly Christian, Truly African*, especially 191–205.
23. Pope Benedict XVI, "Homily for the Eucharistic Celebration for the Opening of the Second Special Assembly for Africa of the Synod of Bishops."
24. Pope Benedict XVI, "Homily for the Eucharistic Celebration for the Opening of the Second Special Assembly for Africa of the Synod of Bishops."
25. Kombo, *Doctrine of God in African Christian Thought*, 12.

and who continues to abide with his church would make to Christian life in Africa.

> It is not enough to enumerate the attributes of God; for theology to be Christian it has also to draw the lessons from scripture and from the Christian tradition on God. What, for example, is the ethical import of the doctrine of the Trinity for Africa? What lessons are there for Africa in the God about whom Jesus Christ taught in the parables? What lesson is there for an African theological ethics that draws on Jesus' saying in John 3:16 and in many other such passages? How would the praxis of Jesus as regards women and the marginalized of society in his day affect the construal of relationships in Christian Africa? What warrant would the teaching of Jesus on forgiveness, personal and communal, provide for the ethics of forgiveness among Africans?[26]

The God of Jesus is yet unknown. Therefore, every renewal of church life and mission must begin by revisiting this God. To the extent that we can get closer to the image of and an understanding of the one Jesus called his Father, we will be able to live right and do right in this world and to construct a church that is truly a family of God. We Christians believe that the God who made heaven and earth has not retired in splendid isolation, leaving the world to its own devices. God continues to journey with us. The fourth Eucharistic Prayer puts it very eloquently when it asserts that even when we sinned and lost his friendship God did not abandon us to the power of death but continued to help us seek and find him. As Joseph Sittler points out, "All Christian speech begins with what God does and gives." What God *does* is that he goes out of himself "in creative and redemptive action" toward human beings.[27] What God *gives* is himself, first through his creative and benevolent acts, but finally and most definitively through the incarnation of Jesus Christ. As the evangelists point out in their stories of the birth of Jesus, "Everything seems to stand still, and all things are bathed in luminous light when the new deed of God occurs in Jesus Christ."[28] The stunning deed of God in Jesus is therefore not only the revelation of God in creation but ultimately his self-disclosure in Christ. This is an engendering deed in that it calls into being lives that are marked by "its originative character."[29]

The church as family of God in Africa needs to hear this message loudly and clearly in this new era of evangelization. In other words, the first project of the church in Africa is to evangelize. This project would have us paint again for ourselves, for our people, and for the world at large a loving portrait of Jesus that gets to the very nature and heart of God. It is no longer enough to claim that our people know God. Indeed, that is not in doubt. The Christian churches in Africa and elsewhere must again in all seriousness take the people back to the God of Jesus Christ, the one who so loved the world that he sent his only begotten son for our salvation. What this entails is a proper catechesis that initiates the people of God into the most fundamental mysteries of the faith.

The Anthropological Challenge

Jesus not only reveals the true nature of God. He also reveals to us the fullness, the nature, and the meaning of the human person. In his post-synodal apostolic exhortation *Africae Munus*, Pope Benedict XVI states that Africa is facing "an anthropological crisis" (§11). Some of the causes and symptoms of the impoverishment and diminishment of the human person that are attendant on this crisis are poverty, conflicts, wars, and violence of all kinds, racist xenophobia, segregation, the division of peoples into classes and castes, and the denial of human rights in various forms. Many people are running around the continent with injured, negative memories of wrongs that have supposedly been done to them or to their ancestors. African societies sometimes appear to be sitting on a powder keg that is ready to explode at the slightest

---

26. See Odozor, *Morality, Truly Christian, Truly African*, 187.
27. Sittler, *Structure of Christian Ethics*, 25.
28. Sittler, *Structure of Christian Ethics*, 29.
29. Sittler, *Structure of Christian Ethics*, 25.

provocation. As Benedict points out, "Africa will have to rediscover and promote a concept of the person and his or her relationship with reality that is the fruit of a profound spiritual renewal" (*AM* §11). Christian tradition in general and Catholic theology specifically offer profound insights that constitute the only real basis for such a renewal.

Anthropological renewal in Africa, especially in the church, must begin with the central Judeo-Christian truth that every human being is made in the image and likeness of God. Creation in the *imago Dei* has far too many anthropological implications to be fully explored here, but let us note a few. It means that every person has an intrinsic worth that is his or hers no matter their circumstances. Every person is essentially equal—equally a son or a daughter of God. Human worth is not something conferred by any government or society or individual, and it cannot be taken away by a person's social, economic, or even moral standing, or by his or her history. Every human being is equally loved by God. As the council put it, "Human begins are the only creatures on earth that God wanted for their own sake."[30] This statement applies to everyone, everywhere. As Pope John Paul II pointed out in his very first encyclical, *Redemptor Hominis*, "The God of creation is revealed as the God of redemption."[31] In his work of redemption, Christ reveals to us the full meaning of the human person. For "in the Redemption man becomes newly expressed and, in a way, newly created. 'There is neither Jew nor Greek, there is neither slave nor free, there is neither male nor female; for you are all one in Christ Jesus'" (§10). The point here is that in Christ and through Christ the human person "has acquired full awareness of his dignity, of the heights to which he is raised, of the surpassing worth of his own dignity and of the meaning of his existence" (§11).

As Pope John Paul II asserts, "For the Church all ways lead to man." Thus, the church cannot abandon man. The reason for this is that the destiny of each and every human person, each man and each woman in every age and place, that is to say, "his election, calling, birth and death, salvation or perdition, is . . . closely and unbreakably linked with Christ" (*RH* §14). Therefore, a central concern of the church as family of God in Africa must be the defense of the human person in all situations in whatever way is possible. Whatever attacks the dignity of anyone anywhere attacks the dignity of us all and must be our concern whether that person is from our village or not, is a Christian or not, or is from my part of the continent or from another region or ethnic group. In this regard, human rights must be a centerpiece of the church's moral crusade—we must insist that everyone has a space to act for himself or herself and that everyone has the right to seek redress when his or her rights are trampled upon. While the African church must attempt to uphold all cultural practices that enhance and reinforce human worth and dignity, we must also be prepared to rise up in revolt to challenge boldly and seek to change all cultural practices that dehumanize people, including practices that demean women, the various caste systems in Igboland and other parts of the continent, and various other systemic practices and issues that challenge or are at variance with the Christian belief in the dignity of the human person. For such a program to be successful, we must immediately initiate processes of dialogue at various levels between Christianity and African traditions, with a view to identifying those aspects of our cultures and traditions that are contrary to the deep Christian belief in the equality and sanctity of all human beings. Such a dialogue is long overdue and must be an essential aspect of the new evangelization in Africa. Cultures and traditions are human creations that can be both noble and sinful, and for this reason must be continually evaluated in the light of the gospel.

The Moral Challenge

For many people, the Christian moral life is simply about dos and don'ts, a situation that often leads to a kind of moral brinksmanship—how far can I go before I fall off the cliff? Christian life must be understood as friendship with God, and this understanding changes everything. For the Chris-

---

30. Vatican II, Pastoral Constitution on the Church in the Modern World (*Gaudium et Spes*) §24.
31. Pope John Paul II, encyclical *Redemptor Hominis* §9 (hereinafter *RH*).

tian, morality is not a dictate given by a master to a servant or by a slave owner to a slave. When Jesus says, "I do not call you servants anymore . . . I call you friends" (John 15:15), this is what he means. "The servant master relationship has little room for the intimacy of friends. Jesus treats them like friends by disclosing who he is and where he is going. Jesus tells them that he is laying down his life for his friends; that is not what a master would do for his slaves."[32] Christian morality is therefore an ethic of response, a response to the stupendous love of a friend; it is an invitation to give back in love to a friend who has shared so much with us. It is never an imposition.

If, in the family of God in Africa we seek to uphold Christian morality, we must do several things. We must seek to foster a community made up of individuals who care about others, that is, people who live justly. Education in virtue is essential for a morally upright Christian community. The church must continue to make its voice heard on moral choices we know from our faith and from human reason to be wrong. Abortion is always wrong, no matter who does it or for whatever reason, and marriage is always an arrangement between a man and a woman. No amount of popular pressure can change these facts. However, even as the church in Africa teaches these truths, it must also act pastorally to help ameliorate those situations that force women into prostitution when they do not want to or to become pregnant when cannot afford to. The church as family of God has a pastoral responsibility to act in coordination with governments and other agencies to find solutions to the scourge of serious problems facing youth all over Africa, which manifests itself in a lack of education, joblessness, and in general a wasting of youth in various ways.

The Pastoral/Catechetical Challenge

As Pope Benedict notes, "The contribution of Christians will be decisive if their understanding of the faith shapes their understanding of the world. For that to happen, education in the faith is indispensable, lest Christ become just one more name to adorn our theories" (*AM* §32). The church in Africa must find a way to retell the Christian story in a coherent manner to our young people, who are bombarded today with so many voices and trends from the media and other sources of information that are very much in opposition to what the church and the Christian faith stand for. The aim would be to present them with healthy alternatives that come from the teaching of the gospel of Jesus Christ. One thing we must no longer do is present Christian morality as merely a set of prohibitions or as a set of joyless options taught for the purpose of taking away human freedom and happiness. This is far from the truth, but our teachings on sex and sexuality, for example, can sometimes appear oppressive to people in this generation, in part because we have not taken the time to find a way to put them in the theological and anthropological settings that animate them and give them meaning in the first place. The Good News is simply that: good news, and Christians must hear it again as a message of joy and deliverance. In this regard, one important challenge is to convince African Christians themselves that they have been given something that is supremely valuable, something the world really needs. How can one give what one does not have or propagate what one does not believe in? Therefore, the church in Africa must find ways to engender a crop of believers who appreciate God's stunning deed in Jesus Christ, people who find in Jesus the Good News of salvation and who are prepared to take risks to share what they believe. I would like to offer several suggestions in this regard.

First, I suggest that the church develop and foster a spirit of volunteerism through carefully planned youth service programs for young Catholics, which would operate in various African contexts. The aim would be to encourage young Catholics to give of their time and talents to serve the cause of the gospel through involvement with the poor. The churches of the West do this, and often Africa is on the receiving end of services provided by these young people. The African church must encourage these types of service-oriented programs across entire regions, countries, dioceses, and local areas as it is feasible. Second, dioceses and religious

---

32. Spohn, *Go and Do Likewise*, 45.

orders must once again encourage and train those willing to engage in door-to-door canvassing for new members just as the Jehovah's Witnesses and the Mormons do. The parish ministry of priests and catechists must include some effort at direct evangelization of those who have not or have only barely heard the faith. Third, adult catechesis must be emphasized. Every priest, every well-trained theologian, and every consecrated religious should be required to give about an hour of their time in any given week to teaching the faith to some segment of the parish community. Fourth, the various episcopal conferences on the continent should aim at providing a national moral instruction guide for schools and for the young in their parishes. Such a guide would situate Catholic moral teaching in the context of the church's beliefs as expressed in, among other sources, the *Catechism of the Catholic Church*, the *Compendium of the Social Doctrine of the Church*, and the Bible. Fifth, to face up to the barrage of atheistic, foreign, and morally questionable propaganda that has been unleashed on Africa, the church must stay vigilant. Although the church may not always be able to match these outside forces "dollar for dollar," it can at least train people to lead an effort to blunt the effect of the propaganda. I suggest in this regard the establishment of a unit of political and policy affairs at the secretariat of every African episcopal conference if none exists already. Such a unit would have to be staffed by people trained in politics, theology, and public affairs and would work collaboratively with the justice and peace commissions to monitor government activity but also to directly influence legislation pertaining to faith, morality, and public policy. Sixth, the church must seek ways to evangelize the culture creators of our day, the segment of society that Pope John Paul II once referred to as the new Areopagus. These are the people in the academy, science, entertainment, and industry. The impact of so-called Nollywood films is now felt worldwide. Some of these films are morally uplifting but many are not. Sometimes hidden in these movies are questionable assumptions about God, the human person, and morality. But the lifestyles of screen actors and other celebrities are emulated and copied by many people, especially the young. The African church must find ways to engage the new Areopagus. We can no longer ignore its impact on the moral formation of Africans, including African Christians. I am not asking that we turn the church into a morality police; I am simply suggesting that we should enter into regular dialogue with culture creators in order to encourage them to practice their arts in a way that brings out the best in us.

The challenges to the church as family of God in Africa are enormous. The two African synods have clearly articulated these challenges and, in fact, have offered solutions that, if followed, would bring the church closer to becoming what it is intended to be.

A Lingering Question

The question is sometimes asked whether the church in Africa is pursuing its social role to the detriment of its more theological one—announcing the Good news. This question is pertinent when we realize, as did the Second Synod of Africa and many African theologians, that despite all these efforts by Christian churches in many African countries, the timbre and tenor of African societies do not appear to change much, that in fact African societies seem to be sinking more and more into chaos and barbarity. What could the church do to further the transformation of Africa? What has it not done, or done well? Let me venture an answer here. The planting of the church in Africa, no matter the historical circumstances of it, is now a reality. The next phase has already begun and must be taken seriously because it is more difficult since it involves more careful theological discernment. Since the church is more fundamentally a theological and religious community, it can help further in the transformation of Africa by addressing some of those specifically theological themes that stand in the way of the transformation of African societies, such as the question of God-language in Africa and the issue of anthropology that were discussed above.

As I have argued in this essay, the one area in which the church must effect transformation in Africa is theological. Although the church's mission is not merely the transmission of doctrine, its effort at social transformation in Africa as elsewhere must come from a well-articulated and openly stated doctrinal core. Unless it focuses with razorlike intensity on this theological task, it cannot any longer be an effective agent of transformation in Africa; it will ultimately become irrelevant in Africa. If the church carries itself merely as another NGO, it will die in Africa. Africa will rise sooner or later to solve its social and economic problems through ingenuous leadership and will therefore find the church an irrelevant voice and in some ways reactionary. Something like this is already happening on the continent. It was once the case that the best hospitals and schools in most of Africa were church-run institutions. This is no longer the case. Today, some of the best hospitals and schools have other proprietors, and church-run institutions are often woefully inadequate. It was the case that once upon a time in Africa the church was the voice for social change and for good governance. That is no longer the case. Other voices, equally articulate and insightful, are arising in various parts of the continent and sometimes drowning out the ecclesial voice on these issues. Does this mean the church should abandon its responsibilities in the social sphere? By no means. It means that the church, family of God in Africa, must be more intentional in its work as agent of transformation by attending to the foundational/theological issues that give credence, grounding, and distinctiveness to its work in society. It must clearly articulate its vision of the God Jesus calls Father, and the implications of this reality for other realities—the human person, ecclesial membership, the natural world, and all reality in general. Even so, the church must never forget that its project is not simply the transformation of this society. Its project is to help people also to reach their ultimate destiny with God. As Galileo once put it, it is not the mission of the church merely to teach people the way the heavens go, but to teach them the way to go to heaven. This is still the case, twenty-five years after the synod.

Conclusion

The church as family of God is both a statement of theological fact and an aspirational call to action for the African church. In both senses, it invites the church to become more and more an authentic witness to the gospel of Jesus Christ. When the Second Vatican Council refers to the church as sacrament of Christ in the world, it means that it is both witness to and cause of the grace of God in the world. Although the synod could have chosen another language and or another organizing metaphor to describe the African church, it did not do so but rather chose the idea of family, which is dear to the African heart, to convey both the importance and the transformative power and potential of the church for Africa. Many years after the First Synod for Africa, it remains for the leaders and members of the church to give wings to this idea. As family, the church can break down the walls of endemic divisions—ethnic, social, political—which characterize the African world today. It can give a sense of personhood to many of Africa's forgotten and marginalized persons. It can also provide a secure haven to all peoples of Africa in their search for identity and relevance both in their own world and in their relationship with the rest of humanity. For the Catholic Church in Africa, despite its flaws,

> is still the one international organization that actually listens to Africa and accepts it and is allowing a center of gravity shift to take place, however slowly. . . . [It] is one of the only truly credible worldwide institutions in Africa, credible locally as local church, not as a global conglomerate. More than any other organization with Western roots, the church seems to have kicked the imperialist addiction in favor of communion. That is why she is so beautiful, and a true locus of renewal, both potential and actual, in Africa and for Africans, even for those who are not Christian.[33]

Bibliography

1971 Synod of Bishops. "Justice in the World." In *Catholic Social Thought: The Documentary Heritage*, edited by David J. O'Brien and Thomas A. Shannon. Maryknoll, NY: Orbis Books, 1992.

---

33. Odozor, *Morality, Truly Christian, Truly African*, 293–94.

Barrett, David, George Kurian, and Todd Johnson, eds. *World Christian Encyclopedia: A Comparative Survey of Churches and Religions in the Modern World*. New York: Oxford University Press, 2001.

Benedict XVI, Pope. *Africae Munus* [Post-synodal Apostolic Exhortation on the Church in Africa in Service of Reconciliation, Justice and Peace; November 19, 2011]. Vatican City: Libreria Editrice Vaticana, 2011. www.vatican.va.

———. [Joseph Cardinal Ratzinger]. *Introduction to Christianity*. Translated by J. R. Foster. San Francisco: Ignatius Press, Communio Books, 1990. Reprinted, 2004.

———. "Homily for the Eucharistic Celebration for the Opening of the Second Special Assembly for Africa of the Synod of Bishops." October 4, 2009.

———. *Jesus of Nazareth*. Translated by Adrian J. Walker. 3 vols. New York: Doubleday, 2007.

Francis, Pope. *Amoris Laetitia* [Post-synodal Apostolic Exhortation on Love in the Family; March 19, 2016]. Vatican City: Libreria Editrice Vaticana, 2016. www.vatican.va.

John Paul II, Pope. *Ecclesia in Africa* [Post-synodal Apostolic Exhortation on the Church in Africa and Its Evangelizing Mission toward the Year 2000; September 14, 1995]. Vatican City: Libreria Editrice Vaticana, 1995. www.vatican.va.

———. *Redemptor Hominis* [Encyclical; March 4, 1979]. Vatican City: Libreria Editrice Vaticana, 1979. www.vatican.va.

Kombo, James Henry Owino. *The Doctrine of God in African Christian Thought*. Leiden: Brill, 2007.

McBrien, Richard P. *The Church: The Evolution of Catholicism*. New York: HarperCollins, 2008.

McCormick, Richard A. "Moral Theology from 1940–1989." In his *Corrective Vision: Explorations in Moral Theology*. Kansas City, MO: Sheed & Ward, 1994.

Nyerere, Julius. "The Christian Rebellion." In *African Christian Spirituality*, edited by Aylward Shorter. Maryknoll, NY: Orbis Books, 1980.

Odozor, Paulinus I. *Morality, Truly Christian, Truly African: Foundational Methodological and Theological Consideration*. Notre Dame, IN: University of Notre Dame Press, 2014.

Okure, Teresa. "Gospel-Based Personal Identity and Life as Recipe for Racism-Free Leadership in the Church." In *One Faith: Many Tongues: Managing Diversity in the Church in Nigeria*, edited by Fortunatus Nwachukwu. Abuja: Paulines Publications Africa, 2017.

Ratzinger, Joseph Cardinal. *See* Benedict XVI, Pope.

Sittler, Joseph. *The Structure of Christian Ethics*. Louisville, KY: Westminster John Knox, 1998.

Spohn, William. *Go and Do Likewise: Jesus and Ethics*. New York: Continuum, 1999.

Tien, Ngo Dinn. "The Church as Family of Development and Implications for the Church in Vietnam." PhD thesis, New South Wales: Faculty of Arts and Sciences, 2006.

Uzukwu, Elochukwu. *A Listening Church: Autonomy and Communion in African Churches*. Maryknoll, NY: Orbis Books, 1996.

Vatican II. *Gaudium et Spes* [Pastoral Constitution on the Church in the Modern World, 1965].

———. *Lumen Gentium* [Dogmatic Constitution on the Church, 1964].

CATHOLIC THEOLOGICAL AND PHILOSOPHICAL TRADITIONS IN AFRICA

The Changing Faces of Roman Catholic Ecclesiology in Sub-Saharan Africa

Josée Ngalula, RSA

Today's Roman Catholic ecclesiology employs various images or metaphors to express the nature and mission of the church. The notion that there is a specifically African ecclesiology often surprises people who ask why the church in Africa needs its own images and metaphors.[1]

Following in the path of the New Testament, the Roman Catholic Church has over the centuries formulated a variety of pictures of the church. The diversity of these pictures has resulted from the multiplicity of challenges posed by different contexts in different historical periods. As an example, in 1985 the Synod of Bishops deemed it important in the context of that time to stress the paradigm of "*koinonia*." African theologians also attempt to systematically elaborate theological reflections on the nature and mission of the church in response to specific challenges facing the continent.

What are the images and metaphors of the church that are being emphasized today in the sub-Saharan church? This chapter will first consider those images and metaphors emanating from scholarly theological work and then move on to discuss current ecclesiological notions being proposed by the official church in Africa. The discussion will then shift to a consideration of the most important ecclesiological challenges facing Africa today.

The Ecclesiological Propositions of Today's African Theologians

An analysis of the ecclesiologies formulated in the African context[2] in recent decades shows that at least four African values have been highlighted as potentially having meaning for deepening Africans' understanding of the nature of the church in their context and for promoting theological formulations that can enrich the other metaphors traditionally employed by the universal church. These values are community, clan, respect for ancestors, and life. They are closely related to and interwoven with each other. African societies have inherited from their ancestral traditions the reality of the community as a structure that fundamentally defines the human being: human identity is founded on belonging to a community and effective participation in it. This communitarian reality is always achieved within the clan (also referred to as the "extended family" or "ethnic group"), which is a large network of people characterized by blood relations with the clan's founder and a responsibility to pass along the life they received from the founder. Ancestors are an important part of the life of the clan, and they are typically shown respect by means of the African cult of ancestors. "Life" is the center of gravity around which these relation-

---

1. Other terms used here that will have approximately the same meaning as "image" and "metaphor" are "model," "paradigm," "formulation," and "picture."
2. See Orobator, "Perspectives and Trends in Contemporary African Ecclesiology"; Nyamiti, *Studies in African Christian Theology*, vol. 3; Lowery, *Identity and Ecclesiology*.

ships between human beings, alive or dead, rotate. The term "life" is understood holistically: living on earth is an ongoing attempt to grab hold of the fullness of life through sustained relationships with both the visible world (including other human beings and nature) and the invisible world (including God the creator, spiritual beings, and virtuous ancestors).

These four values have been used to formulate four ecclesiological metaphors for the African church: church as clan, church as fraternity, church as family and community, and church as family of God.

The Church as Clan

A number of African theologians have drawn a comparison between the African clan and the Christian community, for example, Joseph Thiam in 1956.[3] African theological discussions of the related topic of ancestorship have approached the issue in many different contexts: in studies of traditional African religions, in connection with liturgical celebrations of the communion of saints, and in systematic theology, among others. An investigation of the work of African scholars over the last fifty years shows that their ecclesiological proposals with respect to the notion of clan have approached it from two points of view: Christology and ethics.

Two theologians, Vincent Mulago and Charles Nyamiti, employed Christological reflections to envision the church as clan. In two contributions from 1965 and 1969, Mulago used the metaphor of clan to express the relationship of Christian communities to Jesus Christ.[4] As the members do with respect to the Bantu clan, the church participates in her founder's life and is a community that is united by sharing in Christ's body and blood and in God's Trinitarian life. Mulago also used this clan imagery to stress the church's universality: Jesus Christ is the founder of a new clan, a race or people distinguished by plurality in unity, and for this reason capable of healing the divisions that currently exist among peoples. Along the same lines, Nyamiti suggested in 1984 and 1990 a direct link between what he sees as an ancestor relationship with Christ,[5] who, he asserts, belongs to the "ancestral kinship of the Trinity,"[6] and the nature of the church. In Christian life, it is Jesus who unites all believers into one community worshiping the one supreme God, and for this reason Christ can truly be called "Brother Ancestor."[7] Just as the African clan venerates the bodies of its ancestors, so the church, called the "body of Christ" in the New Testament, is the continuation of the mystery of Christ in living human communities by facilitating a *koinonia* with the Trinitarian God through Christ.[8] In brief, the linkage of the African value of respect for ancestors and Christological reflection underlines the central place of Christ in the life of his church.

Two other African theologians, John-Mary Waliggo and Laurenti Magesa, do not explicitly refer to the church as a clan, but rather look to the ethical values of clans to inspire the creation of better structures in the African society and church. Waliggo became interested in leadership, both in the society and in the church. As an anthropologist, he looked for ethical inspiration from traditional African values and, in 1990, published an analysis of fifty-two clan systems in the Baganda ethnic group. The ethical values of leadership he discovered in these clans, one of which values is eschewing dictatorial behavior, led him to conclude that the clan can be a "true model," not only for African politicians but also for African church leaders.[9] The clan typically features leadership focused on service and avoids leadership that excludes individuals or groups. In 1999, Magesa proposed the African clan as a paradigm that could help develop

---

3. Thiam, "Du clan tribal à la communauté chrétienne."
4. Mulago, *Un Visage africain du christianisme*, 16, 223–24; see also Mulago, "Vital Participation," 157.
5. Nyamiti, *Christ as Our Ancestor*; see also Nyamiti, "Church as Christ's Ancestral Mediation."
6. Nyamiti, "Trinity from an African Ancestral Perspective."
7. Nyamiti, "Church as Christ's Ancestral Mediation," 131.
8. Nyamiti, "African Christologies Today."
9. Waliggo, "African Clan as the True Model of the African Church."

truly democratic leadership in the world and the church.[10] He concluded from his reading of the New Testament that Jesus's entire life was about breaking down pyramidal social structures so that people would understand that authority is service. Magesa had noticed that clans in his native country of Tanzania are characterized by principles of participatory leadership and by mechanisms for preventing the abuse of power. He concluded that the clan is a good model for supporting the principles of subsidiarity, participation, and egalitarian social relations, principles that are already active in the Trinitarian God, but which the church in Africa needed help in practicing.

The Church as Fraternity

Médéwalé-Jacob Agossou published a book in 1987 in which he investigated the notion of and the challenges related to "fraternity" in the African context.[11] He argued that the concept of fraternity involves the related concepts of solidarity, hospitality, communion, and communitarian life, all of which are inspired by the Holy Trinity. Agossou did not, however, call the church a "fraternity."

In 1991, Michel Dujarier published the first volume of his extensive investigation into the history of the notion of the church as fraternity.[12] He is a missionary to, not a native of, Africa, but he was one of the first scholars to strongly propose the ecclesiology of church as fraternity, following in the footsteps laid down by the New Testament and the early church. Dujarier spurred a serious debate in western Africa about the possible usage of this formulation.[13]

At the First Special Assembly for Africa of the Synod of Bishops in 1994, the intervention of Bishop Anselme Titianma Sanon interestingly combined two expressions in saying that, from a Burkinabé perspective, "Church-Family, Church-Fraternity is the same Church born from the Father, the Son and the Holy Spirit."[14] In putting these two formulations side by side, Bishop Sanon was recalling the debate referred to above. Even though Pope John Paul II, in the post-synodal apostolic exhortation *Ecclesia in Africa*, had chosen the metaphor of the church as the "family of God," a theological congress held in Kinshasa shortly after the conclusion of the synod, in 1995, found it interesting to discuss the ecclesiology of the church as fraternity in addition to the church as family.[15] Two exegetes from the school of theology developed in Kinshasa, Atal Sa Agang and Paul Buetubela, investigated the biblical basis and theological significance of church as fraternity and demonstrated that "fraternity" for Christians has always been related to Christ the Son of God as the inaugurator of a new community of adopted children of God through his salvation.[16] This community is a fraternity that calls on a specifically Christian ethics. These two exegetes did not, however, call the church a fraternity—it was presented only as one of the dimensions of Christian identity. In 1996, Alphonse Quenum followed the same intuition by analyzing fraternity as a dimension of the church as family,[17] an important value in the identity of the Christian community as the family of God.

In 2012, Nestor-Désiré Nongo-Aziagbia defended a PhD thesis on the subject of fraternity in Christ in the African context.[18] Following the path of Michel Dujarier and the two exegetes of Kinshasa, he illuminated the notion of fraternity as applied to the faith community described in the Bible and during the patristic period. Nongo-Aziagbia also explored the use of fraternity as a theological concept by African bishops and theologians, in the documents of the Second Vatican

---

10. Magesa, "Theology of Democracy."
11. Agossou, *Christianisme africain: Une fraternité au-delà de l'ethnie*.
12. Dujarier, *L'Église-Fraternité*.
13. This debate occurred especially in a colloquium held after the first African synod in Kinshasa 1995. See Facultés catholiques de Kinshasa, *Église-famille, Église-fraternité*.
14. Bishop Sanon's intervention during the 1994 synod was published in Cheza, *Le synode africain*, 137.
15. Facultés catholiques de Kinshasa, *Église-famille, Église-fraternité*.
16. Facultés catholiques de Kinshasa, *Église-famille, Église-fraternité*, 181–209.
17. Quenum, *L'Eglise-Famille de Dieu*.
18. Nongo-Aziagbia, *La fraternité en Christ*.

Council, in canon law, and in consecrated life throughout church history. The result of his investigation was that only the New Testament and St. Cyprianus in the early church dared to use the term "fraternity" as a paradigm for the Christian communities. He found that, in the history of the church, the term became progressively more narrow in its application, reserved only for some aspects of consecrated life. The texts of Vatican II and canon law have a larger vision of fraternity: they present it as an important value characterizing Christian communities, even humanity as a whole, but only as a value, not an ecclesiological metaphor for the church. Nongo-Aziagbia proposed, alternatively, to concentrate on a "theology of fraternity,"[19] that is, on an idea of the church as a "vector of relations" in the world, proposing to human beings a new society based on the new relationships proposed by Christ. Even when valorizing a theology of fraternity, however, one must be aware also of the potential dangers of fraternity that have been seen in the history of the church, including excommunications, fratricidal violence, and excessive ecclesiastical discipline.

Church as Family and Community

Like Mulago, Nyamiti, Waliggo, and Magesa, Bénézet Bujo used the African value of clan to build his Christology and subsequent ecclesiology. He did not use the term "clan" but instead the terms "family" and "community." In 1992, Bujo completed a careful analysis of the African values of community, respect for ancestors, and life from an ethical point of view.[20] His objective was to read the contemporary social problems of Africa in the light of the Christian faith and to analyze the faith's ability to stimulate African traditions. He discovered that human existence manifests a deep thirst for life that includes an eschatological dimension, and that, for Africans, ancestors are not only the mediators and protectors of this life but also the models and guarantors of the community's moral life. Commemoration of ancestors aims at making the life of the community more full. For Bujo, the title of "proto-ancestor" as applied to Jesus summarizes the way in which many New Testament texts present him as truly God and a source of life. He is not one ancestor among many, not even the first to be born physically, but the "ancestor par excellence," who communicates God's life and salvation as God's unique Son who preexists all of the creation.

For Bujo, the consequence of this for ecclesiology is obvious: the signification Christ gave to the Eucharist during the Last Supper grants to the sacrament the meaning of a "proto-ancestral" communion with Christ the "proto-ancestor," in which Christians receive a "proto-force." The foundation stone of an authentically Christian church is thus a "Church-Family/Church-Community," in which every Christian participates, through baptism, in the wisdom of the proto-ancestor. Such an ecclesiology, concludes Bujo, necessarily has practical implications for the leadership and ministries of the church. For example, the palaver process must be one of the distinctive signs of this church as family and community. In African traditions, a palaver is an interactive dialogue, an open communication dealing with issues of common interest. Its main values are consensus building in tolerance, participation, peaceful truth telling, dialogue, equality, and social solidarity as the basis of reconciliation and promotion of a just social peace. The "palaver tree" is a symbol of peace and reconciliation.[21]

Church as Family of God

The fact that there are more than sixty publications about the ecclesiology of the church as family of God shows the importance of this image in theological research.[22] The emergence of this metaphor in sub-Saharan Africa is interesting: it was used

---

19. Nongo-Aziagbia, *La fraternité en Christ*, 433–35.
20. Many of Bujo's key conclusions are in German. A good summary in English can be found in Bujo and Muya, *African Theology in the 21st Century*, 1:120–40.
21. See Mucherera, *Meet Me at the Palaver*; and Ilo, "The African Palaver Method."
22. See the suggested readings at the end of this chapter.

for the first time in 1975 when the Catholic bishops of Burkina Faso opted for pastoral reasons to abandon a pyramidal ecclesiology and to adopt instead the notion of an ecclesial community living intensively the values of fraternal communion and solidarity.[23] This theological expression reappeared in 1993 during the preparation for the first African synod, and since then many African theologians and biblical specialists have worked to deepen its theological meaning and concrete impact on the church's mission.[24]

But what does it mean exactly that the church is a "family of God"? Several issues have come to the fore. First, concerning the metaphor's biblical and patristic roots,[25] the exact expression "family of God" is rare in the Bible, but some fathers of the church used it to appeal to Christians to exhibit an effective and universal charity in Christ. Some traces of the term can be found in the Roman liturgy and in some of the texts from the council.[26] These texts emphasize the formulation's Trinitarian roots and its roots in the New Testament texts teaching unity in diversity, as well as the specifically Christian fellowship that is formed in Christian baptism with its formula "in the name of the Father, and of the Son, and of the Holy Spirit." The church as family of God must principally be marked by communion because she participates in the Trinity through the person of Jesus Christ.

Second, as has already been noted, there is a strong conception in Africa that the human being is relational and that human life is communal. Using the image of the family appeals to the sensibility of African Christians and therefore has great potential to help them go deeper into the faith to discover the richness of the fraternity God has granted to our humanity in Jesus Christ. The image will help the church in Africa to evangelize their sense of belonging to tribes, ethnic groups, nations, and confessions, while helping them keep in mind that the Trinitarian God and the person of Jesus Christ make all believers into one body, one people in God. This ecclesiology will also help to deepen the evangelization of the realities facing African families, so that the light of the Trinitarian God can deepen within its members an understanding of the dignity of every human being and a sense of solidarity and fraternity with all.

Third, it is important that the term "family" for the church be used prudently: the word is symbolic and metaphorical and its usage must transcend the biological family to embrace the symbolic sense of a communion of grace in God's love, a kinship in Jesus Christ in union with the Holy Spirit. The Christian identity must be greater than tribal, ethnic, and denominational identities.

Finally, many African ecclesiologists have suggested that the image of the family of God can help the African church adjust her exercise of leadership and authority in ways that are more appropriate to a relationship rather than a product of a rigid hierarchical organization. E. E. Uzukwu, for example, argues that the church should be marked by a unity including multiplicity (diversity) because her identity is rooted in the Trinity.[27] Christian identity should include appreciation for diversity; it should not produce conformity. In this way, the ecclesiology of the church as family of God can help in rejecting a monarchical, hierarchical church—the metaphor of family stresses an atmosphere in which each person contributes to the community and to respect and care for others in a collegial, collaborative framework. Following this metaphor, the exercise of church authority must involve a listening process in which authority is not monopolized and every member has a contribution to make and a voice that will be heard. If she becomes a truly "listening church," the African church will help the continent by demonstrating a new way

---

23. Dabiré, "Eglise-Famille de Dieu."
24. Ramazani, *Augustin: Ecclesiologie africaine de famille de Dieu*, 10–89.
25. See, for example, the Proceedings of the 8th and 9th Congresses of the Panafrican Association of Catholic Exegetes, in Matand Bulembat et al., *The Church as Family and Biblical Perspectives*, 1999 and 2002.
26. The phrase "familia Dei" is present in these Vatican II documents: *Lumen Gentium* §§6, 27, 28, 32, 51; *Gaudium et Spes* §§32, 40, 42, 43, 50, 92; *Unitatis Redintegratio* §2; *Christus Dominus* §16; and *Ad Gentes* §1.
27. Uzukwu, *Listening Church*.

of living that is contrary to the present-day tendency of African leaders toward tyranny and the denial of democratic and humane values. In the same way, A. E. Orobator finds that the notion of family, which implies a dynamic and not a static and prefabricated reality, suggests that the proper model of church communication should be the palaver, which places a premium on interpersonal relationships and dialogue and emphasizes participation and listening to the diversity that is a gift of the Holy Spirit.[28] An ideal church leader will be a listener who hears the voices of his people at a grassroots level and incorporates the views of the voiceless, vulnerable, and marginalized persons in society. The different kinds of ministry will enrich the community, and every member will have a place. The laity—the numerical majority of the church—will receive the respect they are due.

An African Ecclesiology of Liberation

Some African ecclesiologists do not focus their attention on metaphors taken from traditional African values. These practitioners of liberation and reconstruction theology use a different terminology in the course of insisting on the urgency of grappling with the social and ethical issues facing contemporary Africa. Their ecclesiology has been variously described: Mubangizi Odomaro has dubbed it the "African ecclesiology of liberation"; Stan Chu Ilo prefers the phrase "ecclesiology of abundant life," while Orobator has identified it as the "church as family at the service of society."[29]

The scholars of this ecclesiological trend insist on the diaconal dimension of the church: in order for the church to promote life in contemporary Africa, it must be in solidarity with the concrete suffering of the peoples of Africa. Following in the path of Jesus Christ, the church in solidarity with a suffering Africa will fight alongside her against every form of evil and death plaguing the continent.

The Ecclesiological Propositions of Today's Official Church

In the current sub-Saharan African theological milieu, new ecclesiological intuitions or formulations do not come only from scholars. African bishops have also contributed to expressing the nature and mission of the church as they face the specific challenges of the continent. Since the two synods on Africa, researchers on African theology have listened to the interventions and analyzed the practices of African bishops in order to understand what might emerge as the trends in and efforts to implement their theologies.[30] Alain Patrick David has summarized the interventions of the African Catholic bishops between 1967 and 2009 as focused on two major and tightly linked ecclesiological affirmations: that there needs to be an "inculturated" church and a "servant" church.[31]

An Inculturated Church

Striving for an inculturated church is a response to two calls by Pope Paul VI: the 1967 message *Africae Terrarum* and the invitation to African bishops at Kampala in 1969 to invest in a true African Christianity.[32] The pastoral option for Small Christian Communities and the choice of the paradigm of

---

28. Orobator, *Church as Family*.

29. Mubangizi, "Church as Liberator"; Ilo et al., *Church as Salt and Light*; Orobator, *Church as Family*; Orobator, *From Crisis to Kairos*; Orobator, *Church We Want*.

30. See, for example, A. G. Kitambala, *Les évêques d'Afrique et le concile Vatican II: Participation, contribution et application du Synode des évêques de 1994* (Paris: L'Harmattan, 2010); B. Muono Muyembe, *Église, évangelisation et promotion humaine: Le discours social des évêques africains* (Fribourg, Switzerland: Universitaires Fribourg, 1995); Jean-Marie H. Quenum, *Les évêques catholiques et la crise africaine (1990–2005)* (Nairobi: Université catholique de l'Afrique de l'Est, 2010); Kalamba Nsapo, *Les ecclésiologies d'épiscopats africains subsahariens*.

31. See the synthesis in Alain Patrick David, "Le rapport Église-monde dans les interventions des évêques d'Afrique noire aux Assemblées du Synode des évêques de 1967 à 2009" (Thèse Doctorat en théologie, Université Laval, Québec, Canada, 2015).

32. Pope Paul VI, Message *Africae terrarum* (the homily of Paul VI during the eucharistic celebration at the conclusion of the symposium organized by the bishops of Africa, Kampala, July 31, 1969). A French version is available in Paul VI, "Voyage de Paul VI en Ouganda," in *La Documentation Catholique* (7 septembre 1969, no. 1546), 764a–b, 765a. English version is available at www.vatican.va.

church as family of God that emanated from the 1994 synod are acts of inculturation following on the Vatican II ecclesiology of communion, which are aimed at a new evangelization of Africa.

Small Christian Communities (SCCs): Church as Communion at the Grassroots and in the Neighborhood

The development of Small Christian Communities in Africa has not followed the same trajectory as in Latin America. In Africa, their impetus came from pastors (including bishops and parish priests) who wanted to breathe life into African Christianity by organizing a new model of church rooted in a communion of believers at the grassroots, in the everyday life of neighborhoods.[33] Various terms are used for these realities in Africa. In English-speaking African Catholic dioceses, they are referred to as Small Christian Communities (SCCs), Basic Christian Communities (BCCs), Basic Ecclesial Communities (BECs), and Ecclesial Basic Communities (EBCs). French-speaking dioceses call them Communautés Ecclésiales de Base (CEBs), Communautés Ecclésiales Vivantes (CEVs), and Communautés Ecclésiales Vivantes de Base (CEVBs).

The first African intuitions of the need for these realities appeared in central and eastern Africa. In the Democratic Republic of the Congo, the Bishops' Assemblies of 1961 and 1967 opened the way for them by opting for a Christianity that would be more deeply involved in the everyday life of African Christians, which gave birth to "small living communities" in the neighborhoods. During the period of 1966–1969, the Tanzanian bishops opted for and initiated the creation of "local ecclesial communities" in order to promote African cultural and social values under the aegis of the church.

After Pope Paul VI's appeal to African Christians to be their own missionaries and to strive for an African Christianity, some bishops in Africa became very creative in devising and promoting pastoral structures that opened new perspectives on Roman Catholic ecclesiology in Africa. Between 1970 and 1980, many archdioceses and dioceses simultaneously put in place pastoral structures that would later become the SCCs, including Eldoret in Kenya, Lilongwe in Malawi, Lusaka in Zambia, and Kinshasa in the DRC. At the same time, some of the episcopal conferences decided that the SCCs would become the basic pastoral unit for the Roman Catholic Church in their countries. These episcopal conferences (including the Episcopal Conferences of the DRC in 1972, the Association of Member Episcopal Conferences in Eastern Africa in 1973, and the Episcopal Conferences of Uganda in 1974, Burkina Faso in 1979, and South Africa in 1978) had come to understand that church life should be based not on parish activities far from everyday life but instead on small local communities where Christians can experience interpersonal relationships in the faith and feel a sense of communal belonging at the grassroots.

Everywhere the SCCs were promoted, the goal was the same: to make effective in Africa the council's ecclesiology of communion by rooting Christianity more firmly in the everyday lives of African Christians. The first steps and the ultimate level of success of the SCCs differed from one diocese to another, even in the same country. Their success depended on the ecclesiological convictions of the pertinent bishops and priests, on the training and dynamism of the laity, and on whether there was peace in the country. It generally took many years to change the minds and lifestyles of a laity used to putting the priest and the parish or mission station at the center of their Christian lives. Through the experience of the SCCs, the lay faithful in Africa slowly began to interiorize Vatican II's valorization of the laity and of the need for every member of the laity to become personally engaged with the Bible. For all the dioceses that encouraged the SCCs, there was the supplementary work of training lay animators and reorganizing parishes. The new reality also implied the training of seminarians and priests in the new spirit of the SCCs so that they would understand the role of parish priest as the servant and promoter of the responsibilities of the laity.

The SCC experience has been successful in the majority of dioceses where it is present. We have

---

33. See the excellent synthesis in Healey, *Building the Church as Family of God*. Also see P. Kalilombe, *From Outstations to Small Christian Communities* (Eldoret: AMECEA Publications, 1984).

now accumulated thirty to forty years of living a new model of church characterized by:

- a communion of the faithful in their everyday lives, at the grassroots, in their neighborhoods
- Bible sharing at the grassroots level
- promotion of lay leadership and the active participation of everyone in the community
- more attention to the evangelization of living culture using the "see–judge–act" method[34]
- a grassroots experience of ecumenism
- valorization of women in the church

Where the experience of the SCCs has been successful, the parish has become a communion of SCCs, in which lay initiatives and pastoral work are valorized. In addition to the classical catechetical ministry, new ministries and services suited to the needs of the church in Africa have emerged in response to various concrete needs of the community, including leadership of the SCCs, local evangelization in the neighborhood, spiritual care of the sick, the promotion of Christian marriage, counseling, local responsibility for justice and peace and ecumenical relationships, care for the poor, the extraordinary ministry of the Eucharist, the ministry of reconciliation, and the ministry of engaging in dialogue with traditional African leaders. With the SCCs, the African church has slowly become local, self-ministering, self-propagating, and self-supporting.

Where the SCCs have worked well, bishops and priests have seen in life and not in books that they can rely on a well-trained, generous, and creative lay faithful for pastoral work. Trusting the lay faithful with and implementing inculturation in ministry in the Roman Catholic Church in Africa began in the mid-1970s with the introduction by Joseph-Albert Cardinal Malula (the then archbishop of Kinshasa in the DRC) of a lay minister called a parish *mokambi*. The bishop officially appoints the *mokambi*, a true lay minister who is not part of the church hierarchy, and entrusts to that person the responsibility of residing in the parish for the purpose of improving parish administration and organizing pastoral activities. The *mokambi* collaborates with a "moderator priest" whose role is to celebrate the sacraments.[35]

The two African synods, held in 1994 and 2009, confirmed the option of the SCCs for the entire Roman Catholic Church in Africa, both as a way of living as church and as a tool for transforming society to conform to values of the kingdom of God.[36] There are, however, at least six remaining challenges facing them.

The first challenge concerns whether there is still strong interest in this model of being church. In some African dioceses, SCCs are still not a priority and do not even exist at all. This is generally the result of lack of interest from bishops and priests. In many dioceses, SCCs are working very well, but there is a lack of interest from the wealthier classes and the youth, which happens where there is poor leadership because of a lack of good leadership training.

The second challenge is the fidelity of SCCs to their initial impulse. In some places, they have been transformed into devotional groups or sodalities, instead of understanding themselves as the church at the grassroots with its foundation in sharing the Word of God and as a phenomenon that transforms believers into witnesses.

The third challenge is related to the economic crisis affecting some countries and churches. People who are financially pressed and who work hard all day long to survive may not have time to participate in the activities of SCCs. In addition, some priests have transformed SCCs into fundraising mechanisms for parish activities.

The fourth challenge concerns the stability of SCCs. Many African countries are facing violent conflicts that force people to flee from their

---

34. "See–judge–act" is an inductive method of analysis developed by Belgian Cardinal Joseph Cardjin. It allows a person or a group within the church to stop, stand back from a situation, and reflect on it in the light of the gospel before jumping in and taking new actions. Pope St. John XXIII recognizes and encourages the use of this method in the encyclical *Mater et Magistra* §§239–41.

35. See Moerschbacher, *Les laïcs dans une Eglise d'Afrique*.

36. See the post-synodal apostolic exhortations by Pope John Paul II (*Ecclesia in Africa* §§28–29) and Pope Benedict XVI (*Africae Munus* §130).

homes, and many SCCs have seen their activities interfered with or even halted because of this violence. In some places, wars have killed people and destroyed villages or parts of cities. On the other hand, camps for refugees or displaced persons have become milieus in which SCCs have been reconstituted or started from scratch. New lay ministries have begun to meet the pastoral needs existing in these camps.

The fifth challenge is the presence of thousands of new religious movements in Africa that promise rapid solutions to life's problems if only people pray and accept Jesus Christ as their savior. Many people have been attracted by these movements, causing some Catholics to abandon their SCCs and parishes for what they see as an opportunity to better their economic circumstances through following the prosperity gospel.

Finally, the sixth challenge is the persistence of a mentality of clericalism, despite the theology that emanated from the council. Decades after the conclusion of the council, there are still clerics in the Roman Catholic Church who believe themselves superior to the lay faithful. For this reason, they do not have a deep understanding of the theological importance of SCCs; they do not appreciate the new lay ministries; and they keep alive some of the structures of the church that discriminate against women. They live in permanent tension with laity in their parishes, tension that sometimes even erupts in violence.

In response to these challenges, the Roman Catholic Church in Africa is urged not only to support and improve the training of both clerics and lay faithful in theology and leadership, but also to be actively involved in issues of justice and peace and in attempts to ensure that Africans can achieve a minimum level of well-being. These commitments would positively impact the evolution of SCCs in Africa.

The Option for Church as Family of God

Another example of a choice in favor of an inculturated church was the decision at the first African synod to adopt the ecclesiological formulation of church as family of God. This metaphor was found pertinent to a deep evangelization of Africa. *Ecclesia in Africa* deems this expression as particularly appropriate for expressing the nature of the church in the African context because it is able to mobilize African Christians by responding to their aspirations for communion and fraternal love in Christ (§63).

The expression "church as family of God," with the theological meaning given it in *Ecclesia in Africa*, has become quite familiar in both theological and pastoral discourses in Africa, with many dioceses using it in everyday pastoral language. The ecclesiology of church as family of God can help African Christians realize that they are called to the reconstruction of their continent and to understand that advocating for justice, peace, and reconciliation is part of inculturation, as was suggested by the second African synod.

The Church as the Servant of Africa in Solidarity

In the dynamic of *Gaudium et Spes*, the Pastoral Constitution on the Church in the Modern World, the church of Christ should interact with modern African society not just by her teaching, but by bolstering the legitimate aspirations of Africans for development, justice, and peace and by sharing her energies and the light of Christ for a better Africa (§§1, 3, 40, 92). This *diakonia* includes dialogue with African societies and the adoption of a sociopolitical ecclesiology in which evangelization, human development, and liberation are linked. The SCCs play a key role in all of this.

Progressively Learning to Serve as a Prophet Who Speaks for the Voiceless

From the beginning of evangelization in Africa in the fifteenth century, the African church has always maintained structures of charity and education. During the period of Africa's colonization, these structures were for many reasons bound to the enterprise of "civilizing" Africans. The first generation of African bishops after the political independence of many African countries would inherit these structures, but decided to keep them for another purpose along the lines set forth in *Gaudium et Spes*: they would be used to further the church's role as a servant of African development. The church would, in the spirit of her mission, serve human beings as part of its work to bring about the reign of God in the world, following in the path of the Lord Jesus Christ. In the decades after independence, the complexity of the African situation would lead to the church's decision to serve Africa as a prophet, by speaking for the voiceless and awakening the consciousness of Africans to take into their own hands the continent's present and future.

During the years 1975–1990, African countries were increasingly plagued by dictatorships and their negative consequences for the liberty of the people and for the quality of education and other social services. In the context of these dictatorships, Christian charitable, educational, and pastoral structures that provided real help for the people, and specifically that provided opportunities for people to exercise free speech, were rare. In some places, priests and bishops suffered persecution for making these structures available to people. In this context, it became important for African Christians to theologically clarify for themselves the links between evangelization and human well-being on the continent.

Following in the path of Paul VI's apostolic exhortation *Evangelii Nuntiandi*, in 1984, 1988, and 2003, the Assemblies of the Symposium of Episcopal Conferences of Africa and Madagascar (SECAM) firmly opted for an ecclesiology of a "church at the service of Africa." The bishops opted for this formulation because the church of Christ does not exist for herself but in order to serve human beings, revealing to them and helping them benefit from the profound dynamic of the kingdom of God in human history.

In the specific context of Africa, serving human well-being cannot be confined to establishing Catholic schools, universities, and health care facilities: it also means being very close to the struggle of African people for peace, real freedom, dignity, and basic human rights. It involves collaborating with all people of goodwill to create structures that can promote the values of the kingdom of God. It also implies a prophetic attitude that denounces the structures of sin present in African societies at all levels and that proposes collective and personal conversion so that African people can live in peace, prosperity, and fraternity.

At the level of the parishes and the SCCs, Justice and Peace Commissions have been put in place to implement the church's commitment to Africa. From these grassroots structures, a flourishing civil society has progressively emerged in some Roman Catholic dioceses in Africa, which has brought the voices of the voiceless into the political debate. In some countries, a network of independent observers monitoring elections has sprung up from the Justice and Peace Commissions.

At the level of the church hierarchy, people in many African countries have seen Roman Catholic bishops regularly write pastoral exhortations and pastoral letters stating their position on various public matters on behalf of suffering or oppressed populations. The Roman Catholic hierarchy in Africa has made strong public commitments to social peace and processes of conflict resolution and reconciliation, for example, in their leadership of the National Conferences in Benin, the DRC, and Togo. In many places, the Roman Catholic Church remains the only moral force advocating for the poor and the voiceless. This prophetic service to Africa has produced African martyrs—bishops, priests, nuns, and lay Catholics, men and women, have been arrested, mistreated, tortured, and even killed for having incarnated in their concrete behavior the ecclesiology of the church as servant of Africa.

The second African synod in 2009 enacted a kind of consecration of this ecclesiological option: it held that, for the Roman Catholic Church in Africa, serving the continent implies a decision to become an actor for justice, peace, and reconciliation. In the Christian faith, peace, justice, and reconciliation go together: that is why the Roman Catholic Church in Africa will continue to be the voice of the voiceless, helping to secure justice and durable peace for suffering Africans. She will not cease her commitment to conflict resolution and reconciliation on the continent. She will also continue inventing new pastoral structures to respond to the various human distresses plaguing Africa, including the tragedy of displaced persons and refugees, the illegal exploitation of African resources, the various forms of trade in and exploitation of human beings, the stigmatization of persons with HIV/AIDS, and the scourge of rape. She will not remain on the level of simply providing help for victims, but will go further by denouncing the root causes of these unjust realities.

Progressively Learning to Serve as a Prophet Who Awakens the Consciousness of Africans

The shadows haunting African history, including the slave trade, colonization, various forms of neocolonialism, dictatorship, and war, have led to a kind of defeatism in the behavior of many Africans. For the church in Africa, serving human beings on the continent involves working to awaken Africans to a consciousness of their fundamental dignity and their responsibility in history. The prophetic behavior of the church in Africa is also a call to Africans to have a positive view of themselves and of their continent, to recognize their own partial responsibility for its historical suffering, to stop begging for all their needs from Western countries, to work hard for the development of Africa, to get rid of their collective inferiority complex with regard to Western culture, and to stop indiscriminately copying everything that originates outside Africa.

Apart from periodic calls to African consciousness contained in general pastoral letters, the African Roman Catholic bishops can use independence and other patriotic celebrations as special occasions to awaken the African people to their responsibility for taking into their own hands the continent's destiny. For example, in 2003, on the occasion of the celebration of the abolition of the slave trade, African bishops made a pilgrimage to Gore and issued, from this very symbolic place, a solemn call to all Africans to assume responsibility for their own role in the human and economic disasters of the continent; they also called on Africans to firmly reject any participation in new forms of slavery on the continent, initiated either by Africans or by foreigners. The bishops confessed the historical sins of Africans and begged the mercy of God.[37] This symbolic gesture was truly prophetic: at first many Africans were shocked to hear that Africans participated in the slave trade and in the violence of the colonial period, but people have progressively recognized the truth of these assertions and the truth about contemporary slavery. This awareness has in some countries led to a dynamic of people acting in the best interests of the present and future Africa.

The church's commitment to Africa has also involved issues of conflict prevention and environmental protection, especially in the last decade. In these areas, SECAM has initiated a liaison with the African Union as a first step toward permanent observer status so that it can be, during meetings of important African leaders, a voice of conscience that may be able to help prevent conflict and institutional abdication of responsibility for the poor. In addition, the church has created a Continental Reconciliation Committee for the purpose of addressing the causes of conflict and dispatching skilled mediators when new conflicts break out. Also noteworthy is the launching of an African Church Network to combat the negative impacts of climate change and to resist assaults on African rain forests.

Some Remaining Ecclesiological Challenges

The first great challenge for ecclesiology in the Roman Catholic Church in Africa today concerns the paradigm of church as family of God. It cannot be a mere slogan in African Christianity, but must progressively become a concrete way of living relationships within the church. This ecclesiology appeals to the evangelization of some problematic aspects of relationships within the African family, such as authoritarianism, gerontocracy, and paternalism. In this sense, Teresa Okure notes that

> The concept of the Church as "the Family of God" emerged from the Synod; it was noted that the family in question is not the African traditional patriarchal family, but one which models itself on the virtues of love, concern, caring, sense of belonging, hospitality and so

---

37. Symposium of Episcopal Conferences of Africa and Madagascar, General Assembly, Regional Episcopal Conference of Francophone West Africa. French text available in *Gorée 2003 Purification de la mémoire africaine: L'église-famille demande pardon* (Dakar: CERAO Editions, 2003).

forth. Many African scripture scholars and theologians elaborated on the significance of this concept and the challenges of its cultural backdrop, which needs to be redeemed by the gospel.[38]

SCCs, parishes, dioceses, and members of consecrated life in Africa are called to implement this ecclesiology in their daily lives so that they can really be salt and light on an African continent divided and at war because of tribal, ethnic, and political affiliations. The ecclesiology of church as family of God poses a real challenge and suggests a program for change, not only for Christians in Africa, but all over the world. Because this ecclesiology emphasizes the original unity of this "family" in the Trinity, all Christians everywhere in the world are challenged to reject certain negative values, including racism, tribalism, ethnicism, any kind of discrimination, a lack of solidarity with other Christians, and violence within the church. In this regard, it is also important to stress the complementary ecclesiology of fraternity.

Ecclesiologies using familial metaphors must be joined by a strong pastoral initiative aiming at education in Catholic Social Teaching (CST). One of the major challenges of the church's mission in Africa today is the promotion of justice, peace, and reconciliation at all levels. In order to become a good witness, the church as family of God in Africa must begin to implement these three things within her own structures: in Catholic families, parishes, dioceses, pastoral institutions, charitable institutions, and other places. If she does this, she will be better heard by politicians and authors of injustice and violence in Africa when she appeals for conversion. That is why it is so important to help all Catholics in Africa at all levels, including bishops, priests, religious, families, SCCs, parishes, youth, and schoolchildren, assimilate CST.

A second great challenge concerns the church as servant. A church that serves Africa may be negatively affected by the many social and economic crises destabilizing portions of the continent—these crises provoke survival reflexes that diminish the church's prophetic dynamism. The reality of fear in the hearts of many Africans, even in the church, is real; to serve them prophetically demands courage, and most people hesitate before the prospect of martyrdom. In both the clerical and lay faithful milieu, many prefer silence to courageous commitment.

Conclusion

This presentation of the changing faces of ecclesiology within the Roman Catholic Church in sub-Saharan Africa has shown the importance of attention to context, both the context of African values inherited from ancestors and the African historical context. Many African theologians have chosen to follow the important recommendation of the Vatican II document *Ad Gentes* (§22) that in-depth theological research be conducted in the contexts of both Christianity and local cultures and religions, in order to discern local values that might help root Christianity more deeply in local contexts. The aim of this research is to bring the gospel of Jesus to the heart of different cultures. The ultimate aim of all the ecclesiological trends analyzed in this chapter is that human beings situated in various cultures encounter Christ.

Why, in conducting Christian theology, begin with human values and human context? Because, as Pope John Paul II notes, it is

> man in the full truth of his existence, of his personal being and also of his community and social being—in the sphere of his own family, in the sphere of society and very diverse contexts, in the sphere of his own nation or people (perhaps still only that of his clan or tribe), and in the sphere of the whole of mankind—this man is the primary route that the Church must travel in fulfilling her mission . . . the way traced out by Christ himself. (*Redemptor Hominis* §14)

This is exactly the point at which contextual African ecclesiologies become universal: when they can be "heard" by any human being who has been, or who will be, touched in his or her mind or body by the common condition of humanity.

---

38. Okure, "Women in the Church," 3.

Bibliography

Agossou, Mèdéwalé-Jacob. *Christianisme africain: Une fraternité au-delà de l'ethnie*. Paris: Karthala, 1995.

Benedict XVI, Pope. *Africae Munus* [Post-synodal Apostolic Exhortation on the Church in Africa in Service of Reconciliation, Justice and Peace; November 19, 2011]. Vatican City: Libreria Editrice Vaticana, 2011. www.vatican.va.

Bujo, Bénézet, and Juvénal Ilunga Muya. *African Theology in the 21st Century: The Contribution of the Pioneers*. Vol. 1. Nairobi: Paulines Publications Africa, 2002.

Cheza, Maurice. *Le synode africain*. Paris: Karthala, 1996.

Dabiré, Jean-Marie Kusiele. "Eglise-Famille de Dieu." *Ricao: Revue de l'Institut Catholique de l'Afrique de l'Ouest* 14–15 (1996): 81–119.

Dujarier, Michel. *L'Église-Fraternité: Les origines de l'expression adelphotès—fraternitas aux trois premiers siècles du christianisme*. Paris: Cerf, 1991.

Facultés catholiques de Kinshasa. *Église-famille, Église-fraternité: Perspectives post-synodales*. Actes de la XXe Semaine Théologique de Kinshasa, 26 novembre–2 décembre 1995. Kinshasa: Facultés catholiques de Kinshasa, 1997.

Healey, Joseph. *Building the Church as Family of God: Evaluation of Small Christian Communities in Eastern Africa*. Eldoret: AMECEA Gaba Publications, CUEA Press, 2012.

Ilo, Stan Chu. "The African Palaver Method: A Model Synodal Process for Today's Church." *Concilium* 2 (2021): 68–76.

Ilo, Stan Chu, et al. *The Church as Salt and Light: Path to an African Ecclesiology of Abundant Life*. African Christian Studies 1. Eugene, OR: Pickwick, 2011.

John XXIII, Pope. *Mater et Magistra* [Encyclical on Christianity and Social Progress; May 15, 1961]. Vatican City: Libreria Editrice Vaticana, 1961. www.vatican.va.

John Paul II, Pope. *Ecclesia in Africa* [Post-synodal Apostolic Exhortation on the Church in Africa and Its Evangelizing Mission toward the Year 2000; September 14, 1995]. Vatican City: Libreria Editrice Vaticana, 1995. www.vatican.va.

———. *Redemptor Hominis* [Encyclical on the Redeemer of Man; March 2, 1979]. Vatican City: Libreria Editrice Vaticana, 1979. www.vatican.va.

Lowery, Stephanie A. *Identity and Ecclesiology: Their Relationship among Select African Theologians*. Eugene, OR: Pickwick, 2017.

Magesa, Laurenti. "Theology of Democracy." In *Democracy and Reconciliation: A Challenge for African Christianity*, edited by Laurenti Magesa et al. Nairobi: Acton, 1999.

Matand Bulembat, Jean-Bosco, et al., eds. *The Church as Family and Biblical Perspectives: Proceedings of the Eighth Congress of the Panafrican Association of Catholic Exegetes*. Kinshasa: APECA/PACE, 1999.

Moerschbacher, Marco. *Les laïcs dans une Eglise d'Afrique: L'œuvre du Cardinal Malula, 1917–1989*. Paris: Karthala, 2012.

Mubangizi, Odomaro. "The Church as Liberator: Towards an African Ecclesiology of Liberation." *Hekima Review* 37 (October 2007): 31–44.

Mucherera, Tapiwa N. *Meet Me at the Palaver*. Eugene, OR: Wipf & Stock, 2009.

Mulago, Vincent. *Un Visage africain du christianisme: L'union vitale bantu face à l'unité vitale ecclésiale*. Culture et religion. Paris: Présence Africaine, 1965.

———. "Vital Participation: The Cohesive Principle of the Bantu Community." In *Biblical Revelation and African Beliefs*, edited by Kwesi A. Dickson and Paul Ellingworth, 137–58. Maryknoll, NY: Orbis Books, 1969.

Nongo-Aziagbia, Nestor-Désiré. "La fraternité en Christ: fondements de l'être ecclésial et son incidence africaine." Doctoral thesis, Université de Strasbourg, 2012. NT: 2012STRAK013.

Nyamiti, Charles. "African Christologies Today." In *Faces of Jesus in Africa*, edited by Robert Schreiter, 3–23. Maryknoll, NY: Orbis Books, 1991.

———. *Christ as Our Ancestor: Christology from an African Perspective*. Gweru, Zimbabwe: Mambo Press, 1984.

———. "The Church as Christ's Ancestral Mediation: An Essay on African Ecclesiology." In *The Church in African Christianity: Innovative Essays in Ecclesiology*, edited by J. N. Kanyua Mugambi and Laurenti Magesa, 129–78. Nairobi: Acton, 1990.

———. *Some Contemporary Models of African Ecclesiology: A Critical Assessment in the Light of Biblical and Church Teaching*. Studies in African Christian Theology 3. Nairobi: CUEA Publications, 2007.

———. "The Trinity from an African Ancestral Perspective." *African Christian Studies* 12.4 (1996): 41–91.

———. *Studies in African Christian Theology*. Vol. 3: *Some Contemporary Models of African Ecclesiology: A Critical Assessment in the Light of Biblical and Church Teaching*. Nairobi: CUEA Publications, 2007.

Okure, Teresa. "Women in the Church." Presentation at SECAM Colloquium in Honor of Popes John XXIII and John Paul II. Rome, April 24–25, 2014.

Orobator, A. E. *The Church as Family: African Ecclesiology in Its Social Context*. Nairobi: Paulines Publications Africa, 2000.

———. *The Church We Want: Foundations, Theology, and Mission of the Church in Africa*. Nairobi: Paulines Publications, 2015.

———. *From Crisis to Kairos: The Mission of the Church in the Time of HIV/AIDS, Refugees, and Poverty*. Nairobi: Paulines Publications Africa, 2005.

———. "Perspectives and Trends in Contemporary African Ecclesiology." *Studia Missionalia* 45 (1996): 267–81.

Paul VI, Pope. "Homily during the Eucharistic Celebration at the Conclusion of the Symposium Organized by the Bishops of Africa." Kampala, July 31, 1969. www.vatican.va.

———. "Message Africae Terrarum." *La Documentation Catholique* 1505 (November 19, 1967): 1937–56.

———. "Voyage de Paul VI en Ouganda." *La Documentation Catholique* 1546 (September 7, 1969): 764a–b, 765a.

Quenum, Alphonse. *L'Eglise-Famille de Dieu: Chemin de fraternité*. Abidjan: ICAO, 1996.

Ramazani, Bishwende. *Augustin: Ecclesiologie africaine de famille de Dieu; Annonce et débat avec les contemporains*. Paris: L'Harmattan, 2007.

Thiam, Joseph. "Du clan tribal à la communauté chrétienne." In *Des prêtres noirs s'interrogent*, edited by Albert Abble et al., 41–56. Paris: Cerf, 1957.

Uzukwu, E. E. *A Listening Church: Autonomy and Communion in African Churches*. Maryknoll, NY: Orbis Books, 1996.

Vatican II. *Ad Gentes* [Decree on the Church's Missionary Activity]. Vatican City: Libreria Editrice Vaticana, 1965. www.vatican.va.

———. *Christus Dominus* [Decree on the Bishops' Pastoral Office in the Church]. Vatican City: Libreria Editrice Vaticana, 1965. www.vatican.va.

———. *Gaudium et Spes* [Pastoral Constitution on the Church in the Modern World]. Vatican City: Libreria Editrice Vaticana, 1965. www.vatican.va.

———. *Lumen Gentium* [Dogmatic Constitution on the Church]. Vatican City: Libreria Editrice Vaticana, 1964. www.vatican.va.

———. *Unitatis Redintegratio* [Decree on Ecumenism]. Vatican City: Libreria Editrice Vaticana, 1964. www.vatican.va.

Waliggo, J. M. "The African Clan as the True Model of the African Church." In *The Church in African Christianity: Innovative Essays in Ecclesiology*, edited by J. N. Kanyua Mugambi and Laurenti Magesa, 111–28. Nairobi: Acton, 1990.

Suggested Reading

Agossou, Mèdéwalé-Jacob. *Christianisme africain: Une fraternité au-delà de l'ethnie*. Paris, Karthala, 1995.

Appiah-Kubi, Francis. *Église Famille de Dieu: Un chemin pour les Églises d'Afrique*. Paris: Karthala, 2008.

Assenga, Petri. *Towards an African Model of Church as Family*. Berlin: Lambert Academic, 2009.

Benedict XVI, Pope. *Africae Munus* [Post-synodal Apostolic Exhortation on the Church in Africa in Service of Reconciliation, Justice and Peace; November 19, 2011]. Vatican City: Libreria Editrice Vaticana, 2011. www.vatican.va.

CUEA. *The Model of Church as Family: Meeting the African Challenge*. Nairobi: CUEA, 1999.

Facultés catholiques de Kinshasa. *Église-famille, Église-fraternité: Perspectives post-synodales. Actes de la XXᵉ Semaine Théologique de Kinshasa, 26 novembre–2 décembre 1995*. Kinshasa: Facultés catholiques de Kinshasa, 1997.

Healey, Joseph. *Building the Church as Family of God: Evaluation of Small Christian Communities in Eastern Africa*. Eldoret: AMECEA Gaba Publications, CUEA Press, 2012.

Ilo, Stan Chu, et al., eds. *The Church as Salt and Light: Path to an African Ecclesiology of Abundant Life*. African Christian Studies 1. Eugene, OR: Pickwick, 2011.

John Paul II, Pope. *Ecclesia in Africa* [Post-synodal Apostolic Exhortation on the Church in Africa and Its Evangelizing Mission toward the Year 2000; September 14, 1995]. Vatican City: Libreria Editrice Vaticana, 1995. www.vatican.va.

Kalamba Nsapo, Sylvain. *Les ecclésiologies d'épiscopats africains subsahariens: Essai d'analyse de contenu.* Brussels: Société ouverte, 2000.

Kanyandago, Peter, et al., eds. *Inculturating the Church in Africa.* Nairobi: Paulines Publications Africa, 2001.

Lowery, Stephanie A. *Identity and Ecclesiology: Their Relationship among Select African Theologians.* Eugene, OR: Pickwick, 2017.

Magesa, Laurenti. *Anatomy of Inculturation: Transforming the Church in Africa.* 1st reprint. Nairobi: Paulines Publications Africa, 2007.

Matand Bulembat, Jean-Bosco, ed. *The Church as Family and Biblical Perspectives: Proceedings of the Ninth Congress of the Panafrican Association of Catholic Exegetes.* Kinshasa: APECA/PACE, 2002.

Matand Bulembat, Jean-Bosco, et al., eds. *The Church as Family and Biblical Perspectives: Proceedings of the Eighth Congress of the Panafrican Association of Catholic Exegetes.* Kinshasa: APECA/PACE, 1999.

Mubangizi, Odomaro. "The Church as Liberator: Towards an African Ecclesiology of Liberation." *Hekima Review* 37 (October 2007): 31–44.

Mugambi, J. N. K., and Laurenti Magesa, eds. *The Church in African Christianity: Innovative Essays in Ecclesiology.* African Challenge. Nairobi: Initiatives, 1990.

Ndongala Maduku, Ignace. *Pour des Eglise régionales en Afrique.* Paris: Karthala, 1999.

Nongo-Azagbia, Nestor-Désiré. *La fraternité en Christ: Fondements de l'être ecclésial et son incidence africaine.* Thèse soutenue à l'Université de Strasbourg, 2012.

Nyamiti, Charles. *Studies in African Christian Theology.* Vol. 3: *Some Contemporary Models of African Ecclesiology: A Critical Assessment in the Light of Biblical and Church Teaching.* Nairobi: CUEA Publications, 2007.

Oluwa, C. Donatus. *The Church as the Extended Family of God: Toward a New Direction for African Ecclesiology.* Bloomington, IN: Xlibris, 2011.

Onwubiko, O. Alozie. *The Church as the Family of God.* Nsukka: Fulladu Publishing, 1999.

Orobator, A. E. *The Church as Family: African Ecclesiology in Its Social Context.* Nairobi: Paulines Publications Africa, 2000.

———, ed. *The Church We Want: Foundations, Theology and Mission of the Church in Africa.* Nairobi: Paulines Publications, 2015.

———. "Perspectives and Trends in Contemporary African Ecclesiology." *Studia Missionalia* 45 (1996): 267–81.

Ramazani, Bishwende. *Augustin: Ecclesiologie africaine de famille de Dieu; Annonce et débat avec les contemporains.* Paris: L'Harmattan, 2007.

———. *Augustin: Eglise-famille-de-Dieu; Esquisse d'ecclésiologie africaine.* Paris: L'Harmattan, 2001.

Uzukwu, E. E. *A Listening Church: Autonomy and Communion in African Churches.* Eugene, OR: Wipf & Stock, 1996.

Key Words

Africa
African theology
church
inculturation
justice and peace
laity
ministry
prophetism
small Christian communities

Who Is Jesus Christ for Us?
Christology in African Catholicism

Chukwuemeka Anthony Atansi

Christ Alive Yesterday, Today, and Tomorrow in Africa

Jesus Christ is experienced by most African Catholics as a living person.[1] The understanding of his identity and mission are expressed in terms that speak of Christ's real presence and power. In other words, Christ is not seen simply as a historical personage, a sociocultural icon, or a figure from the past. He is seen, understood, and, very importantly, worshiped and celebrated as the real, abiding gift of God's own life. Hence, Christ is proclaimed as *Good News*, and as the subject of lived faith and hope in Africa. Furthermore, Christological reflection in African Catholicism is an effort at the creative disclosure of the presence and action of Christ, or the experience of his ongoing self-revelation in the various circumstances of people's life *hic et nunc*. This makes the life of faith in Christ and theological conversations on his person and work in Africa an exciting adventure.

In this chapter, I will discuss the understanding and significance of Jesus Christ in African Catholicism.[2] The discussion will be advanced in three main sections. The first section is devoted to the subject of the proclamation of Christ by many African Catholics, not only in churches but also in homes and on the streets. The proclamation will be treated as grassroots Christologies or what some have rightly described as "lived Christologies," or what I propose to call "celebratory Christologies."[3] The second section will build on the understanding of grassroots Christologies in African Catholicism by offering an overview of the images of Christ as healer, liberator, and king. These are popular Christological images in various Christian communities in Nigeria, Ghana, Kenya, and Uganda. This section presents how these images function in the daily narratives of faith of many African Christians. The third and final section examines some of the enduring themes in contemporary Christological debates in African Catholicism. The selected themes are (1) Christ and the longing for positive transformation of societies in Africa; and (2) Christ and the subject of religious diversity in Africa.

Christ in African Catholicism: A Proclamation

At the heart of Christology is the *proclamation* of the life, work, saving death, and resurrection of Jesus Christ. Therefore, every Christological exploration ought always to begin with an account of how the Christ-event is proclaimed—confessed and cele-

---

1. In this work, the names "Jesus," "Christ," "Jesus Christ," "Jesus the Christ," and "Christ Jesus" are used interchangeably with no theological distinction intended. The creed followed in this essay is faith "in the *one* Lord Jesus Christ," which represents the basic statement of Christian belief in the unity and identity of Christ (cf. 1 Cor 8:6).

2. The focus of this essay is African Catholicism. However, what I say here may also apply to other Christian groups in Africa. Indeed, African Christianity exudes immense commonalities among the different Christian groups in the way Africans answer the question, "Who do you say that I am?" Our modest effort here to highlight the account of a particular African religious tradition—in this case, African Catholicism—is only to cast light on it with a view to illuminating the common faith that Christians share in the Lordship of Jesus Christ in Africa.

3. Bediako, "Guest Editorial: Lived Christology," 1. See also Pénoukou, "Christology in the Village."

brated—among Christians. Aylward Shorter, a pioneer of Catholic Mission in Africa, points to one of the challenges in African Christology that is helpful in the exposition in this first section. Shorter observed that Christology in Africa has often been the outcome of the work of scholars in the libraries of universities and seminaries. He maintains that Christology has been a notional theology that does not always take seriously the embodied experience and imaginative expression of popular faith.[4] For Shorter, this lacuna explains why little progress has been made in bringing the fruits of scholars' Christological engagement to bear in the life of many Christians, and on the social situations of many Africans.[5] This view of Shorter, articulated over three decades ago, still remains a challenge today. Martin Munyao also identified the particular challenge that the lived Christology of Africans has remained largely marginal against the dominant institutional Christological language and symbols of Western missionaries and churches.[6] For this reason I will locate my preliminary Christological discourse in this chapter at the heart of the experience and expressions of Christ's identity and work within grassroots Catholic Christian communities in four English-speaking sub-Saharan African countries—Nigeria, Ghana, Uganda, and Kenya. I have chosen these countries because of the sociological works on the Africans' experience of Christ, particularly at the grassroots level, which are readily available to me.

For my discussion of the African experience and proclamation of Christ, I draw on insights from the sociological findings in the works on African Christologies by respected authors—Donald Goergen, Diane Stinton, Clifton Clarke, and Victor Ezigbo—who have carried out extensive empirical research on the popular images of Christ in sub-Saharan Africa.[7] The contributions of these authors appear prominently in the procedure of their research, or methodology, which aided their identification of the popularity of the images. In each case, the author's research procedures favor qualitative field-based research, which, nevertheless, integrates quantitative research.[8] In their socio-Christological works, the qualitative methods that they employed, according to them, encompass "in-depth interviews, focus groups, participant observation in a number of settings for christological expression, as well as interpretation of song lyrics and visual representations of Christology."[9] This practice enabled each of these authors to gain privileged access to the experiences of their respondents in their specific social context. Thus, in presenting the fruits of their inquiries, they offer a descriptive interpretation and not simply a statistical demonstration of the experiences of their interviewees. However, in order to avoid the danger of overgeneralizations or the risk of personalization, effort was also made to ground the observations in empirical data. These combined methodological procedures served to illustrate similar phenomena about the experience and understanding of Christ's identity and work across sub-Saharan Africa.[10]

---

4. Shorter, "Folk Christianity and Functional Christology," 135.

5. For a similar line of argumentation, see Stan Chu Ilo, "Beginning Afresh with Christ in the Search for Abundant Life in Africa."

6. Munyao, "Christology in Africa," 414.

7. Some of the main works that I rely on in this chapter are Goergen, "Quest for the Christ of Africa"; Stinton, *Jesus of Africa*, as well as some of Stinton's in-depth articles and essays: "Jesus–Immanuel, Image of the Invisible God"; "Encountering Jesus at the Well"; and "Jesus Christ, Living Water in Africa Today"; also Ezigbo, *Re-Imagining African Christologies*, particularly "Grassroots Christologies in Contemporary African Christianity"; and Clarke, *African Christology*. It is important to note that some of the sources derive from theologians beyond African Catholicism. See also my remarks in n. 2 above

8. The qualitative method, as distinguished from the quantitative method, is a unique method that is most appropriate to specific forms of ethnographical research. It prioritizes personal encounter and active conversations between the researchers and the interviewees, who in this case are African Christians.

9. Stinton, "Jesus–Immanuel, Image of the Invisible God," 9; see also Stinton, *Jesus of Africa*, 255–58; Clarke, *African Christology*, 5, 10; Ezigbo, *Re-Imagining African Christologies*, 104–9.

10. Stinton, "Jesus–Immanuel, Image of the Invisible God," 9–10.

Christ, Experienced and Expressed in the Grassroots Christian Communities

In his response to the question "where do we begin?" in the search for the meaning and significance of Jesus Christ, Cameroonian theologian Jean Marc Éla said that "it must be at the grassroots."[11] The search for faith in Jesus Christ, and an attempt to discern, articulate, and appropriate what this faith means and does, according to Éla, must find its roots in and draw upon the Christological imagination of ordinary believers.[12] I suggest here and reflect on two reasons for beginning at the grassroots, drawing from (1) the example of Christ himself in the Gospel; and (2) the ecclesiological principle of *sensus fidelium*. Together, these two reasons substantiate the fact that the experience of Christ originates in and flows from the hearts of believers.

Regarding the first reason given above, there is something of an illumination found in Jesus's approach, which calls for a kind of *ressourcement* (return) to the grassroots Christian communities as the primary locus of Christological reflection in African Catholic Christianity. The approach is important because it takes the context of encounter between Jesus and his African followers seriously, just as the Lord took the historicity of his disciples seriously in his desire to lead them into a deeper understanding of the One in whom they were putting faith and hope. "Who do *people* say that the Son of Man is?" was the very first question Jesus posed to his disciples concerning his person, and accordingly, his ministry (Matt 16:13; Mark 8:27; Luke 9:18).[13] The second question within the same Gospel pericope is "Who do *you* say I am?" (Matt 16:15; Mark 8:29; Luke 9:20). There is no doubt the two questions could be held as closely related. Even though Jesus was conscious of his identity and mission, and even though his words and deeds gave testimony to these, Jesus's question to his followers about who he is and what he does shows the evidential character about his identity and mission required from the *people* he was constituting into a church. The mention of church brings me to the second reason.

This reason is in line with the ecclesiological principle of *sensus fidelium*. This principle is articulated in the document of the Second Vatican Council, the Dogmatic Constitution on the Church, *Lumen Gentium*. The Council Fathers declare:

> The holy people of God share also in Christ's priestly, prophetic, and kingly office; it spreads abroad a living witness to Him, especially by means of a life of faith and charity. . . . The entire body of the faithful, anointed as they are by the Holy One, cannot err in matters of belief. They manifest this special property by means of the whole peoples' supernatural discernment in matters of faith. . . . That discernment in matters of faith is aroused and sustained by the Spirit of truth. Through it, the people of God adheres unwaveringly to the faith given once and for all to the saints, penetrates it more deeply with right thinking, and applies it more fully in its life. (§12)[14]

These conciliar statements support our argument for regarding the experience and expression of faith in Jesus Christ at the grassroots level in African Catholicism as the primary locus in elaborating Christology in Africa. They also mean that who the ordinary Christians believe and proclaim Jesus is, and what he does or can do, should be taken seriously and can never be cast aside. The experience and confession of Christ as "true God and true man," as we shall see further in the second section of this essay, are always the fruit of the life and worship of a believing community.

Notably, Christological experience and expressions "go beyond formal written expressions to include informal expressions, for example, in wor-

---

11. Éla, *My Faith as an African*, 143, 65. Éla further discusses this idea in the second part of the book under the title "Faith at the Grassroots."

12. Éla, *My Faith as an African*, 55. See also Éla's discussion of "A Theology Coming from the People," in *My Faith as an African*, 174–77.

13. Unless noted, all quotations from the scriptures in this work are taken from the New Revised Standard Version (New York: Oxford University Press, 1989). Hereafter NRSV.

14. See also *Catechism of the Catholic Church* §93.

ship, prayer, preaching, artwork, drama, gesture, and symbols."[15] In other words, the sources and methods of the grassroots Christologies are not limited to the sacred scripture and the traditional creedal formulations, as normative and important as these are. This idea is corroborated by Nigerian theologian and ecclesiastic, John Onaiyekan, who asserts that "what the African is saying about Christ is not to be found only in the books and articles published by the few." He maintains that "we must, in characteristic African fashion, listen to the oral expressions of the people: their hymns, sermons, and proverbs." He further refers to his own experiences of having "heard some of the most profound christological insights from the mouths of poor illiterates, rich in nothing but their deep faith in Christ." Onaiyekan then suggests that "the African theologian must count among his primary tasks the effort to listen to, and speak on behalf of our people as they express their life in Christ in the daily circumstances of their lives."[16]

Onaiyekan's recommendation is not new. Veteran Kenyan churchman Henry Okullu had upheld such a view in his explanation of the fundamental criterion for the development of Christology in Africa. In exploring African Christology, Okullu opined that

> we should go first to the fields, to the village church, to Christian homes to listen to those spontaneously uttered prayers before people go to bed. . . . We must listen to the throbbing drumbeats and the clapping of hands accompanying the impromptu singing in the churches; and must look at the way in which faith in Christ is being planted in Africa through music, drama, songs, dances, art, paintings. We must listen to the preaching of the sophisticated pastor as well as that of the simple village vicar.[17]

Then Okullu asks a pointed question, "Can it be that all this is an empty show?" "It is impossible," he rightly responds.

To be sure, the proclamation of Christ in African Catholicism does not occlude theological investigation, systematization, and reconstruction about the meaning and significance of his identity and mission. Many valuable works on the African experience and expressions of Jesus Christ have been produced by African theologians and other theologians outside Africa.[18] They have tried successfully to offer a systematic account of the origins and developments of Christologies in African Christianity. Their Christological contributions are explored as representatives of various trends of theological reflection on Christ in Africa. In an essay of this length, it will be impossible to survey the many rich, though at times complex and confusing, Christological trends in African theology.[19] A more important reason for not surveying the trends here is that the understanding of Christ's identity and work in the grassroots Christian communities could also be traced even in the constructive (academic) Christologies. On this point, Kwame Bediako was right to assert that grassroots

---

15. Ezigbo, *Re-Imagining African Christologies*, 104–5.
16. Onaiyekan, "Christological Trends in Contemporary African Theology," 358.
17. Okullu, *Church and Politics in East Africa*, 53–54, cited in Stinton, "Jesus–Immanuel, Image of the Invisible God," 8.
18. Some of the pertinent ones include Nyamiti, *Christ as Our Ancestor*; Mbiti, "'For Now We See in a Glass Darkly'"; Mugambi and Magesa, *Jesus in African Christianity*; Schreiter, *Faces of Jesus in Africa*; Orobator, "Quest for an African Christ"; Dube, "Who Do You Say I Am?"; Okure, "Jesus and the Samaritan Woman (Jn 1:1-42) in Africa"; Cook, "African Experience of Jesus."
19. Agbonkhianmeghe Orobator, however, argues that, historically, African theology (this could also be said specifically of African Christology) has been interpreted largely under three major categories. The first is "African theology," also referred to as "theology of adaptation, incarnation, or inculturation," or simply "*inculturation* theology." The second category is "Black theology," which is also considered as "African *liberation* theology." The third category, which Orobator identifies as "a third force," that is, "a third major trend in African theological enterprise," is "*reconstruction* theology." See Orobator, "Sky Is Wide Enough," 36–41. For a summary discussion of the trends, see de Jongh, "Contemporary Trends in Christology in Africa."

Christologies are an abiding element of all theology (and Christology) in Africa, and cannot be entirely replaced.[20]

So, then, in what images do the African Catholic Christians—ordinary believers and professional theologians alike—proclaim and reflect on the identity and mission of Jesus Christ? A response to this question is the subject of the next section.

Images of Christ in African Catholicism: "True God and True Man"

A survey of some recent key publications on grassroots Christologies in African Catholic Christology reveals an abundance of images of Christ. An overview of key Christological images shows the richness of African Christologies in general. It also demonstrates the significant contribution to the ongoing development of Christology in African Catholicism and beyond. Some of the images (among many others) that come to the fore include the following: Christ as Healer, Christ as Life-Giver or Abundant Life, Christ as Liberator, Christ as King or Chief, and Christ as Provider. There are minor variations of these images, and at times there is considerable overlap. For this reason, it is possible to trace clear points of convergence that allow a simple but provisional categorization of these sometimes apparently divergent proposals.[21] For example, similar emphases are brought out in the images of Christ as Healer and Christ as Life-Giver. Likewise, there is a considerable overlap between Christ as Liberator and Christ as King or as Provider. There is also a distinction between those images that are more universal and draw on language explicitly found in scripture, and those images that do not utilize explicitly biblical language but are rooted more naturally in the particularity of the African traditional religion and social-cultural context.

Without prejudice to these controversies, I will focus on what I consider the more dominant Christological images—images that are pervasive in the present-day African Christian consciousness. Three such images are of special note: Christ as Healer, as Liberator, and as King. I have chosen to discuss these three Christological images because, as Goergen rightly observed following the empirical study he conducted in Kenya, these images emerge from within context-aware, praxis-oriented, sociopolitically conscious theologies.[22] In other words, the images have the potential to foster a new African Christian and social consciousness within Catholicism and beyond. Stinton herself (like the other authors) also noted that there is manifold evidence from the sociological findings that the experience and proclamation of Jesus Christ, particularly in the three images—healer, liberator, and king—hold "a prime place in the imagination and in the lived experience of vast numbers of Christians."[23] They were by far the most "visible" Christological images, in which Jesus Christ "is clearly perceived in terms of "Immanuel—God with us—in Africa, and in terms of being the 'image of the invisible God,' or the one who puts a human face on the transcendent."[24]

Christ Our Healer

Certainly, healing is a central human concern. It is highly vital in African consciousness and, even more so, given the reality of many preventable and treatable illnesses still killing people in the continent, and the double burden of communicable and non-communicable diseases wearing down the

---

20. Bediako, *Jesus in Africa*, 17.

21. Theologians have grappled with the issue of how to categorize the various images of Christ in the African Christian and theological landscape. It is not my intention to offer a discussion of that issue here. For a quick instructive, though not exhaustive, categorization of some of the images, see Moloney, "African Christology." See also Stinton, *Jesus of Africa*, 49–53 and 54–220.

22. Goergen, "Quest for the Christ of Africa," 11.

23. Stinton, "Jesus–Immanuel, Image of the Invisible God," 38. Apart from ancestor, the images of Christ as healer, liberator, and king are three of the four images Goergen identifies as dominant in his own research. According to him, the images receive much emphasis among African theologians, pastors, and ordinary Christians ("Quest for the Christ of Africa," 6).

24. Stinton, "Jesus–Immanuel, Image of the Invisible God," 38.

continent. So, the quest for healing, wholeness, and human and cosmic flourishing, as Cécé Kolié puts it, is fundamental for the African person.[25]

Many African Catholics proclaim Christ as healer, obviously, because he is also portrayed as such in the Gospels. The vast majority of Catholic Christians, who proclaim Christ as their healer, expect that just as Christ in the Gospels healed all the sick people that were brought to him (see Matt 15:30; Luke 4:40), he would also heal them of *all* diseases and their causes. Stinton particularly narrates some of her personal encounters with Christians who confess such beliefs. She tells, for instance, about Mary Kizito, a lecturer (surprisingly, perhaps, given her views as an intellectual) at Daystar University, Nairobi, who strongly upholds the belief that "Jesus as healer can take away all the diseases, like HIV/AIDS and malaria, which kill people in Africa."[26] Kizito is representative of the vast majority of Christians who not only uphold such a belief but expect that their proclamation of Christ as healer will move him to cure them of their diseases, deliver them of all their ailments, and restore them to physical health and fullness of life.[27]

Stinton also provides some other very vivid data regarding this way of understanding Christ's identity and work as healer.[28] In homes, churches, so-called healing ministries, streets, markets, offices, and, astonishingly, in clinics and hospitals too, Christ is invoked in often loud tones to heal those who are sick. Christ the healer is sought even in unexpected places, as Stan Chu Ilo exposes in a very recent investigation about the search for health, healing, and wholeness among African Christians.[29] Victor Ezigbo's analysis of a number of case studies of healing in Nigeria shows that there is an abundance of healing services with prayers and exorcism, with many healing claims and testimonies.[30] Ezigbo points out the readiness of many Christians across various denominations to locate Jesus-talk and action, largely in terms of and within the framework of healing and the quests to achieve total well-being.[31] One still finds many African Catholic Christians engaging in long nighttime prayer vigils, protracted fasts, exuberant crusades, conventions, and "miraculous meetings" organized by prominent and "powerful men and women of God" purported to be healers in the name of Christ the healer.[32] These Catholic Christians and some of their leaders hope that, by the exercise of their agency in and through these religious means, they will be healed, delivered, and restored to fullness of life. They see these religious exercises as acts of their faith and hope in what Jesus the Healer will do for them.

A constructive or sympathetic assessment reveals that the health gospel forms and informs a particular Christological mindset that recognizes Jesus's identity as a savior and his miraculous power to bestow blessings, particularly of health and wholeness. It seems that such an image of Christ, seen through his saving power to heal, is the way in which Christians strive to make sense

---

25. Kolié, "Jesus as Healer?," 132.
26. Stinton, *Jesus of Africa*, 65.
27. Duke professor of New Testament Craig S. Keener has assembled a massive two-volume work demonstrating that, in fact, millions of Christians in Africa even today hold such confessions and claim to have experienced a miracle through belief in Christ as healer. See Craig S. Keener, "Healing in Mainline Churches: Examples in Africa," in *Miracles: The Credibility of the New Testament Accounts*, 2 vols. (Grand Rapids, MI: Baker Academic, 2011), 1:309–58.
28. Stinton, *Jesus of Africa*, 64–71.
29. Ilo, "Searching for Healing in a Miraculous Stream"; see also Ilo, "Interpreting the Search for Health and Healing among African Charismatic and Pentecostal Groups."
30. Ezigbo, *Re-Imagining African Christologies*, 120–26.
31. Ezigbo, *Re-Imagining African Christologies*, 120–21.
32. For an example of where these so-called charismatic practices are carried out and promoted, see Thomas Landy's account of what Landy, citing Stan Chu Ilo, rightly described as the largest popular Catholic gathering and event in Nigeria (Thomas M. Landy, "All Night at Fr. Mbaka's Adoration Ministry: A Real and Moving Presence in Nigeria," *Catholics & Cultures*, https://www.catholicsandcultures.org/all-night-fr-mbakas-adoration-ministry-real-and-moving-presence-nigeria). Landy's write-up is based on his visits to the adoration ground and his personal conversation with the popular priest Fr. Ejike Mbaka.

of, or as Ezigbo puts it, "to perceive and relate to," the acclamation of Christ as "a prophet mighty in deed and word" (Luke 24:19), as well as the doctrinal formulations about him as "true God and true man."[33] They believe, and I think the Christians are right about this, that as "true man," Christ represents what a good and full life is in the fullest sense. Christ also knows and shares their experiences of brokenness wrought by sickness and disease, becoming through his incarnation an advocate for them and for their well-being. That is why he took on flesh, a humanity that is equipped to feel what human beings feel. For the Gospels portrayed Jesus with perfect human empathy, as always having pity on individuals and people who were sick (see Mark 1:41; Matt 9:36). As "true God," the one "in whom the fullness of God dwells" (Col 2:9), he has the power to take away all the diseases and to restore their physical health.

In addition to this biblical and creedal underpinning for the Christians' narrative about Jesus's healing power, there is also an underlying traditional worldview. The Christian proclamation of Christ as Healer also has an expectation nurtured against the background of the African religious-cultural worldview.[34] In this worldview, health in Africa does not mean only lack of sickness; it connotes well-being in a holistic sense. It touches on the entire constitution of the human person and the whole constellation of his or her environment and social sphere. Health, therefore, is appreciated as encompassing physical, mental, spiritual, and social well-being. For this reason, sickness is not primarily seen to be the result of only physical or psychological symptoms but also of deeply spiritual causes. This is how Stinton presents the view of sickness and the corresponding quest for healing in the context:

> Illness is viewed as a calamity that not only strikes the particular individual, but also indicates a disruption of social relationships, thereby making it a family and communal concern. Where health is viewed as being more than biological, encompassing physical, mental, spiritual, social, and environmental well-being, illness signifies an unfortunate disruption of harmony in these factors. Organic causes may well be recognized, yet the overriding belief attributes sickness to spiritual or supernatural causes.[35]

From this perspective, Catholic Christians, in confessing Christ as Healer, believe and hope that he has the power to also heal the suffering nations of Africa. By the exercise of his healing might, Christ can restore the nations of Africa that have been "wounded by the slave trade, colonization, the post-colonial formation of the nation-states, neo-colonialism's economic dependency, intertribal violence and war, the corruption of many post-independence national leaders."[36] The healing Jesus, as Clifton Clarke both narrates and hopes, "will bring order and integrity into African politics and socio-economic life."[37] Christ's healing power, says Clarke, "transcends and contradicts the distorted image of Africa created by European oppression."[38] This Christological narrative receives more determined expression in the second image that I shall present.

Christ Our Liberator

Also enshrined within the Christological currents in African Catholicism is the image of Christ as Liberator. The image is popular in the ecclesial, social, and intellectual contexts of contemporary African Catholic Christianity. Stinton underscores that Christ the Liberator is a widely confessed image that arose from within the context of her field research in Kenya, Uganda, and Ghana.[39] According to Stinton, "An analysis of the oral Christolo-

---

33. Ezigbo, *Re-Imagining African Christologies*, 139.
34. Ezigbo, *Re-Imagining African Christologies*, 120–22.
35. Stinton, *Jesus of Africa*, 63.
36. Goergen gathers from his findings that the belief and understanding that Jesus the healer will bring about the transformation of things, and that he will bring about the desired social change in Africa, are also dominant.
37. Clarke, "Healer of Africa," 173.
38. Clarke, "Healer of Africa," 173.
39. For a detailed presentation and analysis of the data, see Stinton, *Jesus of Africa*, 205–7.

gies reveals almost unanimous assent to the image of Jesus as liberator, with interpretations generally favouring personal and spiritual dimensions such as deliverance from sin, fear, and evil powers."[40] She tells of how the narratives about Jesus as Liberator are upheld not only by ordinary Christians but also by the leaders. In preaching about Jesus's identity and work as liberator, the Gospel of Luke 4:18–19 (cf. Isa 61:1) is often cited. Here is found the programmatic summary of Jesus's liberating mission:

> The Spirit of the Lord is upon me,
> because he has anointed me
> to bring good news to the poor.
> He has sent me to proclaim liberty to captives,
> And recovery of sight to the blind,
> to let the oppressed go free,
> to proclaim a year of favor
> from the Lord.

For Christians and their leaders, this passage tellingly authenticates the fact that Christ is liberator not just for the people of his time but for those who continue to proclaim him as such in today's Africa. The passage is all the more assuring because, according to the people today, Jesus himself had expressed that this message of liberation is being fulfilled *today*, even as contemporary hearers in Africa are decreeing and listening to it (Luke 4:21). They uphold their firm belief that Christ continues to exercise his liberating power in those specific terms that are underlined in the passage quoted above.

The quest for liberation has also shaped and continues to shape not only the Christians' experience and expression of who Jesus Christ is, but also the Christological constructions of earliest and contemporary thinkers of African Christology.[41] I will draw on insights from a pioneer African theologian, Jean Marc Éla, in order to show how "liberation" has been a major concern in recent and contemporary African Christian Christology. Éla was a renowned Cameroonian sociologist and theologian, who is widely acclaimed for his critical and engaging reimagination of the identity and saving work of Christ, particularly as Liberator. Éla was deeply involved in the "search for faith and experiences of faith in local communities."[42] In his theological reflections and pastoral engagements, he privileges the image of Christ the Liberator, which for him is the comprehensible image that speaks to the struggle for faith and life among those rejected by history, many of whom are found within the local Christian communities, particularly at the grassroots.[43]

Éla presents the meaning of the Christological image of liberator in the light of "three main critical issues or concerns which are interrelated."[44] The first major issue that Éla highlights for understanding the image of Christ as Liberator is the quest by many African theologians for the emancipation of African Christianity and, consequently, Christology from the "ethnocentrism of European theology," which has dominated Christianity and theology for centuries.[45] This dominance, according to Éla, has resulted in the "Babylonian captivity,"[46] or what John Pobee refers to as the "North Atlantic captivity"[47] of African Christianity to Roman structures, doctrines, and practices.[48] In line with this, Éla rightly argues that the image of Christ the

---

40. Stinton, *Jesus of Africa*, 213.
41. See, for example, Magesa, "Christ the Liberator and Africa Today," 79–92; Oduyoye and Amoah, "Christ for African Women," 35–46; Nasimiyu-Wasike, "Christology and an African Woman's Experience," 70–81.
42. Éla, *My Faith as an African*, 55.
43. See, for example, Jean-Marc Éla, *From Charity to Liberation*; *My Faith as an African*; *African Cry*; "Christianity and Liberation in Africa," 136–53; "Memory of the African People and the Cross of Christ," 17–35.
44. Stinton, *Jesus of Africa*, 194. I am indebted to Stinton's analysis of the Christological reflections and contributions of Jean-Marc Éla to the present formulation and dominant expressions of Christ as Liberator in African Christianity.
45. Éla, *My Faith as an African*, 154, cited in Stinton, *Jesus of Africa*, 194.
46. Éla, *My Faith as an African*, 154.
47. Pobee, "Jesus Christ—The Life of the World," 5.
48. See Stinton, *Jesus of Africa*, 194.

Liberator would entail that Christology first be freed from the attendant Christologies that present an "abstract" Christ dispossessed of "a personal and tangible reality," disincarnated and "locked within the conceptual framework of Greco-Latin philosophies and neo-Thomist metaphysically-grounded theologies."[49] He expresses the idea further and points to the urgency of taking the Christological image of Christ the Liberator seriously. He says:

> At a time when the urgent need for Christology is felt in Africa, it is imperative to liberate the faith of the local churches from formulae that have the effect of obscuring Jesus from being recognized by other people because they emanate from a sort of foreign cultural monopoly. Shouldn't we question the validity of approaches that take no consideration at all of the tensions and conflicts in the context of which the people of today hear the gospel in contemporary African societies?[50]

Éla considers this question to be very important, given what he maintains are "faulty Christologies" arising from the collusion of Western Christianity with colonial conquest and the slave trade.[51] These Christologies were also propagated by some of the missionaries to Africa, who formulated and employed "an imperial image of Christ," to justify oppressive powers, and a "slave-trader Christ," "used to promote faith as escapism from present suffering through promise of heavenly bliss."[52] Consequently, against any presentation of Jesus Christ via a theology of the "salvation of souls," Éla continually insists that "salvation in Jesus Christ *is* liberation from every form of slavery."[53] Moreover, according to him, the church ought to witness to this salvation by creating conditions that liberate humans and allow them to thrive.

The second issue that is also helpful for understanding the meaning and implications of the Christological image of liberator is what Éla identifies as "the traps of inculturation"[54] or "the dead-ends of ethno-theology."[55] It is related to the tendency found among many African theologians in their effort to integrate the African pre-Christian religious-cultural heritage with the Christian faith. In order to affirm the unique identity and selfhood of the African Christian, all in the name of inculturation, certain authors continually pay insufficient attention to the African person and to his or her individual and social concrete reality, when such individuals are in fact the concrete subject of history, and they remain at the epicenter of every context. Here, Éla criticizes the attempts to reinterpret Jesus in Africa, which are limited to a theology of simply "digging the sources" found in the traditional African culture. He maintains that inculturation Christologies are insufficient for enabling the Christian faith in Africa to face the challenge of current socioeconomic and political crises.

Along the same lines, Éla notes a third concern

---

49. Éla, "Memory of the African People and the Cross of Christ," 20. For a similar discussion of the meaning of Christ the liberator, and its significance for African Christology, see Magesa, "Christ the Liberator and Africa Today." Magesa, in a large part of the work, offers some methodological and contextual considerations for "liberating Christology." In the light of these considerations he argues that "Jesus as Liberator" in the African situation is therefore much more than just a metaphor." "It is an attempt," he maintains, "to present the only Jesus that can be comprehensible and credible among the African rural masses, urban poor and idealistic youth" (85). On this issue, both Éla and Magesa seem to suggest that the liberation of the African would come about through a liberation of Christology, and consequently of Christianity in Africa.

50. Éla, "Memory of the African People and the Cross of Christ," 20.

51. Éla, *My Faith as an African*, 111, cited in Stinton, *Jesus of Africa*, 194.

52. Jean-Marc Éla, "Le Motif de la liberation dans la theologie africaine," *Les nouvelles rationalités africaines* 2.5 (1986): 43, translated and cited in Stinton, *Jesus of Africa*, 194.

53. Éla, "Christianity and Liberation in Africa," 142.

54. Jean-Marc Éla, "Globalisation et pauperisation: Un défi à la theologie africaine," in *Liberation Theologies on Shifting Grounds: A Clash of Socio-Economic and Cultural Paradigms*, ed. G. De Schrijver (Leuven: Leuven University Press, 1998), 161–65, translated and cited in Stinton, *Jesus of Africa*, 194.

55. Éla, "Memory of the African People and the Cross of Christ," 19–20.

toward a more robust appropriation of the Christological image of liberator. It is what has been referred to as "the irruption of the Third World," precisely, its epistemological rupture from Western Christology.[56] This rupture, according to Éla, is necessary for doing Christology more meaningfully and effectively from within the grassroots Christian communities. For him, it is also vital if we really wish to rediscover the identity and mission of Christ from the "periphery" and its implication for the "actual situation in Africa."[57] Elsewhere, Éla offers a sociopolitical analysis of the situation in Africa with its many unfortunate realities and burden of underdevelopment, which are still prevalent today—and these make his insights relevant for reflecting further on who Jesus Christ is for Africans and in Africa today. According to him, the realities range from the disillusionment with flag independences across the continent, through the international domination that perpetuates injustice in political, economic, social, and cultural spheres, to the internal factors stemming from widespread neocolonialism.[58] It is against these backdrops that Éla questions and responds—as many African Catholic Christians still question and try to respond—to the meaning of Christ as our Liberator. That is why he concludes that, for him, and rightly so, "it is impossible to attempt an overall interpretation of the Good News from our African situation without making liberation the fundamental axis of a theology (Christology) which comes from our people."[59]

Christ Our King

Among the several Christological images appropriated in relation to leadership in contemporary African Catholicism is Christ Our King. It is an image that is in line with the African Christian imagination and quest for authentic leadership—a quest that still prevails in many African societies today. Just as it was in some strands of Jewish socio-religious expectation, the image is used to express the African Christian understanding of Christ as one who will offer imminent access to a domain of unassailable security, well-being, and flourishing. This is understandable given the unfortunate situation of the febrile atmosphere of local, regional, national, and global sociopolitical crises, in which the issue of leadership has been—and still remains—very critical. The failure of the regeneration, renewal, and transformation of many African nation-states is traceable to poor leadership.

African theologians also recognize the problem of leadership as a critical backdrop for Christological exploration in the continent. Ghanaian theologian John Pobee remarks that although the understanding and exercise of authority in various African communities differ, "leadership concept and practice can be very powerful avenues for articulating the answer to the question 'Whom do you Africans say that I am?'"[60] For many Christians and theologians, the image of Jesus as king represents both the fulfillment of leadership expectations in traditional African thought and an ongoing longing for liberation, integral well-being, and common human flourishing. Jesus is seen and understood to embody the people's aspirations for the (re)establishment of God's kingdom and dominion.[61]

Christ as King is not only proclaimed but also celebrated in African Catholicism. This is obvious during the traditional annual liturgical Feast of Christ the King, one of the most celebrated religious events, for instance, among the Igbo Cath-

---

56. See Ecumenical Association of the Third World Theologians, "Final Statement" (Tanzania 1976), in *The Emergent Gospel: Theology from the Developing World*, ed. Sergio Torres and Virginia Fabella (London: Geoffrey Chapman, 1978), 259, referred to in Éla, "Memory of the African People and the Cross of Christ," 18. See also Virginia Fabella and Sergio Torres, eds., *Irruption of the Third World: Challenge to Theology* (Maryknoll, NY: Orbis Books, 1983), cited in Stinton, *Jesus of Africa*, 194–95.
57. Éla, "Memory of the African People and the Cross of Christ," 18–19.
58. See Éla, "Christianity and Liberation in Africa," 137–39, cited in Stinton, *Jesus of Africa*, 195.
59. Éla, "Le Motif de la liberation dans la theologie africaine," 38, translated and cited in Stinton, *Jesus of Africa*, 195.
60. Pobee, "In Search of Christology in Africa," 17.
61. See Agbonkhianmeghe Orobator, "The Idea of the Kingdom of God in African Theology," *Studia Missionalia* 46 (1997): 327–57.

olics of Eastern Nigeria. It offers a good portrait of what lived Christology looks like in a typical Catholic parish in Igboland. During the feast, there are usually throngs of people in long processions moving ahead and following behind the eucharistic Lord in the monstrance lifted on high for adoration. There are many tuneful songs and energetic dancing by what is usually a large crowd of people. As the procession leads on through the towns and villages, the crowd bursts into a thunderous roar each time the Holy Eucharist is lifted higher. They would hail, *Jesus Igweee* . . . Christ the King! During the more sober part of the celebration, the issues of bad governance and poor leadership were always at the fore, in the sermons, in the prayers, and in the vibrating invocations of Christ as King. Jesus is proclaimed as the ideal king whom everyone in positions of leadership should look up to. He is the exemplary king, for he combines religious, social, and political leadership. In fact, in many quarters both during and after the feast, Jesus is petitioned to exercise his kingly might and power in Nigeria, a country in which the problem is considered to be simply and squarely that of leadership and bad governance.[62]

The image of king and its understanding in this sense of expectation is also dominant in other countries of tropical Africa like Ghana, Kenya, and Uganda.[63] Congolese theologian François Kabasélé discusses how the traditional image of the Bantu chiefs informs the Bantu Christian belief that "Christ Jesus is the one to whom the title of king or chief belongs."[64] His work is a good illustration of the approach by some African theologians who begin from the African culture to trace elements that resonate with what the Bible says about the identity and personality of Christ. In the light of this cultural approach, Kabasélé maintains that, for the Bantu Christians, "the prerogatives of a Bantu king are seen to have been fully realized by Jesus Christ."[65] All power belongs to him for he alone is the conqueror, and the greatest "defender and protector of the people."[66] So, as the Jews in the first century had their messianic expectations or hope, African religious people have a certain nationalistic-political understanding of the kingship of Jesus.

They also imagine and express that Jesus's power to heal and liberate consists in his kingship, and that Christ the King is a perfect exemplar of the kind of leaders Africans are in dire need of. Many Christians appreciate the healing activities of Jesus as a definitive affirmation of the all-inclusiveness of God's reign proclaimed by Jesus. Jesus's identity and work as healer and liberator are expressions of his compassion and co-suffering, similar to giving leadership to a people left stranded by their purported leaders (cf. Matt 9:36). Therefore, his healings and other acts of liberation are linked with the coming of the kingdom of God, in which Christ also reigns as king. And his kingship is exercised in his authority and power over all diseases and situations of oppression (Matt 10:1); Jesus could and will heal all diseases and liberate people from all oppression because he is a king. He is the one whom God anointed and commissioned to assist God in the (re)establishment of God's kingdom of well-being, life in freedom, and justice.

As already noted, and it bears repeating here, the response of African Catholic Christians to the identity and mission of Jesus is inspired by their faith in him as the Son of God, true God and true Man—one who is fully divine and fully human. These Christological images at the grassroots level and in the works of academic theologians are grounded in biblical images taken from the sacred scriptures, particularly the Gospels, and inspired by the testimony of the early Christian community, and the church's creedal formulations. African Catholics depend on these sources, wittingly or unwittingly, in order to work out their own experience and understanding of Jesus. Therefore, continually and critically interacting with these sources is important for a deeper appreciation of the legitimacy, and, at the same time, the limits of

---

62. See also Chris Ukachukwu Manus, "Jesu Kristi Oba: A Christology of 'Christ the King' among the Indigenous Christian Churches in Yorubaland, Nigeria," *Asia Journal of Theology* 5 (1991): 311–30.
63. Stinton, *Jesus of Africa*, 177–92.
64. Kabasélé, "Christ as Chief," 103.
65. Kabasélé, "Christ as Chief," 105.
66. Kabasélé, "Christ as Chief," 106.

the imagination of Christ's life and mission in African Catholicism. It is also important for the urgent task of reimagining how the proclamation of Christ in Africa can provide resources for engaging some contemporary issues of life and faith in the continent, two of which I will examine in the next section.

Some Enduring Christological Issues in African Catholicism

Agbonkhianmeghe Orobator argues that one can divide the epochs of African Christian history according to the issues that mean the most for Christian commitment. For instance, the early Catholic missionaries and the pioneers of African theology centered the Christian concern on the doctrine of God and on the status of Christ in the new environment. Contemporary Christians, Orobator observes, set the questions of development, social justice, and inclusion, and rightly so, into the center of their understanding of who Jesus Christ is, what faith in him and its significance are about.[67]

In African Christology, these questions or debates are not just of a philosophical nature or in terms of philosophy's role in clarifying concepts, examining the coherence of ideas, and testing the possibilities of some claims regarding the nature of Christ's identity, personality, and mission. While these are not precluded, the debates are of a substantially experiential nature. They are correspondingly existential since any authentic reflection on the mystery of Christ flows into an engagement with the reality, or even the mystery of human existence.[68] In other words, the Christological debates in African Catholicism touch on the real, concrete experiences of Africans. They are debates that have everything to do with human beings wrestling with faith and hope in Christ, and with the significance of this faith and hope amid the challenges of unimaginable suffering, social dejection, historic racism and its variegated forms today, patriarchal domination and abuse of power, and the confrontation with other legitimate forms of religious beliefs.[69] It is against the backdrop of these realities that African Christians continue today to wrestle with the question of the reality and meaning of Christ's life and work.

What follows is an attempt to flesh out in some bits the Christological content and trajectory of the issues without necessarily trying to resolve them, which lies beyond the scope of the present essay. I have chosen to focus on just two of them here: (1) the social relevance of Jesus's mission; and (2) the unique and universal significance of Jesus Christ as the savior of the world.

Christ and Social Transformation in Africa

The sad and challenging social conditions that are the lot of many Africans, Christians and non-Christians alike, raise the question of the meaning and significance of Jesus Christ as the Redeemer of humankind in the continent.[70] Who is Christ to the poor in Africa, the dying, the migrants, the prisoners, the kidnapped? Who is Christ to the children in Africa who cannot go to school in war-torn countries and in the African Sahel ravaged by radical Islamic asymmetrical warfare and terrorism? Who is Christ for the African seniors who have no retirement benefit? Who is the crucified and risen Christ for the Africans who are hanging on the cross of suffering and pain?

Consequently, there has been an increasing concern among African Catholics, believers and theologians alike, with the sociopolitical relevance of faith in Jesus Christ. This concern is born out of the reality of social inequality and injustice on the continent. Especially relevant to many African Catholics is the socially engaged Jesus of the Gospels, who speaks and acts in God's name and by the power of the Spirit for the transformation of the social situation of people (see Luke 4:18). This has engendered the quest for a socially transformative

---

67. See Orobator, "Quest for an African Christ," 75–76.
68. See Atansi, "Contemplating Christ and/in His People," 283–305.
69. No doubt there are other issues and concerns, but it is beyond the scope of the present contribution to do justice to them all. For a treatment of other themes of debate, see Nicholas Mbogu, *Jesus in Post-Missionary Africa: Issues and Questions in African Contextual Christology* (Enugu: San Press, 2012).
70. Pope John Paul II, Encyclical Letter *Redemptor Hominis*.

Christology and Catholicism in Africa.[71] How can our faith in Jesus Christ provide the transformative insights and practices that may help to dismantle the structures of sin, inequality, and injustice in many African societies?

At the same time, there are a number of challenges to the quest. One is the view that faith in Jesus Christ should have no place in society, and that the church should not get involved in public or social affairs. In addition, there is the challenge of the uncertainty of many African Christians about their role in becoming the architects or agents of a new and hopeful future in the social sphere. This second challenge also stems from the fact that Africa is a complex pluralistic society. It is beyond the scope of this chapter to address these challenges. It suffices to mention that the quest for a socially transformative African Christology moves us toward making space for a Christ-centered vision and ethics in the public domain. The courage or the confidence to advance such a Christological perspective derives from the fact that a transformative Christology allows for encounter with every human person, all human beings, irrespective of one's religious tradition or belongingness. A socially transformative Christology inspires and fosters the dialogue with, openness to, and sharing with even a non-Christian and non-religious other in working for the consolidation of the social order.

African Catholic Christians must, therefore, rise up to the urgent task of embodying, engaging, and enacting the priorities and practices they see in the life of Christ, which are in themselves profoundly humanizing and transforming within the public, cultural, economic, and social spheres. Yet such a recommendation as mine advanced here must face the vexing question already implicitly raised: How does the Christological spirituality or the Christocentric vision of social transformation take into account advances in contemporary social theories, especially concerning the complex pluralism in African societies that challenges any particular religious imagination for its transformation? This question brings us to the second Christological issue in African Catholicism.

Christ and Religious Diversity in Africa

Religious pluralism is often considered to be a challenge in most Christological conversations.[72] Theologians and believers have wrestled seriously with how the divine grace manifest in Christ is mediated to all those who do not belong to the visible Christian community. I share Orobator's sentiment that, rather than seeing religious pluralism as a challenge in African Christianity, it may be seen as the surprising testimony of how Christ has been and continues to be present and active in many and diverse ways in Africa. This is how Orobator beautifully testifies to it:

> Since converting to Christianity I have rediscovered the richness of my African religious heritage in surprisingly new ways as I live and pray as an African Christian. Many years after my conversion, both my African religious heritage and Christian faith come together in a way that I find meaningful, enriching, and deeply satisfying. Contrary to what some writers believe about African Christians, I do not feel torn between two worlds: I have a strong identity as an African Christian. I am at home as an African Christian.[73]

Orobator suggests here the compatibility, for example, between Christian faith and African religious cultures. There is a Christological premise to this compatibility which we shall reflect on shortly.

Before that, I would like to say that, for my part, I often wonder why the debate has to endure in the first place, since what is at the heart of the reflection on the unique and universal salvific significance of

---

71. See, for example, Ilo, "Beginning Afresh with Christ in the Search for Abundant Life in Africa," in *The Church as Salt and Light: Path to an African Ecclesiology of Abundant Life*, ed. Stan Chu Ilo, Joseph Ogbonnaya, and Alex Ojacor (Eugene, OR: Pickwick Publications, 2014), 1–33.

72. See, for example, Mbiti, "Confessing Christ in a Multi-Faith Context with Two Examples from Africa." See also Nicholas Mbogu, *Christology and Religious Pluralism: A Review of John Hick's Theocentric Model of Christology and the Emergence of African Inculturation Christologies* (Münster: LIT, 2007).

73. Orobator, "Preface," in *Theology Brewed in an African Pot*, x–xi.

Jesus Christ is how *divine grace* is mediated to all human beings of all times and places. And "divine grace," according to the *Catechism of the Catholic Church*, is "the free and undeserved help that God gives us to respond to his call to become children of God, adoptive sons, partakers of the divine nature and of eternal life."[74] So to wrestle with the question in the way it is sometimes done appears a bit meddlesome to my mind, since no human being or particular religious institution owns or can be a monopoly of what God chooses to freely give to whomsoever God wishes, and in whatever manner God so desires. The question rather should be approached from the stance of joyful gratitude for what God chose to do, and indeed does with God's gifts of grace for the salvation of all humanity, Catholics and non-Catholics alike. That is why it seems to me the debate is somewhat limited and limiting in the understanding of the meaning and significance of the claim that Jesus is the unique and universal Savior of humankind.

Having said that, to affirm that Christ is the unique and universal savior of humankind is to say that the benefits of the saving event of incarnation are also present in Africa as elsewhere. This idea is not entirely new even though the event of the incarnation—as a unique and universal event—has not always been conceived in this way in the African Catholic Christological landscape. But the early Christians and some of the early Christian writers, persons like Irenaeus of Lyons and Augustine of Hippo, held that the benefits of Christ's saving event accrue to the people of the ancients, our forebears and their children, who also longed and hoped for the redemption of all creation (see Rom 8:22–23).[75] Christ took flesh, no doubt, in the womb of the Blessed Virgin and was born in Bethlehem "under the law" (Gal 4:4). If this unique event is held to bear a universal character and merit, it would mean then that the Christ-event had and still has impact everywhere. Christ's taking flesh transformed the whole of creation, embracing all places, all times, and all peoples. For through the incarnation Christ entered into universal solidarity with all human beings, as well as with the entire created order.

What this implies is that, at the time of the incarnation, the African person, situation, and reality experienced the glorifying and redeeming effect of the incarnation and of the Christ-event.

This Christological understanding calls for an attitude of openness to other religions and cultures. It is an attitude that challenges Catholic Christians to remain open to other spaces of Christological knowing, believing, and living, and, very importantly, to be grateful and joyful about those spaces. The attitude of openness is premised on the fact that Christ—the mystery or the boundless reality of his life and redemptive work—is present and active in the lives of many who may not have offered an explicit confession of faith in him, but whose faith is known to him alone, to paraphrase the wordings of the fourth Eucharistic Prayer of the *Sacramentary for Mass*.

Therefore, in African Catholicism, we appreciate that the particularity of God's self-revelation in Jesus of Nazareth does not preclude the possibility of God's revelatory presence and action in other religious communities and traditions. Thus, the greater challenge is how we as Catholic Christians who claim to know Jesus and to be at home with him in our particular religious tradition should remain grateful, humble, and open and should relate wisely and lovingly to those in other religious traditions in which Jesus might be seen as a stranger. "For I was a stranger and you welcomed me" (Matt 25:35).

Concluding Remarks: Christ Our Joy and Hope in Africa

The question of who Christ is in African Catholicism is a critical question that both Christians and theologians need to continue wrestling with, especially amid the turn of events in Africa today. It is a question one cannot claim to do justice to in a short essay such as this. To claim to have done so will risk making this contribution one of the, sometimes, futile speculations about the identity and work of Christ. It must be noted that in African Catholicism, Christ is not a passive subject to be exhaustively discussed or simply written about, but a living reality to

---

74. *Catechism of the Catholic Church* §1996.
75. See, e.g., Irenaeus of Lyons, *Against Heresies* 5.32–36; Augustine of Hippo, *Retractationes* 1.13.3.

be upheld and turned back to, particularly in such times of great griefs and anxieties in Africa. We uphold and turn back to him always as our joy and hope. He is our joy because we believe he is "God with us" in our lives and situations (Matt 1:23). He is our hope amid all the despair and discouragement that stare Africa and her children in the face. And we keep trusting that our joy and hope in him will not deceive us (Rom 5:5); for they remain sources of the creative vision and energies we always need in order to keep laboring for the manifestation of the redemption Christ has gained for all.

Bibliography

Atansi, Chukwuemeka Anthony. *Christ, the Image of Social Transformation: Towards a Transformative Christology in the African Context*. Doctoral dissertation, Faculty of Theology and Religious Studies, Leuven University, 2020.

———. "Contemplating Christ and/in His People: The Practice of a Social Transformation-Oriented Christology in Africa." In *What Does Theology Do, Actually? Observing Theology and the Transcultural*, edited by Matthew Ryan Robinson and Inja Inderst, 285–307. Leipzig: Evangelische Verlagsanstalt, 2020.

Bediako, Kwame. "Guest Editorial: Lived Christology." *Journal of African Christian Thought* 8.1 (June 2005): 1.

———. *Jesus in Africa: The Christian Gospel in African History and Experience*. Carlisle: Regnum Books International, 2000.

Clarke, Clifton. *African Christology: Jesus in a Post-Missionary African Christianity*. Eugene, OR: Pickwick, 2011.

———. "Healer of Africa." In Clarke, *African Christology: Jesus in a Post-Missionary African Christianity*, 172–73. Eugene, OR: Pickwick, 2011.

Cook, Michael. "The African Experience of Jesus." *Theological Studies* 70 (2009): 668–92.

Dube, Musa. "Who Do You Say I Am?," *Feminist Theology* 15.3 (2007): 346–67.

Éla, Jean-Marc. *African Cry*. Translated by Robert R. Barr. Maryknoll, NY: Orbis Books, 1991. Reprint, Eugene, OR: Wipf & Stock, 2005.

———. "Christianity and Liberation in Africa." In *Paths of African Theology*, edited by Rosino Gibellini, 136–53. Maryknoll, NY: Orbis Books, 1994.

———. *From Charity to Liberation*. London: Catholic Institute for International Relations, 1990.

———. *My Faith as an African*. Translated by John Pairman Brown and Susan Perry. Maryknoll, NY: Orbis Books, 1988. Reprint, Eugene, OR: Wipf & Stock, 2009.

———. "The Memory of the African People and the Cross of Christ." In *The Scandal of a Crucified World: Perspectives on the Cross and Suffering*. Translated and edited by Yacob Tesfai, 17–35. Maryknoll, NY: Orbis Books, 1994.

———. "A Theology Coming from the People." In Éla, *My Faith as an African*, translated by John Pairman Brown and Susan Perry. Maryknoll, NY: Orbis Books, 1988. Reprint, Eugene, OR: Wipf & Stock, 2009.

Ezigbo, Victor. "Grassroots Christologies in Contemporary African Christianity." In Ezigbo, *Re-Imagining African Christologies: Conversing with the Interpretations and Appropriations of Jesus in Contemporary African Christianity*, 103–42. Princeton Theological Monographs 132. Eugene, OR: Pickwick, 2010.

———. *Re-Imagining African Christologies: Conversing with the Interpretations and Appropriations of Jesus in Contemporary African Christianity*. Princeton Theological Monographs 132. Eugene, OR: Pickwick, 2010.

Goergen, Donald J. "The Quest for the Christ of Africa." *African Christian Studies* 17 (March 2001): 5–51.

Ilo, Stan Chu. "Beginning Afresh with Christ in the Search for Abundant Life in Africa." In *The Church as Salt and Light: Path to an African Ecclesiology of Abundant Life*, edited by Stan Chu Ilo, Joseph Ogbonnaya, and Alex Ojacor, 1–33. Eugene, OR: Pickwick, 2014.

———. "Interpreting the Search for Health and Healing among African Charismatic and Pentecostal Groups: A Theological Bio-Social Approach." *Bigard Theological Studies* 38.1 (2018): 1–36.

———. "Searching for Healing in a Miraculous Stream: The Fate of God's People in Africa." In *Wealth, Health, and Hope in African Christian Religion: The Search for Abundant Life*, edited by Stan Chu Ilo, 45–80. Lanham, MD: Lexington Books, 2018.

John Paul II, Pope. *Redemptor Hominis* [Encyclical; March 2, 1979]. Vatican City: Libreria Editrice Vaticana, 1979. www.vatican.va. *AAS* 71.4 (1979).

Jongh, Charles de. "Contemporary Trends in Christology in Africa." *South African Baptist Journal of Theology* (2008): 1–12.

Kabasélé Lumbala, François. "Africans Celebrate Jesus Christ." In *Paths of African Theology*, edited by Rosino Gibellini, 78–94. Maryknoll, NY: Orbis Books, 1994.

———. "Christ as Chief." In *Faces of Jesus in Africa*, edited by Robert Schreiter. Maryknoll, NY: Orbis Books, 1991.

Kolié, Cécé. "Jesus as Healer?" In *Faces of Jesus in Africa*, edited by Robert Schreiter, 128–50. Maryknoll, NY: Orbis Books, 1991.

Magesa, Laurenti. "Christ the Liberator and Africa Today." In *Jesus in African Christianity: Experimentation and Diversity in African Christology*, edited by Jesse Mugambi and Laurenti Magesa, 79–92. Nairobi: Initiatives Publication, 1989.

Manus, Chris Ukachukwu. "Jesu Kristi Oba: A Christology of 'Christ the King' among the Indigenous Christian Churches in Yorubaland, Nigeria." *Asia Journal of Theology* 5 (1991): 311–30.

Mbiti, John. "Confessing Christ in a Multi-Faith Context with Two Examples from Africa." In *Christianity and Other Faiths in Europe—Geneva Documentation No. 37*, 155–69. Geneva: Lutheran World Federation, 1995.

———. "'For Now We See in a Glass Darkly': The Emerging Faces of Jesus in Africa." In *Cristologia e Missioni Oggi*, edited by G. Colanzi, P. Giglioni, and S. Karotemprel, 143–64. Vatican City: Urbaniana University Press, 2001.

Moloney, Raymond. "African Christology." *Theological Studies* 48 (1987): 505–15.

Mugambi, Jesse, and Laurenti Magesa, eds. *Jesus in African Christianity: Experimentation and Diversity in African Christology*. Nairobi: Initiatives Publication, 1989.

Munyao, Martin. "Christology in Africa." In *The Routledge Handbook of African Theology*, edited by Elias Kifon Bongmba, 412–28. New York: Routledge, 2020.

Nasimiyu-Wasike, Anne. "Christology and an African Woman's Experience." In *Faces of Jesus in Africa*, edited by Robert Schreiter, 70–81. Maryknoll, NY: Orbis Books, 1991.

Nyamiti, Charles. *Christ as Our Ancestor: Christology from an African Perspective*. Gweru: Mambo Press, 1984.

Oduyoye, Mercy Amba, and Elizabeth Amoah. "The Christ for African Women." In *With Passion and Compassion: Third World Women Doing Theology*, edited by Virginia Fabella and Mercy Oduyoye, 35–46. Maryknoll, NY: Orbis Books, 1988.

Okullu, Henry. *Church and Politics in East Africa*. Nairobi: Uzima Press, 1974.

Okure, Teresa. "Jesus and the Samaritan Woman (Jn 1:1–42) in Africa." *Theological Studies* 70.2 (2009): 401–18.

Onaiyekan, John. "Christological Trends in Contemporary African Theology." In *Constructive Christian Theology in the Worldwide Church*, edited by William R. Barr, 355–68. Grand Rapids, MI: Eerdmans, 1997.

Orobator, Agbonkhianmeghe. "The Quest for an African Christ: An Essay on Contemporary African Christology." *Hekima Review* 11 (September 1994): 75–99.

———. *Religion and Faith in Africa: Confessions of an Animist*. Maryknoll, NY: Orbis Books, 2018.

———. "The Sky Is Wide Enough: A Historico-Critical Appraisal of Theological Activity and Method in Africa." *Hekima Review* 40 (May 2009): 34–44.

———. *Theology Brewed in an African Pot*. Maryknoll, NY: Orbis Books, 2008.

Pénoukou, Efoé Julien. "Christology in the Village." In *Faces of Jesus in Africa*, edited by Robert Schreiter, 24–51. Maryknoll, NY: Orbis Books, 1991.

Pobee, John. "Jesus Christ—The Life of the World: An African Perspective." *Ministerial Formation* 21 (1983).

———, ed. *Exploring Afro-Christology*. Frankfurt: Peter Lang, 1992.

———. "In Search of Christology in Africa." In *Exploring Afro-Christology*, edited by John Pobee, 9–20. Frankfurt: Peter Lang, 1992.

Schreiter, Robert, ed. *Faces of Jesus in Africa*. Maryknoll, NY: Orbis Books, 1991.

Shorter, Aylward. "Folk Christianity and Functional Christology." *African Ecclesial Review* 24.3 (1982): 133–37.

Stinton, Diane B. "Encountering Jesus at the Well: Further Reflections on African Women's Christologies." *Journal of Reformed Theology* 7 (2013): 267–93.

———. "Jesus Christ, Living Water in Africa Today." In *The Oxford Handbook of Christology*, edited by Francesca Aran Murphy, 425–43. Oxford: Oxford University Press, 2015.

———. *Jesus of Africa: Voices of Contemporary African Christology*. Maryknoll, NY: Orbis Books, 2004.

———. "Jesus–Immanuel, Image of the Invisible God: Aspects of Popular Christology in Sub-Saharan Africa." *Journal of Reformed Theology* 1 (2007): 6–40.

Vatican II. *Lumen Gentium* [Dogmatic Constitution on the Church]. Vatican City: Libreria Editrice Vaticana, 1964. www.vatican.va.

Suggested Reading

Ezigbo, Victor. *Re-Imagining African Christologies: Conversing with the Interpretations and Appropriations of Jesus in Contemporary African Christianity*. Princeton Theological Monographs 132. Eugene, OR: Pickwick, 2010.

Goergen, Donald J. "The Quest for the Christ of Africa." *African Christian Studies* 17 (March 2001): 5–51.

Ilo, Stan Chu. "Beginning Afresh with Christ in the Search for Abundant Life in Africa." In *The Church as Salt and Light: Path to an African Ecclesiology of Abundant Life*, edited by Stan Chu Ilo, Joseph Ogbonnaya, and Alex Ojacor, 1–33. Eugene, OR: Pickwick, 2014.

Jongh, Charles de. "Contemporary Trends in Christology in Africa." *South African Baptist Journal of Theology* (2008): 1–12.

Onaiyekan, John. "Christological Trends in Contemporary African Theology." In *Constructive Christian Theology in the Worldwide Church*, edited by William R. Barr, 355–68. Grand Rapids, MI: Eerdmans, 1997.

Orobator, Agbonkhianmeghe. "The Quest for an African Christ: An Essay on Contemporary African Christology." *Hekima Review* 11 (September 1994): 75–99.

Stinton, Diane B. *Jesus of Africa: Voices of Contemporary African Christology*. Maryknoll, NY: Orbis Books, 2004.

Key Words

African Catholicism
Christology
grassroots
images
Jesus Christ
proclamation

Dei Verbum in African Catholicism: History and Reception

Paul Béré, SJ

Tell the world, Council Fathers, that Jesus Christ is divine revelation, so that hearing, the whole world may believe, believe that it may hope, and hope that it may love. May the happy face of Christ shine in the Church. In that way, you will renew the wonders of love and fidelity that shined in the Early Church.[1]

Paul Cardinal Zoungrana (1917–2000)

A short biographical note about Pope St. John XXIII on the Vatican's website reads, "When on October 20, 1958 the cardinals, assembled in conclave, elected Angelo Roncalli as pope many regarded him, because of his age and ambiguous reputation, as a transitional pope, little realizing that the pontificate of this man of 76 years would mark a turning point in history and initiate a new age for the Church."[2] Less than three months after his election, on January 25, 1959, the newly elected pope called for an ecumenical council of the church. John XXIII, canonized on April 27, 2014, by Pope Francis, who probably shares a similar mission to reform the church, was not expected to make such a historic contribution to it. As many analysts and authors have remarked, he opened up the church to the world, an openness that could be seen in the origins of the participants in the Second Vatican Council, who came from all over the world.[3]

Africa was physically represented, but what was the contribution of the young African church to this historic gathering? The narrative about the African participation in the council emphasized the absence of African voices on historical and theological matters, and highlighted the shallowness of their contributions.[4] Some argued that the African fathers were few in number, and for that reason their voices did not really count.[5] They claimed that the African church was more interested in areas related to the pastoral and organizational aspects

---

1. From the intervention of Bishop Paul Zoungrana at the Second Vatican Council, third period, ninety-second congregation. He spoke on behalf of sixty-seven council fathers: "Dicite mundo, Patres conciliares, *Iesum Christum esse diviniam revelationem*, 'ut mundus universus audiendo credat, credendo speret et sperando amet.' Magis splendeat in Ecclesa festivus vultus Christi. Hoc modo, prodigia amoris et fidelitatis, quae in Ecclesia primaeva splendebant, renovabitis." See *Acta synodalia sacrosanctii concilii oecumenici vaticanii II*, vol. III, part III, 212–14; quotation from 213 (henceforth *AS*).
2. "Pope John XXIII, 1958–1963," www.vatican.va.
3. See Bwidi Kitambala, *Les évêques d'Afrique*, 151; Durand, "Preface to Philippe J. Roy," 5–6.
4. See Hastings, "Council Came to Africa," 315; Patrick A. Kalilombe, "The Effect of the Council on World Catholicism: Africa," in *Modern Catholicism: Vatican II and After*, ed. Adrian Hastings (London: SPCK, 1991), 310–17; de Jong, *Challenge of Vatican II in East Africa*; Laurenti Magesa, *The Post-Conciliar Church in Africa: No Turning Back the Clock* (Nairobi: CUEA Press, 2016); Orobator, "'After All, Africa Is Largely a Nonliterate Continent'"; Orobator, "Look Back to the Future."
5. See the chapters by Orobator and Arabome in this volume.

of its life than in the dogmatic documents that were more in tune with the agenda of the West.[6] It has even been asserted, and rightly so to some extent, that Africa lacked Catholic universities and institutions of higher education that would allow its participants to offer deep insights into the issues raised at the sessions. Finally, it has been asserted that African members were not familiar with the technical procedures used at the council and thus were not able to make their voices heard.[7]

The question of the contribution of the African fathers to the deliberations at the council requires a fresh examination of the data. The above-mentioned views on their contribution may have originated in the fact that most of the interventions at the council were delivered in an unfamiliar idiom—namely, Latin, or in French or English—languages with which not all of the African fathers were sufficiently familiar. Other reasons, such as the narrative of some African fathers on their personal experience of the event, which remained limited in scope, may have affected later representation. The fathers too needed some historical distance between the foundational event and the reflective process, which comes from memory and tradition in order to grasp the reception process of the council's documents. Therefore, even their reports must undergo some historical-critical assessment.[8] I contend that, from the crafting of the council's documents to their reception, the voices of the local and regional African churches, though few, were loud enough to have been heard.[9]

In this chapter, it is my intention to provide an alternative perspective to the dominant view that the contribution of the African fathers to Vatican II was minimal,[10] using as a case study *Dei Verbum* (*DV*) as it relates to the life of the African church. The foundational principle of my argument is that in a process of discernment, which the council definitely was, voices are not counted but weighed.[11] Based on this principle, I will show that the African fathers contributed in a unique way to *Dei Verbum*. To this end, I will first describe the sociopolitical and ecclesial contexts of the Catholic Church in Africa on the eve of Vatican II, then analyze the African fathers' voices and contributions to *Dei Verbum*, and finally offer some concluding remarks.

The Catholic Church in Africa on the Eve of Vatican II

The picture of the church in Africa during the first half of the twentieth century looked pretty much like the African nations themselves under the colonial powers. Most church leaders were missionary bishops or apostolic prefects, usually from the same countries as the colonial powers, but with some exceptions. To paint a clearer picture of the involvement of the entire Catholic world in Vatican II, it seems indispensable to take cognizance of the political and ecclesial environment at the time.

The Missionary and Ecclesial Situation Immediately before Vatican II

In the 1950s, the decade before the council, the world scene was characterized by difficult struggles to achieve peace and liberty. Trapped between the two superpowers, the United States and the Soviet Union, the independent countries from Asia and

---

6. See the following studies: Bwidi Kitambala, *Les évêques d'Afrique*; Appiah-Kubi, *Église, famille de Dieu*; Tshibangu, *Le Concile Vatican II*.

7. Prudhomme, "Les évêques d'Afrique noire anciennement française et le concile"; Bwidi Kitambala, *Les évêques d'Afrique*, chapter 6.

8. See, for instance, Daniel Moulinet's critical edition of Michel Cancouët, *L'Afrique au concile: Journal d'un expert* (Rennes: Presses Universitaires de Rennes, 2013).

9. See de Lubac, *Entretien autour de Vatican II*, 51.

10. See Orobator's summary of the narrative: "Africa's theological memory of Vatican II is sparse, pithy, and uneventful" ("Look Back to the Future," 100).

11. The testimony of Henri de Lubac (see *Entretien autour de Vatican II*, 51) demonstrates this principle in point: "L'impression de ces paroles sur l'Assemblée fut grande. On peut dire que ce jour-là, l'Eglise d'Afrique joua au Concile un rôle de premier plan." ("The impression of these words on the assembly was great. We can say that that day, the church of Africa played a leading role in the Council" [my translation]).

Africa and those still living under colonial rule gathered for the Bandung Conference (April 18–24, 1955) to create a third alternative in postwar international geopolitics, and by doing so, the so-called Third World made its voices heard.

With respect to the ecclesial situation in the 1950s, Angelo Roncalli, the future pope, a former nuncio and a good historian, sensed that the church was closing herself off and alienating herself from the world and was, for this reason, losing missionary ground.[12] From a theological point of view, the dominant missionary concept in pre–Vatican II Africa with emphasis on "the salvation of the souls" slowly gave way to a theology of *plantatio*, which meant planting local churches by promoting local clergy and local religious congregations. This phase of evangelization was pastorally oriented with the goal of enabling locals to carry out the work initiated by the missionaries. The conviction behind this way of proceeding, which was at that time not to be taken for granted, was that Africans could perform the basic tasks that had to that point been performed by missionaries.

We often assume that the leadership of the African church in such a changing context was limited to bishops, priests, and consecrated persons, but the laity was deeply involved in preparing the path of the African fathers to the council.[13] Despite the strict hierarchical structure of the pre–Vatican II church, the African laity were thus not mere observers of the happenings in the church. Just as they were at the forefront of the various struggles for political independence, they promoted a responsible Christianity that would be truly Catholic and truly African. This was evidenced by a conference in Paris on "Negro and African Writers and Artists" convened by a group of Black African intellectuals. The conference took place September 19–22, 1956, under the leadership of Alioune Diop (1910–1980), a Senegalese Muslim who had converted to Catholicism. He was the mind behind the famous book *Les prêtres noirs s'interrogent*,[14] published in 1956 and authored by thirteen Black priests from Africa and the diaspora. This book is considered the first formulation of an African theology. For Diop, the conference in Paris was only a beginning. On the eve of the council, he organized another meeting on "The Unity of Negro-African Cultures," which took place in Rome March 26–April 1, 1959, and would be followed by another on "African Personality and Catholicism" in 1962. The agenda of this intellectual African layperson was to enable the young African church to bring its "Africanness" to the council's deliberations.[15] Those who had long been denied the right to speak for themselves were now ready to voice their vision of the church and its mission in their own context.

These initiatives demonstrated the interest of the church leadership and the laity in the council. Some questioned the authenticity of the motivation behind the movements of the Africans, and it was possible to label the initiatives as "political." It is true that Pope John XXIII called for a pastoral gathering, but did it arouse the same expectations over the entire Catholic Church? For Claude Prudhomme, Vatican II "appeared as an opportunity for decolonized Africa to rise on the international stage. For Catholic intellectuals and priests, the announcement of the council motivated their

---

12. Among the signs of openness, Pope John XXIII traveled out of the Lazio region to Loretto and Assisi; appointed the first African cardinal (Laurean Rugambwa, from Tanzania); and canonized the first black saint, Martin de Porres (Lima, Peru). [Here we are referring to Roncalli and John XXIII as the same person.]

13. See Philippe Verdin's assessment (*Alioune Diop*, 223): "Incontestablement, les évêques africains trouvèrent dans la SAC un soutien opiniâtre, une caisse de résonnance pour leurs souhaits et une aide pour la formulation théologique d'un christianisme africain" ("Undoubtedly, the African bishops found in the SAC [Société Africaine de Culture, Society for African Culture, founded by Alioune Diop in 1956] a stubborn support, a box of resonance for their wishes and a help for the theological formulation of an African Christianity" [my translation]).

14. Société Africaine de Culture, *Les Prêtres noirs*—the book was published by Éditions du Cerf (Paris) in 1956 and was promoted by Alioune Diop, founder and promoter of Présence Africaine.

15. See Charles Becker, Jeanne Lopis-Sylla, and Aloyse-Raymond Ndiaye, "Alioune Diop, le concile et la culture: Les exigences du dialogue des religions," *Présence Africaine* 1 no. 195–96 (2017): 41–62; Verdun, *Alioune Diop*, 223.

struggle to promote black African culture."[16] It was not out of place for Africans to politicize the above-mentioned initiatives; after all, the gospel places "the dangerous memory of Jesus Christ"[17] the liberator within the political realm. This Metzian concept helps avoid disconnecting the gospel from sociopolitical realities.

We now turn to what happened at the council.

The African Council Fathers at the Deliberations

The number of council fathers from Africa was tiny in comparison to that from the West. According to the official record of the council, the number of Africans began at 278 and grew to around 299. This increase came about as the pope appointed new African bishops. By the end of the council, the number of the *periti* (experts) from the continent had increased substantially from one to eighteen. Even though the absolute numbers from Africa were small in comparison to the West, they tell of a strong presence of the young African church at this historic gathering. Some of the African bishops would speak, but did their message contribute anything to the debate? As has already been noted above, some scholars have argued that they offered little substantive input to the deliberations. One African theologian who worked on *Lumen Gentium* remarked that the African fathers expected too much, were poorly prepared, and lacked experience.[18] Does this judgment also apply to the other—and probably more important—dogmatic constitution that came out of the council, *Dei Verbum*?

Before turning to a close examination of the deliberations on *Dei Verbum* specifically, however, it is interesting to remark that the ecclesiological model officially chosen for the church in Africa at the First Special Assembly for Africa of the Synod of Bishops in 1994, the "family of God,"[19] first came to the fore at the council with a sound theological grounding provided through the intervention of a Vietnamese bishop, Simon Hoà Nguyên Van Hien.[20] This image of the church as family of God has biblical roots and was endorsed by the universal church at the council;[21] it particularly resonated with the African worldview.[22] The reception of this biblical image by the African church shows the church's sensitivity to the dogmatic deliberations of Vatican II. *Dei Verbum*, the Dogmatic Constitution on Divine Revelation, exemplifies the emphasis given to the revealed Word in doing theology in a more explicit way. In the deliberations about *Dei Verbum*, an African father of the council, Bishop Paul Zoungrana, the archbishop of Ouagadougou in Upper Volta, made a noteworthy contribution.[23] Zoungrana's contribution should result in a nuancing and qualification of the negative judgment about

---

16. Prudhomme, "Les évêques d'Afrique noire," 164.

17. This phrase was coined by the German theologian Johann Baptist Metz in order to describe Christ's passion. In the midst of injustice and suffering, the followers of Jesus must keep faith in God who works wonders.

18. Appiah-Kubi, *Église, famille de Dieu*, 57.

19. See Pope John Paul II, post-synodal apostolic exhortation *Ecclesia in Africa*.

20. The notion of the church as family of God had previously been proposed in the council by Archbishop Giuseppe d'Avack (1899–1979; Camerino, Italy) and Bishop André Marie Charue (1898–1977; Namur, Belgium), but, unlike Bishop Van Hien (1906–1973; Đà Lat, Viet Nam), neither provided a theological basis for it.

21. See Friedrich Bechina, *Die Kirche als "Familie Gottes": Die Stellung dieses theologischen Konzeptes im Zweiten Vatikanischen Konzil und in den Bischofssynoden von 1974 bis 1994 im Hinblick auf eine "Familia-Dei-Ekklesiologie,"* Analecta Gregoriana 272 (Rome: Editrice Pontificia Università Gregoriana, 1998).

22. The first African synod's use of the ecclesiological image of the family of God came at the end of a long process that began at the local level. Indeed, even before the council, the bishops from Upper Volta (later renamed Burkina Faso) issued a pastoral letter comparing the church to the human family as the best image to help the African faithful understand their belonging to the church. Their concluding sentence was: "The Church is the family of the children of God" ("L'Eglise, c'est la famille des enfants de Dieu"). See Les Evêques de Haute-Volta, *Le chrétien dans l'Eglise* (Bobo-Dioulasso: Imprimerie de la Savane, 1962), 21; quoted by Somé, "Eglise-Famille-de-Dieu," 47.

23. See de Lubac, *Entretien autour de Vatican II*, 51.

the participation of African bishops at the council, especially the claim that they were not able to intervene during the *doctrinal* debates because they had Western theologians who acted as experts for the African bishops.[24] In the case of francophone West African bishops, the regional body was helped by Fr. Michel Cancouët (1931–2012).[25]

Dei Verbum: The Dogmatic Constitution in African Catholicism

Promulgated on November 18, 1965, the Dogmatic Constitution on Divine Revelation, *Dei Verbum*, was the result of a long and difficult process that began with the schema *De Fontibus*. This first draft, whose focus was the relationship between scripture and tradition, was discussed by the fathers on October 14, 1962, but they subsequently rejected it. The redactors of the draft intended to defend Catholic tradition as (1) containing truths that are not contained in scripture; (2) an authoritative interpreter of scripture ("*extra Traditionem, nulla interpretatio*"); and (3) equal in authority to scripture. The Jesuit historian John O'Malley summarizes the evolution of the drafts as follows:

> The revised schema on revelation, still without its final title, *Dei Verbum*, followed for the most part the outline of the original document, though the orientations of the first two chapters were significantly different. The original schema at least implicitly viewed revelation as consisting of truths or doctrines, whereas this one, as set forth in the first chapter, emphasized that it was God's self-manifestation, which expressed itself in God's action in history (*gesta*) as well as in pronouncements (*verba*).[26] Revelation took its ultimate form in the very person of Christ. God is the "source" of revelation—God himself, not Scripture or Tradition as such. Although to the uninitiated this might seem like a theological fine point, it was a significant shift away from ahistorical abstractions, as if God had revealed a collection of timeless propositions.[27]

Revelation was thus removed from the realm of concepts, truths, doctrines, and propositions, so that it would be grounded in life, as was highlighted by the reference to Jesus as *Logos tou Theou* (Word of God).[28] Archbishop Denis Hurley of Durban, South Africa, clearly stated at the council that "the Second Vatican Council finds the Church in the throes of a transition from a theology of concept to a theology of image. The concept was fine for defensive purposes but it is not good for progressive pastoral strategy. In swinging to the image, *the Church finds itself in a back-to-Bible campaign.*"[29] This comment captured the spirit of the council, namely, the need of concreteness at a pastoral level as shown in the constant use of accessible language in the scripture, especially in the communication style of Jesus Christ. Furthermore, in the discussion on divine revelation, the relationship between scripture and (apostolic) tradition was shifted from a diachronic to a synchronic analysis in which tradition is understood as inclusive, an expression of the whole being of the church, a reality that grows with understanding,[30] and is not present only in

---

24. For this opinion, see Appiah-Kubi, *Église, famille de Dieu*, 57. For a better picture of what happened at the council, see some of the *peritis'* memoirs, including those of Henri de Lubac and of Yves Congar, *Mon Journal du Concile, I et II*.

25. See Cancouët's memoirs, *L'Afrique au Concile*.

26. See the exegetical treatment of the pair "*verba/gesta*" by the African exegete Monsengwo Pasinya, "Le Cadre littéraire."

27. O'Malley, *What Happened at Vatican II*, 227.

28. The anthropological term "Word" has been used as an abstract theological concept, but here we are referring to its metaphorical meaning as in *Dei Verbum* 1.

29. See Appiah-Kubi, *Église, famille de Dieu*, 61 (italics mine).

30. See O'Malley, *What Happened at Vatican II*, 228; Gregory the Great stated that "scripture grows with its readers," as quoted by Pier Cesare Bori, *L'interpretazione infinita: L'ermeneutica cristiana antica e le sue trasformazioni* (Bologna: Il Mulino, 1987), 130.

the church's teachings. A dichotomous approach to scripture and tradition in the theological debates could not but generate a sterile conflict. Even a synchronic solution still remains wanting, unless scripture and tradition are understood in the light of divine revelation in the person of Jesus Christ (*DV* §2), as suggested by the African voices in the debate.

The Voices of Africa at the Sessions on Divine Revelation

There were twenty-two interventions by the African fathers at the sessions on divine revelation, comprising five individual oral contributions, two oral interventions in groups, and fifteen written contributions.[31] The record of the debates over what eventually became *Dei Verbum* shows that two Africans made the most significant contributions: Archbishop Zoungrana and Fr. Joâo Ferreira, the apostolic prefect of Portuguese Guinea (now Guinea Bissau). The latter engaged with the inner logic of the document and the biblical citations in the sixth chapter of the first draft, broadening the notion of scripture from being merely a tool for academic theology to something for the whole life of the church, including catechesis, preaching, pastoral life, missiology, liturgy, and even mystical theology. Ferreira advocated for the position that the Word of God should be understood as the soul of the church's life and mission.[32]

Zoungrana praised the biblical flavor of the text and suggested that the person of Christ should be seen as revelation. Scholarly works on *Dei Verbum* rarely mention Zoungrana's contributions at the council. A remarkable exception comes from Hanjo Sauer, an astute Austrian commentator specializing in the subject of revelation as discussed at the council.[33] On this subject, Sauer contributed a chapter entitled "Problems of Doctrine Are Pastoral Problems" to the five-volume *Storia del Concilio Vaticano II*, the monumental work edited by Giuseppe Alberigo of the University of Bologna.[34] The author quotes Zoungrana, who spoke at length on behalf of a group of African bishops[35] concerning his understanding of revelation:

> For all of us, council fathers, it is useful to recall the nature and purpose of this council. The nature is pastoral and the immediate goal is the renewal of the faithful. If the institutions of the Catholic Church are renewed and restored, but the spirit that animates these institutions is not renewed, it would be of little help in our pastoral ministry to the faithful.
>
> In fact a divine revelation that, as they say, is made up of truths to which it is necessary to adhere and precepts that we are bound to fulfil, does not correspond to the contemporary religious mentality, which is predominantly personalistic, and does not arouse love. *Truths of faith and precepts to be lived out need to be considered more in their relationship to a living person.*[36]

---

31. See Bwidi Kitambala, *Les évêques d'Afrique*, 304.

32. Bwidi Kitambala, *Les évêques d'Afrique*, 402. On this point, see the results of the Synod of the Word of God in the Life and Mission of the Church (October 2008) in Pope Benedict XVI, post-synodal apostolic exhortation *Verbum Domini* (September 30, 2010).

33. Sauer, *Glaube und Erfahrung*.

34. Sauer, "I problemi della dottrina sono i problemi della pastorale," 221–58; quotation from 240–41.

35. See *AS* III, III, 212; for the names of those who signed, see *AS* III, III, 214.

36. Alberigo, *Storia del Concilio Vaticano*, 4:240–41 (italics added). The original Latin reads: "Etenim nobis omnibus, Patres conciliares, perutile est meminisse huius Concilii indolis et finis. Indoles pastoralis est, finis vero immediatus Ecclesiae membrorum renovatio. Si Ecclesiae catholicae institutiones renovantur aut restituuntur, si tamen spiritus, qui has institutiones vivificare debet, non renovatur, parum prodest ministerio nostro pastorali ac Ecclesiae membrorum renovationi. Nam revelatio divinia constituta, ut aiunt, veritatibus quibus adhaerere oportet, mandatis quae adimplere tenemur, religiosae menti, praesertim hodiernae, quae eminenter personalis est, non favet et amorem non suscitat. Veritates credendae et mandata adimplenda indigent ut magis relate ad personam viventem considerentur" (*AS* III, 213).

The contributions of Ferreira and Zoungrana call for an in-depth analysis that is beyond the scope of this chapter. A few remarks will have to suffice. First, Fr. Ferreira's suggestion that scripture should function as the soul of the life of the church is strongly affirmed in Pope Benedict XVI's post-synodal apostolic exhortation *Verbum Domini* (§§50–89). The principle for reading and interpreting the scripture put forward by the council in *Dei Verbum* (§24) focuses on "*studium*" (study). The soul of theology is not scripture but the study of the "sacred page," that is, exegesis.[37] The best way to express or bring forth such a perspective would be what Benedict XVI calls "theological exegesis" (*Verbum Domini* §34). This expression implies that the process of scientifically studying scripture remains an enterprise concerning faith seeking understanding that transforms into the development of a theological understanding of the biblical message; this in turn nourishes the pastoral life of the church, pervading all of its activities. This view on how to read, interpret, and apply the scripture to theology, pastoral life, and daily Christian witnessing did not take hold strongly because of the weight of history. As a matter of fact, unlike Protestant theology, Catholic theology has its origins in dogmas rather than the Bible. This difference, together with the Protestant position of *sola scriptura* and Protestant initiatives to engage in a scientific study of the Bible, may have been the cause for the Catholic Church's slow move to adopt critical approaches to the Bible. Groundbreaking papal documents like Pius XII's encyclical *Divino Afflante Spiritu* (1943), which officially opened the way in the Catholic Church for biblical criticism, were still too recent at the time of the council to have a deep impact on the mindset of the church leadership.

Second, Zoungrana's contribution provides a key to understanding the thrust of the final document. It sets divine revelation within the context of relationships: on the one hand, between God and humanity, and on the other, between human beings. The council intended to effect an *aggiornamento* of the church, which Zoungrana understood as its renewal; in this regard, he remarked that hierarchical structures could be good, but that no change would happen unless those who operate the structures are renewed in spirit. At the fiftieth anniversary of the conclusion of the council, the church under Pope Francis has been set on this path of renewal. Francis calls for personal conversion in order to renew the structures. He insists on the centrality of the human person, just as Zoungrana did. Revelation has to do with effective communication and therefore with relationships, not merely abstract concepts and ideas. The quotation above from Zoungrana refers to the personalistic spirit of the times, and the importance of oral communication in the African context might have played a role in his vision of divine revelation as communication through a person. If this connection is right, it shows how cultural sensitivity can help preserve the best of the theological tradition.

Why did very few African fathers speak on the issues raised by the deliberations on *Dei Verbum*, unlike on other topics?[38] I would suggest three reasons. First, the *periti* were very important to the deliberations of the council, and the African delegation did not include many. The pope appointed Fr. Dr. Tharcisse Tshibangu (later a bishop) from the Congo, who had just completed his postdoctoral work, as the only theological expert from sub-Saharan Africa.[39] Second, most Africans were at the time primarily concerned with the independence and self-determination of their people. The book described above, *Les prêtres noirs s'interrogent*, which was the product of the 1956 conference in Paris, voices the concerns of the native intellectual clergy of Africa. It aired their view that they were not full members of the church because their "Africanness" had not found a home in it. And, third, very few native African bishops were able to contribute a theological perspective that was different from that of their Western counterparts. Most of

---

37. The Bible can be read in different ways using different tools. Not every biblical interpretation can be considered "exegetical" in the sense of making meaning out of the text from its historical and cultural context; some are mere "eisegesis," that is, a reading into the Bible of one's own thoughts.

38. Bwidi Kitambala, *Les évêques d'Afrique*.

39. See Tshibangu, *Le Concile Vatican II*.

them were trained in Western theology, and very few, if any, had engaged in theological research. Not until 1970 did an African earn a doctorate in sacred scripture from the Pontifical Biblical Institute.[40] This Jesuit academic institution spearheaded research in scripture, as did the École biblique et archéologique française of Jerusalem run by the Dominicans. The final content of *Dei Verbum* owes a great deal to the debates on exegesis that occurred in these institutions.[41] The challenge, therefore, was to train people who would be able to dialogue on the same footing with others while at the same time offering an African perspective. There was limited general interest in the Africans' repeated statements about the affinity between the world of the Bible and the African world[42]—the broader church and the intelligentsia expected more. Decades would pass before the appearance of a cohort of African Catholic biblical experts. In sum, the insights of the African fathers at the council were highlighted in Western research on *Dei Verbum*, but their contributions have not been significant in past and current theological research in Africa.[43]

The Reception of Dei Verbum in the Life and Mission of the Church in Africa

The sixth chapter of *Dei Verbum* is about the Bible in the life and mission of the church. As O'Malley put it, "For the ordinary Catholic, chapter six, which encouraged the reading of the Bible for spiritual nourishment, was the most important."[44] The first African specialists in biblical sciences created the Pan-African Association of Catholic Exegetes (PACE) in Yaoundé (Cameroon) in 1987 as a development following on the "African Bible Days" (Journées Bibliques Africaines), an initiative started in Kinshasa in 1978. The Association states on its website that "PACE pursues mainly two different, but inseparable objectives: to do scientific exegesis, by means of a rigorous application of the universally recognized methods of biblical studies, and to do contextualized exegesis in order to answer the questions that African Christians pose to the Word of God in their particular contexts."[45] The website continues: "PACE aims thus to serve the Church of Africa in her commitment of being witness to the risen Christ, God's Word become flesh. . . . These objectives are pursued through study congresses that are held . . . every two years." Since its foundation, PACE has convened its members for seminars on a number of important themes, including Christianity and African Identity (Kinshasa, 1978); the Acts of the Apostles and the Young Churches (Ibadan, 1984); Paul and the Churches (Yaoundé, 1987); Johannine Communities (Nairobi, 1989); Universalism and the Mission in the Bible (Abidjan, 1991); the Kingdom of God in the Synoptics (Accra, 1993); Salvation and Revelation (Nairobi, 1995); the Church as Family and Biblical Perspectives I (Ouagadougou, 1997); the Church as Family and Biblical Perspectives II (Abuja, 1999); the New Heavens and New Earth (Rev 21:1) (Dakar, 2001); Prophecy and Prophets in the Bible (Cairo, 2003); Human Wisdom and Divine Wisdom in the Bible (Kinshasa, 2005); Poverty and Riches in the Bible (Johannesburg, 2007); Reconciliation in the Bible (Ouidah, 2009); Women in the Bible (Lusaka, 2011); the Bible and Pastoral Issues (Abidjan, 2013); and Bible and Leadership (Bamenda, 2015).

This listing of the themes of the congresses highlights their development from concerns about African identity to, in recent years, social and contextual issues like poverty and riches, reconciliation, women in the church, and leadership. All the themes have been connected to the social, political, and ecclesial situation of Africa. The scholars involved in PACE strive to read the Bible in the historical context of African societies. They listen, as it were, to the Bible through the real life of their

---

40. See Gilbert, *L'Institut Biblique Pontifical*.
41. See Gilbert, *L'Institut Biblique Pontifical*.
42. See Appiah-Kubi, *Église, famille de Dieu*.
43. Most scholars who have published in-depth research on the sources of *Dei Verbum* are from the West. We are not aware of any such research by African theologians.
44. See O'Malley, *What Happened at Vatican II*, 228.
45. See Pan-African Association of Catholic Exegetes (PACE), http://apeca-pace.org/objectives/.

people. Their study might be said to have a strong pastoral orientation.⁴⁶

In addition, the Biblical Centre for Africa and Madagascar (BICAM) was created by African bishops as part of their work in the Symposium of Episcopal Conferences of Africa and Madagascar (SECAM) in 1981 to promote and coordinate the biblical apostolate on the continent. BICAM traces its roots back to the deliberations of the council fathers: "During the second Vatican Council in 1965, the Fathers of the Council resolved that 'all preaching of the church, as indeed the entire Christian religion should be nourished and ruled by sacred scripture.' The document in which this statement is recorded is known as *Dei Verbum* in Latin or *Divine Revelation* in English."⁴⁷

The Centre's endorsement by Pope St. John Paul II in his post-synodal apostolic exhortation *Ecclesia in Africa* brought to finality the process of recognition of the institution, which displays the fact of this recognition on its website: "Pope John Paul II, in the Apostolic Exhortation *Ecclesia in Africa*, recognized and confirmed the mission of BICAM. He says in nr. 58 of the document: 'to be encouraged is . . . promotion of the Biblical Apostolate with the help of the Biblical Centre for Africa and Madagascar and the encouragement of other similar structures at all levels.' (EIA no. 58)."⁴⁸ The papal document makes room for further initiatives that would help foster a better knowledge of the Bible in African Catholicism when it speaks of "other similar structures at all levels."⁴⁹

As this analysis has shown, the two African voices at the Second Vatican Council on the subject of divine revelation underscored the most important aspects of the final document: Jesus as the Word of God (Zoungrana), and the Word of God as the soul of Christian life, so much so that it permeates all sectors of the church's activities (Ferreira). A close look at these contributions shows that the second idea generated pastoral institutions exemplified by BICAM, while the first inspired academic research in scripture conducted by scholarly associations like PACE, or the Catholic Biblical Association of Nigeria (CABAN). The work in both areas is still in an embryonic stage, and an in-depth study of *Dei Verbum* as a doctrinal document that provides a clear orientation for future African theological works is still needed.⁵⁰

Final Remarks

There are still at least two key hermeneutical principles in *Dei Verbum* that have not yet been fully unpacked. First, the beginning of the document refers to "hearing the word of God with reverence and proclaiming it with faith" (§1). Hearing or listening to the Word of God is the main lesson we should draw from *Dei Verbum*. As Paul wrote in his letter to the Romans, "Faith comes from hearing" (Rom 10:17). It seems rather surprising that this has not been deeply developed in the scholarship, either as a theme present in scripture or as a method of interpreting biblical texts. Listening as a human faculty can unleash its potential in the interpersonal relationship between God and human beings, and the capacity to listen to God's Word can in turn create the capacity to listen to one another: "They have Moses and the prophets; let them hear them! . . . If they do not listen to Moses and the Prophets, they will not be persuaded even if someone rises from the dead" (Luke 16:29). Scripture should teach us to listen before we speak.⁵¹

---

46. For a good analytical survey, see Poucouta, *Quand la Parole de Dieu visite l'Afrique*.
47. See Biblical Centre for Africa and Madagascar (BICAM), http://www.bicam-cebam.org.
48. See Biblical Centre for Africa and Madagascar (BICAM), http://www.bicam-cebam.org.
49. One such initiative would be the biblical seminars at the Institut de Théologie de la Compagnie de Jésus (ITCJ), named after Cardinal Archbishop Laurent Monsengwo Pasinya of Kinshasa, who was the first African to earn a doctorate at the Pontifical Biblical Institute in Rome. These seminars provide a forum for world-class biblical scholars to share the results of their research.
50. However, see the recently published work by Naortangar, *Offenbarung interkulturell*.
51. Theobald (*La réception du concile vatican II*, 1:701–69) develops the methodological concept of *"recadrage"* (reframing) and demonstrates how *Dei Verbum* reframed the documents of the council: "As the latest reports state,

The Bible grew out of a "word culture," usually understood as an oral culture.[52] What I mean by "word culture" is a social way of life that values the spoken word over the written text and believes that if something is written it is meant to be spoken. Writing was intended to compensate for the impossible requirement that speakers always be physically present to their interlocutors, but the Bible as a written text has its roots in oral/aural communication because its target audience originally heard its message aurally.[53] Oral/aural cultures in Africa facilitate the aural reception of the Bible.[54] Yet we should move beyond underscoring an affinity between African and biblical culture[55] to working out effective paradigms that would help bring the two together, for example, by exploring the linguistic and grammatical similarities of Hebrew and Bantu, as discussed by Victor Zinkuratire.[56] Other areas of research along these lines could be the function of African proverbs in the social life of their users and the collections of biblical proverbs whose purpose remains unclear to the scholarship.

The second hermeneutical principle in *Dei Verbum* that needs to be investigated is that "the study of the sacred page is . . . the very soul of sacred theology" (§24). According to this principle, any theological enterprise should begin with a serious exegesis of relevant scriptural texts. The members of PACE have been expending effort on developing better methods of exegesis and developing a theological message that would accomplish the "theological exegesis" that Pope Benedict XVI wished for; however, very few dogmatic and systematic theologians, if any, have grounded their theological work on exegesis.[57] Most works of theology are still controlled by the agendas of culture, identity, liberation, or construction; thus, African theology is much more indebted to anthropology and sociology than to scriptural studies. The two ends or starting points,[58] namely, scriptural studies and theological investigations, have not yet defined a common horizon toward which they must work. The model of the church as family of God, rooted as it is in the world of the Bible, might create an atmosphere conducive to an integrated approach. This will require that the Catholic community become a hearer of the Word of God.

Making the community a theological focus, in which the study of scripture and the hearing of the Word become part of the inner culture of the church, would augur the birth of a genuine African church rooted in the apostolic tradition and in dialogue with the postapostolic traditions of the West and the East. The Catholic Church in Africa will stand on her feet the day she will be able to say, "It is no longer because of what you said that we believe, for we have heard for ourselves, and we know that this is indeed the Savior of the world" (John 4:42). Hearing the Word for oneself implies a long transformative process, and for that to happen, African

---

this dogmatic constitution effectively places us at the theological center of the Council, providing us with the key to all the other texts and the explanation of their ecumenical and pastoral principle" (769; my translation).

52. See Carr, *Writing on the Tablet of the Heart*; van der Toorn, *Scribal Culture and the Making of the Hebrew Bible*.

53. See, for instance, Béré, "Auditor in fabula," for the proposal of "aural criticism" as an approach that takes seriously the historical fact of a listening/aural audience.

54. See Finnegan, *Oral Literature in Africa*.

55. For this idea of affinity in the context of Old Testament scholarship, see Getui et al., *Interpreting the Old Testament*.

56. See Zinkuratire, "Morphological and Syntactical Correspondences," 217–26. Other studies of this kind are needed.

57. Pope Benedict praised exegetical rigor but reminds us "that comparable attention needs to be paid to the theological dimension of the biblical texts, so that they can be more deeply understood in accordance with the three elements indicated by the Dogmatic Constitution *Dei Verbum* [n.12]" (*Verbum Domini* §34).

58. Biblical exegesis and dogmatic theology are at present, on the one hand, "two starting points," but, on the other hand, they seem to be "two ends" with respect to each other in the sense that biblical exegesis tries to become "theological exegesis," while theology (whether dogmatic, moral, or another kind) tries to justify its arguments from the Bible.

churches must come to terms with the legacy of the past as well as the present, a present that is beset by so many serious problems, including homelessness, poverty, ethnic strife, and the misuse of power.

Conclusion

The discussion in this chapter has tentatively shown that *Dei Verbum*, the Dogmatic Constitution on Divine Revelation promulgated at the Second Vatican Council, the deliberations that led to its final form, and its reception in the history of the Catholic Church in Africa have not been a major resource for nourishing theological formulations in Africa. Surprisingly, a voice that contributed immensely to formulating the core message of the document came from Africa—from Archbishop Paul Zoungrana, who would later become a cardinal, and who spoke on behalf of sixty-seven African bishops. No study has ever been done that engages in a full-fledged analysis of the African contribution to *Dei Verbum*. Most studies to date have provided an overview of the African presence at the council and have concluded that African participation in its deliberations was insignificant.

Although *Dei Verbum* has not been studied by African theologians as a key theological document,[59] its principles have impacted the life and mission of the church in Africa. Institutions created to promote the biblical apostolate (such as BICAM) and biblical research in context (such as PACE) have their origin in *Dei Verbum*. There is still much to be done, especially by way of rooting theology in scripture. African sociopolitical struggles have set an agenda oriented toward culture and identity. The Catholic Church in Africa must devise its own agenda along the lines of Pope Paul VI's 1969 invitation: "By now, you Africans are missionaries to yourselves."[60] The church is considered "planted" in the African soil and Africans are responsible for "translating" the gospel message for themselves on their own continent. For that to happen, an ecclesial experience of the incarnation of the Word of God is ever more needed.

Bibliography

Acta synodalia sacrosanctii concilii oecumenici vaticanii II, 4 vols. in 20 parts (Vatican City: Typis Polyglottis Vaticanis, 1970–1977).

Adoukonou, Barthélémy. "Inculturazione della fede in Africa." In *Il Concilio Vaticano II: Recezione e attualità alla luce del Giubileo 2000*, edited by Rino Fisichella, 598–611. Cinisello Balsamo: San Paolo, 2000.

Alberigo, Giuseppe, ed. *Storia del Concilio Vaticano II*. 6 vols. Vol. 4. Bologna: Mulino; Leuven: Peeters, 1999.

Appiah-Kubi, Francis. *Église, famille de Dieu: Un chemin pour les Églises d'Afrique*. Paris: Karthala, 2008.

Benedict XVI, Pope. *Verbum Domini* [Post-synodal Apostolic Exhortation on the Word of God in the Life and Mission of the Church; September 30, 2010). Vatican City: Libreria Editrice Vaticana, 2010. www.vatican.va.

Béré, Paul. "Auditor in fabula—la Bible dans son contexte oral: Le cas du livre de Ruth." *OTE* 19 (2006).

Bwidi Kitambala, Alfred Guy. *Les évêques d'Afrique et le Concile Vatican II: Participation, contribution et application jusqu'à l'Assemblée spéciale du Synode des Évêques de 1994*. Paris: L'Harmattan, 2010.

Carr, David M. *Writing on the Tablet of the Heart: Origins of Scripture and Literature*. Oxford University Press, 2008.

Congar, Yves. *Mon Journal du Concile, I et II*. Paris: Cerf, 2002.

Da Silva, J. A. "African Contributions to the Debate on *Ad Gentes*." *Neue Zeitschrift für Missionswissenschaft* 49.2 (1993): 123–32.

Denis, Philippe. "Archbishop Hurley's Contribution to the Second Vatican Council." *Bulletin for Contextual Theology in Southern Africa and Africa* 4.1 (1997): 5–17.

———. "Vatican II in Southern Africa." *Bulletin for Contextual Theology* 4:1 (1997): 1–2.

---

59. See Naortangar, *Offenbarung interkulturell*.
60. See Pope Paul VI's homily at Kampala on July 31, 1969, www.vatican.va.

Dim, Innocent O. *Reception of Vatican II in Nigeria: Igbo Church with Reference to Awka Diocese.* Frankfurt: Peter Lang, 2004.

Durand, Jean-Dominique. "Preface to Philippe J. Roy." In *Biblie du Concile Vatican II*. Vatican: Libreria Editrice Vaticana, 2012.

Finnegan, Ruth. *Oral Literature in Africa.* Cambridge, UK: Open Book Publishers, 2012.

Getui, Mary, Knut Holter, and Victor Zinkuratire, eds. *Interpreting the Old Testament: Papers from the International Symposium on Africa and the Old Testament in Nairobi, October, 1999.* New York: Peter Lang, 2001.

Gilbert, Maurice. *L'Institut Biblique Pontifical: Un siècle d'histoire (1909–2009).* Rome: Pontificio Istituto Biblico, 2009.

Gribble, Richard. "Vatican II and the Church in Uganda: The Contribution of Bishop Vincent J. McCauley, C.S.C." *Catholic Historical Review* 95.4 (2009): 718–40.

Gundani, Paul. *Changing Patterns of Authority and Leadership: Developments in the Roman Catholic Church in Zimbabwe after Vatican II (1965–1985).* Harare: University of Zimbabwe Press, 2001.

Hastings, Adrian. "The Council Came to Africa." In *Vatican II Revisited by Those Who Were There*, edited by Dom Alberic Stacpoole. Minneapolis: Winston Press, 1986.

Ilunga Muya, Juvénal. "La situazione in Africa." In *Il Concilio Vaticano II: Recezione e attualità alla luce del Giubileo 2000*, edited by Rino Fisichella, 452–79. Cinisello Balsamo: San Paolo, 2000.

Jagoe, Bede. "Vatican II Comes to Africa." *Worship* 79.6 (2005): 544–54.

John Paul II, Pope. *Ecclesia in Africa* [Post-synodal Apostolic Exhortation on the Church in Africa and Its Evangelizing Mission toward the Year 2000; September 14, 1995]. Vatican City: Libreria Editrice Vaticana, 1995. www.vatican.va.

Jong, Albert Herman de. *The Challenge of Vatican II in East Africa: The Contribution of Dutch Missionaries to the Implementation of Vatican II in Tanzania, Kenya, Uganda, and Malawi, 1965–1975.* Nairobi: Paulines Publications Africa, 2004.

Kabasélé Lumbala, François. "L'inculturation et les Églises d'Afrique: Entre Vatican II et le Synode Africain." In *Vatican II and Its Legacy*, edited by Mathijs Lamberigts and Leo Kenis, 351–64. Bibliotheca Ephemeridum Theologicarum Lovaniensium 166. Leuven: Leuven University Press/Peeters, 2006.

Kikoti, William Pascal. *Episcopal Conferences in the Light of Vatican II: The Theological Foundation and Role in the Church. A Case Study of Tanzania Episcopal Conference.* Dissertation, Pontificia Università Urbaniana, 1996.

Kumbu ki Kumbu, Eleuthère. "Le problème de la révélation extra-biblique après Vatican II: Implications pour la mission de l'Église en Afrique." *Revue théologique de Louvain* 38.1 (2007): 41–66.

Lubac, Henri de. *Entretien autour de Vatican II: Souvenirs et réflexions.* Paris: Cerf, 1985.

Messina, Jean-Paul. "L'Église d'Afrique au concile Vatian II: Origines de l'Assemblée spéciale du synode des évêques pour l'Afrique." *Mélanges de sciences religieuses* 51.3 (1994): 279–95.

———. *Évêques Africains au Concile Vatican II (1959–1965): Le cas du Cameroun.* Paris: Karthala, 2000.

———. *Jean Zoa, Prêtre, Archevêque de Yaoundé 1922–1998.* Paris: Karthala, 2000.

Monsengwo Pasinya, Laurent. "Le cadre littéraire de Genèse 1." *Biblica* 57 (1976): 225–41.

———. "Interprétation africaine de la Bible: Racine herméneutique et biblique." *Revue Africaine de Théologie* 1 (1977): 145–64.

Mudiji Malamba, Theodore. "African Cultural Heritage in the Global Encounter of Civilization." In *Multiple Paths to God: "Nostra Aetate," Forty Years Later*, edited by John Hogan, 75–104. Washington, DC: Council for Research in Values and Philosophy and John Paul II Cultural Center, 2005.

Naortangar, Rodrigue. *Offenbarung interkulturell: Die dogmatische Konstitution "Dei verbum" im Dialog mit dem Christus-Modell von Fabien Eboussi Boulaga.* Salzburger Theologische Studien 60. Innsbruck: Tyrolia Verlagsanstalt, 2018.

Njoku, Antony. "Vatican II and the Process of Its Reception in the Igbo Speaking Church of Southeastern Nigeria." Dissertation, Katholieke Universiteit Leuven, 2002.

Oborji, Francis Anekwe. "Revelation in African Traditional Religion: The Theological Approach since Vatican II." *Euntes Docete* 55.3 (2002): 63–78.

Olivier, Bernard. *Chroniques Congolaises: De Lépoldville à Vatican II.* Paris: Karthala, 2000.

O'Malley, John. *What Happened at Vatican II.* Cambridge, MA: Harvard University Press 2008.

Orobator, Agbonkhianmeghe E. "'After All, Africa Is Largely a Nonliterate Continent': The Reception of Vatican II in Africa." *Theological Studies* 74.2 (2013): 284–301.

———. "Look Back to the Future: Transformative Impulses of Vatican II for African Catholicism." *Concilium* 3 (2012): 97–102.

Ponga, Silouane. *L'Écriture, âme de la théologie: Le problème de la suffisance matérielle des Écritures*. Paris: Cerf, 2008.

Poucouta, Paulin. *Quand la Parole de Dieu visite l'Afrique: Lecture plurielle de la Bible*. Paris: Karthala, 2011.

Prudhomme, Claude. "Les évêques d'Afrique noire anciennement française et le concile." In *Vatican II commence . . . : Approches francophones*, edited by Étienne Fouilloux, 162–88. Leuven: Bibliotheek van de Faculteith der Godgeleerdhied, 1993.

Roy, Philippe J. *Bibliographie du Concile Vatican II*. Vatican: Libreria Editrice Vaticana, 2012.

Sauer, Hanjo. *Glaube und Erfahrung: Die Begründung des pastoralen Prinzips durch die Offenbarungskonstitution des II. Vatikanischen Konzils*. Frankfurt: Peter Lang, 1993.

———. "I problemi della dottrina sono i problemi della pastorale." In *Storia del concilio Vaticano II*, vol. 4: *La chiesa come comunione: Il terzo periodo e la intersessione settembre 1964–settembre 1965*, edited by Giuseppe Alberigo, 221–91. Bologna: Mulino, 1999.

Société Africaine de Culture. *Les prêtres noirs s'interrogent*. Paris: Cerf, 1956.

Soetens, Claude. "L'apport du Congo (Zaïre), du Rwanda et du Burundi au concile Vatican II." In *Vatican II commence . . . : Approches francophones*, edited by Étienne Fouilloux, 189–99. Leuven: Bibliotheek van de Faculteith der Godgeleerdhied, 1993.

Somé, Beterbanfo Modeste. "Eglise-Famille-de-Dieu: De la nouvelle genèse d'un concept ecclésiologique à l'époque contemporaine." *Kanien* 1.1 (2013) : 45–62.

Tanner, Norman. ed. *Vatican II: The Essential Texts*. New York: Crown, 2012.

Tessier, Henri. "Vatican II et le Tiers Monde." In *Le Deuxième concile du Vatican (1959–1965)*, 755–65. Rome: École Française de Rome, 1989.

Theobald, Christoph. *La réception du concile Vatican II*. Vol. 1: *Accéder à la source*. Paris: Cerf, 2009.

Toorn, Karel van der. *Scribal Culture and the Making of the Hebrew Bible*. Cambridge, MA: Harvard University Press, 2007.

Tshibangu, Tharcisse. *Le Concile Vatican II et l'Église africaine (1960–2010): Mise en oeuvre du Concile dans l'Église d'Afrique*. Kinshasa: L'Épiphanie; Paris: Karthala, 2012.

Vatican II. *Dei Verbum* [Dogmatic Constitution on Divine Revelation; 1965].

Verdin, Philippe. *Alioune Diop, le Socrate noir*. Paris: Lethielleux, 2011.

Zinkuratire, Victor. "Morphological and Syntactical Correspondences between Hebrew and Bantu Languages." In *Interpreting the Old Testament in Africa: Papers from the International Symposium on Africa and the Old Testament in Nairobi, October, 1999*, edited by Mary Getui, Knut Holter, and Victor Zinkuratire, 217–26. New York: Peter Lang, 2001.

Suggested Reading

Alberigo, Giuseppe, ed. *Storia del Concilio Vaticano II*. 6 vols.; see especially vol. 4. Bologna: Mulino; Leuven: Peeters, 1999.

Bwidi Kitambala, Alfred Guy. *Les évêques d'Afrique et le Concile Vatican II: Participation, contribution et application jusqu'à l'Assemblée spéciale du Synode des Évêques de 1994*. Paris: L'Harmattan, 2010.

Poucouta, Paulin. *Quand la Parole de Dieu visite l'Afrique: Lecture plurielle de la Bible*. Paris: Karthala, 2011.

Theobald, Christoph, *La réception du concile Vatican II*. Vol. 1: *Accéder à la source*. Paris: Cerf, 2009.

Tshibangu, Tharcisse. *Le Concile Vatican II et l'Église africaine (1960–2010): Mise en oeuvre du Concile dans l'Église d'Afrique*. Kinshasa: L'Épiphanie; Paris: Karthala, 2012.

Key Words
aural criticism
Dei Verbum
exegetical theology
inculturation
revelation
scripture
tradition

Bible and Society in Africa: African Exegesis for an Effective Catechesis

Daniel Assefa

This chapter deals with the relationship between the Bible and society in an African context from the perspective of Catholic catechesis. In the teaching of the gospel and instruction in the faith, methods of transmission necessarily vary.[1] There exist today important catechetical materials prepared by Catholic dioceses in various African countries, but their quality depends on how inculturated they are and on their capacity to address essential questions facing African society. Adaptation of catechesis to different cultures in general, and to an African context in particular, is clearly prescribed in the *Catechism of the Catholic Church*.[2]

The following questions will be addressed in this chapter. How much is the centrality of the Bible recognized[3] and integrated into catechetical materials and programs? How important for sustained and authentic Christian service in Africa is an appreciation of the significance of the Bible? How important is such an appreciation for African exegesis and hermeneutics as well as instructional methods and evangelization? How can African values be cherished, promoted, and perfected by the values of the gospel? The chapter aims to show that a biblical approach is fundamental for catechesis and Christian service in Africa. The place of the great African exegetes of antiquity and the experience of Ethiopian biblical hermeneutics will be referred to in the course of the argument.

The Bible in African Languages

The first major translation of the Bible was completed in Africa, in the city of Alexandria.[4] The

---

1. St. Paul's differing missionary approaches toward the Jews (Acts 13) and the Greeks (Acts 17) clearly illustrate how catechesis should be fostered on African soil. Although Paul preaches Christ in both cases, he begins with the biblical history of salvation in Acts 13, while in Acts 17 he discusses the Athenians' altars of worship and cites Greek poetry.

2. The prologue of the *Catechism* states, "By design, this Catechism does not set out to provide the adaptation of doctrinal presentations and catechetical methods required by the differences of culture, age, spiritual maturity, and social and ecclesial condition among all those to whom it is addressed. Such indispensable adaptations are the responsibility of particular catechisms and, even more, of those who instruct the faithful" (§1994, 24). See also Pope John Paul II, apostolic exhortation *Catechesis Tradendae* §53; and Catholic Church Congregation for the Clergy, *General Directory for Catechesis* §§109–11.

3. In his *Anatomy of Inculturation*, Magesa asks, "Without reference to the Bible, to the witness of faith by those who are 'our ancestors in the faith,' to what else would any Christian community go to find the most basic and authentic sources and interpretation of its belief and behaviour? The most authentic link between the church and the Christ the apostles knew is, above all else, the Bible." (180).

4. Mbiti underlines this fact and discusses its significance in his article "The Bible in African Culture," published in 1994.

Septuagint, apart from being a remarkable achievement in itself,[5] became the Old Testament for the early church. One may also consider the translation of the sacred scriptures into Ge'ez, or classical Ethiopic, between the fifth and seventh centuries as another landmark in the reception of the Bible into Africa.[6] In the northeastern part of Africa, at least sixteen centuries have passed in which the Bible has been transmitted by means of a large number of manuscripts,[7] as well as read, meditated upon, venerated, and interpreted.

In more recent times, the translation of the Bible into various African languages, an endeavor of international and local Bible societies, has become a crucial task—catechesis and the celebration of the Christian mysteries in African communities depend on the Bible being translated into local languages. In accomplishing this massive undertaking, semantics and religious figures of speech must be taken into consideration. In the scriptures, God is presented as Lord, creator, savior and redeemer, shepherd, rock, living water, light, shield, and father, to name but a few images. The presentation and explanation of these attributes and images in African languages must make room for African perceptions, interpretations, and usages of the same or similar images. African worldviews and customs, as well as African sociocultural, economic, and political circumstances also need to be taken into consideration.

Hermeneutics

Interpretation is even more essential for those who engage in catechesis. Interpretation is an ancient art—it was already present in the Old Testament in instances of later texts interpreting earlier ones.[8] When the evangelist Matthew says, "I called my son from Egypt" (Matt 2:15), he is interpreting the book of Hosea ("When Israel was a child," Hos 11:2). St. Paul interprets passages from the Old Testament in the light of Christian events. In the First Letter to the Corinthians, he says, "And all drank the same spiritual drink, for they were drinking from the spiritual rock that was following them; and the rock was Christ" (1 Cor 10:4). Here Paul is interpreting and actualizing what we read in the books of Exodus (17:5–6) and Numbers (20:7–11) and in the Psalms (78:15–16): the rock becomes the symbol of Christ. In the fourth chapter of the Letter to the Galatians, Paul compares the heavenly Jerusalem with Sarah and the earthly Jerusalem with Hagar (4:21–31). These are just a few examples among a multitude of New Testament "fulfillment" readings of Old Testament texts.

Throughout history, the church has continued the task of interpreting the scriptures on the basis of the rule of faith it inherited, actualizing what it received. Today's situation is analogous; Christians, wherever they may be, including in Ethiopia, are instructed to interpret the scriptures in order to nourish their faith as well as to respond to the challenges of the time. I will return to what may be learned from traditional patristic and Ethiopian exegesis after a brief look at some modern approaches to interpreting the sacred scriptures in Africa.

An African Approach to the Bible

In *A Handbook on African Approaches to Biblical Interpretation* (2012),[9] Albert Ngengi Mundele proposes two exegetical steps for African scholars to follow. The first step consists of carrying out a literary analysis inspired by modern biblical scholarship. This includes delimiting the text, applying

---

5. In particular, it was a great work of inculturation.
6. For the significance of Ethiopia to Bible translation, see E. Ullendorff, *Ethiopia and the Bible* (Oxford: Oxford University Press, 1967).
7. Thus creating communities of scribal tradition that, even under conditions of hardship, treasured the Word of God. These communities accomplished this by making parchments, preparing inks with different colors from the natural environment, and training scribes in the art of copying.
8. See Fishbane, *Biblical Interpretation in Ancient Israel*.
9. Mundele, *A Handbook on African Approaches to Biblical Interpretation*. The French version of this book, *Manuel d'approches Bibliques en Afrique*, was published in 2014.

textual criticism, exploring the immediate and broader context, analyzing the structure of the biblical passage and its syntax and semantics, and identifying the applicable literary genre. All of this would be followed by choosing the appropriate exegetical method.

With respect to delimitation of the text, we may decide, for instance, that we want to study Mark's Gospel, but we need to narrow the focus of our study, given that we cannot analyze the whole book at one time. Even if we choose to analyze Mark chapter 7, we still need to delimit the text. Mark 7:1–23 deals with the theme of purity, of what defiles a person and what does not, and it also mentions the Pharisees and the scribes; Mark chapter 6 and chapter 7 after verse 23 deal with different themes and characters.

If we choose Mark 7:1–23, we must then keep in mind that different English translations emphasize different information. There is, for example, a significant variation in the rendering of Mark 7:3 in the New Revised Standard Version and the New Jerusalem Bible:

Mark 7:3 (New Revised Standard Version)	Mark 7:3 (New Jerusalem Bible)
For the Pharisees, and all the Jews, do not eat unless they thoroughly wash their hands, thus observing the tradition of the elders.	For the Pharisees, and all the Jews, keep the tradition of the elders and never eat without washing their arms as far as the elbow.

Textual criticism analyzes the variations in the text, attempts to explain the reasons for them, and suggests what may have been the more original reading. Commentaries often discuss these kinds of issues in textual notes, sometimes referring to the original languages, including Hebrew and Greek, and to the relationship among the manuscripts.

It must be kept in mind that no passage is an island; it is part of a whole. With respect to Mark 7:1–23, it should be read in connection with the passages that precede and follow it, even though these treat different themes. It is interesting, for instance, to take note of the division between Jews and gentiles that is reflected in both Mark 7:1–23 and the following passage. In the former, this division is manifested in the debate over what is pure and impure. In the latter, it appears in the privileging of the Jews over the gentiles in the healing story of the Syrophoenician woman (vv. 24–30).

An analysis of the structure of Mark 7:1–23 would involve identifying its various subparts and examining their interrelationship. Thus, verses 1–4 contain introductory information provided by the narrator. Jesus responds in verses 6–13 to a question put by the Pharisees in verse 5, rebuking them. Jesus addresses the crowd in verses 14–15, and in verses 18–23 he replies to a question posed by the disciples. One may thus divide the passage based on Jesus's addresses—to the Pharisees, the crowd, and the disciples. We must then ask, Are the three answers of Jesus similar?

A semantic analysis focuses on the meanings of words. Does the word "Corban" in verse 11 have only one meaning? Does it have other connotations in other contexts? What about the words used in the list of vices in verses 21–22? Scrutinizing the meanings of the words enriches an understanding of the passage.

Identifying the genre of a passage may be useful. Given that Mark 7:1–23 is a Gospel narrative, the meaning of the words are to be taken literally—this would not be the case with an allegory or apocalyptic text. Thus, in verse 4, the words "cups," "pots," and "bronze kettles" refer to the actual material implements people use. This is not the case, of course, for the beast with ten horns of Daniel 7:7 or the slaughtered lamb with seven horns and seven eyes in Revelation 5:6. In those instances we are dealing with apocalyptic passages full of symbolism: the beast with ten horns refers to the Greek empire, while the lamb with seven horns represents Christ.

After these preliminary studies, the African exegete should move to the second step, which consists of analyzing African traditions, cultures, and present-day circumstances as they relate to the biblical passage under study. A number of examples could be taken from Ethiopia; one example is that reconciliation, an important theme in scripture, is also a fundamental value in the Guraghe region located south of the capital city of Addis Ababa. Every September, nearly all the young people return home to celebrate the annual feast of Masqal, which corresponds to the Christian feast of the Exaltation of the Cross. This event coincides with the transition from the rainy season to the season of flowers. Biblical passages on reconciliation may be examined in the light of the Masqal reconciliation ceremony. The ceremony involves recognized elders listening to each person's sins and then blessing them, which encourages the offender to adopt an open attitude and gives the victim some consolation. This ceremony can be compared to biblical readings in which God waits for the repentant sinner. The role of the elders could be evoked and examined when one studies, for instance, Jesus's expression, "Blessed are the peacemakers" (Matt 5:9). The power of parables in the Gospel narratives may be compared with the parables told by elders that result in a change of perspective and attitude among belligerents.

In connection with examining African circumstances in the light of scripture, the book *The Pastoral Use of the Bible* prepared by the Lumko Institute of the Episcopal Conference of Southern Africa is worthy of note.[10] This work has two objectives. The first is to help catechetical leaders design parish-based programs in which participants are given guidelines concerning how to conduct meetings, to pray, to properly read scripture, and to meditate on and discuss biblical passages in relation to their life situations. The second is to provide materials to deepen and improve people's exchange of reflections about biblical texts. Also worthy of note are documents issued by African Catholic ecclesiastical and academic institutions. Among these should be mentioned the Pan-African Association of Catholic Exegetes (PACE), which holds seminars on biblical themes in an African context.[11]

Patristic Exegesis and Ethiopian Commentaries on the Bible

Both *Handbook on African Approaches to Biblical Interpretation* and the *Pastoral Use of the Bible* could be enriched by the use of ancient patristic exegetical writings, which were grounded in the paschal mysteries and the liturgy. Patristic exegesis was masterfully practiced by great African figures, including Origen, Cyril, and Augustine. These exegetes were second to none both in their knowledge of the biblical texts and in theories of reading and interpreting the sacred scriptures. For example, Origen paid close attention to the ancient Hebrew and Greek versions of the text, which is important

---

10. Lumko Institute, *Pastoral Use of the Bible* (3rd ed., 1991). The French version is from 2003. The Episcopal Conference of Southern Africa is composed of church leaders from the countries of South Africa, Botswana, and Swaziland.

11. For more information about these seminars, see the chapter in this handbook authored by Paul Béré, "*Dei Verbum* in African Catholicism: History and Reception."

12. The Hexapla, with the Old Testament text in six columns, is significant with respect to issues related to textual criticism. Origen greatly contributed to textual criticism and to biblical interpretation. In his work *On First Principles*, he offered fundamental principles for approaching the sacred scriptures, including inviting readers to go beyond the text's literal meaning to search for its deeper spiritual significance. According to Origen, doing this work leads to an encounter with Christ, the Word of God (see *On First Principles* 4.2–3, in Bart Ehrman, *After the New Testament: A Reader in Early Christianity* [Oxford: Oxford University Press, 1999], 424–29). See also Simonetti, *Lettera e/o allegoria*, 73–98. Cyril of Alexandria adopted the allegorical interpretation but counseled caution about linking scriptural texts to Christ. See Cyril in *Patrologia Cursus Completus: Series Graeca*, ed. J.-P. Migne, 162 vols. (Paris, 1857–1886), 69:13–677. Simonetti, *Lettera e/o allegoria*, 216–30. For references to Cyril, see Alexander Kerrigan, *St. Cyril of Alexandria, Interpreter of the Old Testament*, Analecta Biblica 2 (Rome: Pontificio Istituto Biblico, 1952); M. Simonetti, "Note sul commento di Cirillo ai Profeti minori," *Vetera christianorum* 14 (1977): 301–30; Robert L. Wilken, *Judaism and the Early Christian Mind: A Study of Cyril of Alexandria's Exegesis and Theology* (New Haven: Yale University Press, 1971). For the importance of patristic exegesis as exemplified in St. Augustine's interpretation of the Psalms, in which an allegorical interpretation leads to an understanding of the essential role of Christology, see Byasse, *Praise Seeking Understanding*, 9–53. For references to Origen, see Rolf Gögler, *Zur Theologie des biblischen Wortes bei Origenes* (Düsseldorf: Patmos, 1963); R. P. C. Hanson, *Allegory and Event: A Study of the Sources and Significance of Origen's Interpretation of Scripture* (London: SCM Press, 1959); N.

in modern exegesis, especially in textual criticism.[12] His great curiosity about nature and cultural contexts is also apparent in his writings. The fact that modern exegesis does not pay enough attention to the patristic approach should not prevent African biblical hermeneutics from nourishing itself from this life source.

The Pontifical Biblical Commission of the Catholic Church has acknowledged the prominent place in modern Christian exegesis of the historical-critical approach but stated that it needs to be supplemented by other methods: "No scientific method for the study of the Bible is fully adequate to comprehend the biblical texts in all their richness. For all its validity, the historical-critical method cannot claim to be totally sufficient in this respect. It necessarily has to put aside many aspects of the writings which it studies."[13] Joseph Putti recognizes that the historical-critical approach enables an appreciation of the "historical sources" of faith, but he also describes its limitations:

> The historical-critical method is inadequate of itself for displaying the meaning of the Biblical texts since it is based on the Romanticist theory of meaning. By trying to locate meaning in the source behind the text—the author, the audience, the context—it fails to attend to the text itself as a source of meaning. This leads to hermeneutical sterility. If the meaning of a text coincides with the author's intention and a later reader must repeat the reading made up by the first addressee, then, we are caught up an exegetical "historicism."
>
> . . . The prevailing gulf between exegesis (what the author meant in the past) and theology (what the text means in the present) has led to questions being raised by many as to whether the Biblical scholars, with all the results of their historical research, can give to the believers some direction about the implications of the Bible for religion in the present.[14]

Other exegetical approaches explore biblical texts without focusing chiefly on history.[15] For example, traditional Ethiopian commentaries for each book of the Bible are available.[16] In addition to providing a historical and literal interpretation of the biblical text, and while always paying close attention to the history of salvation and the Christ-event, these commentaries engage in a constant search for the spiritual meaning of the text. Beyond their affinity with patristic exegesis, especially that of Alexandria and Syria,[17] these commentaries are a remarkable exercise in inculturation, whereby the biblical text is explained with references to indigenous images and stories. Local customs and proverbs, and even local fauna and flora, are used to help the Ethiopian reader appreciate the word of God.

While ancient exegesis begins with faith and with a strong concern for pastoral matters, this does not mean that its practitioners were unaware of historical and critical questions. The introductions to the traditional Ethiopian commentaries are instructive. The four Gospels are preceded

---

R. M. de Lange, *Origen and the Jews: Studies in Jewish-Christian Relations in Third-Century Palestine* (Cambridge: Cambridge University Press, 1976); Henri de Lubac, *Histoire et esprit: L'intelligence de l'Écriture d'après Origène* (Paris: Aubier, 1950); V. Peri, "Criteri di critica semantica dell' esegesi origeniana," *Augustinianum* 15 (1975): 5–27.

13. See Pontifical Biblical Commission, *"The Interpretation of the Bible in the Church": Text and Commentary* (Rome: Pontificio Istituto Biblico, 1995), 50–52.

14. Putti, *Theology as Hermeneutics*, 229.

15. These include synchronic approaches, for example, rhetorical and narrative methods of interpretation.

16. This canon of commentaries is the broadest in scope and the largest numerically among the Christian churches. For studies of Ethiopian biblical hermeneutics, see Andeberhan, *Commentari etiopici sul libro del Profeta Osea*; Cowley, *Traditional Interpretation of the Apocalypse of St. John in the Ethiopian Orthodox Church*; A. Mersha, *Ethiopian Biblical Interpretation: A Study in Exegetical Tradition and Hermeneutics* (Cambridge: Cambridge University Press, 2010); Mersha, *Ethiopian Commentary on the Book of Genesis*; Pedersen, *Traditional Ethiopian Exegesis of the Book of Psalms*; Tedros, *La lettera ai Romani*; Pedersen and Tedros, "Andemta."

17. Because of the presence of common principles and heritage between them, one may also speak of the commentaries' affinity with the work of the Latin fathers.

by a preface called *maqdema wengel* (preface of the Gospel), and Paul's letters are introduced by a *Mekeneyat* (purpose or reason).[18] Some aspects of the historical-critical method are also present in the *Andemtas*. These commentaries deal with questions of authorship, background, content, and canonicity,[19] and a brief sentence after the title of each psalm provides a historical note as a key to understanding the text. It is said, for instance, that Psalms 23, 24, 25, 26, 31, and 40 refer to the time of the Babylonian exile even though the Psalms are attributed to David, who lived long before the exile in 587 BCE. The commentators explain the Babylonian references by taking them as predictions about the time of exile, reading them in light of this now-historical, then-future, event.[20]

For example, the first verse of Psalm 24, "To the Lord belong the earth and its plenitude," is explained in the light of the exile. According to the commentary, the people of Israel said that they had stopped praying because the temple in Jerusalem had been destroyed and because there was no proper sanctuary in Babylon; the people asserted that the priests and prophets told people not to pray in their houses. The commentary stated that the first verse of Psalm 24 was the response of the prophets and priests to the people's failure to pray. The prophets and priests made it clear that they meant to forbid only some types of prayers—they did not forbid all prayers, for "To the Lord belong the earth and its plenitude." In other words, the reasons the people gave for not praying were not adequate—one can pray anywhere, even in the land of the exile, even when there is no temple, no priest, no sacrifice, and no offering.

Faith and Interpretation

The traditional Ethiopian commentaries presuppose faith as the key to biblical interpretation. A sharp distinction between exegesis and theology does not exist in the traditional Ethiopian commentaries, whose content easily gives rise to teachings about the Holy Trinity, Christ, and Mary. The importance of this was underlined by Joseph Cardinal Ratzinger in a lecture delivered on January 27, 1988, at Saint Peter's Church in New York. He stated that the exegete "does not stand in some neutral area."[21] If the exegete ignores the faith of the church, his or her interpretation will never become theology. The Ethiopian commentaries allow their listeners or readers to search the biblical text for a deeper meaning, for what Ethiopian scholars call the *mestir*. The commentaries readily plunge into praise of God and presuppose a spirit of prayer in the listener or reader.

From Scripture to Catechesis

African traditional and cultural values need to be underlined and fostered in the practice of catechesis.[22] Among these values, Pope St. John Paul II underscored a "profound religious sense, a sense of the sacred, the existence of God the creator, and of the spiritual world, the reality of sin, the need

---

18. Cowley, "New Testament Introduction in the *Andemta* Commentary Tradition," 144–92.

19. The Ethiopian commentary on the book of Ezekiel, written in the late nineteenth and early twentieth centuries, is remarkable inasmuch as it includes rabbinic interpretations not found in other Ethiopian biblical commentaries.

20. The exegesis of the Psalms by the Antiochene fathers like Theodore of Mopsuestia, Theodoret of Cyrus, and Diodore of Tarsus, is quite similar to that of the Ethiopian commentaries on the Psalms. See Theodore of Mopsuestia, *Commentary on Psalms 1–81*, translated with an introduction and notes by Robert C. Hill, Writings from the Greco-Roman World 5 (Atlanta: Society of Biblical Literature, 2006); Theodoret of Cyrus, *Commentary on the Psalms*, translated with an introduction and notes by Robert C. Hill, 2 vols., Fathers of the Church 101–102 (Washington, DC: Catholic University of America Press, 2000–2001); Diodore of Tarsus, *Commentary of Psalms 1–51*, translated with an introduction and notes by Robert C. Hill, Writings from the Greco-Roman World 9 (Atlanta: Society of Biblical Literature, 2005).

21. See Thornton and Varenne, *Essential Pope Benedict XVI*, 257–58.

22. Part 2 of Magesa's *What Is Not Sacred?* is focused on how people both in Africa and outside the continent can profit from adopting African values; see 101–97.

23. Pope John Paul II's post-synodal apostolic exhortation *Ecclesia in Africa* §§42–43.

of rites of purification and expiation."²³ An interface between sacramental life, liturgy, prayer, and morality as found in the scriptures, in patristic sources, and in the teachings of the magisterium, on the one hand, and, on the other hand, African traditional rites, prayers, and ethics is needed for an appropriate and fruitful catechesis on the continent.²⁴ Just as the sacred scriptures are rich in symbols and figurative speech, so are African societies. For instance, the motif of the mother symbolizing the earth and the church is used in catechesis. Similarly, the symbolism of water, oil, earth, fire, light, trees, and the cross are so rich that agents of evangelization may use these images to help those being catechized to ponder both the sacred scriptures and their beloved continent. Doing these things is the best way to express transcendence by referring to profound values that are at home in Africa.²⁵ Various African scholars have pointed out that the concept of "life" holds a central role in the African worldview. Thus, underlining that the biblical God is the giver of life is a good start to a catechetical discourse.²⁶ The special place of nature and creation and plants and animals in African societies should also be given this kind of attention.

In addition, ancient methods of biblical interpretation practiced in both ancient North Africa and in present-day Ethiopia are important to effective catechesis. They propose a reading of biblical passages from a holistic and intertextual perspective. They help the reader or listener make a journey of faith, inviting him or her to search for Christ by reading biblical passages in light of Christ's death and resurrection. An integration of these ancient approaches with modern ones is indeed possible, and both African exegesis and African catechesis can profit from such an approach.

Let us take, for instance, the parable of the Good Samaritan. Modern historical exegesis can help us better understand the meaning of the term "Samaritan" and the tensions that existed between Jews and Samaritans at the time of Jesus. Biblical archaeology can help us visualize the place where the story unfolded, and modern narrative analysis can help us analyze character, plot, and narrative tension to enable a clearer understanding of how the story is told and how its meaning is communicated. In contrast, however, Origen and Augustine can inspire the reader to see the Good Samaritan as an image of Christ. Both the Samaritan in the parable and Jesus in the Gospels helped and healed the needy, moved by compassion. Both were rejected and despised by many. The love of neighbor, specifically a robbery victim, illustrated by the Good Samaritan leads to a further and deeper reflection on Jesus's love for humanity. This of course does not mean that the Christological interpretation was part of the literal meaning of the parable, and it is important to consider that finding Christ who heals the wounds of humanity in the story of the Good Samaritan is not an obstacle to a thorough historical and critical study of it. There is no contradiction, but rather a complementarity, as long as one remains within the framework of the history of salvation and Christ's role in it.

From Scripture to Social Life and Ethics

It is important to address briefly certain challenges facing African society. To begin with, the identity of the human being deserves attention in the face of the rapid changes of the technological and digital age. These changes are happening so quickly that distance and pause for critical reflection are crucial. The questions that are raised involve how these changes are affecting African society in general and African Christians in particular and whether they are effecting a change in the African worldview. If they are bringing about such a change, is it for the better or is it having a negative impact on African values?

It is possible to consider issues of poverty and injustice in an African context by looking at the

---

24. Bujo discusses at length how an African morality does not need to refer to Western categories and views of morality (*Foundations of an African Ethic*).

25. The *Gospel Seed: Culture and Faith in Malawi* by Boucher is an example of the use of these images.

26. See here Magesa's *What Is Not Sacred*? In the African worldview, the sacred permeates every dimension of life; it does not include a dualistic vision of what is sacred and profane. The material world becomes a symbol of the divine. This is significant for the doctrine of creation and for any teaching about the sacraments.

condemnation of injustice in the book of Amos. Of course the lessons of this book are to be drawn first in the context of the history of Israel, but the meaning of the text is also applicable to the African context. An analysis of this prophetic book would lead to a full understanding of and condemnation of injustice in a different historical and social situation. In the biblical tradition, the messages of prophets carried a dimension of criticism. They ask for change and a return to God. Edifying criticism needs to be applied to the African context. Can we identify elements of self-criticism in the African worldview? African traditions that need to be critiqued in light of the Word of God implicate questions of peace and the condemnation of violence. People are called to remember that they are created in the image of God, which then evokes respect for the poor, the widow, and the stranger.

According to Musa W. Dube, the African theologian's biblical hermeneutics needs to read African realities as a text.[27] The stories of Bethany of E. Katongole[28] also propose reading Gospel passages in light of current African situations. In this regard, significant help may be obtained from the social teaching of the Catholic Church. If the faithful are well formed in this teaching, they will more clearly understand the relationship between the Bible and social life.[29]

A Lesson from Traditional Ethiopian Biblical Interpretation

The traditional Ethiopian commentaries encourage tolerance of and respect for various approaches to biblical interpretation. There is always an effort to look at a passage, a verse, or a word from different points of view. Usually the deeper meanings are spiritual and Christological. The desire to look for more meanings and to search for more perspectives is by itself inspiring for educators, but even more inspiring is the respect accorded to multiple points of view. This attitude needs to be actualized in present-day Africa. All areas of sociopolitical life in every African country would benefit from accepting various opinions and possible meanings of biblical texts.

This respect for various perspectives is, for example, conspicuous in the commentaries on Psalm 24. There are at least seven levels of meaning offered for the command in verse 7, "O princes open the gates":

1. "O princes of Babylon open the gates of Babylon!" The house of Israel seeks his face at the time of its return. Let the gates unopened for so long be opened. Let the king of glory enter in order to rescue the remnant of Israel from Babylon.
2. "O Cyrus, O Darius, open the gates of Babylon." Let the princes of Babylon who had not been assaulted for so long be attacked. Let the king of glory enter in the persons of Cyrus and Darius and attack Babylon.
3. "O princes of Judea and Samaria open the gates of Judea and Samaria." Let the gates unopened for so long be opened. Let the king of glory, the Lord, bring back the remnant of Israel through Judea and Samaria.
4. "O prophets, princes of prophecy; O priests, princes of teaching, open the gates of prophecy, open the gates of teaching." Let the gates of prophecy, of teaching, unopened for so long, be opened. Let the king of glory, the Lord, reside in the hearts and ears of those who listen.
5. "O prophets, princes of prophecy; O priests, princes of teaching, prophesy saying: 'He will come down, He will be born.'" Let the prophecy, unheard for so long, be announced. Let the king of glory, the Lord, become flesh, incarnated.
6. "Princes of Sheol, devils, open the gates of Sheol." Let the gates of Sheol unopened for so long be opened. Let the king of glory enter to rescue souls from Sheol.
7. "O princes of paradise, cherubim, seraphim, open the gates of heaven." Let the gates of para-

---

27. Dube, "Rereading the Bible."
28. Katongole, *Stories from Bethany*.
29. For the relationship between the Bible and ethics, see the document of the Pontifical Biblical Commission entitled *The Bible and Morality: Biblical Roots of Christian Conduct*. For a thorough study of development in Africa in light of the social ethics of the Catholic Church, see Ilo, *Church and Development in Africa*.

dise unopened for so long be opened. Let the king of glory, the Lord, enter in the company of the souls.[30]

It is interesting to observe the progress from the historical to the metaphorical, Christological, and eschatological levels of meaning.[31]

From the Bible to the Liturgy
We have just seen how Psalm 24 was the subject of a rich traditional commentary that revealed the Christological themes of the incarnation, redemption, and eschatological salvation. The same psalm also plays an important role in the liturgy. It is sung at solemn vespers, in which new theological poems using fresh metaphors related to the feast being celebrated and inspired by biblical themes and stories are uttered.

According to the Ethiopian rite, on Palm Sunday, before the eucharistic celebration, a priest and a deacon dramatize Psalm 24:7–10 in commemoration of the solemn entry of Jesus into Jerusalem. After the distribution of palms, the entire assembly moves in procession outside the church in order to listen to the reading of the Gospel. The priest, however, remains inside the church or sanctuary; the deacon, who stands together with the faithful outside, knocks three times with the processional cross while singing the verse of Psalm 24 that commands, "O princes! Open the gate." The reply to the request, which consists of an inquiry as to the identity of the one who desires entry, is sung by the priest from inside.[32]

One can also explore and admire the role of psalms in the Ethiopian antiphonary, which collects an impressive number of hymns for major Christological feasts[33] occurring throughout the liturgical year. The hymns intertwine biblical verses with theological reflections on the Word of God and creation. The providence of God is praised through the celebration of the beauty of rain, flowers, and fruits.

One visible feature of the Ethiopian eucharistic liturgy is a rich dialogue between the celebrant, the faithful, and the deacon. This not only makes the celebration lively but also gives room to the faithful to express their faith, in addition to confessing doctrinal truths. Often the language is figurative and full of images, sometimes illustrating Christian paradoxes, for example, the one in the Eucharistic Prayer attributed to John Chrysostom: "He who does not die, died; He died in order to cancel death." The poetic language used in the Eucharistic Prayers makes room for the celebrant to wonder and to invite the faithful also to be filled with amazement and admiration. This language is quite helpful and meaningful for catechesis.

From the Bible to Visual Art, Drama, and Media
Commentaries aid the reader or listener in looking for deeper meanings in the Bible, but there are other ways of helping the faithful reflect and meditate on Christian mysteries. One of these is visual art, images, paintings, and icons, which play a significant role in catechesis. Christian visual art has been created for centuries in Egypt and Ethiopia, and these amazing works of art have spoken to people in every age. The doctrine of creation, the history of salvation, and eschatology are represented in the churches with sequential multipanel narrations, as one would see in a comic book. The exercise of painting icons is intimately connected to meditation, prayer, and fasting. Many African communities use visual art to express messages or describe biblical stories. The *Jesus maija* paintings in Cameroon, inspired by plays setting forth the Gospel narratives, are a case in point.

The sacred scriptures are abundant in stories, and we may say the same for African traditions. In addition to employing symbols, hymns, and practical activities, catechesis may be more successful if the content is transmitted through narrated stories and dramas. The storytelling and dramas should be

---

30. Anonymous, *The Psalms: Reading in Ethiopic*, 146–52.
31. For a detailed study of the Ethiopian interpretation of Psalm 24, see Assefa, "Le psaume 24 à la lumière de l'exil babylonien dans le rite éthiopien," 5–18.
32. We have thus seen the multiple functions of this one psalm: interpretation, poetry, and dramatization.
33. Including Marian feasts and feasts of the saints.

inspired by African spirituality and African values. Using stories and dramas effectively implies the creativity and strong formation of the agents of evangelization.

In the contemporary world, the omnipresence of media is a reality, including in African societies. The media can be an effective means of learning about our environment, but modern techniques of using media to improve catechesis are helpful only when the fundamentals of evangelization are kept in mind. Clarity about the essentials at both the theoretical and the practical level comes before discourses about adapting the various elements of modern technology. Catechists must always remember the words of St. Paul: "And we speak of these things in words not taught by human wisdom but taught by the Spirit" (1 Cor 2:13).

The Importance of Testimony

The best method of catechizing is life witness. Catechesis becomes convincing and fruitful when the virtues of faith, hope, and love are not only taught but also practiced and witnessed.[34] A flourishing, renewed, and vibrant church, the result of good catechesis, will in turn serve society well. Any approach to catechesis will bear fruit only when the agents of evangelization transmit the values of the Christian gospel to African society. Christianity in Africa must offer a message that shapes African society for the better, moving it toward peace and justice and development.

In this connection, issues of methodology, audience, and circumstances, including the age and maturity of the persons to be catechized, are important.[35] Although approaches that give room to symbols, narratives, celebrations, drama, and *lectio divina* are valid at every age, the intensity and style of their application may vary according to the maturity of the audience. Catechesis for children obviously needs to take into consideration child pedagogy. The sooner both cardinal and theological virtues are transmitted through life examples, the more effective the catechesis will be. If a child has seen the instructor planting trees during a catechetical program, the message will remain in his or her memory. One example of virtue that should be shown to children is parents paying their debts.[36] The connection between faith and society and between human beings and nature in the context of instruction about creation theology must be implanted at a tender age. Charity and ethics are better shown than recommended, especially by witnessing a style of life that reflects a preferential option for the poor.[37] Similarly, a catechesis that integrates instruction and prayer and teaching and liturgy shows that one believes what one prays, and prays what one believes.

It is important to recognize the challenges that make catechesis among the youth particularly difficult. The challenges of globalization will affect them more than it will older people. Today's adolescent in search of identity is readily attracted by various messages transmitted through the modern media and modern technology. It would be unrealistic and utopian to reject modernity, and the positive elements of globalization should be welcomed. This situation raises a question of discernment. The temptation to imitate the models shown in the modern media without a critical spirit could be challenged by catechesis and the family. Yet families, because they are busy with ever-evolving responsibilities and new lifestyles, may run short of time for listening to their children and attending to their growth in the faith. Especially families, but also the church and the schools in Africa, would benefit from an open and genuine collaboration with other societal actors in order to safeguard and promote African virtues and gospel values.

Where and When to Catechize

Church compounds usually include places where catechesis may be carried out. In small Christian

---

34. In this connection, it is noteworthy that the *Catechism of the Catholic Church* presents the example of various saints as "commentaries" on the sacred scriptures and teachers of prayer (§§113, 2030, 2683–84).
35. See Pope John Paul II, *Catechesi Tradendae* §§46–55.
36. I am indebted for these examples to conversations with Prof. J. N. Mugambi.
37. The church witnesses more by providing examples of holy lives and by prioritizing reality over speculation and theory. See Pope Francis, post-synodal apostolic exhortation *Evangelii Gaudium* §§231–33.

communities, this may also take place within the family, which has the advantage that adults can readily serve as examples to youth and children. The mass media can also be a suitable milieu for instruction. More exposure to the Bible and catechesis is better than less, and regularity is promoted when programs are facilitated by the church. The work of catechesis should give priority to the schedules of the participants—for instance, evenings are often an appropriate time for adults who work during the day.[38]

The commitment of the agents of evangelization is crucial for making catechesis fruitful. Appropriate formation of clergy, religious, and seminarians may also be decisive. As the saying goes, where there is a will there is a way.

Conclusion

This chapter has argued that catechesis in Africa requires a particularly African approach to the Bible. The move from the scriptures to African reality to the Word of God is realized by faith in Jesus Christ. In addition to the historical-critical approach, a reading of the Bible in the context of the church, in the light of faith, as underlined by ecclesiastical documents on exegesis and the available methods of interpreting the sacred scriptures, is needed. The African worldview requires that African exegesis be faith-centered, an approach that was pioneered by the African church fathers. This approach focuses on the celebration of Christian events and reflects the significant place of the Bible in African society, leading to effective catechesis on the continent.

The examples in this chapter have mostly been taken from Ethiopia, but it is not necessary to slavishly copy them. One needs to distinguish between things that are always true and things that are true only in certain situations, between what is truly inspiring and what may be left aside, and between what may be only appreciated and what may and should be adopted. Christians ought to focus on how Christ, the pearl, is confessed, adored, and celebrated. Any engagement with reality that forgets this runs the risk of distracting people from what is really important.

Catechesis in Africa needs to be faithful to African values. Both its content and methods should pay attention to the African context, while always being open to sharing with as well as learning from other realities. The child needs to apprehend the meaning of his or her environment and receive answers to his or her questions in the light of Christ, who welcomes children. The adolescent too needs to be inspired by the call of the gospel in his or her search for meaning and quest for identity. And, finally, the adult needs to see meaning in suffering, injustice, and various social challenges, and be enlightened by the joy of the gospel. A genuinely African catechesis in the Catholic Church should help Africans embrace the Word of God and give hope and meaning to the believer and to society.

Bibliography

Adamo, D. T., ed. *Biblical Interpretation in African Perspective*. Lanham, MD: University Press of America, 2006.

Andeberhan, W. T. *Commentari etiopici sul libro del Profeta Osea: Edizione critica da manoscritti inediti. Principi ermeneutici. Temi teologici*. Äthiopistische Forschungen 40. Wiesbaden: Harrassowitz, 1994.

Anonymous. *The Psalms: Reading in Ethiopic (Ge'ez) with Translation and Commentary in Amharic*. Addis Ababa: Tesfa Gebre Sellassie, 1990.

Assefa, D. "Le psaume 24 à la lumière de l'exil babylonien dans le rite éthiopien." *Histoires & Missions Chrétiennes* 24 (2012): 5–18.

Babendreier, J. *The Faith Explained Today*. Nairobi: Scepter Publishers, 2007.

Benedict XVI, Pope [Ratzinger, Joseph Cardinal]. "Biblical Interpretation in Crisis: On the Question of the Foundations and Approaches of Exegesis Today" (New York, 1988). In *The Essential Pope Benedict XVI: His Central Writings and Speeches*, edited by J. Thornton and S. Varenne, 243–58. New York: Collins, 2008.

---

38. The Ethiopian Orthodox *Tewahido* church, for example, offers instruction daily after 5:00 PM. It takes place outside the church in a public space.

———. *Verbum Domini* [Post-synodal Apostolic Exhortation on the Word of God in the Life and Mission of the Church; September 30, 2010). Vatican City: Libreria Editrice Vaticana, 2010. www.vatican.va.

Böll, V. *"Unsere Herrin Maria": Die traditionelle äthiopische Exegese der Marienanaphora des Cyriacus von Behensa*. Äthiopistische Forschungen 48. Wiesbaden: Harrassowitz, 1998.

Boucher, C. Chisale. *The Gospel Seed: Culture and Faith in Malawi as Expressed in the Missio Banner*. Mua: Kungoni Art Craft Center, 2002.

Bujo, B. *Foundations of an African Ethic: Beyond the Universal Claims of Western Morality*. Nairobi: Paulines Publications Africa, 2003.

Byasse, J. *Praise Seeking Understanding: Reading the Psalms with Augustine*. Grand Rapids, MI: Eerdmans, 2007.

Cowley, R. *Ethiopian Biblical Interpretation: A Study in Exegetical Tradition and Hermeneutics*. Oriental Publication 38. Cambridge: Cambridge University Press, 1988.

———. "New Testament Introduction in the *Andemta* Commentary Tradition." *Ostkirchliche Studien* 26.2/3 (1977): 144–92.

———. *The Traditional Interpretation of the Apocalypse of St. John in the Ethiopian Orthodox Church*. Cambridge: Cambridge University Press, 1983.

Dube, M. W. "Rereading the Bible: Biblical Hermeneutics and Social Justice." In *African Theology Today*, edited by E. Katongole, 57–68. Scranton, PA: University of Scranton Press, 2002.

Fishbane, M. *Biblical Interpretation in Ancient Israel*. Oxford: Clarendon Press, 1985.

Fitzmyer, Joseph A., ed. *The Biblical Commission's Document "The Interpretation of the Bible in the Church": Text and Commentary*. Rome: Pontificia Istituto Biblico, 1995.

Francis, Pope. *Evangelii Gaudium* (The Joy of the Gospel) [Post-synodal Apostolic Exhortation on the Proclamation of the Gospel in Today's World; November 23, 2013]. www.vatican.va.

Garcia, M. A. *Ethiopian Biblical Commentaries on the Prophet Micah*. Äthiopistische Forschungen 52. Wiesbaden: Harrassowitz, 1999.

Holter, K., ed. *Interpreting Classical Religious Texts in Contemporary Africa*. Nairobi: Acton, 2007.

———, ed. *Let My People Stay: Researching the Old Testament in Africa*. Nairobi: Acton, 2006.

Ilo, Stan Chu. *The Church and Development in Africa: Aid and Development from the Perspective of Catholic Social Ethics*. Eugene, OR: Pickwick, 2011.

John Paul II, Pope. *Catechesis Tradendae* [Apostolic Exhortation on Catechesis in Our Time; October 16, 1979]. Vatican City: Libreria Editrice Vaticana, 1979. Nairobi: Paulines Publications Africa, 1991.

———. *Ecclesia in Africa* [Post-synodal Apostolic Exhortation on the Church in Africa and Its Evangelizing Mission toward the Year 2000; September 14, 1995]. Vatican City: Libreria Editrice Vaticana, 1995. www.vatican.va. Nairobi: Paulines Publications Africa, 1995.

Katongole, E. *Stories from Bethany: On the Faces of the Church in Africa*. Nairobi: Paulines Publications, 2012.

Lumko Institute. *The Pastoral Use of the Bible*. 3rd ed. Prepared by the Lumko Institute of the Episcopal Conference of Southern Africa, 1991. French version, 2003.

Magesa, Laurenti. *Anatomy of Inculturation: Transforming the Church in Africa*. Nairobi: Paulines Publications Africa, 2004.

———. *What Is Not Sacred? African Spirituality*. Nairobi: Acton, 2014.

Manus, U. C. *Intercultural Hermeneutics: Methods and Approaches*. Nairobi: Acton, 2003.

Mbiti, J. "The Bible in African Culture." In *Paths of African Theology*, edited by R. Gibellini, 27–39. Maryknoll, NY: Orbis Books, 1994.

Mersha, A. *The Ethiopian Commentary on the Book of Genesis: Critical Edition and Translation*. Äthiopistische Forschungen 73. Wiesbaden: Harrassowitz, 2010.

Mugambi, J. N. *Christianity and African Culture*. Nairobi: Acton, 2002.

———. *From Liberation to the Reconstruction*. Scranton, PA: University of Scranton Press, 2002.

Mundele, Albert Ngengi. *A Handbook on African Approaches to Biblical Interpretation*. Nairobi: Kolbe, 2012.

Oden, T. C. *The Rebirth of African Orthodoxy: Return to the Foundations*. Nashville: Abingdon Press, 2016.

Okure, T., and Paul van Thiel, eds. *32 Articles Evaluating Inculturation of Christianity in Africa*. Eldoret: Gaba, 1990.

Orobator, A. E., ed. *Theological Reimagination: Conversations on Church, Religion, and Society in Africa*. Nairobi: Paulines Publications, 2014.

Pedersen, K. S. *Traditional Ethiopian Exegesis of the Book of Psalms*. Äthiopistische Forschungen 36. Wiesbaden: Harrassowitz, 1995.

Pedersen, K. S., and A. Tedros. "Andemta." *Encyclopedia Ethiopica*, 1:258–59. Wiesbaden: Harrassowitz, 2003.

Pontifical Biblical Commission. *The Bible and Morality: Biblical Roots for Christian Conduct*. Vatican City: Libreria Editrice Vaticana, 2008. www.vatican.va.

———. *The Jewish People and Their Sacred Scriptures in the Bible*. Vatican City: Libreria Editrice Vaticana, 2002. www.vatican.va.

Putti, J. *Theology as Hermeneutics: Paul Ricoeur's Theory of Text Interpretation and Method in Theology*. Bangalore: Kristu Jyoti Publications, 1991.

Ratzinger, Joseph Cardinal. *See* Benedict XVI, Pope.

Simonetti, M. *Lettera e/o allegoria: Un contributo alla storia dell'esegesi patristica*. Rome: Augustinianum, 1985.

Sinton, D. B. *Jesus of Africa: Voices of Contemporary African Christology*. Nairobi: Paulines Publications Africa, 2004.

Tedros, A. *La lettera ai Romani. Testo e commentary della versione Etiopica* Äthiopistische Forschungen (AeF 57). Wiesbaden: Harrassowitz, 2001.

Thornton, J., and S. Varenne, eds. *The Essential Pope Benedict XVI: His Central Writings and Speeches*. New York: Collins, 2008.

United States Catholic Conference. *The Catechism of the Catholic Church*. Vatican City: Libreria Editrice Vaticana, 1994.

Wendland, E. R. *Biblical Texts and African Audiences*. Nairobi: Acton, 2004.

West, G., and M. W. Dube, eds. *The Bible in Africa*. Boston: Brill, 2001.

Yamauchi, E. *Africa and the Bible*. Grand Rapids, MI: Baker Academic, 2004.

Yorke, G., and P. Renju, eds. *Bible Translation and African Languages*. Nairobi: Acton, 2004.

Suggested Reading

Benedict XVI, Pope. *Verbum Domini* [Post-synodal Apostolic Exhortation on the Word of God in the Life and Mission of the Church; September 30, 2010]. Vatican City: Libreria Editrice Vaticana, 2010. www.vatican.va.

Catholic Church Congregation for the Clergy. *General Directory for Catechesis*. Washington, DC: USCCB Publishing, 1998.

Cowley, R. *Ethiopian Biblical Interpretation. A Study in Exegetical Tradition and Hermeneutics*. Oriental Publication 38. Cambridge: Cambridge University Press, 1988.

Cyril of Alexandria. *Commentary on John*. Translated by D. Maxwell. Ancient Christian Texts. Downers Grove, IL: InterVarsity Press, 2013.

John Paul II, Pope. *Catechesis Tradendae* [Apostolic Exhortation on Catechesis in Our Time; October 16, 1979]. Vatican City: Libreria Editrice Vaticana, 1979. Nairobi: Paulines Publications Africa, 1991.

Magesa, Laurenti. *Anatomy of Inculturation: Transforming the Church in Africa*. Nairobi: Paulines Publications Africa, 2004.

McGuckin, J. A., ed. *The Westminster Handbook to Origen*. Louisville, KY: Westminster John Knox, 2004.

Mundele, Albert Ngengi. *A Handbook on African Approaches to Biblical Interpretation*. Nairobi: Kolbe, 2012.

Ratzinger, Joseph Cardinal [Pope Benedict XVI]. "Biblical Interpretation in Crisis: On the Question of the Foundations and Approaches of Exegesis Today" (New York, 1988). In *The Essential Pope Benedict XVI: His Central Writings and Speeches*, edited by J. Thornton and S. Varenne, 243–58. Cambridge: Cambridge University Press, 2008.

Key Words

Bible in Africa
catechesis
Ethiopian biblical hermeneutics
faith and biblical interpretation
historical-critical approach
inculturation
patristic exegesis

African Theologies in Dialogue with the West

Emmanuel-Mary Mbam, MSP

Intraecclesial dialogue between Western and African Catholic theologians is not only possible but necessary. The Catholic Church is a large family of faith featuring diversity and differences, and where there are diversity and differences, dialogue becomes the necessary pathway to unity. It is from this perspective that one should view the need for dialogue between the church in the West and in sub-Saharan Africa. Despite their cultural, economic, and religious differences, we have seen the development of a positive relationship between Africa and the West. For instance, Western forces have intervened, at great material and human cost, to quell fratricidal wars in Africa. There has also been cooperation between the two worlds in the areas of education, science and technology, human rights, environmental preservation, and alleviating poverty, among other things. This work seeks to explore ways in which this ongoing collaboration and dialogue can be transferred to Catholic theology.

At this point, it is pertinent to clarify that, in this work, "dialogue" implies theological exchange between, on the one hand, professional African Catholic theologians—that is, theologians proficient in not only Catholic faith and theology but also in African realities, including the African context, culture, religious orientations and sensitivities, and sociopolitical and economic circumstances—and, on the other, professional Western Catholic theologians, for the purpose of mutual enrichment and advancement of the Catholic faith and the life of the people of God in both Africa and the West. An emphasis on the need for the participants in this intraecclesial dialogue to have solid theological expertise will be elaborated later. It suffices for now to state that, while this dialogue can be carried on at informal levels between believers in both Africa and the West regardless of their theological *savoir-faire*, it demands some level of theological proficiency to succeed.

The discussion begins by clarifying the fundamental terms employed here. Then I will proceed to locate the proposed dialogue within the history of theological and cultural exchange that has already taken place between Western and African theologians. This will be followed by a description of the necessary conditions for dialogue, including the need to heal historical injuries and resolve intercultural misconceptions, the need to preserve ecclesial *koinonia* without allowing unity to degenerate into uniformity, and the need to seek a common meaning from our common sources of theology without jettisoning contextualization. The perichoresal intertwining of the human interests of each person in the future of humanity also provides a solid ground for dialogue.[1] I then examine the approaches and principles that should guide this dialogue if it is to remain authentically Christian and contextual. These include fidelity to the sacred deposit, respecting dialogue partners as equals, a spirit of reciprocity, contextual sensitivity, professionalism, and the use of a dialectic method. Thus, the focus of this work is less on instances of

---

1. I apply the Trinitarian perichoresis—the coinherence of the Trinitarian persons in one another—as both the ground and metaphor for this inextricable intertwining.

theological dialogue and more on methodology. The methodological approach employed here will be narrative and normative—it will tell the story of the challenging history of the relationship between the West and sub-Saharan Africa but will complement this story with a description of the norms that must guide our proposed dialogue, drawing on scriptural, theological, and magisterial sources.

Definition of Terms

The title of this work raises certain questions of meaning. What does the adjectival qualification of a theology or theologies as "African" mean? In other words, when does a theology qualify to be called "African"? Is it when it is done by Africans or when it focuses on issues central to Africa? Why use "theology" in its plural form? Who are those to whom we refer as the "West"? Unpacking these probing questions will highlight the complex nature and significance of this theological adventure.

First, the question of who is an African or a Westerner has been complicated by globalization and immigration. Today, there are Africans naturalized in the West and children of African descent who know no other nationality, language, or even culture than those of the West. Should these people be classified as Africans or Westerners? In addition, many Europeans and Americans now call Africa home: are they Westerners or Africans? Can one say that the theology of people of African descent who are naturalized in the West or have stayed there so long that they identify more with Western than African culture and thought patterns is an African theology? Relatedly, should the theology of Westerners who have settled in Africa or stayed there so long that they are quite knowledgeable, sometimes more than the indigenes, about African reality be called African or Western? Thus, because there are people of European, American, and Asian descent who confidently call themselves Africans just as there are Africans who validly call themselves Westerners, one should guard against a simplistic interpretation of either designation.[2]

A related question is whether non-Africans can do African theology; this is similar to the question that has been raised concerning whether a male can do feminist theology. Stephen Bevans provides an ambivalent answer: on the one hand, he believes that someone who does not wear the shoe does not know where it pinches, and for this reason he calls those who have not shared the African experience and cannot fully understand the wounds, desires, frustrations, and aspirations of Africans "nonparticipants." "Try as they might," Bevans writes, "nonparticipants ultimately bring their own feelings, perceptions, experiences, and privilege into a situation, and however slightly, this foreignness works to distort theology in the other context."[3] On the other hand, Bevans acknowledges that foreigners can sometimes be in the know about a culture and context more than those born into it.[4] The outsider, advantaged by a sense of neutrality, can provide a counterpoint to the traditional narrative that has been made sacrosanct by uncritical reception and long usage. He/she can highlight the strengths and weaknesses of a culture that indigenes are wont to overlook and can uncover covert, unjust, and inhuman cultural practices that are uncritically considered normative.[5]

A similar sentiment is shared by Robert Schreiter, who believes that, without the help of foreign religious leaders, Latin American liberation theology would not have blossomed as rapidly as it did.[6] He argues that, although there is a risk that they will behave paternalistically, expatriates can play a significant role in the development of the local theology where they work.

The expatriate can also be the bearer of the lived experience of other communities, [an] experience that can challenge and enrich a local community. Without the presence of

---

2. Of course, the term "Westerner" normally applies to a person who was born or has been naturalized in Europe, the United States, Canada, or Australia, and it is so used in this chapter.
3. Bevans, *Models of Contextual Theology*, 19.
4. Bevans, *Models of Contextual Theology*, 19.
5. Bevans, *Models of Contextual Theology*, 20.
6. Schreiter, *Constructing Local Theologies*, 19.

outside experience, a local church runs the risk of turning in on itself, becoming self-satisfied with its own achievements. The expatriate, as an outsider, can sometimes hear things going on in a community not heard by a native member of that community.[7]

Therefore, limiting the possible criteria for validating a theology as African to the race of the theologian is circumscribing, myopic, and impoverishing. This is testified to by the efforts of non-African theologians who have contributed to African theology in its various shades.[8] According to Paulinus Odozor, what makes a theology uniquely African "is the content and the context of its preoccupation."[9] Nevertheless, he also recognizes that African theology cannot be limited to its content and context but also, as a Christian theology, must take into consideration the concerns and sources it shares with other theologies.[10] For Schreiter, a theology is African if it arises from the dynamic interaction of the gospel and the church within a particular African cultural context as part of a dialectical process in which the gospel raises questions and challenges the culture and vice versa.[11] Thus, irrespective of who does the theology, as long as it is genuinely focused on issues pertaining to the African continent, it should be regarded as legitimately African. The same applies to theologies done by Africans naturalized in Western countries. Thus, the designations "African" and "Western" as applied to theology should be employed according to the perspective of the theological practitioner. The fact that non-Africans have contributed immensely to the advancement of African theology already demonstrates not only the possibility but also the necessity of theological exchange and collaboration between the local churches in both Africa and the West.

It is also pertinent to clarify that this work uses "theologies" instead of "theology" in order to highlight the diversity of theologies present in Africa. I am aware of the debate about the difference between African theology, which aims at inculturating Christianity into an African setting, and Black theology focused on liberation, as especially employed during the apartheid regime in South Africa. I believe that the distinction between these two forms of theology is no longer necessary in light of the fact that the inculturation or incarnation of the gospel in the African context and the work of liberation and social transformation on the continent are essential elements of the same theological process.[12] Here, "theologies" refers to theological disciplines within broader Catholic theology. The use of "theologies" is also in recognition of the fact that there are other theological ventures on the continent that are not Catholic or even Christian. Hence, it is important to note that "African theology" is not the exclusive preserve of African Christians. Muslims and believers in African Traditional Religion (ATR) also do theology in their own ways. Even within the family of Christian theology, there are various confessional African theologies: Catholic, Coptic, Ethiopic, Protestant, evangelical, that of the African Indigenous Churches (AICs), and others.

It is important to state that my focus in this work is on Catholic theology. Therefore, the dialogue meant here is one between African Catholic theologians and their counterparts in the West. In other words, the chapter discusses an intraecclesial dialogue between Catholic believers who must theologize in their various contexts in order to address their peculiar challenges but who, nevertheless, must seek common meaning and a strengthening of the communion of the one family of faith. But, although this dialogue is envisaged as occurring

---

7. Schreiter, *Constructing Local Theologies*, 22–23.
8. Works by Aylward Shorter, Sergio Torres (who collaborated with Kofi Appiah-Kubi [see Appiah-Kubi and Torres, *African Theology en Route*]), and others demonstrate that non-Africans can contribute enormously to the enrichment of African theology.
9. Odozor, *Morality, Truly Christian, Truly African*, 10.
10. Odozor, *Morality, Truly Christian, Truly African*, 10.
11. Schreiter, *Constructing Local Theologies*, 20–23.
12. See Mushete, "History of Theology in Africa: From Polemics to Critical Irenics," 23–35; Bujo, *African Theology in Its Social Context*, 62–68; Martey, *African Theology*, 7–27.

within the Catholic fold, the principles that will be enunciated here can be applied to other dialogical processes within other Christian confessions.

The use of "theologies" in the plural also highlights the diversity of contexts in which theology is done in Africa. For instance, there is a difference between the history, religion, and sociopolitical and economic development of North and sub-Saharan Africa. There are also linguistic and ideological differences between the francophone and anglophone African countries. Therefore, according to Odozor, it is right to speak of "African theologies" because of the diversity of African contexts and also the diversity of issues to be tackled in the various contexts and historical circumstances.[13]

Finally, the use of "theologies" also underlines the varieties of theological disciplines that are possible loci for theological dialogue, among them systematic theology, moral theology, liturgical theology, biblical theology, liberation theology, and inculturation theology. This underscores the comprehensiveness of this proposed dialogue; that is, the theological dialogue between the West and Africa should include all aspects of Catholic theological endeavor. According to Bénézet Bujo, "Dialogue with foreign cultures should involve all theological and philosophical disciplines, and even and more urgently than ever, all disciplines of humanities."[14] This implies that this dialogue must involve the collaboration of African and Western theologians working in every subdiscipline within the field for the purpose of reformulating and advancing what is today regarded as the official or perennial Catholic theology.[15] On the one hand, there is a clear need for contextualization. The perennial theology needs to be interpreted and communicated in a particular context using local symbols that are more meaningful and accessible to the people. Thus, African theologians need to disambiguate some of the theological jargon used in the various formulations of traditional Catholic doctrine. They also need to foreground the issues pertinent to Africa's interests that were neglected by the architects of this doctrine; the entirety of Catholic doctrine must be reexamined in line with the peculiarly African socioeconomic and cultural situation. As Bujo states, African people are confronted with burning issues that should be answered differently than they are in the economically rich countries of the West.[16] But, on the other hand, theological ghettoization would result if African theologians restricted themselves to contextual theology. Very often, in the name of inculturation or contextual theology, African theologians have contented themselves with adapting theologies "manufactured" in the West. It therefore appears paternalistic and condescending when Stephen Bevans suggests that "in an African culture, for example, the best form of theologizing might be collecting, creating, or reflecting on proverbs."[17] He forgets that Africans like Cyril of Alexandria, Athanasius, Tertullian, and Augustine played a major role in the formulation of what is regarded today as perennial theology. In fact, Alexandria in Egypt

---

13. Odozor, *Morality, Truly Christian, Truly African*, 14.
14. Bujo, *Ethical Dimension of Community*, 226.
15. Perennial theology refers to the theological heritage or the articulation of the faith having an enduring value or validity because it has faithfully communicated the unchanging truths of the sacred deposit. Such a theology gives pride of place to divine revelation, especially as interpreted by the magisterium; dogma; the definitive teachings of the church and the church fathers; and the enduring works of theologians like Thomas Aquinas. It utilizes what has come to be known as traditional classical or scholastic theological terms and conceptions in its articulation of the truths of the faith. For instance, in Trinitarian theology, it employs traditional terms like "Trinity," "persons" (of the Trinity), "perichoresis," "relations" (between the persons of the Trinity), and "processions"; in sacramental theology, especially with respect to the Eucharist, it uses terms like "grace," "form and matter," "transubstantiation," and "real presence." While these terms are not in themselves dogmas, they have become so important for the valid explication of those theological realities that it would be difficult to avoid them irrespective of culture or context. In other words, it is difficult, although not impossible, to do Trinitarian or sacramental theology without employing those terms. Perennial theology is the theological counterpart of *philosophia perennis* (see Vatican II, *Optatum Totius* §15; Pope John Paul II, *Fides et Ratio* [hereinafter FR] §§60, 106).
16. Bujo, *Ethical Dimension of Community*, 226.
17. Bevans, *Models of Contextual Theology*, 17.

was the location of a prominent theological school that played a foundational role in the formulation of Catholic theology. For these reasons, there is an urgent need for collaboration and dialogue between African theologians and their Western counterparts to reexamine what has always been accepted as the sources of Catholic theology.

The diversity of theological issues and disciplines implies that, while it is possible to formulate general principles undergirding the dialogical process, each theological discipline or *locus theologicus* also needs to come up with its own dialogical model, principles, and guidelines. For instance, dialogue between systematic theologians from both Africa and the West where the focus is on the dogmatic and definitive teachings of the church would be guided by different precepts that are slightly different from those guiding theological exchanges focused on culture or on the environment.

Historical Perspectives

This proposed dialogue between Christians in Africa and in the West must be located within the context of the history of the parties' complex relationship, which included slavery and colonialism. This tumultuous relationship was further strained by postcolonial Western meddling in African politics, which sometimes led to the installation of despotic African leaders who gave big Western corporations free rein over Africa's natural resources. There were also cases of Western governments and organizations foisting manipulative politico-economic policies on African countries, which led to further economic woes for Africans. In addition to the ugly realities of slavery and colonialism, the relationship between Africa and the West was further fouled by derogatory misrepresentations of African peoples and their cultures and religion by early Western writers, anthropologists, and ethnologists. The early Western studies of ATR and African cultures were "inadequate, derogatory, and prejudicial."[18] While African cultures were seen as simply primitive, ATR was described in derogatory terms like "animism," "shamanism," "ancestor worship," "black magic," and the like. Some Western thinkers put ATR on the bottom rung of the religious ladder behind monotheistic religions like Christianity, Islam, and Judaism, and even behind some polytheistic Asian religions like Hinduism and Shintoism. Poisoned by such derogatory views of African cultures and traditional religion, many Westerners doubted the possibility that Africans had the capacity for authentic religious and philosophical conceptualization. This deprecatory misconception was epitomized by the now infamous retort of Emil Ludwig to Edwin Smith: "How can the untutored African conceive God.... Deity is a philosophical concept which savages are incapable of framing."[19]

Some of the early Western missionaries have been accused of holding negative and condescending attitudes toward African cultures and traditional religion. Some of them proclaimed an over-Westernized Christian gospel that was highly inimical to African religious traditions. Their approach to evangelization appeared to endorse the negative view that African religious traditions and cultures had nothing to offer with respect to the inculturation of the Christian faith.[20] This reinforced the view of many Africans that Christianity was a foreign, Western religion that brought a strange God whom they came "to identify as the God of the white man."[21] According to Theophilus Okere, in the first era of intellectual encounter between the West and sub-Saharan Africa, "African culture was an object of amused curiosity for foreigners interested in the rude manners of savages, [and] of scholars seeking confirmation for the theory of evolution. It was a descriptive presentation of the way the natives lived."[22]

This disparagement of everything African by Western scholarship and the proclamation of a Christian gospel that Africans believed was contemptuous of them initiated a struggle for Black identity and what Engelbert Mveng calls "the great

---

18. Mbiti, *African Religions and Philosophy*, 7.
19. Smith, *African Ideas of God*, 1. Cf. Dickson and Ellingworth, *Biblical Revelation and African Beliefs*, 10.
20. Dickson and Ellingworth, *Biblical Revelation and African Beliefs*, 9–10.
21. Dickson and Ellingworth, *Biblical Revelation and African Beliefs*, 13.
22. Onwubiko, *African Thought, Religion, and Culture*, vii.

struggle for African Christianity."[23] Beginning in the 1960s with the political independence of many African nations, there emerged a generation of African secular intellectuals and theologians who rose to the defense of African traditional religion and cultures. They responded with a cultural and religious apologetics aimed at not only defending but exalting the autochthonous values of African religion and cultures.[24] This led to a debate that was not only about the worth of African cultures and religion in themselves, but also their appropriateness for conveying Christian values and ethics. In January 1966, a group of African theologians gathered at Immanuel College in Ibadan, Nigeria, to explore the themes of the possible correlations between Christian revelation and faith and African cultures and religious thought and how the Christian faith could be communicated to Africans in a way that would be meaningful and cogent to them. "We seek in effect, to discover in what way the Christian faith could best be presented, interpreted, and inculcated in Africa so that Africans will hear God in Jesus Christ addressing himself immediately to them in their own native situation and particular circumstances."[25]

This debate continued during the 1960s and '70s with African theologians vigorously defending the worthiness and significance of the African religious worldview and African values.[26] It would be a misnomer to call the encounter during this period a "dialogue"; it was rather a monologue, an "us-versus-them" ideological exchange that was highly antagonistic and partisan. This partisanship was manifested in excessive, even fanatical, defenses and exaltation of ATR and African cultures. There could be no real dialogue in the face of mutual misconceptions, prejudices, and adversarial exchanges.[27] Nevertheless, the efforts of these pioneering African Christian writers gave birth to what came to be known as African theology and initiated a sympathetic study of African religions and philosophy.[28] In addition, some expatriate Christian missionaries, in reaction to the early scholars who disparaged African cultures and religion, presented a more accurate account of African religious beliefs in order to demonstrate that "Africans were as civilized as Europeans."[29] According to Odozor, the pioneers of African theology included missionaries and non-African theologians whose writings and insights into African realities have benefited modern African theologians.[30]

This can be seen in works that occasionally embody a dialogue between Christian theology and African traditional life and in thinkers like Placide Frans Tempels (1906–1977), Edward Geoffrey Parrinder (1910–2005), and John Vernon Taylor (1914–2001).[31] But in their efforts to be conciliatory, some of these Western authors went overboard, sometimes defending African religion, philosophy, and cultures to an exaggerated extent.[32] For example, according to Mbiti, Taylor was "too sympathetic and insufficiently critical. He presents everything as if it were so sacred, holy, pure and clean that it is being polluted by Christianity, westernism, urbanization and the ways of technological life. The book has a disturbingly sharp distinction between the 'we' (Europeans) and the 'they' (Africans), seen against the background of what 'we' can learn from 'them.'"[33]

---

23. For a two-volume anthology collecting the work of African theologians from the pioneers to the present, see Bujo and Ilunga Muya, *African Theology in the 21st Century*, 1:67.
24. Bujo and Ilunga Muya, *African Theology*, 1:35; Onwubiko, *African Thought, Religion, and Culture*, vii.
25. Dickson and Ellingworth, *Biblical Revelation and African Beliefs*, 15–16.
26. Bujo and Ilunga Muya, *African Theology in the 21st Century*, 1:8.
27. See Magesa, *African Religion*, 5.
28. Mbiti, *African Religions and Philosophy*, 10–11.
29. Metuh, *African Religions in Western Conceptual Schemes*, viii.
30. Odozor, *Morality, Truly Christian, Truly African*, 25, 26.
31. Placide Tempels, *Philosophie bantoue* (Elizabethville: Lovania, 1945), published in English under the title *Bantu Philosophy* (Paris: Présence Africaine, 1959); Geoffrey Parrinder, *African Traditional Religion* (London: Hutchinson's University Library, 1954); John Vernon Taylor, *Primal Vision* (London: SCM Press, 1963).
32. Mbiti, *African Religions and Philosophy*, 11.
33. Mbiti, *African Religions and Philosophy*, 12.

Eventually, there came a realization that defensiveness and partisanship were counterproductive and that a true dialogue between African and Western worldviews was necessary. Since then, there have been efforts to move away from blind, uncritical defenses of the African worldview. For instance, Laurenti Magesa, in his book *African Religion*, sought to identify as precisely as possible the quintessence of the African religious worldview and life:

> My primary purpose is not to "prove" anything, least of all to argue that African morality is just as rich as Christian or any other religious morality, as many other authors have endeavored to do. I am not engaging in an intellectual argument with any of the many ideological views of African Religion. To my mind, that kind of discussion is no longer very useful; it promotes neither mature ecumenical discussion nor authentic inculturation.[34]

This attitudinal change has highlighted the need for a more dialogical approach to Catholic theology as between African and Western believers, an approach that calls for a clear and precise articulation of one's position and the recognition of one's cultural, religious, and philosophical limitations and prejudices.[35] For instance, there is a need for dialogue to find a common ground between concrete African religious terms and abstract Western concepts so that African theologians can have a meaningful impact on the formation and transmission of universal or perennial Catholic theology.[36]

It therefore appears that the time has come to engage in a more open, critical, and unbiased dialogue that fosters mutual enlightenment. This is especially urgent because Christianity is still seen in some parts of Africa as a Western project.[37] Fortunately, this type of dialogue was envisaged by Michael Kirwen, an American Maryknoll missionary who worked in Tanzania, in his book *The Missionary and the Diviner*. In that work, Kirwen constructs a dialogue between a missionary who represents a Catholic theology that is ethnocentrically Western and an African diviner who represents traditional African religious views and cultural values.[38] The dialogue explores, from the perspectives of both worldviews, theological issues such as monotheism; priesthood; ministry; soteriology; the sources of evil, especially cosmic evil, including evil spirits and witchcraft; and eschatology, especially as it pertains to the ancestors. Both the missionary and the diviner were able to discover points of convergence and divergence and also the strengths and weaknesses of their original positions. This led to a mutual adjustment of positions (which Kirwen describes at the end of each chapter in the form of a commentary). For Kirwen, the fundamental principle of the dialogue was love—love pushes one to understand the beloved and to allow oneself to be influenced and changed by the relationship.[39] The aim, on the one hand, was to help the missionary understand Africa's fundamental religious beliefs, values, ideals, and visions, which Westernized Christianity should not and in fact cannot eradicate. On the other, it was to help the African Christian in search of an African theology that is truly Christian and truly African. Kirwen's book was also aimed at helping both missionaries and African believers to cooperatively find an authentically Christian and African response to significant religious and sociocultural issues arising from African religiosity even in the face of "theological, doctrinal, and pastoral strictures."[40]

It is not possible to envisage dialogue in today's church without locating it within the framework of the Second Vatican Council's overarching promotion of dialogue. The council documents make clear

---

34. Magesa, *African Religion*, 32.
35. See Hans Küng, *Global Responsibility: In Search of a New World Ethic* (New York: Crossroad, 1991), 137–38; Magesa, *African Religion*, 4–5.
36. See Metuh, *African Religions in Western Conceptual Schemes*, ix.
37. Mbiti, *African Religions and Philosophy*, xii.
38. Kirwen, *Missionary and the Diviner*, xxiii–xxiv.
39. Kirwen, *Missionary and the Diviner*, xi.
40. Kirwen, *Missionary and the Diviner*, vii, xiv, xxiii–xxiv; quotation from vii.

that divisions among Christians are both a scandal and an obstacle to the realization of Jesus's will that we be one.[41] Consequently, the council makes dialogue an obligation for every Catholic (*UR* §4); it is the responsibility of the entire church, clergy and laity alike (*UR* §5).[42] Although the council focused more on ecumenical and interreligious dialogue, it appears to have hinted at the need for intraecclesial dialogue by reaching out to the Eastern Orthodox churches, which enjoy the closest intimacy with the Catholic Church; both are bound together by a "communion of faith and sacramental life" (*UR* §14), which means that to some extent, they share common worship (*UR* §15). Poignant in this direction is the council's call for intimate communion between the younger churches (those established during the missionary endeavors in the nineteenth and twentieth centuries) and the universal church. This communion is realized in the concrete, dialogical interactions and solidarity between the young particular churches and the older particular churches for the purpose of ensuring mutual spiritual growth and maturation.[43] Based on these conciliar teachings, one can say that Vatican II provides the context, principles, and impetus for intraecclesial dialogue between Catholics in the West and in sub-Saharan Africa so that the universal church can move toward realizing the perfect ecclesial communion and unity that Christ willed.

The need for dialogue was also emphasized by the Second Special Assembly for Africa of the Synod of Bishops (October 4–25, 2009) when it called on the church in Africa to enter into dialogue "with those with whom we share the same faith" (Proposition 10; cf. *UR* §§14–15). This call was reiterated in Pope Benedict XVI's post-synodal apostolic exhortation *Africae Munus* when the pope exhorted the church in Africa to enter into dialogue with other Christian communities.[44] Even though, like the council, *Africae Munus* focused more on interreligious dialogue, especially with ATR and Islam (*AM* §§92–94), and on ecumenical dialogue, especially with the autochthonous Christian communities of Africa, the AICs (*AM* §89–91), it included the Orthodox and the Coptic Churches, with which we share the same faith (*AM* §89).[45] More importantly, before launching into its treatment of ecumenical and interreligious dialogue, *Africae Munus* emphasized that the church should "promote dialogue as a spiritual disposition, so that believers may learn to work together, for example, in association for justice and peace, in a spirit of trust and mutual help" (*AM* §88). It can be argued that this document encouraged dialogue not only with other Christian bodies and religious communities but also among Catholics, in order to achieve reconciliation, justice, and peace. It is not only the division between the Catholic Church and other Christians but also the division within the one Catholic family that contradicts the will of Christ. There is a great need for dialogue within the church if we want to strengthen Christian unity, undertake works of charity, and also collaborate to protect our common Christian patrimony.[46]

Here, it is important to note that there has been some sort of ongoing dialogue between the church in Africa and the church in the West even though a lot of it has revolved around finances. The church in the West has made enormous financial contributions to the church in Africa, and many African church leaders and theologians were trained thanks to the generosity of Western Christians. There have also been collaborative efforts between the two local churches in the areas of inculturation and social justice. It should also be acknowledged that many Western missionaries have done tre-

---

41. Vatican II, *Decree on Ecumenism* (*Unitatis Redintegratio*) §3 (hereinafter *UR*).
42. Cf. Vatican II, *Christus Dominus* §§11, 16.
43. Vatican II, *Ad Gentes* §§19, 20; Brechter, "Decree on the Church's Missionary Activity," 146, 148.
44. Pope Benedict XVI, *Africae Munus* (November 19, 2011) §§88–89 (hereinafter *AM*). The full quotation is as follows: "Peace in Africa, as elsewhere, is conditioned by interreligious relations. Hence it is important for the Church to promote dialogue as a spiritual disposition, so that believers may learn to work together.... I call upon the whole ecclesial family—particular Churches, institutes of consecrated life as well as lay movements and associations—to pursue this path with ever greater determination."
45. Cf. Vatican II, *Lumen Gentium* §18; *Catechism of the Catholic Church* §838.
46. Second Special Assembly for Africa of the Synod of Bishops, 2009, Proposition 10; cf. *AM* §89.

mendous work, not only in the areas of evangelization, education, and health care but also in the development of African cultures and languages. The Dutch Reformed Church in Nigeria, through their research on cultural anthropology and linguistics, helped the people of Abakaliki in eastern Nigeria to appreciate the significance and beauty of their culture and language. Today, the Abakaliki dialect, which has always been derogated, can be properly written, which has enabled the people to have the Bible in their own tongue.[47]

But, despite the progress already made in achieving mutual understanding and unity between the two local churches, there are still a lot of mutual misgivings and mistrust between African and Western Christians. Some Western theologians have accused the church in Africa of being too conservative and consequently dragging Western Christians back to a religious atmosphere they had overcome after great labors, an atmosphere in which it is difficult for the church in the West to address modern challenges like divorce and homosexuality. This has engendered a debate about how to contextualize the common faith without sundering its unity or devolving into doctrinal and theological sectarianism. Some Western Christians also see African missionaries as economic migrants whose overriding interest is not the salvation of souls but personal economic gain. In addition, some African missionaries to the West have been accused of insensitivity to Western cultures and values and of trying to impose their brand of African spirituality on Western Christians.[48] There is an urgent need for dialogue to address historical hurts and misconceptions on both sides and to encourage theological exchange for the sake of the unity of the universal church. As globalization continues to shrink humanity into a smaller "village," this dialogue becomes ever more indispensable for a church that views itself as one united family.

Grounds for Theological Dialogue

The Communion of Saints

Dialogue is essential for a community of faith marked by its universal character. As previously stated, the dialogue proposed here would be intraecclesial, an exchange between people who share one *koinonia*. The implication of this communion is that Catholic Christians, regardless of race, culture, context, issues of concern, or geographical location, are members of one family united by Trinitarian love. Thus, the local churches, whether in the West or in Africa, have a mutual responsibility for furthering the unity of the universal church through a deeper understanding and living out of the truth they share. This dialogue, therefore, must originate in a collective responsibility to strengthen the Catholic faith through a collaborative search for truth and the promotion of the life and mission of the church in a way that respects the uniqueness of each local or particular church. Following from the communal nature of the church, Catholic "theology is not simply any experience of a community, but that experience of believers coming into encounter with the Scriptures and the authentic experiences of other believing communities."[49] According to Meinrad P. Hebga, African theology cannot withdraw from universal theology: "African theology develops in the bosom of the universal Church. It cannot stop at an allegiance to African particularities. It is an adventure at the core of an increasingly 'globalised' humanity."[50] Thus, African and Western theologies, if they are to remain Catholic, cannot stand in mutual isolation; they must necessarily relate with each other and with the the-

---

47. One of these wonderful anthropological projects involved fieldwork carried out for the doctoral research in cultural anthropology of Gert Guiljam of the University of Utrecht, Netherlands. See *The Izi of North Igboland: A Description of Their Traditional Religion and the Encounter with Christianity* (Woerden, 1993).

48. During the 2014 Extraordinary General Assembly of the Synod of Bishops on the family, some Western bishops, including Walter Cardinal Kasper, accused African prelates of being "impossible" to deal with regarding the issues of homosexuality and those who are divorced and remarried. See "Cardinal Kasper Apologizes for Remarks about Africans; Says He Is Victim of 'Shameful' Attacks."

49. Schreiter, *Constructing Local Theologies*, 19.

50. Hebga, "Églises dignes et Églises indignes," *Concilium* 150 (1979): 127–34; cited in Bujo and Ilunga Muya, *African Theology*, 2:90.

ologies of other local churches. The doctrinal chaos that marred the implementation of *Amoris Laetitia*, especially in regard to the reception of communion by divorced and remarried people, is an obvious example of a situation in which theological collaboration in addressing the universal problems of the church would be helpful.[51] Therefore, theological dialogue is an inevitable corollary of an ecclesial communion that endorses and respects diversity without compromising overall unity.

One of the criticisms of Vatican II is that, while it encouraged dialogue *ad extra*, it did not do much to encourage intraecclesial dialogue. For the Catholic Church to sustain communion as its defining characteristic, there must be such a dialogue in order to address varying cultural, socioeconomic, and political contexts in light of the sacred deposit. Because of immigration and changes in missionary dynamics, there is now a crisscrossing of both ordinary Christians and missionaries between the West and Africa.[52] The proposed dialogue is essential so that African missionaries can appreciate the dynamics of Western Christianity and engage their host communities in a way that is pastorally enriching and respectful. "While African Christians reject Western cultural imperialism and demand that the Good News be communicated to them through the modes of their own cultures, African missionaries working in the West and in Asia should also extend the same gesture to their host Christian communities."[53] This dialogue is also necessary for the Western church to understand the spiritual needs of African Christian immigrants.

Common Sources of Theology

Consequent on the communal nature of the church, Catholic theologians share common sources of theology—scripture, tradition, and magisterial teachings. Both African and Western contextual theologies are but attempts to adapt this foundational Christian patrimony to the various contexts in which theologians work. A dialogue aimed at reaching a common understanding of these common sources is necessary in order to avoid theological and doctrinal sectarianism. Since all Catholics share the same *fides quae*, neither African nor Western Catholic theologians should interpret the scriptures, the sacred tradition, the dogmas, or other church doctrines in a way that is relevant to only their context.[54]

In addition, present-day theological reflection cannot afford to ignore the earlier constitutive insights of previous generations of Christian thinkers. These common sources of theology have often been analyzed and interpreted in the two millennia of the church's existence. The proposed dialogue will allow theologians from both Africa and the West to benefit from the insights of past generations of theologians as well as from their contemporaries, leading to a more comprehensive and balanced understanding of the Christian faith. This is why Odozor insists that African theologians should pay "close attention to the work of

---

51. See Pope Francis, *Amoris Laetitia*, chapter 8, §300. See also Edward Pentin, "'Doctrinal Anarchy' as Bishops' Conflicting Positions on Amoris Laetitia Show," with the subheading "Polish and Belgian bishops have become the latest to issue statements on Communion for civilly remarried divorcees, and both contradict the other," *National Catholic Register*, June 17, 2017, www.ncregister.com.

52. This means that Catholics—lay, clergy, and religious—from both Africa and the West are moving into each other's territory; it is no longer a situation of the one-way traffic of missionaries going from Europe and America to Africa and Asia.

53. Mbam, "Method of Inculturation in Africa," 277.

54. It must be admitted that the Christian patrimony has been culturally mediated, but this was a necessary element of propagating the divine revelation in history. The first recipients of this revelation, the prophets and the apostles, were limited by their cultural and contextual situations, as was, later, the church, as it struggled to understand and articulate the sacred deposit through doctrinal formulations. It is impossible to rediscover divine truth in its original purity because it has been mediated; the most one can do is to identify and excise what can be considered "Western *impedimenta*"; that is, unnecessary Western cultural frills that tend to obscure rather than clarify the faith (see Tharcisse Tshibangu, "Towards an African-Coloured Theology?," in Bujo and Ilunga Muya, *African Theology in the 21st Century*, 1:185). In doing this, the goal is to complement, through collaboration, the common patrimony with African conceptual and cultural treasures. I dealt with this issue in a more comprehensive way in Mbam, "Method of Inculturation in Africa."

other theologians both within and outside Africa."[55] Because of our common faith and common source material, Catholic theology, even though it must speak to particular contexts, cannot help but be collaborative on a global level.

Universal Human Interconnectedness

The grounding for contextual theology has been the socioeconomic, political, and religious differences that distinguish one context from another. It would appear to be denying the obvious to argue that this is not a valuable enterprise, but, upon closer examination, the similarity of our human experiences, desires, aspirations, and challenges is clear, despite differences in context and stages of socioeconomic and technological development. It is unquestionable that the fate of each human person is inextricably intertwined with that of humanity generally and that, because of globalization, humanity has reached a point of interdependence hitherto unknown. Social realities that until now might have been considered problems of a particular context are today global concerns. Thus today, socioeconomic, political, and spiritual events, and even natural disasters in one society in one corner of the globe have ricocheting effects all over the world.[56] The proverb that no person is an island is truer in our age than in any other. Since the world's peoples are interconnected and share common problems, there is a need for solidarity and the collaborative promotion of the common good, both material and spiritual. Thus, *Gaudium et Spes* calls on every part of the church family to take into consideration the needs and legitimate aspirations of the other parts (§26). This solidarity has already been demonstrated in the secular realm among scientists, economists, politicians, military forces, human rights activists, and environmentalists. Why should the same solidarity and dialogue not be possible among theologians? Theological dialogue is necessary if we are going to address our common human problems as one human family and community of faith. The time when theology was "sharply distinguished"[57] from pastoral action has passed; theology must now address the existential reality of the faithful. The world would see a Catholic theology that does not address the contemporary circumstances of believers as sterile.

Principles of Theological Dialogue

In order to be authentic and fruitful, the envisaged theological dialogue should be guided by principles ensuring that it remains Catholic in nature and at the same time open to the needs of particular contexts. Because the dialogue would be Catholic, the dialogical participants need to hark back to the fundamental principles of Catholic theology.[58] This is important because the theologian, as a member of the community of faith, must theologize in a way that ultimately elucidates and promotes the common faith, especially when the doctrine of the faith is in question.[59]

In addition, even though this dialogue is not ecumenical because it is between people of the same faith family, it would be beneficial to glean some methodological principles from the church's teachings on ecumenical and interreligious dialogue, especially as enunciated by Vatican II (*UR* §§2–4). The following should be some of the guiding principles of dialogue between African and Western theologies.

Conversion of Heart

According to the documents of the council, dialogue begins with conversion, a change of heart

---

55. Odozor, *Morality, Truly Christian, Truly African*, 24.
56. Vatican II, *Gaudium et Spes* §25.
57. Vanneste, "True Theology to Begin With," 197.
58. These include: (1) the primacy of divine revelation as transmitted by sacred scripture and the living sacred tradition as interpreted by the church's magisterium as the primary source of Catholic theology; (2) a critical fidelity to the rule of faith and the magisterium; (3) the "analogy of faith"; that is, one aspect of divine revelation cannot contradict another; and (4) the use of reason enlightened by faith and also philosophical, scientific, and cultural conceptual tools. See Congregation for the Doctrine of the Faith, *Instructio Donum Veritatis: On the Ecclesial Vocation of the Theologian* §§10–12, 21–31.
59. See *Instructio Donum Veritatis* §§11, 26.

or inner purification that is an essential premise for peace and reconciliation (UR §7; see also AM §§19–21). This implies the uprooting of feelings and attitudes that tend to demean the other. This renewal must be bilateral for dialogue to be fruitful and begins with an admission by all the involved parties that somehow they have all contributed to the existing divisions (UR §§3, 7). In the case of dialogue between African Catholics and their Western counterparts, this conversion would entail the recognition that, while some Westerners demeaned and exhibited racism in their relationships with Africans, Africans for their part have not always been brotherly and kind toward Westerners. There have been overgeneralizations, blanket condemnations, and a denial of the positive contributions and sacrifices of the missionaries. Moreover, Africans have not always heeded the council's admonition that the present generation should not be charged with the sins of the past (UR §3) when it comes to the horrors of slavery and colonialism. This does not mean we should forget the past; it is rather an invitation to not allow the past to warp our views of the present. This dialogue should be a sincere recognition of and response to the efforts of a modern generation of Western Christians who have sought better relations with the church in Africa, especially in the areas of spiritual growth, theological training, and structural development.

Fidelity to the Sacred Deposit[60]

First, despite the validity and legitimacy of contextual theology, it should be noted that Catholic theology is not an endeavor aimed at only individual believers or parts of the church; it is, rather, oriented toward enhancing the faith of the universal church. Gerald O'Collins, quoting the International Theological Commission, states that "theology can only be done in living community with the Church."[61] According to Joseph Cardinal Ratzinger, Christianity is fundamentally characterized by its indispensable and binding common belief. The "Christian faith affirms truths, the contents of which are not subject to a totally free symbolic interpretation but are to be understood as statements that are valid and true as they stand."[62] This is especially true for Catholic theologians, who belong to a universal church that shares a common rule of faith, or sacred deposit, which must be held by all confessing Catholics irrespective of their different contexts. According to *Fides et Ratio*, belief in universally valid truth is the essential condition for a sincere dialogue (§92)—there can be no authentic Catholic theology that ignores this common patrimony. This also implies that this dialogue should occur in the context of critical cooperation with the magisterium. The history of the church shows that human reason, "wounded and weakened by sin" (FR §51), can and does go wrong. Therefore, the role of the magisterium is to ensure that reason and theological opinion do not stray from the path of revealed truth (FR §§49, 51).

Adherence to the common rule of faith saves contextualization from relativizing theology by engaging in a sectarian pursuit of vested contextual interest. The proposed theological dialogue and collaboration, regardless of whatever else it can achieve, will thus be counterproductive if it ultimately does not lead to a deeper understanding and living out of the shared Catholic faith in every context. Therefore, contrary to Stephen Bevans, theology cannot move away from "*theologia perennis* to a reflection-in-faith on God's revelation in particular situations."[63] Perennial theology must remain a fundamental element of the matrix of contextual theology. As Bernard Lonergan states, Christian theology cannot be divorced from the general history of the Christian religion.[64]

Despite this, a recognition of the significance of the sacred deposit in intraecclesial dialogue should

---

60. The sacred deposit comprises divine revelation as transmitted through scripture and tradition and as dogmatically interpreted by the magisterium. Every Catholic, regardless of culture or context, must adhere to divine revelation, whether contained in the scriptures or in the church's dogmatic teachings. See UR §11.

61. O'Collins, *Fundamental Theology*, 15, quoting International Theological Commission, "The Ecclesiastical Magisterium and Theology," Thesis 8 §2.

62. Ratzinger, *Principles of Catholic Theology*, 326.

63. Bevans, *Modes of Contextual Theology*, 17.

64. Lonergan, *Method in Theology*, 128.

not degenerate into morbid reverence for the past, whereby the articles of faith are simply parroted or received uncritically. Dogmatic teachings, although they are infallibly proposed as irreformable divine mysteries, are communicated through historically conditioned formulations. Without rejecting the substance of the church's dogmatic and definitive teachings, one can, by employing the hermeneutics of suspicion, unravel the contextual, cultural, and historical factors that contributed to their formulation and ask whether those historical-cultural elements are hindering their meaningfulness and adaptability in a particular context. As Pope St. John XXIII makes clear, "The substance of the ancient doctrine of the deposit of faith is one thing, and the way in which it is presented is another."[65] Consequently, when the formulation of a dogmatic teaching threatens to obscure the meaning of the divine mysteries in a particular geographical and temporal context, there is need of reformulation. More importantly, the dogmas, because they address subjects that are ultimately mysteries, are constantly in need of rereading and reinterpretation in light of new developments in biblical and theological scholarship and in the secular sciences, as well as in sociological contexts.

The Hierarchy of Truth

According to Vatican II, a Catholic involved in dialogue should always remember that there is a hierarchy of truth in the church:

> Catholic theologians engaged in ecumenical dialogue, while standing fast by the teaching of the Church and searching together with separated brethren into the divine mysteries, should act with love for truth with charity, and humility. When comparing doctrines, they should remember that in Catholic teaching there exists an order or "hierarchy" of truths, since they vary in their relationship to the foundation of the Christian faith. (*UR* §11 [translation by Walter Abbott])

Even though this dialogical principle is primarily applicable to ecumenical and interfaith dialogue, it can also be useful in intraecclesial dialogue especially in fostering a spirit of flexibility in interpreting and adapting nondogmatic, noninfallible ecclesial teachings. Thus, dialogical agents should distinguish between theological issues and church teachings that can be interpreted elastically for the benefit of a local church and those whose meaning cannot be stretched.

Equality between the Agents Participating in Dialogue

Any dialogue between Western and African theologies must be anchored in the principle of equality between all agents participating in it (*UR* §9). This implies a recognition not only of their ontological and spiritual equality but also of their intellectual equality. This implies that no dialogical partner should treat the other with condescension or set the agenda unilaterally. But to avoid a false egalitarianism based on condescension or concessions, there is a need for African dialogical agents to work hard academically—not to impress their Western counterparts but to be objectively on a par with them with respect to an in-depth and holistic knowledge of Catholic theology. They should engage in extensive research in order to gain a deep, scientific knowledge of their African context. African scholars have occasionally been known to base their knowledge of African contexts on commonsense knowledge that does not stand up to facts and scientific analysis. African dialogical agents should also expend effort to achieve financial independence, because as long as one of the dialogical parties assumes the financial burden of engaging in the process, there is the possibility that the financier will set its agenda and determine its direction, as "He who pays the piper dictates the tune."

Reciprocity

An immediate consequence of the principle of equality is that of reciprocity; that is, all dialogical partners are genuinely open and committed to being mutually enriched by the others' insights. This mutual enrichment should be a pathway to mutual enlightenment, by which each dialogical party gains a deeper insight into the world of the

---

65. Pope John XXIII, *Gaudet Mater Ecclesia*; see Abbott, *Documents of Vatican II*, 715.

other, leading to the shedding of mutual biases and prejudices, the clarification of misconceptions about the others' cultures and traditions, and the sacrifice of unjustifiably triumphalist cultural positions. In other words, there should be no divide between teaching partners and learning partners; all should be teachers and students simultaneously. A situation in which one partner speaks to the other as if the other is an empty vessel would not only lead to the delivery of a monologue but would ultimately generate more animosity and disunity. "Dialogue is a two-way communication. It implies speaking and listening, giving and receiving, for mutual growth and enrichment. It includes witness to one's faith as well as an openness to that of the other."[66] A situation in which one partner considers the other's context, ideas, or practices to be too strange or outmoded to be useful or too progressive or alien to be assimilated would lead to a dialogue of the deaf with each partner holed up in his or her own ideological fortress, engaged in much shouting and little communication.

Therefore, theological dialogue, to be successful, must involve openness to learning and expanding one's horizons; this is a sine qua non for spiritual, intellectual, social, and cultural development. But such openness is possible only for those who view their culture and context not as static and sacrosanct but rather as dynamic and reformable. Therefore, the principle of reciprocity requires not only openness to new ideas but also a reverential yet critical approach to one's context, which would enable the dialogical agent to highlight the context's strengths and weaknesses and to differentiate between positive cultural elements that are conducive to growth and negative ones that are inimical to it.

Contextual Sensitivity
It would be repeating the obvious to emphasize that the dialogue between the West and Africa should be guided by contextual sensitivity. Unless the Christian faith is meaningfully contextualized or incarnated in the host culture, it has not yet been authentically received. According to Lonergan, "Doctrines that are really assimilated bear the stamp of those that have assimilated them and the absence of such an imprint is symptomatic of a perfunctory assimilation."[67] Pope St. John Paul II, in 1982, echoed this sentiment when he stated that a "faith which does not become culture is a faith which has not been fully received, not thoroughly thought through, not fully lived out."[68] One of the great achievements of the council was its respect for the diversity of cultures and contexts in the church. This was based on its understanding of church unity not as a rigid uniformity but as a communion accepting of diversity. The council made clear that the church rejects nothing that is good in any people's culture; rather, it embraces and fosters, insofar as they are good, the abilities, resources, and customs of every people. For the council, the assimilation of the treasures of different cultures and traditions will not only enrich the faith but also make it indigenous to every land.[69] This principle guided the council's liturgical reforms, which allowed for liturgical adaptations to the changeable elements of the liturgy as long as the shared faith and the common good of the universal church is not compromised.[70] The same principle was also applied to the reform of seminary education, which allowed local churches to adapt the form of this education to suit their particular contexts.[71]

Taking a cue from the council, dialogical agents should respect the diversity of cultures and contexts, not only as between the West and Africa but also within both. There is also a need for each dialogical partner to clarify precisely the nature of its culture and context, especially with respect to its values, intellectual frameworks, philosophical and ideological worldviews, and challenges. This clarity can be achieved not only with the help of theology but also by utilizing insights from secular

---

66. Pontifical Council for Interreligious Dialogue (PCID), "Methodology of PCID."
67. Lonergan, *Method in Theology*, 300–301.
68. John Paul II, "Letter to Cardinal Agostino Casaroli, June 28, 1982"; quoted in Mbam, "Method of Inculturation in Africa," 277.
69. Vatican II, *Lumen Gentium* §13; *Gaudium et Spes* §58; *Ad Gentes* §§19, 22.
70. Vatican II, *Sacrosanctum Concilium* §§37–40, 65, 68.
71. Vatican II, *Optatam Totius*, 11.

sciences like sociology, psychology, anthropology, political science, and economics. As I have already shown, a simplistic interpretation of a particular context yields false generalizations. For instance, the Western context might appear to be economically richer, intellectually and culturally more progressive, technologically more advanced, socially more individualistic, and politically more orderly and peaceful than the African context. Despite this, however, a good portion of the Western populace lives in abject poverty, experiences violence and oppression in its various manifestations, espouses religious and moral conservatism, and favors communalism over individualism. The same need to avoid overgeneralization goes for Africa, where poverty exists side by side with opulence, high levels of illiteracy coexist with a highly educated class, and communalism is hemmed in by the socioeconomic individualism and selfishness of a small elite. For this reason, the contexts of both the West and Africa must be defined so that the various orientations and perspectives of all the faithful are included.

Expertise and Professionalism

As has already been hinted at, the dialogue between African and Western theologies must be conducted by experts in theology and in other disciplines such as cultural anthropology, sociology, linguistics, and psychology (*UR* §4). An insistence on the involvement of experts does not in any way imply a denigration of grassroots theological collaboration between Africa and the West—a different level of dialogue that possesses validity in its own right. But the focus here is on the kind of theological dialogue that would enable theologians and church leaders from both Africa and the West to incarnate the faith in their local churches without compromising the orthodoxy and communion of the universal church. This theological collaboration would enable theologians and church leaders from various parts of the Catholic family to share the latest insights and findings in theological scholarship and other sciences. To achieve this, the dialogical agents need theological expertise and in-depth cultural knowledge that may not be available to amateurs. This is where a professional theologian is indispensable—enthusiastic but amateurish dialogical agents may only muddle the situation and create more confusion and misunderstanding between the parties. A professional theologian is a significant resource for the community and can play a significant role in interpreting the community's experience in the light of the Christian faith. He or she is also important in relating local theology to the tradition of the universal church. Although theologians like Bevans have argued that professional or expert theologians should serve only as midwives or in auxiliary roles in contextual theology,[72] it is important to note that sometimes it has actually been professional theologians who have initiated the contextualization of theology. Therefore, as Robert Schreiter observes, "To ignore the resources of the professional theologian is to prefer ignorance over knowledge. . . . In the development of local theologies, the professional theologian serves as an important resource, helping the community to clarify its own experience and to relate it to the experience of other communities past and present."[73]

Dialectical Approach

Dialectics enables the unraveling of points of convergence and divergence and also the resolution of opposites. It is important to reiterate that the purpose of the dialogue proposed here is to strengthen communion without compromising diversity. Through collaborative theological efforts, dialogic agents should strive to expose differences that are only apparent and to find a way to live with real or substantial differences without harming unity. Thus, this dialogical process requires a dialectical approach to uncover the roots and nature of the differences between the two parties concerning their understanding of the deposit of faith and of their spirituality, ideas, worldviews, orientations, and value systems, and of other theological issues. A dialectical process would make it possible to determine whether differences are the result of misconceptions or whether they are inherent in the nature of the reality in question.

---

72. Bevans, *Models of Contextual Theology*, 18.
73. Schreiter, *Constructing Local Theologies*, 18.

According to Lonergan, the various differences that exist between peoples and cultures might be due to differences in worldviews, levels of conversion,[74] or differentiated consciousnesses. Lonergan states further that some of the differences caused by the presence of diverse worldviews follow from the different stages of development at which people find themselves. These differences can be easily resolved through the discovery of further facts and the clarification of the other's positions. But, Lonergan continues, there are differences that are dialectically opposed, involving opposing value judgments and a mutual repudiation of the other's positions. "What in one is found intelligible, in another is unintelligible. What for one is true, for another is false. What for one is good, for another is evil."[75] People can react against these differences by deriding the other's worldview as mythical, fallacious, blind, illusory, backward, immature, or incompatible with God's will and grace.[76] These kinds of differences cannot be resolved through theological argumentation or by mere clarification of the opposing positions. Even further development of facts may not eliminate these differences because proponents of opposing worldviews interpret data tendentiously to support their respective positions.[77] Such inherent differences, according to Lonergan, can be resolved only through a conversion that allows for an encounter between opposing worldviews. By "encounter" Lonergan means "meeting persons, appreciating the values they represent, criticizing their defects, and allowing one's living to be challenged at its very roots by their words and by their deeds."[78] This encounter leads to a new understanding of reality, including that of the opposing worldview.

Applying Lonergan's classification of differences to the theological dialogue between Africa and the West, one can say that a lot of the differences that exist between them may be more related to people being at different stages of development rather than to people being rooted in irremediable opposition. For instance, some of the supposedly well-known distinguishing characteristics of African societies are communalism and family closeness, while the West is seen as characterized by radical individualism. Well, it might turn out that Africans are communal simply because they live in close-knit villages where people are often of the same race, language, and culture. As more and more Africans move into urban environments where people live side by side with total strangers, an environment similar to that of the West, we are beginning to see the dissolution of that communalism and the emergence of Western-style individualism in African societies. Traditional African family ties are also being strained as young people move away from the village setting in search of a more promising future, leaving behind their aged parents and members of their extended families.

Another example may relate to marriage. Stable marriages were once touted as a defining value of African society, while unstable marriages and easy access to divorce were thought to be characteristic of the West. Today, because of the same social pressures as those affecting the West, African societies are experiencing an increased divorce rate. These examples show that Africans might be experiencing today what the West experienced in an earlier time. Thus, the proposed theological dialogue would, by means of a dialectical process, enable Africans to tap into the experiential insights of

---

74. According to Lonergan, conversion means an experience of self-transcendence through which one's worldview and value system are transformed, leading to a radical shift from inauthenticity to authenticity. It also leads to intimacy with, and total surrender to, God. When conversion is holistic, that is, when it is intellectual, moral, and religious, it defines and steers one's knowledge, interests, goals, and criteria for judgment. Such conversion is necessary for objective or scientific or true knowledge, especially in theology. For Lonergan, without conversion, objectivity is an illusion. But this process of conversion is dynamic; that is, it advances but can also collapse due to the forces of falsehood and lustful pleasures. Therefore, people are not often at the same level of conversion, which creates tension and misunderstanding among them. See Lonergan, *Method in Theology*, 244, 339–40.

75. Lonergan, *Method in Theology*, 236.
76. Lonergan, *Method in Theology*, 237.
77. Lonergan, *Method in Theology*, 236; cf. 252, 358.
78. Lonergan, *Method in Theology*, 247.

Western societies and learn from their achievements and missteps. For their part, Western societies, by contemplating African experiences, may, through the dialectical process in dialogue, be able to recover what they lost in the name of progress.

A particular area in which the dialogue with the West could benefit the church in Africa is in managing the boom happening in the present-day African church, which is being manifested in the rapidly increasing number of Christians and vocations to the priesthood and religious life. Many theologians have triumphantly noted the upsurge of Christianity in sub-Saharan Africa and its contrasting decline in the West. According to Lamin Sanneh, Africa has become, or is becoming, a Christian continent in cultural as well as numerical terms, while Western societies have become, or are rapidly becoming, post-Christian.[79] This view was echoed by Philip Jenkins, who believes that the era of Western Christianity has passed and that the day of southern Christianity is dawning. According to Jenkins, by the end of this century, most Catholics will live in Latin America and Africa.[80] It has even been suggested that the growth of Christianity in the Global South may well prove to be a vital source of renewal for Western Christianity.

But such triumphalist exuberance needs to be tempered by a recognition of the cyclic boom and bust that typically attend growth in the church. The growth of Christianity in Africa has reached nowhere near the crescendo it did in the West, with the vast majority of the European continent a mass of Christian faithful for almost two millennia. There have been questions whether the growth of Christianity in Africa can be sustained if socioeconomic and political developments usher in an era of economic prosperity and political stability. As Thomas J. Reese puts it, "When people say Africa is the future, I say 'oh isn't it the past?' I see it as a repeat of the past, what happened in Europe centuries ago. What's going to happen in Africa when everybody gets a television set, when modernity comes?"[81] It is certainly possible that economic prosperity and the advent of modernity might burst the Christian bubble in Africa, but Reese's view may be unduly pessimistic. Africa is not fated to go the way of Europe. Africa has a different religious history that can stand it in good stead should the anticipated economic breakthrough occur. Unlike the West, African societies, especially south of the Sahara, appear averse to atheism. Nevertheless, the gloomy future predicted by Reese can be avoided only if Africans are willing to learn from the experiences of the Western church. The proposed dialogical engagement may enable the church in Africa to manage the current boom by learning from the West why Christianity there went bust.

This dialogue can also deal with differences between the West and Africa by eliminating or minimizing misunderstandings, misrepresentations, and the negative characterization of the other, once both parties become genuinely open and willing to learn and expand their horizons. Of course, as Lonergan remarks, the process of resolving especially intractable differences involves the expansion of our horizons through spiritual, moral, and intellectual conversion. Without such conversion, dialogue leads not to synthesis but to a widening of the gulf between dialogic partners. For this reason, theological dialogue by itself cannot lead to unity or collaboration. There must be a letting go of stubbornness, discrimination, and prejudice and a willingness and commitment to see reality through the prism of the other's worldview.

The Way Forward

It is hoped that the proposed intraecclesial dialogue will help the church in Africa to gain the intellectual progress already achieved by its Western counterpart, especially in the area of producing theological resource materials. As was noted above, intellectual equality is necessary for the success of this theological dialogue. Thus, theological prog-

---

79. Sanneh, *Whose Religion Is Christianity?*, 36.

80. Jenkins, *Next Christendom*, 3, 195. See also Philip Jenkins: "Catholicism's Incredible Growth Story," *Catholic Herald*, September 9, 2016; and St. John in the Wilderness's Adult Education and Formation course, "World Christianity 1. The Christian Revolution: The Changing Demographics of Christianity," http://www.stjohnadulted.org/worldchrist1.htm.

81. Reese, quoted in Nossiter, "Church Helps Fill a Void in Africa."

ress in Africa should be directed toward producing in-depth, well-researched theological works that can become source materials for our seminaries and theological institutes. African theologians must play their part in developing the perennial, universal, Catholic theology. They must do their best not to be mired in a sectarian African theology that simply adapts the universal Catholic theology (principally produced in the West) to African situations. The weakness of the adaptation approach in African theology has been its failure to incarnate the sources of the perennial theology (divine revelation as transmitted through scripture and tradition, conciliar formulations of dogmatic truths, and the classical Christian theological heritage, including the contributions of the church fathers and great theologians like Thomas Aquinas). These sources should be incarnated in Africa by means of African religious, cultural, philosophical, and anthropological concepts.[82] According to Alfred Vanneste, "African theologians must always remember that a great theology, valid for the whole of the Catholic world, is not built up except on the basis of a patient and meticulous scrutiny of the sources of revelation and in permanent contact with the great currents of universal thought."[83] For this reason, African theologians must do more to produce academic works that can make a significant contribution to universal Catholic theology. To achieve this requires more intellectual collaboration and exchange with the church in the West, which possesses more robust academic facilities and programs.

Conclusion

It has been a long and an arduous journey from the days of the *Syllabus of Errors*[84] and *Mortalium Animos*[85]—when dialogue, whether with the separated Protestant brethren or with members of other religions, was forbidden—to the era of the Second Vatican Council, which stressed the great value of such dialogue. Today, dialogue, both inter- and intraecclesial, has been recognized by most Christians as a sine qua non for the realization of Jesus's wish that his followers may be one, as a reflection of Trinitarian unity and as evidence of the divine origin of his mission (see John 17:21–23). Thus, the intraecclesial, intercultural dialogue promoted above is a summons to all Christians, both in the West and in Africa, to work for Christian unity and for the promotion of global catholicity through theological collaboration and the sharing of insights. This chapter has issued a call for positive action to be taken to promote the faith and the common interest of humanity. It is easy for Africans to become mired in mudslinging and cultural wars in which they blame the West for their woes and for the West to despise Africa as a "dark continent" and as a burden. But, ultimately, any true believer who longs for the coming of the kingdom and for a truly universal church that is both a family and a bastion of truth will follow the way of dialogue. In fact, there is no real alternative to dialogue except unending intercultural hatred and mutual contempt fueled by misconception. If Christians in the West and in Africa want peace, progress, and an effective incarnation of the gospel in their various contexts, then dialogue is without question the only solution.

Bibliography

Abbott, Walter M. *The Documents of Vatican II*. Baltimore: Geoffrey Chapman, 1966.

Appiah-Kubi, Kofi, and Sergio Torres. *African Theology en Route*. Maryknoll, NY: Orbis Books, 1983.

Benedict XVI, Pope [Joseph Ratzinger]. *Principles of Catholic Theology: Building Stones for a Fundamental Theology*. San Francisco, CA: Ignatius Press, 1989.

---

82. For the debate over how African theology can appropriate traditional sources of Christian theology, see Martey, *African Theology*, 70–78.
83. See Vanneste, "True Theology to Begin With," 199.
84. On December 8, 1864, the Holy See published the *Syllabus of Errors*, which contained a list (in Latin, *syllabus*) of condemned propositions, that is, theological statements considered to be erroneous.
85. In the 1928 encyclical *Mortalium Animos*, Pius XI forbade Catholics from participating in ecumenical gatherings (§2).

Bevans, Stephen B. *Models of Contextual Theology*. Maryknoll, NY: Orbis Books, 2006.

Brechter, Heinrich Suso. "Decree on the Church's Missionary Activity." In *Commentary on the Documents of Vatican II*, ed. Herbert Vorgrimler. Freiburg: Herder, 1969.

Bujo, Bénézet. *African Theology in Its Social Context*. Nairobi: Paulines Publications Africa, 1992.

———. *The Ethical Dimension of Community: The African Model and the Dialogue between North and South*. Nairobi: Paulines Publications Africa, 1998.

———. *Foundations of an African Ethic: Beyond the Universal Claims of Western Morality*. New York: Crossroad, 2001.

Bujo, Bénézet, and Juvénal Ilunga Muya, eds. *African Theology in the 21st Century: The Contribution of the Pioneers*. 2 vols. Nairobi: Paulines Publications Africa, 2003.

Catholic World Report. "Cardinal Kasper Apologizes for Remarks about Africans; Says He Is Victim of 'Shameful' Attacks." www.catholicworldreport.com.

Congregation for the Doctrine of the Faith. *Instructio Donum Veritatis: On the Ecclesial Vocation of the Theologian* (1990). www.vatican.va.

Dickson, Kwesi A., and Paul Ellingworth, eds. *Biblical Revelation and African Beliefs*. Maryknoll, NY: Orbis Books, 1969.

Fiorenza, Francis S., and John P. Galvin, eds. *Systematic Theology: Roman Catholic Perspectives*. Minneapolis: Fortress Press, 1991.

Francis, Pope. *Amoris Laetitia* [Post-synodal Apostolic Exhortation on Love in the Family; March 19, 2016]. Vatican City: Libreria Editrice Vaticana, 2016. www.vatican.va.

Hebga, Meinrad P. "Églises dignes et Églises indignes." *Concilium* 150 (1979): 127–34.

Ijezie, Luke, et al., eds. *The Church in Nigeria and Ecumenical Question*. Lagos: Cathan Publication, 2015.

Jenkins, Philip. *The Next Christendom: The Coming of Global Christianity*. Oxford: Oxford University Press, 2002.

John XXIII, Pope. *Gaudet Mater Ecclesia* ["Mother Church Rejoices"; Opening Address to the Second Vatican Council; October 11, 1962]. www.vatican.va.

John Paul II, Pope. *Fides et Ratio* [Encyclical on the Relationship between Faith and Reason; September 14, 1998]. Vatican City: Libreria Editrice Vaticana, 1998. www.vatican.va.

Kirwen, Michael C. *The Missionary and the Diviner: Contending Theologies of Christian and African Religions*. Maryknoll, NY: Orbis Books, 1987.

Lonergan, Bernard. *Method in Theology*. Toronto: University of Toronto Press, 2007.

Magesa, Laurenti. *African Religion: The Moral Traditions of Abundant Life*. Maryknoll, NY: Orbis Books, 1997.

Martey, Emmanuel. *African Theology: Inculturation and Liberation*. Maryknoll, NY: Orbis Books, 1993.

Mbam, Emmanuel. "Method of Inculturation in Africa." *Mission* 15.1–2 (2008).

Mbiti, John. *African Religions and Philosophy*. London: Heinemann, 1982.

Metuh, Emefie Ikenga. *African Religions in Western Conceptual Schemes: The Problem of Interpretation*. Ibadan, Nigeria: Pastoral Institute, 1985.

Mushete, Ngindu. "The History of Theology in Africa: From Polemics to Critical Irenics." In *African Theology en Route*, edited by Kofi Appiah-Kubi and Sergio Torres, 23–35. Maryknoll, NY: Orbis Books, 1983.

Nossiter, Adam. "Church Helps Fill a Void in Africa." *New York Times*, February 23, 2013, www.nytimes.com.

O'Collins, Gerald. *Fundamental Theology*. New York: Paulist Press, 1981.

Odozor, Paulinus I. *Morality, Truly Christian, Truly African: Foundational Methodological and Theological Considerations*. Notre Dame, IN: University of Notre Dame Press, 2014.

Onwubiko, Oliver. *African Thought, Religion, and Culture*. Enugu, Nigeria: Snaap Press, 1991.

Paul VI, Pope. *Evangelii Nuntiandi* [Apostolic Exhortation on the Theme of Catholic Evangelization; December 8, 1975]. Vatican City: Libreria Editrice Vaticana, 1975. www.vatican.va.

Pius XI, Pope. *Mortalium Animos* [Encyclical on Religious Unity; January 6, 1928]. www.vatican.va.

Pontifical Council for Interreligious Dialogue (PCID). "Methodology of PCID." www.vatican.va.

Ratzinger, Joseph. *See* Benedict XVI, Pope.

Sanneh, Lamin. *Whose Religion Is Christianity? The Gospel beyond the West*. Grand Rapids, MI: Eerdmans, 2003.

Schreiter, Robert J. *Constructing Local Theologies*. Maryknoll, NY: Orbis Books, 2004.

Smith, Edwin. *African Ideas of God*. London: Edinburgh House Press, 1961.

Tshibangu, Tharcisse. "Towards an African-Coloured Theology?" In *African Theology in the 21st Century: The Contribution of the Pioneers*, edited by Bénézet Bujo and Juvénal Ilunga Muya, vol. 1. Nairobi: Paulines Publications Africa, 2003.

Vanneste, Alfred. "A True Theology to Begin With." In *African Theology in the 21st Century: The Contribution of the Pioneers*, edited by Bénézet Bujo and Juvénal Ilunga Muya, vol. 1. Nairobi: Paulines Publications Africa, 2003.

Vatican II. *Ad Gentes* [Decree on the Church's Missionary Activity; 1965]. www.vatican.va.

———. *Christus Dominus* [Decree on the Bishops' Pastoral Office in the Church; 1965]. www.vatican.va.

———. *Gaudium et Spes* [Pastoral Constitution on the Church in the Modern World; 1965]. www.vatican.va.

———. *Lumen Gentium* [Dogmatic Constitution on the Church; 1964]. www.vatican.va.

———. *Optatam Totius* [Decree on Priestly Formation; 1965]. www.vatican.va.

———. *Sacrosanctum Concilio* [Constitution on the Sacred Liturgy; 1963]. www.vatican.va.

———. *Unitatis Redintegratio* [Decree on Ecumenism; 1964]. www.vatican.va.

Suggested Reading

Bujo, Bénézet, and Juvénal Ilunga Muya, eds. *African Theology in the 21st Century: The Contribution of the Pioneers*. 2 vols. Nairobi: Paulines Publications Africa, 2003.

Kirwen, Michael C. *The Missionary and the Diviner: Contending Theologies of Christian and African Religions*. Maryknoll, NY: Orbis Books, 1987.

Metuh, Emefie Ikenga. *African Religions in Western Conceptual Schemes: The Problem of Interpretation*. Ibadan, Nigeria: Pastoral Institute, 1985.

African Philosophies in Dialogue with the West

Nathanaël Yaovi Soédé

The theme of this chapter requires two observations at the outset. The first is that my analysis of the relationship between "African philosophies" and "the West" is particularly focused on understanding the kind of dialogue that can be developed between these two subjects. This will require a development of what we mean by dialogue, in particular the nature of dialogue and anthropological and philosophical dimensions of dialogue. The second observation is anthropological: dialogue between African philosophies and the West demands an in-depth study of African philosophies insofar as they are not closed in on themselves but rather are in conversation with each other.

In this chapter, "the West" refers to Western peoples and their culture. This means Europe, North America, and Australia, and specifically includes Western thinking about African people and African philosophies. Africa refers to the so-called Black people living south of the Sahara and in the African diaspora and their cultural, anthropological, and philosophical thought.

The chapter will focus on a broad overview of the past and present meaning, objectives, content, and importance of the dialogue between African philosophies and the West. It would also be possible to employ a method that analyzes this dialogue through the lens of particular topics linked to particular historical periods, such as the Atlantic slave trade, colonization,[1] culture, development, peace, and the person. This latter method, however, does not allow us to look at history to develop an in-depth understanding of the foundations of the dialogue between the West and African philosophies. Moreover, this method does not make clear that this dialogue was first unilaterally conducted by the West to assert and spread the theory that the "Negro" is wild and uncivilized, without history or culture. Western anthropology created an ideology that it was the absolute master of the "Black" or the "Negro" before Africans could reply. Katrin Flikschuh reveals the weakness of this ideology when she asserts that "to date, Western philosophical thinking has engaged very little with African traditions of thought."[2] However, she does not reach beyond her argument in order to think in-depth about the foundations of the West's view of Africa. She states only that "when it comes to personhood, the Western tradition has for long periods of time barely accorded Africans the status of persons at all. Kant has been implicated in that failure."[3] The concept of the person is the framework for Flikschuh's reflection on the dialogue between the West and African philosophical thought. Flikschuh represents the West through Kant and Africa through Menkiti. In short, the analytical method of focusing on particular topics, as seen in Flikschuh's work, fails

---

1. The slave trade and colonization has been the subject of numerous studies. See W. H. Worger, E. A. Alpers, and N. L. Clark, *Africa and the West: A Documentary History*, vol. 1: *From the Slave Trade to the Conquest*; vol. 2: *From Colonialism to Independence, 1875 to the Present* (Oxford: Oxford University Press, 2010).
2. Flikschuh, "Arc of Personhood."
3. Flikschuh, "Arc of Personhood."

to consider the ideological foundations of the dialogue among African philosophies.

Whichever method is chosen, however, any discussion of the dialogue between African philosophies and the West should consider two things. The first is that the West has described, made statements about, and characterized Africa without having actually met or listened to her. The second is that Africa has been called to enter a dialogue with the West in order to respond to the West's allegations about her. These two things are the basis of and constitute the necessary starting point for the dialogue between the West and Africa.

What is the nature of the relationship between Africa and the West that led to the existence of this dialogue? Answering this question will require a study of the meaning of this dialogue in order to understand its anthropological scope. The first part of this chapter will focus on the meaning and requirements of true dialogue, and on the main ideas advanced by the West in its initial discourse about Africa. The second part will reflect on the West's reconsideration of its discourse about Africa and the latter's response. The third section will analyze the ongoing dialogue by employing a critical approach to the West's ideology of domination with respect to Africa. However, even though the dialogue in its current form continues to promote the West's ideas over Africa's, Africa does not despair; instead, she uses the dialogue as an opportunity to understand her responsibility to build her own future as well as that of the world. The chapter concludes by proposing a real and renewed dialogue between African philosophy and the West, inviting both Africa and the West to welcome the demands of a real dialogue. This proposal is made in the light of Enrique Dussel's works about various issues that must be considered before a dialogue between the Global North and the Global South can occur. A real and productive dialogue would be rooted in the world's oldest philosophical traditions and in the present-day social contexts of the people of both North and South.

The Meaning and Requirements for True Dialogue and the West's Initial Discourse about Africa

What is meant by the concept of "dialogue"? What are the requirements of true dialogue?

The Meaning of Dialogue

It must first be emphasized that dialogue is of an anthropological order because it connects people through the mediation of speech at the primary level. Dialogue means communication, an exchange of words (*logos*, i.e., speech, discourse, reason, thought) between (*dia*, i.e., between, through) two or more people. Dialogue presents the human being as a being of speech, rational communication, a quest for meaning, a sharing of experiences, and a search for truth in collaboration with others.

The concept of dialogue also implies that the human being is a speaking, rational, and relational subject. Because speech is inherent in the living person—that is, according to African anthropology, the human being as fundamentally manifesting life or as a "living-being" (*être-vie* in French)[4]—we would say that dialogue involves the human being as a being of word, relationship, and rationality.

Dialogue is the level at which the relationship of two or more alterities enters into intercommunication and is thus asserted as a relationship between persons. Thus, Emmanuel Levinas, following Martin Buber, conceived of dialogue as fundamental to being human:[5] it imposes itself through the face of the other whom I am bound to recognize as another self, to love him or her, to speak to him or her, to do him or her good. Dialogue is the sublime moment of the conscious encounter of the living subject with another living subject.

As interpersonal communication, dialogue is authentic only if it generates life and constructive human, social, and cosmic relationships. It expresses speech and must, like it, follow the Dogon (Mali) and Aja-Ewe and Aja-Fon (South Benin, Togo, and Ghana) anthropologies,[6] which

---

4. Magesa, *African Religion*; Mveng, *L'Afrique dans l'Eglise*; Soédé, *Sens et enjeux de l'éthique*.
5. Levinas, *Totality and Infinity*; Levinas, *Altérité et transcendance*; Buber, *I and Thou*; Friedman, *Martin Buber*.
6. Griaule, *Conversations with Ogotemmêli*; Guédou, *Xó et gbè*; Soédé, "Parole et vérité dans la culture et les comportements actuels des Africains."

hold that speech is fertile when it is true. The African palaver as a collective dialogue finds its essential foundations here.

The African palaver is, indeed, a collective exchange of speech undertaken to discuss and share reflections on a problem or on good or bad news with a view toward finding and implementing a life-enhancing solution that supports fraternal relationships and constructive rationality among all. Thus, the speech, or the dialogue of the palaver, leads to the truth by a consensual method and by choosing a consensual solution.[7] Decisions are not made for the benefit only of the one who is right—African culture takes into account the interest of everyone in a community. Dialogue does not emerge simply because of conflict; rather, it is a way of being with others intersubjectively to promote the collective interest. Of course, joy and suffering are present in every community, and the African communitarian ideal focuses on reconciliation, reconstruction of life, and achieving a peaceful relationship between people in conflict, people who often have divergent views on how to solve problems.

Dialogue makes it possible to seek and walk together toward the truth. Truth reflects reality as it is and cannot be denied. Thomas Aquinas defines truth as *adaequatio intellectus et rei*, that is, the adequacy of the intellect to reality. From the African anthropological perspective of palaver, reality is what is, what exists, and what cannot be denied. Reality is what makes the human being alive, here and now, which means that he is not dead—he is happy or may seek to be. This is the truth that fulfills all the hopes of humankind and protects against all error, a truth that unites and rallies all people in search of well-being and an enriching relationship to the world, to others, and to God.

According to Jürgen Habermas, in intercommunication all interlocutors must seek the truth and be convinced by the best argument,[8] by the voice that leads objectively to the truth. By understanding the truth in its relation to the aim of African palaver, the truth to be sought is rational speech, which promotes the life of those speaking and of the entire human group, as well as the development within them of constructive relations with their social, cosmic, and ecological environment.

The Requirements of Dialogue

Dialogue implies mutual recognition that the interlocutors are equal subjects, as well as humility, honesty, and sincerity in seeking and acknowledging the truth in collaboration with others, even when it does not arise from the exercise of our own rationality, but from that of others. Dialogue is ultimately based on the ability to prioritize the interests of others over the self.

This is possible only if the interlocutors recognize the human dignity of all men and women and respect their freedom of expression. Each interlocutor must also demonstrate an open relational rationality and avoid engaging in monologues that close individuals in on themselves. Monologues and soliloquies are in fact the product of monads who are denying alterities. They create a world, at the center of which they live, withdrawn into themselves or dominating others. They place themselves in a position in which they cannot assert fully and authentically their identity as human beings. They alienate and impoverish themselves and others.

To summarize, dialogue between people rests, first, on the respect for others insofar as they are worthy human beings and free, autonomous, and solidary subjects; second, on certain conditions of exchange; and, third, on the common good. Dialogue is based on whatever expresses the expectations and mutual demands that arise from the quest for a fulfilling life and cohesive relationships with the human and ecological environment.

Any act that expresses itself in terms of exchange and fully touches and engages human beings in their identity, essence, and existence can be expressed in terms of dialogue. The relationship between the elements such an act brings together may be called dialogue. It is from this perspective that dialogue between African philosophies and the West is discussed in this chapter.

We can distinguish between two types of dialogue as they relate to the interaction of African

---

7. Bidima, *La palabre*; Bujo, *Ethical Dimension of Community*.
8. Habermas, *Theory of Communicative Action*, vol. 1.

philosophies with the West: truncated dialogue and true dialogue. The latter respects the conditions of a genuine and ongoing exchange between persons. It is always constructive and always under construction because it is called to perfection, to come ever closer to the truth. It develops and continues as long as the partners are living and expressing their rational faculties.

When it began, the dialogue between African philosophies and the West did not respect these conditions. It was a truncated dialogue because of the West's view of Africans. But, despite its weaknesses, this first step toward an exchange of ideas and constructive thought-sharing laid the groundwork for a better dialogue between African and Western philosophies. What do we mean by truncated dialogue? How has this dialogue opened the way for a true dialogue between African philosophies and the West?

Truncated Dialogue: Listening to Oneself and to What One Says about the Other

The past relationship of the West to Africa was based on the West's imagined cultural superiority and on conceiving of Africa as a continent of barbarians. François de Medeiros, a historian specializing in the Middle Ages, describes the historical relationship between Africa and the West in his book *L'Occident et l'Afrique*.[9] He shows that Europeans have always seen Africa as a land of uncivilized peoples, having neither culture nor philosophy. This view was based on an ideology grounded in ignorance, racism, and a quest for hegemony in defiance of the human dignity of others, going all the way back to five centuries before Christ.

When the first navigators, traders (including slave traders), settlers, and missionaries arrived in Africa, they brought with them this mentality that negated and dehumanized Africans and their cultural heritage, referring to the African as "the Negro" or "the Black." Some of the works denigrating Africans written from the fifteenth to the nineteenth century by missionaries, philosophers, and politicians, regardless of whether they visited Africa, continue to be influential into the third millennium. Not everything written about Africans was bad, however. The ethnological study of African societies was born in the years of the slave trade and colonization. Travelers, missionaries, and men and women in love with the customs and practices of the sub-Saharan peoples would become African specialists among their own people, then among the Africans themselves and elsewhere in the world.

In general, however, Westerners did not question their views of African morals and cultural traditions that they did not understand, especially at first. Westerners continue to make statements about Africa without having previously entered into dialogue with it. When the need arises, they will give Africa the floor as they ask questions that are generally designed to acquire information supporting what they already intend to say about it. Unfortunately, many Westerners still believe that they cannot enter into a true dialogue with Africans and exchange ideas with them as equals because they are subhuman and their societies and countries are underdeveloped.

Slavery and colonization would last more than four centuries based on these views; colonization in particular would be conceived of as a civilizing mission of the West in Africa. The same is true of evangelization, which was seen as the work of missionary "heroes" who came to the tropics to deliver Africans from their congenital curse.

The West's Reconsideration of Its Discourse about Africa and Africa's Response

The rejection of Africa would not be total. A number of Westerners and Africans were able to combat the West's unidimensional perspective that considered Africans to be savage and uncultured people. Two Western missionaries in Benin (formerly Dahomey) and the Congo (DRC), Joseph Monney and Placide Tempels, responded in 1941 and 1945, respectively, to the West's erroneous view of Africa,[10] opening another front in the dialogue

---

9. De Medeiros, *L'Occident et l'Afrique (XIII–XVè siècle)*. See also Yancy, *Black Bodies, White Gazes*; Bindman, *Image of the Black in Western Art*, vol. 1; see also vols. 2 and 3.

10. Monney, *La vie profonde des Houedah*; Tempels, *Bantu Philosophy*. The latter book was written in French in 1945 under the title *La philosophie bantoue* and translated into English fourteen years later.

with Africa. Here, we briefly reflect on the thought of Tempels, the best known of these missionaries.

The Work of Placide Tempels

Placide Tempels was a Belgian Franciscan missionary who was in search of a better understanding of the culture, mentality, and behavior of Africans. His immediate objective was not to investigate African philosophies and the possibilities for mutual enrichment between them and Western philosophies; rather, it was to find ways to accelerate the slow growth of evangelization in the Congo. To do this, he went to the Bantu people to ask them questions about their traditions, values, and practices. He wanted to know the Bantu and to make them known to his compatriots.

Tempels's book following on his inquiries, *The Bantu Philosophy*, represents a Copernican revolution in the West's encounter with Africa. It replaces the view of Africans as savage people without a culture or civilization with one holding that a philosophical dialogue between the West and Africa was possible. Tempels sought to understand whether Africa has an indigenous philosophy and what kind of relationship there should be between this philosophy and the philosophy of the West.

Tempels's work wrought an epistemological change. But is the meaning it gives to philosophy relevant to dialogue? With a view toward grounding and justifying his thesis, he observes that Africa has a philosophy like the West's, and he compares African and Western philosophical categories. He shows that Africans have their own ontology, culture, ethics, religion, law, moral values, moral conscience, notion of property rights, and so on, just as Westerners do. In short, Africa has a civilization that is not dissimilar to that of the West.

Unfortunately, Tempels views the African use of Western conceptions as referencing and mirroring those conceptions—he accepts the Western worldview that sees the West as the primary existent reality, providing the benchmark of all cultural values and representing a universally valid model to be reproduced everywhere in the world. In effect, Tempels affirms that Africa has philosophy because her culture displays characteristics that mirror Western philosophy.

Dialogue Based on the West's Understanding of Rationality

Is a dialogue genuine when one party to the dialogue seeks to find characteristics in its interlocutor's culture, institutions, thought, laws, and practices that are the same as its own? Is it not rather the differences that must be seen in otherness that would create a fruitful exchange? The logic of sameness promoted by the West puts it in a position of superiority. According to this logic, the characteristic features of philosophy are determined in relation to the West's conception of it and of rationality; generally, however, the rationality concerns human beings' identity.[11]

In works critical of Tempels, Fabian Eboussi Boulaga (1968), Henry Odera Oruka (1971), and Paulin J. Hountondji (1974)[12] would especially invite Africa not to be flattered for having a philosophy bestowed upon her. The philosophy Tempels identified as "African philosophy" is based on generalized assertions about a particular ethnic group that were extended to the continent generally. According to these authors, Tempels expresses his own understanding of the constitutive elements of Bantu culture, which he then compares to philosophy in the West.

Eboussi Boulaga, Odera Oruka, and Hountondji reject the notion that what Tempels designates as Bantu philosophy is philosophy at all. They argue that nowhere in the world is philosophy based on an exposition of ideas, myths, stories, proverbs, values, beliefs, and collective practices, as Tempels describes Bantu "philosophy," and that it must not be otherwise in the case of Africa. These authors insist that, at the risk of creating an ethnophilosophy, Africa must realize that philosophy requires the development of personal reflections and not the presentation of myths, visions of the world, and

---

11. Our reflection on the characteristic traits of African philosophy is based on the research of Hubert Mono Ndjana (*La philosophie négro-africaine*).

12. Eboussi Boulaga, "Le bantou problématique"; Odera Oruka, "Mythologies as African Philosophy," *East Africa Journal* 9.10 (1972), quoted by Mono Ndjana, *La philosophie négro-africaine*, 208; and Hountondji, *Sur la "philosophie africaine."*

the collective values of a people. The philosophical heuristic approach is developed on the basis of discussion, critical analysis, argumentation, objectivity in debate, and the search for truth. We speak of the "philosophy" of a people when we consider the thought of individual members of this people who are seekers of meaning and truth, and who raise fundamental questions and make original contributions based on argued, rigorous discussion.

The work of Tempels and the reactions it provoked explain why we speak of "African philosophy" singular and "African philosophies" plural. "African philosophy" is related to the philosophical thought of African scholars. "African philosophies" refers to the various perspectives on philosophy presented by African thinkers expressing their own reflections and points of view on a problem.

Let us return to our analysis of Tempels's thought and expand it to other philosophies that followed from it. The dialogue initiated by Tempels refers to issues that would provoke dialogue among Africans and then between Africans and the West.

Africa's Response to the West's Discourse Using Various Philosophical Perspectives

The dialogue between Africa and the West about philosophy now involves African philosophers trained in Western universities as well as learned African theologians. A group of African theologians from the continent and the Caribbean wrote in 1956: "Our problems have for a long time been thought about for us, without us, and even in spite of us."[13] William Jones echoes this perspective for African Americans: "Is the white philosopher to be the sole definer of the reality?"[14] The West cannot continue to ignore African thought nor to think on Africa's behalf. In their dialoguing among themselves, Africans' reflections have involved topics that relate to their relationship with the West; thus, this African dialogue is a debate among Africans and with the West, directly and indirectly.

Direct and Indirect Dialogue

Direct dialogue aims at clarifying the terms of exchange between Africa and the West and allowing Africans to challenge false assumptions about philosophy. In this form of dialogue, Africans communicate about a challenge they are facing and invite Westerners to contribute to an ongoing reflection. The dialogue proceeds indirectly when the subject of African philosophical reflections is a response to a Western idea.[15] This indirect dialogue also refers to African investigation of the West's history in Africa without the West being a direct interlocutor listening and reacting in the moment.

Schools of African Philosophy and Western Rationality

On the basis of Odera Oruka's works, I will distinguish six schools of African philosophy:[16]

1. The ethnographic school of Tempels and his disciples, including Mbiti[17]
2. The rationalist school of Eboussi Boulaga, Hountondji, K. Wiredu, and others who emphasize that philosophy is based on rationality and logic and must be distinguished from general, collective, and popular assertions about culture[18] and mystical remarks
3. The historical school, which presents the thoughts and works of African rational philosophy (Claude Sumner, the author of the five-volume *Ethiopian Philosophy*, is representative of this school)[19]
4. The hermeneutical school of V. Ocaya, Wiredu, Odera Oruka, and others, which concerns the

---

13. Collectif, *Des prêtres noirs s'interrogent*, 16 (my translation).
14. Jones, "Legitimacy and Necessity of Black Philosophy," 157.
15. Africa's indirect dialogue with the West began when a number of African scholars made it clear that African philosophy is something other than Tempels's "Bantu philosophy." Odera Oruka is one of the most important protagonists in this debate; see his *Trends in Contemporary African Philosophy* and *Sage Philosophy*. See also Mono Ndjana, *La philosophie négro-africaine*, 210–18.
16. See Mono Ndjana, *La philosophie négro-africaine*, 210–18.
17. Mbiti, *African Religions and Philosophy*.
18. Mono Ndjana, *La philosophie négro-africaine*, 211.
19. Sumner, "Light and the Shadow"; and Sumner, *Ethiopian Philosophy*, vol. 1.

epistemological resources of language aiming at reflecting on a subject individually and personally by making use of the art of logical, critical, and inventive thought[20]

5. The school of sage philosophy, which is based on the principle that one can "seek and . . . find philosophy in traditional Africa without falling into the error of ethnophilosophy"[21] (this school reflects the thought of wise men and women at the local level who devised autonomous, critical, and logical solutions to problems; it can be considered a strand of present-day African philosophical thought, albeit in oral form)
6. The philosophical sagacity school, which is the work of "wise philosophers" who engage in critical reflections on beliefs and culture in order to develop original personal thought that "produces a system in a system and an order in an order"[22]

Two things can be said of these various schools. The first is that African philosophy is not univocal or uniform; it is plural in its content and perspectives. The horizons of each can lead to the others. These perspectives are places of encounter and dialogue with the concrete human being, all the peoples of the earth, and especially the West.

The second point is that the philosophical dialogue that has been initiated with the West and among African philosophers themselves revolves around two major ideas: first, the role of myths, collective narratives, and personal reflection, and, second, rationality. Even if the existence of myths and narratives is not enough to conclude that a people has a philosophy, it is important to understand, as Meinrad Hebga has pointed out, that myths, narratives, and reflections are not *contrary* to philosophy but rather must be subjected to a process of critical thinking. Odera Oruka's school of philosophical sagacity must be subjected to this process.

What about the six other philosophical perspectives on the dialogue they are helping to establish with the West? When we remain within the framework of our observation that relates to rationality, it must be emphasized that the rationality which characterizes the other forms of philosophy is not peculiar to it, neither to Cartesian thought nor to Western philosophy as a whole. It is universally true. Logic, critical analysis, argumentation, and objectivity are tools through which any human thought worthy of the name can be expressed, that is, any thought that strives for a knowledge of the truth and the good of the person. An analysis that proceeds by means of argumentation and enunciates theses and antitheses, and in which the Cartesian "I think" is determinant, is not the only mode of critical expression and rationality at the philosophical level. This kind of critical thought, by insisting on the "I think," often results in individuals being closed in on themselves. Individuals are called upon to affirm their individuality principally in reflection even when they talk about other peoples' thought and work. Human beings are capable of engaging in another kind of rationality, one that considers the person as an individual but also as a member of a community and of a particular social environment. For this reason, there is not just one kind of rationality, but many forms applicable to particular cultures, languages, and fields of knowledge and research.[23]

Dialogue through African Rationality

True critical reflection leads individual human beings to understand that they cannot through their own reason alone comprehend all of reality and promote life in all its dimensions. Their critical reflection must be transformed by "palaver" or "African palaver." This fruitful process gives life because it provides the conditions for individuals to break out of themselves by soliciting the contributions of all members of the community and other creatures inhabiting the cosmos. The community instructs individuals through the use of images, signs, and symbols. It is up to the indi-

---

20. Wiredu, "Concept of Truth in the Akan Language."
21. Mono Ndjana, *La philosophie négro-africaine*, 215.
22. Mono Ndjana, *La philosophie négro-africaine*, 217.
23. D'Avray, *Medieval Religious Rationalities*; d'Avray, *Rationalities in Histories*; Leibenstein, "From Substantive to Procedural Rationality"; Hountondji, *La rationalité: Une ou plurielʔ*; Hebga, *La rationalité d'un discours africain sur les phénomènes paranormaux*.

vidual to decipher their meaning, and fulfilling this responsibility provides him or her with the energy to struggle against the predominance of impoverishment and the reign of death in the world, a world that is seen in African culture as a field of conflict between life and death, a conflict that in the African worldview necessarily leads to the triumph of life over death.

Because it is rational, the palaver involves a critical debate[24] that takes into account the concrete problems of human existence and aims at responding to them by asking questions and offering solutions that do not consider only the rights of the just and the duties of guilty parties. It considers these rights and duties together and as a whole, as well as the rights and duties of the relevant human and ecological environment, which must always be an environment promoting life, reconciliation, and coexistence in peace for all. This kind of rationality uses critical thinking to reconcile and create cohesion so that life, existence, and well-being are possible for all creatures no matter the problems and situations they encounter.

Philosophy must accommodate the logic of the palaver by developing a kind of critical thought that, no matter the philosophical perspective, can incorporate appropriate proverbs and myths. These proverbs and myths give rise to questions that lead to the deepening of affirmations and arguments. This approach involves parties to a dialogue introducing new symbolic languages and cosmic images that lead them to consider all the relevant aspects of a problem and whose interpretation opens the intelligence to incomprehensible events and situations. In this way, the palaver often revives moribund dialogue.

In the African culture, the true masters of rationality use a discursive language that is nourished by proverbs and myths, which provoke critical personal reflections that draw on experiences, the reasoning of others, and teachings and laws inscribed in living beings. This process provides evidence of a truth that reconciles and commits individuals to promote life-generating well-being within and around them. The human being is a communitarian and cosmological being. Thus, the dialogue does not take place between "I" and "you," but between "I" and "we." The "we" includes the "I" and the other members of the community where he/she lives as well as the visible and invisible world that surrounds them. The person, in Africa, dialogues both with his/her fellows and with plants, minerals, and so on. The latter are signs and symbols of the sacred. Concerning this communitarian dimension of the human being as thinker, Barthélemy Adoukonou called the ancient or African sage a "community intellectual."[25] This description or even that of "cosmic intellectual" can be applied to the philosopher participating in the palaver.

There are numerous currents in African philosophy, and one is therefore justified to speak about African philosophies, plural. Western philosophers have extensively studied the nature, and especially the diversity, of African philosophy, giving rise to both direct and indirect dialogue between Africa and the West. These dialogues have led to the view that African philosophy is first-rate, and African philosophers like Odera Oruka, Hountondji, Wiredu, Eboussi Boulaga, and others have received international recognition, even though there are not yet many African philosophers who are credited with creating original systems of thought or a large body of scholarship.

Many Africans have received doctoral degrees in philosophy, but mainly in the philosophy of the West. Universities in Africa tend to teach Western philosophy, not an African philosophy that might better address African problems using African forms of rationality. It is evident, however, that the dialogue about philosophy is no longer one-sided, with the West speaking about African philosophy while Africa remains silent. Now, Africa is speaking about Western philosophy, but the West is not listening, especially about what Africa is saying about the West's erroneous picture of Africa and the West's harmful political and economic praxis on the continent. In general, the West promotes an ideology of white hegemony over Africans and does not consider African thought to be enriching. It does not integrate African thought into the academic curricula of schools and universities.

This problem is particularly evident in the case

---

24. See Hountondji, *La rationalité: Une ou pluriel?*
25. Adoukonou, "Le Sillon Noir."

of African Americans. George Yancy notes that African American philosophers are not included in the listed names of philosophers in the entry for "philosophy" in *The World Book Encyclopedia*. He wrote that "even under the 'Other' category, the names of African American philosophers were nowhere to be found."[26] The African American philosopher Robert Birt explains the reason for this: "Philosophy is often regarded as among the highest of human intellectual activities and manifestations of human intellectual excellence, a superior endeavor suited for 'superior' (i.e. 'white') minds. . . . To this day a 'black philosopher' is commonly regarded as a contradiction in terms, an anomaly or an undesired intruder into a realm that does not concern him or her."[27] There is some reason for hope in the U.S., however, because the marginalization of African philosophies is being contested by many African American scholars. Yancy has noted the importance of "the maintenance and the continual nurturance of an African-American philosophical identity [and] the contestation of philosophic literary hegemony as this is expressed in canonical exclusionary power."[28] As a corrective to this marginalization, Yancy has suggested "the restructuring of philosophical syllabi; and the power to define and institutionalize African Americans domains of philosophical concern, interest, and value."[29]

Dialogue and the West's Ideology of Domination

Africa has become critical of the political, economic, and cultural thinking of the West and has sought paths toward liberation and development. Its exchange with the West has made it possible to consolidate the foundations of a critically based, original African philosophy.

Dialogue and the Response of African Philosophy to the West's Ideology of Domination

Advocates of the notion of "negritude," including Hebga, Léopold Sédar Senghor, and Aimé Césaire,[30] are responding to ideologies that hold to the savage nature of the "Negro" or the "Black," ideologies that can even be found among some of the great Western philosophers, including G. W. F. Hegel.[31] The protagonists of this African response to the Western discourse assert that Africans need to take pride in the color of their skin, their culture, and their history, and that they share in the human dignity inherent in all persons everywhere. According to the notion of "negritude," Africans are masters of their history and must assume responsibility for their own destiny by achieving political, economic, cultural, and spiritual liberation. On the other hand, some authors, like Stanislas Spero Adotévi (*Négritude et négrologues*) and Wole Soyinka, have denounced the concept of negritude because it involves an unrealistic quest for cultural identity and a preference for the verbal affirmation of African cultural values over action aimed at development.[32]

African thinkers have looked to the philosophical discourse and experience of the West to find political ideologies that might pave the way to independence and development. The first African political philosophies dealt particularly with the choice between liberalism and Marxist socialism,[33] although they distanced themselves from Marxist-Leninist notions of communism and a classless society. They proposed an African socialism based

---

26. Yancy, *African-American Philosophers*, 3.
27. Birt, "Negation of Hegemony," 116.
28. Yancy, *African-American Philosophers*, 9.
29. Yancy, *African-American Philosophers*, 9.
30. Senghor, *Négritude et civilisation de l'universel*; Césaire, *Notebook of a Return to the Native Land*.
31. See Wright, *Racism Matters*.
32. Adotévi, *Négritude et négrologues*. Soyinka pointed out with irony about negritude that "a tiger does not proclaim his tigritude—he pounces": quotation attributed to multiple sources including *Time* magazine, November 17, 1967.
33. Nkrumah, *Freedom and Development*; Nkrumah, *Freedom and Socialism*; Nkrumah, *Class Struggle in Africa*; Dieng, *Hegel, Marx, Engels et les problèmes de l'Afrique*.

on the fundamental African values of community and solidarity (the *ujaama* of Julius Nyerere). Hountondji criticizes Kwame Nkrumah's consciencism because it advocates an African collectivism, and Abdul Rahman Mohammed Babu denounces its idealistic character.[34]

The position taken in relation to Western thought on living beings, existence, and the conception of the person, presents the same approach.

These approaches, inspired by the problematic of Tempels, have been criticized for being ethnophilosophical. Their insistence on the spiritual and religious dimension of African culture and its pluralistic conception of being has also been employed in more in-depth works, including historical, scientific, anthropological, and philosophical research aimed at the reconstruction of historical truth and ultimately at Africa's liberation and development. For example, Anta Diop and Théophile Obenga argue that Africa is not savage and without culture—they demonstrate that in fact Western civilization was inspired by African Egyptian civilization. The West was in dialogue with African Egypt through its philosophers, especially Plato and Aristotle,[35] who traveled to Egypt to learn from its knowledge. Engelbert Mveng argues against Tempels's vital force theory because the African notion of being and life does not recapitulate in the category of vital force. Using the Egyptian-Pharaonic myth of Isis and Osiris, Mveng asserts that African anthropology is based on the concept of the fullness of life. The vocation of the human being in the world is to ensure that life triumphs over death in all areas of existence. Hebga shows that the Western dualism between body and soul and matter and spirit is contrary to a proper and full view of rationality.[36] He demonstrates that the pluralistic African conception of being implies a better approach to human existence—and a proper understanding of the link between the visible and the invisible, as well as the natural and the paranormal—than the dualistic Western approach toward being.

The debate among African philosophies as represented in the work of a new generation of researchers supports a critical approach to Western thought. These researchers are important interlocutors in the dialogue between Western and African philosophy. Among the protagonists in this debate are the American thinker Laird Scranton and the French thinker Geneviève Calame-Griaule.[37] They condemn a Eurocentric and imperialist approach to African culture, presenting it in a more positive light than does Tempels in *The Bantu Philosophy*. They show that African culture is able to promote the well-being and human fulfillment of Africans.

A true dialogue has begun between Western and African thinkers, which can be seen in the fact that some Western philosophers, anthropologists, and ethnologists are offering commentary on African culture without immediately comparing it to that of the West. The value of African culture and its contributions to renewing the world's civilizations is the touchstone for this Western participation in a dialogue with African thought. For instance, in his book *The Science of the Dogon: Decoding the African Mystery Tradition*, Scranton argues for the scientific value of Dogon culture by showing the similarities between its myths and symbolic language and the Egyptian and Hebrew religious traditions, as well as its relevance to "scientific concepts from atomic theory to quantum theory and string theory."[38] Calame-Griaule's *Words and the Dogon World* describes the sacred, anthropological, ecological, and cosmic dimensions of words in the Dogon culture.[39] It is important to note, however, that there are very few white scholars engaged in research from this perspective and that most

---

34. See Mono Ndjana's presentation of this topic in *La philosophie négro-africaine*, 206.

35. See Diop, *Antériorité des civilisations nègres*; Obenga, *L'Egypte, la Grèce et l'école d'Alexandrie*; Mveng, *L'Art d'Afrique noire*.

36. Hebga, *La rationalité d'un discours africain sur les phénomènes paranormaux*.

37. For the seminal works of these researchers, see Calame-Griaule, *Words and the Dogon World*; Scranton, *Science of the Dogon*.

38. Scranton, *Science of the Dogon*. See also Simon & Schuster, "About the Book," www.simonandschuster.com.

39. Ibid.

of them are anthropologists, not philosophers. In addition, these white researchers are usually engaged only with African specialists, not with the scholarly community more generally.

A Dialogue Promoting Western Philosophy over African Philosophy

The dialogue between African and Western philosophers has to date contributed more to Western culture than to African culture because it has focused on the legacy of Western philosophy as reflected in thinkers like René Descartes, G. W. F. Hegel, Baruch Spinoza, Martin Heidegger, Henri Bergson, Edmund Husserl, and others. Many African scholars have written their doctoral dissertations on Western philosophers, for example, Paulin Hountondji's thesis was on the German philosopher Husserl. On the other hand, other African scholars, especially Hebga, have, as we have noted, advocated for the rationality of a peculiarly African discourse revolving around myths, the values of life, spirituality, and theories of communication, time, and space. In advancing this position, these authors have drawn on both their knowledge of Western philosophy and the historical and cultural realities of their people.

Hubert Mono Ndjana's summary of African philosophy presents two further examples in the work of Antoine-Guillaume Amo and Robert Ntebi Biya. The first, a Ghanaian brought to the West as a slave in the eighteenth century, was given an opportunity to pursue higher education and defended a doctoral thesis in philosophy written in Latin. In this work, entitled *Dissertatio de humanae mentis apatheia* (1734), Amo discussed the conflict between mechanists and vitalists. He demonstrated the internal contradictions in the thought of Descartes concerning the relationship between the body and the mind when it affirms that the immortal soul feels as the body does,[40] thus siding with the vitalists. The second, Ntebi Biya, demonstrated that African metaphysics thinks about being through myth. He responded to ethnophilosophy's detractors that it is not contrary to reason, highlighting the intrinsic link between myth and reason. He employed the resources of both "traditional African thought and the most modern thought"[41] to make clear that being means not only "difference" (which goes beyond Heidegger) and that it may be the result of "generation" (correcting Plato's thesis). Biya employs the concepts of space, time, the human being, word, and God to support his argument about generation.[42]

Dialogue and Africa's Responsibility: Philosophy in Service of Building the Future

Does the dialogue as described in the preceding reflections give rise to mutual listening? It is not clear that the importance that many African authors ascribe to the philosophical thought of Westerners is reciprocated by Western philosophers as concerns African philosophy, a reciprocation that is necessary to establish authentic dialogue. The West's history of cultural domination and the learned response that often leads Africans to deny the value of their culture are key factors in this disconnect. Thus, it needs to be asked whether Western philosophers want to be in a true dialogue with African philosophers.

African philosophies such as those of Eboussi Boulaga, Hountondji, V. Y. Mudimbe, and others, as well as those of African Americans, including Yancy and W. D. Wright, are known by only a limited number of Western philosophers. African philosophers are generally not studied in Western universities except in African studies programs, to which very few Westerners are attracted. In contrast, Western philosophers, starting with the pre-Socratics, are included in the curricula of many African institutions of higher learning. For these reasons, it can be said that at present the dialogue is very one-sided.

Addressing Issues of Concern to the Future of Africa and Other Societies

I will briefly consider two African philosophers who have studied the issue of the future of Africa and other societies with a focus on the themes of

---

40. Mono Ndjana, *La philosophie négro-africaine*, 343–44.
41. Mono Ndjana, *La philosophie négro-africaine*, 370.
42. Mono Ndjana, *La philosophie négro-africaine*, 370.

autonomy, openness to the needs of humanity, and creativity: Fabien Eboussi Boulaga and Kä Mana. According to the Cameroonian philosopher Eboussi Boulaga, human beings must reflect on how they relate with and act toward one another in order to construct and reconstruct the present and the future, for their own benefit and that of their larger societies. Thus, in the face of the omnipresence of the West, Africans do not need to look for themselves in a lost authenticity or renounce themselves. On this point, Eboussi Boulaga's thought contrasts with other problems considered by African philosophies dialoguing with the West.

Eboussi Boulaga invites the *muntu*, the Africans, to think about themselves and their future in terms of freeing themselves from the servitude of tradition when it looks backward to maintaining "the ancient passivity," which results in the triumph of cultural, political, and economic impoverishment over Africa. Emancipation must help Africans understand culture and tradition as "being-together and a having-in-common that call for a common destiny and action."[43] Emancipation is a "critical utopia" because it carries within it "creative and recreational possibilities."[44] Eboussi Boulaga rereads the history of missionary Christianity through this lens,[45] and it appears as a "fetish" with its institutions, dogmas, morals, canon law, and liturgy. These features have led Africans to reproduce and repeat the material productions and words of a faith that they have not confessed, thought about, or in any way expressed in their own lives and social and religious institutions. Eboussi Boulaga demands a "missionary departure"—the programmatic and orderly departure of European missionaries from Africa—as the necessary condition for Africans to learn and commit themselves to creating a Christianity[46] that expresses their own response to the question of Christ: "Who do you say that I am?" (Matt 16:13).

Without addressing the West directly, the work of these scholars has led to significant repercussions in international, missionary, and ecclesiastical universities worldwide, so much so that Eboussi Boulaga's two most important books have been translated into English.[47] He contributed to a better understanding of African culture and tradition, and specifically the concept of *muntu*, especially with respect to creativity. The political dimension of his thinking led him to address contemporary political issues of democracy, "sovereign national conferences," human rights, and state power, as did Habermas and John Rawls.[48]

Kä Mana focuses his reflections on political ethics and specifically on how to overcome crises resulting from the reconstruction of African societies. He brings together certain epistemological and hermeneutical tools available from African history, in particular the myth of Isis and Osiris, in constructing a dialogue with Hannah Arendt, Gilbert Durand, and Bronislaw Baczko (imaginary).[49] Prolific, profound, original, and impressive, his thinking, expressed in more than twenty books, describes the causes, manifestations, and solutions to the African crisis.[50] His thought revolves around myth, the imagination, the ethical action of reconstruction, and the spirituality of responsibility. He highlights the myth of passivity and resignation, which provokes crises and paralyzes the imagination and creative action of Africans. He suggests that the problems caused by this myth could be addressed by the reconstruction of other myths, so that Africans can recover the inventiveness, spirituality, commitment, and ethical behavior necessary to change and develop their societies.

Addressing Issues of Globalization and Gender

Globalization and postmodernity present issues of concern to both Africa and the West. Global-

---

43. Eboussi Boulaga, *La crise du muntu*, 145 (my translation).
44. Eboussi Boulaga, *La crise du muntu*, 152.
45. Eboussi Boulaga, *Christianity without Fetishes*.
46. Eboussi Boulaga, *A contretemps*.
47. See Eboussi Boulaga, *Muntu in Crisis* and *Christianity without Fetishes*.
48. Yamb, *Droits humains, démocratie*.
49. See Kä Mana, *L'Afrique va-t-elle mourir?*
50. See particularly Kä Mana, *Théologie africaine pour temps de crise*; and Kä Mana, *L'Afrique va-t-elle mourir?*

ization is generally defined as the free movement of people and economic, financial, political, cultural, scientific, technological, digital, industrial, and informational goods and services from one part of the world to the other. As has been noted by the *Handbook for Globalization Studies*[51] and by David Harvey, Roland Robertson, David Held, Thomas Pogge, and Simon Caney,[52] Western philosophies go beyond a phenomenological and social approach. They raise problems that would make globalization suicidal for humanity if forgotten: the risk of domination of one culture over all the others on a planetary scale—that is, a quest for a hegemonic assertion of identity and linguistic imperialism, problems of governance and justice, and the enrichment of some and impoverishment of others. Western philosophical reflections identify the meaning, dangers, and requirements of postmodernity, and the alter-globalist movement is welcome as a response to the various challenges of globalization and postmodernity.

On these points, African philosophies have established a genuine dialogue with those of the West. They have recognized that globalization and postmodernity are imposing themselves on the planet, even in Africa where people have benefited from these phenomena less than the peoples of the West. Gwoda advocates "creating a more humane globality"[53] in order to reconcile the forces of globalization and alter-globalization. Roger Mondoué has admonished his Black brothers and sisters not to complain about or let themselves be carried away by the forces of globalization, but to become its new protagonists: "Can we become rational so as not only to break the nets of Globalization, but also and above all to serve as a locomotive for other peoples?"[54] In order to respond to this challenge so that Africans can solve Africa's problems in the age of globalization, Africans need to enter into a dialogue among themselves. They need to avoid Western materialism and moral decadence and put an end to egoism, corruption, and occult practices whose purpose is solely to gain wealth,[55] among other things. Teresa Washington affirms that in Africa "for many people, ego-fluffing and money-grubbing are more important than problem-solving and nation-building."[56]

I conclude with some comments about gender. There is a debate about this issue among African philosophers: some have reacted against the idea that ancestral African traditions oppress women, emphasizing rather the importance of such traditions to the continent's cultural, religious, and political realities and in general their inescapable place in African society; others have stressed that in Africa as in the West and elsewhere, women are exploited even as they are respected as first educators. Among the authors stressing the need for a constructive approach to and responsible perspectives on the status of women are Henri Ngoa, Barnabé Bilongo, Aminata Traore, Tanella Boni, and Béatrice Faye. These authors are open to cooperation with national and international laws and initiatives aimed at the liberation of women, but they do not engage with Western theories and practices that do not adequately balance equality and difference and autonomy and complementarity as respects the relationship between men and women.

Senegalese philosopher Béatrice Faye has proposed an inclusive approach to gender,[57] arguing that liberation is not total if achieved only by women; both men and women must be freed from every tendency that results in the oppression of the latter. For Faye, the end of the oppression of women would be a source of equality, affirmation, and integration between both women and men at every level of social life. This end to oppression will be fully realized if the specific gifts of women

---

51. Bryan S. Turner, ed., *The Routledge International Handbook of Globalization Studies* (Hoboken, NJ: Taylor and Francis, 2013).
52. Caney, *Justice beyond Borders*; Harvey, *Condition of Postmodernity*; Held, *Democracy and the Global Order*; Pogge, "Priorities of Global Justice"; Robertson, *Globalization*.
53. On Gwoda's thought, see Mono Ndjana, *La philosophie négro-africaine*, 275.
54. Mondoué, *Logique et irrationalisme modern*, quoted by Mono Ndjana, *La philosophie négro-africaine*, 302.
55. Armah, *Beautiful Ones Are Not Yet Born*.
56. Washington, *African World in Dialogue*, 11.
57. Faye, "Difference in the System of the Self," 13–42.

are employed for the benefit of society, the church, religion, and humanity in general. This means the participation of women in the decision-making and exercises of power that determine the life and future of the world.

Drawing on the resources of traditional African culture, Faye describes the relationship between the placenta and the earth. Through the former, woman is the first to welcome within her and to protect and nurture every human being in the world. After birth, the earth becomes the new home of every human being and continues the work that the woman began in her genius. The earth can achieve its mission efficiently and well thanks to the woman's commitment to the education and the fulfillment of each person. Thus, according to Faye, humanity will not be the center of life, and the future of life of every human being on the planet cannot be guaranteed without the work of the woman and without a recognition and promotion of the wealth that the earth specifically carries in her. Gender-based criticism must free women and men without causing women to give up their specific nature and role and the rights and duties attached to it.

Concluding Remarks: Toward a Real Dialogue

The path we have followed in this chapter reveals the existence of a dialogue between African philosophies and the West. Each of the perspectives on African thought discussed here nourishes a dialogue with the West according to its own approach to philosophical problems. The vicissitudes of the historical relationship between Africa and the West have had the effect of making African philosophies a bit too dependent on those of the West—Africans living both on the continent and elsewhere in the world have often been trained in academic Western philosophy. As the work of all the authors cited in this study shows, African philosophers tend to learn more about the philosophical thought of the West than that of their own people. Fortunately, young African philosophers like Hountondji, Eboussi Boulaga, Okure, Wiredu, Mudimbe, and others are interested in the thought of their forebears, focusing their reflections on the challenges facing Africa. But their work often has little impact globally because of the social, cultural, economic, political, and religious situation in which it is carried out.

Despite the various obstacles separating them from each other, African and Western philosophies have the same objectives—promoting reflection on human existence and the world—which should promote a real dialogue between them. This dialogue will be achieved only if both sides respect the conditions that would favor a constructive relationship. Concerning African philosophies, these conditions include (1) the duty of responding, as Eboussi Boulaga suggests, to the crisis of the *muntu*, of the African, that is, to lead Africans to ask themselves questions about the construction of their own destiny in a relationship with the West that is neither mimetic nor inhibitory in relation to the past but efficient and inventive in building the present and the future; (2) the responsibility to help Africans escape from situations of misery that do not favor their emergence as a people; and (3) urgently working toward a philosophy that is universally applicable to all peoples everywhere.

For the Western philosophies, these conditions include (1) the duty to enrich their own philosophy with that of African and other non-Western thinkers, acknowledging their contributions to the debates over the problems facing humanity; (2) the duty to reject cultural domination as well as people's tendencies to think, act, and judge in their dialogue and relationship with other peoples and nations by referring only to their own culture, points of views, and interests; and (3) the same duty as African philosophies to work urgently toward a philosophy that is universally applicable to all peoples everywhere.

The proposals of Enrique Dussel concerning philosophical training and teaching are useful for the achievement of these conditions.[58] I conclude by presenting the essential points of Dussel's thought, which aims at promoting an inter-philosophical dialogue not only with the West but with all regions, cultures, and civilizations of the world.

---

58. Dussel, "Pour un dialogue mondial entre les traditions philosophiques."

Like the African-American philosopher George Yancy, Dussel denounced the economic, political, cultural, and philosophical colonialism of the Global South (Africa, Latin America, Asia, and Eastern Europe) by the Global North. He calls for a philosophical dialogue between North and South and between the countries of the South. In a global context in which "the philosophical communities of the postcolonial countries (as well as their problems and their philosophical responses) are not accepted by metropolitan hegemonic communities,"[59] the principles of this dialogue need to be clarified. Dussel asserts that we must think and speak about the future of the world not in terms of postmodernity, "the universe," and capitalism but rather in terms of "trans-modernity," the "pluriverse," and "transcapitalism."[60] The world is plural, and thus there can be no postmodernity that designates "a still partial European–North American criticism of modernity."[61] Modernity must involve "a global project" that goes beyond North America and Europe.

Dussel proposes that the orientation and content of the teaching of philosophy to future generations be redefined to incorporate a multidisciplinary and transmodern perspective based on knowledge and respect of and dialogue with all philosophical traditions. He argued that philosophical formation should proceed in three stages. It would begin with "the first great philosophers of humanity . . . in Egypt (Mesopotamia), Mesopotamia (including the prophets of Israel), Greece, China, Meso-America or among the Incas,"[62] then move to the great ontologies of history, and end with the development of later philosophical thought (including its religious content) and reflections on logic, politics, ethics, and other matters, from a global perspective.

With Dussel, we can conclude that, in the future, the most important dialogue will no longer be that of the African philosophies with the West, but one that turns them both toward all of the philosophical traditions of humankind. If African philosophies manage to move more in line with the direction indicated by Eboussi Boulaga and Kä Mana, that is, by distancing themselves from the concerns of the West, Africa will be able to offer many original and relevant contributions to this dialogue: it will be able to ask its own questions of these traditions.

Bibliography

Adotévi, Stanislas Spero. *Négritude et négrologues*. Paris: Union générale, 1972.

Adoukonou, Barthélemy. "Le Sillon Noir: La théologie africaine comme œuvre de l'intellectuel communautaire." *Communio* 11.67 (1986).

Armah, Ayi Kwei. *The Beautiful Ones Are Not Yet Born*. London: Heinemann, 1968.

Bidima, J.-G. *La palabra: Une juridiction de la parole*. Paris: Michalon, 1997.

Bindman, David. *The Image of the Black in Western Art*, vol. 1: *From the Pharaohs to the Fall of the Roman Empire*. Cambridge, MA: Harvard University Press, 2010.

Birt, Robert E. "Negation of Hegemony: The Agenda of *Philosophy Born of Struggle*." *Social Science Information* 26.1 (March 1987): 115–27.

Bodunrin, P. O. *Philosophy in Africa: Trends and Perspectives*. Ife: University of Ife Press, 1985.

Buber, Martin. *I and Thou*. Translated by Ronald Gregor Smith. New York: Penguin Classics, Kindle edition, 2011.

Bujo, Bénézet. *The Ethical Dimension of Community: The African Model and the Dialogue between North and South*. Nairobi: Paulines Publications Africa, 1997.

Calame-Griaule, Geneviève. *Words and the Dogon World*. Philadelphia: Institute for the Study of Human Issues, 1979.

Caney, Simon. *Justice beyond Borders*. Oxford: Oxford University Press, 2005.

Césaire, Aimé. *Notebook of a Return to the Native Land*. Translated by Clayton Eshleman. London: Wesleyan Poetry Series, 2001.

---

59. Dussel, "Pour un dialogue mondial entre les traditions philosophiques" (my translation).
60. Dussel, "Pour un dialogue mondial entre les traditions philosophiques," paragraphs 44–45 in the online version.
61. Dussel, "Pour un dialogue mondial entre les traditions philosophiques," paragraph 44.
62. Dussel, "Pour un dialogue mondial entre les traditions philosophiques," paragraph 36.

Collectif. *Des prêtres noirs s'interrogent.* Paris: Présence Africaine, 1956.

d'Avray, D. L. *Medieval Religious Rationalities: A Weberian Analysis.* Cambridge: Cambridge University Press, 2010.

———. *Rationalities in Histories: A Weberian Essay in Comparison.* Cambridge: Cambridge University Press, 2016.

Dieng, A. *Hegel, Marx, Engels et les problèmes de l'Afrique.* Dakar: Sankoré, 1978.

Diop, Cheikh Anta. *Antériorité des civilisations nègres: Mythe ou vérité historique.* Paris: Présence Africaine, 1967.

Dussel, Enrique. "Pour un dialogue mondial entre les traditions philosophiques." *Cahiers des Amériques latines* 62 (2009): 111–27. http://cal.revues.org/1619.

Eboussi Boulaga, Fabien. *A contretemps: L'enjeu de Dieu en Afrique.* Paris: Karthala, 1991.

———. "Le bantou problématique." *Présence Africaine* 66 (1968): 4–40.

———. *Christianity without Fetishes: An African Critique and Recapture of Christianity.* Maryknoll, NY: Orbis Books, 1984.

———. *La crise du muntu.* Paris: Présence Africaine, 1980.

———. *Muntu in Crisis: African Authenticity and Philosophy.* New York: Penguin Classics, Kindle edition, 2014.

Faye, Béatrice. "The Difference in the System of the Self: A Philosophical Contribution to the Gender Approach." In *Global Exchanges and Gender Perspectives in Africa*, edited by J.-M. Ouedraogo and R. M. Achieng', 13–42. Dakar: Codesria; Kampala: Fountain, 2011.

Flikschuh, Katrin. "The Arc of Personhood: Menkiti and Kant on Becoming and Being a Person." *Journal of the American Philosophical Association* 2.3 (October 2016): 437–55.

Fløistad, Guttorm, ed. *Contemporary Philosophy: A New Survey.* Vol. 5. Dordrecht: Springer, 1987.

Friedman, M. S. *Martin Buber: The Life of Dialogue.* Chicago: University of Chicago Press, 1955.

Griaule, M. *Conversations with Ogotemmêli: An Introduction to Dogon Religious Ideas.* Uppsala: International African Institute, 1975.

Guédou, G. A. G. *Xó et gbè: Langage et culture chez les Fon (Bénin).* Paris: SELAF, 1985.

Habermas, Jürgen. *Theory of Communicative Action.* Vol. 1: *Reason and the Rationalization of Society.* Translated by Th. A. McCarthy. Boston: Beacon Press, 1984.

Harvey, David. *The Condition of Postmodernity: An Enquiry into the Origins of Cultural Change.* Oxford: Blackwell, 1989.

Hebga, Meinrad P. *La rationalité d'un discours africain sur les phénomènes paranormaux.* Paris: L'Harmattan, 1998.

Held, David. *Democracy and the Global Order: From the Modern State to Cosmopolitan Governance.* Stanford, CA: Stanford University Press, 1995.

Hountondji, Paulin J. *La rationalité: Une ou pluriel?* Dakar: Codesria, 2007.

———. *Sur la philosophie africaine.* Paris: Maspéro, 1977.

Jones, William R. "The Legitimacy and Necessity of Black Philosophy: Some Preliminary Considerations." *Philosophical Forum* 9 (Winter–Spring 1977–1978): 149–60.

Kä Mana. *L'Afrique va-t-elle mourir? Essai d'éthique politique.* Paris: Karthala, 1993.

———. *Théologie africaine pour temps de crise.* Paris: Karthala, 1993.

Levinas, Emmanuel. *Altérité et transcendence.* Montpellier: Fata Morgana, 1995.

———. *Totality and Infinity: An Essay on Exteriority.* Translated by Alphonso Lingis. Pittsburgh: Duquesne University Press, 1969.

Leibenstein, H. "From Substantive to Procedural Rationality." In *Method and Appraisal in Economics*, edited by Spiro J. Latsis, 129–48. Cambridge: Cambridge University Press, 1976.

Magesa, Laurenti. *African Religion: The Moral Traditions as Abundant Life.* Maryknoll, NY: Orbis Books, 1997.

———. *African Religion in the Dialogue Debate: From Intolerance to Coexistence.* Zurich: Lit, 2010.

Massole, D. A. *African Philosophy in Search of Identity.* Bloomington: Indiana University Press, 1994.

Mbiti, John S. *African Religions and Philosophy.* London: Heinemann, 1969.

Medeiros, François de. *L'Occident et l'Afrique (XIII–XVè siècle): Images et representations.* Paris: Karthala/CRA, 1985.

Mlilo, Luke G., and Nathanaël Y. Soédé, eds. *Doing Theology and Philosophy in the African Context:*

Faire la théologie et la philosophie en contexte africain. Frankfurt/London: IKO-Verlag für Interkulturelle Kommunikation, 2003.

Mondoué, Roger. *Logique et irrationalisme modern: Essai sur la théorie de la proposition de Ludwig Wittgenstein*. Thèse de doctorat/PhD, Université de Yaoundé, 2007.

Monney, Joseph. *La vie profonde des Houedah: Contribution à une meilleure compréhension de l'âme noire*. Lyon: Imprimerie des Missions Africaines, 1941.

Mono Ndjana, Hubert. *La philosophie négro-africaine: Essai de présentation générale*. Paris: L'Harmattan, 2016.

Mveng, Engelbert. *L'Afrique dans l'Eglise: Parole d'un croyant*. Paris: L'Harmattan, 1985.

———. *L'Art d'Afrique noire: Liturgie cosmique et langage religieux*. Tours: Mame, 1964.

Nkrumah, Kwame. *The Class Struggle in Africa*. New York: International Publishers, 1970.

———. *Consciencism: Philosophy and Ideology for Decolonization*. London: Heinemann, 1964.

———. *Freedom and Development*. Oxford: Oxford University Press, 1974.

———. *Freedom and Socialism*. Oxford: Oxford University Press, 1968.

Obenga, Théophile. *L'Egypte, la Grèce et l'école d'Alexandrie: Histoire interculturelle dans l'antiquité. Aux sources égyptiennes de la philosophie grecque*. Paris: L'Harmattan, 2005.

Odera Oruka, Henry. *Sage Philosophy: Indigenous Thinkers and Modern Debate on African Philosophy*. Leiden: Brill, 1990.

———. *Trends in Contemporary African Philosophy*. Nairobi: Shirikon, 1990.

Ouedraogo, J.-M., and R. M. Achieng', eds. *Global Exchanges and Gender Perspectives in Africa*. Dakar: Codesria; Kampala: Fountain, 2011.

Pogge, Thomas. "Priorities of Global Justice." *Metaphilosophy* 32 (2001): 6–24.

Robertson, Roland. *Globalization: Social Theory and Global Culture*. London: Sage, 1992.

Scranton, Laird. *The Science of the Dogon: Decoding the African Mystery Tradition*. Rochester, VT: Inner Traditions, 2002.

Senghor, Léopold Sédar. *Négritude et civilisation de l'universel*. Paris: Seuil, 1977.

Soédé, Nathanaël Yaovi. "Contextualiser et inculturer la philosophie et la théologie dans les programmes de formation." In *Doing Theology and Philosophy in the African Context: Faire la théologie et la philosophie en contexte africain*, edited by Luke G. Mlilo and Nathanaël Y. Soédé, 145–57. Frankfurt/London: IKO-Verlag für Interkulturelle Kommunikation, 2003.

———. "Parole et vérité dans la culture et les comportements actuels des Africains." *RUCAO* 24 (2005): 133–52.

———. "Perspectives éthiques pour la renaissance de l'Afrique." In *La théologie et l'avenir des sociétés: Cinquante ans de l'Ecole de Kinshasa*, edited by Léonard Santedi, 495–516. Paris: Karthala, 2010.

———. *Sens et enjeux de l'éthique*. Paris: L'Harmattan, 2005.

Sumner, Claude. *Ethiopian Philosophy*. Vol. 1: *The Book of the Wise Philosophers*. Addis Ababa: Central Printing Press, 1974.

———. "The Light and the Shadow: Rera Yacob and Walda Heywat; Two Ethiopian Philosophers of the Seventeenth Century." In *A Companion to African Philosophy*, edited by K. Wiredu and W. E. Abraham. Malden, MA: Blackwell, 2004.

Tempels, Placide. *Bantu Philosophy*. Paris: Présence Africaine, 1959.

Washington, Teresa N., ed. *The African World in Dialogue: An Appeal to Action*. N.p.: Oya's Tornado, 2016.

Wiredu, K. "The Concept of Truth in the Akan Language." In *Philosophy in Africa: Trends and Perspectives*, edited by P. O. Bodunrin. Ife: University of Ife Press, 1985.

Wiredu, K., and W. E. Abraham, eds. *A Companion to African Philosophy*. Malden, MA: Blackwell, 2004.

Wright, W. D. *Racism Matters*. London: Praeger, 1998.

Yamb, G. D. *Droits humains, démocratie: Etat de droit chez Rawls, Habermas et Eboussi Boulaga*, Paris: L'Harmattan, 2011.

Yancy, George, ed. *African-American Philosophers: 17 Conversations*. New York/London: Routledge, 1998.

———. *Black Bodies, White Gazes: The Continuing Significance of Race*. Plymouth: Rowman & Littlefield, 2008.

Suggested Reading

Calame-Griaule, Geneviève. *Words and the Dogon World*. Philadelphia: Institute for the Study of Human Issues, 1979.

d'Avray, D. L. *Medieval Religious Rationalities: A Weberian Analysis*. Cambridge: Cambridge University Press, 2010.

Eboussi Boulaga, Fabien. "Le bantou problématique." *Présence Africaine* 66 (1968): 4–40.

Faye, Béatrice. "The Difference in the System of the Self: A Philosophical Contribution to the Gender Approach." In *Global Exchanges and Gender Perspectives in Africa*, edited by J.-M. Ouedraogo and R. M. Achieng', 13–42. Dakar: Codesria; Kampala: Fountain, 2011.

Hountondji, Paulin J. *La rationalité: Une ou pluriel?* Dakar: Codesria, 2007.

Magesa, Laurenti. *African Religion in the Dialogue Debate: From Intolerance to Coexistence*. Zurich: Lit, 2010. See especially 19–26 and 131–48. The first section (19–26) is entitled "Dialogue, Identity and Choice" and the second (131–48), "African Religion in Scholarship."

Massole, D. A. *African Philosophy in Search of Identity*. Bloomington: Indiana University Press, 1994. See especially chapter 7, "Excavating Africa in Western Discourse," 147–93.

Odera Oruka, Henry. "African Philosophy: A Brief Personal History and the Current Debate." In *Contemporary Philosophy: A New Survey*, edited by Guttorm Fløistad, 5:45–77. Dordrecht: Springer, 1987.

———. *Sage Philosophy: Indigenous Thinkers and Modern Debate on African Philosophy*. Leiden: Brill, 1990. See especially 1–26.

Yancy, George, ed. *African-American Philosophers: 17 Conversations*. New York/London: Routledge, 1998.

Key Words

African communitarianism
African palaver
African philosophy
alternity
anthropology
capitalism
colonialism
communitarianism
consciencism
dialogue
education
environment
ethnophilosophy
gender
globalization
intercommunication
modernity
negritude
philosophy
pluriverse
postmodernity
rationality
sagacity
sage
sage philosophy
solidarity
spirituality
tigritude
trans-capitalism
trans-modernity
ujaama
Western philosophy
woman/women

From Vatican II to the Second African Synod: Themes, Traditions, and Transitions

Anne Arabome, SSS, and Agbonkhianmeghe E. Orobator, SJ

A precious treasure is to be found in the soul of Africa, where I perceive a "spiritual 'lung' for a humanity that appears to be in a crisis of faith and hope," on account of the extraordinary human and spiritual riches of its children, its variegated cultures, its soil and sub-soil of abundant resources. However, if it is to stand erect with dignity, Africa needs to hear the voice of Christ who today proclaims love of neighbour, love even of one's enemies, to the point of laying down one's life: the voice of Christ who prays today for the unity and communion of all people in God (cf. Jn 17:20–21).[1]

The title of this essay might appear misleading; in fact, we have searched in vain for a straight historical line from the Second Vatican Council (1962–1965) to the Second Special Assembly for Africa of the Synod of Bishops (2009).[2] Yet, upon closer examination, there are grounds to suggest an implied connection in the nature of the inspiration of both the council and the synod; beyond this, nothing more can be concluded or inferred. This chapter considers the themes, traditions, and transitions arising from this elusive connection.

The council, which addressed matters of pertinence to the world church, was, appropriately, held in Rome, an important seat and symbol of Catholic Christian unity. Even though the African continent would have offered the most fitting location for the synod, which was focused on the mission and identity of the church in Africa, it was also held in Rome, ostensibly to highlight the importance of Africa for the world church.

One simple criterion for establishing and measuring any evidence of continuity or connection between the council and the African synod is the latter's use of the resources generated by the former. Pope Benedict XVI's post-synodal apostolic exhortation *Africae Munus* (November 19, 2011) quotes extensively from Pope St. John Paul II's own post-synodal apostolic exhortation that followed the first African synod, *Ecclesia in Africa* (September 14, 1995).[3] *Africae Munus* also contains copious quotations from a number of encyclicals, exhortations, and apostolic letters of Popes Paul VI, John Paul II, and Benedict XVI.[4] With respect to the teachings and documents of the council, however, the link

---

1. Pope Benedict XVI, post-synodal apostolic exhortation *Africae Munus* §13 (hereinafter *AM*).
2. This was the second of two African synods, and was convened under the theme "The Church in Africa in Service to Reconciliation, Justice and Peace: 'You are the salt of the earth . . . You are the light of the world' [Matt 5:13, 14]." The First Synod occurred in 1994 under the theme "The Church in Africa and Her Evangelising Mission towards the Year 2000: 'You Shall Be My Witnesses' [Acts 1:8]."
3. Pope John Paul II, post-synodal apostolic exhortation *Ecclesia in Africa* (hereinafter *EA*).
4. It does not, however, make any significant reference to any documents originating from any of the African bishops' conferences, including the continental Symposium of Episcopal Conferences of Africa and Madagascar (SECAM).

between *Africae Munus* and the council appears tenuous. *Africae Munus* references the Dogmatic Constitution on the Church *Lumen Gentium* five times, the Decree on the Missionary Activity of the Church *Ad Gentes* twice, and there is one reference each to the following three conciliar documents: the Decree on the Apostolate of the Laity *Apostolicam Actuositatem*, the Pastoral Constitution on the Church in the Modern World *Gaudium et Spes*, and the Declaration on the Relation of the Church to Non-Christian Religions *Nostra Aetate*. Thus, while Benedict XVI expressed a desire that the second synod "should continue the work" of the First Synod of 1994, "'which was intended to be an occasion of hope and resurrection, at the very moment when human events seemed to be tempting Africa to discouragement and despair'" (*AM* §2, quoting *EA* §1), it is far from obvious that there was the same objective of continuity from the council to the second synod.

Notwithstanding the lack of an obvious link, Pope St. John XXIII intended Vatican II to be a moment of *aggiornamento* for the universal church, and Benedict XVI and the bishops of Africa similarly aimed for a "profound spiritual renewal" for a continent "experiencing a culture shock which strikes at the age-old foundations of social life, and sometimes makes it hard to come to terms with modernity," living "through . . . traumas and conflicts," and facing an "anthropological crisis" (*AM* §11). The challenge of responding effectively to this continental crisis defines the scope and objectives of the second synod. According to the *Message to the People of God of the Second Special Assembly for Africa of the Synod of Bishops,* reconciliation, justice, and peace constitute "a theme of the greatest urgency for Africa . . . a continent that is very much in dire need of these graces and virtues."[5] In his preface to the *Instrumentum Laboris* of the synod, the general secretary of the Synod of Bishops, Archbishop Nikola Eterović, underlined the pressing and urgent character of the work of reconciliation on a continent "torn by many conflicts and ethnic, social and religious divisions, which oftentimes erupt into hateful and violent happenings."[6] The mission of peace "has never been more timely in Africa, because of her conflicts, wars and violence."[7] These considerations aptly demonstrate that the objectives and aims of the second African synod form part of a wider scope of concern for the "joys and the hopes, the griefs and the anxieties" of the "People of God," as stated by *Gaudium et Spes* (§1). In general, however, historical and contextual factors warrant the conclusion that the council's impact on Africa can be seen only in certain vestiges and traces. There is in fact a broad consensus among commentators that the impact of the council essentially bypassed Africa.

In response to the question, "Was the African theological and pastoral view present at the council?," the eminent African theologian Laurenti Magesa responds, "Quite frankly, not really!"[8] A number of observations justify Magesa's comment. First, the insignificant number of African-born representatives at the council was striking: of the roughly 2,200 participants in the council, only "260 (11.81%) came from Africa. The majority of these bishops were white missionaries, while sixty-one were native Africans."[9] Second, both the expatriates and African-born representatives were assigned or assumed only secondary roles at the council. It cannot be said that African bishops exerted any decisive influence on the proceedings and outcomes of the council;[10] while not entirely muted, their voices were heard only sporadically and were ultimately inconsequential.[11] Thus, while not totally absent and passive at the council, neither was the African church fully present.

---

5. Synod of Bishops, *Message to the People of God of the Second Special Assembly for Africa of the Synod of Bishops*, no. 1.

6. Synod of Bishops, Second Special Assembly for Africa, *Instrumentum Laboris*, "Preface."

7. Synod of Bishops, Second Special Assembly for Africa, *Instrumentum Laboris*, "Preface."

8. Magesa, *Post-Conciliar Church in Africa*, 1. Magesa devotes the first chapter of this book to this question (1–5).

9. De Jong, *Challenge of Vatican II in East Africa*, 10.

10. De Jong, *Challenge of Vatican II in East Africa*, 10.

11. Kalilombe, "Effect of the Council on World Catholicism: Africa," 311.

The third observation supporting Magesa's view relates to the status of the African church in the 1960s. Quite clearly, as a mission church at the time of the council, Africa possessed a marginal status and, therefore, could not raise matters of substance concerning the issues it addressed. The conclusion drawn by the late Bishop Patrick Kalilombe underscores the extent of this ecclesial irrelevance: "It is obvious from an examination of the sixteen documents that the Council was largely a forum for the concerns of the Churches of Europe and America in the 1960s. . . . Africa's problems and preoccupations, therefore, came only indirectly: they did not determine the central perspective from which the Council's deliberations were moving."[12] The fact that the council fathers had a narrowly Eurocentric outlook lies beyond doubt. John O'Malley corroborates Kalilombe's claim: "Europe, its concerns and the legacy of its history, provided the framework within which Vatican II operated. The story of the Council is almost exclusively the story of Europeans fighting over issues arising out of European history."[13]

The fourth and final observation concerning Magesa's comment relates to the dearth of scholarly materials devoted to the study of the council's impact on and significance for Africa. With the exceptions of Albert de Jong's study focusing on the role in and contribution of Dutch missionaries to the implementation of the council in East Africa, and Magesa's recent work *The Post-Conciliar Church in Africa*, no solid, comprehensive studies exist in English combining a sustained appraisal of the council's impact on the African church with a scholarly examination of its original documents from the perspective of the history, identity, and mission of the African church.[14] This can be understood in light of the fact that, as mentioned above, the central issues addressed by the council touched only indirectly on Africa. To this should be added the challenges created by the theological illiteracy and dogmatic resistance to change that characterized the ecclesiastical hierarchy in Africa during and after the council, although we should not glibly and gratuitously castigate the African participants at the council without taking into account the council's historical context, particularly with regard to Africa.[15]

In light of the foregoing, this essay undertakes a brief retrospective study identifying and assessing the themes, traditions, and transitions, which we also refer to as "vestiges and traces," connecting Vatican II to the second African synod, relying on the benefit of a certain methodological hindsight. This chapter asserts that the link between the former and the latter lies not in the council's actual material content, but rather in the subtle, indirect way in which it has inspired some of the key developments in the African church's theological self-understanding and mission in the wake of the second synod.

The reaction of the African church to the theological developments following from the council can be appropriately described as "delayed." Kalilombe put it starkly when he argued that, in the wake of the council, "The African Church seemed simply to follow the Western responses to the conciliar programme. Only later, especially beginning with the mid-1970s, and thanks to the growing influence of SECAM, has there begun to emerge a specifically African response to Vatican II."[16] As optimistic as his assessment may have sounded on the twenty-fifth anniversary of the close of the council, this "specifically African response to Vatican II" still needs to be clearly demonstrated and characterized more than fifty years after the coun-

---

12. Kalilombe, "Effect of the Council on World Catholicism: Africa," 310.
13. O'Malley, *What Happened at Vatican II*, 13.
14. The commemoration of the council's fiftieth anniversary and the sundry anniversaries of the documents of the council have, however, provided valuable impetus for renewed interest in the general topic of Vatican II and Africa. See, for example, Orobator, "'After All, Africa Is Largely a Non-Literate Continent'"; Orobator, "Look Back to the Future"; Hurley, *Vatican II: Keeping the Dream Alive*; Gribble, *Implementation of Vatican II in Eastern Africa*; Bwidi Kitambala, *Les évêques d'Afrique et le Concile Vatican II*; Messina, "L'Église d'Afrique au concile Vatican II"; Tshibangu, *Le Concile Vatican II et l'Église africaine*; Jagoe, "Vatican II Comes to Africa."
15. Orobator, "'After All, Africa Is Largely a Non-Literate Continent,'" 291–92.
16. Kalilombe, "Effect of the Council on World Catholicism: Africa," 317.

cil. The second African synod (and other sources) offers rich terrain for exploring the status of this response.

In light of the factors outlined above, this assessment calls for the exercise of caution. It is impossible to exaggerate the lack of participation and underrepresentation of the African church at the council. However, the perspective provided by the last fifty years has made clear that the council set in motion a series of processes deliberately envisioned to define and shape—doctrinally and pastorally, globally and locally—the identity and mission of the African church for decades to come. Accordingly, the council should justifiably not be thought of merely as an event or moment in history, monumental as it was, but rather as the beginning of a historical process and as an inspiration for ongoing theological and ecclesial progress. In this way, the effect of the council could not be controlled by the dominant actors and churches, with their Eurocentric mindset, that shaped its agenda, conducted its debates, fought its conflicts, and produced its documents. Instead, this process of ecclesial growth and maturation has unfolded over five decades, validating Karl Rahner's insight that the council's enduring legacy would best be perceived and appreciated by the emergence of a truly world church.[17] Approaching the matter from a sociological and demographic perspective, John Allen Jr. commented perceptively, "If I were asked to offer a history of Roman Catholicism in the twentieth century in one sentence, I would reply: 'The center of gravity shifted from North to South.'"[18] Africa is at the heart of this demographic shift and hence an integral part of the historical process initiated by the council.

A study of some of the themes, traditions, and transitions pertinent to Africa having their origin in the council allows us not only to revisit the council's historical trajectory, but also to discover the African church's role in the historical process and theological progression it inspired. The question then arises: Where do we look for themes, traditions, and transitions generated by the council, or the vestiges and traces of the council, in the African church? As de Jong puts it, this is a question of assessing the issues raised by the implementation "in the Church in practice [of] the results of the Council."[19] To answer this question, we focus on four examples of themes, traditions, and transitions applicable to the African church that have been inspired by the council.

The "Ray of Truth" and "Shadows and Images" of African Religion[20]

In the aftermath of the council there was a growing recognition that African religious traditions possessed a genius that could in fact generate a unique variety of Christianity, at once attuned to centuries of Christian tradition, beliefs, and practices and consciously and carefully adapted to a local context. This development, which has spawned a series of theological and liturgical experimentations, owes its origin to the change of attitude initiated by Vatican II. In *Africae Munus*, while acknowledging that "the problem of 'dual affiliation'—to Christianity and to the traditional African religions—remains a challenge," Benedict quotes *Nostra Aetate* to underline the imperative of "a theological study of those elements of the traditional African cultures in conformity with Christ's teaching" in order to further the mission of reconciliation on the continent (*AM* §§92–93).

Two years after the close of the council, Pope Paul VI issued his programmatic message *Africae Terrarum*. In extolling the "ancient glories of Christian Africa," the pope argued strongly in favor of giving "attentive consideration" to the "moral and religious values" of "ancient African religious cultures" (§7). Paul VI's insightful document lies within the slow but conscious axis of fundamental attitudinal change initiated by Vatican II. In fact, a close study of *Africae Terrarum* reveals unmistakable resemblance to the central tenets of *Nostra Aetate*, especially in the latter's revolutionary declaration that "the Catholic Church rejects nothing that is true and holy in these religions. She regards

---

17. Rahner, *Concern for the Church*, 80.
18. Allen, *Future Church*, 17.
19. de Jong, *Challenge of Vatican II in East Africa*, 90.
20. See Vatican II, *Lumen Gentium* §16; *Nostra Aetate* §2.

with sincere reverence those ways of conduct and of life, those precepts and teachings which, though differing in many aspects from the ones she holds and sets forth, nonetheless often reflect a ray of that Truth which enlightens all men" (*Nostra Aetate* §2). Although the referents of this positive valuation of "non-Christian" religions did not include African religions explicitly, Paul VI seemed to have translated this attitude into the African context, thus upending the prevailing beliefs and practices of missionary Christianity, which summarily demonized African religious traditions and cultures. Paul VI declared that

> the Church views with great respect the moral and religious values of the African tradition, not only because of their meaning, but also because the Church sees them as providential, as the basis of spreading the Gospel message and beginning the establishment of the new society in Christ. . . . And that is why the African, who becomes a Christian, does not disown himself [or herself], but takes up the age-old values of tradition "in spirit and in truth." (*Africae Terrarum* §14)

As Magesa demonstrated in his study of the history and practice of inculturation in Africa, many African Christians attribute this "new attitude" to "the Second Vatican Council as the watershed between strict intolerance and a limited official acceptance of aspects of an African spirituality in the church."[21] In light of the teachings of *Nostra Aetate*, Magesa employs the vivid imagery of opening a door to describe the council's positive assessment of African religious traditions: the council "slightly opened the door for consideration of African Religion as a dialogue partner."[22] In the last fifty years, that door has opened wider as African theologians have undertaken penetrating analyses and studies of the "age-old values" of African religion, attempting to correlate them with the core beliefs of Christianity. The single most important step in walking through this door has been the move toward inculturation, which focuses on and investigates the "encounter between gospel and culture in Christian life," a process by which "the gospel discovers itself in a culture, accepting the elements that reveal the face of God already present, and rejecting those that do not."[23] As a movement and theological methodology, inculturation has thrived in Africa since the council, albeit with some strong criticism of its achievements and usefulness.[24]

Africae Munus revisited the theme of inculturation in its discussion of reconciliation. It conceded the continued relevance of African cultures as repositories of "traditional pedagogical forms of mediation" (§33) and African values as "traditional formulae for peaceful coexistence" (§38). In light of this, the pope notes that "it would be helpful if the bishops were to commission a serious study of traditional African reconciliation ceremonies in order to evaluate their positive aspects and their limitations" (§33). Such an objective evaluation of African realities is a direct outcome of a change in attitude initiated and inspired by the council.

Innovation and Adaptation in Worship and Liturgy

A rather curious lack of consensus exists among scholars and commentators on the legacy of Vatican II with respect to liturgical adaptation, reform, and inculturation in the African church. In the wake of the promulgation of *Sacrosanctum Concilium* (Constitution on the Sacred Liturgy) and the key liturgical reforms it mandated, drawing on "the qualities and talents of the races and nations" (§37), Africa appeared strategically positioned to take full advantage of the favorable conditions and

---

21. Magesa, *Anatomy of Inculturation*, 10.
22. Magesa, "On Speaking Terms," 26.
23. Magesa, *Anatomy of Inculturation*, 144; see also 154.
24. See Martey, *African Theology: Inculturation and Liberation*. Martey identifies inculturation and liberation as the two dimensions of African theology; they are in dialectical tension, with the latter often being employed to criticize the former for not taking seriously the issue of African oppression. In turn, proponents of inculturation criticize African liberation theology (or "Black theology") for dissipating the core of the gospel in political activism.

to lead the liturgical innovations and transformations encouraged by the council. The spectrum of appraisal of Africa's response to this mandate ranges from "relatively insignificant adaptations"[25] to a liturgical revolution of immense practical and pastoral significance.[26] The evidence leads us to adopt a sympathetic position toward the latter view.

In the post–Vatican II period, there was no room for diffidence in initiating and accomplishing the liturgical reforms of the council. What the council mandated for the universal church Pope Paul VI explicitly permitted for the church in Africa. As he declared two years after the council, "You may, and you must, have an African Christianity. Indeed, you possess human values and characteristic forms of culture which can rise up to perfection such as to find in Christianity, and for Christianity, a true superior fulness, and prove to be capable of a richness of expression all its own, and genuinely African."[27]

Although the theme of liturgical adaptation and creativity did not feature highly on the list of priorities of the second African synod, it is noteworthy that the synod proposed some liturgical innovations adapted to the needs of the African continent and its theological context. As Pope Benedict enjoined the church in Africa,

> In order to encourage reconciliation in communities, I heartily recommend, as did the Synod Fathers, that each country celebrate yearly "a day or week of reconciliation, particularly during Advent or Lent." SECAM will be able to help bring this about and, in accord with the Holy See, promote a continent-wide *Year of Reconciliation* to beg of God special forgiveness for all the evils and injuries mutually inflicted in Africa, and for the reconciliation of persons and groups who have been hurt in the Church and in the whole of society. This would be an extraordinary Jubilee Year "during which the Church in Africa and in the neighbouring islands gives thanks with the universal Church and implores the gifts of the Holy Spirit," especially the gift of reconciliation, justice and peace. (*AM* §157)

From all indications, this call does not seem to have initiated a lasting tradition of celebrating a continent-wide "day or week of reconciliation, particularly during Advent or Lent."

Notwithstanding the tendency to detect and decry an apparent timidity in the ranks of the African ecclesiastical hierarchy in leading the liturgical innovations authorized by Vatican II, the available evidence supports the view that at least modest and sometimes important innovations, rather than insignificant adaptations, have taken place.[28] The existing evidence of constructive experimentation and creativity in liturgical celebration and worship in the wake of the second African synod can be traced directly to the impetus of the council.

Small Christian Communities: Places of Reconciliation, Justice, and Peace

In the 1970s the Association of Member Episcopal Conferences in Eastern Africa (AMECEA), which consists of the national episcopal conferences of the nine English-speaking countries of eastern Africa, adopted Small Christian Communities (SCCs) as a pastoral strategy for advancing the mission of evangelization. In 2002, the AMECEA bishops "renewed their confidence in SCCs and gave to them an indispensable role in the new and deeper evangelization of Africa."[29]

The origin, development, and practice of SCCs drew inspiration from the emphasis on the local church prevalent in the council documents. We concur with de Jong's assessment that "the redis-

---

25. Chima, "Africanising the Liturgy," 290.
26. Hastings, "Council Came to Africa," 320.
27. Pope Paul VI, Homily (Eucharistic Celebration at the Conclusion of the Symposium Organized by the Bishops of Africa), Kampala, Uganda, July 31, 1969, §2.
28. See examples of innovative liturgical experimentation in sub-Saharan Africa in Uzukwu, *Worship as Body Language*, 270–317.
29. Cieslikiewicz, "Pastoral Involvement of Parish-Based SCCs in Dar es Salaam," 99–100.

covery of the local Church in the ecclesiology of Vatican II exercised a strong influence on the young Churches of Africa. . . . These young Churches of Africa were moving out of the missionary period and engaged in finding their own ecclesial identity as local Churches within the universal Church."[30] In the understanding of the AMECEA bishops, "SCCs were meant to be cells where the Christian faith would be intensely lived and shared. They were in fact seen as the ecclesiastical extension of the African extended family or clan."[31] Understood in this sense, SCCs have emerged and flourished as the most concrete and visible manifestations of the church in its local context, especially in eastern Africa.

According to Joseph Healey, whose authority on the theology of SCCs is considerable, there are 120,000 SCCs in the AMECEA countries; in Kenya alone, there are 45,000.[32] Seen in some places as the "church in the neighborhood,"[33] SCCs embody and fulfill the ecclesiology of the local church following Vatican II, in particular the understanding that the "Church of Christ is really present in all legitimately organized groups of the faithful, in so far as they are united to their pastors and are also quite appropriately called Churches in the New Testament" (*Lumen Gentium* §131). The second African synod recognized the importance of such communities in shaping "Christian conscience" and advancing "the struggle for justice and peace" (*AM* §131), One of the propositions of the synod explicitly states that SCCs are "a place for concretely living out reconciliation, justice and peace."[34]

In the wake of the second African synod, the ecclesiological import of SCCs can be viewed in a variety of ways. The assessment of theologians is generally positive, especially when SCCs are seen as "today's new way of being church from the bottom up" and a "church on the move" under the inspiration of the Holy Spirit.[35] Yet the successes of SCCs cannot mask their shortcomings, including the clericalist control often imposed on them, their patriarchal leadership even when the majority of members are women, and the near-total absence of youth participation.[36]

An Inspiration for the African Synodal Process and African Theology

The two decades following the council witnessed a flurry of activities aimed at disseminating the teachings of the council in various dioceses in sub-Saharan Africa.[37] An oft-overlooked outcome of the council in Africa was a series of diocesan synodal assemblies held to "discuss the consequences of Vatican II" and so that local dioceses could "draw up a plan of pastoral renewal of the Church."[38] Although these assemblies turned out to be short-lived, with the passage of time two significant ecclesial undertakings can be traced directly to the process begun by the council, namely, the two Special Assemblies for Africa of the Synod of Bishops.

Magesa is quite categorical in his positive appraisal of the importance and inspiration of Vatican II for the development of the synodal process in Africa: "Perhaps the most important consequence of Vatican II for African Catholicism was the convocation in 1994 of the Special Assembly of the Synod of Bishops for Africa or African Synod, almost three decades after the closing of the

---

30. De Jong, *Challenge of Vatican II in East Africa*, 39.
31. Magesa, *Anatomy of Inculturation*, 43.
32. Healey, "Small Christian Communities (SCCs) Promote Family Ministry in Eastern Africa."
33. Mejia, *Church in the Neighborhood*.
34. Synod of Bishops, *Message to the People of God of the Second Special Assembly for Africa of the Synod of Bishops* §37.
35. Healey, "Twelve Case Studies of Small Christian Communities in Eastern Africa," 96; see also Healey and Hinton, "Introduction: A Second Wind," in Healey and Hinton, *Small Christian Communities Today*, 4, 6.
36. See Healey, "Small Christian Communities: Promoters of Reconciliation, Justice, and Peace in Eastern Africa," 59–70; Orobator, "Small Christian Communities as a New Way of *Becoming* Church"; Cieslikiewicz, "Pastoral Involvement of Parish-Based SCCs in Dar es Salaam," 101–2; Nasimiyu-Wasike, "Role of Women in Small Christian Communities."
37. Orobator, "'After All, Africa Is Largely a Non-Literate Continent,'" 284–301.
38. De Jong, *Challenge of Vatican II in East Africa*, 91.

Council."³⁹ Magesa offered this assessment before the second African synod, and, as the quotation below demonstrates, he holds the same opinion about the significance of Vatican II for the second synod as well.

The First Synod considered the ecclesiology of the new model of the "church as family." In *Ecclesia in Africa*, Pope John Paul II stated that "not only did the Synod speak of inculturation, but it also made use of it, taking the Church as God's Family as its guiding idea for the evangelisation of Africa. The Synod Fathers acknowledged it as an expression of the Church's nature particularly appropriate for Africa" (*EA* §64). As has already been discussed, the second synod focused its attention on the mission of the church in Africa to foster reconciliation, promote justice, and build peace (*AM* §10). Accordingly, the synodal fathers affirmed, "In this light, we accept our responsibility to be instruments of reconciliation, justice and peace in our communities, 'ambassadors for Christ' (2 Cor 5:20), who is our peace and reconciliation."⁴⁰ Both synods have spawned considerable progress in African theology, including in ecclesiology, Christology, and social ethics. Magesa is unequivocal in his assessment:

> If there is one gift that emerged from the spirit of the Council which Africa can genuinely celebrate, it is the possibilities that it opened up for the development of African Theology. . . . The two synods of Africa, in 1994 and 2009, and the apostolic exhortations following each of them in 1996 and 2011, respectively issued by Popes John Paul II and Benedict XVI, attest to the importance of African Theology for the development of the Church on the continent.⁴¹

What we have designated as the "inspiration"—and Magesa calls the "spirit"—of the council bears significant importance for the development of theological research and scholarship on the themes prioritized by the second African synod.⁴²

A Synod of Men in the Tradition of a Council of Men

By all accounts, the deliberations of the Second Vatican Council were characterized by the near absence and even exclusion of the voices of women. Although this is not the place for an extended analysis of this issue, the fact is that only a negligible number of women were invited to the council. Perhaps unsurprisingly, "The only speech by a female, economist Barbara Ward, had to be read by a man. Even the wives of reporters covering the event were not allowed to approach the altar for communion during daily Mass."⁴³ Since Vatican II, a number of important ecclesial gatherings have perpetuated this exclusion of women. The second African synod was no exception.

A handful of African women, notably members of religious communities, were invited to address the synod. One of the women invitees was Sr. Felicia Harry, the Superior General of Our Lady of Apostles. She focused her address on the incontrovertible reality of women's presence in and contribution to the church, as well as the importance of mutual and meaningful collaboration between men and women in the church, collaboration that often grants women direct access to decision-making and leadership roles. Another invitee, Zambian Sister Mary Ann Katiti, the Provincial Superior of the Kasisi Sisters, asserted that "women have no real voice when it comes to their places and rights, and their contribution to evangelisation."⁴⁴ Other women speakers underlined the sad reality that women in Africa bear a disproportionate share of the burden arising from the various crises affecting the continent.⁴⁵

---

39. Magesa, *Anatomy of Inculturation*, 130.
40. *Message to the People of God of the Second Special Assembly for Africa of the Synod of Bishops* §15.
41. Magesa, *Post-Conciliar Church in Africa*, 19.
42. See Orobator, *Practising Reconciliation, Doing Justice, Building Peace*.
43. Fletcher, "How Women Benefited from Vatican II without Even Being There."
44. McCabe, "Second African Synod: Major Emphases and Challenges."
45. McCabe, "Second African Synod: Major Emphases and Challenges."

From Vatican II to the Second African Synod

On the face of it, the second African synod struck a positive and hopeful note in response to trenchant statements delivered by the women auditors. The final message of the synod recommends that the local churches in Africa "put in place concrete structures to ensure real participation of women at appropriate levels." Quite significantly, proposition 47 of the synod pledges "greater integration of women into Church structures and the decision making process."[46] In *Africae Munus,* Pope Benedict XVI challenged the church in Africa "to be a model for society as a whole" and offered an admission of monumental proportions:

> Women in Africa make a great contribution to the family, to society and to the Church by their many talents and unique gifts. As John Paul II said: "woman is the one in whom the order of love in the created world of persons takes first root." The Church and society need women to take their full place in the world "so that the human race can live in the world without completely losing its humanity." (*AM* §55–56)

Questions remained after the synod about whether this stirring rhetoric and these pledges would be redeemed with bold and concrete action.[47] Unfortunately, the reality of the lives of many women, often characterized by silence and oppression in both the African church and society, continues to the present day. Understandably, African women theologians continue to call the church to break from its tradition of gender bias and to conduct itself not merely as God's mouthpiece or as a proclaimer of reconciliation, justice, and peace to the world, but as a credible embodiment and authentic practitioner of these virtues at all levels of the ecclesial community. Unfortunately, the persistent existence of gender bias in Africa represents a continuing state of affairs dating back to the council (and of course before the council) through the time of the second synod and up to the present.

Concluding Remarks

At the end of the chapter in which he analyzes the influences that shaped Vatican II, Magesa poses the question: "Was, therefore, Vatican II completely lost on Africa?" "Part of the answer," he argues, "lies in the dynamics of the Council-event itself. Despite the precise planning and some attempts at stage-management, once begun, the Council took its own course, some of whose consequences were unexpected and, in diverse ways, affected the Church in every part of the world."[48] These unexpected consequences are particularly visible in churches in the Global South.

According to O'Malley, "What is striking about Vatican II is not any prominent role played by 'the new churches' of former colonies but its dominance by Europeans."[49] On the basis of this observation it is easy to draw the conclusion that Vatican II had little or no significance for Africa, but this conclusion would be a product of an understanding of the council primarily as an event or moment in history. Seen from a different point of view, however, and understood as the initiation of a historical process, the council served as a catalyst for theological developments and changes that continue to define the identity and shape the mission of the African church more than fifty years after its close. Thus to the questions "How did these changes come about?" and "What made possible the birth of the SCCs, the use of the vernacular and secular music, and the rise of participatory leadership?," the response is unequivocal: "It was the Second Vatican Council that officially initiated the process."[50]

The examples presented in this essay are illustrative rather than exhaustive. Together, they offer indications about how to judge and interpret the significance of the council for Africa in the wake of the second African synod. We have not discussed all the possible themes, traditions, and transitions bridging the council and the synod. What this essay offers is a perspective on the council's inspiration for the ongoing development of the church

---

46. *Message to the People of God of the Second Special Assembly for Africa of the Synod of Bishops.*
47. McCabe, "Second African Synod: Major Emphases and Challenges."
48. Magesa, *Anatomy of Inculturation,* 42.
49. O'Malley, *What Happened at Vatican II,* 13.
50. Magesa, *Anatomy of Inculturation,* 42.

in Africa. Evidence of this inspiration is not to be adduced solely from references to the conciliar documents in the synodal documents. Rather, this evidence is grounded in the fact that the situation and context of the African church have changed dramatically since the close of the council, from a mission church that was too timid to assert its identity and raise its voice in the grand assembly of the world church to a vibrant church that "constitutes an immense spiritual 'lung' for a humanity that appears to be in a crisis of faith and hope."[51]

In sum, one of the key conclusions that we can draw from this study is the conviction that, far from being unintended consequences, the exponential expansion, the vibrancy of ministry, the liturgical creativity, and the theological development—while not forgetting entrenched patriarchal proclivities and conservative leanings—that now characterize the church in Africa owe their original impetus to the process, influence, and spirit of Vatican II, which continue to "animate, motivate, and support the demographic and theological flourishing of the African Church."[52] The approach adopted, the examples considered, and the arguments offered in this essay make clear that these developments now constitute permanent features, themes, and traditions of a lively and dynamic African church. As the synodal fathers noted, "Africa is not helpless. Our destiny is still in our hands. All she is asking for is the space to breathe and thrive. Africa is already moving; and the Church is moving with her, offering her the light of the Gospel."[53]

The transition from Vatican II to the second African synod traces the trajectory of a steadily maturing theology of the nature and mission of the church in Africa. The traces of continuity or implicit transitions between the former and the latter reflect the vitality of theological reflection in Africa, its implications for the self-understanding of the community called church, and the vital importance of reconciliation, justice, and peace as clear imperatives for ecclesial renewal and social transformation.

Furthermore, the second African synod opened a new path for the church in Africa in its quest to bring gospel values to bear on a crisis-prone and traumatized continent, following the methodology adopted by the council, especially in *Gaudium et Spes,* its document pertaining specifically to the church in the modern world. Rather than seeing the modern world through the lens of secularism, relativism, materialism, and atheism, the church should, as was often repeated at the second African synod, play the role of a facilitator of dialogue among competing but complementary claims, ideologies, and institutions. The measure to which the church in Africa succeeds in undertaking this role will confirm its mission as a humble yet authentic servant of reconciliation, justice, and peace. The themes and traditions of Vatican II are not ossified in the conciliar documents; rather, they continue to inspire movements that shape, guide, and animate the unfolding theological narrative of the self-understanding and mission of the African church as a community of reconciliation, justice, and peace on a divided, conflicted, and turbulent continent.

Bibliography

Allen, John L., Jr. *The Future Church: How Ten Trends Are Revolutionizing the Catholic Church.* New York: Doubleday, 2009.

Benedict XVI, Pope. *Africae Munus* [Post-synodal Apostolic Exhortation on the Church in Africa in Service of Reconciliation, Justice and Peace; November 19, 2011]. Vatican City: Libreria Editrice Vaticana, 2011. www.vatican.va.

———. Homily: "Eucharistic Celebration for the Opening of the Second Special Assembly for Africa of the Synod of Bishops," 2009.

Bwidi Kitambala, Alfred Guy. *Les évêques d'Afrique et le Concile Vatican II. Participation, contribution et application jusqu'à l'Assemblée spéciale du Synode des Évêques de 1994.* Paris: L'Harmattan, 2010.

---

51. Pope Benedict XVI, Homily: "Eucharistic Celebration for the Opening of the Second Special Assembly for Africa of the Synod of Bishops."
52. Orobator, "'After All, Africa Is Largely a Non-Literate Continent,'" 301.
53. *Message of the Bishops of Africa to the People of God at the Conclusion of the Second African Synod* §42.

Chima, Alex. "Africanising the Liturgy: Where Are We Twenty Years after Vatican II?," *African Ecclesial Review* 25.5 (October 1983): 280–91.

Cieslikiewicz, Christopher. "Pastoral Involvement of Parish-Based SCCs in Dar es Salaam." In *Small Christian Communities Today: Capturing the New Moment*, edited by Joseph Healey and Jeanine Hinton, 99–100. Nairobi: Paulines Publications, 2005.

Fletcher, Peggy. "How Women Benefited from Vatican II without Even Being There." *The Salt Lake Tribune*, October 12, 2012, www.sltrib.com.

Gribble, Richard. *The Implementation of Vatican II in Eastern Africa: The Contribution of Bishop Vincent McCauley, CSC*. Lewiston, NY: Edwin Mellen Press, 2009.

Hastings, Adrian. "The Council Came to Africa." In *Vatican II by Those Who Were There*, edited by Alberic Stacpoole. London: Geoffrey Chapman, 1986.

Healey, Joseph. "Small Christian Communities: Promoters of Reconciliation, Justice, and Peace in Eastern Africa." In *Reconciliation, Justice, and Peace: The Second African Synod*, edited by Agbonkhianmeghe E. Orobator, 59–70. Maryknoll, NY: Orbis Books, 2011.

———. "Small Christian Communities (SCCs) Promote Family Ministry in Eastern Africa." *Hekima Review* 50 (2014): 54–67.

———. "Twelve Case Studies of Small Christian Communities in Eastern Africa." In *How Local Is the Local Church? Small Christian Communities and the Church in Eastern Africa*, edited by Agatha Radoli. Eldoret, Kenya: AMECEA Gaba Publications, 1993.

Healey, Joseph, and Jeanine Hinton. *Small Christian Communities Today: Capturing the New Moment*. Nairobi: Paulines Publications, 2005.

Hurley, Dennis. *Vatican II: Keeping the Dream Alive*. Pietermaritzburg, South Africa: Cluster Publications, 2005.

Jagoe, Bede. "Vatican II Comes to Africa." *Worship* 79.6 (2005): 544–54.

John Paul II, Pope. *Ecclesia in Africa* [Post-synodal Apostolic Exhortation on the Church in Africa and Its Evangelizing Mission toward the Year 2000; September 14, 1995]. Vatican City: Libreria Editrice Vaticana, 1995. www.vatican.va.

Jong, Albert de. *The Challenge of Vatican II in East Africa: The Contribution of Dutch Missionaries to the Implementation of Vatican II in Tanzania, Kenya, Uganda, and Malawi 1965–1975*. Nairobi: Paulines Publications, 2004.

Kalilombe, Patrick A. "The Effect of the Council on World Catholicism: Africa." In *Modern Catholicism: Vatican II and After*, edited by Adrian Hastings. London: SPCK, 1991.

Magesa, Laurenti. *Anatomy of Inculturation: Transforming the Church in Africa*. Maryknoll, NY: Orbis Books, 2004.

———. "On Speaking Terms: African Religion and Christianity in Dialogue." In *Reconciliation, Justice, and Peace: The Second African Synod*, edited by Agbonkhianmeghe E. Orobator. Maryknoll, NY: Orbis Books, 2011.

———. *The Post-Conciliar Church in Africa: No Turning Back the Clock*. Nairobi CUEA Press, 2016.

Martey, Emmanuel. *African Theology: Inculturation and Liberation*. Maryknoll, NY: Orbis Books, 1993.

McCabe, Michael. "The Second African Synod: Major Emphases and Challenges." *Missiologia* (2009). http://www.missiologia.org.br/cms/UserFiles/cms_artigos_pdf_73.pdf.

Mejia, Rodrigo. *The Church in the Neighborhood: Meetings for the Animation of Small Christian Communities*. Nairobi: St. Paul Publications-Africa, 1992.

Messina, Jean-Paul. "L'Église d'Afrique au concile Vatican II: Origines de l'Assemblée spéciale du synode des évêques pour l'Afrique." *Mélanges de sciences religieuses* 51.3 (1994): 279–95.

Nasimiyu-Wasike, Anne. "The Role of Women in Small Christian Communities." In *The Local Church with a Human Face*, edited by Agatha Radoli, 181–202. Eldoret, Kenya: AMECEA Gaba Publications, 1996.

O'Malley, John W. *What Happened at Vatican II*. Cambridge, MA: Harvard University Press, 2008.

Orobator, Agbonkhianmeghe E. "'After All, Africa Is Largely a Non-Literate Continent': The Reception of Vatican II in Africa." *Theological Studies* 74 (June 2013): 284–301.

———. "Look Back to the Future: Transformative Impulses of Vatican II for African Catholicism." *Concilium International Journal of Theology* (2012/13): 97–102.

———, ed. *Practising Reconciliation, Doing Justice, Building Peace: Conversations in Catholic Theological Ethics in Africa*. Nairobi: Paulines Publications, 2013.

———, ed. *Reconciliation, Justice, and Peace: The Second African Synod.* Maryknoll, NY: Orbis Books, 2011.

———. "Small Christian Communities as a New Way of *Becoming* Church: Practice, Progress and Prospects." In *Small Christian Communities: Fresh Stimulus for a Forward-Looking Church,* edited by Klaus Kramer and Klaus Vellguth, 113–25. Quezon City, Philippines: Claretian Publications, 2013.

Paul VI, Pope. *Africae Terrarum* [Message to the Countries of Africa; 1967].

———. Homily: "Eucharistic Celebration at the Conclusion of the Symposium Organized by the Bishops of Africa," Kampala, Uganda, July 31, 1969.

Radoli, Agatha, ed. *How Local Is the Local Church? Small Christian Communities and the Church in Eastern Africa.* Eldoret, Kenya: AMECEA Gaba Publications, 1993.

Rahner, Karl. *Concern for the Church: Theological Investigations XX.* Translated by Edward Quinn. New York: Crossroad, 1981.

Synod of Bishops, Second Special Assembly for Africa. *Instrumentum Laboris* (2009).

———. *Message to the People of God of the Second Special Assembly for Africa of the Synod of Bishops* (2009).

Tshibangu, Tharcisse. *Le Concile Vatican II et l'Église africaine (1960–2010): Mise en oeuvre du Concile dans l'Église d'Afrique.* Kinshasa: L'Épiphanie; Paris: Karthala, 2012.

Uzukwu, E. Elochukwu. *Worship as Body Language: Introduction to Christian Worship. An Orientation.* Collegeville, MN: Liturgical Press, 1997.

Vatican Council II. *Gaudium et Spes* [Pastoral Constitution on the Church in the Modern World; 1964]. www.vatican.va.

———. *Lumen Gentium* [Dogmatic Constitution on the Church; 1964]. www.vatican.va.

———. *Nostra Aetate* [Declaration on the Relation of the Church to Non-Christian Religions; 1965]. www.vatican.va.

———. *Sacrosanctum Concilium* [Constitution on the Sacred Liturgy; 1963]. www.vatican.va.

Suggested Reading

Magesa, Laurenti. *The Post-Conciliar Church in Africa: No Turning Back the Clock.* Nairobi: CUEA Press, 2016.

O'Malley, John W. *What Happened at Vatican II.* Cambridge, MA: Harvard University Press, 2008.

Orobator, Agbonkhianmeghe E. *Religion and Faith in Africa: Confessions of an Animist.* Maryknoll, NY: Orbis Books, 2018.

———, ed. *Reconciliation, Justice, and Peace: The Second African Synod.* Maryknoll, NY: Orbis Books, 2011.

Schultenover, David, ed. *50 Years On: Probing the Riches of Vatican II.* Collegeville, MN: Liturgical Press, 2015.

Key Words

Africa
African church
African religion
African spirituality
African Synod
culture
inculturation
justice
liturgy
peace
reconciliation
Small Christian Communities
women
worship

From *Ecclesia in Africa* to *Africae Munus*: The Synodal Traditions in African Catholicism

Anthony Adawu

> We announce a message of hope . . . to you, Family of God in Africa, to you, the Family of God all over the world: Christ our Hope is alive; we shall live!
>
> —The Bishops of Africa[1]

The above proclamation of a message of hope by the African bishops not only sums up the goals, deliberations, and fruits of the two synods of Africa, but also charts a course for theological conversation and pastoral action for the African church. The theme of the First Special Assembly for Africa of the Synod of Bishops, convened in Rome from April 10 to May 8, 1994, was "The Church in Africa and Her Evangelizing Mission towards the Year 2000: 'You Shall Be My Witnesses' (Acts 1:8)." The Second Special Assembly, again in Rome, convened as a follow-up to the first, took place on October 4–25, 2009, with the theme "The Church in Africa in Service to Reconciliation, Justice and Peace: 'You Are the Salt of the Earth . . . You Are the Light of the World' (Mt. 5:13–14)." These themes underscore the nature and mission of the church in Africa as the bearer of the hope we have in Christ. The synods culminated in the publication of two interconnected post-synodal apostolic exhortations: *Ecclesia in Africa* by Pope St. John Paul II in 1995 and *Africae Munus* by Pope Benedict XVI in 2009.

The objectives of the First Special Assembly were twofold: first, to celebrate the communion and collegiality of the African bishops with the pope and the universal church and, second, to promote renewed pastoral efforts for the church in Africa. A major objective of the Second Special Assembly was "to give a new impulse, filled with evangelical hope and charity, to the Church of God on the African continent and the neighboring islands."[2] The synods for Africa were located within the larger synodal tradition of the universal church, and the hope born out of them exemplified the nature of the church as a communion of the Holy Spirit.

This chapter discusses the relationship between these two synods, highlighting Christian hope as a theological lens for reading the two resulting documents in the context of God's mission for Africa. The purpose of the discussion is to propose an appropriate theological methodology for an ongoing reading of these documents and of the whole synodal process. The discussion will invite readers to engage with the documents as texts of hope and with the synodal process and in doing so to confront the reality of millions of Africans, whose cries "for abundant life, for food, housing, health care, and peace have become the new text for African theology" as well as engage with "the new narratives of God's revelation to which African theologians [and pastors] must listen."[3] The concrete daily lives of Africans served as the context and background for both the 1994 and

---

1. Bishops of Africa, *Message of the First Synod of Africa*, 2.
2. Pope Benedict XVI, *Africae Munus* §3 (hereinafter *AM*).
3. Ilo, "*Africae Munus* and the Challenges," 121.

2009 synods. The synodal process has not ended; the "people of God" in Africa continue to journey together to find the path of abundant life made manifest in the event of Christ—namely, the incarnation, death, and resurrection of the Lord Jesus—and through the action of the Holy Spirit.

I propose the development of a theological praxis of hope as an overarching theological lens for reengaging the African synodal traditions and suggest four significant strands of thought as a starting point for this effort. The first is a historical and methodological survey of the African synodal traditions, including a discussion of the historical and social contexts of the two synods, the planning of the synods, the actual synodal events, and the implementation of the decisions taken. A second strand provides a theological survey focusing on the movement from seeing the recent African synods as events of resurrection and hope to seeing them also as synods of a new Pentecost, and includes a discussion of the intentional turn of African Catholic theologians toward theological praxis as part of the ongoing process of implementing the synodal decisions. The third strand of thought discusses the nature and mission of the church in light of the African synodal traditions, with specific emphasis on the African church's self-understanding as the "family of God" seeking communion, reconciliation, justice, and peace. The fourth and concluding line of thought explores the notion of the church as the servant of families and children. In particular, I argue that a commitment to children is critical to the future of the church's mission in Africa.

African Synodal Traditions: Historical and Methodological Survey

Historical Survey: The Synodal Tradition of the World Church as Context

The 1994 and 2009 African synods do not stand in isolation—they are situated firmly within the church's long synodal tradition. The practice of convening synods as a means of church administration goes back to the earliest centuries of the church's life. The African or Carthaginian synods, which began in the early third century, are good examples.[4] St. Cyprian, who became a bishop of Carthage in 249 CE, presided over a number of general synods. The Carthaginian synods focused largely on matters of interest to the African church; however, the focus often transcended local issues in order to deal with topics affecting the universal church.

For instance, the Synods of Hippo (393) and Carthage (397) drew up the final list of the books of the Bible, that is, the canons of both the Old and New Testament. St. Augustine participated in both synods and was one of forty-four bishops who formally approved the proceedings at Carthage. He was also present at the Synod of Carthage in 420, which refuted and condemned the heresy of Pelagius. The Carthaginian synods were well attended and continued into the eighth century, by which time the growth and influence of the church of Roman Africa had waned as the result of Arab domination.[5] While there is no direct connection between the early-century synods and contemporary ones, the understanding of synod as an instrument of church administration at both the local and universal levels holds true even in present times.[6]

The contemporary understanding of a synod of bishops is a legacy of the Second Vatican Council. At the council, the bishops sought to identify affective and effective means of caring for all the churches and began to plan suitable structures at the national, regional, and continental levels. Pope Paul VI officially established the Synod of Bishops on September 15, 1965, in response to the desire of the bishops to keep alive the positive spirit engendered by their experience at the council, and particularly as a permanent body in service to the communion and collegiality of the world's bishops with the Holy Father. As an instrument of episcopal

---

4. In the early centuries of the church, the notion of *synod* sometimes overlapped with the notion of *council*. See Hefele, *History of the Christian Councils*, 1:1–27. The contemporary understanding makes a clear distinction between synod and council. The latter refers to ecumenical councils, which necessarily address matters concerning the universal church. They are extensive in terms of participation, duration, and outcome. Synods are narrower in focus and address topics impacting the whole church or the church in specific regions.

5. See Havey, "African Synods."

6. See Hefele, *History of the Christian Councils*, 1:1–27.

collegiality, the Synod of Bishops has the duty to advise the pope in governing the universal church, particularly concerning the tasks entrusted to him to protect the church, increase faith and strengthen traditions, maintain and confirm church discipline, and study the consequences of the church's activities in the world. The pope's decision to seek this collaboration and collegiality was an effort to adapt the means and methods of the papal apostolate to the needs of the church and of the world.[7] The event of the synod is intended to bear something sacred within it, which at once manifests the earthly and ethnic reality of the church, as well as its mystery as the body of Christ. The bishops and other synod participants endeavor to keep this reality and mystery in mind in their deliberations and interventions, which occur in a spirit of mutual love, reciprocal assistance, and "fraternal correction."[8] The Synod of Bishops can meet in ordinary general session, extraordinary session, or special session, depending on the purpose and scope of the subject matter and the number and characteristics of the individuals or groups invited to attend. These sessions are also called "assemblies." Ordinary and extraordinary sessions address topics impacting the universal church; for example, the First Ordinary Assembly (1967) concerned "The Preservation and Strengthening of the Catholic Faith," and the Extraordinary General Assembly of October 2014 and Ordinary General Assembly of October 2015 concerned the family. Special sessions, such as the special assemblies for Africa, address concerns of the church in specific regions or countries.

The initial experience of the African bishops at the council inspired them to create a forum where they could discuss the church's evangelizing mission on the continent. They established their own general secretariat with the task of coordinating their interventions at the council so that they could speak with one voice. In July 1969, barely four years after the conclusion of Vatican II and during Pope Paul VI's visit to Africa, the initial cooperation between the bishops of Africa at the council became permanent in the creation and launch of the Symposium of Episcopal Conferences of Africa and Madagascar (SECAM). In 1975, SECAM held a plenary meeting in Rome in order to explore ways of promoting evangelization. The cooperation among the African bishops at the continental level increased in subsequent years, as did the desire for an African council or synod. The goal was to find ways of working together to address the religious problems that concerned the entire continent, particularly with respect to how the church's work of evangelization might help shape its future. The convocation of the first African synod was in response to the African church's expressed desire "to promote an *organic pastoral solidarity* within the entire African territory and nearby Islands."[9]

Other synods of bishops for various regions of the world have been held in the manner of the African synods—that is, as special sessions—such as for Europe (1991 and 1999); the Americas (1997); Asia (1998); Oceania (1998); and the Middle East (2010). There have also been synods for specific countries for special reasons, including the Netherlands (1980) and Lebanon (1995). What all these synods have in common is that they are events of the universal church called in response to specific needs of specific churches in various regions of the world, and thus the title of "special sessions" makes perfect sense. We understand the assembly or assemblies of the Synod of Bishops for the church in Africa as the action of the universal church on behalf of, and in solidarity with, the church in Africa. The synods are therefore not African events, but rather events of the world church. Thus, while the African synods were "authentically and unequivocally African," they were at the same time "in full communion with the universal church" (*EA* §19).

Crisis and Progress in Africa as Context

The existence of both crisis and progress in Africa provides another context for the synods of Africa. The First Synod (1994) took place at a time of untold suffering in Africa, including fratricidal hate resulting from political unrest in many parts of the continent, the crushing devaluation of currencies,

---

7. Pope Paul VI, *Apostolica Sollicitudo* [Apostolic Letter Issued *Motu Proprio* Establishing the Synod of Bishops for the Universal Church], Introduction (www.vatican.va).
8. Holy See Press Office, *General Information on Synod of Bishops*, Introduction.
9. Pope John Paul II, *Ecclesia in Africa* §5 (emphasis in the original) (hereinafter *EA*).

and the growing burden of international debt. This unrest could be seen in the wars and genocides in Rwanda, Sudan, Angola, Liberia, Sierra Leone, Somalia, and parts of central Africa. There was also tribal conflict between the Nanumba and Konkomba of northern Ghana. However, the preparatory document (the *Lineamenta*) for the First Synod identified pertinent "signs and reasons for hope" that served as the background of the African church's evangelizing mission. These included (and include) the relative freedom of action for the church's work of evangelization; the openness of traditional African religion to Christianity; the presence of Islam, which simultaneously presents a challenge and an opportunity for dialogue; and the ongoing changes in the political, economic, social, and cultural life of the people.[10]

At the time the bishops and other participants gathered with the Holy Father for the second synod for Africa (2009), the situation on the continent had changed in many ways. In his analysis of the changed situation, Peter Cardinal Turkson observed that

> although forms of the miseries of hunger, poverty, bad governance, and conflict persisted in certain areas, views about the continent were more positive: the continent was now generally considered to occupy the tenth position in the world economy. Africa was the second emerging world market after China; and the G8 summit (in L'Aquila, Italy 2009) labeled it a continent of opportunities. The great African challenge at the inception of the [second] synod was how these opportunities could become real for its people! What role could the Church play?[11]

Cardinal Turkson's analysis shows that, while the challenges facing the African continent were formidable, there were compelling reasons to engage in a new evangelization, which required a new zeal, methodology, and fervor akin to the dynamism exhibited by the early disciples. The 2009 synod emphasized that the African church had come of age. It had moved from being a mission church to assuming its role as a missionary church. The African synods were thus a way to examine the African church's missionary work in response to the needs of Africa and as a contribution to the growth of the universal church.

Methodological Survey: Engaging the People of God in a Synodal Process

Two terms are of great importance to our discussion at this point: synodal tradition and synodal process. Synodal tradition refers to the concept and practice of convening synods. It explores and explicates the theological meaning and pastoral practice of synods. Synodal tradition includes the notion of synodal process, which refers to all the stages involved in convening a synod, including its planning, the actual event, and the implementation of its decisions.

The methodology for the synodal process is based on collegiality and ecclesial community. The process emphasizes the relationship among bishops and the bond between the bishops and the Holy Father. This is good for the church. However, the collaboration among bishops is meaningful only in the context of the communion of the church and of church leadership engaging the voices and experiences of the entire people of God. Synods are consultative in character. When prepared well, synods are able to involve all interested parties at "all levels of the Christian community: individuals, small communities, parishes, Dioceses, and national and international bodies" (*EA* §23). This methodology of engagement and consultation allows the Synod of Bishops to become the point of convergence of a listening process—"a mutual listening in which everyone has something to learn."[12] One sees the application of this methodology in the two African synodal processes—from the planning of the synods to the ongoing implementation of their decisions—as evidenced, for instance, in the work

---

10. The General Secretariat of the Synod of Bishops, "Lineamenta for the First Special Assembly for Africa" §11.

11. Turkson, "Keynote Address: The New Evangelization for the Transmission of the Christian Faith in Ghana in the Light of Africae Munus," 31.

12. Pope Francis, "Address at the Fiftieth Anniversary of the Synod of Bishops," 3.

of SECAM and specific episcopal conferences, as well as in significant theological conversations taking place among African scholars, pastors, and the faithful. Some African theologians and pastors, however, have not been not satisfied with this process. For example, there were some who hoped for a council for Africa held on African soil. For them, holding a synod on Africa outside Africa (in Rome) was not only a disappointment but also a way to control the conversation about and the vision of the African church. These concerns are addressed when one understands the African synods as events of the universal church in solidarity with the church in Africa.

The process for the first African synod began with Pope John Paul II's announcement convoking it on January 6, 1989. On that same day, he nominated a number of African bishops to form a pre-preparation commission to conduct an initial discussion about the synod's details. The commission was expanded in June 1989 to form the Council of the General Secretariat, which was entrusted with the actual preparation of the synod. Consultation with bishops and other persons of interest started before and continued throughout the synodal process. Prior to the inauguration of the First Synod in 1994, the pope had paid ten pastoral visits to Africa and Madagascar, going to thirty-six countries. Four of these trips preceded his announcement convoking the synod, and six took place after it. These visits allowed the pope to listen to the people of Africa and to forge a dynamic relationship with them. He also used the occasions to encourage all the faithful to prepare for the synod. On three different occasions during the pope's pastoral visits, he held working sessions with the Council of the General Secretariat, at Yamoussoukro, Ivory Coast (1990), Luanda, Angola (1992), and Kampala, Uganda (1993), in order to galvanize support for and encourage participation in the synod. The pope also took advantage of the *ad limina* visits of African bishops to ask for the cooperation of everyone in the synod's preparation. The consultations on African soil signaled the pope's interest in making sure that the synodal process was not far removed from the people. The repeated visits and growing connection with the African people during the preparatory stage was a way of addressing some of the criticisms of those who felt that holding the synod in Rome potentially hijacked it, stifling African voices. It is important to note that these criticisms focused solely on the location of the synod did not fairly judge the entire synodal process, which involved the African people at various levels.

The church in Africa received the news of the announcement of the synod with enthusiasm. The percentage of responses to the *Lineamenta* was, at the time, "the highest [percentage] ever recorded for a synod."[13] The pope praised this enthusiastic response in his post-synodal exhortation: "The response of the African peoples to my appeal to them to share in the preparation of the synod was truly admirable. The replies given to the *Lineamenta*, both within and outside the African Ecclesial Communities, far exceeded every expectation" (*EA* §25). A key component of the preparatory document was its associated eighty-one-item questionnaire, which invited the African church to reflect on the theme of evangelization. It was organized into five subthemes: the proclamation of the Christian message, inculturation, dialogue within the church and among religions, justice and peace, and the means of social communication. The Council of the General Secretariat held several meetings with selected African bishops and theologians to consider the responses to the *Lineamenta* and to draft the working paper (the *Instrumentum Laboris*). This document, published in February 1993, constituted the reference point for the synod's agenda. Its purpose was to guide the discussions at the synod and help the bishops' conferences and delegates in their ongoing preparation and in their evaluation of the priorities they would propose at the synod.

Consultation, collegiality, and ecclesial communion continued at the synod through the interventions of bishops and other delegates and through smaller discussion groups. The fruits of these discussions were twofold: they helped produce

---

13. Schotte, "Preface to the Instrumentum Laboris for the First Special Assembly for Africa." Bracketed insertion mine.

several propositions presented to the Holy Father and helped the bishops craft their messages to their people. The final report with the propositions formed the basis for *Ecclesia in Africa*. This apostolic exhortation outlined the five major proposals of the First Synod: (1) the proclamation of the gospel of salvation realized in Christ and offered to all; (2) inculturation of the Christian life; (3) dialogue within the church as well as with other Christian and non-Christian faith traditions, particularly with traditional African religions and Islam; (4) the search for justice and peace for the people of Africa and the world; and (5) use of the means of social communication in fostering dialogue and sharing the faith.

Clear recommendations and decisions to be implemented emanated from the synod. For instance, it proposed the model of the church as "family of God" as a guide for the activity of the African church. It also set down a number of conditions to add credibility to the church's witness, including working on reconciliation, justice, and peace. The church in Africa was to assert its prophetic role by forming Christians in justice and peace, including the establishment of Justice and Peace Commissions, and by advocating for just salaries for workers.

An evaluation of the extent of the implementation of these decisions formed the basis for the initial conversation about the second African synod, which was convened to accomplish at least two purposes. The first was to keep alive the event of the First Synod by arousing renewed interest in the objectives of *Ecclesia in Africa*, and the second was to begin a synodal process that would help the African church address and overcome the situations of crisis on the continent and assist her in her work of evangelization amid both challenging and hopeful circumstances. With these goals in mind, the preparatory document (*Lineamenta* 2) of the second synod aimed at taking inventory of what the African church had done in response to *Ecclesia in Africa* and understanding what remained to be done. A majority of responses indicated that *Ecclesia in Africa* had been put into action and continued to serve as a guide; for example, a number of bishops' conferences had organized pastoral congresses and devised plans for pastoral action based on the document. Many conferences had also established Justice and Peace Commissions as instruments of evangelization and as a means of forming Christian consciences that would defend human rights and encourage good governance. In collaboration with government and nongovernmental organizations, a number of conferences had also created opportunities to combat the scourge of HIV/AIDS. The focus on the biblical apostolate, Small Christian Communities, integral development, and self-sufficiency had also been encouraging. SECAM's efforts at keeping the objectives of *Ecclesia in Africa* in the forefront were also significant, including in its plenary meetings in South Africa (1997) and Rome (2000), which focused on the church as family of God as the place and sacrament of reconciliation, pardon, and peace in Africa.

Similar implementation efforts followed the second African synod and the publication of Pope Benedict XVI's post-synodal exhortation *Africae Munus*. These implementation efforts focused on the five major proposals outlined in *Africae Munus*. First, the document proposes the centrality of Christ as the source of reconciliation, justice, and peace. The second proposal focuses on various paths to achieve reconciliation, justice, and peace, particularly relating to care for the human person, harmony among peoples, the protection of and respect for life, and dialogue and communion among people. Third, the pope proposes the significance of promoting reconciliation, justice, and peace through the work of the faithful, through the Word of God, and through the church's sacraments and social teaching. Fourth, the document gives particular attention to major areas of the church's apostolate, including its work in education and health care and its efforts to harness the available resources in the world of technology and in new forms of communication. The church in Africa must approach these tasks with the understanding that she is the sacrament of Christ—it is through her presence and activities that people encounter the risen Lord and the source of peace. Finally, the apostolic exhortation proposes a new evangelization as a way to achieve reconciliation, justice, and peace. In this proposal, the Holy Father tasks the church in Africa to find renewed vitality in her identity and mission as the bearer and witness of the risen Christ, walking in the savior's footsteps.

The implementation of the decisions of both African synods is an ongoing process. An assessment of this process reveals that important areas continue to demand the church's attention. This assessment also shows, however, that the two synods have launched a praxis of hope that has shaped the theological conversation and the pastoral life of the church in Africa in quite significant ways. Together with their fruits *Ecclesia in Africa* and *Africae Munus*, the African synodal traditions have injected a renewed vigor into the deliberations and actions of the people of God on the continent. These two events of grace continue to invite and encourage African Catholic Christians to dare to give an account of the hope that is in us, and to do so with gentleness and respect, following the apostle Peter's exhortation (see 1 Pet 3:15). This exhortation is a call to the church in Africa to develop a theology of hope that responds to the realities and laments of the African people.[14]

Theological Survey: The Synods of Africa and the Praxis of Hope

The focus on the praxis of hope is not an accident or an ad hoc theological decision. On the contrary, a focus on hope addresses "a key question of our time," as Carlos Granados states in his introduction to an interview with Gerhard Cardinal Müller on the state of the church. In an effort to discern the deep questions our contemporaries might have for the church and the believer, Granados noted that

> people today do not see their lack of faith as a tragedy, but what does worry them profoundly is their lack of hope, for which—making matters worse—they try to make up with substitutes like optimism.... [Our] contemporaries wonder whether there is hope for the "now," they wonder whether they can find it in Christianity—and they wonder above all: What is the foundation of Christian hope?[15]

The interview—described as "A Report on Hope"—addresses the questions of what we can hope for from Christ, the face and incarnation of God's mercy, and from the church, the family, and the society. In addressing these questions, the report underscores the significance of seeing Christ as the source of Christian hope. It also unravels the mystery of the hope we find in communion, in particular the communion of the church, family, and society, all of which find their true meaning in the communion of the Trinity.

Emmanuel Katongole argues that a focus on hope is a "much-needed and urgent theological task," especially for Africa, where the connection between suffering and hope is unmistakable.[16] Seen in light of suffering and lament, "hope takes the form of arguing and wrestling with God ... [and] a way of acting in the midst of ruins."[17] Katongole's view underscores at least two complementary dimensions of hope: a vertical dimension and a horizontal dimension. First, hope looks toward God and is salvific. Hope is a way of actively engaging God about God's offer of redemption and about the realities of the human situation. Pope Benedict XVI opens his encyclical letter *Spe Salvi* (saved in hope; November 30, 2007) with the words of St. Paul: "*Spe salvi facti sumus*—in hope we are saved" (Rom 8:24). With these words, the Holy Father focuses our attention on a theological and pastoral discourse on Christian hope. The goal is to exhort all persons to embrace a kind of hope that has the power to transform from within, and in which we are saved. Benedict explains that the hope that saves is a faith-based hope and that by virtue of this trustworthy hope we can face our present situation, which is often arduous and challenging (*Spe Salvi* §1). His explanation shows that Christian hope takes God seriously as a faithful God, as One who keeps the covenant made with humanity, a covenant of fidelity and of love—"I will be your God and you will be my people" (see Exod 6:7; Lev 26:12; Jer 30:22). For the Christian, the hope expressed in and through this covenant comes to fulfillment in Christ and through the action of the

---

14. See Katongole, *Born from Lament*, 2017. For a similar argument, see also Metz, *Faith in History and Society*.
15. Müller, with Carlos Granados, *Cardinal Müller Report*, vii (bracketed insertion mine).
16. Katongole, *Born from Lament*, xvi–xx.
17. Katongole, *Born from Lament*, xvi (bracketed insertion mine).

Holy Spirit. It is in Christ and through the Spirit that we find the hope that does not disappoint. Paul calls it "the hope of glory" (Rom 5:1–5). It keeps our focus on a God who is present to humanity and to all of creation and has pledged fidelity and love for all eternity. In short, "we boast in hope of the glory of God" (Rom 5:2).

The second, horizontal dimension sees hope as a transformative force. Christian hope is the basis of our actions that are aimed at transforming our lives and our communities. As Benedict puts it, "The one who has hope lives differently; the one who hopes has been granted the gift of a new life" (*Spe Salvi* §2). This statement highlights not only the salvific nature of Christian hope but also its ethical character as a force for change. Hope is not optimism. It is neither blind nor passive. It opens the eyes to see with clarity the realities of our human situation—both personal and communal—and provides the endurance and courage to act justly to bring about positive change. Christian hope tells us that God takes seriously our mission to bring about a desired transformation in our world—to be agents of God's abundant life in a world accustomed to death. Hope does not look away when our sisters and brothers suffer economic, political, social, and even religious injustices. It challenges us to seek communion and stand in solidarity with them. Christian hope, then, is solidaristic hope. It addresses "the concrete historical-social situation in which [all persons] find themselves: their experiences, their suffering, struggles, and obstacles."[18] Accounting for this kind of hope is not a purely intellectual exercise but a meaningful praxis—a theological and pastoral responsibility to articulate a practical reason for our hope in Christ, and to act in the power of the Spirit to bring about a desired transformation.[19]

From a Synod of Resurrection and Hope to a Synod of a New Pentecost

For the participants in the African synods as well as theologians and pastors who continue to engage the synodal traditions, hope serves as the principle for actions that sustain a belief in the rich possibilities of Africa's present moment as well as its future.[20] This sense of hope was felt from the very beginning of the African synodal process. On January 6, 1989, when Pope John Paul II made the surprise announcement to convoke a Special Assembly for Africa of the Synod of Bishops, he intended it "to be an occasion of hope and resurrection, at the very moment when human events seemed to be tempting Africa to discouragement and despair" (*EA* §1). He later prayed that the synod "may result in a deep renewal of the church in Africa, so that Christians on that continent may be filled with zeal to live the Gospel fully and to share Christ's salvation and liberation with humanity."[21] Also, as noted above, the *Lineamenta* of the First Synod, in pointing to the sharing of the Good News as a source of hope and strength, highlighted pertinent "signs and reasons for hope" for the African church's evangelizing mission.

At the end of the First Synod in 1994, the bishops of Africa sent a message of hope to the church and people of Africa and to the world describing the synod as "the Synod of Resurrection, the Synod of Hope."[22] Elsewhere I wrote that "the basis of the expressed hope is the Resurrection, which breathes life into the present difficult situation of the people of Africa even as it beckons them toward the fulfillment of all things in Christ at the end of time."[23] The joy experienced at the synod, as expressed through African songs, instruments, and dance, therefore, marked a "rhythm of the struggle between life and death."[24] But hope will prevail because "Christ our Hope is alive, [and] we shall live!"[25]

---

18. Metz, *Faith in History and Society*, 1 (bracketed insertion mine).
19. Metz, *Faith in History and Society*, 29.
20. Ojacor, "Church in Africa and the Search for Abundant Life," 88–98.
21. John Paul II, "Address to the 6th Meeting of the General Secretariat of the Synod of Bishops."
22. Bishops of Africa, *Message of the Synod*.
23. Adawu, "Witnessing to a Just Hope," 7–9.
24. Bishops of Africa, *Message of the Synod*, 6.
25. Bishops of Africa, *Message of the Synod*, 6 (bracketed insertion mine).

The vocation to witness to hope belongs to all—the lay faithful, including men, women, and young people, men and women of the consecrated life, and the clergy. John Paul II rearticulated the theme of hope in *Ecclesia in Africa*, in which he called on Africans not only to have hope but also to celebrate, live, and share the hope they have in Christ. Thus, the synod allows the church in Africa to "celebrate with joy and hope its faith in the Risen Christ" and to critically examine the "lights and shadows" that serve as the context for the mission of God's people in Africa (*EA* §§1, 13, 57).

The second synod for Africa in 2009 also echoes the theme of hope. In particular, Pope Benedict XVI describes the continent as a "spiritual 'lung' for a humanity that appears to be in a crisis of faith and hope."[26] He invites the church in Africa to remain "an ever greater blessing" (*AM* §17) for the African continent and for the entire world. This vision of hope is both refreshing and challenging. It encourages Africans to see the hope they carry and can share with the world. Africa can confidently share her stories of hope with all who care to listen. However, this vision of hope also challenges Africa to take hopeful actions to address her many difficulties.[27] The metaphor of a "spiritual lung" breathing life into the difficult situations of Africa and the world conjures an image of health. A lung must stay healthy if it is to perform its functions properly. Africa, however, is a lung that needs healing, even as it continues to breathe life and hope; she breathes with difficulty but also with an ever-renewed hope about her own painful situations and those of the world: "Christians in Africa witness to hope not *in spite of* their suffering. Rather, they do so *because of* their many challenges, thereby holding suffering and hope in creative tension."[28] In the words of Katongole, Africans possess a kind of hope that is born from lament: "The starting point of any discussion of hope is the valley of lament."[29] These observations are deeply rooted in scripture and in the reality of painful human experience. The Psalms of lamentation are a good example, as they feature cries that erupt from the depth of pain and hope.[30] The apostle Paul also indicates that, in the chain of spiritual development, affliction produces enduring hope (Rom 5:2–5).

The description of the second assembly for Africa as a "Synod of a New Pentecost"[31] further underscores its focus on Christian hope. A new Pentecost is a new beginning, a rebirth of the church in Africa, a renewed opportunity to bring the gospel of life to the people of Africa and to the world in its fullness. In a keynote address at the Second National Pastoral Congress of the church in Ghana in 2014, Peter Cardinal Turkson recalled Pope Benedict XVI's introductory prayer at the first sitting of the second African synod, in which the Holy Father asked "the Lord to give us the Holy Spirit, that he may inspire a new Pentecost and help us to be servants in the world at this time."[32] Cardinal Turkson concludes that one lesson from the synodal traditions that the church in Africa cannot forget is that its members should be "servants of the Spirit [on the continent] and in the world."[33] The life of the African church is an ongoing celebration of a new Pentecost—a new freedom and an unquenchable thirst for reconciliation, justice, and peace.[34]

African Synodal Traditions and the Intentional Turn toward Theological Praxis

The African synods have had significant influence on African Catholic theological conversation and pastoral action. In the face of the numerous challenges facing the African continent, the synodal

---

26. Pope Benedict XVI, "Homily at the Opening Mass of the Second Assembly for Africa."
27. Adawu, "Witnessing to a Just Hope," 7.
28. Adawu, "Witnessing to a Just Hope," 8. Italics in original.
29. Katongole, *Born from Lament*, xvii.
30. Katongole, *Born from Lament*, 103–42; see also Brueggemann, *Message of the Psalms*; and Brown and Miller, *Lament*.
31. General Secretariat of the Synod of Bishops, *Elenchus Finalis Propositionum*, 2.
32. Turkson, "Keynote Address," 32.
33. Turkson, "Keynote Address," 32.
34. Turkson, "Keynote Address," 30–33.

traditions call for a new approach, a "transforming theology into pastoral care" (*AM* §10). This call challenges African Catholic theologians to place more emphasis on praxis—theological action—and to relate theological conversation more closely to pastoral action. Post-synodal theological conversation places faith and transformative action together in more intentional and more significant ways. More than ever, African theologians are moving away from a form of theology that focuses mostly on doctrinal explications and toward how theology (our "God-talk") informs and is informed by the daily experiences of the ordinary person in the contemporary African context, especially those who find themselves on the margins of society. Theologians have assumed more prophetic and personal approaches to their task and have become "concerned more with proposing concrete theological and realistic pastoral solutions and recommendations for the church in Africa than simply enunciating doctrinal truths or validating theological positions."[35] This renewed theological methodology is not only descriptive and explanatory but also rooted in quantitative and qualitative approaches to the critical study of the African context. Its focus is on how gospel values become concrete norms for the life of the people and for churches in Africa, and on how gospel values and the life of Christ have impacted the way in which the church collaborates with others "in building a better society where the abundant life is available to everyone."[36] Beginning afresh with Christ,[37] and solidly rooted in scripture,[38] the new and emerging theological approaches take seriously the complex economic, political, social, and cultural systems of injustice in Africa and call for "vigilance and full engagement in the very structures that assail the human condition."[39] These approaches involve creatively reading the reality of our times and acting upon it not out of fear and hopelessness but with inventive strategies grounded in confidence and hope. That is, they focus theologians' attention and energy on being "channels of life and hope" so as to transform the historically based sufferings of our time.[40] The goals, then, are renewed faith and hope, and the transformation of troubled situations.

Stan Chu Ilo's proposed transformative missional theological praxis is a good example of the intentional and emerging methodology that characterizes the post-synodal theological landscape.[41] Taking the theme of *Africae Munus* on reconciliation, justice, and peace as a starting point, Ilo's proposed approach examines the "deeper concern on how to bring about the fruits of the eschatological harvest of God's kingdom to bear on the present complex African social context."[42] Achieving this objective requires a sociotheological analysis of the concrete realities characterizing the African social context and a way of mining the rich resources—religious, spiritual, cultural, and human—available on the continent. Such an analysis will hold suffering and hope in creative tension, seeing what needs to change as well as the giftedness and resourcefulness Africa offers, which can serve as a springboard for needed changes.

Works that make use of theological praxis have addressed specific issues in Africa in the light of the gospel, including the complex issues of poverty, HIV/AIDS, refugees, and integral and sustainable human development.[43] It is important to mention that the church in Africa has focused on development from the very beginning of its activities on the

---

35. Ilo and Ogbonnaya, "Introduction," xvi–xvii.
36. Ilo and Ogbonnaya, "Introduction," xvii.
37. See Ilo, "Beginning Afresh with Christ in the Search for Abundant Life in Africa," 1–33.
38. See Béré, "Word of God."
39. Opongo, "Inventing Creative Approaches."
40. Opongo, "Inventing Creative Approaches."
41. See Ilo, "*Africae Munus* and the Challenges"; Ilo, "Second African Synod and the Challenges," part 1, 195–204; Ilo, "The Second African Synod and the Challenges," part 2, 249–60.
42. Ilo, "*Africae Munus* and the Challenges," 116.
43. For a discussion and application of an intentional theological praxis, see Orobator, *From Crisis to Kairos*; Ogbonnaya, *Lonergan, Social Transformation, and Sustainable Human Development*; Ogbonnaya, *African Catholicism and Hermeneutics of Culture*; Ilo, *Church and Development in Africa*; Adawu, "Witnessing to a Just Hope"; Mucherera and Lartey, *Pastoral Care, Health, Healing, and Wholeness in Africa*.

continent. Improved education and health care are major developmental strategies. Tens of thousands of schools established by the church have made a significant difference in the lives of millions of primary, secondary, and tertiary students. There are also hundreds of hospitals, orphanages, and homes for the elderly, chronically ill, and persons with various disabilities.[44] The various steps taken by the church in Africa to address the concrete needs of the people have recently captured the attention of many African theologians and have begun to shape their theological discourse, especially after the two synods for Africa. The concrete issues most African theologians have recently paid attention to intersect with specific themes of the African synods, particularly the nature and mission of the church in Africa and questions of ethics.

African Synodal Traditions and the Church as Family of God

From Church as Family to Church as Servant of Reconciliation, Justice, and Peace

The African synodal traditions present us with a church whose nature and mission continue to serve as a source of hope for Africa and for the world. The First Synod presents the church as the family of God. In her nature as the family of God, the church seeks communion with God and with all peoples through dialogue, proclamation of the gospel, communication, and a deep appreciation of how her cultural values intersect with the enduring message of Christ. In the second synod, the church understands herself as a servant of reconciliation, justice, and peace, and as "salt of the earth and light of the world" (Matt 5:13–14). Together, the two synods present a church that sees itself as a servant of the Spirit tasked with the mission of addressing "issues of human society, living in society, and . . . the challenges and exigencies of inter-personal relationships."[45] But it is also a church that constantly invites all persons to fix their gaze on God, who loves us now and for all eternity. After the synods, the task of African theologians and pastors has been to use the vibrant Christian imagination inspired by the synods to create a new African ecclesiology aimed at bringing abundant life to the suffering people of Africa—in other words, to understand how the church can be an oasis of hope on a continent long off the global radar of developmental efforts. These theologians and pastors are seeking a church that begins afresh with Christ in addressing the needs of Africans today, a church with a renewed focus on integral human development, as well as the development of the African continent as a whole.[46] It is a church in which its social teachings do not remain on bookshelves, a church that engages, integrates, and applies them to real-life situations, and allows them to be enriched by these concrete experiences. The church in Africa is vibrant and youthful, "a citadel of hope" for the future of Christianity, with a great potential to significantly contribute to the evangelization of the universal church.[47]

Church as Family and the Hope of Communion

The use of the concept of family in defining the church is faithful to both the best values of the African cultural context and the church's understanding derived from scripture and tradition. The understanding of the concept of family in Africa is rooted in the African concept of humanity[48] and is captured by notions of relationality and communalism. It emphasizes the relationship between the divine and the human, between the communal and the individual, and between the material and the spiritual.[49] Most Africans are of the view that "humanity is a creation of God," that all human beings are children of God, and that all persons have an intrinsic value that ought to be respected.[50] Human beings also carry in their nature an

---

44. See Ogbonnaya, "Church in Africa: Salt of the Earth?," 74–79.
45. Turkson, "Keynote Address," 33.
46. Ilo and Ogbonnaya, "Introduction," xiv–xv.
47. Ogbonnaya, "Church in Africa: Salt of the Earth?," 68–69.
48. See Muzorewa, *Origins and Development of African Theology*, 16–18.
49. Adawu, "Witnessing to a Just Hope," 28–32.
50. Gyekye, *African Cultural Values*, 24.

aspect of God—a speck of the divine, that is, the soul—which "constitutes all human beings into one human family or humankind."[51] Thus, humanity's ontological relationship with God provides the basis for African communal relationships. In addition, the ties that unite Africans are not limited to one's biological parents and immediate family but rather embrace the entire community of humanity. That means that those connected through kinship ties include the living, the dead, and those who are yet to be born.[52] This explains the emphasis on extended family relationships involving networks of multiple lineages. But the circle is even wider. Recognizing their common humanity, people learn to embrace others beyond their limited geographical, ethnic, and religious boundaries.[53] When boundaries are erected, painful and destructive things happen, as seen in multiple wars fueled by tribal, ethnic, and even religious loyalties on the continent.[54] And, finally, Africans are united in their attempt to live a "worthy and bearable life in this world."[55] They are united in their capacities, limitations, successes, failures, frustrations, sufferings, and good-naturedness. In this shared life, the individual stands in need of the community and the community in need of the individual.[56]

Christian theology echoes similar understandings about the human person and human relationships. For instance, Vatican II's Pastoral Constitution on the Church in the Modern World, *Gaudium et Spes*, provides a brief but profound discourse on the human person in communion with God and others. Its teaching highlights three key theological insights: (1) the dignity of the human person; (2) the community of the human person; and (3) the vocation of the human person (§§12–39). First, the human person is created in the image and likeness of God, and therefore his or her dignity is rooted and perfected in God. This means that one cannot adequately think about the human person without reference to God (§22). Second, the human person is created for communion, for relationship with God and with fellow human beings. Therefore, human nature is by definition relational, reflecting a Trinitarian theology of relationships.[57] And, third, the proper vocation of the human person is to know and love God, to participate in God's creative action, and, as a faithful steward and wise builder, to govern creation and the world with justice and holiness (§34).

Rooted in these cultural, anthropological, and theological foundations, the formulation of the church as family enriches, reconstructs, and contributes to a new way of relating with others that leads to a civilization of love, community, and service.[58] The image of family emphasizes care for others, solidarity, warmth in human relationships, acceptance, and dialogue. In this sense, the concept of the church as a family of God's people highlights the liberating, ethical, and compassionate principles needed to reach our suffering brothers and sisters in Africa (see *EA* §63). It also allows the church to see herself as rooted in the daily struggles and hopes of the people, offering the light of Christ and constantly committing herself to their integral and sustainable development.

Church as Family and the Hope of Reconciliation, Justice, and Peace

Both the first and second African synods address the question of how the church as the family of God and servant of the Spirit might contribute to the mission of the church in the public sphere. The nature of this mission reveals the church's theological self-understanding and allows for her more effective participation in the promotion of reconciliation, justice, and peace, both within the church and in society.[59] Reconciliation begins with authen-

---

51. Gyekye, *African Cultural Values*, 24.
52. See Uzukwu, *God, Spirit, and Human Wholeness*, 154–58; Snyper, *Akan Rites of Passage*, 70–75.
53. Gyekye, *African Cultural Values*, 27.
54. Adawu, "Witnessing to a Just Hope," 7–8.
55. Gyekye, *African Cultural Values*, 24.
56. Gyekye, *African Cultural Values*, 24.
57. For an engaging discussion on a Trinitarian theology of relationships, see Ouellet, *Divine Likeness*; Thatcher, *Theology and Families*.
58. See Obiezu, "Church in Africa and the Search for Integral and Sustainable Development," 34–64.
59. Elenga, "Toward a New Social Configuration?"

tic conversion at the personal and communal level (*AM* §32). A personal conversion involves a sustained healing of the individual's relationship with God and neighbor through regular acts of penance and a commitment to charity. It is an openness to the healing of the wounds of division caused by our actions taken against others (and therefore against God) as well as the actions of others against us. At the communal level, reconciliation takes the form of a spirituality of communion focused on establishing all persons in "a love that heals through the working of God's word" and actions (*AM* §34). A spirituality of communion helps us to perceive the light of God "shining on the faces of brothers and sisters around us . . . in order to share their joys and sufferings, to sense their desires and attend to their needs, to offer them deep and genuine friendship" (*AM* §35).

Reconciliation is rooted in justice, understood as the development of right relationships[60] and as the grounds for upholding the inherent rights of all persons.[61] Justice as right relationships reflects a state of affairs in which we relate to God, to our neighbor, and to the rest of creation in a way that honors God and supports human flourishing.[62] Justice as the protection of inherent rights complements relational justice. "Rights are normative social relationships. . . . A right is a right *with regard to someone*."[63] Recognizing the inherent rights of others strengthens the relationship ties that individuals in society seek to develop.[64] In traditional African thought and practice, the responsibility to develop right relationships, as expressed through the notion of communalism, is not at variance with individual rights. "It is indeed the exercise of individual rights . . . that enhances cultural development and ensures the material and political success of the community."[65]

The model for the church as family becoming just and building a just social order is Christ, from whom the church receives her mission of truth and love. The task of the church as family is to be a sentinel of truth and an exemplar of love. The church carries out this task within the church and in the society as a whole. An example of practicing truth in love within the church is to seek communal conversion and reconciliation. The task of the church as family in this regard, as Teresa Okure observes, involves taking sustainable, gospel-based actions to ensure that all obstacles to authentic communion are removed. Specific actions include addressing the divide between the laity and the clergy, addressing the issue of women occupying positions of responsibility in the church, and the use of language that tends to subvert the gospel, such as dissociating the "sacred" from the "secular."[66] A church as family that consciously works toward healing its own wounds caused by long-standing divisions among its members will serve as a clear-sighted sentinel, a stronger voice for reconciliation, justice, and peace, and a better exemplar of love in society. Another example from African ecclesial history involves the way the church in Africa connects her identity as the family of God to her mission to pursue truth and justice.[67] In many parts of Africa, the church commits herself to speaking out for social justice and showing concern for the poor. In many instances, the church constitutes the light of truth and a clear voice in opposing social evils, particularly political machinations and decisions that threaten the sanctity of life and the well-being of all people. In their message to the people after the first African synod, the bishops spoke out against anti-life plans and decisions taken at the 1994 International Conference on Population

---

60. Humbach, "Towards a Natural Justice of Right Relationships," 41–61.
61. See Wolterstorff, *Justice: Rights and Wrongs*; Wolterstorff, *Justice in Love*.
62. Adawu, "Witnessing to a Just Hope," 4.
63. Wolterstorff, *Justice: Rights and Wrongs*, 4–6.
64. Humbach prioritizes justice as right relationships over justice as the recognition of rights: "Rights are at best a means to right relationships, a way of providing background conditions in which right relationships can be established and developed" ("Towards a Natural Justice of Right Relationships," 41).
65. Gyekye, *African Cultural Values*, 151.
66. Okure, "Church Family."
67. By encouraging "reconciliation and true communion" (*EA* §63), the church as family of God favors solidarity not only among its members but also with society at large, particularly where justice and the light of truth are sorely needed.

and Development (also known as the Cairo Conference). The bishops condemned in no uncertain terms plans that put pressure "on the poor nations to force them to choose options . . . which are contrary to life and morality."[68] At the same time, they highlighted areas of collaboration between the church and the United Nations in the promotion and development of peoples and asked, against the background of the International Year of the Family, that the decisions taken at the conference "not allow the African family to be ridiculed on its own soil," and that that year (1994) not "become the year of destruction of the family."[69] Without the light of truth, corrupt and unjust systems remain under the cover of darkness and the work of justice remains futile. Similarly, without love, justice degenerates into a mechanical and legalistic effort to heal relationships. For the Christian, true justice is *"the justice of love,"* . . . a revolution of love brought about by [Christ's] complete self-giving through his death and resurrection" (*AM* §§25–26).[70] By this justice of love, the poor are "consoled and admitted to the banquet of life" (*AM* §26) here and now and in the reign of God, which is to be fully realized at the end of time.

Peace is the fruit of reconciliation and justice and of relationships healed and restored in love and truth. Like reconciliation and justice, peace is rooted in Christ, whose person and work opened up a new horizon for a new order of peace, a horizon that surpasses the minimum demands of justice, namely, to give others their due. The peaceful order opened up in Christ invites the disciple to stand in solidarity with suffering humanity, even to the point of "laying down one's life for one's friends" (*AM* §28). The desire for peace leads the church as family "to be present wherever human suffering exists and to make heard the silent cry of the innocent who suffer persecution, or of peoples whose governments mortgage the present and the future for personal interests" (*AM* §30). The church's concrete works of love, which restore "peace to human hearts" (*AM* §29), are also signs of hope and revival. Over the years, the African church has been involved in restoring peace to the continent. Her enthusiastic faith and work toward development have contributed significantly to the establishment of peace on the African continent, as seen in the independence of states, the end of apartheid, the growing intolerance of dictatorships and human rights abuses, and the formation of governing bodies that allow Africans to address African political, economic, social, and cultural issues.[71] There remains much work to be done in reconciling peoples and achieving lasting peace on the continent, and so the church as family of God continues its works of peace through the *justice of love*.

Christian Ethics and the Praxis of Hope

The church's ongoing work of reconciliation, justice, and peace deepens and flourishes in the way she addresses the moral issues of our time. This work is particularly important because it is through addressing concrete moral issues that hope comes alive: "The church can only be the salt and light of African societies by how she shapes the minds and morals of African Christians, imbuing them with a sense of hope and transformative grace."[72] Christian hope follows from a real encounter with God, and it is life changing. In the words of Pope Benedict XVI, "The one who has hope lives differently; the one who hopes has been granted the gift of a new life" (*Spe Salvi* §2), and "All serious and upright human conduct is hope in action" (*Spe Salvi* §35). With these statements, Benedict highlights not just the salvific nature of Christian hope but also its ethical character. The hope that saves is not individualistic but creates opportunities for ethical awareness and moral decision-making, compelling the Christian to reach out in charity to the whole of humanity. The focus on the connection between morality and hope is especially applicable to the African context, as evidenced in the works of Paulinus Odozor and Katongole discussed below.

---

68. Bishops of Africa, *Message of the Synod*, 30.
69. Bishops of Africa, *Message of the Synod*, 30.
70. Bracketed insertion is mine.
71. Ojacor, "Church in Africa and the Search for Abundant Life," 88–90.
72. Ilo and Ogbonnaya, "Introduction," xix.

Pope Benedict emphasizes that the moral well-being of the world cannot be guaranteed by material structures alone. It requires that the freedom of all persons be acknowledged and that all are invited to assent freely to the social order. In other words, Christian hope seeks to transform not only the external material structures of society but also the inner moral structures of every person. Christian hope engages our human agency and freedom and commits us to live for others. It is in hope, rooted in the certainty of God's love, that we can act uprightly and courageously, even in the face of hostility and failure: "Only the great certitude of hope that my own life and history in general, despite all failures, are held firm by the indestructible power of Love, . . . only this kind of hope can then give the courage to act and to persevere" (*Spe Salvi* §35).

The connections between works of hope and Christian ethics underpin the call of the African synods to the church as family to seek communion, reconciliation, justice, and peace. This is evidenced in the works of a number of African theologians. Paulinus Ikechukwu Odozor, for example, discusses the African synodal traditions in the light of Christian ethics. He draws a close connection between ecclesiology and moral theology, describing the church as family in Africa as "a community of moral discourse—that is, . . . a community that deliberates on and teaches about what should be done or left undone in Africa and by African Christians in light of the teachings, deeds and life of Jesus."[73] He highlights moral issues associated with leadership and governance and with the way women are treated on the continent. Citing Cardinal Turkson's report after the discussions at the second African synod (*Relatio Post Disceptationem*), Odozor observes that, although some women in Africa are making great strides for themselves and in their work on issues facing the continent, many women remain "underdeveloped resources, suffering exclusion from social roles, inheritance, education, and decision-making places."[74]

Emmanuel Katongole also draws our attention to the centrality of hope in transforming the dire circumstances on the African continent. Katongole points to the second African synod's emphasis on hope as critical in mobilizing "spiritual energies and material resources to relieve Africa's burden, and so to open Africans to the fullness of life in Christ."[75] He further points to Pope Benedict XVI's claim that there are "grounds for hope in Africa's rich intellectual, cultural and religious heritage."[76] For Katongole, however, such claims of hope remain prescriptive, as they do not offer narratives that might shed light on how hope actually and concretely works to bring about desired transformation. He calls for a narrative theological praxis of hope and actually demonstrates how such hope can highlight the voices of individuals whose life experiences speak to and show the connection between hope, suffering and lament, and transformation.[77]

Conclusion: The African Church as the Servant of Families and Children

The African synods apply the image of the family to the church. The primary focus of the discussion in both synods is not the family per se but how to understand the identity and mission of the church in Africa and in the world. Surely, there are discussions about the family and even recommendations for making family life better, but the focus of these discussions is related to how families serve the church. Staying true to their focus on the church, the African synodal traditions regard the family primarily as an agent of evangelization and promoter of reconciliation, peace, and justice in service to the church.

---

73. Odozor, *Morality, Truly Christian, Truly African*, 271.
74. Odozor, *Morality, Truly Christian, Truly African*, 288.
75. Katongole, *Born from Lament*, 25.
76. Katongole, *Born from Lament*, 25.
77. Katongole, *Born from Lament*, 25. For example, Katongole tells the deeply wrenching stories of courageous Christian activists working for change in East Africa and calls on the church and all people of good will to enter into lament and hope with them.

The time has come, however, to take a closer look at the concrete experiences of families and to discuss the notion of a church in service to families in Africa and in the world; that is, we must not only ask about the role of the family in the life of the church but also about the role of the church in the life of the family. The questions are similar and complementary, but their starting points and emphases differ. The synodal traditions ask about the meaning and mission of the church and how the family contributes to an understanding of this meaning and mission. The new questions we need to ask are about the nature of the family and how the church can help families everywhere thrive. It would require more space than we have in this chapter to adequately answer these new questions, but it is important to make some concluding recommendations that might help guide future research on some of the key themes discussed in this chapter.

First, the hope offered through an understanding and practice of the church as the family of God will be short-lived if the African church does not resist the negative influences bearing down on the family both from within and from outside the borders of Africa, especially policies that threaten Africa's openness to life and her efforts to safeguard the dignity and role of marriage (*EA* §§83–85). The church in Africa must also address certain negative tendencies that are part of the idea and reality of family life in Africa, such as ethnocentrism and injustices against children and women.[78] By way of addressing these tendencies from a theological standpoint, Pope John Paul II put forward the Holy Family of Jesus, Mary, and Joseph as an example for all families (*EA* §81). The example of the Holy Family provides a solid biblical understanding for how families discern and respond to God's plans for their lives. There is great benefit in looking at the example of the Holy Family in light of the realities of families burdened with suffering yet filled with hope. Such a perspective will allow us to pursue justice for families in Africa, especially for children and women, and for families whose work and livelihood are threatened by corrupt leadership and harmful foreign trade policies.[79]

Second, seeking the well-being of families requires a revision of our understanding of family in Africa, both theologically and pastorally. It requires that we diligently seek the plan of God for families, take seriously the complex experiences of families, and faithfully and creatively place the teachings and resources of the church at their service. When we consider the many questions that surround the changing nature and life of families in Africa, it is imperative that we begin to shift the way we theologize about and pastorally respond to families. Issues of poverty, polygamy, single parenthood, separation, divorce, infidelity, violence in families, and abuse of children compel us to discern the will of God for families in Africa and take positive action to bring about desired change.[80] The model for this paradigm shift is Christ's own approach to attending to the wounds and hopes of humanity, captured in his words that "the Son of Man came not to be served but to serve and to give his life as a ransom for many" (Mark 10:45). The church must continue to develop the same attitude toward families. The 2014 and 2015 synods on the family, which resulted in Pope Francis's apostolic exhortation *Amoris Laetitia* (March 19, 2016), provide the foundation and context for envisioning a church that serves families, not just a church that is served by families. The African bishops not only contributed to the conversation at these synods but also dedicated the seventeenth plenary meeting of SECAM in Luanda, Angola (July 18–25, 2016), to addressing the challenges facing families in Africa in light of the gospel, providing the African church a way forward.

Finally, our theological and pastoral focus on families in Africa should pay radical attention to the continent's children. That Africa is a continent of children, who make up more than 40 percent of its population, is a fact that our theological discourse cannot and must not overlook. In our efforts to seek an understanding of our faith in the African context, we can no longer be silent about their experiences, anxieties, and hopes. The second

---

78. Obiezu, "Church in Africa and the Search for Integral and Sustainable Development," 46–57.
79. Obiezu, "Church in Africa and the Search for Integral and Sustainable Development," 46–47.
80. Orobator, "State of the African Family," 41.

synod for Africa began a conversation about children, even if briefly, describing children as a source of hope for their families, the church, and society. It also highlights the plight of children on the continent and pledges strongly, and with urgency, to protect each one of them. In spite of the urgency articulated in the synodal documents, an intentional focus on children as a theological theme remains conspicuously absent from African Catholic theological scholarship. In many instances, not even essays about the values of and challenges facing the African family make a specific case for a committed focus on children. As a church, our theology as it relates to children has, for the most part, focused on the protection of life from conception, and on questions about parenting and faith formation. These are absolutely critical matters and we must continue discussing them, but our theology and pastoral practice need to expand to many other issues pertaining to children, including their beauty, mystery, and spirituality, and, unfortunately, their vulnerability and the abuse, rejection, and enslavement they experience through trafficking. There is in Africa the child on the street, the child accused of witchcraft, and the child abandoned because of physical or mental disability. A theological silence about these children imperils their lives, the lives of families, and the continent as a whole. In short, we must embrace children in our theological praxis with tenacity if the African synodal traditions are to have relevance for people in Africa and elsewhere. We cannot develop a theological praxis of hope based on the two African synods without at the same time developing a theology of children and their well-being in Africa. Theological methodologies that place praxis at the center, rather than on the peripheries, of what theologians are trying to achieve can strengthen the church's witness and make the fruits of the synods available and relevant to families, especially to children, and to the African society as a whole.

Bibliography

Adawu, Anthony. "Witnessing to a Just Hope: A Theology of the Child in Contemporary Africa." PhD diss., St. Thomas University, Miami Gardens, FL, 2017. ProQuest.

Benedict XVI, Pope. *Africae Munus* [Post-synodal Apostolic Exhortation on the Church in Africa in Service of Reconciliation, Justice and Peace; November 19, 2011]. Vatican City: Libreria Editrice Vaticana, 2011. www.vatican.va.

———. "Homily at the Opening Mass of the Second Special Assembly for Africa of the Synod of Bishops" (2009).

———. *Spe Salvi* [Encyclical "Saved in Hope"; November 30, 2007]. www.vatican.va.

Béré, Paul. "The Word of God as Transformative Power in Reconciling African Christians." In *Reconciliation, Justice, and Peace: The Second African Synod*, edited by Agbonkhianmeghe Orobator, chapter 4. Maryknoll, NY: Orbis Books, 2011. Kindle edition.

Bishops of Africa. *Message of the Synod: First Special Assembly for the Church in Africa* (1994).

———. *Message to the People of God of the Second Special Assembly for Africa of the Synod of Bishops* (2009).

Brown, Sally, and Patrick Miller, eds. *Lament: Reclaiming Practices in Pulpit, Pew, and Public Square*. Louisville, KY: Westminster John Knox, 2005.

Brueggemann, Walter. *The Message of the Psalms: A Theological Commentary*. Minneapolis: Fortress Press, 1984.

Elenga, Yvon Christina. "Toward a New Social Configuration? The Role of the Catholic Church in the Public Sphere." In *Reconciliation, Justice, and Peace: The Second African Synod*, edited by Agbonkhianmeghe E. Orobator, chapter 7. Maryknoll, NY: Orbis Books, 2011. Kindle edition.

Francis, Pope. "Homily at the Celebration of Palm Sunday of the Passion of the Lord, XXVIII World Youth Day" (March 24, 2013).

General Secretariat of the Synod of Bishops. *Lineamenta*: Preparatory Document for the First Special Assembly for Africa (2006).

———. *Elenchus Finalis Propositionum*: Final List of Propositions of the Second Special Assembly for Africa of the Synod of Bishops (2009).

Gyekye, Kwame. *African Cultural Values: An Introduction*. Accra, Ghana: Sankofa, 2003.

Havey, Francis. "African Synods." In *The Catholic Encyclopedia*, vol. 1. New York: Robert Appleton Company, 1907. http://www.newadvent.org/cathen/01199a.htm.

Hefele, Charles Joseph. *A History of the Christian Councils: From the Original Documents*. Vol. 1: *To the Close of the Council of Nicaea, A.D. 325*. 2nd rev. ed. Translated and edited by William R. Clark. Edinburgh: T. & T. Clark, 1883.

Humbach, John A. "Towards a Natural Justice of Right Relationships." In *Human Rights in Philosophy and Practice*, edited by Burton M. Leiser and Tom D. Campbell, 41–61. Burlington, VT: Ashgate, 2001.

Ilo, Stan Chu. "*Africae Munus* and the Challenges of Transformative Missional Theological Praxis in Africa's Social Context." *Transformation* 31.2 (2014): 116–31.

———. "Beginning Afresh with Christ in the Search for Abundant Life in Africa." In *The Church as Salt and Light: Path to an African Ecclesiology of Abundant Life*, edited by Stan Chu Ilo, Joseph Ogbonnaya, and Alex Ojacor, 1–33. Eugene, OR: Pickwick, 2011.

———. *The Church and Development in Africa: Aid and Development from the Perspective of Catholic Social Ethics*. 2nd ed. Eugene, OR: Pickwick, 2014. Kindle edition.

———. "The Second African Synod and the Challenges of Reconciliation, Justice, and Peace in Africa's Social Context: A Missional Theological Praxis for Transformation. Part 1." *Missiology: An International Review* 11.2 (April 2012): 195–204.

———. "The Second African Synod and the Challenges of Reconciliation, Justice, and Peace in Africa's Social Context: A Missional Theological Praxis for Transformation. Part 2." *Missiology: An International Review* 11.3 (July 2012): 249–60.

Ilo, Stan Chu, and Joseph Ogbonnaya. "Introduction." In *The Church as Salt and Light: Path to an African Ecclesiology of Abundant Life*, edited by Stan Chu Ilo, Joseph Ogbonnaya, and Alex Ojacor, xiii–xxi. Eugene, OR: Pickwick, 2011.

Ilo, Stan Chu, Joseph Ogbonnaya, and Alex Ojacor, eds. *The Church as Salt and Light: Path to an African Ecclesiology of Abundant Life*. Eugene, OR: Pickwick, 2011.

John Paul II, Pope. "Address to the 6th Meeting of the General Secretariat of the Synod of Bishops for the Special Assembly for Africa." June 9, 1992.

———. *Ecclesia in Africa* [Post-synodal Apostolic Exhortation on the Church in Africa and Its Evangelizing Mission toward the Year 2000; September 14, 1995]. Vatican City: Libreria Editrice Vaticana, 1995. www.vatican.va.

Katongole, Emmanuel. *Born from Lament: The Theology and Politics of Hope in Africa*. Grand Rapids: Eerdmans, 2017.

———. "The Church of the Future: Pressing Moral Issues from *Ecclesia in Africa*." In *The Church We Want: African Catholics Look to Vatican III*, ed. Agbonkhianmeghe E. Orobator, 161–73. Maryknoll, NY: Orbis Books, 2016.

Metz, Johann Baptist. *Faith in History and Society: Toward a Practical Fundamental Theology*. New York: Crossroad, 2007.

Mucherera, Tapiwa N., and Emmanuel Y. Lartey, eds. *Pastoral Care, Health, Healing, and Wholeness in Africa: Methodology, Context, and Issues*. African Practical Theology Series 1. Eugene, OR: Wipf & Stock, 2017.

Müller, Gerhard, with Carlos Granados. *The Cardinal Müller Report: An Exclusive Interview on the State of the Church*. San Francisco: Ignatius Press, 2017.

Muzorewa, Gwinyai H. *The Origins and Development of African Theology*. Eugene, OR: Wipf & Stock, 1987.

Mwale, Jones Chitalu. *Relationality in Theological Anthropology: An African Perspective*. Saarbrücken: Lambert, 2013.

Obiezu, Emeka Xris. "The Church in Africa and the Search for Integral and Sustainable Development of Africa: Toward a Socio-Economic and Politically Responsive Church." In *The Church as Salt and Light: Path to an African Ecclesiology of Abundant Life*, edited by Stan Chu Ilo, Joseph Ogbonnaya, and Alex Ojacor, 34–64. Eugene, OR: Pickwick, 2011.

Odozor, Paulinus I. *Morality, Truly Christian, Truly African: Foundational, Methodological, and Theological Considerations*. Notre Dame, IN: University of Notre Dame Press, 2014.

Ogbonnaya, Joseph. *African Catholicism and Hermeneutics of Culture: Essays in the Light of African Synod II*. Eugene, OR: Wipf & Stock, 2014.

———. "The Church in Africa: Salt of the Earth?" In *The Church as Salt and Light: Path to an African Ecclesiology of Abundant Life*, edited by Stan Chu Ilo, Joseph Ogbonnaya, and Alex Ojacor, 65–87. Eugene, OR: Pickwick, 2011.

———. *Lonergan, Social Transformation, and Sustainable Human Development*. Eugene, OR: Pickwick, 2013.

Ojacor, Alex. "The Church in Africa and the Search for Abundant Life: Signposts for Renewal and Transformation for God's People in Africa." In *The Church as Salt and Light: Path to an African Ecclesiology of Abundant Life*, edited by Stan Chu Ilo, Joseph Ogbonnaya, and Alex Ojacor, 88–98. Eugene, OR: Pickwick, 2011.

Okure, Teresa. "Church Family as the Place of God's Reconciliation, Justice and Peace." In *Reconciliation, Justice and Peace: The Second African Synod*, edited by Agbonkhianmeghe E. Orobator, chapter 1. Maryknoll, NY: Orbis Books, 2011. Kindle edition.

Opongo, Elias Omondi. "Inventing Creative Approaches to Complex Systems of Injustice: A New Call for a Vigilant and Engaged Church." In *Reconciliation, Justice and Peace: The Second African Synod*, edited by Agbonkhianmeghe E. Orobator, chapter 6. Maryknoll, NY: Orbis Books, 2011. Kindle edition.

Orobator, Agbonkhianmeghe E. *From Crisis to Kairos: The Mission of the Church in the Time of HIV/AIDS, Refugees, and Poverty*. Nairobi: Paulines Publications, 2005.

———, ed. *Reconciliation, Justice, and Peace: The Second African Synod*. Maryknoll, NY: Orbis Books, 2011.

———. "The State of the African Family: A Layman's Appraisal." In *African Family Today*, edited by Giuseppe Caramazza and Beatrice Churu, 40–50. Nairobi: Paulines Publications, 2015.

Ouellet, Marc. *Divine Likeness: Toward a Trinitarian Anthropology of the Family*. Translated by Philip Milligan and Linda M. Cicone. Grand Rapids: Eerdmans, 2006.

Schotte, Jan P. "Preface to the Instrumentum Laboris for the First Special Assembly for Africa." February 7, 1993.

Snyper, Robert C. *Akan Rites of Passage and Their Reception into Christianity: A Theological Synthesis*. Frankfurt am Main: Peter Lang, 2003.

Thatcher, Adrian. *Theology and Families*. Malden, MA: Blackwell, 2007.

Turkson, Peter K. A. "Keynote Address: The New Evangelization for the Transmission of the Christian Faith in Ghana in the Light of Africae Munus." In Ghana Catholic Bishops' Conference, *Acts of the 2014 National Pastoral Congress*. Accra, Ghana: GCBC, 2016.

Uzukwu, E. Elochukwu. *God, Spirit, and Human Wholeness: Appropriating Faith and Culture in West African Style*. Eugene, OR: Pickwick, 2012.

———. *A Listening Church: Autonomy and Communion in Africa Churches*. Eugene, OR: Wipf & Stock, 2006.

Vatican Council II. *Gaudium et Spes* [Pastoral Constitution of the Church in the Modern World; 1965]. www.vatican.va.

Wolterstorff, Nicholas. *Justice: Rights and Wrongs*. Princeton, NJ: Princeton University Press, 2008.

———. *Justice in Love*. Grand Rapids: Eerdmans, 2011.

Suggested Reading

African Bishops. *Christ's New Homeland—Africa: Contribution to the Synod on the Family*. Translated by Michael J. Miller. San Francisco: Ignatius Press, 2015.

Browning, Don S. *Equality and the Family: A Fundamental, Practical Theology of Children, Mothers, and Fathers in Modern Societies*. Grand Rapids: Eerdmans, 2007.

Dillen, Annemie, and Didier Pollefeyt, eds. *Children's Voices: Children's Perspectives in Ethics, Theology, and Religious Education*. Leuven: Peeters, 2010.

Francis, Pope. *Amoris Laetitia* [Post-synodal Apostolic Exhortation on Love in the Family; March 19, 2016]. Vatican City: Libreria Editrice Vaticana, 2016. www.vatican.va.

Imoh, Afua Twum-Danso, and Nicola Ansell, eds. *Children's Lives in an Era of Children's Rights: The Progress of the Convention on the Rights of the Child in Africa*. New York: Routledge, 2014.

Pontifical Council for the Family. *Compendium on the Family and Human Life*. Vatican City: Libreria Editrice Vaticana, 2015.

Key Words

children as sources of hope
Christian ethics and the praxis of hope
Church as family of God
Church as servant of families and children
hope of communion
synodal process
synodal tradition
theological praxis of hope

Epilogue: Dreaming about the Future of the Church in Africa

Laurenti Magesa

The Ongoing Task of "Inventing" Church Tradition

Attempting to predict a possible, or even probable, profile of the future African Christian church from the present vantage point is something of a perilous task. Yet it should be seen neither as necessarily a naïve undertaking nor a futile exercise in futurology. On the contrary, the endeavor is quite rational and useful, particularly when guided by empirical data and other reliable indicators within the life of the church itself. Based on the environment in which the church lives, in which the pace of change can be overwhelming, to profile the future of the African church is an essential endeavor if the church is not to be overtaken by events. Even though, precisely because of the rapid transformations happening in the church and in the world, a completely accurate prognosis of the nature of the church to come may not be possible, it is still prudent to prepare for and plan for possible eventualities. A certain degree of "dreaming" about the future of the church is an unavoidable necessity.

Just like any other human organization, the church as a visible institution necessarily comprises clear structures of leadership. Its internal life is organized around and guided by certain teachings, rituals, regulations, and practices or customs that are informed and shaped by a system of ideas and beliefs called "theology." As it exerts its influence upon the visible structures and the inner life of the church, theology is itself, in turn, simultaneously and continually informed and shaped by them. The practical, day-to-day life of the church, its "tradition," is thus constructed or "invented" on an ongoing basis.[1]

The church's external structures and its inner life and theology are dynamic and evolving—again, even more so in today's world than ever before. Paradoxically, the homogeneity that the globalization movement aims to foster in the areas of economics, politics, and general culture also promotes diversity. The unconstrained and massive flow of global travel and globally available information has, in an unprecedented way, made diversity evident as a value to be guarded and preserved. Globalization has rendered social interactions very complex—nothing like those the world knew only a half century ago.

Globalization has thrown church structures, teachings, and practices in Africa and elsewhere into constant flux. Theological propositions that were thought perpetually settled are now being challenged by developments in practically all areas of knowledge. New scientific findings, technological discoveries, and developments in the fields of physics, chemistry, biology, anthropology, psychology, geography, and paleontology, among many others, are raising new and hitherto unimagined ethical questions. As various African peoples of faith become more and more aware of their cultural identities and cultural dignity and rights within the church, they are questioning certain long-standing theological positions, rituals, regulations, and practices as these have been inculcated on the continent for more than the two centuries that have passed

---

1. See Tilley, *Inventing Catholic Tradition*.

since Africa's third encounter with the gospel. Pope Francis has recently commented that

> today's vast and rapid cultural changes demand that we constantly seek ways of expressing unchanging truths in a language which brings out their abiding newness. "The deposit of the faith is one thing . . . the way it is expressed is another." There are times when the faithful, in listening to completely orthodox language, take away something alien to the authentic Gospel of Jesus Christ, because that language is alien to their own way of speaking to and understanding one another. With the holy intent of communicating the truth about God and humanity, we sometimes give them a false god or a human ideal which is not really Christian. In this way, we hold fast to a formulation while failing to convey its substance. This is the greatest danger. Let us never forget that "the expression of truth can take different forms. The renewal of these forms of expression becomes necessary for the sake of transmitting to the people of today the Gospel message in its unchanging meaning."[2]

Consequently, an attempt to paint a portrait of the future of the church in Africa necessarily involves a consideration or reconsideration of as many aspects of the organism that is the church as possible, including its past positions, present mutations, and possible future condition. In a word, it requires some invention of tradition. Urgent questions have to be faced, such as, Why was the church the way it was in the past in Africa? Why and how is it different today? What are the forces that constrain it to take on a different expression in order to meet the future?

In this reflection, I wish to consider the shifts in the African church's self-understanding and tradition over the last few decades based on three major pivots: first, the church's very recent and phenomenal numerical growth on the continent; second, the structural transformations that this growth has necessitated; and, third, the theological thinking that has emerged to authorize and legitimize these transformations.

Remarkable Shifts: The Movement of Christianity into Europe

From the time of the church's founding up to about the seventh century CE, Africa contributed tremendously to the development of the church's thought and structures. It is not actually possible to discuss the shape of the Christian church today without accounting for the impact of the ancient patriarchate of Alexandria in Egypt and the episcopal see of Carthage in present-day Tunisia with their renowned catechetical schools and teachers. Omitting the names of figures like Clement of Alexandria and Origen and the stories of the courageous martyrs Perpetua, Felicity, and their companions, produces an incomplete history of Christianity. The pastoral zeal of Cyprian, Carthage's bishop-martyr, who coined the maxim *Extra ecclesiam nulla salus* ("Outside the church there is no salvation"), remains legendary in the annals of the universal church.

Numerous other individuals and movements in Africa that put an indelible mark on the Christian tradition come easily to mind. Special mention must be made of Tertullian of Carthage and Augustine of Hippo (modern Annaba in Algeria, North Africa). The monastic movement that historian John Baur characterizes as "the greatest contribution of the African continent to the universal Church"[3] had its origins and took shape in Egypt under the tutelage of such towering spiritual figures as Anthony and Pachomius. The origins of Gnosticism and monophysitism, philosophical and theological orientations that have deeply marked the shape and character of Christianity and the church throughout the world, can also be traced to Africa.

But, at a certain point, there was a shift in the tradition, impelled by political necessities. Joseph H. Lynch notes that there is "no precise date" at which to fix the movement of Christianity from the Middle East and Africa to Europe—it was "a

---

2. Francis, post-synodal apostolic exhortation *Evangelii Gaudium* §41 (hereinafter *EG*).
3. Baur, *2000 Years of Christianity in Africa*, 24. For an examination of the first encounter of the church with Africa, see 99–240.

long process" strongly connected to the decline of the Roman Empire, with which "Christianity had allied itself."[4] Without imperial protection, Christianity had to find ways to relate to invaders from the north if it was to endure. As a matter of the survival of the church, Pope Gregory I (also known as "the Great" [pope 590–604]) and his successors, as well as the emerging Christian missionaries, cultivated relations with the "pagan" Spanish Visigoths, the Germanic peoples, and the Celtic, Anglo-Saxon, and Frankish tribes, who were gradually assimilated into a new "Christian" culture. Now shaped by a mixture of Roman customs and those of these converts, the Christian tradition had changed considerably by the dawn of the second millennium.

Understandably, after the chaos accompanying the collapse of the Roman Empire, there was, according to Lynch, "a desire for order and hierarchy" among those shaping this tradition.[5] The Carolingian dynasty in Western Europe (750–850) "set the religious life . . . [there] on a new course,"[6] a new tradition, different from the earlier one born in Palestine and northern Africa. As a consequence, there emerged in the European church novel structural and attitudinal realities: "A growing respect for the prestige and authority of the papacy, a sharper separation of the clergy from the laity, a Benedictinization of monasticism and an incorporation of the laity into a sturdy parish framework in which they received the sacraments, paid their tithes and shaped their moral behaviour and social lives."[7]

An elaborate new ecclesiology developed based on this need for order—Christ was invested with "kingly" powers, and the pope and bishops were seen to carry Petrine and apostolic authority as their "successors." Numerous rural parishes administered by priests (the lower clergy) were created that were under the authority of bishops. Religious houses, guided almost exclusively by the Benedictine rule, concerned themselves with worship. Up to the end of the late Middle Ages (1301–1500) this became the accepted framework that governed the church of Europe, and, despite intermittent interruptions, it proved extremely resilient.

Even though the unity of institutional Christianity was seriously fractured by the Protestant Reformation of the sixteenth century, much of the theological and structural legacy invented during the Middle Ages remained substantially intact and was inherited by the various denominations in the wake of the Reformation, including Catholicism, Lutheranism, Calvinism, and Anglicanism. In the main, it was this legacy that was carried over into Africa by European missionaries, initially in a limited way, in the sixteenth and seventeenth centuries, which Baur describes as the second meeting of Africa with Christianity, and then from the nineteenth century onward, what Baur terms the third encounter.[8]

Remarkable Shifts: The Movement of Christianity into Africa

Christianity's second encounter with Africa failed to leave a significant and lasting impression on the continent. Usually accompanying the slave traders as chaplains, the missionaries made little meaningful contact with—or sense to—the indigenous populations. The missionaries harbored certain deeply held uncertainties concerning the African peoples' dignity as human beings as well as concerning the value of their cultures. Even in the kingdoms of Kongo (comprising parts of the modern Democratic Republic of the Congo and Angola), where some conversions were made, the Christian influence was minimal. During the third encounter, however, Christianity has had an extraordinary impact on Africa, necessitating a novel and more positive outlook on African cultures that, to some in the church, has been rather difficult to accept on account of the previous historical mentality and practices vis-à-vis Africa.

The numerical growth of Christianity in sub-Saharan Africa since the end of the nineteenth century has been variously described by sociologists of

---

4. See Lynch, *Medieval Church*, 19–34.
5. Lynch, *Medieval Church*, 83.
6. Lynch, *Medieval Church*, 83.
7. Lynch, *Medieval Church*, 83.
8. See Baur, *2000 Years of Christianity in Africa*.

religion as "explosive," "massive," and "soaring." In just over 150 years, the center of Christianity has, at least in statistical terms, moved from Europe to Africa, Asia, and Latin America, with Africa being at the forefront of the shift. Research conducted by the Pew Research Center shows that, from making up only 1.4 percent of the Christian population worldwide in 1900, Christians in Africa increased to 23.6 percent of the total in 2010. This research shows that "the fastest growth in the number of Christians in the past century has been in sub-Saharan Africa (a roughly 60-fold increase, from fewer than 9 million in 1910 to more than 516 million in 2010)."[9]

The tradition has shifted on another front as well. From bearing the demeaning status of an exclusively "mission field" or "mission territory" in terms of personnel and resources only a few decades ago, Africa is now sending missionaries to the Global North and, with them, its brand of Christianity. Missionary congregations of African origin have pastoral agents serving as far afield as the United Kingdom and the United States. Immigration of African Christians to other parts of the world, where they establish themselves and need spiritual care that is comprehensible to them, has contributed to the growth of a new tradition in the church.[10] Thus, whereas barely a century ago the Christian church in all its forms was exclusively European, by the mid-twentieth century the African church had become vocal in demanding modifications to the theology, structures, and practices applied to it.

The "moratorium" debate in Africa in the 1970s provides an interesting example. In 1971, Rev. John Gatu, the general secretary of the Presbyterian Church of East Africa, proposed that there be a halt to Western personnel and funds provided to the African churches. He saw this as necessary so that the latter could learn to stand on their own feet. Understandably, the idea received a mixed reception, even among the African churches themselves, but it did not die. It surfaced again in 1974 as a subject of discussion at the All Africa Conference of Churches (AACC) in Lusaka, Zambia. Even if the proposal had a limited influence, the fact that the idea was broached at all indicated a shift in tradition. It showed that Christianity in Africa was developing a new level of self-awareness and identity, requiring a new understanding.

The elevation of indigenous Africans to positions of high leadership in the churches, which happened around this time, was an indication of the impact of this awareness on the structures of the African church and society and made it possible for the voice of the African church to be heard in some important global church forums, even if as yet feebly and cautiously. In the mid-twentieth century, an increasing number of African churches gained membership in the World Council of Churches (WCC), and in 1963 the AACC was established, bringing together numerous mainline Protestant denominations as well as some African Initiated or African Independent Churches (AICs) to deliberate on global issues of mutual interest. Gradual though it was, this development began to affect the conversation in the universal church, even though, as Ian Linden notes, the African churches at the time were, regardless of the color of the faces of their leaders, still fundamentally "European."[11]

For the Catholic Church, which is not a member of the WCC, the most significant shift in ecclesiological tradition happened with the Second Vatican Council (1962–1965). Both the council's process and conclusions were important for this change. There were very few indigenous African representatives present at the council, and the representatives who were present had undergone European theological formation and held a Europe-centered understanding of Christianity. The view that "Christianity is Europe and Europe is Christianity" still largely held sway at the council's conclusion. Yet, in what may be described as the working of the spirit of God, who "can write straight with crooked lines" as the saying goes, the bishops from Africa made a significant impression on their colleagues at the council. They got the continent noticed. John W. O'Malley reports that they were "particu-

---

9. Pew Research Center, "Global Christianity," lines 97–100.
10. See Leys, "African Missionaries"; see also ter Haar, *Halfway to Paradise*.
11. Linden, *Global Catholicism*, 33.

larly well organized," "tended to sympathize with the majority," and "voted almost unanimously on issues." And so, "Although they, like other non-Europeans, had a generally low profile at the council, their coherence made them a strong influence."[12]

Remarkable Shifts: Dreaming a Future African Church

The presence of the African churches on the worldwide ecclesiastical scene as members of the WCC and participants at Vatican II fostered a general shift in ecclesiology and theology. It strengthened the dream of a truly African church in several ways, including the need for a deeper integration of theology into the spiritual *Weltanschauung* of the peoples of the continent, an expression of the Christian faith that is part and parcel of and responsive to their spiritual and religious imagination and practice, and structures founded on the continent's sociopolitical culture.

At these encounters on the world stage, the gap between the Christianity of the missionaries, inspired by and rooted in the West, on the one hand, and the indigenous African "language" of the faith on the other, was becoming increasingly evident. Whereas it was incontestable that the presence of the Christian faith in Africa had, even at this time, generated strong witnesses of faith in Christ, it remained arguable whether this was in spite of, rather than fundamentally because of, Africa's intrinsic spiritual and theological gifts, informed by the gospel, for inspiring individuals and groups toward heroic Christian virtue. In any event, the dichotomy between the European and African "languages" of faith was increasingly recognized by perceptive Christian faithful in the world church as being undesirable. The phenomenal quantitative growth of Christianity on the continent together with its theological shallowness was raising serious concerns.

What kind of Christian faith practices exist among African Christians, and how, if at all, do they differ from those bequeathed to the African church by the missionary pioneers, practices that were embedded in and informed by a philosophical and material culture alien to the continent? Taking into account contemporary ecclesiological understandings, what should be the orientation of the church with respect to its formulation and expression of the faith, its relationship to the public square, and its attitude toward interreligious relations? These questions call for a reflection about how the future African church should be constructed and how its new tradition should be oriented. Because of its phenomenal growth, the impetus toward building a church sensitive to the realities and needs of the African faithful has always been inevitable.

That some of these concerns had caught the attention of church authorities by the middle of the last century corroborated the strength of the need for the African church to branch out in new directions. In Catholic Christianity, for example, Pope John XXIII addressed this need in 1959 by encouraging African artists to bring their talents to the service of the faith in the continent. Though the church had for centuries been associated with Europe, the pope averred that it "is not bound to any culture." Presaging the council's Declaration on the Relation of the Christian to Non-Christian Religions (*Nostra Aetate*), he noted that, in its mission of salvation, the church "remains disposed to recognize, to accept, and even to animate whatever is to the honour of the human mind and heart in any part of the world other than the Mediterranean basin, notwithstanding that here stood the providential cradle of Christianity."[13] More recently, reflecting the same understanding, Pope Francis wrote in *Evangelii Gaudium* that "the faith cannot be constricted to the limits of understanding and expression of any one culture. It is an indisputable fact that no single culture can exhaust the mystery of our redemption in Christ" (*EG* §118) and also:

The history of the Church shows that Christianity does not have simply one cultural expression, but rather, "remaining completely true to itself, with unswerving fidelity to the

---

12. O'Malley, *What Happened at Vatican II*, 122.

13. Pope John XXIII, "Allocution to African Writers & Artists," 13. This sentiment was reflected in *Nostra Aetate* §2.

proclamation of the Gospel and the tradition of the Church, it will also reflect the different faces of the cultures and peoples in which it is received and takes root." In the diversity of peoples who experience the gift of God, each in accordance with its own culture, the Church expresses her genuine catholicity and shows forth the "beauty of her varied face." In the Christian customs of an evangelized people, the Holy Spirit adorns the Church, showing her new aspects of revelation and giving her a new face. Through inculturation, the Church "introduces peoples, together with their cultures, into her own community," for "every culture offers positive values and forms which can enrich the way the Gospel is preached, understood and lived." In this way, the Church takes up the values of different cultures and becomes *sponsa ornata monilibus suis*, "the bride bedecked with her jewels." Cf. Is. 61:10. (*EG* §116)

But perhaps the most striking and direct statement with reference to Africa came in 1967 in a message to the church in Africa by Pope Paul VI, the immediate successor to John XXIII. After listing a number of African cultural values he deemed to be divinely inspired, he stated that "the teaching of Jesus Christ and his redemption are, in fact, the complement, the renewal, and the bringing to perfection of all that is good in human tradition," and, after describing certain African values, Pope Paul further affirmed that Africa possesses salvific traditions. "*And that is why*," he concluded, "*the African, who becomes a Christian, does not disown himself [or herself], but takes up the age-old values of tradition 'in spirit and in truth,'*"[14] and, guided by faith in Jesus, constructs a new African Christian tradition.

Two years later, in 1969, Pope Paul VI emphasized the importance of Africans retaining their cultural identity within the church while inaugurating the Symposium of Episcopal Conferences of Africa and Madagascar (SECAM), the continent-wide organization of Catholic bishops, in Kampala, Uganda. Foreshadowing the already mentioned moratorium debate that was to take place a few years later, he urged Africans to be their own missionaries with a distinctive expression of the gospel. "*The expression, that is, the language and mode of manifesting this one Faith [in Christ], may be manifold,*" he affirmed. "Hence, it may be original, suited to the tongue, the style, the character, the genius, and the culture of the one who professes this one Faith."[15] And so,

> From this point of view, a certain pluralism is not only legitimate, but desirable. An adaptation of the Christian life in the fields of pastoral, ritual, didactic and spiritual activities is not only possible, it is even favoured by the Church. The liturgical renewal is a living example of this. *And in this sense, you may, and you must, have an African Christianity.* Indeed you *possess* human values and characteristic forms of culture which can rise up to perfection, such as to find in Christianity, and for Christianity, a true superior fullness, and prove to be capable of a richness of expression all its own, and genuinely African.[16]

This trend toward a true African Christianity cannot be reversed. The seeds of a future authentic African Christianity are in its soil. Though not universal, there is a widespread understanding that the African church must move away from what Efoe-Julien Penoukou describes as the threefold dilemma it formerly suffered as a legacy of missionary Christianity: it was a "dependent" church, a "wait-and-see" church, and an "outmoded" church. These characteristics fed into one another, Penoukou argues. Dependence robbed the African church of its imagination, dynamism, and daring, as it was always waiting for directions from outside; in turn, dependence encouraged a wait-and-see attitude that lacked vision. Dependence and a wait-and-see attitude contributed to a fossilization of the African church's structural, doctrinal, moral, and pastoral development. The result was a church

---

14. Pope Paul VI, *Africae Terrarum* §14 (italics in original).
15. Pope Paul VI, "To the Inaugural 1969 SECAM," 35 (italics in original).
16. Pope Paul VI, "To the Inaugural 1969 SECAM," 35 (italics in original).

that was out of touch with the realities of the times, an outmoded church.[17]

Because of initiatives begun in the mid-twentieth century, the future looks different and much more hopeful. Practical plans for an authentic future African church are based on the "three selfs": self-government, self-support, and self-propagation. To be sure, these emphases may not be new, but rather a rediscovery of what some farsighted Protestant missionaries strongly advocated as the proper missionary method in China, India, and the Philippines, among other places. Henry Venn (1796–1873), Rufus Anderson (1796–1850), and Anthony N. Groves (1795–1853) deserve mention in this respect.[18] From Africa itself, the best-known proponent of inventing Christian tradition in and for the continent is David J. Bosch (1929–1992), in his masterpiece *Transforming Mission: Paradigm Shifts in Theology of Mission* (1991). Bosch put forward the "three-selfs" insight as the most relevant approach to mission in postcolonial Africa.

As Robert Reese explains, emphasis on the "self" in constructing the local church negates neither the need for unity or catholicity nor the need for the churches to interact with each other. Rather, it facilitates these things by promoting authentic adult relationships. The accent on the "self" is "not meant to indicate self-centeredness or absolute autonomy, but rather responsibility and maturity," he notes. "It did not mean to exclude reliance on God, but indicated that these churches had no need to remain dependent on outsiders."[19] According to Archbishop Jean Zoa, the formula helps make African religious values "explicit in order to elaborate a true kerygma, a meaningful theology, an appropriate catechism, an Inculturated theology."[20] If applied seriously, the formula stimulates the church's imagination and helps preserve in new social structures some important indigenous African spiritual and religious ideals, some of which are threatened with extinction.

African Theological Imagination: Social and Ecclesiastical Structures

Social structures are a product of collective imagination, but the converse also holds true: social structures play a role in either encouraging or stifling intellectual creativity. In Christian terms, this is to say that structures partake in shaping the theological development of and therefore forming the shape of the local church. And so, although the history of theology and that of the institutional church cannot be said to have been always identical, they are nevertheless often closely related, even intertwined.[21] Not infrequently, the content of theology mirrors existing socio-structural arrangements, as we showed above in the discussion about the various epochs of the church. We have shown that historically the (symbolic) language and actual behavior of the church have mirrored existing social movements and demands. Political, economic, and cultural realities invariably exert profound influence over the intellectual and physical shape of the church.

Accordingly, for some time after Pentecost, arguably the founding event of the church, Christian believers lived, behaved, and prayed in the manner of their originating Jewish traditions, observing most Jewish religious laws, and frequented the synagogue for worship (Acts 2:43–3:26; Gal 2:11–14). Understandably, they initially insisted that doing so was part and parcel of faith in Jesus. Their encounter with non-Jewish Christians, people who lived by different customs, however, was bound to cause tension; it changed this exclusive theological perspective and propelled the invention of a new tradition. Far from being restricted to only Jewish religious and social points of view, the saving power of Jesus was now expanded to include other and different cultural practices, including changed dietary rules, something that has often seemed impossible in the history of the church, including recently.

---

17. Penoukou, "Churches of Africa," 40–41.
18. Other important figures were John L. Nevius (1829–1893), Hudson Taylor (1832–1905), Dixon E. Hoste (1861–1946), Roland Allen (1868–1947), Alice Luce (1873–1955), Nicholas Zamora (1875–1914), and Melvin Hodges (1909–1988).
19. Reese, "Surprising Relevance," lines 59–62.
20. Zoa, "Preserving Africa's Traditional Religious Values," 279.
21. See Lynch, *Medieval Church*, xiii.

Dreaming about the Future of the Church in Africa

The church in Africa has gained inspiration from this foundational experience of the church in terms of its overall theology and organization. While prayer must remain a central practice of the Christian faithful everywhere, it cannot be uniform in every location. Varieties of prayer experience and ministries should not be seen as a threat to church unity. When the church spread out from Jerusalem, the synagogue or temple officials no longer stood as the indispensable facilitators of religious life and worship. Christian assemblies assigned these roles to households and heads of households, both men and women, wherever common prayer took place. Some of these new ministers were appointed or confirmed by the apostles, usually on an ad hoc basis, to head the churches they founded. Generally called "presbyters," these church leaders were created according to need. They had the responsibility of overseeing the day-to-day life of the church and were occasionally visited by or counseled by letters from the apostles, as the letters of Paul to the various churches he founded indicate.

A similar situation should mark the African church of the future. There appears to be no need to completely overhaul in Africa the church structures inherited from the Middle Ages (ca. 500–1300 CE). But some of the Roman imperial political and cultural symbols and the language adopted by the church clearly call for reform in African ecclesiology—specifically, the view of Jesus Christ as an "emperor" who "reigns" from his "throne" in heaven. Apart from the fact that this image is obviously a departure from the overall New Testament Christology that consistently depicts Jesus as poor and lowly, a "servant" rather than a king (e.g., Matt 20:27–28; Mark 10:42–45; Luke 9:46–48), it distorts the structures of the church in Africa. Thus, the monarchical episcopate that developed from an ecclesiology of power and domination must be rethought in Africa. African bishops must be at the service of the local churches, counseling and confirming them in the faith.

The theological importance of the local Christian community in its basic, parish, or diocesan forms, must not be allowed to continue to play second fiddle to that of the church's leadership, specifically the clergy. The principle of subsidiarity must be upheld. The constitution of the church needs to reemphasize the ecclesiological validity of the Basic Christian Communities, what the New Testament characterizes as "household" churches. But acknowledgment of this will relativize some of the claims of current ecclesiology. Pope Boniface VIII's assertion in his bull *Unam Sanctam* (1302),[22] that it is "a truth necessary for salvation that every human being is subject to the Roman pontiff," for example, must be reconsidered. Similarly dubious theologically is Pope Clement VI's claim in his papal bull *Unigenitus Dei Filius* (1713) that "the Pope, as the Vicar of Christ on earth, possesses the same full power of jurisdiction that Christ himself possessed during his human life."[23]

Although the Council of Trent and the First Vatican Council essentially reaffirmed these positions, there has been a sense in the church since the Second Vatican Council that it should go back to the theological and legislative authority of regional bishops, as was the situation in the church up to the sixth century. Before the centralization and concentration of power in Rome, regional synods could define doctrine and even legislate for their churches. There is therefore no reason that the national and regional conferences of bishops in Africa, as well as their continental body, SECAM, should not enjoy a similar status. However, the cardinal prefect of the Congregation for the Doctrine of the Faith, Joseph Ratzinger, the future Pope Benedict XVI, asserted that national and regional episcopal conferences were associations without "theological basis" and that they did not "belong to the structure of the Church, as willed by Christ."[24] This was contrary to what, as a professor of theology, he had previously argued, asserting the "theological and evangelical reality" of episcopal collegiality through bishops' conferences.[25] At any rate, his former stance is more in line with the official documents of Vatican II, including, most prominently, the Decree on the Bishops' Pastoral Office in the Church, *Christus*

---

22. Pope Boniface VIII, *Unam Sanctam*; https://www.papalencyclicals.net/bon08/b8unam.htm.
23. Clement VI, *Unigenitus Deus Filius*.
24. Ratzinger, *Ratzinger Report*, 48.
25. Ratzinger, "Pastoral Implications," 59. See Granfield, *Limits of the Papacy*, 82.

Dominus (§37). This idea is also found in the personal edict or *motu proprio* of Pope Paul VI, *Ecclesiae Sanctae*, which mandated the establishment of episcopal conferences in every region.[26]

For Africa, centralized ecclesiastical power resulted in severe diminishment and in some cases even a lack of theological imagination and pastoral initiatives, making it impossible to think without or outside of the hierarchical "box," as it were. The time-honored counsel to always "be at one" with the universal church (*sentire cum ecclesia*) may have been distorted to imply uncritical loyalty to the hierarchy's line of thinking. This tended to create mere superficial uniformity rather than true inner solidarity, reciprocity, communion, and unity. Jean-Marc Éla decries this situation, which is characteristic of the church in Africa. He laments that it does not reflect the reality of a truly local church, with a theology and ministries that respond to the people's real needs. In the main, African particular churches remain "extensions" of churches elsewhere—the still so-called mother churches—in organization, doctrine, language, and rituals.[27] Éla concurs with Fabien Eboussi Boulaga's sentiments that

> torpor reigns in the churches of the southern hemisphere. Priests and bishops sit dozing over the scholastic catechism of their adolescence, stroked by canonical reassurances. They stir to life only when pricked by the needles of mammon, luxury, and perquisites. When they are unwilling to "play up to important people," as this would be "vain" and "self-seeking," they lose themselves in the institutional casuistry of attempts to "apply the Council." Their docile application of the Council gives birth to nothing but wind or stillbirths, because ultimately it merely mimics the life that is perhaps unfolding elsewhere. Structures, even post-conciliar ones, will never be able to replace message, will never be able to replace the soul that invents its own body.[28]

Centralization of ecclesiastical power and the resulting lack of imagination can sideline the work of the spirit of God found in the popular church, ignoring an equally ancient ecclesial principle that the voice of the people is indeed the voice of God (*vox populi vox Dei*). This principle cannot be trivialized; its importance must be recaptured in the tradition of the contemporary church. It is the practice of consultation in church leadership structures that is at stake: in serious matters of faith, no church leader must act on his or her "own authority," but legitimately only when united with the people of God, with the church community. It is essential to keep in mind that whatever is asserted by Vatican II about the authority of the teaching office of the pope and the bishops, the hierarchical magisterium, it is important to be aware that it "is not above the word of God, but serves it, teaching only what has been handed on, listening to it devoutly, guarding it scrupulously, and explaining it faithfully by divine commission and with the help of the Holy Spirit" (*Dei Verbum* §10). Because the word of God that the magisterium must explain, guard, listen to, and serve is first of all expressed in the faith life of all of the faithful, the *sensus fidelium fidei* (the sense of the faith of the faithful) or the *consensus fidelium* (the agreement of the faithful) must be taken very seriously indeed in the new tradition of the church. It is to the *consensus fidelium* that the entire church must loyally defer.

From this point of view, the two-dimensional and dichotomous model of church—the teaching church (*ecclesia docens*) and the learning or listening church (*ecclesia discens*)—though valid, must be nuanced. It must be understood in the context of the sense of the faith of the faithful, as just explained. As in the early church, the bishop should play the role of a facilitator, an elder, a unifier, and an exemplar of the faith of the whole church.

Liberating Inculturation

It is by paying serious attention to the sense of the faith of the church that true inculturation—with-

---

26. See Granfield, *Limits of the Papacy*, 97.
27. See Éla, *African Cry*, 105–20.
28. Eboussi Boulaga, "Metamorphoses africaines," 38; Éla, *African Cry*, 106–7.

out doubt the greatest need for an authentic *African church*—will happen. In the paradigmatic experience of Israel, the people's attempt, with God's assistance, to make sense of the divine presence in their lives is what made Israel truly a "people of God." This is a recurring theme in the Hebrew scriptures: if you follow my ways and keep in mind what I did for you, God tells the people of Israel, "I shall be your God and you will be my people" (Exod 6:6–8; Lev 26:10–14; Jer 11:4; Ezek 36:28; 37:27).[29]

With God at the helm, how should we live? This was and remains the perennial question for inculturating the faith throughout the history of the church. The answer to it, in the Christian faith, has been fully and finally manifested by the Incarnation: the life, teaching, and death of Jesus Christ. As Jesus's Incarnation traverses time and space through the growth of the church, it must be concretized in contingent situations, unavoidably giving it faces appropriate to each situation.[30] As we indicated above, Pope Francis has underlined the fact that "we cannot demand that peoples of every continent, in expressing their Christian faith, imitate modes of expression which European nations developed at a particular moment of their history" (*EG* §118). Again, Pope Paul VI asserted the same thing to the bishops of SECAM in Kampala in 1969.

The official rhetoric has certainly changed, but it must be said that the practical expression of the Christian faith in Africa remains largely alien to the continent, as Éla has noted. As things now stand, African Christians bear a heavy yoke because the spirituality which forms their religious language and understanding of the world is still largely sidelined in the church. What it means to realistically dream of a future African church involves recapturing this spirituality, this indigenous language that still forms the root of the African person's self-understanding. This cannot be done in an outmoded manner, though, as if we were engaged in an archaeological, fossil-finding exercise: in the search for African identity, we must recognize and take into account the dynamism of culture. However, despite various necessary developments and changes in African culture, there are still, in the words of Pope Paul VI already cited, existent "human values and characteristic forms of [African] culture which can rise up to perfection, such as to find in Christianity, and for Christianity, a true superior fullness, and prove to be capable of a richness of expression all its own, and genuinely African."[31] Culture should not, however, be accepted uncritically: when the gospel encounters culture, it challenges it, often radically. Authentic inculturation cannot be insensitive to any abuses of human rights and dignity that may be inherent in African (as, indeed, any) culture.

The process of true inculturation, of dreaming into existence an African church, needs to be based on essential African cultural ideals as reflected in a desire for physical, mental, and spiritual health, wholeness, relationality, community and communion, harmony, cooperation, sharing, and participation. It is not an exaggeration to say that, regardless of educational or social status, African peoples cherish most of these dimensions of existence. The more the church incorporates them, perceptibly, in its structures and ways of living, the more it will touch the roots of the spirituality of the people. To the extent this is done, Christians will more easily identify with the church, and the church will, in turn, be better able to influence them more profoundly. All of these elements are related in the lives of African people; they constitute their most central aspiration: abundance of life.

The Christian churches have attracted and continue to attract the African person because of their concern for his or her complete well-being. The hospitals and schools that missionary evangelizers established along with the churches captured very well the African ideal of harmonious wholeness. The future African church cannot afford to sideline these initiatives; on the contrary, it must underline them as a key component of its evangelizing mission. The fact that no government in sub-Saharan Africa will be able to satisfy these needs in the foreseeable future intensifies them. Julius K. Nyerere, the former president of Tanzania, described the

---

29. See Magesa, *Anatomy of Inculturation*, 103–16.
30. Magesa, *Anatomy of Inculturation*, 117–72.
31. Paul VI, "To the Inaugural 1969 SECAM," 35.

predicament of the church of the future in precise terms: unless the church engages itself "actively in the rebellion against those social structures and economic organizations which condemn men to poverty, humiliation and degradation," he stated, "then the Church will become irrelevant . . . and the Christian religion will degenerate into a set of superstitions accepted by the fearful."[32]

Bernhard Udelhoven offers wise advice on the process of inculturation in pastoral practice related to spiritual healing. The best approach for church leaders, he says, is "to follow the lead of cultural insights into human life and notions of selfhood, always trying to meet . . . people on their own ground."[33] As an instance, he notes that

> witchcraft, spirits and unseen worlds are posing grave problems in Africa that call for prudent engagements. Priests and pastors are approached by people who fall victim of such forces but also by people who fall victim of wrongful accusations. These are important issues. Ignoring them means that the Christian Church excludes itself from important discernment processes that affect the souls; people struggling with such problems go somewhere else. Tackling the issues presented at face-value can entangle the pastor in a minefield of suspicions and accusations. Reflection and evaluation are hallmarks of a prudent approach that sets up long-term goals shaped and challenged by the Christian message.[34]

When one reads the New Testament, it is clear that this was actually the approach of Jesus: he accepted people as they were and proceeded to liberate them. Thus, he dismissed no claims, no matter how absurd they seemed to some. The daily stuff of his preaching and activity ranged from assertions of spirit possession (e.g., Matt 4:23–25; 8:28–34; Mark 1:21–28; 16:9; Luke 13:10–17, 31–32) to the cultural practice of wife inheritance (Matt 22:25–28; Luke 20:29–33) to questions of mutual assistance (Luke 10:25–37). Christian liberation happens within these all-too-human conditions.

Wholeness, relationality, community and communion, harmony, cooperation, sharing, and participation still enjoy a firm place in the cultures of Africa. But do they in the present-day tradition of the church? When Christians worship together, for instance, does their unity last much longer than the service? Sadly, most often in many churches it does not. This is unsatisfactory to African peoples, who value community and communion as the essence of being human, described as *ubuntu* by many of them. For African peoples it is clear, as John V. Taylor observed, that "men and women who do not live in a community and feel that they really belong to it are not completely human. Something essential is missing, something which God has ordained for them as necessary for their true life."[35]

For African peoples the human wholeness produced by authentic community and communion, harmony, cooperation, sharing, and participation is not merely something sociological; it is a deep spiritual need. Structures of the future church in Africa must take the need for this wholeness into account more earnestly than before. The ecclesiastical institution of Small or Basic Christian Communities that is emerging all across the continent is trying to address this need. It would seem that church communities that facilitate mutual contact and personal knowledge among the faithful of a given locality are the promise of a desirable African future church. Such ecclesiastical organizations are helping to preserve valuable indigenous modes of living which, unfortunately, some forms of Christian pedagogy and modern social structures have often inadvertently contributed to dismantling.

Conclusion

From its emergence in Palestine in the early first century CE, faith in Jesus as the "savior of the world," which was shortly afterward constituted as the Christian religion and church, has been a dynamic reality, adapting to various circumstances

---

32. Nyerere, *Freedom and Development*, 215–16.
33. Udelhoven, *Unseen Worlds*, xi.
34. Udelhoven, *Unseen Worlds*, xi.
35. Taylor, *Christianity and Politics in Africa*, 35.

and adopting mystical and intellectual values as well as institutional forms[36] that at any given time could best express the sense of its basic treasure, the life and message of Jesus. History shows clearly how, extending beyond its Jewish roots, the early church borrowed liberally, albeit very selectively and judiciously, from the Roman imperial culture that was dominant at the time.

As it spread to and established itself also in Egypt and North Africa in the following six centuries, it received intellectual and spiritual contributions from a variety of personalities and philosophies, which enabled it to clarify its beliefs and teachings. The rise of monasticism in the third and fourth centuries as part of the spirituality of the church illustrates this dynamism of openness. In medieval Europe, church structures, teachings, and rules emerged that reflected the changing political, economic, social, and religious environments of the region. With European missionary incursion into sub-Saharan Africa toward the end of the nineteenth century, Christian vitality continued to grow through the contribution of African spirituality, often unconsciously and, in fact, frequently against the wishes of the missionaries. African Christians could not but instinctively become adapters of the Christian faith to the religious ideals of their cultures.

This process must today take on a more proactive and deliberate character so that it can fuel the dream of a future African church. As it becomes more and more probable that at some time in the present century "Christians in Africa will become more numerous than Christians in any other single continent," they will be "more important than ever before in articulating a global Christian identity in a pluralist world."[37] Perhaps this is the *kairos* of Christianity and the church in Africa.

Bibliography

"African Missionaries Take Religion to the West." http://www.churchshift.org/index.php?option=com_contents&view=article&id=70:african-missionaries-take-religion-to-the-west&catid=39:press-room&Itemid=60.

Baur, John. *2000 Years of Christianity in Africa: An African Church History.* Nairobi: Paulines Publications Africa, 2009.

Benedict XVI, Pope [Joseph Ratzinger]. "The Pastoral Implications of Episcopal Collegiality." In *The Church and Mankind*, edited by Edward Schillebeeckx. Glen Rock, NJ: Paulist Press, 1965.

———. [Joseph Ratzinger], with Vittorio Messori. *The Ratzinger Report: An Exclusive Interview on the State of the Church.* San Francisco: Ignatius Press, 1985.

Boniface VIII, Pope. *Unam Sanctam* [Papal bull: One God, One Faith, One Spiritual Authority; November 18, 1302].

Bosch, David J. *Transforming Mission: Paradigm Shifts in Theology of Mission.* Maryknoll, NY: Orbis Books, 1991.

Clement VI, Pope. *Unigenitus Deus Filius* [Papal bull; September 8, 1713].

Eboussi Boulaga, Fabien. "Metamorphoses africaines." *Christus* 77 (1973).

Éla, Jean-Marc. *African Cry.* Maryknoll, NY: Orbis Books, 1986.

Francis, Pope. *Evangelii Gaudium* (The Joy of the Gospel) [Post-synodal Apostolic Exhortation on the Proclamation of the Gospel in Today's World; November 23, 2013]. www.vatican.va. Nairobi: Paulines Publications Africa, 2013.

Granfield, Patrick. *The Limits of the Papacy: Authority and Autonomy in the Church.* New York: Crossroad, 1987.

Haar, Gerrie ter. *Halfway to Paradise: African Christians in Europe.* Cardiff: Cardiff Academic Press, 1998.

Hügel, Friedrich von. *The Mystical Element of Religion: As Studied in Saint Catherine of Genoa and Her Friends.* London: Dent, 1908.

Jenkinson, William, and Helene O'Sullivan, eds. *Trends in Mission: Toward the 3rd Millennium.* Maryknoll, NY: Orbis Books, 1991.

John XXIII, Pope. "Allocution to African Writers & Artists." In *32 Articles Evaluating Inculturation of Christianity in Africa*, edited by Teresa Okure et al., 13. Eldoret, Kenya: AMECEA Gaba Publications, 1990.

Linden, Ian. *Global Catholicism: Toward a Networked Church.* London: Hurst, 2012.

---

36. See von Hügel, *Mystical Element of Religion*, 65.
37. Ward, "Africa," 235.

Lynch, Joseph H. *The Medieval Church: A Brief History*. London: Longman, 1992.

Magesa, Laurenti. *Anatomy of Inculturation: Transforming the Church in Africa*. Nairobi: Paulines Publications Africa, 2004.

Nyerere, Julius K. *Freedom and Development: Uhuru na Maendeleo. A Selection from Writings and Speeches, 1968–1973*. Dar es Salaam: Oxford University Press, 1973.

Okure, Teresa, et al., eds. *32 Articles Evaluating Inculturation of Christianity in Africa*. Eldoret, Kenya: AMECEA Gaba Publications, 1990.

O'Malley, John W. *What Happened at Vatican II*. Cambridge, MA: Harvard University Press, 2008.

Paul VI, Pope. "*Africae Terrarum* (Land of Africa): Message to the Countries of Africa (1967)." In *32 Articles Evaluating Inculturation of Christianity in Africa*, edited by Teresa Okure et al., 14–32. Eldoret, Kenya: AMECEA Gaba Publications, 1990.

———. *Ecclesiae Sanctae* [Apostolic letter; 1966].

———. "To the Inaugural 1969 SECAM, Kampala." In *32 Articles Evaluating Inculturation of Christianity in Africa*, edited by Teresa Okure et al., 32–36. Eldoret, Kenya: AMECEA Gaba Publications, 1990.

Penoukou, Efoe-Julien. "The Churches of Africa: Their Identity? Their Mission?" In *Trends in Mission: Toward the 3rd Millennium*, edited by William Jenkinson and Helene O'Sullivan, 39–45. Maryknoll, NY: Orbis Books, 1991.

Pew Research Center. "Global Christianity: A Report on the Size and Distribution of the World's Christian Population." http://www.pewforum.org/2011/12/19/global-christianity-exec/

Ratzinger, Joseph. *See* Benedict XVI, Pope.

Reese, Robert. "The Surprising Relevance of the Three-Self Formula." *Mission Frontiers* (July–August 2007). http://missionfrontiers.org/issue/article/the-surprising-relevance-of-the-three-self-formula.

Taylor, John V. *Christianity and Politics in Africa*. Harmondsworth: Penguin, 1957.

Tilley, Terrence W. *Inventing Catholic Tradition*. Maryknoll, NY: Orbis Books, 2000.

Udelhoven, Bernhard. *Unseen Worlds: Dealing with Spirits, Witchcraft, and Satanism*. Lusaka: FENZA Publications, 2015.

Vatican II. *Christus Dominus* [Decree on the Bishops' Pastoral Office in the Church; 1965].

———. *Dei Verbum* [Dogmatic Constitution on Divine Revelation; 1965].

———. *Nostra Aetate* [Declaration on the Relationship of the Church to Non-Christian Religions; 1965].

Ward, Kevin. "Africa." In *A World History of Christianity*, edited by Adrian Hastings. London: Cassell, 1999.

Zoa, Jean. "Preserving Africa's Traditional Religious Values." In *Trends in Mission: Toward the 3rd Millennium*, edited by William Jenkinson and Helene O'Sullivan, 277–79. Maryknoll, NY: Orbis Books, 1991.

Contributors

Anthony Adawu is a priest of the Archdiocese of Cape Coast, Ghana. He has doctoral degrees in practical theology and second language education. His research focuses on the theology of children and families in the world church, African Catholicism, and the theology of hope. He serves as a chaplain and lecturer at the University of Education, Winneba, Ghana, as well as the founder and executive director of Africa Youth-Now Foundation (AYNF), a Christian organization working to promote the integral development of children and youth in Africa.

Rev. Godswill Agbagwa is a priest of the Catholic Archdiocese of Owerri, Imo State, Nigeria. He holds a PhD in moral theology and ethics from the Catholic University of America, Washington, DC; a licentiate in the theology of new evangelization from the University of St. Thomas Aquinas, Rome; and an MA in legal and ethical studies from the University of Baltimore, Maryland. He doubles as ethics adjunct professor at Frostburg State University and the executive director of the Center for Social Awareness, Advocacy, and Ethics (CSAAE), both in Maryland. He is also the coordinator of Catholic Social Teaching in Action (CASTINA). His ministerial, research, teaching, and consultancy interests are in the areas of social and human development; he is the author of several books and articles and the editor of *C-Journal, the African Journal of Development*.

Anthony A. Akinwale, OP, is a Nigerian Dominican. A past president of the Catholic Theological Association of Nigeria, he has also served as an expert at the Symposium of Episcopal Conferences of Africa and Madagascar (SECAM), the Catholic Bishops' Conference of Nigeria (CBCN), and the 2012 Synod on New Evangelization. He is professor of systematic theology and vice-chancellor of the Dominican University in Ibadan, Nigeria, and visiting professor at Institut St. Thomas d'Aquin de Yamoussoukro in the Ivory Coast. His publications include *The Congress and the Council: Towards a Nigerian Reception of Vatican II* and *Sowing in the Desert: Birth and Growth of the Catholic Diocese of Sokoto* (coauthored with Emmanuel Akubor), in addition to numerous essays in academic journals.

Ebere Bosco Amakwe, HFSN, holds a PhD in communication and sociology from the Pontifical Gregorian University in Rome. In addition, she holds an MA in social communication from the Pontifical Salesian University in Rome, a bachelor's in missionary spirituality, and a diploma in media studies and social communication from the Pontifical Urban University in Rome. Sr. Amakwe also has a masters in international relations and diplomacy, a graduate certificate in post-conflict state reconstruction and sustainable development, and a certificate in the study of the United Nations, all from the School of Diplomacy and International Relations, Seton Hall University, South Orange, New Jersey (2017). She earned a certificate in interfaith conflict resolution (2016) and another in conflict analysis (2015) from the United States Institute of Peace. Since 2019, Sr. Amakwe has served as an adjunct professor of Christianity and culture in dialogue in the Department of Core Curriculum at Seton Hall University.

Anne Arabome, SSS, is a member of the Sisters of Social Service in Los Angeles, California. She holds a doctor of ministry degree in spirituality from the Catholic Theological Union in Chicago, Illinois, and a PhD in systematic theology from the University of Roehampton in London. She is presently associate director of the Faber Center for Ignatian Spirituality at Marquette University in Milwaukee, Wisconsin. She has published several articles and book chapters on gender and women, including "Who Is Christ for African Women?," in *Catholic*

Contributors

Women Speak: Bringing Our Gifts to the Table, edited by The Catholic Women Speak Network (2015); and "Dreams from My Mother, Prayers to My Father: Rethinking the Trinity of God, Woman, and Church," in *Feminist Catholic Theological Ethics: Conversations in the World Church*, edited by Linda Hogan and A. E. Orobator (2014).

Daniel Assefa is director of Tibeb Research and Retreat Center, under the Eparchy of Addis Ababa, Ethiopia, and assistant professor in the Department of Linguistics and Philology at Addis Ababa University. He obtained a licentiate in biblical sciences from the Pontifical Biblical Institute of Rome, a PhD in biblical theology from the Catholic Institute of Paris, and a PhD in literature and philosophy from the University of South Africa. He has published mainly on the Ethiopic book of Enoch, including *L'Apocalypse des Animaux (1 Hen 85–90): Une propagande militaire? Approches narrative, historico-critique, perspectives théologiques* (2007); "Matthew's Day of Judgment in the Light of 1 Enoch," in *Enoch and the Synoptic Gospels*, edited by L. Stuckenbruck and G. Boccaccini (2016); and "The Cry of the Earth in 1 Enoch and Environmental Theology," in *The Blessing of Enoch: 1 Enoch and Contemporary Theology*, edited by Philip F. Esler (2017). His research interests include Second Temple Judaism, Ethiopian biblical hermeneutics, the textual history of the Ethiopic Bible, and apocalyptic literature.

Chukwuemeka Anthony Atansi is a priest of the Roman Catholic Diocese of Awka, Nigeria. He obtained a Doctor of Sacred Theology (PhD and STD) from the Catholic University of Leuven, Belgium. His doctoral dissertation is entitled *Christ, the Image of Social Transformation: Towards a Transformative Christology in the African Context*. Atansi was a research fellow at the Center for World Catholicism and Intercultural Theology (CWCIT) at DePaul University, Chicago, Illinois. He is presently a research fellow and chaplain of the Newman Centre of McGill University, Montreal, Quebec, Canada, as well as adjunct professor at the McGill School of Religious Studies. His latest publication is "Contemplating Christ and/in His People: The Practice of a Social Transformation-Oriented Christology in Africa," in *What Does Theology Do, Actually? Observing Theology and the Transcultural*, edited by Matthew Ryan Robinson and Inja Inderst (2020), 285–307. He can be reached at chukwuemeka. atansi@mcgill.ca or anthonyatansi@yahoo.com.

Richard Benson, CM, is a Vincentian Father, a member of the Congregation of the Mission, Western Province, ordained in 1978. He has a B.A. in philosophy, a master of divinity degree, a master of arts degree in theology, and a master of arts degree in the biological sciences. He has a license in sacred theology (STL), a PhD, and an STD from the Katholieke Universiteit Leuven in Belgium. He served at St. John's Theology Seminary (Archdiocese of Los Angeles, California) for eighteen years as vice-rector, academic dean, and chair of the Moral Theology Department. Later he was appointed mission superior of the Vincentians in East Africa. He has also served in Chicago, Illinois, as an instructor at DePaul University and as academic dean of the Catholic Theological Union.

Paul Béré, SJ, a Jesuit from Burkina Faso, lectures at the Pontifical Biblical Institute (Rome). He graduated from the same Institute after carrying out research on the figure of Joshua in the Hebrew Bible. His research concentrates on the exegesis of biblical texts in a word-based culture. He served as consultor to the Secretariat of the Synod at the Vatican for five years. He has been consultor to the Pontifical Council for Culture at the Vatican since 2014, to the Anglican-Roman Catholic International Commission since 2018, and to the Pontifical Biblical Commission since 2020. He is a member of the Pan-African Association of Catholic Exegetes (PACE) and the Association of African Theologians (AAT).

Patrick C. Chibuko is a priest of the Enugu, Nigeria, diocese and emeritus professor of practical theology (sacred liturgy) at the Catholic Institute of West Africa (CIWA) (Port Harcourt, Nigeria). Currently, he is at Haltern am See in the Diocese of Muenster, Germany. He attended the Pontifical University of St. Anselm in Rome and served as rector of St. Paul's International Institute of Evangelization, Enugu (affiliated with Godfrey Okoye University, Enugu). At CIWA, he served as academic dean and as head of the Department of

Contributors

Sacred Liturgy. In 2016, he was awarded a research fellowship at the Center for World Catholicism and Intercultural Theology (CWCIT), DePaul University, Chicago, Illinois. A specialist in liturgical inculturation, he has published seven books, fifteen monographs, and many articles.

Beatrice Wairimu Churu, a teacher by profession, holds a PhD in religious studies with a focus on Catholic education. She currently teaches in the Tangaza College of the Catholic University of Eastern Africa, where she also serves as dean of the School of Arts and Social Sciences. In her studies, publications, teaching, and leadership, she endeavors to promote the proactive consciousness of communities in their own development. She lives in the Rift Valley of Kenya with her husband and three teenage children.

Zorodzai Dube is a senior lecturer in New Testament studies at the University of Pretoria in South Africa. He is the author of "Jesus's Death and Resurrection as Cultural Trauma" (2013) and many other works.

Benedict Ndubueze Ejeh is a priest of the Catholic Diocese of Okigwe in southeastern Nigeria. He is a professor and the president and doctoral degree coordinator at the St. Pius X Faculty of Canon Law, Venice, Italy, and a judge on the Regional Ecclesiastical Tribunal of Triveneto, Italy. He has authored a number of works on the canon law of persons, church organization, and matrimonial law.

Michael Onyebuchi Eze teaches African political theory at Institute of Philosophy, Leiden University, and is a research associate to the SA-UK Bilateral Research Chair in Political Theory, Universities of the Witwatersrand and Cambridge. He was formerly a graduate fellow of Trinity Hall, University of Cambridge, and visiting scholar at the Center for African Studies and research associate at the Martin Luther King Jr. Institute, both at Stanford University. He received a PhD in history and cultural reflection from Universität Witten-Herdecke, Germany, an MA in philosophy from the University of Pretoria, South Africa, and a BA, with honors, in philosophy and classics from the Jesuit School of Philosophy (now Arrupe Jesuit University), Zimbabwe. He has taught at universities in Africa, Europe, and the United States, and he has published two books: *The Politics of History in Contemporary Africa* (2010) and *Intellectual History in Contemporary South Africa* (2010). Selected recent academic articles include: "I Am Because You Are: Cosmopolitanism in the Age of Xenophobia" (2017); "Menkiti, Gyekye and Beyond: Towards a Decolonization of African Philosophy" (2018); "Cultural Appropriation and the Limits of Identity: A Case for Multiple Humanity(ies)" (2018); and "African Philosophy as a Cultural Resistance" (2018).

Anne Béatrice Faye, CIC, is a Senegalese member of the Congregation of the Sisters of Our Lady of the Immaculate Conception of Castres (CIC). She holds a PhD and is currently professor at Al Mowafaqa in Rabat, Morocco, and a member of the Commission of Theologians for the next synod (2023).

Elizabeth A. Foster is author of *African Catholic: Decolonization and the Transformation of the Church* (2019) and *Faith in Empire: Religion, Politics, and Colonial Rule in French Senegal* (2013), which won the Andrew Alf Heggoy Prize of the French Colonial Historical Society. An associate professor of history at Tufts University, she has been a visiting scholar at Harvard's Minda de Gunzburg Center for European Studies and has received Fulbright, ACLS, and NEH Fellowships.

Joseph G. Healey, MM, is an American Maryknoll missionary priest who lives in Nairobi, Kenya. He came to Kenya in 1968 and founded the Social Communications Office of the Regional Catholic Bishops Association (AMECEA) in Nairobi. Presently he teaches a full semester core course entitled "Small Christian Communities (SCCs) as a New Model of Church in Africa Today" at Tangaza University College (of the Catholic University of Eastern Africa) in Nairobi, and a similar elective course at Hekima University College (also of CUEA) in Nairobi. He authored *Building the Church as Family of God: Evaluation of Small Christian Communities in Eastern Africa* (2020), and coedited *Small Christian Communities Today: Capturing the New Moment* (2005). The moderator of the Small Christian Communities' global collaborative website, he is a member of the Eastern Africa Small Christian Communities Training Team and of the St. Kizito Small Christian Community in St. Austin's Parish in the Archdiocese of Nairobi.

Rev. Walter Chikwendu Ihejirika is a priest of the Catholic Diocese of Ahiara Mbaise, Imo State, Nigeria. He holds a doctorate degree in the sociology of communication from the Pontifical Gregorian University in Rome, as well as master's degrees in missiology from the Gregorian University and in pedagogy and social communication from the Pontifical Salesian University in Rome. In 2003, he was a member of the team of communication experts commissioned by the Catholic Bishops' Conference of Nigeria to set up the Centre for the Study of African Culture and Communication (CESACC) at the Catholic Institute of West Africa, Port Harcourt, Nigeria. He is currently professor in as well as the first dean of the Department of Communications and Media Studies at the Federal University of Port Harcourt, Rivers State, Nigeria. He has published extensively in the field of communications and media in both local and international journals and has participated in local and international conferences. He has a special research interest in the field of media, religion, and culture. He is president of SIGNIS–Africa and sits on the board of SIGNIS, the World Catholic Organization for Communication. He is founder and administrator of the online evangelization group FaceGod.

Stan Chu Ilo is research professor of world Christianity and African studies at the Center for World Catholicism and Intercultural Theology at DePaul University, Chicago, Illinois. He is an honorary professor of religion and theology at Durham University in England and the 2017 recipient of the Afro-Global Excellence Award for Global Impact. He is a member of the board of directors of *Concilium* International, where he is also an editor of the *Concilium* Catholic International Journal. He is the coordinator of the Pan-African Theology and Pastoral Network. Some of his most recent books are *Church and Development in Africa* (2014); *A Poor and Merciful Church* (2018); *Wealth, Health, and Hope in African Christian Religion* (2019); *Someone Beautiful to God: Finding the Light of Faith in a Wounded World* (2020); and *365 Days Walk with God: African Biblical Reflection for a Good Christian Life* (2021). He also co-edited the three-volume work *Faith in Action in Africa*.

Eunice K. Kamaara is professor of religion at Moi University, Kenya, and an international affiliate of Indiana University–Purdue University Indianapolis (IUPUI), in Indiana. She holds a PhD in African Christian ethics and an MSc degree in international health research ethics. Her research expertise is in interpretive methods of applying transdisciplinary perspectives to religion, gender, and health in contemporary Africa. She is particularly interested in translating research findings into the practical development of policy and community uptake. She is widely published and has been a research consultant for various national and international organizations, including the World Bank, Church World Service (CWS), the United States Agency for International Development (USAID), the United Nations Population Fund (UNFPA), the Templeton World Charity Foundation, Inc. (TWCF), and the World Council of Churches (WCC). Eunice currently serves as a director of Church World Service and as a member of the Ethics Review Board of Médecines San Frontières.

Emmanuel Katongole is a Catholic priest, ordained in the Archdiocese of Kampala, Uganda (1987). He currently serves as professor of theology and peace studies in the Keough School, University of Notre Dame, Notre Dame, Indiana. Before joining Notre Dame in 2013, he served as associate professor of theology and world Christianity at Duke University, Durham, North Carolina, and as founding co-director of the Duke Center for Reconciliation. He is the author of several books, including *Reconciling All Things* (with Chris Rice, 2008); *The Sacrifice of Africa: A Political Theology for Africa* (2010); *Born from Lament: The Theology and Politics of Hope in Africa* (2017); and *The Journey of Reconciliation: Groaning for New Creation in Africa* (2017).

Paul V. Kollman, CSC, is a priest of the Congregation of Holy Cross and associate professor of theology at the University of Notre Dame, Notre Dame, Indiana. He is the author of *The Evangelization of Slaves and Catholic Origins in Eastern Africa* (2005) and co-author of *Understanding World Christianity: Christianity in Eastern Africa* (2018). A scholar of missiology and world Christianity and a historian of Christianity in Africa, Kollman has lived and taught in eastern Africa, and carried out research in Africa as well as in archives in Europe and the United States. He previously served as executive director of Notre Dame's Center for Social Concerns as well as president of the American Society of Missiology; currently, he is president of the International Association of Mission Studies. He is presently working on a historical study of the Catholic missionary evangelization of eastern Africa.

Laurenti Magesa is a Catholic priest from Tanzania. He has taught theology in various institutions in Africa and abroad, and his main area of interest is African studies. His publications include *African Religion: The Moral Traditions of Abundant Life* (1997); *Anatomy of Inculturation: Transforming the Church in Africa* (2004); and *What Is Not Sacred? African Spirituality* (2013). He lives and works in Kenya.

Clement Majawa is a priest of the Archdiocese of Blantyre in Malawi. He holds a sacred doctorate in dogmatic theology from the Urbaniana Pontifical University in Rome, a licentiate in dogmatic theology from the Catholic University of Eastern Africa (CUEA) in Nairobi, a master's in spirituality and counseling from the St. Thomas Aquinas Pontifical University in Rome, a postgraduate diploma in education from Hythrop University in London, and a diploma in pastoral and church management from St. John's University in New York. He has published fifteen books, eighteen book chapters, and numerous articles in international and local peer-reviewed journals. His books on higher education include *The Holy Spirit and Charismatic Renewal in Africa and Beyond* (2007); *Patristic Education* (2014); and *A Handbook on Borderline between Christianity and Witchcraft (Foundations, Anthropology, Theories and Trends)* (2 vols., 2017, 2018). His research and teaching interests include the identification of new paradigms of doing theology; the inculturation of the Catholic faith in Africa and beyond; the exploration of theology to respond to the present needs of the public interest; the deconstruction and optimization of the patristic intellectual heritage in schools and universities; and the realignment of pneumatology with Pentecostal and charismatic experiences. He formerly served as dean of the Ecclesiastical Faculty of Theology and director of the School of Graduate Studies at CUEA and is a member of a number of professional bodies and associations.

Wilfred Mamah is a child protection specialist and justice-sector reform practitioner for UNICEF, with experience in child justice, development law, corrections, human rights, and sociolegal research. He holds a PhD in international development law from the University of Westminster and an LLM in international law and legal studies from City, University of London; he currently works in Kaduna, Nigeria.

Emmanuel-Mary Mbam, MSP, is a Nigerian priest and a member of the Missionary Society of St. Paul. He currently teaches systematic theology at the National Missionary Seminary of St. Paul in Abuja, Nigeria. He is a member of Alpha Sigma Nu, the honor society of Jesuit institutions of higher learning. His publications include the three-volume work *You Shall Know the Truth: Explaining the Catholic Faith* (2003); *Nwiboko Obodo Onyike* (2003); "Method of Inculturation in Africa: A Critique of Peter Schineller's 'How of Inculturation,'" *Mission: Journal of Mission Studies* 15.1–2 (2008); "Pastoral Response or Ecumenical Dialogue? *Africae Munus* and African Independent Churches," *Abuja Journal of Philosophy and Theology* 2 (2012); and "Vatican II, 50 Years After: Lessons for the Church in Africa," *Abuja Journal of Philosophy and Theology* 6 (2016).

Patrick J. McDevitt, CM, a Vincentian priest, has served since 2020 as provincial of the Congregation of the Mission Western Province. Previously, he was rector and superior of the Vincentian seminary, DePaul Centre, in Nairobi, Kenya; president of All Hallows College, a Catholic, Vincentian third-level institution in Dublin, Ireland; and an associate professor in the Department of Counseling and Special Education in the College of Education at DePaul University in Chicago, Illinois. He has written on education, leadership development, the psycho-social influences on ministry and education in today's society, and on aspects of community mental health.

Philomena Njeri Mwaura is associate professor in the Department of Philosophy and Religious Studies and former director of the Center for Gender Equity and Empowerment at Kenyatta University, Nairobi, Kenya. She is a former president of the International Association for Mission Studies, the Africa region co-coordinator of the Theology Commission and the Women's Commission of the Ecumenical Association of Third World Theologians, and a member of the Circle of Concerned African Women Theologians. Mwaura has published extensively on various aspects of African Christianity, new religious movements, gender and theology, and gender and religion. Her latest publication is "Reconstructing Mission: The Church in Africa in the Service of Justice, Peace and Reconciliation," in *Religion and Social Reconstruction in Africa*, edited by Elias K. Bongmba (2018).

Josée Ngalula, RSA, is a nun from the Democratic Republic of the Congo (DRC) belonging to the Sisters of St. Andrew. She has a PhD in theology from the Université Catholique de Lyon and teaches dogmatic theology in various Catholic institutions in Kinshasa, DRC. She is cofounder of the Association of African Theologians (AAT) and has published works on the Christian theology of languages and translations in the African context, new religious movements in Africa, African theology, and religion and violence against women in Africa. She is the founder of the *Bible and Women in Africa* collection.

†Mary Gloria C. Njoku, DDL (1972–2018), belonged to the Daughters of Divine Love Congregation and was a professor of clinical psychology at Godfrey Okoye University in Enugu, Nigeria. Her research interests included chronic illness, invisible illness, coping behavior, and spirituality.

MarySylvia Nwachukwu, DDL, is a Nigerian-born sister of the Daughters of Divine Love Congregation. She holds a PhD in biblical theology from the Pontifical Gregorian University in Rome and a licentiate (SSL) from the Pontifical Biblical Institute in Rome. Since 2002, she has taught theology at tertiary ecclesiastical institutions and seminaries. She is presently the deputy vice chancellor of Godfrey Okoye University, Enugu, Nigeria. Her research interest areas include the Pentateuch, St. Paul's letters, and contextual theology. She is the author of *Creation-Covenant Scheme and Justification by Faith* (2002); *Consecrated: A Vision of Religious Life from the Viewpoint of the Sacred* (2010); and many articles in scholarly journals. Her next book will be *Vessels of Mercy: An Idea of Universal Salvation in Romans 9–11*.

Sampson K. Nwonyi is experimental psychologist and lecturer in the Department of Psychology and Sociological Studies at Ebonyi State University Abakaliki, Nigeria.

Jordan Nyenyembe is a pastoral theologian and priest from the Mbinga diocese in Tanzania. He teaches at the AMECEA Pastoral Institute of the Catholic University of Eastern Africa, Gaba Campus in Eldoret, Kenya.

Edward Osang Obi, MSP, is a Nigerian priest and social ethicist who advocates for good governance, safe environments, and secure livelihoods. He is a member of the Catholic Theological Association of Nigeria (CATHAN) and teaches moral theology at the Catholic Institute of West Africa (CIWA), Port Harcourt, Nigeria. In addition to his academic work, Obi is active in Nigeria as an advocate of social inclusion, peace, and environmental justice, and works to curb violence in the Niger Delta region of Nigeria. In this capacity, he runs a technical agency for the Niger Delta Catholic Bishops' Forum of the Catholic Bishops' Conference of Nigeria (CBCN), which is dedicated to following and influencing developments toward a transition to renewable energy sources in Nigeria. Some of his more recent publications include: "Fragile Ecosystems and the Pressures of Anthropogenia: Recovering a Theo-Ethic of Relationality in Our Common Home," in *Fragile World: Ecology and the Church*, edited by William T. Cavanaugh (2018); "Creational Solidarity Strengthens the Weakest Link: Energy Ethics and Climate Change in Sub-Saharan Africa," in *Light for a New Day: An Interfaith, Global Energy Ethics Essay Collection*, edited by Erin Lothes Biviano (2016); and "The Exploi-

Contributors

tation of Natural Resources: Reconfiguring Economic Relations toward a Community-of-Interests Perspective," in *Just Sustainability: Technology, Ecology, and Resource Extraction*, edited by Christiana Z. Peppard and Andrea Vicini (2015).

Paulinus I. Odozor, CSSp, is a priest of the Congregation of the Holy Spirit (Spiritans), professor of moral theology/theology of the World Church, and professor of Africana Studies at the University of Notre Dame, Notre Dame, Indiana. He received his initial formation in Nigeria and did his graduate studies at St. Michaels College, Toronto; Regis College, Toronto; and the University of Toronto. Fr. Odozor's scholarly interests are in foundational issues in Christian ethics; history of Catholic moral theology; contextual theological issues, including questions pertaining to inculturation; theology and society; African Christian theology; and the theology of marriage. Fr. Odozor is also an Africanist with interests in African history, African literature, African politics, and questions relating to change and contemporary African societies. In addition to being the author of many articles in peer-reviewed publications in Africa, Asia, Europe, and North America, Fr. Odozor has also authored or edited nine books, including *Morality Truly Christian, Truly African: Foundational, Methodological and Theological Considerations* (2014). He has held numerous academic, administrative, and pastoral positions in Nigeria and Canada; was president of the Governing Council of Spiritan International School of Theology in Enugu, Nigeria (2005–2017); and was appointed by Pope Benedict XVI as expert assistant to the 2009 Synod of Bishops for Africa.

Aloys Ojore lectures at the Institute for Social Transformation (IST) of Tangaza University College, Nairobi. He holds a diploma in philosophy, a bachelor of education, and a master of arts in religious studies from the Catholic University of Eastern Africa. He also holds a professional doctorate in practical theology from Cambridge Theological Federation and Anglia Ruskin University, United Kingdom. Aloys is the author of *Ministerial Formation in Africa Today: A Layman's Perspective* (2009), and many other works. Currently he is the MA program leader and coordinator of research and quality assurance at IST.

Ikenna Paschal Okpaleke is a priest of the Catholic diocese of Aba, Nigeria. He obtained a doctorate in theology and religious studies (PhD; STD) from the Catholic University Leuven, Belgium. A past visiting researcher at the Institute of Hermeneutics, University of Bonn, Germany, he is currently a postdoctoral research associate at the Theologische Fakultät Trier, Germany. He is the author of *Ecumenical and Interreligious Identities in Nigeria: Transformation through Dialogue* (2021) and published in many international peer-reviewed journals, including *Exchange*; *Ecumenical Review*; *Journal of Ecumenical Studies*; *Transformation*; and *International Bulletin of Mission Research*, among others.

Vincent J. O'Malley, CM, was born in Philadelphia, Pennsylvania, and raised in South Jersey. He entered the Vincentian seminary in 1963, completing his theological studies at Mary Immaculate Seminary at Northampton, Pennsylvania, prior to ordination to priesthood in 1973. He has served in a variety of ministries: high school; university teaching and administration; vocation and formation ministries; parish ministry at Bedford-Stuyvesant in Brooklyn, New York, and at St. Joseph Parish, Emmitsburg, Maryland; and retreat ministry. Currently, he serves as university chaplain at Niagara University in Niagara Falls, New York. He has researched and written five books on the saints: *Saintly Companions* (1995); *Ordinary Sufferings of Extraordinary Saints* (2000); *Saints of Africa* (2001); *Saints of North America* (2004); and *Saints of Asia* (2007). He has authored more than a dozen articles, mostly on promoting vocations and pastoral topics, which were published in *The Priest* magazine and in vocation journals. He has served on the Board of Catholic Education for the Diocese of Buffalo, New York, and the Board of Trustees for Mount St. Mary's University in Emmitsburg, Maryland, and currently serves on the Board of Trustees for the St. Vincent de Paul Society of Western New York.

Agbonkhianmeghe E. Orobator, SJ, is a member of the Society of Jesus (the Jesuits) and president of the Jesuit Conference of Africa and Madagascar. He received his PhD from the University of Leeds in England. Among other books, he is the author of

Theology Brewed in an African Pot (2008) and *Religion and Faith in Africa: Confessions of an Animist* (2018).

Florence Adetoun Oso, EHJ, was born in 1966 in Lagos, Nigeria, and attended UNA Mission School and Our Lady of Apostles Girls Secondary School Ijebu-Ode. She made a first profession of vows in the Congregation of the Sisters of the Eucharistic Heart of Jesus in 1986, and obtained a doctoral degree in missiology from the Pontifical Urbaniana University, Rome, in 1993, and a postgraduate diploma in education from the University of Jos (Nigeria) in 2002. She began her teaching career at St. Augustine's Major Seminary in 1996, where she lectured for eleven years before moving to Ibadan in 2008. She is currently senior lecturer and assistant head of the Department of Theology at the Seminary of SS. Peter & Paul, Bodija, Ibadan, Nigeria.

Idara Otu, MSP, a member of the Missionary Society of St. Paul, teaches dogmatic theology at the National Missionary Seminary of St. Paul, in Abuja, Nigeria. He is the author of *Communion Ecclesiology and Social Transformation in African Catholicism: Between Vatican Council II and African Synod II* (2020).

Cosmas Ebo Sarbah studied at the Pontifical Institute of Dar Comboni for Arabic and Islamic Studies in Cairo and received an MPhil from the Pontifical Institute of Arabic and Islamic Studies in Rome and a PhD from the Centre for Christian-Muslim Relations at the University of Birmingham (UK). He is director of interreligious dialogue for the Catholic Archdiocese of Cape Coast, Ghana, and since 2012 has been a lecturer in both the Department for the Study of Religions at the University of Ghana and at St. Peter's Regional Seminary in Pedu. He also took part in a study conducted by the US Institute on Religious Pluralism at the University of California, Santa Barbara, in 2016. His articles have appeared in *Studies in Interreligious Dialogue*, the *Journal of Ecumenical Studies*, the *Trinity Journal of Church and Theology*, and the *Journal of Applied Thought*.

Nicholaus Segeja is a diocesan priest from the Archdiocese of Mwanza, Tanzania. He holds a master's degree, licentiate (STL), and doctorate in theology (PhD/STD) with a specialization in pastoral theology from the Catholic University of Eastern Africa (CUEA), Kenya. Fr. Segeja is a professor in pastoral theology and a member of the International Theological Commission, Vatican City, Rome. The former head of the Department of Pastoral Theology at CUEA, he is currently director of its Eldoret Gaba Campus. He teaches courses in fundamental pastoral theology; methods in pastoral theology; strategic pastoral planning; team/collaborative (reverential dialogical) ministry in the church; laity, religious, and ordained ministers; the social teaching of the church from a pastoral theological perspective; and church leadership and management, among others. He is chief editor of the *Good Shepherd Journal of Pastoral Theology*. He has coedited and written several books and articles, especially in the areas of research methodologies, contextual theology, and ecclesial synodality.

Hellen Sitawa Wanyonyi is lecturer in the Department of Social Sciences at the University of Eldoret, Kenya. She holds a PhD in religious studies from Moi University in Kenya. Her chief research interest is moral values and ethics for young people, and her doctoral research investigates how traditional African values may be integrated with Christian values, especially in the development of modern initiation rites in western Kenya, a study that is part of the broader work of the African Christian Initiation Project (ACIP).

Nathanaël Yaovi Soédé holds PhDs in theology from St. Paul University in Ottawa, Canada, and in philosophy from the University of Ottawa. He is a priest from the Diocese of Lokossa in Benin. He was a full-time professor in the Department of Theology at the Catholic University of West Africa in Abidjan from 1991 to 2009 and at the Institut Catholique Missionnaire d'Abidjan from 2010 to 2017. He has been a visiting professor at the Jesuit Institut de Théologie in Abidjan at the Catholic University of the Congo in the Democratic Republic of the Congo (DRC) and also served as a visiting research fellow with the Center for World Catholicism and Intercultural Theology (CWCIT), DePaul University, Chicago, Illinois. He is president of the Association of African Theologians and sits on the theological committee of the

Symposium of Episcopal Conferences of Africa and Madagascar. He has mentored various international research programs (Iwalehaus, University of Bayreuth [2005–2008]; and the Nagel Institute of Chicago [2015–2017]); and oversaw publication of the *Dictionary of African Theology* (2012–2017). He is author of many books and articles focusing on African ethics, anthropological and philosophical ethics, Christian ethics, African Christian theology, Christianity, crisis, reconstruction, and the African renaissance.

✠**George Desmond Tambala, OCD,** is the archbishop of Lilongwe, Malawi (Zomba, Malawi), and a member of the Order of the Discalced Carmelites. He studied philosophy at the Intercongregational Institute in Balaka, Malawi, and received a BA in theology from Tangaza College, Nairobi. He also received a diploma of specialization in mysticism and Carmelite spirituality from Centro Internacional Teresiano Sanjuanista, Ávila, Spain, and a licentiate in theology from Facultad de Teologia del Norte de España, Vitoria, Spain, where his research topic was "African Theology in Engelbert Mveng, SJ." He was a member of the General Council of the Order of the Discalced Carmelites in Rome (2009–2015). He is the author of *History of Religious Life in Africa: Shift of Paradigm*; and *Prophetic African Religious Life in the 21st Century* (both 2017). His research interests are the history of spirituality, mysticism/spirituality, theology of the consecrated life, and psychology/formation to religious life.

Bernhard Udelhoven, MAfr, born in 1968 in Germany, is a member of the Missionaries of Africa (the White Fathers) and has worked in Zambia since 1989. He studied social anthropology in London. At present he ministers in Lumimba parish in Zambia's Luangwa Valley and is also affiliated with the Faith & Encounter Centre (FENZA) in Lusaka.

Dorris van Gaal was born and raised in the Netherlands. She received her master's in theology from the Katholieke Universiteit in Nijmegen and worked as a lay pastor for Roman Catholic parishes with large migrant communities. In 2006, she emigrated with her husband and children to Baltimore, Maryland. She continued working for the Roman Catholic Church, while also teaching theology courses at Loyola and Notre Dame Universities in Baltimore, Maryland. Her main theological interests are migration theology and world Christianity. She received her PhD in theology from her alma mater, the (now) Radboud University in Nijmegen, the Netherlands.

Gabriel T. Wankar is a Catholic priest of the Diocese of Gboko, Nigeria, and is currently involved in pastoral ministry in the Archdiocese of San Francisco, California. He earned his doctoral degree in systematic theology at the Jesuit School of Theology in Berkeley, California. He also holds a master of science degree in development studies. His research interests are in the areas of church and society, ecclesiology, and community organizing and development.

Quentin Wodon is a lead economist at the World Bank. Previously, he managed the Bank's work on faith and development and served as lead poverty specialist for Africa and senior economist for Latin America. His focus has been on policy analysis and dialogue in over fifty countries. He previously taught at the University of Namur, as well as at American University and Georgetown University, both in Washington, DC. Trained in business engineering, he worked in brand management for Procter & Gamble before shifting careers and joining a nonprofit working with the extreme poor. He has tried to remain faithful to the cause of ending extreme poverty ever since. A lifelong learner, he holds four PhDs and has authored more than five hundred publications, a few of which have been carried by leading international news media. Awards include the Prize of Belgium's Secretary for Foreign Trade, a Fulbright grant, the Dudley Seers Prize, and the World Bank President's Award for Excellence. He served as president of two economics associations and two Rotary clubs. In 2020, he launched the Global Catholic Education project, an effort to provide resources on Catholic education and integral human development.

Index

AACC (All Africa Conference of
    Churches), 170, 170n38
  established, 719
  and Moratorium Declaration, 87
  moratorium of missionaries of,
    353
  and vernacular translations of
    Bible, 169
Abakaliki dialect (Nigeria), 655
abolitionist movement(s)
  and African church, 156
  church's involvement with (19th
    century), 156–57
  See also slavery; slave trade
abundant life
  aspects of, 511
  as basis for African anthropology,
    676
  Christ as, 608
  theology of, 525–26
abuse
  and family, 574
  See also Africa, challenges facing
accountability, 58n89
Acholonu, Catherine
  Motherism of, 552
ACIP (African Christian Initiation
  Project), and modern initiation
  rites, 459, 462
ACP (African Catholicism Project)
  and idea of *Handbook*, xxi–xxii
  objectives of, xxii
Ad Gentes (Vatican II, Decree on the
  Church's Missionary Activity),
  12
  on catechumenate, 58
  and diversity of customs, 170
  on indigenous theologies, 172
  on missionary work, 269
  quoted by *Africae Munus*, 685
  on seeds of the word in Islam, 373
  on task of developing a local
    church, 24
  theological research and, 600
  See also evangelization; mission;
    missionaries; Vatican II
adaptation
  and incarnation, 90
  and inculturation, 83

rejection of, 90
superficiality of, 90
weakness of, 664
Adogame, Afe
  on African immigrants, 71, 77
  on liminality, 68
  on migration, 65
Adotévi, Stanislas Spero, and denun-
    ciation of negritude, 675
Adoukonou, Barthélemy, on African
  sage as community intellectual,
  674
AEA (Association of Evangelicals in
  Africa), 170, 170n39
  biblical interpretation of, 176n80
AECAWA (Association of Episcopal
  Conferences of Anglophone
  West Africa), 51
Aedesius (youth), story of, in Ethiopia,
  9
Afan, Mawuto, OP, on ethics in a
  multidisciplinary framework,
  144
Afonso I (king of Kongo; ruled
  1506–1543), 30
  conversion of, to Catholicism, 150,
    226
  and cult of ancestors, 85
  and denunciation of European
    slave merchants, 151–52
  and development of Catholicism,
    34
  as modernizer, 151
  as patron and defender of mission-
    aries, 150
  viewed as mystic, 150
Afonso V (king of Portugal), right of,
  to enslave Muslims, 155
Africa
  anthropology of, 225
  challenges facing, xxi, 16, 705–6
    (*see also under* individual
    issues)
  Christianity in (*see* Christianity in
    Africa)
  cultural realities of, as challenge to
    faith, 80
  cultural values of, 140–41
  European view of, 670

exploration of, by European pow-
    ers, 264
future of: philosophy and, 677–78
geographical meaning of term in
    early church, 166n1
income inequality in, 88
independence of nations in, 86
Latin Roman: canon law in,
    258–60; celebration of martyrs
    in, 34
meaning of, 127
micro-nations in, 128
philosophy of, 671
postcolonial Christian: history of,
    166–67
as "radio continent," 210–11
seminary training in, 292
songs and dances in, 316
suffering in, 610, 610n36
vibrant religiosity of, 88
viewed as lacking history, 157
viewed as nonrational culture,
    157
and West, 668, 670
West's discourse about, 670–75
West's erroneous picture of, 674
Africae Munus (Pope Benedict XVI,
    post-synodal apostolic exhor-
    tation; 2011)
  agenda of, 223–38
  on anthropological crisis, 580–81
  on apostolate of women, 559
  on candidates for priesthood, 293
  on Catholic Social Teaching, 363
  on church as family of God,
    102n23
  on church presence in media,
    210–11
  on development, 349
  on dialogue, 102, 369
  and *Ecclesia in Africa*, 684–85,
    697–715
  five major proposals of, 702
  implementation of, 235–37,
    702–3
  on importance of education, 234
  inculturation and, 689
  on interreligious dialogue, 654,
    654n44

739

Index

Africae Munus (cont.)
   on magisterium and inculturation, 140–41
   on new form of leadership, 109
   objectives of, 225–26
   on recognition of women, 362
   on reconciliation, justice, and peace, 225, 355, 355n43, 356–59, 702–3
   on SCCs, 190–91
   on soul of Africa, xviii, 685
   See also Benedict XVI, Pope
Africae Terrarum (papal message of Paul VI), 352, 352n35
   on African religion, 431
   on attention to ancient African religious cultures, 688–89
   See also Paul VI, Pope
African, meaning of term, 648, 649
African Book of Blessings, need for, 58
African church. *See* Catholic Church in Africa
African Ecclesiastical/Ecclesial Review, 353
African identity. *See* identity, African
African Independent Churches. *See* AICs
African Indigenous Churches. *See* AICs
African Indigenous Religions
   efforts of Muslims to proselytize, 375
   See also ATR
African Initiated Churches. *See* AICs
African Instituted Churches. *See* AICs
African interests, issues in, 58n89
African migrants to the U.S. *See* migrants to the U.S., African
African Missal, need for, 58
African names, and implication of theophoric names, 175
African nationalism, 87
African people
   characterized as savages (15th century), 262
   misrepresentations of, by Western writers, 651
African religion. *See* religion, African; *see also* AICs; ATR
African Society of Culture. *See* SAC
African theologians. *See* theologians, African
African theology. *See* theology, African
African thought
   and community, 726
   and connection between belief and practice, 22–23
   and connection between spiritual and material worlds, 20, 22–23

African Traditional Religion. *See* ATR
African traditional rites, and catechesis, 639–40
Africana, use of term, 552
Africana womanism. *See* womanism, Africana
Africanization, racial overtones of term, 83–84
Africans
   absence of, at Vatican II, 719
   as active historical agents, 149
   as descendants of Ham, 268
   and high leadership posts in churches, 719
   as masters of their history, 675
   viewed as irrational and nonhistorical, 158
Agamben, Giorgio, on idea of "bare life," 521–22
Agang, Atal Sa, on church as fraternity, 591
Age of Enlightenment. *See* Enlightenment, Age of
Age of Exploration, 10
agency, African
   and challenges to development, 357
   destruction of, 345
   in growth of African Christianity, 31
   of poor people, 350
aggiornamento, 96, 627
   as spirit of Vatican II, 12
   Vatican II and, 468, 685
   See also John XXIII, Pope; Vatican II
Agossou, Médéwalé-Jacob, on "fraternity" in African context, 591
agriculture, decline of, 340
Agrippinus, Bishop, and Council of Carthage (3rd century), 258
Ahmadiyya Movement (Muslim missionary movement), 375
Ahmed Sékou Touré (ruler in Guinea), 227, 228
Ahmed, Nahed Mohammed
   on African womanism, 552
   on centrality of family, 561
AICs
   abuse of, 407
   and beginning of SCCs, 186
   and charismatic Christianity, 482
   and Ethiopianism movement, 86
   and gifts of the Holy Spirit, 468
   and global issues, 719
   healing ministries of, 172
   and inculturation, 89–90
   as models and signs of hope, 89–90
   problems of, 90

   and recovery of African traditions, 91
   role of, in politics, 407
   spiritual components of sickness and, 516
Akong'a, Joshua, on information and communication in family planning, 457
Alamano, Blessed Giuseppe (founder of Missionaries of the Consolata), 310
Alexander VI, Pope, bull *Inter Caetera* (1493), 155, 261 (*see also Inter Caetera*)
Alexandria (Egypt)
   as center of ancient academic life, 32, 650–51
   and Coptic apostolic throne, 148
   as early center of Christendom, 130, 331
   Mark the evangelist as first bishop of, 4
   surrender of, to Islamic Arab army, 7
All Africa Conference of Churches. *See* AACC
Allen, John, Jr.
   on African church, 556
   on Vatican II from sociological perspective, 688
al-Qaeda, against Western and Christian dominance in Africa, 377
al-Shaba'ab (Kenya and Somalia), and dysfunctional government, 374
Alston, Phillip, on Millennium Development Goals and human rights, 421–22
alterity
   planetary living and, 438–39
   spirituality and, 440–41
Alufuo, Rev. Mother Patricia, OSB, 559n85
Alumuku, Patrick, on radio stations in Africa, 210–11
Alva, Reginauld, on good fruits of Catholic Charismatic Renewal, 486
Alvaro I (grandson of Afonso)
   expansion of African church under, 152
   recognition of papal primacy by, 152
Alvaro II (son of Alvaro I)
   claim to throne by, 152
   dealings of, with Rome, 152–53
Ambrose of Milan, Saint
   denial of communion by, to Emperor Theodosius II (390), 410
   and inculturation, 85

Index

AMECEA (Association of Member Episcopal Conferences in Eastern Africa)
  on BCCs and SCCs, 186–89, 690–91
  Bible sharing and reflection of, 192–93
  on laity, 479
  in nine English-speaking countries of eastern Africa, 186n5
  and priority of building SCCs, 188
  vision of, focused on communion, 193
AMECEA Pastoral Institute (Gaba, Eldoret, Kenya), 188
Ammah, Rabiatu, on implementation of Sharī'a law, 376
Ammon (d. ca. 356), monasticism and, 6
Amo, Antoine-Guillaume, on contradictions of Descartes, 677
Amoris Laetitia (Pope Francis, post-synodal apostolic exhortation; 2016)
  on pastoral challenges related to family, 460
  problems of implementation of, 656
  vision of church serving families in, 712
  See also Francis, Pope
analogy of faith, as principle of Catholic theology, 657n58
anamnesis
  meaning of, 48n44
  as memorial of paschal mystery, 41n5, 47, 48–49
ancestor(s)
  Africans bound to, 429
  and African notion of life, 432
  criteria for veneration of, 433
  cult of, 85
  hierarchy of, 433
  and naming ceremonies, 55–56
  as model of moral life, 433
  role of, 432–33
  social continuity and, 427
  spirituality of belief in, 466
  veneration of and inculturation, 276
Anderson, Allan
  on African spirituality and global Pentecostalism, 473
  on Holy Spirit revisiting Africa, 466
  on rise of Pentecostalism in Africa, 485
Anderson, Benedict, on racism in Asia, 158

Anderson, Rufus, on proper missionary method, 722
Anglican-Roman Catholic International Commission, 383
Angola, evangelization programs in, 10
animistic mentality, 333
anointing of the sick
  as church's continuation of Jesus's healing ministry, 503
  healing character of, 523
Ansar Dine (Mali), and dysfunctional government, 374
Anselm, Saint, and faith seeking understanding, 144
Anthony of Egypt, Saint
  as founder of religious life in Latin church, 309
  monastic movement and, 717
anthropocentrism
  as bane of ecological rectitude, 437
  negative interpretation of, 436
anthropogenia, 437, 437n58
anthropology
  African: based on concept of fullness of life, 676; conception of person in, 417–18
  challenge of, 580–81
  theological, 419; as ground of theology of development, 355
  Western, 667
Anti-Balaka (Christian militia groups), in Central African Republic, 374
antijuridicalism, 278
Antonian movement, and indigenous religion, 85–86
Antony, Saint
  monks and, 5–6
  and solitary desert life, 5
Anyanwu, Mother Mary Charles, OSB, 559n85
Aparecida Document, 137, 137n27
  on popular piety in Latin America, 480–81
Apiarius of Sicca, excommunication of, 259
apostasy, during Roman persecution, 33
Apostolicam Actuositatem (Vatican II, Decree on the Apostolate of the Laity)
  on proper discernment in Pentecostal churches, 472
  quoted by *Africae Munus*, 685
  See also laity; Vatican II
Aquiar, Rui de (1516), on King Afonso of Kongo, 333
Archdiocese of Baltimore, and categories of U.S. census, 64

Archdiocese of Kampala (Uganda), ordinations in, 22
Archdiocese of Kinshasa, and SCCs, 187, 196
Archdiocese of Mwanza (Tanzania), and SCCs, 189
architecture, modern: examples of, in churches in Africa, 213
  Assumpta Cathedral (Owerri, Nigeria), 213
  Basilica of the Uganda Martyrs (Namugongo, Uganda), 213
  Don Bosco Catholic Church (Nairobi, Kenya), 213
  Igreja Santana (Caxito, Angola), 213
  Mater Ecclesia Cathedral (Ahiara, Nigeria), 213
  Shrine of Mary Help of Christians (Nairobi, Kenya), 213
  St. Gabriel's Chaplaincy Church (Abuja, Nigeria), 213
ARCIC (Anglican-Roman Catholic International Commission), ecumenism and, 383
Arendt, Hannah, Kä Mana's dialogue with ideas of, 678
Arianism, 7–8
Aristotle, 100
  influence of, Egypt on, 676
  on leadership, 115
  Nicomachean Ethics of, 115–16
  Politics and human being as political animal, 232–33
Armstrong, Dave, on church's position on sex, 452
Arrupe, Pedro (Father), on inculturation, 81–82
Arusha Declaration, 405
Asamoah-Gyadu, J. Kwabena
  on Africa as hot-bed of charismatic Christianity, 482
  on AICs, 482
  on Pentecostals, 348–49
Ascension Health, 502
Ashanti (people; Ghana)
  Ashanti Mass, 53
  Corpus Christi celebration, 53
  Odwira festival, 53
Asia
  Christian theologies in, 168–69
  as new center of Christianity, 168
Asika, Ukpabi
  as beneficiary of Catholic education, 234
  leading takeover of schools in Nigeria, 229
Association of Episcopal Conferences of Anglophone West Africa, 51

741

Index

Association of Evangelicals in Africa. *See* AEA
Association of Member Episcopal Conferences in Eastern Africa. *See* AMECEA
Association of St. Anne, education of laity and, 479
Association of St. Monica, education of laity and, 479
Athanasius, Saint (patriarch of Alexandria), 6, 21, 30, 32
 as African church father, 166n4
 as doctor of the church, 6
 and early Christianity in Africa, 81, 309
 and evangelization of Ethiopia, 6
 on life as festival, 526
 preaching in Coptic language, 84
 role of, in formulating perennial theology, 650–51
 theological anthropology of, 437
atheism, African aversion to, 663
Atingas (peasant majority), industrialization and, 341
ATR (African Traditional Religion), 429
 advocacy and, 424
 African theologies and, 649
 and Christian message, 173
 defense of, 652
 derogatory descriptions of, by Westerners, 651
 ethical perspectives of, 443
 as *preparatio evangelica*, 172
 as source of African studies on the New Testament, 172
Atyam, Angela (northern Uganda), courage of, 34
Audollent, Auguste, on early councils of church, 260
Augustine, Saint (bishop of Hippo), 5, 6, 21, 30, 331
 as African church father, 166n4
 and ancient church in Africa, 81
 on benefits of Christ's saving event, 617
 and biblical interpretation, 174–75
 on Christian empire as mirror of heavenly one, 332
 on Christian religion among the ancients, xxv
 Christian tradition and, 717
 as doctor of the church, 6
 and Latinate Africans, 33
 on parable of Good Samaritan, 640
 as patristic exegete, 637
 on politics, 397
 referred to as *Romanus Augustinus* of Hippo, 43

reverence for personal sanctity in, 34
 role in formulating perennial theology, 650–51
 and sexual morality, 450–51, 454, 462
 at synods of Hippo and Carthage, 698
 as theologian of African church, 148
 on unanimity of heart and mind, 105
Augustinians, 10
austerity, in Catholic Church of North Africa, 331–32
authority, and respect, 121
Ave Maria Pastoral Center (Tzaneen, South Africa), 188
Ayittey, George, on postindependence Africa, 340–41
Ayyudid dynasty, tolerance of Christians in, 8
Azana, King, in Ethiopia, 6

Babangida, Ibrahim, leader of military junta (1990), 230
Babu, Abdul Rahman Mohammed, on Kwame Nkrumah's conscienticism, 676
Bacteriological Revolution, 518
Baczko, Bronislaw, Kä Mana's dialogue with ideas of, 678
Bakhita, Josephine, Saint (Sudan), 21
Bakongo kingdom, 226
Balandier, Georges, Alioune Diop and, 301
Balokole Movement, 483
Baltimore City, northeast, Catholic community of, 69–71
Bamat, Thomas, on colonization, 19
Bamubamu, Brighton (street preacher) on charism, 469
Banakar, Reza, on idea of universal human rights, 422
Banana, Canaan (Reverend; first president of Zimbabwe), 405
Bandung Conference (1955), Third World voices and, 623
baptism
 and celebration of thanksgiving for child, 57
 development of rite of, 85
 of married converts by missionaries, 262
Bardy, G., on early synods and councils, 259–60
Barney, G. L., on inculturation, 82
Basic Christian Communities. *See* BCCs

Basic Ecclesial Communities. *See* BECs
Basukuma of Tanzania, and *shikome*, 102
Bauman, Whitney, on planetary perspective, 439
Baur, John
 on education in Congo, 226
 on foreignness of Christian faith, 86
 on King Afonso of Kongo, 333
 on mission and colonization, 19
 on missionary movement of 16th and 17th centuries, 718
 on monastic movement, 717
BCCs (Basic Christian Communities), 185n2, 595
 ecclesiological validity of, 723
 as model of church, 185
BECs (Basic Ecclesial Communities), 185n2, 595
 as model of church, 185
Bediako, Kwame
 on Christianity as African experience, 172
 on grassroots Christologies, 607–8
Belgian Congo, Western education in, 226
Belgian orders, in DRC, 17
Bellarmine, Robert, 153
Benedict XV, Pope, beatification of Uganda Martyrs (1920), 305
Benedict XVI, Pope (Joseph Cardinal Ratzinger)
 on African sisters, 558
 on African women, 561
 on Catholic involvement in civic activities, 336
 on charismatic gifts, 471
 on church's mission in Africa, 98
 on communication of gospel, 208–9
 on condom use, 460
 on contraception, 455, 462
 on education in the faith, 582
 encyclical *Caritas in Veritate* (2009), 358
 encyclical *Deus Caritas Est* (2005), 335
 encyclical *Spe Salvi*, 703, 704, 710, 711
 on families in Africa, 561–62
 on God as personal, 578–79
 on *Humanae Vitae*, 455 (*see also* *Humanae Vitae*)
 on Jesus bringing light and salt to Africa, xxv
 on Jesus's sense of God, 578–80

INDEX

on liturgy as education to the gospel, 49n47
on media, 210
on popular piety in Latin America, 481
on school of Alexandria and church in Africa, xxv
on special faculties in China, 272
on spirituality of communion, 216
on use of media for church, 409
on women, 559, 567–68
post-synodal apostolic exhortation *Verbum Domini* (2010), 209, 627
See also Africae Munus
Benedictine Word Incarnate Abbey, 559n85
Benedictines, in DRC, 17
Benin
  Christian activity in early modern period in, 30
  evangelization programs in, 10
Berbers, resistance to Islam by, 8
Berger, Peter, market model of religion of, 348
Berger, Teresa, on women and Vatican II, 559
Bergson, Henri, legacy of Western philosophy and, 677
Berlin Conference (1884–1885), 19
  initiated colonial era in Africa, 264, 311
Berman, Edward, on missionary schools in Africa, 245
Bertone, Tarcisio Cardinal, on authentic charisms, 471–72
Bevans, Stephen
  on contextualization, 84, 137
  on expert theologians, 661
  on non-Africans doing African theology, 648
  on *theologia perennis* (perennial theology), 104, 658
  on theologizing in African culture, 650
Biafra, war against secession (1967–70), 229, 229n20
Biayenda, Cardinal, murdered in political strife, 354
Bible
  as accomplice in colonialism, oppression, and racism, 170
  African approach to, 635–37
  in African languages, 18, 169, 634–35
  African traditions and, 636–37
  as central to the mission of SCCs, 192–93

ecumenical translations of, 388
Ethiopian commentaries on, 637–39
genre of works in, 636
holistic reading of, 640
in life and mission of church, 628–29
liturgy and, 642
messages of prophets in, 641
misuse and misinterpretation of, 472
as normative framework, 415
pastoral use of, 637
relation of, to liturgy, 44n20
scribal traditions of, 635, 635n7
semantic analysis and, 636
social life and ethics and, 634–46
spiritual meaning of, and Ethiopian commentaries, 638–39
textual criticism and, 636
theological meaning of, 630n57
and visual arts, drama, and media, 642–43
See also biblical exegesis/interpretation; biblical studies, African; *see also* Index of Scripture Passages *below*
Biblical Centre for Africa and Madagascar. *See* BICAM
biblical exegesis/interpretation
  African, for effective catechesis, 634–46
  catechesis and, 635
  contextualized, 628
  and dogmatic statements, 177
  dogmatic theology and, 630n58
  faith and, 639–44
  historical-critical approach to, 638, 644
  meaning of, 168, 168n12
  methods of, 635–36, 638, 638n15
  patristic: and Ethiopian commentaries on Bible, 637–39; as faith-centered, 644; catechesis and, 640
  tools of, 627n37
  on Western model, 173–74
  See also Bible; biblical studies, African; biblical theology
biblical scholars, African, as praxis-oriented, 166, 168
biblical studies, African, 169–71
  ATR as source of, 172
  deposit of faith as source of, 172
  and hermeneutics of church fathers in, 174–75
  history and methods of, 166–82
  living experience of church as source of, 172–73

methodological considerations relating to, 174–77
nature of, 172–74
sources of, 171–72
thematic approach to, 174
See also New Testament studies in Africa
biblical theology, 168, 168n13
BICAM (Biblical Centre for Africa and Madagascar), 629, 631
  roots of, at Vatican II, 629
  training workshops at, 196
Bieringer, Reimund, on revelation and dialogue, 387–88
Bigard Memorial Seminary (Enugu, Nigeria), 22
  visit of John Paul II to, 51
Bill, Fr. (Vincentian Congregation of India), 486–88
Bilongo, Barnabe, on status of women, 679
Biney, Moses, on African immigrants, 71, 77
biomedical model, and transformative understanding of healing, 523–25
Biondi, Fabio (papal envoy), praise of Kongolese by, 153
biopolitics, privileged populations and, 520–21
biopsychosocial model
  implementation of, 500
  of Mary Gloria C. Njoku, 500
biopsychosospiritual, meaning of term, 498n9
biopsychosospiritual health care
  curriculum for training medical professionals and, 508
  team approach to, 508
Birt, Robert (African American philosopher), 675
bishops
  African: in 3rd and 4th centuries, 5
  governing authority of, 272
  growth in ethnic and cultural diversity of, 143
  regional: authority of, 723
Bishops' Conference of Zaire, and inculturation, 85n30
Biya, Robert Ntebi, on African metaphysics, 677
Black, as description of African American in census, 63–64
Black internationalism, 299, 301
Black liberationist discourse, 353–54
Black nationalism, and independence of African nations, 86
Black people
  viewed as cursed race, 156
  viewed as lacking souls, 158

743

INDEX

Black people (*cont.*)
    viewed as uncivilized in West, 667
Black theology
    focus of, on liberation, 91
    and God as liberator, 170
    and New Testament studies, 172
    North American, 91
    relationship of, to African theology, 91
    of South Africa, 169–72
Blyden, Edward, and development of African nationalism, 87
Bobbio Missal, 41
body of Christ
    and church, 410, 590, 699
    and Eucharist, 296, 297
    expressing reality of communion, 99
    and inclusiveness, 99
    and inculturation, 136
    incorporation through baptism, 575
    and the laity, 22
    and liturgy, 45
    unity of, 60
    worship of, 40n2
Boeije, Hennie, on qualitative research and grounded theory, 66–67
Boesak, Allan, on Black theology, 172
Boff, Leonardo
    on church as authoritarian system, 361
    on grace, 320
Boko Haram (Nigeria and Cameroon)
    begun as peaceful movement, 374
    and dysfunctional government, 374
    and poor human rights image of Nigeria, 419–20
    violence of, 374
Bolt, Cawley, on positive aspects of syncretism, 89
Bongmba, Elias
    on crisis of postcolonial state, 340–41
    on critical dialogue with state, 360
    on Katongole's *Sacrifice in Africa*, 360
Bonhoeffer, Dietrich, on cheap grace, 288
Boni, Tanella, on status of women, 679
Boniface VIII, Pope
    bull *Unam Sanctam* (1302), 723
    every human subject to Roman pontiff, 723
Bonnke, Reinhardt, leader of Christ for All Nations, 486
Bosch, David J.
    on contextualization, 84

    on mission approach in postcolonial Africa, 722
Botha, P. W. (president; South Africa), and Zion Christian Church, 407
Botswana, Catholic mission hospitals and clinics in, 372
Bradshaw, Paul F., on result of Arab conquest, 43
Bresillac, Blessed Melchior Marion de, founder of Society of African Missions, 310
Breviarum Hipponense, legislation promulgated at Council of Hippo, 259
Breviatio canonum (6th century), canons of early Greek and African councils, 259
Brigit, Sr. (charismatic preacher from Ireland), 486
British Congo, colonized by Great Britain, 11
British East Africa, colonized by Great Britain, 11
broadcast media, as tool of evangelization, 210–11
Brothers of St. John of God, 10
Buber, Martin
    on dialogue, 668
    on dialogical character of human person, 233
Buetubela, Paul, on church as fraternity, 591
Bujo, Bénézet
    on African values of community, ancestors, and life, 592
    on ancestral beliefs, 427, 429, 432, 433
    on communal dimension in African view, 432, 434
    on dialogue, 650
    ecclesiology of, 592
    on Fourth Gospel, 172, 176–77
    on fundamental structures of African religiosity, 432
    on Jesus as "proto-ancestor," 592
    on natural family planning, 456
    on Placide Tempels as starting point for African theology, 170
    on seminary training, 294
    social analysis of, 353
Burkina Faso
    and SCCs, 187 (*see also* SCCs)
    parental choice in education in, 248–49
Burns, J. Patout, Jr., on Roman North Africa, 32–33
Burns, James MacGregor, and transformational leadership model, 115–17

Burundi, risks of poverty in, and education, 249, 251 (figure)
Buthelezi, Manas
    on Black theology, 172
Buthelezi, Mangosuthu (chief), seeking political support from Zion Christian Church, 407
Byzacena, part of Latin North Africa, 32

CABAN (Catholic Biblical Association of Nigeria), 629
    and inculturation, 60, 60n92
Cairo Conference (International Conference on Population and Development), 709–10
Calame-Griaule, Geneviève
    dialogue between Western and African philosophy and, 676
    on Dogon culture, 676
Calisi, Matteo, on antecedents to Catholic Charismatic Renewal, 483–84
Calixtus, Pope (1456), ordinance of, prohibiting enslavement of Catholics, 154
CAMECO (Catholic Media Council), 211n31
Cameroon
    appearances of Blessed Virgin in, 12
    colonized by Germany, 11
    enrollment of students from privileged households in, 250
    refugees from Central African Republic, 374
    relief initiatives by Catholic Church in, 377
    and SCCs, 187 (*see also* SCCs)
    vocations in, 16
Cameroonian Mass, 52n60
Campese, Gioacchino, on migration theology, 66
Camus, Albert, and Alioune Diop, 301
Cancouët, Father Michel, and assistance to West African bishops at Vatican II, 625
Caney, Simon, on globalization, 679
canon law
    adaptation of, to diverse circumstances, 272
    contextualizing of, 276
    current phase of, impacted by Vatican II, 258
    and custom in Africa, 276–77
    definition of, 257, 257n1
    development, challenges, and prospects of, 257–83
    and good governance, 270

Index

and growth of church in Africa, 270
holistic consideration of, 278–80
inadequate knowledge of, 270–71
institutions granting degrees in, 279nn 132–33
jurisprudence and, 279–80
legislation and, 278
and legislative canonical autonomy, 258
missionary activity and, 258, 262
and missionary law, 258
particular circumstances allowed by, 271–77
and religious life, 324
in Roman Africa, 258–60
and Roman law, 280
science of, 278–79
synchronic historical approach to, 257
universal and particular, 269–77
as vehicle for dialogue between faith and life, 278
and Westernization of particular churches, 271–72
widespread apathy to, 271
Canon Law, Code of, 91–92
and authority of bishop, 273
first (1917), 268
on scholastic method, 101n21
See also canon law
canon law in Africa
during era of royal patronage, 260–63
historical phases of, 258–69
present state of, 269–77
scholarship of, 278–79
Canon Law Society of Nigeria, and inculturation, 50, 60n92
canonical norms, collections of, 259–60
Cão, Diogo (Portuguese explorer of Congo basin; 1482), 150
Cape Verde, Catholic diocese established in, 10
capitalism
as challenge to African Catholicism, 143
effect of, on environment, 428
and global economy, 98
rejection of, in *Populorum Progressio*, 352
Capuchins, and evangelization of sub-Saharan Africa, 10–11
CARA (Center for Applied Research in the Apostolate), on population growth in Africa, xix
Carey, James, on ritual model of communication, 213

Carey, William (1792), role of Christian, 110
Carmelites, 10
Carpenter, Joel, on Roman Catholic Church in Africa, xix
Carthage (Tunisia)
conquest of, 258
early Catholic faith in, 331
falling to Islam, 8
as root of Christian faith in North Africa, 258
Carthage, Council of (256), 260n19
Carthage, Council/Synod of (397)
and *Breviarum Hipponense*, 259
canon of Bible and, 698
on prayers suspected of containing false doctrine, 42n8
Carthage, Councils of (3rd century–5th century), 258–59
Carthage, Synod of (407), on prayers under supervision of hierarchy, 42n8
Carthage, synods of, on matters of interest to African church, 698
Castillo Guerra, Jorge
on liminality, 68
on migration theology, 66
Castlereagh, Lord, as abolitionist, 156
catechesis
African exegesis and, 634–46
and African traditional rites, 639–40
African values and, 644
appropriate to audience, 643
children and, 643, 644
importance of testimony in, 643
liturgy as, 45
patristic exegesis and, 640
proclamation and, 368
setting for, 643–44
and translation of Bible into local languages, 635
visual arts and, 642
youth and, 643
Catechetical School of Alexandria
on procreation, 454
Catechism of the Catholic Church (CCC)
on adaptation of catechesis to different cultures, 634, 634n2
on conjugal love, 453
on creation, 439
on divine grace, 617
on healing ministry, 523, 523n56
on health care, 501
on offenses against chastity, 451–52
on procreative purpose of sex, 452
on solidarity, 439

catechists
lack of appreciation for, 22
pastoral leadership of, 21–22
catechumenates, and RCIA, 57–58
CATHAN (Catholic Theological Association of Nigeria), 170, 170n42
and inculturation, 60, 60n92
CATHCA (Catholic Health Care Association of Southern Africa), 502, 506–7
Cathedral of the Holy Savior (1596; Kongo), 153
Catholic Action, and education of laity, 479
Catholic Apostolic National Church (Uganda), 296
Catholic Biblical Association of Nigeria. *See* CABAN
Catholic chaplaincy in universities, and agenda of *Africae Munus*, 236
Catholic Charismatic Renewal. *See* Charismatic Renewal, Catholic
Catholic Church
Africa hurt by, 346
antislavery policies of, 154–60
Bible sharing and, 596
centralization of power in, 724
as church of poor and marginalized, 16
as collegial, 576
as communion, 99–100
corruption in governance of, 361
councils of (*see under individual location*)
development and, 346, 354–59
diaconal dimension of, 594
emerging theological thinking of, 717
as eschatological, 576
as family and community, 592 (*see also* Catholic Church as family of God)
as family, and SCCs, 193–94 (*see also* SCCs)
foundational experience of, 722–23
as fraternity, 591–92
gestures and symbols in, 208
grassroots and, 596
growth in number of African cardinals in, 143
growth of, and future, 717
growth of, in Africa, xix–xx, 720 (*see also* Catholic Church in Africa)
health care and, 497–98
as historical subject, xxiii

Catholic Church (*cont.*)
  history of, 717–18, 727
  and human rights, 416
  images and metaphors of, in sub-Saharan Africa, 589, 589n1
  images of, 99, 576
  inculturation and, 594–95, 597
  as *koinonia*, 383
  lack of transparency in governance of, 361
  lay leadership and, 596
  as listening church, 593–94
  ministerial function in, 96
  mission of, 335–36, 343; in African development, 347; and right to development, 422; as salvific, 329
  new model of, 596
  nonverbal communication in, 208
  patriarchy in governance of, 361–62
  politics and, 397–414 (*see also* church and state)
  post-Vatican II revival of, 20
  prophetic attitude of, 598
  public relations and, 215
  and public sphere, 616 (*see also* church and state)
  radio stations operated by (table), 211
  and relationship of hierarchy to missionaries, 268
  as sacrament, 584
  see-judge-act and, 596
  separation of church and state, 334 (*see also* church and state)
  as servant, 576, 597–99, 600
  sexual morality and, 449–65
  as sign and instrument of communication, 202
  social agency of, 343–50
  social paideia of, 363–64
  in solidarity with suffering, 594
  as spiritual force in world Christianity, xix
  spirituality of, 727
  structures of, 716–23
  Trinitarian understanding of, 193–94
  universal and particular, 269, 658
  valorization of women and, 596
  and Vatican II, 576 (*see also* Vatican II)
  as visible institution, 716
Catholic Church as family of God, 355, 388, 389, 592–94, 624nn20, 22
  in Africa, 573–85
  African synodal traditions and, 707–11
  African value of communal life and, 593, 708
  Catholic Social Teaching and, 600
  and Catholic studies in Africa, 95
  challenges of, 573–74, 582–83
  ecclesiology of, 575–77, 599–600
  and hope of communion, 707–8
  as inculturated church, 597
  kinship of multiple generations and, 708
  and leadership and authority, 593–94
  meaning of, 593–94
  as metaphor, 573–77, 593, 624
  and mission of church, 708–9
  and New Testament studies, 174
  reconciliation, justice, and peace and, 598, 600, 707, 708–10
  social implications of, 390
  as sociological reality, 575–76
  solidarity and, 709n67\
  specific actions of, 709–10
  in sub-Saharan Africa, 592–94
  as theme of First Synod, 574 (*see also* First Synod)
  as theological hope and guide, 575
  and unity of Trinity, 600
  universalism of, 579
Catholic Church in Africa
  anthropology and, 578, 580–81
  as agent of transformation, 584
  challenges facing, 16, 23–24, 109, 577–78
  conservatism of, 655
  criticisms of, 655
  dysfunctional situations in, 577
  ecclesiological propositions of, 594–99
  evangelization and, 580
  future of, 409–11, 716–28
  and global network of Catholic schools, 248
  growth of, 12, 119, 577–78, 663
  history of, 33, 81, 274: barbarian invasion and occupation, 6–7; in early centuries, 3–6; periodization in, xxiv
  holiness of, 33–34
  and Islamic expansion, 7–9; missionary revival in, 10–11
  as missionary church, 700
  as most important NGO, 354
  negative tendencies in organization of, 121
  pastoral needs of, 212
  postcolonial identity of, 131
  problem of self-determination of, 359
  prophetic role of, 408–9
  regular synodal assemblies of, 259–60
  relationship with West: history of, 651–55
  renewal and reform of structures of, 361–64
  role in development, 351
  as servant of families and children, 711–13
  sexuality morality and, 655, 655n48
  social mission of, 351–54
  statistics of, 312
  universal law in, 269–71
  and Vatican II, 621–25, 686, 687
  and vocations in, 663
Catholic faith, teaching of, in Catholic schools, 248
Catholic Health Association (CHA), 541–44
Catholic Health Association of the United States, 502
Catholic Health Care Association of Southern Africa (CATHCA), 502, 506–7
Catholic Higher Institute of East Africa (CHIEA). 51
Catholic Institute for Development, Justice, and Peace (CIDJAP), health care program of, 507
Catholic Institute of West Africa (CIWA), 51–52
Catholic intellectual tradition, 224
Catholic Media Council(CAMECO), 211n31
Catholic schools
  achievements and challenges of, 239–56
  benefit to communities of, 241
  educational advantage in, 250n45
  enrollment in, 371–72; data of, by country, 243–45, 246–47 (table); diversity of (Muslims and Christians), 371–72; growth in, 243 (table), 253; statistics for, 241–43, 252–53
  factors to improve quality of, 250–52
  and fundamental option for poor, 240–41, 249, 250
  funding of, 250
  impact of COVID on, 240
  interventions for improvement in, 253
  location of, 251–52
  parental demand and, 248

Index

quality education in, 240, 248–49
strengthening identity of, 251
and teaching of the faith, 248
See also education
Catholic social imagination
  in antiquity, 331–32
  history and development of, 329–39
  and integral world approach, 330, 333
  in Middle Ages, 332–33
  in modern era, 333–37
  and steering clear of social and political issues, 332
  structural approach to, 331, 335
  See also Catholic Social Teaching
Catholic social ministry, and the poor, 423
Catholic Social Teaching (CST), 340, 351–66
  and African voiceless, 415
  application of, in Africa, 351
  in curricula of African seminaries and universities, 353
  and dehumanization of the poor, 417
  and developmental methodologies, 342–43
  and ecclesiologies using family metaphors, 600
  and health care programs, 507
  and informing faithful of faith tradition, 357
  planetary and, 439
  and preferential option for poor, 240, 523n56, 538
  principles of, 419
  and right to development, 418–20
  on role of laity, 479
  and SCCs, 353 (*see also* SCCs)
  supposed neutrality of, in political matters, 354
  theological development of, 353
Catholic studies
  in Africa, 95–108
  and church as communion, 99–100
  and dialogue, 102–3
  and illuminated research, 104–5
  importance of context in, 103
  and listening and learning, 106
  methodology in, 95–96, 100–102
  and ministerial function of church, 96
  and reverential dialogue, 103
  social sciences and, 101
Catholic Theological Association of Nigeria. *See* CATHAN

Catholic Theological Ethics in the World Church (CTEWC), and ecumenism, 381n2
Catholic universities
  and concept of popular university, 410
  corruption and, 410
Catholic University of Eastern Africa (CUEA), 51n56
Catholic University of Ghana, 51n56
Catholic University of Ivory Coast, 51n56
Catholic voice, global, 141–42
Catholic Women's Organizations (CWOs) 559–60
  leadership roles of, 567
Catholicae Fidei Propagatione, and missionary activity, 264
Catholicism
  ambivalence of Africans toward, 19
  church and development in, 340–66
  as church of poor and marginalized, 16
  definition of, 39–40
  in early centuries in Africa, 331
  gestures and symbols in, 208
  as global religion, xxiii
  growth of, in Africa, xix–xx (*see also* Catholicism, African)
  harm to Africa by, 346
  healing ministry of, 497–98
  and human rights, 416
  inculturation and, xxiii–xxiv
  indigenization of, 556
  and Islam, 373–77
  as most important NGO in Africa, 354
  nonverbal communication in, 208
  post-Vatican II revival of, 20
  radio stations operated by (table), 211
  rural vs. urban varieties of, 21
  sacramental vs. non-sacramental versions of, 21
  sexuality morality and, 449–65
  social mission of, and Right to Development, 422
  as spiritual force in world Christianity, xix
  traditional vs. charismatic expressions of, 21
  universal and particular, 269, 302, 303
  vs. Protestantism, 10; in missions, 264–65
  See also Catholic Church; Catholic Church in Africa; Catholic Social Teaching

Catholicism, African, 15–26
  canon law and, 257–83
  challenges to development of, 96–97
  Christology in, 604–20
  as church of missionaries, 143
  colonial heritage of, 19–20
  communication of faith in, 202–22
  complexity of, 17
  confidence of, 16
  contextuality of, 141–42
  Dei Verbum and, 621–33
  and early Christianity, 17, 130
  ecumenism and, 381–96
  as embodied experience, 22–23
  and evangelical and Pentecostal Christianity, 143
  and freedom from European Enlightenment, 162
  fringe movements in, 20
  future of, 36–37, 57–58
  global context of, 127–46
  global impact on, 140–44
  growth of, 16, 18, 133, 142
  health care and, 497–510
  history of, 28–38, 130–31
  impact of laity on, 299–308
  impact of, outside Africa, 142
  inculturation and, 80–94
  influence of, on Roman liturgies, 43
  and intellectual history in Africa, 147–65
  Islam and, 367–80
  in Kenya, 478–96
  Kongolese, 34–35
  and liberative historiography, xxiii
  liturgies in, 39–62
  method and models for studies in, 95–108
  missionary achievements in, 35–36
  official and popular, 20–21 (*see also* Catholicism, popular)
  Pauline principle of universal access and, 442–43
  planetary living and, 427–45
  religious life in, 309–25
  right to development and, 415–26
  and sectarianism, 43–44
  social ethics and, 449–65
  as story of powerlessness, 19–26
  as story of success, 16–19
  and Western Catholicism, 134
  women in, 551–72
Catholicism, contextual, 137–40
Catholicism, institutionalized, 20
Catholicism, popular
  meaning of, 479–82
  models of, 485–86, 493–94

747

Index

Catholicism, popular (*cont.*)
   in Kenya, 492–93
   and social change in Africa, 493
Catholicism, Western, hierarchical structure of, 141
catholicity, and unity in diversity, 272
Cavell, Stanley, on medicine, 518
CCC. *See Catechism of the Catholic Church*
CEAC (Center for Early African Christianity)
   founded by Thomas Oden, 31
CEBs (Communautés Ecclésiales de Base), 185n2, 595
CECOTAPS (Centre for Conflict Transformation and Peace Studies), 377
Celestine I, Pope. absolution of Apiarius by, 259n15
celibacy, clerical, 451
   as detriment to forming clergy, 34
census, U.S. (2010), 63–64
   and African migrants, 63–64
Center for Applied Research in the Apostolate (CARA), on population growth in Africa, xix
Center for Early African Christianity (CEAC), founded by Thomas Oden, 31
Central Africa, charismatic prayers to combat witches in, 53
Central African Republic
   refugees from violence in, 374
   tribalism and, 101
   violence in, between Muslims and Christians, 374
Centre for Conflict Transformation and Peace Studies (CECOTAPS), 377
CEP (Congregation for the Evangelization of Peoples), 80
   acting on behalf of pope, 270
   African dioceses hurt by control by, 346
   establishment of, 153–54
   on missionaries to China, 80, 272
   and mission territories, 272
Césaire, Aimé, and negritude movement, 301, 675
CEVBs (Communautés Ecclésiales Vivantes de Base), 185n2, 595
CEVs (Communautés Ecclésiales Vivantes), 595
CHA (Catholic Health Association), 541–44
   government funding and, 543
Chalcedon, Council of (451), 6, 32, 42n11
   rejected by Ethiopian and Coptic Christianity, 6, 32, 149

chama (small group), and SCCs, 186
   (*see also* SCCs)
Charismatic Renewal, Catholic
   education of laity and, 479
   emergence of, 483
   emphasis of, on experience of Holy Spirit, 485
   and global Pentecostal renewal movement, 482
   healing ministry of, 511, 513
   in Kenya, 484–85, 487n59
   literature about, 482–85
   ministries of, 486
   socioeconomic and political context of, 485
   in Uganda, 487–88, 487n59
   and Vatican II, 468
   See also Pentecostalism
charismatic revival, dismissal of, 348
charismatics, experience of worship of, 525
charisms
   affirmed by Vatican II, 471
   criteria for good or bad, 471–72
   manifestations of, 483
   Pentecostal: different contexts of, 475
   religious life and, 324
Charlemagne, first Christian emperor of Holy Roman Empire, 397
Charles Lwanga, Saint, 21
chastity, sexual morality and, 451–52
CHIEA (Catholic Higher Institute of East Africa), 51
childbearing, early, impact of education on, 240–41
children
   issues pertaining to, 713
   as supreme gift of marriage, 453
   theology of, 713
children, African
   church as servant of, 711–13
   as source of hope for families, 712–13
Chimbotosya, Aluko, on gospel of prosperity, 470
chrism oil, and ordination, 286
Christ. *See* Jesus Christ
Christ-event, proclamation of, 604–5
Christ for All Nations, 486
Christ the King, Feast of, in Igboland, 613–14
Christian
   meaning of, 577
   non-Chalcedonian, 32
Christian Association of Nigeria, 382
Christian century, xx
Christian Council of Ghana, peace committees of, 377

Christian Councils of Kenya (1943), 382n7
Christian Councils of Zambia (1945), 382n7
Christian faith
   local expressions of, 170
   pioneers of, 430–32
Christian initiation, development in Uganda, 36
Christian person, as theologian, 40
Christian social ethics, task of, 358
Christian university, as achievement of ancient African Christianity, 31
Christianity
   demographic shifts of, xix–xx
   early centuries of, in Roman Empire in Africa, 5, 29, 167, 167n8, 205, 258, 717–20
   evangelizing in Africa of (18th century), 258
   factors in 19th-century decline of, 30
   growth of, 718–19
   missions of (19th and 20th centuries), 205, 258
   movement of, into Europe and Africa, 717–20
   near elimination of, under Islam expansion, 7–9
   racialization of, 158–60
   racism of, 154
Christianity, charismatic
   in Africa, 482
   challenges facing, 469 (*see also* Charismatic Renewal, Catholic Pentecostalism)
Christianity, Ethiopian, differences from Coptic Christianity of, 32
Christianity, evangelical, as challenge to African Catholicism, 143
Christianity, Western, and first collection of canonical norms, 259
Christianity in Africa, 721–22
   Catholic perspective on history of, 31–36
   deconstruction of, 169
   dependency and, 721–22
   missionary efforts in 19th and 20th centuries, 205, 258
   modern missionary movement of, 29
   under Portuguese (15th century), 29
   in sub-Saharan Africa, 205, 718–19
   as substratum of African philosophy, 170
   three stages or "plantings" of, 29–30, 258

Index

Christianization, in sub-Saharan Africa, 10–14
Christians, African
 and missionary activity, 29
 and West, 651–55
Christians and Muslims
 dialogue weakened by conflict, 391n46
 holistic development of, 371–73
Christifideles Laici (John Paul II, post-synodal apostolic exhortation; 1988)
 on vocation and mission of the lay faithful, 479
 See also John Paul II, Pope; laity
Christology
 academic, 607–8
 in African Catholicism, 604–20
 and African New Testament studies, 174
 and African quest for liberation, 611–12
 African Traditional Religion and, 172
 African vs. Western, 613
 African women's, 564–65
 grassroots, 606–8
 issues and debates in, 604, 615–17
 proclamation of Christ and, 604–8
 qualitative and qualitative methods in, 605, 605n8
 and religious pluralism, 616–17
 as socially transformative, 615–17
 sociology and, 605
Christus Dominus (Vatican II, Decree on the Bishops' Pastoral Office in the Church), 723–24
 on authority of bishops, 272
 See also bishops; Vatican II
Chupungco, Ansgar J., on challenges to African church, 43–44
church
 abuse of, by politicians, 407–8
 African values and, 589–91
 models of, and SCCs, 197–98
 and Roman state, 397
church and state
 crises of, 340–43
 relations of, 397, 411–12
 separation of, 332, 338
 ways to improve, 409
church fathers
 African, in early centuries, xx
 fusion of faith and culture in, 174
 inculturation and, 82–83
 recourse to, in hermeneutics, 174–75
churches, African
 decolonialization of, 138

outreach programs of, 350
 role of, in reconciliation, 406
 social roles of, 348
 theological importance of local churches, 723
CIDJAP (Catholic Institute for Development, Justice, and Peace), health care program of, 507
Circle of Concerned African Women Theologians, 173, 564
 and ecumenism, 381n2
 method of theology of, 66
civil unrest, as challenge in Africa, 16
clan
 church as, 589–91
 leadership values of, 590–91
clannishness, in church organization, 121
Clarke, Clifton
 on African Christology, 605, 605n7
 on Christ's healing power, 610
Clarke, John H., on relations between Africans and Portuguese (17th century), 154
Clarke, Juanne, on behavior of medical personnel, 525
Clement of Alexandria, Saint, 30, 32
 as African church father, 166n4
 and church in 3rd century, 6, 717
 as theologian of African church, 148
 and tradition of Mark the evangelist, 4
Clement VI, Pope
 bull *Unigenitus Dei Filius* (1731), 723
 pope having authority of Christ, 723
clericalism, and SCCs, 597, 691 (*see also* SCCs)
climate change, effect of, on most vulnerable, 442
Codex Apiarii Causai (ca. 419), and case of Apiarius of Sicca, 259
Cold War, effect of, in Africa, 228
collegiality, and synodal process, 699, 700
colonial powers, territorial wars of, 10
colonialism
 Bible as accomplice in, 170
 canon law and, 263–65
 and character of indigenous African leaders, 111
 church's role in, 301
 as civilizing mission, 160
 and decline of indigenous African culture, 87
 education in European culture and, 158

Enlightenment and, 157
 era of, 334
 and evangelization, 19
 and history of relationship between Africa and West, 651
 and "humanization" of Black subjects, 158
 and nation-states, 128
 as part of past, 658
 residue of, in directives about attending Catholic schools, 161–62
 tribalism and, 129
 Western domination through, 169
 See also colonization
colonization, 88
 of Africa by European powers, 264
 Berlin Conference and, 311
 and Christianization of Africa, 11
 ethnography and, 670
 and European nationalism, 312–13
 missionary schools as instruments of, 245
 and racialization of Christianity, 159–60
 See also colonialism
Columbus, Christopher, and patronage, 261
Comboni Missionaries
 Comboni Sisters as female counterpart of, 310
 founded by St. Daniel Comboni, 310
 in northern Uganda, 17
Comboni Sisters, female counterpart of Comboni Missionaries, 310
Comboni, Daniel, Saint
 and appeal for young missionaries, 267–68
 founder of Comboni Missionaries, 310
 and holistic evangelization, 18
commissions, in missionary territories, 265–67
Commodus, persecution under, 4
common good
 dialogue and, 669
 and planetary living, 439
 social conditions and, 419
communal conflict, as challenge to ecumenism, 393
communalism
 African concept of the family and, 707
 and communication, 205–6
Communautés Ecclésiales de Base (CEBs) 185n2, 595

749

Communautés Ecclésiales Vivantes (CEVs), 595
Communautés Ecclésiales Vivantes de Base (CEVBs), 185n2, 595
communication
  approaches to research in, 203, 207
  in Catholic universities and institutes, 217
  church as sign and instrument of, 202
  church documents dealing with, 204
  cross-cultural, 207
  evangelization as goal of, 203–5
  of faith, 203
  goals of, in Catholic Church, 203–5
  human, 202
  intercultural, 207
  liturgical, 213–15
  and media, 209–12
  models of, 205–6, 213
  nonverbal, 208–9
  oral: and evangelization, 205–8
  pastoral, 203–5, 212–17 (*see also* Communio et Progressio)
  stereotyping in, 207–8
communio, family as expression of, 574
Communio et Progressio (pastoral instruction on social communications; 1971)
  and church's public relations, 215
  on training of priesthood and religious, 216
communion, hope of, church as family of God and, 707–8
Communion of Saints, as grounds for theological dialogue, 655–56
communitarianism, as theory of human rights, 417
community
  and African notion of life, 432
  African value of, 429
  and social nature of human person, 416
  universality of, 435
Comoro, Christopher, on pre-Vatican II Catholicism, 20
comparison, as problem of pastoral ministry, 122
Compendium of Catholic Social Doctrine, 329
Concilia Africae, collection of canonical norms, 259
condom use
  church opposition to, 459–62
  for contraception and prevention of HIV, 458–63

in married couples with one infected partner, 462
problems of, 460–61
See also contraception; sexual intercourse; sexual morality
Cone, James
  on African feminism, 91
  on debate about African theology vs. Black theology, 91
Conference of Women Religious (Nigeria), 558
Congo
  colonized by Belgium, 11
  evangelization programs in, 10
  under Mobutu Sese Seko, 225–27, 225n7, 228
  See also Democratic Republic of the Congo
Congolese Episcopal Conference, 185, 186
Congregation for Catholic Education
  on education as service to poor, 240–41
  on social communication and ministerial priesthood, 216
Congregation for Divine Worship, and Zairean Mass, 52
Congregation for Evangelization in Africa, 263–65
Congregation for the Evangelization of Peoples. *See* CEP
Congregation for the Propagation of the Faith
  activities of, 263–64
  and missionary law, 258
  missionary period of, 263
  new missionary norms of, 333
Congregation of the Holy Spirit (Holy Ghost Fathers; Spiritan Fathers and Brothers), 310
Consalvi, Ercole (cardinal), and abolitionist movement, 156
conscienticism, 676
consecrated life
  biblical models of, 316
  limitations of, 316
  and preferential option for poor, 319–20
  surrounded by misery, 316–17
  vow of poverty in, 317
consensus fidelium (agreement of the faithful), 724
Consolata Missionaries, Consolata Sisters as female counterpart of, 310
Consolata Sisters, female counterpart of Consolata Missionaries, 310

Constance, Councils of (1414–1418), and ties between Ethiopian rulers and Europe, 149
Constantine, triumph of Christianity and, 397
Constantinople, First Council of, 6
consumption, sustainable and thoughtful, 438
context
  African, 87–90, 706
  definition of, 40
  global: Africa and, 142–44; diversity and, 134; meaning of, for Africa, 133–34; as opportunity to "be church," 132; as primarily cultural, 137
  importance of, in Catholic studies, 103
  liturgical assembly as, 40
  religious, 130–31
  and theological discoveries, 40
contextual sensitivity, as principle of theological dialogue, 660–61
contextual theology, 95, and SCCs, 198
contextualization
  in adapting gospel, 96
  of biblical text, 177
  of Christian faith, 660
  dialogue and, 650
  and inculturation, 84
  preserving message in, 96
  problems of, 84
contraception
  condom use and, 458
  flexibility concerning, 456
  history of church teaching on, 454–56
  opposition of church to, 453–56, 462
  population and, 455
  poverty and, 456–58
  youth sexual activity and, 458–59
  See also condom use; sexual intercourse; sexual morality
conversational theology, and SCCs, 198
conversion
  of heart, and theological dialogue, 657–58
  meaning of, 662n74
  moral: inculturation and, 235
Cooper, Frederick, on development programs in Africa, 343
Cooper, Matthews, on church founded through Holy Spirit, 473
cooperation, as principle of dialogue, 369
Coptic Christianity, differences from Ethiopian Christianity, 32

750

Index

Coptic Church, 8, 31
Cordes, Paul (archbishop), on charismatic gifts, 467
Cornelius, Pope, on *lapsi*, 5
Corpus Christi celebration, in Igboland, 53–54
corruption
    in Africa, 88, 419–20
    as challenge to church in Africa, 109
    as challenge to ecumenism, 393
    in church governance, 361
    as detriment to church services to people, 409–10
    equivalent to genocide, 410
cosmology, African, anthropocentrism of, 436–38
Coulombe, Harold, on Catholic health facilities in Ghana, 546–47
council, meaning of, in relation to synod, 698n4
council fathers, African, at Vatican II, 624–25 (*see also* Vatican II)
councils, ecumenical, impact of, in missionary law, 267–69
councils, local, use of, in Africa, 274
COVID-19
    impacts of, 240
    and inequality in health outcomes, 538
    negative effects of, 538
creation
    human person as apex of, 436–38
    relationship of God to, 441
    solidarity and, 443
    See also imago Dei
credendi, primacy of *orandi* over, 46
Crow, Paul A., on ecclesiology, 383
crucifix, and Kongolese Catholic art, 35
CTEWC (Catholic Theological Ethics in the World Church), and ecumenism, 381n2
CUEA (Catholic University of Eastern Africa), 143
Cullinane, Tim, on priesthood as gift, 285
cultural repositioning, and global Catholicism, 134
cultural specificity, and human rights, 417
culture
    conflated with race, 159–60
    fossilization of, 140
    nature of, 90
    relationship of, to history, 163
culture, African
    anthropocentric approach to life in, 431
    attitude of missionaries to, 87
    centrality of community in, 434–35
    Christian values and ethics and, 420, 652
    diversity of, respect for, 660–61
    effect of globalization on, 88
    integration of Christian message into, 172
    pluralism in, 168–19, 168n22
    similar across continent, 329
    theological study of, 688
    traditional values of, 473
curse of Ham, and view of Black people, 156
custom, as best interpreter of laws, 276–77
customs, African, destroyed by missionaries, 262
CWOs (Catholic Women's Organizations), 559–60
    leadership roles of, 567
Cyprian, Saint (bishop of Carthage), 6, 21, 30
    as African church father, 6, 81, 148, 166n4
    on African liturgy, 42
    on bishops, 237
    and Councils of Carthage, 258, 260n. 19
    and "fraternity" as paradigm for Christian communities, 592
    and heretics, 5
    and idea that outside the church there is no salvation, 717
    and Latinate Africans, 33
    martyrdom of, 5
    as presider over general synods, 698
Cyrenaica (Libya)
    early Catholic faith in, 331
Cyril of Alexandria, Saint
    at Council of Ephesus, 6
    as doctor of the church, 6
    as patristic exegete, 637, 637n12
    role of, in formulating perennial theology, 650–51
    as theologian of African church, 148

D'Souza, Radha, on human rights, 422
da'wah (proselytizing non-Muslims), 375–77
Dalmais, I. H., on liturgy as ecclesial event, 44–45
Damas, Léon-Gontran, and negritude movement, 301
Darfur, tribalism and, 101
dark night, blessings of, 76
Dark Night of the Soul, quotations from, 76–77
Daughters of the Sacred Passion Congregation, 559n86
David, Alain Patrick, on interventions of bishops, 594
Davies, Colin, MHM (bishop), on SCCs, 191
Davis, Jefferson, on biblical justification for slavery, 159
Deane-Drummond, Celia, on Gaia hypothesis, 436
death
    causes of, in Africa, 504 (table)
    as issue of interest, 58n89
Decius, persecution under, 4, 5
decolonization
    move away from Eurocentrism, 306–7
    suffering and persecution and, 352
Dei Verbum (Vatican II, Dogmatic Constitution on Divine Revelation), 193
    in African Catholicism, 621–33
    African interventions in, 626–28
    contribution of African fathers to, 621–33, 622n11
    first draft of, 625
    on God as communication, 387
    on hearing word of God, 629
    reception of, in church in Africa, 628–29
    See also revelation; Vatican II
Dei Verbum Institute, 559n85
Delgado, Jesus, on popular Catholicism, 480
Democratic Republic of the Congo (DRC)
    beginning of SCCs in, 185
    Catholic schools established in, 226
    conference on Basic Living Ecclesial Communities (2011), 189–90
    differences in types of Catholicism in, 17
    enrollment of students in poverty in, 249–50
    inculturation in, 85n30
    micro-nations in, 128–29
    and refugees from Central African Republic, 374
    risks of poverty in, and education, 249, 251 (figure)
    and SCCs, 187, 595
    statistics for enrollment in Catholic schools in, 244
    years of schooling in, 250
    and Zairean missal, 139
    See also Congo

demonic, meaning of, 530
demonic possession, person-centered approach to, 530
demonology, church teaching on, 514
demons
   belief in existence of, 512n5
   illness and, 529–30
   inner psychic constellations and, 530
   moral dialogue and, 527
   Pentecostal ministries and, 530–32
   social structures and, 527
   See also evil spirits; exorcism; witchcraft
dependency
   cycle of, and Western economic orthodoxies, 345
   and development, 358, 421
   as legacy of missionary Christianity, 721–22
deposit of faith, as source of African New Testament studies, 172
Descartes, René, 673
   on human identity, 157n59, 158
   legacy of Western philosophy and, 677
Deus Caritas Est (Pope Benedict XVI, encyclical; 2009)
   on church and state, 335
   on lay Catholics engaging in civic life, 337–38
   See also Benedict XVI, Pope
development
   African Christian notion of, 346–47
   African theology of, 347
   areas of requiring additional research, 364
   Catholicism and rights to, 415–26
   church's official approach to, 354–55
   context education and, 358
   destruction of people's agency and, 345
   and environmental destruction, 345
   functional, building on assets of ordinary Africans, 358
   illiteracy as obstacle to, 357
   meaning of, 343
   methods pertaining to, 359–61
   and North–South relations, 345
   participatory approaches to, 358–59
   as principle of Catholic Social Teaching, 419
   right to self-determination as basis for, 359
   role of religion in, 340–41, 343
   theologies of, 345, 355–59
   voices of poor ignored in, 354–55
   Western ideas of, 343, 346
   See also RTD
development decades, 421
development discourse, 343–50
dhimma (People of the Book), Christians as, 375
diakonia
   and SCCs, 193
   as selfless Christlike service, 46n38, 48
dialogue
   between African philosophies and West, 667–84
   and African rationality, 673–75
   Africa's responsibility and, 677–80
   anthropologies and, 668–69
   and Catholic studies, 102–3
   between church and culture creators, 583
   as communication, 668
   Christian unity and, 664
   communion and, 654
   and community of faith, 364
   conditions for constructive relationship of, 680
   contextualization and, 650
   contributions of, to Western culture, 677
   dialectical approach to, 661–63
   direct and indirect, 672–73
   ecclesiology and, 388
   education and, 371–72
   equality of agents in, 659
   in Ethiopian Eucharistic liturgy, 642
   etymology of, 668
   family life and, 102–3
   future of, 663–64
   of inner and outer worlds, 531–32
   interreligious, 654; meaning of, 368; obstacle to, 377
   intraecclesial, 654; and Vatican II, 656
   between local churches and universal church, 655–56
   love as fundamental principle of, 653
   meaning of, 368, 647, 668–69
   and method in theology, 102
   with Muslims, 369–70
   mutual enrichment and, 659–60
   as necessary pathway to unity, 647
   as obligation of every Catholic, 654
   principles for, 647–48
   process of, 391
   Protestant and Catholic, 166–82
   purpose of, 661
   and reconciliation, justice, and peace, 654
   requirements of, 669–70
   reverential, 101–6
   rooted in revelation, 387
   socially transformative Christology and, 616
   theological, 655–63
   theological proficiency and, 647
   three principles of, 369
   transformation as objective of, 386
   two types of (truncated and true), 669–70
   and Vatican II, 653–54
   vertical and horizontal dimensions of, 388
   weakened by Christian–Muslim conflict, 391n46
   and West's ideology of domination, 675–77
   West's understanding of rationality and, 671–72
Dibie, Josephine, on dependence of family on mother, 561
Dibie, Robert, on dependence of family on mother, 561
Dickson, Kwesi
   and debate about African theology, 90
   ecumenism and, 383
dicta probantia (examining the sayings/words), 103–4
didascalia (teaching), liturgy as, 44
Dignitatis Humanae (Vatican II, Declaration on Religious Freedom), 11 (*see also* Vatican II)
Dilthey, Wilhelm, on Enlightenment methods, 518
diocesan synodal assemblies, following Vatican II, 691–92
Diocese of Diebougou (Burkina Faso), Moore ritual, 53
Diocese of Enugu
   eucharistic celebration for peace, 56
   Igbo Christian Rite of Marriage of, 54–55
Diocese of Musoma (Tanzania), beginning of SCCs in, 186
Diocese of Ndola (Zambia), pastoral priority of SCCs in, 189
Diocese of Yaounde (Cameroon), and *ndzon-melen* Mass, 52
Dioceses of Zaire, and Zairean Mass, 52–53
Diocletian, persecution under, 4–5
Diop, Alioune
   activism of, 302–6
   biographical facts of, 300–302

Index

conference of Black African intellectuals convened by, 623
on dialogue between peoples, 301–2
as founder of *Présence africaine*, 299
legacy of, 306–7
and modern African Catholicism, 299–308
Vatican II and, 304–6
Diop, Anta, on Western civilization inspired by Egyptian civilization, 676
Dioscorus of Alexandria, at Council of Chalcedon, 6
Discalced Carmelites, 10
discernment
of charismatic manifestations, 475
pastoral guidelines for, 472
in Pentecostalism, 471
spirituality of
disease
biomedical model of, 518–19
as challenge to ecumenism, 393
social factors affecting, 519
understanding of, 498–99
See also health care; illness; sickness
disputatio
as element of scholastic method, 100
and needs of people, 101
diversity
church as community of, 388
global context and, 134
and inculturation, 81–82
religious: in Africa, 369–70
respect for, 122
divination, spirituality of, 172
Divino Afflante Spiritu (Pope Pius XII, encyclical; 1943)
Catholic biblical criticism and, 627
Djamba, Yanyi, on sexual abuse of wives, 459
Djintcharadzé, Anna, on African fathers and Latin church, 148
dogma
notion of, as achievement of ancient African Christianity, 31
reinterpretation of, 659
Dom Henrique (son of Afonso) appointed bishop of Utica, 151
Dom Henrique of the Congo, first native sub-Saharan bishop, 10
domination, ideology of, 668, 675–77
Dominicans, 10
Donatism, in Latin church, 6, 8, 33, 309

Donatists, 7
bishops in North Africa, 332
forbidden to be primate, 260n20
Dorr, Donal, on preferential option for poor, 319
Douzinas, Costas
on idea of universal human rights, 422
on problem of universal human rights, 422
DOV (Decade to Overcome Violence) of WCC, 384
DRC. *See* Democratic Republic of the Congo
dreams, witchcraft and, 527–28
drought, problem discussed in Catholic Social Teaching, 353
Droz, Yvan, on songs and the revival, 483
Dube, Kenneth Okomatani, on zeal of first evangelizers, 470
Dube, Musa W., on African biblical hermeneutics, 641
Dujarier, Michel, on church as fraternity, 591
Dulles, Avery, SJ, on models of church, 198, 210
Dupuch (bishop), prohibited from evangelizing in Algiers, 10–11
Durand, Gilbert, Kä Mana's dialogue with ideas of, 678
Dussel, Enrique
on dialogue between Global North and Global South, 668
on philosophical training and teaching, 680–81
on "trans-modernity," 681
Dutch, and colonization of Africa, 10

EACUC (East Africa Church Union Consultation), 382n7
earth
attachment to: in African thought, 435–36
stewardship of, 436
See also ecology; environment; planetary; planetary living
East Africa, charismatic prayers to combat witches in, 53
East Africa Church Union Consultation (EACUC), 382n7
East African Revival Movement, 483
Eastern Catholic churches
and inculturation, 139
as model for African Catholicism, 59, 59n90
EATWOT (Ecumenical Association of Third World Theologians), 170, 170n40

EBCs (Ecclesial Basic Communities), 595
Ebira Christian Marriage Rite (Nigeria), 54n71
Ebola, Catholic medical care and, 505
Eboussi Boulaga, Fabien
on convocation of church in Africa, 305
criticism of Tempels by, 671
and debate about African theology, 90
on future, 678, 680
international recognition of, 674
not widely known by Western philosophers, 677
rationalist school of African philosophy of, 672
on structures versus message, 724
Ebunoluwa, Sotunsa Mobolanle, on research on women's issues, 563
ecclesia discens (listening church), 724
ecclesia docens (teaching church), 724
Ecclesia in Africa (Pope John Paul II, post-synodal apostolic exhortation; 1995), 13, 18
and *Africae Munus*, 684–85, 697–715
on church as family of God, 25, 95n2, 102n23, 573–85
on communication, 215
on dialogue, 102; with Muslims, 369
ecclesiology of, 388
endorsing BICAM, 629
on evangelization and church in Africa, 16, 355–59
five proposals as basis for, 702
and gap between faith and culture, 355
on Holy Family, 712
implementation of, 702
on importance of education, 234
on language barriers in early missionary efforts, 207–8
on magisterium and inculturation, 140–41
on mission challenges facing church in Africa, 573
on need to apply gospel to concrete life, 336
on role of church in human development, 336
on SCCs, 188–89
and signs of the times, 197
on solidarity, 191
on task of theologians in Africa, 198
on training in use of mass media, 216

753

Index

Ecclesia in Africa (cont.)
  three-part framework in, 30
  See also Africae Munus; First Synod; John Paul II, Pope
ecclesia semper reformanda (the church always reforming), 392
ecclesial associations, and involvement of faithful, 270
Ecclesial Basic Communities (EBCs), 595
ecclesial communities, as alternatives to civil society, 332
ecclesiastical circumscriptions in Africa, statistics for, 270
ecclesiology
  binary approach to, 110–11
  challenges facing, 599–600
  church as family of God and, 599–600
  as *communio*, 388
  Eucharist and, 592
  illuminative, 110
  leadership and ministries and, 592
  of liberation, 594
  and reform of structures from Middle Ages, 723
  of SCCs, 193–94
  serving social transformation of society, 388
  shift in, after Vatican II, 720
  in sub-Saharan Africa, 589–603
  See also Catholic Church; Catholic Church in Africa; Catholicism
ecology
  African Catholicism and, 427–45
  morality of, 443
  planetary living and, 439–40
economic distress, as challenge in Africa, 16
economic inequality, 24–25
economic recession, impact of, in Africa, 43
economics, ecological, and anthropology of economism, 438
Ecumenical Association of Third World Theologians (EATWOT), 170, 170n41
ecumenical associations, 170–71
Ecumenical Catholic Church (Kenya), 296
ecumenical councils
  as achievement of ancient African Christianity, 31
  following African conciliar patterns, 331
  See also under individual locations
ecumenical initiatives, as second stream of ecumenism, 382

ecumenical learning, as openness to Holy Spirit, 387
ecumenical movement
  commitment to justice and peace of, 383
  history of, 382–83
  See also ecumenism
ecumenical projects, 383
ecumenical scholarship
  as one stream of ecumenism, 382
ecumenical spirituality, 391–93
Ecumenical Symposium of Eastern Africa Theologians (ESEAT), 170, 170n44, 171, 171n45
ecumenical theology, and intercultural hermeneutics, 381
ecumenism
  apathy for, 382
  constructive works of, 382n6
  ecclesial denominational arrogance as challenge to, 393
  friendship and, 390–91
  future of, 387–90, 393–94
  grassroots: and new model of church, 596; in Pentecostalism, 383
  and internal diversity, 394
  methodologies and, 394
  methods and trajectory of in African Christianity today, 381–83
  mistrust of, 389
  participation and, 390–91
  social, 383
  solidarity and, 390–91
  tension between institutional and grassroots, 383
  three main steps needed, 389–90
  and Trinitarian life, 391–92
  two operative streams of, 382
ecumenism, receptive
  acting *in spe* (in hope), 386
  in African context, 386–87
  and dialogue, 386n31
  as form of ecumenical learning, 386–87
  grounded in intercultural hermeneutics, 385
  on institutional and grassroots levels, 386–87
  and *other*, 385, 387
Edict of Milan, 5
Edinburgh Conference (1910), 382
education
  as achievement of missionary practice, 35
  actualization of right to development and, 424
  civility and, 232
  and common good, 232

construction of mission schools, 18
development and, 358
effect of COVID-19 on, 240
and formation of human person, 233–35
goal of, 235
and inculturation, 235
and interreligious dialogue (Muslims and Christians), 371–72
mainly Western theological concepts, 24
missionary and colonial, 253
parental demand in, 248–49
popular universities and, 410
post-independence, 253
and schools for girls in Sudan, 18
state monopoly on, 228–29
three areas for improvement, 253
in virtue, 582
as way to defeat slavery, 18
education, Catholic
  in Africa: and *Africae Munus*, 223–38
  in Africa: future of, 223, 232–34
  church–state partnership in, 228–29
  and cultivation of Catholic intelligence, 234–35
  goal of, 223
  history of, 223,
  meaning of, 223
  and struggles for independence, 228
education, Western, brought by missionaries, 226
Edwards, Denis, on humans made in image of God, 436–37
efficiency/effectiveness, as element of pastoral ministry, 100
Egbulefu, John, on need for plural African cultures, 90
Egypt
  ancient church of, 84–85
  appearances of Blessed Virgin in, 12
  as birthplace of Septuagint, 166
  as central pillar of Islam, 7
  colonized by Great Britain, 11
  Coptic churches in, 7, 31
  Holy Family in, 3
  and introduction of Christianity, 167
  Mark the evangelist and, 4
  in New Testament, 3
  occupations of, 8
Eikwe Catholic Hospital (Ghana), 372
Eilers, Franz-Josef
  on communication, 204, 207, 212

Index

instructions for preachers by, 214
on nonverbal communication, 208
on public's perceptions of church, 215

Éla, Jean-Marc
as African theologian, 173
on alien Christian faith, 725
on Christ as liberator, 611–12
on development of theologies, 25
on faulty Christologies, 612
on language of symbolism in African theology, 177
on liberation from ethnocentrism of European theology, 611–12
social analysis of, 353
on superficial uniformity in the church, 724

Ella Amida, King, in Ethiopia, 6
Ellacuría, Ignacio, migrant theology and, 66
Elsbernd, Mary, on social paideia of church, 363–64
emigration, meaning of, 67 (*see also* migration; migrants to U.S.)
Emume Uka Nwa (Igbo Rite of thanksgiving for a child), 57
encounter, meaning of, 662
Engel, George, on biopsychosocial medicine, 499–500, 519
English, and colonization of Africa, 10
Enlightenment, Age of
Christianity subjected to, 159–60
cultural impact of, 10
and domination of non-Western cultures, 158
as intellectual harbinger of colonialism, 157
project of "humanization" of, 161
racism of, 157n59, 158
residue in directives about attending Catholic schools, 161–62
view of Black people in, 156–59
view of non-European peoples in, 157

Enugu Diocese (Nigeria), administration of health insurance in, 506–7
environment
and African notion of life, 432
globalism and, 437
warning of science about, 443
See also earth; ecology; planetary; planetary living

Ephesus, Council of, 6
Ephphatha, charismatic healing ministry, 484
Ephphatha Movement, 514
epidemics, as challenge to church in Africa, 109

episcopal conferences, mandated by Paul VI, 723–24
episcopate, monarchical, to be rethought in Africa, 723
equality
church as community of, 388
as principle of Catholic Social Teaching, 419
as requirement of dialogue, 669
Equatorial Africa, colonized by France, 11
Esack, Farid, criticism of Christian–Muslim dialogue as continuing colonialism, 376
ESEAT (Ecumenical Symposium of Eastern Africa Theologians), three symposia of, 170, 170n44, 171, 171n45
Esua, Cornelius Fontem (archbishop; Bamenda, Cameroon), on SCCs, 188
Eterović, Nikola (archbishop), on reconciliation, 685
ethical behavior, three determinants of, 452–53
ethics, Catholic, applied in Catholic health centers, 372
ethics, Christian, praxis of hope and, 710–11
Ethiopia
ancient monasteries as centers of faith, 84–85
Catholic diocese established in, 10
Christian churches in, 31
first evangelization efforts in, 6
importance of, in early Latin Ethiopia
Italian missionaries in, 11
and Jewish religion of Old Testament, 9
in New Testament, 3
Ethiopian, in names of AICs, 30
Ethiopian church
and Africans as active historical agents, 149
rejected by Council of Chalcedon, 149
Ethiopian commentaries
ethical lessons from, 641–42
inculturation and, 638–39
levels of meaning in, 641–42
method of, 638–39
presupposition of faith in, 639
Ethiopian eucharistic liturgy, dialogue in, 642
Ethiopian Orthodox Church, surviving Islamization, 167
Ethiopianism, and political and religious independence, 86, 86n34

Ethiopians
described by Isidore of Seville, 147–48
described by Pliny, 147
ethnic cleansing, of Igbo people in Nigeria, 230
ethnic conflicts, negative human rights image of Nigeria and, 419
ethnic tension, 578
ethnocentrism
as challenge to ecumenism, 393
family life in Africa and, 712
Eucharist
and African culture, 51
almost magical view of, 20
as anamnesis of cross, 296
and Ashanti Mass, 53
celebration of, in Igboland, 56
ecclesiology and, 592
foremost expression of church, 43n15, 46
healing character of, 523
and indigenization, 83
as sacrament of love and communion, 286, 296–97, 394
and transformation of God's people, 45
Zairean rite of, 139
See also liturgy
Eucharistic Prayer(s)
in Ashanti Mass, 53
fourth, 580, 617
published by CIWA, 52
in Zairean rite, 139
eudaimonia (happiness), 115
Eugenius IV, Pope, on excommunication of enslavers of Catholics in Canary Islands, 154
Eurocentrism, criticism of, by Alioune Diop, 302–3, 307
Europe
movement of Christianity into, 717–18
racist mindset of, 343
Eusebius of Caesarea, *Ecclesiastical History* of, 4, 343
evangelical counsels, 322
evangelical revival, dismissal of, 348
evangelicals. *See entries under* Pentecostal; Pentecostalism
Evangelii Gaudium (Pope Francis, post-synodal apostolic exhortation; 2013)
and call to holiness for whole community, 481
on church not bound to any culture, 720–21
on connection between theological anthropology and Christian vocation, 347

755

INDEX

Evangelii Gaudium (cont.)
  on evangelizing community, 195
  on faithful as God's instrument to help the poor, 424
  four principles of, 391
  on popular piety and inculturation, 481
  on preaching, 214–15
  on quest for justice and peace, 389
  on SCCs, 191
  See also Francis, Pope
Evangelii Nuntiandi (Pope Paul VI, apostolic exhortation; 1975)
  on ecclesiology of church at the service of Africa, 598
  on evangelization, 237n36, 368–69
  on homilies, 214
  on popular piety, 480
  See also evangelization; Paul VI, Pope
evangelists, lay, as storytellers, 18
evangelization
  of Africa by Africans, 623
  coinciding with colonial occupation, 19
  dialogue and, 367–68
  as first project of church in Africa, 580
  and First Synod, 355
  as goal of communication in church, 204
  grassroots, 346
  health care facilities and, 515
  holistic, 18–19
  parish ministry and, 583
  patronage as hindrance to, 261–62
  Pentecostal religiosity and, 470
  as "pneumocentric," 470
  proclamation and, 367–69
  role of laity in, 479
  and SCCs, 195
  task of, 204
  tensions resulting from, 375–77
  three phases of, in Africa, 16–17
  transformational approach to, 358
  and Western missionaries in Africa, 17–18
  See also missionaries; missionary activity
evangelization, new, 204–5, 356
  and Catholic studies, 99–100
  laity and, 494–95
  pneumatic movements and, 468
  women's qualities needed for, 566
  as vocation of all people, 109–10, 481
Evans, David, on interventions to improve Catholic schools, 251
evil, as independent and external object, 434

evil spirits
  belief in, and illness 526–27
  evil effects of, 177
  See also demons; exorcism; illness; witchcraft
exclusion
  globalism and, 442
  health care facilities and, 522
  medicalization and, 521
  and societal ills, 442
exegesis. *See* biblical exegesis/interpretation
exorcism, 513n12
  healing ministries and, 513
  purpose of, 514
  as traditional practice, 20
Extraordinary Synod for the Twentieth Anniversary of the Closing of the Second Vatican Council, 81
Eze, Emmanuel Chukwudi, on Enlightenment methods, 518
Ezigbo, Victor
  on acclamation of Christ, 610
  on African Christology, 605, 605n7
  on healing services and prayers, 609

Facultés Catholiques de Kinshasa (DRC), 51
faith
  interpretation and, 639–44
  through personal and communal hearing, 106
faith and life, and intercultural hermeneutics, 385
Faith and Order Commission, 383
faith seeking understanding, 174n69
  methodology for, 97
  and signs of the times, 96
  and study of globalization, 144–45
  theological exegesis and, 627
false equivalence, global mentality and, 439
Familiaris Consortio (Pope John Paul II, post-synodal apostolic exhortation; 1981)
  affirming stand against artificial contraception, 455
  See also contraception; family
families, African, church as servant of, 711–13
family
  African idea of, 431
  breakdown of, in Africa, 458–59
  change and uncertainty in, 25
  as foundation for values, 458–59
  negative characteristics of metaphor, 574

  negative influences on, 712
  problems of, 574
  respect for life in, 574
  symbolic sense of, 593
  See also church as family of God
family planning programs (Kenya), contraceptives provided by, 457 (*see also* contraception)
Fanon, Frantz, on demon possession, 512n4
Farmer, Paul
  on management of global health programs, 500–501
  on "reasonable" treatment options, 522
Fashole-Luke, Edward
  on African theology vs. Black theology, 91
  and development of African nationalism, 87
  on task of biblical interpretation, 176n79
fasting, as traditional practice, 20
Fatimids, as tolerant of Christians, 8
favoritism
  in African politics, 119
  in church organization, 121
Faye, Béatrice
  on inclusive approach to gender, 679–80
  on relationship between placenta and earth, 680
Feierman, Steve, on lay therapy management and sickness, 529
Felicity. *See* Perpetua and Felicity
Fellowship of Christian Councils and Churches in West Africa (FOCCIWA), 382–83
feminism
  African, 91, 551–52
  Black, 551–52
  in contrast to womanism, 554
  negative connotation of, 554
  as problematic for African women, 563
  replaced by African womanism, 563
  as theory of human rights, 417
  See also womanism; women
feminist theologians, African, as praxis-oriented, 168n17
feminist theology, 175n73
Ferreira, Father João
  contribution of, to *Dei Verbum*, 626–28
  on Word of God as soul of Christian life, 629
fides (faith), and Catholic education, 224

Index

First and Second Synods, xxvi–xxvii
   and church's social mission, 355–59
   praxis of hope and, 703–7
   on SCCs, 596
   spirit of Vatican II and, 692
First Cross-Cultural Conference of Catholic Theological Ethics, 144
first development decade, dependency theory and, 421
First Special Assembly for Africa of the Synod of Bishops (Rome; 1994). *See* First Synod
First Synod (First Special Assembly for Africa of the Synod of Bishops [Rome; 1994]), 12–13, 30, 204, 355, 355n43, 573–85
   and church as family of God, 13, 25, 355, 486, 624, 692, 702
   and evangelization, 188, 355–56, 369
   five major proposals of, 702
   on fundamental challenges of church, 336
   on human beings as family of God, 233
   on importance of training, 216
   inculturation and, xxvi, 276
   Instrumentum Laboris for, 701
   Lineamenta for, 701, 704
   objectives of, 697
   and pastoral needs of church in Africa, 215
   period of progress following, 353
   process for, 701–2
   on proper understanding of Pentecostalism, 473
   reception of Vatican II and, xxvi
   recommendations of, 702
   relationship to Second Synod, 697–98
   on respect for human life and family, 355n43
   on right of women to be involved in church ministries, 355n43
   as Synod of Resurrection, Synod of Hope, 704
   at time of great crisis, 699–700
FitzGerald, Constance, on John of the Cross, 68, 76n79
Flikschuh, Katrin, on Western philosophical thinking, 667–68
Florence, Council of (1431–1449), and ties between Ethiopian rulers and Europe, 149
FOCCISA (Fellowship of Christian Councils in Southern Africa), 382–83
Focolare, education of laity and, 479
food insecurity, in sub-Saharan Africa, 538
foreign aid, and Catholic Social Teaching, 353
Foucault, Michel
   on "medical gaze," 518
   on power, 520
Fourth Roman Synod of Bishops (1974), on self-definition of local churches, 87
France
   and colonization of Africa, 10
   effect of politics on colonialism, 302–6
Francis, Pope
   on Africa as continent of hope, xviii
   apostolic exhortation *Amoris Laetitia* (2016), 460
   apostolic exhortation *Evangelii Gaudium* (2016), 191
   apostolic exhortation *Gaudete et Exsultate* (2018), 466
   on authentic human development, 418–19
   and call to be missionary disciples, 195
   and canonization of John XXIII, 621
   on church as family of families, 574
   on church as poor and merciful, 36, 110
   on church not bound to any culture, 720–21
   on connecting with people, 110, 120
   on contemporary Gnosticism, 466
   on contraception, 455–56, 460, 462
   on ecumenical dialogue, 389–91
   encyclical *Laudato Si'* (2015), 136–37
   on fifteen ailments of Roman Curia, 114
   on globalization, 136–37
   and golden jubilee of Charismatic Renewal movement, 484
   on inculturation, 725
   on integral ecology, 443
   on leadership, 112
   on poor, 424
   on popular piety, 481
   on preaching, 214–15
   on priestly vocations, 293, 294
   principles of solidarity and interdependence, 389, 391
   on renewed joy of priests, 284
   on renewing forms of expression in church, 717
   on responsible parenthood, 457
   on sex in marriage, 452
   on social conditions in Africa, 109
   on theme of synodality, 195
   on theological anthropology and Christian vocation, 347
   on world of social communications, 50
Franciscans, 10
fraternity, church as, 591–92
Fredman, Sandra, on idea of universal human rights, 422
Fredriksen, Paula, on church's concept of sin, 451
free market, imperialism of, 428
French colonies, rights of Africans in, 300n9
French Revolution
   and emergence of nation-states, 334
   hostility of, to church, 10, 263–64, 263–64n39, 398
French West Africa, colonized by France, 11
Freud, Sigmund, on demonic possession, 512
Friar Mauro (1459), on discovery in Africa, 147, 148
Friedman, Milton, on goal of making money, 428
Friedman, Thomas, on globalization, 131–32, 133, 134, 136, 142–43
Fromont, Cécile, on Kongolese Catholic art, 34–35
Frumentius, Saint
   first bishop of Ethiopia, 6
   and first evangelization efforts in Ethiopia, 6
   story of, in Ethiopia, 9
Fry, Louis, on spiritual leadership, 113
Fuchs, Erich, on sexuality in Reformation, 452
Fukuyama, Francis
   on evolution of institutions toward liberal democracy, 343–44
   on Western reading of history, 343
Fulgentius Ferandus of Carthage, and *Breviatio canonum*, 259
Full Gospel Businessmen's Fellowship International, 383
fundamental option for poor
   and Catholic Social Teaching, 240–41
   See also liberation theology; preferential option for the poor; poor
funeral rites, need for Afro-Christian rites, 57
Furman, Rev. Richard, on biblical justification for slavery, 159

Index

Gaba, Christian, African theologian, 173
Gadamer, Hans-Georg, on Enlightenment methods, 518
Gaia hypothesis, 436
Gallican liturgy. *See* liturgy, Gallican
Gallienus, persecution under, 4
Gambia
    colonized by Great Britain, 11
    slave trade and, 155
Gambia Christian Council, 382
Gamble, Michael, on communicative cultural clashes, 207
Gamble, Teri Kwal, on communicative cultural clashes, 207
Ganye, Antoine, on polygamy in Africa, 277n131
Garcia II, King (Kongo; ruled 1641–1661), 154
Garden of Eden, according to Word of Faith movement, 524, 524n58
Gardner, Howard, on leaders, 114
Gatu, John (Rev.), moratorium debate and, 719
Gaudete et Exsultate (Pope Francis, apostolic exhortation; 2018), 523n56
    on Christian community called to holiness, 479
    on contemporary Gnosticism, 466
    on new Pelagianism, 466
    See also Francis, Pope
Gaudium et Spes (Vatican II, Pastoral Constitution on the Church in the Modern World), 96
    on artificial contraception, 455
    on challenges facing church, 393
    diakonia and, 597–98
    on human person, 708
    on human rights, 416
    quoted by *Africae Munus*, 685
    on solidarity in human interconnectedness, 100, 657
    See also Vatican II
Ge'ez (classical Ethiopic), translation of Bible into, 635
Gelasius, Pope, African, 148
Gelmer (Vandal king), 7
gender
    globalization and, 678–80
    as theme in African New Testament studies, 174
    See also feminism; womanism; women
gender relations, 459 (*see also* family; womanism)
Gendlin, Eugene, on "focusing," 531
Genesis, creation narratives, 233
genital mutilation, 362–63

Genseric (Vandal king), 6
German East Africa, colonized by Germany, 11
German Southwest Africa, colonized by Germany, 11
gestures, understanding meaning of, 58
Getui, Mary, African theologian, 173
Ghaemi, N., on eclecticism of biopsychosocial model, 500
Ghana
    addressing concerns of marginalized, 375
    as case study of Catholic health facilities, 546–47
    Catholic hospitals and clinics in, 354, 372, 542–43
    holistic evangelization in, 18
    Kwame Nkrumah as dictator in, 228
    missionary "castle" schools in, 245
    northern: Catholic mission by White Fathers in, 375
    parental choice in education in, 248–49
    peaceful coexistence between Catholics and Muslims in, 370, 375
    SCCs as pastoral priority in, 196
    southern: tensions between Muslims and Christians in, 373–74
Gichuhu, George, on spirituality of SCCs, 191–92
Gichure, Peter, on research in Catholic studies, 106
Gifford, Paul
    on African Catholics and spirit world, 513
    on churches under Moi, 404
    on involvement of African churches in public sphere, 335–36
    on religious women in Uganda, 23
    on worldview of African Christianity, the world of spirits and demons, 360–61
girls, education of, 240–41
Glaser, Barney, on complex social phenomena, 66
global context. *See* context, global
Global North
    branches of African churches in, 31
    or Minority World, 28
    planetary living as protest to greed in, 439
Global South
    growth of Christianity in, 663
    growth of SCCs in, 185
    or Majority World, 28

    as new center of Catholic population, 133
    planetary living and, 439
globalization
    and African Catholicism, 127–46
    and African culture, 88
    African philosophies and, 679
    and catechesis of youth, 643
    church structures and, 141, 716–17
    cross-disciplinary methodology and, 144–45
    dangers of, 679
    definition of, 679
    as dialogue, 143–44
    and environmental destruction, 437–38
    exclusion and, 442
    as feature of modernity, 97
    forces of, 143–44
    gender and, 678–80
    as new paradigm, 131–34
    as postcolonial reality, 137
    and sharing of ideas, 136–37
    and subsidiarity and solidarity, 134–37
    technology and, 131
    as a virtue, 134
    weakening of family system and, 562
Gnosticism
    Christian history and, 717
    sexual practices in, 454
    theological discourse against, 331
God
    Christian understanding of, 578–80
    as original ancestor, 432
    relationship of, to creation, 441
    whiteness of, 162–63
Godfrey Okoye University (Enugu, Nigeria), 51n56
Goergen, Donald, on African Christology, 605, 605n7, 608
Gold Coast, colonized by Great Britain, 11
Good News
    Christ as, 604
    proclamation of, in global context, 143
    See also gospel
Good Samaritan, parable of, interpretation of, 640
gospel
    communicated in African languages, 177
    connected with quality of life, 356
    implications of adaptation of, 96
    and inculturation, 40
    proclamation and, 368

Index

gospel of prosperity. *See* prosperity gospel
gospel values, and social sciences, 101
gospel, social, and praxis of social transformation, 347
Gospels, depiction of Jesus in, in concrete historical contexts, 174
governments
  dictatorial: and Catholic Social Teaching, 353; and state monopoly on education, 228; negative impact of, 225
  dysfunctional: and religious tensions, 374–75
  failing: as challenge to church in Africa, 109
  good: elements of, 362
  role of, 233
Gowon, Yakubu, leader of Nigerian military, 229
Grail, The, education of laity and, 479
Granados, Carlow, on hope, 703
Grant, Jacquelyn, on African feminism, 91
Grashow, Alexander, on attributes of leadership, 115
Gratian, *Concordance of Discordant Canons* (12th century), on Pauline privilege, 262
graveyard monuments, inscriptions on, 42
Gravissimum Educationis (Vatican II, Declaration on Christian Education), 240–41.
  See also catholic schools; education; Vatican II
Gray, Richard
  on decree against slave trade, 156
  on evangelizing from Ethiopia, 149
Great Turkish War (1683–1699), as context of church condemnation of slave trade, 156
Greater Northwood Community Council, in Baltimore, 70
greed, capitalist, opposed to planetary living, 439 (*see also* capitalism)
Green Revolution, social and ecological costs of, 421
Greenleaf, Robert K., on qualities of servant leader, 117
Gregory I, Pope (504–605)
  and Donatists, 260n20
  relationships with Visigoths and others of, 718
Gregory XIII, Pope, constitution *Populis* (1585), allowing slaves to remarry, 263
Gregory XV, Pope
  bull *Inscrutabili Divinae Providentiae arcano*, establishing institution for spreading Catholic faith, 153–54
  Congregation for the Propagation of the Faith instituted by, 263
  and expansion of church's missionary movement in Africa, 10
Gregory XVI, Pope, bull *In Supremo Apostolatus* (1839) condemning enslavement of Africans, 156
Grinker, R. R., on biopsychosocial medicine, 499–500
Groody, Daniel G.
  on characteristics of migrant spirituality, 65
  on John Chrysostom, 292
Groves, Anthony N., on proper missionary method, 722
Guinea, Catholic education in, 227
Gunthamund (Vandal king), 7

Haar, Gerrie ter, on charismatic healing, 484
Habermas, Jürgen, on seeking truth, 669
Hamid, Mustapha Abdul, on efforts in Ghana to address concerns of marginalized, 375
Harding, Vincent, on horrors of slave trade, 160
Harries, Jim, on privileging of Western languages and thought in early missionary efforts, 207–8
Harry, Sr. Felicia, addressing Second Synod, 692
Harvey, Davie, on globalization, 679
Hastings, Adrian
  on Catholic Church in Portugal, 332
  on colonization and Christianization, 19–20
  on conversion of kings, 332–33
  on separation of church and state, 334
  social analysis of, 353
  on Western missionary movement in 19th century, 18
healer
  Christ as, 608–10
  exploitation by, 514–15
healers
  charismatic, 609, 609n32
  traditional African, 516
Healey, Joseph
  on reverential dialogue, 103
  on SCCs, 691
healing
  African Traditional Religion and, 172
  Catholic, 511–36
  Catholic theology of, 523–24, 532–33
  contests, 515–16
  dialogue on, 517
  discourse: translating Western medical terms into local languages, 516n24
  Jesus's example of, 503
  and miracles, 517
  missiology and, 511
  as mystery, 529
  as paradigm for God's salvific actions, 511
  and popular movements, 20
  as related to moral response, 523
  as theme in African New Testament studies, 174
  theological concept of, 524–25
  transformative paradigm of, 523–25, 523n57, 533
healing ministry
  blame and, 527
  and Catholic Charismatic Renewal, 484
  Catholic understanding of, 515
  CCC on, 523
  centrality of joy in, 525, 532–33
  church's continuation of Christ's, 502–3
  and establishment of Catholic health facilities, 372
  of Jesus, 502
  otherworldly dimension of, 524
  political acquiescence and, 524–25
  prophetic voice in, 524–25
  of Protestant pastors, 172
  restorative approach of, 525
  sacraments and, 503
  transformative approach of, 523–25
healing paradigms, plurality of, 511–36
healing practices, spirituality of, 172
healing prayers, people's expectations and, 514
health
  abundant life and, 511–36
  African: statistics concerning, 503–4, 504 (table)
  biblical interpretation of, 502
  challenges in Africa to, 497
  definitions of, 497
  holistic model of, 497, 499–500, 508, 610
health care
  as achievement of missionary practice, 35
  anthropological model of, 500–501

759

healh care (*cont.*)
    and belief in spiritual forces, 508
    biopsychosospiritual model of, 498
    Catholic Church and, 501–2, 504–8
    eye care services, 372
    holistic approach to, 499–500, 519–23
    as human right, 501–2, 522
    and *igbaafa* (divination) as traditional practice of, 499
    and *ikwaaja* (offerings to spirits) as traditional practice of, 499
    inadequate resources for, 501, 503–4, 508
    inculturation and, 508
    and mystery of Christ, 502
    and native African medicine, 499, 508, 516n23
    privileged populations and, 521
    quality of, in Ghana, 546–47
    sustainability model of, 500–501
health care facilities
    African Catholic, 537–50: achievements of, 542–44, 548; data by country, 540–42, 542 (table); limited resources of, 538; poverty and, 538; quality of care in, 538
    established by missionaries, 504–5
    evangelization and, 515
    faith-based: challenges facing, 544–47, 545 (figure); as basis for peaceful coexistence between Christians and Muslims, 372; and good health outcomes, 544, 546–47, 548; and health of all citizens, 372
    as hallmark of holistic mission, 18
    operated by Catholic Church, 505–6, 506 (tables)
    people's failure to make use of, 522
    services provided by, 507
    statistics about, 537, 539–42, 547–48
health centers, Catholic, application of Catholic ethics in, 372
health discourse
    exclusion and, 522–23
    as force for regulating social life, 520–21
    moral hegemony over, 520
    problems of, 519–23
health gospel, 609–10
health outcomes, inequality in, 538
health problems
    biomedical (or biological) model of, 499
    biopsychosocial model of, 499–500
    supernatural forces and, 498
    understanding of etiology of, 498–501
    See also disease; illness; sickness
health training services, 507 (table)
Hearne, Brian, DSSp, on SCC way of life, 191–92
Hebga, Meinrad (Jesuit; Cameroon)
    on construction of African Christian theology, 173
    on Enlightenment methods, 518
    and Ephphatha healing ministry, 484
    as exorcist, 513–14
    on illness and witchcraft, 513–14
    on multidisciplinary approach to health care, 514
    on myths and philosophy, 673
    on negritude, 675
    on power of Holy Spirit, 514
    on Western dualism, 676
Hegel, G. W. F.
    and political philosophy, 343, 677
    view of Blacks by, 675
Heidegger, Martin
    on idea of worldview, 440
    legacy of Western philosophy and, 677
Heifetz, Ronald, on attributes of leadership, 115
Held, David, on globalization, 679
Henn, William, on "receivability" of ecumenical documents, 392
Henriot, Peter
    on insufficient attention to contributions of women, 362
    social analysis of, 353
Herder, Johann Gottfried, on language as key component of humanism, 157n59
hermeneutics, intercultural
    definition of, 385
    and ecumenical theology, 381
    as ground for receptive ecumenism, 385
hermeneutics of suspicion, dogmatic teachings and, 658
Hien, Simon Hoà Ngyuên (bishop), church as family of God and, 624
Higden, Ranulf (1350), on Africans, 147, 148
Hilderic (Vandal king), 7
Himes, Kenneth, on human rights, 415–16
Hippo (Algeria), early Catholic faith in, 331
Hippo, Council of (393), and *Breviarum Hipponense*, 259
Hippo, Synod of (393)
    canon of the Bible and, 698
    on prayer at the altar, 42n8
Hippolytus, and inculturation, 85
historical-critical method, for theology, 144–45
historiography, liberative, xxiii
history
    African, negative developments in, 599
    brought by colonizers, 160
    as characteristic of highest humanity, 157
    context of, 163
    Eurocentric conception of, 343
    interpretation of, 344
    postcolonial theories of, xxvi
    relationship of, to culture, 163
    viewed as lacking in Africa, 157
HIV
    among African youth, 458
    condom use and, 458, 463
    management of, and biopsychosocial model of medicine, 519
    and sexual activity in Africa, 449–50
HIV/AIDS, 21
    Catholic medical care and, 505
    Catholic sexual morality and, 450, 462
    as challenge in Africa, 16, 25
    church's position on, 459–62
    statistics about, 459
    stigmatization and, 526
Hochschild, Adam
    on Afonso I, 151
    on colonial past, 358
    on *King Leopold's Ghost*, 334
    on role of missionaries in Congo, 333–34
holiness
    Christians called to, 479
    personal, and Pentecostalism, 33
    as quality of Christian leader, 124
Hollenbach, David, on linking human rights and human nature, 416–17
Hollenbach, Paul
    on demonic possession, 512n4
    on illness healed by Jesus, 512
    on Jesus's exorcisms, 524n63
Holy Ghost Fathers (Congregation of the Holy Spirit; Spiritan Fathers and Brothers), 10, 310
    and evangelization of sub-Saharan Africa, 11
    and holistic evangelization in Tanzania, 18
Holy Rosary Sisters, maternity hospital of (Nigeria), 505

Index

Holy Spirit
    experience of, in Charismatic Renewal movement, 485
    as theme in African New Testament studies, 174
holy water, use of, as traditional practice, 20
Homo consumens, 436
Homo sapiens, origin of, in Africa, 127–28n1
homosexual practices, church view of, 453
homosexuality, acceptance of, as challenge to African Catholicism, 143
honesty, as requirement of dialogue, 669
Hoover, Theresa, on African feminism, 91
hope
    Africa as continent of, xviii
    African, in face of dehumanizing experiences, 473
    biblical theology of, 703–4
    church as family of God and, 707–8
    complementary dimensions of, 703
    as context for mission, 705
    ethical character of, 704, 710–11
    First and Second Synods and, 703–7
    new Pentecost and, 704–5
    offered by African church, 21
    resurrection as basis for, 704
    salvific nature of, 703–4
    theology of, 360
    as transformative force, 704
    witness to, 705
hospitals and clinics. *See* health care facilities
Hountondji, Paulin J.
    on challenges facing Africa, 680
    criticism of Tempels by, 671
    international recognition of, 674
    on Kwame Nkrumah's conscienticism, 676
    not widely known by Western philosophers, 677
    rationalist school of African philosophy and, 672
    thesis of, on Husserl, 677
Houphouët-Boigny, Félix (president; Togo), on politicians courting churches, 407
house churches, as predecessors of SCCs, 192n26. *See also* SCCs
Hudson-Weems, Cleonora, 563
    Africana womanism of, 552–54, 555n48, 561, 568
    Afrocentricity of, 566
    on concept of collectivism, 558
    on CWOs, 560
    on gender relations, 554–56
    on women theologians, 565–66
human dignity, recognition of, as requirement of dialogue, 669
human interconnectedness, as ground for theological dialogue, 657
human person(s)
    African understanding of, 707–8
    centrality of, in Catholic Social Teaching, 419
    as created in *imago Dei*, 416
    in creation narratives, 233
    dignity of: elevated by incarnation, 416; and right to development, 418–19
    diminishment of, 580
    nature of, 232–33
    proper vocation of, 708
    relationship of, to state, 233
    rights and duties of, 233
    social and communitarian nature of, 416
    Vatican II on, 708
    See also imago Dei
human rights
    African perspective on, as communal and communitarian, 417
    Catholic teachings on, 415–16, 581
    as inherent and inalienable, 416
    legal norms concerning on, 415
    relativist approach to, 417
    religion and, 415
    theological understanding of, 416
    theories of, 417
Humanae Vitae (Pope Paul VI, encyclical; 1968), 452
    careful interpretation of, 456
    on church's teaching on sexual morality, 453, 455, 462
    rights of women and, 362
    See also contraception; Paul VI, Pope
humanism, African, values of, 346–47
humanity, dominance of Western view of, 157
Hume, David, on inferiority of Black people, 157
humility, and wise leaders, 122
Huneric (Vandal king), 6
Hurley, Denis (archbishop), on transition from theology of concept to theology of image, 625
Huruma, Bishop, as example of mercy, 289–91
Husserl, Edmund
    on Enlightenment methods, 518
    legacy of Western philosophy and, 677
Ibhawoh, Bonny, on human rights, 422
Ibiam, Francis Akanu, Sir (governor of colonial eastern Nigeria), 384
ICAO (Institut Catholique d'Afrique de l'Ouest [Ivory Coast], 51
identity
    African, 91n68, 648; local context of, 129; negated by missionaries and colonizers, 89
    social and cultural: supported by missionary practice, 35
    tribal: importance of, 129
ideology of domination
    response of African philosophy to, 675–77
    in West, 668
Idi Amin Dada
    despotic regime of, 403
    ordering murder of Archbishop Luwum, 354
IDLC-ISAN (Inter-Diocesan Liturgy Commission of the Igbo Speaking Area of Nigeria), 60, 60n92
Idowu, Bolaji
    on construction of African Christian theology, 173
    on traditional African religion as a unified system, 91
Idowu-Fearon (bishop of Sokoto), on Muslim concern about state and Christian faith, 376
Igba ndu (Igboland), 55
igbaafa (divination), as traditional practice of health care, 499
Igbo Mass, in Baltimore, 70
Igbo people, ethnic cleansing of, in Nigeria, 230
Ige, Bola, Nigerian representative to WCC in 1968, 384
Ihejirika, Walter C.
    on methods in communication research, 203
    on televangelism in Pentecostal churches in Nigeria, 211
ikwaaja (offerings to spirits), as traditional practice of health care, 499
Ilesanmi, Simon, on universalist approach to human rights, 417
Illich, Ivan, on health discourses, 520
illiteracy, as obstacle to development, 357
illness
    acceptance and, 526–30
    becoming sickness, 524

761

Index

illness (*cont.*)
  blame and, 526–30
  distinction from sickness, 524n61
  listening and, 531
  moral dimension of, 526–30
  mystical experiences during, 532–33
  as mystery, 529
  support groups in, 529
  See also disease; health; health care; sickness
Ilo, Stan Chu
  on approaches to development, 359–60
  on context-driven education, 360
  on ecclesiology of abundant life, 594
  on intercultural hermeneutics of friendship and participation, 390
  on ministries of Charismatic Renewal, 486
  on search for health and healing, 609
  on transformative theological praxis, 358, 706
imago Dei
  anthropological implications of, 581
  Athanasius on, 437
  and Catholic theological anthropology, 355
  and church as family of God, 575
  and dignity of human person, 416, 436–37
  and human rights, 416
  human sexuality and, 452
  and right to development, 418–19
  ubuntu and, 474
IMBISA (Inter-Regional Meeting of the Bishops of Southern Africa), conferences and workshops of, 196
IMC (International Missionary Council), meeting in Ghana (1957), 384
immigration, meaning of, 67 (*see also* migration; migrants to U.S.)
imperialism, versus missionary activity, 261–62
imprimi potest, for printed materials, 210
incarnation
  and adaptation, 90
  as beginning of inculturation, 81, 82–83
  and dignity of human person, 416
  inculturation and, 176, 725

inclusion
  at core of Christ-event, 442
  and planetary living, 439
income inequality, in Africa, 88
inculturation, 80–94, 95, 177
  abuse of, 176
  and adaptation, 83, 177
  and AECAWA, 51
  and African languages, 83, 83n12
  and African religious traditions, 689
  and African theology, 24, 167, 175
  authentic, 138
  Christological character of, 176
  church and, 235, 594–95
  and contextualization, 40, 84, 175
  and creative reinterpretation of gospel and culture, 81–82
  definitions of, 40, 81–82
  and developments in faith and culture, 82–84
  diversity and, 81–82
  Dutch Reformed Church (Nigeria) and, 654–55
  in early church, 82–83
  in early modern Kongo, 35
  and education, 235
  elements of, 81–82
  and evangelization in ancient churches in Africa, 84–85
  following Western models, 24
  gestures and, 58
  goal of, 176, 177
  and gospel, 40
  health care and, 508
  historical development of, in Africa, 84–87
  and imposition of faith, 83
  and incarnation, 81, 82–83, 176, 725
  and indigenization, 83–84, 86–87
  issues related to, 90–92
  language and, 40, 40n1
  liberating, 724–27
  and liturgy, 86
  and local churches, 140
  as mark of subsidiarity, 136
  methodology of, 175–77
  missionaries and, 82–83
  and mutual disclosure and dialogue, 81–82
  need for, in curricula, 59
  orthodoxy as issue for, 90
  pedagogical method of, 82–83
  Pentecostalism and, 475
  popular piety and, 481
  as postcolonial phenomenon, 89
  priority of biblical revelation in, 175

  resistance to, 86, 91, 91n67
  in sub-Saharan Africa, 86–87
  theological and ecclesial investigation of, 138
  as theological program endorsed by Vatican, 35
  traps of, 612
  universality and, 81–82
  Vatican II and, 556
  and Zairean rite of Eucharist, 139
inculturation, liturgical
  in Cameroon, 52–53
  in West Africa: Burkina Faso, 53; Ghana, 53; Igboland, 53–57; Yoruba and Igboland, 55–56; Zaire, 52–53
indigenization
  of church leaders, 86–87
  as focus of African theology, 91
  and inculturation, 83–84
indigenous cultural practices
  diversity of, 81
  and faith in Africa, 80
individualism
  as challenge to African Catholicism, 143
  in contrast to nature of human person, 416
  as hindrance to religious life, 322
industrialization, and first development decade, 421
infidelity, as problem in family, 574
Information Communications Technology (ICT), and liturgy, 50
Ingoli, Francesco, on missionary norms, 333
inheritance, as issue of interest, 58n89
Innocent XI, Pope, decree against transatlantic slave trade, 156
instability, as challenge in Africa, 16, 88
Institut Catholique d'Afrique de l'Ouest (Ivory Coast) (ICAO), 51
Institut Catholique de Yaoundé, Cameroon, 51
intellectual conversion, inculturation and, 235
intellectus (intuition), and human knowing, 223–24
intelligence, Catholic, meaning of, 223–24
intention, of sexual act, 452
Inter Caetera (Pope Alexander VI, papal bull; 1493)
  division of regions given to Portugal and Spain, 151n26, 261
  on overthrowing barbarous nations, 155

762

Index

interculturation, 95
interdependence, church as community of, 388
Inter-Diocesan Liturgy Commission of the Igbo Speaking Area of Nigeria (IDLC-ISAN), 60, 60n92
International Missionary Council (IMC), meeting in Ghana (1957), 384
International Theological Commission (ITC), on relationship between humans and other creatures, 439–40
International Year of the Family, 13, 710
Inter-Regional Meeting of the Bishops of Southern Africa (IMBISA), conferences and workshops of, 196
Interreligious Council of Liberia, set up by Muslims and Christians, 377
Inter-Religious Dialogue Commission of AECAWA (IRDC), sessions for Muslims and Christians at, 370–71, 370–71n24
intersectionality, oppression of women and, 567
Iran, and Islamicization of Africa, 376
IRDC (Inter-Religious Dialogue Commission of AECAWA), sessions for Muslims and Christians at, 370–71, 370–71n24
Irenaeus of Lyons, Saint
  on benefits of Christ's saving event, 617
  and tradition of Mark the evangelist, 4
Isichei, Elizabeth, on catechetical school of Alexandria, 331
Isidore of Seville, Saint, 6
  on Ethiopians and Libyans, 147–48
Islam
  African Catholicism and, 367–80
  experienced as threat to church, 43
  growth of, 578
  hegemony of, over North Africa, 8
  invasion of, and destruction of liturgical materials, 42–43
  not a homogenous entity, 367
  regarded as a Christian heresy, 8
  Sharīʿa law of, 376
  spread of (7th century), and decline of Christianity, 30, 167
Islamicization, and oil boom of the 1970s, 376
ITC (International Theological Commission), on relationship between humans and other creatures, 439–40
ius commissionis, and missionary activity, 312
Ivory Coast
  Catholic mission hospitals and clinics in, 372
  Institut Catholique d'Afrique de l'Ouest, 51

Janzen, John, on therapy management group and sickness, 529
Jenkins, Philip, on decline of Western Christianity, 663
Jensen, Robin, on Roman North Africa, 32–33
Jerome, Saint, and tradition of Mark the evangelist in Egypt, 4
Jesuit Centre for Theological Reflection (Lusaka, Zambia), guided reflection pamphlets from, 195
Jesuits, 10
  and evangelization of sub-Saharan Africa, 11, 17
  suppression of, in Portugal, 10
Jesus Christ
  African understanding of, 174, 604
  as brother ancestor, 590
  dangerous memory of, 624, 624n17
  as founder of new clan, 590
  as Good News, 604
  grassroots experience of, 606–8
  as healer, 498, 501, 610, 614
  identity and mission of, 614
  images of, 604, 605, 608–15
  as joy and hope in Africa, 617–18
  as king, 613–15
  as liberator, 610–13, 612n49
  as *Logos tou Theou,* 625
  proclamation of, 604, 607
  as proto-ancestor, 592
  as savior, 615–17
  social relevance of mission of, 615–16
  sociopolitical relevance of faith in, 615–16
  as true God and true man, 610, 614
  as white, 160, 162, 162n84
Jesus maija paintings (Cameroon), 642
John Cassian, Saint, view of Islam as Christian heresy, 8
John Chrysostom
  concern for church of his time, 292
  Eucharistic Prayer attributed to, 642
John of the Cross, Saint, and *Dark Night of the Soul,* 68, 75–77

John Paul II, Pope
  on Africa and sign of the times, xviii
  on African religious culture, 429
  on African spirituality, 473
  on African values and catechesis, 639–40
  at anniversary of closing of Vatican II, 81
  apostolic exhortation *Christifideles Laici* (1988), 479
  apostolic exhortation *Familiaris Consortio* (1981), 455, 462
  apostolic exhortation *Vita Consecrata* (1996), 318–19
  and Archbishop Tchidimbo, 227
  on chastity and marriage, 451
  on church as family of God, 574
  on common good, 338
  on conducting Christian theology, 600
  encyclical *Redemptor Hominis* (1979), 204, 581
  encyclical *Redemptoris Missio* (1990): on witness and evangelization, 376
  on evangelization, 368
  on First Synod as occasion of hope, 704
  on inculturation, 81–82, 84n21, 138–39, 660
  on mercy, 287
  on new Areopagus, 583
  on organic pastoral solidarity, xxvi
  on Pentecostal awareness, 467, 469
  post-synodal apostolic exhortation *Ecclesia in Africa* (1995), 13
  on solidarity as a virtue, 134–35
  support for Charismatic Renewal by, 484
  Synod of Africa (1994) convened by, 12
  on technology, 212
  on women, 561, 567
  visits to Africa by, 701
John XXIII, Pope (Angelo Roncalli), 623
  on church not bound to any culture, 720
  encyclical *Mater et Magistra* (1961): on Christianity and social progress, 523n56
  encyclical *Pacem in Terris* (1963), 501
  on new Pentecost, 483–84
  on presentation of deposit of faith, 659
  on reliving Pentecost, 468

763

Index

John XXIII, Pope (*cont.*)
  support of African intellectuals by, 303–4
  and theological understanding of human rights, 416
  Vatican II and, 621
Jones, William, on African philosophy, 672
Jong, Albert de
  on local church and Vatican II, 690–91
  study on implementation of Vatican II in East Africa, 687, 688
justice
  meaning of, 709–10
  as one of three duties of church, 225
  recognition of rights as, 709, 709n64
  reconciliation rooted in, 709
  right relationships and, 709
  social order and, 709
Justice and Peace Commissions, 598, 702
  as area for church attention, 410–11
justice, peace, and reconciliation. *See* reconciliation, justice, and peace
Justin de Jacobis, Saint, as model of evangelization, 138, 139
Justin Martyr, Saint, as African church father, 166n4
Justinian, heresy of, 260

Kä Mana
  ecumenism and, 383
  on political ethics, 678
Kabasélé, François. *See* Lumbala, François Kabasélé
Kabila, Joseph (president; DRC), arresting Catholic worshipers, 408
Kagame, Alexis (Rwanda), on construction of African Christian theology, 173
Kajabe Conference, 382
Kalilombe, Patrick (bishop; Diocese of Lilongwe, Malawi)
  exiled, 408
  on inculturation of African spirituality, 468
  one of founding fathers of SCCs in eastern Africa, 191
  on Vatican II as predominantly concerned with Europe, 687
Kalu, Ogbu
  on inculturation, 86
  on Pentecostal Christianity in Africa, 483, 485–86

on reappropriating African traditions of abundant life, 344
on turmoil of 20th and early 21st centuries, 493
Kamanga, Eugene (former archbishop of Lubumbashi, DRC), on African conception of life and Holy Spirit, 466
Kamau, David (auxiliary bishop of Nairobi), 488
Kant, Immanuel, on inferiority of Black people, 157, 667
Kanyari, Victor (televangelist; Kenya), abuses of, 472
Kanyoro, Musimbi R. A.
  African theologian, 173
  on traumatic situation of women, 362
  on women theologians, 565–66
Kasomo, Daniel, on Catholic Charismatic Renewal movement, 484–85, 484n41
Kasper, Walter (cardinal)
  on corporal and spiritual works of mercy, 287
  on dialogue, 517
  on Jesus Christ, the merciful Judge, 288
Kassimir, Ronald, on popular religion, 481–82
Katiti, Sister Mary Ann, on exclusion of women from evangelization, 692
Katongole, Emmanuel (Uganda)
  on approaches to development, 359
  on church during missionary and colonial era, 334
  on dependency of Africa on the West, 359–60
  ecumenism and, 383
  on hope, 297, 360, 703, 705, 710–11
  on reading Gospel passages in African situations, 641
  retelling story of Africa, 358
  theologian, 34
Kattarath, Father Varkey, Vincentian Congregation of Kerala, India, founded by, 487
Kavanagh, Aidan, on primacy of worship over belief, 46
kayamba (traditional musical instrument), 284
Keenan, James, SJ, and global conference on theological ethics and world church, 142
Keener, Craig S., on belief in Christ as healer, 609n27

Keim, Curtis, on imaginary Africa, 128
Kenema Pastoral Center (Kenema, Sierra Leone), 188
Kenya
  appearances of Blessed Virgin in, 12
  Catholic mission hospitals and clinics in, 372
  Christian activity in, in early modern period, 30
  on churches and political crises, 404
  churches obsessed with ethnic loyalties in, 404
  church–state relations in, 398, 403–4, 406, 407
  ethnic cleansing in, 404
  lay Catholic associations in, 478–79
  new constitution drafted under leadership of Bishop Philip Sulumeti, 406
  peaceful coexistence between Catholics and Muslims in, 370
  popular Catholicism in, 478–96
  risks of poverty in, and education, 249, 251 (figure)
  SCCs in, 595
  tribalism in, 129
  years of schooling in, 250
Kenyan Women's Prayer Group, in Baltimore, 71
Kenyatta, Jomo (president; Kenya), on church as conscience of society, 403
Kerr, Richard, on leader, 116
kerygma, proclamation and, 368
Kevin, Mother, hospital for lepers established by (Uganda), 505
Kibicho, Samuel, African theologian, 173
Kikuyu Conference (1913), 382n7
Kimuna, Sitawa, on sexual abuse of wives, 459
king, Christ as, 608, 613–15
King João III (1526), letter from Afonso about Portuguese kidnapping citizens of Kongo as slaves, 151
Kirwen, Michael, on dialogue between African Christianity and Western, 653
Kiwanuka, Joseph (first African Catholic bishop in modern times [1939]), 16
Kizito, Mary, on Christ as healer, 609
Klerk, Frederick W. de, seeking political support from Zion Christian Church, 407

764

Index

Knoblecher, Ignatius, in Sudan mission, 18
knowledge, power and, xxiii
Kobia, Samuel (bishop)
    on church and politics, 408–9
    ecumenism and, 383
koinonia (communion), 202
    church as, 383
    dialogue and, 647, 655
    paradigm of, 589, 590
    and SCCs, 193
    as selfless Christlike service, 46n38, 48
    Trinity and, 590
Koka, Kgalushi, on *ubuntu*, 474
kola nut
    breaking of: as act of welcoming guests, 54
    as symbolic object, 55
Kolawole, Mary Modupe, on African women scholars, 563
Kolié, Cécé, on quest for healing, 609
Kongo, Kingdom of, 30
    and European imagination, 150
    inculturation in, 34, 35
    location of, 149n6
    Portuguese period of, 34
    Protestant missionaries in, 333
    relationship of, with Holy See, 152
    Roman church in, 149–54
    See also Congo; Democratic Republic of the Congo
Kooistra, Nelli, on Roman Catholic Church in Africa, xix
Kouzes, James, on transformational servant leadership, 117–18
Kraemer, Hendrik, on communicating Christian message, 204
Kraft, Charles H., on communicative approaches from different cultures, 207
Krause, Donald, on nature of leadership, 115
Kuh, George, on education and values, 410
Kuhnen, Frithjob, on development decades, 421
Kuruppamparambil, Joseph, Fr. Dr. (Fr. Bill), and origin of Vincentian Ministries Kenya, 487
Kwok Pui-lan, on planetary living and alterity, 438–39
Lactantius, as theologian of African church, 148
Lado, Ludovic, on Catholic Pentecostalism, 484
laicization, as improper term, 295
laity
    apostolate of, 494, 595
    and *Apostolicam Actuositatem*, 472
    associations of, and popular piety, 481
    and collaboration with ordained ministers, 284
    and new evangelization, 494–95
laity, formation of, 236–37
Lamont, Donal (Catholic bishop; Zimbabwe), 405
land
    community ownership of, 435
    as gift of supreme being, 435
    sacred character of, 435
Lange, Glenn-Marie
    on investment in children's education, 241
language
    African: call for use of African, 86–87; as means of communicating gospel, 177
    as first means of communication, 205–8
    and inculturation, 40, 83, 83n12
    and vernacular translations of Bible, 169
languages, African, 128n6, 206
Lao Tzu, on leader, 112
lapsi (returning lapsed Christians), 260
Latin America, as new center of Christianity, 168–69
Latin church
    Africa's encounter with, 148–49, 148n5
    history of, 309
Laudato Si' (Pope Francis, encyclical; 2015), 136–37
Laurie, Emma Whyte, on justifications for certain medical interventions, 521
Lavigerie, Charles Martial Allemand (bishop of Nancy)
    appointed archbishop of Algiers, 11
    inspired by early church in northern Africa, 36
    Society of Missionaries of Africa (White Fathers) founded by, 11, 310
lay associations, popular piety and, 481 (*see also* laity)
Lay Carmelites, education of laity and, 479
leaders
    Christian: description of, 124
    mentoring of, 126
    qualities of, 114–15
    skills needed by, 120
    training of, 351
    transformational, 116–17
leadership
    of all people, 110
    of bishops, and agenda of *Africae Munus*, 237, 237n35
    challenge of, in Africa, 109–12
    as Christian witness, 110
    church structures of, 112–13
    communal, 112
    damaged by military regimes, 111–12
    and ecclesiology, 592
    and history of Africa, 111
    image of Christ as king and, 613–15
    importance of, 58n89
    lack of succession plans in, 111
    lay: in church before Vatican II, 623; and new model of church, 596
    marginalization of women in, 120–21
    master–slave pattern of, 111
    nature of, 112–15
    organizational aesthetics and, 115–16
    oriented toward common good, 116
    and power and privilege, 112–13
    of priests and religious, 110
    qualities of, 112–13
    spiritual, 113–14
    starting from the grassroots, 112
    training for, 117, 119–20
    transactional, 116
    transformational servant, 109–26
lectio, as element of scholastic method, 100
lectionary cycle, and SCCs, 193, 193n30
Legion of Mary, education of laity and, 479
Leibniz, Gottfried Wilhelm, on human identity, 157n59
Leiris, Michel, and Alioune Diop, 301
Leo III, Pope (795–816), Charlemagne declared as first Christian emperor of Holy Roman Empire by, 397
Leo the Great (400–461), on proliferation of dioceses and bishops in early African church, 260n18
Leo XIII, Pope
    encyclical *Rerum Novarum* (1891): on capital and labor, 523n56
Leonor Nzinga a Nlaza (wife of King Nzinga), as convert to Catholicism, 150

Index

Leopold, and Catholic missionaries, 334
Levinas, Emmanuel, on dialogue, 668
Lewis, C. S., on education and teachers, 120
lex credendi, 46
lex orandi, 46
lex orandi, lex credendi, and Zairean missal, 139
libelli missarum (prayer forms for particular occasions), 42, 42n9
liberal democracy, triumph of, 343–44
liberalism, as theory of human rights, 417
liberation
    African ecclesiology of, 594
    African Traditional Religion and, 172
    as focus of Black theology, 91
    inclusive of men and women, 679–80
    as theme in African New Testament studies, 174
liberation theology, 95
    in Africa, 353–54
    and Black theology, 172
    emergence of, in Latin America, 352
    in South Africa, 175n73
Liberia, ex-slaves returning to, 264n42
Libermann, Francis, founder of society of priests for the emancipation of black slaves, 310n5
libertarianism, as theory of human rights, 417
Libya, as part of Latin North Africa, 32
Libyans, described by Isidore of Seville, 147–48
Life and Work Movement, 383
Likonde Minor Seminary, emphasis on intellectual formation in, 292n42
liminality, and experience of migration, 68–69
Linsky, Marty, on attributes of leadership, 115
listening, dialogue and, 660
liturgy
    as act of prayer, 45
    as anamnestic, 48–49
    and Bible, 44n20, 642
    and catechesis, 45
    celebrative nature of, 41, 213
    as center of Catholicism, 44–50
    definition of, 40–41
    Ethiopian Eucharistic, 642
    and inculturation, 86
    innovation and adaptation in, 689–90
    as *locus theologicus*, 44
    as mission-oriented, 49–50
    nature of, 45–50
    Roman North African, 43
    and salvation history, 45
    as source and norm of faith, 46
    symbols of, foreign to African experience, 89
    as teaching (*didascalia*), 44, 45
    and technology, 50
    and theological discourse, 44
    and theology, 44–47
    as transformative, 49
liturgy, African
    and celebration, 22
    future Catholic, 47–50
    historical survey of, 42–44
    need for, 92
    in post-Nicene period, 42–43
    spirituality of, 43
    in 21st century, 22
liturgy, Gallican, influenced by North African liturgy, 42
liturgy, Mozarabic, influenced by North African liturgy, 42
liturgy, Roman
    influenced by North African liturgy, 42
    influence of African Catholicism on, 43
Livingstone, David, xviii, evangelizing in sub-Saharan Africa, 10
Löblich, M., on historical research in communication studies, 203
locus liturgicus, theology as, 44
locus operandi (place of operation), and theological research, 40
locus theologicus
    African experience as, 172
    each theological discipline as, 651
    human needs as, 104
    liturgy as, 44
    migration as, 65–66
    popular piety as, 481
    and signs of the times, 96
    world as, 96–97
logos (speech, discourse, reason, thought), meaning of dialogue and, 668
Logos tou Theou, Jesus as 625
Lonergan, Bernard
    on academic theology, 223
    on assimilation of doctrines, 660
    on conversion, 235, 662, 662n74, 663
    on differences between peoples and cultures, 662
    on encounter, 662
    on theological method, 95–96, 99, 202
    on theology and history of Christian religion, 658
Lopes, Duarte, Kongo's ambassador to papal court, 152
Louvanium University at Kinshasa, on possibility of African theology, 86
love, and abundant life, 415
Lovelock, James, Gaia hypothesis of, 436
low-cost care in, 543–44; periods of conflict and, 546; and poor, 544–45; reasons for choice of, 544; satisfaction of patients in, 544
Lowery, Stephanie, on ecclesiological models inspired by Vatican II and two African Synods, 388
Ludwig, Emil, derogatory remarks of, 651
Lukken, Gerard, on liturgy as first theology and first orthodoxy, 45–46
Lumbala, François Kabasélé
    on Christ as King, 614
    on concept of consecration and vows, 315
Lumen Gentium (Vatican II, Dogmatic Constitution on the Church), 96–97n7
    on charisms, 472
    on church as one body, 575
    on cultural dialogue, 224–25
    on governing authority of bishops, 272
    on human beings as people of God, 233, 388
    on local churches, 691
    and notion of church as people of God, 193–94
    quoted by *Africae Munus*, 685
    See also church; Vatican II
Lumko Institute, work of, on pastoral use of the Bible, 637
Lumko Missiological Institute (Germiston, Delmenville, South Africa), and SCCs, 187–88
Lumko program, on social justice, 195
Lumumba, Patrice, antichurch policies of, 226
Luo ethnic group, and beginning of SCCs, 186
Lupton, Robert D., on toxic charity, 346
Luther, on separation of church and state, 397–98
Luwum, Janani (archbishop of Kampala; Uganda), tortured and murdered on orders of Idi Amin, 354, 403, 408

Index

Luzbetak, L., on contextualization, 84
Lynch, Joseph H., on movement of Christianity to Europe, 717–18

M'Baye, Kéba (Senegal), on development as a right, 418
Maathai, Wangari, on modern Africa, 128
Macarius, Saint, and monasticism, 6
Madagascar
    Christian activity in early modern period, 30
    colonized by France, 11
Madonna University (Okija, Nigeria), 51n56
Magesa, Laurenti
    African theologian, 173
    on African experience and theology, 172
    on African religious worldview, 640n26, 653
    on Africans and Vatican II, 686, 691–93
    on balance in life, 440–41
    on Bible as most authentic link between church and Christ, 634n4
    on church and politics, 397
    on church's concern for justice and truth, 410
    on deconstruction of church in Africa, 169
    on ethical values of clans, 590–91
    on ethics, 443
    on inculturation, 689
    on natural family planning, 456
    on SCCs, 192–93, 193n32, 197
    on separation of church and state, 408
    social analysis of, 353
magisterium
    authority of, 724
    dialogue in cooperation with, 658
    fidelity to: as principle of Catholic theology, 657n58
    role of, 658
    as source of theology for Africa and West, 656
Mahumbulele, Baison, on need for spiritual gifts, 467
Maina, John, on Eucharist and Patrick and Rosalia Family Prayer Group, 491
Maistre, Joseph de, on inferiority of Black people, 158
malaria, prevalence of, 499
Malawi
    risks of poverty in, and education, 249, 251 (figure)
    SCCs in, 595

Maldonado, Alonso, and Teresa of Avila, 310
Mali, Modibo Keita as dictator in, 228
Malula, Joseph-Albert (cardinal; archbishop of Kinshasa)
    and appointment of *mokambi*, 596
    authority of Mobutu recognized by, 408
    in exile, 227
    on imposing Western ways on African culture, 12
    political class denounced by, 226–27
    and SCCs, 187
Mameluke rule, least tolerant of Christians, 8
mandates, system of missionary cooperation between bishops and Roman pontiff, 267
Mandela, Nelson, 359
    on leadership, 112
    and Zion Christian Church, 407
Manichaeism
    and Christian sexual morality, 450
    heresy of, 5
Mantiero, Sr. Eletta (Uganda), dispensary founded by, 505
Manunga, Godefroid (Father), on SCCs in South Africa, 190
Marcionists, on procreation, 454
Marcus Aurelius, persecution under, 4
Marian piety, in fringe movements, 20
Marianhill Fathers, and evangelization of sub-Saharan Africa, 11
Mark the Evangelist
    and ancient church of Africa, 81, 130, 331
    as first bishop of Alexandria, 4, 30, 166n2
market, health industry and, 521
marriage
    African customary norms and practices of, 277, 662–63
    child: impact of education on, 240–41
    Christian rite of, in Igboland, 54–55
    inculturation and, 276
    not treated in First Synod, 12
    as sacrament, 574
    sexual intercourse in, 453
    as vocation, 453
    Western practices of, 662–63
Marsili, Salvatore, on liturgy as theology, 81
Marteau, Marguerite, 301
Martín de Agar, José Tomás, on rules in first Christian communities, 257

martyrdom, in 2nd and 3rd centuries, 4–5
martyrs
    celebration of, in Roman Africa, 34
    as witnesses to paschal mystery, 43
    See also Scillitan Martyrs; Uganda Martyrs
martys (witnessing), 48
Marxism, as theory of human rights, 417
Mary, Blessed Virgin, appearances of, 12
Mary, the Star of Evangelization, and evangelizing mission in Africa, 13
Maryknoll missionaries, and SCCs, 186
Mass according to the Zairean Rite, 52, 139
Massignon, Louis, and Alioune Diop, 301
Masson, Joseph, on inculturation, 82
Mater Misericordiae Hospital (Nigeria), 505
material world, as symbol of divine, 640n26
materialism, religious life and, 318–19
matrimony, sacrament of, 574 (*see also* marriage)
Mauretania, part of Latin North Africa, 32
Mawagali, Noa, as martyr, 18
Maxwell, John, in influencing others, 114
Maydieu, Jean-Augustin, and education of Alioune Diop, 300–301
Mbaka, Fr. Ejike, healing ministry of, 609n32
Mbiti, John (Kenya)
    on Africa and the West,, 168
    on African Christian theology, 90, 173
    on African theology vs. Black theology, 91
    on Christian theology and African traditional life, 652
    on church's inability to solve problems, 23–24
    as disciple of Tempels, 672
    on modern Christian Africa, 167
    on pan-African culture, 90
    on solidarity, 318
Mbonu, Mother Dorothy, 559n86
McDougal, Serie, on intersectionality and oppression of women, 567
McEnroy, Carmel, on women prior to Vatican II, 558, 560
McFague, Sallie, on ecological economics, 438

INDEX

McGahan, A., on management of global health programs, 50–501
McGilvray, James, on CHAs and faith-based health facilities, 543
McQuail, Denis, on models of communication, 205
MDGs (Millennium Development Goals), and right to development, 421
Medeiros, François de, on historical relationship between Africa and West, 670
mediation, African concept of, 172
medicalization
    and mechanisms of exclusion, 521
    programs of, 520–21
medicine
    biological model of, 518
    biopsychosocial model of, 519
    colonial, 521n45
    dilemmas of paradigm of, 517–19
    holistic, and biopsychosocial model, 519
    independent of religion, 518
    as system of knowledge, 518
    See also health; health care
Méjan, François
    denouncing Vatican, 299
    on "de-occidentalization," 299
Mejia, Rodrigo
    on interpretation of human situations, 104
    on method in theology, 98
    on theology and Catholic studies, 100
Mendonça, Lourenço da Silva de (1684), on horrors of slave trade, 156
Menkiti, Ifeanyi, African philosophy and, 667
mercy
    meaning of, 285
    and pastoral work among poor, 287
    and priestly vocation, 285
    two case studies of, 288–91
Merleau-Ponty, Maurice, on Enlightenment methods, 518
metaxy (participation), in paschal mystery, 49
method
    meaning of term, 99, 99n15
    and real needs of people, 99
    relevance of, in doing Catholic studies, 100–102
    theological, and listening and learning, 106

methodology
    for approaching Africa's future, 411–12
    divine intervention in, 104
    implied intention in, 98–99
    inductive and deductive, 103–4
    motivations and drivers of, 98–99
    in theology, as challenge to SCCs, 198
Metuh, Emefie Ikenga
    on African worldview, 440
    on human harmony with nature, 441
Metz, J. B., on theological method, 95–96
Metzler, Josef, on synods and councils in missionary period, 266–67
micro-nations, in Africa, 128
Middle Ages
    popular devotions in, 480n12
    sexual morality in, 450–51
migrants to U.S., African
    challenges of, 71–74
    diversity of, 63–64
    experience of loss of, 71–74
    invisibility of, 63
    language barrier of, 72
    loss of socioeconomic status of, 73
    migration theology and, 64–65
    stories of, 65, 70–77
    understanding of God of, 74–76
    and U.S. census, 63–64
migration
    African Catholic migrants to U.S., 63–79
    as challenge to church in Africa, 109
    changes of identity and, 67–68
    and dark night, 67
    as experience of liminality, 67–68
    global and local networks of, 65
    God's presence and purpose in, 65
    and increases in Muslim population in Zongo communities, 374
    liminality and, 68–69
    as *locus theologicus*, 65–66
    as process, 67–68
    and religion, 64–65
    role of faith and church communities in, 65
    terms related to, 67n32
    theology of, 63–67
    transitions in, 69
    See also immigration; migrants to U.S.
Miguda, Edity
    on gender relations, 555
    on idea of womanism, 554

Milingo, Emmanuel (archbishop of Lusaka)
    founded Divine Providence Community, 484
    healing ministry of, 20–21
    leader of married priests in Africa, 296
    ministry of, 514
Milingo Affair
    idea of spirit world and, 513
    popular healing ministry of, 513
military forces, African, misadventures of, 228
Militiades, Pope, African, 148
Mill Hill Missionaries, founded by Henry Vaughan, 17, 310
Millennium Development Goals (MDGs), and right to development, 421
mimēsis (imitation), in paschal mystery, 49
ministry/ministries
    and ecclesiology, 592
    varieties of, 723
Minucius Felix, as theologian of African church, 148
miracles, as theme in African New Testament studies, 174
misericordia (mercy), 286
missio Dei (mission of God), and global context, 137–38
missiology, as compulsory topic in formation of religious, 323
mission
    church as family of God and, 708–9
    communicative aspect of, 204
    hope as context for, 705
mission, life
    illness and, 526
    moral dimension of, 526–30
mission territories
    in Africa, 272
    under jurisdiction of CEP, 272
missionaries, 718
    from Africa to elsewhere, 143, 306–7, 367, 719
    African Christians as own, 595
    attitude of, toward African culture, 87
    belief in demonic possession and, 512n5
    biomedical model of health problems and, 499
    book of the catechism used by, 210
    concern for Christian doctrine of, 615
    early negative attitudes of, 651
    and ecclesiastical hierarchy, 268

Index

exchanges between West and Africa, 656, 656n52
faulty Christologies and, 612
French, and ideas of conquest, xxvi
and ideology of domination, 670, 306
and inculturation, 82–83
and indigenous African leaders, 111
in modern era, 334
and native African medicine, 499
paternalism of, 35
as people of their time, 19
as pioneers of African theology, 652
politics and, 398
racism of, 35
schools established by, 245
schools founded by, 36
shaped by Western values and history, 19
sociopolitical contributions of, 335
and Western medicine in Africa, 504–5, 515
See also evangelization
Missionaries of Africa (White Fathers), evangelization efforts of, 36
Missionaries of the Consolata, founded by Blessed Giuseppe Alamano, 310
missionary activity
 and canon law, 262
 as challenge of SCCs, 196
 during era of royal patronage, 260–61
 failure of, 10
 goals of, 311–12
 versus imperialistic interests, 261–62
 in negative manner, 376
 under Propaganda Fide, 264–65
 providing education and health care, 35
 religious life as, 309–10
 rivalries in, 264–65
 slave trade and, 167
 in sub-Saharan Africa, 30
 success of, 10, 91
 three dimensions of, 470
 trade as, 332
 See also evangelization
missionary Christianity, legacy of, 721
Missionary Daughters of Blessed Michael Iwene Tansi, 559n85
missionary expansion, in Africa (19th and 20th centuries), 310
missionary law
 canon law and, 263–65
 impact of ecumenical councils on, 267–69

missionary life, model of, 311
missionary movement, in 19th century, 17–18
missionary religious orders and congregations, growth of, 264
missionary schools, as instrument of colonization, 245
Missionary Servants of Our Lady of Roses Congregation, 559n86
Missionary Sisters of Divine Mercy, 559n85
Missionary Sisters of Our Lady of Africa, female counterpart of White Fathers, 310
missions
 ecclesiastical structure of, in Africa, 265–67
 independent, 268
 racist mindset of, 343
Mitchell, Bob, on marginalization of religion, 347–48
Mitchell, Patrick, on Pentecostal and charismatic values, 473
Mnangagwa, Emmerson (president of Zimbabwe following Mugabe), 406
Mobutu Sese Seko (DRC)
 as ally of church at first, 226
 authenticity philosophy of, 186–87, 226
 and Catholic education, 225–27, 234
 and confrontation with Catholic Church, 186–87
 government of President Kasavubu (1965) overthrown by, 226
 nationalization of schools by, 244
 repression of church under, 227
modernity
 challenges of, 97–98
 definition of, 97
 features of, 97
 and methodology for Catholic studies, 101
 social transformation of, 98
Modisane, Bloke, on Black people as despised, 158
Moemeka, Andrew, on communalism and communication, 205–6
Moerschbacher, Marco, on beginning of SCCs in 1961, 1984–85
Moi, Daniel arap (dictatorial president; Kenya)
 opposition between church and state under, 403–4
 stoking ethnic tensions, 404
mokambi (lay minister), role of, 596
Moltmann, Jürgen, theology of joy of, 525–26

monasteries, populations of, 6
monasticism
 and ancient African Christianity, 31
 Christian tradition and, 717
 and deserts, 5–6
 discipline and, in Africa, 331
 in 2nd and 3rd centuries, 4–5
Mondoué, Roger, on globalization, 679
Monney, Joseph (missionary; Benin), on West's erroneous view of Africa, 670
Monod, Théodore, and Alioune Diop, 301
Monomotapa, evangelization programs in, 10
monophysitism
 Christian history and, 6, 7, 717
 in Latin church, 309
Montanism, 5, 6
Montesquieu, Baron de, on inferiority of Black people, 157–58
Montini, Giovanni Cardinal. *See* Paul VI, Pope
Moore Ritual, 53
morale, and pastoral agents, 121
morality
 Christian, 581–82
 ecological, 443
 as theme in African New Testament studies, 174
Moratorium Declaration, 87
Moriarty, Declan, on men who have left priesthood, 295
Morrison, Toni, as Africana womanist, 553
Mossi (people; Burkina Faso), and Moore Ritual, 53
Mounier, Emmanuel, and Alioune Diop, 301
Mouvement Populaire de la Révolution (MPR), as Mobutu's agents, 227
Movement for the Restoration of the Ten Commandments of God (Uganda), 20
Mozambique
 Christian activity in, in early modern period, 30
 evangelization programs in, 10
 Portuguese missionaries in, 11
Mozarabic liturgy. *See* liturgy, Mozarabic
Mpalanyi, Gerald Maxwell (scholar; Uganda), on Pentecostal reality in Africa, 474–75
MPR (Mouvement Populaire de la Révolution), as Mobutu's agents, 227

Index

Mudimbe, V. Y.
  challenges facing Africa and, 680
  not widely known by Western philosophers, 677
Mugabe, Robert
  atrocities committed under, 405
  brutal forces used against churches by, 405
  placed under house arrest by military (2017), 406
  as president of Zimbabwe, 405
  and War of Liberation in Zimbabwe, 405
Mugambi, J. N. K. (Jessie)
  ecumenism and, 383
  on new centers of Christianity, 168
Mulago, Vincent (Congo)
  on ancestors, 430, 432
  anthropomorphic ethical framework of, 430–31
  on church as clan, 590
  on construction of African Christian theology, 173
  hierarchy of beings and, 430
  on *ntu*, 430, 431, 432
  on participation, 432–33
  on traditional African religion as a unified system, 91
Müller, Gerhard Cardinal, on hope, 703
Mulumba, Matthias, as martyr, 18
Mundele, Albert Ngengi, on African biblical interpretation, 635–36
Munemo, Douglas, on theological formation of pastors, 411
Munier, C., *Concilia Africae*, 259
muntu (Africans), 678, 680
Munyao, Martin
  on Christology, 605
Munzihirwa Christophe (archbishop; eastern Congo), assassination of, by Rwandan troops, 21, 34, 354
Murray, Paul
  on African feminism, 91
  on receptive ecumenism, 386
Museveni, Yoweri (president; Uganda)
  and Christian churches, 403
  and condom use in Uganda, 461–62
Mushete, Ngindu, and debate about African theology, 90
Musisi, Nakanyike, on health care in Africa, 504–5
Musisi, Seggane, on health care in Africa, 504–5
Muslim invasion, and decline of Christianity in North Africa, 85
Muslims
  African theology and, 649
  in Catholic schools, 371–72
  dialogue with, 367, 369–70
  not protected from enslavement, 154–55
  pastoral needs of, 371
  prevailing over Latin Christianity, 309
Muslims and Catholics
  holistic development of, 371–73
  peaceful relations between, 370
  spiritual growth and, 373
  tensions between, 373–77
Mutesa, Edward, II (first president of Uganda), 403
Muthigani, Augusta, on global network of Catholic schools, 248
Muzorewa, Abel (bishop; second president of Zimbabwe), 405
Mveng, Engelbert (Father)
  on poverty, 316–17
  social analysis of, 353
  on struggle for Black identity, 651–52
  against Tempels's vital force theory, 676
Mwanga, Kabaka (king; Uganda), and Uganda Martyrs, 403
Mwaura, Philomena Njeri
  Catholic Charismatic Renewal in Kenya, 486–87
  on Catholic Women Association in Kenya, 559
  on liturgical roles of women, 558
  on Pentecostalism in Kenya, 482–83
Mwoleka, Christopher (bishop; Diocese of Eulenge, Tanzania), one of founding fathers of SCCs in eastern Africa, 191
mystic, true sense of, 320
mysticism, prophetic, and religious life, 320

N'zeki, Raphael Ndingi Mwana, as first patron of Charismatic Renewal movement in Kenya, 484
Nairobi, Archdiocese of
  fieldwork in, on Catholic Charismatic Renewal in Kenya, 486–90
  popular Catholic groups in, 479–96
naming
  act of, for women, 553–54
  ceremony of, in Yoruba and Igboland, 55–56
  significance of, for Africans, 556
National Catholic Health Services (NCHS), 372
National Council for Population and Development (NCPD), family planning programs of, 457
National Council of Churches of Kenya (NCCK). apologized to Kenyans, 404
nation-states
  created by colonial powers, 128
  emergence of, 334
  Western model of, 140
natural disasters, as challenge to church in Africa, 109
natural family planning, 457–58 (*see also* contraception)
nature, harmony in, 427–28
NCCK (National Council of Churches of Kenya), apologized to Kenyans, 404
Nchimbi, John (Father; d. 2012), story of practice of mercy of, 288–89
NCHS (National Catholic Health Services), 372
Nciizah, Elinah, on theological formation of pastors, 411
NCPD (National Council for Population and Development), family planning programs of, 457
Ncube, Pius Alick Mvunda (archbishop of Bulawayo; Zimbabwe), challenging Mugabe, 406
Ndigbo (collective noun for the Igbo people), 55n74
Ndjana, Hubert Mono, summary of African philosophy of, 677
Ndubuisi Community Mutual Based Health Insurance (NMBHI), 506–7
Ne Vunda, Antonio Emanuele Nsaku
  detained by Spanish authorities, 153
  first Kongolese ambassador to papal court, 153
NECC (Northeast Catholic Community), 69–71
NECO (Northeast Community Organization), 70
negritude movement, 299
  and Aimé Césaire, 301
  idea of, 675
  Léon-Gontran Damas and, 301
Neoplatonism, Christian, as achievement of ancient African Christianity, 31
nepotism
  in African politics, 119
  in church organization, 121

Index

Network of Small Christian Communities in Africa, workshops of, 196
new evangelization. *See* evangelization, new
new Pentecost, and Second Synod, 705
New Testament
    African characters in, 171n47
    African studies of, 166–82
    contextualized study of, 175
New Testament studies
    in Africa, 169–71: and contextualized theology, 168; and independence of African nations, 169–70; and themes of liberation, inequality, and reconciliation, 168; as conversational, 168, 168n16; as praxis-oriented, 168; characteristics and scope of, 167–68; identity of, 168–69; and African religio-cultural ideas, 167
    modern critical methods of, 167
Newman, John Henry Cardinal, and Catholic intellectual tradition, 224
Ngango, Georges (Cameroon), 300, and Paul VI, 304–5
Ngoa, Henri, on status of women, 679
NGOs
    and health care, 500–501
    involvement of women in, 558
Ngumu Pie-Claude (Father), and *Ndzon-melen* Mass, 52
Nicaea, Council of (325), 6, 42n11
Nicholas V, Pope
    bull *Dum Diversas* (1452): promoted conquest and enslavement of pagans, 155
    extending privilege of patronage to African territories, 261
Nida, Eugene, on communication model of Western missionaries, 205
Nigeria
    and 2021 Human Rights Watch World Report, 419
    Bigard Memorial Seminary in, 22
    Boko Haram in, 374
    and Catholic education, 225, 225n7, 227–32
    Catholic political engagement in, 337–38
    as colonized by Great Britain, 11
    constitutions in, 230–31
    ethnic cleansing in, 230
    health care services in, 505
    human rights abuses in, 419
    influence of Catholic vote in, 337
    as microcosm of Africa, 419–20
    military coup in (1966), 228
    Miss World competition in (2002), 377
    missionaries and new visa regime in, 229n21
    priestly vocations in, 16, 293
    radio industry in, 211
    and right to development, 415, 419–20
    rise of Catholic universities in, 232, 232n30
    schools established by missionaries in, 227–28
    state takeover of education in, 229–30
    as underdeveloped nation, 419–20
Nigeria, northern
    legacy of slave trade in, 373
    tensions between Muslims and Christians in, 373
Nigeria, southwestern, peaceful coexistence between Catholics and Muslims in, 370
Nigerian–Biafran War (1967–70), 384
nihil obstat, for printed materials, 210
Niles, Preman, on WCC goal of Christian unity, 384
Njagi, Margaret, on Patrick and Rosalia Family Prayer Group, 492
Njalula, Sister Josée, RSA (DRC), BCCs reflective of desire for Christianity to be rooted in African reality, 185
Njoya, Timothy (Kenya), beaten, 408
Njui, John Cardinal (archbishop of Nairobi), on Charismatic Renewal movement as threat, 484
Nkadi Mpemba, supreme being and sky spirit in Congo, 85
Nkalanga, Gervase (bishop; Tanzania), on SCCs, 191
Nkemnkia, Martin Nkafu
    on anthropocentric approach to life, 431
    on community, 435
    notion of "vitalogy" of, 435
nkisi ("fetish"), 34
Nkosi, Z. (South Africa), on land as gift of God, 435–36
Nkrumah, Kwame (Ghana), Marxist-leaning leader, 408
NMBHI (Ndubuisi Community Mutual Based Health Insurance), 506–7
Nnukwu njo (big sins), 161
non-Chalcedonian Christians, 32
Nongo-Aziagbia, Nestor-Désiré, on fraternity in Christ in African context, 591–92
North Africa
    African school of theology in, 32–33
    and canon law, 257
    Catholic Church in, 331–32
    centers of early Christianity, 32, 130
    Christological discussions in, 32
    colonized by France, 11
    Coptic churches in, 32, 130
    as cradle of Latin Christianity, 42
    Ethiopian Christianity in, 32
    Greek speakers in, and philosophical speculation, 33
    Islamic landscape of, xx
    juridical tradition of church in, 259
    Latin culture and languages in ancient churches in, 32–34, 42, 85
    Muslim invasion and decline of Christianity in, 85, 85n25
    persecution of, 33
    prefiguring Western Christianity, 32
    rejection Chalcedon in, 32
    Roman churches in, 130
    speculative theology and philosophy in, 32
    theological legacy of, 33
Northeast Catholic Community (NCC), in Baltimore, 69–71
Northeast Community Organization (NCO), in Baltimore, 70
Northouse, Peter, on transformational leadership, 116
Nostra Aetate (Vatican II, Declaration on the Relationship of the Church to Non-Christian Religions), 11
    on ecumenism, 388
    and indigenous theologies, 170
    on non-Christian religions, 688–89
    quoted by *Africae Munus*, 685, 688
    and *Salus extra ecclesiam non est*, 161n80
    See also ecumenism; Vatican II
Nouwen, Henri, on spiritual leader, 124
Nthamburi, Zabbon, on challenge of Islam in North Africa, 85n25
ntu (vital force), 430–32
Nubia
    early Christianity in, 8–9, 30, 130
    and treaty with Muslim leaders, 9
Numidia, as part of Latin North Africa, 32
Nyamiti, Charles
    on church as clan, 590

771

Index

Nyamiti, Charles (*cont.*)
  on inculturation, 86
  on pan-African culture, 90
  on scholastic method, 101n21
  on syncretism and inculturation, 89
  on truly African church, 91–92
Nyarombo Parish, and SCCs, 186
Nyerere, Julius (first president of Tanzania)
  and idea of community and solidarity, 676
  and need for close links between church and state, 404
  on predicament of church of the future, 725–26
  on responsibility of church to combat social ills, 578
Nzeki, Raphael Ndingi Mwana'a (bishop; Kenya), on African grassroots communities, 186
Nzinga a Nkuwu (João I), and Portuguese explorers, 150
Nzinga Mbemba (future King Afonso I), sent to Portugal, 150
Nzinga Nkuwu, king, 226

Oba Ozolua (Benin Empire; 1514) emissary to Portugal, 155–56
Obasanjo, Olusegun (leader of military government in Nigeria) and state takeover of schools, 230
obele Njo (small sins), 161
Obenga, Théophile
  on Western civilization inspired by Egyptian civilization, 676
Obineli, Rev. Mother Dr. Susana Uzoamaka, 559n85
object language
  as nonverbal communication, 208
Oblates of Mary Immaculate, and evangelization of sub-Saharan Africa, 11, 18
Obote, Milton (first prime minister of Uganda), 403
Obstetric Fistula Centre (Mankessim, Ghana), 372
Ocaya, V., hermeneutical school of African philosophy and, 672–73
O'Collins, Gerald, on theology in living community with church, 658
O'Connor, Edward, on Duquesne University Bible study, 483
Oden, Thomas
  on achievements of ancient African Christianity, 31
  on African faith shaping Western Christianity, 331

Odomaro, Mubangizi, on African ecclesiology of liberation, 594
Odongo, James (archbishop; Uganda), on SCCs, 191
Odozor, Paulinus Ikechukwu
  on African synodal traditions and Christian ethics, 710–11
  on African theology, 649, 652, 656–57
  on diversity of African contexts, 650
  on women as underdeveloped resource, 711
Oduyoye, Mercy Amba
  on African story, xxii
  African theologian, 173
  on listening to people's questions, 175
  on need for plural African cultures, 90
  on women theologians, 565–66
OECD (Organization for Economic Co-operation and Development), 345
Ofala Jesu (Corpus Christi), 53
ofo (consecrated stick), as symbolic object, 55
ogirise leaf, as symbolic object, 55
Ogundipe-Leslie, Molara, Stiwanism of, 552
Ogunu, Michael, on constitutions in Nigeria, 230–31
O'Halloran, James, SDB, on antiquity of SCCs, 186
Okello, Irwa and Daudi (Gulu in northern Uganda), 21
Okere, Theophilus, on Western view of African culture, 651
Okogie, Olubunmi (Lagos; cardinal), heroism of, 354
Okonjo Ogunyemi, Chikwenye
  African womanism of, 552–55
  on male–female relationship, 554–55
  on naming, 553–54
Okoth, Yona, succeeding Wani, 403
Okoth, Zacchaeus (archbishop; Archdiocese of Kisumu, Kenya), on SCCs, 188
Okullu, Henry (bishop)
  on church as conscience of society, 403
  on life experience and Christology, 607
  on relation of church to governments, 408–9
Okure, Teresa
  challenges facing Africa and, 680
  on church as family of God, 576–77, 599–600, 709

Olpade, Dayo, optimism for Africa's future, 88, 88n51
Olukoshi, Adebayo, on eroded autonomy of African states, 341
O'Malley, John
  on reading the Bible, 628
  on Vatican II, 625, 687, 693, 719–20
Omego, Christy U., on methods in communication research, 203
Onaiyekan, John (cardinal; Nigeria)
  on African life experience of Christ, 607
  on peaceful coexistence between Catholics and Muslims, 370
Ondiek, Stephen (archbishop; Kenya) appointed to cabinet by Moi, 407
Onitsha, Albert Obiefuna (archbishop), on ethnicity in Africa, 577
Opoku, K. A., on necessity of inculturation, 89
Opongo, Elias
  and ethical pubic officials, 410
  on future of African church, 409
Optatam Totius (Vatican II, Decree on Priestly Formation)
  on candidates to seminaries, 293
  on scholastic method, 101n21
  See also priest; priestly formation; priestly ministry; Vatican II
Optatus, Saint, as theologian of African church, 6, 148
oral tradition, in African cultures, 172–73, 175
orandi, primacy of, over *credendi*, 46
Organization for Economic Co-operation and Development (OECD), 345
Orientalium Ecclesiarum (Vatican II, Decree on Eastern Catholic Churches)
  and distinct liturgical rites, 83, 83n14
  See also ecumenism; liturgy; Vatican II
Origen
  as African church father, 6, 30, 32, 81, 148, 166n4, 331, 637
  exegesis of, 637–38, 637n12
  history of church and, 717
  on parable of Good Samaritan, 640
  and tradition of Mark the evangelist, 4
Orobator, Agbonkhianmeghe E., SJ
  on African theology and Christology, 607n19
  on church as conscience of society in Kenya, 403
  on church under Moi, 403–4

Index

on community, 434
on complexity of Africa, 431–32
on creation, 436–37
on epochs of African Christian history, 615
on four traits of African ancestorship, 433
on method of critical collaboration, 412
on palaver as model of church communication, 594
on religious pluralism, 441, 616
on reverential dialogue, 103
on SCCs, 197
Orsuto, Donna, on radical following of Christ, 314
orthodoxia prima, liturgy as, 45–46
orthodoxia seconda, as right teaching, 45–46
orthodoxy, doing right things, 100
orthopraxis, right way, 100
Oruka, Henry Odera
criticism of Tempels by, 671
international recognition of, 674
school of philosophical sagacity of, 672–73
Osegbo, Mother Amaka, 559n85
Osler, William, on science and art applied to health care, 500
Otene, Matungulu (DRC), on concept of consecration and vows, 315
Other, the
rejection of, 385
as threat to privileged populations, 520–21
Otu, Idara
on Catholic social ministry, 423
on poor in Africa, 423–24
outside the church there is no salvation, 332
Ozman, Agnes, receiving power of Holy Spirit, 482

Pacca, Bartolomeo (cardinal), and abolitionist movement, 156
PACE (Pan-African Association of Catholic Exegetes; Cameroon), 170, 170n43, 628
congresses convened by, 628, 631
and contextualized exegesis, 171
objectives of, 628
proceedings of, 168n15
research objectives of, 170–71
seminars on biblical themes of, 637
theological exegesis and, 630
Pacem in Terris (Pope John XXIII, encyclical; 1963)
and Catholic vision of human rights, 416
on health care, 501

Pachomius, monasticism and, 6, 717
padroado, ecclesiastical rights granted to Portuguese kings, 153–54
Palacios, Joseph, on Catholic social imagination, 329, 333, 335, 336
palaver (interactive dialogue), 102, 669, 673–74
of African women, 551
consensus building and, 592
as model of church communication, 594
palaver theology, and SCCs, 198
palaver tree, as symbol of peace and reconciliation, 592
palm kernel oil, as local element for liturgy, 58
Palm Sunday, liturgy of, in Ethiopian rite, 642
Pan-African Association of Catholic Exegetes (Cameroon). *See* PACE
Pan-African Catholic Congress on Theology, Society, and Pastoral Life, and ecumenism, 381n2
pandemics, in Africa, 88
Papias, and tradition of Mark the evangelist, 4
Parankimali, Fr. Anthony, Vincentian prayer houses and, 488
parish groups, roles of, 350–51
Parratt, John
on new centers of Christianity, 168
on Placide Tempels as starting point for African theology, 170
Parrinder, Edward Geoffrey
on Christian theology and African traditional life, 652
on pan-African culture, 90
and Yoruba creation myth, 431
Parsons, Talcott, functionalist sociology of, 524
participation
philosophy of, 432–33
and planetary living, 439
participation-sharing
African worldview and, 440–41
meaning of, 441
particular law
and conference of bishops, 275–76
and plenary and provincial councils, 274–75
sources of, 272–73
topics addressed by, 273–74
paschal mystery
anamnesis of, 47, 48–49
liturgy and, 41, 41n5, 47
sacraments as memorial of, 47

witnesses of saints and martyrs to, 43
past
dealing with, 59
importance of studying, 36–37
pastoral centers, promoting SCC model of church, 188
pastoral cycle, 284–85n8
methodology of, 284–85
pastoral leadership, and *Africae Munus,* 236
pastoral ministry
in areas of poverty, 287
dominated by clerics, 110
elements of, 100
and encountering God, 123
friendship model of, 123
goal of, 123
problems of, 121–23
skill sets for, 123
theology and, 103, 356
transformational servant leadership in, 109–26
transformational, 123
pastoral model, SCCs as, 194, 195, 195n37
paternalism, and Roman Missal for the Dioceses of Zaire, 139–40
patriarchy
in church organization, 121, 361–62
women and, 555
Patrick and Rosalia Family Prayer Group, 487, 491–92
patronage
as hindrance to evangelization, 261–62
and leadership, 111
and missionary activity in Africa, 260–62
rights and duties involved with, 261
royal, 260–63
slave trade and, 262
patron–client relationship, in politics, 119
Paul III, Pope, bull *Altitudo Divini Consilii* (1537): on polygamy, 262
Paul the First Hermit, 5
Paul V, Pope, and Kongolese, 153–54
Paul VI, Pope
Africae Terrarum, 688 (*see also Africae Terrarum*)
on African values, 721
on Africans as their own missionaries, 595, 721
on *aggiornamento,* 12
and Alioune Diop, 304–5

773

Index

Paul VI, Pope (*cont.*)
  apostolic exhortation *Evangelii Nuntiandi:* on evangelization, 138, 142 (*see also Evangelii Nuntiandi*)
  and canonization of Uganda Martyrs, 21, 212
  on Charismatic Renewal, 467, 484
  on church in Africa, 429, 721–22
  on development of peoples, 305, 523n56 (*see also Populorum Progressio*)
  encyclical *Ecclesiam Suam* (1964), 96
  encyclical *Humanae Vitae* (1968), 362 (*see also Humanae Vitae*)
  encyclical *Populorum Progressio* (1967), 305 (*see also Populorum Progressio*)
  episcopal conferences mandated by, 723–24
  on inculturation, 725
  on plurality of theologies, 86–87
  on role of church in African development, 351–54
  speech of, in Kampala, 352
  on spirituality of Africa, xviii
  Synod of Bishops established by, 698–99
  on task of evangelization, 204
  on women, 551, 558, 562
Paul, Saint
  as apostle of the Gentiles, 4
  and principle of universal access, 442–43
Pauline privilege, 262–63
Pavy, Louis-Antoine-Augustin (bishop), prohibited from evangelizing in Algiers, 10–11
peace
  as fruit of reconciliation and justice, 710
  meaning of, 710
  as one of threefold duty of church, 225
  See also reconciliation, justice, and peace
Pelagia's snake, story of, 527–30
Pellerin, Marquita, on Africana womanist methodology, 554
penance, sacrament of, healing character of, 523
Pengo, Polycarp (cardinal; archbishop of Dar es Salaam, Tanzania), on SCCs, 197
Penoukou, Efoe-Julien, on legacy of missionary Christianity, 721
Pentecost event, in Acts of the Apostles, 166

Pentecostal and charismatic movements, 485–86
Pentecostal Christianity, as challenge to African Catholicism, 143
Pentecostal churches
  diversity of, 469, 474–75
  enthusiasm in, 28
  healing and, 516
  spirits and witchcraft and, 516–17
Pentecostal ministries, sick people attracted to, 525
Pentecostal renewal movement, global, and Catholic Charismatic Renewal, 482
Pentecostal revival, 348–49
Pentecostalism, 466–77
  in Africa, models for, 485
  attraction of, 33, 468, 470, 484–85
  catechesis and spirituality of, 475
  Catholic vs. Protestant, 474–75
  charismatic expressions of, 467–68
  demons and witchcraft and, 528–32
  diversity in, 474–75
  dualistic framework of, 514
  fellowship meetings and, 483
  foundations of, 468–69
  and grassroots ecumenism, 383
  growth of, 467, 485, 578
  inculturation and, 475
  as new African Reformation, 341
  personal holiness and, 33
  public nature of, 471
  second wave of, 483
  as source for socio-moral-pastoral praxis, 474
  spirituality of discernment in, 471
  televangelists and sham pastors in, 469–70
  and theology of abundant life, 525
  traditional African spirituality and, 468, 471, 473–74
people of God
  church as, 576
  meaning of term, 193–94n33
perichoresis, Trinitarian, 647n1
Perpetua and Felicity, Saints, 21
  acts of, 42
  history of church and, 717
  Latin narratives in honor of, 33
  martyrdom of, 4
  and reverence for personal sanctity, 34
persecution
  of Christians under Islam, 7, 166–67n5
  of Christians under Roman emperors, 4–5, 166–67n5

and colonial powers (19th century), 166–67n5
of Roman Africans, 33
by Vandals, 309
person, concept of, 667–68
Peschke, Karl
  on artificial methods of family planning, 457
  on sexual act, 452
Peterson, Anna, on popular Catholicism, 480
Pew Research Center, population figures from, 131, 132
Phan, Peter, on migrants, 64
Philemon, Letter to, as justification for slavery, 160
Philip (apostle), in Ethiopia, 3, 9
philosophers, African
  on globalization, 679
  not studied in Western universities, 677
  and philosophies of West, 667–84
philosophies, African
  pluralism of, 673
  schools of, 672–73
philosophies, Western
  enrichment of, by African philosophies, 680
  having same objectives as African philosophies, 680
philosophy
  formation in, 681
  meaning of, 671–72
  multidisciplinary perspective on, 681
  or philosophies, 671
philosophy, African
  role of myths, narratives, and personal reflection in, 673
  role of rationality in, 673
philosophy, political, as choice between liberalism and Marxist socialism, 675
philosophy, Western, legacy of, 677
Phipps, William, on West Africa as source of slaves, 155
phronesis (practical wisdom), 115
  and wise leaders, 121–22
Picasso, Pablo, Alioune Diop and, 301
piety, popular
  definitions of, 479–80
  inculturation and, 481
  lay associations and, 481
  as *locus theologicus*, 481
  as spirituality, 481
Pio-Benedictine code, 268
Piper, John, theology of joy of, 525–26
Pius II, Pope (1462), excommunication of those enslaving Catholics by, 154

774

Index

Pius IX, Pope (1873), on natural curse of African race, 156
Pius V, Pope
 bull *Romani Pontificis* (1571) on polygamy, 262
Pius VII, Pope
 and abolitionist movement, 156
 reconstituting Propaganda Fide (1817), 264
Pius XI, Pope
 encyclical *Casti Connubii* (1930): on procreation, 455, 462
 encyclical *Divini Illius Magistri* (1929): on Christian education, 161–62
 encyclical *Vigilanti Cura* (1936): on electronic media, 210
Pius XII, Pope
 encyclical *Divino Afflante Spiritu* (1943), 627 (*see also Divino Afflante Spiritu*)
 encyclical *Mediator Dei* (1947): definition of liturgy in, 40n2
 encyclical *Miranda Prorsus* (1957): on electronic media, 210
 encyclical *Quadragesimo Anno* (1931), 135
 encyclical *Summi Pontificatus* (1939): on solidarity, 136
 on natural method of contraception, 455 (*see also* contraception)
placebos, and treatment of disease, 519
planetarity, 439
planetary living
 African Catholicism and, 427–45
 African relational ethic and, 440–41
 alterity and, 438–39
 Catholic social thought and, 439
 characteristics of, 438–39
 common good and, 439
 ecology and, 439–40
 effects of globalization on, 438
 greed opposed to, 439
 participation and inclusion and, 439
 See also earth; ecology
plantatio, planting local churches, 623
Plato
 influence of Egypt on, 676
 on leadership, 115
plenitudo potestatis, claim of Roman pontiff, 260
Pliny the Elder, *Natural History,* 147
pluralism, religious, Christology and, 616–17
pneumatic experience, attraction to Pentecostalism and, 470

pneumatology, African Traditional Religion and, 172
Pobee, John
 on captivity to Roman doctrines, 611–12
 on Fourth Gospel, 172, 176–77
 on leadership, 613
Pogge, Thomas, on globalization, 679
political unrest, in Africa, 16, 88
politics, African, 119
 Western meddling in, 651
polygamy
 acceptance of, 90
 and canon law, 262
 contrary to Christian view of conjugal love, 453
 as issue of interest, 58n89
 spirituality of, 172
 and women, 363
polytheism, as issue of interest, 58n89
Pontifical Biblical Commission, on historical-critical approach, 638
Pontifical Commission/Council for Justice and Peace
 and *Compendium of Catholic Social Doctrine,* 329, 329n1
 created by Paul VI, 352
Pontifical Council for Interreligious Dialogue, and evangelizing mission, 368
Pontifical Council for Social Communication
 on church's public relations, 215
 on internet, 212
Pontifical Council for the Family, on condoms and HIV, 460
poor
 advocacy for, 424
 health care of, in Ghana, 546–47
 humanity of, 423–24
 as members of the community, 423
 mission to, and church structures, 361–64
 neglect of, 356
 objectification of, in approach to development, 354–55
 solidarity with, and religious life, 318
 See also fundamental option for poor; liberation theology; poverty; preferential option for the poor
pope, authority of, 6
Popova, Anna, on interventions to improve Catholic schools, 251
popular devotions, 479, 480n12
popular religion. *See* religion, popular

population
 of Catholics, 11, 16: in 1910, 132; in 2010, 132; in Africa, 1980 to present, 133; in Africa by 2040, 133; in sub-Saharan Africa in 2017, 132
 changes in Continental Catholic population, 1980–2012 (table), 133
 of Christians: in Africa, 14; in 1900, 28; in 4th century, 5; in Africa by 2060, 131; in sub-Saharan Africa, 28
 data from Nigeria, 419–20
 growth of Catholic, 143
 growth of, in Africa, xix
 socioeconomic impacts of high growth, 456–57, 462
population, Christian, statistics of, 719
population, Muslim, increasing due to migration, 374
population, sub-Saharan Africa, by religion, 367
Populorum Progressio (Pope Paul VI, encyclical; 1967), 305
 on church's social ministry in world, 352–54
 See also Paul VI, Pope
Portugal, conquests of Africa (15th century), 260–61
Portuguese
 and Afonso, 152
 and colonization of Africa, 10
 and slave trade, 151, 155
Portuguese missionaries, activities of, 333
Portuguese traders, and sub-Saharan Africa, 130
Portuguese West Africa, Portuguese missionaries in, 11
Posner, Barry, on transformational servant leadership, 117–18
postcolonial Christianity, in sub-Saharan Africa, 131
postcolonial states
 crisis of, 340–43
 lack of cohesion in, 341
postindependence Africa, problems facing, 340–41
postmodernity
 and church in Africa, 97–98
 dangers of, 679
 and methodology for Catholic studies, 101
 social transformation of, 98
post-Western missionary Christianity
 crisis of, 340–42
Poullart des Places, Claude-François, as founder of Spiritan Fathers, 310n5

775

Index

poverty, 21, 24
  in Africa, 88
  and African Catholic health facilities, 538
  anthropological challenge of, 580
  anti-contraception position of church and, 456–58
  in Bible, 317–18
  biblical interpretation and, 640–41
  Catholic sexual morality and, 450, 462, 463
  and Catholic Social Teaching, 353
  as challenge in Africa, 16, 109
  as challenge to ecumenism, 393
  as challenge to faith-based health facilities, 544–47
  consecrated, 317, 321–22
  ecological, 437
  effects of, in Africa, 456–58
  Hebrew and Greek terms relating to, 317, 317n18
  implication of, for human rights, 417
  as issue of interest, 58n89
  nature and causes of, 356
  pastoral work in, 287
  as problem in family, 574
  risk of, as educational challenge, 249, 251 (figure)
  in spiritual sense, 317–18
  sickness and, 522
  spiritual, and New Testament beatitudes, 317–18
  vow of, 312, 317–18
  See also fundamental option for poor; poor; preferential option for poor
power
  abuse and misuse of, 340–41
  coercive, 113–14
  definition of, 113
  knowledge and, xxiii
  leadership and, 112–13
prayer
  communal: diversification of, 486
  varieties of, 723
  worship and, 46n38
prayer centers, by Catholic priests, 172
preachers, training of, 214
preaching, as liturgical communication, 214–15
preferential option for poor
  Catholic Social Teaching and, 538
  consecrated life and, 319–20
  and structural elements of societies, 347
premarital sex, viewed negatively by church, 453 (*see also* sexual intercourse; sexual morality)

Premonstratensians, in DRC, 17
Presbyterorum Ordinis (Decree on the Ministry and Life of Priests):
  on scholastic method, 101n21
Présence africaine
  leading journal of negritude movement, 299
  religious discussion in, 302
Prester John, legend of, 150
priest(s)
  as agents of mercy, 285–88
  alienated from day-to-day realities, 293
  changing image of, 284
  continuous formation of, 292–94, 296
  defections of, 296
  effectiveness of, 284
  laicized, 295–96
  ministry of, 288
  mission of, 285
  need for, in places of suffering, 294
  office-bound, 298–94
  and religious, serving in the West, 22
  responsibility of, to serve, 287
  shortage of, 286–87
  special favor of mercy granted to, 286
priesthood
  African vocations to, 16
  reasons for leaving, 296
priestly formation, women as teachers in, 294
priestly ministry
  in Africa, 284–98
  an office of love (*amoris officium*), 287
  personal sacrifice and, 287
  practical proposals for, 291–96
priestly ordination, indelible character of, 295
priestly vocation(s)
  in Africa, 284–98
  corrosion of, 293
  as gift from God, 285–87
  gratitude of faithful for, 297
  as mystery, 286
  need to pray for, 291–92
  new character conferred by, 286
  vertical and horizontal dimensions of, 287
principium et finis, supreme being as, 430
printed materials, authenticity of, 210
proclamation
  in African Catholicism, 607
  baptism and, 368
  catechesis and, 368
  institutional objective of, 368

Proconsularis, part of Latin North Africa, 32
procreation
  church teaching on, 455
  population and, 455
production, and consumption, 98
Propaganda Fide. *See* Congregation for the Propagation of the Faith
property, as bondage, 319–20
prosperity gospel, 472, 525
  critics of, 525
  as lucrative business, 470
  rise of, 424
  and roots of poverty, 424
Protestants vs. Catholics in missions, 10, 264–65
provider, Christ as, 608
Prudhomme, Claude, on Vatican II and Africa, 623–24
Putti, Joseph, on historical-critical approach to Bible, 638

Quadragesimo Anno (Pope Pius XI, encyclical; 1931): on subsidiarity, 135
quaestio
  in African context, 102
  in Catholic studies, 103
  as element of scholastic method, 100
  and needs of people, 101
qualitative method of research, Christology and, 605, 605n8
quality of life, gospel and, 356
quantitative method of research, Christology and, 605, 605n8
Queen of Peace Benedictine Monastery, 559n85
Quenum, Alphonse, on fraternity as dimension of church as family, 591

race, conflated with faith or culture, 158–60
racism
  anthropological challenge of, 580
  Bible as accomplice in, 170
radical, meaning of word, 314
radicalism
  evangelical, 314–15
  of Jesus, 314
  of religious life, 313–14
  saints as examples of, 314
Rahner, Karl
  on future Christian as mystic, 320
  on legacy of Vatican II, 688
  on theological method, 95–96

Index

Raniero, Father
  sent by John Paul II to strengthen Charismatic Renewal movement in Kenya, 484
ratio (discursive thought), and human knowing, 223–24
rationality
  African, 673–75
  as characteristic of highest humanity, 157, 157n59
  viewed as lacking in Black people, 157
  West's understanding of, 671–72
Ratzinger, Joseph Cardinal
  on biblical exegesis, 639
  on common belief of Christianity, 658
  against regional episcopal conferences, 723
  See also Benedict XVI, Pope
Rausch, Thomas, on misunderstandings of Pentecostalism, 469
Ravenna liturgy, 41
Ray, Benjamin, on need for plural African cultures, 90
RCIA (Rite of Christian Initiation of Adults), 36, 57–58
reason, as principle of Catholic theology, 657n58
reciprocity, as principle of theological dialogue, 659–60
reconciliation
  African Traditional Religion and, 172
  day or week of, 690
  description of, 708–9
  as one of threefold duties of church, 225
  rooted in justice, 709
  as theme in African New Testament studies, 174
reconciliation, justice, and peace, 234
  and *Africae Munus*, 355–59, 598–99, 685, 697
  and church as family of God, 600, 707
  SCCs as places of, 690–91
RECOWA (Regional Episcopal Conference of West Africa), 51n57
Redemptor Hominis (Pope John Paul II, encyclical; 1979), 600
  on full meaning of human person, 581
Redemptoris Missio (Pope John Paul II, encyclical; 1990)
  on Christian witness, 376
  on new evangelization, 204–5
Redemptorists, in DRC, 17

Reed, Pamela Yaa Asantewaa
  on African women scholars, 563–64
  on women naming and defining themselves, 553
Reese, Robert, on emphasis on "self," 722
Reese, Thomas J., on modernity coming to Africa, 663
Reformation, view of sex in, 452, 462
refugees, as challenge to church in Africa, 109
Regional Episcopal Conference of West Africa (RECOWA), 51n57
relativism, and human rights, 417, 422
relevance
  as attribute of leadership, 115
  as element of pastoral ministry, 100
  and scholastic method, 100
religion
  corrupted state of, 177
  effect of, on state, 348
  in guise of white Christianity, 162–63
  and human rights, 415
  importance of, in society, 249–50
  market model of, 348
  and racialized savior, 162
  relation to commerce and politics, 333
  role of, in development, 340–41, 343
  as social capital, 349
  tied to race, 158
  worldview and, 440
religion, African
  anthropocentrism of, 436–38
  centrality of community in, 434–35
  diversity of, 429
  fundamental structures of, 432
  God as original ancestor in, 432
  multiple intermediaries in, 431
  plural or singular, 90–91
  ray of truth in, 688–89
  as unified system, 90–91
religion, indigenous
  destruction of, by missionaries, 333
  expressions of, 12
  See also African Traditional Religion; religion, popular
religion, popular, 481–82
  meaning of, 479–80
  official, 482
  respect for, 12
religion, traditional, practice of, 12

religiosity
  as issue of interest, 58n89
  transgenerational, in Africa, 470
religious articles, wearing of, as traditional practice, 20
religious congregations, 309–11
religious consecration, African concept of, 314–16
religious conversion, inculturation and, 235
religious crises, in Africa, 88
religious life, 309–25
  and African spirituality and mysticism, 322–23
  African vocations to, 16
  canonical setting for, 324
  charism and, 324
  and common ownership, 319–20
  and community life, 322
  as European enterprise, 312–13
  future of, in Africa, 322–23
  and global solidarity, 323
  Gospels and, 322
  hindrances to, 321
  indigenous forms of, in Africa, 323
  as individual response, 315
  and materialism, 318–19
  as missionary enterprise, 309–10
  and prophetic mysticism, 316–21, 323
  radicalism of, in Africa, 313–16
  and rediscovery of evangelical inspiration, 322
  and solidarity with poor, 318, 323
  as state of perfection, 315, 315n14
  theology and, 324
  vows of, 314–15
religious orders
  in Africa, 10
  local, founded by women, 558–59
religious terms, African, and abstract Western concepts, 653
religious traditions, African, inculturation and, 689
Renan, Ernest, on identity and roles of races, 160
Rerum Novarum (Pope Leo XIII, encyclical; 1891), bringing social concerns to the forefront, 336
Resource Centre for Women (Benin City), 558
respect, as principle of dialogue, 369, 669
restoration, theology of, 523–24
revelation
  grounded in life, 625
  relationships and, 627
  in scripture and tradition, 657n58

Index

rhetoric, Christian, as achievement of ancient African Christianity, 31
Rhodesia, colonized by Great Britain, 11
Right to Development. *See* RTD
rights, Catholic theology of, 423
Rite of Christian Initiation of Adults (RICA), 36, 57–58
ritualization
   definition of, 41
   and reenactment and, 41
   synergy of elements of, 41
   in theological studies, 44
Robertson, Roland, on globalization, 679
Rogers, Carl
   person-centered method of, 515
   on transformative way, 531
Roman Curia, fifteen ailments of, 114
Roman Missal for the Dioceses of Zaire, 139–40
Romanus Pontifex
   donating Africa to Portuguese king Alphonsus V, 261
   papal bull (1454)
Roncalli, Angelo. *See* John XXIII, Pope
Rossetti, Stephen
   on human weakness and power of God, 286
   on priesthood as gift, 285
Rousseau, Jean-Jacques, on notion of "noble savage," 157n59
RTD (Right to Development)
   and Catholic social teaching, 418–19
   Catholic vision of, 419, 422
   church's role in promoting, 420, 423–24
   communal dimension of, 418
   historical context of, 415
   history of, 421–22
   as inalienable human right, 418
   multilevel interdisciplinary approach to, 424
   obstacles to, 420
   overcoming barriers to implementation of, 423
   role of Christian faith in, 415
   as universal right, 422
   See also development
Rugambwa, Laurean (Tanzania), first Black cardinal, 303–4
Rusch, William, on reception as transgenerational, 392
Rutechura, Pius (Father), on SCCs, 189–90
Rwanda
   1994 genocide in, 16, 21, 25, 88, 195
   appearances of Blessed Virgin in, 12
   Kibuye school girls in, 21
   risks of poverty in, and education, 249, 251 (figure)
   tribalism and, 101
Ryan, Patrick, on religious and real-life situations, 321

SAC (African Society of Culture)
   Alioune Diop and, 302
   and Vatican II, 304
SACC (South African Council of Churches), 382
Sacra Congregatio de Propaganda Fide. *See* CEP
Sacrament of Reconciliation, communal celebration of, 58
sacraments
   efficacy of, 33
   as foreign to African experience, 89
   and healing ministry of church, 503, 523
   as memorial of paschal mystery, 47
sacred deposit, fidelity to, as principle of theological dialogue, 658–59
Sacred Heart Hospital (Nigeria), 505
Sacrosanctum Concilium (Vatican II, Constitution on the Sacred Liturgy), 40n2
   on Eucharist, 43n15, 49
   on limitations of Roman liturgical books, 57
   on liturgical creativity, 56
   liturgical reform and, 689–90
   on marriage rite, 54–55
   on relationship between liturgy and other theological sciences, 46–47
   on teaching of liturgy in seminaries, 46–47
   See also liturgy; Vatican II
Safi, Catholic diocese established in, 10
saints
   African, 21
   as witnesses to paschal mystery, 43
Salus extra ecclesiam non est ("there is no salvation outside the church"), 161
salvation
   no salvation outside the church, 161
   as theme in African New Testament studies, 174
   universality of, 442
salvation history
   Africa's central place in, 352
   liturgy and, 45
San Salvador, Catholic diocese established in, 10
sangamentos (martial dances; Kongo), 35
Sankara, Thomas, 359
Sanneh, Lamin
   on Africa as Christian continent, 663
   on globalization of Christianity, 132–34
   on importance of translation, 83n12
   on translation into African languages, 35–36
Sanon, Anselme Titianma (bishop), on church as family and fraternity, 591
Sant'Egidio (ecumenical project), 196, 383
Sarah, Robert (archbishop/cardinal)
   on laity, 479
   successor to Tchidimbo in Guinea, 227
Sarpong, Peter (archbishop of Kumasi, Ghana)
   composer of Ashanti Mass, 53
   on participation as central value of African society, 191
Sartre, Jean-Paul, and Alioune Diop, 301
satanism, explanations for misfortune and, 527 (*see also* demons; evil spirits)
Saudi Arabia, and Islamicization of Africa, 376
Sauer, Hanjo, on revelation as discussed at Vatican II, 626
Sawyerr, Harry
   on community aspect of sin, 434
   on debate about African theology vs. Black theology, 91
Scannone, Juan Carlos, migrant theology and, 66
SCCs (Small Christian Communities), 185–201
   application of term, 185n2
   as basic pastoral unit, 595
   biblical foundations of, 192–93
   called "local church communities," 186
   Catholic Social Teaching and, 353
   challenges facing, 196–98, 596–97
   and church as family, 189, 193
   concept and praxis of, 186
   contextual character of, 194–95
   development of, in Africa, 195–96
   as devotional groups, 596
   in DRC, 185–87, 595
   and ecclesiology, 185, 187, 197–98, 691

INDEX

essential characteristics of, 187
and evangelization, 690–91
formation and training in, 195–96, 595
as fundraising mechanisms, 596
in Ghana, 196
and growth of local churches, 105
historical development of, 185–91
and idea of people of God, 191, 193–94
in Kenya, 595
lack of interest in, 596
in Malawi, 595
mentality of clericalism and, 597
missionary activity of, 195
model of church at the grassroots, 595–97
new ministries of, 596
and new religious movements, 597
and outreach programs, 350–51
as pastoral priority, 103, 187, 196
patriarchal leadership of, 691
as places of reconciliation, justice and peace, 690–91
and reconciliation and healing ministry, 195
shortcomings of, 691
and Small Christian Communities Global Collaborative Website, 197
and social capital, 350–51
stability of, 596–97
in South Africa, 196
success of, 595–96
in Tanzania, 595
themes of, 191–95
in Zambia, 595
in Zimbabwe, 196
Scheu, A. M., on historical research in communication studies, 203
Scheut Fathers, and evangelization of sub-Saharan Africa, 11
Schindler, David, on community life as expression of love, 105
Schlegel, August Wilhelm, on language and human identity, 157n59
Schluter, M. G. G., on method in theology, 101
Schmemann, Alexander, on liturgical theology, 46
Schoffeleers, Matthew, on healing churches in Africa, 524
scholastic method, 100–101
    characteristics of, 100
    major drawback of, 101
    persistence of, 98
    relevance and, 100, 101n21
schools
    attendance at non-Catholic, 161

as first targets of repression by dictators, 228
Islamic, 248–49
private, and student performance, 252
See also Catholic schools; education
Schor, Naomi, on women theologians, 565
Schreiter, Robert, CPPS
    on African theology, 649
    on experience of liminality, 68
    on Latin American liberation theology, 648–49
    on local theologies of SCCs, 198
    on professional theologians, 661
science, warning of, about environment, 443
science and technology, reliance on, as feature of modernity, 97–98
Scillitan Martyrs, 4
    Latin narratives composed in honor of, 33
    and reverence for personal sanctity, 34
Scranton, Laird
    dialogue between Western and African philosophy and, 676
    on Dogon culture, 676
scripture
    catechesis and, 639–40
    exegesis of, in Africa, 331
    methods of interpretation of, 175
    as soul of the life of the church, 627
    as source of theology for Africa and West, 656
    study and interpretation of, 627, 630
    and tradition and, 625–26
    See also Bible; biblical exegesis/interpretation; biblical studies; New Testament
SDGs (Sustainable Development Goals), 422
Seabrook, Jeremy, on globalization, 88
SEC (European Society of Culture). Alioune Diop and, 301–2
SECAM (Symposium of Episcopal Conference of Africa and Madagascar)
    on challenges facing families, 712
    and church at the service of Africa, 598
    on importance of training, 216
    inauguration of, 212, 699, 721
    influence of, on responses to Vatican II, 687
    and pastoral strategy of SCCs, 188

and synodal process, 700–701
on plurality of theologies, 87
Second Special Assembly for Africa of the Synod of Bishops (Rome, 2009). *See* Second Synod; *also* First Synod; First and Second Synods
Second Synod, 355, 355n43
    call for dialogue by, 654
    evangelization and, 369
    on importance of training, 216
    Lineamenta for, 702
    liturgical adaptation and, 690
    major objective of, 697
    and pastoral needs of church in Africa, 215–16
    progress in theology and praxis preceding, 353
    prophetic function of church and, xxvi–xxvii
    on reconciliation, justice, and peace, 355, 355n43, 356–59, 598–99, 685, 697
    relationship to First Synod, 697–98
    and SCCs, 189, 691
    as Synod of a New Pentecost, 705
    theme of hope in, 705
    twofold purpose of, 702
    and Vatican II, 685–96
    women auditors at, 692–93
Second Vatican Council. *See* Vatican II
sectarianism, as enemy of Catholicism in Africa, 43–44
secularization, and relationship between church and world, 97
see, judge, act
    methodology and SCCs, 194–95, 194n36
    as methodology for theology, 144–45
    and new model of church, 596
segregation, anthropological challenge of, 580
Seleka (Islamic rebel group), in Central African Republic, 374
self, emphasis on, in authentic African church, 722
self-determination
    as basis for true development, 359
seminaries
    candidates in, 293
    and Catholic Social Teaching, 353
    contemporary curricula in, 36
    and formation, 292–94
    and indigenous clergy, 268
Senegal
    Catholic mission hospitals and clinics in, 372
    colonized by France, 11
    slave trade and, 155

779

Index

Senghor, Léopold Sédar (Senegal), 300
    Alioune Diop and, 301
    education of, 300n7
    and idea of negritude, 675
    and John XXIII, 304
sensus communis, whole community affected by events, 434
sensus fidelium fidei (the sense of the faith of the faithful), magisterium and, 724
Septuagint
    Egypt as birthplace of, 166
    translation of Bible, 634–35
Setiloane, Gabriel, African theologian, 173
sex education, need for, 461
sexual act, consequences of, 452
sexual intercourse
    abstaining from, 451
    marital unity and, 452
    morality of, 452–53
    outside marriage, 453–54
    procreative purpose of, 450–52, 462
    spiritual function of, 452
    twofold purpose of (procreation and unity), 455, 462
sexual morality
    controversies related to, in African Catholicism, 454–62
    history of church teaching on, 450–54
sexual violence, 453, 449–50
sexuality, positive dimension of, 452
Seymour, William J. (Pentecostal preacher), and spread of Pentecostalism, 482
shade tree theologies, 25–26
Shagari, Shehu (president; Nigeria)
    courting Archbishop Runcie, 407
    courting John Paul II, 407
shalom
    and abundant life, 511
    and African humanism, 346–47
    lack of, during illness, 532
Shanahan, Joseph (bishop), father of Catholicism in eastern Nigeria, 228
Sheldon, Kathleen, on African women's studies, 567
Shenk, Wilbert, on contextual theology, 137–38
shikome ("reverential dialogue"), 102, 102n25
Shillington, Kevin, on Christianity in sub-Saharan Africa, 130–31
Shinagel, Michael, on leadership, 112
Shorter, Aylward
    and African theology, 90

    on Christology as notional theology, 605
    on consecrated poverty, 317–18
    on meaning of inculturation, 81
    on need for plural African cultures, 90
sickness, 21
    belief in demons and, 512–13, 516 (*see also* evil spirits; exorcism)
    biological model of, 518
    biomedical perspective on, 511
    as deviance from societal expectations, 524
    different understandings of, 511–12
    as issue of interest, 58n89
    moral dimension of, 512
    multiple causes of, 517
    person-centered approach to, 533
    popular notions of, 516
    poverty and, 522
    social sciences and, 512
    spiritual concerns and, 512
    See also disease; health; illness
Sierra Leone
    abductions of children into rebel armies in, 25
    school enrollment in, 250
sign language, as nonverbal communication, 208
signs of the times
    as challenge for SCCs, 197
    church and, 573
Siloto, Francisco Joao (bishop; Diocese of Chimoio, Mozambique), on SCCs, 188
Simeon the Stylite, radicalism and, 314
Simon of Cyrene, 3
sin
    and African culture, 51
    community perspective on, 434
Sindima, Harvey
    on African worldview in contrast to Western, 440
    on spiritual implications of worldview, 440
Sittler, Joseph, on what God does and gives, 580
Sivalon, John, on pre-Vatican II Catholicism, 20
Sixtus II, Pope, martyrdom of, 5
Sixtus V, Pope, relationship with Kongo, 152–53
Skelton, Kenneth (Anglican bishop; Zimbabwe), 405
Skete, desert at, monastaries in, 6
Slattery, Denis, on takeover of schools in Nigeria, 231, 231n27
slave trade, 88
    abolition of, 599

    church's indifference to, 154, 156
    collusion of Western Christianity in, 612
    condemnation of, by Rome (1686), 156
    creating master–slave pattern of leadership, 111
    ethnological study of African societies and, 670
    historical context of, 154–60
    missionary involvement in, 262
    participation of Africans in, 599
    Portuguese and, 155
    rise of, 30
    sanctioned by church, 262
    tragic impact of, on African Christianity, 35
    transatlantic, church and, 154–60
    and unraveling of Kongolese Catholicism, 34
slavery
    abolition of, in America, 264
    and history of relationship between Africa and West, 651
    missionary approaches to, 18
    as part of past, 658
    and racialization of Christianity, 159–60
    and social life in Africa, 111
slaves
    bringing Christianity with them, 31
    captured in war, 151
    catechetical instruction banned for, 159
    exchanged as gifts, 151
    returning to Africa, 264, 264n42
    separated from spouses (16th century), 263
Small Christian Communities Global Collaborative Website, 197 (*see also* SCCs)
Smart, Barry, on charismatic religiosity and witness in Africa, 471
Smith, Barbara, on African feminism, 91
Smith, Edwin, derogatory remarks of, 651
Smith, Ian, and independence of Zimbabwe, 405
Sobrino, Jon, on doing theology, 66
SOCADIDO (Soroti Catholic Diocese Integrated Development Organization), 19
social capital
    idea of, in early church, 350
    and local parish groups, 350–51
social distress, as challenge in Africa, 16

INDEX

social injustice, in Africa, 88
social justice, health care and, 501
social media, as mediated communication, 209–12
social order, justice and, 709
social sciences
  and gospel values, 101
  needed for Catholic studies, 101
social theory, Christological spirituality and, 616
socialism, African, 675–76
society
  African, and Bible, 634–46
  African, communalism of, 662
  problems of, 345
  three elements of, 231–32
  Western, individualism and, 662
Society for the Propagation of the Gospel, banning catechetical instruction for slaves, 159
Society of African Missions
  and evangelization of sub-Saharan Africa, 11
  founded by Blessed Melchior Marion de Bresillac, 310
  holistic evangelization in Ghana, 18
Society of Missionaries of Africa (White Fathers), founded by Charles Martial Allemand Lavigerie, 11
sociology, Christology and, 605
socioeconomic and political realities, as challenge to ecumenism, 393
Sofala, evangelization programs in, 10
soil, Africans bound to, 429
sola scriptura, Protestant theology and, 627
Solemnity of Christ the King, in Igboland, 53–54
solidarity
  African Catholicism and, 128
  application of, 346
  and call to communion, 135
  as challenge to tribalism, 134
  church as community of, 388
  church as family of God and, 709n67
  corporate, and ethical conduct, 434
  creation and, 442–43
  and dignity of individuals, 135
  as existential openness, 391
  global, and religious life, 323
  and globalization, 134–37, 142
  with poor, 318, 323
  pursued in spite of conflict, 389
  as virtue, 134–35

Somaliland, Italian missionaries in, 11
Songhai Farms (Benin), as model outreach program, 350
Soroti Catholic Diocese Integrated Development Organization (SOCADIDO), and Catholic social services in Uganda, 19
Souraphiel, Berhaneyesus (cardinal; archbishop of Addis Ababa, Ethiopia), on evangelization, 197
South Africa
  Black theology of, 169–70
  colonized by Great Britain, 11
  holistic evangelization in, 18
  Muslims and Christians united against apartheid in, 377
  and SCCs, 187, 196
South African Council of Churches (SACC), 382
South America, expansion of church into, 309–10
South Sudan, tribalism and, 101
Southern African Regional Network of Catholic Health Care Providers, 506
Soviet Union, as "friend" to Africa, 228
Spain, conquests of Africa (15th century) by, 260–61
Speich, Jean-Marie (archbishop), on SCCs as African invention, 186
Spinoza, Baruch, legacy of Western philosophy and, 676
spirit world, inculturation and, 276
Spiritan Fathers and Brothers (Congregation of the Holy Spirit; Holy Ghost Fathers), 310
spirits
  and demons, and worldview of African Christianity, 360 (*see also* evil spirits)
  moral dimension of, 533
  pastoral dilemmas in dealing with, 513–15
spiritual forces
  connected to problems in life, 20
  and diseases, 508
  See also demons; evil spirits
spiritual integrity, attraction to Pentecostalism and, 470
spiritual realities, person-centered approach to, 530–32
spiritual world, African, demonization of, 514
spirituality
  of discernment in Pentecostalism, 471
  laity and, 479

  of openness, 392–93
  popular piety as, 481
  transformation and, 69–77
spirituality, African, 727
  goals of, 473
  rooted in social and public life, 471
  as socioreligious phenomenon, 474
  ubuntu and, 474
spirituality, Pentecostal, 474
sponsor, as euphemism in sexual activity, 449n3, 458, 459
St. Dominic Catholic Hospital (Akwatia, Ghana), 372
St. Francis Xavier Hospital (Assin Fosu, Ghana), 372
St. Gerard's Hospital (Nigeria), 505
St. Leo's Catholic Church (Ikeja, Nigeria)
St. Luke Catholic Hospital (Apam, Ghana), 372
St. Luke's Hospital (Nigeria), 505
St. Matthew Social Action committee in Baltimore, 70
Stanley, Brian, on climactic millennial age, xx
state
  effect of religion on, 348
  relationship of, to human person, 233
  social issues as responsibility of, 335
  See also church and state; nation-states
Stephen, Pope, against rebaptism of heretics, 5
stewardship, responsibilities of, 297
Stinton, Diane
  on African Christology, 605, 605n7
  on images of Christ, 608–11
  on sickness and quest for healing, 610
STIWA (Social Transformation Including Women in Africa), 552n8
Stiwanism, 552, 552n8
storytelling, migration and, 65–66
Strauss, Anselm, on complex social phenomena, 66
structures
  ecclesiastical: African theological imagination and, 722–24
  and shape of local church, 722
  social: African theological imagination and, 722–24
subjective reclamation
  African intellectual history as, 148–49
  and understanding of the colonizer, 158

Index

sub-Saharan Africa
  Bantu culture in, 430n15
  beginnings of church in, 260
  canon law in, 257–58
  Catholic health care facilities in, 505–6
  Catholic schools in, 239–40
  Christianity in, 10–14, 29, 30, 130, 205, 718–19
  Christology in, 605
  church as family of God in, 592–94
  church in, 167
  colonization of, 10
  data of health facilities in, 537–38
  in dialogue with West, 647–66
  ecclesiology in, 589–603
  educational challenges in, 249–52
  as epicenter of HIV/AIDS, 459
  food insecurity in, 538
  images and metaphors of church in, 589, 589n1
  impact of education on child marriage and early childbearing, 240–41
  inculturation in, 86–87
  Muslims and Christians in, 367
  participation-sharing and, 441
  Portuguese activity in, 30
  primary evangelization of, 212
  religious tensions in, 374–75
  sexual activity in, 449–50
  years of schooling in, 250
subsidiarity
  African Catholicism and, 128
  application of, 346
  disregarded by dictators, 228
  and globalization, 134–37, 142
  and good government, 362
  and inculturation, 136
  principle of, 723
  as virtue, 135
Sudan
  civil war in, 376
  colonized by Great Britain, 11
  slave trade in, 18
Suenens, Leo Joseph Cardinal
  head of a commission to study Charismatic Renewal, 484
  on Pentecostal believers, 467
Sumner, Claude, historical school of African philosophy and, 672
superstition, sickness and, 512
supreme being, in African thought, 430–32
Sustainable Development Goals
  fourth, 240
  third, 538

Symposium of Episcopal Conferences of Africa and Madagascar. *See* SECAM
syncretism
  as challenge to inculturation, 89–90
  fears of, 91n67
  movements of, 85–86
  oral theology and, 172
synod of bishops (1994)
  approval of inculturation of, 87
  collegiality and, 699
  established by Paul VI, 698–99
synod(s)
  African: crisis and progress as context for, 699–700
  in earliest centuries of church, 698
  meaning of, in relation to council, 698n4
  responding to specific needs, 699
  in various regions, 699
synodal process, methodology of, 700–703
synodal tradition, as concept and practice of convening synods, 700
synodal traditions, African
  Christian ethics and, 710–11
  church as servant of families and children and, 698
  four strands of thought pertaining to, 698
  historical and methodological survey of, 698–703
  nature and mission of church and, 698
  synods as new Pentecost, 698
  theological praxis and, 705–7
synodality, and SCCs, 195

Taban, Paride (bishop; South Sudan), courage of, 34
Tangier, Catholic diocese established in, 10
Tanner, Ralph, on need for plural African cultures, 90
Tansi, Cyprian Michael Iwene (Nigeria), 21
Tanzania (Trust Territory of Tanganyika)
  Basukuma people in, 102, 102n26
  Catholic church support of independence in, 404
  Christian activity in early modern period in, 30
  church–state relations in, 398, 404–5
  holistic evangelization in, 18

  SCCs in, 189, 595
  Wanamawombi in, 20
Taylor, John Vernon
  on AICs, 482
  on community, 726
  on dialogue between Christian theology and African traditional life, 652
Tchidimbo, Raymond-Marie (archbishop; Conakry), arrested in Guinea, 227
technology
  Catholic Church and, 211–12
  as challenge to SCCs, 196–97
  and evangelization, 212
  and globalization, 131
televangelism, 472
Tempels, Placide Frans
  Bantu culture and, 671, 672n15
  on Christian theology and African traditional life, 652
  on dialogue between West and Africa, 670–71
  ethnographic school of African philosophy of, 672
  problematic of, 676
  publications of, in field of ethnophilosophy, 170
  as starting point for African theology, 170
  vital force theory of, 676
Teresa of Ávila, Saint, founder of Order of Discalced Carmelites, 309–10
Teresa Okure
  African theologian, 173
  on theological interpretation, 168n17
terra nullius ("land belonging to no one"), mandate to dominate non-European lands, 155
Tertullian, 6, 21, 30
  as African church father, 148, 166n4
  on African liturgy, 42
  on blood of martyrs, 5, 21
  on Christian expansion in North Africa, xx
  Christian tradition and, 717
  and formation of perennial theology, 650–51
  and inculturation, 85
  linked to Latinate Africans, 33
  on pagans and heretics, 5
  reverence for personal sanctity in, 34
testimony, importance of, 643 (*see also* witness)
Tévoéjdrè, Albert (Benin), 300

INDEX

theologia prima, liturgy as, 45–46
theologia seconda, dogmatic speculation as, 45–46
Theological Colloquium on Church, Religion, and Society in Africa (TCCRSA), and ecumenism, 381n2
theological discourse
    and liturgical celebration, 44
    shaped by concrete issues, 706–7
theological imagination, African, social and ecclesiastical structures and, 722–24
theological imperialism, struggle against, 170
theological praxis, 705–7
theologies, as different disciplines, 650
theologies, African
    in dialogue with West, 647–66
    diversity of contexts for, 650
    instead of singular theology, 649–50
theology
    absence of well-developed local theology, 23–24
    authentic, beginning with faith, 174
    biblical, 168, 168n13
    Black, 607n19; focused on liberation, 649
    Catholic: and human rights, 415–18; principles of, 657, 657n58
    common sources of, 656
    doctrine of God and, 577
    dogmatic: biblical exegesis and, 630n58
    European: ethnocentrism of, 611–12
    of hope, 360
    and human values and context, 600
    inductive methods of, 97
    intercultural, 385n22
    as *locus liturgicus*, 44–47
    natural, 442
    as need of church in Africa, 583–84
    new methodologies and, xxiii
    pastoral, and worship, 46
    pastoral care and, 356, 706
    patristic, and sexuality morality, 450–51
    qualitative and quantitative approaches to, 706
    reconstruction, 607n19
    reduced to religious anthropology, 173
    research in, 664
    scholastic, and sexual relations, 451–52
    separating content from practice, 96
    shift in, after Vatican II, 720
    study of scripture as soul of, 627, 630
    temporal impact of, 357–58
    Western: as paternalistic, 650
theology, African, 95, 607n19
    absence of, 92
    and abundant life, 344
    adaptation approach to, 664
    anthropology and sociology and, 630
    authentic identity of, 169
    beginnings of, 652
    of development, 347
    and First and Second Synods, 692
    growth and development of, xxvi–xxvii, 143
    importance of, 86–87
    and indigenization, 91
    and liberation, 607n19
    meaning of, 648
    moving beyond Western theological systems, 167
    non-Africans and, 648–49
    and prophetic proclamation, 344
    relationship of, to Black theology, 91
    and religious life, 324
    and trajectory of history, 344
theology, perennial
    content of, 650n15
    contextual theology and, 658
    incarnation of, in Africa, 664
    meaning of, 650n15
Thérèse of Lisieux, Saint, honored for teaching, 100
Thiam, Joseph, on church as clan, 590
Third World, Alioune Diop and, 305
Thomas Aquinas, Saint
    on analysis of human situations, 104, 104n35
    on charismatic religiosity, 467
    on charisms, 472
    on chastity as important virtue, 451
    influence of, on church's view of sexual intercourse, 451
    on justice and mercy, 288
    perennial theology and, 650n15, 664
    on politics, 397
    on state of perfection, 315n14
    on truth, 669
Thomas, Lewis, on biomedical model of health problems, 499
Thornton, John K., on practice of Kongolese kings, 152
thought, African
    anthropocentric belief in, 432
    centrality of community in, 434–35
    human person as apex of creation in, 436–38
    notion of life in, 432
Thrasimund (Vandal king), 7
Tien, Ngo Dinn, on church as family of God, 573–74
Tobin, Mary Luke, as one of conciliar women, 560
Tomko, Jozef Cardinal, on inculturation and African liturgy, 50–51
TOT (Training of Trainers), workshops, 196
Touré, Ahmed Sékou, Marxist-leaning leader, 408
tradition
    as inclusive, 625–26
    scripture and, 625–26
    as source of theology for Africa and West, 656
transcendent, consideration of, in methodology, 101
transformation
    and dark night, 75–76
    empowerment through, 76–77
    as objective of dialogue, 386
    and presence of God, 75–77, 75n76
    and spirituality, 69
transformative theological praxis, 358
trans-modernity, future and, 681
transparency, lacking in church governance, 361
Traore, Aminata, on status of women, 679
Trappist monks, and evangelization of sub-Saharan Africa, 11
Trent, Council of, 100
    on abstaining from sexual intercourse, 451
    on ecclesiastical governance in territories, 265, 266
    and formalization of seminary training, 294
tribalism
    in church organization, 121
    colonialism and, 129
    as different from tribe, 129–30
    exclusivity and, 130
    meaning of term, 130
    solidarity as challenge to, 134
    threat to African religion, 88, 101
tribe
    and experience of community, 129
    meaning of term, 129

Index

Triduum, 49, 49n46; in Igboland, 55
Trinity
   as communication, 202
   koinonia and, 590
   as model for social nature of human person, 416
Tripathi, Deepak, on sexual violence, 449
truth
   dialogue and, 670
   hierarchy of, as principle of theological dialogue, 659
   meaning of, 669
Tshibangu, Fr. Dr. Tharcisse (DRC), *periti* at Vatican II, 627
Tsvangirai, Morgan (leader of opposition party in Zimbabwe), 406
Tucker, Mary Evelyn, on globalism and environmental destruction, 437
Tulud Cruz, Gemma, on characteristics of migrant spirituality, 65
Turkson, Peter Cardinal
   new Pentecost and, 705
   on Second Synod, 700, 711
Tutu, Desmond
   on Black theology, 172
   on debate about African theology vs. Black theology, 91
   spirit of *ubuntu* and, 441, 532
   and Truth, Justice and Reconciliation Commission, 406
Tveit, Olav Fyske, on WCC pathway of prayer and action, 384

ubuntu ("I am because we are")
   African philosophy of, 390–91
   anthropology of, expressing interconnectedness, 418, 532
   description of, 390n44, 474
   discernment and, 475
   as essence of being human, 726
   and participation-sharing, 441
   and Pentecostal formation, 468, 474
Udelhoven, Bernhard, on inculturation, 726
Uganda
   Anglican church in, 403
   breakaway sect of Catholic Apostolic National Church, 296
   Catholic Church as provider of education, 354
   Catholic hospitals in, 354
   church–state relations in, 398, 400–403, 406
   colonized by Great Britain, 11
   devotion to the Sacred Heart in, 17
   educational analysis of, 251–52
   government takeover of schools in, 244
   grants for health facilities in, 538
   health services in Diocese of Soroti in, 19
   lay catechists in, 18
   low levels of proficiency for students in primary schools, 252
   Marian devotion in, 17
   mission priests sent by Lavigerie, 11
   ordinations in Archdiocese of Kampala, 22
   processes of Christian initiation developed in, 36
   risks of poverty in, and education, 249, 251 (figure)
   rivalry between Catholic and Protestant missions in, 18, 403
   schools reaching the poor in, 251–52
   secondary education in, 252
   statistics for enrollment in Catholic schools in, 244–45
   vocations in, 16
   years of schooling in, 250
Uganda, northern, abductions of children into rebel armies in, 25
Uganda Martyrs, 305
   annual feast on June 3, 34
   canonization of, 21, 212, 352, 352n34
   devotion to, 34
   killing of, 403
Uganda Martyrs Guild, witch-hunting activities of, 514n18
Uganda Martyrs Shrine, 34
Ujamaa (villagization), system of government in Tanzania, 405, 676
Ukah, Asonzeh, on market model of religion, 348
Ukpong, Justin, on biblical interpretation, 176
Umeh, Mother Maryann Chinazo, 559n86
umunthu (African humanness), 474
umuntu ngumuntu ngabantu (a person through other persons), Zulu, 418
Unam Sanctam (Pope Boniface VIII, bull; 1302), every human subject to Roman pontiff, 723
underdevelopment, identification of victims of, and RTD, 423
unemployment, as challenge to ecumenism, 393
UNESCO Institute of Statistics, on enrollment in primary and secondary schools, 242
Unigenitus Dei Filius (Pope Clement VI, bull; 1731), on pope having authority of Christ, 723
Unitatis Redintegratio (Vatican II, Decree on Ecumenism), 381, 388 (*see also* ecumenism; Vatican II)
United Nations Conference on Families (Cairo, 1994), viewed negatively by Pope John Paul II, 13
United Nations Conference on Trade and Development, on industrial nations and poor nations, 421
United Nations Declaration on the Right to Development, 418
United States Bishops, pastoral letter *Economic Justice for All*: subsidiarity and, 135
United States Conference of Catholic Bishops (USCCB), on health and healing apostolate, 501
unity of origin and shared destiny, as principle of Catholic Social Teaching, 419
Universal Declaration of Human Rights, 415
universal destination of the goods of earth, as principle of Catholic Social Teaching, 419
universal human rights, 422
universalism, as approach to human rights, 417
universality, and inculturation, 81–82
usable past, 29
   meaning of term, 29n4
Utica, Diocese of, 151n20
Uwalaka, Mother Angela, DDL, 559n85
Uzukwu, E. Elochukwu
   on African liturgy, 52
   on ecstasy with social agenda, 527
   on listening church, 209
   on metaphor of family, 574
   social analysis of, 353

Vagaggini, Cipriano, on liturgy and mystery of faith, 45
Vähäkangas, Auli, on African missiologists, 566
Valignano, Alexandre, and racism in Asia, 158–59
values, traditional African, charismatic belief and, 473
values education, promotion of, 462
Vandals
   defeat of by Romans, 7
   invasion of, 258

Index

persecution by, 260, 309
rule of, in North africa, 6–7
treatment of Christians by, 6–7
Vatican, First Council of (1869–1870), on missions, 267–69
Vatican, guidelines for healing ministry and, 513
Vatican, Second Council of. *See* Vatican II
Vatican II
 and African Catholicism, xxvi–xxvii, 143, 556, 687–88, 693–94
 African council fathers at, 624–25
 and *aggiornamento*, 96, 468
 Alioune Diop and, 304
 anniversary of, 39
 on authority of diocesan bishops, 272
 as beginning of historical process, 688, 693
 as catalyst for theological developments, 693
 and Catholic Pentecostalism, 483–84
 changes brought about by, 20, 568
 and Charismatic Renewal movement, 468
 on charisms, 471
 on Christian mission, 479
 communion ecclesiology of, 96–97, 185
 contribution of African church to, 621–22, 686, 688
 on dialogue, 664
 and dialogue between Christian theology and African traditional life, 653–54
 and ecumenism, 387–90
 emphasis of, on local church, 690–91
 historical context of, 687
 on importance of family, 561
 and inculturation, 82, 83, 556
 and intraecclesial dialogue by, 656
 languages used at, 622
 on liturgy, 50, 54–57, 213
 metaphors for church of, 576
 and method in theology, 101
 on missionary activity, 269
 on natural family planning, 455, 462
 as new Pentecost, 468
 as pastoral and ecumenical event, 95
 on pastoral vigilance of church, 96
 on plurality of theologies, 86–87
 renewal of church by, 556
 respect for diversity of cultures of, 660
 and Second Synod, 685–96
 shift in ecclesiological tradition of, 719
 on synods of bishops, 698–99
 on theological understanding of human rights, 416
 universalist message of, 170
 valorization of laity at, 595
 women and, 560–62
 See also Ad Gentes; Apostolicam Actuositatem; Christus Dominus; Dei Verbum; Dignitatis Humanae; Gaudium et Spes; Gravissimum Educationis; Lumen Gentium; Nostra Aetate; Optatam Totius; Orientalium Ecclesiarum; Presbyterorum Ordinis; Sacrosanctum Concilium; Unitatis Redintegratio
Vaughan, Henry, founder of Mill Hill Missionaries, 310
Venn, Henry, on proper missionary method, 722
Ventegodt, Søren, on medicine and life mission, 526
Venter, Dawid, on new religious groups, 349
Verbum Domini (Pope Benedict XVI, post-synodal apostolic exhortation; 2010)
 on importance of silence, 209
 on reading and interpreting scripture, 627
 See also Benedict XVI, Pope
Veritas University (Abuja, Nigeria), 51n56
Verona Fathers, and evangelization of sub-Saharan Africa, 11
Victor, Pope (African), 148
Vieira, Antonio (1594), leader of Kongolese diplomatic delegation to Rome, 152–53
Villa-Vicencio, Charles, ecumenism and, 383
Vincentian Prayer House (VPH; Nairobi), 488
Vincentian Congregation of Kerala, India, founded by Father Varkey Kattarath, 487
Vincentian Fathers and Brothers, 10
 and evangelization of sub-Saharan Africa, 11
Vincentian Ministries Kenya (*see* VMK)
Vincentian Retreat Centre (VRC; Thika), 488
violence, 21, 24
 as challenge to church in Africa, 109
 as challenge to SCCs, 596–97
 gender-based sexual, 449–50, 459–62
 as problem in family, 574
virtue, ecological, 443
visual arts, 642
Vita Consecrata (Pope John Paul II, apostolic exhortation; 1996)
 on detachment, 321–22
 on materialism, 318–19
 on participation in life of people, 321
 on preferential option for poor, 319
 on solidarity, 318–19
 See also John Paul II, Pope
Vita, Dona Beatriz Kimpa, leader of Antonian movement, 85–86
vitality, 431
VMK (Vincentian Ministries Kenya)
 activities of, 488–89
 eucharistic life of, 489–90
 ministry of, in media, 488n64
 origin and spread of, 487–88, 488n61
 retreats held by, 488–89
 testimonials concerning, 490–91
Voconius (bishop of Castellum in Mauretania), sacramentary composed by, 42
Voltaire, on human identity, 157n59
volunteerism, youth service programs and, 582–83
vows, misunderstanding of, 316

Waaijman, Kees, on experience of liminality, 68
Wabukala, Eliud (Anglican archbishop; Kenya), on Ethics and Anti-Corruption Commission, 406
Wakahiu, Jane, on women religious, 557, 559
Waliggo, John Mary (on Uganda Constitution Commission), 406
 on ethical values of clans, 590
Walker, Alice, womanism and, 551–52
Wall, Barbara Mann, on challenges for health care, 508
Walls, Andrew, on history of Christianity in Africa, 30–31
Wambui, Regina, on transformative power of gospel, 491–92
Wanamawombi (Tanzania), 20
wananchi (common men and women)
 empowering of, 424
 giving voice to, 423–24
Wani, Silvanus, succeeding Luwum, 403

Index

Wanjala, Frederick, on noetic approach to theologizing, 103
Wanjau, Michael, on lack of engagement of church with real problems, 491–92
war
 anthropological challenge of, 580
 and Catholic Social Teaching, 353
 as challenge in Africa, 16, 88
Ward, Barbara, speech of, at Vatican II, read by man, 692
Wariboko, Nimi, on Pentecostal groups, 348–49
Washington, Teresa, on problems of globalization, 679
Wasike, Godfrey Shiundu, and Ecumenical Catholic Church, 296
WCC (World Council of Churches)
 commitment of, to unity, 383–84
 and commitment to justice and peace, 383–85
 Fifth Assembly (Nairobi, 1975), 384
 on human rights, 384
 incorporation of Africa into, 381–82
 number of African churches in, 719
 Sixth Assembly (Vancouver, 1983)
 Tenth Assembly (Busan, 2013)
 theme of justice and peace, 384
 Uppsala (1968)
 on work for justice and peace, 384
Weber, Max
 on "enchanged world," 513
 on traditional authority, 112
Werner, Dietrich
 on healing, 511
 on necessity of dialogue, 517
West
 African theologies in dialogue with, 647–66
 idea of, as center of global progress, 343
 and idea of Black people as uncivilized, 667
 ideology of domination in, 668, 675–77
 relationship to Africa, 668, 670
 and white hegemony over Africans, 674
West Africa, slave trade and, 155, 672–75
Western
 characteristics of, 440
 conceptual frameworks, and African theology, 169
 meaning of term, 648, 649
Western civilization, inspired by Egyptian civilization 676

Western paradigms, and African context, 175, 175n73
Western philosophy, legacy of, 677
Western worldview
Whelan, William Patrick (Catholic bishop), argued in favor of apartheid, 407
White Fathers
 and evangelization of sub-Saharan Africa, 11
 founded by Charles Cardinal Lavigerie, 310
 mission in northern Ghana of, 375
 Missionary Sisters of Our Lady of Africa as female counterpart of, 310
 in southern Uganda, 17
white hegemony, ideology of, 674
White, Robert A., SJ, and communications formation in church, 217
wholeness (*katholos*), 234
 and Catholic education, 223, 225
 and catholicity, 223–24
Wiest, Jean Paul, on colonization, 19
Wilberforce, William, as abolitionist, 156
Wilkens, Katharina (Tanzania), healing ministry and, 484
Wilks, Tammy, on market model of religion, 348
Willebrands, Cardinal, on devotional practices of faithful, 392
Williams, Rowan (retired archbishop of Canterbury), visit to Zimbabwe, 407
Wilmore, Gayraud, on debate about African theology vs. Black theology, 91
Winters, Mark, on East African Revival Movement, 483
Wiredu, K.
 on challenges facing Africa, 680
 on hermeneutical school of African philosophy, 672–73
 international recognition of, 674
 rationalist school of African philosophy and, 672
wisdom, as quality of Christian leader, 124
witchcraft
 discourses of, 533
 evil effects of, 177
 illness and, 527, 529–30
 as issue of interest, 58n89
 pastoral engagement with, 513
 Pentecostal ministries and, 530–32
 as preoccupation of African Catholics, 33
 relief from, 514

 spirituality of, 172
 story of Pelagia's snake and, 527–30
 See also demons; evil spirits; exorcism
witches, charismatic prayers against, 53
witness
 to hope, 705
 prophetic: in African Christian communities, xx–xxi
 as testimony, 643
Wodon, Quentin, on Catholic health facilities in Ghana, 546–57
Wolfensohn, James D., on importance of religion in society, 249
Wolof kingdom, 300
womanism, 551–52
 in contrast to feminism, 554
 meaning of term, 554
womanism, Africana
 as family-oriented, 561
 gender relations and, 554, 555, 566
 holistic and complementary nature of, 554, 555
 man–woman complementarity in, 555, 566
 methodology and, 554
 replacing feminism, 563
 as theoretical framework, 552–56
women
 absence of, at Vatican II, 692–93
 in academia, 567
 ancestral African traditions and, 679
 bibliographies of works by, 567
 as cloistered religious, 310
 commitment of, to education, 680
 contributions of, to church, 568
 employed in agriculture, 363
 empowering of, 57
 exploitation of, 679
 honoring of, 57n84
 and *Humanae Vitae*, 362
 Igboland rites to honor, 57n84
 as issue of interest, 58n89
 leadership of, 23, 120–21, 566–67
 marginalization of, 120–21, 362
 as mothers, 23
 oppression of, 362–63, 567, 679, 693
 as pillars of the church, 23
 and peacemaking, 195
 place of, in African Catholicism, 551–72
 polygamy and, 363
 positions of responsibility in the church and, 709
 prior to Vatican II, 557–59

Index

recognition of, in *Africae Munus*, 362
research about and by, 567
right of, to be involved in church ministries, 355n43
role of: in church, 57n84; in family, 561; in priestly formation, 294
scholarship of, 568
seen as inferior in African cultural mentality, 568
valorization of, and new model of church, 596
as victors, 554, 568
vocations of, to religious life, 23
women, African
   absence of, from positions of power, 566
   advocacy for, 566–68
   agency of, 553, 563
   contribution of, 693
   eighteen descriptors of, 553
   role of: in African church, 557–60; in society, 560–62
   state of research on, 562–66
   transformative impact of, 568
women, religious
   activities of, 558
   and health care facilities, 505
   as missionaries, 558
   role of, in African church, 557–58
women theologians, African, gender bias and, 693
women's studies, African, 567–68
Wong, Briana, on mission and development, 360–61
word culture, Bible and, 630
Word of Faith Movement, 524
World Christian Database, 132
world Christianity, southern shift of, 16
World Development Report, on improving education, 253
World Health Organization (WHO), definition of health of, 497
World Reader (NGO), renovating schools in Ghana, 375

World Synod of Bishops (Rome 1971), and SCCs, 187
worlds, inner and outer, 531–32
worldview
   African: anthropocentric, 441; elements of, 440–41
   meaning of, 440
   religion and, 440
worship, prayer and, 46n38
Wresinski, Joseph (priest), founder of Fourth World Movement in France, 410
Wright, W. D., not widely known by Western philosophers, 677
Wrong, Michela, on tribalism, 129

Yago, Cardinal (Abidjan), heroism of, 354
Yancy, George
   denouncing colonialism of Global South, 681
   neglect of African American philosophers, 675
   not widely known by Western philosophers, 677
Yang, A., on management of global health programs, 500–501
Yeboah, Kwame, on globalization, 88
Yoruba creation myth, 431
Young Christian Students, education of laity and, 479
Young, Josiah, on colonialism, 87
youth
   absence of, in SCCs, 197, 691
   African: failures of church and society and, 346; high instance of HIV among, 458
   of African church, 143
   challenges to catechesis for, 643
   education in the faith of, 582–83
   sexual activity of, statistics about, 458–59, 462
   unemployment of, as challenge to church in Africa, 109

Zahan, Dominique, on pan-African culture, 90
Zairean Mass (Mass according to the Zairean Rite), 52
Zairean Rite, 85n30
   as model of inculturation, 139
Zakahlana, Jameson (charismatic theologian; South Africa), on "New Pentecost," 466–67
Zalot, Jozef D.
   on liberation ecclesiology, 359
   on temporal impact of theology, 357–58
Zambia, SCCs in, 595
Zaphwanyika, Paul Oliver, on *ubuntu*, 474
Zerbo, Joseph Ki, activist against colonial order, 300
Zimbabwe (formerly Southern Rhodesia)
   church–state relations in, 398, 405–7
   independence of, 405
   rigged elections in, 406
   SCCs in, 196
Zinkuratire, Victor, on reception of Bible, 630
Zion Christian Church, millions of followers in South Africa, 407
Zithatha, Maxwell George, on globalism and socioreligious identity, 466
Zoa, Jean (archbishop), on emphasis on self, 722
Zosimus, Pope, absolution of Apiarius of Sicca by, 259n15
Zoungrana, Paul (bishop, cardinal; Ouagadougou)
   contribution of, to *Dei Verbum*, 624–25, 626–28, 631
   heroism of, 35
   intervention of, at Vatican II, 621, 621n1
   on Jesus as Word of God, 629

Index of Scripture Passages

Old Testament

Genesis
1:26–28   436
1:26–27   355, 016
1:27   474
1:31   452
2:5   350
38:8–10   454

Exodus
6:6–8   725
6:7   703
17:5–6   635

Leviticus
11:44–45   475
19:2   475
20:7   475
20:26   475
26:10–14   725
26:12   703

Numbers
20:7–11   635
21   528–29

1 Samuel
13:14   292

Job
16:12–16   76

Psalms
10:2   317
18:28   317
24   639, 641–42, 642n31, 32
37:10   317
68:31   86
78:15-16   635
86:14   317
137:1–4   316

Ecclesiastes
4:9-12   192

Isaiah
6:1-13   285

53:5   511
61:1   611

Jeremiah
1:5   285
3:15   292
11:4   725
30:22   703

Lamentations
3:1-20   76

Ezekiel
36:28   725
37:27   725

Hosea
11:1   3
11:2   635

Amos
           640–41

Zephaniah
2:3   317
3:12   317

Malachi
2:7   124

New Testament

Matthew
1:23   618
2:13–15   166
2:13   3
2:15   3
2:25   635
4:23–25   726
5:9   637
5:13–14   425
6:21   319
7:15–29   471
8:1–4   502
8:19–22   314
8:28–34   726
9:20–22   502
9:27–31   502
9:35   502

9:36   610, 614
9:38   291
10:1   614
10:8   127, 323
11:28–30   502
13:7   43
13:11   123
15:30   609
16:13   678
18:20   192
20:26–28   314
20:27–28   723
22:25–28   726
25:31–46   415
25:34–40   503
25:35   617
27:32   3
28:16–20   368
28:20   60

Mark
1:21–28   726
1:41   610
4:11   123
7:1–23   636
8:35   314
9:43–48   523
10:13–16   57
10:21–22   314
10:42–45   723
10:42   113
10:45   712
14:51–52   4
15:21   3
16:9   726
16:15–20   368

Luke
2:21–40   57
4:18–19   611
4:18   615
4:21   611
4:40   609
5:17–26   502
5:31   295
8:3   559
8:14   43
9:23   314
9:46–48   723

Index of Scripture Passages

10:8–9	503	8:27–38	9, 166	Philippians	
10:25–37	726	8:30–38	368	3:8	124
13:10–17	726	11:25	84		
13:31–32	716	12:12	4	Colossians	
16:29	629	12:25–13:13	4	2:9	610
17:10	297	13	634	4:10	4
18:13	206	13:1	3		
20:29–33	726	15	84	1 Thessalonians	
23:26	3	17	634	5:12	472
24	195	18:25–28	3	5:19–21	472
24:19	610				
		Romans		1 Timothy	
John		10:12	159	3:15	574
1:2	209	10:17	106, 629		
1:14	81	2:11	442	2 Timothy	
1:38–39	314–15	3:22	442	4:11	4
3:8	467	3:23	442		
3:16	92	5:2–5	705	Titus	
3:17	295	5:5	618	3:13	3
4:41–42	502	8:19	442		
4:42	630	8:22–23	617	Philemon	
5:1–14	523	8:24	703	24	4
6:37	123				
9:2	526	1 Corinthians		Hebrews	
10:10–11	526		3	4:12	190, 193
10:10	494	2:13	643	5:4	286
10:10b	511	3:9	3		
12:32	473	3:22–23	3	1 Peter	
13:34	391	4:1–2	297	1:15–16	475
14:27	502	7:3–5	453	1:22–25	190
15:11	526	10:4	635	2:9–10	193–94n33
15:15	123, 582	15:54–55	49	2:18	160
15:16	286, 291			2:24	511
17:21–23	664	2 Corinthians		3:15	189, 703
17:21	471	5:20	692	5:13	4
17:22–23	416	8:1–24	350		
				1 John	
Acts of the Apostles		Galatians		4:1	471
1:8	92	2:11–14	722		
2:1–13	468	2:12–13	442	Revelation	
2:5–41	368	3:27–29	126	2:7	195
2:5	3	3:28	159, 442	3:15–16	314
2:8	59	4:4	617	5:9	126
2:10	3, 166	4:21–31	635	7:9	126
2:42–47	192				
2:43–3:26	722	Ephesians			
4:32–35	350	2:14	442		
4:32	192	2:19–22	442, 574		
4:43	105	3:8	124		
8:27–39	3	4:1–7	442		